MW01598377

MACQUARIE
ESSENTIAL THESAURUS

MACQUARIE

MACQUARIE
ESSENTIAL THESAURUS

Based on the Fourth Edition of

MACQUARIE DICTIONARY

AUSTRALIA'S NATIONAL DICTIONARY

Macquarie Dictionary

at

The University of Sydney

Published by Macquarie Dictionary Publishers Pty Ltd
The University of Sydney, NSW 2006 Australia

Copyright © Macquarie Dictionary Publishers Pty Ltd 1984, 2008

First edition published 1984
Second edition published 2008

Cover design: Bland Design
Typeset by Macmillan India Ltd, Bangalore-25
Printed in China

National Library of Australia Cataloguing-in-Publication Data

  Title: Macquarie essential thesaurus.
  Edition: 2nd ed.
  Publisher: Sydney : Macquarie Dictionary Publishers, 2008.
  ISBN: 9781876429706 (pbk.)
  Notes: Includes index.
  Subjects: English language – Australia – Synonyms and antonyms
         – Dictionaries.
         English language – Synonyms and antonyms – Dictionaries
  Dewey Number: 423.1

A number of words entered in this thesaurus are derived from trademarks. However, the presence or absence of indication of this derivation should not be regarded in any way as affecting the legal status of any trademark.

Contents

Editorial staff

First edition:

General editor: JRL Bernard
Executive editor: Susan Butler
Senior editor: Richard Tardif

Second edition:

General editors: Richard Tardif
Susan Butler
Ann Atkinson

Senior editor: Alison Moore

Editors: Tim Miller
Maree Frakes

Proof editors: Margaret McPhee
Victoria Morgan

Database editors: Scott Fitzgerald
Sarah Ogilvie

Manuscript consultant: Colin Yallop

Editorial assistants: Eric Smith
Ben Smoker
Jeremy Swain
Ryan Wittingslow
Lachlan Young

Database management: Richard Tardif

Botany consultant: Dr Murray Henwood, School of Biological Sciences, University of Sydney

Zoology consultant: Dr Elizabeth May, School of Biological Sciences, University of Sydney

Preface

In 1852 Dr Peter Mark Roget published the first edition of his *Roget's Thesaurus*, creating an entirely new way of recording language. Instead of the useful but meaningless alphabetic ordering of the dictionary, he offered words *ordered* by meaning.

Part of the philosophical basis of Roget's ordering system goes back at least to Aristotle, though the version presented in his thesaurus belongs entirely to Roget himself. He divided the world of words into six broad classes: Abstract Relations, Space, Matter, Intellect, Will, and Affections and Morality. These were further divided into various categories and sub-categories, leading to a progressive evolution from simple existence in the abstract all the way to the temple of religion.

It is debatable whether these broad categories represent some sort of natural division of meaning in language, or whether a particularly Victorian sensibility is at work. What is beyond debate is the very great usefulness of bringing together words of similar meaning, and the delight that readers find in discovering new words and expressions from such an arrangement. No other kind of book makes the rich and subtle semantic distinctions of the English language so evident, and for this all lovers of English are forever in Roget's debt.

In the *Macquarie Thesaurus* we have abandoned the large-scale abstract structure of Roget, but retained the idea of collecting words under broad areas of meaning, which we call *keywords*. We hope that this method brings together the full diversity of expressions related to a particular concept, without imposing on the reader the need to navigate an unnecessary philosophical superstructure.

As it happens, there are 809 keywords in the *Macquarie*. Roget had 1000 entries at this keyword level, and most comparable works published since tend to have between about 800 and 1000 entries. It is tempting to speculate that this number, rather than the six general classes of Roget's large-scale structure, represents some sort of natural division of the language. That is, there seem to be 800 or so categories of meaning within which the great majority of English words can be encompassed.

Within this range of keywords, certain concepts stand out as being the most productive fields for the creation of expressions of similar meaning. For example, English is particularly rich in terms for stupidity and craziness. We have over 200 synonyms for *fool*, compared to eighteen for *wise person*. It seems that when we encounter someone whose language fails, either through incompetence or disorder, we are greatly stimulated to display our own wit.

The 200 synonyms for *fool* probably do not indicate subtle gradations of foolishness – does a *twerp* rank higher or lower on the scale of stupidity than a *boofhead*? In other areas of meaning, though, the productiveness of English is expressed precisely in these subtle gradations. Something which is beautiful might be attractive, pretty, elegant, voluptuous, delicate, radiant, or picturesque, and each of these has its own set of finely graded synonyms, again amounting in all to over 200 expressions, but this time with significant differences of definition. We hope that the way we have organised and presented entries in this thesaurus will make these distinctions clear.

Of course, being a *Macquarie*, this thesaurus reflects English as it is used in Australia. Australian English has not produced entirely new categories of meaning at the level of our keywords. I would nominate *Clayton's* as one of Australia's most useful linguistic contributions, providing an expression for a meaning that was previously very poorly catered for in English, but it does not constitute a broad new concept for our language. (It can be found in this thesaurus within the keywords *exchange* and *imitation*.) Usually the words and meanings that are unique to Australia enrich existing areas of meaning with new colours and a culturally specific perspective. Particularly interesting are the contributions of Aboriginal English, the inclusion of which is a special feature of this new edition.

A thesaurus can be a quick way to find a forgotten word, or a leisurely way to explore a language. Both paths are well provided for in this book.

Richard Tardif
General Editor

How to use this book

The *Macquarie Essential Thesaurus* is divided into two main parts: the keywords section and the index. To explore our language in a general way, you can browse through the keywords. To bring to mind a particular word, the index will guide you to the right place in the keywords section.

Keywords

As described in the Preface, a keyword denotes a broad area of meaning, within which related words are grouped. For a summary of the 809 keywords included in this Thesaurus, see the list on page x. The keywords are presented in alphabetical order, with headings at the top right and left of each double page to serve as a guide. For the style of alphabetisation used, see under *Index* below.

Each keyword is divided into a number of sections, firstly by part of speech using the following abbreviations:

n. = noun; *adj.* = adjective; *v.* = verb; *adv.* = adverb; *prep.* = preposition; *conj.* = conjunction; *interj.* = interjection; *phr.* = phrase.

Within each part of speech there are numbered paragraphs and subparagraphs, arranged to reflect levels of meaning within the main concept. In the main, words with a general or abstract meaning are grouped before words with a more specific meaning. Each subparagraph has a summary word in bold type which serves as an indication of the area of meaning of the following words. Although the words within each subparagraph are close in meaning, they are not necessarily exact synonyms. They may be similar in meaning but have varying nuances. In some cases, a subparagraph may not contain synonyms at all, but may be a list of examples of a particular category. For more information about such lists, see under *Special lists* below.

The words and phrases following each summary word are in alphabetical order, except for those used in informal language, which are grouped separately at the end of a subparagraph, themselves in alphabetical order, after the subheading *Informal*. Other labels indicating that a word is restricted in use by reason of region, time or level of language appear in italic type in brackets after the word. These labels include, for example, *Archaic, Obsolete, Obsolescent, Rare, Poetic, Literary, US* (United States), *Brit.* (Britain), *NZ* (New Zealand) and those indicating an Australian regional usage.

References to related keywords appear in small capitals at the end of selected keywords.

Index

What do you do when want to use a word with a particular meaning but cannot bring the exact word to mind? For example, you want to describe a meal you have enjoyed and the only word you can think of is 'nice'. This is when you use the index section of the Thesaurus.

The index lists most of the words and phrases that appear in the Thesaurus in strict alphabetical order, that is, a particular word can be located by taking each successive letter in alphabetical order, ignoring capital letters, hyphens, apostrophes, brackets and word spaces. For example, the words **bush-feller** and **bushfire** are found between **bush** and **bush telegram**. A special case is the treatment of numbers as, for example, in **catch 22**. For the purpose of alphabetical ordering the number is regarded as spelt out (as **catch twenty-two**), so that **catch 22** comes between **catch someone's eye** and **catchup**. Note that phrases are alphabetised by the first word in the phrase, rather than by the main word in the phrase. For example, **by hook or by crook** appears at the alphabetical place for 'by', rather than at 'hook' or 'crook'.

Each such word or phrase in the index is in bold type, followed by its part of speech in abbreviated form as listed under *Keywords* above. If a word has more than one part of speech, there are separate entries in the index for each part of speech. Then follows a list of references to the places in the Thesaurus where the word occurs. The references give keyword name, then paragraph and subparagraph number.

So if you look up **nice** in the index, you will find:

> **nice** *adj.*
> competence 5.1
> discernment 4.2, 4.3
> goodness 5.1
> kindness 3.1
> pleasant flavour 2.1
> pleasantness 2.1, 2.2
> pleasure 4.2
> precision 3.10

As you want to describe food, the best choice in this list is *pleasant flavour*. Your next step is to locate this keyword in its alphabetical position in the keywords section, where you will find the following.

PLEASANT FLAVOUR

n. **1.** **1. pleasant flavour** deliciousness, lusciousness, mellowness, niceness, palatability, palatableness, sapidity, savour, savouriness, tastiness, toothsomeness. **2. relish** life, tang, zest.

adj. **2.** **1. delicious** ambrosial, ambrosian, delectable, epicurean, fit for the gods, flavorous, lipsmacking, luscious, mouth-watering, nectareous, nice, succulent, sweet, tasty, yum. *Informal:* delish, goluptious, more-ish, nummy, scrummy, scrumptious, yummy. **2. delicate** dainty, minikin, nice. **3. savoury** appetising, enticing, flavourful, flavoursome, mouth-watering, palatable, piquant, sapid, savorous *(Chiefly US)*, savory, tangy, tasty, toothsome, zestful, zesty.

v. **3.** **1. savour** lap up, lick one's fingers, smack the lips. **2. taste good** tickle the palate.

interj. **4.** **1. yummy** *Informal:* delish, mmm, scrummy, scrumptious, what a feast, yum, yum-o.

RELATED KEYWORDS: PUNGENCY, FOOD, SWEETNESS, TASTE

Following the index reference to paragraph 2.1, you will find a range of alternative terms to 'nice', including several informal words, all under the subheading **delicious**. A wider choice of words can be found by reading the whole of paragraph 2, that is, including the words listed in 2.2 and 2.3 under the headings **delicate** and **savoury**.

Special lists

As mentioned under *Keywords*, some subparagraphs in the Thesaurus consist of groupings of specific examples of certain categories. The summary words for these lists are itemised alphabetically at the end of the index in the special lists section.

So if you are searching, for example, for the name of a particular dog breed, a kind of spanner, a type of cheese, consult this section, which gives references to keywords with paragraph and subparagraph numbers, in the same way as in the index. If you look up **dog breeds,** you will be directed to *animals 73.3*; **spanners** will take you to *machine 14.1*; **cheeses** to *food 12.1*, and so on.

List of keywords

abandonment
absence
abstinence
accomplishment
accord
accounting
accusation
acquirement
acquittal
action
actuality
addition
adequacy
advance
affectedness
afterworld
agent
agreement
air
alcohol
alleviation
allure
alphabet
amusement
analysis
anarchy
anger
animal noise
animals
annoyance
answer
anticipation
anxiety
apathy
appearance
approval
aristocracy
arrangement
arrival
arrogance
artist
artlessness
ascent
assertion
atom
attack
attempt
attention
attraction

authority
avoidance
award
badness
bareness
beauty
behaviour
belief
bend
black
blemish
blue
bluntness
bodily discharge
body
bombast
book
boredom
bottom
bragging
brevity
bribery
brittleness
brown
bubbliness
bulge
the bush
busyness
buying
calculation
callousness
cancellation
carefulness
cause
cautiousness
centre
certainty
change
changeableness
changelessness
change of allegiance
channel
character
cheapness
choice
city
clarity
classification
cleanliness

closeness
closure
clothes
cloud
coldness
colour
colourlessness
combination
coming after
coming before
command
commerce
communication
companionship
comparison
compensation
competence
complexity
composure
computing
conditionality
conformity
confusion
congratulation
conjecture
contact
container
contentedness
contest
continuation
contract
contraction
controlling device
convergence
cookery
cooling
cooperation
copy
cord
cost
council
counteraction
courage
courtesy
court of law
covering
cowardice
creation
crossing

cunning
curiosity
curve
custom
cut
damage
dancing
danger
dark
day
deafness
death
deception
decoration
decrease
defeat
defence
deficiency
delusion
denial
departure
dependence
depth
descent
desire
despair
destruction
deterioration
deviation
diagram
difference
difficulty
digging
direction
dirtiness
disagreement
disappearance
disapproval
disbelief
discernment
discontentedness
discord
discouragement
discourtesy
disenchantment
dishonesty
dismissal
disobedience
disorder

dispersion
display
displeasure
disrepute
dissonance
distortion
disuse
dive
divergence
drug
dryness
dullness
dwelling
earliness
easiness
edge
effort
electricity
eloquence
emblem
emission
emotion
employment
emptiness
enclosure
encouragement
energy
entertainer
entertainment
enthusiasm
entrance
entreaty
equality
erectness
error
escape
essay
essence
eternity
evidence
evolution
exaggeration
excess
exchange
excitement
exclusion
exit
expectation
expedience
expensiveness
explosion
extinguishing

extraction
extravagance
factory
failure
fairness
faithfulness
fantasy
farming
fashion
fastening
faulty sight
faulty speech
feather
fertility
a few
fighter
figure of speech
finance
finding
fine arts
finish
fire
five and over
flattery
flood
flow
flying
fold
food
fool
foolishness
force
foreignness
forgetting
forgiveness
formality
four
frequency
friendliness
fright
front
fuel
fullness
funeral rites
furniture
furrow
the future
gambling
gap
gas
gathering
generality

generosity
giving
god
good fortune
goodness
good taste
government
gradation
grammatical error
gratefulness
greatness
green
grey
grief
growth
guidance
guilt
habitation
hair
hanging
happiness
hardness
harshness
hate
healing
health
hearing
heat
heating
heaviness
height
help
hiding
high regard
hindrance
hissing
hitting
hold
hollow
homogeneity
honesty
hope
humanity
humour
idea
idleness
ignorance
ill health
illogicality
imitation
immorality
impenitence

imperfection
importance
imposition
impossibility
imprecision
imprisonment
improvement
impulsiveness
imputation
inadequacy
inattention
inclusion
incompetence
increase
indebtedness
indecision
independence
inequality
inevitability
inexpedience
inferiority
infertility
infinity
influence
informality
information
innocence
insanity
insertion
inside
insipidity
insistence
intake
intangibility
intellectual
intelligence
intention
interaction
interpretation
interruption
interval
intolerance
invisibility
irregularity
irreverence
irritableness
jealousy
job
joining
joy
judge
judgement

List of keywords *cont.*

remnant
remoteness
removal
repair
repetition
representation
repression
reproduction
repulsion
repute
resonance
rest
restraints
result
retaliation
reticence
retreat
revelation
reverence
revolution
rhythm
right
rights
robbery
rock
romance
room
roughness
roundness
route
rubbing
rule
ruler
safety
sanity
satisfaction
school
scripture
sea
season
secrecy
selfishness
selling
separation
servant
sex
shallowness
shape
shapelessness
sharing
sharpness
shelter

shop
shortness
shouting
showiness
shrillness
side
sight
sign
silence
similarity
simplicity
simultaneity
single state
size
skin
sky
slander
sleep
slope
slowness
sludge
smallness
smell
smoothness
sociability
society
softness
solidity
solitude
sombreness
sound
sourness
space
speech
speed
spin
sport
start
state
steadiness
stickiness
stoppage
straightness
strangeness
strength
stubbornness
student
stupidity
subject matter
subtraction
suggestion
superiority

the supernatural
supernatural being
supply
support
surety
surprise
surroundings
swamp
swearing
sweetness
taking
talkativeness
taste
teacher
teaching
telecommunications
temporariness
test
textiles
thickness
thief
thinking
thinness
three
thrift
throw
time
timeliness
time measurement
tiredness
tobacco
tolerance
top
touch
trade union
transparency
transport
travel
traversing
truth
turbulence
twist
two
ugliness
uncertainty
unconditionality
unconsciousness
undertaking
unfairness
unfaithfulness
unfriendliness
ungratefulness

unhappiness
unimportance
unkindness
unlawfulness
unlikelihood
unpleasant flavour
unpleasantness
unpreparedness
unrelatedness
unselfishness
untimeliness
untruthfulness
unwillingness
use
uselessness
vanity
vehicle
verbosity
vibration
victim
violence
visibility
visit
voluptuousness
vulgarity
waking
wall
war
warning
watercraft
weakness
wealth
weapon
weather
wetness
white
whole
willingness
wind
winning
wise person
woman
word
work
worker
working class
writing
wrongdoing
youth

ABANDONMENT

n. **1.** **1. abandonment** defection, dereliction, desertion, desolation, evacuation, exposure, relinquishment, resignation, surrender, vacation, waiver. **2. renunciation** abdication, abnegation, rejection, shedding. **3. forsakenness** desolateness, forlornness, lovelornness.

2. **1. abandoner** betrayer, defector, deserter, evacuator, relinquisher, seceder, traitor. *Informal:* quitter, rat. **2. jilt** jilter. **3. abnegator** forgoer.

adj. **3.** **1. abandoned** derelict, deserted, desolate, forlorn, forsaken, lovelorn, stranded, unredeemed, unutilised, vacant. *Informal:* high and dry, like a shag on a rock.

v. **4.** **1. abandon** defect, desolate, discontinue, dish, disown, forsake, give over, give up, give up as a bad job, jettison, leave someone to their own devices, let down, let go, throw up, toss on(to) the rubbish heap, write off, yield. *Informal:* ditch. **2. renounce** abdicate, abjure, abnegate, discard, disclaim, dismiss, dispense with, forgo, have (or be) done with, quit, quit claim, reject, release, relinquish, repudiate, waive, yield. **3. desert** betray, decamp, defect, leave in the lurch, run out on, squib on, walk out on. *Informal:* bugger off, leave someone holding the baby, pike on, rat on, shoot through. **4. jilt** cast off, drop, throw over. **5. strand** expose, maroon.

5. **1. back out** back down, back off, back-pedal, backtrack, bolt *(US)*, cut one's losses, pass, scratch, stand down. *Informal:* bail out, chuck it (in), chuck one's hand in, flunk, pike out, pull out, sling it in. **2. withdraw** evacuate, give the game away, lay down one's arms, quit, relinquish, resign, retire, secede, sign off, strike (or lower) the flag, submit, surrender, throw in the towel (or sponge), vacate. *Informal:* be out of here, sky the rag, sky the towel.

adv. **6.** **1. forsakenly** desolately, forlornly.

RELATED KEYWORDS: IMPULSIVENESS, CHANGE OF ALLEGIANCE, UNFAITHFULNESS, INDECISION

ABSENCE

n. **1.** **1. absence** blank, blankness, default, deficit, dumbness, emptiness, lack, lacuna, loss, non-access, short, vacuity, want, wantage *(US)*. **2. leave** absence, accrued day off, ADO, break, furlough, holidays, leave of absence, leavers *(Perth Region)*, long service leave, long vacation, maternity leave, R and R, RDO, rec leave, rostered day off, sabbatical, shore leave, vacation *(Chiefly US)*. *Informal:* hollies, hols, sickie, vac. **3. absenteeism** non-appearance, truancy.

2. **1. absentee** absenter, exile, interstater, truant.

adj. **3.** **1. absent** absent without leave, away, missing, off, truant. *Informal:* A.W.L., A.W.O.L., ack-willie, ack-willy. **2. bereft** bankrupt, blank, broken, dry, dumb, empty-handed, unprovided for, vacant, wanting. *Informal:* broke, bust, minus, stumered. **3. used up** out of stock.

v. **4.** **1. be absent** be nowhere, flex, flex off, give something a miss, miss out on. *Informal:* go bush, shoot through. **2. go missing** bale, beg off, jump bail, play the wag, play truant, truant. *Informal:* go AWOL, go walkabout, jig, jig it, jig school, play hooky, shoot the moon, wag, wag it.

adv. **5.** **1. away** abroad, afield, awa *(Scottish)*, off, out, overseas. *Informal:* o.s. **2. behind someone's back** in absentia.

6. **1. absently** blankly, dumbly, vacantly.

prep. **7.** **1. without** less, minus, senza, sine, wanting.

RELATED KEYWORDS: NON-EXISTENCE, REST, EMPTINESS, ESCAPE

ABSTINENCE

n. **1.** **1. abstinence** abstinency, austerities, denial, eschewal, mortification, penance, self-abnegation, self-command, self-control, self-denial, self-discipline, self-mastery, self-restraint. *Informal:* cold turkey. **2. asceticism** austereness, austerity, monachism, monasticism, puritanism. **3. abstemiousness** abnegation, abstention, abstinence, forbearance, frugality, sparingness, spartanism, temperateness. **4. celibacy** chastity, continence, honour, innocence, intactness, maidenhead, maidenhood, radical celibacy, virginity, virtue. **5. teetotalism** Prohibition, soberness, sobriety, temperance, the pledge. *Informal:* wowserdom. **6. dieting** banting, fasting, weight reduction.

2. **1. fast** hunger strike. **2. diet** biblical diet, bread and water, iron rations, short commons, starvation diet, starvation rations. **3. fast day** Friday, Lent, Ramadan, Yom Kippur.

3. **1. abstainer** eschewer, faster, forgoer, Lysistratan, monk, nun, old maid, prude, spartan, Victorian. **2. ascetic** anchoress, anchoret, anchorite, eremite, fakir, flagellant, hermit, incluse, monastic, monk, mortifier, penitent, puritan, recluse, sadhu, seclusionist,

solitary, stylite. **3. celibate** maiden, vestal virgin, virgin, virgo intacta. *Informal:* cherry.
4. teetotaller prohibitionist, total abstainer. *Informal:* dry *(US)*, lemon avenue, water-bag. **5. dieter** weight watcher. **6. wowser** *(Informal)* jeremiah, killjoy, party pooper, snufflebuster, wet blanket.

adj. **4.** **1. abstinent** abstemious, abstentious, puritanical, self-denying, steady, temperate, Victorian, wowseristic. **2. ascetic** ascetical, austere, Calvinistic, dour, puritan, severe, stern, straitlaced, strict. *Informal:* straight-arrow. **3. celibate** chaste, clean, continent, dovelike, honest, honourable, immaculate, impeccant, incorruptible, innocent, irreproachable, lamblike, lily, lilywhite, maidenly, moral, prudish, pure, respectable, righteous, sinless, unsullied, untouched, upright, virgin, virginal, virtuous, white, white-handed. **4. virgin** chaste, honest, intact, vestal, vestal virgin, virginal. **5. frugal** abstemious, provident, spare, sparing, spartan. **6. teetotal** demure, dry, heavy, sober, sober as a judge. *Informal:* on the (water) wagon, on the square, stone-cold sober. **7. on a diet** on short commons.

v. **5.** **1. abstain** be on the wagon, deny oneself, forbear, forego, forgo, hold back, mortify oneself, refrain, resist, restrain oneself. **2. renounce** avoid, eschew, forswear, give up, go on the (water) wagon, swear off. *Informal:* cut, go cold-turkey, kick the habit. **3. diet** count calories, fast, reduce, watch one's waistline, watch one's weight.

adv. **6.** **1. abstinently** abstemiously, frugally, sparingly. **2. ascetically** austerely, self-denyingly. **3. chastely** continently. **4. soberly** teetotally, temperately.

RELATED KEYWORDS: MODERATION, RELIGION, REVERENCE

ACCOMPLISHMENT

n. **1.** **1. accomplishment** achievement, act, attainment, completion, creation, discharge, dispatch, effectuation, execution, fulfilment, implementation, performance, procurance, production, transaction. **2. feat** achievement, coup, deed, effort, exploit, fait accompli, last hurrah, masterstroke, performance, res gestae, stroke, success, tour de force. **3. completion** accomplishment, arrival, climax, close, conclusion, culmination, determination, effect, end, ending, execution, expiry, finale, finish, fruition, fulfilment, head, parti pris, rounding off, termination, wind-up. **4. realisation** completion, consummation, entelechy, fulfilment, performance, self-realisation.

2. **1. accomplisher** achiever, completer, concluder, discharger, effecter, expediter, finisher, fulfiller, succeeder.

adj. **3.** **1. accomplished** all over, complete, done, finished, over, well-done. *Informal:* all over bar the shouting, in the can, over the hump, wrapped up.

4. **1. accomplishable** actable, attainable, compassable, dischargeable, doable, performable, surmountable.

v. **5.** **1. accomplish** achieve, attain, attain to, break the back of, compass, complete, discharge, dispatch, dispose of, do, effect, effectuate, execute, expedite, finish, follow out, fulfil, make, manage, perfect, perform, procure, realise, satisfy, transact. *Informal:* deliver the goods, produce the goods, turn the trick. **2. bring off** bring about, carry out, carry through, effect, fix up, get over, hurdle, make, make a good job of, put over *(US)*, put through, surmount, work. *Informal:* bang over, button up, chalk up, knock off, make short work of, pull off, work the oracle. **3. complete** bring to a head, cap, cast off, cease, clinch, close, conclude, consummate, crown, culminate, end, finalise, finish, fulfil, make up, polish off, round off, settle, sign on the dotted line, stop, succeed, terminate. *Informal:* ace, bang it over, put the capper on *(NZ)*, wind up, wrap up.

RELATED KEYWORDS: ATTEMPT, COMPETENCE, ACTION, UNDERTAKING, WINNING

ACCORD

n. **1.** **1. accord** accordance, affinity, agreement, coherence, coherency, concurrence, concurrency, conformableness, conformance, conformity, congruence, congruency, congruities, congruity, congruousness, consentaneousness, consistency, consonance, consonancy, correspondence, fit, sympathy. **2. harmony** accord, balance, concert, concinnity, concord, concordance, congeniality, harmoniousness, harmonisation, rapport, sympathy, syntonisation, syntony. **3. unity** oneness, unison. **4. equivalence** coincidence, commensurability, correspondence, equivalency, parallelism, parity, sameness. **5. homology** homonymy, homophony, isomerism, synonymity, synonymousness, synonymy.

2. **1. aptness** applicableness, application, appositeness, appropriateness, aptitude, becomingness, competence, competency, concord, consonance, eligibility, felicitousness, fittingness, happiness, pertinency, relevance, relevancy, suitableness. **2. propriety** decorum, rightness, suitableness, towardness. **3. compatibleness** reconcilableness, togetherness.

    3.   **1. equivalent** actinomere, antimere, coequal, compeer, correspondent, equal, fellow, homograph, homologue, homonym, homophone, isologue, isomer, match, parallel, peer, synonym.

    4.   **1. conformation** accommodation, adjustment, compromise, reconcilement, reconciliation, settlement, settling, standardisation, synchronisation, uniformity.

adj.   **5.**   **1. accordant** accordable, agreeable, agreeing, commeasurable, commensurate, concurrent, conformable, congruous, consentaneous, consistent, consonant, correlative, corroborant, felicitous, happy, natural, pursuant to, sympathetic, sympathising. **2. harmonious** all one, concordant, cosmic, harmonic, homonymous, homophonic, homophonous, in accord, one, symphonious, true, unanimous, unisonant, unisonous. **3. equivalent** actinomeric, consubstantial, correspondent, even, homological, homologous, isomeric, parallel, same, synonymous, syntonic, syntonical. **4. congruent** coincidental, coincidental.

    6.   **1. apt** applicable, apposite, appropriate, cut out for (or to be), fit, germane, in point, pertinent, relevant, to the point. **2. congenial** acceptable, to someone's taste, unobjectionable, up one's street. **3. fitting** appropriate, apropos, becoming, befitting, condign, congruous, decent, due, felicitous, fit, perfect, proper, ready-made, right, suitable. *Informal:* just the job. **4. compatible** assorted, coherent, consistent, en rapport, made for, matched, self-consistent, typical.

v.   **7.**   **1. accord** agree, chime, concur, consort, correspond, dovetail, go with, harmonise, key in, live up to, match, sympathise, tone (in) with. **2. fit** assort, comport with, consist with, get along (or on), get on (or along), go with, interlock, intermesh, match, mate, mesh, satisfy, suit. **3. correspond** agree, answer, answer to, check, cohere, coincide, come (or fall) into line, concur, conform, consort, follow, jibe with, match, meet, parallel, quadrate. **4. add up** cohere, commeasure, hang together, square, tally. **5. apply** pertain. *Informal:* be the ticket. **6. befit** be one's cup of tea, belong to, beseem, fit the bill, suit.

    8.   **1. adjust** adapt, configure, correct, phase in, regularise, shape. **2. accommodate** accommodate to, attune, move with the times, reconcile. *Informal:* get it together. **3. match** find one's level, register, synchronise, track. *Informal:* sync.

adv.   **9.**   **1. accordingly** accordingly, answerably, compatibly, concurrently, conformably, congenially, congruously, consentaneously, consistently, consonantly, happily, harmoniously, sympathetically, sympathisingly, unobjectionably. **2. correspondingly** coincidentally, coincidently, commensurably, correspondently. **3. equivalently** just the same, the same, typically, uniformly.

   10.   **1. aptly** applicably, appositely, appropriately, apropos, felicitously, pertinently, relevantly. **2. fittingly** becomingly, befittingly, coherently, condignly, congruously, duly, in order, meetly, properly, right, rightly, suitably, truly. **3. in accordance** in chime, in compliance with, in concert, in keeping, in phase, in register, in step, in tram. **4. adjustably** reconcilably. **5. thereunder** according to, allegedly, pursuant to, pursuantly.

RELATED KEYWORDS: AGREEMENT, EQUALITY, HOMOGENEITY, SIMILARITY

ACCOUNTING

n.   **1.**   **1. accounting** accountancy, bookkeeping, cost accounting, money matters, reckoning. **2. budgeting** allocation, batch costing, costing, factoring, job costing, periodising, process costing. **3. audit** auditing.

    2.   **1. account** active, bank account, budget account, capital account, capital accounts, cash account, charge account, cheque account, contra account, credit account, debtor and creditor account, deposit account, drawing account *(US Banking)*, expense account, joint account, nostro account, running account, savings account, suspense account, vostro account. **2. passbook** bank passbook, bankbook, tally. **3. statement** balance sheet, bank statement, contract note, group certificate, P and L account, profit and loss account, return. **4. entry** balance, credit, debit, double entry, fudge factor, single entry, tally, trial balance, write-off. **5. bill** account, bill of lading, dun, invoice, itemised bill, reckoning, score, statement, tab, tally, tax invoice, ticket. *Informal:* Jack-'n'-Jill. **6. receipt** docket, warrant. **7. ledger** book of prime entry, budget, cashbook, daybook, folio, inventory, journal, receipt book, stock book, the books. **8. National Accounts** balance of payments, current account.

    3.   **1. accountant** certified accountant, chartered accountant, cost accountant, public accountant. *Informal:* bean counter. **2. bookkeeper** balancer, purser, tallier. **3. auditor** Auditor-general, comptroller, controller.

v. **4.** **1. keep accounts** account, audit, bank, budget, inventory, keep books, keep the books, take stock. *Informal:* count beans. **2. make an entry** bill, capitalise, credit, debit, enter, journalise, post, register, ring up. **3. balance the books** adjust, balance, cast up, equalise, liquidate, make square, make up, pay, post, set off, settle, slicker, square, square one's account, square up, tally, tot up. **4. liquidate** amortise, wind up, write off.

RELATED KEYWORDS: FINANCE, RECORD

ACCUSATION

n. **1.** **1. accusation** attack, impeachment, indictment, personal action, presentment *(Victoria)*, prosecution. **2. charge** accusation, allegation, arraignment, complaint, count, crimination, gravamen, imputation, incrimination, inculpation, indictment, laying of charges, matter, plaint, quantum meruit, reproach. *Informal:* frame, frame-up, rap. **3. countercharge** answer, appeal, plea, recrimination, retort. **4. denunciation** delation, denouncement. **5. allegation** implication, innuendo, insinuation. **6. bill of indictment** bill.

2. **1. accuser** alleger, arraigner, attacker, complainant, complainer, demandant, impeacher, incriminator, indicter, plaintiff, taxer. **2. prosecutor** district attorney *(US)*, fiscal, public prosecutor, state's attorney *(US)*. **3. recriminator** countercharger. **4. denouncer** approver, delator, denunciator, framer, oppugner.

3. **1. accused** appellee, co-respondent, codefendant, defendant, libellee, respondent, suspect.

adj. **4.** **1. accusatory** accusatorial, accusing, condemnatory, criminative, denunciatory, invective, recriminatory. **2. incriminating** inculpatory.

v. **5.** **1. accuse** complain, inculpate. *Informal:* finger, fit, frame, have the wood on someone, point the bone at, put the finger on. **2. blame** accuse, censure, denounce, oppugn, tax. **3. denounce** delate, denunciate, hammer, turn queen's (or king's) (or state's) evidence. *Informal:* put someone's pot on. **4. allege** imply, insinuate. **5. incriminate** implicate, inculpate.

6. **1. lay charges** accuse, arraign, arrest, article, book, bring to book, charge, cite, criminate, crust, give in charge, hang something on, impeach, implicate, impute, incriminate, inculpate, indict, involve, lay a complaint, name, prefer charges, press charges, swear out. *Informal:* have up, lag, put on the mat, throw the book at. **2. countercharge** recriminate.

RELATED KEYWORDS: DISAPPROVAL, SLANDER, LITIGATION, DISREPUTE

ACQUIREMENT

n. **1.** **1. acquirement** acceptance, acquisition, attainment, collection, obtainment, procuration, procurement, purchase, receipt, receival, reception, recipience, recipiency. **2. inheritance** alienation, appanage, bequest, birthright, coinheritance, devise, entail, gift, heirdom, heirloom, heirship, hereditament, heritage, jointure, koha *(NZ)*, legacy, patrimony, taluk.

2. **1. acquirer** abandonee, acceptor, alienee, appointee, assignee, beneficiary, cessionary, concessionaire, concessionary, conferee, consignee, donee, earner, endorsee, gainer, grantee, indorsee, payee, presentee, receiver, recipient, retriever. **2. heir** assigns, beneficiary, coheir, coheirship, coinheritor, devisee, distaff, haeres, heir apparent, heir by custom, heir presumptive, heir-at-law, heiress, heritress, inheritor, inheritress, inheritrix, jointress, legatee.

adj. **3.** **1. acquirable** adoptable, collectable, hereditable, heritable, inheritable, obtainable, receivable. **2. receptive** acceptant, hospitable to, recipient. **3. hereditary** inherited, patrimonial, testamentary.

v. **4.** **1. acquire** accept, accrue, adopt, annex, be in receipt of, buy, collect, come by, come into, earn, gain, gather, get, have, obtain, pocket, procure, purchase, realise, receive, secure, take, take off someone's hands, take possession. *Informal:* cop, git, land, rake in, scrounge, sub. **2. receipt** sign for. **3. come to hand** fall into one's hands, fall to one's lot. **4. conquer** win, wrest. **5. inherit** become heir to, come into, come into one's own, heir, step into a fortune, succeed.

RELATED KEYWORDS: BUYING, FINDING, TAKING, OWNERSHIP, PROFIT

ACQUITTAL

n. **1.** **1. acquittal** absolution, acquittance, act of grace, clearance, discharge, dismissal, exoneration, pardon, pardoning, purgation, quittance, release, remission, remittal, reprieve. **2. excusal** exculpation, vindication. **3. nolle prosequi** autrefois acquit, autrefois attaint, non pros., non prosequitur. **4. amnesty** immunity.

adj. **2.** **1. acquitted** blameless, clear, exonerated, guiltless, inculpable, innocent, irreproachable, not guilty, reproachless, uncondemned, unsullied, white-handed. **2. absolvable** exculpable, excusable, vindicable, vindicatory.

v. **3.** **1. acquit** absolve, acquit oneself, amnesty, compound, discharge, exculpate, exonerate, forgive, let off, pardon, purge, remit, reprieve, spare. **2. absolve** acquit, affranchise, clear, exculpate, excuse, free, justify, legitimate, let out, pardon, release, shrive, unburden, vindicate. **3. be acquitted** get off, get up.

RELATED KEYWORDS: COMPENSATION, FORGIVENESS, INNOCENCE, JUSTIFICATION, LITIGATION

ACTION

n. **1.** **1. action** doing, execution, exercise, performance, perpetration, pursuance.

2. **1. act** action, affair, affirmance, deed, factum, initiative, manoeuvre, measure, move, play, proceeding, transaction. **2. feat** deed, doing, exploit, performance, stunt. **3. practice** exercitation, hands-on experience, praxis. **4. process** function, operation. **5. reaction** reflex.

3. **1. doer** actor, engager, executant, executioner, executor, executrix, exerciser, johnny-on-the-spot, performer, perpetrator, practitioner, transactor. **2. activator** actionist, activist, actuator, agent provocateur, agitator, animater, arouser, catalyst, initiator, initiatrix, provocateur, provocative, provoker, wakener. *Informal:* stirrer. **3. agent** agency, applier, fulfiller, wreaker. **4. pragmatist**.

4. **1. activation** actuation, animation, arousal, galvanisation, initiation, institution, mobilisation, operation, provocation, reanimation, recrudescence, revival.

v. **5.** **1. do** accomplish, carry out, carry through, commit, cut, effect, execute, exercise, follow out, get round to, make, perform, perpetrate, run, transact, wreak. *Informal:* chuck. **2. perform** discharge, fill, fulfil, satisfy. **3. proceed** act, go, go on, practise, take steps. *Informal:* do one's stuff, do one's thing. **4. engage in** deal with, play, wage. **5. do vigorously** get one's teeth into, put one's shoulder to the wheel, take the bit between one's teeth, take the bull by the horns, throw oneself into. *Informal:* get cracking, get stuck into, hoe into, hop into, make a meal of, sail in, whale into.

6. **1. activate** actuate, energise, galvanise, initiate, provoke, put into commission. **2. animate** arouse, awake, awaken, excite, pique, rev, rouse, waken. **3. revive** reactivate, reanimate, recall *(Poetic)*, recrudesce. **4. get things moving** start (or set) the ball rolling. *Informal:* crack the whip.

phr. **7.** **1. actions speak louder than words**.

RELATED KEYWORDS: BUSYNESS, EFFORT, WORK, WORKER

ACTUALITY

n. **1.** **1. actuality** actualness, case, concreteness, entelechy, fact of life, immediacy, objectivity, reality, realness, solidness, substance, substantiveness, the real, truth, verity. **2. being** ens, existence, life, pre-existence, presence, self-existence. **3. subsistence** survival, sustentation.

2. **1. object** creature, entity, existent, fact, noumenon, realia, subject, substantial, substrate, substratum, thing, thing-in-itself. *Informal:* thang.

adj. **3.** **1. actual** concrete, de facto, existent, existential, factual, incarnate, objective, original, positive, real, real-life, solid, substantial, substantival, substantive, tangible, true. **2. existent** current, extant, going, ingenerate, living, pre-existent, self-existent, surviving, uncaused.

v. **4.** **1. actualise** crystallise, exteriorise, externalise, hypostasise, hypostatise, objectify, objectivise, realise.

5. **1. be** exist, inhere, pre-exist. **2. live** keep body and soul together, subsist. **3. occur** come to pass, happen, lie, take place. **4. continue** endure, go on, last, prevail, remain, stay, survive.

adv. **6.** **1. actually** as a matter of fact, concretely, existentially, factually, in fact, in reality, in substance, in truth, indeed, quite, really, solidly, substantively. *Informal:* for real.

RELATED KEYWORDS: CREATION, LIFE, MATTER, OCCURRENCE, START, TRUTH

ADDITION

n. **1.** **1. addition** accession, accruement, admixture, aggregation, amalgamation, amplification, annexation, appendance, attachment, augmentation, enlargement, expansion, increase, interpolation, mixture, prolongation, subjunction, superaddition, superimposition, superinduction, supplementation. **2. accumulation** accompaniment, accretion, accrual, addition, admixture, appreciation, build-up, expansion, extension, increase, increment. **3. something added** additive, adjunct, affix, alts and adds, annexe, appendant, appurtenance, appurtenant, attachment, bonus, increment, makeweight, postfix, postscript. **4. appendage** appendicle, arm, cirrus, fin, flagellum, flap, label, lappet, tab, tag, tailpiece, wing. **5. accessory** accessories, trappings.

    2. 1. total aggregate, all up, count, lump, subtotal, sum, summation, tot, totality.

    3. 1. more allowance, another, extra, margin, over, seconds. *Informal:* a bit on the side, anotherie, gash. **2. extra** etceteras, extras, plus, sundries, supernumerary, supplement, supplementary.

    4. 1. postscript allonge, annex, annexure, appendix, codicil, embolism, endorsement, rider, schedule, subjunction, subscription. **2. epilogue** addendum, addition, corollary, envoy, excursus, follow-up. **3. footnote** adversaria, annotation, comment, end note, epexegesis, gloss, interlineation, marginalia, note, protocol, scholium, scholiums, sidenote, subtitle.

adj. **5. 1. additional** another, follow-up, fresh, incidental, more, new, second, supernumerary. **2. extra** add-on, additional, bonus, further, over, plus, surplus. **3. supplementary** additional, adjunct, ancillary, auxiliary, codicillary, subsidiary, supernumerary, supplemental. *Informal:* sup. **4. annexed** accessorial, accessory, ancillary, appendant, appertaining, appurtenant, attached, incident, subsidiary. **5. additive** accretive, adjunctive, incremental, interpolative.

    6. 1. appended caudate, cirrate, cirriped, cirrose, flagellate. **2. appendiculate** extensional. **3. armlike** brachial, caudal, finlike, twiglike, winglike.

v. **7. 1. add** admix, affix, annex, append, attach, enlarge, heap, lend, piggyback, postfix, subjoin, suffix, superimpose, superinduce, tack on, tag, throw in. **2. add to** accessorise. **3. supplement** accrete, round out, superadd, superimpose. **4. interpolate** grangerise, intercalate, interject, interlay, interleaf, interleave, interline, interlineate, interpose, interstratify, sandwich. **5. footnote** annotate, note. **6. be additional** go along with, supervene.

adv. **8. 1. additionally** adjunctively, caudally, extensionally, in addition, subscriptively, supplementally, supplementarily. **2. moreover** again, at that, besides, beyond, by the bye, by the way, farther, further, furthermore, incidentally, more. **3. in addition** all, also, and all, as well, beside, besides, either, else, even, for good measure, further, furthermore, into the bargain, likewise, moreover, nay, tae *(Scottish)*, to boot, too, yet. **4. and so on** and all that, and so forth, and then some, and what not, et al., et cetera, etc., etc.. *Informal:* and all that jazz.

conj. **9. 1. and** 'n, along with, ampersand, an', as well as, in addition to, let alone, plus, together with, with. **2. plus** alongside, besides, forbye *(Chiefly Scottish)*, not to mention, over and above.

    RELATED KEYWORDS: INCREASE, CALCULATION

ADEQUACY

n. **1. 1. adequacy** adequateness, all that could be desired, competence, enough, full measure, reasonableness, satisfaction, sufficiency. **2. quorum** complement, right number. **3. repletion** fill, fullness, one's fill. *Informal:* bellyful. **4. minimum** no less, the least one can do. **5. competence** adequacy, competency, effectuality, worthiness.

    2. 1. abundance ampleness, bounteousness, bountifulness, copiousness, fulsomeness, plenitude, plenteousness, plentifulness, plenty, prodigality, profusion, prolificacy, prolificness, store. **2. plenty** abundance, bonanza, cornucopia, flood, horn of plenty, luxuriance, milk and honey, more where it came from, outpouring, overabundance, profusion, wealth. *Informal:* lashings. **3. generousness** heartiness, lavishness.

adj. **3. 1. adequate** enough, equal to one's needs, sufficient. **2. satisfactory** alright, decent, fair, good-enough, passable, reasonable. *Informal:* good enough, good-o, tolerable. **3. barely sufficient** bare, meagre, scant, scanty, scrimpy, skimpy, spare, sparing, sparse, stingy. **4. competent** effectual, equal to the task, useful.

    4. 1. abundant ample, aplenty, bounteous, bountiful, copious, cornucopian, enough and to spare, galore, liberal, lousy, opulent, overabundant, plenteous, plentiful, plenty, polycarpic, profuse, prolific, rampant, rich, superabundant, teeming, wealthy. **2. hearty** copious, generous, good, lavish, plenteous. **3. rich** bumper, copious, fat, luxuriant, plenteous, plentiful, pregnant with, prodigal, profuse, rich in (or with).

v. **5. 1. be adequate** be sufficient, cut the mustard, superabound in (or with). **2. suffice** answer, answer for, be enough, cover, do, last, make do, run to, serve. **3. qualify** fill the bill, make the grade, measure up, pass, pass muster.

adv. **6.** **1. adequately** duly, enough, reasonably, satisfactorily, sufficiently. **2. abundantly** amply, bounteously, bountifully, copiously, fulsomely, plenteously, plentifully. **3. generously** lavishly. **4. effectually** competently.

RELATED KEYWORDS: GOODNESS, MANY, EXCESS, SATISFACTION

ADVANCE

n. **1.** **1. advance** advancement, course, going forward, headway, leap forward, march, movement, passage, process, progress, progression, way. **2. encroachment** intrusion, invasion, trespass. **3. surge** current, efflux, effluxion, flood tide, flow, flowage, flux, onrush, pour, press, push, rush, stream, sweep, wave, whirlwind. **4. forward position** cutting edge, forefront, forwardness, front, head, lead, van, vanguard. **5. head start** lead, lead time, start. **6. advance person** apostle, forerunner, leader, outrider, outrunner, pioneer, spearhead, trailblazer, van, vanguard.

adj. **2.** **1. advanced** advance, ahead of one's time, first, fore, forehand, foremost, forward, headmost, high, in the forefront, in the lead, leading, prime, up, uppermost. **2. advancing** coming, forward moving, go-ahead, ongoing, onward, proceeding, processional, progressing, progressional, progressive, sweeping.

v. **3.** **1. advance** amble, come a (good) distance, continue, cover the ground, follow, gain ground, go on, jog, jog along, lump, make headway, make one's way, make progress, make strides, march, move, move forward, nose, nose forward, precede, press, proceed, progress, pull ahead, shoot along, stalk, thread, travel, travel on, walk. *Informal:* make tracks, shoot through. **2. bring forward** advance, bring on, bring up. **3. encroach** advance on, approach, bear down, close, close in, close with, come up to, draw, gain, impinge on (or upon), infringe on (or upon), invade, near, reach, rise, sap, trench on (or upon), walk up. **4. pull ahead** beat, burn ahead, drop, dust *(Aboriginal English)*, forereach, gain ground, lap, make up leeway, outdistance, outgo, outpace, outride, outrun, outstrip, overhaul, overtake, pass, plough through, ride down, stem, street. **5. advance relentlessly** forge ahead, juggernaut, steamroller. *Informal:* thrash along. **6. press** crowd, hustle. **7. surge** flood, roll, rush, sweep.

adv. **4.** **1. forwards** ahead, before, fore, forth, forward, frontwards, in advance, on, onward, onwards, to the fore. **2. onwards** ahead, along, en route, forth, forward, forwards, henceforth, onward, thence.

RELATED KEYWORDS: COMING BEFORE, IMPROVEMENT, MOVEMENT, TRAVEL

AFFECTEDNESS

n. **1.** **1. affectedness** affectation, artificiality, artificialness, factitiousness, forcedness, hypocrisy, overelaborateness, studiedness, theatricality, unnaturalness. **2. pretentiousness** bombast, condescendence, flatulency, graciosity, grandiosity, magniloquence, pomposity, snobbery, stiltedness, verbiage. **3. foppery** coquetry, coxcombry, foppishness, prudery. **4. preciosity** coyness, preciousness. **5. pedantry** preciseness, precision, punctiliousness. **6. genteelness**. **7. priggery** priggishness, primness, sanctimony. **8. sentimentality** soppiness, treacliness, unctuousness. **9. affected piety** religionism.

2. **1. affectation** beau geste, dramatisation, foppery, mannerism, postiche, pretence, pretence to, pretension. *Informal:* frill. **2. act** manner, pose. *Informal:* side. **3. show** pedantry, shoddy, varnish, veneer. **4. airs** foppery, graces. **5. melodrama** dramatics, histrionics, melodramatics. **6. bathos** crocodile tears, simper, snivel. *Informal:* schmaltz, sob-stuff, treacle.

3. **1. affected person** actor, actress, affecter, alarmist, artiste, attitudiniser, drama queen, dramatiser, exhibitionist, hypocrite, poser, poseur. **2. dandy** adonis, beau, coxcomb, fop, gay blade, jackanapes, macaroni, peacock, prancer, spark. *Informal:* lair, mug lair, ponce, show pony, teddy bear, turkey cock, two-bob lair. **3. arty person** *Informal:* arty, culture-vulture. **4. snob** buckeen, bunyip aristocracy, his lordship, Lady Muck, Lord Muck. *Informal:* boiled shirt, pannikin snob, snoot, snot, snot-nose, snotty nose, stuffed shirt. **5. pooh-bah** panjandrum. **6. pedant** *Informal:* Barcoo lawyer, bush lawyer. **7. sniveller** crocodile, simperer. **8. pharisee** Tartuffe.

adj. **4.** **1. affected** artificial, dramatic, exhibitionistic, factitious, forced, hammy, histrionic, laboured, mannered, missish, over-produced, prudish, studied, theatrical, unnatural. **2. pretentious** arty-crafty, bombastic, bombastical, dramatic, flashy, flatulent, high-flown, inflated, ostentatious, prestige, puffy, swollen, up-market. *Informal:* arty, arty-farty, flash, highfalutin, puffed-up, swank, toplofty. **3. snobbish** arrogant, conceited, condescending, consequential, full of oneself, gracious, grand, grandiose, high-sounding, overweening, Pecksniffian, pompous, pretentious, puffy, self-important, showy, stuffy, superior, upperty, uppish. *Informal:* hifalutin, highfalutin, jammy, jumped-up, la-di-da, la-di-dady, lah-di-dah, pluty *(NZ)*, snooty, snot-nose, snot-nosed, snotty, snotty-nosed, stuck-up, toffee-nosed. **4. dandyish** buckish, coxcombical, mincing, minikin, niminy-piminy, peacocky, poncy, sparkish, strutting. *Informal:* all ponced up. **5. precious** coy, cutsie-pie, finicky, foppish, mincing, niminy-piminy, rosewater, simpering, trifling. *Informal:* twee. **6. pedantic** donnish, hypercorrect, precise. **7. priggish** dandy, fine, genteel, mealy-mouthed, missish, old-maidish, prim, prudish, superfine. *Informal:* goody-goody, prissy. **8. facetious** hypocritical, ironic, playful, sly, tongue-in-cheek. **9. mawkish** crocodilian, maudlin, misty-eyed, namby-pamby, sentimental, sickly, soft, soupy, treacly, unctuous. *Informal:* cheesy, corny, gooey, hokey *(US)*, mushy, sawney, schmaltzy, soppy, sorney, syrupy.

v. **5. 1. act pretentiously** give oneself airs, show off. *Informal:* bung on, put (or pile) (or turn) on the agony, put on (the) dog, put on (the) jam, strut one's stuff, swank. **2. dandify** *Informal:* lairise. **3. dramatise** overact, overdo, overdress, overwrite, theatricalise.

6. 1. attitudinise act, affect, assume, dissemble, emote, fake, feign, go through the motions, keep up appearances, masquerade, peacock, play-act, pose, posture, posturise, prance, pretend, profess, put on an act, sham, swagger. **2. simper** mince, prim, smirk. **3. snivel** snuffle. *Informal:* turn on the waterworks.

adv. **7. 1. affectedly** artificially, factitiously, forcedly, histrionically, studiedly, theatrically, unnaturally. **2. pretentiously** flatulently, ostentatiously, swankily. **3. foppishly** coyly, daintily, mincingly, prancingly, preciously, simperingly. **4. pedantically** donnishly. **5. priggishly** genteelly, primly.

RELATED KEYWORDS: ARROGANCE, SHOWINESS

AFTERWORLD

n. **1. 1. afterworld** afterlife, future life, hereafter, other world, the beyond, the other side. **2. underworld** hades, hell, lower world, nether regions, nether world, shade. **3. the Dreaming** alchera, alcheringa, Dreamtime.

2. 1. heaven Elysium, paradise, sky. **2. abode of the good** Asgard, Avalon, Elysian plains, Elysium, empyrean, happy hunting grounds, Hesperides, kingdom come, New Jerusalem, Olympus, Pearly Gates, Promised Land, Sion, Valhalla, Zion. **3. higher state of being** ananda, atman, nirvana. **4. heavenliness** bliss, divineness, glory, heaven.

3. 1. hell Acheron, Gehenna, hades, Hades, hellfire, inferno, Niflheim, pandemonium, Pandemonium, sheol, Sheol, Tartarus. **2. purgatory** limbo, Limbo, limbus. **3. damnation** perdition. *Informal:* tarnation. **4. abyss** the bottomless pit, the pit.

adj. **4. 1. heavenly** blissful, celestial, divine, Elysian, empyreal, empyrean, ethereal, paradisaical, paradisiacal, supernal, superterrestrial. **2. other-worldly**.

5. 1. hellish chthonian, infernal, nether, pandemonic, purgatorial, stygian, sulphurous. **2. Dantean** Dantesque.

adv. **6. 1. celestially** blissfully, divinely, paradisiacally, supernally.

RELATED KEYWORDS: GOD, DEATH, RELIGION, THE SUPERNATURAL

AGENT

n. **1. 1. agent** apparatchik, clerk of works, depositary, depository, deputy, executor, executor de son tort, man, mandatary, mandatory, proctor, receiver, representative, subagent, tort, trustee. **2. deputy** appointee, commissary, fill-in, spokesman, spokesperson, spokeswoman, stand-in, substitute, surrogate, vice-chairman, vice-chairperson, vice-chairwoman, viceroy. **3. executor** coexecutor, coexecutrix, executrix, public trustee. **4. viceroy** crown agent, governor, governor-general, lieutenant governor, Lord Lieutenant, nawab, state governor, vice-regent, vicegerent.

2. 1. delegate agent, ambassador, deputy, emissary, envoy, go-between, intermediary, mediator, middleman, negotiator, palatine, proxy, secondary, spokesman, spokesperson, spokeswoman, substitute. *Informal:* delo.

3. 1. body of delegates delegacy, delegation, deputation, mission. **2. diplomatic corps** corps diplomatique, diplomatic body. **3. embassy** chancellery, chancery, consulate, legation, mission, vice-consulate.

4. 1. ambassador career diplomat, chargé d'affaires, diplomat, diplomatist, envoy, high commissioner, legate, minister plenipotentiary, minister resident, persona grata, persona non grata, plenipotentiary, resident *(British)*. **2. attaché** commissioner, consular agent, cultural attaché, first secretary, minister, second secretary. **3. consul** consul general, legate, proconsul, representative, vice-consul. **4. papal envoy** ablegate, apostolic delegate, internuncio, legate, nuncio, papal nuncio.

5. 1. power to act agency, charter *(British)*, commission, delegacy, delegation, empowerment, licence, permit, power of attorney. **2. delegation of responsibility** appointment, assignment, delegacy, installation, nomination, ordination. **3. commission** brevet, errand, mission.

6. 1. ambassadorship commissionership, consulate, consulship, executorship, legateship, nunciature, surrogateship, trusteeship, vicarship, vice-chairmanship, vice-consulship. **2. vice-regency** vicegerency, viceroyalty, viceroyship.

adj. **7. 1. agential** proctorial, representational, representative. **2. acting** delegated, deputy, substitute, vicarious. **3. ambassadorial** commissarial, consular, diplomatic, legatine, legationary, magisterial, official, plenipotentiary, proconsular, vice-consular. **4. viceregal** vicegeral, vicegerent.

v. **8. 1. depute** accredit, appoint, assign, authorise, charge, commission, commit into the hands of, commit into the keeping of, consign, delegate, designate, employ, empower, entrust, give into the hands of, give into the keeping of, hire, mandate, name, nominate, place in charge.

9. 1. act for act on behalf of, deputise, represent, stand in, subcontract.

phr. **10. 1. on behalf of** in the name of.

RELATED KEYWORDS: EXCHANGE, POLITICS

AGREEMENT

n. **1. 1. agreement** accord, agreeance, complaisance, compliance, concord, concurrence, consensus, unanimity. **2. pact** accord, agreement, compact, concordat, contract, covenant. **3. accord** accordance, agreement, amity, common ground, compatibleness, concert, concord, concordance, congeniality, consentaneousness, consentience, consonance, empathy, esprit de corps, fellow feeling, harmony, meeting point, oneness, rapport, solidarity, spirit, sympathy, team spirit, understanding, unity. **4. acquiescence** accordance, according to, agreement, along, coexistence, compliance, conformance, conformity, congruence, correspondence, facility. **5. reconciliation** accommodation, agreement, compromise, détente, rapprochement, reconcilement.

2. 1. agreeableness compliableness, conformableness, reconcilableness.

3. 1. assent affirmation, approval, attestation, confirmation, corroboration, endorsement, homologation, ratification, sanction. **2. approval** accession, approbation, assent, authorisation, clearance, consent, endorsement, go-ahead, green light, imprimatur, leave, permission, royal assent, sanction, support, the call, warrant. *Informal:* ok, okay. **3. avowal** acknowledgement, admission, allowance, confession, recognition. **4. acceptance** accession, acquiescence, adoption, conformity, consent, courtesy, resignation, sanctification, submission, subscription. **5. the affirmative** affirmative, affirmatory, amen, ay, aye, placet, pro, the nod, yea, yes.

4. 1. assenter acceder, acceptor, accorder, acknowledger, admitter, affirmant, affirmer, approver, conceder, conformer, consenter, covenanter, endorser, ratifier, sanctifier, signatory, signer, subscriber, upholder. *Informal:* rubber stamp, yes-man. **2. reconciler** arranger, compromiser. **3. confirmer** verifier.

adj. **5. 1. in agreement** accordant, according, ad idem, agreeable, close-knit, compatible, concordant, concurrent, congenial, consensual, consentaneous, consentient, consonant, en rapport, harmonious, in accord, like-minded, of one accord, of one mind, simpatico, solidary, sympathetic, unanimous. **2. allied** associate, in cahoots, in league.

6. 1. assenting consenting, signatory. **2. acquiescent** agreeable, agreed, amenable, complacent, complaisant, compliable, compliant, complying, conformable, conventional, obedient, pliant, resigned, resigned to, submissive, willing, yielding. **3. affirmative** confirmatory, corroborative, ratifying, recognitive.

7. 1. reconcilable accordable, compliant, compoundable, conformable.

v. **8. 1. agree** arrange, close with, cohere, coincide, concur, consort, harmonise, meet, run parallel, see eye to eye, settle, shake, shake hands, unite. **2. sympathise** empathise. **3. accord** act together, attune, concert.

9. 1. compromise coexist, come to terms, come to terms with, compound, live and let live, meet someone halfway, split the difference, strike a bargain, swim with the stream. **2. go with the fashion** bend with the breeze, climb (or jump) on the bandwagon, go with the flow.

10. 1. assent accede, accept, accord, acknowledge, admit, agree, agree to, approbate *(Scottish Law)*, comply, concede, concur, confess, consent, embrace, fall in with, give one's vote to, go along with, grant, grant consent to, hear, lend oneself to, recognise, say yes to, turn a willing ear. *Informal:* be a sport, buy, give the nod to, wear. **2. confirm** accept, accredit, adopt, affirm, amen, approbate *(Chiefly US)*, approve, attest, authorise, bear out, certify, corroborate, countersign, endorse, fortify, homologate, indorse, ratify, sanction, sign, subscribe, testify, uphold, verify. **3. approve** initial, rubber-stamp, seal. *Informal:* okay. **4. acquiesce** come around, come around to, come to terms, come to terms with, give in, give in to, have no objection to, lie down under.

adv. **11.** **1. agreeably** accordingly, at one, compliantly, conformably, congenially, consentaneously, emphatically, in tune with, nem. con., nem. diss., pro, sympathetically, unanimously, with one accord. **2. assentingly** affirmably, affirmatively, approvingly, concededly, consensually, consentingly, reconcilably.

interj. **12.** **1. yes** ae, all right, alright, amen, by all manner of means, by all means, exactly, no problem, of course, quite, quite so, rather *(Chiefly British)*, right, so be it, to be sure, true *(Especially Aboriginal English)*, very well. *Informal:* alrighty, fair enough, mmm, ok, okay, righto, sure thing, sweet, that's the stuff, yair, yeah, yeh. **2. certainly** absolutely. *Informal:* abso-bloody-lutely, blood (or bloody) oath, can do, dicken *(Chiefly SA and Far West NSW)*, my bloody oath, no problemo, no risk, no sweat, not half, okey-doke, right on!, you bet, you betcha.

RELATED KEYWORDS: ASSERTION, CONFORMITY, ACCORD, CONTRACT, FRIENDLINESS, SOCIETY

AIR

n. **1.** **1. air** air mass, liquid air. **2. fresh air** open air, out of doors, sea air, the great outdoors. *Informal:* ozone. **3. skies** azure, canopy, ether, firmament, heaven, the blue. **4. thin air** etherealness, rarity. **5. gas** compressed air, nitrogen, oxygen.

2. **1. airflow** advection, air cushion, airstream, crosswind, current, down draught, draught, headwind, in-draught, jet stream, slipstream, standing wave, tailwind, thermal, up draught, updraught, wind. **2. turbulence** air pocket, airhole, backwash, backwind, bump, burble, dirty wind, downwash, wash.

3. **1. airway** air duct, air-intake, airdrive, airshaft, airwell, breezeway, louvre, port, porting, schnorkle, slot, snorkel, upcast, uptake, vent, ventiduct, ventilator, windsail. **2. air conditioner** demister, exhaust fan, extractor fan, fan. **3. inflator** aerator, airpump, bicycle pump, pump. **4. air chamber** air bladder, air cushion, air jacket, swim bladder.

4. **1. aerology** aerodynamics, aerography, aeromechanics, aerometry, aerostatics, anemometry, barometry, pneumatics, pneumodynamics, spherics.

5. **1. breathing** air-breathing, aspiration, expiration, inspiration, insufflation, respiration. **2. rough breathing** spiritus asper, stertor, windedness. **3. smooth breathing** eupnoea, spiritus lenis. **4. artificial respiration** expired air resuscitation, kiss of life, mouth-to-mouth. **5. inhalation** draw, puff, whiff. **6. exhalation** aspirate, blow, gasp, halitus, hiss, pant, sibilation, sigh, steam, suspiration. **7. gasp** cough, croup, graveyard cough, rattle, sneeze, sniff, sniffle, snore, snort, snuff, snuffle, sternutation, wheeze. *Informal:* graveyard bark. **8. the breath** atman, spirit, wind.

6. **1. breathing apparatus** aqualung, CPAP, diving bell, iron lung, octopus regulator, oxygen mask, oxygen tent, rebreathing apparatus, scuba, self-contained underwater breathing apparatus.

7. **1. airing** air conditioning, flowthrough ventilation, ventilation.

8. **1. suffocation** apnoea, asphyxia, asphyxiation, breathlessness, choking, drowning, sleep apnoea, smothering.

adj. **9.** **1. airy** elemental, elementary, ethereal. **2. well-aired** air-conditioned, breezy, fresh, well-ventilated. **3. pneumatic** aerologic, aeromechanic, aeromechanical, aerometric, aerostatic. **4. aerobiotic** aerobic. **5. aerial** airborne, flying, volant, volitant.

10. **1. aerated** aeriferous, bubbly, carbonated, effervescent, oxygenated. **2. inflated** puffy.

11. **1. open-air** alfresco, exposed, plein-air.

12. **1. airless** breathless, close, ill-ventilated, stuffy, windless. **2. breathless** apnoeic, asphyxiated, choked, gasping, out of breath, panting, puffed, puffy, short-winded, smothered, winded, windless.

v. **13.** **1. air** expose, give an airing to. **2. ventilate** air-condition, freshen. **3. aerate** activate, carbonate, oxygenate, oxygenise. **4. blow up** inflate, insufflate. **5. puff up** balloon, blouse out, puff.

14. **1. breathe** draw breath, inbreathe, inhale, respire. **2. inhale** breathe in, inbreathe, inspire, suck the breath. **3. exhale** breathe, breathe out, respire. **4. puff** aspirate, huff, snuffle. **5. sniff** snuff, snuffle, whiff, whiffle. **6. wheeze** cough, hiccup, sneeze. **7. gasp** blow, breathe hard, breathe heavily, heave, pant.

15. 1. suffocate asphyxiate, choke, drown, jugulate, overlie, smother, stifle, strangle, strangulate.

adv. **16. 1. in the open air** abroad, alfresco, en plein air, in the fresh air, out-of-doors, outdoors, under the stars.

RELATED KEYWORDS: BUBBLINESS, GAS, INTANGIBILITY

ALCOHOL

n. **1. 1. alcohol** aqua vitae, ardent spirits, bootleg *(Chiefly US)*, brewage, cordial *(US)*, drink, ethyl alcohol, grain alcohol, home-brew, liquor, pot, spirits, spirits of wine, the bottle. *Informal:* booze, bouse, firewater, gravedigger *(British Military)*, grog, gutrot, hard stuff, hooch *(US)*, ink, juice, La Perouse, lunatic soup, lush, one's poison, pink-eye, plonk, purge, rotgut, shicker, slosh, snake juice, stagger juice, swipes *(British)*, waipiro *(NZ)*, wallop. **2. intoxicant** inebriant, stimulant. **3. type of alcoholic beverage** beer, cocktail, fermented drink, liqueur, spirits, wine. **4. illegal liquor** Old Hokanni, poteen, potheen. *Informal:* hooch *(US)*, hootch, moonshine, mountain dew, sly grog. **5. methylated spirits** *Informal:* bush champagne, elephant juice, jungle juice, metho, white angel, white lady.

2. 1. drink aperitif, chaser, dram, draught, drop, lace, lacing, nightcap, nip, nobbler, potation, shot, stirrup cup, sundowner *(Chiefly British)*, the other half, tipple, toast, tot. *Informal:* bevie, bracer, charge, chug-a-lug, drop of the doings, drop of the needle, drop of the old religion, gargle, hair of the dog (that bit you), heart-starter, hooker *(Chiefly US, Canadian)*, Jimmy Woodser, Johnny Woodser *(NZ)*, leg opener, long-sleever, mickey, mickey finn, one for the bitumen, one for the gutter, one for the road, pick-me-up, pipe-opener, quickie, reviver, rosiner, slug, snifter, snort, snorter, spot, sting, swig, tonic, woodser.

3. 1. beer ale, amber liquid, ball of malt, bitter *(Chiefly British)*, bock beer, boutique beer, brown ale, chicha, craft beer, draught, draught beer, handle *(Tasmania, NSW, ACT, WA, NT, some Qld, Victoria, SA)*, ice beer, lager, light ale, lube, malt, malt liquor, mild, mild ale *(Chiefly British)*, new beer, old, old beer, packaged beer, pale ale, pilsener, porter, portergaff *(Especially SA)*, shandygaff, shandy, small beer, stout, tap, wassail. *Informal:* a cold one, amber fluid, Bishop Barker, brownie, coldie, cruiser, fifty *(Chiefly NSW)*, fifty-fifty, frosty chop, hops, ice-cold, liquid lunch, paroo sandwich, pig's ear, poultry lunch, rabbit, senator, sheepwash, sherbet, shypoo, slops, stringybark, suds, swipes *(British)*.

4. 1. wine bulk wine, dessert wine, house red, house white, marsala, quaffing wine, red wine, table wine, vin blanc, vin ordinaire, vin rouge, vino bianco, vino rosso, white wine. *Informal:* bombo, goon, gooner *(Chiefly WA)*, nelly, pinky, plonk, quaffer, steam, the grape, vino. **2. champagne** fizz. *Informal:* bubbly, champers.

5. 1. alcoholicity alcoholic strength, beeriness, proof, vinosity. *Informal:* kick.

6. 1. drunkenness bacchanalianism, bibulousness, ebriety, fuddle, inebriation, inebriety, insobriety, intoxication, sottishness, tightness, tipsiness, wooziness. *Informal:* load. **2. alcoholism** d.t.'s, delirium tremens, dipsomania. *Informal:* blue devils, heebie-jeebies, horrors, Joe Blakes, pink elephants, shakes, the dingbats. **3. hangover** morning after.

7. 1. drinker alcoholic, bacchanal, bacchant, bacchante, bibber, compotator, dipsomaniac, drunkard, hard case, hard drinker, imbiber, indulger, inebriate, sot, swigger, tippler, toper, winebibber, winedot. *Informal:* Adrian Quist, Alderman Lushington, alkie, alky, bar fly, beer swiper, booze artist, booze hound, boozer, boozican, cheap drunk, dipso, drinking school, drunk, grog artist, guzzle-guts, hophead, Jimmy Woodser, juice-freak, lolly legs, lush, lushington, metho, plonko, pot-walloper, shicker, soak, souse, stiff, tos-spot, two-pot screamer, wineskin, wino. **2. wine connoisseur** oenophile, wine-lover.

8. 1. drinking session bacchanalia, bowl, compotation, happy hour, jamberoo, spree. *Informal:* barney, bash, bat, beer-up, bender, binge, blind, blinder, boatrace, booze, booze up, booze-up, boozeroo *(NZ)*, bouse, bust, drinkies, drunk, grog-on, grog-up, jag, lush, pub crawl, rort, scatter, six o'clock swill, soak. **2. drinks** cocktail party, wine-tasting, winebibbing.

9. 1. pub beer house, beer-hall, drinking house, free house *(British)*, hotel, inn *(British)*, local, public house, tap, taproom *(British)*, tavern, tied house *(British)*. *Informal:* boozer, boozeroo *(NZ)*, grog shop, opera house, rubberdy, rubbidy, shypoo joint, watering hole, watering-place. **2. bar** beer garden, bistro, bodega, bunny club, cocktail bar, cocktail lounge, hot spot, ladies' lounge, ladies' parlour, lounge, lounge bar, nightclub, night-spot, private bar, public, public bar, saloon, saloon bar, taproom *(British)*, wine bar.

Informal: clipjoint, groggery, nineteenth hole, swill. **3. shanty** gin palace. *Informal:* bloodhouse, dive, joint. **4. liquor store** bottle department, bottle shop, bottle store *(NZ)*, cellar door, cellars, off-licence, wine cellar, wineshop. *Informal:* bottlo. **5. illegal liquor store** shebeen, speak-easy *(US)*. *Informal:* grog tent, honky-tonk *(Chiefly US)*, sly-grog shop. **6. brewery** boutique brewery, boutique winery, craft brewery, distillery, microbrewery, still, winery.

10. **1. type of alchohol container** baby, balthazar, beer bottle, cask, demijohn, double magnum, eighteen, flagon, hogshead, jeroboam, keg, kilderkin, magnum, methuselah, nebuchadnezzar, nine, pipe, quarter cask, rehoboam, shot glass, sixpack, tun, wineskin, wood. *Informal:* aristotle, dead marine, goon bag, goon box, pig *(NZ)*, square bear. **2. type of beer glass** blackjack, bobby, butcher, cruiser, half, handle *(Tasmania, NSW, ACT, WA, NT, some Qld, Victoria, SA)*, jar, Lady Blamey, lady's waist, long'un, middy, pint, pint-pot, pixie, pony *(Especially WA, Qld, NSW, ACT)*, pot, pottle, schooner, tankard, ten *(Tasmania, Qld, NSW, ACT, WA, NT, some Qld, Victoria, SA)*. *Informal:* long-sleever. **3. stubby** echo. *Informal:* Darwin stubby, frostie, frosty, glass can. **4. beer can** can, tally *(Chiefly Qld)*. *Informal:* slab, throwdown *(Brisbane Region, Sydney Region)*, tinnie, tube. **5. wine measure** jigger, noggin, tot.

11. **1. winemaking** oenology, viniculture. **2. winemaking process** bottom fermentation, carbonic maceration, champagne method, estufado system, fining, maderisation, malolactic fermentation, tirage, top fermentation, vinification, working. **3. yeast** barleycorn, dosage, finings, hops, John Barleycorn, malt, oenocyanin, wort. **4. barm** beeswing, bottle sickness, casse, crust, slops, suds, tartar, wash. **5. alcoholic strength** spirituousness. **6. vintage** bin, bottle age, brew, tirage. **7. woodiness** stalkiness, velvetiness.

12. **1. brewer** distiller, distilling apparatus, wet. **2. seller of illegal liquor** bootlegger. *Informal:* moonshiner, sly grogger. **3. oenologist** wine-taster, winegrower, winemaker.

13. **1. alcotest** Alcolmeter, breathalyser. *Informal:* bag test, blue balloon, booze bus.

14. **1. type of wine** amontillado, asti spumante, barolo, barsac, beaujolais, blanquette, Bordeaux, burgundy, canary, chablis, champagne, chateau wine, chian, chianti, cider, claret, cream sherry, cyder, gewurztraminer, gluhwein, Hermitage, hermitage, hock, lachryma Christi, médoc, madeira, malaga, malmsey, malvoisie, manzanilla, marsala, Marsanne, mistelle, moselle, muscadet, muscat, muscatel, must, pernod, perry, pink champagne, pinot blanc, porphyry, port, retsina, Rhine riesling, Rhine wine, riesling, rosé, ruby port, sack, sangaree, sauterne, sauvignon blanc, sercial, sherry, solero sherry, sparkling wine, spumante, sticky, sweet cider, tawny port, tokay, vermouth, vinho verde, viognier, white shiraz. *Informal:* red ned, sloshing wine.

15. **1. grape variety** cabernet sauvignon, chardonnay, chenin blanc, Frontignac, grenache, Müller Thurgau, Malbec, malvasia, Malvoisie, Mataro, Merlot, Muscat, Palomino, Pedro Ximenez, sauvignon blanc, semillon, Sercial, shiraz, sylvaner, traminer, trebbiano, verdelho.

16. **1. type of spirit** absinthe, amaretto, angostura bitters, applejack, apricot brandy, aqua vitae, aquavit, arak, Armagnac, bitters, bourbon, brandy, brindabella, cherry brandy, Cognac, cognac, corn *(US)*, eau de vie, feints, gin, grappa, Hollands gin, hospital brandy, Irish whiskey, John Barleycorn, kirsch, liqueur brandy, low wine, marc, mescal, OP, proof spirit, raki, rum, rye, schnapps, Scotch, Scotch whisky, slivovitz, snort, tafia, tequila, vodka, whisky. *Informal:* aunty's downfall, boilermaker, Bundy, dad and mum, hokonui *(NZ)*, hooker *(Chiefly US, Canadian)*, mother's ruin, mountain dew.

17. **1. type of fermented drink** hydromel, kava, koumis, kumis, kvass, mead, methaglyn, quass, rice wine, sake. *Informal:* rosiner.

18. **1. type of liqueur** advocaat, anisette, benedictine, calvados, chartreuse, cointreau, cordial *(US)*, crème de menthe, creme de cacao, curaçao, galliano, grand marnier, hippocras, kümmel, liquid lamington, maraschino, noyau, ouzo, parfait amour, pear William, ratafia, slivovitz, sloe gin.

19. **1. type of cocktail** alcopop, B & D, barmaid's blush, black and tan, black velvet, bloody mary, brandy alexander, claret cup, cobbler, daiquiri, dry martini, eggnog, fizz *(Chiefly US)*, frappé, gin-sling, grog, harvey wallbanger, highball, mai tai, maiden's blush, manhattan, margarita, martini, mint julep *(US)*, negus, nog, peg, pina colada, pink gin, portergaff *(Especially SA)*, posset, punch, sangria, shandy, shrub, Singapore sling, sling, sour, stinger *(US)*, strawberry blonde, swizzle, toddy, Tom and Jerry *(US)*, Tom Collins. *Informal:* paroo sandwich, white lady.

20. **1. publican** innkeeper, lamber-down, licensee, shanty-keeper, vintner. **2. bartender** bar hostess *(SE Asian English)*, bar useful, barkeep *(US)*, barkeeper, barmaid, barman, cellarmaster, drink waiter, skimpy *(WA, NT)*, useful, wine waiter. *Informal:* bar girl *(SE Asian English)*.

adj. **21.** **1. drunk** blind, charged, drunk with, drunken, fighting drunk, in one's cups, inebriate, inebriated, intoxicated, tipsy, winy. *Informal:* blasted, blotto, blued, cast *(NZ)*, chocker, cockeyed, corked, cut, elephants, full, groggy, half-seas-over, high, high as a kite, inked, jagged, legless, lit, lit up, lushy, maggoted, molo, oiled, on the barbed wire *(Qld)*, pickled, pie-eyed, pinko, pixilated, plastered, potted *(US)*, primed, ripe, rolling drunk, screwed, shickered, shot, slewed, sloshed, sodden, sozzled, spiflicated, spliced, stewed, stiff, stinking, stinko, stoked, stonkered, stung, tanked, the worse for wear, three sheets in (or to) the wind, tight, tired and emotional, under the weather, well-oiled. **2. extremely drunk** dead drunk, fuddled, full as a boot (or goog) (or tick), unconscious. *Informal:* dead to the world, drunk as a lord, drunk as Chloe, far gone, flakers, full as a state school, loaded, non compos, not be able to scratch oneself, off one's face, paralytic, ripped, rotten, smashed, stoned, under the table. **3. slightly drunk** elevated, maudlin, tipsy. *Informal:* lushy, merry, muzzy, on the bottle, squiffy, tiddly, tight, woozy. **4. hung-over** *Informal:* gone to Gowings *(NSW)*, morning-after. **5. given to drinking** alcoholic, bacchanalian, bacchic, beery, bibulous, dipsomaniacal, sottish. *Informal:* boozy, bousy, dipso, in the grip of the grape.

22. **1. alcoholic** beery, hard, inebriant, intoxicant, intoxicating, intoxicative, spirituous, vinaceous, vinic, vinous, winy. **2. strong** heady, high-proof, nappy *(British)*, neat, overproof, short, stiff, underproof. *Informal:* gutsy.

23. **1. winy** oenological, vinicultural, viniferous, vintage, winebibbing, winey. **2. vintage** auslese, beerenauslese, cru, estate, flor, oloroso, rancio, rounded, spätlese, velvety. **3. woody** beeswinged, fat, malty, pricked, stalky. **4. dry** brut, fini, petillant, spritzig. **5. home-brewed**.

24. **1. licensed** BYO, BYOG, dry, off-licence, wet. *Informal:* honky-tonk *(US)*.

25. **1. teetotal** abstinent, alcohol-free, grog-free *(Aboriginal English)*.

v. **26.** **1. drink alcohol** down, drink, fuddle, imbibe, quaff, tipple, wassail. *Informal:* booze, get a drink across one's chest, grog, lush, sink, soak it up, sock away, stop one, swig, tip the little finger, wet one's whistle. **2. drink heavily** carouse, indulge, mix one's drinks, tope. *Informal:* bash the turps, bend (or raise) one's elbow, bend the elbow, booze, drink like a fish, get into it, give it a bash, give it a nudge, go on the squiff, go on the stun, go on the tank, grog on, have a skinful, hit the booze, hit the bottle, iron oneself out, lay into it, nudge the bottle, shicker, souse, tank up, write oneself off. **3. shout** *Informal:* be in the chair, carry the mail, sneeze, splice the mainbrace. **4. toast** bumper, wassail. **5. grog run** *Informal:* run the rabbit.

27. **1. intoxicate** befuddle, besot, fuddle, go to someone's head, inebriate, wine. *Informal:* liquor up, souse.

28. **1. brew** distil, maderise, malt, moonshine, rack, vinify, work. **2. alcoholise** lace. *Informal:* spike.

adv. **29.** **1. drunkenly** bibulously, groggily, maudlinly, merrily, sottishly, tipsily, woozily. **2. intoxicatingly** headily. **3. on the drink** *Informal:* on the booze, on the ran-tan, on the razzle *(Chiefly British)*, on the shicker, on the tank, on the turps.

interj. **30.** **1. bottoms up** down the hatch, here's looking at you, here's mud in your eye, here's to, here's to you, prost, skol, to your health. *Informal:* cheers, chug-a-lug.

RELATED KEYWORDS: OVERINDULGENCE, CONTAINER, DRUG, FOOD

ALLEVIATION

n. **1.** **1. alleviation** abatement, assuagement, easement, mitigation, palliation, relaxation, relief, remission, remittal. **2. respite** deliverance, disburdenment, disembarrassment, redemption, reprieve, rescue, rest, truce. **3. solace** appeasement, comfort, consolation, easing, mollification, solacement, soothing. **4. ease** analgesia, comfort, facility, lightness, sedation.

2. **1. alleviator** allayer, assuager, comforter, easer, mitigator, pacifier, palliator, reliever, solacer, soother. **2. salve** alleviant, alleviative, anodyne, balm, balsam, comfort, palliative, solace. **3. analgesic** anodyne, painkiller, paregoric, sedative.

adj. **3.** **1. alleviant** alleviative, alleviatory, assuasive, balmy, balsamaceous, balsamic, demulcent, emollient, lenitive, palliative, soothing. **2. analgesic** anodyne, antineuralgic, antirheumatic, calmative, depressant, paregoric, sedative.

4. **1. soothed** comfortable, easeful, easy, quiet, restful, sedate.

v. **5.** **1. alleviate** abate, adulce, allay, appease, assuage, bate, ease, facilitate, lighten, milden, mitigate, moderate, modify, modulate, mollify, palliate, preside, qualify, relieve, remit, season, slack, soften, sugar the pill, sweeten, tame, tone down, turn down. **2. soothe** allay, assuage, calm, comfort, console, give comfort, hush, mollify, palliate, pat on the back, pour oil on troubled waters, salve, smooth over, smooth the ruffled brow of care, solace, temper, tranquillise. **3. relieve** deliver, disburden, discharge, disembarrass, disencumber, reprieve, rescue, respite.

6. **1. be relieved** breathe more freely, draw (or take) comfort from, respire, take a deep breath.

RELATED KEYWORDS: DECREASE, COMPOSURE, REPAIR, REST, HAPPINESS, IMPROVEMENT, MEDICATION

ALLURE

n. 1. **1. allure** allurement, amiability, animal magnetism, appeal, attraction, bait, charisma, charm, cynosure, enticement, fascination, glamour, magic, sex appeal, sunny disposition, winning ways, zest. *Informal:* fetch, glam, it, mojo *(Chiefly US)*, oomph. **2. draw** crowd-puller, drawcard. **3. lure** allurement, animal magnetism, attractant, attraction, bait, captivation, charm, counterattraction, enchantment, engagement, enticement, fascination, inducement, magnetism, spell. *Informal:* come-on. **4. seduction** allurement, attraction, bait, cajolery, enticement, honeyed words, inveiglement, invitation, palaver, solicitation, temptation. **5. entanglement** ensnarement, entrapment. **6. trap** birdlime, booby trap, butterfly net, drawnet, hook, lime, lure, mantrap, meshes, rat-trap, snare, springe, tin hare, toils, wire.

2. **1. alluringness** attractiveness, buxomness, charm, desirableness, engagingness, invitingness, irresistibleness, kittenishness, lushness, seductiveness, sexiness, sugariness, temptingness, winsomeness, witchery.

3. **1. allurer** attracter, bewitcher, captivator, charmer, desirable, enchanter, engager, enthraller, enticer, fascinator, forbidden fruit, inviter, magnet, magnetiser, object of desire, object of lust, seducer, sex object, sex symbol, tempter. *Informal:* a good sort, dish, dreamboat, good-looker, honey, knockout, looker, stunner. **2. siren** Circe, Delilah, enchantress, femme fatale, houri, Mata Hari, minx, nymphette, seductress, sexpot, temptress, vamper, witch. *Informal:* bit of fluff, foxy lady, mantrap, pin-up, sex kitten, vamp. **3. stud** Casanova, Don Juan, ladies' man, Lothario, rake. *Informal:* daddy, hunk, lady-killer, stud muffin, sugar daddy, wolf. **4. ensnarer** entrapper, inveigler, spider, trapper, waylayer.

adj. 4. **1. alluring** amorous, appealing, appetising, attractive, beautiful, becoming, Circean, come-hither, come-hitherish, concupiscent, delectable, desirable, eligible, enchanting, enticing, enviable, fair, flirtatious, glamorous, good, graceful, intriguing, invitatory, inviting, kissable, kittenish, mouth-watering, much in demand, piquant, popular, preferable, provocative, racy, ravishing, seductive, sensual, sexy, siren, succulent, tempting, thrilling, winsome, zesty. *Informal:* cheeky *(Singaporean and Malaysian English)*, glam, kinky, lush, oomphy, pin-up, plummy, to die for. **2. charismatic** alluring, bewitching, captivating, catching, charming, enchanting, engaging, fascinating, fetching, impressive, interesting, irresistible, magic, magnetic, mesmeric, prepossessing, striking, taking, tempting, winning, winsome, witching. **3. voluptuous** bosomy, busty, buxom, callipygian, comely, cuddlesome, cuddly, curvaceous, curvy, full-bodied, shapely, sonsy *(Scottish, Irish)*, well-proportioned, well-rounded.

5. **1. captivated** carried away, enamoured, enchanted, enthralled, fascinated, much taken by, overcome, seduced, smitten, spellbound, struck by, tempted. **2. aroused** libidinous, lustful, on heat, rampant, sexually excited.

v. 6. **1. allure** attract, becharm, beckon, beguile, bewitch, captivate, charm, court, enchant, enmesh, ensorcel *(Poetic)*, entice, fascinate, intrigue, inveigle, invite, magnetise, mesmerise, seduce, smite, spellbind, tantalise, tempt, titillate, vamp, wheedle, witch. **2. lure** allure, bait, catch, ensnare, entice, entrap, mesh, waylay.

7. **1. enchant** allure, appeal to, appetise, arouse, attract, be (much) in demand, becharm, beguile, bewitch, bowl someone over, captivate, charm, create desire, engage, enrapture, ensorcell *(Poetic)*, enthral, entrance, excite desire, have a way with one, ravish, stimulate, take one's fancy, tempt, wile. *Informal:* fetch, knock sideways, knock someone's eye out, make one's mouth water.

adv. 8. **1. alluringly** attractively, buxomly, desirably, enticingly, glamorously, intriguingly, invitingly, kittenishly, piquantly, ravishingly, seductively, sexily, temptingly, witchingly, zestily. **2. appealingly** bewitchingly, charismatically, enchantingly, engagingly, fascinatingly, fetchingly, irresistibly, magically, magnetically, strikingly.

RELATED KEYWORDS: ATTRACTION, BEAUTY

ALPHABET

n. **1.** **1. alphabet** ABC. **2. type of alphabet** abecedary, Cyrillic alphabet, futhorc, Greek alphabet, International Phonetic Alphabet, IPA, phonetic alphabet, roman alphabet, runic alphabet. **3. alphabetisation** acrophony, charactery, kana, notation, syllabary, transliteration.

2. **1. letter** alphanumeric, character, digraph, grapheme, hieroglyphic, ideogram, ideograph, numeral, rune, sign, sphenogram, stenograph, trigraph. **2. cipher** cuneiform, lettering, monogram, ogham, script, stencil, stenotype. **3. sound** allophone, cardinal vowel, consonant, continuant, diphthong, homophone, phone, phoneme, polyphone, vowel. **4. print type** character face, print, typeface. **5. style of print type** block capital, block letter, block type, Gothic, initial, italics, roman. **6. capital letter** capital, caps, majuscule, small capitals, uncial, upper case. **7. small letter** lower case, minuscule. **8. superscript** adscript, cock-up, subindex, subscript, superior. **9. letter part** ascender, descender.

adj. **3.** **1. alphabetical** abecedarian, alphanumeric.

v. **4.** **1. alphabetise** put into alphabetical order.

RELATED KEYWORDS: PRINTING, WRITING, SIGN, WORD

AMUSEMENT

n. **1.** **1. amusement** dissipation, distraction, diversion, divertissement, entertainment, fun, game, hobby, pastime, play, recreation, relaxation, sport. **2. romp** buffoonery, caper, cheer, frolic, fun, gaieties, horseplay, lark, prank, spree. *Informal:* shine. **3. sportiveness** frolicsomeness, gamesomeness, rompishness, sportfulness. **4. fun and games** amusement, enjoyment, fun, play, pleasure. **5. revelry** carnival, celebration, festivities, frolic, gaieties, gaudy *(British)*, good cheer, jollification, merrymaking, revel, revels, shindy. *Informal:* whoopee. **6. carnival** festival, Mardi Gras. **7. playtime** break. **8. toy** plaything, puzzle.

2. **1. player** gamer, gamesman. **2. enjoyer** dabbler, dilettante. **3. frolicker** larker, reveller. **4. card player** banker, dealer, discarder, dummy, elder hand, lone hand, maker, pairs, pone.

3. **1. amusement park** carnival, fair, fun fair, fun park, theme park. **2. fairground amusement** amusement, Aunt Sally *(Chiefly British)*, big dipper, bouncy castle, carousel, coaster *(US)*, coconut-shy, Ferris wheel, fun castle, ghost train, hall of mirrors, helter-skelter, hurdy-gurdy, jumping castle, merry-go-round, river caves, roller-coaster, roundabout, scenic railway, sideshow, swing boat, switchback, water slide, whirlabout, whirligig. **3. play centre** creative leisure centre, leisure centre. **4. fun parlour** amusement arcade, casino, midway *(US)*, penny arcade, poolroom. **5. playroom** cubbyhouse, nursery, playhouse, rumpus room, Wendy house *(Chiefly British)*. **6. playground** adventure playground, park, passive open space, sandpit. **7. playground equipment** jungle gym, monkey bars, seesaw, slide, slippery dip, slippery slide, swing.

4. **1. card game** écarté, all-fours, ante-up, auction bridge, baccarat, banker, beggar-my-neighbour, bezique, blackjack, bridge, canasta, canfield, cassino, chemin de fer, cinch, conquian, contract bridge, cooncan, cribbage, euchre, faro, five hundred, gin, gin rummy, grab, happy families, hearts, lansquenet, loo, manilla, monte, nap, napoleon, old maid, ombre, pam, patience, pedro *(US Cards)*, penuchle, pinochle, piquet, pitch, poker, pontoon, quadrille, rouge et noir, rummy, seven-up, sevens, skat, slapjack, snap, solitaire *(US)*, solo, strip poker, stud, stud game, stud poker, tarots, Texas hold 'em, trente et quarante, twenty-one, vingt-et-un, whist. *Informal:* chemmy. **2. playing card** ace, bower, cards, court card, deck *(Chiefly US)*, face card, high, honour, jack, joker, king, knave, low, major arcanum, matador, nob, pack, pam, pedro *(US Cards)*, pentagram, picture card, pinochle, quart major, queen, quint, side card, soda, talon, tierce, trump, wild card. **3. card hand** barmaid's blush, book, crossruff, discard, double, finesse, flush, four of a kind, four-flush, full house, goulash, grand slam, lay-down misère, little slam, make, meld, misère, no-trumper, overtrick, pair, quick trick, re-entry, redouble, round, routine, royal flush, royal routine, rubber, ruff, seesaw, sequence, slam, slough, square deal, stop, straight, straight flush, sweep, tenace, trick, triplets, undertrick, Whitechapel, widow, Yarborough. **4. suit** club, clubs, diamond, diamonds, heart, hearts, long suit, major suit, minor suit, spade, spades.

5. **1. board game** backgammon, chequers, chess, Chinese chequers, correspondence chess, draught, gammon, go, halma, ludo, Monopoly, pachisi, parcheesi, postal chess, Scrabble, shovelboard, shuffleboard, snakes and ladders, solitaire, tricktrack, trictrac. **2. chess piece** bishop, castle, chequer, chessman, draught, draughtsman, king, knight, man, pawn, piece, queen, rook. **3. chess terms** check, checkmate, en passant, end-game, endplay, mate, middle game, opening, self-mate, stalemate.

6. 1. billiards bar billiards, pocket billiards, pool, pyramids, snooker. **2. billiards terms** baulk line, break, bricole, bridge, cannon, carom, cue ball, follow, frame, in baulk, in-off, jigger, mace, massé, plant, rest, side, spot-ball, string, string line, White-chapel.

7. 1. parlour game beetle, bo-peep, charades, consequences, crambo, crossword puzzle, flapdragon, forfeits, hunt the slipper, I-spy, magic square, musical chairs, nim, noughts-and-crosses, O'Grady says, peekaboo, quiz, Simon says, snapdragon, tick-tack-toe *(US)*, tit-tat-toe, word association, word game.

8. 1. arcade game air hockey, claw machine, coconut shy, fuss ball, pin ball, shooting gallery, the clowns. *Informal:* pong.

9. 1. electronic game arcade game, computer game, console game, video game. *Informal:* spacies.

10. 1. children's game blindman's buff, brandings, brandy, British bulldog, cat's cradle, cherrybobs, cockylora, conkers *(British)*, dibs, dress-ups, ducks and drakes *(British)*, elastics, fiddlesticks, five-stones, fly, follow-the-leader, hide-and-go-seek, hide-and-seek, hidey, hidey-seek, hidings, hopscotch, jacks, jackstraw, keepings off, paperchase, pass the parcel, pepper, piggy-in-the-middle, Queenie, sardines, scavenger hunt, skipping, skipping stones, spin the bottle, stacks on the mill, string game, tag, tiggy touchwood.

11. 1. ball game captain ball, drawings-back, forcings-back, kingpin, pelota, punch ball *(US)*, pushball, T-ball, tunnel ball.

12. 1. marble acker, agate, aggie, alley, American, bottler, darts, domino, doog, doogs, fat, glassey, glassie, glassy, peewee, taw, taws.

13. 1. games – miscellaneous all-fives, bagatelle, bingo, candlepins, cat, deck tennis, diabolo, dice, fan-tan, fivepins, hazard, hob, hoopla, horseshoe *(US)*, housie-housie, hoy, lotto, mahjong, muggins, ninepin, ninepins, pinball, pinnie, pitch-and-toss, poker dice, pussy, quoit, skittles, table skittles, tiddlywinks, tipcat, tombola, trivia, war game.

14. 1. toy action figure, alphabet block, babushka doll, ball, balloon, beanbag, building block, cockhorse, disc, doll, doll's house, dolly, Dutch doll, fizgig, frisbee, glove puppet, golliwog, golly, hobby, hobbyhorse, hoop, hula hoop, jack-in-the-box, jigsaw puzzle, jumping jack, jumprope, Lego, matchbox toy, meccano set, moppet, peashooter, peg top, plush toy, pogo stick, popgun, puppet, rattle, rocking horse, Rubik's cube, Russian doll, skipping-rope, slinky, squirt gun *(Chiefly US)*, teddy, teddy bear, teetotum, tin soldier, top, tumbler, water pistol, whipping top, whirlabout, whirligig, yoyo.

adj. **15. 1. amused** distracted, diverted, entertained. **2. sportive** frisky, frolicsome, game-some, jesting, jocose, larksome, playful, rompish, scherzando, sportful.

16. 1. amusing cheerful, distractive, diversionary, diverting, divertive, entertaining, light, recreational. *Informal:* fun.

v. **17. 1. amuse oneself** disport oneself, have fun, play, recreate, sport. **2. trifle with** dabble, dally, toy, toy with. **3. romp** fool around, frisk, frolic, gambol, play up, skylark. *Informal:* horse about (or around), play silly (or funny) buggers.

18. 1. amuse distract, divert, entertain, tickle.

adv. **19. 1. playfully** friskily, frolicsomely, gamesomely, sportively. **2. for fun** for kicks, in fun. **3. amusingly** enjoyably.

RELATED KEYWORDS: HUMOUR, JOY, SOCIABILITY, SPORT

ANALYSIS

n. **1. 1. analysis** appraisal, appraisement, assay, assessment, breakdown, criticism, critique, diagnosis, diagnostic, test. **2. inquiry** enquiry, examination, investigation, probe *(US)*, review, reviewal, scan, scrutiny, study. **3. methodology** analytical procedure, classifi-cation, exhaustive study, graphing, ordering, random sampling, reductionism, sifting, sorting, SWOT analysis, systematisation, tabulating. **4. microanalysis** biodiscovery, chromatography, destructive distillation, dry distillation, gas chromatography, gas-liquid chromatography, on-stream analysis, paper chromatography, vapour-phase chromato-graphy, volumetric analysis. **5. dissection** anatomisation, anatomy, autopsy, biopsy, post-mortem examination, segmentation. **6. analytics** critical-path analysis, input-output analysis, marginalism, operations research, principal components analysis, systems analysis, variable rule analysis. **7. analytical display** distribution, frequency distribu-tion, graph, histogram, isothermal line, pie chart, pie graph, plot *(Chiefly US)*, record, register, scattergram, table.

2. **1. analyst** analyser, appraiser, assayer, assessor, deriver, dissector, prosector, reductionist, scanner, tester. *Informal:* nuts-and-bolts man.

v. 3. **1. analyse** anatomise, appraise, arrange, assay, assess, break down, catalogue, classify, codify, derive, digest, distinguish, evaluate, file, group, interpret, list, problematise, pull apart, pull to pieces, rank, reduce to order, sift, sort, test, unravel, winnow. **2. dissect** prosect, randomise, segment. **3. inquire into** canvass, examine, explore, investigate, look into, probe, research, review, scan, scrutinise, search, sound, study.

RELATED KEYWORDS: CLASSIFICATION, CALCULATION, MEASUREMENT, ORDER, QUESTION, TEST

ANARCHY

n. 1. **1. anarchy** blackboard jungle, cataclysm, chaos, civil disobedience, disorder, pandemonium, tumult, turbulence, turmoil. **2. lawlessness** brute force, disorderliness, lynch law, misrule, unruliness, Wild West. **3. irresponsibility** arbitrariness. **4. anarchism** nihilism, ruffianism, seditiousness.

2. **1. rebellion** act of defiance, commotion, counter-revolution, insurgence, insurgency, insurrection, mutiny, outbreak, palace revolution, putsch, resistance, revolt, revolution, rising, sedition, unauthorised march, unauthorised stoppage, uprising, violation of the law, wildcat strike.

3. **1. anarchist** destructionist, nihilist, revolutionary, revolutionist *(US)*. **2. despiser of the law** Hell's Angel, irresponsible, outlaw, ruffian, seditionary. *Informal:* mad mullah. **3. street fighter** urban guerilla.

adj. 4. **1. anarchic** anarchistic, chaotic, disobedient, insubordinate, insurgent, mutinous, nihilistic, rebellious, recalcitrant, revolutionary, seditionary, seditious. **2. lawless** disorderly, headless, helmless, illegal, riotous, turbulent, unattended, unchartered, unregulated, unruly. **3. unruly** dissolute, fractious, incontrollable, lawless, libertine, licentious, loose, obstreperous, pandemonic, rampageous, riotous, turbulent, uncontrollable, ungovernable, wanton. *Informal:* rambunctious *(US)*. **4. irresponsible** impetuous, lawless, ruffian, runaway, unbitted, unbounded, unbridled, uncontrolled, wild. *Informal:* tearaway. **5. arbitrary** absolute, tyrannical, unilateral, unwarranted.

v. 5. **1. rebel** anarchise, destabilise, disobey, mutiny, resist, ride roughshod over, run riot, take the law into one's own hands, transgress, violate.

adv. 6. **1. anarchically** arbitrarily, high-handedly, irresponsibly, lawlessly, out of order, seditiously, unwarrantedly.

RELATED KEYWORDS: MISBEHAVIOUR, UNLAWFULNESS, DISORDER, REVOLUTION

ANGER

n. 1. **1. anger** annoyance, blood and thunder, choler, fury, ill temper, indignation, infuriation, ire, pique, rage, resentment, temper, vehemence, vexation, wrath. **2. angriness** crankiness, furiousness, furore, fury, hastiness, incensement, irefulness, lividness, passion, resentfulness, savageness, savagery, shrewishness, vehemence, violence, wrathfulness. **3. irascibleness** passionateness, prickliness. **4. road rage** water rage. *Informal:* hose rage.

2. **1. acrimony** acrimoniousness, asperity, bitterness, enmity, hatred, ill feeling, intolerance, rancorousness, rancour, resentment, sourness, verjuice. **2. sullenness** sulkiness, sulks.

3. **1. tantrum** act, blow-up, explosion, fireworks, flare, flare-up, huff, outburst, pelter, rage, ramp, rampage, tear. *Informal:* hissy fit, paddy, paddywhack, tanter, wax, wobbly. **2. dirty look** frown, glare, glower, lour, scowl, sneer. **3. diatribe** rant, yap.

4. **1. angry person** angry young man, crabstick, hellcat, maenad, menad, ranter, scold, shrew, spitfire, termagant, thunderbolt, virago, vixen, wildcat, xanthippe.

adj. 5. **1. angry** ablaze, blazing, blowzy, choleric, cranky, cross, cross as two sticks, furious, hopping, hot under the collar, ill-tempered, indignant, infuriate, infuriated, irate, ireful, like a bear with a sore head, livid, mad, mad with rage, rampant, ranting, red-faced, spiteful, sulky *(Aboriginal English)*, up in arms, vexed, wrathful, wroth, wrought. *Informal:* aggro, cheesed-off, crooked on, dark, dirty, fit to be tied, full up, grumpy, hairy, lemony, mad as a hornet, mad as a maggot, mad as a meataxe, maggoty, on the warpath, red-hot, ropeable, snaky, snotty, spewing, steamed-up, tooshie, uptight, wally. **2. fed up** huffy, sick to death. *Informal:* browned off, fed up to the back teeth, fed up to the gills, jack of, shirty, sick. **3. bad-tempered** apoplectic, black-browed, cantankerous, choleric, cranky, cursed, dark, easily aroused, evil, fiery, hasty, ill-tempered, irascible, irritable, mean, prickly, quick-tempered, savage, short-tempered, verjuice. *Informal:* ornery *(US)*, scotty. **4. glaring** lowering, wild-eyed.

6. **1. acrimonious** acerbate, angry, bitter, caustic, fierce, heated, irascible, maenadic, passionate, peppery, quick-tempered, rancorous, shrewish, vehement, virulent, warm. *Informal:* lemony. **2. resentful** aggrieved, beetle-browed, dark, dour, hurt, indignant, peeved, sulky, sullen. *Informal:* narked.

7. **1. vexing** annoying, inciting, invidious, irritating, odious, provocative, provoking.

v. 8. **1. be angry** bite, bite back, boil, boil over, bridle, bristle, flame, flare up, flash, growl, lash out, let fly, let go, let off steam, lose one's temper, rage, rampage, rant, rear, see red, storm, throw a fit, throw a tantrum, thunder, yap. *Informal:* arc up, blow a fuse, blow a gasket, blow one's top, blow up, bung (or stack) on an act, do one's bun *(NZ)*, do one's cruet, do one's lolly, do one's nana, do one's nut, do one's quince, do one's scone, flip one's lid, fly off the handle, fly out, foam at the mouth, fume, get off one's bike, get one's back up, get one's Irish up, get one's monkey up, give curry, gnash one's teeth, go ballistic, go bananas, go crook, go crook at (or on), go hostile *(NZ)*, go off one's brain, go off pop, go off the deep end, go postal *(Chiefly US)*, go psycho, go spare, hit the ceiling (or roof), let rip, lose (or blow) one's cool, lose (or do) one's block, lose it, lose one's wool, perform, ramp, sound off, spit chips, tear one's hair out, throw (or chuck) a micky, throw a willy. **2. be fed up** broil, grudge. *Informal:* have a skinful. **3. glower** darken, glare, lour, sulk.

9. **1. anger** annoy, enrage, huff, incense, inflame, infuriate, irritate, madden, pique, provoke, put someone's back up, rile, rouse, vex. *Informal:* get (or take) a rise out of. **2. irritate** aggravate, anger, provoke, vex.

10. **1. be angry with** *Informal:* be crook on, be crooked on, be dirty on, come the acid over *(NZ)*, get one's knife into, go butchers (hook) at, go crook at (or on), look daggers at, roar someone up, snap someone's head off, take it out on, tell off. **2. resent** take amiss, take exception to. *Informal:* sweat.

adv. 11. **1. angrily** apoplectically, furiously, in a fury, in a huff, in a rage, in high dudgeon, indignantly, irately, irefully, lividly, rampantly, red-facedly, with one's hackles up, wrathfully. **2. crankily** hastily, irascibly. **3. acrimoniously** rancorously, shrewishly, virulently. **4. gloweringly** loweringly. **5. resentfully** huffily, sulkily, sullenly, umbrageously. **6. fiercely** passionately, savagely, vehemently, warmly. **7. infuriatingly** provocatively, provokingly. **8. invidiously** odiously.

RELATED KEYWORDS: ANNOYANCE, EXCITEMENT, DISCONTENTEDNESS, EMOTION, UNHAPPINESS, IRRITABLENESS, HATE, VIOLENCE

ANIMAL NOISE

n. 1. **1. animal noise** call, cry. **2. roar** bell, bellow, roaring, trumpet. **3. howl** caterwaul, hoot, screech, ululation. **4. growl** grunt, snarl, snort. **5. bark** bay, bow-wow, howl, whine, woof, yap, yelp, yip *(Chiefly US)*. **6. mew** miaow, purr. **7. bray** heehaw. **8. bleat** baa. **9. whinny** neigh, nicker *(Scottish)*. **10. moo** low. **11. whimper** squeak, whine. **12. oink**.

2. **1. bird call** birdsong, charm, cheep, chirm, chirp, chirr, chirrup, chitter, coo, cuckoo, peep, roll, screech, squawk, toot, trill, tweet, twitter, warble. **2. cackle** caw, clack, clang, clink, clucking, croak. **3. song** note, pipe, piping, woodnote. **4. dawn chorus** matin song, matins *(Poetic)*, mattin. **5. crowing** cock-a-doodle-doo, cockcrow, gobble, hiss, honk, quack, swan song.

3. **1. buzzing** buzz, chirp, chirr, drone, hum, humming, whine. **2. croak** ribbit.

4. **1. barker** bellower, bleater, brayer, growler, grunter, howler, roarer, snarler, yelper. **2. croaker** honker, squawker, whooper. **3. chirruper** cackler, chirper, hooter, twitterer.

v. 5. **1. call** cry, laugh, screech, sing, speak, talk, whistle. **2. roar** bell, bellow, blare, trumpet. **3. howl** caterwaul, hoot, ululate, wail. **4. bark** bay, bay at the moon, challenge, give tongue, growl, grunt, snap, snarl, woof, yap, yelp. **5. bray** heehaw. **6. baa** bleat. **7. whinny** neigh, snicker, snort, whicker. **8. mew** meow, miaow, pur, purr. **9. moo** low. **10. whimper** squeak, whine. **11. oink**.

6. **1. chirp** bill and coo, cheep, chirk, chirm, chirrup, chitter, coo, cuckoo, peep, pip, roocoocoo, screech, squeak, trill, tweet, twitter, warble. **2. cackle** caw, clack, clang, cluck, gabble, gaggle, gobble, squark, squawk, waul, wawl. **3. crow** cock-a-doodle-doo, croak, gobble, hiss, honk, quack, whoop. **4. cluck** chuck, chuckle, clack.

7. **1. buzz** chirp, chirr, drone, hum, whine.

RELATED KEYWORDS: ANIMALS, SHOUTING, SHRILLNESS, SOUND, SPEECH

ANIMALS

n. **1.**   **1. animals** animal kingdom, animality, fauna. **2. animal** animalculum, beast, brute, creature, zooid. *Informal:* critter *(US).* **3. wild animal** wilding, wildlife, wildling. **4. livestock** farm animals, stock. **5. crossbred** bitser, cross, crossbreed, grade, half-blood, half-breed, hybrid, mongrel, mule. *Informal:* bitzer, mong. **6. vermin** varmint. **7. game** big game. **8. carnivore** herbivore, insectivore, omnivore. **9. pet. 10. zoo** animal park, deer-park, insectarium, menagerie, vivarium, zoological gardens, zoological park.

2.   **1. animal kingdom phylum** Acanthocephala, Annelida, Arthropoda, Bivalvia, Brachiopoda, Bryozoa, Caudofoveata, Cephalochordata, Cephalopoda, Chaetognatha, Chelicerata, Chordata, Cnidaria, Crustacea, Ctenophora, Cycliophora, Echinodermata, Enteropneusta, Gastropoda, Gastrotricha, Insecta, Kinorhyncha, Loricifera, Mollusca, Monoplacophora, Myriapoda, Nematoda, Nematomorpha, Nemertea, Onychophora, Phoronida, Placazoa, Platyhelminthes, Polyplacophora, Porifera, Priapulida, Pterobranchia, Pycnogonida, Rotifera, Scaphopoda, Sipuncula, Solanogastres, Tardigrada, Urochordata, Vertebrata.

3.   **1. megafauna. 2. Australian megafauna** diprotodont, giant short-faced kangaroo (Procoptodon goliath), monitor lizard (Megalania prisca), saltwater crocodile, thunder bird (Genyornis).

4.   **1. microfauna** microbe, mite. **2. protozoa – amoebae** amoeba, endamoeba, foraminifer, heliozoan, nummulite, protozoan. **3. ciliates** ciliate, paramecium, vorticella. **4. sporozoa** gregarine, sporozoan. **5. flagellates** dinoflagellate, euglena, flagellate, karlodinium micrum, noctiluca, trichomonad.

5.   **1. Porifera – sponges** bath sponge, glass sponge, sponge, Venus' flower basket.

6.   **1. Cnidaria** coelenterate. **2. anemones** actinia, actinozoan, alcyonarian, anthozoan, bloodsucker, sea anemone, sea pen, sea waratah, sea-feather, sertularian, waratah anemone. **3. soft corals** dead men's fingers, gorgonian, sea fan. **4. hard corals** coral, coralline, gorgonian, madrepore, millepore, stony coral. **5. jellyfish** hydra, hydroid, hydromedusa, hydrozoan, jelly blubber, medusa, medusan, polyp, polypus, sallee rover, scyphozoan. **6. box jellyfish** marine stinger, sea stinger, sea wasp. **7. hydrozoans** bluebottle, by-the-wind sailor, man-of-war, Portuguese man-of-war *(British, US)*, sallee rover, siphonophore.

7.   **1. Ctenophora** comb jelly, ctenophore, sea gooseberry, Venus's girdle.

8.   **1. worms. 2. Annelida** annelid. **3. Acanthocephala** acanthocephalan. **4. Platyhelminthes** platyhelminth. **5. Echiura** anchor worm, echiuran. **6. Sipuncula** peanut worm, sipunculid. **7. Nemertea** nemertean, ribbon worm. **8. Aschelminthes** gastrotrich, penis worm, priapulid, rotifer. **9. Nematoda** ascarid, eelworm, filaria, gapeworm, guinea worm, heartworm, hookworm, kidney worm, lungworm, nemathelminth, nematode, pinworm, roundworm, stomach worm, strongyle, threadworm, trichina, vinegar eel, wheatworm, whipworm, wireworm. **10. horsehair worms** hairworm.

9.   **1. Onychophora** onychophoran, peripatus.

10.   **1. Chelicerata – Arachnida** acarid, acaridan, arachnid, arachnoid, bird-eating spider, bird-spider, black house spider, black widow, book scorpion, brown spider, cattle tick, cheese mite, chigga, chigger, crab spider, daddy-long-legs, diadem spider, fiddleback, funnel-web, harvest mite, harvest tick, harvester, harvestman, huntsman, itch mite, jockey spider, jumping spider, katipo, ked, mite, money spider, mouse spider, orb-weaver, red mite, red-back, redbug *(US)*, retiarius spider, Saint Andrew's Cross spider, scorpion, spider, tarantula, tick, trapdoor spider, triantelope, vinegarroon, water spider, whip scorpion, white-tailed spider, wolf spider.

11.   **1. Chelicerata – horseshoe crabs** eurypterid, horseshoe crab, king crab, limuloid, limulus, xiphosuran.

12.   **1. Crustacea** amphipod, anomuran, Balmain bug, banana prawn, barnacle, beach flea, blue manna *(WA)*, blue swimmer, bluey, brachyuran, branchiopod, cirriped, coconut crab, copepod, crab, crawbob *(NSW, Qld)*, crawchie *(Coastal Qld and North-Eastern NSW)*, crawfish *(Chiefly US)*, craybob *(Especially NSW and Southern Qld)*, craydab *(NSW, ACT)*, crayfish, crustacean, cuttlefish, decapod, euphausiasiid, fairy shrimp, fiddler crab, fish-louse, freshwater crayfish, frog crab, ghost nipper, gilgie, gribble, hermit crab, isopod, jilgie, king crab, king prawn, koura *(NZ)*, krill, land crab, langouste, lobby *(Chiefly Qld)*, lobster, macruran, malacostracan, mandibulate, mantis crab, Moreton Bay bug, mud crab, opossum shrimp, oyster crab, pagurian, pea crab, phyllopod, pink nipper *(Qld)*, prawn, robber crab, rock lobster, sand crab *(Especially Qld)*, sandflea, sandhopper, schizopod, school prawn, sea crayfish, sea spider, shellfish, shovel-nosed lobster, shrimp, slater, soft-shelled crab, soldier crab, sowbug *(US)*, spanner crab, spider crab, spiny lobster, squilla, stomatopod, tiger prawn, trilobite, water flea, wood-borer, woodlouse, yabby. *Informal:* cray, kingie, muddie, sandie *(Chiefly Qld)*, schoolie.

13.   **1. Uniramia – centipedes**   centipede, chilopod, house centipede, myriapod. **2. millipedes**   diplopod, millepede, myriapod, wireworm.

14.   **1. insect**   bitie, bloodsucker, borer, bug, grub, hexapod, imago, zonkerpede. *Informal:* creepy-crawly. **2. larva** instar. **3. insect colony** hive, termitarium, vespiary. **4. invertebrate** arthropod, segmented invertebrate. **5. cicada** black prince, double drummer, green Monday, greengrocer, Union Jack, yellow Monday. *Informal:* floury baker, red-eye. **6. worm** annelid, earthworm, helminth, leech, tube worm, vermicule.

15.   **1. insect part**   aculeus, austellum, proboscis, sting, stinger. **2. feeler** antenna, palp, palpus, tentacle. **3. compound eye** ommateum, ommatidium. **4. segment** abdomen, head, mesothorax, metathorax, prothorax, thorax. **5. insect wing** elytron, elytrum, forewing, hemelytron, hemielytron, wing-case, wing-sheath.

16.   **1. Uniramia – insects**   Africanised bee, alderfly, Amazon ant, American cockroach, ant lion, aphid, Argentine ant, army ant, assassin bug, bedbug, bee, beef ant, black beetle *(NZ)*, blowfly, blue ant, bluebottle, booklouse, bookworm, borer, bristletail, bronze orange bug, bug, bull ant, bulldog ant, bumblebee, caddis fly, caddis worm, carpenter bee, chalcid fly, chigger, chigoe, chinch bug, chironomid, cicada, cicada hunter, cimex, click beetle, coccid, cochineal, cockroach, collembolan, cootie, cottony-cushion scale, crab, crablouse, cricket, cuckoo-spit, culex, culicid, damsel fly, dayfly, demoiselle, devil's darning needle, dor, dragonfly, driver ant, dun, earwig, ephemera, ephemerid, ergate, false acacia, field cricket, firebrat, flea, flower wasp, froghopper, gall midge, gall wasp, gallfly, gnat, grasshopper, greenfly, greenhead, grub, hexapod, hive bee, honey locust, hornet, horntail, humblebee, hymenopter, hymenopteron, ichneumon, ichneumon fly, insect, isopteran, jigger, jumper ant, jumping plant louse, katydid, killer bee, lac insect, lacewing, leaf-hopper, leaf-miner, lepidopteron, locust, longicorn, louse, maggot, mantis, Maori beetle, mason bee, mason wasp, mayfly, mealworm, mealy bug, meat ant, midge, mole cricket, mosquito, mound ant, mud dauber, mud eye, myrmecophile, naiad, nit, nymph, orthopteron, phylloxera, plague locust, plant-louse, policeman fly, pond-skater, praying mantis, psyllid, roach, Rutherglen bug, sandflea, sandgroper, sawfly, scale insect, scorpion-fly, silverfish, skater, skipper, slave ant, snapping beetle, soldier, soldier ant, spittle insect, squeaker, stick insect, stonefly, swarm, sweat bee, termite, thrips, thynnid, thysanuran, tick, vespid, walking-stick *(US, NZ)*, wasp, water scorpion, water strider, wax insect, white ant, wingless grasshopper, wood ant, woodworm, worker, yellow jack, yellow jacket, zonkerpede, zygopteran. *Informal:* blowie, bull, bull Joe, butcher's canary, cocky, creepy-crawly, dunny budgie, horse-stinger, pisser, pisswhacker, skeeter, skitterbug. **2. insect life stages** bloodworm, chrysalis, cocoon, drone, imago, instar, larva, maggot, nymph, pupa, queen, worker, wriggler.

17.   **1. Australasian insects**   awheto *(NZ)*, black prince, blowfly cicada, bollworm, cherry nose, coon bug, cotton-feed bug, double drummer, emperor gum moth, greengrocer, Hexham grey, honey ant, honey-pot ant, huhu, kootchar, magnetic termite, pink bollworm, sawyer *(NZ)*, taipo *(NZ)*, thynnid, vedalia, weta, witchetty grub, yellow Monday. *Informal:* floury baker, pisswhacker, red-eye.

18.   **1. moths and butterflies**   admiral, army worm, Atlas moth, bag moth, bagworm, bardi, bee moth, bentwing swift moth, blue fanny, blue triangle, bogong, bogong moth, bollworm, bombycid, brimstone, bugong, burnet, burnet moth, cabbage butterfly, cabbage moth, cabbage white butterfly, cabbage worm, cactoblastis, Camberwell beauty, cankerworm, case moth, caseworm, caterpillar, chrysalid, chrysalis, cinnabar, clothes moth, codling moth, comma, comma butterfly, corn earworm *(US)*, cup moth, cutworm, death's-head moth, diamondback moth, double-headed hawk, eggar, egger, emperor moth, Etiella moth, forester, fritillary, geometrid, ghost moth, giant wood moth, grayling, ground beetle, gypsy moth, hairstreak, hawkmoth, hepialid, hornworm, hummingbird moth, inchworm, Io, Io moth, lepidopteron, looper, luna moth, measuring worm, meloid, monarch, moth, mountain blue butterfly, mourning cloak, noctuid, nymphalid, painted applemoth, painted lady, painted woman, pyralid, red admiral, saturniid, satyr, Saunder's case moth, silkworm, skipper, sphinx moth, spitfire, sting moth, swallowtail, swift moth, tent caterpillar, tineid moth, tortoiseshell, tussock moth, Ulysses butterfly, wanderer, wax moth, whistling moth, white, white admiral. *Informal:* cacto, flutter-by, woolly bear.

19.   **1. beetles**   ambrosia beetle, bardi, bark beetle, bee-beetle, beetle, black beetle, blister beetle, boll weevil, bombardier beetle, borer, buprestid, burying beetle, cadelle, cane-beetle, cantharidin, carpet beetle, chafer, clavicorn, click beetle, cockchafer, coleopteron, Colorado beetle, curculio, deathwatch beetle, diamond beetle, dorbeetle, dung beetle, elaterid, fiddleback, fiddler beetle, firefly, flea-beetle, glow-worm, goldsmith beetle, jewel beetle, June bug, kurrajong-pod beetle, ladybird, ladybug *(US)*, lamellicorn, lightning bug, meloid, pie-dish beetle, potato beetle, rhinoceros beetle, rove-beetle, scarab, scarabaeid, scarabaeus, snapping beetle, snout beetle, soldier beetle, Spanish fly, stag-beetle, tiger beetle, water beetle, whirligig beetle, wireworm.

20. **1. flies and mosquitoes** aëdes, anopheles, bee-fly, bee-killer, beetfly, black fly, blowfly, bluebottle, botfly, bush fly, cabbage fly, cleg, cranefly, drosophila, flesh-fly, flies, fly, fruit fly, fungus fly, gadfly, glow-worm, gnat *(Chiefly British)*, greenfly, Hessian fly, horsefly, housefly, hoverfly, march fly, mosquito, mossie, muscid, robber fly, sandfly, screw-worm, sheep tick, syrphid, tabanid, tachina fly, tsetse fly, tzetze fly, vinegar fly, warble fly. *Informal:* blowie, blue-arsed fly, butcher's canary, dunny budgie, mozzie, sandie, skeeter.

21. **1. Platyhelminthes – free-living flatworms** flatworm, planarian, platyhelminth, turbellarian. **2. flukes** bilharzia, cercaria, fluke, liver fluke, redia, schistosome, trematode. **3. tapeworms** bladder worm, cestode, cysticercoid, cysticercus, hydatid, stomach worm, taenia, tenia *(US)*, wireworm.

22. **1. Ectoprocta** bryozoan, lophophorate, retepore, sea moss.

23. **1. Brachiopoda** brachiopod, lamp-shell, lophophorate.

24. **1. Mollusca – chitons** chiton, mollusc. **2. gastropods** abalone, australwink, cockle, conch, concha, cone shell, cowry, dogwhelk, drill, ear fish, gasteropod, gastropod, Glavert's land snail, keyhole limpet, limpet, murex, mutton-fish, nudibranch, opisthobranch, paua, periwinkle, pulmonate, sea butterfly, sea ear, sea hare, sea lemon, shellfish, slug, snail, tooth shell, towershell, triton, trochus, volute, wentletrap, whelk, winkle. *Informal:* shellback *(Chiefly Tasmania)*. **3. bivalves** cherry stone *(US)*, clam, eugarie *(Chiefly Qld)*, Goolwa cockle *(SA)*, lamellibranch, mussel, oyster, oyster white, pearl oyster, piddock, pipi, pippy, potato scallop, razorshell, rock oyster, scallop, scollop, shipworm, spat, surf clam, Tasmanian scallop *(Chiefly NSW)*, teredo, toheroa, ugari, univalve, wood-borer, yugari. **4. cephalopods** ammonite, argonaut, blue-ringed octopus, cephalopod, decapod, devilfish, dibranchiate, nautilus, octopod, octopus, paper nautilus, pearly nautilus, sepia, spirula, squid, vampire squid. *Informal:* ockie.

25. **1. Annelida** annelid, baitworm, beachworm, bloodworm, bluey, chaetopod, fan worm, feather worm, giant beachworm, kingworm, lob, lobworm, lug, lugworm, palolo worm, polychaete, pump worm, sandworm, sea mouse, slimy, tube worm, wiry, wood-borer. *Informal:* bungum worm *(SA)*, hairy Mary, kingie. **2. earthworms** angleworm, annelid, brandling, chaetopod, earthworm, lug, lugworm, oligochaete. **3. leeches** bloodsucker, Hirudinea, horseleech, leech, medicinal leech.

26. **1. Echinodermata – sea-lilies** crinite, crinoid, echinoderm, encrinite, feather-star, sea fan, sea lily, sea-feather. **2. starfish** asteroid, asteroidean, brittle-star, crown-of-thorns starfish, sea star, star. **3. urchins** echinoid, echinus, kina, sand-dollar, sea hedgehog, sea urchin, urchin. **4. sea cucumbers** bêche-de-mer, holothurian, sea cucumber, trepang.

27. **1. fish** food fish, free-swimmer, freshwater fish, ichthyoid, mouth-breeder, Pisces, saltwater fish. **2. benthos** groundling. **3. plankton** nekton. **4. tiddler** fingerling. **5. shoal** school.

28. **1. fish part** branchia, branchiae, gill. **2. fin** anal fin, dorsal fin, finlet, pelvic fin, pinnula, pinnule, ventral fin. **3. flipper** fin, paddle.

29. **1. fishes** acanthodian, acanthopterygian, albacore, alevin, amberjack, anabantid, anabas, anchovy, anemone fish, angel shark, angelfish, angler, anglerfish, anthias, arapaima, archerfish, armed bullhead, Arthurs paragalaxias, Atlantic salmon, Australian salmon, Australian shad, baitfish, baldfish, ballahoo, balloo, barb, barbel, barracouta, barracuda, barramundi, bass, batfish, bay trout *(Chiefly Victoria)*, beardie, beluga, belut, bib, bichir, billfish, black bass, black bream, black drummer, black kingfish, black perch, blackfish, bleak, blenny, blindfish, blue-bonnet, blue-eye, blue-throated parrot fish, bluecap, bluefin tuna, bluefish, bluegill, bluenose, boarfish, bonefish, bonito, bony bream, bowfin, box fish, bream, brill, brisling, brit, broadbill, brown trout, brown-banded mullet, bull-trout, bullhead, bullrout, bullseye, bully mullet, bumblebee, bummalo, burbot, butterfish, butterfly cod, butterfly fish, callop, candlefish, capelin, carangid, cardinal fish, carp, cat, catfish, cavally, ceratodus, cero, char, characin, chimaera, chub, cichlid, cisco, climbing perch, clingfish, clownfish, clupeid, coalfish, cobbler, cobia, cockabully *(NZ)*, cockney bream, cod, codfish, codling, coelacanth, conger, conger eel, congolli, coral trout, coralfish, count-fish, couta, cowfish, crossopterygian, cuckoo wrasse, cyprinid, cyprinodont, dab, dace, damselfish, dart, dealfish, Derwent smelt, dewfish, dhufish, diamond fish, dipnoan, doctor fish, dog shark, dog-tooth tuna, dogfish, doggie, dolphin, dory, dragonet, drum, drummer, eel, eelpout, electric eel, elver, emperor,

eulachon, fantail, fighting fish, filefish, fingerling, fishing frog, flat-tail mullet, flatfish, flathead, flounder, fluke, flying fish, flying gurnard, fortescue, four-eyes, freshwater bream, freshwater flathead, freshwater herring, frogfish, fugu, gadid, gadoid, galaxias, game fish, gar, garcon, garfish, garpike, gemfish, giant perch, gilthead, globefish, goatfish, gobbleguts, goby, golden perch, goldfish, gourami, grayling, greenbone *(NZ)*, grenadier, grilse, groper, grouper, grunt, grunter, gudgeon, gunnel, guppy, gurnard, haddock, hake, halfbeak, halibut, hapuku, harder, herring, herring cale, hogfish, hoki, horse mackerel, houting, imperial, inanga, jack, jackass fish, jackfish, javelin fish, jewelfish, jewfish, John Dory, jollytail, kabeljou, kahawai *(NZ)*, kelpfish, killifish, king barracouta, king of the herrings, kingfish, labroid, lake herring, lancet fish, lantern fish, latchet, launce, lax, leatherjacket, lemon sole, ling, lizard fish, loach, long tom, luce, luderick, lumpfish, lumpsucker, lungfish, mackerel, mado, mahi mahi, mahseer, mangrove jack, marble fish, marlin, meagre, menhaden, milkfish, miller's thumb, minnow, mirror carp, mirror dory, moki, molly, mooneye, moonfish, moorish idol, moray, morwong, mudskipper, muley, mulie, mullet, mulloway, Murray cod, Murray perch, nannygai, native salmon, native trout, needlefish, neopterygian, nigger, oarfish, opah, osteoglossid, ox-eye herring, paddlefish, paradise fish, parore *(NZ)*, parr, parrotfish, Patagonian toothfish, patiki *(NZ)*, pearl perch, peppermint cod, perch, pickerel, pig drummer, pigfish, pike, pike eel, pikeperch, pilchard, pilot fish, pipefish, piranha, plaice, poddy mullet, pogge, pollack, pomfret, pompano, pope, porae *(NZ)*, porcupine fish, pout, powan, puffer, pumpkin seed, Queensland halibut, Queensland kingfish, Queensland lungfish, Queensland trumpeter, rabbit-fish, rainbow trout, red bream, red emperor, red firefish, red mullet, red rock cod, redfin, redfish, remora, ribbonfish, river blackfish, roach, robalo, rock bass, rock blackfish, rock cod, rock whiting, rock-hopper, rockfish, rockling, roughie, rudd, ruff, ruffe, sailfish, saithe, salmon, salmon catfish, salmon trout, salmon-bass, samlet, samson fish, sand eel, sand launce, sand trout, sand-dab, saratoda, sardine, sauger, saury, scabbard fish, scalare, scalyfin, schnapper, school mackerel, sciaenoid, scorpion-fish, scratch, scrod *(US)*, sculpin, sea bass, sea bream, sea dragon, sea fox, sea hedgehog, sea leopard, sea mullet, sea perch, sea pike, sea raven, sea scorpion, sea trout, sea wife, sea wolf, seacock, seahorse, sergeant baker, sergeant fish, serranoid, sewermat, shad, sheatfish, shiner, Siamese fighting fish, sibyl, sild, silurid, silver belly, silver biddy, silverfish, skipjack, skipper, skippy, sleepy cod, slippery, smelt, smolt, snapper, snoek, snook, snub-nosed dart, sockeye, sole, Spanish mackerel, sparling, spearfish, spinefoot, spoonbill, sportfish, spotted mackerel, sprat, springer, squeteague, squire, squirrelfish, stargazer, stickleback, stinkfish *(SA)*, stone-bass, stonefish, stranger, sturgeon, sucker, suckerfish, sunfish, surgeon, surgeonfish, surmullet, sweep, sweetlips, swellfish, swordfish, swordtail, tailer, tailor, tambour, tandan, tang, tarakihi *(NZ)*, tarpon, tarwhine, Tasmanian kingfish, tasselfish, tautog, taylor, tench, teraglin, terakihi, tetra, threadfin, tigerfish, tilefish, tinker, toadfish, tommy rough *(Especially SA)*, top minnow, topknot, torsk, tramontane, trevalla, trevally, triggerfish, tripletail, trout, trumpet fish, trumpeter, trunkfish, tuna, tunny, tupong, turbot, turrum, tusk fish, vendace, wahoo, walleye, warehou, weever, whitebait, whitefish, whiting, wirra, wirrah, witch, wolf, wolf-fish, wollomai, wrasse, Yarra herring, yellow jack, yellow jacket, yellow-belly, yellowfin tuna, yellowtail, yellowtail kingfish, zebra fish. *Informal:* barra, coota, darkie, darky, flat *(NZ)*, flattie, jewie, kelpie, kingie, pillie, sawbones, toady.

30. **1. sharks and rays** angel shark, angelfish, basking shark, blue pointer, blue shark, bronze whaler, bull-head shark, carpet shark, devil ray, devilfish, dog shark, dogfish, electric ray, ghost shark, great white shark, grey nurse shark, gummy shark, hammerhead, leopard shark, mackerel shark, mako, manta, manta ray, monkfish, numbfish, nurse shark, Port Jackson shark, ray, saw shark, sawfish, scalare, school shark, scutch, sea fox, selachian, seven-gill shark, shark, shovel-nose ray, skate, stingaree, stingray, thrasher, thresher, tiger shark, torpedo, tuatini, whale shark, whaler, whaler shark, white pointer, white shark, wobbegong, zebra shark. *Informal:* Joan of Arc, munchie, Noah's Ark, schoolie.

31. **1. Agnatha** ammolecete, borer, cyclostome, hag, hagfish, lamper eel, lamprey, marsipobranch.

32. **1. Chordata – Protochordata** chordate, protochordate. *Informal:* cunjei. **2. tunicates** ascidian, cunjevoi, doliolid, salp, salpa, sea squirt, tunicate. **3. lancelets** amphioxus, cephalochordate, lancelet.

33. **1. Amphibia** aglossa, amphibian, anuran, arrow-poison frog, axolotl, batrachian, bufo, bullfrog, caecilian, cane toad, congo snake, dendrobates, escuerzo, frog, frogspawn, goliath frog, mud puppy, natterjack, newt, pipa, platanna, polliwog, pollywog, rana, salamander, siren, tadpole, toad, tongueless frog, tree frog, triton, xenopus. *Informal:* taddie.

34. **1. Reptilia** reptile, reptilian. **2. snake** ophidian, serpent. *Informal:* Joe Blake, wriggler. **3. lizard** saurian.

35. **1. Australasian lizards** bearded dragon, bearded lizard, bicycle lizard, black skink, bloodsucker, blue-tongue, bobtail, bobtail lizard *(WA)*, bungarra *(Northern WA, NT)*, Burton's legless lizard, Cunningham's skink, cycling lizard, double-ender, dragon, dtella, fence lizard, frill-necked lizard, frilled dragon, frilled lizard, garden lizard, giant skink, goanna, Gould's goanna *(NSW)*, ground goanna, illchiljera, jacky lizard, jew lizard, knob-tailed gecko, lace monitor, lance-head lizard, land mullet, moloch, mountain devil, perentie, pine-cone lizard, racehorse goanna *(WA)*, sand goanna, scaly foot, shingleback, sleepy lizard, sun lizard, thorn lizard, thorny devil, tree dragon, tree goanna, water dragon, water goanna. *Informal:* frillie, go.

36. **1. non-Australasian lizards** agama, anole, basilisk, blindworm, bloodsucker, chameleon, chelonian, chuckwalla, cycling lizard, draco lizard, dragon, fence lizard, flying dragon, flying lizard, garden lizard, gecko, giant, Gila monster, glass snake, horned toad, iguana, iguanid, iguanodon, komodo dragon, lacertilian, lance-head lizard, legless lizard, lizard, monitor, sand lizard, scincoid, skink, slow worm, snake-lizard, swift, three-toed skink, tokay, varan.

37. **1. Australasian snakes** amethystine python, amphisbaena *(mythical)*, bandy-bandy, black snake, black-headed python, blind snake, blindworm, blue-bellied black snake, broad-headed snake, brown snake, carpet snake, cockatrice *(mythical)*, common brown snake, coral snake, deaf adder, death adder, diamond python, diamond snake, dugite, fierce snake, gwardar, king brown, mallee snake, mulga snake, myall snake, night tiger, red-bellied black snake, rock python, saltbush snake, Schneider python, slow worm, snake-eater, spotted black snake, taipan, tarpot, tiger snake, water snake, woma, worm snake.

38. **1. non-Australasian snakes** adder, anaconda, asp, aspic *(Poetic)*, banded sea snake, boa, boa constrictor, bushmaster, Cape cobra, cobra, constrictor, copperhead, cottonmouth, diamondback, elapid, fer-de-lance, gopher, grass snake, hamadryad, harlequin, herald snake, hognose snake, horned viper, king cobra, king snake, krait, mamba, massasauga, moccasin, ophidian, pit viper, puff adder, python, rattler, rattlesnake, ringed sea snake, ringhals, serpent, sidewinder, spitting snake, viper, water moccasin, whip snake, worm snake. *Informal:* hoop snake.

39. **1. Australasian tortoises** flatback turtle, long-necked tortoise, mullentypery, pig-nosed turtle, saw-tooth tortoise, snake-necked tortoise, ware, water tortoise.

40. **1. non-Australasian tortoises** chelonian, green turtle, hawk's bill, hawkbill, leatherback, leathery turtle, loggerhead, luth, matamata, mud turtle, snapper, snapping turtle, soft-shelled turtle, terrapin, turtle.

41. **1. crocodiles** alligator, caiman, cayman, croc, crock, crocodilian, garial, gavial, gharial, mugger. *Informal:* gator.

42. **1. Aves** bird, cock, dicky bird, feathered friend, hen. *Informal:* birdie. **2. songbird** songster. **3. poultry** Australorp, Aylesbury duck, Bantam, brahma, broiler, capon, chicken, cochin, cockerel, domestic fowl, fowl, griller, leghorn, Muscovy duck, musk duck, Orpington, Pekin, Plymouth Rock, poulard, poussin, pullet, quail, Rhode Island Red, rooster, rumper, Sussex, turbit, turkey, turkey cock, white leghorn, Wyandotte. **4. chick** flapper, fledgling. **5. flock** bevy, clutch, covey, flight, gaggle, murmuration, wisp. **6. kookaburra** alarm bird, barking jackass, blue-winged kookaburra, breakfast bird, bushman's clock, clockbird, giant kingfisher, great brown kingfisher, ha-ha pigeon, howling jackass, Jack, jackass, Jacky Jacky, Johnny, kooka, laughing Jack, laughing jackass, laughing John, laughing Johnass, laughing Johnny, laughing kingfisher, laughing kookaburra, settler's clock, settler's kingfisher, shepherd's clock, woop woop pigeon. *Informal:* ha-ha duck, Jacko, Jacky.

43. **1. bird part** beak, bill, neb, nib. **2. comb** caruncle, cockscomb, coxcomb, crest, crown, rose-comb. **3. snood** crop, wattle. **4. wing** ala. **5. talon** claw, pounce. **6. wishbone** fourchette, furcula, furculum.

44. **1. indigenous Australasian birds** alarm bird, Albert's lyrebird, Alexandra's parrot, amadavat, anvil bird, apostlebird, apteryx, Asian frogmouth, auctioneer bird, Australasian bittern, Australasian robin, Australian brush turkey, Australian bustard, Australian chat, Australian courser, Australian fernwren, Australian finch, Australian frogmouth, Australian ground thrush, Australian owlet-nightjar, Australian pipit, Australian pratincole, Australian raven, Australian shoveler, Australian warbler, Australian wren, Australo-Papuan robin, avocet, avoset, axebird, babbler, baldyhead, banana bird, banded tintac, barking jackass, barn owl, barn swallow, Bassian thrush, bee-eater, bell miner, bellbird, berrin-berrin, bird of paradise, black cuckoo, black-eared miner, black-faced cuckoo-shrike, black-headed honeyeater, blackcap, blackhead, blightbird, blue jay, blue wren, blue-eye, blue-faced honeyeater, boatbill, boobook, bowerbird, brain-fever bird, bristlebird, broad-billed roller, broadbill, brolga, bronze-cuckoo, bronzewing, brown fieldlark, brush turkey, bubbly Jock, bubbly Mary, buff-breasted pitta, bullbat, buln-buln, bush canary, bush hen, bush robin, bush stone-curlew, bush turkey, bush wren, bushlark, bustard, bustard quail, butcher bird, button quail, cassowary, catbird, caterpillar-eater, channel-billed cuckoo, chat, chatterer, chestnut-quilled rock pigeon, chiffchaff, chimney swallow, chimney swift, chockalott, chowchilla, cicadabird, clamorous reed-warbler, coach-whip bird, coachman, cobblers awl, comb-crested jacana, comedo, cooee bird, corbie *(Scottish)*, corncrake, coucal, courser, crested bellbird, crested shrike-tit, crow, cuckoo, cuckoo-dove, cuckoo-shrike, culver *(Poetic)*, desert chat, diamond bird, diamond firetail, diamond sparrow, dollarbird, dove, dow-itcher, dragoon bird, drongo, dwarf cassowary, eastern spinebill, emu, emu-wren, fairy-wren, fantail, fernbird, fernwren, fieldwren, fig-parrot, figbird, finch, finfoot, firetail, flock pigeon, flycatcher, flying coachman, forty-spotted pardalote, four-o'clock, fowl, friarbird, frogmouth, fruit-dove, gallinacean, gerygone, giant kingfisher, giant moa, gibberbird, gnow *(WA)*, golden-headed cisticola, goldfinch, Gouldian finch, grass-finch, grassbird, grasswren, great brown kingfisher, green catbird, greenfinch, grey-crowned babbler, groundlark, grouse, halcyon, happy family, Happy Jack, heathwren, honeyeater, hon-eysucker, Horsfield's bushlark, howling jackass, huia, hylacola, imperial pigeon, jackass, Jacky Winter, jay, junglefowl, Kangaroo Island emu, kereru, King Island emu, kite, kite hawk, kiwi, koel, kokako, kookaburra, korimako *(NZ)*, kotuku, kuku, landrail, large-tailed nightjar, lark, laughing kookaburra, leatherhead, Lewin's honeyeater, Lewin's rail, lily trotter, long-tailed finch, lotus bird, lowan, lyrebird, magpie, magpie lark, makomako, malleefowl, mannikin, Maori hen *(NZ)*, martin, masked lapwing, masked plover, matata, matuhitui, matuku *(NZ)*, megapode, metallic starling, micky, miner, mistletoebird, moa, mockingbird, monarch, monarch flycatcher, monkey-faced owl, moonbird, mopoke, morepork, mosquito hawk, mound bird, mudlark *(Chiefly Victoria, SA and WA)*, mul-berry bird, Murray magpie *(Chiefly SA)*, native companion, native hen, native pheasant, needletail, New Holland honeyeater, New Zealand thrush, nighthawk, nightjar, noisy friarbird, noisy miner, noisy pitta, northern cassowary, northern chowchilla, nun, olive-backed oriole, orange-footed scrubfowl, orange-winged sittella, oriental pratincole, oriole, owlet-nightjar, painted finch, pallid cuckoo, paradise kingfisher, pardalote, parson-bird, peaceful dove, peewee *(Especially Qld, NSW and ACT)*, phalarope, pheasant coucal, pictorella mannikin, pie, pied goose, pigeon, pilotbird, pintail, piopio, pipit, pitta, piwa-kawaka, plain turkey, plains-wanderer, plover, poll, pratincole, pukeko, purple-breasted finch, pygmy-goose, quail, quail-thrush, rail, rainbird, rainbow bee-eater, raven, red grouse, red-necked avocet, redbill, redhead, redthroat, reeve, regent bowerbird, regent honeyeater, restless flycatcher, Richard's pipit, riflebird, rifleman, ringdove, riroriro, roband, robbin, robin, robin redbreast, rock pigeon, rockwarbler, roller, ruff, ruru *(NZ)*, russet-tailed thrush, sacred kingfisher, saddleback, satin bowerbird, satin flycatcher, satin sparrow, scalebird, scissors grinder, screech owl, scrub turkey, scrub-bird, scrub-robin, scrubfowl, scrubhen, scrubtit, scrubwren, semitone-bird, settler's clock, shining starling, shoveler, shrike-thrush, sicklebill, silvereye, singing bushlark, sittella, soldier bird, son-glark, southern boobook, southern cassowary, southern chowchilla, southern figbird, southern stone-curlew, spangled drongo, spine-tailed chowchilla, spinebill, spinifexbird, spotted nightjar, spotted pardalote, spur-winged plover, squeaker, star finch, starling, stone-curlew, sugarbird, sunbird, superb fairy-wren, superb lyrebird, swallow, swamp pheasant, swiftlet, tailorbird, takahe *(NZ)*, tang, Tasmanian emu, tawny frogmouth, teal, thick-knee, thickhead, thornbill, thrush, thunderbird, tit, titi *(NZ)*, topknot pigeon, tree runner, treecreeper, triller, trumpet manucode, tui, tullawong *(Coastal Qld, Northern NSW, Tasmania)*, turkey quail, twelve apostle bird, tyrant flycatcher, varied sittella, wagtail, warbler, water pipit, wattlebird, wattled crow, waxeye, waybung, wedgebill, wee juggler, weebill, weka, welcome swallow, whipbird, whistler, white-breasted finch, white-browed babbler, white-eye, white-fronted chat, white-naped honeyeater, white-quilled rock pigeon, white-throated gerygone, white-throated nightjar, white-winged chough, white-winged triller, whiteface, widgeon, wild turkey, willaroo, willie wagtail, wompoo pigeon, wonga pigeon, woodhen *(NZ)*, woodpecker, woodpigeon, woodswallow, wren, wrybill, yellow-throated miner, yellowhead, zebra finch. *Informal:* bifcus, greenie, Jacko, kelly, maggie, mocker *(NZ)*.

45. **1. Australasian parrots** Australian ringneck, blue-winged parrot, Bourke's parrot, budgerigar, buln-buln, chockalott, Cloncurry parrot, cockatiel, cockatoo, cockatoo-par-rot, cocklerina, corella, Coxen's fig-parrot, double-eyed fig-parrot, eclectus parrot, elegant parrot, galah, gang-gang, golden-shouldered parrot, grass parrot, ground parrot, hooded parrot, kaka, kakapo, kea, Leadbeater's cockatoo, lorikeet, lorilet, lory, lovebird, lowry,

Major Mitchell, mallee ringneck, Marshall's fig-parrot, mulga parrot, night parrot, orange-bellied parrot, palm cockatoo, paradise parrot, parakeet, parrakeet, parrot, poll, Port Lincoln parrot, princess parrot, quarrion *(NSW)*, rainbow lorikeet, red-capped parrot, red-rumped parrot, regent parrot, ringneck, ringneck parrot, rock parrot, rock pebbler, rosella, scarlet-chested parrot, sulphur-crested cockatoo, superb parrot, turquoise parrot, twenty-eight parrot, wee juggler, weero *(WA)*, white cockatoo. *Informal:* 'keet, budgie, cocky.

46. 1. Australasian birds of prey Australian goshawk, Australian hobby, Australian kestrel, Australian king parrot, black-breasted buzzard, brown goshawk, buzzard, chickenhawk, collared sparrowhawk, duckhawk, eagle, eaglehawk, erne, falcon, goshawk, harrier, hawk, hawk-owl, hobby, kestrel, king parrot, marsh harrier, nankeen kestrel, osprey, ossifrage, peregrine, peregrine falcon, red goshawk, rufous-bellied buzzard, sea eagle, sparrowhawk, wedge-tailed eagle, wedgie, white-bellied sea eagle.

47. 1. Australasian ocean birds Australasian gannet, booby, commic tern, crested tern, darter, diving petrel, fairy penguin, fairy prion, fairy tern, frigatebird, fulmar, gull, jäger, jaeger, king mutton-bird, korora *(NZ)*, little penguin, little tern, mallemuck, man-o'-war bird, mollymawk, Mother Carey's chicken, mutton-bird, oystercatcher, penguin, petrel, prion, rockhopper, sea swallow, seagull, shearwater, short-tailed shearwater, silver gull, skua, sooty shearwater, storm-petrel, stormy petrel, takapu *(NZ)*, Tasmanian mutton-bird, titi *(NZ)*, tropicbird, wandering albatross, whalebird, Wilson's storm-petrel, yager. *Informal:* stinker.

48. 1. Australasian shorebirds beach stone-curlew, cob, curlew, dotterel, eastern curlew, godwit, greenshank, grey plover, knot, kuaka *(NZ)*, little whimbrel, plover, red-necked stint, sanderling, sandpiper, snipe, sooty oystercatcher, stint, stone-curlew, superb fairy-wren, Tasmanian native hen, tattler, thick-knee, turnstone, wader, wading bird, whimbrel.

49. 1. Australasian water birds Australasian bittern, Australasian grebe, Australasian shoveler, Australian coot, Australian crake, Australian pelican, Australian shelduck, Australian shoveler, Australian spotted crake, Australian white ibis, Australian wood duck, bald coot, baldyhead, banded landrail, banded lapwing, bittern, black duck, black swan, black-necked stork, blue crane, blue duck, boomer, Burdekin duck, Cape Barren goose, cattle egret, cormorant, crake, crane, dabchick, didapper, diver, duck, dusky moorhen, egret, freckled duck, gallinule, glossy ibis, goose, great crested grebe, great egret, grebe, greenhead, hardhead, heron, hoary-headed grebe, ibis, jabiru, jacana, Kangaroo Island emu, King Island emu, landrail, Lewin's rail, loom, loon, magpie goose, marsh hen, moorhen, nankeen night heron, night heron, night raven, northern shoveler, Pacific black duck, paradise duck, pelican, pink-eared duck, policeman bird, purple swamphen, putangitangi, radjah shelduck, rail, reed-warbler, rufous night heron, sacred ibis, shoveler *(US)*, shoveller, snakebird, spoonbill, spotted crake, stilt, stork, straw-necked ibis, swamphen, swan, Tasmanian emu, water crake, waterhen, whio, whistling duck, white-eyed duck, white-faced heron, wood duck.

50. 1. introduced Australian birds blackbird, bulbul, Eurasian tree sparrow, house sparrow, Indian myna, laughing turtledove, mallard, myna, ostrich, quail, red-whiskered bulbul, Senegal turtledove, song thrush, sparrow, spotted turtledove, starling, tree sparrow, turtledove. *Informal:* spadger, spag, spoggy *(Chiefly SA)*, sprag *(Chiefly Qld)*.

51. 1. birds (general) auk, bay duck, besra, bishop, black-bellied plover *(Chiefly US)*, blue jay, bobwhite, boobook, brown owl, chat, chick, chicken, chukar, cicadabird, comb-crested jacana, coot, cuckoo, cuckoo-dove, dabbling duck, diving duck, Eurasian coot, fig-parrot, flycatcher, fowl, frogmouth, fruit-dove, game bird, game fowl, garganey, gerygone, giant petrel, glossy ibis, golden whistler, great egret, hanging parrot, jacana, junglefowl, killdeer, lily trotter, magpie, manucode, megapode, monarch, myna, northern cardinal, northern gannet, northern shoveler, oriental pratincole, painted snipe, parakeet, peach-faced lovebird, percher, pintail, purple swamphen, pygmy-goose, raven, red junglefowl, red-whiskered bulbul, ringdove, roller, rosy-faced lovebird, sarus crane, sea eagle, shikra, shoveler, singer, snipe, solan, solitaire, sparrowhawk, spotted crake, swiftlet, ternlet, trumpet manucode, tyrant, waterfowl, weep, whalebird, whistling duck, wildfowl, willow warbler, wood duck, wood stork. *Informal:* chook. **2. particular birds** accentor, accipiter, adjutant, aigrette, albatross, American eagle, anhinga, ani, archangel, argus, auk, auklet, Australasian grebe, avadavat, avocet, babbler, bald coot, bald eagle, banana bird, banded landrail, banded tintac, barb, barbet, barebelly, barn owl, barn swallow, barnacle, barnacle goose, bateleur eagle, bearded parrotbill, bearded tit, bearded vulture, beccafico, bee-eater, bell magpie, bernicle goose, bird of peace, bird of prey, black cuckoo, black grouse, blackbird, blackcap, blackhead, blue crane, blue tit, blue-bonnet, blue-winged teal, bluebird, bluecap, boatbill, bobolink, booby, brain-fever bird, brambling, brant *(Chiefly US)*, brent, broad-billed roller, broadbill, bufflehead, bulbul, bullbat, bullfinch, bunting, burrowing owl, bushtit, bustard, butterball, button quail, buzzard, cacique, cagebird, Canada goose, canary, canvasback, Cape Sparrow, Cape wren-warbler, capercaillie, capercailzie, caracara, cardinal, carrier, carrier pigeon, carrion crow, catbird, caterpillar-eater, cattle egret, chaffinch, channel-billed cuckoo, chanticleer, chaparral cock, chat, chatterer, chickadee, chipping sparrow, chough, clamorous reed-warbler, cliff swallow, cob, cock-of-the-rock, cockatoo, collared sparrowhawk, coly, condor, conure, coot, corbie *(Scottish)*, cormorant, corncrake, cotinga, coucal, courser, cowbird, crake, crane, crested flycatcher, crested shrike-tit, crested tern, crocodile bird, cropper, crossbill, crow, crow blackbird, cuckoo, cuckoo-shrike, culver *(Poetic)*, curassow, curlew, cygnet, dabchick, darter, daw, demoiselle, didapper, dipper, diver, diving petrel, dodo, dollarbird, dotterel, dove, dovekie, drongo, duck, duckhawk, duckling, dunlin, dunnock, dusky moorhen, duyker, eagle, eagle-owl, eaglet, eastern curlew, egret, eider, emperor penguin, erne, eyas, fairy penguin, fairy prion, falcon, falconet, fantail, feral pigeon, fighting cock, finch, firebird, firecrest, firetail, fowl, francolin, frigatebird, fulmar, gallinacean, gallinule, gamecock, gannet, garden warbler, garefowl, gerfalcon, glaucous gull, goatsucker, gobbler, godwit, goldcrest, golden eagle, golden pheasant, golden-headed cisticola, goldfinch, goliath heron, goony bird *(US)*, goosander, goose, gosling, grass parrot, grassbird, great auk, great crested grebe, great egret, great white heron, grebe, green duck, greenfinch, greenhead, grey duck, grey parrot, grey plover, greylag, griffon, grosbeak, ground owl, grouse, guacharo, guan, guillemot, guinea hen, guineafowl, gull, gyrfalcon, hadada, halcyon, hamerkop, hammerhead, hangbird, hardhead, harlequin duck, harpy eagle, harrier, hawk, hedge accentor, hedge sparrow, heron, herring gull, hoactzin, hoatzin, hobby, homing pigeon, honey buzzard, honeyeater, hoopoe, hornbill, house martin, house sparrow, hummingbird, ibis, Indian myna, Indian runner, indigo bunting, ivory gull, jabiru, jacamar, jack snipe, jackdaw, Jacobin, jaeger, Java sparrow, jay, junglefowl, juvenal, juvenile, kestrel, king mutton-bird, kinglet, kite, kittiwake, knot, koel, kokako, lammergeyer, landrail, lanner, lanneret, large-tailed nightjar, lark, leucosticte, limpkin, linnet, lintwhite *(Chiefly Scottish)*, little auk, loggerhead, loom, loon, lorikeet, lory, lourie, lovebird, macaw, magpie, mallard, mallemuck, man-o'-war bird, manakin, mandarin duck, manikin, marabou, marsh harrier, marsh hen, martin, martlet, mavis,meadowlark, merganser, merle *(Chiefly Scottish or Poetic)*, mew, missel thrush, mistle thrush, mockingbird, mollymawk, monkey-faced owl, moorhen, mosquito hawk, mossie, Mother Carey's chicken, motmot, mound bird, mousebird, murre, murrelet, musket, mutton-bird, nestling, night heron, night raven *(Poetic)*, night-bird, nightingale, nightjar, noddy, northern cardinal, northern hawk-owl, Numidian crane, nutcracker, nuthatch, oilbird, old squaw, oldwife, organ bird, oriole, ortolan, osprey, ossifrage, ostrich, ousel, ouzel, owl, owlet, oxpecker, oystercatcher, parrot, partridge, peaceful dove, peacock, peafowl, peahen, pecker, peetweet *(US)*, pelican, pen, penguin, percher, peregrine, peregrine falcon, petrel, phalarope, pheasant, philomel *(Poetic)*, pie, pigeon, pigeon-hawk, pileated woodpecker, pipit, plantain-eater, plover, poll, popinjay, poult, pouter, prairie chicken, pratincole, prion, ptarmigan, puffin, purple swamphen, pyrrhuloxia, quail, quetzal, rail, raptor, razorbill, red hat, red-necked stint, red-whiskered bulbul, redbill, redbreast, redpoll, redshank, redstart, redwing, reed-warbler, reedbird, reedling, reeve, rhea, Richard's pipit, ring ouzel, ring-necked pheasant, ringdove, roadrunner, roband, rock dove, rock thrush, rockhopper penguin, rockjumper, roller, rook, sacred ibis, sacred kingfisher, saddlebill, saker, sand martin, sanderling, sandpiper, sawbill, scarlet robin, scaup, scoter, screamer, screech owl, scrubfowl, scutch, sea duck, sea fox, sea mew, sea swallow, seabird, seafowl, seagull, secretary bird, sedge warbler, seed-eater, seriema, serin, shag, shearwater, sheathbill, sheldrake, shelduck, shoebill, shorebird, short-tailed shearwater, shovelbill, shrike, shrike-tit, sicklebill, silver gull, siskin, skimmer, skua, skylark, smew, snakebird, snipe, snow bunting, snow goose, snowy owl, song thrush, sooty shearwater, sparrow, spoonbill, spotted turtledove, squab, starling, stilt, stint, stitchbird, stock dove, stonemarten, stork, storm-cock, storm-petrel, sugarbird, sultana bird, sun bittern, swamphen, swallow, swamphen, swan, swordbill, tailorbird, tanager, tattler, tawny owl, teal, tercel, tern, thick-knee, thrasher, thresher, throstle, thrush, tick-bird, tiercel, tinamou, tinktinkie, tit, titlark, titmouse, tody, toucan, tragopan, tree sparrow, treecreeper, triller, trochilus, trogon, tropicbird, troupial, trumpet, trumpeter, tumbler, turaco, turkey buzzard, turnstone, turtledove, umbrella bird, vulture, wading bird, wagtail, wall creeper, wandering albatross, warbler, water ouzel, water rail, water wagtail, waterbird, waterhen, wattled crow, waxbill, waxwing, waybung, weaver, weaverbird, wheatear, whidah, whimbrel, whippoorwill, whistler, whistling swan, white-eye, white-eyed duck, white-faced heron, white-winged chough, whitethroat, whooper, whydah, widgeon, widowbird, wigeon, wild goose, willet, willow warbler, Wilson's storm-petrel, wood stork, woodchat, woodcock, woodgrouse, woodlark, woodpecker, woodpigeon, woodswallow, wren, wryneck, wydah, yellowbird, yellowhammer. *Informal:* cocky, guinea, kelly, spadger, spag, stinker, wank, wood duck. **3. birds by gender** cob, cock, cock sparrow, falcon-gentle, gander, hen.

52. 1. Mammalia artiodactyl, carnivore, cetacean, chiropter, chiropteran, edentate, elephant, insectivore, lagomorph, mammal, marsupial, monotreme, perissodactyl, pholidote, placental, primate, rodent, sirenian.

53. 1. animal part proboscis, snout, trunk. **2. horn** antler, attire, hartshorn, ivory, point, scur, spike. **3. pincers** chela, forceps, nipper, pinchers. **4. tooth** carnassial, denticle, fang, tush, tusk. **5. cheek pouch** bell, dewlap, jowl, pouch. **6. forelimb** arm, brachium, foreleg. **7. paw** foot, forefoot, forepaw, pad, pettitoes, podium. **8. hoof** unguis, ungula. **9. claw** nail, unguis. **10. tail** brush, bush, flag, fox brush, scut. **11. shell** plastron, scutcheon, scute, shuck *(US)*, tortoiseshell, turbinate.

54. 1. Australasian mammals – monotremes anteater, duckbill, echidna, giant anteater, ornithorhynchus, platypus, spiny anteater. **2. carnivorous marsupials** anteater, banded anteater, Canning's little dog, cynocephalus, Darling Downs dunnart, devil, dibbler, dunnart, kowari, kultarr, larapinta, mardo, marsupial cat, marsupial mole, marsupial mouse, native cat, native mouse, ningaui, northern native cat, numbat, phascogale, pitchi-pitchi, planigale, quoll, satanellus, sminthopsis, spotted native cat, Tasmanian devil, Tasmanian tiger, Tasmanian wolf, thylacine, tiger cat, tuan, ursine dasyure, wambenger, wild cat, wuhl-wuhl, yellow-footed antechinus. **3. bandicoots and bilbies** bandicoot, barred bandicoot, bilby, brindled bandicoot, brown bandicoot, dalgyte, desert bandicoot, golden bandicoot, Gunn's bandicoot, long-eared bandicoot, long-nosed bandicoot, Malabar rat, marl, northern brown bandicoot, pig rat, pig-rat, pinkie *(SA)*, quenda, rabbit-eared bandicoot, short-eared bandicoot, short-nosed bandicoot, southern brown bandicoot, Tasmanian barred bandicoot, wintarro, yallara. *Informal:* bandy. **4. koalas and wombats** badger *(Tasmania)*, hairy-nosed wombat, koala, naked-nose wombat, native bear, wombat. *Informal:* monkey bear. **5. possums and gliders** bobuck, brush-tailed possum, burramys, cuscus, feather-tail glider, fluffy glider, flying mouse, flying phalanger, flying possum, gliding possum, greater glider, green ringtail possum, Herbert River ringtail possum, mongan, mountain possum, mountain pygmy possum, mundarda, noolbenger, phalanger, pygmy glider, pygmy possum, ringtail, ringtail possum, rock possum, squirrel glider, striped possum, sugar glider, tait, tollah, toolah, wogoit, yellow-bellied glider. **6. kangaroo** big red, blue flyer, boomer, doe, joey, kanga cricket, old man, red. *Informal:* kanga, roo. **7. kangaroos and wallabies** agile wallaby, antelope kangaroo, antilopine wallaroo, Bennett's tree kangaroo, Bennett's wallaby, bettong, big red, biggada, black wallaby, black-faced kangaroo, black-tailed wallaby, blue flyer, boodie, boodie rat, boongary, bridled nail-tail wallaby, brush kangaroo, brush-tailed bettong, brush-tailed wallaby, burrowing rat-kangaroo, crescent nail-tail wallaby, dama, desert rat-kangaroo, eastern brush wallaby, eastern grey kangaroo, euro, great grey kangaroo, grey kangaroo, Grey's brush wallaby, hare-wallaby, joey, jungle kangaroo, kanga cricket, kangaroo rat, karrabul, Lesueur's rat-kangaroo, Lumholtz's tree kangaroo, mala, mallee kangaroo, marlu *(Aboriginal English)*, merrin, munning, musk rat-kangaroo, nail-tail wallaby, northern nail-tail wallaby, paddymelon, pademelon, parma wallaby, plains kangaroo, potoroo, pretty-face wallaby, quokka, rat-kangaroo, red, red kangaroo, red wallaby, red-necked wallaby, river wallaby, rock wallaby, rufous hare-wallaby, rufous rat-kangaroo, rufous wallaby, sandy wallaby, scrub wallaby, sooty kangaroo, squeaker, swamp wallaby, tammar, tcharibeena, toolache, tree kangaroo, tungoo, uroo, wallaby, wallaroo, western grey kangaroo, whiptail wallaby, woylie, wurrung, wurrup, yellow-footed rock wallaby. *Informal:* kanga. **8. rats and mice** broad-toothed rat, bush rat, dargawarra, false swamp-rat, false water-rat, fawn hopping mouse, hopping mouse, jerboa rat, kiore, Maori rat, mosaic-tailed rat, native rat, oorarrie, rock rat, spinifex hopping mouse, stick-nest rat, tillikin, tree-rat, water rat, wilkintie. **9. marine mammals** Australian fur seal, wig. **10. dogs and dingos** dingo, Maori dog, native dog, warragul, warregal, warrigal.

55. 1. Artiodactyla addax, African buffalo, alpaca, ammon, anoa, antelope, aoudad, Arabian camel, argali, ariel, artiodactyl, Asian water buffalo, Asiatic mouflon, aurochs, axis, babiroussa, babirusa, Bactrian camel, Bali cattle, banteng, Barbary sheep, barking deer, bharal, bighorn, bison, blackbuck, blue sheep, bongo, brocket, bubal, bushbuck, camel, Cape buffalo, carabao, caribou, cattle, chamois, chevrotain, chital, deer, dik-dik, dinoceras, doe, dromedary, duiker, eland, elk, European bison, fallow deer, gazelle, gemsbok, gerenuk, giraffe, gnu, goa, goat, goat antelope, goral, grysbok, guanaco, hart, hartebeest, hind, hog deer, ibex, impala, Indian buffalo, inyala, izard, Javan rusa deer, klipspringer, koodoo, kudu, llama, markhor, moose, mouflon, mountain goat, mountain ibex, mountain sheep, mouse deer, mule deer, muntjac, musk deer, nilgai, nyala, nylghai, okapi, oont *(Indian English)*, oribi, oryx, Père David's deer, peccary, pig, pronghorn, puku, red deer, reedbuck, reindeer, river-horse, Rocky Mountain goat, roe, roebuck, roedeer, royal, rusa deer, sable antelope, saiga, sambar, sasin, sassaby, serow, sheep, spiker, spotted deer, springbok, stag, steenbok, steinbok, swine, tahr, tamarau, thar, topi, tufted deer, uintatherium, urus, vicuña, Virginia deer, wapiti, wart-hog, water buffalo, water ox, waterbuck, Weddell seal, white-tailed deer, wild boar, wildebeest, wisent, yak, yeanling.

56. 1. Primates anthropoid ape, ape, australopithecine, aye-aye, baboon, Barbary ape, bushbaby, capuchin, chacma, chimpanzee, colugo, cynocephalus, douc, douroucouli, drill, entellus, flying lemur, gelada, gibbon, gorilla, great ape, green monkey, grivet, guenon, hanuman, howler, howling monkey, indri, jocko, langur, lemur, lemuroid, loris, macaque, man, mandrill, mangabey, marmoset, monkey, orangutan, pithecanthrope, pongid, Pongo, potto, proboscis monkey, rhesus monkey, saki, sapajou, siamang, simian, spider monkey, talapoin, tamarin, tarsier, titi, uakari, vervet, wanderoo. *Informal:* chimp.

57. 1. Edentata ai, ant bear, anteater, armadillo, edentate, pichiciago, shrewmouse, silky anteater, sloth, tamandua, tatouay, two-toed anteater, unau. **2. Tubulidentata** aardvark, ant bear, anteater.

58. 1. Carnivora aardwolf, African wild dog, arctic fox, badger, bear, binturong, black bear, black buck, blue fox, bobcat, brock, brown bear, brown hyena, bruin, cacomistle, canis, caracal, carcajou, catamountain, cheetah, chetah, cinnamon bear, civet, coati, cougar, coyote, creodont, dhole, earthwolf, ermine, eyra, felid, fennec, ferret, ferret badger, fisher, fitch, genet, glutton, golden cat, grey wolf, grison, grizzly, grizzly bear *(Chiefly North America)*, honey bear, honey-badger, honey-ratel, hyaena, hyena, ichneumon, jackal, jaguar, jaguarundi, jennet, kinkajou, Kodiak bear, kolinsky, laughing hyena, leopard, liger, linsang, lion, lioness, lobo, lynx, maned wolf, margay, marten, meerkat, mink, mongoose, mountain cat, mountain lion, ocelot, olingo, oncilla, otter, ounce, painter *(US)*, palm civet, panda, panther, pantheress, pine marten, polar bear, polecat, prairie wolf, puma, raccoon, racoon, ratel, red fox, red wolf, sable, sea otter, serval, silver fox, skunk, sloth bear, snow leopard, spotted hyena, stoat, striped hyena, suricate, tayra, teledu, tiger, tiger cat, tigon, tigress, timber wolf, viverrine, weasel, white bear, wildcat, wolf, wolf note, wolverine, zoril. *Informal:* coon *(US)*.

59. 1. Rodentia acouchi, agouti, beaver, cane rat, capybara, castor, cavy, chickaree, chinchilla, chipmunk, coypu, deer mouse, desert rat, dormouse, fat mouse, fieldmouse, flying squirrel, gerbil, golden hamster, gopher, grey squirrel, ground hog, ground squirrel, groundhog, guinea pig, hamster, harvest mouse, jerboa, jerboa pouched mouse, jerboa rat, kultarr, lemming, marmot, mouse, murine, muskrat, musquash, nutria, paca, pocket gopher, porcupine, prairie dog, rabbit, rat, red squirrel, spermophile, squirrel, suslik, taguan, trade rat, tree-mouse, viscacha, vizcacha, vole, waltzing mouse, water rat, water vole, white rat, wood rat, woodchuck. *Informal:* bunny *(US)*.

60. 1. Perissodactyla ass, barrow, black rhinoceros, eohippus, hippopotamus, horse, jackass, jennet, kiang, mule, onager, perissodactyl, pygmy hippopotamus, quagga, rhinoceros, river-horse, sea-cow, tapir, tarpan, white rhinoceros, zebra *(US, British also)*. *Informal:* hippo, rhino.

61. 1. Cetacea baleen, bay whale, beluga, black whale, blackfish, blower, blue whale, bottlenose, bowhead, cachalot, cetacean, crookback, dolphin, dolphinfish, finback, finner, finwhale, grampus, humpback, killer whale, leveret, narwhal, orca, pika, pilot whale, porpoise, right whale, rorqual, sea canary, sea unicorn, sei whale, sperm, sperm whale, sulphur-bottom, unicorn, whale, white whale. **2. dugongs** dugong, manatee, sea cow, sirenian.

62. 1. Chiroptera bat, chiropter, false vampire, flying fox, fox-bat, fruit bat, kalong, noctule, pipistrelle, serotine, vampire bat.

63. 1. Pinnipedia bladdernose, clapmatch, eared seal, elephant seal, fur seal, hair seal, harbour seal, hooded seal, leopard seal, sea elephant, sea leopard, sea lion, sea-dog, seahorse, seal, walrus.

64. 1. Insectivora desman, elephant shrew, hedgehog, hedgepig, insectivore, mole, moonrat, otter shrew, shrew, solenodon, tana, tenrec, tree shrew, water shrew.

65. 1. Proboscidea African elephant, dinothere, elephant, Indian elephant, mammoth, mastodon, pachyderm. *Informal:* jumbo. **2. Hyracoidea** daman, hyrax, tree hyrax.

66. 1. Lagomorpha cony, hare, jack, jack rabbit, lagomorph, pika, rabbit. *Informal:* bunny.

67. 1. Pholidota pangolin, scaly anteater.

68. 1. domestic animal pet. **2. stable** stud.

69. 1. horse bay, bloodhorse, bloodstock, bolter, broncho, bronco *(Chiefly US)*, brumby, bucker, buckjumper, cob, cocktail, colt, courser *(Chiefly Poetic)*, creamy, cuddy *(Chiefly Scottish)*, dun, entire, equine, fencer, filly, foal, galloway, gee-gee, gelding, grey, hack, hinny, horsey, horsy, jade, jarung, juvenile, ladino, mare, mount, nag, nanto, night horse, pad, padnag, palomino, piebald, pit pony, pony, racehorse, ridgeling, rig, roadster, roan, scrubber, sheltie, shire horse, sorrel, speeler, stallion, steed, stud *(US)*, Thoroughbred, warrigal, yarraman, yearling. *Informal:* apple sauce, boom galloper, fizzer, hayburner, neddy, prad, rip. **2. workhorse** bucker, buckjumper, carthorse, Clydesdale, coach-horse, coacher, dobbin, draught horse, dray-horse, drayhorse, furrow horse, hack, hackney, high horse, hunter, pacer, pole horse, poler, post-horse, quarter horse, saddle-horse, shaft-horse, sledder, stockhorse. *Informal:* clumper, moke, plug, rip, wheel-horse *(US)*. **3. warhorse** charger, garron, high horse, trooper. **4. beast of burden** ass, burro, dicky, donkey, llama, mule, packhorse, packtrain. *Informal:* donk, moke *(British)*. **5. team** four-in-hand, pair, span. **6. horse breeds** Appaloosa, Arab, barb, Falabella, jennet, mustang, Nubian, paint horse, Palouse pony, Percheron, pinto *(US)*, Przewalski's horse, quarter horse, Shetland pony, skewbald, tarpan, Thoroughbred, Timor pony, Turk, Waler, Welsh mountain pony.

70. **1. cattle** beef, beef cattle, beefalo, beefer, bobby calf, bovine, bull, bullock, bush cattle, cattalo, cow, four-legged kangaroo, heifer, horny, Longhorn, moo-cow, muley, ox, ruminant, sook, sookie, springer, steer, vealer. *Informal:* micky, snaily. **2. cow breeds** Aberdeen Angus, Afrikander, Alderney, Australian Illawarra Shorthorn, Australian lowline, Ayrshire, beefalo, Beefmaster, Blonde d'Aquitaine, Braford, Brahman, Brangus, catalo, Charbray, Charolais, chopper, Devon, Droughtmaster, Friesian, gaur, Hereford, Holstein, Illawarra shorthorn, Jersey, Limousin, Longhorn, Murray Grey, Poll Hereford, Redpoll, Santa Gertrudis, Shorthorn, Simmental, Sussex, Wagyu cattle.

71. **1. sheep** barebelly, bellwether, carry-over lamb, cobbler, cosset, cracker, crock, double fleecer, doubler, ewe, fat lamb, flock ewe, flock ram, freezer, full-mouth, hermit sheep *(NZ)*, hogget, Judas sheep, land lice, mountain maggot, off-shears, prime lamb, ram, sandy cobbler, shear-hog, shearer, snob, sound-mouth, spring lamb, teg, treble fleece, tup, two-tooth, wet sheep, woolly. *Informal:* concertina, ground lice, gummy, joe, jumbuck, monkey, rosella, shornie, woolly back, yeo. **2. sheep breeds** aoudad, argali, bharal, Border Leicester, Cheviot, Comeback, Damara sheep, Devon, Dorset Horn, down, karakul, Leicester, Lincoln, long wool breed, Merino, mouflon, mountain sheep, Oxford, Polwarth, Rambouillet, Romney, Ryeland, Scotch blackface, Shetland, Short Wool breed, Shropshire, Texel. *Informal:* maggot taxi. **3. goat** Anglo-Nubian goat, billy, billy goat, kid, nanny goat, Nubian goat.

72. **1. pig** backfatter, baconer, barrow, boar, bush pig, Captain Cooker *(NZ)*, gilt, grunter, hog, kunekune, landrace, piggie, piglet, pigling, porker, razorback, shoat, shote, sow, sucking-pig, superporker, swine. **2. pig breeds** Berkshire, Wessex saddleback.

73. **1. dog** barker, bitch, bow-wow, canine, canis, cur, doggie, doggy, hound, pup, puppy, tyke. *Informal:* dawg, dishlicker, mutt, pooch, tripehound, woofer. **2. guide-dog** bandog, heading dog, hearing dog, housedog, leading dog, sled dog, sniffer dog, tracker dog, watchdog. **3. dog breeds** Afghan, Airedale, Akita, Alsatian, Australian cattle dog, Australian silky terrier, Australian terrier, barb, basenji, beagle, beardie, bird dog *(US)*, bloodhound, blue cattle dog, blue heeler, bluey, boarhound, border collie, borzoi, Boston terrier, boxer, bruiser, buckhound, bull-mastiff, bull-terrier, bulldog, cairn terrier, camp-dog, cardigan, cattle dog, chihuahua, chow, clumber, coachdog, cocker, cocker spaniel, collie, corgi, dachshund, Dalmatian, Dandie Dinmont, deerhound, Doberman pinscher, draghound, elkhound, English setter, English springer spaniel, Eskimo dog, eye dog, forcing dog, fox terrier, foxhound, gazehound, German shepherd, golden retriever, Gordon setter, Great Dane, greyhound, gun dog, harrier, heel, heeler, heeling dog *(NZ)*, housedog, husky, Irish setter, Irish terrier, Irish water spaniel, Irish wolfhound, kangaroo dog, keeshond, kelpie, Kerry blue, King Charles spaniel, kuri, labradoodle, labrador, lakeland terrier, lap-dog, Lhasa apso, lurcher, malamute, Maltese dog, Manchester terrier, Maori dog, maremma sheepdog, mastiff, Mexican hairless, Molosser dog, newfoundland, Norwegian elkhound, Norwich terrier, Old English sheepdog, otterhound, papillon, pariah, pariah dog, Pekingese, pharaoh hound, pi-dog, pig dog, pit bull terrier, pointer, police dog, Pom, Pomeranian, poodle, pug, pye-dog, Queensland Blue Heeler, raccoon dog, red setter, retriever, Rhodesian ridgeback, Rottweiler, Russian wolfhound, Saint Bernard, saluki, Samoyed, schipperke, schnauzer, schnoodle, Scotch terrier, Scottish terrier, Sealyham, setter, sheepdog, shepherd dog, Shih tzu, silky, Skye terrier, sleuth, sleuthhound, spaniel, spitz, spotted dick, springer, springer spaniel, Staffordshire terrier, staghound, stumpy-tailed cattle dog, Sussex spaniel, Sydney silky, terrier, toy dog, tumbler, turnspit, water dog, water spaniel, Welsh corgi, Welsh springer spaniel, Welsh terrier, whippet, wire-haired terrier, wolf-dog, wolfhound, Yorkshire terrier. *Informal:* bullie, foxie, foxy, Newfie, peke, roo dog, rottie, sausage dog, Scottie, Scotty, spotted dog.

74.   **1. cat** alley cat, feline, grimalkin, kitten, kitty, marmalade cat, mog, mouser, puss, pussy, tabby, tom, tomcat, tortie cat, tortoiseshell. *Informal:* ballarat, moggy *(British)*. **2. cat breeds** Abyssinian, Angora, Archangel, Burmese, Cheshire, Egyptian, Havana brown, Himalayan, Maltese, Manx, Persian, Russian blue, Siamese, Turkish.

75.   **1. prehistoric animals – fossil reptiles** allosaurus, brachiosaur, brontosaurus, dinosaur, diplodocus, ichthyosaur, ichthyosaurus, megalosaur, ornithopod, plesiosaur, protoceratops, psittacosaurus, pterodactyl, rhamphorhyncus, sauropod, stegosaurus, titanosaurus, triceratops, tyrannosaurus. **2. fossil mammals** archaeohippus, aurochs, eohippus, imperial mammoth, Irish elk, mammoth, mastodon, northern woolly mammoth, protohippus, sabre-toothed tiger. **3. fossil birds** archaeopteryx, archeopteryx, ichthyornis, teratorn, thunder bird. **4. fossil invertebrates** ammonite, trilobite. **5. prehistoric Australian animals** Austropelor, Austrosaurus, Blinasaurus, Deltasaurus, Diprotodon, Dromornis, Genyornis, Kronosaurus, Megalania, Ngapakaldia, Nototherium, Pallimnarchus, Paracyclotosaurus, Phascolonus, Procoptodon, Quipollornis, Rhoetosaurus, Sthenurus, Thylacoleo, Zygomaturus.

76.   **1. zoology** bacteriology, biology, cryobiology, ecology, entomology, ethology, helminthology, ichthyology, malacology, marine biology, microbiology, myrmecology, ophiology, ornithology, palaeontology, parasitology, pisciculture, sociobiology, zoogeography. **2. zoolatry** animal worship, hippomania, ophiolatry, zoophilism.

77.   **1. zoologist** bacteriologist, biologist, cryobiologist, ecologist, ethologist, helminthologist, ichthyologist, malacologist, marine biologist, microbiologist, myrmecologist, ophiologist, ornithologist, palaeontologist, parasitologist, sociobiologist, zoogeographer. **2. aquarist** aviculturist, pisciculturist. **3. animal-lover** ailurophile, bird-fancier, dogfancier, hippomaniac, zoophile. **4. birdwatcher** birder, birdman. *Informal:* birdo, twitcher. **5. lepidopterist** butterfly catcher. **6. entomologist** *Informal:* bug-hunter.

adj. 78.   **1. animal-like** beastlike, bestial, brutal, brute, brutish, faunal, zooid, zoological, zoomorphic. **2. subhuman** theriomorphic, theroid. **3. animalcular** rotiferous. **4. warm-blooded** endothermic, homeothermic, homoeothermic, homoiothermic. **5. wild** brumby, ferae naturae, feral, ferine, untamed. **6. mammalian** mammiferous. **7. bovine** canine, cervine, equine, erinaceous, feline, hircine, leonine, lupine, ovine, phocine, sciurine, simian, taurine, therian, ursine, vaccine, vituline.

79.   **1. birdlike** ornithoid. **2. avian** avifaunal, ornithic. **3. winged** alar, alary, alate, aliform, pennate, volant. **4. anatine** anserine, aquiline, columbine, corvine, gallinaceous, grallatorial, halcyon, hirundine, larine, pavonine, rasorial, strigiform, struthious, turdine, vulturine.

80.   **1. fishy** finned, finny, fishlike, ichthyic, ichthyoid, piscine.

81.   **1. amphibian** amphibiotic, amphibious, batrachian. **2. froglike** anuran, salientian, toadlike.

82.   **1. reptilian. 2. snake-like** anguine, colubrine, ophidian, serpentine, snaky, viperine, viperish, viperous. **3. cold-blooded** ectothermic, heterothermic, poikilothermic. **4. lizard-like** lacertilian, saurian.

83.   **1. insect-like** apian, coleopterous, culicid, entomic, hexapodous, muscid, vespine.

ANNOYANCE

n. **1.**   **1. annoyance** aggravation, chafe, exacerbation, exasperation, fret, irritation, nuisance, peeve, trouble, vexation. **2. annoyingness** importunacy, importunateness, irksomeness, offensiveness, troublesomeness. **3. harassment** aggravation, bedevilment, persecution, pinpricking, tease. **4. irritant** aggravation, pinprick, torment, vexation. **5. nuisance** bind, bore, bother, pain, pest, plague, thorn, thorn in someone's flesh (or side), trial. *Informal:* face-ache, menace, terror. **6. trouble** difficulty, problem, the last straw, the matter, worry. *Informal:* the (dizzy) limit.

    2.   **1. annoyer** aggravator, exasperator. *Informal:* stirrer. **2. harasser** baiter, nagger, niggler, persecutor, plaguer, tease, teaser, tormentor, troubler.

adj. **3.**   **1. annoying** abrasive, aggravating, irritant, irritating, offensive, tiresome, trying, vexatious. *Informal:* pesky *(Chiefly US)*, pestiferous. **2. troublesome** annoying, bothersome, importunate, importune, irksome, mischievous, narky, niggling, pestilent, thorny, vexatious, worrisome. *Informal:* pesky *(Chiefly US)*, pestiferous. **3. exasperating** galling, infuriating, insufferable, insupportable, maddening. *Informal:* wicked.

    4.   **1. annoyed** aggravated, cross, infuriated, irritated, vexed. *Informal:* bushwhacked. **2. exasperated** *Informal:* browned off, fed up (to the back teeth), fed up to the gills. **3. harassed** hassled, hot and bothered, tormented, troubled.

v. **5.** **1. annoy** aggravate, chafe, chagrin, displease, exasperate, fester, gall, get on someone's nerves, get to, get under someone's skin, goad, irk, irritate, jangle, nettle, niggle, pip, pique, provoke, put out, put someone out, rankle, rasp, ruffle. *Informal:* get (on) someone's goat, get across, get in someone's hair, get on someone's quince, get on someone's wick, get up someone's nose, give someone the irrits, give someone the pip, peeve, rub (up) the wrong way, stick in someone's craw. **2. exasperate** acerbate, chevy, chivvy, exacerbate, fray, gall, infuriate, irritate, madden, nag, rile, roil, sting, vex. *Informal:* drive someone up the wall. **3. irritate** aggravate, antagonise, bug, fret, gall, nark, niggle, offend, play cat and mouse, provoke, rile, torment, try the patience of, vex. *Informal:* get (or take) a rise out of. **4. harass** badger, bait, bedevil, bullyrag, harry, haze *(US)*, heckle, hound, keep at, nag, needle, peck at, persecute, pester, pick on, plague, stir, taunt, tease, torment. *Informal:* be on someone's back, devil, gig, hassle, rag, rib. **5. trouble** bother, chivvy, fret, fuss, pester, plague, worry. *Informal:* hassle.

6. **1. be annoyed** be sick (and tired) of, have had it. *Informal:* burr up *(Chiefly NSW and Qld),* go off the deep end, have had a bellyful, have had an eyeful. **2. express annoyance** *Informal:* spew, spew on.

adv. **7.** **1. annoyingly** aggravatingly, irksomely, offensively, tiresomely, tryingly. **2. exasperatingly** gallingly, infuriatingly, insupportably, maddeningly.

interj. **8.** **1. for Pete's sake** *(Informal)* bother, drat, heavens (above). *Informal:* (for) Christ's sake, (God) stiffen the crows (or lizards), botheration, bugger, Christ, for Chrissake, for God's sake(s), for pity's sake, for the love of Mike, for the love of Pete, heavens to Murgatroyd, hell, Jesus wept!, phut, rats, sod it, spare me days, spewing, stone the crows, that does it, wouldn't it rot your socks, wouldn't it rotate you.

RELATED KEYWORDS: ANGER, DISCONTENTEDNESS, BADNESS, IRRITABLENESS, PAIN, UNPLEASANTNESS

ANSWER

n. **1.** **1. answer** acknowledgement, countersign, echo, feedback, redoublement, rejoinder, repartee, replication, reply, report, rescript, respond, respondence, response, return, RSVP. *Informal:* comeback. **2. reaction** a Roland for an Oliver, back talk, bite, contradiction, countercharge, counterclaim, defence, repartee, retort, riposte. *Informal:* comeback. **3. conditioned response** conditioned reflex. **4. responsive singing** antiphon, antiphony, gradual.

2. **1. solution** answer, conclusion, deduction, determination, explanation, generalisation, illation, inference, key, proof, solvent, technofix.

3. **1. answerer** rebutter, replier, respondent.

adj. **4.** **1. answering** respondent, responsive. **2. providing a final answer** conclusive, decisive, definitive, last, peremptory. **3. answerable** capable of being answered, extractable, resolvable, soluble, solvable. **4. antiphonal** amoebaean.

v. **5.** **1. answer** acknowledge, reciprocate, rejoin, reply, respond, retort, return, RSVP. **2. retort** answer, back-answer, confute, contradict, countercharge, counterclaim, rebut, reply, return, riposte. *Informal:* bite back. **3. reduce to silence** cut the ground from under someone's feet, not leave someone a leg to stand on, silence, still.

6. **1. solve** deduce, draw, explain, figure out, find the key to, get out, hammer out, infer, puzzle out, thrash out, turn the scales, work out, zero in. *Informal:* crack. **2. resolve** clear up, conclude, extract, find. **3. answer a need** meet a requirement, satisfy.

ANTICIPATION

n. **1.** **1. anticipation** aforethought, calculation, forecast, forefeel, foretaste, forethought, hunch, long-sightedness, premeditation, presage, prognostic. **2. forward planning** looking ahead, precaution, preparation, preparative, prudence. **3. foresight** augury, cartomancy, chiromancy, clairvoyance, divination, ESP, extrasensory perception, foreknowledge, futurology, hand-reading, hydromancy, metagnomy, palmistry, precognition, prediction, prescience, prevision, prophecy, second sight, soothsaying. **4. foreboding** adumbration, bodement, boding, foreshadowing, forewarning, premonition, presage, presentiment. **5. omen** harbinger, portent, sign.

adj. **2.** **1. anticipatory** aforethought, precautionary, premeditated. **2. anticipative** adumbrative, precognitive. **3. forward-looking** designing, forehanded *(US)*, pre-emptive, pre-emptory, precautious, prepared, provident, provident of, prudent, thrifty. **4. foresighted** clairvoyant, far-seeing, far-sighted, long-headed, long-sighted, onlooking, prescient, psychic.

v. **3.** **1. anticipate** expect, look ahead, pre-empt, preconceive, see how the land lies, sniff the morning air. **2. prepare** arrange, gear up, gird (up) one's loins, gird oneself (up) for, lay in stocks, make allowance(s), prepare for, see one's way ahead to. *Informal:* prep. **3. foresee** feel in one's bones, forefeel, foreknow, foretaste, prefigure, previse, see one's way ahead. **4. foreshadow** adumbrate, foretell, foretoken, prefigure. **5. foretell** augur, bode, forebode, forecast, forewarn, omen, portend, predict, presage, previse, prophesy.

adv. **4.** **1. anticipatively** adumbratively, against the time when, anticipatorily, designingly, far-sightedly, presciently, providently, prudently.

RELATED KEYWORDS: EXPECTATION, PREDICTION, PREPAREDNESS

ANXIETY

n. **1.** **1. anxiety** anxiousness, concern, disquiet, disquietude, franticness, fussing, nervousness, overanxiety, unrest, worry. *Informal:* jimjams. **2. trepidation** agitation, consternation, distress, feverishness, perturbation, tremulousness. **3. nerves** flutter, goose flesh, goose pimples, tremor. *Informal:* butterflies, the yips. **4. the twitches** *(Informal)* fidgets. *Informal:* jumps, shakes, the creeps, the jitters, the shivers, willies. **5. tenseness** self-consciousness, tension, tensity. **6. jumpiness** boggle, dysphoria, edginess, fidgetiness, restlessness, skittishness, twitchiness, uneasiness. **7. fuss** ado, bother, flurry, fluster, frustration, needle, trouble, worriment. **8. flap** *Informal:* dither, fever, funk, in a tizz, stew, sweat, tizzy, twitter. **9. stage fright** performance anxiety. **10. separation anxiety disorder**.

2. **1. worrier** basket case, fidget, flutterer, fusser, jitterbug, nervous wreck, panic merchant. *Informal:* fusspot, old woman, worrywart.

adj. **3.** **1. anxious** apprehensive, concerned for, drawn, exercised, overanxious, worried. *Informal:* fussed, on pins and needles, toey. **2. trembly** shaky, tremulant, tremulous, twittery, wobbly. **3. tense** fraught, high-strung, highly strung, highly-wrought, nervous, on tenterhooks, overstrung, uptight. **4. nervous** anxious, apprehensive, edgy, fidgety, fretful, hypersensitive, jittery, jumpy, skittish, supersensitive, twitchy, uneasy, unquiet. *Informal:* hyper, like a cat on a hot tin roof, like a cat on hot bricks, nappy, nervy, scratchy, toey, uptight. **5. fraught** anxious, distressful, emotional, feverish, frantic, frenetic, frenzied, overwrought, unstrung, upset. *Informal:* hag-ridden, het-up, on the rack, toey. **6. agitated** flustered, fluttery, hot and bothered, in a flap, in a tizz. *Informal:* thingy. **7. ill-at-ease** uncomfortable, uneasy, unquiet. **8. self-conscious** paranoid.

4. **1. worrying** disquieting, distressing, disturbing, niggling, upsetting.

v. **5.** **1. be anxious** bother, busy about, fash *(Chiefly Scottish)*, flurry, fluster, flutter, fret, fuss, lose sleep over, overreact, panic, pother, worry. *Informal:* come unstuck, fiddle-faddle, flap, get one's knickers in a knot (or twist), have the jitters, pop one's cork, stew, sweat. **2. startle** jump, shy, start. *Informal:* be in a funk, boggle, funk, go to pieces, have (or take) a willy. **3. fidget** *Informal:* have ants in one's pants, have got 'em bad, hop up and down. **4. jitter** chatter, rattle. **5. sweat blood** *(Informal)* agonise over (or about). *Informal:* go hot and cold all over, tear one's hair out.

6. **1. alarm** consternate, disquiet, distress, unhinge, unnerve, unsettle, unstring, upset. **2. trouble** eat, eat away at, exercise.

adv. **7.** **1. anxiously** fretfully, nervously, overanxiously, self-consciously, uneasily, worriedly. **2. agitatedly** distressfully, feverishly, feverously, franticly, frenetically, in trepidation. **3. tensely** disquietly, skittishly, uncomfortably.

RELATED KEYWORDS: EXCITEMENT, COWARDICE, FRIGHT

APATHY

n. **1.** **1. apathy** accidie, acedia, depression, mopishness, purposelessness, spiritlessness. **2. torpor** inertia, languidness, languor, lethargy, listlessness, numbness, stupor, torpidness. **3. indifference** aloofness, bloodlessness, detachment, disinterest, half-heartedness, impassivity, incuriousness, indifferentism, lack of involvement, lukewarmness, perfunctoriness, unconcern, unconcernedness, uninterestedness. **4. nonchalance** carelessness, casualness, easiness, insouciance, jemenfoutisme, pococurantism.

2. **1. apathetic person** armchair Norm, indifferentist, mope, moper, pococurante, yawner, zombie.

adj. **3.** **1. apathetic** ambitionless, bloodless, dead-and-alive, depressed, depressive, mopey, mopish, passive, phlegmatic, purposeless, spiritless, unaspiring. **2. torpid** benumbed, coasty, comatose, dreamy, dull, inactive, indolent, inert, languid, lethargic, listless, numb, remiss, sleepy, slow, sluggish, stagnant, supine. *Informal:* moony. **3. uninterested** aloof, disinterested, distanced, impassive, insensible, nonpartisan, switched-off, turned off, unaffected, unmoved, unresponsive, unruffled, untouched. **4. uncommitted** apolitical, uninvolved. **5. indifferent** detached, half-hearted, incurious, irresponsive, lukewarm, uncaring. *Informal:* half-pie. **6. nonchalant** airy, careless, casual, cavalier, easygoing, free and easy, insouciant, laid-back, offhand, pococurante, relaxed, throwaway, unconcerned.

v. **4. 1. be indifferent** be left cold, not blink at, shrug off, take for granted. *Informal:* give someone (or something) the go-by, not bat an eye, not care a straw, not give a damn, not give a darn, not give a hang, not give a stuff, not give a tinker's cuss, not give a tinker's damn, not give a twopenny damn, not give a twopenny dump. **2. mope** dream, moon. *Informal:* switch off.

adv. **5. 1. apathetically** bloodlessly, languidly, listlessly, lukewarmly, mopingly, mopishly, perfunctorily, spiritlessly. **2. nonchalantly** casually, cavalierly, phlegmatically, unconcernedly. **3. indifferently** aloofly, by halves, half-heartedly, impassively, incuriously, uninterestedly.

interj. **6. 1. so what** che sarà sarà, do tell, for aught one cares, it's all one to me, what of it, who cares. *Informal:* big deal, hard cheddar, hard cheese, stiff cheddar, stiff cheese, that's the way the cookie crumbles, what the hell.

RELATED KEYWORDS: BOREDOM, DISCOURAGEMENT, UNWILLINGNESS

APPEARANCE

n. **1. 1. appearance** air, aspect, bearing, cast, colour, complexion, countenance, dimension, facies, figure, form, guise, image, light, look, looks, mien, outward, presence, semblance, show. *Informal:* get-up, the cut of someone's jib. **2. face** appearance, aspect, contour, countenance, facade, features, lineament, physiognomy, profile, visage. **3. phenomenon** mode, phase, phasis. **4. manifestation** apparition, appearance, emergence, emersion, fade-in, forthcoming, loom, materialisation.

2. 1. appearances apparentness, colouring, externals, gloss, guise, pretence, seeming, semblance, show, superficiality, superficies, surface structure.

adj. **3. 1. apparent** external, manifest, ostensible, ostensive, outward, seeming, specious, superficial, surface, visible.

v. **4. 1. appear** arise, bob up, come, come across, come into view, come to light, come up, crop up, drop in, emerge, figure, gleam, glimpse *(Poetic)*, heave in sight, loom, materialise, on view, peek, peep, peer, present, report, rise, shoot, show, surface, turn up, unroll. *Informal:* front, show a leg, show one's face, show the flag, show up. **2. seem** appear, look, look like, sound.

adv. **5. 1. apparently** at (the) first blush, at face value, from the look of the thing, manifestly, on the face of it, ostensibly, prima facie, seemingly, superficially, to all appearances, to the eye.

phr. **6. 1. all that glitters is not gold** all that glisters is not gold, you can't judge a book by its cover. *Informal:* don't judge a sausage by its shiny overcoat.

RELATED KEYWORDS: ARRIVAL, ACTUALITY, BODY, DECORATION, REVELATION, OUTSIDE, SIGHT, VISIBILITY

APPROVAL

n. **1. 1. approval** a good press, admiration, appreciation, appreciativeness, approbation, backing, endorsement, esteem, green light, opinion, regard, support, sympathy. **2. recommendation** a good word, advocacy, approbation, commendation, espousal, rave, testimonial. *Informal:* rap-up, wrap-up. **3. praise** acclaim, acclamation, celebration, emblazonment, exaltation, extolment, glory, laudation, puffery. **4. acceptance** acceptation, agreement, assent, countenance, favour, okay. **5. sanction** confirmation, endorsement, ratification, recognition.

2. 1. applause a round of applause, acclaim, acclamation, applauding, bouquet, cheer, clap, curtain call, eclat, hand, handclap, ovation, plaudits, salvo, three cheers. **2. tribute** compliment, encomium, eulogium, eulogy, hymn, laud, paean, panegyric, pean, toast. **3. admiring look** eye-service.

3. 1. admirableness acceptability, commendableness, exemplariness, favourableness, laudableness, praiseworthiness, splendidness, unobjectionableness.

4. 1. approver acclaimer, admirer, applauder, appreciator, caroller, cohort, favourer, follower, supporter, sympathiser. **2. praiser** encomiast, eulogiser, eulogist, exalter, lauder, panegyrist, tributary, tributer. **3. barracker** cheerer, claque, fan. *Informal:* groupie, rooter. **4. recommender** advocate, advocator, countenancer, extoller, promoter.

adj. **5.** **1. approving** applauding, applausive, approbative, approbatory, commendatory, favourably disposed, lost in admiration, praising, recommendatory, recommending, shook on. **2. praising** acclamatory, complimentary, encomiastic, eulogistic, flattering, laudatory, panegyrical, rave, tributary. **3. favourable** acceptant, accepting, adoptive, appreciative, appreciatory, rapt, receptive, recognitory, susceptive, sympathetic, tolerant, uncritical. *Informal:* wrapped.

6. **1. approved** commended, recommended. **2. praiseworthy** admirable, approvable, commendable, excellent, exemplary, laudable, prepossessing. *Informal:* schmick, sick. **3. acceptable** all right, alright, cleared, passable, passed, uncensored. *Informal:* 10-4, fair enough, okay. **4. favourite** best, darling, favoured, in favour, in someone's good books, popular.

v. **7.** **1. approve** accept, acknowledge, advocate, approbate *(Chiefly US, Scottish Law)*, back, bless, encourage, endorse, give one's blessing, hold a brief for, hold with, recognise, set one's seal on (or to), support, sympathise. *Informal:* give the thumbs up. **2. acclaim** adore, applaud, carol, celebrate, commend, cry up, emblazon, eulogise, exalt, extol, glorify, hail, hymn, laud, panegyrise, praise, proclaim, worship. *Informal:* big-mouth, plug, polish, rap up. **3. compliment** commend, exalt, give the green light, recommend, sing someone's praises, speak well of. **4. admire** appreciate, favour, prize, smile on (or upon), take to, think the world of, value. **5. give full (or top) marks** give points to, give someone a good mark, hand it to, pass, throw a bouquet at. **6. applaud** clap, huzza. **7. cheer** barrack for. *Informal:* root for *(US)*. **8. toast** bumper, raise one's glass, wassail. **9. endorse** approve, countenance, ratify, recognise, sanction, second, support.

8. **1. be approved** get the nod, pass muster. **2. grow on** get in good with, prepossess. *Informal:* be in big with. **3. impress** affect, make an impact on, take by storm. *Informal:* bring down the house, grab, grab them by the balls, knock their eyes out, lay them in the aisles, wow them.

adv. **9.** **1. approvingly** admiringly, appreciatively, appreciatorily, complimentarily, encouragingly. **2. eulogistically** panegyrically. **3. favourably** in a good light, smilingly, sympathetically, sympathisingly. **4. tolerantly** uncritically. **5. in favour of** pro.

interj. **10.** **1. well done** good for you, good on you, good show. *Informal:* (you) (little) beauty, attaboy, attagirl, beaut, bewdy, bully, bully for ..., curl the (or a) mo, good egg, good iron, great, man, nice one, onya, that's the shot, your blood's worth bottling. **2. good** *Informal:* good-o, goodo, great, hot dog. **3. hear hear** touché. *Informal:* no risk, right on!, spot-on, thumbs up, too right!. **4. solid** *Informal:* classic, groovy, hoo, okay, sweet. **5. hip hip hooray** alleluia, hallelujah, hooray, hurray, huzza, three cheers, viva. *Informal:* kapai *(NZ)*, pie, pie on *(NZ)*. **6. bravo** encore. **7. yummo** *(Informal)*.

RELATED KEYWORDS: AGREEMENT, FLATTERY, GOODNESS, HIGH REGARD, PLEASURE

ARISTOCRACY

n. **1.** **1. aristocracy** ancien régime, daimyo, elite, ermine, high society, nobility, patriciate, peerage, purple, ruling class, society, the haves, top drawer, upper class, upper crust. **2. gentry** county *(British)*, gentlefolk, squattocracy, squirearchy, squiredom. **3. noble birth** blue blood, ennoblement, gentility, gentle birth, grandeur, noblesse. **4. pedigree** ancestry, birth, descent, extraction, family, line, lineage, origin, strain, succession, witan. **5. royalty** kingliness, majesty, princeliness, queenliness. **6. lordship** baronage, barony, dukedom, earldom, emperorship, kinghood, kingship, ladyship, marquisate, princedom, queendom, queenhood, sultanate, sultanship, thanage, viscountcy, viscounty. **7. kingcraft.**

2. **1. aristocrat** blue blood, boyar, Brahman, eupatrid, hidalgo, life peer, lordship, noble, nobleman, noblewoman, patrician, peer. *Informal:* nob, swell *(Chiefly US)*. **2. noblewoman** archduchess, baroness, countess, crown princess, czarevna, dame, Dame, dauphiness, dowager, duchess, grand duchess, infanta, lady, Lady, landgravine, life peeress, marchesa, marchioness, margravine, marquise, miladi, milady, peeress, princess, princess royal, queen consort, queen dowager, sultana, tsarevna, tzarevna, vicereine, viscountess. **3. nobleman** archduke, atheling, baron, count, count palatine, crown prince, czarevitch, daimyo, dauphin, don, Don, duke, earl, emeer, emir, grand duke, grandee, infante, jarl, Junker, landgrave, lord, Lord Spiritual, Lord Temporal, lordling, magnifico, marchese, margrave, marquess, marquis, mense lord, mirza, monseigneur, prince, prince consort, prince imperial, prince regent, prince royal, princeling, rangatira, robber baron, seigneur, Sir, thane *(Scottish History)*, thegn, tsarevitch, tzarevitch, viscount. **4. sovereign** czar, czarina, emperor, Kaiser, king, kinglet, maharajah, maharani, majesty, monarch, prince, queen, queen regent, queen regnant, rajah, rani, regent, regina, rex, shah, sultan, tsar, tsarina, tsaritsa, tzar, tzarina, tzaritza. **5. esquire** armiger, country gentleman, laird, landlord, landowner, squatter, squire, yeoman *(British)*. **6. lady-in-waiting** maid of honour. **7. royal family** dynasty, noble family.

adj. **3.** **1. aristocratic** blue-blooded, gentle, highborn, highbred, nobiliary, noble, patrician, pedigreed, thoroughbred, upper, upper-class, well-born. *Informal:* toffee-nosed, toney, tonky *(NZ)*, top-drawer. **2. titled** archducal, baronial, coroneted, ducal, lordly, seigneurial. **3. royal** basilic, every inch a king, imperial, kingly, monarchal, monarchical, noble, princely, purple, queenly, regal, regius, regnal, sovereign.

adv. **4.** **1. aristocratically** imperially, nobly.

RELATED KEYWORDS: ARROGANCE, WEALTH

ARRANGEMENT

n. **1.** **1. arrangement** accord, accordance, agreement, compact, composition, concord, contra deal, contract, deal, indenture, pact, set-up, settlement, settling, understanding. *Informal:* prenup. **2. assignation** anniversary date, appointment, blind date, boogie, date, double date, engagement, get-together, interview, introduction, meeting, note in one's diary, rendezvous, tryst. **3. booking** invitation, prearrangement. **4. place of assignation** meeting place, trysting place.

2. **1. procurer** arranger, fixer, go-between, maquereau, pander, panderer, pimp, procuress. *Informal:* fancy man, ponce, poofter rorter.

adj. **3.** **1. arranged** agreed, planned, prearranged, set-up.

v. **4.** **1. arrange** agree, appoint, decide on (or upon), determine, fix, hold, settle, settle on (or upon), work it. *Informal:* jack *(NZ)*. **2. arrange to meet** ask someone out, invite, make a date, prearrange, preconcert. **3. rendezvous** date, tryst *(Chiefly Scottish)*.

RELATED KEYWORDS: CONTRACT, ROMANCE, SEX

ARRIVAL

n. **1.** **1. arrival** advent, coming, homecoming, incoming, influx. **2. disembarkation** landfall, landing, set-down. **3. check-in** registration.

2. **1. arriver** comer, landing party. **2. immigrant** émigré, black hat, boat people, emigrant, illegal immigrant, incomer, migrant, new arrival, newcomer, nominated migrant, refugee. *Informal:* chum, cloggie, ethno, Jimmy Grant, new chum, Pom, Pommy. **3. newcomer** stranger. *Informal:* blow-in, griffin, new chum.

3. **1. destination** bourn, goal, haven. **2. arrival point** air terminal, airport, airstrip, anchorage, bus station, bus stop, dropzone, halt, harbour, helipad, heliport, landing ground, landing strip, port, railway station, station, stop, terminal, terminus.

v. **4.** **1. arrive** be along, bob up, come, fetch up, make it, roll in, roll up, show up, surface, turn up. **2. reach** arrive at, attain, attain to, come at, come to, come up, end up, fetch, get, hit, join, make, put in at, reach to, regain, strike, summit, top. **3. check in** register. **4. make land** beach, berth, bring up, cast anchor, come in, dock, drop anchor, land, make landfall, pull in, put down, touch down. **5. settle on** light. **6. disembark** alight, debark, debus, deplane, detrain, dismount, get down, get off, get out, go ashore, jump ship, light.

RELATED KEYWORDS: ARRANGEMENT, ENTRANCE, TRAVEL, VISIT

ARROGANCE

n. **1.** **1. arrogance** airs, airs and graces, arrogancy, disdainfulness, haughtiness, hubris, hybris, loftiness, pride, self-importance, smugness, stuffiness, superciliousness, toploftiness, uppishness. **2. disdain** affectation, haughtiness, hauteur, pomposity, scorn, vainglory. **3. insolence** arrogance, assumption, assurance, audacity, effrontery, gall, impertinence, impudence, presumption, temerity. *Informal:* cheek, chutzpah, crust, face, hide, nerve, sauce. **4. self-assertion** bounce, conceit, face, front, pretension, swagger, swashbuckling. *Informal:* brass, cheek, ego, hide, nerve, side, swank. **5. insult** a slap in the face, affront, contumely, indignity, snub. **6. snobbery** elitism, ethnocentrism, inverted snobbery, superiority complex.

2. **1. audaciousness** assuredness, audacity, barefacedness, bumptiousness, effrontery, forwardness, gall, hardihood, insolence, presumptuousness, shamelessness. *Informal:* cheek, moxie *(US)*. **2. cockiness** cockishness, sauciness. **3. high-handedness** dictatorialness, domineeringness, high-mindedness, imperiousness, officiousness.

3. **1. arrogant person** assumer, loudmouth, peacock, presumer, swaggerer, upstart. **2. bully** fascist, pusher, swashbuckler, tin god, upstart. *Informal:* bastard from the bush, rugger-bugger, two-bob boss. **3. know-all** *(Informal)* dogmatiser, dogmatist, wiseacre. *Informal:* alec, smart alec, smartie, smartypants, wise guy *(Chiefly US)*. **4. squirt**

Informal: cock sparrow, cut-lunch commando. **5. snob** elitist, patroniser. *Informal:* boiled shirt, his nibs, pannikin snob, snoot, snot, snot-nose, snotty nose, stuffed shirt.

adj. **4.** **1. arrogant** assured, audacious, autocratic, barefaced, cavalier, condescending, contemptuous, full of oneself, gracious, grandiose, haughty, high and mighty, hoity-toity, impertinent, impudent, inconsiderate, insolent, lofty, loudmouthed, overweening, Pecksniffian, pompous, pretentious, proud, saucy, smug, snobbish, snubby, supercilious, thoughtless. *Informal:* arty-farty, high-hat, highfalutin, jumped-up, la-di-da, lah-di-dah, pluty *(NZ)*, puffed-up, snooty, snot-nose, snot-nosed, snotty, toplofty. **2. disdainful** conceited, haughty, hoity-toity, lofty, offhand, proud, supercilious, superior, too big for one's britches, unashamed. *Informal:* highfalutin, sniffy, snooty, toffee-nosed. **3. overconfident** big-headed, cocksure, conceited. *Informal:* cockish, cocky, stuck-up. **4. snobbish** elitist, ethnocentric. **5. self-important** conceited, consequential, puffy, self-opinionated, stuffy, upperty, uppish. *Informal:* toney, tonky *(NZ)*, toplofty, uppity.

5. **1. presumptuous** assuming, assumptive, audacious, blushless, bold, bold-faced, brash, brazen, brazen-faced, bumptious, familiar, flash *(Aboriginal English)*, forward, hoity-toity, hubristic, immodest, pert, precocious, shameless, unblushing. *Informal:* cheeky. **2. high-handed** dictatorial, doctrinaire, dogmatic, domineering, imperious, magisterial, officious, opinionated, opinionative, overbearing, positive, pushy, self-assertive, swashbuckling. *Informal:* bossy, on one's high horse. **3. dismissive** dismissory.

v. **6.** **1. be arrogant** be too big for one's boots, boast, cavalier, flaunt, overween, queen it, strut, swagger, swash, swell. *Informal:* be up oneself, fancy oneself, get a big (or swelled) head, get on one's high horse, have more front than Mark Foys, have tickets on oneself, put on (the) jam, swank. **2. presume** assume, have a nerve, have the cheek, perk. *Informal:* have oneself on. **3. patronise** overbear. **4. disdain** despise, look down on, look down one's nose at, scorn, sneer, spurn. *Informal:* cock a snook (or snoot). **5. dogmatise** lay down the law. **6. bully** browbeat, bullyrag, domineer, hector, lord it over someone, overlord. *Informal:* rib.

adv. **7.** **1. arrogantly** assuredly, autocratically, barefacedly, impertinently, impudently, overweeningly, swaggeringly, swashingly. **2. audaciously** bumptiously, forwardly, presumedly, presumptuously, self-importantly, shamelessly, vaingloriously. **3. cavalierly** cockily, cockishly, saucily. **4. high-handedly** dictatorially, dogmatically, domineeringly, imperiously, magisterially, overbearingly, patronisingly. **5. superciliously** disdainfully, haughtily. **6. snobbishly** stuffily, uppishly.

RELATED KEYWORDS: AFFECTEDNESS, BRAGGING, VANITY

ARTIST

n. **1.** **1. artist** aesthetician, depicter, limner, old master. **2. painter** aquarellist, colourist, dauber, frescoer, genre painter, impressionist, landscape painter, marine painter, portraitist, watercolourist. **3. illustrator** caricaturist, commercial artist, copyist, illuminator, vignettist. **4. designer** architect, cartoonist, delineator, drafter, draftsman, draughtsman, sign-painter, sign-writer. **5. drawer** crayonist, pastellist, penciller, sketcher. **6. black-and-white artist** monochromist. **7. bohemian** dilettante.

2. **1. craftsman** artisan, craftsperson, handicraftsman, mosaicist, technician, tradesman. **2. woodworker** ebonist, woodcraftsman. **3. sculptor** carver, modeller, sculptress. **4. potter** ceramicist. **5. metalworker** brazier, enamellist, goldsmith, silversmith. **6. jeweller** lapidary. **7. photographer** retoucher.

3. **1. engraver** burinist, cerographist, chalcographer, chaser, embosser, pyrographer, scrimshander, tattooist, wood engraver, woodcutter, xylographer. **2. etcher** lithographer, printer, tinter.

RELATED KEYWORDS: FINE ARTS, PHOTOGRAPHY, WORKER

ARTLESSNESS

n. **1.** **1. artlessness** childlikeness, dupability, greenness, guilelessness, gullibility, immaturity, inartificiality, ingenuousness, innocence, lack of sophistication, literality, naivety, naturalness, plainness, rusticity, simple heart, simple-mindedness, simplicity, unaffectedness, unpretentiousness, unsophisticatedness, unworldliness, viridity.

2. **1. forthrightness** bluffness, bluntness, candidness, candour, directness, downrightness, foursquareness, frankness, genuineness, honesty, openness, plain dealing, single-mindedness, straightforwardness.

3. **1. artless person** a babe in the woods, cat's paw, dupe, gudgeon, gull, ingenue, innocent, lamb, lamb to the slaughter, primitive, shlemiel, tool. *Informal:* fall guy, mug, patsy, sitting duck, sucker. **2. unsophisticated person** backwoodsman *(Chiefly US)*, philistine, rough diamond, rustic. *Informal:* hayseed, hick, redneck *(US)*, rube *(US)*.

adj. **4.** **1. artless** aw-shucks, childlike, dewy-eyed, dupable, green, gullible, inartificial, inexperienced, ingenuous, innocent, naive, natural, open-faced, simple, simple-minded, single-hearted, single-minded, trusting, unaffected, uncalculating, undesigning, unguarded, unpretentious, unsophisticated, unsuspecting, unsuspicious, untaught, untutored, unvarnished, unworldly, verdant, wide-eyed, without guile. *Informal:* blue-eyed, new-laid. **2. unsophisticated** Arcadian, backwoods, hillbilly, insular, narrow, provincial, rustic, simple-minded, up-country, verdant. *Informal:* hick, stringy-bark.

5. **1. forthright** above, aboveboard, bluff, blunt, candid, commonplace, direct, downright, extroverted, foursquare, frank, genuine, guileless, honest, ingenuous, literal, man-to-man, matter-of-fact, open, outspoken, plain, plain dealing, plain-spoken, prosaic, simple-hearted, sincere, straight, straightforward, unreserved, up-front, upstanding. *Informal:* open as the day (is long), straight-out.

v. **6.** **1. be forthright** call a spade a spade, have nothing to hide, say what one thinks. *Informal:* let it all hang out.

adv. **7.** **1. artlessly** guilelessly, gullibly, ingenuously, naively, simple-mindedly, simply, unaffectedly, unpretentiously, unsophisticatedly.

8. **1. forthrightly** bluffly, bluntly, candidly, downrightly, forthright, foursquare, foursquarely, genuinely, plainly.

RELATED KEYWORDS: MEEKNESS, HONESTY, INNOCENCE, SIMPLICITY

ASCENT

n. **1.** **1. ascent** acclivity, ascension, Ascension, assurgency, climb, escalade, escalation, mount, rise, rising, up, uphill, uprise, uprising, upswing. **2. upthrust** upheaval, upstroke, upthrow. **3. upsurge** ridge lift, zoom. **4. slope** acclivity, ascent, bank, chute, gradient, ramp, side, talus, tilt, upgrade *(US)*, uphill, upsweep, upthrow. **5. mountaineering** alpinism, clambering, layback, rockclimbing.

2. **1. climber** ascender, clamberer, escalader. **2. mountaineer** alpinist, cragsman, mountain climber.

3. **1. stairs** back steps, backstairs, companionway, escalator, flight, front steps, spiral staircase, staircase, stairway, steps. *Informal:* apples and pears. **2. stair** curtail step, doorstep, footstep, gradin, horseblock, step. **3. tread** going, nosing, riser. **4. ladder** accommodation ladder, rope ladder, set of steps, stepladder, steps, turret, wall bars. **5. rung** ratline, rundle.

4. **1. lifting** Assumption, cranage, elevation, Elevation, erection, exaltation, leverage, levitation, take-up, upheaval, uplift, upliftment, uptake. **2. boost** leg-up, raise. **3. lift** bench press, dead lift, deep knees bend, heave, jerk, press, snatch.

5. **1. lift** cable lift, dumb waiter, elevator, fork hoist *(NZ)*, forklift, goods lift, grain elevator, hoist, ladder lift, manlift, noria, service lift, ski lift, T-bar lift. **2. pulley** block and tackle, capstan, cat, garnet, parbuckle, winch, windlass. **3. crane** derrick, goliath crane, luffing crane, tower crane. **4. lever** jack, jackscrew, screw-jack, sweep, wallaby jack, well sweep.

6. **1. lifter** booster, exalter, heaver, hoister, levitator, raiser, uplifter. **2. wincher** jacker.

adj. **7.** **1. ascending** ascendant, assurgent, emergent, rising, up, upcast. **2. climbing** epigeal, epigeous, positively geotropic, running, scandent. **3. uplifting** anabatic. **4. upward** heavenward, skyward.

8. **1. risen** emersed, uplifted. **2. erect** jessant, rampant. **3. erectile** erective. **4. scansorial**.

9. **1. ascendable** climbable, climbing, scalable, surmountable.

v. **10.** **1. ascend** arise, levitate, overtop, rise, upswing. **2. gain height** air, hurdle, jump, mount, skyrocket, soar, take off, zoom. **3. tower** erect, ramp, rear, spire, stand up. **4. surmount** culminate, overbuild, top. **5. climb** clamber, escalade, scale, shin, swarm up, walk up, work one's way up, work up. *Informal:* shinny. **6. mount** get up, horse, reascend, remount, scale. **7. mountaineer** back up, herringbone, sidestep *(Skiing)*, sidle *(NZ)*.

11. **1. lift** elevate, hoist, lever, lever up, prise, pry *(Chiefly US)*, raise, up-end, upheave, uplift, upraise. **2. hoist** advance, crane, exalt, fly, masthead, raise, run up, sway up, up. **3. erect** build, set up. **4. boost** heighten, prop, stilt, underlay. **5. heave** heft, hoick, hoist, lift, pick up. **6. toss** chuck, fling, fork, launch, let fly, lob, loft, pitch, sling, throw. *Informal:* hoick, peg, sky. **7. hitch** hitch up, kilt, perk up, take up. **8. pull up** dredge, fish up, haul, jack, winch, wind, windlass. *Informal:* haul up. **9. weigh anchor** trip anchor.

12. **1. be lifted** scend.

adv. **13.** **1. up** above, airwards, erect, heavenward, heavenwards, skyward, skywards, sunward, sunwards, upstairs, upward, upwardly, upwards.

RELATED KEYWORDS: ERECTNESS, FLYING, HEIGHT, JUMP, SLOPE, THROW, TOP

ASSERTION

n. **1.** **1. assertion** advisory, affirmation, allegation, asseveration, assurance, attestation, averment, avouchment, avowal, claim, contention, declaration, dogmatisation, enouncement, enunciation, ipse dixit, offer, pretension, profession, pronouncement, protestation, restatement, statement, submission. *Informal:* say-so. **2. proposition** affirmative, predicate, predication, premise. **3. affidavit** stat dec, statutory declaration.

2. **1. assertiveness** peremptoriness, positive thinking, self-development. **2. insistence** avowedness, dogmatism, insistency. **3. emphasis** accent, stress. **4. assertiveness training** positive thinking course, self development course.

3. **1. asserter** affirmant, affirmer, alleger, assuror, claimer, declarant, declarer, dogmatiser, dogmatist, enunciator, insister, maintainer, protester, submitter.

adj. **4.** **1. assertory** affirmative, affirmatory, affirming, declarative, declaratory. **2. assertive** assured, dogmatic, outspoken, positive, strong. **3. insistent** categorical, dogmatic, dogmatical, emphatic, insisting, peremptory, persistent, urgent.

5. **1. avowed** declared, predicate, predicative, professed, sworn.

v. **6.** **1. assert** affirm, allege, announce, argue, asseverate, aver, avow, claim, contend, declare, dogmatise, enunciate, insist, maintain, pose, posit, predicate, press, proclaim, profess, pronounce, pronounce on, protest, purport, restate, state, submit, swear, vouch, vouch for, vow. **2. propose** advance, initiate, move, propound, put forward, suggest. **3. assert oneself** be confident, speak up for oneself, stand up for oneself.

RELATED KEYWORDS: AGREEMENT, EVIDENCE, PUBLICITY, SPEECH

ATOM

n. **1.** **1. atom** corpuscle, exotic atom, hot atom, isodiaphere, molecule, nucleide, nuclide, radionuclide, Rutherford-Bohr atom. **2. ion** anion, cation, free radical, kation, negative ion, positive ion, thermion, zwitterion. **3. atomic structure** electron orbit, nucleus. **4. atomic mass** atomic number, atomic weight, electrochemical equivalent, isotopic number, mass number, neutron excess, packing fraction, relative atomic mass, weight. **5. quantum number** charm, colour, flavour, isotopic spin, spin, strangeness. **6. rutherford** gray.

2. **1. elementary particle** . **2. fermion** . **3. quark** bottom quark, charm quark, down quark, strange quark, top quark, up quark. **4. lepton** electron, muon, positron, tau lepton. **5. neutrino** electron neutrino, muon neutrino, tau neutrino. **6. boson** gluon, Higgs boson, photon, W, Z. **7. composite particle** glueball, hadron, hyperon, kaon, meson, neutron, nucleon, pentaquark, pion, proton, tetraquark.

3. **1. chemical bond** bond, cohesion, coordinate bond, coordinate covalent bond, covalent bond, dative bond, donor bond, double bond, duplet, electrovalent bond, exchange force, ionic bond, polar bond, semipolar bond, triple bond, valency bond. **2. bond energy** chemical affinity, ionisation potential, work function. **3. energy state** ground state, stationary state.

4. **1. atomic energy** atomic power, nuclear energy, nuclear power. **2. nuclear reactor** atomic pile, boiling-water reactor, breeder, converter, fast breeder reactor, fast reactor, FBR, fusion reactor, pile, power reactor, pressurised water reactor, production reactor, propulsion reactor, reactor, thermal reactor, ZETA. *Informal:* nuke. **3. nuclear core** absorber, crystal lattice, lattice, moderator, reflector, space lattice. **4. particle accelerator** accelerator, betatron, bevatron, cosmotron, cyclotron, doughnut, electronuclear machine, stellarator, storage ring, synchro-cyclotron, synchrotron, tokamak. *Informal:* atom-smasher.

5. **1. atomic radiation** alpha radiation, background radiation, beta radiation, calorescence, cascade shower, delta radiation, gamma radiation, ray, re-radiation, secondary emission, soft shower, twenty-one centimetre line. **2. ray** alpha ray, beta ray, delta ray, electron beam, gamma ray, molecular beam, molecular ray. **3. radioactivity** alpha decay, artificial radioactivity, beta decay, beta transformation, induced radioactivity, photodisintegration, stimulated emission. **4. radiation level** absorbed dose, ambient dose, background count, background radiation, chronic dose, gray count, rad count, rem count, strontium unit. **5. fallout** buffer distance, fallout contour, fallout pattern, nuclear freeze, nuclear winter, rainout, yield. **6. half-life** becquerel, curie, roentgen. **7. X-rays** roentgen ray, thermal X-rays, X-radiation.

6. **1. radioactivation** activation, breeding, capture, conversion, excitation, induction, initiation, ionisation, multiplication, spallation, transformation, transition. **2. fission** binary fission, photofission. **3. fusion** cold fusion, fusion reaction, nuclear fusion, thermonuclear reaction. **4. nuclear reaction** chain reaction, pair production, reaction. **5. meltdown** critical mass. *Informal:* China syndrome.

7. **1. atomic bomb** A-bomb, fission bomb, nuclear bomb. **2. hydrogen bomb** fusion bomb, H-bomb. **3. neutron bomb** clean bomb, clean weapon. **4. nuclear weapon** nuclear warhead.

8. **1. atomic theory** atomics, microphysics, nuclear physics, nucleonics, quantum electrodynamics, quantum mechanics, quantum theory.

9. **1. Geiger counter** cloud chamber, counter, counter tube, dosimeter, drop meter, Geiger-Müller counter, scintillation counter, scintillometer.

adj. **10.** **1. atomic** corpuscular, molecular, nuclear. **2. intermolecular** interatomic, intraatomic, intramolecular, subatomic.

11. **1. chain-reacting** multiplicational, subcritical, supercritical. **2. radioactive** actinic, charged, hot, irradiated, radiogenic, radiological. **3. fissile** fertile, fissionable, scissile. **4. nuclear** atomic, endoergic, endothermic, exoergic, exothermic, thermonuclear.

RELATED KEYWORDS: FUEL, SMALLNESS, MATTER, WEAPON

ATTACK

n. **1.** **1. attack** aggression, assault, attempt, drive, forage, foray, interdiction, offensive, onset, pillage, push, raid, rush, sally, sortie, storm, strafe, strike, surprise, thrust. **2. invasion** attack, attempt, incursion, infiltration, ingress, inroads, irruption, onset, raid, strafe. *Informal:* bust. **3. ambush** ambuscade, stake-out, trap. *Informal:* set-up. **4. air raid** air strike, assault, attack, blitz, Blitz, bombardment, broadside, first strike, plastering, strafe. *Informal:* prang, stoush. **5. charge** course, flèche. **6. counterattack** counteroffensive, escalation, fight-back, retaliation. **7. assailment** assault, attempt on one's life, battery, blow, feint, offence, onset, onslaught, salvo. **8. indecent assault** assault, date rape, interference, molestation, pack-rape, rape, ravishment, sexual assault, statutory rape *(US)*, violation.

2. **1. firing** bombing, cannonade, enfilade, field gunnery, fire, friendly fire, fusillade, pot shot, salvo, shellfire, shot, strafe, volley.

3. **1. attacker** aggressor, assailant, assailer, assaulter, bludgeoner, harasser, hawk. **2. raider** air raider, invader, space invader. **3. ambusher** ambuscader. **4. marauder** forager, forayer, mosstrooper, pillager. **5. front line** advance party, shock troops, spearhead, storm troops.

adj. **4.** **1. aggressive** assailant, belligerent, combative, hawkish, militant, persecutory, pugnacious, spoiling for a fight, truculent. *Informal:* aggro. **2. predatory** depredatory, incursive, invasive, offensive.

v. **5.** **1. attack** assail, assault, attempt someone's life, batter, beat up, carry the fight, din, fall on (or upon), fly at, go at, go for, hit, horsewhip, knuckle, lunge, make at, maul, pelt, pitch into, prey on or upon, punch, round on (or upon), sabre, savage, set about, set on, set upon, sic, sool, take off the gloves, turn on, visit, weigh into. *Informal:* bash, clobber, get, get (stuck) into, go the knuckle, hoe into, jump, jump down someone's throat, jumperpunch, lace *(British)*, lace into, larrup, let someone have it, make mincemeat of, mug, put in the boot, tear into, wade in (or into), whale into. **2. go on the offensive** aggress, be spoiling for a fight, come to blows, draw first blood, strike the first blow, take the offensive. **3. invade** besiege, blockade, lay siege to, leaguer, move in on, overrun, siege, stake out. **4. beset** beleaguer, besiege, declare open season on, harass, invest, lay siege to, leaguer, mob, press. *Informal:* gang up on. **5. ambush** ambuscade, descend, descend on (or upon), spring, surprise, swoop down. *Informal:* bushwhack, jump. **6. maraud** depredate, forage, foray, loot, pillage, pirate, plunder, prey, raid, ransack, spoliate. **7. charge** advance against, advance upon (or on), bear down on, erupt, lunge, remise, run at, rush, sally, tilt, tilt at. **8. counterattack** retaliate.

6. **1. fire** ack-ack, open up, pepper, shoot, shoot down, snipe. *Informal:* fill someone full of lead, ping, pot. **2. bomb** bombard, dive-bomb, saturate. *Informal:* lay an egg, nuke, plaster, prang. **3. strafe** pelt, shell, storm. *Informal:* zap. **4. fusillade** cannonade, enfilade. **5. raid** air raid, blitz. **6. feint** demonstrate.

adv. **7.** **1. aggressively** belligerently, harassingly, offensively, truculently.

8. **1. under attack** between two fires, on the receiving end, under fire, under seige.

RELATED KEYWORDS: DISAGREEMENT, DISAPPROVAL, CONTEST, FIGHTER, HITTING, HATE, RETALIATION, VIOLENCE, WAR, WEAPON

ATTEMPT

n.   **1.**   **1. attempt** assay, bid, effort, endeavour, essay, fling, long shot, lucubration, offer, run-through, shot, stroke, trial, try. *Informal:* burl, crack, fly, go, pop, stab, try-on, whack. **2. venture** adventure, experiment, gamble, speculation. **3. first chance** first-up. **4. second chance** two bites of (or at) the cherry. **5. striving** assailment, assay, conation, struggle, trial.

     2.   **1. attempter** aimer, assailant, assailer, assayer, endeavourer, essayer, essayist, mover, seeker, trier. **2. struggler** battler, do-it-yourselfer, striver. *Informal:* goer. **3. gambler** hazarder, punter. **4. candidate** appellant, applicant, applier, aspirant, postulant, pretender, probationer.

adj.   **3.**   **1. striving** conative, effortful, essayistic, grasping, struggling. **2. last-ditch** all-out, desperate.

v.   **4.**   **1. attempt** aim, assail, assay, endeavour, essay, seek, take on, try, undertake. *Informal:* have a lash at. **2. try for** aim, aim at, aim for, assay, attempt, endeavour, essay, pursue, seek, seek to, strive, study, tackle, undertake. **3. strive for** attack, exert oneself, grasp at, make so bold as to, push hard for, put (some) effort into, scrabble for, struggle for, work towards. **4. audition for** apply, read for, throw one's hat into (or in) the ring, try out for. **5. try one's luck** adventure, experiment, gamble, hazard, push one's luck, risk, speculate, take one's chance, tempt fortune, try one's fortune, venture on (or upon). *Informal:* chance. **6. try one's hand at** chance one's arm, make an attempt, take time out. *Informal:* give it a bash, give it a buck, give it a go, give it a go (or whirl), give it a nudge, have a bash, have a buck at, have a crack at, have a go, have a smack at, take (or have) a punt. **7. keep on trying** battle on, hammer away at. **8. go all out** bend over backwards, do one's level best, leave no stone unturned, move heaven and earth, put one's best foot forward, sink or swim. *Informal:* bust a gut, do one's darnedest, give it everything one has got, go for the doctor, shoot one's bolt.

RELATED KEYWORDS: ACCOMPLISHMENT, EFFORT, UNDERTAKING

ATTENTION

n.   **1.**   **1. attention** awareness, engagement, focalisation, heed, interest, note, notice, regard, remark.

     2.   **1. attentiveness** advertency, alertness, curiousness, heedfulness, mindfulness, regardfulness, watchfulness. **2. engrossment** absorbedness, absorption, fascination, intentness, interestedness. **3. assiduousness** application, assiduities, carefulness, sedulity, sedulousness. **4. fastidiousness** finicalness.

     3.   **1. interestingness** conspicuousness, deepness, fascination, juiciness, newsworthiness, readableness, remarkableness, savour, showiness, spice, zest.

     4.   **1. centre of attraction** centre of attention, concern, cynosure, eye-catcher, fascinator, focal point, focus, focus of attention, lodestar, spellbinder.

adj.   **5.**   **1. attentive** advertent, alert, alerted, argus-eyed, awake, careful, curious, heedful, interested, keen-eyed, mindful, observant, open-eyed, vigilant, watchful. **2. aware** alive to, awake up, on the ball, sharp, switched-on, vigilant, wakeful, wary. **3. absorbed** concerned, deep in, earnest, engrossed, intent, involved, preoccupied, preoccupied with, rapt, spellbound, wrapped up in. **4. assiduous** attentive, careful, diligent, mindful, painstaking, sedulous. **5. fastidious** chary, finical, finicky, selective. *Informal:* fernickety, pernickety.

     6.   **1. attention-getting** absorbing, arresting, conspicuous, curious, engrossing, eye-catching, fascinating, gripping, interesting, juicy, newsworthy, noteworthy, noticeable, ostentatious, readable, remarkable, showy, striking.

v.   **7.**   **1. pay attention** address oneself to, advert to, attend, be all ears, be glued to, concentrate, consider, focalise, focus, get down to, get on with, hang on the lips of, hang upon, heed, keep an eye on, listen, look, look at, look to, mark, mind, note, notice, regard, see about, see to, sink into, stand by, study, watch for. **2. notice** animadvert, be awake-up, enter into, eye, get with it, observe, observe on (or upon), remark, sit up and take notice.

     8.   **1. call attention to** agitate, engage, enkindle, point out, publicise. *Informal:* ram (or thrust) something down someone's throat. **2. draw attention to oneself** catch someone's eye, feature, make a splash, upstage. *Informal:* draw the crabs.

     9.   **1. engross** absorb, amuse, consume, devour, enwrap, fascinate, grip, hold the stage, interest, intrigue, involve, lose, occupy, preoccupy, spellbind.

adv.   **10.**   **1. attentively** absorbedly, advertently, alertly, fixedly, heedfully, interestedly, mindfully, on the alert, on the edge of one's seat (or chair), regardfully, with one's ears flapping. **2. assiduously** carefully, earnestly, intently, vigilantly.

11. **1. engrossingly** absorbingly, devouringly, fascinatingly, grippingly, interestingly, intriguingly, juicily, remarkably. **2. noticeably** conspicuously, showily, strikingly.

interj. **12.** **1. hey** ahem, ahoy, cooee, cop this, hallo, halloo, hallow, heigh, hello, hem, hey there, hi, hist, ho, hollo, hoy, hullo, hulloo, I say, look here, NB, nota bene, oi, there, yack-ai, yo-ho, yoo-hoo. **2. look out** fore, look here, timber, watch that last step (it's a doozy).

RELATED KEYWORDS: CAREFULNESS, CURIOSITY, PRECISION, SIGHT

ATTRACTION

n. **1.** **1. attraction** adduction, allurement, appetence, attractiveness, counterattraction, draw, enticement, magnetism, pull. **2. gravity** gravitation. **3. chemical affinity** chemotaxis, Van der Waals' forces.

2. **1. attracter** attractant, bait, decoy, draw, lure, teaser. **2. centre of attraction** centre of attention, cynosure, eye-catcher, fascinator, focal point, focus, focus of attention. **3. magnet** electromagnet, field magnet, loadstone, lodestone, magnetite, permanent magnet. **4. magnetiser** centre of attraction, keeper.

3. **1. magnetism** archaeomagnetism, archeomagnetism, earth magnetism, electro-magnetism, palaeomagnetism, terrestrial magnetism. **2. ferromagnetism** diamagnet-ism, ferrimagnetism, paramagnetism. **3. magnetisation** magnetic moment, magnetic permeability, magnetic susceptibility, remanence, retentivity. **4. magnetic force** coercive force, coercivity, electrovalent bond, flux, flux density, ionic bond, Lorentz force, magnetic field strength, magnetic flux, magnetic flux density, magnetic induction, mag-netic induction field, magnetic intensity, magnetic potential, magnetic vector potential, magnetomotive force, maxwell, polar bond. **5. magnetic field** electromagnetic field, electromagnetic wave, gravitational field. **6. magnetic pole** magnetic dipole, magnetic element, magnetic monopole, pole, unit pole. **7. magnetic bottle** magnetic mirror.

4. **1. magnetometry** magneto-chemistry, magnetohydrodynamics. **2. electromagnetic unit** gamma, gauss, magneton, tesla. **3. gravitational theory** Einstein theory, general theory of relativity, Newton's law of gravitation, special theory of relativity, unified field theory. **4. magnetometer** fluxgate, fluxmeter, magnetograph, variometer.

adj. **5.** **1. attractive** adducent, adductive, alluring, appetent, appetising, arresting, come-hither, seductive. **2. magnetic** aclinic, aeromagnetic, electromagnetic, geomagnetic, magneto-chemical, magnetomotive, magnetostatic, polar, pyromagnetic. **3. ferromagnetic** dia-magnetic, ferrimagnetic, paramagnetic. **4. gravitational** gravitative.

v. **6.** **1. attract** adduct, allure, bring towards, decoy, draw, draw to, engage, gather, lure, magnetise, pull. **2. be attracted to** be drawn to, cluster, gravitate, gravitate to (or towards).

RELATED KEYWORDS: ALLURE, BEAUTY, CONVERGENCE, SEX

AUTHORITY

n. **1.** **1. authority** accreditation, authorisation, carte blanche, commission, jurisdiction, last word, mandate, manus, mastership, officiation, order, power, prerogative, procuration, roving commission. **2. authoritativeness** arbitrament, control, dominance, dom-inancy, governance, jurisdiction, masterfulness, potence, potency, power, rule, supremacy, supremeness, supremity. **3. authoritarianism** absolutism, bumbledom, despotism, divine right of kings, domination, domineeringness, Fascism, officialism, peremptoriness, totalitarianism, tyranny. **4. dominion** command, commission, condominium, domin-ium, imperium, reign, rule, sway. **5. sovereignty** governance, government, headship, hegemony, kingship, leadership, lordship, magistracy, masterdom, mastery, seigniory, signory, supremacy, suzerainty. **6. rule** command, control, governance, government, jurisdiction, law, martial law, mastery, regulation, sway. *Informal:* say-so. **7. emblem of authority** arms, chair, crown, crownpiece, diadem, fasces, mayoral chain, regality, rod, sceptre, sovereignty, throne.

2. **1. the authorities** Big Brother, elite, Establishment, faceless men, officialdom, the administration, the elite, the powers that be, the ruling classes, them.

3. **1. the police** constabulary, filth, force, gendarmerie, police, police force, police service, the law, the long arm of the law, the thin blue line. *Informal:* ducks and geese, fuzz, the Bill *(British)*, the boys in blue, the filth. **2. police unit** Armed Constabulary, CIB, CID, coastguard, consorting squad, Customs, dog squad, drug squad, FBI, field police, flying squad, military police, mounted police, Scotland Yard, secret police, strike force, vice squad, water police.

4. **1. policeman** booliman *(Aboriginal English)*, bulldog, chief superintendent, commis-sary, constable, convict constable, customs officer, detective, farm constable, gendarme, gunjabal *(Aboriginal English)*, inspector, lawman *(US)*, marshal, operative *(US)*, patrolman, pointsman *(NZ)*, police constable, police officer, policewoman, prisoner constable, proctor, provost, provost marshal, ranger, roundsman *(US)*, sergeant, super, superintendent, trooper. *Informal:* bobby *(Chiefly British)*, cop, copper, crime buster, demon, flat, flatfoot, heavy, jack, Joe, john, John Hop, jonnop, Mickey, Mounty, narc, pig, provo, rozzer, speed cop, traps, walloper. **2. prison officer** deathwatch, gaoler, jailer, turnkey, warden *(Chiefly US)*, warder, wardress. *Informal:* four-by-two, screw, trump. **3. vigilante** posse *(Chiefly US)*, posse comitatus, vigilance committee, vigilance man *(US)*. **4. peace officer** marshal *(US)*, sheriff *(US)*, special, special constable. **5. parking policeman** parking inspector, traffic warden *(British)*. *Informal:* grey ghost *(Victoria, NSW, WA)*, grey meanie *(Victoria)*, meter maid *(British)*. **6. ticket inspector** *Informal:* snapper, ticket snapper. **7. attendance officer** truant officer.

5. 1. police station *Informal:* cop shop, gendarmerie.

adj. **6. 1. authoritative** commanding, competent, dominant, dominative, imperative, imperial, in the saddle, master, official, predominant, prepotent, sceptred, sovereign, superintendent, supreme. **2. official** authentical, cathedral, ex-cathedra, ex-officio, oracular.

7. 1. autocratic authoritarian, autocratical, dictatorial, domineering, fascist, feudal, feudalistic, imperial, imperious, lordly, magisterial, masterful, overbearing, peremptory, totalitarian, tsarist.

v. **8. 1. authorise** accredit, clear, crown, empower, enable, establish, legitimate, license, mandate, privilege, revest, sanction, seal, swear in, warrant. *Informal:* give the nod to.

9. 1. pronounce on have the final word, have the last say, lay down the law, speak ex cathedra.

adv. **10. 1. officially** authoritatively, ex cathedra, from the horse's mouth. **2. in the name of** by (or in) virtue of, by the authority of.

RELATED KEYWORDS: COMMAND, FORCE, JUDGE, GOVERNMENT, REPRESSION, MANAGEMENT, MANAGER, RULER

AVOIDANCE

n. **1. 1. avoidance** buck-passing, escapism, evasion, evasiveness, obliqueness, tokenism. **2. abstention** abstinence, eschewal, forbearance, self-restraint. **3. escape** dodge, duck, flight, shuffle, sidestep. *Informal:* a moonlight flit.

2. 1. loophole bypass, conscience clause, doubletalk, escape clause, escape mechanism, fine print, sidestep, small print. **2. tax shelter** tax dodge, tax haven, tax lurk. **3. quibble** chicane, chicanery, equivocation, evasion, excuse, fencing, hedge, prevarication, procrastination, quibbling, quip, quirk, run-around, runround, subterfuge, temporisation.

3. 1. avoider absconder, abstainer, averter, chicaner, deserter, dodger, escaper, escapist, eschewer, evader, shunner, truant. *Informal:* draft dodger. **2. fleer** blencher, boggler, ducker, fugitive, runaway. *Informal:* fly-by-night. **3. shirker** bilker, buck-passer, hedger, malingerer, shirk, skulker. *Informal:* bludger, dingo, quitter, slacker. **4. quibbler** equivocator, fencer, prevaricator, procrastinator, temporiser.

adj. **4. 1. evasive** elusive, elusory, escapist, slippery. **2. fugitive** in flight, runaway. *Informal:* fly-by-night. **3. aloof** noncommittal, stand-offish, unforthcoming. **4. quibbling** equivocal, equivocating, evasive, oblique, prevaricating.

v. **5. 1. avoid** avert, back away from, blench from, blink at, deconflict, duck, evade, fight shy of, give a wide berth to, jib, miss, shrink from, shun, shy away from. *Informal:* dip out, not touch with a (ten foot or forty foot) barge pole, steer clear of. **2. bypass** boycott, cold-shoulder, eschew, fob off, get off, leave, let sleeping dogs lie, put on one side, shun. *Informal:* ditch. **3. shirk** bilk, dodge, elude, evade, shuffle out of, weasel out on *(Chiefly US)*. *Informal:* bludge, dingo, funk, pass the buck, sell the dump. **4. quibble** avoid the issue, beat about the bush, beg the question, deflect, equivocate, evade, fence, hedge, hem and haw, parry, prevaricate, procrastinate, put on the back burner, shelve, sidestep, skate round (or over), stall, temporise.

6. 1. evade elude, get away from, give someone the run-around, give someone the slip, shake off, throw off. **2. flee** abscond, beat a retreat, bilk, bolt, do a bunk, escape, flit, fly, make a getaway, run, run away, take (to) flight, take to one's heels, turn tail. *Informal:* blow through, cut, do a get, take it on the lam *(US)*, take to the hills.

adv. **7. 1. quibblingly** avertedly, equivocatingly, evadingly, evasively, prevaricatingly, shrinkingly, temporisingly. **2. obliquely** elusively, equivocally. **3. on the run** in flight. *Informal:* on the lam *(US)*.

RELATED KEYWORDS: RETREAT, IDLENESS, ABANDONMENT, ESCAPE

AWARD

n. **1.** **1. award** a feather in one's cap, accolade, blue riband, blue ribbon, cordon bleu, credit, distinction, laurels, prize. **2. honorarium** gold watch. **3. accolade** dub. **4. laurel wreath** crown, garland, palm. **5. prize** booty, door prize, lucky door prize, spoil, spoils, stakes, sweep, sweepstake. **6. entertainment award** Awgie Awards, BAFTA, Emmy, gold record, Grammy, Logie, Mo, Oscar, platinum record, Sammy. **7. writing award** Age Book Award, Booker Prize, Miles Franklin Award, Patrick White Award, Pulitzer Prize, Vogel Award, Walkley Award. **8. painting award** Archibald Prize, Blake Prize, Sulman Prize, Wynne Prize. **9. general award** Churchill Fellowship, Fulbright scholarship, Harkness Fellowship, Nobel prize, Rhodes scholars, Rotary Scholarship, ZONTA Fellowship. **10. sporting award** America's Cup, Ashes, Davis Cup, FA Cup, Melbourne Cup, Sheffield Shield, Stawell Easter Gift, Stawell Gift, The Auld Mug, World Cup. **11. best and fairest** Allan Border Medal, Brownlow Medal, Dally M.Award, fairest and best *(Especially WA)*, Magarey Medal, Sandover Medal. **12. trophy** belt, black belt, blue, bronze medal, colours, Cup, first prize, gold medal, Grand Prix, loving-cup, pendant, pennant, premium, ribbon, silver medal. *Informal:* pot. **13. honours list** birthday honours, roll of honour. **14. medal** bar, citation, cluster *(US Army)*, decoration, honour, medallion. *Informal:* fruit salad, gong. **15. knighthood** dubbing. **16. booby prize** *Informal:* wooden spoon.

2. **1. award winner** awardee, diplomate, honoree *(US)*, laureate, licentiate, prizewinner. **2. medallist** gold medallist. **3. honour roll** honours system, roll of honour.

v. **3.** **1. award** adjudge, afford, bestow, grant, present. **2. decorate** crown, garland, laurel, medal, reward. **3. diploma** cap *(NZ)*. **4. knight** dub.

RELATED KEYWORDS: EMBLEM, ENTERTAINMENT, FINE ARTS, WRITING, SIGN, SPORT, TEACHING, WAR

BADNESS

n. **1.** **1. badness** damnableness, dismalness, egregiousness, grievousness, lousiness, miserableness, peccancy, preciousness, shamefulness, sinfulness, unfortunateness, woefulness, wretchedness. **2. awfulness** abominableness, atrociousness, contemptibleness, deplorability, despicableness, detestableness, devilishness, diabolicalness, dreadfulness, fiendishness, infernality, monstrousness, terribleness, vileness. **3. adverseness** direfulness, portentousness, sinisterness, undesirableness. **4. squalidness** insalubrity, seaminess, shoddiness, sleaziness, unhealthiness. **5. worthlessness** paltriness, unworthiness.

2. **1. bad thing** abomination, atrocity, bane, bastard, blemish, botch, bungle, detestation, horror. *Informal:* fizzer. **2. trash** brum, garbage, goats, mess of pottage, pulp, rubbish. *Informal:* brummy, el cheapo, quickie, rag. **3. the worst** low tide, the (living) end. *Informal:* the pits. **4. jonah** evil omen, evil star, hex. *Informal:* hoodoo, jinx, mozz.

3. **1. bad person** black sheep, good-for-nothing, idler, ne'er-do-well, undesirable, waster, wastrel. *Informal:* bad apple, bad egg, bad hat, bad lot, bad penny, baddie, rag, whatnot. **2. bastard** *(Informal)* coyote *(US)*, cur, dunghill, pimp, swine, the (living) end. *Informal:* bathplug, blister *(British)*, bugger, bum, cow, dog, drop kick, hound, mongrel, scumbag, so-and-so, sod, stinker. **3. louse** *(Informal)* cad, dastard, recreant, reptile, runt, serpent, skulk, snake, sneak, sneaker, squib, varmint, vermin, viper, wretch. *Informal:* blighter, bounder *(British)*, dingo, fink, heel, insect, pussy-footer, rat, ratfink, rotter *(Chiefly British)*, shocker, skunk, swab, toad. **4. creep** *Informal:* creeping Jesus, drip, jerk. **5. cadger** bushranger, leech, parasite, ranger, sponge, sponger, vampire. *Informal:* bastard from the bush, bloodsucker, bludger, bot, droog, knight of the road, scab, ten-per-center. **6. bitch** *(Informal)* carline *(Chiefly Scottish)*, crone, gorgon, hag, harpy, harridan, hellcat, scold, witch. *Informal:* cow, fleabag, old cow, rich bitch. **7. fiend** animal, beast, brute, demon, devil, hellhound, lost soul, vulture. **8. monster** Frankenstein, ogre, ogress, savage. **9. scum** trash, white trash *(US)*, worthless lot.

adj. **4.** **1. bad** abject, deplorable, dismal, egregious, grievous, hopeless, ill, inadequate, mean, miserable, paltry, pathetical, pernicious, poor, sad, shameful, short, sorry, substandard, terrible, weak, woeful, wretched. *Informal:* measly, not much chop, not much cop, pathetic. **2. worthless** base, botchy, brum, cheap, cheapjack, good-for-nothing, inferior, low, low-grade, low-rent, mean, ne'er-do-well, nugatory, rubbishy, scrubby, shoddy, sleazy, tin, twopenny, unacceptable, unsatisfactory, unworthy, useless, vagabond, valueless. *Informal:* bodgie, brummy, bum, crook, crummy, dud, el cheapo, grotty, mongrel, no-good, not worth a tinker's cuss (or damn), not worth a whoop *(British)*, oncus, onkus, punk, queer, scummy, tacky, tin-pot, up to putty. **3. awful** abhorrent, abominable, abysmal, abyssal, appalling, atrocious, beastly, chronical, contemptible, currish, deplorable, despicable, detestable, disastrous, disgraceful, dreadful, enormous, execrable, filthy, grievous, heinous, hideous, ignominious, inexcusable, inexpiable, lamentable, loathsome, monstrous, outrageous, pitiful, repugnant, rotten, shocking, terrible, unmentionable, unspeakable, vile. *Informal:* bastard, bastardly, chronic, God-awful, ungodly, unholy, unreal. **4. adverse** cross, detrimental, dire, direful, disadvantageous, hard, ill, impossible, inimical, malevolent, malign, portentous, thwart, undesirable, unfavourable, unfortunate. **5. evil** black, dark, depraved, ill, malefic, malevolent, pernicious, sinful, sinister, ungodly, unholy, wicked. **6. worst** of the deepest (or blackest) dye. **7. devilish** cloven-footed, cloven-hoofed, diabolic, diabolical, fiendish, hellish, infernal, satanic, stygian. **8. damned** anathema, cursed, curst, damnable. **9. squalid** insalubrious, seamy, sordid. **10. stinking** *(Informal)* cankerous, filthy, foul, frightful, horrid, noisome, odious, putrid, rank, revolting, septic. *Informal:* feral, festy, lousy, rotten.

adv. **5.** **1. badly** bad, dismally, ill, miserably, shamefully, undesirably, unfortunately, woefully. **2. awfully** abominably, abysmally, appallingly, atrociously, damnably, deplorably, despicably, dreadfully, egregiously, execrably, shockingly, terribly, unspeakably.

RELATED KEYWORDS: BLEMISH, INEXPEDIENCE, DETERIORATION, UNLAWFULNESS, MEDIOCRITY, IMMORALITY, IMPERFECTION, INFERIORITY

BARENESS

n. **1.** **1. bareness** blankness, bleakness, denudation, leaflessness. **2. nudity** décolletage, dishabille, nakedness, nudeness, undress. *Informal:* birthday suit. **3. nudism** naturism.

2. **1. undressing** dismantlement, disrobement, divestiture, divesture, exposure, indecent exposure, lap dance, striptease. *Informal:* full monty, hambone, poppy show.

3. **1. nudist** Adamite, artiste, disrober, naturist, skinny-dipper, stripper. *Informal:* jaybird, streaker. **2. nude** centrefold, full-frontal. *Informal:* beefcake, cheesecake, pin-up.

4. **1. hairlessness** alopecia, alopecia areata, baldness, beardlessness, calvities, exposedness, exposure, mange, manginess, tonsure. **2. baldhead** baldpate. *Informal:* baldy, eggshell blonde, nude nut.

5. **1. clearance** circumdenudation, clearage, defloration, defoliation, deforestation, denudation, disafforestation, disforestation, disfurnishment, excoriation. **2. burn-off** back-burn, burn, burn-back, bush-burn *(NZ)*, control burn. **3. paring** decortication, excortication, exfoliation. **4. clearing** clears *(NZ)*, landing field.

6. **1. depilation** deplumation, ecdysis, epilation, exuviation, moulting.

adj. **7.** **1. bare** bleak, defoliate, denudate, exposed, hypaethral, leafless, nudicaul, nudicaulous, open, uncovered. **2. featureless** blank, open. **3. unpainted** unvarnished. **4. revealing** décolleté, low, low-necked, peekaboo. **5. nude** en déshabillé, full frontal, full-frontal, naked, stark, stark-naked, unclad, unclothed, uncovered. *Informal:* bollocky, nudy, starkers. **6. girlie** *(Informal)*.

8. **1. undressed** barefaced, barefoot, barefooted, barehanded, bareheaded, barelegged, low-cut, topless.

9. **1. bald** baldheaded, baldish, baldpated, thatchless, tonsured. *Informal:* bald as a bandicoot. **2. hairless** clean-shaven, furless, glabrate, glabrous, smooth, smooth-faced. **3. featherless** callow, impennate, unfledged. **4. depilatory** exfoliative.

v. **10.** **1. bare** clear out, debark, disfurnish, dismantle, divest, expose, open, uncase, uncover, undrape, unshroud, unswathe, unveil, unwrap. **2. clear** burn off, bush, deforest, disafforest, disforest. *Informal:* bushwhack *(NZ)*. **3. strip** clear, deplume, disfurnish, dismantle, disrobe, uncase, undress, unshroud, unswathe. **4. pare** bark, decorticate, excoriate, excorticate, flype, hull, peel, pod, skin, unhusk. **5. deflower** defoliate, denudate, denude, exfoliate, strip. **6. depilate** clip, deplume, epilate, fleece, grain, pink, pull, shave, shear, tonsure, unhair. **7. moult** exuviate, mew, shed.

11. **1. undress** bare, disrobe, divest, expose oneself, strip, uncover, unhood, unrobe. *Informal:* peel. **2. go naked** *Informal:* flash, jaybird, skinny-dip, streak.

adv. **12.** **1. nakedly** au naturel, in the nude, nudely. *Informal:* in one's birthday suit, in the altogether, in the bollock, in the bollocky, in the buff, in the nick, in the nuddy, in the raw.

RELATED KEYWORDS: CUT, ENTERTAINER, ENTERTAINMENT, FARMING, FIRE, REMOVAL, SKIN

BEAUTY

n. **1.** **1. beauty** beauteousness, comeliness, gorgeousness, heavenliness, loveliness, pulchritude. **2. good looks** attractiveness, handsomeness, jauntiness, picturesqueness, seemliness, sexiness, smartness, spunkiness. **3. prettiness** bonniness, fairness. **4. physical beauty** the body beautiful. **5. glory** braveness, brilliance, gloriousness, grandeur, grandiosity, grandness, impressiveness, lustrousness, magnificence, resplendence, resplendency, showiness, splendidness, splendour, sumptuousness, superbness.

6. radiance bloom, brightness, brilliance, gloss. **7. elegance** charm, elegancy, exquisiteness, flair, fluency, grace, gracefulness, gracility, style, symmetry. **8. delicacy** daintiness, lightness. **9. voluptuosity** buxomness, shapeliness. **10. aesthetics** esthetics.

2. **1. beautiful person** adonis, angel, Aphrodite, Apollo, arm candy, bathing beauty, bathing belle, beau ideal, beauty, beauty queen, belle, bombshell, dream, English rose, goddess, houri, nymph, peri, phoenix, picture, swan, Venus *(Poetic)*. *Informal:* a bit of alright, a good sort, corpus delicti, dish, doll, dolly, dreamboat, eyeful, good-looker, honey, hunk, knockout, looker, perv, smasher, sort, stunner.

adj. **3.** **1. beautiful** Adonic, angelic, apollonian, aureate, beauteous, exquisite, fair, gorgeous, heavenly, lovely, lustrous, marvellous, nymphean, ornamental, personable, pulchritudinous, splendid, statuesque, sumptuous. *Informal:* dreamy, stunning. **2. attractive** beautiful, becoming, bosker, comely, decorative, fair, good-looking, jaunty, piquant, sightly, smart, soignée, striking, tottymungous. *Informal:* bonzer. **3. good-looking** comely, fine, good, handsome, seemly, well-favoured. *Informal:* babelicious *(Chiefly US)*, drop-dead, easy on the eyes, phat. **4. pretty** beautiful, blooming, bonny, bright-eyed, dainty, dinky, dishy, dollish, fair, mignon, pretty-pretty, prettyish. **5. elegant** civilised, cultivated, cultured, exquisite, fine, genteel, good, polished, polite, refined, silken, thoroughbred. **6. voluptuous** bosomy, busty, buxom, callipygian, comely, curvaceous, curvy, deep-bosomed, full-bodied, Rubenesque, sexy, shapely, sonsy *(Scottish, Irish)*, well-formed, well-proportioned. *Informal:* pneumatic. **7. picturesque** aesthetic, aesthetical, artistic, charming, esthetical, pleasant. **8. glorious** adorable, aureate, brilliant, dashing, flamboyant, gorgeous, grand, grandiose, imperial, lustrous, magnificent, majestic, marvellous, palmy, regal, resplendent, splendid, splendorous, stately, sumptuous, superb. **9. graceful** aerial, aery *(Poetic)*, ethereal, flowing, fluent, gracile, lissom, lithe, lithesome, supple. **10. radiant** blooming, bright, ravishing, rosy, rosy-cheeked, ruddy, splendent. **11. delicate** dainty, minikin.

v. **4.** **1. beautify** decorate, glamorise, prettify, pretty, refine, set off. **2. smarten** brighten, brighten up. *Informal:* posh up, slick up *(US)*, tart up. **3. be beautiful** be dressed to the nines, be tarted up, be well turned out, look good.

adv. **5.** **1. beautifully** angelically, beauteously, becomingly, gorgeously, stunningly. **2. decoratively** attractively, bravely, handsomely. **3. prettily** bonnily, dollishly. **4. gloriously** grandiosely, grandly, imperially, lustrously, resplendently. **5. splendidly** regally, statuesquely, sumptuously, superbly. **6. gracefully** aerially, daintily, delicately, elegantly, ethereally, exquisitely, flowingly, fluently. **7. radiantly** bright, brightly. **8. voluptuously** buxomly.

RELATED KEYWORDS: ALLURE, ATTRACTION, DECORATION, PERFECTION, PLEASANTNESS

BEHAVIOUR

n. **1.** **1. behaviour** action, actions, conduct, course, dealing, demeanour, form, front, manner, mode of conduct, observance, proceeding, treatment. *Informal:* goings-on. **2. behaviour pattern** collective behaviour, course of action, culture complex, method, MO, modus operandi, path, procedure, response, standards. **3. custom** convention, foreignism *(US)*, habit, habitude, living, manner, mannerism, meme, practice, praxis, role, trick, usage, way, way of acting, ways. **4. conduct** air, appearance, bearing, carriage, comportment, demeanour, deportment, mien. **5. manners** breeding, finish.

adj. **2.** **1. well-behaved** couth, good, good-mannered, law-abiding, polite, respectable, seemly, well-mannered. *Informal:* as good as gold, pukka, straight-arrow.

v. **3.** **1. behave** acquit oneself, act, bear oneself, behave oneself, carry oneself, comport oneself, conduct oneself, deal, demean oneself, deport oneself, do, do by, mind one's p's and q's, sit (up) like Jacky. **2. perform** paddle one's own canoe, play one's part, shift for oneself. *Informal:* play the game. **3. live** lead one's life, run one's race. **4. react** respond, treat.

RELATED KEYWORDS: CHARACTER, COURTESY, LAWFULNESS, MORALITY, OBEDIENCE, PROPRIETY, PSYCHE

BELIEF

n. **1.** **1. belief** acceptance, acceptation, assumption, confidence, credence, credit, credulity, credulousness, dependence, faith, fondness, presumption, suspension of disbelief, trust, trustfulness, trustingness. **2. popular belief** folk myth, folk remedy, folk story, folklore, myth, old wives' tale, oral tradition, superstition, urban myth. *Informal:* bug. **3. misbelief**.

2. **1. opinion** apprehension, concept, conception, conjecture, conviction, editorial, estimate, idea, impression, judgement, mind, notion, preconception, prejudice, prenotion, prepossession, rooted opinion, sentiment, surmise, theory, thinking, thought. **2. public opinion** groundswell, vox pop, vox populi. **3. viewpoint** perspective, point of view, position, school of thought, stance, stand, standpoint, view, Weltanschauung, world view.

3. **1. creed** articles of faith, belief, canon, catechism, credendum, credo, doctrine, dogma, doxy, faith, gospel, ideology, ism, philosophy, plank, platform, principle, standards, teaching, tenet. **2. ism** absolutism, agnosticism, animism, asceticism, atheism, Averroism, Baha'ism, Buddhism, Calvinism, Catholicism, Confucianism, Congregationalism, Conservative Judaism, creationism, deism, demonism, diabolism, ditheism, dualism, episcopalism, evangelicalism, evangelism, existentialism, fatalism, fideism, Foism, fundamentalism, heathenism, henotheism, Hinduism, humanism, idealism, illuminism, illusionism, immaterialism, immersionism, indifferentism, infralapsarianism, Islamism, Jacobinism, Jainism, Jansenism, Judaism, Lamaism, materialism, Methodism, Mithraism, Mohammedanism, monotheism, moral relativism, Moslemism, Muslimism, mysticism, naturalism, neo-paganism, nihilism, occultism, ontologism, Orphism, Orthodox Judaism, paganism, panentheism, pantheism, papism, perfectionism, polytheism, Presbyterianism, Protestantism, Pure Land Buddhism, Quakerism, Rastafarianism, Reform Judaism, resurrectionism, Roman Catholicism, Romanism, sacerdotalism, Saivism, Salvationism, scientism, Shaivism, shamanism, Sikhism, spiritism, spiritualism, sublapsarianism, Sufism, supralapsarianism, Tantrism, Taoism, theanthropism, theism, Tractarianism, traducianism, transcendentalism, Trinitarianism, tritheism, Zoroastrianism.

4. **1. believability** accreditation, credential, credibility, credibleness, credit. *Informal:* cred.

adj. **5.** **1. believing** assured, confident, confiding, credent, credulous, superstitious, trustful, trusting. **2. credal** doctrinal, ideological, mythical.

6. **1. believable** authentic, credible, fiducial, plausible, reliable, swallowable, true, trustworthy, worthy of belief.

v. **7.** **1. believe** accept, accredit, adjudge, adopt, assume, believe in, credit, deem, have confidence in, hold, imagine, opine, pin one's faith on, presume, profess, put one's trust in, rely on (or upon), suppose, take (or put) stock in *(Chiefly US)*, take for granted, take someone at their word, think, trust, trust in, understand. *Informal:* swallow. **2. misbelieve**

adv. **8.** **1. believingly** confidently, credulously, superstitiously, trustfully, trustingly. **2. in my opinion** to the best of one's belief.

RELATED KEYWORDS: CERTAINTY, CONJECTURE, JUDGEMENT

BEND

n. **1.** **1. bend** angle, bent, bow, corner, crook, curve, dogleg, elbow, flection, flexion, flexure, fold, fork, hairpin bend, inflection, inflexion, notch, S-bend, S-shaped bend, sinus, switchback, winding, zigzag. **2. angularity** acuteness, angularities, angularness, angulation, bifurcation, crookedness, flexure, forkedness, obliqueness, obliquity, perpendicularity.

2. **1. inclination** altitude, angle of attack, attitude, azimuth, bank, bearing, camber angle, cant, codeclination, declination, depression, deviation, dip, elevation, elongation, grid magnetic angle, grid variation, grivation, heading, magnetic declination, magnetic variation, polar distance, solar parallax, stalling angle.

3. **1. angle in geometry** oblique angle, obtuse angle, reflex angle, right angle, salient angle, spherical angle, straight angle. **2. adjacent angle** allied angles, alternate angles, co-interior angles, complementary angle, corresponding angles, exterior angle, plane angle, re-entrant angle, supplementary angle, vertical angle. **3. angle of light** angle of incidence, angle of reflection, angle of refraction, angular diameter, critical angle. **4. type of angle** axil, beam, bite, fleam, quarter point, quirk, steeve, stop, wedge. **5. degree** centigrade, complement, mil, minute, pitch, radian, second, steradian, supplement.

4. **1. instrument measuring an angle** astrolabe, clinometer, declinometer, gradiograph, gradiometer, inclinometer, octant, protractor, set square, sextant, square, theodolite, transit *(US Surveying)*, triangle *(Chiefly US)*, trigonometer, try square, variometer, vertical circle.

adj. **5.** **1. bent** antrorse, biflex, crooked, flectional, flexional, flexural, forked. **2. angular** angulated, equiangular, isogonic. **3. acute** askew, aslant, cant, oblique, out of square, skew. **4. perpendicular** contrary, decussate, normal, on the beam, orthogonal, plumb, square, vertical. **5. angled** forked, inclined, inflexed, jagged, notched, serrated, zigzag.

v. **6.** **1. bend** bow, circumflex, couch, crouch, flex, incline, jackknife, obvert, sag, spring, stoop, turn. **2. angle** square, square away, stagger.

7. **1. turn** corner, quarter, tack. **2. zigzag** wind, wind one's (or its) way.

adv. **8.** **1. angularly** antrorsely, crookedly, diagonally, forkedly, obliquely, orthogonally, perpendicularly, rectangularly. **2. at an angle** abeam, athwart, athwartships, cornerways, cornerwise, crabways, crabwise, square, zigzag. **3. aslant** akimbo, askew.

RELATED KEYWORDS: DIVERGENCE, DEVIATION, SHARPNESS, SLOPE

BLACK

n. **1.** **1. black** blue-black, jet, jet black, sable, sloe. **2. blackness** darkness, inkiness, lividness, nigritude, obscurity, pitchiness, shadow, sootiness, swarthiness. **3. nigrescence** nigrification. **4. shadowing** chiaroscuro, crosshatching, hatching, shading, shadow.

2. **1. blackener** animal black, black, blacking, carbon black, charcoal, ivory black, kohl, lampblack, nigrosine. **2. liquid black** black ink, Indian ink, japan, printer's ink.

adj. **3.** **1. black** black as jet, black as pitch, black as the ace of spades, coal-black, dusky, inky, piceous, pitch-black, pitch-dark, pitchy, raven, sable *(Poetic)*, sombre, swarthy. **2. blackish** coaly, nigrescent. **3. blackened** corked. **4. ebony** ebon *(Poetic)*, jet, jetty. **5. black-browed** black-headed.

v. **4.** **1. blacken** black, black-lead, blot, darken, denigrate, nigrify, smudge. **2. darken** charcoal, cork, smoke. **3. ebonise** japan.

RELATED KEYWORDS: COLOURLESSNESS, HAIR, DARK

BLEMISH

n. **1.** **1. blemish** defect, deformity, disfigurement, fault, flaw, imperfection, mutilation, tarnish, vice. **2. birthmark** beauty spot, blemish, discolouration, lentigo, macula, mole, Mongolian spot, naevus, nevus *(US)*, stigma, stork mark, strawberry mark. **3. freckle** age spot, blotch, dot, fleck, lentigo, liver spot, maculation, speckle, splotch, spot, variole. **4. pimple** acne, blackhead, comedo, milium, papilla, pustule, whelk, whitehead. *Informal:* crunchie, zit, zits. **5. sore** blister, blood blister, bruise, canker, cold sore, ecchymosis, fester, phlyctena, proud flesh, ulcer, water blister. **6. cyst** boil, carbuncle, furuncle, sty, wen. **7. wart** condyloma, corn, verruca. **8. scar** cheloid, cicatrice, furunculosis, granulation, granulation tissue, keloid, pit, pock, pockmark, scratch. **9. wale** weal, welt. **10. lovebite** *Informal:* hickey *(Originally US)*. **11. spottiness** imbruement, imbuement, patchiness, scratchiness.

adj. **2.** **1. blemished** blotchy, patchy, scabby, scabious, splotchy. **2. bruised** black-and-blue, blebby, blistery, blue, ecchymotic. **3. freckled** dapple, freckly, macular, maculate, naevoid, spotted. **4. pimply** spotty. **5. scarred** cheloidal, cicatrised, keloidal, pockmarked, pocky, scarified. **6. bloody** blood-spattered, bloodstained, gory, sanguinary, sanguine. **7. disfigured** crooked, deformed, grotesque, miscreated, misshapen.

v. **3.** **1. blemish** blot, blotch, dapple, discolour, ensanguine, fleck, imbue, mackle, mottle, scratch, splotch, spot, stain, sully. **2. freckle** maculate, speckle, spot. **3. disfigure** deface, deform, distort, mar, misshape, mutilate.

RELATED KEYWORDS: UGLINESS, DAMAGE, IMPERFECTION

BLUE

n. **1.** **1. blue** azure, caerulean, cerulean, cornflower, forget-me-not, lapis lazuli, sapphire, sky blue. **2. light blue** Copenhagen blue, pearl blue, pearl grey, powder blue, Wedgwood blue. **3. deep blue** anil, Bristol blue, gentian blue, indigo, perse, royal blue, ultramarine, violet. **4. navy** blue-black. **5. electric blue** peacock blue. **6. slate** steel blue. **7. blue-green** aqua, aquamarine, beryl, Nile blue, Nile green, saxe blue, sea, sea green, turquoise.

2. **1. blue pigment** bice, Brunswick blue, cobalt blue, cyanine, indican, indophenol, induline, pastel, Prussian blue, sapphirine, smalt, Thenard's blue, true blue, verditer, viridian, woad, zaffre. **2. washing blue** blue, blue-bag. **3. blue light** Bengal light, Bengal match. **4. blueing.**

3. **1. blueness** bluishness. **2. lividity** cyanopathy.

adj. **4.** **1. blue** cold, cyanic, ice-blue, pavonine, periwinkle, royal blue, sapphire, sapphirine, woaded. **2. azure** azury, caerulean, cerulean, skiey, sky-blue, skyey *(Chiefly Poetic)*, skylike. **3. bluish** aquamarine, blue-green, blueish, bluey, glaucous. **4. blue-grey** blue-black, cyanotic, griseous, livid, slaty.

RELATED KEYWORDS: COLOUR, GREEN, PURPLE

BLUNTNESS

n.　**1.**　　**1. bluntness** dullness, obtuseness, pointlessness. **2. blunting** hebetation.

adj.　**2.**　　**1. blunt** arcuate, convex, curved, dull, dullish, flat, obtundent, obtuse, pointless, round, worn. *Informal:* flat as a tack. **2. rounded** hebetate, obtuse. **3. club-shaped** clavate, claviform.

v.　**3.**　　**1. blunt** dampen, deaden, dull, hebetate, obtund, opiate, turn.

adv.　**4.**　　**1. bluntly** dully, obtusely, opacity.

　　　　　RELATED KEYWORDS: LEVEL, SMOOTHNESS

BODILY DISCHARGE

n.　**1.**　　**1. bodily discharge** eccrisis, egestion, excretion. **2. discharge** defluxion, flow, gleet, ichor, lochia, matter, maturation, pus, suppuration, swab. **3. perspiration** diaphoresis, exudate, exudation, foam, lather, sudor, sweat, transpiration. **4. menstruation** catamenia, menses, period. *Informal:* girl's week, monthlies, the curse. **5. gore** grume. **6. excrement** excreta. **7. sewage** effluent, nightsoil, soil.

　　　　2.　　**1. secretion** blood serum, chalone, incretion, internal secretion, juice, recrement, sebum, serous fluid, serum, smegma, synovia. **2. blennorrhagia. 3. bile** gall. **4. semen** ejaculation, emission, seed, sperm, spermatic fluid. **5. hormone** autacoid, corticosteroid, enzyme, histamine, insulin, leptin, lymph, steroid. **6. mucus** expectoration, phlegm, snivel, spittle, sputum. *Informal:* bogey, boo-boo, booger, drool, snot. **7. saliva** salivation, slaver, slobber, spit, spittle. *Informal:* drool, slag. **8. cerumen** earwax. **9. tear** sleep, teardrop. **10. lactation** beastings, beestings, biestings, colostrum, milk. **11. animal secretion** cast, castor, cuckoo-spit, flyspeck, manna, meconium, pheromone, royal jelly, spit, spittle, toad spittle, trehala. **12. seborrhoea** blennorrhoea.

　　　　3.　　**1. defecation** business, evacuation, movement, passage. *Informal:* big job, crash, jobbies, number two. **2. diarrhoea** dysentery, incontinency, scouring, scours. *Informal:* Bali belly, collywobbles, Montezuma's revenge, squitters, the runs, the trots. **3. faeces** egesta, excrement, faecal pellets, feces, meconium, motion, ordure, stool, weenies. *Informal:* borrie *(Chiefly Victoria)*, cack, poo, pooh, poop. **4. scatology** coprology.

　　　　4.　　**1. dung** coprolite, cow cake, cow pat, dungheap, dunghill, manure, mess, muck, pat, scat, top dressing. *Informal:* meadow cake, Taranaki topdressing *(NZ)*.

　　　　5.　　**1. urination** micturition. *Informal:* hey-diddle-diddle, hi-diddle-diddle, Jimmy Riddle, leak, mimi *(NZ)*, number one, pee, piddle, twinkle, wee-wee, werris. **2. urine** stale, water. *Informal:* piddle, wee, wee-wee, widdle. **3. diuresis** bed-wetting, enuresis, frequency.

　　　　6.　　**1. toilet** bathroom, closet, euphemism, head, hole-in-the-floor toilet, latrine, lavatory, low-down suite, Mary's room, pan, pedestal, pit toilet, roundhouse, squat toilet, urinal, urinary, water closet, WC. *Informal:* brasco, can *(US)*, did, diddy, dub, dumpty, dunny, dyke, jerry, john, khazi, la, la-di-da, lav, lavvy, long-drop, loo, smallest room in the house, the throne, toot. **2. outhouse** backhouse *(Chiefly US)*, cloaca, earth closet, porta-potty, portaloo, privy, skillion, stool. *Informal:* dunny, little house. **3. public toilet** ablutions block, amenities, amenity, convenience, facilities, gents, ladies, lavatory, mens, powder room, public convenience, rest room. **4. sanitary can** chemical toilet. *Informal:* dry pan, dunny can, honey pot, thunderbox. **5. bedpan** bottle, chamber, chamber-pot, commode, po, pot. *Informal:* bedroom mug, gazunder, gozunder, jerry, Melbourne Cup *(NZ)*, potty, thunder-mug, tub. **6. cesspool** cess, cesspit. **7. sewer** cloaca, sep, septic, septic system, septic tank, sewage farm, sewerage, sink. **8. sanitary man** *Informal:* Dan, dunny man, sanny man, sano man. **9. sanitary cart** sanitary wagon. *Informal:* dunny cart, honey cart, night cart, sanny cart, seventeen-door sedan. **10. kitty litter** deep litter.

　　　　7.　　**1. purgative** aloe, cathartic, diuretic, eccritic, laxation, laxative, lenitive, loosener, mannitol, physic, purge, purger. **2. enema. 3. sudorific** diaphoretic. **4. snuff** errhine.

adj.　**8.**　　**1. excremental** cacky, excrementitious, faecal, scatological, stercoraceous, stercorous. **2. excretal** emunctory, evacuative, excretive, excretory, waste. **3. urinary** cloacal, genito-urinary, urinative, uriniferous, urinogenital, urinous, urogenital, urogenous. **4. perspiratory** sudoral, sudoriferous, sudorific, sudoriparous, sweaty, transpiratory. **5. menstrual** catamenial, menstruous.

　　　　9.　　**1. secretory** exudative, mucosal, recremental, runny, secernent, secretionary, secretive, serous. **2. glandular** biliary, bilious, endocrine, galactic, galactopoietic, hormonal, lacteal, lactiferous, salivary, sialoid. **3. watery** lochial.

　　　　10.　　**1. purgative** cathartic, diuretic, eccritic, errhine, evacuant, laxative. **2. sudorific** diaphoretic, hidrotic.

v. **11.** **1. excrete** effuse, exude. **2. perspire** exude, foam, lather, sweat, swelter, transpire. *Informal:* feel like a grease-spot. **3. slaver** cough, dribble, drivel, expectorate, gob, hawk, salivate, slobber, snivel, spit, spittle, water. *Informal:* golly, gooby, hoick, slag. **4. ejaculate** masturbate, orgasm. *Informal:* get one's rocks off. **5. discharge** matter, maturate, run, spew, suppurate, weep. *Informal:* bogey. **6. menstruate** flood. *Informal:* be on the rags, have the flags out, have the painters in, see the flowers, see the roses, see the visitors. **7. purge** physic, scour, void. *Informal:* go through like a dose (or packet) of salts. **8. secrete. 9. lactate** express milk, give milk.

12. **1. defecate** cack, evacuate, loosen, move, move the bowels, open the bowels, pass, pass excrement, scour. *Informal:* crash, do a job, do a poo, drop a load, dump, dump a load, lay an egg, poo, poop, see a man about a job. **2. go to the toilet** answer the call of nature. *Informal:* be caught short, kangaroo, spend a penny, visit aunty, visit Mary.

13. **1. urinate** make water, micturate, relieve oneself, stale. *Informal:* have a pee, leak, pee, piddle, pot, powder one's nose, see a man about a dog, spend a penny, spike the keg, splash the boots, tinkle, wash one's hands, water the horse, wee, wee-wee, wet one's pants, wet oneself, wet the bed, widdle.

RELATED KEYWORDS: EMISSION, FLOW, ILL HEALTH, USELESSNESS

BODY

n. **1.** **1. body** carcass, corpse, corpus, flesh, frame, soma, system. **2. anatomy** figure, physique. *Informal:* vital statistics. **3. corporality** corporealness, physicality. **4. physiology** endocrinology, hormonology, neuroanatomy, neurology, neurophysiology, organology, otology.

2. **1. head** crown, pate, top. *Informal:* bean, block, chump, cruet, crumpet, dome, loaf, lolly, melon, nob, noddle, noggin, noodle, nut, onion, sconce, scone. **2. skull** brainpan, calvaria, cranium, inion. **3. scalp** poll, vertex. **4. brow** forehead, front, temple. **5. brain** encephalon, grey matter, little grey cells, white matter. **6. forebrain** cerebral hemisphere, cerebrum, corpus callosum, cortex, end brain, hemisphere, hippocampus, infundibulum, prosencephalon, sensorium, telencephalon. **7. midbrain** corpora quadrigemina, diencephalon, hypothalamus, interbrain, mesencephalon, optic thalamus, peduncle, thalamencephalon, thalamus. **8. afterbrain** cerebellum, epencephalon, hindbrain, medulla oblongata, metencephalon, myelencephalon, pons Varolii. **9. convolution** gyrus, lobe, sulcus, ventricle. **10. fontanelle** foramen magnum. **11. craniology** cephalometry, craniometry, phrenology. *Informal:* bumpology.

3. **1. face** aspect, countenance, features, front, metope, physiognomy, visage. *Informal:* dial, moosh, mug, pan, phiz, puss. **2. jowl** cheek, dewlap. **3. jaw** chin, jowl, point, underjaw. *Informal:* chops.

4. **1. eye** eyeball, orb *(Chiefly Poetic)*, orbit, white. *Informal:* lamps, peepers, winker. **2. eyelid** lid. **3. pupil** apple of the eye, retina, yellow spot. **4. eyelash** lash. **5. eye socket** eyehole, orbit. **6. eyebrow** brow, superciliary.

5. **1. nose** *Informal:* beak, boko, bracket, bugle, button, conk, hooter, nozzle, proboscis, schnozzle, smeller, snoot, snout, snoz. **2. nostril** nares, olfactories.

6. **1. ear** cauliflower ear, earlap. *Informal:* lug, shell-like. **2. earlobe** earlap, lappet, lobe. **3. external ear** auditory canal, auricle, concha, ear canal, pavilion, pinna. **4. middle ear** anvil, atrium, ear bone, eardrum, Eustachian tube, hammer, incus, malleus, ossicle, oval window, round window, stapes, stirrup bone, syrinx, tympan, tympanic membrane, tympanum. **5. internal ear** basilar membrane, ear stone, inner ear, labyrinth, organ of corti, otolith, saccule, sacculus, semicircular canal, utricle.

7. **1. mouth** jaw, maw. *Informal:* cakehole, chook's bum, gob, hole, kisser, moosh, mug *(British)*, north and south, puss, rattletrap, trap. **2. lip** labium, labrum. **3. tooth** denticle, dentition, snag, snaggle-tooth, teeth, tusk. *Informal:* choppers, fang, pearly gates, tatts. **4. type of tooth** baby tooth, bicuspid, canine, carnassial, cheektooth, cuspid, eyetooth, grinder, incisor, laniary, microdont, milk tooth, molar, premolar, wisdom tooth. **5. false teeth** denture, plate. *Informal:* clackers, falsies, tatters. **6. tongue** glossa, lingua. *Informal:* clapper. **7. gums** alveolar ridge, alveolus, faucal pillars, fauces, gingiva, hard palate, palate, soft palate, teethridge, uvula, velum.

8. **1. neck** nape, nucha. *Informal:* scrag, scruff. **2. throat** gorge, gullet, maw, pharynx. *Informal:* little red lane. **3. air passage** bronchi, bronchial tubes, bronchiole, bronchus, lung, trachea, tube, windpipe. *Informal:* pipes. **4. larynx** Adam's apple, epiglottis, glottis, vocal cords, voice box.

9. **1. limb** appendage, extremity, member.

10. **1. arm** brachium, forearm, shoulder, shoulders. *Informal:* fin, warwicks, wing. **2. elbow** ancon, crazy bone, funny bone. **3. hand** carpus, manus, metacarpus, mutton-fist, palm, thenar, wrist. *Informal:* bunch of fives, duke, fin, fist, flipper, mitt, paw. **4. finger** annular, digit, forefinger, index finger, little finger, minimus, phalange, phalanx, pinky, pointer, pollex, ring finger, thumb. *Informal:* hooks, onka, onkaparinga, pinkie. **5. nail** claw, fingernail, onyx, unguis. *Informal:* talon. **6. armpit** axilla. **7. underarm cleavage** *(Informal)*.

11. **1. chest** breast, bust, diaphragm, front, thorax. *Informal:* brisket. **2. torso** trunk. **3. rib** costa. *Informal:* slat, slats. **4. bosom** breast, bust, cleavage, dug, heart, mamma. *Informal:* boob, Bristols *(British)*, bub, charlies, fun bags, knockers, norks, tit, titty. **5. nipple** areola, dug, mamilla, mammilla *(Chiefly US)*, pap, teat, tit, titty. *Informal:* diddy.

12. **1. abdomen** belly, hypochondrium, hypogastrium, middle, midriff, pubes, stomach, venter, waist, waistline. *Informal:* guts, puku *(NZ)*. **2. stomach** belly, maw, tum, vitals. *Informal:* bingy, breadbasket, tummy. **3. paunch** *Informal:* bay window, beer belly, beer gut, bow window, corporation, muffin top, pot, potbelly, pukunui *(NZ)*, spare tyre. **4. solar plexus** mark. *Informal:* wind. **5. entrails** gizzard, innards, internals, intestines, inwards, viscera. *Informal:* comic cuts, guts, insides. **6. alimentary canal** appendix, back passage, bowels, caecum, colon, duodenum, enteron, epigastrium, esophagus, foregut, gullet, gut, ileum, intestine, jejunum, large intestine, midgut, oesophagus, omentum, pylorus, rectum, small intestine, vermiform appendix. **7. navel** omphalos, umbilication, umbilicus. *Informal:* bellybutton, innie, outie.

13. **1. back** dorsum, small of the back. *Informal:* paddywhack. **2. spine** backbone, chine, lumbar, rachis, rhachis, spinal column, spinal cord, vertebra, vertebral column. **3. hunchback** convex, crookback, dowager's hump, gibbosity, hump, humpback, hunch, scoliosis, widow's hump.

14. **1. buttocks** beam, behind, bottom, breech, cheek, fundament *(US, British)*, nates, posterior, rear, rump, seat, tail. *Informal:* acre, backside, base, big A, bot, bum, butt, can *(US)*, chuff, clacker, derrière, ding, dinger, jacksy *(NZ)*, Khyber, slats. **2. haunch** ham, hams, hip, hock, hunkers, loins. **3. anus** fundament. *Informal:* acre, ring. **4. natal cleft**.

15. **1. groin** crotch, mons, mount (or mound) of Venus, pubes, pubic hair. **2. genitals** genitalia, loins *(Bible and Poetic)*, perineum, private parts, privates, pudendum. *Informal:* gear. **3. female genitalia** cervix, clitoris, G spot, glans, gonad, hymen, labia, labium, maidenhead, nymphas, ovary, phallus, tubes, uterus, womb. *Informal:* cherry. **4. vulva** prepuce, pudendum, vagina. *Informal:* michael, mickey. **5. male genitalia** epididymis, foreskin, glans, gonad, lingam, manhood, phallus, prepuce, prostate, prostate gland, scrotum, vas deferens. *Informal:* cod. **6. testicle** spermary, testis. *Informal:* ball. **7. testicles** gonads, testes. *Informal:* aggots, bollocks, cobblers, fun bags, goolies, knackers, Niagara falls, nuts. **8. penis** member, the virile member. *Informal:* dickie, ding, dong, donger, John, John Thomas, old boy, old fellow, old man, Percy, tassel, willie. **9. erection** phallus. **10. camel toe** *Informal:* moose knuckle.

16. **1. leg** calf, crus, femur, lap, shank, shin, thigh, thighbone. *Informal:* gam, pin, props, stumps. **2. knee** genu, kneecap, kneepan, marrowbones, pan, patella. **3. foot** ankle, heel, instep, pettitoes, podium, sole, tarsus. *Informal:* dogs, footsy, hoof, mundowie *(Northern Qld, NSW)*, tootsy. **4. toe** big toe, hallux, little toe, minimus. *Informal:* pinkie. **5. toe cleavage** *(Informal)*.

17. **1. bone** anatomy, bones, frame, framework, os, skeleton. **2. caput** capitulum, condyle, diaphysis. **3. joint** articulation, ball-and-socket joint, diarthrosis, enarthrosis, ginglymus, gomphosis, hinge, knuckle, pivot joint, symphysis. **4. bones of the skull** ethmoid, frontal, hyoid, malar, nasal, occipital, palatine, parietal, renal, sphenoid, temporal, zygomatic, zygomatic bone. **5. jawbone** mandible, maxilla, vomer. **6. cheekbone** jugal, malar. **7. bones of the pectoral girdle** blade, clavicle, collarbone, pectoral arch, pectoral girdle, scapula, shoulderblade. **8. rib** breastbone, sternum. **9. bones of the pelvic girdle** cervical vertebra, coxa, haunchbone, hip, hipbone, ilium, innominate bone, ischium, pelvis, pubis, thoracic vertebra. **10. bones of the vertebral column** atlas, axis, coccyx, lumbar, sacrum, spine, vertebra, vertebral column. **11. bones of the arm** carpus, humerus, metacarpus, phalanges, radius, ulna. **12. bones of the leg** anklebone, astragalus, femur, fibula, hucklebone, malleolus, metatarsus, patella, shinbone, talus, tarsus, thigh, thighbone, tibia, tibiale. *Informal:* splinter-bone.

18. **1. flesh** fat, lean, tissue. *Informal:* flab. **2. gristle** cartilage. **3. marrow**. **4. muscle** brawn, thews. **5. connective tissue** aponeurosis, facia, fascia, isthmus, membrane, peritoneum, pons, stroma, tunic, tunica. **6. tendon** Achilles tendon, hamstring, ligament, sinew. *Informal:* hammy. **7. muscle** bicep, biceps, costal, deltoid, gluteus, hamstring, intercostal, quadricep, quadriceps, rectus, rectus abdominis, sartorius, splenius, tricep, triceps.

19. **1. bladder** ureter, urethra, vesica. *Informal:* waterworks. **2. vesicle** blister, blood blister, bulla, bursa, capsule, cistern, cyst, phlyctena, pustule, sinus. **3. duct** tube, vas, vessel.

20. **1. heart** pump. *Informal:* ticker. **2. parts of the heart** aortic valve, atrium, auricle, endocardium, epicardium, mitral valve, myocardium, pacemaker, pulmonary valve, semilunar valve, tricuspid, ventricle.

21. **1. blood vessel** arteriole, artery, capillary, vein, vena, venule. **2. blood vessels** aorta, axillary, brachial, brachiocephalic, carotid, coeliac, coronary, femoral, gastric, hepatic, iliac, jugular, mesenteric, portal, pulmonary vein, saphenous, splenic, subclavian, vena cava.

22. **1. blood** plasma, serum. *Informal:* claret. **2. blood cell** corpuscle, erythrocyte, haemocyte, haemoglobin, haemoleucocyte, leucocyte, lymph cell, lymphocyte, macrocyte, neutrophil, phagocyte, platelet, red blood cell, red cell, white blood cell, white cell.

23. **1. nervous system** central nervous system, parasympathetic nervous system. **2. nerve** funiculus, ganglion, nerve fibre, pathway, reflex arc, synapse, synapsis, tract. **3. neuron** brain cell, nerve cell, neuroendocrine cell. **4. neuron component** AMPA receptor, axon, dendrite, ionotropic receptor, receptor.

24. **1. organs (miscellaneous)** bladder, brain, gall bladder, gonad, heart, kidney, lien, liver, lung, organ, ovary, spleen.

25. **1. glands** adrenal gland, epiphysis, hypophysis, lachrymals, pancreas, parathyroid, parotid, pineal body, pineal gland, pituitary gland, salivary gland, suprarenal gland, thymus gland, thyroid gland. **2. lymph gland** amygdalas, lymphatic gland, tonsil. **3. sebaceous gland** sweat gland.

adj. 26. **1. bodily** animal, corporal, corporeal, fleshly, physical, skeletal, systemic. **2. anatomical** anatomic, audiological, gastrological, ophthalmological, topical. **3. anterior** inferior, posterior, sagittal, superior. **4. organic** biliary, cardiac, hepatic, lymphatic, pancreatic, renal, splenetic, splenetical, thyroid.

27. **1. cranial** auricular, buccal, cerebral, facial, frontal, mandibular, maxillary, narial, narine, nasal, ocular, ophthalmic, parietal, temporal. **2. oral** alveolar, dental, faucal, gingival, labial, lingual, palatal, palatine, uvular, velar.

28. **1. trunk** abdominal, acetabular, costal, diaphragmic, dorsal, iliac, pectoral, pelvic, pubic, sacral, thoracal, thoracic, umbilical.

29. **1. brachial** carpal, clavicular, digital, humeral, manual, metacarpal, palmar, scapular. **2. pedal** astragalar, femoral, fibular, geniculate, patellar, tarsal, tibial.

30. **1. gastric** anal, caecal, colonic, digestive, duodenal, esophageal, excretory, ileac, intestinal, oesophageal, pyloric, rectal, stomachic.

31. **1. urinogenital** ejaculative, ejaculatory, genital, genito-urinary, penile, prostate, scrotal, testicular, urethral, urinary, urogenital, vaginal, vulviform.

32. **1. respiratory** bronchial, glottal, laryngal, laryngeal, pharyngal, pharyngeal, tracheal.

RELATED KEYWORDS: HUMANITY, ORGANISM, REPRODUCTION, SEX

BOMBAST

n. **1.** **1. bombast** balderdash, blather, blether *(British)*, blither, bluff, boasting, braggadocio, bravado, bunkum, claptrap, fanfaronade, fustian, gasconade, jactation, rant, rodomontade, skiting, talk, wind. *Informal:* blah, guff, hot air, put-on. **2. turgidness** grandiloquence, Johnsonese, magniloquence, orotundity, pomposity, pompousness, pretentiousness, sesquipedalianism, swollenness, tumidness. **3. demagoguery** demagoguism, demagogy, oratory, rhetoric.

2. **1. harangue** diatribe, exhortation, lecture, philippic, screed, sermon, tirade.

3. **1. haranguer** demagogue, phrase-monger, rabble-rouser, ranter, rhetorician, soapbox orator, stump orator *(Chiefly US)*, word-monger. *Informal:* pooh-bah, raver, stuffed shirt, tub-thumper.

adj. **4.** **1. bombastic** big, circumlocutory, demagogic, fustian, grandiose, infelicitous, inflated, mouthy, orotund, overblown, pompous, puffed-up, puffy, swollen, tub-thumping, tumid, turgid. **2. affected** consequential, flamboyant, flashy, high-flown, ostentatious, pompous, pretentious, showy, stilted. *Informal:* flash, hifalutin, highfalutin, jammy, toplofty. **3. sententious** Johnsonian, pedantical, rhetorical.

adv. **5.** **1. bombastically** loftily, pretentiously, tumidly, turgidly, windily.

RELATED KEYWORDS: VERBOSITY, GRAMMATICAL ERROR, FAULTY SPEECH, TALKATIVENESS

BOOK

n. **1.** **1. book** booklet, e-book, publication, rare book, tome, volume. **2. manuscript** autograph, codex, document, draft, inedita, Ms., palimpsest, parchment, script, scroll, treatise, typescript, vellum. **3. edition** casebound, coedition, conflation, extra-special, first edition, hardback, hardcover, incunabula, issue, library edition, limited edition, paperback, softcover, three-decker, trade edition, vanity edition, variorum, yearly. **4. series** collection, library, range, set, varia. **5. bestseller** *Informal:* potboiler. **6. blockbuster** airport novel. **7. reprint** offprint, reissue. **8. remainder** *Informal:* dog. **9. slim volume** booklet, brochure, chapbook, fascicle, fascicule, fasciculus, pamphlet, part work. **10. large volume** elephant, folio. **11. compilation** anthology, belles-lettres, collectanea, festschrift, garland, memoirs, miscellanea, miscellanies, omnibus, Parnassus, potpourri, recollections, sketchbook, travels. **12. notebook** black book, casebook, commonplace book, diary, exercise book, flight log, jotter, journal, log, logbook, personal organiser, ringbinder, tickler *(US)*, workbook. *Informal:* dole diary. **13. pocketbook** book of prime entry, daybook, notepad, scratchpad *(US)*, table-book, writing pad, writing paper. **14. work** autonym, classic, magnum opus, opus, opuscule, wonderwork. **15. talking book** audio book. **16. serial** partwork.

2. **1. book part** binding, board, case, demy, full binding, half-binding, half-leather, headband, library binding, mull, perfect binding, ream, rib, spine, thermoplastic binding, three-quarter binding, yapp. **2. jacket** cover, wrapper. **3. page** bastard title, blocking, carpet page, centrefold, centrespread, contents page, doublure, endpaper, fillet, flyleaf, frontispiece, half-title page, headpiece, home page, imprint page, leaf, panel, recto, reverso, tailpiece, title, titlepage, verso. **4. gathering** section, signature. **5. quarto** eighteenmo, folio, octavo, octodecimo, sextodecimo, sixteenmo, twenty-fourmo, twentymo, vigesimo, vigesimo-quarto. **6. divisions of a book** addendum, appendix, body, colophon, corrigendums, dedication, end matter, exordium, foreword, front matter, index, induction, introduction, lead-up, preamble, preface, preliminary, prelims, proem, prolegomenon, prologue, prolusion, protasis, recitals, subindex, text, trial run, vermiform appendix. *Informal:* intro. **7. title** bastard title, caption, crosshead, half-title, heading, letterhead, long title, masthead, rubric, running head, running title, subheading, subtitle. *Informal:* cap.

3. **1. work of fiction** novel. **2. penny dreadful** chiller, dime novel *(US)*, dreadful, thriller. *Informal:* shocker, whodunnit. **3. pillow book** curiosa *(Chiefly US)*, erotica, facetiae, yellowback. **4. children's book** picture book, pop-up book, storybook.

4. **1. reference book** almanac, atlas, calendar, cyclopedia, dictionary, digest, directory, encyclopedia, fauna, gazette, gazetteer, gradus, key, lapidary, lexicon, linguistic atlas, map book, menology, source book, telephone directory, thesaurus, wordbook, yearbook. *Informal:* phone book. **2. cookbook** cookery book, recipe book. **3. guidebook** companion, guide, itinerary, roadbook. **4. schedule** playbill, program, TV guide. **5. handbook** bench book, companion, enchiridion, guide, manual, phrasebook, stylebook, vade mecum, workbook. **6. bibliography** reading list.

5. **1. textbook** ABC, arithmetic, catechism, crammer, geography, grammar, hornbook, institutes, primer, reader, schoolbook, special, speller, spelling book, text. **2. workbook** copybook.

6. **1. prayer book** antiphonal, antiphonary, bible, breviary, catechism, diglot, diurnal, family Bible, hours, hymnal, hymnbook, lectionary, mahzor, missal, ordinal, ordo, passional, passionary, polyglot, Psalter, rubric, service book, testament, vesperal.

7. **1. newspaper** biweekly, black and white, blatt, daily, journal, mouthpiece, news-sheet, newsletter, newsweekly, organ, paper, print, publication, review, semiweekly, sheet, soft news, softcover, supplement, tabloid, triweekly, weekly. *Informal:* kiss-and-tell, kite, local, rag. **2. magazine** annals, annual, bimonthly, bulletin, comic book, dreadful, ezine, fanzine, fashion journal, fashion magazine, fortnightly, girlie magazine, glossy, house journal, house magazine, illustrated, journal, periodical, pictorial, quarterly, semiannual, semiyearly, trade journal, trade magazine, webzine. **3. section** comic, comics, editorial, feature, feuilleton, fiction, horror comic, review, roto *(US)*, strip. *Informal:* funnies. **4. fourth estate** bad press, electronic media, good press, press, print journalism, print media, print press, printed press, yellow press. *Informal:* the daily blatts.

8. **1. book trade** bibliopegy, micropublishing, publishing, samizdat, self-publishing, vanity publishing. **2. editing** copy tasting, copyediting, proofreading. **3. publisher.** **4. bookseller** bibliopole, newsagent, newsdealer *(US)*, newsvendor. **5. bookshop** book store, second-hand bookshop. **6. printer** book designer, bookbinder, compositor, copyboy, copyeditor, copyholder, copytaker, editor-in-chief, layout artist, lithographer, pressman, printmaker, proofreader, reader, stonehand, typefounder, typesetter, typographer. *Informal:* clicker. **7. newsagent's shop** newsagency, newsstand, paper shop, paperstand.

9. 1. booklover bibliophile. **2. book collector** antiquarian. **3. librarian** acquisitions librarian, bibliographer, cataloguist. **4. bibliomania** bibliophilism.

10. 1. library bibliotheca, bookmobile, circulating library, clipping service, databank, dossier, file, indices, lending library, lyceum, mobile library, public library, reading room, reference library, research library, subscription library, teletext, term bank. **2. library book** *Informal:* floater. **3. catalogue** card file, card index, tickle box, union catalogue. *Informal:* platter log. **4. database** relational database, search engine. **5. Boolean search** Boolean operator.

RELATED KEYWORDS: KNOWLEDGE, NEWS, PRINTING, WRITING

BOREDOM

n. **1.** **1. boredom** discontent, dissatisfaction, ennui, indifference, languor, lethargy, listlessness, satiety, surfeit, taedium vitae, tedium vitae, weariness. *Informal:* seven-year itch.

2. **1. boringness** drabness, dreariness, dullness, irksomeness, pointlessness, stupidness, tediousness, tedium, wearifulness, wearisomeness. **2. monotonousness** everlastingness, humdrum, monotony, sameness, uniformity, uniformness. **3. insipidness** jejunity, lifelessness, staleness, tameness, vapidness. **4. pedantry** pedestrianism, prosaicism, prosaicness, prosaism, prosiness, stodginess, stuffiness, unreadableness. **5. dreariness** aridness, barrenness, blankness, desolation, tastelessness. **6. leadenness** ponderosity.

3. **1. bore** humdrum, plebeian. *Informal:* alf, bromide, drag, drip, fish head, pain, party pooper, pill, shmo, vegetable, wet, wet blanket. **2. pedant** Dryasdust, sermoniser. *Informal:* lugger. **3. cliché** banality, commonplace, platitude, triteness. **4. sermon** litany. **5. stodge** *(Informal)* purple prose. **6. dullsville** bind, bore, the daily grind, treadmill, wet weekend. *Informal:* drag, the nine to five, yawn.

adj. **4.** **1. boring** arid, dragging, dry, dry as dust, dull, featureless, flat, ho-hum, slow, tasteless, tedious, uninteresting. *Informal:* dull as dishwater. **2. tedious** boring, everlasting, irksome, mind-numbing, tiresome, unrelieved, weariful, wearing, wearisome, weary, wearying. **3. insipid** anodyne, humdrum, incurious, institutional, lethargic, lethargical, lifeless, pedestrian, pointless, sapless, tame, undramatic, unsatisfying. **4. pedantic** pedantical, platitudinous, sermonic, sermonical, stodgy, stuffy. **5. commonplace** banal, clichéd, common, common-or-garden, hack, hackneyed, jejune, mundane, musty, ordinary, pedestrian, plebeian, practical, prosaic, prosaical, prosy, run-of-the-mill, stale, stereotyped, stock, stupid, threadbare, tired, trite, trivial, unimaginative, uninspired, uninspiring, unreadable, vapid, vulgar, world-weary. **6. monotonous** monotone, repetitious. **7. drab** arid, barren, blank, bleak, desolate, dreary, soul-destroying. **8. leaden** leady, plodding, ponderous, soggy.

5. **1. bored** apathetic, blasé, full of ennui, incurious, indifferent, musty, tired of, uninterested, weary of. **2. listless** coasty, lethargic, lethargical, stale, tired, weariful, weary, well-worn. **3. fed up (to the back teeth)** *(Informal)* huffy, sulky *(Aboriginal English)*. *Informal:* browned off, cheesed-off, fed up to the gills, jack of, sick, sick and tired, sick to death.

v. **6.** **1. bore** hackney, irk, leave flat, pall on (or upon), stale, test one's patience, tire, try, try one's patience, wear, weary. *Informal:* bore the socks off, take someone cold, make one yawn, send one to sleep. **2. be tedious** dull, jade, preach. **3. protract** do to death, drag out, linger, outstay one's welcome. **4. drag on** go on ad nauseam, linger on, wear away (or on), wear thin. *Informal:* chunter on.

7. **1. be bored with** be weary of, tire, tire of. *Informal:* be fed up with, be sick (and tired) of.

RELATED KEYWORDS: INATTENTION, BOMBAST, WRITING, REPETITION

BOTTOM

n. **1.** **1. bottom** base, basis, bed, bedrock, floor, flooring, seat. **2. foundation** baseboard, basement, bedding, cordon, drum, groundwork, hardcore, podium, roadbed, sea-floor, stereobate, stylobate, sub-base, substrate, substratum, substruction, substructure, tholobate, understratum. **3. bottom part** foot, footing, heel, heelpiece, skirts, sole, tail. **4. stump** base, dado, pedestal, plinth. **5. underside** underbody, undercarriage, underlay, underlayer, underneath, underpart, undersurface. **6. basement** cellar, crypt, downstairs, souterrain, sub-basement, subcellar, undercroft, vault. **7. low level** base, base level, baseline, low, low tide, low-water mark, nadir, rock bottom.

adj. **2.** **1. bottom** basal, base, basic *(Chiefly US)*, basilar, bass, bottommost, downstairs, ground, hypogeal, hypogeous, low, lowermost, lowest, nethermost, radical, stereobatic, sub-basal, under, underground, underlaid, undermost. **2. underlying** inferior, low, lower, nether, subjacent, under, underneath, ventral. **3. low** depressed, flattened, lowly, prostrate, sunken, surbased.

v. **3.** **1. underlie** base, bottom, found, underlay.

adv. **4.** **1. below** infra, thereunder, under, underneath. **2. low** down. **3. basally** below, beneath, underground, underneath, ventrally.

prep. **5.** **1. under** adown, after, beneath, neath *(Poetic or Scottish)*, underneath.

RELATED KEYWORDS: DEPTH, SHORTNESS

BRAGGING

n. **1.** **1. bragging** blustering, boasting, name-dropping, vapouring. *Informal:* ego-tripping, skiting. **2. bluster** boasting, bounce, bravado, fanfaronade, puff, self-advertisement, swagger. *Informal:* blow. **3. braggadocio** brag, bragging, bravado, fanfaronade, gasconade, jactation, jactitation, rodomontade. *Informal:* blow, bull, skite. **4. brag** boast, vaunt. *Informal:* blow, ego trip, skite.

2. **1. braggartism** egoism, egomania, egotism, narcissism, self-absorption, self-conceit, self-love, vainglory. *Informal:* ego. **2. boastfulness** swankiness, vaingloriousness.

3. **1. braggart** bloviater, boaster, brag, braggadocio, fanfaron, grandstander, name-dropper, pup, puppy, vaunter. *Informal:* big mouth, big noter, bighead, hoon, show-off, skite. **2. blusterer** blower, bouncer. *Informal:* bull artist, storyteller, tinhorn *(US)*. **3. egotist** egoist, egomaniac, narcissist.

adj. **4.** **1. bragging** big, blustering, boastful, boasting, braggart, grandiloquent, rodomontade, vainglorious. **2. self-opinionated** big-headed, blusterous, conceited, thrasonical, vainglorious. *Informal:* spread-eagle *(US)*, stuck-up, swanky, swollen-headed. **3. egoistical** egotistical, narcissistic.

v. **5.** **1. brag** bloviate, blow one's own trumpet, bluster, boast, bounce, crow, gasconade, pitch a line, puff, rodomontade, show off, swagger, trumpet, vapour, vaunt. *Informal:* big-mouth, bull, bulldust, shoot a line, shoot one's mouth off, skite, swank, talk big. **2. ego-trip** *(Informal)* blow one's own trumpet, boast, brag, glory in, grandstand, sell oneself. *Informal:* big-mouth, big-note, blow, bull. **3. have a swollen head** pat oneself on the back, think oneself someone, think oneself something. *Informal:* have tickets on oneself, think one is Christmas.

adv. **6.** **1. braggingly** blusteringly, boastfully, boastingly, swankily, thrasonically, vapouringly, vauntingly. *Informal:* big. **2. egoistically** egotistically.

RELATED KEYWORDS: AFFECTEDNESS, ARROGANCE, SELFISHNESS, SHOWINESS, VANITY

BREVITY

n. **1.** **1. brevity** briefness, compactness, compendiousness, conciseness, concision, crispness, curtness, economy, shortness, succinctness, terseness. **2. pithiness** Atticism, epigrammatism, laconicism, laconism, sententiousness, straightness, trenchancy.

2. **1. abridgement** abbreviation, compression, condensation, encapsulation, shortened version. **2. summary** abstract, analysis, argument, compend, compendium, conspectus, digest, epitome, formularisation, formulation, formulisation, highlights, outline, outlines, pandect, precis, résumé, run-down, sum, summarisation, summing-up, synopsis, thumbnail, thumbnail sketch. **3. concise piece of writing** apophthegm, cameo, capsule, epigram, epitaph, essay, haiku, limerick, maxim, monostich, mot, novella, short story, vignette. **4. jotting** adversaria. **5. ellipsis** abbreviation, acronym, blend, brachylogy, elision, initialism, portmanteau word, postnominal, syncope.

adj. **3.** **1. brief** compact, concise, laconic, laconical, of few words, short, short-spoken, short-winded, succinct, to the point. **2. abbreviated** abridged, compressed, condensed, elliptic, elliptical, potted, summarised, telescoped. **3. abstractive** compendious, epitomical, summarised, synoptic. **4. pithy** compact, crisp, epigrammatic, sententious. **5. curt** clipped, monosyllabic, terse.

v. **4.** **1. abbreviate** abridge, condense, cut, cut a long story short, epigrammatise, shorten, telescope. **2. summarise** put in a nutshell, abstract, boil down, digest, encapsulate, formularise, formulate, formulise, make a synopsis of, outline, precis, sum up, summate.

adv. **5.** **1. briefly** compendiously, concisely, laconically, short, summarily, synoptically. **2. in brief** in a few words, in a nutshell, in a word, in essence, in fine, in short. **3. pithily** crisply, direct, directly, elliptically, epigrammatically, shortly, straight, to the point. **4. curtly** tersely.

RELATED KEYWORDS: ELOQUENCE, SPEECH, RETICENCE

BRIBERY

n. **1.** **1. bribery** corruption, embracery, graft, oil, protection, subornation. *Informal:* dollar diplomacy, envelopmental journalism *(Philippine English)*, pork *(US)*, pork barrel.

2. **1. bribe** pay-off, sop, tong *(Philippine English)*, under-the-table payment. *Informal:* backhander, backsheesh, baksheesh, bonus, boodle *(Chiefly US)*, fix, kickback, spiff, sweetener, you'lldo. **2. hush money** inducement allowance, protection, protection money, slush fund, subsidisation. *Informal:* cigarette money *(Philippine English)*, coffee money *(Singaporean and Malaysian English)*, drugola, payola, sling, spiff. **3. inducement** bait, bribe, carrot, douceur, incentive, instigation. *Informal:* backhander, bonus, fix, spiff, sweetener.

3. **1. bribability** corruptibleness, purchasability, venality.

4. **1. briber** embraceor, suborner, subsidiser. *Informal:* bagman, boodler. **2. receiver of bribes** *Informal:* bent cop, crooked cop, crooked politician.

adj. **5.** **1. bribable** buyable, corrupt, purchasable, venal. *Informal:* all right, alright, bent, crooked.

v. **6.** **1. bribe** buy, buy off, purchase, suborn, subsidise, tamper with. *Informal:* cross (or grease) (or oil) someone's palm, fix, get at, give someone a backhander, give someone a sweetener, make it right with, nobble, oil, pay off, sling, sweeten, throw a sop to.

RELATED KEYWORDS: ENCOURAGEMENT, DISHONESTY, UNLAWFULNESS, PAYMENT

BRITTLENESS

n. **1.** **1. brittleness** crispness, glassiness, vitreosity, vitreousness, vitrification. **2. breakability** fragileness, fragility, frailness, frailty, frangibility, tenderness.

adj. **2.** **1. brittle** brashy, calcareous, china, crisp, crispy, crispy-crunchy, eggshell, glass, glasslike, glassy, red-short, semivitreous, shivery, splintery, vitreous. **2. breakable** brashy, brittle, crumbly, delicate, fragile, frail, frangible, friable, shatterable, short, tender.

RELATED KEYWORDS: DAMAGE, HARDNESS, SEPARATION, SOLIDITY

BROWN

n. **1.** **1. brown** nutbrown. **2. light brown** almond, amber, beige, biscuit, bisque, buff, café au lait, camel, caramel, coffee, drab, dun, ecru, fallow, fawn, hazel, khaki, oak, putty, raw sienna, sienna, tan, tawny, teak, walnut. **3. dark brown** chocolate, cocoa, mocha, mouse-dun, puce, seal brown, sepia, umber, Vandyke brown. **4. reddish-brown** auburn, bay, brick red, bronze, burnt sienna, chestnut, cinnamon, copper, ginger, henna, liver, mahogany, maple, orange-brown, roan, russet, rust, sinopia, sorrel, terracotta, titian. **5. browning** tanning. **6. melanin. 7. brunette** *Informal:* bitumen blonde.

2. **1. brownness** rustiness, suntan, tan, tawniness.

adj. **3.** **1. brown** brown as a berry, brownish, brunette, nutbrown, spadiceous. **2. light brown** almond, amber, beige, biscuit, bisque, buff, cacky-coloured, café au lait, camel, caramel, cervine, coffee-coloured, drab, dun, ecru, fallow, fawn, fulvous, khaki, musteline, oak, putty, raw sienna, tan, tawny, teak, unbleached, walnut. **3. dark brown** chocolate, cocoa, fuscous, mocha, mouse-dun, puce, seal brown, sepia, umber, Vandyke brown. **4. reddish-brown** auburn, bay, brick red, bronze, bronzy, burnt sienna, chestnut, cinnamon, copper, copper-coloured, coppery, cupreous, dapple-bay, ferruginous, foxy, ginger, gingery, hazel, henna, hepatic, liver, mahogany, maple, roan, rubiginous, russet, rust-coloured, rusty, sinopia, sorrel, terracotta, testaceous, titian. **5. snuff-coloured** nicotine-stained. **6. sun-tanned** bronzed, sunburned, sunburnt, tanned. **7. brunette.**

v. **4.** **1. brown** blanco, bronze, embrown, tan, toast. **2. rust.**

RELATED KEYWORDS: COLOUR, HAIR, ORANGE, RED

BUBBLINESS

n. **1.** **1. bubbliness** effervescence, effervescency, fizz, foaminess, frothiness, gassiness, life, liveliness, prickle, spumescence, yeastiness. **2. carbonation** carbon dioxide, carbonic acid gas.

2. **1. bubble** air pocket, air-bell, bead, blob, globule. **2. blister** bulla, pustule, seed. **3. artificial horizon** false horizon. **4. speech bubble.**

3. **1. bubbling** burble, burbling, cavitation. **2. foam** barm, bead, froth, head, lather, sea foam, soapsuds, spindrift, spoondrift, spray, spume, suds, surf, white horse, yeast. **3. bubble bath. 4. bubblegum.**

4. **1. aerator** carbonator, latherer, soda siphon. **2. bubble chamber.**

adj. **5.** **1. bubbly** aerated, bubbling, carbonated, ebullient, effervescent, effervescing, fizzing, fizzy, foamy, frothing, frothy, gassy, lathery, spumescent, spumy, sudsy, with a head on, yeasty. **2. sparkling** brisk, effervescent, lively, petillant, prickly, spritzig. **3. blistered** blebby, blistery.

v. **6.** **1. bubble** bead, boil, burble, effervesce, foam, froth, intumesce, lather, sparkle, spume. **2. gargle** gurgle. **3. aerate** carbonate, ferment, leaven, yeast.

adv. **7.** **1. bubblingly** ebulliently, effervescently, foamily, foamingly, frothily, yeastily.

    RELATED KEYWORDS: GAS

BULGE

n. **1.** **1. bulge** ball, billow, mushroom, pout, swell, swelling. **2. protuberance** cusp, excrescence, outgrowth, ridge, shoulder, snout, spine, spur, tenon, torus. **3. knob** bunch, head, knobble, knop, nub, nubbin *(US)*, nubble, pinhead, prominence, spur, stub, umbo. **4. burr** Aleppo gall, burl, emergence, gall, gallnut, gnarl, knot, knur, node, nodule, nutgall, trabecula, tubercle, whelp. **5. process** apophysis, berry, bosset, calcar, calk, caruncle, condyle, cornu, coronoid process, horn, hyperostosis, nose, osteophyte, spur, vibraculum, villus. **6. jut** bucktooth, cog, dent, dentation, denticle, denticulation, fang, finger, flange, horn, joggle, languet, pallet, ratchet, ratchet wheel, serration, serrature, serrulation, snag, tappet, tongue, tooth. **7. crest** comb. **8. projection** aculeus, gargoyle, jag, limb, lip, point, prickle, snag, spade, spine, spout, tentacle, thorn, toe, tusk. **9. saddlebow** horn, pommel, pummel.

2. **1. swollenness** billowiness, rotundness, tuberosity, tumefaction, tumescence, tumidness, turgor. **2. lumpiness** bumpiness, gibbousness, nodality, nodosity, tuberculation, verrucosity, vesication, vesiculation. **3. convexity** crenation, crenature, entasis, ventricosity. **4. protrusion** evagination, exophthalmia, exophthalmos, exsertion, extrusion, herniation, protraction, salience, saliency.

3. **1. bodily protuberance** angioma, bubo, bump, bunion, chondroma, desmoid, goitre, hernia, node, puff, scrofula, struma, swelling, tragus, tumescence, tumour, turgescency. *Informal:* outie. **2. belly** bloat, potbelly, venter. *Informal:* bay window, beer gut. **3. hump** convex, dowager's hump, gibbosity, humpback, hunch, hunchback, widow's hump. **4. lobe** bud, button, lobation, lobule, mamilla, nipple, stud, teat, tit. *Informal:* titty. **5. lump** air sac, anbury, bedeguar, boss, capped hock, cheloid, condyloma, cyst, diverticulum, fibroid, fibroma, ganglion, growth, keloid, knob, knot, macrocyst, node, nodule, papilla, papilloma, polyp, sebaceous cyst, spavin, tuber, tubercule, verruca, wart, wen. **6. blister** barbs, bighead, blain, blood blister, bog spavin, boil, bulla, carbuncle, gathering, head, papilla, papule, pimple, pock, pustule, tubercle, vesicle, water blister, whelk, whitehead. *Informal:* crunchie, zit. **7. goose pimples** goose bumps, goose flesh, heat rash, horripilation. **8. welt** wale, weal, wheal.

adj. **4.** **1. bulgy** bosomy, bulbaceous, bulbous, bulging, bunchy, busty, chubby, mushroom, round, turgescent, turgid, ventricose. **2. protuberant** beetle, beetling, exsert, exserted, extrusive, imminent, obtrusive, overhanging, pendent, prognathic, prognathous, projectile, projecting, prominent, protractile, protrusible, protrusive, rostral, salient, tumular. **3. raised up** eminent, erect, proud. **4. spiny** acanthaceous, acanthoid, calcarate, calcarated, hornlike, horny, muricate, prickly, spinelike, spiniferous, spinous, spurred, thorny. **5. popeyed** exophthalmic. *Informal:* bug-eyed. **6. tentacled** tentacular, tentaculate, vibracular.

5. **1. knobby** bony, bossy, burled, burly, condylar, condyloid, gangliate, gangliated, ganglionic, gnarled, gnarly, jointed, knobbly, knoblike, knurled, knurly, moniliform, nodal, nodose, nodular, nodulose, nodulous, nubbly, osteophytic, ridged, torose, umbonal, umbonate, umbonic, warty. **2. cusped** bicorn, bicornuate, bicuspid, calcariferous, corniculate, cornuted, cuspate, cuspidal, cuspidate, cuspidated, tricorn, tricuspid, tricuspidal. **3. goose-pimply** goosy. **4. bumpy** hummocky, lumpy, pebbly, snaggy. **5. jagged** biserrate, dentate, denticulate, denticulated, dentirostral, jaggy, peaked, pointed, pointy, projective, saw-toothed, serrate, serrated, serriform, serrulate, toothed. **6. clumpy** clumpish, lobate, lobated, lobular, multilobular, stubbed, stubby, tussocky. **7. crested** carunculate, carunculated, carunculous, cristate, cristated.

6. **1. swollen** bloated, blubber, blubbery, distended, inflated, puffy, strumose, strumous, tumefacient, tumescent, tumid, tumorous. **2. billowy** balloon, bloused, blown, bursiform, saccate. **3. potbellied** *Informal:* poddy *(British)*. **4. humped** gibbous, humpbacked, humpy, hunchbacked. **5. blistery** blebby, blistered, bullate, condylomatous, eruptive, knoblike, nodose, scabby, scabrous, torose, vesicular, vesiculate. **6. tuberous** tubercular, tuberculate, tuberculoid, tuberculose, tuberculous, tuberose, verrucose.

v. **7.** **1. bulge** bag, balloon, belly, bilge, billow, bloat, distend, fill, fill out, heave, inflate, mushroom, puff up, swell, tumefy. **2. hump** hunch, knot, lump, pod. **3. butt** dome, point. **4. blister** gather, vesicate, vesiculate. **5. emboss** pounce, raise, stud. **6. extrude** evaginate, herniate.

8. **1. jut** basset, beetle, exsert, flange, outcrop, outgrow, point out, poke out, thrust out. **2. protrude** pout, project, protract, shoot out. **3. stand out** start, stick out, stick up. **4. bunch** calk, clump, spike.

RELATED KEYWORDS: ADDITION, BODY, BLEMISH, ILL HEALTH, ROUGHNESS, ROUNDNESS, SHARPNESS, SUPPORT

THE BUSH

n. **1.** **1. the bush** countryside, meadows and pastures, the country, the land, the open, the provinces, the soil. **2. bush country** brush, bush, bushland, mallee district, mulga, the brigalow, the bush, the mallee, the mulga, the saltbush, tiger country. **3. back country** backblocks, backwoods, high country, hinterland, out beyond, outback, the inland, the outback, the wayback *(NZ)*. *Informal:* back of beyond, booay, boohai, boondocks *(Chiefly US)*, cactus, goat country, outside country, Snake Gully, Speewah, the back of beyond, the back of Bourke, the booay, the cactus, the donga *(Chiefly SA)*, the never-never, the sticks. **4. dead heart** dead centre, the Centre, the red centre, the red heart. **5. woods** woodlands.

2. **1. ruralism** agrarianism, bucolicism, pastoralism. **2. rusticity** provincialism, provinciality, rurality, swainishness. **3. ruralisation** bushwhacking, countrification, pastoralisation, rustication.

3. **1. countrydweller** back-countryman, backwoodsman, bushman, country cousin, countryman, countrywoman, hatter, peasant, plainsman, provincial, ruralist, rustic, villager, yokel. *Informal:* bushie, bushwhacker *(US)*. **2. peasant** bumpkin, clown, country bumpkin, hillbilly *(Chiefly US)*, moujik, muzhik, ploughboy, ploughman, plowboy *(US)*, plowman *(US)*, ryot, villager, yeoman *(British)*, yokel. *Informal:* bogtrotter *(Chiefly British)*, hayseed, redneck *(US)*, rube *(US)*. **3. country people** country folk, peasantry. **4. rustic** bucolic, swain *(Chiefly Poetic)*.

adj. **4.** **1. rural** agrarian, agrestic, agricultural, country, from the sticks, rustic, village, villatic. **2. outback** back-country, backwoods, high, highland, inland, up-country. **3. country-style** countrified, country-fashion, countryfied. **4. pastoral** agrarian, agricultural, Arcadian, bucolic, rural, rustic, sylvan, woodland.

5. **1. provincial** boorish, churlish, cloddish, clodhopping, hayseed, hillbilly, peasant, rube, stringy-bark, yeoman, yeomanly, yokelish. *Informal:* hick. **2. country-born** country-bred. **3. folksy** *(Informal)* Dad'n'Dave. **4. rustic** bucolic, swainish.

v. **6.** **1. ruralise** go bush, rusticate. **2. bushwhack** *(Informal)* be on the land.

adv. **7.** **1. rurally** bucolically, pastorally, provincially, rustically. **2. outback** *Informal:* back of beyond, beyond the black stump, up (in) the mulga, up the booay.

RELATED KEYWORDS: REMOTENESS, FARMING, HABITATION, NATURE

BUSYNESS

n. **1.** **1. busyness** activeness, aliveness, lissomness, pertness, warmness. **2. activity** action, ado, exertion. *Informal:* goings-on, movement at the station, the action. **3. bustle** coil, hustle, rush, stir, to-do. *Informal:* merry-go-round, razzamatazz, razzle-dazzle. **4. burst of activity** flurry, sally, sprint, spurt, start, tornado. **5. fuss** ado, bother, carry-on, commotion. *Informal:* botheration, song and dance, stink. **6. much ado about nothing** all froth and bubble, boondoggle, sound and fury signifying nothing.

2. **1. sprightliness** alacrity, animation, brilliance, briskness, dapperness, dash, enlivenment, fastness, go, hurriedness, liveliness, quickness, raciness, spryness, verve, vivacity. **2. vigour** animation, brilliance, dash, eagerness, elan, energy, gusto, heartiness, life, liveliness, nerve, pizazz *(Chiefly US)*, red-bloodedness, spirit, spiritedness, sprightliness, sthenia, vigorousness, vim, vivacity, zest. *Informal:* bang *(US)*, kick, pep, snap, zap, zing, zip *(Chiefly US)*. **3. restlessness** exhaustiveness, inquietude, nervous energy, potter, skittishness, tinker, unquietness. **4. hyperactivity** overactivity.

3. **1. centre of activity** beehive, hive, hive of activity, madding crowd, madhouse, Mecca, thick. **2. peak hour** rush hour. **3. period of activity** session, shift, spell.

adj. **4.** **1. busy** active, alive, at work, engaged, hard at work, hearty, hectic, lissom, occupied, smart. *Informal:* humming, up to one's armpits in. **2. sprightly** active, agile, alive, animated, brisk, dapper, fast, full of go, hurried, live, lively, pert, prompt, quick, racy, spirited, spry, vigorous, vivacious, warm. *Informal:* peppy, zippy. **3. vigorous** bustling, cracking, energetic, go-ahead, jazzy, lively, lusty, pushing, red-blooded, spirited, spirituoso, vigoroso, vivacious. **4. dashing** dashy, dynamic, dynamical, lively, showy, slashing. *Informal:* peppy. **5. tireless** exhaustless, indefatigable, inexhaustible, never-tiring, persevering, sedulous, unresting, unstinting, untiring, unwearied, weariless. **6. hardworking** businesslike, diligent, industrious, methodical, operose, painstaking, practical, systematic, vigilant.

   5. **1. excitable** feisty, nervous, skittish, volitant. **2. restless** excited, unquiet, unresting. **3. hyperactive** on the go, overactive.

   v. **6.** **1. be busy** burn the candle at both ends, burn the midnight oil, not have a moment to call one's own. **2. be active** bustle, busy, busy oneself, buzz about, gad about (or around), hum, hum with activity, hurry-scurry, rush, rush around.

   7. **1. belt into** buckle (down) to, bury oneself in, get into the swim, get into the swing, get on with the job, go at, go to it, lay about oneself mightily, make short work of, make the most of one's time, make time, persevere, pull one's weight, put one's shoulder to the wheel, stick at, swing into action, take the bit between one's teeth, turn one's hand to. *Informal:* dig in, get a go on, get cracking, get stuck into, go all out, go at something baldheaded, go to town, have a go, hoe into, hop into, hop to it, not let the grass grow under one's feet, peg away, pull one's finger out. **2. fuss** carry on, fidget, make a fuss of, run riot. *Informal:* fiddle-faddle, make a song (and dance) about.

   adv. **8.** **1. busily** actively, hectically. **2. actively** briskly, energetically, lively, pertly, spiritedly, warmly, with might and main. **3. sprightly** bustlingly, dapperly, hurriedly, hurryingly, racily, spryly. **4. vigorously** dashingly, dynamically. **5. restlessly** exhaustlessly, inexhaustibly, skittishly, unquietly, unrestingly. **6. flat out** *(Informal)* (at) full tilt, full blast, in full swing, in the swim, like nobody's business, on a hurdy-gurdy, on the hop, on the wing. *Informal:* flat out like a lizard drinking, in everything bar (or but) a bath, like a cut snake, on the trot, up to one's ears, up to the elbows, up to the eyes in. **7. in the press of business** in medias res, in the middle of things, in the thick of it. **8. in action** in use, on active service, on the job.

   RELATED KEYWORDS: EXCITEMENT, ACTION, EFFORT, ENCOURAGEMENT, ENERGY, UNDERTAKING, WORKER

BUYING

   n. **1.** **1. buying** acquisition, consumption, mail order, marketing, pre-emption, purchase, shopping, shopping spree. *Informal:* retail therapy. **2. monopolisation** buyout, coemption, engrossment. **3. repurchase** buyback, redemption, retirement. **4. hirepurchase** HP, lay-away *(US)*, lay-by. *Informal:* the never-never. **5. buy** a good buy, acquisition, bargain, covering, deal, purchase. **6. management buyout** MBO. **7. internet shopping** comparison shopping.

   2. **1. buyer** cash buyer, consignee, consumer, hire purchaser, homebuyer, impulse buyer, purchaser, transferee, vendee. *Informal:* peacocker. **2. customer** bargainer, bearer, buyer, client, end user, haggler, marketer, patron, shopper, user. *Informal:* shopaholic. **3. clientele** carriage trade, clientage, market. **4. patronage** custom.

   adj. **3.** **1. buyable** convertible, marketable, purchasable, redemptive. **2. redemptory** redeemable.

   v. **4.** **1. buy** acquire, bulk buy, buy into, buy up, forestall, get, have, hive off, mail-order, make a purchase, obtain, overbuy, pay, pay for, pay off, pay up, pre-empt, procure, purchase, regrate, secure, take, traffic, underbuy. *Informal:* shout. **2. monopolise** buy out, buy up, corner, corner the market, engross, gridiron. *Informal:* peacock. **3. repurchase** buy back, ransom, redeem. **4. buy on credit** hire-purchase, lay-by, use plastic. **5. be in the market for. 6. hire** book, buy, rent. **7. shop** bargain, drive a hard bargain, get one's money's worth, go on a shopping spree, go shopping, patronise, shop around, strike a bargain. **8. be in the chair** *Informal:* shout. **9. pay cash** pay C.O.D.

   RELATED KEYWORDS: COST, EXPENSIVENESS, CHEAPNESS, FINANCE, LOAN, MONEY, OWNERSHIP, PAYMENT, PROFIT, SHOP, COMMERCE

CALCULATION

   n. **1.** **1. calculation** cast, computation, compute, figure work, figures, numeration, reckoning, workings. *Informal:* number crunching. **2. count** aggregate, headcount, loss, recount, sum, summation, tally, total. *Informal:* tot. **3. estimate** approximation, cast-off, guess. *Informal:* guesstimate. **4. demography** capitation, census, demographics.

   2. **1. mathematics** algebra, analysis, analytical geometry, analytics, arithmetic, binary arithmetic, calculus, combinatorial analysis, complex analysis, coordinate geometry, differentiation, ethnomathematics, Euclidean geometry, floating point arithmetic, geometry, higher mathematics, infinitesimal calculus, integral calculus, math *(US)*, maths, number theory, plane geometry, quadratics, quaternions, set theory, theoretical arithmetic, topology, trigonometry. **2. applied mathematics** analysis of variance, biometrics, biometry, Boolean algebra, critical-path analysis, dead reckoning, factor analysis, Fourier analysis, mathematical logic, mensuration, Monte Carlo method, numerical analysis, statistics.

3. 1. mathematical operation addition, combination, derivation, division, enumeration, evolution, factorisation, integration, involution, long division, multiplication, permutation, quadrature, rationalisation, short division, subtraction, times, transform, transposition, variation. **2. algorithm** algorism. **3. equation** cubic equation, differential equation, identity, quadratic, simultaneous equations, wave equation. **4. formula** empirical formula, golden rule, rule, structural formula. **5. statistical distribution** binomial distribution, decile, Gaussian distribution, mathematical expectation, Maxwell-Boltzmann distribution, normal curve, normal distribution, ogive, ordinate, pentile, percentile, Poisson distribution, probability curve, quartile, range, relative frequency, standard deviation, standard error, variance. **6. matrix** array, Latin square, magic square.

4. 1. mathematician algebraist, arithmetician, geometrician. **2. statistician** actuary, demographist, statist. **3. counter** adder, calculator, computer, figurer, integrator, numerator, scorer, tallier, teller. *Informal:* numbers person, walking calculator.

5. 1. elements of computation addend, amount, argument, augend, base, carryover, coefficient, common multiple, derivative, differential coefficient, dividend, divisor, factor, greatest common divisor, highest common factor, integrand, least common multiple, lowest common multiple, minuend, modulus, multiple, multiplicand, multiplier, operand, power, primitive, product, radical, reciprocal, root, submultiple, subtotal, subtrahend, sum, term.

adj. **6. 1. mathematical** algebraic, algebraical, arithmetic, arithmetical, geometric, geometrical, trigonometrical. **2. statistical** demographic, statistic. **3. computable** calculable, countable, denumerable, enumerable, integrable, numerable.

v. **7. 1. compute** calculate, cast up, figure, find, reckon, recount, work out. **2. count** add, add up, card, cash up, cast, differentiate, enumerate, number, numerate, re-count, reach, score, sum, sum up, tally, tell, tell off, total. *Informal:* tot up. **3. divide** add, cube, factor, factorise, integrate, multiply, permute, quantise, raise, rationalise, reduce, square, subtract, transpose. **4. borrow** carry. *Informal:* dot and carry one. **5. estimate** make, measure. *Informal:* guesstimate.

RELATED KEYWORDS: ADDITION, SUBTRACTION, LIST, NUMBER, COMPUTING

CALLOUSNESS

n. **1. 1. callousness** hard-heartedness, hardness of heart, harshness, heartlessness, induration, lovelessness, obdurateness, pitilessness, rigour, rockiness, severity, steeliness, stoniness, tactlessness, unfeelingness. **2. ruthlessness** barbarity, brutality, cold-bloodedness, cruelness, cruelty, inhumanity, mercilessness, savagery. **3. relentlessness** inexorableness, remorselessness. **4. coldness** frigidness, frostiness, iciness. **5. insensitivity** impassivity, indifference, insensitiveness, irresponsiveness, stoicism, unconcern. *Informal:* a thick hide. **6. unfeeling person** block, emotional cripple, stoic.

adj. **2. 1. callous** cold-blooded, conscienceless, cruel, flinty, hard, hard-baked, hard-hearted, hard-nosed, hardened, heartless, indurate, indurative, inhumane, inured, loveless, merciless, obdurate, rocky, steely, stony, stony-hearted, tough, unfeeling, unmerciful, unsparing, unsqueamish. **2. ruthless** cutthroat, draconian, hard-hitting, harsh, heavy-handed, iron, iron-fisted, merciless, pitiless, severe, stony, unkind, unpitying. **3. brutal** bestial, cruel, hard-hearted, harsh, inhuman, pitiless, soulless, unfeeling. **4. unrelenting** firm, grim, hard-hearted, implacable, inexorable, inflexible, pitiless, relentless, remorseless. **5. cold-hearted** bloodless, clinical, cold, draconian, frigid, frosty, frozen, hard, harsh, hostile, icy, marble, marbly, rigid, severe, sharp, soulless, stern, uncompassionate, unfeeling, unkind, unsympathetic. **6. insensitive** clumsy, heavy-footed, insensible, outspoken, overbearing, tactless, thick-skinned, unconsidered. **7. unmoved** apathetic, blasé, cold, dry-eyed, impassible, impassive, impervious, passionless, stoic, stoical, tearless, unemotional. *Informal:* unfazed.

v. **3. 1. be callous** give short shrift, have no heart, have no mercy, have no pity, know no mercy, not be moved, not care less, stick to the letter of the law, turn a deaf ear. *Informal:* play hardball. **2. be ruthless** give no quarter, have one's pound of flesh. **3. be insensitive** *Informal:* have a hide like a rhinoceros, have a hide like an elephant, have a thick skin. **4. harden** case-harden, deaden, dehumanise, sear.

adv. **4.** **1. callously** brutally, hard-heartedly, heartlessly, inhumanely, inhumanly, lovelessly, obdurately, pitilessly, soullessly, stonily, unfeelingly, unsympathetically. **2. ruthlessly** harshly, mercilessly, relentlessly, unrelentingly. **3. cold-heartedly** bloodlessly, clinically, cold-bloodedly, coldly, cruelly, frigidly, frostily, frozenly, icily, in cold blood, without turning a hair. **4. insensitively** clumsily, tactlessly.

RELATED KEYWORDS: UNFAIRNESS, UNFRIENDLINESS, UNKINDNESS, VIOLENCE

CANCELLATION

n. **1.** **1. cancellation** annulment, cancel, cassation, countermand, deletion, deregistration, dissolution, invalidation, nullification, renege, rescission, reversal, revoke, voidance. **2. suspension** discontinuance, disuse, recall, repudiation, revocation, undoing, withdrawal, withdrawment. **3. repeal** abatement, abolishment, abolition, abrogation, ademption, avoidance, bar, suppression. **4. renunciation** abdication, abjuration, demission. **5. abolitionism**.

2. **1. canceller** abator, abjurer, abolisher, abrogator, invalidator, repealer, rescinder, revoker, withdrawer.

v. **3.** **1. cancel** abolish, annihilate, annul, break, break off, defeat, dele, delete, derecognise, deregister, disaffirm, disannul, dissolve, do away with, invalidate, nullify, precancel, quash, rescind, vacate, void. *Informal:* scrub. **2. revoke** abjure, annul, avoid, change one's tune, climb down, countermand, disaffirm, disanoint, eat one's words, forswear, recant, renege, renounce, repeal, repudiate, rescind, resile from, retract, reverse, sing another (or a different) tune, unsay, unspeak, unswear, withdraw. **3. repeal** abate, abolish, abrogate. **4. recall** call back, recede, undo, withdraw.

RELATED KEYWORDS: DENIAL, REFUSAL, PROHIBITION

CAREFULNESS

n. **1.** **1. carefulness** application, assiduity, assiduousness, attention, attentiveness, care, deliberativeness, diligence, fussiness, heedfulness, intentness, mindfulness, solicitousness, thought, vigilance, wariness, watchfulness. **2. solicitude** attendance, care, cherishment, consideration, ministration, tendance, tender loving care, thoughtfulness, tough love. *Informal:* TLC. **3. custody** adoption, care, charge, fosterage, guardianship, keeping, ministry, observance, protection, providence, superintendence, trust, ward, wardship. **4. nurture** bringing-up, upbringing, upkeep.

2. **1. carer** amah, attendant, ayah *(Originally Indian English)*, babysitter, caregiver, careworker, childcare worker, childminder, dry nurse, duenna, fosterer, guard, guardian, housefather, housemother, houseparent, keeper, minder, ministrant, mother's help, nanny, nurse, nursemaid, OOSH worker, parent, protector, sitter, warden, watchman, yaya *(Philippine English)*. **2. pamperer** cherisher, mollycoddler. **3. caring profession** helping profession.

3. **1. nursery** after-school care centre, before school care centre, childcare centre, creche, day nursery, kindergarten, kindie, nursery school, preschool. *Informal:* kinder *(Chiefly NSW)*, kindy.

4. **1. child care** after-school care, before-school care, day care, family day care. **2. minding** baby sitting. **3. fostering** foster care.

adj. **5.** **1. careful** advertent, attentive, diligent, heedful, intent, mindful, painstaking. **2. caring** considerate, heedful, mindful, ministrant, ministrative, regardful, respectful, solicitous, thoughtful. *Informal:* clucky.

v. **6.** **1. be careful** be at pains to, be sure, pay attention to detail, take care, take pains. **2. care for** care, keep an eye on, look after, look out for, minister, shepherd, take care of, tend, tend to. **3. keep** guard, safeguard, save, secure. **4. nurture** bring up, foster, groom, nurse, raise, rear. *Informal:* fetch up *(US)*. **5. mind** attend, babysit, guard, parent, sit, take care of, tend, watch. **6. pamper** cherish, coddle, lap, mollycoddle, mother, nurse, room in, suckle. **7. fuss over** dance attendance, make a fuss of.

adv. **7.** **1. carefully** attentively, diligently, heedfully. **2. solicitously** thoughtfully.

RELATED KEYWORDS: ATTENTION, CAUTIOUSNESS, HELP

CAUSE

n. **1.** **1. cause** aetiology, agent, causality, causation, determinant, evocation, grounds, matter, occasion. **2. reason** cause, cofactor, factor, incentive, matter, motive, rationale, secret, the whys and wherefores, wherefore, why. **3. engenderment** beginning, breeding. **4. catalysis** induction, precipitation.

2. **1. causer** evoker, mainspring, pivot, prime mover, primum mobile, principle. **2. provoker** begetter, beginner, breeder, engenderer, inducer, inspirer, instigator, producer. **3. catalyst** casus belli, catalyser, precipitator. **4. incentive** carrot, causative, instigation, provocative, stimulus. **5. causation** instigation, provocation.

3. **1. causality** aetiology, causation, determinism, etiology, final causes, finalism, teleology.

adj. 4. **1. causal** aetiological, determinant, evocable, occasional. **2. causative** efficient, inductive, inductive to, precipitative, productive. **3. agentive** causative, ergative, responsible for. **4. provocative** catalytic, deterministic, evocative, instigative, provoking.

v. 5. **1. cause** bring about, bring into effect, bring on, bring to bear, bring to pass, do, effect, induce, materialise, occasion. **2. produce** action, adduce, arouse, be inductive to, bring forth, call forth, catalyse, conduce to, educe, elicit, evoke, excite, give rise to, incur, inspire, instigate, motivate, precipitate, provoke. *Informal:* kick up, spark off. **3. make** act, cause, effect, get, have, let, occasion, perform, render. **4. engender** be responsible for, beget, breed, cause, create, occasion, play a part, procreate, produce, sire.

adv. 6. **1. causally** aetiologically, catalytically, causatively, deterministically, efficiently, inductively, provocatively, provokingly.

conj. 7. **1. why** how, whence, wherefore. **2. because** 'cause, 'cos, and so, as, because of, by reason of, considering, for, in the light of, in view of, insofar as, on account of, owing to, since. **3. for the sake of** for the love of, in order to, so as to, so that. **4. consequently** accordingly, an, ergo, hence, in consequence, in that, then, thence, therefore, thus. **5. thereat** hereat.

interj. 8. **1. why?** how come?, what for?.

RELATED KEYWORDS: COMING BEFORE, CREATION, REPRODUCTION, START

CAUTIOUSNESS

n. 1. **1. cautiousness** caution, circumspection, circumspectness, discreetness, wariness. **2. care** caginess, carefulness, caution, chariness, conservativeness, guardedness, heed, heedfulness, mindfulness, vigilantness, wariness. **3. prudence** aforethought, calculation, canniness, discretion, forethought. **4. tentativeness** gingerliness, hesitancy, hesitation, pause. **5. instinct (of or for) self-preservation**.

adj. 2. **1. cautious** canny, careful, chary, circumspect, circumspective, deliberate, discreet, heedful, measured, mindful, solicitous, thoughtful, vigilant, wary, watchful. *Informal:* cagey. **2. guarded** careful, cautious, chary, conservative, safe, safety-conscious, solicitous. **3. prudent** circumspect, discreet, forethoughtful, provident, well-advised. **4. tentative** gingerly, hesitant, wary.

v. 3. **1. be cautious** be on the safe side, err on the safe side, look twice, mind one's tongue, play (it) safe, see which way the cat jumps, take care, take no risks, think twice, tread warily (or softly), watch one's step. **2. feel one's way** be tentative, tiptoe, tread on eggshells, tread softly. **3. beware** be on one's guard, guard against, keep a weather eye open, look out, mind, watch out for. **4. cover oneself** cover one's tail, insure.

adv. 4. **1. cautiously** cannily, carefully, charily, circumspectly, conservatively, discreetly, measuredly, mindfully, plunge in, vigilantly, warily. **2. guardedly** on (one's) guard, safely. **3. tentatively** charily, gingerly, warily. **4. prudently** forethoughtfully.

RELATED KEYWORDS: ANXIETY, ATTENTION, CAREFULNESS, COWARDICE, PREPAREDNESS, PROTECTION, SAFETY

CENTRE

n. 1. **1. centre** centring, centrum, core, heart, heartwood, hub, kern, kernel, marrow, nave, node, nucellus, nucleus, pith, pivot, yolk. **2. middle** golden mean, halfway house, intermediate, mean, media, median, medium, midfield, midpoint, midriff, midst, waist. *Informal:* hey-diddle-diddle. **3. navel** omphalos, umbilicus. **4. bullseye** blank, bull. **5. centre of gravity** barycentre, centre of inertia, centre of mass, centroid, dead centre, dead point. **6. centre of buoyancy** metacentre. **7. focus** apple of the eye, bunt, epicentre, eye, fess point, focal point. **8. headquarters** ganglion, HQ, nerve centre. *Informal:* oicery. **9. storm centre** eye of the storm. **10. centralisation** concentration.

2. **1. centre-line** axis, caudex, columella, fulcrum, hinge, longitudinal axis, newel, pivot, point of rest, polar axis.

adj. 3. **1. central** axial, centric, centrical, core, intranuclear, nuclear, nucleate, pivotal, umbilical, uniaxial. **2. middle** betwixt and between, halfway, intercalary, mean, medial, median, mesial, mezzo, mid, Middle, middlemost, midmost, midway.

3. intermediate intermediary, medium, mezzo. **4. epicentral** epifocal. **5. centripetal** centrifugal, focal, outflung. **6. concentrical** concentric, homocentric. **7. pivotal** axial.

v.   **4.**   **1. centralise** centre, concentrate, concentre, focalise, focus, funnel, middle, zoom.

adv.   **5.**   **1. centrally** axially, centrically, centripetally, focally. **2. intermediately** amidships, medially, medianly, midmost, midships. **3. in midstream** in medias res, in the middle, inter alia. **4. dead-centre** *Informal:* bang-on.

prep.   **6.**   **1. amid** 'mid, amidst, among, between, in, mid, midst *(Poetic)*.

RELATED KEYWORDS: ESSENCE, INSIDE, ORDINARINESS, WALL

CERTAINTY

n.   **1.**   **1. certainty** assurance, certitude, decidedness, definiteness, inerrancy, positivism, secureness, sureness, surety. **2. conviction** assurance, assuredness, belief, cocksureness, confidence, surety. **3. doctrinarism** bigotry, dogmatism. **4. firm belief** conviction, fixed belief.

  2.   **1. certain thing** bird in the hand, certainty, dead certainty, inevitable, open and shut case, safe bet, sure thing. *Informal:* bird, cert, dead cert, knocktaker, monte, monty, moral, shoo-in, sure cop. **2. clincher** clencher, convincer, decider. **3. dictum** gospel.

adj.   **3.**   **1. certain** apodictic, doubtless, incontrovertible, indisputable, indubitable, irrefragable, irrefutable, sure, unchallengeable, undeniable, undisputed, undoubted, unfailing, unimpeachable, unquestionable, unquestioned. **2. guaranteed** assured, rock-solid, sealed, signed, sealed and delivered. *Informal:* deadset, in the bag, sure-fire. **3. cast iron** absolute, indefectible, infallible, perfect, proven, sure, unfailing. **4. unequivocal** as plain as a pikestaff, unambiguous, unanswerable, univocal, unmistakable. **5. self-evident** axiomatic. **6. inevitable** bound to, certain, sure, unavoidable. *Informal:* sure as death and taxes.

  4.   **1. sure** certain, confirmed, decided, definite, determinate, determined, fixed, given, positive, resolute, resolved, risoluto, stated, unquestioning. *Informal:* sorted. **2. confident** assured, certain, decisive, poised, secure, self-assured, self-confident, self-sufficient. **3. cocksure** bold as brass, cool as a cucumber, overconfident, positive. **4. doctrinaire** bigoted, dogmatic, dogmatical, opinionated, opinionative, thetic, thetical, unshakable.

v.   **5.**   **1. be certain** be sure, dare say, have no doubt. *Informal:* bet London to a brick (on), bet one's boots. **2. be cocksure** dogmatise, know all the answers, lay down the law. **3. be self-evident** go without saying.

adv.   **6.**   **1. certainly** assuredly, beyond a shadow of doubt, beyond question, doubtless, doubtlessly, for a certainty, for a monte, for certain, for sure, indubitably, surely, to be sure, undoubtedly, unimpeachably, unquestionably, without doubt, without fail, without question. **2. definitely** apodictically, clearly, decidedly, demonstrably, determinately, incontestably, positively, undeniably, unmistakably. **3. inevitably** bound to be, unavoidably. *Informal:* sure *(US)*.

RELATED KEYWORDS: BELIEF, EVIDENCE, INEVITABILITY, KNOWLEDGE, LIKELIHOOD, TRUTH

CHANGE

n.   **1.**   **1. change** alteration, amendment, arrangement, becoming, changeover, fluctuation, flux, metamorphism, metamorphosis, modification, mutation, permutation, perversion, physical change, reaction, reformation, renounce, reorganisation, reshuffle, revisal, revise, revision, sea change, shake-up, shift, switch, switch-over, transformation, transit, transition, turn, turnabout, twist, variation, variegation, vicissitude, vicissitudes. *Informal:* switcheroo. **2. sudden change** break, cataclysm, crisis, cut, jump cut, metastasis, revolution. **3. transformation** alchemy, bioconversion, change of state, conversion, denaturation, denaturisation, dialectic, differentiation, diversification, endomorphism, fossilisation, heteromorphy, metaplasm, metastasis, phase change, radicalisation, transfiguration, transfigurement, transmogrification, transmutation, transubstantiation, xenogenesis. **4. modification** adaptation, adaption, adjustment, alts and adds, dissimilation, inflection, makeover, maladjustment, modulation, mutagenesis, mutation, rectification, rehash, saltation, vicissitude. **5. morphosis** anabolism, carbonation, carbonisation, catabolism, cytokinesis, dissimilation, karyokinesis, katabolism, metabolism, metaplasia, oxidation. **6. turning point** climacteric, climacterical, crisis, great divide, moment of truth, tipping point, watershed.

  2.   **1. changer** alembic, alterant, catalyser, catalyst, catalytic, catalytic converter, converter, modifier, modulator, philosopher's stone, transducer, transformer.

2. modifier adaptor, adjuster, finetuner. **3. transformer** alchemist, converter, transmuter. **4. reviser** amender, manipulator, revisionist, turner, varier.

adj. **3.** **1. changing** heteromorphic, on the turn, transformative, transmutative, variant, vicissitudinous, xenogenic. **2. adaptive** acculturative, modificative, modificatory. **3. modulative** alterant, alterative, amendatory *(US)*, manipulatory, revisionary, revisory.

4. **1. variable** adaptable, adjustable, alterable, amendable, changeable, convertible, deformable, flexible, flexile, malleable, modifiable, permutable, pervertible, rectifiable, temperable, transformable, transmutable. **2. variational** adaptational, conversionary, differential, dissimilative, gradational, metabolic, mutational, mutative, revisional, sportive, transmutative, variable. **3. transformational** alchemical, alchemistical, metamorphic, metamorphous, transilient, transitionary, transitive.

v. **5.** **1. change** acculturate, affect, alter, amend, catalyse, chequer, contort, counterchange, dissimilate, interchange, leave one's mark, leaven, make over, manipulate, modify, mutate, permutate, permute, pervert, reconstruct, remodel, reorientate, revise, revolutionise, ring the changes, touch, transfer, twist, variegate, vary. **2. modify** adapt, adjust, configure, correct, edit, fair, finetune, modulate, phase in, proportion, qualify, recast, reconfigure, rehash, reshape, shape, specialise, tone, trim. **3. differentiate** diversify, mutate, shift, switch, turn, variegate. **4. transform** arrange, change, colour, convert, deform, metamorphose, radicalise, rectify, repurpose, restructure, transcribe, transfigure, translate, transmogrify, turn. **5. be transformed** become, change into. **6. transmute** alchemise, alkalify, alkalise, denature, elaborate, fossilise, metabolise, transubstantiate.

adv. **6.** **1. variably** adaptively, adjustably, alterably, convertibly, flexibly, transitionally, transitively.

RELATED KEYWORDS: CHANGEABLENESS, EVOLUTION, REVOLUTION, TEMPORARINESS

CHANGEABLENESS

n. **1.** **1. changeableness** alterableness, changefulness, mutableness, transmutableness, variableness. **2. unsteadiness** astaticism, fluidity, insecurity, instability, lability, sandiness, treacherousness, unsettlement, unsoundness, unstableness. **3. adaptableness** adaptiveness, elasticity, mobility, suppleness. **4. volatileness** versatileness. **5. allomerism** allomorphism, metastability. **6. inconstancy** indefiniteness, indeterminateness, indetermination, uncertainness, unsteadiness, vertiginousness. **7. capriciousness** fickleness, flightiness, freakiness, freakishness, levity, mercurialness, waywardness. **8. vacillation** fluctuation, indetermination, oscillation, tergiversation. **9. transitoriness** caducity, temporality.

2. **1. waverer** acrobat, chameleon, erratic, flibbertigibbet, oscillator, tergiversator.

adj. **3.** **1. changeable** alterable, ambulatory, changeful, convertible, mutable, transmutable, unstable, variable. **2. unstable** astatic, cheeky *(Aboriginal English)*, floating, fluid, fluidic, hydrokinetic, insecure, instable, labile, precarious, rootless, sandy, slippery, treacherous, unsettled, unsound, unsteady, vagrant. **3. adaptable** adaptive, elastic, flexible, flexile, malleable, mobile, protean, supple, variform, versatile. **4. inconstant** indefinite, indeterminate, movable, vertiginous. **5. wavering** erratic, fluctuant, fluctuating, meandering, roller-coaster, stop-start, uncertain, unsettled, unsteady, up-and-down, vacillating. **6. capricious** amphibolic, arbitrary, crank, cranky, errant, erratic, fickle, flighty, freakish, freaky, frivolous, irresolute, Jekyll-and-Hyde, light, mercurial, quick-change, quicksilver, rickety, shaky, skittish, slippery, temperamental, unreliable, unsteady, variable, varying, volatile, wayward, whimsical. **7. chameleonic** kaleidoscopic, phantasmagorical. **8. transitory** caducous, short-life, short-lived.

v. **4.** **1. be changeable** blow hot and cold, change horses in midstream, change one's tune, chop and change, dicker *(Chiefly US)*, fluctuate, oscillate, sway, swing, tergiversate, vacillate, waver, wobble.

adv. **5.** **1. unstably** astatically, uncertainly, unsteadily. **2. capriciously** errantly, erratically, fickly, flightily, freakishly, mercurially, temperamentally, uncertainly, waywardly. **3. indefinitely** inconstantly, indeterminately, unsteadily, vertiginously. **4. waveringly** acrobatically, meanderingly, vacillatingly.

RELATED KEYWORDS: UNCERTAINTY, CHANGE, IRREGULARITY

CHANGELESSNESS

n. **1.** **1. changelessness** immutableness, inadaptability, inalterability, incommutableness, invariableness. **2. inflexibleness** inexorableness, infrangibleness. **3. constancy** continuance, enduringness, eternalness, invariability, permanence. **4. immortality** deathlessness, immortalisation, imperishableness. **5. permanency** indefeasibility, indelibleness, indissolubleness, ineffaceability, irreducibleness, irremovability, irreversibleness, permanence, stability, stableness, unfadingness, unfailingness. **6. fixedness** consistency, determinateness, fixity, permanence, stability, steadfastness. **7. entrenchment** establishment, fixation, ossification, settlement, settling.

adj. **2.** **1. changeless** invariable, invariant, unchanging, unfading, unfailing, unflagging, unregenerate, unvarying. **2. unchangeable** immobile, immovable, immutable, inadaptable, inalterable, incommutable, indecomposable, indelible, indissoluble, ineffaceable, ineradicable, insoluble, irrecoverable, irreducible, irremovable, irrepealable, irreversible, unalterable, unshakable. **3. hardcore** chronic, deep-rooted, deep-seated, dyed-in-the-wool, hardline, ingrained, inveterate, through-and-through. **4. constant** continual, continuous, daylong, endless, enduring, eternal, everlasting, frequent, indefeasible, inerasable, interminable, lasting, perdurable, perennial, permanent, persistent, quenchless, regular, stable, standing, steady, unbroken, unending, uninterrupted, unswerving, yearlong. *Informal:* 24/7. **5. fixed** cast-iron, chronic, confirmed, determined, fast, immovable, inexorable, inflexible, infrangible, ingrain, ingrained, inveterate, resolute, resolved, rigid, risoluto, set, static, steadfast, unalterable, unbending, unwavering, unyielding. **6. immortal** aeonian, amaranthine, deathless, eternal, everlasting, imperishable, incorruptible, lifelong, perdurable, perpetual, timeless, undying.

adv. **3.** **1. changelessly** immovably, immutably, inalterably, incommutably, incorruptibly, indissolubly, inexorably, inflexibly, infrangibly, invariably, irrecoverably, irreducibly, irrepealably, irreversibly, unfadingly, unfailingly, unflaggingly, unregenerately, unshakably. **2. constantly** consistently, continuously, persistently, steadfastly. *Informal:* 24/7. **3. eternally** always, enduringly, forever and a day, immortally, imperishably, interminably, perdurably, perennially, perpetually, undyingly, unendingly. *Informal:* for keeps. **4. permanently** indefeasibly, indelibly, ineffaceably, ineradicably, inerasably, irremovably, stably.

RELATED KEYWORDS: CONTINUATION, ETERNITY, FASTENING, INFINITY, STEADINESS

CHANGE OF ALLEGIANCE

n. **1.** **1. change of allegiance** about-face, alienation, apostasy, backslide, backsliding, changeover, defection, desertion, renunciation, secession, tergiversation, transfer, treason, turnabout, volte-face. **2. conversion** naturalisation, proselytism, rebirth, redemption, reformation, regeneracy, regeneration, renaissance, renascence. **3. rehabilitation** reeducation, reconditioning, repatriation. **4. brainwashing** indoctrination.

2. **1. defector** apostate, backslider, deserter, renegade, reneger, traitor, turncoat. **2. vacillator** acrobat, floating voter, swinging voter, tergiversant, tergiversator. **3. convert** born-again, catechumen, changed person, disciple, neophyte, new man, new woman, novice, proselyte, separatist.

adj. **3.** **1. renegade** apostate, murtad, tergiversant, traitorous. **2. converted** born-again, reborn, redeemed, reformed, regenerate. **3. naturalised**.

v. **4.** **1. change one's allegiance** change one's mind, change one's spots, change one's tune, defect, do an about face, go back on one's word, renege, sing another (or a different) tune, tergiversate, unthink. **2. be converted** change one's ways, convert, go over, go straight, mend one's ways, regenerate, repent, see the light, turn, turn over a new leaf. **3. apostatise** backslide, fall away, renegade, throw over. **4. lose one's faith** fall from grace, turn away from God.

5. **1. convert** bring over, bring round, episcopise, reclaim, reform, regenerate, repurpose. **2. proselytise** brainwash, convert, evangelise, missionise, proselyte, teach.

RELATED KEYWORDS: DISBELIEF, IMPULSIVENESS, UNFAITHFULNESS, INDECISION, RELIGION

CHANNEL

n. **1.** **1. channel** aqueduct, canal, conduit, ditch, duct, dyke, fairway, fishway, fosse, irrigator, lane, lateral, lead, navigable water, navigation, nullah *(Indian English)*, reach, river, river basin, riverbed, runlet, runnel, seaway, ship canal, stream channel, swash, thoroughfare, tideway, trench, trough, wash, watercourse, waterway. **2. stormwater channel** floodway, gutter, spillway. **3. moat** fosse. **4. tunnel** water tunnel, wind tunnel. **5. dry creek** donga, wadi, winterbourne. **6. strait** euripus, gat, neck, sound. **7. valley** arroyo, channel, chine, gulch *(Chiefly US)*, gullet, gully, nullah *(Indian English)*, pass *(US)*, ravine, strath, water gap. **8. furrow** crevice, flute, fulgurite, gouge, groove, rebate, rut, sulcus.

2. **1. passageway** adit, crosscut, draft tube, drift, heading, lateral, shaft, tunnel. **2. airway** air duct, airdrive, airshaft, breezeway, port, porting, schnorkle, slot, snorkel, umbilical cord, upcast, uptake, vent, ventiduct, windsail. **3. chimney** chimneypot, flue, funnel, smokestack, stack, tallboy.

3. **1. drain** bore drain, conduit, culvert, ditch, downcomer, downpipe, drainpipe, gutter, guttering, limber, ponding board, sewer, sink, spitter, spout *(Chiefly Victoria and Tasmania)*, spouting *(Chiefly Victoria and Tasmania)*, spreader, table drain, wastepipe, watertable. **2. wastepipe** gully trap, S trap, soil pipe, stench trap, trap. **3. spout** gargoyle, spile *(US)*, waterspout. **4. catheter** cannula.

4. **1. borehole** artesian bore, artesian well, bore, subartesian bore, well, wellpoint. **2. funnel** tundish. **3. sinkhole** pothole, sink, soakage pit, sump, swallow-hole.

5. **1. chute** chinaman, feed, feedpipe, gravity feed. **2. sluice** drain, flash, floodgate, lock, penstock, plughole, sluicegate, tide gate, water gate, weir. **3. race** flume *(US)*, headrace, leat, millrace, millrun, raceway, sluiceway, spillway, tailrace.

6. **1. piping** air-cock, blowpipe, conduction, gas main, gas pipe, pipage, pipe, pipeline, service pipe, steampipe, the mains, tubing, water main, waterworks. **2. agricultural pipe** ag pipe, boom spray, sprinkler system. **3. exhaust pipe** stinkpipe, tailpipe. **4. navel pipe** spurling pipe. **5. hose** hosepipe. **6. tube** siphon, straw, sucker, syphon, tubulure.

adj. **7.** **1. channelled** ducted, vascular, veined. **2. tubular** cannular, capillary, fistulous, funnel-like, gutterlike, lumbricoid, pipelike, pipy, tubate, tubulate. **3. irrigational** irrigative.

v. **8.** **1. channel** canal, canalise, gutter. **2. pipe** intubate, reticulate, siphon, spile, tube, tubulate. **3. irrigate** subirrigate.

RELATED KEYWORDS: BODY, FLOW, ROUTE

CHARACTER

n. **1.** **1. character** complexion, constitution, ethos, fibre, genius, identity, image, mindscape, nature, persona, personality, psychology, self, self-identity. **2. temperament** character, constitution, crasis, disposition, ethos, fibre, frame of mind, grain, humour, kidney, mind, mood, spirit, temper, tone, vein. **3. type** blood, breed, cast, character, colour, complexion, cut, disposition, feather, kidney, make, make-up, manner, mien, mould, quality, sort, stamp, style, timber, worth. **4. grain** strain, streak, stripe *(Chiefly US)*, vein. **5. soul** anima, animus, essence, heart, inner man, inner nature, inner woman, inscape, inside, libido, psyche, vital force. **6. backbone** calibre, character, fibre, heart, mettle, pith, principle, resolution, spirit, strength. **7. aura** air.

2. **1. characteristics** aspects, attributes, endowment, features, inheritance, instincts, manner, physiognomy, properties, qualia, qualities, stuff, vein. **2. characteristic** difference, distinction, habit, idiolect, idiosyncrasy, individualism, lineament, mark, peculiarity, touch, trait, way.

3. **1. attitude** opinion, outlook, point of view, pose, position, stance, stand, standpoint, view, viewpoint. **2. inclination** bent, bias, cast, fancy, impulse, lean, leaning, liking, penchant, ply, preference, prejudice, set, slant, tendency, tenor, turn. **3. predisposition** diathesis, disposition, habit, liability, liableness, susceptibility, susceptibleness, susceptiveness, tendency, weakness. **4. affinity** affection, appetence, aptitude, favour, inclination, liking, partiality, predilection, proclivity, proneness, propensity, readiness. **5. trend** climate, course, current, direction, drift, gravitation, motion, movement, stream, tide, undercurrent, wave, wind.

adj. **4.** **1. characteristic** discriminating, discriminative, distinctive, typical. **2. inherent** baseline, basic *(Chiefly US)*, congenital, connate, connatural, constitutional, core, essential, fundamental, idiosyncratic, inborn, inbred, inherited, innate, inner, native, pre-existing, unconditioned. **3. dispositional** constitutional, temperamental.

5. **1. predisposed** apt to, capable of, disposed, given to, in a fair way to, inclined, minded, oriented, prone, ready, tempered, tending, wont. **2. partial** biased, one-eyed, partisan, prejudiced, tendentious. **3. susceptible** accessible, amenable, annihilable, diathetic, exposed, liable, open, subject to, susceptive, vulnerable. *Informal:* come-at-able, get-at-able.

v. **6.** **1. be characteristic of** characterise, epitomise, exemplify, typify.

7. **1. tend** go, gravitate to (or towards), have in the blood, incline, lean towards, look, look towards, propend, trend.

adv. **8.** **1. characteristically** at bottom, au fond, idiosyncratically, in character, temperamentally, typically.

RELATED KEYWORDS: EMOTION, ESSENCE, INFLUENCE, PSYCHE

CHEAPNESS

n. **1.** **1. cheapness** inexpensiveness. **2. valuelessness** worthlessness. **3. depreciation** amortisation, devaluation, dirty float, price-cutting, undervaluation. **4. concession** corporate rate, cut rate, discount, discount rate, trade discount, undercharge. *Informal:* mates rates. **5. depression** recession, slump.

2. **1. bargain** good deal, special. *Informal:* buy, dicker *(Chiefly US)*, go *(US)*, steal. **2. budget edition** catchpenny, cheapie. *Informal:* brummy, rip. **3. sale** boot sale, car boot sale, clearance sale, clearing sale, fire sale, garage sale, jumble sale, lawn sale *(NT)*, reduction sale, rummage sale, yard sale. **4. op shop** Vinnie's.

3. **1. bargaining** chaff, chaffer, haggling.

4. **1. bargainer** chafferer, haggler, shaver.

adj. **5.** **1. cheap** affordable, cheap at the price, dirt-cheap, economic, economical, economy, frugal, inexpensive, low-priced, no-frills, sixpenny. *Informal:* cheap as chips (or dirt), mickey mouse. **2. marked down** cut-price, cut-rate, depreciated, discounted, half-price, nominal, on special, reduced. **3. free** complimentary, costless, gratis, gratuitous, honorary, interest-free. *Informal:* buckshee. **4. untaxed** duty-free, scot-free, tax-free. **5. worthless** fustian, valueless. *Informal:* not worth a button, not worth a cracker, not worth a crumpet, not worth a tinker's cuss (or damn). **6. cheap and nasty** brum, catchpenny, cheap, gaudy, gimcrack, rubbishy, tawdry, tinsel, tinselly, trashy, trumpery. *Informal:* brummy, el cheapo, tinhorn *(US)*, tizzy. **7. depreciative** depreciatory, depressive. **8. economy-class** third-class, tourist-class.

v. **6.** **1. be cheap** cost little. **2. slump** collapse, fall in price.

7. **1. cheapen** beat down, depreciate, depress, devalue, discount, knock down, reduce, undervalue. **2. underbuy** buy for a song. **3. undercharge** underquote. **4. undercut** undersell.

adv. **8.** **1. cheaply** at a discount, cheap, economy, for a song, for next to nothing, inexpensively. *Informal:* on the cheap, on the smell of an oily rag. **2. for free** for nothing, gratis, gratuitously.

RELATED KEYWORDS: BUYING, THRIFT, PAYMENT, COMMERCE, POVERTY

CHOICE

n. **1.** **1. choice** alternative, discretion, elective, first refusal, marque, option, preference, refusal, selection. *Informal:* druthers. **2. preference** affect, affinity, fancy, favourite, inclination, leaning, liking, predilection, tendency. **3. selection** adoption, choice, cull, lot, pick. **4. preselection** cooptation, nomination, preferment, selectness. **5. free will** preferentialism, self-determination, voluntariness, will. **6. smorgasbord** menu, olla podrida, variety. **7. eclecticism** dilettantism.

2. **1. election** by-election, exit poll, general election, hustings, indirect election, khaki election, plebiscite, poll, presidential primary *(US)*, primary *(US Politics)*, primary election, public opinion poll, referendum, tanistry. **2. vote** a show of hands, acclaim, ballot, blackball, division, majority, voice. **3. kind of vote** absence vote, abstention, alternative vote, Australian ballot *(Chiefly US, British)*, ballot, card-vote, casting vote, compulsory voting, conscience vote, cumulative voting, d'Hondt system, declaration vote, deliberative vote, donkey vote, exhaustive ballot, exhaustive preferential voting, first-past-the-post voting, free vote, Hare electoral system, Hare-Clarke system, informal vote, postal vote, preferential voting, proxyholder, second ballot. **4. suffrage** ballot, franchise. **5. polling booth** ballot box, ballot paper, booth, voting machine *(US)*, voting paper. **6. psephology**.

3. **1. chooser** endorser, nominator, plumper, preferentialist, preferrer, selector. **2. voter** absentee vote, aspirational voter, balloter, blackballer, caster, constituent, elector, electoral college *(US)*, electorate, floating voter, quorum, swinging voter. **3. suffragist** suffragette. **4. decider** determiner, resolver. **5. eclectic**. **6. psephologist**.

4. **1. the chosen** seed, the elect, top seed. **2. nominee** candidate.

adj. **5.** **1. optional** alternative, discretional, discretionary, elective, facultative, permissive, selective, volitionary, voluntary, votive. **2. multiple-choice** either-or, two-way. **3. eclectic**.

6. **1. chosen** choice, elect, favourite, hand-picked, pet, picked, preferred, select. *Informal:* fave. **2. eligible** adoptable, votable.

v. **7.** **1. choose** fix on (or upon), hand-pick, mark out, opt for, pick, pick out, pitch on (or upon), select, take. **2. prefer** fancy, favour, have rather, like best, opt for, plump for, preference, single out. **3. pick and choose** *Informal:* peacock, pick the eyes out of.

4. determine agree, arbitrate, conclude, decide, make up, resolve. **5. suit oneself** work one's will.

    8. **1. elect** put in, return, vote into office. **2. vote** ballot, blackball, cast a vote, coopt, divide, go to the polls. **3. appoint** adopt, affect, preselect.

adv.   **9.** **1. optionally** ad lib, ad libitum, alternatively, at one's discretion, discretionarily, electively, volitionally. **2. eclectically** preferentially, selectively. **3. rather** by choice, first, preferably, sooner, voluntarily.

    RELATED KEYWORDS: POLITICS, INTENTION, WILLINGNESS

CITY

n.   **1.** **1. city** burgh, capital, conurbation, federal capital, free city, main centres, megalopolis, metropolis, multifunctionpolis, open city, state capital, system city, the federal capital. *Informal:* burg *(US)*, concrete jungle, the big smoke. **2. inner city** business area, business section, CBD, central business district, civic centre, downtown, shopping area, the City *(British)*, the docks, tin-pan alley, uptown, waterfront, waterfrontage. **3. suburb** barrio, borough, built-up area, dormitory, faubourg, municipality, parish, precinct *(US)*, residential district, subdivision, ward. **4. suburbia** commuter belt, ribbon development, urban sprawl. *Informal:* the burbs. **5. slum** ruin, ruins, shantytown, skid row, slums. **6. native quarter** casbah, Chinatown, ghetto, kasbah. **7. decadent city** Babylon, Gomorrah, Sodom.

    2. **1. town** boom town, borough *(British, British History)*, closed town, company town, exurbs, fishing town, ghost town, growth centre, home town, market town, mining town, outport, port, rail town, satellite town, seaport, township. **2. country town** Bandywallop, Bullabakanka, Bullamakanka, clachan, county town *(British)*, hamlet, kainga, kampong, kraal, Oodnagalahbi, pa *(NZ)*, settlement, Speewah, subtopia *(British)*, village, whistlestop *(US)*. *Informal:* one-horse town, one-pub town. **3. shopping complex** high street, main street, mall, market, pedestrian plaza, shopping centre, shopping mall, shopping precinct *(British)*, shoppingtown. **4. outskirts** city surrounds, exurbia *(US)*, greenfields. *Informal:* backblocks, boondocks *(Chiefly US)*.

    3. **1. townsfolk** burgess, burgher, citizen, fringe dweller, town, townsman, townspeople, townswoman. **2. urbanite** citizen, city slicker, city-slicker, cityite, exurbanite, metropolitan, slicker, suburban, suburbanite, suburbia. *Informal:* townie.

    4. **1. urbanisation** suburbanisation, urban renewal. **2. civics** topography, town planning.

adj.   **5.** **1. urban** brownfield, burghal, citied, civic, intercity, interurban, megalopolitan, metropolitan, urbanite. **2. citified** townish. **3. suburban** cross-town, downtown, slummy, uptown. *Informal:* brick venereal. **4. exurban** fringe.

v.   **6.** **1. urbanise** municipalise, suburbanise.

    RELATED KEYWORDS: HABITATION

CLARITY

n.   **1.** **1. clarity** clearness, cognisability, legibleness, limpidness, lucidness, pellucidness, perspicuity, perspicuousness, plainness, preciseness, precision, transparency. **2. intelligibility** apprehensibility, comprehensibleness, intelligibleness, interpretability, luminousness.

    2. **1. clarification** elucidation, illumination, illustration. **2. explanation** elaboration, exegesis, explication, exposé, interpretation, meaning. **3. exposition** discourse, summa, treatise. **4. decipherment** cryptanalysis, decryption, demystification, unravelment. **5. reductionism** oversimplification. **6. annotation** adversaria, apostil, comment, commentary, crib, end note, epexegesis, footnote, gloss, marginalia, note, schedule, scholium, scholiums, sidenote. **7. key** appendix, caption, cipher, legend.

    3. **1. clarifier** elucidator, explainer, exponent, expositor, expounder, illustrator, luminary. **2. decipherer** cryptanalyst, decoder, solver, unraveller, unscrambler. **3. annotator** commenter, exegete, glossator, scholiast.

adj.   **4.** **1. clear** apparent, articulate, crystal clear, definite, distinct, easy, evident, explicit, fair, legible, limpid, lucid, luculent, manifest, obvious, pellucid, perspicuous, plain, precise, readable, straightforward, transparent, unambiguous, uncomplicated, unequivocal, univocal, unmistakable. **2. intelligible** apprehensible, cognisable, cognoscible, comprehensible, decipherable, explainable, explicable, fathomable, graspable, interpretable, knowable, luminous, perceivable, perceptible, recognisable, scrutable, understandable.

    5. **1. explanatory** declarative, declaratory, elucidatory, explicative, explicatory, exponential, expository, illuminating, illuminative, illustrational, illustrative, interpretational, interpretative, interpretive. **2. annotative** commentarial, epexegetic, exegetic, exegetical, expository, glossarial, scholiastic.

v. **6.** **1. clarify** clear, clear the air, clear up, demystify, elucidate, explain, rationalise, shed (or throw) light on, speak for itself, speak plainly, unfold. **2. explain** allegorise, amplify, bring home to, elaborate on, explicate, expound, flesh out, give the rhyme and reason, illuminate, illumine, illustrate, interpret, parabolise, set out, spell out, translate. **3. decipher** decode, decrypt, explain, expound, make out, puzzle out, resolve, see, solve, translate, unravel, unscramble, untangle. **4. annotate** comment, interpret, note.

adv. **7.** **1. clearly** articulately, clear, distinctly, limpidly, lucidly, luculently, perspicuously, plain, plainly, precisely, simply. **2. intelligibly** cognisably, comprehensibly, luminously, perceivably, perceptibly.

RELATED KEYWORDS: INTERPRETATION, KNOWLEDGE, LOGICALITY, MEANING

CLASSIFICATION

n. **1.** **1. classification** assortment, categorisation, codification, coordination, dichotomisation, distribution, rating, reclassification, schematisation, systematisation, systematism, systemisation, tabularisation. **2. typology** architectonics, systematics, systematology. **3. system** hierarchy, method, nomenclature, systematics, tabulation, taxonomy. **4. catalogue** code, digest, index, inventory, key, ladder, schedule, sequence, subject catalogue, synchronism, table, timetable.

2. **1. class** bracket, branch, category, compartment, denomination, description, designation, fashion, genre, group, kidney, kind, persuasion, range, school, set, sort, subcategory, subgroup, subordinate set, subset, subtype, tier, type, variety. **2. taxon** alliance, allopatric, class, family, generic, genus, kind, kingdom, life form, order, phylum, sort, species, strain, subclass, subfamily, subgenus, subkingdom, suborder, subphylum, subspecies, superclass, superfamily, superorder, tribe, variety. **3. tribe** breed, brood, genus, group, house, kind, kindred, lineage, phratry, race, social class, social subset, stirps, stock. **4. rank** caste, category, class, degree, estate, grade, grading, league, mark, order, place, standard, stratum, stream.

3. **1. classer** adjuster, categorist, classifier, codifier, digester, grader, identifier, indexer, ranger, ranker, sorter, systematiser, systematist, tabulator. **2. typologist** systemiser, taxonomer. **3. wool classer** fleece-oh, fleece-picker, fleecy, picker, picker-up, piecepicker, stapler, wool sorter.

adj. **4.** **1. classificatory** categorical, diachronic, hierarchical, Linnean, monothetic, physiographical, polythetic, synchronic, synchronous, systematic, systemic, tabular, taxonomical, typological. **2. classifiable** classable, identifiable, sortable. **3. classified** assorted, class, coordinative, discriminative, generic, ordinal, phyletic, representative, subgeneric, subordinal, subspecific, true, typical, under the one umbrella, varietal.

v. **5.** **1. class** assort, categorise, classify, code, codify, compartment, compartmentalise, coordinate, departmentalise, digest, distinguish, distribute, divide, factionalise, fire-rate, gradate, grade, identify, label, lemmatise, mark, methodise, order, organise, parcel out (or up), pigeonhole, position, range, rank, rate, reclassify, schematise, size, sort, staple, stratify, stream, systematise, systemise, zone.

RELATED KEYWORDS: HOMOGENEITY, LIST, ORDER, PARENTAGE, RELATIVE

CLEANLINESS

n. **1.** **1. cleanliness** cleanness, freshness, immaculateness, pureness, purity, spotlessness. **2. sanitariness** asepsis, disinfection, hygiene.

2. **1. cleansing** ablutions, bath, bathing ghat, bubble bath, douche, footbath, lavage, lavation, rinse, rinsing, sauna, shampoo, shower, sitz bath, spa bath, sponge, sponge bath, sponge-down, steam bath, toilet, Turkish bath, wash, washing. *Informal:* annual, brasco, bushman's breakfast, sluice. **2. quick wash** strip bath *(British)*. *Informal:* a lick and a promise, APC bath, birdbath, catlick, Mary Pickford in three acts, Pommy wash. **3. scour** brush, careen, careenage, careening, decarbonisation, decarburisation, scrub, ultrasonic cleaning. *Informal:* decarb, decoke. **4. housework** housekeeping, sweep, sweeping, wash-up, washing-up. **5. cleaning of clothes** dry-cleaning, shoeshine. *Informal:* bull. **6. clean-up** emu parade, spring-clean, spring-cleaning. **7. washing** banjoing, box sluicing, surfacing. **8. purification** depuration, elutriation, expurgation, filtration. **9. sterilisation** antisepsis, chlorination, fumigation. **10. decontamination** bioremediation, desalination, remediation, sanitisation. **11. religious cleansing** ablution, baptism, lavabo, luster, lustration, lustrum.

3. **1. bathroom** bagnio, bath, bathhouse, baths, comfort station, ensuite, facilities, lavatory, rest room, sauna, shower recess, shower room, sudatorium, sudatory, thermae, washroom. *Informal:* lav, lavvy.

4. **1. bath** basin, bathtub, bidet, birdbath, bush shower, douche, footbath, handbasin, hipbath, hot tub, jacuzzi, kitchen sink, shower, shower-bath, sink, sitz bath, spa, spa pool, tub, wash tub, washbasin, washbowl. **2. vanity unit** commode, vanity, washstand. **3. font** baptistery, lavabo, laver, stoup. **4. laundry** laundrette, laundromat, utility room, washhouse, washshed. **5. sluice** banjo, cradle, launder, long tom, rocker, rumble, strake, tumbling box, V-box. **6. copper** kier, laundry tub *(Especially Qld and NSW)*, trough, tub. **7. car wash**. **8. sheep dip** dip, plunge dip, sheep wash, washpool.

5. **1. washer** face cloth, face flannel, face towel, face washer, flannel, loofah, sewermat, washcloth, washrag. **2. toothbrush** dental floss, dentifrice, floss, tooth-stick, toothpaste, toothpick. **3. swab** cotton bud. **4. napkin** dinner napkin, serviette, table napkin. **5. nappy** diaper *(US)*, napkin, pilchers, swaddle, swaddling clothes. **6. handkerchief** bandanna, bushman's hanky, pocket handkerchief. *Informal:* hanky, nose rag, snotrag. **7. toilet paper** bumf, lavatory paper. *Informal:* bum fodder, bumph, dunny paper. **8. doormat** foot-scraper. **9. dishcloth** bottlebrush, dishrag, dishwasher, dolly mop, scourer, sponge, steel wool, wash-leather, wettex, wire wool. **10. pull-through** electric eel, four-by-two, pipe-cleaner, ramrod. **11. syringe** syrette.

6. **1. brush** banister brush, bootbrush, comb, currycomb, dandy-brush, duster, feather duster, fitch, floor polisher, hairbrush, nailbrush, scrubber, scrubbing-brush, wire brush. **2. comb** afro comb, hatchel, heckle. *Informal:* bug rake, flea rake. **3. broom** besom, push broom, Turk's head broom. **4. carpet-sweeper** hoover, vacuum, vacuum cleaner. **5. mop** floorcloth, scrim, squeegee, squeegee mop, swab. **6. scraper** nailfile, strigil. **7. fibre cleaner** gin, linter, rippler, scutch.

7. **1. cleanser** amole, cold cream, quillai bark, salts of lemon, shampoo, shower gel, soap, soap flakes, soap powder, soapbark, soapsuds, toiletry, Windsor soap. *Informal:* Bob Hope. **2. detergent** abluent, abstergent, cleaner, degreaser, detersive, rinser, saddlesoap, sugar soap, washing powder, washing soda. **3. mouthwash** gargle, rinse. **4. face pack** face mask, facial mask, mask. **5. purge** aperient, catharsis, cathartic, croton oil, depurative, detergence, physic, purgation, purgative. **6. disinfectant** antiseptic, argyrol, boric acid, carbolic acid, chloramine, chlorination, chlorine, Dakin's solution, eusol, fumigant, hexachlorophene, hexylresorcinol, hydroxybenzene, ichthammol, iodoform, Javel water, lysol, mercuric oxide, orthoboric acid, phenol, pickle, sheep dip, silver fluoride, surgical spirit, white vitriol. **7. cleansing agent** ammonium chloride, ammonium hydroxide, antifouling, borax, flux, whiting. **8. sandsoap** holystone, sandblast. **9. purifier** chlorinator, disinfector, fumigator. **10. steriliser** autoclave. **11. filter** alembic, distilling apparatus, elutriator, filter bed, filter cloth, filter paper, filter press, filter tip, scrubber, separator, still. **12. sandblaster**. **13. separator** desalinator.

8. **1. cleaner** au pair, charlady, charwoman *(British)*, cleaning lady, daily, domestic, domestic help, duster, helper, home aid, home help, houseboy, maid. *Informal:* char *(British)*, cleaner upper, greasy, old Dutch, sadie. **2. sweeper** chimneysweep, streetsweeper. *Informal:* broomie, picker-up. **3. launderer** dhobi *(South Asian English)*, drycleaner, laundress, laundryman, laundrywoman, spotter, washerman, washerwoman, washwoman. **4. purifier** clarifier, purger, refiner. **5. washer** careener, currier, depurator, scourer, sudarium. **6. sanitary inspector** sanitarian.

adj. **9.** **1. cleansing** abluent, abstergent, aperient, depurative, detergent, detersive, disinfectant, purgative, purging, saponaceous, soap-like, soapy. **2. ablutionary** balneal, cleanly, lavational, sudatory. **3. self-cleaning** antifouling, dirt repellent, dust repellent, dustproof. **4. purificatory** baptismal, expiatory, lustral, piacular, purgatorial, purgatory.

10. **1. clean** clean as a whistle, dustless, immaculate, pristine, pure, snowy, spick-and-span, spotless, unspotted. *Informal:* kempt, squeaky-clean. **2. pure** candid, chaste, clean, fresh, lily, pristine, stainless, uncorrupted, undefiled, unmixed, unsoiled, unstained, unsullied, untainted, virgin, virginal. **3. uncontaminated** alembicated, aseptic, axenic, refined, sterile. **4. sanitary** antiseptic, hygienic, sanitarian.

v. **11.** **1. clean** char *(British)*, clean out, clean up, cleanse, expurgate, furbish, mop up, muck out, polish, scavenge, sponge, sponge off (or away), spot, spot-clean, spring-clean. **2. wash** floss, flush, freshen up, gargle, kier, shampoo, soft-soap, swill, syringe, wash away, wash down, wash out, wash up. **3. bathe** bath, bogey *(Chiefly Eastern Mainland)*, lave *(Poetic)*, rinse, shower, wash. *Informal:* tub. **4. sweep** broom, brush, hoover, mop, swab, swingle, vacuum, vacuum-clean. **5. scrub** black, buff, dust, rub, scour. **6. degrease** soap, soft-soap. **7. comb** card, heckle. **8. launder** dry-clean. **9. filter** cohobate, distil, elutriate, filtrate, refine. **10. purify** anele, baptise, heal, lustrate, purge, purify of (or from), sanctify. **11. sluice** cradle, hush, pan, surface. **12. pickle** scavenge, scrub. **13. decarbonise** decarburise, decoke. **14. sandblast** careen, grave, holystone. **15. currycomb** curry. **16. dag** ring. *Informal:* chase marguerites.

12. 1. disinfect antisepticise, chlorinate, dip, fog, fumigate, sanitise, smoke, sterilise. **2. cleanse** depurate, deterge, douche, physic, purge. **3. decontaminate** purify.

adv. **13. 1. cleanly** cleanlily, immaculately, spotlessly. **2. aseptically** antiseptically, hygienically, sanitarily, sterilely. **3. purely** clean, cleanly, fresh, immaculately, virginally.

RELATED KEYWORDS: WHITE, ESSENCE, HEALTH, ORDER

CLOSENESS

n. **1. 1. closeness** adjacency, contact, contiguousness, immediacy, immediateness, nearness, propinquity, proximity. **2. close position** nearness, neighbourhood, presence, propinquity, proximity, vicinage, vicinity. **3. accessibility** approachableness, attainableness. **4. approach** advent, approximation, coming, oncoming. **5. conjunction** abutment, apposition, cluster, juxtaposition. **6. near thing** close call, dead draw, photo finish, squeaker. **7. closest point** pericynthion, perigee, perihelion, perilune.

adj. **2. 1. close** approximate, dead, hither, hithermost, hot, near, nearby, proximate, silly. *Informal:* a hop, step (or skip) and a jump away, warm. **2. adjacent** adjoining, appositional, approximal, bordering, bumper-to-bumper, circumlittoral, close-order, connivent, conterminous, contiguous, coterminous, end on, immediate, nearby, nearest, neighbour *(US)*, neighbouring, next, next door, next-door, proximate, ringside, surrounding, vicinal. **3. approaching** coming, oncoming. **4. accessible** approachable, attainable. *Informal:* get-at-able.

v. **3. 1. come close** advance on, approach, bear down, close, close in, close with, come near, come up to, confront, draw near, draw on, gain, lay aboard, near, overtake, reach, rise, sap, shave, trench on (or upon), verge, walk up. **2. approximate** be in the neighbourhood of, be in the vicinity of, be on the point of, border on (or upon), neighbour on, verge on (or upon).

4. 1. be close adjoin, appose, border, burn, juxtapose, lie off, neighbour, subjoin.

adv. **5. 1. closely** a hop step and a jump away, a step away, as near as damn it, as near as makes no difference, at close quarters, at one's elbow, at one's fingertips, at someone's heels, bumper to bumper, cheek by jowl, close, eyeball to eyeball, hard by (or against), just round the corner, near at hand, on the back of, on the heels of, on the tip of one's tongue, on top of, under one's nose, within a hair's-breadth of, within a stone's throw, within an inch of, within cooee, within earshot, within hearing, within range, within reach, within spitting distance. **2. together** adjacently, appositionally, chock, conterminously, contiguously, next door. **3. nearby** about, around, by, here, hereabout, hither, in view, near.

6. 1. almost about, about to, all but, approximately, for all practical purposes, going on, most *(Chiefly US)*, nearly, nigh on, on (or upon) the point of, practically, proximately, pushing, rising, thereabouts, upon the point of, well nigh, within an ace of.

prep. **7. 1. near** 'pon, aboard, about, around, beside, by, circa, forbye *(Chiefly Scottish)*, on, round, touching, towards, upon.

RELATED KEYWORDS: CONTACT, CONVERGENCE, JOINING, IMPRECISION

CLOSURE

n. **1. 1. closure** barricade, blockade, blockage, impedient, impediment, obstacle, obstruction, obturation, occlusion, stop. **2. impenetrability** impenetrableness, impermeability, impermeableness, imperviousness.

2. 1. plug bathplug, bung, cock, cork, faucet *(Chiefly US)*, gasket, jackass, pillar cock, shive, spigot, spile, stop, stopper, stuffing box, tap. **2. top** bottle cap *(US)*, bottle top, cap, crown cap, crown seal, screw-top. **3. sealing wax** cachet, cane, seal, wax. **4. sealing strip** weather strip, weather-stripping. **5. wad** tampion, tampon, tamponade, tompion. *Informal:* plug.

3. 1. door back door, bulkhead, deadlight, drop, Dutch door, fly, fly door, folding doors, French door, French window, jib door, louvre, paddle, port, portal, portcullis, postern, screen door, shutter, stable door, stern door *(US)*, swing door, storm door, trap, trapdoor, vampire, wing, wire door. **2. gate** bogan gate, boom gate, drafting gate, droprail, floodgate, headgate, hurdle gate, lock-gate, sluicegate, swing gate, Taranaki gate *(NZ)*, tollgate, water gate, water-gate, wicket.

adj. **4. 1. closed** barred, blind, close, drawn, fast, occluded, occludent, occlusive, pent, shut, unopened. **2. stopped** corked, screw-top, ventless. **3. impenetrable** airproof, airtight, dustproof, gastight, hermetic, hermetically sealed, impermeable, impervious, proof, watertight.

v. **5.** **1. close** bang, marry, shut, slam. **2. shutter** board up. **3. blockade** clench, occlude, shut in, shut up, stop down, wall in, wall up. **4. stop** airproof, bung, close, cork, obturate, plug, spile, stem, stop up, stopper, top. **5. seal** air trap, plumb, wafer, weatherstrip. **6. gag** pad, stuff, tampon, wad.

adv. **6.** **1. impermeably** closely, hermetically, impenetrably, imperviously.

RELATED KEYWORDS: COVERING, ENCLOSURE, FASTENING, HINDRANCE

CLOTHES

n. **1.** **1. clothes** apparel, array, attire, caparison, clothing, dress, garb, garment, garments, get-out, habiliment, habiliments, maternity clothes, menswear, outfit, rig-out, robes, slip-on, slops, streetwear, things, trappings, trim, wardrobe, wear, wearable, wearing apparel, womenswear. *Informal:* civvies, clobber, gear, get-up, mocker, rig, scungies, toggery *(British)*, togs. **2. clothwork** dart, fly, gore, peplum, tuck.

2. **1. finery** best, black tie, cocktail dress, court dress *(British)*, creation, dress, evening dress, fallal, fallalery, formal dress, formals, frippery, full dress, gala outfit, going-away outfit, smart clothes, Sunday best, tails, white tie. *Informal:* glad rags, one's best bib and tucker, war paint.

3. **1. uniform** cap and gown, full dress, gown, habit, livery, robe, silks, sweatband, vestment. **2. military clothing** battle fatigues, battle jacket, battledress, class A's, combat fatigues, dress uniform, fatigue dress, fatigues, mess kit, order, regimentals, service dress, tropical dress, tropical whites, tunic, undress. *Informal:* gigglesuit, number ones. **3. pressure suit** G-suit, spacesuit. **4. religious clothing** alb, canonicals, cassock, chasuble, chimar, chimer, cope, cotta, dalmatic, ephod, epitrachelion, fanon, Geneva gown, maniple, mantelletta, omophorion, pall, pallium, pluvial, pontificals, rochet, scapular, soutane, stole, surplice, tunic, tunicle, undervest, vestment. *Informal:* clericals. **5. prison clothing** *Informal:* magpie clothing. **6. hairshirt** sanbenito.

4. **1. sportswear** activewear, all-in-one, bloomers, casuals, creams, cycle pants, habit, jersey, jogging suit, jumpsuit, playsuit, slipsuit, sports uniform, sunsuit, sweatpants *(US)*, sweatsuit, trackpants, tracksuit, tunic, whites. *Informal:* strip, trackie daks, trackies, trog suit. **2. rompers** crawlers, romper suit.

5. **1. swimwear** bandeau bikini, bathers, bathing suit, bathing trunks, beachwear, bikini, costume, dive boot, diving suit, maillot, monokini, neck-to-knees, one-piece, stinger suit, string bikini, swimmers *(Especially Qld, NSW, ACT, and Tasmania)*, swimming costume, swimming trunks, swimsuit, tankini, trunks *(Chiefly Eastern States)*. *Informal:* ballhuggers, budgie-smugglers, cock jocks, cod jocks, cossie, cozzie, dick pointers, dick stickers, dick togs, dikdaks, DTs, knobbies, lollybags, meat-hangers, nylon disgusters, sluggos, swimming togs, togs, toolies, vees.

6. **1. nightwear** nightclothes. **2. dressing-gown** bathrobe, beach robe, brunch coat, kimono, negligee, nightrobe, peignoir, robe, shave coat, shaving coat, shaving jacket. **3. pyjamas** nightdress, nightgown, nightie, nightrobe, nightshirt, nighty, pajamas *(US)*, shirt. *Informal:* jamas, jamies, PJs.

7. **1. costume** cap and bells, catsuit, domino, fancy dress, masquerade, motley. *Informal:* drag.

8. **1. graveclothes** breasting, cerecloth, cerements, shroud, winding sheet. **2. mourning clothes** armband, black, black armband, half-mourning, hatband, mourning, sables, weed, weeds, weeper.

9. **1. dressmaking** corsetry, tailoring. *Informal:* rag trade.

10. **1. clothier** cobbler, corsetiere, costumier, couturière, couturier, dresser, dressmaker, equipper, fashion designer, furrier, glover, haberdasher *(US)*, hatter, hosier, milliner, modiste, outfitter, seamstress, sempstress, sewer, slopworker, stylist, tailer, tailor, taylor. **2. clothing store** boutique, furriery, haberdashery, hosiery, jeanery, millinery, slop-shop.

11. **1. outfit** change, ensemble, layette, separates, trousseau, turnout. **2. suit** costume, dinner suit, dress suit, evening suit, lounge suit, morning dress, pants-suit, safari suit, Sidcot, slacks suit, three-piece, trouser suit, tuxedo, two-piece. *Informal:* bag of fruit, monkey suit, penguin suit, tux. **3. overalls** boilersuit, coogans, dungarees.

12. **1. headgear** millinery. **2. headdress** commode, cornet, crown, pinner, pouf, puggaree, tiara, turban. **3. hood** amice, balaclava, calash, capuche, capuchin, cowl, headcloth, sapajou, wimple.

13.   **1. hat** akubra, bearskin, beaver, bell-topper, beret, billycock, boater, borsalino, bowler, bowler hat, broadbrim, busby, cabbage-tree, cabbage-tree hat, caddie, cartwheel hat, chapeau, cocked hat, deerstalker, derby *(US)*, digger's hat, Dolly Varden, fedora *(US)*, hard-hitter, hard-knocker, high hat, homburg, miter *(US)*, mitre, mortarboard, opera hat, panama, Panama hat, petasus, picture hat, pillbox, pork-pie hat, red hat, sailor hat, shovel hat, slouch hat, snap-brim, sombrero, stetson, taj, tall hat, tarpaulin, ten-gallon hat, top hat, toque, trencher, trilby, turban, wide-awake. *Informal:* barrel, bun hat *(NZ)*, cady, chimneypot, lemon squeezer, lid, stovepipe, stovepipe hat, titfer, topper. **2. sunhat** pith helmet, sun helmet, sunbonnet, topee, topi.

14.   **1. cap** balmoral, baseball cap, beanie, beaver, berretta, billycock *(British)*, biretta, black cap, bonnet *(Chiefly Scottish)*, calotte, calpac, castor, coif, Cossack hat, dunce's cap, fez, fool's cap, glengarry, jockey cap, kalpak, kepi, kippah, nightcap, shako, skullcap, sou'-wester, tam, tam-o'-shanter, tarboosh, tricorn, tuque, yarmulke, zucchetto. *Informal:* the baggy green. **2. bonnet** blue-bonnet, bluecap, capote, cloche, coif. **3. bathing cap** cap, shower cap.

15.   **1. helmet** basinet, beaver, burgonet, casque *(Poetic)*, crash hat, crash helmet, crest, hard hat, headpiece, morion, safety helmet, sallet, tin hat. *Informal:* bash hat, bump cap, skid lid, stackhat.

16.   **1. headband** bandeau, chaplet, fillet, snood, sweat rag, sweatband. **2. veil** fly net, flyveil, loup, mask, veiling, yashmak. **3. earflap** earlap, earmuff, lug. **4. hairnet** net, snood.

17.   **1. neckwear** boa, comforter, fichu, fraise, muffler, neckband, neckerchief, neckpiece, ruff, shirt band. **2. collar** air collar, bertha, collaret, collet, dicky, Eton collar, facings, fraise, front, guimpe, jabot, lapel, mandarin collar, peter pan collar, revers, roll-collar, ruff, stock, Vandyke, Vandyke collar, wing collar. *Informal:* choker, dog-collar. **3. tie** black tie, bow tie, cravat, necktie, old school tie, white tie, Windsor tie. *Informal:* choker. **4. clerical collar** bands, Geneva bands, Roman collar. *Informal:* dog-collar. **5. scarf** agal, babushka, bandanna, barb, fascinator, four-in-hand, headscarf, head-square, hijab, keffiyeh, kerchief, madras, mantilla, nubia, tippet, tudung *(Singaporean and Malaysian English)*, victorine. **6. neckline** décolletage, halter, halter-neck, poloneck, scoop neck, sweetheart neckline, turtleneck, V-neck.

18.   **1. cloak** aba, abaya, blanket *(North America)*, burnous, cape, capote, chaddar, chador, chuddar, cope, cowl, dolman, joseph, kaross, korowai, manta, mantelet, mantilla, mantle, mantua, mat *(NZ)*, mozzetta, muffle, opera cloak, palatine, pallium, pashmina, pelerine, pelisse, plaid, pluvial, poncho, serape, shahtoosh, shawl, surplice, tallith, wrap, wraps.

19.   **1. overcoat** balmacaan, box coat, buff, cutaway, frockcoat, gabardine, gaberdine, greatcoat, guernsey frock, jubbah, matinee jacket, pelisse, peplos, peplum, petersham, Prince Albert, raglan, redingote, surcoat, topcoat, ulster. **2. overgarment** frock, outer garments, overclothes, overdress, paletot, smock, tabard, toga, vestment, wrapper. *Informal:* woollies. **3. coverall** cover-up, dustcoat, duster *(US)*, housecoat, overall. **4. apron** bib, dickey, dicky, feeder, pinafore, smock. *Informal:* pinny.

20.   **1. raincoat** burberry, camlet, Drizabone, mackintosh, oilers *(US)*, oilskins, rubbers *(US)*, slicker, trench coat, waterproof. *Informal:* mac.

21.   **1. jacket** banian, bedjacket, blazer, blouse, camisole, cassock, coat, doublet, Eton jacket, jerkin, jupon, monkey jacket, Norfolk jacket, sack, sack coat, sacque, safari jacket, slops, smoking-jacket, soutane, spencer, sports jacket, tunic, undercoat, waistcoat, weskit. *Informal:* bumfreezer *(Chiefly British)*, hoodie. **2. heavy jacket** anorak, battle jacket, Bermuda jacket, cagoule, donkey jacket *(British)*, duffel coat, lumber-jacket, parka, pea jacket, reefer, reefer jacket, tabard. **3. dress coat** coat-tails, dinner jacket, hacking jacket, mess jacket, monkey jacket, morning coat, swallow-tailed coat, tail coat, tails. *Informal:* claw-hammer coat. **4. cardigan** twin-set. *Informal:* cardie. **5. bodice** basque, bolero, vest, waistcoat. **6. straitjacket** straightjacket. **7. life jacket** Mae West.

22.   **1. dress** A-line, caftan, caparison, chemise, cheongsam, dirndl, Dolly Varden, evening gown, exclusive, frock, gown, halter-neck, hostess gown, jumper *(US)*, kaftan, kimono, mantua, maternity dress, Mother Hubbard, muu-muu, pinafore, pinafore frock, polo-naise, princess line, robe, sack, sarung kebaya, sheath, shift, shirtmaker, slip dress, suit, sundress, tea-gown, topless, tunic, tunica, underdress, wedding dress. *Informal:* pinny. **2. wrapround** cummerbund, haik, ihram, lava-lava, pareu, sari, sarong, tapis, wrap-around. **3. skirt** A-line, bubble skirt, culottes, dirndl, filibeg, fillibeg, hobble skirt, hoop, hoop skirt, hula skirt, kilt, lehenga, maxi, maxiskirt, micro skirt, midi, mini, miniskirt, overskirt, patadyong, peg top, peplum, philibeg, piupiu, ra-ra skirt, rah-rah skirt, tutu. **4. tunic** gym tunic, mantoo.

23. **1. jumper** guernsey, jersey, pullover, skinny rib, skivvy, sloppy joe, sweater, turtleneck, vest, windcheater, windjammer. *Informal:* pullie, woolly, woolly pully.

24. **1. shirt** baju melayu, banian, body shirt, byrnie, cilice, Crimean shirt, jac shirt, sports shirt, sweatshirt, T-shirt, tank top, tee-shirt, top. *Informal:* boiled shirt. **2. blouse** chemisette, choli, guimpe, kebaya, overblouse, stomacher. *Informal:* boob tube. **3. shirt tail** *Informal:* Australian flag, flag.

25. **1. sleeve** arm, batwing sleeve, bishop sleeve, dolman sleeve, oversleeve, shirtsleeve.

26. **1. glove** boxing glove, doeskins, gantlet, gauntlet, kid gloves, mitt, mitten, muff, wristlet. *Informal:* mittens. **2. cuff** finger, palm, thumb.

27. **1. trousers** bags, bell-bottoms, breeches, buckskins *(US)*, calzoneros, capri pants, cargo pants, chaps, corduroys, cut-offs, flannels, flares, galligaskins, gauchos, harem pants, hipsters, jeans, jodhpurs, knee breeches, knickerbockers, knickers, knicks, Oxford bags, palazzo pants, pant, pants, pedal pushers, peg tops, plus-fours, pyjamas, riding breeches, slacks, stirrup pants, trews, trunk hose, velveteens. *Informal:* applecatchers, baggies, britches, cords, dacks, daks, denims, drainpipes, duds, long'uns, strides, tweeds. **2. shorts** bermuda shorts, board shorts, boxer shorts, hotpants, lederhosen, stubbies, walk shorts. *Informal:* boardies, Bombay bloomers, bum shorts. **3. loincloth** breechcloth, breechclout, dhoti, futah, G-string, lap-lap, loin-clout, longee, lungi, naga, thong *(US)*, waistcloth.

28. **1. pocket** fob, hip pocket, pouch *(Chiefly Scottish)*, sporran. *Informal:* bin.

29. **1. footwear** footgear. **2. shoe** balmoral, block, blocked shoe, boat shoe, boot, brogan, brogue, chopin, clodhoppers, desert boot, flat, gillie *(Scottish)*, goditcha shoes, kadaitja shoes, kadaitjas, kurdaitcha shoes, loafer, moccasin, Oxford, Oxford shoe, point, point shoe, pump, wingtip *(US)*, winklepicker. *Informal:* brothel boots, creepers, flattie, flatties. **3. clog** patten, sabot, wooden shoe. **4. spats** puttee, putty, spatterdashes. **5. shoe part** air cushion, bootleg *(Chiefly US)*, counter, galosh, half-sole, heel, heelpiece, heeltap, innersole, insole, lift, platform, rand, sole, stiletto, stiletto heel, tongue, upper, vamp, wedge heel. **6. sandshoe** gym shoe, jogger, plimsoll *(British)*, runner, sneaker, tennis shoe. **7. spikes** running spikes, sprigs, track shoe. **8. rollerskate** ice skate, inline skate, rollerblade, skate. **9. snowshoe** racquet.

30. **1. boot** 'lastic-sides, blucher, buskin, Docs, elastic sides, gambado, half-boot, jackboot, riding boot, shoe *(US)*, sock, steelcap, surgical boot, top-boot, ugg boot, workboot. *Informal:* bovver boot *(British)*. **2. gumboot** galoshes, goloshes, gumshoe, overshoes *(Chiefly US)*, rainboot, rubber boot, rubbers *(US)*, waders, water boot, wellington boot. *Informal:* wellies.

31. **1. sock** ankle sock, bedsock, bobbysocks *(Chiefly US)*, bootee, bootie, gaiters, gambado, leggings, slipper sock, sox, stocking *(US)*, toe sock. *Informal:* alberts, almonds.

32. **1. sandal** espadrille, flip-flop, getta, jandal *(NZ)*, reef sandal, surf thong, thong, zori. *Informal:* double plugger, Japanese safety boot, rubber, slaps. **2. slipper** carpet slipper, mule, pantofle, pantoufle, scuff, ugg boot. *Informal:* uggies.

33. **1. tights** bodystocking, leg warmers, leotard, maillot. **2. hose** nylons, pantihose, pantyhose, stocking.

34. **1. underwear** camiknickers, chiton, combinations, dishabille, lingerie, teddy, underclothes, undergarment, underthings, unmentionables. *Informal:* long johns, smalls *(Chiefly British)*, undies. **2. camisole** bodice, chemise, hoop, hoop skirt, singlet, spencer, undershirt *(US)*, undersleeve. *Informal:* shimmy. **3. petticoat** balmoral, bustle, crinoline, farthingale, half-slip, slip, underskirt. **4. foundation garment** bra, brassiere, busk, corselet, corsetry, corsets, cup, easies *(NZ)*, girdle, maternity bra, pasty, push-up bra, rollons, stays, step-ins. *Informal:* boob tube, falsies, sheepdog bra. **5. singlet** undervest, vest. *Informal:* Jacky Howe, Jimmy Howe, wife-beater. **6. underpants** briefs, cachesexe, jockey shorts, jockeys, jocks, knickerbockers. *Informal:* grundies, reggies, reginalds, underdaks, underdungers, Y-fronts. **7. panties** bloomers, briefs, drawers, gorgeous gussies, knickers, pantalets, pants, underpants, witches' britches. *Informal:* grundies, gussies, scanties, scungies, underdaks.

35. **1. fig leaf**.

adj. 36. **1. clothed** apparelled, arrayed, dressed. **2. dressed up** all dressed up, dollish, done up, tricked out. *Informal:* done up like a sore finger (or toe), dressed (up) to the nines, dressed to kill, dressed to the nines, dressed up like a pox doctor's clerk, in one's Sunday-go-to-meeting clothes *(US)*. **3. well-dressed** fashionable, smart, stylish. **4. badly-dressed** dowdy, frumpish, ill-dressed, unfashionable, unstylish. **5. sartorial** vestiary.

v. 37. **1. clothe** array, attire, costume, cover, dress, endue with, equip, frock, garb, garment, gown, habit, invest, prink, robe, smock, suit, swaddle, vest. *Informal:* deck out, rig out (or up), tog out, trick out (or up). **2. style** tailor.

38. **1. wear** dress in, have on, sport. **2. get dressed** attire oneself, clothe oneself, don, dress, dress oneself, huddle on, put on, try on. *Informal:* doll up, hop into. **3. rug (oneself) up** bundle up, cover up, do up, enrobe, get oneself up, muffle, muffle oneself up, re-dress, scarf, wrap up. **4. change** disarray, undress. **5. dress up** scrub up, spruce up. *Informal:* mocker up, tog up. **6. overdress** dress up. *Informal:* lair up. **7. be well-dressed** have good dress sense. **8. be badly-dressed** be a fashion victim, have a wardrobe malfunction, have no dress sense.

RELATED KEYWORDS: COVERING, FASHION, FASTENING

CLOUD

n. **1.** **1. cloud** anvil, cloudbank, cloudlet, hogsback *(NZ)*, low cloud, mare's tail, nimbus, rack, rain cloud, storm cloud, thundercloud, thunderhead, woolpack. *Informal:* clag. **2. cloud-type** altocumulus, altostratus, cirrocumulus, cirrostratus, cirrus, cu-nim, cumulonimbus, cumulus, cumulus fractus, false cirrus, fractocumulus, fractostratus, funnel cloud, nimbostratus, orographic clouds, scud, stratocumulus, stratus, stratus fractus. **3. puff** scud, whiff. **4. mist** brume, fog, gauze, haze. **5. steam** effluvium, fumes, gas, live steam, reek, vaporescence, vapour, wet steam. **6. vapour trail** condensation trail, contrail. **7. fog** aerosol, anthelion, brume, fogbank, sea fog, smoke. *Informal:* pea soup, pea souper. **8. smoke** dust, fug, nuclear cloud, pother, smog, smother, smoulder, smudge.

 2. **1. cloudiness** fogginess, gauziness, haziness, hydrometeor, mackerel sky, mistiness, nebulosity, nebulousness, steaminess. **2. smokiness** dustiness, murkiness. **3. vaporosity** vapourishness. **4. vaporisation** fumigation. **5. sunlessness** sullenness.

 3. **1. cloud study** hydrometeorology, nephanalysis, nephology. **2. isoneph** nephogram, nephograph, nephoscope.

adj. **4.** **1. cloudy** cloud-capped, foggy, heavy, nubilous, overcast, sunless. **2. cirrose** cirrostrative, cumuliform, cumulous, mammatus, stratiform. **3. cloud-like** cloudy, hazy, nebulose, nebulous, nubilous. **4. sunless** grey, heavy, overcast, sullen. **5. steamy** foggy, misty, thick, vaporescent, vaporific, vaporous, vapour-like, vapouring, vapourish, vapoury. **6. misty** gauzelike, hazy. **7. smoggy** dusty, foggy, fuggy, hazy, mirky, misty, murky, nebulose, nubilous, smoky, smudgy, soupy, thick. **8. foggy** brumous, misty, nubilous, thick. **9. smoky** fuliginous, fumy.

v. **5.** **1. cloud** becloud, cloud over, overcast, overcloud, shadow. **2. smoke** reek. **3. mist** fog, gauze. **4. vaporise** steam, vapour. **5. fumigate** smoke out.

adv. **6.** **1. cloudily** nebulously, sullenly, sunlessly. **2. foggily** hazily, mistily. **3. smokily** dustily, murkily, smudgily. **4. steamily** vaporously.

RELATED KEYWORDS: GAS, RAINFALL, WEATHER

COLDNESS

n. **1.** **1. coldness** bleakness, cold, coolness, wintriness. **2. chilliness** chill, chillness, nip, sharpness. **3. frozenness** clamminess, frigidity, frost, frostiness, gelation, gelidness, glaciation, iciness, regelation. **4. absolute zero** degrees of frost, freezing point, frost point.

 2. **1. chill** ague, algidity, algor, rigor. **2. shiver** horripilation, shudder, tremble, tremor. **3. goose pimples** goose bumps, goose flesh, the shivers. **4. frostbite** chilblains. **5. cold snap** cold change, cold front, cold wave. *Informal:* brass monkey weather, perisher. **6. winter** freeze, nuclear freeze, the dead of winter. **7. ice age** glacial epoch.

 3. **1. snow** firn, névé, snow cap, snow country, snowdrift, snowfall, snowfield, snowfields, snowflake, snowline, virga. **2. sludge** slosh, slush. **3. snowstorm** avalanche, blizzard, flurry, hailstorm, sleet, snow shower, snowfall. **4. snowball** snowman. **5. frost** black frost, freeze, glaze ice, glazed frost, hoar, hoarfrost, Jack Frost, permafrost, rime, silver frost, white frost.

 4. **1. ice** brash, dry ice, fast ice, floe, frazil, glacier, icecap, icefall, icefield, icefloe, icepack, icesheet, iceshelf, sea ice, water ice. **2. glaze ice** dead ice, drift ice, glaze *(US)*, ground ice, icefoot, icefront, pack ice, pancake ice. **3. ice needles** frost flower, graupel, hail, hailstone, sleet, soft hail, stone. **4. icicle** bollard, serac. **5. iceberg** berg. **6. ice cube** iceblock, party ice. **7. rink** icerink. **8. glaciology**.

adj. **5.** **1. cold** Antarctic, Arctic, freezing, frigid, frigorific, frosty, frozen, glacial, hyperborean, ice-cold, icy. *Informal:* nipping, nippy, perishing, sharp. **2. stone-cold** marble. **3. cool** coldish, coolish, fresh. **4. chilled** agued, algid, hypothermal, shivering, trembly. **5. blue** frostbitten. **6. wintry** bleak, brumal, chill, chilly, cold, hibernal, icy, raw, winter, winterly. *Informal:* cold enough to freeze the balls off a brass monkey, parky. **7. snowy** niveous, white. **8. slushy** sleety. **9. frosted** frostlike, frosty, hoar, iced, rimy. **10. frozen** gelid, glacé *(US)*, icicled. **11. glacial** englacial, glaciered, glaciological, subglacial, superglacial.

v. **6. 1. be cold** freeze, frozen. *Informal:* do a freeze, do a perish. **2. chill** freeze, frost, glaciate, ice, regelate, rime, snap-freeze. **3. snow** hail, sleet. **4. shiver** get goose pimples, shudder, tremble. **5. become cold** cloud over, freshen.

adv. **7. 1. coldly** bleakly, fresh, freshly, wintrily. **2. icily** chillily, chillingly, frigidly, frostily, frozenly, gelidly, glacially. **3. tremblingly** aguishly.

RELATED KEYWORDS: COOLING, WEATHER

COLOUR

n. **1. 1. colour** complementary colour, hue, primary colour, prismatic colours, secondary colour, tertiary colour. **2. hue** cast, colouring, nuance, patina, shade, tinge, tint, tone, undertint, undertone. **3. spectrum** palette, pallette, prism, rainbow. **4. areola** areolation, areole, sunbow, sundog. **5. colour scheme** decorator colour, fashionable colours. **6. colours** GT stripes, military colours, national colours, racing colours, team colours. *Informal:* strip. **7. complexion** bloom, rubicundity, skin colour. **8. skin pigmentation** age spot, chloasma, fleck, freckle, lentigo, liver spot, melanin, melanism, speckle. **9. chromophore** chlorophyll, chromatoplasm, chromogen, chromoplasm, chromoplast, chromoprotein, haemoglobin, oxyhaemoglobin. **10. camouflage** countershading, protective colouring. **11. colouring** colouration, pigmentation. **12. colour quality** chroma, gradation, intensity, purity, saturation, tone, value. **13. chromatics**.

2. 1. colourfulness floridness, iridescence, richness. **2. brightness** brilliance, fieriness, gaudiness, glaringness, liveliness, vividness. **3. glow** blare, flame, highlight, highlights.

3. 1. dyeing chrome tanning, colouring in, imbuement, impasto, painting, staining. **2. colour reproduction** chromolithography, colour photography, four-colour process, photochromy, process printing, technicolour, three-colour process. **3. colour print** acidfast, aquatint, chromo, chromolithograph, colour proof, halftone, monochrome, oleograph.

4. 1. colourist brightener, chromolithographer, colourer, dyer, painter, stainer, tinter, toner. *Informal:* seagull.

5. 1. dye acid dye, alizarin, aniline dye, azo dye, chromogen, colorant, colour fast, dyestuff, hypercolour, ink, lake, madder, marking-ink, mordant, natural dye, opaque, pigment, reactive dye, rinse, stain, vat dye, wash. **2. counterstain** stain. **3. paint** acrylic, acrylic colour, body colour, colourwash, distemper, duco, emulsion paint, gouache, luminous paint, oil, oil colour, pigment, plastic paint, polymer colour, poster colour, poster paint, primer, scumble, stain, tempera, undercoat, undercoating, underglaze, watercolour, waterpaint. **4. make-up** blusher, eye shadow, eyeliner, face powder, foundation, greasepaint, highlighter, kohl, liner, lip gloss, lipstick, mascara, pencil, rouge, vanishing cream. *Informal:* lippie, lippy, paint, war paint. **5. pencil** ballpen, ballpoint pen, biro, chalk, crayon, dip-pen, felt pen, fountain pen, graphos, nib, pen, permanent marker, quill, stylograph, texta.

adj. **6. 1. colourful** brilliant, deep, glowing, iridescent, lustrous, purple, rich, saturated, strong, vivid. **2. bright** brilliant, candescent, colouristic, fiery, gay, hot, incandescent, live, lively, lustrous, rich, technicolour, vivid. *Informal:* jazzy, psychedelic, snazzy. **3. gaudy** garish, glaring, loud, lurid.

7. 1. coloured high-coloured, hued, rosaceous, roseate, rosy, self-coloured, three-colour. **2. florid** rubicund. **3. dyed** acidophilic, double-dyed, fumed, hypercolour, piece-dyed, tinct *(Poetic)*, yarn-dyed. **4. mordant** adjective, substantive, sunfast. **5. colourable** stainable.

8. 1. colorific chromatic, chromogenic, tinctorial. **2. monochromatic** immaculate, monochroic, monochrome, monochromical, unicolour. **3. isochromatic** isochrous, orthochromatic. **4. metachromatic** amphichroic, apatetic, panchromatic, polychromatic.

v. **9. 1. colour** chrome, counterstain, distemper, dye, illuminate, ink, marble, mordant, ochre, overdye, paint, pencil, raddle, reddle, repaint, spray-paint, stain, stencil, tie-dye, tinge, umber. **2. tint** colour, imbue, tincture, tinge, wash. **3. brighten** highlight, tone up. **4. tone** tone (in) with, tone down.

adv. **10. 1. colourfully** fierily, floridly, gaudily, glaringly, glowingly, iridescently, richly, vividly.

RELATED KEYWORDS: BLUE, BROWN, FINE ARTS, GREEN, MULTICOLOUR, ORANGE, PHOTOGRAPHY, PRINTING, PURPLE, RED

COLOURLESSNESS

n. **1.** **1. colourlessness** achromaticity, achromatism, lack of colour. **2. fading** blanching, decolouration, discolouration, etiolation, tarnish. **3. paleness** delicateness, lightness, thinness, whiteness. **4. dullness** soberness, sobriety, sombreness. **5. pallor** anaemia, anemia, bloodlessness, cadaverousness, ghastliness, mealiness, paleness, pallidness, pastiness, sallowness, sickliness, wanness. **6. albinism** alphosis.

2. **1. decolourant** blancher, bleacher, decolouriser, diluter. **2. bleach** chlorine, hydrogen peroxide, oxalic acid.

adj. **3.** **1. colourless** achromatic, achromatous, achromic, neutral, pallid, untinged. **2. neutral** achromatic, delicate, grey, light, mousey, mousy, pastel, thin. **3. black-and-white** greyscale, sepia. **4. anaemic** anemic, green, mealy, pale, pallid, pasty, pasty-faced, peaky, sallow, sallowish, sick, sickly, tired-looking, wan, wannish, washed-out, wheyfaced, white, white-faced, white-livered, yellow. **5. cadaverous** bloodless, ghastly, ghostlike, lurid, pale, pallid. **6. pale** ash-coloured, ashy, blank, palish. **7. dull** dim, drab, dreary, dullish, lacklustre, muddy, muted, old, sad, sober, sombre, subdued. **8. watery** wheylike. **9. bleached** etiolated, faded.

v. **4.** **1. lose colour** blanch, blench, change colour, discolour, etiolate, fade, go white, go white at the gills, sallow, tarnish, turn pale, wan. **2. dull** dilute, pale, subdue. **3. decolour** achromatise, bleach, decolourise, peroxide, whiten.

RELATED KEYWORDS: BLACK, WHITE, ILL HEALTH, GREY

COMBINATION

n. **1.** **1. combination** addition, aggregate, aggregation, amalgamation, assemblage, association, coalescence, coalition, commixture, composition, confection, conglomeration, conjugation, conjunction, consociation, consolidation, coordination, fusion, incorporation, interfusion, intermingling, interweaving, meeting, mergence, mixture, polysynthesism, summation, synergism, synergy, synthesisation, synthesism, synthetisation, totalisation, unification, union, unity, zygosis. **2. desegregation** acculturation, assimilation, integration. **3. symbiosis** mutualism.

2. **1. combine** aggregate, amalgam, assemblage, assembly, collective, combination, compound, condensate, conglomeration, consolidation, consortium, ensemble, fusion, melting pot, merger, mix, mixture, synthesis, system, tie, union, web. **2. duo** nonet, octet, quartet, quintet, septet, sestet, sextet, trio. **3. twins** octuplets, quadruplets, quintuplets, septuplets, sextuplets, triplets. **4. couplet** duplet, pair, triplet.

3. **1. combiner** amalgamator, assembler, blender, catalyst, compounder, conjoiner, consolidator, coordinator, fusionist, incorporator, synthesiser, synthesist, synthetiser, unifier, unionist. **2. mingler** integrationist, integrator. **3. weaver** interweaver, twiner.

adj. **4.** **1. combined** allied, associate, associated, coalescent, confederate, conjoint, conjugate, conjunct, coordinate, joint, synthetic, tight-knit, unified, united, unsegregated. **2. composite** aggregate, coalition, complex, compound.

5. **1. combinative** aggregate, aggregative, amalgamative, collective, combinational, conjunctional, conjunctive, federative, integrative, joint, syndetic, syndetical. **2. connective** copulative, syndetic.

v. **6.** **1. combine** associate, club, coalesce, commingle, compound, conjoin, consociate, consolidate, decompound, hang together, lump, merge, mingle, organise, syncretise, synergise, unify, unite. **2. synthesise** assemble, compose, constitute, make up, synthetise. **3. blend** commix, fuse, immingle, incorporate, interblend, interfile, interfuse, interlace, intermingle, intermix, meld, mingle, mix. **4. amalgamate** aggregate, ankylose, blend, coalesce, compact, conflate, conglomerate, consolidate, coordinate, join, join up, solid. **5. desegregate** assimilate, integrate.

adv. **7.** **1. together** at one blow, jointly. **2. collectively** associatively, conjointly, conjunctionally, coordinately.

RELATED KEYWORDS: ADDITION, COOPERATION, JOINING, MIXTURE, SOCIETY

COMING AFTER

n. **1.** **1. coming after** consecutiveness, posteriority, postposition, subsequence, successiveness. **2. consequentialness**. **3. supersedure** follow, supersession, supervention. **4. consequence** after-effect, aftermath, aftertaste, attendant, butterfly effect, consequent, corollary, effect, fallout, flow-on, legacy, repercussion, result, resultant, secondary, sequel, sequent, train. *Informal:* pay-off.

2. **1. sequence** catena, chain, concatenation, consecution, consequence, continuance, continuation, continuity, course, cycle, progression, prolongation, round, rounds, sequel, series, succession, suit. **2. following** cavalcade, column, cortege, procession, progression, retinue, string, trail, train. **3. single file** file, Indian file, tandem. **4. sequel** threequel. **5. postpositive** object.

    3. **1. successor** coheir, descendant, follower, heir, heir apparent, heir-at-law, heiress, incomer, inheritor, inheritrix, legatee, succeeder, superseder, supplanter.

adj.   **4.** **1. following** in tow, incoming, proximate. **2. next** immediate, junior, second, second-best. **3. consecutive** alternate, back-to-back, continued, following, progressive, running, sequacious, sequent, sequential, subsequent, succeeding, successional, successive. **4. consequent** attendant, consecutive, consequential, ex post facto, resultant, supervenient. **5. after** later, latter, posterior, postposed, postpositive, ulterior.

v.   **5.** **1. come after** ensue, follow, result, succeed, supervene. **2. supersede** supplant.

adv.   **6.** **1. after** last, next, proximately, proximo, second, secondarily, secondly. **2. afterwards** anon, since, then, thereon, thereupon, therewith. **3. behind** in the tracks of, in the wake of, posteriorly, postpositively, ulteriorly. **4. hereunder** below, et seq., hereinafter, thereinafter. **5. consequently** ex post facto, in consequence, subsequently, thus.

    7. **1. successively** in array, in file, in line, in tandem, one by one, sequentially, seriatim, successively, tandem.

    RELATED KEYWORDS: AUTHORITY, LATENESS, THE FUTURE, UNTIMELINESS

COMING BEFORE

n.   **1.** **1. coming before** antecedence, antecedency, anteriority, lead, precedence, precedency, precession, prevenience, priority, right of way. **2. head start** advantage, handicap, law, start.

    2. **1. forerunner** advance guard, anticipator, apostle, cutting edge, forebears, forefather, foregoer, harbinger, herald, introducer, leader, outrider, outrunner, pioneer, precursor, predecessor, primogenitor, progenitor, prophet, spearhead, trailblazer, trendsetter, usher, van, vanguard. *Informal:* early bird, first cab off the rank.

    3. **1. antecedent** antecedents, archetype, exemplar, master, mock-up, model, original, precedent, protocol, protoplast, prototype, working model.

    4. **1. introduction** exordium, foreword, front matter, frontispiece, intro, lead-up, preamble, preface, preliminary, prelims, proem, prolegomenon, prologue, prolusion, protasis, recitals, trial run. **2. prelude** overture, praeludium, voluntary. **3. prefix** forepart. **4. curtain-raiser** prerelease, teaser. **5. promo** leader, run-in groove, trailer.

adj.   **5.** **1. preceding** antecedent, anterior, early, former, pre-existing, precedent, precessional, precursive, prevenient, previous, prior. **2. aforesaid** above, abovementioned, aforementioned, foregoing, foresaid, said, which. **3. prefixal** preposed, prepositive.

    6. **1. prototypic** archetypical, embryo, first, primary, prime, primitive, protoplastic. **2. introductory** inaugural, introductive, isagogic, precursory, prefatory, preliminary, prelusive, prelusory, preparative, preparatory, proemial, prolegomenous, prolusory, propaedeutic. *Informal:* prep. **3. advance** advanced, fore, forehand, foremost, headmost, leading, up-front. **4. anticipatory** anticipant, anticipative. **5. avant-garde** ahead of one's time, at the bleeding edge, at the cutting edge, at the sharp end.

v.   **7.** **1. come before** antecede, antedate, beat, foredate, forego, forerun, precede, predate, preface. **2. anticipate** look ahead, look for, pre-empt, predict, presage, prophecy, second-guess, think.

    8. **1. introduce** herald, preface, prelude, premise, usher in. **2. pioneer** blaze a trail, go ahead, guide, head, lead the way.

adv.   **9.** **1. before** antecedently, anteriorly, formerly, heretofore, previously, prior to. **2. hereinbefore** above, thereinbefore, ubi supra. **3. yesterday** ult., ultimo, ulto, yesteryear *(Chiefly Poetic).*

   10. **1. first** ahead, ahead of time, first-up, firstly, foremost, in advance, primarily *(Chiefly US)*, up front, up-front. **2. introductorily** prefatorily, preliminarily, prelusively.

prep. **11.** **1. before** afore.

    RELATED KEYWORDS: EARLINESS, NEWNESS, THE PAST, START

COMMAND

n.   **1.** **1. command** adjuration, behest, bidding, call, calling, caution, charge, commandment, commission, demand, dictate, enjoinment, imperative, injunction, instruction, jussive, mandate, order, order of the day, placet, prescript, prescription, regulation, request, requisition, rubric, rule, sanction, signal, solicitation, standing order, summons, testament, threat, ultimatum, will, word, word of command. *Informal:* bung, say-so. **2. decree** accrue, act, ancient, appointment, ban, brevet, bull, closing order, commandment, decretal, dictate, dictum, directive, dispensation, edict, fatwa, fiat, instruction, instructions, law, letters of credence, mandate, mitzvah, ordinance, precept, pronouncement, regulation, rescript, rule, ukase. **3. countermand** caveat, recall, revocation.

2. **1. legal order** acquittance, bench warrant, breve, call-up, capias, capias ad satisfaciendum, certiorari, citation, commitment, court order, death warrant, decree absolute, decree nisi, default summons, deportation order, detainer, duces tecum, enactment, execution, extradition order, fieri-facias, garnishment, habeas corpus, law, mandamus, mittimus, monition, originating summons, prerogative order, prerogative writ, process, rule nisi, sanction, scire facias, statute, subpoena, summons, supersedeas, ticket, warrant, writ, writ of execution, writ of prohibition, writ of right *(US)*. *Informal:* blister, blue, bluey.

3. **1. commander** adjurer, bidder, demander, enjoiner, exactor, mandator, orderer, prescriber.

adj. **4.** **1. commanding** adjuratory, authoritative, decisive, decretal, decretive, decretory, edictal, imperatival, imperative, in command, in control, injunctive, instructional, mandatory, official, preceptive, prescriptive. **2. jussive** imperative. **3. dictatorial** authoritarian, dictatory, dogmatic, domineering, imperious, masterful, peremptory, tsarist.

v. **5.** **1. command** adjure, appoint, bid, boss, call the tune, call upon, captain, charge, commission, conjure, demand, dictate, direct, domineer, enjoin, entail, force, give orders, give the command, insist on, instruct, ordain, order, prescribe, require, tell. **2. summon** call to account, require someone's presence, send for. **3. commit** remand, subpoena, summon. **4. decree** appoint, enact, legislate, ordain, set.

adv. **6.** **1. commandingly** at the stroke of a pen, imperatively, officially, preceptively, prescriptively.

RELATED KEYWORDS: DESIRE, FORCE, INSISTENCE, MANAGEMENT, INTENTION

COMMERCE

n. **1.** **1. commerce** brokage, brokerage, business, commercialism, m-business, m-commerce, marketing, mercantilism, merchandising. *Informal:* biz. **2. trade** agiotage, barter, buying and selling, dealings, exchange, market, trading, traffic. **3. transaction** operation, trade. **4. overseas trade** shipment, shipping. **5. export** exportation, re-exportation. **6. importation. 7. smuggling** bootlegging, drug running, gun running, running, trafficking. **8. commercialism** mercantilism, shipment.

2. **1. commodity** artefact, goods, staple, wares. **2. stock** cargo, commodities, consumer goods, freight, freightage, merchandise, stock-in-trade.

n. **3.** **1. economy** demand economy, macro economy, market economy. **2. free trade** free enterprise, mercantile system. **3. private enterprise** capitalism, economic rationalism. **4. mixed economy** welfare state. **5. planned economy** communism, socialism, statism. **6. monopoly** corner, duopsony, monopsony, oligopoly, oligopsony. **7. black economy** black market, cash economy, shadow economy.

4. **1. business** adventure, concern, venture. **2. company** dot-gov, dotcom, holding company, joint-stock company, limited company, non-government organisation, private company, private enterprise, proprietary limited company, straw company, subsidiary company, unlimited company. **3. conglomerate** amalgamation, big business, cartel, chaebol, conference, cooperative, cooperative society, empire, firm, group, house, industry, interest, mixed business, mixed industry, multinational, partnership, pool, pyramid, syndicate, transnational. **4. chamber of commerce. 5. market** exchange, futures exchange, Stock Exchange. **6. commercial centre** bazaar, entrepot, fair, fort *(North American History)*, marketplace, mart, souk, suq. **7. office** shop.

5. **1. businessman** adventurer, businessperson, businesswoman, chevalier, commercialist, entrepreneur, little man, mercantilist, merchandiser, small businessman, speculator, technopreneur, tycoon. *Informal:* wheeler-dealer. **2. trader** bourgeois, broker, cash and carry, chandler, dealer, distributor, kerb broker, kulak, marketeer, merchant, merchant prince, monger, wholesaler. **3. tradespeople** private sector, trade. **4. broker** agent, commission agent, forwarding agent, middleman, representative, ship-broker, single desk, syndic. **5. barterer** bargainer, exchanger, stag. **6. smuggler** bootlegger, contrabandist, courier, drug-runner.

6. **1. economics** classical economics, demand-side economics, econometrics, macro, macro-economics, micro-economics, monetarism, motivational research, political economy, supply-side economics. **2. economist** cambist, chartist, dry, econometrician, free-trader, Keynesian, Marxist, monetarist, physiocrat, wet.

adj. **7.** **1. commercial** commercialistic, entrepreneurial, mercantile, merchant, trading.

v. **8.** **1. economic** econometric, econometrical, economical, Keynesian, macro-economic, Marxist, micro-economic, socioeconomic.

v. **9.** **1. trade** barter, bootleg *(Chiefly US)*, deal, dicker *(Chiefly US)*, do business, exchange, export, go offshore, handle, import, market, mass-market, merchandise, overtrade, re-export, recapitalise, smuggle, trade in, traffic, transact, truck, wheel and deal. **2. negotiate** bargain, broker, chaff, chaffer, haggle, higgle, huckster, palter, truck. **3. operate** conduct, run.

RELATED KEYWORDS: BUYING, SELLING, FINANCE, SHOP

COMMUNICATION

n. **1.** **1. communication** categoric contact, commerce, communications, communion, congress, connection, conveyance, dialogue, discourse, fellowship, impartment, information, intelligence, interchange, intercommunication, intercommunion, intercourse, liaison, propagation, total communication, transmission, transmittal, transmittance, understanding. **2. discourse** chitchat, commune, conversation, converse, cued speech, dialogue, duologue, exercitation, interlocution, mag, small talk, table talk, talk. *Informal:* chinwag, yabber. **3. afflatus** afflation, gift of tongues, glossolalia, tongues. **4. nonverbal communication** body language, morse, morse code, semaphore, sign language, signalling, speech bubble, tick-tack. **5. telepathy** mind-reading, thought transference, thought-reading.

v. **2.** **1. communicate** broadcast, convey, disseminate, get across, give, impart, newscast, pass on, project, put across, put over, relate, relay, report, rumour, televise, tell, transmit. **2. link up** converse, get in touch, get on to (or onto), intercommunicate, liaise, look someone up, normalise relations, stay in touch with. **3. make contact** connect, contact, get, get through to, raise. **4. signal** flag, tick-tack, wave to.

RELATED KEYWORDS: HEARING, MESSAGE, SIGN, SPEECH, THE SUPERNATURAL, TALKATIVENESS, TELECOMMUNICATIONS

COMPANIONSHIP

n. **1.** **1. companionship** association, coexistence, commensality, company, comradeship, consociation, fraternity, partnership, presence, society, togetherness. **2. concomitancy** conjunction. **3. partnership** buddy system, mateship.

2. **1. companion** associate, beau, bedfellow, brother *(Aboriginal English)*, colleague, comate, commensal, companion animal, compeer, comrade, copartner, fellow, fellow traveller, helpmate, mate, offsider, partner, playmate, running mate, schoolmate, sister, track mate, yokefellow. *Informal:* significant other, sparring partner. **2. company** association, band, circle, clique, coterie, crowd, fellowship, outfit, retinue, social subset. *Informal:* rat pack. **3. follower** camp follower, hanger-on, henchman, inseparables, satellite, shadow, trencherman. **4. wedding party** best man, bridal party, bridesmaid, flower girl, groomsman, maid of honour, matron of honour, pageboy, paranymph, trainbearer. **5. accompanist** backing group, backing musician. **6. accompaniment** backing, obbligato, support, vamp.

adj. **3.** **1. accompanying** appendant, attached, attendant, collateral. **2. companionate** associate, associational, consociate.

v. **4.** **1. accompany** affiliate, associate, associate with, bear (or keep) someone company, chaperone, companion, consociate, consort, join with, mate, rub shoulders with, run (around) with. **2. escort** conduct, convoy, guide, walk. **3. follow** dangle, hang (around) with someone, hang about (or around). *Informal:* go around with, string along with. **4. partner** see, squire, take out.

adv. **5.** **1. in company with** arm in arm, in convoy, side by side. **2. together** jointly, unitedly, with. *Informal:* in each other's pockets. **3. in waiting** in attendance.

RELATED KEYWORDS: FRIENDLINESS, HELP, PARTNER, MARRIAGE, SOCIABILITY, SOCIETY

COMPARISON

n. **1.** **1. comparison** allegory, analogy, apologue, balance, collation, compare, likening, parallel, simile, similitude.

2. **1. contrast** antipathy, antithesis, contradiction, contraposition, contrariety, difference, discrepancy, disparity, dissimilarity, inequality, inversion, oppositeness, variance. **2. contrary** antonym, converse, counterpart, foil, opposite, opposite pole, reverse, the other side.

3. **1. comparer** collator, comparator, measurer, standardiser, typologist.

adj.	**4.**	**1. comparable** analogous, assimilable. **2. comparative** allegorical, collative, parallel, relative, typological. **3. contrastable** compared with, contrasted with, contrastive, contrasty.
v.	**5.**	**1. compare** balance, cf., collate, draw a parallel, liken, mate, measure, parallel, weigh.
	6.	**1. contrast** be at odds with, be contrary to, invert, oppose, reverse, set against.
adv.	**7.**	**1. comparably** by analogy, comparatively, in proportion, relatively.
	8.	**1. in contrast** against, au contraire, but then, by way of contrast, contrarily, contrariwise, contrary, conversely, on the contrary, on the other hand, rather, vice versa.

RELATED KEYWORDS: ANALYSIS, EQUALITY, MEASUREMENT, SIMILARITY

COMPENSATION

n.	**1.**	**1. compensation** accord and satisfaction, act of grace, amends, apology, atonement, guerdon *(Poetic)*, indemnification, indemnity, payment, quittance, recession, recompense, redress, reparation, reparations, requital, requitement, restitution, restoration, satisfaction. **2. recoupment** recaption, recoup, recovery, replevin, resumption, retrieval. **3. remuneration** attachment, compensation, offset, pay in hand, pay-off, payment, quittance, recompense, refund, reimbursement, repayment, requital, return, reward, reward claim, salvage. *Informal:* compo, golden handshake. **4. damages** blood money, distrainment, indemnification, recompense, requital, square-off. *Informal:* hoot *(Chiefly NZ)*. **5. penalty rate** allowance, attraction money, climatic allowance, dirt money, disability allowance, district allowance, field allowance, heat money, height money, industry allowance, isolation allowance, living allowance, loading, locality allowance, lost time allowance, meal allowance, mess allowance, mileage, pension, per diem, percentage, separation allowance, shift allowance, shift premium, subsistence allowance, subsistence money, tea money, time allowance, tool allowance, war loading, weighting, workers compensation, zone allowance.
	2.	**1. atonement** contrition, expiation, penance, penitence, purgation, purge.
	3.	**1. requiter** indemnifier, redressor, restorer, satisfier. **2. penitent** atoner, expiator, mourner *(US)*, purger.
	4.	**1. Lent** Day of Atonement, jubilee, Yom Kippur.
adj.	**5.**	**1. compensatory** apologetic, apologetical, compensative, conciliative, conciliatory, offset, propitiatory, reparative, reparatory, restoring. **2. redemptive** expiatory, lenten, lustral, piacular, purgatorial, purgatory, redemptory. **3. penitent** contrite, reformed, repent of, repentant, repenting, self-accusing.
v.	**6.**	**1. compensate** expiate, indemnify, make amends, make good, make up, overcompensate, pay back, recompense, redeem, refund, render back, repay, requite, restitute, reward, satisfy, square off with. **2. offset** allow for, countervail, cover. **3. recoup** get back, ransom, recover, regain, replevy, retrieve. **4. refund** guerdon *(Poetic)*, reimburse, remit, remunerate, replace, restore, return, revest, reward.
	7.	**1. atone** confess, expiate, purge, shrive. **2. reform** apologise, be on good behaviour, conciliate, heal, live down, make one's peace, pray, propitiate, redress, repair. **3. excuse** condone.
adv.	**8.**	**1. in compensation** back, in return. **2. on compo** on the suss.

RELATED KEYWORDS: GIVING, OBLIGATION, PAYMENT, PENITENCE, RETALIATION

COMPETENCE

n.	**1.**	**1. competence** accomplishment, capableness, capability, competency, completeness, dexterity, efficiency, goodness, handiness, nimbleness, proficiency, resourcefulness, skilfulness, skill, workmanship. **2. adeptness** ability, adroitness, art, craft, craftiness, cunning, cunningness, deftness, dexterity, dexterousness, expertness, facility, featliness, hand, skill, sleight. **3. experience** colonial experience, know-how. **4. expertise** address, craftsmanship, expertness, masterfulness, masterliness, mastership, mastery, professionalism, proficiency, skill. **5. ability** capability, capacity, competence, endowment, flair, grasp, grip, knowledge, prowess, talent. **6. aptitude** bent, faculty, flair, forte, genius, gift, innate ability, intelligence, knack, sense, strong point, talent, the right stuff, the stuff. *Informal:* the smarts. **7. skills** abilities, capabilities, capacity, cleverness, creativity, giftedness, powers, skill set. **8. versatileness** enterprise, resource, versatility. **9. dexterity** ambidexterity, ambidextrousness, dexterousness. **10. athleticism** ball sense, gross motor skills, suppleness, sure-footedness.
	2.	**1. artistry** art, craft, delicacy, delicateness, felicity, fineness, finesse, handicraft, lightness, niceness, power, savoir faire, subtleness, subtlety. **2. style** elegance, elegancy, flair, grace, handsomeness. **3. technique** execution, technic. **4. virtuosity** bravura,

brilliantness, display, fireworks, sparkle, technical skill. **5. verve** dash, elan, nerve, panache, pizazz *(Chiefly US)*, vigour, zest. *Informal:* bang *(US)*, kick, pep, zing. **6. specialty** pièce de résistance, speciality, stock-in-trade.

3. 1. expert ace, good hand, master hand, old hand, pundit, right-hand man, sensei, specialist. *Informal:* boffin, crack, dab hand, gun, hot dog *(US)*, hot shot, old chum, old stager, ringer, supermum. **2. master** adept, artisan, artist, authority, craftsman, engineer, expert, fabricant, master hand, master workman, master-craftsman, past master, professional, proficient, specialist, stager, technician, tradesman. *Informal:* the doctor. **3. virtuoso** ace, expert, genius, giant, high priest, king, maestro, old master, thoroughbred, wizard. *Informal:* crack, hepcat, the greatest, whiz. **4. talent** child prodigy, enfant terrible, good material, prodigy, wunderkind. *Informal:* natural, whiz-kid. **5. allrounder** ambidexter, generalist, Renaissance man, universal genius. *Informal:* one-man band. **6. dream team**. **7. go-to man**.

adj. **4. 1. able** accomplished, active, adept, adroit, capable, capable of, clean, competent, deft, efficient, expert, extraordinaire, fully-fledged, good, good at, habile, practical, practised, professional, proficient, resourceful, skilful, skilled, sure, trained, workmanlike. *Informal:* great at. **2. dexterous** apt, crafty, deft, dextrous, fit, habile, handy, ingenious, neat, nimble, skilful, skilled, smart, sure-footed, unerring, wristy. **3. cunning** apt, daedal *(Chiefly Poetic)*, deft, dexterous, expert, ingenious, neat, skilful, slick. **4. versatile** all-round, ambidextral, ambidextrous. **5. clever** gifted, heaven-born, peart, talented. **6. best** top. *Informal:* gun.

5. 1. masterful accomplished, artful, artistic, crafty, dexterous, expert, fine, good value, graceful, handsome *(US)*, hot shot, light-handed, master, master hand, masterly, nice, practised, specialistic, stylish, subtle, virtuoso. *Informal:* ace. **2. experienced** au fait, blooded, educated, old, practised, qualified, savvy, thoroughbred, thoroughpaced, up-to-date, versed in, veteran. *Informal:* ofay, salted.

v. **6. 1. be competent** be good value, be great at, be no slouch at, be worth one's salt, come into one's own, excel, have (or get) something down to a fine art, have a way with, have been (a)round the ridges, have the game sewn up (or by the throat), have the knack, know what's what, make a good fist of, not put a foot wrong, pull off a hat-trick, rise to the occasion, shine at, sparkle. *Informal:* know a thing or two, know how many beans make five, know one's onions, rock at. **2. master** learn, perfect, rise above oneself. *Informal:* get on top of. **3. be one's strong suit** be in one's bailiwick, be up one's alley.

RELATED KEYWORDS: INTELLIGENCE, KNOWLEDGE, POWER

COMPLEXITY

n. **1. 1. complexity** complexness, complicacy, complicatedness, complication, complicity, convolution, fussiness, intricacy, intricateness, involution, knottiness, nonplus, overelaborateness, overelaboration, perplexity, sophistication, winding. **2. inextricability** inextricableness. **3. compositeness** multifariousness. **4. maziness** mazement, tortuousness. **5. complication** complicacy, embellishment, embranglement, enmeshment, entanglement, node, ravel, ravelment.

2. 1. tangle bob, clutter, confusion, difficulty, disarrangement, disarray, disorder, distemper, fuddle, gallimaufry, hash, hubble-bubble, huddle, hugger-mugger, jumble, knot, litter, mat, mess, mishmash, moil, muddle, node, nodus, rat-trap, ravel, shakings, snarl, twine. *Informal:* can of worms, dog's breakfast, dog's dinner, frig-up, muss *(Chiefly US)*, snafu. **2. turmoil** anarchy, bedlam, bouleversement, chaos, derangement. **3. maze** Chinese puzzle, labyrinth, wheels within wheels. **4. imbroglio** fracas, mayhem, melee, uproar. **5. rigmarole** ins and outs, involution. **6. complex** composite, compound, network, reseau, structure, system, tissue.

adj. **3. 1. complex** complicate, complicated, higher, intricate, involved, perplexed, sophisticated. **2. intricate** anfractuous, crabbed, elaborate, entangled, flexuous, Gordian, involute, involutional, knotty, perplexing, reticular, serpentine, sinuate, sinuous, snaky, tortuous, winding. *Informal:* gnarly. **3. compound** composite, decompound. **4. overelaborate** fernickety, finicky, fussy, Heath Robinson, over-produced, overworked, overwrought, pernickety, rhetorical. *Informal:* anal. **5. elaborated** developed, elaborative, inwrought, wrought.

4. 1. tangled afoul, convolute, cotted, disordered, entangled, foul, inextricable, intricate, kaleidoscopic, knaggy, knotted, knotty, matted, perplexed, tangly. **2. mazelike** byzantine, intricate, labyrinthine, mazy.

v. **5. 1. complicate** develop, elaborate, embarrass, embellish, embroil, entangle, involve, ornament, overelaborate, overwork, thicken. **2. confound** baffle, bamboozle, becloud, bedazzle, befog, bemuse, bewilder, bother, buffalo, confuse, daze, dazzle, discomfit, disorientate, disturb, embrangle, flurry, flutter, fog, fox, fuddle, hobble, jumble, mither *(Chiefly British)*, muddle, mystify, nonplus, obfuscate, perplex, puddle, puzzle, ravel, stick, stump, stun. *Informal:* discombobulate, floor, flummox, rattle, throw.

6. 1. tangle confuse, convolute, derange, disarrange, disarray, discompose, disorder, embrangle, enmesh, entangle, entrammel, fall foul of, foul, immesh, jumble, knot, litter, mat, mess, mix, overset, ravel, shuffle, snarl, wind. *Informal:* balls something up.

adv. **7. 1. complexly** complicatedly, elaborately, intricately, involutedly, kaleidoscopically, overelaborately, perplexingly.

RELATED KEYWORDS: DIFFICULTY, DISORDER, TWIST

COMPOSURE

n. **1. 1. composure** balance, coolness, equanimity, equilibrium, even-mindedness, level-headedness, levelness, poise, presence of mind, sangfroid, savoir faire, self-possession, steadiness. *Informal:* cool. **2. imperturbableness** blandness, equableness, stolidness, unflappableness. **3. ease** assurance, confidence, easefulness, repose, reposefulness, secureness, security. **4. calmness** ataraxia, ataraxy, calm, imperturbation, placidness, quiet, quietude, rest, sedateness, tranquillity, tranquilness. **5. restraint** control, docility, moderation, self-command, self-control, self-mastery, temperance. **6. mildness** lenience, leniency, lenity. **7. patience** submission. **8. detachment** dispassionateness, impassivity, indifference, nonchalance, uninvolvement.

adj. **2. 1. composed** calm, controlled, cool, cool-headed, dégagé, deliberate, detached, imperturbable, level-headed, poised, possessed, self-assured, self-composed, self-contained, self-possessed, stable, steady, unflappable, unfussed, unhurried, unruffled. **2. placid** ataractic, bland, calm, clear, composed, even, level, quiet, secure, sedate, serene, sober, subdued, tranquil, tranquillo, undisturbed, untouched. **3. easygoing** balanced, easy, equable, even-minded, even-tempered, lackadaisical, lenient, mild, philosophic, philosophical, slap-happy. **4. impassive** deadpan, inscrutable. **5. phlegmatic** blasé, cool, imperturbable, stoic, stolid, unemotional, unfazed, unfired, unimpassioned, unmoved. **6. blasé** bland, jaded, smooth, sophisticated, suave, unblinking, world-weary. **7. reposeful** calm, docile, easeful, sedative, tractable.

v. **3. 1. compose oneself** calm down, recover oneself, relax, unbend, unwind. *Informal:* cool it, cool off (or down), play it cool, simmer down. **2. keep calm** get the better of oneself, hold on, keep one's temper. *Informal:* get a hold on oneself, keep (or stay) cool, keep one's hair on, keep one's shirt on. **3. be indifferent** not bat an eye (or eyelid), take it or leave it. **4. be unenthused** leave someone cold. *Informal:* not to go nap on. **5. endure** be patient, submit.

adv. **4. 1. composedly** calmly, coolly, deliberately, imperturbably, level-headedly, placidly, sedately, steadily, tranquilly, unhurriedly. **2. blandly** philosophically, stoicly, stolidly, suavely, unblinkingly, without turning a hair.

RELATED KEYWORDS: CONTENTEDNESS, MODERATION, NEUTRALITY

COMPUTING

n. **1. 1. computing** ADP, automatic data processing, batch processing, data capture, data processing, data retrieval, EDP, electronic data processing, systems analysis, systems engineering.

2. 1. computer AI, analog computer, artificial intelligence, control computer, data-handling system, digital computer, digital controller, electronic computer, macro-computer, mainframe, mainframe computer, micro, microcomputer, microprocessor, PC, personal computer, processor, quantum computer, supercomputer, synchronous computer, Turing machine, word processor. **2. adding machine** adder, calculator, cash register, comptometer, counter, integrator, tab key, taximeter, totalisator, totaliser. **3. slide rule** calculator, difference engine, ready reckoner. **4. abacus** ball-frame, Cuisenaire rods, Napier's bones, Napier's rods, quipu.

3. 1. computer elements accumulator, arithmetic unit, backing store, central processing unit, chip, circular store, comparator, core, core memory, core store, counter, CPU, data bus, decoder, disk, drive, drum, ferrite, flip-flop, half-adder, interpreter, logical element, magnetic core, magnetic disk, magnetic drum, memory, memory bank, microcircuit, microcircuitry, microprocessor, RAM, random-access memory, read-only memory, register, ROM, semiconductor, semiconductor memory, shift register, silicon chip, storage, storage device, store, translator, UART, VRAM, working memory.

4. 1. software assembler, code, computer program, disk operating system, DOS, firmware, high-level language, instruction, interrupt, jellyware, language, low-level language, machine code, machine language, malware, menu, object, program, ransomware, routine, source, statement, subroutine, utility. **2. programming language** ALGOL, BASIC, C, C++, COBOL, FORTRAN, Java, JavaScript, Lisp, Pascal, Perl, Python, Visual Basic. **3. hardware** A-D converter, analog-to-digital converter, bar code reader, bar code scanner, cable modem, card, card punch, computer graphic terminal, computer terminal, console, control panel, converter, D-A converter, digital-to-analog converter, disc, disk, diskette, floppy, floppy disk, groupware, hard disk, hard drive, head, joystick, key punch, keyboard, light-pen, line, magnetic ink, magnetic tape unit, menu-driven device, modem, mouse, OCR, optical character reader, optical mouse, optical scanner, paddle, paper tape, peripheral, peripheral device, peripheral unit, printer, printout, punch card, punched paper tape, scanner, sensor, sorter, stand-alone, tape drive, terminal, VDT, VDU, verifier, visual display terminal, visual display unit, workstation.

5. 1. computer terms address, array, band, bit, bootstrap, buffer, byte, carriage return, character, click-through, cold boot, communications protocol, compatible, computer graphics, cursor, data retrieval, database, database language, dataset, default, digital display, digital encoding, digital-to-analog conversion, direct memory access, direct memory channel, directory, disc file, disk storage, down time, downlink, dropout, editor, facsimile, facsimile machine, fax, field, file, filler, frame, ftp, function, hypertext transfer protocol, I/O, ident, index, indicator, input, input/output, intelligence, interface, Kbyte, key, kilobyte, logical design, macro, macro command, macro instruction, meg, megabyte, menu, MICR encoding, MIPS, mips, multi-tasking, network, output, p2p, PCM, peer-to-peer, program, protocol, pulse code modulation, random number, random-access, readout, real-time, record, response time, run time, scratch file, sequential processing, sign digit, subroutine, switch, system, throughput, time-sharing, toggle, turnaround, utility program, vector, warm boot, window, word, WYSIWYG.

6. 1. computer applications automatic data processing, batch processing, CAD, CAI, CAT, computer animation, computer art, computer graphics, computer typesetting, computer-aided design, computer-aided instruction, computerised axial tomography, computerised tomography, data processing, desktop publishing, digital imaging, DTP, fluidics, photoshopping, programmed art, simulation, teleprocessing, word processing.

7. 1. computer programmer liveware, logical designer, operator, programmer, systems analyst, systems engineer.

adj. **8. 1. analog** analogue, digital. **2. programmable** dedicated, intelligent, interactive, userfriendly.

v. **9. 1. computer terms** access, back up, batch, boot, boot up, call, chain, code, cold boot, compress, computerise, copy, debug, dump, edit, encode, enter, execute, feed, format, generate, index, key, load, log on, maintain, manipulate, map, output, pack, print, process, program, protect, randomise, read, scan, verify, warm boot, write.

RELATED KEYWORDS: CALCULATION, TELECOMMUNICATIONS

CONDITIONALITY

n. **1. 1. conditionality** contingency. **2. condition** but, catch 22, if, limitation, margin, modification, provision, proviso, qualification, qualifier, rider. *Informal:* strings. **3. precondition** hinge, hypothesis, premise, prerequisite. **4. reservation** afterthought, arrière-pensée, reserve. **5. conditional clause** article, codicil, condition subsequent, fine print, in terrorem clause, small print, stipulation, tail.

adj. **2. 1. conditional** contingent, dependent, eventual, hypothetic, hypothetical, interlocutory, nisi, precarious, provisional, provisionary, provisory.

v. **3. 1. qualify** condition, limit, provide, stipulate.

4. 1. be contingent on depend on, hang on, hinge upon, rest on (or upon).

adv. **5. 1. conditionally** provisionally, qualifiedly.

conj. **6. 1. on condition that** as, if, insofar as, on the understanding that, provided, provided that, providing, so (or as) long as, so as to, tho, though. **2. unless** lest, nisi, save, saving, without *(British)*. **3. if and only if** iff.

CONFORMITY

n. **1. 1. conformity** accordance, adjustment, agreement, assimilation, coincidence, conformableness, conformation, correspondence, keeping, straightness, tradition, uniformity, uniformness. **2. conformance** abidance, appropriateness, felicitousness, good form, observance, order, propriety. **3. typicalness** commonness, normalcy, normality, ordinariness, regularity, the ordinary. **4. rightness** fitness, legitimacy, legitimateness, propriety. **5. classicism** academicism, academism, classicalism, classicality, formalism. **6. adaptation** adjustment.

    2. **1. regularisation** acculturation, enculturation, justification, normalisation, regimentation, self-justification, social control, socialisation. **2. conventionalisation** ordering, stylisation.

    3. **1. conformist behaviour** a matter of form, accepted behaviour, ceremony, convention, conventionalism, conventionality, custom, form, formality, good form, orthodoxy, usage. **2. stereotype** cliché, set piece, type, type genus, yardstick. **3. clannishness** desire to conform, herd instinct. **4. conservatism** amenity, Babbittry, conservativeness, conventionality, political correctness, reaction, the conventionalities, WASP-ishness.

    4. **1. conformer** a stickler for …, adherer, Babbitt, capitalist roader, classicist, conformist, conservative, conventionalist, formalist, observer of conventions, reactionary, reactionist, right wing, right-winger, stick-in-the-mud, suburban, suburbanite, suburbia, traditionalist, WASP. *Informal:* schoolmarm, straight. **2. normaliser** adjuster, aligner, regulator, styliser. **3. yes-man** *(Informal)* company man, party man.

adj. **5.** **1. conventional** academic, accepted, accustomed, appropriate, bread-and-butter, customary, decorous, felicitous, habitual, in keeping, matter-of-fact, practical, prosaic, set, trad, traditional, usual. *Informal:* straight-up. **2. commonplace** common-or-garden, copybook, day-to-day, everyday, familiar, household, normal, ordinary, philistine, plebeian, prosaic, ready-made, run-of-the-mill, stereotyped, stock, trivial, unexceptional, unremarkable. **3. typical** entopic, in character, prime, stereotypical, true. **4. conformable** acquiescent, adjustable, agreeable, assimilative, assimilatory, complacent, complaisant, pliable.

    6. **1. conservative** Biedermeier, blue-rinse, fogram, fusty, reactionary, right, right-wing, square, suburban, WASP. *Informal:* daggy, straight, straight-arrow, twin-set and pearls, uptight. **2. clannish** closely adhering, loyal. **3. arbitrary** overbearing, procrustean, right. **4. orthodox** canonical, classic, classical, conformist, fundamentalist, law-abiding, strict.

v. **7.** **1. conform** accommodate, accommodate to, act, act (or be) one's age, adapt, adapt oneself, adjust, agree, agree with, answer, be guided by, behave properly, bend with the breeze, come (or fall) into line, comply, comply with, do as others do, follow, follow the beaten track, follow the precedents, go by the book, jibe with, keep up appearances, move with the times, obey, observe, observe conventions, observe proprieties, observe the rules, play the game, quadrate, run with the herd, run with the mob, swim with the tide, toe the line.

    8. **1. regularise** gauge, normalise, right, set to rights, socialise, standardise. **2. stylise** classicise, conventionalise, reduce to order, stereotype, style. **3. adjust** align, arrange, bowdlerise, bring into line, expurgate, fit, measure, regiment, regulate, set, systematise.

adv. **9.** **1. conventionally** appropriately, as a matter of course, as a matter of form, fitly, in line, in step, pro forma, properly, rightly, traditionally, true. **2. conservatively** classically, formally, straightly. **3. orthodoxly** according to, by rule, conformably, in accordance with, in conformity with, in keeping with, in the natural order of things, strictly. **4. commonly** as usual, generally, invariably, normally, ordinarily, regularly, typically, unexceptionally, uniformly, unremarkably.

RELATED KEYWORDS: CHANGELESSNESS, CUSTOM, FASHION, ORDINARINESS, PROPRIETY, REGULARITY, RULE

CONFUSION

n. **1.** **1. confusion** bamboozlement, bedevilment, bewilderment, consternation, daze, discomfiture, discomposure, disconcertedness, disconcertion, disconcertment, dismay, disorientation, distraction, dizziness, embarrassment, fog, maze, mazement, muddle-headedness, muzziness, mystification, nonplus, obfuscation, perplexity, perturbation, wilderment, wooziness. **2. dither** bother, flurry, fluster, flustration, flutter, fuss, ruffle. *Informal:* flap, flat spin, muss *(Chiefly US),* spin, tailspin, tizzy.

    2. **1. muddle** limbo, mess, mess-up, mix-up, no-man's-land, shambles, topsy-turvy. *Informal:* ball-up, balls-up, kettle of fish, muck-up, shemozzle. **2. disturbance** babel, bouleversement, brouhaha, commotion, furore, hullabaloo, jungle, madhouse, maelstrom, melee, pother, riot, shindig, shindy, tumult, turmoil, uproar, upset. **3. disorder** chaos, clutter, confusedness, confusion, derangement, hugger-mugger, jumble, messiness, pandemonium, tumultuousness, turbidness, turbulence. **4. entanglement** embranglement, embroilment, enravelment, ravelment, tangle. **5. maze** anfractuosity, labyrinth.

adj. **3.** **1. confused** adrift, aflutter, at a loss, at one's wits' (or wit's) end, at sea, bemused, bewildered, boxed, confounded, disconcerted, distracted, distrait, distraught, fluttery, mixed-up, muddle-headed, muddled, perplexed, shambolic, taken aback, topsy-turvy.

Informal: bushed, mixed up, up a gum tree, up the wall, woozy. **2. muddle-headed** dithery, dizzy, unbalanced. **3. blank** in limbo, lost.

4. 1. in a muddle at sixes and sevens, in a mess, in disorder, messy. **2. chaotic** disorderly, hectic, pandemonic, riotous, tumultuary, tumultuous, turbid, turbulent, wild. *Informal:* snafu.

5. 1. confusing bewildering, distracting, distractive, perplexing. *Informal:* clear as mud. **2. mazelike** labyrinthic, labyrinthine, mazy.

v. **6. 1. confuse** baffle, becloud, bedazzle, befog, bemuse, bewilder, bother, bowl over, buffalo, confound, daze, dazzle, discomfit, discompose, disconcert, discountenance, disorient, disorientate, distract, disturb, dizzy, flurry, fluster, flutter, fog, fuddle, hobble, mither *(Chiefly British),* muddle, mystify, nonplus, obfuscate, perplex, perturb, puddle, puzzle, shake up, stick, stump, stun, unsettle. *Informal:* discombobulate, faze, floor, flummox, flustrate, knock (or throw) someone for a loop, rattle, throw.

7. 1. muddle embrangle, embroil, entangle, jumble, make a mess of, mess, mix up, overset, ravel. *Informal:* balls something up.

8. 1. become confused blunder, dither, flounder, lose one's head, not know which way to look, wander. *Informal:* flap, get one's knickers in a knot (or twist), go off the deep end, not to know whether one is Arthur or Martha.

adv. **9. 1. confusedly** bewilderedly, discomposedly, disconcertedly, distractedly, distraughtly, dizzily, flutteringly, hectically, perplexedly, wanderingly, wildly.

10. 1. confusingly bewilderingly, blunderingly, discomposingly, disconcertingly, disturbingly, perplexingly.

RELATED KEYWORDS: INATTENTION, OBSCURITY, DISORDER

CONGRATULATION

n. **1. 1. congratulation** compliment, compliments, congratulations, felicitation, salutation. **2. best wishes** good wishes, happy returns, regards. **3. salute** a pat on the back, cheer, handshake, health, salvo, toast.

2. 1. congratulant toaster. **2. toast**.

adj. **3. 1. congratulatory** congratulant, gratulatory, well-wishing.

v. **4. 1. congratulate** cheer, compliment, drink to, felicitate, pat someone on the back. **2. wish someone joy** wish happy returns. **3. show one's respect** dip one's lid, shake hands. **4. salute** applaud, cheer, toast. **5. honour** fete, grace, lionise, make much of. *Informal:* duchess. **6. congratulate oneself** thank one's lucky stars, thank one's stars.

interj. **5. 1. congratulations** felicitations. *Informal:* congrats. **2. bravo** cheers, hooray, to your health.

RELATED KEYWORDS: APPROVAL

CONJECTURE

n. **1. 1. conjecture** bush reckoning, extrapolation, forecast, glimpse, guess, guesswork, inkling, intuition, shot, surmisal, surmise, suspicion. *Informal:* guesstimate, hunch, shot in the dark. **2. theory** abstraction, first principle, ideology, ism, philosophy, principle, school of thought, view. **3. assumption** axiom, hypothesis, postulate, postulation, premise, presumption, presupposition, presurmise, proposition, speculation, supposal, supposition.

2. 1. theorisation abstractness, speculativeness, supposititiousness, theoretics.

3. 1. theorist armchair philosophiser, armchair revolutionary, assumer, conjecturer, doctrinaire, doctrinarian, philosophe, philosopher, philosophiser, presumer, supposer, surmiser, theoretician, theoriser.

4. 1. type of philosophy Andersonianism, anthroposophy, Averroism, Baconism, Benthamism, Berkeleianism, Buddhism, Cartesianism, Confucianism, critical philosophy, Epicureanism, hedonism, Hegelianism, Heracliteanism, humanism, juche, Kantism, logical positivism, Marxism, monadism, Nietzscheism, Platonism, Stoicism, Taoism, Thomism, traditionalism, transcendentalism, utilitarianism. **2. branch of philosophy** aesthetics, axiology, epistemology, ethics, logic, metaethics, metaphysics.

adj. **5. 1. conjectural** abstract, academic, baseless, doctrinaire, groundless, hypothetical, idle, notional, speculative, theoretic, theoretical, ungrounded. **2. supposed** assumptive, axiomatic, axiomatical, ballpark, estimated, hypothetical, presumptive, putative, quasi, reputed, so-called, suppositional, supposititious, supposititious, suppositive. **3. conjecturable** assumable, guessable, supposable, surmisable. **4. postulated** assumed, conjectured, given, mooted, presumed.

v.   **6.**   **1. conjecture** augur, expect, extrapolate, guess, imagine, presume, presuppose, suppose, surmise, suspect. *Informal:* guesstimate, smell a rat, tip. **2. postulate** assume, give, posit, presume, presuppose, suppose, take for granted.

      7.   **1. theorise** hypothesise, philosophise. **2. propound** argue, moot, move, offer, propose, put up a case, say, submit, suggest.

adv.   **8.**   **1. conjecturally** academically, doctrinally, hypothetically, on paper, presumptively, putatively, speculatively, suppositionally, suppositively, theoretically.

RELATED KEYWORDS: IDEA, JUDGEMENT, THINKING

CONTACT

n.   **1.**   **1. contact** brush, contingence, dab, graze, interface, kiss, osculation, tag, touch. **2. junction** abutment, abuttal. **3. meeting** link-up, occlusion. **4. meshing**. **5. contiguity** contiguousness, tangency.

adj.   **2.**   **1. contacting** adjoining, valvate. **2. contiguous** adjacent, adjoining, conterminal, conterminous, impingent, meeting, osculatory, semidetached, striking, tangent, tangential, touching.

v.   **3.**   **1. contact** apply, hit, join, join up, make contact, meet, touch. **2. join** be tangent to, board, butt, join up, link up, occlude, touch. **3. abut** adjoin, border, border on (or upon), bound on, join, juxtapose, march on (or upon), neighbour, subjoin. **4. intertwine** be in mesh, braid, dovetail, entwist, fay, interlock, intermesh, intervolve, mesh, pin, plait, tooth, twine, twist, weave. **5. come upon** alight on (or upon), chance on (or upon), hit. **6. brush** button, dab, graze, kiss, nose, nuzzle, osculate, pat, shave, tongue.

RELATED KEYWORDS: CLOSENESS, COMMUNICATION, CONVERGENCE, FASTENING, JOINING

CONTAINER

n.   **1.**   **1. container** case, frame, holder, receiver, receptacle, repository. **2. cover** enclosure, wrapper. **3. frame** casing, framework, framing, shell.

      2.   **1. box** bunker, carton, chest, crate, egg carton, packing case, pyxis, shoebox, tea-chest, toolbox. **2. trunk** Gladstone bag, imperial, port, portmanteau. **3. hatbox** bandbox. **4. casket** chest, coffer, pyxis. **5. safe** moneybox, piggy bank, strongbox, till. *Informal:* peter. **6. jewellery box** jewel case. **7. locker** glove box, glove compartment, medicine box, medicine chest, seachest. **8. letterbox** ballot box, mailbox, pillar-box, post, post-office box, postbox. **9. snuffbox** pillbox. **10. matchbox** tinderbox. **11. window box** fernery, flowerbox, flowerpot, jardinière, planter box, polyhouse, terrarium. **12. woodbox** coalscuttle, hod, woodbin. **13. sandbox**. **14. lunch box** canteen, crib tin *(NZ)*, crib-box, tuckbox, tuckerbox. **15. canister** breadbin, caddy, firkin, tea caddy. **16. refrigerator** car fridge, car refrigerator, cool safe, cooler, cooler house, esky, gas refrigerator, ice bucket, ice chest, icebox, kerosene refrigerator, meat safe, stubby cooler, stubby holder, wine cooler. *Informal:* bush refrigerator, chillybin *(NZ)*, Coolgardie cooler, Coolgardie safe, fridge, frig, reefer. **17. hot box**.

      3.   **1. case** attaché case, beauty case, briefcase, dispatch box, dispatch case, papeterie, portfolio, skippet, vanity bag, vanity case, writing case. **2. suitcase** bag, case, port, valise. **3. purse** bag, billfold *(US)*, bumbag, burse, cardcase, clutch bag, handbag, moneybag, notecase, pochette, pocket-book, pocketbook, pouch, reticule, wallet. *Informal:* whippy, willy. **4. compact** smelling bottle. **5. workbox** ditty bag, ditty-box, etui, housewife, kit. **6. sheath** encasement, holster, quiver, sabretache, scabbard. **7. magazine** cartouche, cartridge, cassette, powder flask. *Informal:* mag. **8. specimen case** solander, vasculum.

      4.   **1. bag** billum, blister pack, carpetbag, carrier bag, carry bag, carryall, cod, dilly, dillybag, ditty bag, duffel bag, garbag, gladbag, grip, gunny, holdall, jiffy bag, kitbag, musette bag *(US)*, paper bag, plastic bag, sack, seabag, shoulder bag, sponge bag, string bag, tote bag, workbag. *Informal:* plackie bag. **2. swag** backpack, bluey, cigarette swag, drum, frame pack, haversack, knapsack, musette bag *(US)*, packsack *(US)*, rucksack, satchel, shiralee. *Informal:* matilda. **3. saddlebag** dosser, pannier. **4. sack** cornsack, flourbag, gamebag, honeybag, mailbag, post bag, ragbag, sugarbag. **5. package** bundle, Christmas stocking, packet, parcel, sachet. **6. doggie bag** feedbag, nosebag, tuckerbag, waterbag. **7. sac** air bladder, air cell, air sac, bladder, bulla, cistern, conceptacle, crop, cupule, cyst, cystoid, macrocyst, saccule, utricle, vesica, vesicle. **8. bladder** air bladder, air chamber, air cushion, air sac, balloon, gasbag, swim bladder, vesica. **9. pod** algarroba, capsule, integument, peasecod, shell, skin, theca.

      5.   **1. basket** basketry, breadbasket, chip basket, clothes basket, crate, creel, crib, dirty clothes basket, flasket, frail, gondola, hamper, hanaper, kit *(NZ)*, laundry basket, linen basket, Maori basket, punnet, rice steamer, scuttle, shopping basket, skep, trug, work-basket. **2. bassinette** car basket, carry basket, carrycot, cradle, crib, Moses basket.

6. 1. cupboard ambry, aparador *(Philippine English)*, armoire, cabinet, chiffonier, clothes press, dresser, filing cabinet, glory hole, hot-water cupboard, lazy Susan, linen cupboard, locker, lowboy, pantry, press, robe, wall unit, wardrobe. **2. reliquary** ark, burse, chrismatory, cist, monstrance, phylactery, pix, pyx, shrine, tabernacle.

7. 1. rack dish rack, hack. **2. stand** dump bin, inkstand, penholder, tantalus, umbrella stand, whatnot. **3. grate** brazier, chauffer, firebox, hay oven, haybox, hearth.

8. 1. rubbish bin ash can *(US)*, ashtray, car tidy, dustbin *(Chiefly British)*, dustpan, garbage bin, hell, hellbox, kitchen tidy, litter basket, litter bin, otto bin, pedal bin, pig bin, pig bucket, rubbish tin, tidy, trash can *(US)*, wastebasket, wastepaper basket. *Informal:* w.p.b., w.p.b. file. **2. catchpit** catch-basin, silt pit. **3. spittoon** cesspit, cuspidor, grease trap, slop basin, slop bowl, slop bucket, slop pail, sullage pit.

9. 1. basin baptistery, font, handbasin, lavabo, piscina, piscine, sink, washbasin, wash-bowl. **2. laundry tub** copper, dolly pot, dolly tub, trough, tub *(Especially Qld and NSW)*, wash tub *(Especially Qld and NSW)*. **3. bath** bathtub, bidet, footbath, hipbath, hot tub, sitz bath, spa bath, tub. **4. tank** boiler, cistern, reservoir, sump, well. **5. inkwell** ink-horn. **6. eyebath** eyecup, eyeglass.

10. 1. barrel breaker, butt, cask, eighteen, firkin, hogshead, keg, kilderkin, nine, pin, pipe, puncheon, quarter cask, scuttlebutt, tierce, tun, water butt, wine cask, wineskin, wood. **2. vat** bin, cane bin, churn, drum, hopper, keeve, kier, lauter tun, tank.

11. 1. vessel amphora, ampoule, ampulla, creamer, cruse, ewer, greybeard, hydria, jug, pitcher, potiche, pyxis, samovar, toby jug, urn, vase. **2. jar** Canopic vase, pipkin, pot. **3. crock** pithos. **4. coffeepot** percolator, tea urn, teapot. **5. sauce boat** boat, gravy boat. **6. bucket** bail, bailer, ice bucket, ice-cream bucket, kibble, pail, piggin, pipkin *(US)*, stoup *(Scottish)*, water carrier, watering-can. **7. dipper** clamshell. **8. jerry can** carboy, kerosene tin, milk can. **9. chamber-pot** bedpan, bottle, chamber, po, pot, sanitary can, urinal. *Informal:* bedroom mug, dry pan, gazunder, gozunder, jerry, Mel-bourne Cup *(NZ)*, potty, thunder-mug, tub. **10. rocker** banjo, cradle, launder, puddling box, puddling tub, rumble, sluice, strake, tumbling barrel, tumbling box, V-box. **11. test tube** balloon, beaker, pipette.

12. 1. bottle aris, baby, balthazar, beer bottle, demijohn, double magnum, echo, flagon, half-bottle, jeroboam, king brown, longneck, magnum, methuselah, nebuchadnezzar, rehoboam, tally, throwdown. *Informal:* aristotle, dead marine, glass can, pig *(NZ)*, square bear. **2. stubby** echo. *Informal:* Darwin stubby, frostie, glass can. **3. beer pack** six-pack. *Informal:* slab. **4. flask** canteen, carafe, costrel, decanter, feeding bottle, fiasco, flasket, hipflask, phial, water bottle, water monkey. **5. retort** alembic, matrass, still. **6. measuring cup** burette, dispenser, Erlenmeyer flask, measuring cylinder, pipette, pycnometer, pyknometer. **7. thermos** Dewar flask, thermos flask, vacuum bottle, vacuum flask. **8. hot-water bottle** bedpan, hot-water bag, warming pan. *Informal:* hottie. **9. cylinder** aerosol, aerosol container, air-spray, aqualung, gas cylinder, plenum, pressure pack, siphon, soda siphon.

13. 1. drinking vessel beaker, blackjack, bowl, calix, can, cannikin, chalice *(Poetic)*, ciborium, coffee cup, cup, cylix, demitasse, goblet, grace cup, Grail, Holy Grail, loving-cup, mug, noggin, pannikin, pint-pot, pottle, quart pot, rhyton, rummer, scyphus, skin, stein, tallboy, tankard, taster, teacup, toby jug. **2. drinking glass** balloon, balloon glass, beer glass, bobby, brandy balloon, butcher *(SA)*, champagne flute, flute, handle, middy *(NSW, ACT, WA, NT, some Qld, Tasmania, Victoria, SA)*, pony *(Especially WA, Qld, NSW, ACT)*, pot, schooner *(Chiefly NSW, ACT, NT and Qld, some WA and Tas-mania)*, shot glass, snifter, ten, tumbler, vegemite jar, waterglass, wineglass. *Informal:* cruiser, half, jar, Lady Blamey, lady's waist, long'un, long-sleever, pint *(British)*. **3. glassware** stemware. **4. gourd** calabash, horn, wineskin. **5. can** ring-pull, tin, tin can, tinny. *Informal:* tinnie, tube.

14. 1. tableware china, chinaware, crockery, dinner service, dinner set, earthenware, ironware, oven-to-tableware, tea service, tea set. **2. bowl** coupe, dariole, eggcup, epergne, fingerbowl, mortar, porringer, ramekin, rice bowl, soup plate, sugar basin, sugar bowl, tazza. **3. saucer** bonbonnière, coquille, scallop, shell. **4. tureen** crater, mon-teith, punchbowl, terrine. **5. plate** bombe, butterdish, dish, sizzle plate. **6. platter** ashet *(Chiefly Scottish)*, charger, paten, patin, patina. **7. tray** salver. **8. cone** cornet, cornucopia, horn of plenty. **9. coolamon** pitchi.

15. 1. cargo container container, I.S.O., loose container load, seatainer, tank, tanker, W-box.

16. **1. animal enclosure** beehive, birdcage, cage, coop, crib, enclosure, fishbowl, goldfish-bowl, hencoop, hutch, pen, skep, stall, terrarium.

17. **1. contents** cargo, content, freight, lading, load, pack, payload, wealth. **2. capacity** bulk, capaciousness, cubage, cubature, gross tonnage, mass, net tonnage, register tonnage, tonnage, tunnage, volume.

RELATED KEYWORDS: ENCLOSURE, HOLD, IMPRISONMENT, SUPPLY

CONTENTEDNESS

n. **1.** **1. contentedness** content, contentment, peace of mind, satisfaction. **2. comforta-bleness** comfort, ease, featherbed, heavenliness, wellbeing. *Informal:* cotton wool. **3. happiness** bliss, blissfulness, eudemonia, felicity, gaiety, glory, heaven, honey-moon, joy, paradise, seventh heaven. **4. complacency** gratification, satisfaction, self-complacency, self-content, self-contentment, self-satisfaction.

adj. **2.** **1. content** contented, easy, satisfied. **2. comfortable** at home, at one's ease, cosy, dégagé, in one's element, snug, well-to-do. *Informal:* comfy, cotton wool, snug as a bug (in a rug). **3. complacent** relaxed, self-complacent, self-contented, self-satisfied, sitting pretty. **4. happy** delighted, enchanted, eudemonic, felicific, glad, happy as a lark, happy as a sandboy, joyful, joyous, on top of the world, overjoyed. *Informal:* chuffed, happy as Larry, tickled to bits.

v. **3.** **1. be content** be a box of birds, be in heaven, make no complaint, purr, walk (or tread) on air, wouldn't be dead for quids. *Informal:* grin (or smile) like a Cheshire cat.

adv. **4.** **1. contentedly** comfortably, cosily, snugly. **2. complacently** self-complacently, self-contentedly, smugly.

RELATED KEYWORDS: HAPPINESS, PLEASANTNESS, PLEASURE, WEALTH

CONTEST

n. **1.** **1. contest** battle, competition, concurrence, conflict, confliction, contention, contesta-tion, engagement, game, infighting, match, match race, match-up, ring, stake, straight fight, struggle, trial, tug of war, war. *Informal:* clash, comp, go. **2. tournament** carnival, challenge, grudge match, jousts, knockout, local derby, meet, meeting, round robin. **3. boxing match** arm bending, arm wrestling, arm-wrestle, prize fight, sciamachy, sciomachy, spar. **4. animal contest** bear-baiting, bullfight, bullfighting, cockfight, cockfighting, main, tauromachy. **5. rodeo** bareback bronc riding, barrel race, buck-jumping, bull riding, bulldogging, campdraft, carousel, dressage, gymkhana, saddle bronc riding, steer wrestling. **6. jousts** carousel, joust, lists, pool, tilt, tilting, tournament. **7. panel game** game show, quiz, spelling bee. **8. boatrace** *(Informal)* stew. **9. mis-cellaneous contest** arms race, belt race, eisteddfod, goanna pulling, log-chop, roller derby, sheaf tossing, sheepdog trial, shoot, shooting match, spider, surf carnival, wood-chop. **10. championship** Cup, cup final, cup tie, decider, final, finals, grand final, match-of-the-day, open, prelim, preliminary final, premiership, quarterfinal, replay, rub-ber, run-off, semi, semifinal, test, test match, tie breaker.

2. **1. competitiveness** combativeness, emulation, keenness, rivalry.

3. **1. fight** battle, bout, broil, brush, chance-medley, combat, dogfight, encounter, grapple, passage, pillow-fight, rencounter, running battle, scrape, scrimmage, scuffle, set-to, skirmish, spat, struggle, tug, tug of war, tussle, wrestle. *Informal:* barney, biff, bingle, blue, boil-up, box-on, ding, ding-dong, dust-up, go-in, mix-up, punch-up, rough-house, rough-up, rumble, scrap, stink, stoush, turn-in, turn-up, yike. **2. quarrel** altercation, argument, bicker, contest, contretemps, cut and thrust, debate, difference, disaccord, disagreement, discord, dispute, dissension, dissent, friction, fuss, jangle, jar *(Aboriginal English)*, logomachy, misunderstanding, row, slanging match, splutter, squabble, unpleasantness, upset, variance, war of nerves, words, wrangle. *Informal:* argy-bargy, ding, hassle, high words, kafuffle, Mexican stand-off, ruckus, run-in. **3. free fight** affray, battle royal, boilover, brawl, donnybrook, fray, free-for-all, gang-fight, melee. *Informal:* donny *(NZ)*, pitched battle, shebang. **4. feud** blood feud, gang warfare, vendetta. **5. duel** affaire d'honneur, duello, gunfight, shoot-out.

4. **1. race** trial. **2. footrace** Bay to Breakers, City to Surf, cross-country, dash, egg-and-spoon race, fun run, hare and hounds, marathon, middle distance, obstacle race, paperchase, relay, running race, sack-race, scurry, sprint, the hurdles, three-legged race, ultra-marathon, walking race, wheelbarrow race. **3. ski race** dauerlauf, downhill, sla-lom. **4. swimming race** aquathlon, iron-man race, medley relay, relay, surf race. **5. boatrace** bumping race *(British)*, head of the river, regatta, repechage, sculls. **6. car race** car rally, drag, drag race, Grand Prix, gymkhana, hill climb, motocross, motor cross, motorkhana, MX, rally, rallycross, scramble, stock-car race, street race. **7. cycle**

race devil take the hindmost, madison, miss and out, prime, pursuit, roller race, scramble, stage race, tour, Tour de France, Tour Down Under. **8. soapbox derby** billycart race, derby.

5. 1. contestant adversary, backmarker, challenger, combatant, combater, competitor, contender, contester, duellist, emulator, entrant, entry, feudist, field, intrant, logomachist, principal, racer, rival, selection, starter, striver, struggler, tourneyer, vendettist. **2. finalist** quarterfinalist, semifinalist. **3. dark horse** also-ran, frontrunner, hotpot, outsider, reserve champion, runner-up. *Informal:* roughie, skinner.

6. 1. racing flat racing, greyhound racing, horseracing, point-to-point, races, the trots, the turf, trot. *Informal:* red hots, the dogs, the gallops. **2. horserace** advanced, advanced handicap, advanced horse, approved, approved handicap, barrier trial, boilover, chase, classic *(British Horseracing)*, derby, encourage, encourage handicap, eventing, feature double, flat, flying handicap, futurity, futurity race, graduation stakes, Grand Prix, improver, improver handicap, intermediate, intermediate handicap, juvenile, juvenile handicap, maiden, maiden handicap, meeting, novice, novice handicap, nursery handicap, picnic races, plate, point-to-point, produce stakes, progressive, progressive handicap, race meeting, restricted race, sires' produce stakes, steeplechase, sweep, sweepstake, transition, transition handicap, trial, trial handicap, welter.

7. 1. racehorse approved, approved class horse, approved horse, creeker, encourage, encourage horse, encourage-class horse, improver, improver horse, improver-class horse, intermediate, intermediate horse, intermediate-class horse, maiden, maiden horse, maiden-class horse, progressive, progressive horse, progressive-class horse, rogue, running mate, steeplechaser. *Informal:* boom galloper, donk, morning glory.

8. 1. racecourse birdcage, collecting ring, dromos, flat, home straight, racetrack, ring, sandtrack, stretch, track, winning post.

adj. **9. 1. competitive** agonistic, agonistical, combatant, combative, conflictive, dog-eat-dog, emulative, emulous, gladiatorial, mean, vying. **2. hand-to-hand** fistic, pugilistic, stand-up. **3. knockout** elimination, sudden-death.

v. **10. 1. contest** be at daggers drawn, compete, contend, emulate, look to one's laurels, play, race, rival, run, run close, run hard, strive, try out, vie. **2. challenge** draw, throw down the gauntlet. **3. enter the lists** take up the cudgels, take up the gauntlet, throw one's hat into (or in) the ring. **4. walk over** *Informal:* run rings round. **5. edge out**. **6. quarrel** argie-bargie, argle-bargle, argue, bandy words, bicker, chaffer, dispute, haggle, join issue, joust, squabble, tiff, wrangle. *Informal:* argy-bargy, have words with, make the fur fly, row.

11. 1. fight be rowing *(Aboriginal English)*, box, brawl, broil, buffet, come to blows, dispute, fight like Kilkenny cats, fisticuff, skirmish, spar, spat. *Informal:* barney, biff, blue, box on, go the knuckle, go the thump, mix it (up) with, rough-house, rumble, scrap, thump. **2. wrestle** arm-wrestle, buckle, grapple, scuffle, struggle, tussle. **3. set to** assay, close with, combat, cross swords, draw first blood, encounter, fight, join, match, meet, take arms, take on. **4. duel** joust, tilt. *Informal:* have someone on. **5. campaign** battle, conflict, feud, fight it out, wage war.

adv. **12. 1. competitively** agonistically, combatively, vyingly.

RELATED KEYWORDS: DISAGREEMENT, SPORT, WAR

CONTINUATION

n. **1. 1. continuation** abidance, abidingness, continuance, continuativeness, continuity, continuousness, duration, long standing, maintenance, progress, subsistence, sustainment. **2. protraction** prolongation, prolongment. **3. incessantness** endlessness, uninterruptedness, unremittingness. **4. successiveness** consecutiveness, perseverance, seriation. **5. unbrokenness** solidity, solidness.

2. 1. enduringness durableness, endurance, everlastingness, lastingness, perpetuality, survival, unfailingness. **2. persistence** assiduity, assiduousness, diligence, persistency, steadiness.

3. 1. continuer continuator, maintainer, prolonger, protractor. **2. survivor** abider, laster, perennial, relict, survivalist. *Informal:* Stuart Diver.

4. 1. series concatenation, consecution, continuum, gradation, gradations, one thing after another, progression, sequence, succession. **2. line** chain, column, file, Indian file, procession, queue, rank, row, run, single file, stream, string, train. **3. arithmetical progression** arithmetic series, geometric progression, geometric series.

adj. **5. 1. continual** abiding, constant, continuative, continuous, enduring, incessant, lasting, long-time, nonstop, ongoing, persistent, round-the-clock, standing, unbroken, uninterrupted, unrelenting, unrelieved, year-round. *Informal:* 24/7. **2. everlasting** amaranthine, ceaseless, continuing, deathless, endless, eternal, immortal, perdurable, perennial, perpetual, timeless, unbroken, unceasing, undying, unending. **3. unfailing** assiduous, incessant, unflagging, unremitting, unresting, unwearied. **4. extended** continued, drawn-out, interminable, long-term, longstanding, persistent, prolonged, protracted, protractive. **5. continuable** maintainable, retainable.

6. **1. sequential** back-to-back, consecutive, following, on end, processional, progressional, running, sequent, serial, seriate, subsequent, successive. **2. unbroken** direct, entire, flowing, indiscrete, run-on, solid, steady, straight, successive, uniform, uninterrupted, whole.

v. **7.** **1. continue** endure, flow, go on, keep on, keep the ball rolling, keep up, last, proceed, push on, soldier on, survive, wear, weather. *Informal:* kick on. **2. flow on** attacca, segue with. **3. remain** abide, continue, dwell, keep, rest, stay, wait. **4. persist** continue, endure, hold on, hold out, keep going, last, persevere, sit out, stick around, stick on.

8. **1. protract** prolong, string out. **2. maintain** keep, preserve, retain, sustain. **3. resume** renew, take up. **4. outlast** outlive, outwear, survive.

adv. **9.** **1. continually** all along, constantly, continuatively, continuously, incessantly, momently, persistently, sempre, unceasingly, week in, week out, year in, year out. *Informal:* 24/7. **2. unremittingly** abidingly, assiduously, at a run, ceaselessly, on end, unfailingly, unflaggingly, unrelentingly, unrelievedly, unrestingly, unswervingly, unweariedly. **3. always** abide, aye, aye *(Poetic)*, constantly, e'er *(Poetic)*, ever, still *(Poetic)*, yet. **4. successively** back-to-back, consecutively, in succession, one after another, sequentially, serially, seriately, seriatim. **5. unbrokenly** flowingly, on, solidly, steadily, straight, uninterruptedly. **6. forever** age-long, day in, day out, endlessly, eternally, ever and again, everlastingly, evermore, for an age, forever and a day, in perpetuum, on and on, perennially, perpetually, without a break.

prep. **10.** **1. during** round, since, through, throughout, under.

RELATED KEYWORDS: ETERNITY, REGULARITY, STEADINESS

CONTRACT

n. **1.** **1. contract** agreement, arrangement, bargain, bond, compact, composition, convention, covenant, deal, dicker *(Chiefly US)*, gentlemen's agreement, indenture, mise, settlement, testament, truck, understanding. **2. promise** assurance, commitment, earnest, engagement, gage, guarantee, homage, insurance, oath, obligation, parole, pledge, sacrament, security, simple vow, solemn vow, swear, the pledge, undertaking, vow, warrant, warranty, word, word of honour. **3. pact** concord, concordat, entente, league, protocol, treaty, truce. **4. bond** cartel, charter. **5. booking** pre-engagement. *Informal:* gig.

2. **1. type of contract** affreightment, aleatory contract, assumpsit, award, binder, bottomry, carryover, collateral agreement, collective agreement, comprehensive home building contract, consent agreement, consent award, futures contract, immoral contract, implied contract, implied term, indenture, industrial award, knock-for-knock agreement, lease agreement, lend-lease, mandate, nudum pactum, prenuptial agreement, quasi contract, restrictive covenant, social contract, subcontract, sweetheart agreement, sweetheart deal, turnkey contract, wager, wagering contract. *Informal:* prenup.

3. **1. deed** articles, articles of association, escrow, guarantee, indent, indenture, instrument, memo, memorandum, memorandum of association, quit claim deed, specialty, statute, submission, title deed, trust deed, warranty deed, will, written contract. **2. article** clause, condition, consideration, fine print, in terrorem clause, provision, proviso, small print, stipulation. **3. escalation clause** escalator clause, exclusion clause, habendum, reddendum, rollover provision, wet-weather clause.

4. **1. contractor** agent of necessity, arranger, bargainer, binder, covenantor, engager, guarantee, guarantor, indenter, obligor, subcontractor, undertaker. *Informal:* subbie. **2. promisor** pledger, swearer, vower.

v. **5.** **1. contract** affiance, arrange, bind, commit, engage, guarantee, lend-lease, oblige, preengage, precontract, subcontract, tie, undertake. **2. promise** agree, give, give one's word, mortgage, obligate *(US)*, pledge, plight, stipulate, swear, vow, wager. **3. article** bind, bind over, indent, indenture. **4. bargain** come to terms with, covenant, dicker *(Chiefly US)*, do a deal, go in with, settle, strike a bargain, tut. **5. stipulate** give terms, make conditions. **6. league** accede, ally, ally to (or with), associate.

RELATED KEYWORDS: AGREEMENT, OFFER, MARRIAGE, SURETY

CONTRACTION

n. **1.** **1. contraction** constriction, crumple, detumescence, gather, gathers, intake, retraction, shrink, shrinkage. **2. spasm** peristalsis, plasmolysis, systole, tetanus, vaginismus, vasoconstriction. **3. atrophy** amyotrophic, marasmus, myasthenia, phthisis, tabefaction, wasting. **4. astringency** constringency. **5. contractedness** contractibleness, contractility, contractiveness, retractility.

adj. **2.** **1. contracted** constricted, cramped, tense. **2. withered** atrophied, blasted, dried-up, marasmic, marcescent, shrivelled, shrunken, stunted, tabescent, tabetic, wasted, wizen, wizened. **3. retractive** astringent, constrictive, constringent, contractile, contracting, contractive, retractile, styptic, subastringent. **4. spasmodic** spasmodical, spastic. **5. systolic** systaltic. **6. retractable** contractible, foldaway.

v. **3.** **1. contract** astringe, constrict, constringe. **2. shrink** atrophy, blast, blight, contract, draw, dwindle, ebb, retract, shrivel, waste, wither, wither on the vine, wizen. **3. crumple** cockle, corrugate, crease, crimp, crimple, crinkle, crush, furrow, pucker, rumple, scrumple, wrinkle. **4. take in** pleat, tuck. **5. sanforise** shrink. **6. shrink-fit** shrinkwrap.

RELATED KEYWORDS: DECREASE, SMALLNESS

CONTROLLING DEVICE

n. **1.** **1. controlling device** checker, controller, controls, curb, damper, dedicated computer, dedicated server, governor, guide, monitor, regulator, rein. **2. automatic control** automation, computer control, gate, process control, remote, remote control, servocontrol, timer. *Informal:* auto.

2. **1. tap** bung, cock, faucet *(Chiefly US)*, pillar cock, plug, spigot, spile, stop, stopper. **2. valve** air valve, ball valve, butterfly valve, check valve, cistern valve, clackvalve, induction valve, inlet valve, mixing faucet, mixing valve, needle valve, piston, radio valve, seacock, slide valve, stop, throttle, throttle valve, thyratron, valvelet, valvule. **3. cock** ballcock, bib cock, float valve, petcock, stopcock, turncock.

3. **1. dam** conduit, flood bank, floodgate, gate, levee, lock, lock-gate, penstock, retaining wall, revetment, sluice, sluicegate, spillway, tank, tide gate, water gate, weir.

4. **1. type of vehicle control** accelerator, brake, choke, choking coil, clutch, cruise control, pedal, steering wheel, treadle. **2. type of aircraft control** aerofoil, aileron, elevator, flap, joystick, rudder, tab, throttle. **3. type of ship control** engine-room controls, helm, rudder, ship's wheel.

5. **1. type of computer control** cursor box, glidepoint trackpad, joystick, keyboard, light-pen, mouse, optical mouse, stick pointer, trackball, trackpad. *Informal:* nipple mouse.

adj. **6.** **1. controlling** checking, dedicated, governing, regulating, regulatory.

7. **1. controlled** automated, computer-controlled, monitored, regulated.

v. **8.** **1. control** bit, check, constrain, curb, damp, govern, handle, keep in check, keep under control, manage, monitor, regulate, rein, repress, restrain.

adv. **9.** **1. under control** in check. **2. in control** at the helm, at the wheel.

RELATED KEYWORDS: CLOTHES, MACHINE, MANAGEMENT, RESTRAINTS, TEXTILES

CONVERGENCE

n. **1.** **1. convergence** accession, affluence, afflux, approach, assembly, concentration, concourse, confluence, conflux, congress, convergency, flection, flexion, flocking together, huddling together, intersection, junction. **2. encounter** collision, engagement, meeting. **3. assembly** concentration, concourse, meeting.

2. **1. point of convergence** crunode, cusp, focus, hub, node, vanishing point. **2. line of convergence** asymptote, confluent, spoke.

adj. **3.** **1. convergent** asymptotical, connect, flexional, synclinal. **2. confluent** centring, centripetal, cusp-like, cuspated, cusped, cuspidal, cuspidate, cuspidated.

v. **4.** **1. converge** be on a collision course with, centralise, coalesce, come together, come up to, concentrate, concentre, focalise, focus, intercept, intersect, join, meet, merge, unite. **2. meet up with** bump into, collide with, come across, come upon, encounter, fall in with, meet, rendezvous. **3. concentrate** assemble, bring together, collect, congregate, convene, forgather, funnel, gather, gather together.

RELATED KEYWORDS: ATTRACTION, CENTRE, CLOSENESS, CONTACT

COOKERY

n. **1.** **1. cookery** catering, cooking, cuisine, domestic science, gastrology, home economics, home science. **2. haute cuisine** cordon bleu cookery, fusion food, nouvelle cuisine. **3. baking** boiling, broiling, grilling, infusion, kindling, marination, red cooking, roasting, scorching, simmering, steaming, stewing, toasting. **4. peeling** paring. *Informal:* kitchen patrol *(US)*, KP *(US)*, spud-bashing. **5. cookbook** cookery book, recipe book. **6. recipe** receipt.

2. **1. cook** baker, chef, confectioner, kitchen hand, kitchener, kitchenman, pastrycook, restaurateur, short-order cook. *Informal:* doc, doctor. **2. bush cook** *Informal:* babbler, babbling brook, baitlayer, belly punisher, blacksmith, crippen, doughbanger, doughpuncher, greasy, grub pusher, gutstarver, poisoner, water burner.

3. **1. stove** charcoal-burner, cooker, cooktop, fuel stove, gas cooker, gas range, gas ring, gas stove, kitchener, oil stove, one-fire stove, pot-belly stove, primus, range, spirit stove, stovette, wetback *(NZ)*, wood stove. **2. oven** colonial oven, convection microwave oven, convection oven, Dutch oven, fan-forced oven, gas oven, hangi, hay oven, haybox, Maori oven, micro-oven, microwave, microwave oven, two-fire stove, umu *(NZ)*. **3. spit** rotisserie. **4. griller** broiler, grill, salamander, toaster. **5. camp fire** barbecue, hibachi, kettle barbecue, primus, salamander, weber. *Informal:* barbie. **6. hotplate** element. **7. burner** backburner.

4. **1. cookware** corningware, enamelware, kitchenware, oven to table ware, ovenware, pyrex. **2. pressure cooker** autoclave, olla, steamer. **3. frying pan** deep-frier, frier, fryer, frypan, pan, popper, sizzle plate, skillet, wok. *Informal:* banjo. **4. casserole** bedourie, camp oven, cocotte, crockpot, Dutch oven, fondu dish, marmite, ramekin, terrine. **5. egg coddler** poacher. **6. griddle** gem iron, girdle *(Scottish)*, jaffle iron, waffle iron. **7. baking dish** roaster. **8. saucepan** bain-marie, billy, billy can, broiler, caldron, cauldron, dixie, double boiler, double saucepan, fish kettle, goashore *(NZ)*, kettle, pan, pot, steam-boiler, steamboat, steamer, stockpot, teakettle. **9. mess tin** dixie. **10. cake tin** dariole, patty pan, ring tin. **11. bombe** coquille, scallop. **12. blender** beater, egg beater, eggwhisk, food processor, mincer, rotary beater, whisk. **13. liquidiser** vitamiser. **14. skewer** brochette. **15. percolator** cappuccino machine, coffee plunger, dripolator, espresso machine, plunger, plunger pot.

adj. **5.** **1. cooked** à la mode, baked, billy, boiled, broiled, en cocotte, en daube, flambé, fried, grilled, roast, sauté, stewed, stir-fried. **2. underdone** au naturel, blue, green, half-baked, medium, rare, raw, soft-boiled. **3. done** done to a turn, hard-boiled, overdone, well-done. **4. rich** cream, short, shortcrust, sickly, suety, unleavened. **5. sugared** glacé. **6. cured** alcoholic, corned, double-smoked, dried, pickled, potted, recalesce, salt, salted, smoked, soused, sun-cured, sun-dried. **7. culinary** cordon bleu, home-cooked. **8. type of cooking style** à la orly, au bleu, au citron, au gratin, au jus, au lait, au naturel, au poivre, au vin, bonne femme, cacciatore, catalane, chasseur, en brochette, gratin, julienne, lyonnaise, maître d'hôtel, marengo, marinara, mariniere, orly, parmentier, paysanne, soufflé.

v. **6.** **1. cook** fix *(US)*, get, hash, microwave, pan *(US)*, pick, precook, prepare. *Informal:* nuke. **2. grill** barbecue, broil, carbonado, chargrill, griddle, toast. **3. beat** blend, fold in, mix, process, stir, whip, whisk. **4. bake** blind-bake, plank *(US)*, roast, shirr. **5. fry** brown, deep-fry, dry-fry, French-fry, frizzle, pan-fry, parch, sauté, scramble, sear, shallow-fry, stir-fry. **6. boil** coddle, hard-boil, parboil, poach, seethe, simmer. **7. braise** casserole, fricassee, ragout, ragu, scallop, stew. **8. blanch** scald. **9. steep** brew, draw, filter, infuse, percolate, soak. **10. dredge** bread, breadcrumb, coat, crumb, egg, flour. **11. mince** bone, chip, chop, dice, filet, fillet, spatchcock, spitchcock. **12. tenderise** hang, macerate, marinate, soak. **13. crackle** decrepitate. **14. strain** tammy. **15. season** flavour, pepper, salt, savour, spice. **16. marinate** marinade. **17. curry** devil, korma. **18. preserve** brandy, corn, cure, jerk, jug, kipper, pickle, pot, put up, salt, salt away (or down), smoke, souse. **19. garnish** dress, sauce, stuff. **20. baste** bard, lard. **21. make tea** *Informal:* boil the billy. **22. truss** collar. **23. cream** blend, puree, whip, whisk. **24. candy** caramelise, crystallise, sugar, thread. **25. prove** raise, shorten. **26. deglaze**.

RELATED KEYWORDS: HEATING, FOOD

COOLING

n. **1.** **1. cooling** cold storage, cryonics, thermolysis. **2. refrigeration** ventilation. **3. air conditioning** air, aircon, regenerative cooling. **4. cryogenics**.

2. **1. coolant** refrigerant. **2. cooler** cooling tower, radiator, ultracooler, water cooler, water jacket. **3. refrigerator** car refrigerator, creamer, crisper, frigidaire *(US, Philippine*

English), frost-free refrigerator, gas refrigerator, kerosene refrigerator. *Informal:* fridge, frig, reefer. **4. freezer** chiller, deep freeze, freezing chamber, ice machine, icebox. **5. esky** chillybin *(NZ)*, cooler, ice chest, icebox. **6. Coolgardie safe** cool safe, meat safe. *Informal:* bush refrigerator. **7. cooler house. 8. ice bucket** car fridge, stubby cooler, wine cooler. **9. freezing works** coolstore, icehouse. **10. freezing mixture** carbon dioxide snow, cryogen, cryohydrate, isobutane, rhigolene. **11. ice cube** iceblock. **12. air conditioner** fan.

adj. **3.** **1. cooled** chilled, iced, on the rocks. **2. refrigeratory** refrigerant, thermolytic. **3. air-conditioned** air-cooled, water-cooled. **4. frozen** frappé, quick-frozen, snap-frozen.

v. **4.** **1. cool** air-condition, air-cool, fan, water-cool. **2. refrigerate** chill, ice, supercool. **3. freeze** deep-freeze, quick-freeze, snap-freeze.

RELATED KEYWORDS: COLDNESS

COOPERATION

n. **1.** **1. cooperation** collaboration, combined operation, concurrence, concurrency, connivance, consensus, cooperativeness, coopetition, coordination, give and take, helpfulness, joint effort, mutuality, participation, reciprocation, reciprocity, synergism, synergy, teamwork, working together. **2. team spirit** clannishness, esprit de corps, fellowship, party spirit, solidarity, unitedness.

2. **1. acquiescence** compliance, compliancy, conformity, consent, obedience. **2. amenableness** corrigibility, ductility, tractableness. **3. passiveness** meekness, nonresistance, resignation, resignedness, tameness, yieldingness.

3. **1. obsequiousness** humbleness, self-abasement, servility, slavishness, sliminess, submissiveness, subserviency, suppleness. *Informal:* slime, smarm. **2. deference** congé, genuflection, homage, kowtow, obeisance, prostration, salaam. **3. sycophancy** toadyism.

4. **1. alliance** cabal, clique, coalition, combine, confederacy, confederation, conspiracy, federacy, federation, league, pie.

5. **1. cooperator** collaborator, cooperationist, coworker, fellow worker, participant, participator, partner. **2. ally** associate, cobelligerent, confederate. **3. accomplice** accessary, accessory, accessory before the fact, confederate, conniver, conspirator, particeps criminis, partner in crime, plotter. *Informal:* pal. **4. coordinator** combiner, matchmaker, organiser, uniter.

adj. **6.** **1. cooperative** coefficient, collaborative, concurrent, coordinative, solidary, synergetic, synergic, synergistic. **2. allied** coalition, cobelligerent, confederate, confederative, united, unitive.

7. **1. obsequious** abject, menial, parasitic, parasitical, servile, slavish, subservient, supple, sycophantic, toadyish, wormlike, wormy. *Informal:* slimy, smarmy. **2. submissive** acquiescent, amenable, biddable, complacent, compliable, compliant, concessionary, concessive, conformable, corrigible, deferent, deferential, ductile, easily managed, easy, flexible, flexile, manageable, meek, obedient, obsequious, pliant, resigned, tame, tractable, weak-kneed, yielding. **3. bowed** broken, browbeaten, cowed, crushed, down, downtrod, downtrodden, henpecked, humbled, prostrate, tamed.

v. **8.** **1. cooperate** club together, collaborate, combine, concur, confederate, conspire, coordinate, pull together, synergise, team, team up with, unite, work together. **2. participate** club in, contribute. *Informal:* pitch in. **3. concur** assist, go along with, help. *Informal:* play ball, string along with. **4. conspire** cabal, collaborate, collude, complot, connive, connive at, contrive, plan, plot, scheme, tick-tack with.

9. **1. capitulate** abandon, back down, bend the knee, bow, buckle under, cave in, cede, defer, fall, give ground, give in, give way, give way to, go under, haul down the flag, knuckle under, lay down one's arms, lose, lose ground, sag, strike (or lower) the flag, submit, succumb, surrender, take lying down, throw in one's hand, throw in the towel (or sponge), throw up, yield. *Informal:* drop one's bundle, run scared, sky the rag, sky the towel, throw it in. **2. submit** accede, accept, acquiesce, admit, appease, comply, comply with, concede, draw (or pull) one's horns in, give, lump it, resign, resign oneself, submit to, temporise, turn the other cheek.

10. **1. grovel** be at someone's beck and call, bend before, bow and scrape, bow to, chum up to, eat humble pie, eat one's words, eat out of someone's hand, fawn, kneel to, kotow, kowtow, pocket one's pride, prostrate, slaver, toady, truckle to. *Informal:* eat crow, get gravel rash, lick the dust, smarm.

adv. **11.** **1. cooperatively** collaboratively, concurrently, coordinately, in cahoots, in league. **2. unitedly** jointly, together.

12. 1. obsequiously cap in hand, deferentially, in obedience to, meekly, menially, slavishly, slimily, subserviently, tamely, trucklingly. **2. submissively** acquiescently, amenably, compliably, compliantly, corrigibly, flexibly, in compliance with, on bended knee, resignedly, yieldingly.

RELATED KEYWORDS: AGREEMENT, CONDITIONALITY, OFFER, MARRIAGE, SURETY

COPY

n. **1.** **1. copy** autotype, blind copy, clone, counterpart, double, dubbing, dummy, duplicate, duplication, ectype, exemplar, facsimile, fax, image, imitation, match, model, reconstruction, remake, repeat, replica, reproduction, transcription. *Informal:* ditto, mini-me. **2. counterfeit** Chinese copy, forgery, imitation, replicar, semblance. *Informal:* phoney. **3. tracing** transfer. **4. transcript** copy, engrossment, estreat, exemplification, fair copy, transcription, typescript. **5. carbon copy** flimsy, manifold. **6. plate** cut, electro, electrotype, offset, photoelectrotype, photoengraving, photogravure, stereotype, zincograph. **7. photocopy** autotype, blueprint, cyanotype, facsimile, microcopy, photostat, xerograph, xerox, zincograph. **8. offprint** decal, decalcomania, galley, galley proof, print, proof, slip. **9. woodblock** intaglio, wood engraving, woodcut. **10. cast** death mask, mould, squeeze. **11. magnification** reduction.

2. 1. copying copy, duplicate, duplication, gemination, quotation, repetition, replication, reproduction, transcript, transcription. **2. reprography** autography, autotypy, decal, decalcomania, intaglio, zincography.

3. 1. copier imitator, printmaker, reproducer. **2. transcriber** copyist, exemplifier. **3. manifolder** copier, cyclostyle, diagraph, duplicator, electrotyper, facsimile machine, fax machine, fordigraph, gestetner, hectograph, mimeograph, pantograph, photocopier, polygraph, telecopier, tracer.

adj. **4. 1. copied** duplicate, duplicative, ectypal, facsimile, reproductive. **2. transcriptive** word for word.

v. **5. 1. copy** download, dub, duplicate, facsimile, imitate, match, replicate, reproduce, rerecord, simulate, upload. *Informal:* ditto. **2. transcribe** engross, estreat, exemplify, take down word for word. **3. trace** calk, calque, cyclostyle, generate, prick. **4. mould** squeeze. **5. photostat** autotype, blueprint, decal, electrotype, fordigraph, gestetner, hectograph, manifold, mimeograph, offprint, roneo, xerox.

RELATED KEYWORDS: IMITATION, PHOTOGRAPHY, PRINTING, REPETITION, SHAPE, SIMILARITY

CORD

n. **1. 1. cord** bond, cable, cablet, line, rope. **2. leash** breeching, creance, dog run, lariat *(US)*, lashing, lasso, lead, leading rein, leading string, leg-rope, lune, lunge, lunging rein, rope *(US)*, slip, tether. *Informal:* leggy. **3. towrope** grabrope, guestrope, guide rope, lifeline, tow, towline. **4. tightrope** highwire, slackwire, tightwire. **5. whip** cat, cat-o'-nine-tails, colt, crop, flagellum, horsewhip, knout, lash, quirt *(US)*, rawhide, rope's end, scorpion, scourge, sjambok *(South African)*, stockwhip, tawse *(Chiefly Scottish)*. *Informal:* gully-raker. **6. rigging** bight, boltrope, boom vang, brail, breeching, buntline, cable, cablet, clew line, colt, cordage, downhaul, earing, footrope, forestay, gantline, grabline, grabrope, guestrope, guy, guy rope, halliard, halyard, handy billy, hawser, inhaul, inhauler, jackstay, knife lanyard, lashing, line, messenger, monkey rope, outhaul, painter, parbuckle, pendant, preventer, ratlin, ratline, reef point, roband, robbin, running rigging, seizing, sennit, sheet, shrouds, sinnet, slings, spring, standing rigging, stay, stirrup, stop, stopper, sweep, swifter, tack, tackle, thrum, traveller, triatic stay, tripping line, vang, warp. **7. miscellaneous cords** baulk, bellpull, chalk-line, clothes line, dragline, dragrope, guide rope, heddle, idiot tape, leg-rope, lifesaving reel, line, marline, match, moorings, octopus strap, plumbline, recovery strap, ripcord, rope's end, sashcord, skipping-rope, snatch strap, snatchem strap, spider, stringline, surf-lifesaving reel, surf-line, tagrope, taper, topping lift, trail rope, trip-wire, wick. *Informal:* ockie strap.

2. 1. string aglet, aiglet, apron strings, bootlace, bride, cordon, drawstring, fillet, lace, lacing, latchstring, petersham, shoelace, shoestring, streamer, tie. **2. twine** cordelier, pearl, purl, spun yarn, tatting, torsade, whipcord, whipping. **3. ornamental cord** aiguillette, braid.

3. 1. tape durex, ferret, inkle, marking tape, masking tape, red tape, ribbon, sticky tape, strapping. **2. band** chinstrap, crupper, hatband, jess, sandal, shoulder strap, sling, snood, stirrup leather, strap, strop, thong. **3. bandage** blindfold, brace, bracing, ligature, tourniquet. **4. belt** belting, cestus, cincture, girdle, tie.

4. 1. harness bearing rein, bellyband, bridle, britchen, check rein, halter, martingale, noseband, rein, surcingle, trace, tug.

5. **1. thread** cabling, chenille yarn, combed yarn, hank, noil, oakum, pack-thread, pick, pile, ply, rope yarn, rove, roving, sleave, sliver, slub, strand, thrum, thrums, tops, tram, twist, yarn. **2. fibre** fibril, filament, filum. **3. artificial fibre** acetate, acetate fibre, carbon fibre, Kevlar, lurex, lycra, maxxam, monofil, monofilament, nylon, parasilk, poly-cotton, poly-wool, polyester, PVC, rayon, tactel, teflon, tinsel, vulcanised fibre. **4. floss** dental floss. **5. tendril** byssus, chalaza, chord, cirrus, cobweb, cord, cross-hair, crosswire, gossamer, neurofibril, promycelium, string, tentacle, vegetable silk, web, wire. **6. skein** ball, clew, clue, cop, hank. **7. fishing line** dropline, gut line, line, tackle, trawl.

6. **1. wire** barbed wire, barbwire, cheese cutter, chicken mesh, chicken wire, crosshair, crosswire, haywire, luff wire, piano wire, razor wire, string, tie-wire, wire rope. **2. electric cord** automotive wire, cable, cablet, cabling, coaxial cable, cord, earth, extension cord, figure eight flex, flex, fuse wire, lead, line, mains cable, pigtail, ribbon cable, speaker wire, the mains, three core flex, wire, wiring. **3. chain** chain cable, slings.

adj. **7.** **1. stringed** corded, corduroy, funicular, ropy. **2. cable-laid** hawser-laid, right-hand-ed, shroud-laid, twice-laid. **3. stringy** desmoid, sinewy, wirey, wiry, wiry. **4. fibrous** fibred, fibriform, fibrillar, fibrilliform, fibrillose, fibroid, filamentary, filamentous, filar, filiform, filose, piled, piliform, tendrilous, tentacular, threading, threadlike, thready, unifilar, wir-ewove. **5. silky** byssaceous, cobwebby, sericeous, silk.

v. **8.** **1. tie** cord, lace, rope, string, wire. **2. rein in (or back)** lasso, rope in. **3. thread** intertwine, interweave, string, thrum, twine, weave. **4. spin** strand, wiredraw. **5. fibrillate** rove, sleave.

RELATED KEYWORDS: FASTENING, RESTRAINTS

COST

n. **1.** **1. cost** charge, expenditure, expense, outgo, price, rate, score. *Informal:* damage. **2. cost price** floor price, net price, trade price, wholesale price. **3. unit cost** cost unit, unit price. **4. overheads** burden, oncost, operating costs, outlay. **5. production cost** opportunity cost, prime cost. **6. market price** going price, market, retail price, spot price. **7. asking price** knockdown price, reserve, reserve price, upset price. **8. offer** ante, bid, nearest price. **9. fee** common fee, contract sum, cost-plus, honor-arium, most common fee, refresher, transfer fee. **10. commission** bank charge, per-centage. *Informal:* cut. **11. admission fee** admission, entrance, entrance fee, gate, gate money, gate takings, takings. **12. corkage** cover charge, service charge. **13. brassage** seigniorage.

2. **1. tax** cess, clawback, company tax, dues, geld, progressive taxation, regressive taxation, tallage, taxation, tithe, tithes, tithing, uniform taxation. **2. direct taxation. 3. indirect taxation** stealth tax. **4. pay-as-you-earn tax** flat rate tax, pay-as-you-go tax, PAYE tax, provisional tax. **5. income tax** capital gains tax, capital transfer tax, gift tax, indirect taxation, payroll tax, supertax, surtax, wealth tax, withholding tax. **6. duty** countervailing duty, custom, death duties, droit, estate duty, reprises, stamp duty. **7. excise** customs, customs duties, fair trade *(British)*, primage, protective tariff, pur-chase tax *(British)*, sales tax, tariff. **8. consumption tax** goods and services tax, GST, value added tax, VAT. **9. levy** capital levy, contribution, custom, imposition, impost, tax, toll, tribute. **10. poll tax** capitation, head money, poll. **11. miscellaneous taxes** bed tax, departure tax, energy tax, graduate tax, inheritance tax, land tax, ship money *(British History)*, tertiary tax.

3. **1. freight** airfreight, carriage, cartage, expressage, freightage, haulage, pipage, portage, porterage, postage, towage, trackage *(US)*, truckage, waterage. **2. storage** cellarage, poundage, stowage, tankage, yardage. **3. dockage** anchorage, average, demurrage, dock dues, ground, groundage, keelage, metage, pilotage, tonnage, tunnage, wharfage.

4. **1. price control** fair trade *(US)*, orderly marketing, price-fixing, resale price main-tenance, valorisation. **2. price index** basket, consumer price index, cost of living, cost-of-living index, CPI, tax indexation. **3. price war** price discrimination, price-cutting.

5. **1. value** money's worth, the full two bob, worth. **2. nominal value** book figure, book value, par value. **3. assessment** appraisal, appraisement, appreciation, duty, estimate, transvaluation, valuation. *Informal:* VG. **4. quotation** best ask, estimate, forward price, forward quotation, quote. **5. exchange rate** cable rate, foreign exchange rate, rate of exchange, ratio, spot rate.

6. **1. tax collector** assessor, farmer, inspector, publican, taxman. **2. customs officer** exciseman.

7. **1. valuer** appraiser, appreciator, estimator, valuator, valuer general.

v. **8.** **1. cost** bring, fetch, sell for, set one back. **2. be worth** close, close at. **3. amount to** add up to, come to, run to. **4. valorise** fix a price, set. **5. change in value** bull, demonetise, devaluate, devalue, down-value, fall, rise, transvalue, upvalue.

9. **1. appraise** assess, capitalise, cost, esteem, evaluate, means test, price, prize, quote, rate, revalue, tag, tariff, undervalue, value. **2. offer** bid.

10. **1. tax** assess, cess, excise, levy, overtax, rate, surtax, tariff, tithe.

RELATED KEYWORDS: ACCOUNTING, BUYING, SELLING, EXPENSIVENESS, CHEAPNESS, FINANCE, PAYMENT

COUNCIL

n. **1.** **1. council** assembly, board, caucus *(British)*, comitia, commission, committee, conclave, conference, convocation, divan, executive, gathering, panel, shop committee, synod. **2. administrative council** agora, council, divan, gemot, junta, local council, municipal council, politburo, presidium, soviet, witenagemot, zemstvo. **3. executive council** executive. *Informal:* exec. **4. board** directorate, syndicate. **5. forum** conference, discussion group, panel, round table, workshop. **6. parliament** assembly, congress, Diet, duma, legislature, moot. *Informal:* talking shop. **7. house of parliament** chamber, house. **8. federal and state houses of parliament** House of Assembly, House of Representatives, Legislative Assembly, Legislative Council, Senate. **9. cabinet** camarilla, council of war, court, genro, inner cabinet, Privy Council, shadow cabinet, shadow ministry. **10. committee** board of reference, Committee of the Whole House, joint committee, select committee, sessional committee, standing committee, steering committee, subcommittee. **11. ecclesiastical council** assembly, conclave, conference, consistory, convocation, duma, Ecumenical Council, house, parish council, presbytery, Sanhedrin, synod, vestry.

adj. **2.** **1. parliamentary** congressional, senatorial. **2. consistorial** convocational, synodal.

RELATED KEYWORDS: COMPANIONSHIP, COOPERATION, GUIDANCE, HELP, GOVERNMENT, SOCIETY

COUNTERACTION

n. **1.** **1. counteraction** bite, counter, counter-reformation, counter-revolution, counter-attack, counterblast, countercheck, counterclaim, countermove, counteroffensive, counterpressure, cross-claim, fight-back, neutralisation, reaction, recoil, retroaction. **2. repeal** abolishment, abolition, abrogation, annulment, avoidance, cancellation, cassation, countermand, disaffirmance, discharge, frustration, nullification, recall, rescission, revocation, self-contradiction, voidance.

2. **1. counterbalance** balance, balancer, check, counterpoise, counterweight, counterwork, equilibrant, offset, set-off, tare. **2. antidote** antacid, antalkali, antitoxin, antivenene, antivenom, buffer, counterirritant, counterpoison, neutraliser.

3. **1. counterworker** abrogator, annihilator, canceller, counter-revolutionary, counterclaimant, dissolver, nullifier, repealer, revoker, voider.

adj. **4.** **1. counteracting** antidotal, counter-revolutionary, counteractive, diriment, remedial, rescissory, revocatory.

v. **5.** **1. counteract** antagonise, cancel, counter, countercheck, counterclaim, countermand, countervail, counterwork, frustrate, negative, neutralise, overturn, remedy, slap down, undo. **2. balance** compensate, counterbalance, counterpoise, counterweigh, equilibrate, equiponderate, match, offset, write off.

6. **1. repeal** annihilate, annul, avoid, cancel, derecognise, disaffirm, dissolve, do away with, invalidate, nullify, rescind, set aside, think better of, vacate, void.

RELATED KEYWORDS: DISAPPROVAL, DENIAL, UNLAWFULNESS, RETALIATION

COURAGE

n. **1.** **1. courage** braveness, bravery, courageousness, fortitude, game, gameness, gaminess, grit, grittiness, hardihood, intestinal fortitude, moral courage, pluck, pluckiness, prowess, stomach, valiance, valiancy, valiantness, valorousness, valour. *Informal:* balls, bottle, guts, pecker *(British)*, ticker. **2. daring** adventurousness, crest, daringness, derring-do, enterprise, liveliness, venturesomeness, venturousness. **3. heroism** chivalrousness, chivalry, gallantness, gallantry, heroicness, knight-errantry, valour. **4. boldness** audaciousness, audacity, effrontery, forwardness, gall, nerve, temerity. *Informal:* balls, cheek, chutzpah, face, hide, moxie *(US)*. **5. fearlessness** dauntlessness, defiantness, doughtiness, great-heartedness, indomitableness, intrepidity. **6. spirit** heart, mettle, pluck, spiritedness, sportsmanship, spunkiness, stomach. *Informal:* spunk.

7. undauntedness heart of oak, unshrinkingness. **8. stalwartness** hardiness, manliness, spartanism, stoutness. **9. pot-valiance** Dutch courage.

2. **1. heroic story** épopée, epic, epos, legend, saga.

3. **1. hero** champion, daredevil, dreadnought, heroine, lion, spartan, stalwart, the brave, the good guys, tiger. *Informal:* goodie, legend. **2. darer** Promethean, sportsman, venturer.

adj. 4. **1. courageous** brave, game, gamey, gamy, gritty, lion-hearted, mentioned in dispatches, plucky, valiant, valorous. *Informal:* ballsy, game as a pebble, game as Ned Kelly, gutsy. **2. daring** adventuresome, adventurous, venturesome, venturous. **3. heroic** chivalric, chivalrous, determined, epic, gallant, herculean, lion-hearted, quixotic. **4. bold** audacious, bold as brass, defiant, nervy. **5. fearless** dauntless, doughty, great-hearted, inapprehensive of, indomitable, intrepid, unblinking. **6. spirited** feisty, full of fight, great-hearted, high-spirited, mettled, mettlesome, yang-yang. *Informal:* spunky. **7. undaunted** fortitudinous, unblinking, undismayed, unflinching, unshrinking, unyielding. **8. stalwart** hardy, manly, spartan, stout, stout-hearted, strong, sturdy. **9. pot-valiant**.

v. 5. **1. be courageous** be man enough, brave, face up to, look someone in the face, outbrave, square up to. *Informal:* bite the bullet, grasp the nettle. **2. dare** bell the cat, go through fire and water, venture, venture on (or upon). **3. put on a bold front** brazen out, keep a stiff upper lip, keep the flag flying, put on a brave face, take it on the chin. *Informal:* crack hardy (or hearty). **4. pluck up courage** take heart.

6. **1. embolden** arouse, buoy, encourage, hearten, inspire, inspirit, nerve. *Informal:* psych, psych up.

adv. 7. **1. courageously** bravely, gamely, gamily, grittily, nobly, pluckily, valiantly, valorously. **2. daringly** adventurously, venturesomely, venturously. **3. heroically** chivalrously, epically, gallantly. **4. boldly** audaciously, defiantly. **5. fearlessly** dauntlessly, doughtily, indomitably, intrepidly. **6. spiritedly** spunkily. **7. undauntedly** hardily, stalwartly, stout-heartedly, stoutly, unblinkingly, unflinchingly, unshrinkingly.

RELATED KEYWORDS: ARROGANCE, BRAGGING, RASHNESS, ENCOURAGEMENT, GOODNESS, NARRATIVE

COURTESY

n. 1. **1. courtesy** civility, comity, complacence, decency, good manners, manners, p's and q's, politeness, respect. **2. chivalry** gallantry. **3. attentions** attention, complacence, courtesy, devoir, devoirs. **4. deference** regard, respect. **5. curtsy** beck *(Scottish)*, bob, bow, curtsey, genuflection, kowtow, obeisance, salaam. **6. salutation** greeting, greetings, hail, hongi, mihi, red carpet, respects, salaam, welcome. **7. suavities** amenities, urbanities.

2. **1. courteousness** decorousness, decorum, diplomacy, gentility, gentleness, graciosity, mannerliness, mildness, politeness, politesse. **2. attentiveness** chivalrousness, debonairness, decentness, errantry, gallantness. **3. suaveness** breeding, decorum, sleekness, slickness, suavity, urbaneness, urbanity.

3. **1. courteous person** cavalier, chevalier, diplomatist, gentleman, gentlewoman, lady, retrosexual, rye, señor, señora. *Informal:* gent, snag.

adj. 4. **1. courteous** accomplished, attentive, chivalric, chivalrous, civil, debonair, decent, decorous, diplomatic, fair, fair-spoken, gallant, gracious, kind, polite, proper, well-mannered. **2. well-mannered** civilised, couth, cultivated, educated, good, good-mannered, mannered, mannerly, refined, tasteful, well brought up, well-behaved, well-bred, well-educated, well-spoken, well-tried. **3. gentlemanlike** gentlemanly. **4. ladylike** gentlewomanly. **5. genteel** euphemistical, soft-spoken. **6. suave** bland, polished, sleek, slick, smooth, smooth-spoken, sophisticated, urbane.

v. 5. **1. show respect** bend the knee, bob, bow, curtsy, dip one's lid, genuflect, hail, kotow, kowtow, make obeisance, salaam, salute, uncap.

6. **1. be polite** have good manners, mind one's p's and q's.

adv. 7. **1. courteously** attentively, cavalierly, chivalrously, civilly, considerately, debonairly, decently, decorously, gallantly, graciously, politely, properly, well, with (a) good grace. **2. gently** genteelly, mildly. **3. suavely** sleekly, slickly, urbanely.

RELATED KEYWORDS: BEHAVIOUR, HIGH REGARD, PROPRIETY

COURT OF LAW

n. 1. **1. court of law** assizes, bar, board, closed court, court, divan, durbar, forum, inquest, judicatory, law court, open court, tribunal. **2. level of court** higher court, inferior court, intermediate court, lower court, superior court. **3. courts** administrative tribunal, arbitration court, banco court, chancery *(British Law)*, common court, conciliation and arbitration commission, coroner's court, coronial court, county court, court of appeal, court of common pleas, court of disputed returns, court of exchequer *(British)*, court of petty sessions, court of record, court of summary jurisdiction, crown court *(British)*, district court, exchequer, family court, full court, high court, high court of justice, industrial court, juvenile court, local court, magistrate's court, oyer and terminer, petty sessions, police court, probate court, sessions. **4. court martial** drumhead court martial. **5. moot court** moot *(English History)*. **6. royal commission** board of inquiry. **7. courthouse** bar table, cell, chambers, courtroom, dock, judge's chambers, jury box, witness box, witness stand. **8. inquisition** Star Chamber *(English History)*.

    2. **1. trial** appeal, coronial inquiry, court case, court martial, double jeopardy, hearing, impeachment *(US)*, inquest, inquiry, inquisition, mistrial *(US)*, nisi prius, prosecution, retrial, show trial, state trial, trial by jury.

    3. **1. court session** assizes, quarter sessions, session, sitting. *Informal:* high jump, woodpeckers' day.

adj. **4.** **1. judicial** adjudicative, cognisable, forensic, judiciary.

v. **5.** **1. be in session** sit. **2. stand trial** go to court. **3. bring to trial** arraign, court-martial, try. **4. hand down (or deliver) a judgement** sentence.

adv. **6.** **1. before the court** sub judice. **2. in court** in camera, in closed court, in open court.

    RELATED KEYWORDS: JUDGE, LAWFULNESS, LAWYER, LITIGATION

COVERING

n. **1.** **1. covering** armour, carpet, cladding, cloak, clothing, cover, coverlet, covert, coverts, gilding, housing, integument, involucre, mantle, overlay, panoply, sheet, shell, shroud, skin, tegmen, tegument, umbrella, veil. **2. sheath** case, casing, casing shoe, jacket, scabbard, sheathing. **3. capsule** calyptra, epicarp, husk, integument, investment, peasecod, pericarp, pod, rind, seed capsule, seed vessel, shell, tunic, utricle. **4. coating** coat, crust, encrustation, eschar, film, incrustation, plaque, scab, scale, sheathe, skin. **5. icing** frosting, spread, topping. **6. scum** cap, dusting, fur, fuzz, fuzziness, head, scurf. **7. antimacassar** facing, lambrequin, loose cover, pallium, pillow sham, runner, shower, slip cover, throwover, tidy *(Chiefly US)*, trim. **8. tablemat** damask, duchesse set, tablecloth. **9. drapery** altarpiece, dosser, frontal, frontlet, lambrequin, scrim. **10. cover glass** bell glass, bell jar, cloche, crystal, watch-glass. **11. tea-cosy** egg-cosy. **12. hatch** booby hatch, calash, grate, lid, shutter. **13. umbrella** beach umbrella, parasol, sunshade.

    2. **1. wrapper** envelop, envelope, enveloper, envelopment, folder, shrink-wrap, wrappings. **2. wrapping paper** alfoil, aluminium foil, cellophane, giftwrapping, silver foil, silver paper, tinfoil. **3. book cover** binder, binding, board, bookbinding, case, doublure, dust cover, dust jacket, dustcover, dustsheet, full binding, headband, jacket, mull, self-cover, spine, wrapper.

    3. **1. roof** cupola, curb roof, decking, dome, drop ceiling, gambrel roof, hip roof, hipped roof, mansard, mansard roof, northlight roof, pop-top, roofing, rooftree, saddle roof, sawtooth roof, shell, skillion roof, southlight roof, span roof. **2. pergola** marquee *(US)*, marquise, penthouse. **3. canopy** baldachin, ciborium, tester. **4. tarpaulin** dustcover, dustsheet, fly, oilcloth, pool blanket, throwover, tilt, tonneau. *Informal:* tarp.

    4. **1. paving** clinker, cobble, cobblestone, pavement, paver, paviour, quarry tile, tile, tiling. **2. asphalt** blacktop, macadam, metal road, mineral pitch, seal, surface dressing, tarmac, tarmacadam, tarseal *(NZ)*, the bitumen. **3. concrete** cement, Leichhardt grass. *Informal:* Italian lawn, Leichhardt lawn.

    5. **1. flooring** decking, duckboard, floor, floor covering, malthoid, planking, stringboard. **2. mat** bath mat, beach mat, doormat. **3. carpet** Aubusson carpet, Axminster carpet, body carpet, broadloom carpet, brussels carpet, carpet tile, carpeting, Persian carpet, red carpet, shag pile, stair-carpet, velvet carpet, wall-to-wall carpet, Wilton carpet. **4. rug** hearthrug, Kashmir rug, kazak, Kirman, oriental rug, prayer mat, prayer rug, runner, scatter rug, tapis. **5. seagrass matting** coconut matting, coir matting, matting, rush, Vietnamese matting. **6. linoleum** lino, linotile, vinyl, vinyl tile.

    6. **1. bedclothes** bed linen, bed-roll, bedding, pillowcase, pillowslip, sheet, slip. *Informal:* nap. **2. blanket** afghan, bunny-rug, electric blanket, kaross, rug, throw. **3. eiderdown** bedcover, bedspread, comfort *(US)*, comforter *(Chiefly US)*, continental quilt, counterpane, coverlet, coverlid, doona, duvet, quilt, spread. **4. swagman's blanket** wagga. *Informal:* bagman's two-up. **5. sleeping-bag** *Informal:* fart sack, farter, fleabag. **6. saddlecloth** caparison, housing, housings, trapping, trappings.

7. **1. plating** case, casing, electroplating, enamel, enamelling, enamelwork, foliation, galvanisation, gilding, glaze, gold plate, leading, lustre, nickel plate, overlay, oxidation, oxidisation, patina, plate, porcelain enamel *(US)*, rolled gold, silver plate, silvering, tarnish, vitreous enamel.

8. **1. paint** acrylic colour, antifouling, clobber, colourwash, couch, daub, distemper, dope, duco, emulsion paint, estapol, gesso, glair, glaze, glazing, graining, ground colour, impastation, japan, kalsomine, lacquer, luminous paint, lustre, metalflake duco, oil-paint, overglaze, paintwork, plastic paint, polymer colour, poster colour, poster paint, size, slip, spirit varnish, splash coat, tempera, thixotropic paint, tiger's eye, tigereye, varnish, wash, waterpaint, whitewash. **2. undercoat** primer, sealant, undercoating, underglaze, underseal.

9. **1. plaster** cement render, drummy, facing, gibraltar board *(NZ)*, gyprock, parget, pargeting, plasterboard, plastering, pricking coat, render, rendering, revetment, roughcast, setting coat, skimming coat, wattle and daub. **2. veneer** brick veneer, burlwood veneer, panelling, wainscot. **3. wallpaper** dado, flock paper, lining paper, paper.

adj. 10. **1. covered** covert. **2. hooded** cowled, cucullate, veiled. **3. tegminal** tegumentary. **4. jacketed** armour-plated, ermined, ironclad, loricate, loricated, panoplied.

11. **1. coated** chromed, copper-bottomed, electroplated, galvanised, gilded, gilt, plated, tinned. **2. bitumenised** sealed, tar, tarred, tarry. **3. sugar-coated** candied, farinose, frosted, glacé, glaireous, glairy, iced, powdery, sugared.

v. 12. **1. cover** coat, face, invest, pall, shroud, throw something over, web. **2. shroud** drape, enshroud. **3. jacket** blanket, caparison, cloak, cushion, mantle, trap, tuck, vest. *Informal:* tarp. **4. mask** blindfold, cowl, hood, hoodwink. **5. swathe** bandage, bind, cocoon, enfold, enswathe, enwrap, insulate, inswathe, involve, inwrap, muffle, smother, swaddle. **6. wrap** bundle, fold, giftwrap, pack, package, packet. **7. bind** fother, parcel, serve, whip. **8. overlay** bespread, carpet, litter, perfuse. **9. line** brattice, face, fettle, resurface, revet, wainscot. **10. upholster** overstuff, trim. **11. roof** canopy, cope, embower, plash, rafter, shade, shingle, thatch, tile. **12. grass** loam, sod, sward, top, topdress, topsoil, turf.

13. **1. coat** anoint, bedaub, besmear, flock, lather, powder, smear, spread, wipe. **2. batter** breadcrumb, candy, frost, glair, glaze, ice, white frost. **3. paint** calcimine, clobber, daub, distemper, duco, dye, glaze, japan, kalsomine, lacquer, prime, shellac, spray-paint, undercoat, varnish, whitewash. **4. plate** anodise, braze, copper, electroplate, ferrotype, foil, galvanise, metal, nickel, nickel-plate, oxidate, oxidise, platinise, sherardise, silverplate, sputter, tin, veneer, zinc. **5. gild** foliate, overgild. **6. bitumenise** asphalt, pave, seal, tarmac, underseal. **7. cement-render** bag, cement, clay, daub, flush, impaste, paper, parget, paste, pay, plaster, puddle, putty, render, roughcast.

RELATED KEYWORDS: CLOTHES, HAIR, LAYER, PROTECTION, SKIN

COWARDICE

n. 1. **1. cowardice** baseness, cowardliness, cravenness, dastardliness, faint-heartedness, fearfulness, fearsomeness, nervelessness, poltroonery, pusillanimity, recreancy, spinelessness, timidity, timidness, yellow streak.

2. **1. coward** chocolate soldier, craven, dastard, faint-heart, milksop, poltroon, recreant, sheep, skulk, skulker, squib, wheyface. *Informal:* a nervous Nellie, chicken, cissy, cowardy custard, cream puff, creamer, cry-baby, dingo, fraidy-cat, funk, gutless wonder, limp-dick, poof, poofta, poofter, ringtail, scaredy-cat, sis, sissy, softie, softy, sook, sop, weakie, wimp, wuss, yellow-belly.

adj. 3. **1. cowardly** base, chicken-hearted, coward, craven, dastard, dastardly, faint, faint-hearted, fearful, fearsome, frightened, gritless, gun-shy, lily-livered, mealy-mouthed, meek, milky, nerveless, pavid, pigeon-hearted, poor, poor-spirited, pusillanimous, recreant, shy, spineless, spiritless, tame, terrified, timid, timorous, unheroic, unknightly, unmanly, weak-kneed, white-livered. *Informal:* chicken, gutless, sooky, yellow, yellowbellied.

v. 4. **1. lack courage** wouldn't say boo to a goose. **2. behave in a cowardly way** go to water, have cold feet, malinger, show the white feather, skulk. *Informal:* chicken out, dingo, funk, pike out. **3. quail** back up, blench, boggle, cower, flinch, shrink, shy, waver.

adv. 5. **1. timidly** basely, cravenly, faint-heartedly, fearfully, fearsomely, nervelessly, pusillanimously, recreantly, spinelessly, tamely. *Informal:* in a blue funk, in a funk.

RELATED KEYWORDS: MEEKNESS, CAUTIOUSNESS, FRIGHT

CREATION

n. **1.** **1. creation** coinage, composition, conception, derivation, design, devisal, excogitation, fabrication, generation, genesis, innovation, invention, origin, origination, procreation, production, reproduction. **2. abiogenesis** abiogenetic, autogenesis, autogeny, continuous creation, paedogenesis, parthenogenesis, spontaneous generation, virgin birth. **3. improvisation** extemporisation. **4. establishment** constitution, engenderment, institution. **5. re-creation** destructive distillation, palingenesis, recast, reconstitution, reconstruction, regeneracy, regeneration.

2. **1. creating** building, construction, contrivance, crystallisation, development, elaboration, erection, fabrication, facture, formation, forming, make, making, manufacture, manufacturing, output, prefabrication, preparation, production, synthesis, synthesisation, turning, turnout, twinning, working. **2. structure** architecture, arrangement, build, composition, constitution, construction, contexture, form, layout, macrostructure, make, make-up, microstructure, ordination, ordonnance, plan, reconstruction.

3. **1. creativity** creativeness, formativeness, imagination, innovation, inventiveness, originality, parturiency, productiveness, productivity. **2. workmanship** craft, craftsmanship, handcraft, handicraft. **3. authorship** creatorship.

4. **1. industry** cottage industry, primary industry, secondary industry, sunrise industry. **2. technology** high tech, high technology, industrialisation, industrialism.

5. **1. creator** architect, artificer, author, coiner, composer, conceiver, constituter, designer, deviser, engenderer, excogitator, fabricator, framer, generator, hatcher, inventer, inventor, originator, parent, procreator, source. **2. author** authoress, co-author, littérateur, pen, penman, scribe, wordsmith, writer. **3. maker** artificer, artisan, blacksmith, builder, constituter, constructor, contriver, craftsman, craftsperson, developer, erecter, fabricant, fabricator, former, framer, handicraftsman, luthier, manufacturer, master-craftsman, producer, smith, tradesman, wright. **4. innovator** idea-monger, innovationist, mastermind. **5. founder** establisher, father, first cause, fons et origo, founding father, fountainhead, instituter, institutor, mainspring, matriarch, mother, parent, patriarch, prime mover, progenitor. **6. improviser** extemporiser, improvisator.

adj. **6.** **1. creative** excogitative, generative, groundbreaking, imaginative, ingenious, innovational, innovative, innovatory, inventive, omnific, original, originative, productive, Promethean. **2. seminal** primordial, procreative. **3. constructive** formative, tectonic. **4. creational** authorial, conceptional, genetic, institutive, parturient.

7. **1. made** artificial, compacted of, factitious, man-made, manufactured, wrought. **2. industrial** factorial, factory-like, handmade. **3. ready-made** prefabricated, readyrolled. **4. custom-built** bespoke, custom-made, made-to-measure, made-to-order, rollyour-own, tailor-made.

v. **8.** **1. create** author, bring into being, call into being, compose, conceive, constitute, father, float, form, give birth to, give rise to, indite, initiate, materialise, poetise, trigger, utter. **2. devise** brew, cast, cogitate, compass, concoct, contrive, hatch, machinate, make up, scheme. *Informal:* cook up. **3. invent** adlib, coin, compose, extemporise, fabricate, forge, imagine, improvise, innovate, manufacture, mint, originate, think up, turn, vamp. *Informal:* toss off. **4. develop** be responsible for, beat out, bring about, contrive, design, devise, draw, engineer, evolve, excogitate, formulate, frame, incubate, instigate, pioneer, stage, think out. **5. establish** constitute, erect, found, ground, inaugurate, institute, institutionalise, make, open the door to, plant, set up. **6. breed** birth, bring forth, bring into the world, engender, father, generate, germinate, get, mother, procreate, produce, sire, spawn. **7. re-create** re-form, recast, recompose, reconstitute, reconstruct, regenerate.

9. **1. make** assemble, compound, create, develop, do, effect, effectuate, fashion, form, frame, generate, machine, mould, prepare, produce, set, shape, synthesise, synthetise, think, work, write. **2. construct** build, do, erect, fabricate, forge, form, frame, knock together, knock up, loop, make up, manufacture, mock up, prefabricate, put up, raise, throw together, turn out, whip up. **3. constitute** compose, form, make, make up.

adv. **10.** **1. creatively** institutively, inventively, originally, originatively, productively. **2. constructively** formatively, tectonically. **3. industrially** technologically.

RELATED KEYWORDS: FERTILITY, RESULT, REPRODUCTION, SHAPE

CROSSING

n. **1.** **1. crossing** intersection, junction, overlap, overlapping. **2. interlacement** enlacement, entanglement, intertwinement, interweavement, matting, mesh, meshes, meshwork, net, netting, network, reseau, retic, reticulation, reticulum, wattling, webbing. **3. type of mesh** bird netting, chain mesh, chain wire, chainmesh, chicken wire, dragnet, fish-net, mesh, mosquito net, net, netting, netting wire, network, purse seine, screen, seine, stinger net, wire gauze, wire netting, wirecloth. **4. grid** gauntlet, grating, gridiron, grillage, grille. **5. latticing** lattice, latticework, treillage, trellis, trelliswork, wicker, wickerwork. **6. trellis** espalier, latticework, trelliswork, wattle. **7. plait** braid, plat, wreath. **8. skein** cat's cradle. **9. crisscross** crackle, craze, frostwork. **10. shutter** jalousie, wicket. **11. crosshair** crosswire, graticule, reseau, reticle.

2.   **1. type of cross** ankh, cross, crosslet, crux ansata, swastika, tau cross, tee, X. **2. crucifix** Agnus Dei, Celtic cross, cross, Cross, Greek cross, Holy Rood, holy rood, Jerusalem cross, Latin cross, Maltese cross, papal cross, Red Cross, rood, Saint Andrew's Cross, Saint Anthony's Cross, Saint George's Cross, Saint Patrick's Cross. **3. decussation** chiasm, chiasma, X-shape.

3.   **1. crosspiece** buttock, crossbar, crossbeam, crosscut, crosstree, fess, thwart, transversal, transverse, traverse.

4.   **1. intersection** circus *(Chiefly British)*, cross-street, crossing, crossroad, crossway, interchange, junction, level crossing, pedestrian crossing, roundabout, traffic circle *(US)*, zebra crossing.

adj. 5.   **1. overlapping** crossing, equitant. **2. intersectional** secant. **3. transversal** athwart, cross, crosscut, jessant, lyrate, thwart, transverse, traverse. **4. cruciform** chiasmic, cross-shaped, crucial, cruciate, decussate, tee, tee-shaped, X-shaped.

6.   **1. crossed** crisscross, cross-grained, cross-legged. **2. netlike** arachnoid, clathrate, crazed, cross-grained, mesh, meshy, net, reticulate, retiform.

v. 7.   **1. cross** crosscut, cut, decussate, gauntlet, interlace, intersect, overlap, traverse. **2. crisscross** craze. **3. bestraddle** bestride, overstride. **4. cross** bless.

8.   **1. interlace** braid, enlace, enmesh, entangle, intercross, intertwine, intervolve, interweave, plait, plash, pleach, reticulate, twine, weave. **2. mat** mesh. **3. trellis** wattle.

adv. 9.   **1. crosswise** across, crisscross, fesswise. **2. transversally** athwart, on the cross, transversely. **3. cruciformly** crucially, decussately.

RELATED KEYWORDS: TEXTILES, TRAVEL, TRAVERSING

CUNNING

n. 1.   **1. cunning** art, artifice, chicanery, craft, double-dealing, duplicity, finesse, fraud, gimmickry, guile, guilefulness, hocus-pocus, Jesuitism, Machiavellism, nimbleness, sharp practice, shrewdness, subtleness, subtlety, supersubtlety, trickery. *Informal:* hanky-panky, jiggery-pokery. **2. machination** engineering, enginery, insinuation, machinations, manipulation, politicking. **3. politics** fancy footwork, footwork, intrigue, manoeuvring, strategy. **4. craftiness** archness, artfulness, cleverness, deviousness, diabolicalness, insidiousness, shiftiness, slyness, trickiness, trickishness, tricksiness, wiliness, wryness. **5. astuteness** canniness, cuteness, foxiness, knowingness, sharpness, shrewdness.

2.   **1. stratagem** artifice, arts, catch, con, contrivance, craft, deceit, deception, double, fetch, finesse, fraud, game, gimmick, hoax, jugglery, legerdemain, manoeuvre, plot, roughy, ruse, scheme, shift, sleight of hand, trick, trickery, wile, wiles. *Informal:* angle, caper, dodge, fake, fastie, flim-flam, hanky-panky, have, little game, lurk, roughie, sell, shenanigans, shrewdie, slanter, swiftie, wangle, wheeze *(British)*, wrinkle. **2. bluff** avocation, diversion, evasion, feint, ploy, stew, subterfuge. *Informal:* all smoke and mirrors, put-on, rort. **3. trap** ambuscade, ambush, contrivance, meshes, net, pitfall, web. *Informal:* set-up.

3.   **1. cunning person** artful dodger, dodger, Jesuit, wangler. *Informal:* bag of tricks, shrewdie. **2. confidence man** bluff, bluffer, entrapper, false-pretencer, fraud, grifter *(US)*, illywhacker, lurk man, magsman, paperer, share-pusher, slicker. *Informal:* balancer, bushranger, con, con man, con woman, dud-dropper, fake, faker *(US)*, gypster, mouthman, paperhanger, rorter, shyster, spiv *(Chiefly British)*. **3. machinator** carpetbagger, crimp, insinuator, Machiavellian, political animal, shaver, trophy hunter. *Informal:* downy bird. **4. fox** gamesman, juggler, serpent, trepanner, tricker, trickster, wangler, weasel. *Informal:* duckshover, finagler, slyboots. **5. cheat** bilk, double-dealer, palmer, rook, sharper, trickster. *Informal:* gyp, shicer, spieler, schemer. **6. intriguer** plotter, politician, schemer.

adj. 4.   **1. cunning** calculating, diabolic, guileful, insidious, insinuative, Machiavellian, mephistophelian, oversubtle, sly, subtle, supersubtle, wily. *Informal:* Ikey Mo. **2. crafty** artful, carney, clever, conniving, daedal *(Chiefly Poetic)*, deep, deep-laid, devious, dodgy, hard-headed, Jesuitic, Jesuitical, nimble, serpentine, smart, sneaking, tricksy, wry. **3. astute** canny, foxlike, foxy, knowing, sharp, shrewd, smart. *Informal:* all there. **4. underhand** arch, carney, furtive, shifty, sleekit, sleeky, slick, sly, underhanded, weasely. *Informal:* leery, shoofty, spivvy. **5. tricky** catchy, gimmicky, rorty, slippery, sneaky, trick, trickish, tricksy. **6. diversionary** distracting, feinting. **7. politic** manipulatory, strategic, strategical.

v. **5.** **1. beguile** beguile someone of something, bluff, deceive, delude, fluff, trick into, wile, wrong-foot. *Informal:* con, do someone brown, handle, sell someone the dummy. **2. hook** catch, catch out, inveigle, mislead. *Informal:* rope in. **3. wangle** *Informal:* finagle. **4. outsmart** circumvent, outfox, outjockey, outmanoeuvre, outwit, overreach, steal a march on, undercut. *Informal:* euchre, pull a fast one (or a swiftie), stonker. **5. machinate** brew, cast, compass, concoct, contrive, engineer, feint, manipulate, mastermind. *Informal:* cook up, wangle. **6. insinuate** fish, wheedle, wriggle. **7. intrigue** cabal, collude, conspire, contrive, plan, plot, scheme. **8. be quick-witted** live by one's wits. *Informal:* know a thing or two, not (or never) miss a trick. **9. cheat** *Informal:* doublecross, sell, take for a ride, two-time. **10. ambush** crimp, ensnare, entrap.

RELATED KEYWORDS: DECEPTION, INTELLIGENCE, PLAN

CURIOSITY

n. **1.** **1. curiosity** curiousness, inquisitiveness, nosiness. **2. thirst for knowledge** inquiring mind. **3. morbid curiosity** pruriency, voyeurism. **4. curio** conversation piece, peepshow.

     2. **1. curious person** busybody, eavesdropper, inquisitive, nosy parker, peeping Tom, prier, pry, pryer, quidnunc, stickybeak, voyeur. *Informal:* butt, buttinski, earwig, gig, rubberneck.

adj. **3.** **1. curious** agog, agog with, inquiring, interrogatory, questioning. **2. inquisitive** curious, meddlesome, prying. *Informal:* nosy, rubberneck, squizzy.

v. **4.** **1. be curious** ferret, have a good look (around), make inquiry (or inquiries), nose about, nose after (or for), nose into, nose out, poke about (or around), poke one's nose into, pry, root around, smell out, stickybeak, wonder. *Informal:* dig into, rubberneck, snoop.

adv. **5.** **1. inquisitively** agog, curiously, nosily, pryingly, questioningly.

RELATED KEYWORDS: ATTENTION, SURPRISE, PARTICIPATION

CURVE

n. **1.** **1. curve** arc, arch, bow, camber, crispation, crook, hook, roll, scallop, sinus, tumblehome, undulation, wave. **2. arithmetic curve** bell curve, cardioid, catenary, cissoid, conchoid, conic section, cycloid, envelope, epicycloid, folium, geodesic, geodesic line, gradient, hyperbola, hypocycloid, inflection, inflexion, locus, parabola, quadrant, rhumb, rhumb line, segment, sine wave, sinusoid, synergic curve, trajectory, trochoid. **3. caustic** catacaustic, diacaustic. **4. figure eight** analemma, lemniscate. **5. bend** bight, flexure, gooseneck, heel, inflection, inturn, offset, ogee, quirk, S-bend, S-shaped bend, sheer, sigmoid flexure, sinuosities, swan neck, turn, twist, winding. **6. loop** folium, hank, lug, picot. **7. crescent** half-moon, lune, lunette, lunula, lunule, meniscus, semicircle. **8. horseshoe** shoe, U-bolt. **9. hook** butcher's hook, carlisle, crook, crotchet, falx, fishhook, fleshhook, ganghook, sickle, uncinus, uncus.

     2. **1. curvature of the spine** gibbousness, humpback, hunchback, kyphosis, lordosis, roach back, scoliosis, stoop, sway-back.

     3. **1. type of arch** acute arch, arcade, arch, arching, archlet, archway, extrados, flying buttress, fornix, Gothic arch, haunch, intrados, lancet arch, ogive, pointed arch, Roman arch, skew arch, soffit, squinch. **2. type of dome** calotte, cloche, cupola, dome, geodesic dome, hemicycle, hemisphere, hemispheroid, pericline, radome, semidome, thole, tholus. **3. type of vault** arcade, barrel vault, fornix, vault, vaulting. **4. beading** bead, cavetto, echinus, ovolo, quad, quadrant moulding, torus. **5. foil** foliation, multifoil, trefoil.

     4. **1. curvature** arcuation, bent, concaveness, concavity, convexity, convexness, curvedness, spiling. **2. curling** assurgency, curl, flexure, incurvature, inversion, resupination, retroflexion. **3. waviness** damascene, damask, sinuosity.

adj. **5.** **1. curved** bent, bow, bowed, bowlike, cambered, crooked, incurvate, loopy, rounded, saddle-backed, sigmoid, sigmoidal. **2. U-shaped** horseshoe. **3. hooked** crooked, crotchety, falcate, falciform, hamate, hook-shaped, hooky, quirky, scorpioid, sickle-shaped, unciform, uncinate, uncinated. **4. convex** biconcave, biconvex, concave, concavo-convex, convexo-concave, convexo-convex, lenticular. **5. crescent** crescent-shaped, horned, lunar, lunarian, lunate, lunular, lunulate, lunulated, meniscoid, semilunar. **6. heart-shaped** bell-shaped, cordate, flabellate, flabelliform, obcordate, pear-shaped. **7. semicircular** hemicyclic, semielliptical.

6. **1. curvilinear** conchoidal, curvilineal, epicycloidal, hypocycloidal. **2. geodesic** caustic, geodetic, geodetical, toric, toroidal. **3. wavy** damascene, gyrose, marcel, repand, undulative, undulatory, wavelike. **4. parabolic** catenary, hyperbolic, hyperbolical, paraboloidal, sinusoidal, trochoidal. **5. blunt** lobate, obtuse. **6. recurvate** assurgent, resupinate, retroflex, retrorse, retroussé, revolute, tip-tilted.

7. **1. domed** arched, arcuate, arcuated, beehive, domelike, round, testudinate, vaulted, vaultlike, waggon-headed, wagon-headed. **2. hemispherical** hemispheric, hemispheroidal.

v. **8.** **1. curve** arch, bend, bow, camber, circumflex, curl, flex, hog, incurve, loop, overarch, sag, stoop, sweep, turn. **2. recurve** retroflect. **3. hook** crook, incurvate. **4. wave** scallop, undulate.

adv. **9.** **1. curvedly** wavily. **2. convexly** archwise, concavely.

RELATED KEYWORDS: BULGE, FOLD, ROUNDNESS, SLOPE, TWIST

CUSTOM

n. **1.** **1. custom** a matter of course, cliché, common practice, constitution, consuetude, convention, course, established custom, habit, habitude, institute, institution, practice, praxis, second nature, usage, usual practice, wont. **2. routine** beaten track, commonplace, daily round, groove, rut, the daily grind, the ordinary, the usual, treadmill. **3. protocol** etiquette, good form, manners, the (done) thing. **4. mores** the conventionalities, the proprieties, ways. **5. tradition** culture, culture complex, folklore, folkways, oral tradition, survival, traditionalism, unwritten law, way of our forebears. **6. procedure** fashion, manner, mode, way, way of doing things. **7. ceremony** ceremonial, exercises *(US)*, observance, rite, rite of passage, ritual.

2. **1. customariness** accustomedness, generalness, normality, ordinariness, regularity, staidness, triteness, usualness. **2. habitualness** inveteracy, inverterateness, wontedness.

3. **1. habituation** acclimatisation, conditioning, hardening, inurement, naturalisation, seasoning, training.

adj. **4.** **1. customary** accustomed, consuetudinary, habitual, habitudinal, usual, wont. **2. traditional** accepted, conventional, time-honoured, trad, traditionary, traditive. **3. approved** de rigueur, established, recognised, settled. **4. regular** common, commonplace, familiar, general, normal, ordinary, plebeian, run-of-the-mill, simple, stock, trivial, usual. **5. stereotyped** banal, clichéd, common, commonplace, hack, hackneyed, stale, threadbare, tired, trite, unoriginal. **6. rooted in tradition** folkloristic, passed on by word of mouth, unwritten.

v. **5.** **1. be accustomed to** be always at, be given to, be in the habit of, be used to, be wont to, do regularly, go in for, make a habit of, make a practice of, perform regularly, practise, take to, take up.

6. **1. habituate** acclimate *(US)*, acclimatise, accustom, condition, enure, familiarise, harden, inure to, naturalise, season, wont.

adv. **7.** **1. customarily** as a rule, commonly, generally, in general, normally, ordinarily, regularly, usually. **2. habitually** by force of habit, by habit, inveterately, wontedly. **3. as usual** according to habit, as can be expected.

8. **1. ritually** ceremonially, ceremoniously, ritualistically, traditionally.

RELATED KEYWORDS: FASHION, FORMALITY, MEDIOCRITY, ORDINARINESS, REGULARITY

CUT

n. **1.** **1. cut** fissure, gash, incision, kerf, laceration, lancination, nick, rent, score, scotch, slash, slit, snick, snip, stab, tear. **2. notch** box, chip, cleft, crenature, crop, dap, gain, hack, incisure, indent, indentation, indention, indenture, nock, undercut. **3. scarification** chatter marks, graze, scoring. **4. cross-section** crosscut, exsection, microtomy, section, transection. **5. haircut** shave. *Informal:* Dad'n'Dave. **6. shear** long blow, second cut.

2. **1. cutting** bushing, clipping, mowing, pruning, rod pruning, xylotomy. **2. severance** curtailment, decapitation, decerebration, dissection, disseveration. **3. carving** engraving, rifling, tapping, turnery, whittling. **4. surgery** abscission, amputation, circumcision, excision, microsurgery, necrotomy, nephrotomy, trepanation, vivisection. **5. timber-getting** bush bashing, bush-falling, clear-felling, logging, lumbering *(Chiefly US, Canadian)*, scrub bashing.

3. **1. knife** balisong, barong, bowie knife, breadknife, budding knife, butterfly knife, butterknife, carver, carving knife, case-knife, clicking knife, corer, drawknife, drawshave, fish knife, French knife, fruit knife, hunting knife, kukri, leilira, palette knife, pallet knife, paperknife, parang, pigsticker, putty knife, sheath-knife, skean, sock knife, steel, ulu. *Informal:* shiv *(British)*. **2. dagger** anlace, crease, creese, dirk, keris, knife, kris, misericord, poniard, skean, stiletto, stylet. **3. clasp knife** dover, flick-knife, jackknife, penknife, pigsticker, pocketknife, Stanley knife, Swiss Army knife, switchblade. **4. heavy knife** cleaver, cradle, cradle scythe, froe, machete, panga, pruning hook, pruning knife, runner, scythe, sickle, swingle. **5. scalpel** bistoury, guillotine, lance, lancet. **6. razor** cutthroat, safety razor, shaver. **7. blade** edge, edge tool, knife, knife edge, runner, slice bar, tool.

4. **1. sword** épée, anlace, ataghan, backsword, bayonet, blade, broadsword, claymore, cold steel, cutlass, estoc, Excalibur, falchion, foil, hanger, katana, knife, kris, lil-lil, prog, rapier, sabre, scimitar, sgian dubh, simitar, smallsword, steel, sticker, sword bayonet, tanto, Toledo, wakazashi, yataghan.

5. **1. axe** battleaxe, broadaxe, celt, chopper, cleaver, Douglas, fasces, hack, hatchet, iceaxe, kelly, meataxe, mogo, palstave, poleaxe, sax, scutch, tomahawk, tommyaxe, twibill, vouge. *Informal:* tommyhawk.

6. **1. saw** back-saw, bandsaw, bowsaw, breakdown saw, bucksaw, bush saw, bushman's saw, buzz-saw, chainsaw, circular saw, cold saw, compass saw, coping saw, crosscut saw, crown saw, diamond saw, docking saw, framesaw, fretsaw, gangmill, gangsaw, goose saw, grubsaw, hacksaw, handsaw, hargan, hargan saw, jigsaw, muley saw *(US)*, panel saw, pitsaw, planer saw, ripsaw, scroll-saw, tenon saw, trepan, trephine, whipsaw.

7. **1. scissors** clippers, nail scissors. **2. shears** b-bows, blades, bog-eye, bogghi, bows, clips, daggers, dover, hand shears, handpiece, lizard, shear, wool shears. *Informal:* jingling Johnnies, swords, tongs. **3. clipper** bill, billhook, clippers, grass-clipper, pinking shears, pruning shears, secateurs, snips, tinsnips.

8. **1. chisel** adze, boaster, bolster, burin, cold chisel, crosscut chisel, drove, firmer chisel, gouge, graver, hack hammer, hardy, icebreaker, leilira, neolith, osteotome, pitching tool, quarrel, set chisel, sett, spud.

9. **1. cutter** cheese cutter, cigar-cutter, glass-cutter, guillotine, microtome. **2. cutting machine** burr, capstan lathe, chaser, chipper, decapitator, dicer, die, guillotine, lathe, machine tool, milling machine, mincer, scarificator, scarifier, scorer, skiver, tap. **3. mower** header, lawnmower, reaper, reaping machine, ride-on mower, sit-on mower, slasher.

10. **1. woodcutter** axeman, bush-faller *(NZ)*, bush-feller, busher, bushman, cedar-getter, chopper, cutter, faller, feller, gooseman, hewer, jacker, logger, lumberjack *(Chiefly US, Canadian)*, lumberman, scrub-cutter, skiddy, sleeper cutter, splitter, stumper, swamper *(US)*, tiersman *(SA)*, timber-getter, top dog, topnotcher, underdog, woodman, woodsman. *Informal:* bushwhacker *(NZ)*, jarrah jerker *(WA)*, slabby *(NZ)*, stick-picker. **2. sawyer** breaker-down, crosscutter *(NZ)*, sawer.

adj. **11.** **1. cut** cleft, cloven, cut-up, incised, split. **2. clipped** trimmed. **3. diced** brunoise, fine-cut, julienne. **4. carved** carven *(Poetic)*, chiselled, engraved, step-cut, table-cut, trap-cut. **5. clear-cut** clear-felled.

12. **1. cutting** slashing. **2. jagged** jaggy, lacerate, lacerated, laciniate, retuse. **3. scissile** cleavable, dissectible, fellable, fissile, lacerable, sectile, severable.

13. **1. bladed** carinal, carinated, serrated, two-edged. **2. knife-edged** cutthroat. **3. incisive** carnassial, keen, mordacious, sharp. **4. sectorial** incisory, laniary. **5. bladelike** carinate, ensiform, gladiate, sword-shaped, xiphoid.

v. **14.** **1. cut** bite, bite into, carve up, chine, gash, gride, heckle, hew, knife, lance, prick, scissor, scotch, shear, slash, slit, snip, tool, trench, vivisect. **2. slice** carve, cross-section, crosscut, section, skive, thickness, transect. **3. scratch** carbonado, claw, crimp, graze, hack, hackle, overscore, rake, rase, scarify, score, scribe. **4. notch** blaze, chase, crenel, crenellate, gain, indent, jag, nick, nock, pink, serrate, snick, trench, undercut. **5. carve** chisel, engrave, etch, gouge, incise, rough-hew, sculp, whittle. **6. whittle** edge, hew, snig. **7. bevel** cant, chamfer, countersink, facet, rake. **8. thread** die, rifle, tap. **9. sliver** dice, flitch, hash, mince, ribbon. **10. saw** break down, crosscut, lumber, quartersaw, rip, stave, whipsaw. **11. axe** adze, chip, chop, hack, hew, pickaxe, tomahawk. *Informal:* swing kelly. **12. ringbark** girdle, sap-ring. **13. fell** clear-cut, clear-fell, coppice, cut, dock, hew, knock down *(NZ)*, log, poll, pollard. **14. mutilate** grangerise, lacerate, mangle, rip, slash. **15. cut out** core, excide, excise, exscind, exsect. **16. circumcise** cut *(Aboriginal English)*, decerebrate, resect. **17. behead** decapitate, decollate, guillotine.

15. **1. clip** abridge, abscind, bang, bobtail, crop, curtail, cut short, disbranch, dock, head, hog, manicure, pinch, prune, sever, trim. **2. barber** cut, poll, razor, scalp, shave, shingle.

3. shear barrow, channel, crutch, dag, pink, poll, razor, shave, tomahawk. *Informal:* undress. **4. mow** cut, head, make hay, reap, scythe.

adv. **16.** **1. cuttingly** incisively, keenly, sharply.

RELATED KEYWORDS: FARMING, HEALING, SEPARATION, MACHINE, SHARPNESS

DAMAGE

n. **1.** **1. damage** defacement, disablement, disfeaturement, disfiguration, disfigurement, ill-treatment, molestation. **2. wounding** concision, forging, maiming, mutilation. **3. wreckage** arson, breakage, rack, ruination, sabotage, vandalism, wrack, wreck. **4. wear and tear** wear. **5. disrepair** brokenness, disruption, rack and ruin, ruin, ruination, ruins, unsoundness, waste. **6. shabbiness** dilapidation, raggedness, seediness, worminess, wornness.

2. **1. harm** damage, hurt, ill, injury, mayhem, trespass. **2. detriment** disadvantage, disservice, evil, loss, mischief, prejudice. **3. ruin** havoc, ravage, scaith, waste. **4. bomb damage** blast effect, collateral damage, cratering, ground-shock effect.

3. **1. injury** flesh wound, hurt, lesion, microtrauma, trauma, traumatism, wound. *Informal:* Blighty *(British Military)*. **2. specific injury** bite, black eye, break, bruise, burn, contusion, fracture, graphospasm, greenstick fracture, march fracture, scratch, sprain, stab, stitch, strain, subluxation, welt, writer's cramp. *Informal:* mouse, shiner. **3. grievous bodily harm** GBH. **4. disability** handicap, impediment. **5. limp** claudication, cork leg, flatfoot. *Informal:* corky.

4. **1. harmfulness** corrosiveness, deleteriousness, hurtfulness, injuriousness, nocuousness, noxiousness.

5. **1. damager** blinder, maimer, mangler, molester, mutilator, ravager, ruiner, vandal, waster, wrecker. **2. spoiler** adulterator, contaminator, tarnisher, vitiator. **3. saboteur** diversionist, marplot, underminer.

6. **1. casualty** the walking wounded, wounded, wreck. *Informal:* write-off. **2. amputee**. **3. handicapped person** cripple, defective, paraplegic, quadriplegic, slow worker, the disabled. *Informal:* quad.

adj. **7.** **1. damaged** broken, cracked, defective, disrupt, disserviceable, impaired, on the turn, out of joint, out of order, out of plumb, ruined, screwed, worn-out. *Informal:* buggered, bung, bust, cactus, clapped-out, gone to Gundy, in dock, kaput, on the blink, on the fritz, on the skids, pakaru *(NZ)*. **2. unsound** affected, sick, stricken, unhealthy, unwholesome. **3. discoloured** foxy, stained.

8. **1. injured** battle-scarred, bruised, cork, harmed, maimed, marred, winged *(especially Poetic)*, wounded. *Informal:* corked, in dock. **2. frozen** frostbitten. **3. handicapped** crippled, developmentally disabled, disabled, flat-footed, hipshot, incapacitated, lame, loppy. *Informal:* game, gammy.

9. **1. dilapidated** attrited, beat-up, broken-down, derelict, dog-eared, down at heel, gnarled, moth-eaten, mothy, old, out at elbows, ragged, ramshackle, ratty, ruinous, rusty, scrubby, second-hand, seedy, shabby, shopsoiled, the worse for wear, third-hand, time-worn, toilworn, tumbledown, used, weather-beaten, weathered, weatherworn, well-worn, worn. *Informal:* flea-bitten, grungy, scruffy, tacky.

10. **1. harmful** cariogenic, corrosive, damaging, deleterious, detrimental, evil, hurtful, injurious, mephitic, mischievous, mutilative, nocent, nocuous, noisome, noxious, pernicious, prejudicial, ruinous, scorching, virulent, wearing. **2. bruising** contusive. **3. pestilent** baneful, pernicious, pestiferous, pestilential, putrefactive, saprogenic, saprogenous.

v. **11.** **1. damage** annoy, damnify, grangerise, hack, ill-treat, ill-use, impair, mar, pinch, play hell with, play the (very) devil with, prejudice, vandalise, wrong. **2. devastate** desolate, eat, harry, lay waste to, ravage, smite, waste. **3. undermine** put the skids under, sabotage, white-ant.

12. **1. injure** backstab, break, cut to the quick, harm, hurt, traumatise. **2. wound** beat up, break, concuss, disfeature, draw first blood, fracture, lacerate, run over, shatter, sprain, strain, wing, wrench. **3. maim** bemaul, contort, deface, deform, disfigure, distort, give someone a facial, make mincemeat of, mangle, mutilate. **4. bruise** contuse, jam. **5. stab** bayonet, bite, feather, impale, knife, lance, pike, pink, prick, run through, spear, spit, spur, stick. *Informal:* carve up. **6. cripple** disable, hamstring, hock, incapacitate, lame, nobble, scotch. **7. cut one's (own) throat** cut off one's nose to spite one's face, self-harm, self-injure, shoot oneself in the foot.

13. **1. break** burst, crack, crash, fracture, fragment, hole, rupture, shatter, smash, snap, stave, stave in, tear, wrench. *Informal:* bust, ding, prang. **2. crush** chew, chew up, scrumple, scrunch, smash.

14. **1. spoil** addle, befoul, blast, blight, canker, contaminate, defile, deflower, deprave, empoison, infect, pervert, poison, soil, sully, taint, tarnish, vitiate. *Informal:* doctor. **2. corrupt** adulterate, bastardise, commercialise, debase, empoison, prostitute. **3. wreck** abort, blunder, botch, botch up, break, bungle, butcher, dig one's own grave, fail, flub, foozle, graunch *(Chiefly NZ)*, hinder, make a hash of, mull, puckeroo, pukaru, ruin, scupper *(British)*, trip. *Informal:* balls something up, bitch, blow, bugger up, cook, cruel, cruel (or queer) someone's pitch, dud up, foul up, gum up, gum up the works, louse up, make a muck of, make a muff of, muck, muck up, muff, pakaru *(NZ)*, queer.

adv. 15. **1. harmfully** damagingly, hurtfully, injuriously, nocuously, noxiously, pestiferously, pestilently, ruinously. **2. detrimentally** corrosively, deleteriously, for the worse.

RELATED KEYWORDS: ATTACK, DESTRUCTION, BADNESS, DETERIORATION, IMPERFECTION

DANCING

n. 1. **1. dancing** ballet, light fantastic, modern dance, old-time dancing, performance art, the dance. **2. frisk** caper, frolic, gambol, leap, saltation, skip. **3. choreography** ballet, choreology.

2. **1. dance** ball, dance party, dinner dance, factory party, fancy-dress ball, fandango *(US)*, formal, masked ball, rave, rave party, ridotto, warehouse party. *Informal:* fifty-fifty, hop, knees-up, prom *(US)*. **2. breakdance** rap dance. **3. disco** blue-light disco.

3. **1. dancer** almah, alme, B-boy, B-girl, belly dancer, bootscooter, breakdancer, clog-dancer, crowd surfer, exotic dancer, frisker, glider, go-go girl, groovers and shakers, jitterbug, line dancer, macho dancer, male stripper, pole dancer, prancer, rapdancer, rope-dancer, shuffler, square-dancer, stripper, tangoist, tap dancer, terpsichorean, wiredancer. *Informal:* hoofer *(US)*. **2. ballet dancer** ballerina, ballet, corps de ballet, coryphée, danseur, danseuse, figurant, figurante, prima ballerina. **3. partner** gentleman dance host, gigolo, hostess, taxi dancer *(US)*. **4. choreographer** choreologist, dance arranger.

4. **1. types of dance** écossaise, adagio, allemande, apache dance, barn dance, batucada, beguine, belly dance, bergamasque, blue-light dance, bolero, boogaloo, bootscooting, bossa, bossa nova, bourrée, branle, brawl, breakdancing, breakdown *(US)*, bridal waltz, bugaku, bump, bus stop, cachucha, cakewalk, Canadian twostep, cancan, capoeira, carioca, carmagnole, ceroc, cha-cha, cha-cha-cha, chaconne, charleston, chorus, clog dance, clown dance, conga, contredanse, cotillion, courante, crowd-surfing, csardas, cucaracha, czardas, dance of death, danse macabre, dirty dancing, disco, disco dancing, dragon dance, drongo, eightsome, eurhythmics, excuse-me *(British)*, exhibition dancing, fan dance, fandango, farandole, flamenco, fling, foxtrot, frug, fruit, gagaku, galliard, gallo-pade, galop, gavotte, gigue, gopak, habanera, haka, havanaise, hay, headbanging, hey, Highland fling, hoedown, hokey-pokey, hop, hornpipe, house funk, hula, hula-hula, hustle, international dancing, jazz, jazz ballet, jig, jitterbug, jive, joget, jota, juba, kan-garoo dance, knees-up, krump, ländler, lambada, lancers, lap dance, Latin American, lavolta, limbo, linedance, linedancing, liturgical dancing, locomotion, macarena, madison, malaguena, mambo, mashed potato, mazurka, minuet, moshing, nautch, onestep, pas, pas de deux, pas seul, paso doble, passacaglia, passepied, pavan, penguin, petronella, polacca, polka, polonaise, poussette, Pride of Erin, pyrrhic, quadrille, rap dance, rap dancing, redowa, reel, rigadoon, rock'n'roll, rope-dance, round dance, roundel, roundelay, rumba, sacred dancing, salsa, saltarello, salterello, samba, saraband, schottische, seguidilla, shake, shimmy, shuffle, sicilienne, Sir Roger de Coverley, slam dancing, snowball, soft-shoe shuffle, square dance, stage diving, stomp, strathspey, street dancing, strip the willow, sun dance, swim, sword dance, tambourin, tango, tap dance, tarantella, techno-dancing, time warp, touch dancing, trance dancing, turkey trot, twist, twostep, Tyrolienne, valeta, valse, variation, veleta, Virginia reel, vogueing, volta, waltz, war dance, watusi, whiddershins, wiredancing, zapateado. **2. bush dancing** clogdancing, folk dancing, morris, morris dance, square dancing. **3. barn dance** B & S, B & S ball, bush dance, country dance, hoedown, moondance, woolshed hop. **4. whitefella dancing** *(Aboriginal English)* disco dancing *(Aboriginal English)*.

5. **1. dance movements** allemande, arabesque, assemblé, attitude, balance, battement, cabriole, chassé, dosido, elevation, entrechat, figure, figure of eight, flicflac, glide, glissade, maze, mirror exercise, pas, pigeonwing, pirouette, plié, position, poussette, promenade, quickstep, shuffle, step, telemark, tittup. *Informal:* bump and grind. **2. routine** phrase, set.

6. 1. dance hall ballroom, disco, discothèque, discotheque, palais, palais de danse. *Informal:* honky-tonk *(Chiefly US)*.

adj. **7. 1. terpsichorean** dance, dancing.

v. **8. 1. dance** boogie, bootscoot, dance the night away, frisk, jig, prance, shuffle, tread, tread a measure, trip, trip the light fantastic. *Informal:* cut a rug *(Chiefly US)*, have a bop, hoof it, hop, skank. **2. jive** alemana turn, bop, frug, jitterbug, rock, shimmy, stomp, twist. *Informal:* bump and grind. **3. foxtrot** cakewalk, dosido, mambo, polka, square-dance, tango, twostep, waltz. **4. pirouette** balance, chassé, glissade, poussette, promenade, set. **5. breakdance** break, rapdance. **6. choreograph**.

RELATED KEYWORDS: ENTERTAINER, ENTERTAINMENT, MUSIC

DANGER

n. **1. 1. danger** a matter of life and death, hazard, jeopardy, peril. **2. risk** adventure, chance, gamble, hazard, lottery, throw. **3. threat** menace, sabre-rattling, shadow, sword of Damocles. *Informal:* dynamite. **4. hazard** awkwardness, blind alley, dilemma, double bind, hot spot, impasse, pit, pitfall, predicament, quandary, risk, vicious circle. *Informal:* a trap for young players, catch 22, hot seat, pickle, spot, three-day night. **5. safety risk** black spot, deathtrap, fire hazard, fire risk, firetrap, trap, vigia. *Informal:* snorter. **6. minefield** no-man's-land.

2. 1. dangerousness chanciness, criticalness, desperateness, forbiddingness, imperilment, ominousness, perilousness, precariousness, seriousness, venturesomeness. **2. endangerment** imperilment, obnoxiousness.

3. 1. vulnerability indefensibility, indefensibleness, insecurity, nakedness, susceptibility, unguardedness, unsafeness, unsafety, untenability, unwariness, vulnerableness. **2. weak spot** Achilles heel, chink in one's armour, hazardousness, incertitude, insecurity, soft underbelly. **3. black spot** no-man's-land, open ground.

4. 1. hazarder brinkman, dice man, equilibrist, hellraiser, soldier of fortune, stunt double, stuntman, thrillseeker, tightrope-walker. *Informal:* shark bait. **2. brinkmanship**.

adj. **5. 1. dangerous** critical, forbidding, hazardous, parlous, perilous, precarious, risky, touch-and-go, unsafe, venturous. *Informal:* dicey, kamikaze, unhealthy. **2. risky** awkward, equilibristic, hazardous, kittle *(Scottish)*, parlous, perilous, ticklish, touchy, unreliable, venturesome. *Informal:* chancy, dicey, dodgy, hard-hat, iffy, tropical. **3. ominous** black, boding, critical, fatal, fateful, fatidic, foreboding, grave, heavy, illboding, imminent, impendent, impending, inauspicious, malignant, menacing, oracular, pendent, portentous, predictive, prophetic, sinister, threatening. **4. suicidal** banzai, breakneck, dangerous, desperate, forlorn, forlorn hope, hazardous, last-ditch. *Informal:* kamikaze.

6. 1. vulnerable bareheaded, defenceless, derelict, insecure, naked, obnoxious, solitary, unarmed, unassured, unattended, uncovered, undefended, unguarded, unprotected, unsafe, unsecured, unwary. **2. indefensible** untenable. *Informal:* dicky.

v. **7. 1. risk** adventure, chance, gamble, give a hostage to fortune, hazard, tempt fortune, try one's fortune, try one's luck. **2. dare** adventure, brave, chance one's arm, court disaster, enter the lion's den, gamble, live dangerously, play a dangerous game, presume, risk, run the gauntlet, tempt fate, tempt providence, venture, walk into the dragon's mouth. *Informal:* buy into trouble. **3. play with fire** be between Scylla and Charybdis, be in danger, be in dire straits, be in harm's way, be on the brink, be on the precipice, be out on a limb, bell the cat, dice with death, hang by a thread, ride for a fall, run the gauntlet, run the risk of, sail too near the wind, skate on thin ice, take one's life in one's hands, walk a slackwire, walk a tightrope. *Informal:* play chicken.

8. 1. endanger catch, compromise, ensnare, entrap, expose, imperil, insnare, jeopardise, net, peril, put the skids under, risk. **2. menace** bode ill, intimidate, overshadow, terrorise, threaten. *Informal:* put the heat on.

adv. **9. 1. dangerously** adventurously, critically, desperately, hazardously, ominously, parlously, perilously, precariously. **2. threateningly** forbiddingly, malignantly, menacingly. **3. vulnerably** indefensibly, insecurely, unguardedly, unwarily. **4. riskily** at hazard, awkwardly, venturously. **5. on the spot** on thin ice.

RELATED KEYWORDS: RASHNESS, MENACE, WARNING

DARK

n. **1. 1. dark** darkness, gloom, shades, shadows. **2. night** hours of darkness, moonset, night-tide, night-time, the dead of night. **3. nightfall** candlelight, crepuscule, dusk, evening, gloaming *(Poetic)*, half-light, sundown, sunset, twilight. **4. eclipse** annular eclipse, occultation, partial eclipse, solar eclipse, total eclipse. **5. blackout** brownout, dim-out *(US)*, lights out, outage.

2. 1. shade penumbra, shadow, umbra. **2. cloud** fog, lour, mirk, mist, murk, smog, smoke. **3. pall** covering, shroud.

3. 1. darkness blackness, gloominess, greyness, pitchiness, sootiness. **2. opacity** obscureness, obscurity, opaqueness. **3. shadiness** sunlessness, umbrageousness. **4. dimness** bleariness, cloudiness, dullness, duskiness, sombreness. **5. murkiness** dirtiness, fogginess, mistiness, smokiness.

4. 1. darkening obfuscation, obscuration, occultation, overshadowing, shadowing. **2. shading** chiaroscuro, crosshatching, hatching.

5. 1. darkener blackener, dimmer, eclipser, fader. **2. blind** shade. **3. type of blind** holland blind, jalousie, roman blind, venetian, venetian blind. **4. sunglasses** dark glasses. *Informal:* polaroids, shades.

adj. **6. 1. dark** aphotic, benighted, cimmerian, darkish, darkling *(Poetic)*, darksome *(Poetic)*, gloomy, lightless, midnight, obscurant, obscure, pitch-black, pitch-dark, rayless, starless, stygian, unilluminated. **2. dark-coloured** black, blackish, coal-black, dusky, fuliginous, grey, infuscate, inky, piceous, pitchy, raven, sable *(Poetic)*, sombre, sooty. **3. dark-skinned** coloured, swarthy. **4. ecliptic** blinding, ecliptical, opaque, umbral.

7. 1. shadowy adumbral, bosky, bowery, darkened, gloomy, obscure, penumbral, shaded, shady, tenebrific, tenebrous, umbrageous, umbriferous. **2. twilight** crepuscular, dusk, duskish. **3. dim** darkish. **4. dull** bleary, cloudy, dingy, dirty, dismal, foggy, gloomy, hazy, heavy, lacklustre, lowering, mirky, misty, murky, nubilous, overcast, sad, smoky, sombre, subfusc, sunless, thick.

v. **8. 1. darken** black, blacken, dusk, embrown, nigrify, opaque. **2. become dark** darken, darkle, dim, dusk, fade, fog, grow dark, lour. **3. obscure** adumbrate, becloud, befog, blanket out, blind, blot, cloud, cover, darken, eclipse, enshroud, envelop, obfuscate, overcast, overcloud, overshade, overshadow, shade, shroud. **4. black out** brown out, turn down the lights, turn out the lights. **5. shade** crosshatch, hatch, shadow, silhouette.

adv. **9. 1. darkly** blackly, gloomily, greyly. **2. in the dark** darkling *(Poetic)*, in the shadows. **3. ecliptically** blindingly. **4. dimly** duskily. **5. murkily** cloudily, foggily, loweringly, smokily. **6. obscurely** opaquely.

RELATED KEYWORDS: DISAPPEARANCE, INVISIBILITY

DAY

n. **1. 1. day** broad daylight, daylight, daytime, light.

2. 1. morning a.m., ack-emma, ante meridiem, forenoon, midmorning, morn *(Poetic)*, morning time *(Aboriginal English)*. **2. dawn** break of day, cockcrow, cockcrowing, dawning, daybreak, daylight, dayspring *(Poetic)*, light, morning, piccaninny dawn, piccaninny daylight, sun-up, sunrise. *Informal:* sparrow fart. **3. small hours** matins, prime. **4. breakfast-time** brunch, elevenses *(British)*. **5. morning song** aubade, dawn chorus, dawn serenade.

3. 1. noon mean noon, midday, midnoon, noonday, noontide, noontime. **2. lunchtime** big lunch *(Chiefly Qld, NSW and ACT)*, dinnertime, lunch.

4. 1. afternoon afternoons, dinnertime, evening *(Qld)*, midafternoon, p.m.. *Informal:* aftie, afto, arvo.

adj. **5. 1. daily** diurnal. **2. auroral** dawnlike. **3. morning** antemeridian, breakfast-time, forenoon, matin, matutinal, midmorning. **4. midday** lunchtime, meridian, midnoon, noon, noonday. **5. afternoon** midafternoon, postmeridian.

adv. **6. 1. daily** all day, day by day, diurnally, morning, noon, and night, overday. **2. a.m.** ante meridiem, matutinally. **3. p.m.** post meridiem.

RELATED KEYWORDS: EARLINESS, LIGHT, PERIOD

DEAFNESS

n. **1. 1. deafness** anacusis, anakusis, deaf-mutism, faulty hearing, tone-deafness. **2. deaf person** deaf-mute, the Deaf.

2. 1. hearing aid acoustic, all-in-the-ear hearing aid, audiphone, deaf-aid, dentiphone, ear trumpet, trumpet. **2. hearing dog**. **3. sign language** American Sign Language, Ameslan, Auslan, Australian Sign Language, dactylology, deaf-and-dumb language, fingertalk. **4. signing** fingertalking, lip-reading.

adj. **3. 1. deaf** deaf and dumb, deaf-mute, hard of hearing, hearing-impaired, stone-deaf, tone-deaf. *Informal:* deaf as a doorpost, deaf as a post. **2. deafened** unable to hear. **3. deaf to** not listening, unhearing.

v. **4.** **1. be deaf** have a hearing problem, not hear. **2. turn a deaf ear** be deaf to, not listen. **3. fall on deaf ears. 4. deafen** split the eardrums.

5. **1. sign** fingertalk, lip-read, read someone's lips, use sign language.

RELATED KEYWORDS: SILENCE

DEATH

n. **1.** **1. death** biolysis, decease, demise, dissolution, dying, end, ending, grave, great divide, mort, one's hour, parting, passing, passing away, release, sticky end, time. **2. megadeath** massacre, slaughter. **3. lifelessness** cadaverousness, coldness, deadness, defunctness, exanimation, inanimateness, moribundity, mortification, rigor mortis. **4. means of death** asphyxiation, brain death, choking to death, crucifixion, drowning, famishment, freezing to death, hanging, heart attack, natural death, starvation, strangulation, suffocation. **5. cot death** SIDS, sudden infant death syndrome. **6. stillbirth. 7. euthanasia** active euthanasia, mercy killing, passive euthanasia. **8. suicide** race suicide, self-murder. **9. martyrdom** supreme sacrifice. **10. doom** bane, death sentence, fate, Götterdämmerung, sentence of death. **11. death penalty** black cap, capital punishment, death cell, death sentence, execution. **12. personification of death** Death, the grim reaper. **13. death's-head** black, crossbones, marrowbone, marrowbones, skull and crossbones. **14. dance of death** danse macabre. **15. deathwatch** death bell, death knell, passing bell, wake. **16. death throes** at death's door, death rattle, deathbed, dying day, last agony, last breath, last gasp, last hour, last words, swan song. **17. death-wish** death wish, thanatophobia, thanatopsis. **18. necromania** necrophilia, necrophilism, necrophobia. **19. coup de grâce** death blow. **20. death machine** electric chair.

2. **1. last resting place** catacombs, cist, confession, crypt, cubiculum, grave, hypogeum, mastaba, mausoleum, samadhi *(Indian English)*, sepulchre, tomb, vault. **2. deathbed. 3. mortuary** morgue. **4. death certificate.**

3. **1. the dead** dearly departed, ghosts, loved ones, shades, the deceased, the defunct, the departed, those who have gone before. **2. corpse** ashes, body, cadaver, carcase, carcass, last remains, mummy, relics. *Informal:* stiff. **3. casualty** fatality. **4. zombie** walking dead. **5. death rate** casualty list, death register, death toll, deathroll, mortality, mortality rate, necrology, road toll. **6. war dead** casualties, losses, the fallen, the slain.

adj. **4.** **1. dead** cold, deceased, defunct, departed, exanimate, fallen, gone, inanimate, lifeless, no more, stillborn, stone-cold, stone-dead. *Informal:* dead as a dodo, dead as a doornail, deadybones, done for, sleeping with the fishes. **2. deceased** asleep, at rest, departed, lamented, late, mourned, regretted, sainted. **3. mortal** earthborn, ephemeral, evanescent, fleeting, fugacious, passing, perishable, short-lived, transient, transitory. **4. doomed** condemned to death, fey. **5. dying** done for, moribund, sick unto death. *Informal:* far gone. **6. extinct** defunct, moribund.

5. **1. deathlike** biolytic, deathful, deathly, funeral, ghastly, macabre. **2. corpselike** cadaveric, cadaverous. **3. posthumous** defunctive, post-mortem, post-obit.

6. **1. deadly** anaplastic, deathful, deathly, fatal, fateful, killing, lethal, malignant, mortal, pernicious, sublethal, terminal.

v. **7.** **1. die** be gathered to one's fathers, breathe one's last, decease, depart, die off, die on someone, drop, end, exit, expire, go, go the way of all flesh, go to one's account, part, pass away, pass by on the other side, pass on, perish, predecease, stop, succumb, terminate. *Informal:* be carried out feet first, buy it, buy the farm *(US)*, cark, cark it, cash in one's chips, chuck a seven, conk out, croak, croak it, do a perish, fall off the perch, flatline, give up the ghost, go west, hop (or fall off) the twig, kark, kick off *(US)*, kick the bucket, pass in one's marble, peg out, pop off, snuff it, throw a seven, turn up one's toes. **2. fall** drop, kiss the dust. *Informal:* bite the dust, lick the dust. **3. lose one's life** asphyxiate, catch one's death, choke, drown, famish, feed the fishes, freeze, smother, starve, stifle, suffocate, walk the plank. *Informal:* swing. **4. commit suicide** die a martyr's death, die for the cause, kill oneself. **5. die down** die, die back, die off, fade, fade away, fade out, fall away, miff, wither, wither away. **6. receive one's death warrant** die the death. **7. be at the point of death** be as good as dead, be at death's door, be written off. *Informal:* be a goner, be curtains, have had it. **8. be dead** be dead and buried, be dead and gone, be no more, lie six feet under. *Informal:* be history, push up daisies. **9. sleep** lie in state, repose, rest. **10. execute** crucify, line up in front of a firing squad, put to death, send to the electric chair, send to the gallows, send to the gas chambers, sign someone's death warrant, stone. **11. kill** assassinate, do away with, murder, slay. *Informal:* bump off, do in, eliminate, rub out, stiff, take out.

RELATED KEYWORDS: NON-EXISTENCE, FUNERAL RITES, KILLING

DECEPTION

n. **1.** **1. deception** abuse of trust, bamboozlement, beguilement, chenanigans, cozenage, craft, cunning, deceit, defraudation, delusion, dupery, equivocation, fast-talking, fraud, guile, hocus-pocus, indirection, intrigue, monkey tricks (or business), sharp practice, stealth, trickery. *Informal:* eyewash, hanky-panky, shenanigans. **2. false pretences** impersonation, personation. **3. deceitfulness** archness, duplicity, humbug, sneakiness, speciousness, stealthiness, surreptitiousness. **4. fraud** artifice, forgery, trick. **5. legerdemain** hocus-pocus, hokey-pokey, jugglery, misdirection. *Informal:* four-flush, jiggery-pokery.

2. **1. act of deception** bilk, bubble, capriccio, cheat, confidence game, confidence trick, deceit, effect, feint, fetch, finesse, juggle, shift, smokescreen, stew, swindle, trickery. *Informal:* caper, chizz *(British)*, con, con job, con trick, do, dodge, fastie, fiddle, fix, flim-flam, frame-up, frost, gyp, have, plant, put-on, racket, rip-off, roughie, sell, set-up, skin game, slanter, snow job, sting, swiftie, swiz, swizzle, take, take-down. **2. hoax** leg-pull, leg-pulling, practical joke, prank, prankery. *Informal:* berley, kid-stakes, sell. **3. legerdemain** hocus-pocus, sleight of hand, trick. *Informal:* hanky-panky. **4. bluff** *Informal:* four-flush. **5. stratagem** line, wile, wiles. *Informal:* angle, wheeze *(British)*, wrinkle. **6. excuse** pretext, subterfuge.

3. **1. deceiver** gay deceiver, Mata Hari. **2. trickster** adventurer, adventuress, bamboozler, beguiler, bluffer, cheat, cheater, conjurer, cozener, defrauder, deluder, diddler, duper, feigner, finagler, flim-flammer, frontman, gypper, hoodwinker, hotpointer, humbug, impersonator, impostor, juggler, personator, rook, sharper, stealer, swindler, swizzler, trepanner, tricker, twister, welsher. *Informal:* fiddler, gyp, shicer, slyboots. **3. confidence man** bushranger, false-pretencer, fraud, grifter *(US)*, illywhacker, lurk man, paperer, share-pusher, slicker, thimblerigger. *Informal:* balancer, con man, dud-dropper, gypster, mouthman, paperhanger, rorter. **4. leg-puller** kidder, ragger. **5. dissembler** actor. **6. hoaxer** gagster, joker, practical joker, prankster, spoofer.

v. **4.** **1. deceive** abuse someone's trust, bamboozle, befool, bluff, catch, cheat, cheat on, delude, dupe, equivocate, fast-talk, foist, foist on (or upon), fool, fox, gull, hocus-pocus, hoodwink, humbug, impose on (or upon), lead the dice, misinform, mislead, swift-talk, take in, throw dust in someone's eyes, trick, wrong-foot. *Informal:* bull, cog the dice, come the double on, come the raw prawn, come the uncooked crustacean, handle, have, have a lend of, have someone on, lead up the garden path, pull (or put over) a fastie, pull (or put over) a swiftie, pull a fast one, pull the wool over someone's eyes, put it across someone, put one over, put over a fast one, sell, string along (or on), suck in, take for a ride, two-time. **2. hoax** fool, joke, make, make a fool of, mock, play a joke on, pull someone's leg, send on a fool's errand, sport with, trifle with. *Informal:* gag, gammon, kid, rag. **3. counterfeit** act, fabricate, fake, fudge. **4. sneak** lurk, sidle, skulk, slink, steal, tiptoe. *Informal:* gumshoe *(US)*, mooch. **5. feint** sell someone the dummy.

5. **1. cheat** beat *(US)*, bilk, bite, brass, clip, cog, con, cozen, defraud, fudge, gudgeon, hoozle, jockey, mountebank, overreach, palm, point, quack, rogue, rook, smuggle, swindle, take down, trick out of, victimise. *Informal:* chisel, diddle, do, do down, do in the eye, do out of, do someone brown, finagle, flim-flam, gyp, hotpoint, nick, ringbolt *(NZ)*, scam, short-change, sting, swizzle, take the palm, welsh, work a slanter.

6. **1. fall for** be deceived, have been had. *Informal:* be sold a pup, bite, have oneself on.

RELATED KEYWORDS: CUNNING, ERROR, DISHONESTY, ROBBERY, THIEF, UNTRUTHFULNESS

DECORATION

n. **1.** **1. decoration** adornment, beautification, bedecking, blazonry, decking, decor, embellishment, embossment, embroidery, encrustation, enrichment, figure, frost, frostwork, garnish, garnishment, garniture, incrustation, moiré, motif, openwork, ornament, ornamentation, pattern, quilling. **2. figuration** arabesque, cuspidation, foliation, gammadion, toreutics, vermiculation. **3. decorativeness** ornamentality. **4. floridness** over-elaboration. **5. interior decoration** paperhanging. **6. bunting** Christmas tree, festoonery, paperchain, streamer. **7. pokerwork** pyrography. **8. scroll** curlicue, flourish, quirk, volute. **9. fretwork** fret, meander, scrollwork. **10. centrepiece** epergne. **11. figurehead** fiddlehead.

2. **1. moulding** Aaron's rod, astragal, baguette, bead, beading, beadwork, bed moulding, bilection, bolection, cable moulding, cabling, cavetto, chain-moulding, chainwork, chaplet, chevron, congé, cordon, dancette, dogtooth, echinus, egg and anchor, egg and dart, fillet, gadroon, gorgerin, necking, ovolo, quad, quadrant moulding, reed, reglet, scotia, string-course, surbase, torus. **2. boss** crocket, knob, pellet, pendant, stud. **3. spur** cusp, finial, griff, poppy, poppyhead, terminal. **4. frieze** ancon, cordon, cornice, dancette, guilloche. **5. crest** antefix, bratticing, brattishing, cresting. **6. fluting** glyph, strigil, triglyph. **7. tablet** banderol, bannerol, cartouche, medallion, metope, plaque. **8. facing** panelling. **9. architrave** archivolt, cased frame, epistyle. **10. roundel** bezant, ovum, rose. **11. tracery** fan tracery. **12. iron lace**.

3. 1. inlay buhl, buhlwork, cross-banding, damascene, intarsia, marquetry, marquetry, mosaic, niello, parquetry, purfle, tarsia. **2. enamelwork** cellulose lacquer, champlevé, cloisonné, enamel, enamelling, Fabergé, japan, japanning, lacquer, tole, varnish.

4. 1. tapestry altarpiece, arras, dossal, dosser, frontlet, hangings, reredos, wall-hanging.

5. 1. trimming border, clock, edging, fringe, lace, orfray, orphrey, passementerie, piping, torsade, trim, trimmings, whipping. *Informal:* fixings. **2. flounce** caparison, falbala, frill, furbelow, gathering, pelmet, ruff, ruffle, shirr, valance. **3. braid** binding, braiding, galloon, gimp. **4. loop** picot, purl. **5. tassel** bobble, pompom, zizith. *Informal:* fandangle. **6. spangle** gilding, gilt, glitter, gold foil, gold leaf, mosaic gold, ormolu, paillette, sequin, tinsel. *Informal:* pearly. **7. gold braid** aiguillette, bullion, cordon, epaulet, gimp, lace, sword knot. **8. plume** aigrette, crest, panache. **9. wheel trim**.

6. 1. jewellery bijouterie, body jewellery, costume jewellery, estate jewellery, paste. *Informal:* tomfoolery. **2. jewel** bijou, brilliant, gem, gemstone, pearl, precious stone, scarab, scarabaeus, solitaire, stone. *Informal:* rock, sparkler. **3. brooch** anaglyph, breastpin, breastplate, broach, cameo, fibula, pin, scatter pin, stickpin, tiepin. **4. bracelet** anklet, armlet, bangle, tennis bracelet, wristlet. **5. ring** circle, circlet, engagement ring, eternity ring, nose-ring, wedding band, wedding ring. **6. necklace** beads, chain, chaplet, choker, collar, collaret, locket, mala, peag, rivière, rope, rosary, strand, string, tennis necklace, torque, wampum. *Informal:* dog-collar. **7. bead** bugle bead, charm, drop, girandola, girandole, pear drop, pendant. **8. earring** chandelier earring, ear stud, eardrop, labret, sleeper. **9. crown** circlet, coronal, coronet, crownpiece, diadem, frontlet, tiara. **10. parure** equipage. **11. filigree** engrailment, filagree, fillagree, gadroon, godroon.

7. 1. ornament bauble, bibelot, bijou, bric-a-brac, falderal, fallal, garden gnome, gaud, gee-gaw, gewgaw, gimcrack, gingerbread, knick-knack, nick-nack, pretties, scrimshaw, toy, trinket, trumpery. *Informal:* doodads. **2. bric-a-brac** pedlary, Victoriana.

8. 1. bookbinding blocking, border, carpet page, coat of arms, crest, dinkus, doublure, fillet, frontispiece, headpiece, illumination, initial, logo, logotype, marbling, panel, rib, tailpiece, tooling, vignette.

9. 1. cosmetic beauty spot, blusher, court plaster, eye shadow, eyeliner, face powder, foundation, greasepaint, highlighter, kohl, liner, lip balm, lippy, lipstick, mascara, nail polish, nail varnish, pancake, pencil, rouge, vanishing cream. *Informal:* lippie, paint. **2. make-up** face paint, maquillage. *Informal:* war paint.

10. 1. decorator adorner, beautifier, detailer, dresser, embellisher, garnisher, window-dresser. **2. interior decorator** interior designer, paperer, paperhanger. **3. carver** embosser, engraver, medallist. **4. jeweller** enamellist, goldsmith, silversmith.

adj. **11. 1. decorative** Christmassy, dressy, elaborate, embroidered, fancy, fine, frosted, highly-wrought, non-functional, ornamental, rich, worked, wrought. **2. florid** alhambresque, baroque, clinquant, flamboyant, luxuriant, ornate, overelaborate, overwrought, plater-esque, rococo, trumpery. **3. bannered** beribboned, cockaded. **4. annular** floreated, floriated, foliate, foliated, geometric, multifoil, runic. **5. enamelled** champlevé, cloi-sonné, gilt-edged, ormolu. **7. cut** engraved, glyptic, incised, step-cut, toreutic, trap-cut. **8. fluted** repoussé. **9. inlaid** inwrought.

v. **12. 1. decorate** adorn, beautify, boss, dress, embellish, emblaze, enrich, fret, frill, frost, furbish, garnish, make up, mould, ornament, titivate, trim. **2. array** attire, bedeck, bespangle, deck out, dress, dress up, habit, lair up, overdress, preen, primp, prink, titivate, trim. *Informal:* rig out (or up). **3. bejewel** bespangle, powder, set, stud. **4. over-elaborate** *Informal:* pansy up, tart up. **5. pattern** detail, dice, figure, trace, vermicu-late, wreathe. **6. festoon** dress ship, flag. **7. pink** engrail.

adv. **13. 1. decoratively** adorningly, dressily, glitteringly, ornamentally, richly. **2. luxuriantly** floridly, overelaborately.

RELATED KEYWORDS: BEAUTY, CLOTHES, SHAPE, SHOWINESS, TEXTILES

DECREASE

n. **1. 1. decrease** abatement, contraction, damping, decrement, depletion, detumescence, diminution, lessening, maceration, miniaturisation, minimisation, reduction, shrinkage, shrinking, taper. **2. depreciation** break, cut, deflation, devaluation, discount, disinflation, drop, markdown, sag, subtraction. **3. mitigation** abatement, alleviation, attenuation, extenuation. **4. decline** declination *(Chiefly US)*, decrescendo, diminution, downswing, downturn, ebb, fall, lowering, subsidence, wane. **5. abridgement** abbreviation, curtailment. **6. cutback** redundancy, retrenchment, short-time. *Informal:* the axe. **7. depression** recession.

adj.   **2.**   **1. decreased** diminished, less, lesser, miniature, miniaturised, under. **2. abridged** censored, cut, expurgated, reduced, watered-down.

     3.   **1. decreasing** damping, decrescent, detumescent, dwindling, reducing, waning. **2. depreciative** alleviant, deflationary, depreciatory. **3. alleviative** extenuatory, mitigative.

v.   **4.**   **1. decrease** abate, bate, cut, cut down, diminish, lessen, lower, miniaturise, minify, minimise, reduce. **2. depreciate** belittle, bring down, cheapen, deflate, degrade, devalue, discount, disparage, down-value, downgrade, hammer, laugh off (or away), lower, make little of, mark down, play down, pooh-pooh, pull down, sink. **3. mitigate** allay, alleviate, assuage, ease, extenuate, lighten, moderate, temper. **4. weaken** attenuate, damp, depress, dilute, relax, slack, underdamp. **5. shorten** abbreviate, abridge, clip, condense, curtail, cut, diminish, lessen, precis, telescope, truncate. **6. cut back** clip, downsize, draw (or pull) one's horns in, lop, pare down, pare off (or away), prune, retrench, scale down, scant, slash, step down, taper, whittle, whittle away at, whittle down, wind down. *Informal:* axe. **7. shrink** contract, sanforise.

     5.   **1. wane** abate, fade out, fall, fall off, lag, peak, peak and pine, peter out, tail away (or off), trail off. **2. depreciate** break, drop, drop off, lower, sag, sink, slip, tumble. **3. decline** crumble, decay, die away, dwindle, ebb, fade away, go soft, subside, waste, wear away.

adv.   **6.**   **1. decreasingly** diminishingly. **2. less** at a discount, down, off, under. **3. on the wane** at a low ebb, at low ebb, decrescendo, in decline, less and less.

RELATED KEYWORDS: SUBTRACTION, SMALLNESS, CONTRACTION, A FEW, MODERATION

DEFEAT

n.   **1.**   **1. defeat** annihilation, conquest, discomfiture, downfall, downthrow, elimination, loss, overthrow, overturn, pulverisation, rout, ruin, subdual, subjection, subjugation, vanquishment. **2. drubbing** beating, checkmate, confutation, demolition, flogging, hiding, thrashing. *Informal:* hammering, pasting, shellacking. **3. reversal** check, rebuff, repulse, reverse, upset.

     2.   **1. loser** a bad loser, a good loser, also-ran, defeatist, has-been, non-starter, underdog. *Informal:* wooden spooner.

     3.   **1. defeater** conqueror, conquistador, drubber, subjugator.

adj.   **4.**   **1. defeated** beaten, bested, down, down-and-out, downfallen, frustrated, lost, outclassed, outmanoeuvred, pipped at the post, subdued. *Informal:* beat, creamed, dished, dished up, done like a dinner, euchred, gone a million, stonkered, whacked.

v.   **5.**   **1. lose** be all up, come off second best, come off worst, get the worst of it, go down, go under, lose out, meet one's match, overreach, take a beating, take a tumble. *Informal:* bite the dust, luck out, meet one's Waterloo. **2. give in** back down, bow, break down, buckle under, cave in, give ground, give way, give way to, knuckle under, lay down one's arms, lose ground, resign, run scared, sag, strike (or lower) the flag, submit, succumb, surrender, throw in one's hand, throw in the towel (or sponge), throw it in, throw up, yield. *Informal:* drop one's bundle, say uncle, sky the rag, sky the towel. **3. fail** be among the also-rans, collapse, come to grief, come undone (or unstuck) (or unglued), crack, crash, crumple, fizzle out, flop, go, go down, go under, have had it, lose out on, misfire. *Informal:* bomb, bomb out, come a cropper, come a gutser, conk out, fall flat on one's (or its) face, get the thumbs down, get the wooden spoon, give up the ghost, go down like a lead balloon, go down the tube(s), go phut, go to the wall, have had one's chips, have had the sword, not to be able to take a trick, win the wooden spoon.

     6.   **1. defeat** annihilate, break, come all over, conquer, crush, do for, master, overcome, overmaster, overpower, overthrow, overturn, overwhelm, prostrate, rout, subdue, subjugate, take by storm, tame, triumph over, upset, vanquish. *Informal:* floor, go through like a dose of salts, go through like a packet of salts, slaughter. **2. beat** clobber, down, drub, flog, pulverise, punish, thrash, trounce, whip. *Informal:* beat the stuffing out of, beat the tripe out of, cream, do like a dinner, floor, knock the stuffing out of, make mincemeat of. **3. checkmate** confute, euchre, master, outargue, outfox, outjockey, outmanoeuvre, outplay, outstare, outwit, shoot down, stump, undercut, whipsaw *(US)*. **4. stop** check, upset. **5. best** better, bowl over, dismiss, get ahead of, get the best of, get the better of, have the best of, outbox, peg, polish off, shout down, steal a march on, trump, worst. *Informal:* donkey-lick, get the drop on, have the drop on, knock off, knock spots off, lick, roll, skunk *(US)*, stonker, whitewash, wipe the floor with.

RELATED KEYWORDS: FAILURE, CONTEST, SPORT, INFERIORITY, WAR

DEFENCE

n. **1.**   **1. defence** border protection, brickwall defence, defense *(US)*, muniment, resistance, security, self-defence, self-preservation, self-protection. **2. protection** armour, barrage balloon, buffer, bulwark, defensive, fortification, rampart, safeguard, shield. **3. sentry-go. 4. civil defence** national service. **5. defence policy** Fortress Australia, forward presence, scorched earth policy. **6. air cover** air picket, umbrella. **7. flak** balloon barrage, barrage, creeping barrage, screen, smokescreen. **8. early warning system** dumaresq, radar.

2.   **1. fortification** fieldwork, flèche, flanker, gabionade, lunette, muniment. **2. parapet** barbican, bulwark, rampart, redan, walls. **3. barricade** parallel, salient, traverse. **4. battlement** battery, blockhouse, casemate, crenellation, embrasure, emplacement, field battery, pillbox. **5. stockade** abatis, air base, base, fastness, fraise, palisade. **6. spike** barbwire, caltrop, crowfoot, gabion. **7. movable shelter** manta, mantelet, mantlet, testudo, tortoise. **8. earthworks** breastwork, contravallation, counterscarp, entrenchments, escarp, escarpment, glacis, mound, outwork, parados, ravelin, redoubt, retrenchment, scarp, sconce, vallation, vallum, works. **9. trench** ditch, dugout, dyke, enfilade, fire trench, fosse, foxhole, moat, slit trench. *Informal:* doover. **10. screen** blindage, cover, shield. **11. trap** ambush, booby trap.

3.   **1. fortress** acropolis, Acropolis, bastille, castle, citadel, donjon, dun, fastness, fort, fortalice, fortifications, garrison, hillfort, keep, kremlin, Martello tower, motte, motte and bailey, peel, presidio, quadrilateral, stronghold, tower. **2. blockhouse** belfry, bridge-house, gatehouse, sentry box, watch-house *(Chiefly British)*, watchtower. **3. garrison town** burg. **4. defensive position** anchor, approaches, bastion, bridgehead, outpost.

4.   **1. defender** bastion, champion, crusader, protector. **2. sentry** bodyguard, coast-watcher, conductor *(US)*, doorkeeper, guard, hired gun, lifeguard, safeguard, security police, sentinel, sky marshal. **3. army reserve** Home Guard, reserve, territorial army. *Informal:* Dad's Army. **4. reservist** *Informal:* weekend warrior. **5. deliverer** rescuer, saviour.

adj. **5.**   **1. defended** armed, armoured, bastioned, battlemented, entrenched, fortified, protected, ready, walled. **2. defendable** bombproof, bulletproof, defensible, impenetrable, proof. **3. alerted** warned. **4. defensive** protective.

v. **6.**   **1. defend** fence, fend, forefend, stand up for, take someone's part. **2. protect** guard, keep, safeguard, shield, watch over. **3. entrench** dig in, intrench, retrench, sap, trench. **4. barricade** bulwark, circumvallate, crenel, crenellate, embattle, fortify, garrison, palisade, rampart, rearm, stockade. **5. repel** beat off, drive back, drive off, fight off, repulse, ward off. **6. be on the defensive** be on guard, steel oneself.

RELATED KEYWORDS: PRESERVATION, FIGHTER, PROTECTION, SAFETY, SHELTER, WAR, WEAPON

DEFICIENCY

n. **1.**   **1. deficiency** default, defect, deficit, depletion, failing, insufficience, insufficiency, lack, loose end, missing link, need, omission, requirement, shortage, shortcoming, shortfall, underage, want, wantage *(US)*. **2. incompletion** incomprehensiveness. **3. perfunctoriness** paucity, scrappiness, sketchiness, superficialness.

adj. **2.**   **1. deficient** barren of, chary of, in short supply, insufficient, lacking, meagre, out of, rationed, short, short of, shy, sparse, strapped, wanting, weak. **2. incomplete** bitty, broken, fragmental, fragmentary, imperfect, incomprehensive, perfunctory, scant, scrappy, sketchy, superficial, touch-and-go. **3. unfinished** aborning, cut short, half, incomplete, part, partial, truncated, uncompleted. **4. unaccomplished** blank, unbegun, undone, unexecuted, unfinalised, unrealised. **5. rudimentary** abortive, rudimental, vestigial.

v. **3.**   **1. be wanting** be lacking, not suffice, run dry, run low, run out, run short, want.

adv. **4.**   **1. deficiently** by halves, imperfectly, incompletely, partially, partly, rudimentarily, scrappily, sketchily.

RELATED KEYWORDS: INADEQUACY, PART

DELUSION

n. **1.**   **1. delusion** error, false impression, misconception, superstition, warped notion. **2. illusion** bubble, delusion, dream, fantasy, fata morgana, figment, fixed idea, hallucination, mirage, myth, pink elephant, reverie. **3. daydream** chimera, fancy, idle fancy, imagining, make-believe, phantasm, phantasma, phantasmagoria, phantasmagory, play-acting, pretence, reverie, vision. **4. dream world** castle in Spain, castles in the air, cloud-cuckoo-land, cloudland, dreamland, fantasy land, fool's paradise, pie in the sky. **5. will-o'-the-wisp** friar's lantern, ignis fatuus, marsh light, wildfire.

2. 1. trickery false perspective, FX, hocus-pocus, hokey-pokey, illusion, legerdemain, sleight of hand, special effects, trompe l'oeil. **2. trick** gimmick. *Informal:* flim-flam, have. **3. trick of the light** aberration, corposant, distortion, optical illusion, reflection, refraction, St Elmo's fire, virtual image.

adj. **3. 1. delusive** airy, deceptive, delusory, dreamlike, dreamy, false, fatuous, illusional, illusionary, illusive, illusory, insubstantial, oneiric, quixotic, spurious, unreal. **2. delusional** artificial, barmecidal, chimeric, chimerical, fancied, fantastic, feigned, fictitious, imaginary, imagined, make-believe, moonshiny, phantasmagorical, phantasmal, phantasmic, pretend, visional, visionary. *Informal:* never-never. **3. phantom** apparitional, ghostly, shadowy, shady, spectral. **4. hallucinatory** psychedelic, transcendental. *Informal:* spaced-out, spacey.

v. **4. 1. be deluded** labour under a false impression, misapprehend, misunderstand. **2. delude oneself** deceive oneself. *Informal:* have oneself on. **3. dream** daydream, imagine, live in dreamland, make as though, make believe. **4. hallucinate** flashback, hear things, see pink elephants, see things. *Informal:* trip.

RELATED KEYWORDS: ERROR, FANTASY, PSYCHE, INSANITY

DENIAL

n. **1. 1. denial** apophasis, contradiction, disavowal, disclaimer, nay, negative, non est factum, rebuttal, traverse. **2. repudiation** denial, disaffirmation, disavowal, disclamation, disowning, disownment, negation, palinode, recantation, renouncement, renunciation, retraction. **3. nullification** abolishment, abolition, abrogation, annulment, avoidance, cancellation, cassation, countermand, disaffirmance, discharge, frustration, repeal, rescission, revocation, self-contradiction, voidance.

2. 1. denier contradictor, controverter, gainsayer, negativist. **2. repudiator** abjurer, disavower, disclaimer, disowner, forswearer. **3. nullifier** abrogator, annihilator, canceller, counterclaimant, counterworker, dissolver, repealer, revoker, voider.

adj. **3. 1. denying** abjuratory, adversative, contradictive, contradictory, negative, negatory, repudiative.

4. 1. repealable rescindable, rescissible, revocable.

v. **5. 1. deny** contradict, controvert, disaffirm, disavow, disown, gainsay, give the lie to, negate, negative, rebut, repudiate, traverse. **2. repudiate** abjure, abnegate, deny, disavow, disclaim, disown, forswear, recant, renounce, retract. **3. annul** abate, abolish, abrogate, annihilate, avoid, break, cancel, derecognise, disaffirm, dissolve, do (or make) away with, invalidate, nullify, quash, repeal, rescind, reverse, revoke, set aside, vacate, void.

RELATED KEYWORDS: DISAGREEMENT, CANCELLATION, REFUSAL, PROHIBITION

DEPARTURE

n. **1. 1. departure** debarkation, decampment, embarcation, embarkation, emigration, exit, exodus, farewell, going, issue, parting, pullout, retirement, walk-off, walkout, withdrawal. **2. take-off** lift-off, sailing, start. *Informal:* blast-off. **3. French leave** *Informal:* moonlight flit, skedaddle. **4. dismissal** cavel-out, cavil-out, lay-off, retrenchment, run-out, the (old) heave-ho, wrongful dismissal. **5. leave** congé, early mark, early minute *(SA, Tasmania),* nunc dimittis. *Informal:* nick.

2. 1. farewell adieu, goodbye, goodnight, valedictory. **2. parting** farewell, goodbye, leave, leave-taking, parting of the ways, valediction. **3. valedictory dinner** despedida *(Philippine English).* *Informal:* send-off. **4. parting shot**.

3. 1. leaver émigré, emigrant, migrant, valedict, voider. **2. absconder** deserter, fugitive, runaway.

adj. **4. 1. departing** farewell, going, goodnight, parting, recessional, valedictory. **2. retired** outgoing, retiring. **3. emigrating** emigrant, emigrational, outbound, outward-bound. **4. departed** absent, gone. *Informal:* gone for a Tosca, gone to Gowings *(NSW).*

v. **5. 1. depart** absquatulate, buzz along, buzz off, eloign, evacuate, exit, get along, get away, go, go away, go bush, go off, hop, leave, make off, move out, part, pull out, push along, push off, quit, remove oneself, retire, retreat, shuffle off, take an early mark. *Informal:* be out of here, beat it, blow, bug off, choof off, clear out, disappear, get lost, hook, hook it, hop it, mooch off, move, nick off, nick out, p.o.q., push off (or along), shove off, skive off, tie a knot in one's bluey, tootle off. **2. set off** cast off, get under way, go on board, go to sea, loose, make sail, make tracks, put forth, put off, put out, put to sea, sail, sally, sally forth, set forth, set out, set sail, shake the dust from one's feet, step out, take off, take the road for, take to the road, take wing, up, weigh anchor. *Informal:* blast off, hit the road, sling one's hook *(British)*. **3. embark** embus, entrain, go on board. **4. walk out** bounce out, flounce, storm out. *Informal:* vote with one's feet. **5. break camp** decamp, saddle up. *Informal:* check out, make tracks, pull up stakes. **6. run off** beat a retreat, decamp, flee, flight, fly, put to flight, run, run out, strike, take (to) flight, take to one's heels, tear off, turn tail, wing. *Informal:* be outta here, bugger off, cut, cut and run, do a flit, hightail it *(Chiefly US)*, imshi, lam *(US)*, light out, micky quick, nip, pop off, rack off, scat, scram, shoot off, shoot through like a Bondi tram, skedaddle, skidaddle, skiddoo *(US)*, split, take a powder, tear, vamoose, zot. **7. abscond** abandon, absent, decamp, defect, desert, desolate, do a bunk, do a disappearing act, do a moonlight flit, do a sneak, escape, forsake, get off, go missing, jump, leave in the lurch, make a getaway, play truant, run away, run off, run out on, slope off, take French leave, truant, walk out on. *Informal:* blow, blow through, go AWOL, jig, jig it, jig school, leave someone holding the baby, make oneself scarce, nick off, pike on, rat on, scarper, shoot the moon, shoot through, skip, sneak, squib on, take to the hills. **8. withdraw from** abandon, evacuate, leave, pull back from, quit, secede, vacate. **9. withdraw** bow out, fall back, fall off, go down *(British)*, make (or stage) an exit, retire, separate from, take one's leave. **10. emigrate** migrate, transmigrate.

    6. 1. farewell bundle off (or out), ring out, see off, see out, see someone to the door, see to the door, send off, show someone the door.

interj. **7. 1. goodbye** a rivederci, adieu, adios, aloha, arrivederci, au revoir, auf Wiedersehen, bon voyage, bonsoir, bye, cheerio, farewell, good afternoon, good day, good evening, good morning, goodnight, haere ra *(NZ)*, khuda hafiz, night-night, see you (later), see you anon, vale, yickadee *(NT)*. *Informal:* Abyssinia, bye-bye, ciao, hooroo, ooroo, pip-pip *(British)*, so long, ta, ta-ta, toodle-loo, tooroo. **2. all aboard** all ashore that's going ashore.

    8. 1. away away with …, be off, go away, off. *Informal:* beat it, bugger off, buzz off, get knotted, get lost, get nicked, get ripped, go jump (in the lake), go to billyo, go to blazes, go to buggery, hop it, nick off, on your bike, rack off, hairy-legs, scat, scram, skedaddle, vamoose. **2. exeunt** exeunt omnes, exit.

RELATED KEYWORDS: RETREAT, AVOIDANCE, DIVERGENCE, EXIT, ESCAPE

DEPENDENCE

n. **1. 1. dependence** clientship, dependency, entrustment, faith, reliance, trust, vassalage. **2. guardianship** custody, fosterage, matronage, tutelage, wardship.

  2. 1. dependant camp follower, client, hanger-on, satellite. **2. ward** adoptee, charge, client, clientele, constituency, dependant, dependent *(Chiefly US)*, foster, foster-child, fosterling, parasite, protégé, satellite, trencherman. *Informal:* mother's boy. **3. vassal** feudatory, henchman, liegeman, man, vavasor. **4. pensioner** annuitant, pensionary. **5. contingent** appendant, contingency.

adj. **3. 1. dependent** at the mercy of, conditioned, contingent, dependant *(Chiefly US)*, in chancery *(British Law)*, in the hands of, parasitic, reliant, semiparasitic, tied to the apron-strings. **2. contingent** appendant, conditional, dependent, nisi, provisory.

v. **4. 1. depend on** hinge on, turn on (or upon). *Informal:* hang on. **2. bank on** bargain on, depend, pend, reckon, rely on, repose. *Informal:* figure on, lean on. **3. live for** hope, swear by, trust to.

RELATED KEYWORDS: REPRESSION, POWERLESSNESS, SERVANT

DEPTH

n. **1. 1. depth** deepness, lowness, profoundness, profundity. **2. abyss** abysm *(Poetic)*, chasm, deep, depth, depths, gulf, profound *(Poetic)*, ravine. **3. soundings** bathometry, cast, echo sounding, plumbing. **4. bathometer** bathymeter, echo sounder, flashboard, lead line, sonar. **5. depth measurement** deep, isobath, mark.

adj. **2. 1. deep** abysmal, abyssal, bottomless, cavernous, fathomless, profound, unsounded, yawning.

v. **3. 1. plumb the depths** go deep. **2. plumb** fathom, heave the lead, sound, take soundings.

adv. **4. 1. deeply** profoundly.

RELATED KEYWORDS: HEIGHT, LENGTH, MEASUREMENT, BOTTOM

DESCENT

n. **1. 1. descent** decadence, declension, declination, decline, down, downswing, downwardness, drop, dropping, gravitation. **2. landing** bellylanding, crashlanding, dead-stick landing, hard landing, instrument landing, soft landing, three-point landing, touchdown. **3. slide** chute, ramp, slippery dip, slippery slide *(Qld, Tasmania)*, water slide, waterfall. **4. abseil** BASE-jump, bungee jump, rappel, skydiving.

2. 1. bow droop, sag, stoop. **2. prolapse** lapse.

3. 1. fall crash, dive, false step, flop, plop, plump, plumper, pratfall, precipitation, prostration, slip, slump, stumble, trip, tumble. *Informal:* flump, purler, whop, wipe-out. **2. pounce** downrush, swoop. **3. free fall** flat spin, jump, nosedive, sideslip, skydive.

4. 1. landslide ash fall, ash flow, avalanche, cave-in, earthflow, landslip, mudslide, rockfall, slide, snowslide, snowslip, soil creep. **2. sinkage** settlement, settling, subsidence.

5. 1. faller autumn leaf, flopper, stumbler. **2. windfall** *Informal:* sailer *(NZ)*.

adj. **6. 1. descending** cataclinal, declivitous, descendant, descendent, down, downgrade, downhill, downward, katabatic, positively geotropic. **2. deciduous** caducous. **3. fallen** bowed, cast, downcast, droopy, drop, sunken. **4. free fall**.

v. **7. 1. descend** alight, coast, dip, drop, glissade, go down, lapse, pitch, set, slip down. **2. free-fall** bail out, bungee-jump, jump, parachute, smoke-jump. **3. abseil** classic, climb down, rap-jump, rappel, scale. **4. land** bellyland, crash, ditch, flop, pancake, put down, touch down.

8. 1. dismount get down, get off. **2. alight** debark, debus, deplane, detrain, disembark, get out, go ashore, land, light, perch, settle.

9. 1. fall crash-land, drop, fall off, flop, knuckle over, lose one's balance, measure one's length, overbalance, pitch, slide, slip, stumble, topple, trip, tumble, tumble over. *Informal:* bite the dust, come a cropper, come a gutser, flump, go for a sixer, go for six, hit the deck, keel over, take a dive, take a toss. **2. flop** plump, plunk, whop, whump. **3. collapse** avalanche, cave in, subside. **4. slump** droop, prolapse, sag, sink. **5. sink** bog, founder, mire, settle, subside, swamp, touch bottom. **6. bow** bob, crouch, curtsy, dip, duck, nod, stoop.

10. 1. lower bring down, douse, let down, pull down, strike, take down. **2. set down** drop off. **3. knock down** bring down, down, drop, fell, floor, grass, lay, level, overthrow, run down, sling, throw, topple, tumble, wooden. *Informal:* deck, iron out. **4. dump** deposit, ditch *(US)*, plonk, precipitate, throw down. **5. scuttle** run down, scupper, send to the bottom, sink, torpedo.

11. 1. shower beat, cascade, hail, pelt, pepper, plop, rain, rain cats and dogs, snow.

adv. **12. 1. down** adown, below, beneath, downstairs, over, overboard, overside, underneath. **2. downwards** downgrade, downhill, downward, downwardly, face-downwards.

RELATED KEYWORDS: DIVE, JUMP, OVERTURN, SLOPE, BOTTOM

DESIRE

n. **1. 1. desire** achage, ache, appetence, appetency, appetite, craving, demand, eagerness, famishment, hunger, hungriness, keenness, longing, mania, need, passion, pleasure, rage, thirst, thirstiness, will, wish, yearning. **2. ardour** ardency, concupiscence, desire, fervency, fire, flame, glow, lechery, libido, lust, passion, passionateness, zeal. *Informal:* hotpants. **3. obsession** a monkey on one's back, compulsion, insane desire. **4. desires** sighs, wishes. **5. wish** conation, desideration, fancy, hankering, itch, mind, urge, velleity, volition, want, whim, whimsy, will, willingness, yen. **6. propensity** appetence, bent, bias, inclination, leaning, partiality, penchant, ply, predilection, proclivity, propension, set, turn. **7. aspiration** ambition, ambitiousness, arrivism, arrivisme, zeal. **8. languishing** nostalgia, wistfulness. **9. fondness** adoration, liking, love, relish, stomach, taste. **10. avarice** acquisitiveness, avariciousness, avidity, covetousness, cupidity, graspingness, greed, greediness, insatiableness, insatiateness, mammonism, rapacity, selfishness, voracity. **11. gluttony** bulimia, edacity, gluttonousness, sitomania.

2. 1. object of desire ambition, attraction, big game, consummation greatly to be desired, desiderata, desideratum, desire, fantasy, goal, lure, magnet, mecca.

3. 1. desirer coveter, hankerer, mammonite, thirster, wanter, wisher. **2. lover** admirer, buff, devotee, enthusiast, votary. **3. languisher** sigher. **4. glutton** trencherman. *Informal:* garbage guts, greedy-guts, guzzle-guts. **5. social climber** arriviste, careerist, company man, company woman, pothunter. *Informal:* go-getter. **6. aspirer** aspirant, candidate, intender, pretender, seeker.

adj. **4. 1. desirous of** affected, apt to, desiderative, disposed, inclined, inclined to, minded, partial, ready, solicitous, volitionary, volitive, willing, wishful, would-be. **2. eager** agog, all agog, breathless, impatient, keen, raring, sharp-set, solicitous, voracious. *Informal:* toey. **3. ardent** ablaze, athirst, avid, eager, fervent, fiery, glowing, impassioned, keen, libidinal, on fire, passionate, sharp, warm-blooded. **4. keen on** dying to, fixated, longing for, mad, partial to, set on. *Informal:* nuts about (or on) (or over), nutty over (or about), queer for. **5. aspiring** ambitious. **6. longing** languishing, lovesick, nostalgic, sentimental, wistful, yearning. **7. lustful** aroused, concupiscent, fruity, hot, lascivious, libidinous, lusty, on heat, rampant, raunchy, salacious. *Informal:* toey. **8. votive**.

5. **1. desirable** appetising, covetable, eligible, enviable, in demand, inviting, mouth-watering, popular, preferable, sought after, succulent, tantalising, top. *Informal:* plummy, to die for. **2. attractive** alluring, fascinating, kissable, nubile, seductive, sexy, siren, voluptuous. *Informal:* beddable, cute, hot.

6. **1. appetitive** appetent, conative, orectic.

7. **1. avaricious** acquisitive, covetous, extortionate, grasping, greedy, hungry, insatiable, insatiate, open-mouthed, rapacious, selfish.

8. **1. hungry** edacious, empty, esurient, famished, hollow, hungry as a hunter, hungry as hell, peckish, ravening, ravenous, sharp-set, starving, voracious. **2. gluttonous** bulimic, greedy. *Informal:* gutsy.

9. **1. thirsty** droughty, drouthy, dry, dry as the Nullarbor, parched. *Informal:* dry as a bone, dry as a pommy's towel, dry as the Gobi Desert, dry as the Simpson Desert.

v. 10. **1. desire** admire *(US)*, be all for something, be hell-bent on, covet, crave, crave for (or after), desiderate, hanker, hanker after (or for), hunger, hunger for, long, want, wish, yearn. *Informal:* be dying for. **2. seek** court, look after, make eyes, make eyes at, make sheep's eyes at, moon over, solicit, woo. **3. wish** care for, choose, covet, desire, fancy, feel like, have (half) a mind to, have a heart to, incline towards, intend, like, need, require, take a fancy to, take to, want, would be glad to. **4. pine for** ache, languish, long, pant, sigh, starve, starve for, thirst, yearn. **5. have high ambitions** aim high, aspire, aspire to, raise one's sights, set one's cap at, want the earth. **6. run after** be gasping for (or after), die for, have eyes only for, itch, itch for, lust for (or after), pant after, run mad after, scream for, set one's hat at, set one's heart on, slaver, yen. *Informal:* (would) give one's eyeteeth for. **7. flame** burn, fire, rage. **8. offer oneself** be in for, throw one's hat into (or in) the ring.

11. **1. be hungry** famish, have a good appetite, starve. *Informal:* could eat a horse, could eat a horse and chase the rider, eat like a horse, eat the crutch out of a low-flying duck, have the munchies.

12. **1. be thirsty** be dry, feel parched, thirst.

adv. 13. **1. desirously** achingly, longingly, nostalgically, yearningly. **2. aspiringly** acquisitively, ambitiously, avariciously, covetously, cravingly, gluttonously, graspingly, greedily, insatiably, insatiately, rapaciously. **3. eagerly** agog with, ardently, avidly, hungrily, thirstily. **4. willingly** gladly, lief, with good will.

RELATED KEYWORDS: ENTHUSIASM, INTENTION, WILLINGNESS

DESPAIR

n. 1. **1. despair** desolateness, desolation, desperateness, desperation, distress, hopelessness, inconsolableness. **2. pessimism** defeatism, demoralisation. **3. melancholy** blues, damp, dejection, depression, despondency, gloom, misery, oppression, prostration, slough of despond. *Informal:* blue devils, dumps.

2. **1. hopelessness** irrecoverableness, irredeemableness, irremediableness, irreparableness, irretrievableness. **2. bleakness** blackness, comfortlessness, dismalness, oppressiveness, unbearableness, wretchedness. **3. hopeless situation** hell, living death, worst case scenario. **4. vain hope** chimera, illusion, mirage.

3. **1. pessimist** bear, cynic, demoraliser, melancholiac. *Informal:* glumbum. **2. doom-watcher** Cassandra, doomsdayman. **3. doomsaying** counsel of despair.

adj. 4. **1. despairing** broken-down, desolate, desperate, distressed, forlorn, inconsolable, miserable, past hope or caring. **2. pessimistic** defeatist, dyspeptic, gloom-and-doom, resigned. **3. melancholy** Byronic, crestfallen, depressed, downcast, low, low-spirited, melancholiac, melancholic, world-weary, wretched. *Informal:* down.

5. **1. hopeless** beyond remedy, capital, forlorn, immedicable, incurable, inoperable, irrecoverable, irredeemable, irremeable, irremediable, irreparable, irretrievable, irreversible. **2. desperate** dead-end, futureless. **3. inevitable** defeated, unavoidable. **4. bleak** black, comfortless, depressive, desolate, funereal, gaunt, intolerable, unbearable.

v. 6. **1. despair** buckle under, despond, give it away, give up, go to the pack, lose heart, lose hope. *Informal:* drop one's bundle, give up the ghost. **2. be pessimistic** look on the worst side. **3. write off** hope for nothing more from.

7. **1. have no hope** be doomed to failure, have no chance, have one's fate sealed. *Informal:* have a fat chance, have Buckley's, have Buckley's chance.

    8. **1. desolate** cast down, chill, demoralise, drive to despair, leave no hope.

adv.   **9.** **1. despairingly** desperately, pessimistically. **2. without hope** bleakly, defeatedly, hopelessly.

    RELATED KEYWORDS: FAILURE, EMOTION, DISCOURAGEMENT, MISFORTUNE, UNHAPPINESS

DESTRUCTION

n.   **1.** **1. destruction** abolishment, abolition, bane, consumption, death, decimation, decomposition, demolishment, demolition, dissolution, extermination, naught, pulverisation, ruin, shipwreck, smash, wreck. **2. desolation** depredation, devastation, havoc, ravage, ruin, waste. **3. eradication** deracination, extirpation. **4. annihilation** extinction, liquidation. **5. erasure** defacement, effacement, erasion, expunction, obliteration. **6. disintegration** breakdown, dissipation, dissolution. **7. chemical breakdown** autodigestion, autolysis, bacteriolysis, biodegradation, biolysis, breakdown, catabolism, chromatolysis, decomposition, digestion, dissimilation, electrolysis, histolysis, lysis, radiolysis. **8. destructivity. 9. perniciousness** fatalness, fellness. **10. vandalism** arson, hoodlumism.

    2. **1. ruination** belial, comedown, defeat, doom, downfall, fall, fate, labefactation, labefaction, loss, overthrow, perdition, ruin, ruinousness, undoing. *Informal:* watergate, waterloo. **2. collapse** crash. **3. smash** destruct, shipwreck. *Informal:* prang. **4. conflagration** holocaust, incineration. **5. blast effect** ground-shock effect, scorched earth. **6. ruins** ashes, rack, shipwreck, wrack, wreck, wreckage. **7. disaster** apocalypse, avalanche, calamity, cataclysm, catastrophe, debacle, fatality, plague. **8. the end** last straw, moment of truth, the (living) end, the beginning of the end, the crunch, the finish, the last straw, the road to ruin.

    3. **1. destroyer** abolisher, bane, decimator, demolisher, destructor, juggernaut, pulveriser, razer, unmaker. **2. desolater** barbarian, depredator, havocker, Hun, ravager, ruiner, Visigoth, waster, wrecker. **3. annihilator** annihilationist, exterminator, extirpator. **4. scourge** incinerator, poison, sword, thunderbolt. **5. bane** blight, cancer, canker, devil, mould, must. **6. defacer** hoodlum, vandal. **7. arsonist** fire-raiser, firebug, incendiary, pyromaniac. **8. destructive agent** ablative, acid, autolysin, caustic, cauter, cautery, corrosive, hazmat. **9. eraser** effacer, eradicator, expunger. **10. nihilist** anarchist, assassin, iconoclast, subversive, subverter.

adj.   **4.** **1. destructive** depredatory, despoiling, devastating, ruinous, vandal, vandalic, vandalistic, wasteful, wasting. *Informal:* destructo. **2. annihilative** abolitionary, eradicative, exterminative, exterminatory, extirpative, obliterative. **3. biodegradable** biolytic, catabolic. **4. apocalyptic** apocalyptical, black, cataclysmic, holocaustic. **5. pernicious** baneful, cancerous, cankerous, consumptive, gnawing, pestiferous, pestilent, pestilential, poisonous.

    5. **1. ruined** beaten, broken, defeated, destroyed, downfallen, fallen, had it, lost, stuffed, undone. *Informal:* buggered, bust, cactus, done for, done up, down the plughole, gone to Gundy, jiggered, kaput, pakaru *(NZ)*, shagged, stonkered, up the spout. **2. annihilated** decimated, eradicated, exterminated, extirpated, liquidated, nuked, obliterated.

v.   **6.** **1. destroy** decimate, demolish, destruct, finish off, kill, make short work of, obliterate, pull down, pulverise, ride down, ruin, slay, smash, smite, take out, tear down, wipe out. *Informal:* frag, hit for six, knock for six, make mincemeat of, spifflicate, wipe the floor with, zap. **2. ravage** bite, corrode, desolate, devastate, eat, harry, lay waste to, rape, waste. **3. eradicate** deracinate, exterminate, extirpate, get rid of, outroot, root up, uproot, wipe off the map. **4. erase** blank out, blot out, efface, expunge, obliterate. **5. abolish** do (or make) away with, liquidate, unmake. **6. overthrow** bring down, defeat, do for, subvert, undo, unhorse. **7. deface** depredate, mar, undermine, vandalise. **8. consume** cremate, gut, incinerate, put to the torch, raze. **9. poison** blight, canker, empoison. **10. annihilate** extinguish. *Informal:* nuke.

    7. **1. ruin** havoc, lose, play havoc with, put paid to, shipwreck, sink. *Informal:* bugger up, bust up, cook, cook someone's goose, do in, frig up, jigger. **2. break down** break, graunch *(Chiefly NZ)*, malfunction, shatter, wreck. *Informal:* pakaru *(NZ)*. **3. scuttle** run down, scupper, shipwreck, sink, torpedo, wreck.

    8. **1. collapse** come undone, crash, crumple, fall, give way, go (or end) up in smoke, go by the board, go under, perish. *Informal:* be history, bite the dust, come unstuck, go belly up, go down the tube(s), go for a burton *(Chiefly British)*, go phut, go to the dogs, have had it, have had the sword. **2. disintegrate** degrade, dissipate, dissolve, tetter.

adv.   **9.** **1. destructively** devastatingly, ruinously, wastefully. **2. perniciously** banefully, pestiferously, poisonously.

    RELATED KEYWORDS: DAMAGE, DETERIORATION, KILLING

DETERIORATION

n.   **1.**   **1. deterioration** cytolysis, debasement, declension, declination *(Chiefly US)*, decline, degeneracy, degenerateness, degeneration, impairment, involution, pejoration, regression, retrogradation, retrogression. **2. contamination** adulteration, bastardisation, corruption, rancidity, sophistication, spoilage, taint, tarnish, vitiation. **3. rottenness** carrion, corruptness, putrefaction, putrescence, putridity, putridness, putrilage. **4. decay** atrophy, breakdown, decadence, decomposition, deterioration, disintegration, retrogradation, rot, rotting, waste, wasting. **5. erosion** corrasion, crumbling, fading, wearing away, weathering. **6. rustiness** ablation, corrosion. **7. rot** black rot, blight, canker, curl, dry rot, wet rot. **8. rust** corrosion, fret. **9. bottle sickness** casse.

adj.   **2.**   **1. deteriorated** atrophic, atrophied, decadent, degenerate, degenerative, degraded, manky, retrograde, retrogressive, waste, wasted, worn. **2. rotten** acetified, adulterate, bad, cankerous, carrion, corrupt, corrupted, decadent, decayed, frowsty, frowzy, high, ill-smelling, infected, pricked, putrescent, putrid, putrilaginous, rancid, spoiled, tainted, vitiated. *Informal:* off, on the nose. **3. flyblown** blown, corrupt, fly-struck, maggoty, vermiculate, worm-eaten, wormy. **4. rusty** corroded, eroded, faded, weathered, worn away. **5. decayed** bad, carious.

     3.   **1. deteriorating** declining, failing, flagging, getting worse, in decline, no better, on the decline, on the downward path, sinking, slipping, weakening, wilting, worse.

     4.   **1. deteriorative** contaminative, corrosive, corruptive, degenerative, ulcerous.

v.   **5.**   **1. deteriorate** aggravate, decline, degenerate, degrade, dilapidate, disintegrate, ebb, get worse, go backwards, go downhill, go from bad to worse, macerate, pejorate, retrograde, retrogress, sicken, sink, slide, slip, waste, wear out, worsen. *Informal:* go to pot, go to seed, go to the pack. **2. wear** eat, erode, fray, frazzle, fret, ravel, scab, scuff, weather. **3. decay** age, atrophy, caseate, decline, deteriorate, dilapidate, ebb, fade, shank, shrivel, wither, wizen. **4. rot** biodegrade, decay, decompose, ebb, fester, gangrene, go bad, go off, mortify, perish, putrefy, rot away (or off), stagnate, turn, wither. **5. rust** corrode, nitrify, oxidise.

     RELATED KEYWORDS: DAMAGE, BADNESS, ILL HEALTH

DEVIATION

n.   **1.**   **1. deviation** aberration, declension, deflection, departure, digression, divergence, divergency, excursion, perturbation, swerve, variation. **2. reflection** backscatter, refraction, refringence. **3. diversion** circumvention, circumvolution, divagation, indirection, sheer.

     2.   **1. byroad** back road, backtrack, bypass, bypath, bystreet, byway, crossroad, crossway, detour, side road, sidetrack, sideway, turn-off. **2. siding** pinch, shunt, sidetrack *(US)*, tram pinch.

     3.   **1. deflector** circumventor, deviator, diverter, inflector, refractor, shyer, swerver, switcher, tacker.

     4.   **1. indirectness** aberrancy, anfractuousity, circuitousness, circularity, deviousness, obliqueness, obliquity, refractiveness, tortuosity, tortuousness, wryness.

adj.   **5.**   **1. deflective** aberrant, aberrational, deviating, divergent, inflective, sideward, sideways, sidewise, tangental, tangential, transverse, veering. **2. refractive** reflectional, refractional, refringent. **3. indirect** anfractuous, circuitous, circular, circumventive, devious, diversionary, dogleg, errant, erratic, periphrastic, roundabout, serpentine, sinuate, sinuous, tortuous, twisting, winding, wry. **4. off-course** askew, oblique, sharp, skew, straggly, wide. *Informal:* squiffy.

     6.   **1. wandering** itinerant, meandering, migratory, noctivagant, nomadic, peripatetic, rambling, roaming, roving, vagarious, vagrant.

v.   **7.**   **1. deflect** deviate, divert, perturb, turn aside. **2. reflect** backscatter, refract, reverberate. **3. hook** cut, edge, nick, seam, slice, snick, swing. **4. deviate** depart from, digress, divagate, diverge, fly off at a tangent, lose, pull over, sheer, shunt, sidetrack, stray, turn off. **5. sidle** move aside, oblique.

     8.   **1. swerve** jink, lurch, pitch, prop, sidestep, skew, skid, slew, twist, wheel, whirl. **2. veer** broach, gripe, hang in, hang out, haul, haul off, jib, jibe, run off the track, shy, stay, tack, wear, weathercock, yaw. *Informal:* run via the Cape. **3. turn away** angle, bear away, bend, claw, corner, face, fade, fall away, fleet, head, put about, square, turn, warp. **4. turn round** about-face, about-ship, back, back water, boxhaul, bring about, go about, reverse, stem. *Informal:* box, chuck a U-ey.

     9.   **1. divert** canalise, flume *(US)*, head off, inflect, switch.

adv. **10.** **1. deflectively** across, aside, athwart, athwartships, away, collaterally, divergently, obliquely, off, sidelong, sideward, sidewards, sideway *(US)*, sideways, transversely. **2. astray** afield, agley *(Chiefly Scottish)*, askew, awry, go wide, indirectly, off the track, wide of the mark, wild. *Informal:* off to billyo, off to buggery. **3. circuitously** circularly, deviously, round, tortuously.

RELATED KEYWORDS: REPULSION, DIVERGENCE, DIRECTION, HITTING, MISPLACEMENT

DIAGRAM

n. **1.** **1. diagram** atlas, chart, delineation, figure, graph, histogram, hook-up, map, plat *(US)*, plot *(Chiefly US)*, schema, schematic, scheme, spectrum. *Informal:* charts. **2. blueprint** cross-section, delineator, design, draft, draught, drawing, elevation, ground plan, illustration, layout, lines, outline, pattern, plan, profile, rough draft, section, skeleton, sketch, visual. **3. formula** prescription, receipt, recipe, scrip, script. **4. projection** azimuthal projection, conic projection, conical projection, cylindrical projection, map projection, Mercator's projection, trimetric projection, zenithal projection.

2. **1. planner** architect, delineator, designer, draftsman, draughtsman, heritage architect, landscape architect, nomographer, photogrammetrist, plotter. **2. cartographer** map-maker, mapper, surveyor.

3. **1. chart making** air base, cartography, chartography, cosmography, drawing, map projection, nomography, photo relief, photogrammetry, phototopography, uranography.

4. **1. type of map or diagram** cadastral map, circuit, contingency table, contour map, control chart, detail, detail drawing, dialect atlas, electronic chart, elevation, exploded view, family tree, flight plan, floor plan, flow chart, flow sheet, Gaussian distribution, genealogical tree, hemisphere, histogram, horoscope, hydrograph, indicator diagram, linguistic atlas, mimetic diagram, mosaic, mud map, nativity, nephanalysis, nomogram, nomograph, normal distribution, phrase marker, pie chart, planisphere, population pyramid, relief map, scattergram, scheme, sonogram, spectrogram, spectrograph, speech spectrogram, sphygmogram, stereogram, stratigraphic column, tree diagram, veduta, Venn diagram, weather map, wind rose, work sheet, working drawing, working model, zodiac.

adj. **5.** **1. diagrammatic** cosmographical, delineative, diagrammatical, graphic, nomographical, photogrammetric, spectrographic. **2. architectonic** architectonical.

v. **6.** **1. map** blueprint, chart, contour, crayon, diagram, diagrammatise, draft, graph, outline, plat *(US)*, plot, protract, represent, schematise, trace.

RELATED KEYWORDS: FINE ARTS, IMITATION, REPRESENTATION

DIFFERENCE

n. **1.** **1. difference** discord, dissimilarity, dissimilitude, dissonance, distinctness, inequality, unlikeness. **2. contrast** antithesis, contradistinction, contraposition, contrariety. **3. disparity** discrepancy, error, variance. **4. spectrum** broad spectrum, cline, range, set. **5. diversity** disparateness, diverseness, heterogeneity, variety, variousness. **6. disparateness** incommensurableness, incomparableness, incompatibility, nonconformity, otherness, unlikeness, variation, variedness. **7. asymmetry** dissymmetry. **8. generation gap** age gap, class divide, cultural divide.

2. **1. dissimilarity** a fine distinction, a nice distinction, contrast, dissimilitude, diversity, variation. *Informal:* diff. **2. something different** horse of another colour, something else, something else again, this that or the other. **3. deviation** discrepancy, divergence, gap, variance. **4. a clean slate** a whole new ball game, change of scene. **5. another** change, choice, tertium quid. *Informal:* otherie. **6. hybrid** modification, variety.

adj. **3.** **1. different** alien, aliunde, as like as chalk and cheese, cast in a different mould, contradistinctive, discrepant, disparate, dissimilar, divergent, foreign, heterogamous, heterologous, incommensurable, incomparable, other, otherly, otherwise, poles apart, removed, unequal, unlike, unusual. *Informal:* blue seal *(Philippine English)*. **2. diverse** all kinds of, all manner of, chequered, daedal *(Chiefly Poetic)*, diversified, heterogeneous, heterogenous, manifold, many-sided, multicultural, multiform, of all kinds, pluralist, polytypic, varied, variegated, various. **3. distinct** another, apart, disconnected, discrete, disjointed, disjunct, divided, segregate, segregated, separate, unattached, unconnected, unrelated. **4. asymmetric** asymmetrical, dissymmetric, dissymmetrical. **5. contrastive** contrastable, contrasting, contrasty, distinguishable. **6. modified**. **7. incongruous** clashing, discordant, discrepant, disharmonious, dissociable, dissonant, inconsistent, inconsonant, inharmonious, mismatched, noncongruent, off-key, parataxic.

v.   **4.**   **1. differ** diverge, divide, go different ways, speak a different language, vary. **2. contrast** be of a different kidney, bear no resemblance, foil, mismatch. **3. discriminate** separate the men from the boys, separate the sheep from the goats, sort, tell one from the other. **4. cause to differ** dissever, modify, rearrange.

adv.   **5.**   **1. differently** disparately, dissimilarly, incommensurably, incomparably, inconsistently, otherwise. **2. diversely** manifoldly, variously. **3. asymmetrically** dissymmetrically.

RELATED KEYWORDS: CHANGE, NONCONFORMITY, DISCORD, COMPARISON, SEPARATION

DIFFICULTY

n.   **1.**   **1. difficulty** awkwardness, complexity, complicity, perplexity, thorniness. **2. arduousness** onerousness, painfulness, toughness. **3. refractoriness** bloody-mindedness, intractableness, obstinacy, perverseness, perversity, prickliness, recalcitrance, stubbornness. **4. problem** coil, complicacy, complication, crux, difficulty, entanglement, knot, node, stymie, trouble. *Informal:* bugger, catch, fair cow, fun and games, headache, nigger in the woodpile, the devil to pay, tickler. **5. difficult task** an uphill battle, challenge, chore, long haul. *Informal:* a bastard of a job, a big ask, a bugger of a job, a cow of a job, a devil of a job, a hard (or long) row to hoe, a hard nut to crack, a hell of a job, a tall order, ballbreaker, job, stinker, the devil's own job. **6. burden** a millstone around someone's neck, an albatross around one's neck, care, charge, cumbrance, dead weight, encumbrance, hardship, onus, weight. **7. teething problems** growing pains. **8. hardship** asperity, rigour, tribulation.

    2.   **1. dilemma** blind alley, catch 22, double bind, impasse, predicament, quandary, vicious circle. *Informal:* pickle, spot. **2. difficult predicament** corner, dire straits, fix, quagmire. *Informal:* death seat, hole, hot seat, hot water, pickle, spot, squeeze, sticky wicket, tight corner, tight spot. **3. mess** rat-trap, scrape. *Informal:* can of worms, dog's breakfast, fine kettle of fish, frig-up, hobble, hot potato, how-do-you-do, pretty kettle of fish.

adj.   **3.**   **1. difficult** awkward, complex, complicated, diabolical, dilemmatic, hard, hellish, intricate, involved, knotty, problematised, tough, troublesome. *Informal:* crook, curly, diabolic, dodgy, fiddly, gnarly, graunchy *(NZ)*, hairy. **2. painful** distressful, distressing, trying. **3. arduous** backbreaking, formidable, herculean, laborious, painful, stiff, sweaty, toilsome, troublesome, uphill. **4. burdensome** bothersome, cumbersome, cumbrous, heavy, heavy-handed, leaden, onerous, oppressive, overburdensome, troublesome, weighty. **5. harsh** rugged, scabrous, severe, unforgiving. **6. difficult to handle** awkward, kittle *(Scottish)*, tight, tricky. *Informal:* dicky, dodgy, hairy, icky, spooky, sticky, ticklish. **7. challenging** confronting, demanding, formidable, testing. *Informal:* graunchy *(NZ)*. **8. prickly** spiny, thorny.

    4.   **1. unmanageable** contrary, fractious, hard-mouthed, impossible, incontrollable, intractable, obstinate, obstreperous, perverse, recalcitrant, refractory, restive, self-willed, strong-willed, stubborn, uncontrollable, ungovernable. *Informal:* bloody, bloody-minded.

v.   **5.**   **1. be difficult** be a long hard pull. *Informal:* be no picnic, be rocket science.

    6.   **1. have difficulty** buy into trouble, catch a Tartar, fall foul of, have difficulty with, have one's work cut out, wrestle with. **2. make it difficult** do it the hard way, flounder, go through the mill, make heavy weather of, scratch along.

    7.   **1. cause difficulties** clog, complicate, embarrass, encumber, entangle, hamper, harry, hinder, impede, incommode, involve, mire, perplex, straiten, stymie. **2. be a difficult person** be a handful, try someone's patience. **3. mess someone around** lead someone a chase, mess someone about, put through the hoops. *Informal:* lead someone a merry dance, make it hot for.

adv.   **8.**   **1. in difficulties** hard put, hard put to it, hard-set, in a jam, in deep (or hot) water, in dire straits, in trouble, on one's beam-ends, on the hook, on the spot, over a barrel, with one's back to the wall. *Informal:* behind the eight ball, in hot water, in strife, in the cactus, in the cart, in the poo, in the soup, on a sticky wicket, up against it, up the creek (without a paddle), up the pole. **2. in a fix** between Scylla and Charybdis, between the devil and the deep blue sea, between wind and water, in a cleft stick, on the horns of a dilemma.

    9.   **1. with difficulty** awkwardly, cumbersomely, ill, painfully, stiffly, troublesomely.

RELATED KEYWORDS: EFFORT, MISFORTUNE, HINDRANCE

DIGGING

n.   **1.**   **1. digging** banjoing, shovelling. **2. mining** black-sanding, coalmining, deep sinking, drift mining, fossicking, longwall mining, reefing. **3. excavation** magmatic stoping, shallow sinking, stoping, wet sinking. **4. gold-digging** goldmining. **5. gum-digging**

2. **1. digging implement** bogger, digger, digging stick, grubber, mattock, pick, pick-axe, scoop, shovel, spade, spud, trowel, V-box. *Informal:* banjo. **2. hoe** dutch hoe, grub hoe, rotary hoe. **3. mechanical shovel** front-end loader, post-hole digger, steam shovel, tractor shovel. **4. dredge** dredger, dredging machine. **5. grad-er** bulldozer, calfdozer, crawler, dozer, earthmover. **6. plough** chain harrow, chisel-plough, disc plough, drag, drill, gang plough, harrow, plow *(Chiefly US)*, rotary plough, rotary tiller, seed drill, stump-jump plough. **7. excavator** backhoe, drott. **8. jack-hammer**.

3. **1. digger** bogger, boodler, burrower, fossicker, harrower, shoveler *(US)*, shoveller. **2. miner** alluvial miner, black-sander *(NZ)*, coalminer, collier, Cousin Jack, digger, gold-digger, goldfielder, goldminer, gouger, grass captain, gum-digger *(NZ)*, mineworker, opal gouger, opal miner, pitman, pitworker, reefer, sand miner, tributer *(Chiefly SA)*. **3. excavator** bore sinker, ditcher, gravedigger, navvy, sapper, tank-sinker, tunneler.

4. **1. diggings** coalface, dig, workings. **2. mine** alluvial, bal, chalkpit, coal pit, excava-tion, goldmine, gunny, open cut, open pit mine, open-cut mine, pit, quarry, salt mine, wheal. *Informal:* show. **3. reef** alluvial, deep ground, ledge, lode, mother lode, mullocky reef, vein. **4. face** coalface, prospect, workface. **5. trench** ditch, entrenchments, fire trench, fosse, retrenchment, sap, slit trench, sondage, tunnel. **6. tunnel** cross-drive, crosscut, drift, lateral. **7. pit** downcast, mineshaft, monkey shaft, shaft, stope, well. **8. tailings** dump, leavings, slagheap, spoil.

adj. **5.** **1. digging** burrowing, fossorial. **2. mining** coalmining, open-cut.

v. **6.** **1. dig** ditch, dredge, fossick out, gouge, harrow, hoe, plough, shovel, spade, spud, subsoil, unearth. **2. mine** cut, drive, excavate, gad, open-cut, quarry, scratch, sink, spud, stope, surface, undermine. **3. tunnel** burrow, channel, sap. **4. dig up** burrow, grub, root up, rout, scratch, undermine, uproot. *Informal:* bandicoot. **5. scoop** cave, cave in, crater, dibble, dish, hole, hollow, hollow out, pit.

RELATED KEYWORDS: HOLLOW, FARMING, LAND, METAL, OIL, ROCK

DIRECTION

n. **1.** **1. direction** aim, alignment, bearing, bearings, beat, course, current, drift, eye, fly *(US)*, heading, line, line of sight, magnetic bearing, orbit, orientation, path, set, stream, streamline, streamline flow, stretch, sweep, tack, track, trajectory, trend, way. **2. aspect** bearings, lie, sense. **3. navigational course** azimuth, loxodromic curve, rhumb, rhumb line. **4. direct course** beeline, crosscut, geodesic, great circle.

2. **1. navigation** astronavigation, celestial navigation, contact flight, GPS, radio-navigation, teleran.

3. **1. directness** pointedness, straightness, sureness, unerringness.

4. **1. signpost** anchor light, arrow, beacon, beam, beckon, checkpoint, EPIRB, finger-post, guide, guidepost, guiding light, landmark, lighthouse, localiser, lodestar, pharos, pole star, pylon, riding light, traffic sign, vane, weathercock, weathervane, windvane.

5. **1. direction-finder** alidade, astrocompass, automatic direction finder, compass, GPS, gyro, gyrocompass, gyroscope, gyroscopic compass, gyrostat, gyrostatic compass, mag-netic compass, navaid, radio direction-finder, telltale compass. **2. compass card** compass rose, lubber line, magnetic needle, needle, pointer, quarter, rose. **3. point of the compass** cardinal point, rhumb.

6. **1. steerer** aimer, cockswain, cox, coxswain, driver, guide, helmsman, leader, man-oeuvrer, pilot, steersman, wheelman *(US)*. **2. automatic pilot** automatic flight control system, autopilot, beam-riding, celestial guidance, command guidance, inertial guidance, inertial navigation, radio control, talkdown.

adj. **7.** **1. directional** omnidirectional, omnirange, unidirectional, vaned. **2. steer-able** dirigible. **3. geotropic** apogeotropic, chemotropic, positively geotropic.

8. **1. direct** downright, geodesic, on the beam, one-way, point-blank, rectilineal, recti-linear, straight, straightforward, true, undeviating, unerring.

v. **9.** **1. direct** aim, channel, con, cox, helm, lay, lead, level, luff, make, pilot, point, present, steer, turn, up. **2. guide** beacon, beckon, gesticulate, home in on, induce, influence, lead, lull, motion, pilot, point, set, show, signal, talk someone down. **3. orientate** do, orient, point towards, quarter, range, redirect, reorientate, run, set, sight, train, traverse. **4. be oriented** bear, face, give on to, lie, look, look out on, present, tail.

10. **1. make for** bear down, carry on, course, fetch, fetch about, head, strike out towards. **2. ply a course** fly (or ride) the beam, follow, go by, ply, pursue, pursue a course, run a course, stand, track, wend.

adv. **11.** **1. directly** as the crow flies, blankly, due, point-blank, right, slam-bang, straight, unerringly. *Informal:* slap-bang.

RELATED KEYWORDS: FLYING, MARINER, MOVEMENT, POSITION, TRAVEL, VEHICLE

DIRTINESS

n. **1.** **1. dirtiness** feculence, filthiness, foulness, nastiness. **2. grubbiness** griminess, miriness, muckiness, muddiness, sliminess, sloppiness. **3. impurity** impureness, insanitariness, insanitation, uncleanliness, verminousness. **4. dustiness** sootiness. **5. smeariness** greasiness, smudginess, stickiness. **6. mouldiness** mucidness, mustiness. **7. pollution** carrion, contamination, corruption, corruptness, defilement, putrefaction, putrescence, putridness, stagnancy, stagnation. **8. squalor** dinginess, sleaziness, sordidness, squalidness. **9. messiness** frowziness, lousiness, manginess, scruffiness, slovenliness, untidiness. **10. piggishness** hoggishness, piggery.

2. **1. dirt** filth, grime, mess, muck, soil. *Informal:* grot, scuzz, toe jam. **2. smudge** blot, blotch, dirt, greasespot, grime, maculation, muck, pick, smear, smirch, smut, smutch, soil, spot, stain. **3. dust** cinders, cobweb, fallout, soot. **4. waste** putrilage, sewage, sullage. **5. swill** bilge, drainage, effluent, rinsing, slop, slops, slush, wash. **6. muck** grease, grunge, ooze, scum, slime, sludge, slush, spume, sullage. *Informal:* cack, guck, guk, gunk, scunge. **7. dandruff** furfur, scurf. **8. mould** fungus, mildew, mold *(US)*, must, rot, wet rot. **9. sweepings** garbage, refuse. **10. dag** daglock, dagwool.

3. **1. pigsty** Augean stables, pigpen, sty. **2. fleapit** *(Informal)* plague spot. **3. rubbish heap** dunghill, garbage bin. **4. cesspool** cess, cloaca, gutter, sewer, slough.

4. **1. dirty person** drab, draggletail, mucker, sloven, trollop. *Informal:* dag, scruff, scunge, slummock, warb, waub. **2. polluter** defiler, pollutant. **3. guttersnipe** gamin, urchin. *Informal:* mudlark *(British)*. **4. piggish person** beast, wallower. *Informal:* hog, pig. **5. litterbug** litterer.

adj. **5.** **1. dirty** black, dingy, dusty, grimy, skungy, smoky, smutty, sooty, thick with dust, unswept. *Informal:* grotty, scungy, scuzzy. **2. unclean** dirty, impure, insalubrious, insanitary, maculate, polluted, squalid, uncleanly, unsanitary. **3. smeary** cacky, clarty, greasy, miry, muddy, smeared, smudgy, smutchy. **4. grubby** shopsoiled. **5. messy** dishevelled, disordered, slovenly, trashy *(US)*, untidy. *Informal:* daggy. **6. foul** cacky, daggy, feculent, filthy, mucky, nasty, offensive. **7. stagnant** festering, septic. **8. rotting** maggoty, tainted, verminous. **9. slimy** slimey, sloppy, slushy. *Informal:* goozy *(WA, SA)*. **10. mucid** mouldy, musty.

6. **1. unkempt** bedraggled, blowzy, dishevelled, down at heel, draggletailed, frowzy, grubby, ragged, raggle-tailed, scrubby, shaggy, sleazy, slipshod, slovenly, sluttish, untidy, wretched. *Informal:* daggy, scruffy, warby, wild and woolly. **2. dirty** scabby, scabious, scrofulous, scurfy, unwashed. *Informal:* scruffy, snot-nose, snotty, snotty-nosed. **3. squalid** buggy, crawling, dingy, flea-bitten, lousy, mangy, pedicular, pediculous, ratty, shabby, sordid, tatty, verminous, weevilly, wretched. *Informal:* chatty, grungy, scruffy. **4. piggish** beastlike, hoggish, hoglike.

v. **7.** **1. dirty** befoul, begrime, besmear, besmirch, clog, defile, foul, grime, pollute, poop, smirch, soil, soot. **2. smear** bedaub, besmear, blot, blur, clart *(Scottish)*, daub, fuzz, mackle, slime, smudge, smut, smutch, spot, stain, thumb. **3. contaminate** corrupt, desterilise, flyblow, infect, maculate, pollute, spoil, sully, taint, tarnish. **4. mire** bemire, bespatter, muddy, puddle, slop, splash. **5. mess** litter up, muck, muss, untidy.

8. **1. get dirty** collect dust, foul. **2. mildew** moulder. **3. stagnate** decompose, fester, go bad, putrefy, rot. **4. draggle** drabble. **5. pig it** *(Informal)* live in a pig sty. **6. wallow** make mud pies, roll in the mud.

adv. **9.** **1. dirtily** dingily, dustily, grimily, smudgily. **2. filthily** foully, hoggishly, nastily, piggishly. **3. greasily** muddily, slimily, sloppily. **4. impurely** stagnantly, uncleanly. **5. squalidly** frowzily, grubbily, sleazily, sordidly. **6. sootily** smokily.

RELATED KEYWORDS: BODILY DISCHARGE, ILL HEALTH, DISORDER, IMPERFECTION, DISUSE

DISAGREEMENT

n. **1.** **1. disagreement** argument, conflict, contention, contest, controversy, difference, disaccord, discord, dissension, dissent, dissentience, dissidence, division, friction, misunderstanding, noncompliance, strife, variance. **2. argument** altercation, bicker, contretemps, disagreement, disputation, dispute, feud, fight, jangle, quarrel, row, set-to, squabble, strife, unpleasantness, upset, wrangle. *Informal:* argy-bargy, barney, bust-up, ding, hassle, high words, jar *(Aboriginal English)*, run-in. **3. objection** cavil, contradiction, contrasuggestion, demur, demurral, demurrer, denial, difficulty, point of order.

4. denial denegation, disallowance, nay, negative, no, traverse. **5. protest** expostulation, remonstrance, remonstration.

2. **1. argumentativeness** contentiousness, contrariness, disputatiousness, divisiveness, negativity, pettifoggery. **2. discord** disharmony, disunion, disunity.

3. **1. disputant** arguer, bickerer, contester, controversialist, disputer, eristic, pettifogger, troublemaker, wrangler. *Informal:* stirrer. **2. dissenter** anti, contradictor, controverter, demurrer, denier, dissentient, dissident, maverick, objector, protestant, protester, remonstrant, remonstrator.

adj. **4.** **1. dissenting** anti, disagreeing, dissentient, dissident, divergent, diverging, remonstrant, remonstrating, tangential. **2. argumentative** adversarial, belligerent, cantankerous, contentious, contradictory, contrary, contrasuggestible, contrasuggestive, disputant, disputatious, disputative, dissentious, oppugnant, polemical, quarrelsome.

5. **1. controversial** conflictive, contentious, divisive, eristic. **2. at variance** inconsonant. **3. arguable** contestable, contradictable, disputable, exceptionable, objectionable, questionable.

v. **6.** **1. disagree** conflict, deviate, differ, disaccord, dissent, diverge, vary, wrangle. **2. argue** altercate, bicker, chaffer, contend, contest, demur, disaccord, disagree, dispute, fall out, haggle, have words, join issue, joust, pettifog, quarrel, squabble, stickle, tiff, wrangle. *Informal:* argie-bargie, argle-bargle, argufy, argy-bargy, cook up a storm, have words with, make the fur fly, row, stir the possum. **3. object** buck at, confound, contradict, controvert, demur, disagree with, dispute, oppose, protest, question, reluct to, remonstrate, shake one's head, take exception to, take issue with. *Informal:* pay out.

adv. **7.** **1. argumentatively** belligerently, contentiously, controversially, disputatiously, divisively. **2. contradictorily** contrarily.

8. **1. in question** at issue, at variance, under discussion.

interj. **9.** **1. no** absolutely not, by no means, nae *(Scottish)*, nay, never, nix, no such luck, no way, not a bit of it, not by a long sight, noway, nowise, scarcely. *Informal:* (in a) pig's ear, baal, like fun, like hell, no way José, nope, not (bloody) likely, not for quids, not on your life, not on your nelly, nuts, phooey, pigs, uh-uh.

RELATED KEYWORDS: DENIAL, NONCONFORMITY, DISCORD, CONTEST

DISAPPEARANCE

n. **1.** **1. disappearance** blackout, dematerialisation, departure, dispersion, evanescence, evaporation, exit, fade-out, fading, passing, vanishing. **2. eclipse** occultation, total eclipse. **3. black hole** Bermuda Triangle.

2. **1. extinction** dying out, expiration, expiry, petering out.

adj. **3.** **1. disappearing** evanescent, evaporating, evasive, fading, fleeting, vanishing. **2. dispersive** evaporative.

4. **1. disappeared** into (or in) thin air, lost to view. *Informal:* gone for a Tosca. **2. extinct** departed, expired, extinguished.

v. **5.** **1. disappear** dematerialise, disperse, dissipate, dissolve, drop, evanesce, evaporate, fade away, leave no trace, melt, melt away, peter out, vanish. **2. melt into thin air** become lost to sight, become lost to view, do a vanishing trick, pass out of sight. *Informal:* blackhole, go into smoke, take a powder. **3. go missing** be stolen, be taken, get lost.

6. **1. become extinct** be curtains for, depart, die out, exit, expire, fizzle out, give out, wither away.

RELATED KEYWORDS: RETREAT, DEPARTURE, NON-EXISTENCE, HIDING, ESCAPE, INVISIBILITY

DISAPPROVAL

n. **1.** **1. disapproval** disapprobation, discountenance, disesteem, disfavour, dislike, disrelish, distaste, odium. **2. censure** abuse, blame, commination, condemnation, criticism, denunciation, detraction, disapprobation, flak, headshaking, invective, obloquy, rebuff, reprobation, reproof, vitriol, vituperation. **3. remonstration** admonition, execration, expostulation, protest, protestation, remonstrance. **4. chastisement** castigation, censure, condemnation, disapprobation, disapproval, objurgation, rebuke, reprehension, reprobation, reproof, reproval. **5. denunciation** condemnation, crimination, damnation, denouncement, fulmination. **6. criticism** animadversion, depreciation, dispraise, growling *(Aboriginal English)*, reflection, stricture. **7. contempt** contumely, disdain, disgrace, dishonour, disparagement, ignominy, opprobrium, scorn, shame. **8. fault-finding** captiousness, carping, censoriousness, nitpicking, quibbling. **9. self-criticism** self-reproach.

2.   **1. reprimand** admonishment, lecture, rebuke, reproach, reproof, reproval, scolding, upbraiding. **2. tongue-lashing** a piece of one's mind, bashing, counterblast, derision, dressing-down, lashing, mockery, rating, rub, scorn, slap. *Informal:* a kick in the pants, bagging, blast, chip, curtain lecture, earful, flea in someone's ear, jaw, pasting, payout, razz, roast, roasting, rocket, scorcher, serve, slam, talking-to, the rough side of one's tongue, the rounds of the kitchen, the treatment, trimming *(British)*, wigging *(British)*. **3. tirade** diatribe, jeremiad, philippic. **4. attack** air raid, broadside, onslaught.

3.   **1. boo** catcall, groan, handclap, hiss, slow handclap. *Informal:* bird, brickbat, Bronx cheer, raspberry, thumbs down. **2. sneer** frown, lour, scowl. **3. demerit** black mark, blackball.

4.   **1. disapprover** booer, deprecator, hisser. **2. censurer** carper, caviller, censor, complainer, critic, criticiser, cynic, fault-finder, hypercritic, nitpicker, quibbler. *Informal:* basher, knocker, niggler, whingeing Pom, whinger. **3. denouncer** condemner, denunciator, jeremiah, vituperator. **4. scolder** admonisher, chider, rebuker, reproacher, reprover, scold, upbraider. **5. chastiser** castigator, chastener. **6. protester** expostulator, objector, remonstrant, remonstrator.

adj.   **5.**   **1. disapproving** admonitory, monitory, remonstrant, remonstrative, reproving, scolding. **2. censorial** censorious, critical, hypercritical, overcritical. **3. fault-finding** captious, carping, derogatory, nitpicking, quibbling, snide. *Informal:* picky. **4. deprecatory** contemptuous, contumelious, insinuating, pejorative, sarcastic. **5. denunciatory** comminatory. **6. disapprobatory** dyslogistic, opprobrious. **7. condemnatory** censorious, damnatory, damning, objurgatory, reprehensive, reprobative, uncharitable, upbraiding, vituperative. **8. scathing** biting, blistering, blistery, caustic, cutting, sarcastic, scorching, scornful, slashing, withering.

v.   **6.**   **1. disapprove of** be unimpressed, deprecate, discommend, discountenance, frown on (or upon), look daggers at, look down on, object, take a dim view of. **2. condemn** animadvert on (or upon), blame, censure, criminate, damn, disapprove, fault, tax. *Informal:* pick to pieces. **3. criticise** boo, cast (or throw) the first stone, scarify, scathe, scorch, score *(US)*, slam, slate, snipe at, vituperate. *Informal:* bag, bash, dump on, knock, monster, pan, pooh-pooh, roast, slag, tear strips off, throw off at. **4. boo** catcall, hiss, slow clap. *Informal:* burl.

7.   **1. scold** admonish, berate, blame, censure, chasten, chastise, chide, find fault, lambaste, name, rebuke, remonstrate with, reprehend, reprimand, reproach, reprobate, reprove, tongue, tongue-lash, twit, upbraid. *Informal:* chew out, give someone a bad mark, go crook at (or on), go on at, lay it on, rag, rouse on (or at), tick off, wig *(British)*. **2. lecture** admonish, chat, lesson, reprimand, tutor. *Informal:* jaw, rag, read someone a lecture. **3. scold severely** attack, baste, berate, castigate, chide, denounce, denunciate, flay, fulminate against, objurgate, pelt, rail, rate, reprimand, scold, scourge, take to task, tongue-lash, upbraid, whip. *Informal:* bawl out, be on at, blast, blast (the) hell out of, blow up, bore it up someone, carpet, dress down, give a pay, give someone beans, give someone gip, give someone heaps, give someone hell, give someone Larry Dooley, give someone what for, give the rough side of one's tongue, give the rounds of the kitchen, go to town on, haul over the coals, hoe into, keelhaul, lash, make mincemeat of, mat, paste, play hell with, put on the mat, put the boot into someone, rap someone over (or on) the knuckles, roust hell out of, sally up *(NZ)*, take a piece out of, tear (or take) strips off. **4. jump on (or upon)** *Informal:* jump down someone's throat, pull up. **5. cop flak** *(Informal)*.

adv.   **8.**   **1. disapprovingly** askance, deprecatingly, deprecatorily, discouragingly, pejoratively. **2. chidingly** admonishingly, reproachfully, reprobatively, reprovingly, scoldingly, upbraidingly. **3. censoriously** captiously, carpingly, condemningly, contemptuously, critically, damningly, despiteously, dyslogistically, hypercritically, reprehensively, vituperatively. **4. scathingly** ad hominem, bitingly, scorchingly, scornfully, sneeringly, uncharitably, witheringly. **5. in someone's black books** in someone's bad books.

RELATED KEYWORDS: DISAGREEMENT, SLANDER, BADNESS, LOW REGARD, DISPLEASURE

DISBELIEF

n.   **1.**   **1. disbelief** denial, discredit, distrust, incredulity, incredulousness, unbelief, unbelievingness. **2. doubt** credibility gap, distrust, distrustfulness, dubiety, misgiving, mistrust, mistrustfulness, scepticalness, suspicion, uncertainty. **3. scepticism** agnosticism, nescience, nihilism, pyrrhonism.

2.   **1. disbeliever** agnostic, atheist, distruster, doubter, doubting Thomas, infidel, kafir, mistruster, nihilist, nullifidian, questioner, sceptic, skeptic *(US)*, unbeliever.

adj.   **3.**   **1. disbelieving** agnostic, distrustful, doubtful, doubting, dubitative, inconvincible, incredulous, mistrustful, sceptical, suspicious, unbelieving.

v. **4.** **1. disbelieve** call in (or into) question, deny, doubt, entertain doubts, harbour suspicions, have one's doubts, question, suspect, take with a grain of salt. *Informal:* smell a rat. **2. distrust** disbelieve, discredit, mistrust. **3. query** bring into question, challenge, raise doubts.

adv. **5.** **1. disbelievingly** agnostically, distrustfully, doubtingly, inconvincibly, incredulously, mistrustfully, mistrustingly, sceptically, unbelievingly.

interj. **6.** **1. nonsense** don't make me laugh, eh, fiddle-de-dee, fiddlesticks, get out, go on, ha, humph, my hat, pah, pshaw, rubbish, sure, um, what. *Informal:* ... has got to (or must) (or has to) be kidding, (all) my eye and Betty Martin, (in a) pig's ear, apple sauce, as if, bollocks, bosh *(Chiefly British)*, bull, bullswool, gammon, get along with you, get away, get away with you, heifer dust, in a pig's eye, like fun, my foot, my sainted aunt, oh yeah, phooey, pigs might fly, pull the other leg, pull the other one (it has bells), tell that (or it) to the horse marines, tell that to your grandmother, that'll be the day, that's a good one, try another, yeah right.

RELATED KEYWORDS: UNCERTAINTY

DISCERNMENT

n. **1.** **1. discernment** cultivation, culture, delicateness, discretion, finesse, preciosity, refinement, selectivity, tact, taste. **2. perspicacity** clear-headedness, clear-sightedness, insight, penetration, perspicuity, sagaciousness, sagacity. **3. differentiation** difference, discrimination, distinction, hairsplitting.

2. **1. distinction** nicety, nuance, quiddity, subtlety.

3. **1. discerner** differentiator, discriminator, distinguisher, hairsplitter. **2. connoisseur** aesthete, cognoscente, critic, esthete. *Informal:* maven *(US)*.

adj. **4.** **1. discerning** clear-eyed, clear-headed, clear-sighted, discriminate, discriminating, discriminative, penetrating, perspicacious, perspicuous, sagacious. **2. subtle** fine, fine-drawn, fine-spun, hairsplitting, nice, overcritical, refined. **3. selective** cultured, dainty, delicate, discerning, fastidious, nice, refined. **4. discreet** considerate, diplomatic, judicious, prudent, sage, tactful. **5. discretional** discretionary, judicial.

v. **5.** **1. discern** have an ear for, have an eye for, know, know chalk from cheese, know the difference. **2. differentiate** characterise, contradistinguish, difference, discern, discriminate, distinguish, distinguish between, pick out, resolve, separate the sheep from the goats, tell, winnow. **3. split hairs** fine-draw, refine, refine on (or upon).

adv. **6.** **1. discerningly** clear-sightedly, discriminately, discriminatingly, discriminatively, penetratingly, perspicaciously, sagaciously. **2. subtly** delicately, finely, nicely.

RELATED KEYWORDS: COMPARISON, GOOD TASTE, INTELLIGENCE

DISCONTENTEDNESS

n. **1.** **1. discontentedness** affluenza, cold comfort, disappointment, discontent, dissatisfaction, distemper, ennui, heartburning, moods, restlessness, unrest. *Informal:* seven-year itch. **2. grumpiness** bitchery, disgruntlement, fretfulness, grouchiness, grumbles, murmuring, querulousness, sourness, sulkiness, verjuice.

2. **1. complaint** bleat, cavil, dissent, gravamen, grievance, gripe, grizzle, grouse, grumble, grumbles, kick, lamentation, moan, murmur, objection, peeve, plaint, protest, regret, repining, squawk, squeal, whine, whinge, yammer. *Informal:* beef *(Chiefly US)*, bellyache, bitch, chip on the shoulder.

3. **1. complainer** a bad loser, bleater, carper, crab, fault-finder, fuss-budget *(Chiefly US)*, fusspot, griper, grouch, grouser, growler, grumbler, grump, malcontent, moaner, murmurer, mutterer, squawker, squealer, whiner, whinger, yammerer. *Informal:* bitch, bite *(NZ)*, grizzleguts, grumblebum, lemon, miseryguts, mopoke, nark, sorehead, whingeing Pom.

adj. **4.** **1. discontented** aggrieved, cast down, discontent, disgruntled, dissatisfied, fretful, fretting and fuming, ill-conditioned, ill-humoured, injured, malcontent, moody, never satisfied, not happy, offended, out of humour, querulous, restless, seething, soured, troubled, uneasy, ungruntled, weary, wronged, wry. *Informal:* browned off, sore. **2. grouchy** bad-tempered, bleating, broody, carping, crabby, cranky, cross, crusty, griping, grumbling, grumpy, huffy, ill-tempered, in a mood, in high dudgeon, in the sulks, like a bear with a sore head, moaning, murmuring, murmurous, narky, peevish, snarly, snuffy, sulky, surly, temperamental, whingeing, with one's face tied in a knot. *Informal:* pippy, snitchy.

v. **5.** **1. be discontented** bitch and bind, feel blue, feel sad, get upset, take in bad part, take on. **2. complain** bleat, carp, cavil, chew the rag, croak, fret, fuss, gripe, grizzle, grouch, grouse, growl, grumble, moan, murmur, mutter, pine, protest, repine, seethe, squawk, squeal, whine, whinge, yammer. *Informal:* beef *(Chiefly US),* bellyache, bitch, fratch, scream (or yell) (or cry, etc.) blue murder.

6. 1. make discontented annoy, begrudge, bite, chagrin, discomfort, discontent, disgruntle, displease, dissatisfy, irritate, nag, nark, put out, put out of countenance, rile, roil, worry.

adv. **7. 1. discontentedly** carpingly, complainingly, dissatisfiedly, fretfully, grouchily, grumblingly, grumpily, murmurously, querulously, sulkily, wryly.

RELATED KEYWORDS: EXCITEMENT, UNHAPPINESS, UNPLEASANTNESS

DISCORD

n. **1. 1. discord** contention, discordance, discordancy, disharmony, disunity, inconsonance. **2. incongruity** anomalousness, incongruence, oddness, unnaturalness. **3. unaptness** improperness, impropriety, infelicity, unbecomingness, unfitness, unseemliness, unsuitableness. **4. disaccord** antinomy, contradictoriness, disagreement, nonconformity, repugnance, repugnancy. **5. irreconcilableness** incompatibleness. **6. antibiosis** disoperation.

2. 1. anomaly discrepance, discrepancy, inconsistency, irreconcilable, variance. **2. misfit** mismatch, mockery. *Informal:* square peg in a round hole.

adj. **3. 1. discordant** disharmonious, dissonant, inconsonant, inharmonious, off-key, out of phase, parataxic. **2. incongruous** absonant, absurd, anomalistic, anomalous, incongruent, odd, unnatural. **3. discrepant** contradictory, differing, incongruous, inconsistent, repugnant. **4. incompatible** alien to, ill-assorted, incoherent, indecent, indecorous, irreconcilable, off, unapt, unbecoming, unconformable, unfitting, unfortunate, unhappy, unseemly, unsuitable, unsuited. **5. unapt** de trop, impertinent, improper, inappropriate, inapt, incorrect, inept, infelicitous, irrelevant, misplaced, out of character, out of keeping, out of place, unfit, unhappy, unseasonable, unsuitable, unsuited, wrong. **6. at variance** at issue, at odds, contentious, controversial, disputatious, eristic, in question.

adv. **4. 1. discordantly** discrepantly, dissonantly, inconsistently, inconsonantly, irreconcilably, out of step. **2. incongruously** anomalously, incongruently. **3. unaptly** improperly, inappropriately, incoherently, incompatibly, infelicitously, malapropos, unfitly, unhappily, unsatisfactorily, unseemly, unsuitably.

RELATED KEYWORDS: DISAGREEMENT, INEQUALITY, DIFFERENCE

DISCOURAGEMENT

n. **1. 1. discouragement** demoralisation, determent, deterrence, disenchantment, disheartenment, dispiritedness, dissuasion, negative reinforcement. **2. remonstrance** expostulation, protest, protestation, warning.

2. 1. discourager block, check, damp, dampener, dash, demoraliser, deterrent, discouragement, disincentive, dissuader, obstacle, restraint, setback, stop, throwback. **2. remonstrant** expostulator, protester. **3. killjoy** spoilsport, wet blanket. *Informal:* party pooper, wowser.

adj. **3. 1. discouraging** deterrent, dispiriting, dissuasive, off-putting, soul-destroying. **2. remonstrative** expostulatory, warning. **3. forbidding** prohibitive.

v. **4. 1. discourage** dash, daunt, demoralise, disenchant, dishearten, disillusion, dismay, dispirit, get someone down, repel. *Informal:* beat the stuffing out of, knock the stuffing out of, slap down. **2. dissuade** advise against, block, check, chill, damp, dampen, demotivate, deter, discourage from, put a damper on, put off, quench someone's enthusiasm, restrain, talk out of, throw cold water on, wet-blanket. **3. remonstrate** expostulate, protest. **4. stop** frustrate, thwart.

adv. **5. 1. discouragingly** dishearteningly, dispiritingly, dissuasively. **2. remonstratively** expostulatingly.

RELATED KEYWORDS: REPULSION, WARNING, UNWILLINGNESS

DISCOURTESY

n. **1. 1. discourtesy** bad form, bad manners, conduct unbecoming, discourteousness, disobligingness, disrespect, ill-breeding, impoliteness, incivility, inurbanity, rudeness, solecism, tactlessness, ungraciousness, unhandsomeness, unknightliness, unmannerliness. **2. brusqueness** abruptness, bluffness, bluntness, briefness, brusquerie, curtness, shortness, terseness. **3. insolence** brassiness, brazenness, dumb insolence, forwardness, freshness, gall, impertinence, impudence, impudency, more hide (or cheek) than Jessie, sauciness, temerity. *Informal:* cheek, chutzpah, crust, face, hide, nerve, sauce. **4. coarseness** bastardry, boorishness, crudeness, crudity, immodesty, improperness, impropriety, indecency, savageness, unseemliness, vulgarity. **5. surliness** bearishness, churlishness, crustiness, grouchiness, moroseness.

2. 1. discourteous person barbarian, bear, blackguard, blaggard, boor, buffoon, bull in a china shop, churl, clown, Goth, hooligan, insolent, lout, nouveau riche, vulgarian. *Informal:* bastard, gremmie, hoon, ocker, pleb, roughie, yahoo, yob, yobbo. **2. minx** fishwife, hoyden. **3. insulter** knocker, snubber.

adj. **3. 1. discourteous** badly-behaved, boorish, caddish, churlish, disobliging, hoyden, hoydenish, ignorant, ill-bred, ill-mannered, impolite, inurbane, mannerless, rude, tactless, unceremonious, uncivil, uncourteous, uncourtly, ungentlemanly, ungracious, unhandsome, unknightly, unladylike, unmannered, unmannerly, unseemly. **2. brusque** abrupt, bluff, blunt, brief, curt, short, short-spoken, terse. **3. insolent** abusive, audacious, bold, bold-faced, brash, brazen, brazen-faced, flash *(Aboriginal English)*, forward, fresh, impertinent, impudent, insulting, pert, precocious, presumptuous, saucy. *Informal:* brassy, cheeky, sassy. **4. coarse** barbarian, barbarous, brutish, coarse-grained, common, common as muck, crude, dead common, foul-mouthed, improper, inelegant, low, rorty, rough, rude, thersitical, uncivil, uncivilised, uncouth, unmannerly, unpolished, unrefined, unseemly, vulgar. **5. haughty** cavalier, contemptuous, contumelious, disdainful, inconsiderate, offhand, overbearing, presumptuous, snubby, supercilious, superior, thoughtless. *Informal:* snooty, toplofty. **6. surly** bearish, boorish, churlish, crusty, gruff, grumpy, ill-conditioned, immodest, moody, morose, savage, sulky, sullen.

v. **4. 1. act discourteously** blackguard, blaggard, commit a solecism, forget oneself, speak out of turn, take a liberty, tread on someone's corns, tread on someone's toes. *Informal:* drop a brick, put one's (big) foot in it. **2. be insolent** answer back, give someone a short answer, give someone cheek, talk back. *Informal:* give someone lip.

adv. **5. 1. discourteously** disobligingly, ill-manneredly, impolitely, inurbanely, rudely, tactlessly, ungraciously, unhandsomely, with (a) bad grace. **2. brusquely** abruptly, bearishly, bluffly, bluntly, boorishly, briefly, churlishly, crustily, curtly, shortly, surlily, tersely. **3. impudently** brassily, brazenly, forwardly, freshly, impertinently, insultingly, saucily. **4. coarsely** crudely, immodestly, improperly, unseemly. **5. haughtily** cavalierly.

RELATED KEYWORDS: MISBEHAVIOUR, LOW REGARD, WRONGDOING

DISENCHANTMENT

n. **1. 1. disenchantment** chagrin, disheartenment, disillusion, disillusionment, dismay, frustration, tantalisation. **2. disappointment** anticlimax, bathos, baulk, blow, comedown, dash, hitch, let-down, lowlight, mare's nest, setback. *Informal:* bummer, fizzer, sell, swiz.

adj. **2. 1. disenchanted** baffled, chagrined, disappointed, foiled, frustrated, let down, thwarted. *Informal:* gutted, stuffed.

v. **3. 1. disenchant** betray, betray one's hopes, dash, daunt, disappoint, dishearten, disillusion, dismay, mock, mock one's hopes. **2. frustrate** baffle, baulk, bilk, defeat, foil, stymie, tantalise, thwart. **3. be a disappointment to** be less than one's hopes, disappoint, fall short of the goal, not come up to expectations, not come up to scratch, not come up to the mark. **4. be disappointed** *Informal:* come a thud.

RELATED KEYWORDS: FAILURE, DISCONTENTEDNESS, DESPAIR

DISHONESTY

n. **1. 1. dishonesty** crookedness, fraudulency, improbity, knavery, knavishness, lubricity, rascality, roguery, shiftiness, trickery, wickedness, wile. **2. insincerity** deceitfulness, duplicity, faithlessness, prevarication. **3. corruption** bribery, corruptibleness, corruptness, graft, jobbery, jobbing, malversation, nepotism, payola, pork-barrelling, racketeering, venality. *Informal:* dirty pool, jobs for the boys. **4. cheating** barratry, champerty, chicane, chicanery, double dip, double-dealing, guile, pettifoggery, sharp practice, shifty business, skulduggery, sophistry. *Informal:* funny business, jiggery-pokery, skin game. **5. swindle** bilk, cheat, confidence trick, cozenage, fraud, gerrymander, graft, legerdemain, medifraud, phishing, ramp, roguery, rook, rookery, ruse, scheme, shift, subreption, trick, trickery, wile. *Informal:* caper, chizz *(British)*, con, con job, con trick, do, dodge, fastie, fiddle, fix, flim-flam, frost, gyp, have, lurk, racket, rip-off, roughie, scam, sell, set-up, shenanigans, shrewdie, skin game, snow job, stew, swiftie, swiz, swizzle, take, take-down, tax lurk, wangle, wrinkle. **6. crime** foul play, lawlessness.

2. 1. dishonest person adventurer, adventuress, barrator, confidence man, corrupter, dodger, false-pretender, fraud, grifter *(US)*, illywhacker, knave, picaro, picaroon, racketeer, rascal, rogue, scamp, shark, spalpeen, twister, wangler. *Informal:* con man, crook, fake, faker *(US)*, fiddler, ratbag, rorter, slyboots, wrong 'un. **2. swindler** bilker, chicaner, confidence man, double-dealer, front man, pettifogger, sharp dealer. *Informal:* con artist, con man, faker *(US)*, pie-eater, shicer, shyster, twicer. **3. cheat** bilk, blackleg, cheater, palmer, rook, sharp, sharper, short-changer, swindler, trickster. *Informal:* fink, gyp, gypper, gypster, shicer, spieler. **4. criminal** felon, lawbreaker. **5. corrupt offi-cial** dishonest politician, jobber, security risk. *Informal:* bent cop. **6. self-seeker** company man, sycophant.

adj.   **3.**   **1. dishonest** crafty, crooked, cross, deceitful, double-dealing, fraudulent, knavish, pettifogging, picaresque, rascally, roguish, shifty, slippery, two-faced, unfaithful. *Informal:* bent, crook, dodgy, shady, shonkie, shoofty. **2. corrupt** open to bribery, rotten, Tammany-Hall, venal. *Informal:* bent, in it up to the hilt, shonky. **3. fraudulent** cross, dishonest. *Informal:* cronk, fixed, lurky, set-up. **4. self-seeking** beggar-my-neighbour.

v.   **4.**   **1. swindle** beat *(US)*, chicane, fleece, gudgeon, job, pettifog, racketeer, take in, thim-blerig. *Informal:* chisel, do, do in the eye, dud, gyp, hoozle, lamb down, make a fast buck, nobble, rip off, screw, swizzle, wangle, work a ready. **2. cheat** play with marked cards, rig, tamper. *Informal:* brass, fix. **3. deceive** deliberately mislead, sophisticate, speak with double tongue, speak with forked tongue, trick out of. *Informal:* gee someone up. **4. be self-seeking** feather one's nest, look after number one, look out for number one, take care of oneself.

adv.   **5.**   **1. dishonestly** cheatingly, corruptly, crookedly, fraudulently, knavishly, on the cross, on the fiddle, shadily, shiftily.

     RELATED KEYWORDS: DECEPTION, UNFAIRNESS, UNLAWFULNESS, IMMORALITY, ROBBERY, UNTRUTHFULNESS

DISMISSAL

n.   **1.**   **1. dismissal** cavel-out, lay-off, lockout, retrenchment, stand-down, wrongful dismissal. **2. marching orders** dehiring, notice, the (old) heave-ho, walking papers. *Informal:* bullet, bum's rush, DCM, order of the boot, the axe, the can, the chop, the chuck, the push, the sack, walking ticket. **3. deposal** comedown, deplumation, deposition, dethronement, disrobement, downfall, overthrow, removal. **4. resignation** abdication, demission, retirement, spill.

     2.   **1. dismisser** deposer, dethroner, hatchet man, ouster, unmaker. *Informal:* axeman.

     3.   **1. demotion** abasement, debasement, degradation, relegation.

adj.   **4.**   **1. dismissed** axed, dooced, jobless, retrenched, sacked, time-expired, unemployed. **2. raddle-marked** for the chop, on the skids.

v.   **5.**   **1. dismiss** amove, boot out, discharge, displace, fire, give someone notice, hunt, lay off, relieve one's duties, remove, retrench, shelve, stand down, strike off. *Informal:* axe, bounce, can, chop, jeff *(Victoria)*, put out to grass, sack, tramp *(WA)*. **2. discharge** board out, cashier, decommission, demob, demobilise, drum out, muster out, pension off. *Informal:* give someone (or something) the boot. **3. disbar** disbench, drop, give someone the red card. **4. defrock** deprive, disfrock, disordain, disrobe, unfrock. **5. suspend** stand off. **6. oust** disseat, put the skids under, unseat. **7. depose** deplume, dethrone, overthrow, uncrown.

     6.   **1. be dismissed** be given the golden handshake, fall, get one's ticket. *Informal:* get the boot, get the chop, get the sack, get the shunt, get the spear.

     7.   **1. resign** bow out, go into retirement, leave, quit, retire, sign off, step down, take off, tender one's resignation, vacate, vacate a position. *Informal:* chuck it in, give the tube away, roll over, snatch one's time. **2. abdicate** give up the throne, lay down the burden of office.

     8.   **1. demote** abase, break, debase, declass, degrade, disrate, relegate. *Informal:* bust.

     RELATED KEYWORDS: DISUSE

DISOBEDIENCE

n.   **1.**   **1. disobedience** breach, civil disobedience, contempt, fault, filibusterism, infraction, infringement, misconduct, non-compliance, non-cooperation, offence, passive resistance, rebeldom, transgression, violation, wrong. **2. delinquency** contu-maciousness, contumacy, disesteem, disrespect, fractiousness, mutinousness, naughtiness, rudeness, unruliness. **3. rebelliousness** incompliancy, insubordination, recalcitrance, recalcitrancy, recalcitration, recreance, recreancy. **4. incorrigibleness** frowardness, incorrigibility, indocility, perverseness, perversity, refractoriness, ungovernableness.

2. **1. disobeyer** bandit, infringer, insubordinate, looter, non-complier, outlaw, rioter, violator. **2. rebel** anarchist, apostate, dissenter, dissentient, dissident, diversionist, insurgent, maverick, mutineer, protestant, recalcitrant, recreant, renegade, street fighter, traitor, transgressor, urban guerilla. **3. delinquent** juvenile delinquent, urchin. *Informal:* hellion, tearaway.

adj. **3.** **1. disobedient** incompliant, insubordinate, non-compliant, transgressive, unyielding. **2. rebellious** anarchic, contumacious, insurgent, lawless, mutinous, renitent, treasonable, treasonous. **3. disorderly** anarchistic, dishevelled, haywire, restive, riotous, turbulent, unchartered, unregulated. **4. badly-behaved** cantankerous, contrary, froward, ill-behaved, improper, perverse, problem, rampageous, robustious, rude, uncivilised, unruly, wayward, wild. **5. delinquent** hard case, mischievous, naughty, rebel, urchin. **6. incorrigible** fractious, headstrong, incontrollable, inordinate, intractable, obstreperous, strong-willed, stubborn, unbroken, uncontrollable, undisciplined, ungovernable, unmanageable, wilful. *Informal:* rambunctious *(US)*. **7. intransigent** recalcitrant, refractory, self-willed.

v. **4.** **1. disobey** attaint, break, contravene, defile, disgrace, dishonour, drag one's feet, foul, infract, infringe, rebel, recalcitrate, sin, stray, transgress, trespass, violate. **2. take the law into one's own hands** go under someone's neck, kick over the traces, mutiny, run riot.

adv. **5.** **1. disobediently** incompliantly, incorrigibly, insubordinately, naughtily, ungovernably, unmanageably. **2. rebelliously** contumaciously, delinquently, fractiously, frowardly, mutinously, perversely, recreantly, refractorily, transgressively, treasonably, treasonously.

RELATED KEYWORDS: DISAGREEMENT, UNLAWFULNESS

DISORDER

n. **1.** **1. disorder** anarchy, bedlam, bouleversement, chaos, complication, difficulty, discord, disharmony, distemper, disturbance, fuddle, mayhem, moil, ravel, shakings, trouble, turbulence, turmoil. *Informal:* can of worms, snafu. **2. disorderliness** confusedness, confusion, derangement, disarrangement, disarray, dislocation, disorganisation, entanglement, labyrinth, messiness, misarrangement, sprawl, topsy-turviness, twine. *Informal:* hubble-bubble, hugger-mugger. **3. riotousness** rampageousness, rowdiness, rowdyism, tumultuousness, uproariousness.

2. **1. untidiness** dishabille, dishevelment, dowdiness, frowziness, sleaziness, sloppiness, slovenliness, sordidness, unkemptness. *Informal:* sleaze. **2. pigsty** dump, pigpen, shambles. *Informal:* brothel, disaster area, fleapit.

3. **1. commotion** agitation, alarums and excursions, blare, brawl, brouhaha, brush, cataclysm, catastrophe, clamour, clangour, clatter, coil, confusion, convulsion, corroboree, cry, din, disquiet, distraction, disturbance, ferment, flurry, grapple, hubble-bubble, hubbub, hurly, hurly-burly, inquietude, madhouse, maelstrom, much ado about nothing, noise, outcry, perturbation, racket, roar, rowdiness, screech, shindy, shivaree *(US)*, skirmish, spat, three-ring circus, trouble, turmoil, welter. *Informal:* bunfight, bust-up, ding, ding-dong, domestic, mix-up, row, ruckus, shemozzle, shindig, squall, stink, yike. **2. hullabaloo** ballyhoo, bobsy-die, bustle, carry-on, furore, fuss, pother, scandal, to-do. *Informal:* ballyhooly, hoo-ha, kafuffle, kerfuffle, rhubarb, song and dance. **3. riot** bluster, breach of the peace, broil, outbreak, pandemonium, pell-mell, race riot, rout, tempest, tumult, unrest, uproar. *Informal:* boil-up, bovver *(British)*, merry hell, rough-house, rumpus. **4. free-for-all** affray, battle, chance-medley, dogfight, dust, encounter, fight, fracas, melee, passage, rencounter, running battle, scrape, scrimmage, scuffle, set-to, struggle, tussle, wrestle. *Informal:* barney, biff, bingle, blue, box-on, dust-up, go-in, punch-up, rough-up, rumble, scrap, turn-in, turn-up. **5. jungle** blackboard jungle, no-man's-land, wilderness. **6. babel** bear garden. *Informal:* bloodhouse. **7. troubled waters**.

4. **1. jumble** bob, clutter, confusion, disarray, hash, hubble-bubble, huddle, hugger-mugger, knot, litter, mat, mess, mix, muddle, node, nodus, snarl, tangle, tumble, upset. *Informal:* dog's breakfast, dog's dinner, muss *(Chiefly US)*. **2. mess-up** baulk, blunder, bone, boss-shot, botch, bug, bungle, error, false step, fault, faux pas, fiasco, foot-fault, foul-up, Freudian slip, gaffe, GIGO, howler, hugger-mugger, inaccuracy, kettle of fish, lapse, malapropism, mess, misapprehension, miscarriage, misconception, miscount, mishap, mismove, mistake, mix-up, muddle, oversight, parapraxis, slip, solecism, stumble, trip. *Informal:* a fine kettle of fish, a pretty kettle of fish, bad, ball-up, balls-up, barry, bloomer, blooper, blue, boggle, boner, boo-boo, boob, clambake *(US)*, clanger, fizzer, fluff, foozle, glitch, muck-up, shemozzle, shocker, slip-up, stuff-up.

3. hotchpotch catch-all, fantasia, farrago, flotsam and jetsam, gallimaufry, grab bag, hodgepodge, macedoine, medley, mishmash, mixed bag, motley, odds and ends, olio, omnium gatherum, patchwork, pell-mell, potpourri, rummage, salmagundi, shandigaff, smorgasbord. *Informal:* bag of tricks. **4. bustle** ado, bun rush, helter-skelter, hurry-scurry, scramble, to-do.

5.   **1. untidy person** chat, derelict, dowdy, drab, draggletail, mucker, ragamuffin, ragbag, scarecrow, scrubber, slattern, slommock, sloven, tatterdemalion, trollop, urchin. *Informal:* dag, dero, derro, scruff, scunge, sleaze, slummock, warb, waub. **2. rowdy** apache, brute, ruffian, thug. *Informal:* boyo, bull, chokeman, goon, gorilla, harum-scarum, he-man, muscle man, nightrider *(US)*, plug-ugly *(US)*, tough, yegg *(US)*. **3. rabble** doggery, mob. **4. disarranger** disorganiser, disturber, jumbler, rifler.

adj.   **6.**   **1. disorderly** boxed, chaotic, confused, deranged, disordered, haywire, headless, higgledy-piggledy, hugger-mugger, in (a state of) mayhem, inordinate, jumbled, messy, out of joint, sprawly, topsy-turvy, trashy *(US)*, unattended, untidy, upside down, wild. *Informal:* daggy, mussy *(Chiefly US)*, snafu. **2. unorganised** desultory, immethodical, random, unbusinesslike, unclassified, undisciplined, unjustified, unmethodical, unregulated, unruly, unstructured, unsystematic. **3. disorganised** broken, disconnected, disjointed, disjunct, dislocated, fragmented, inarticulate, incoherent. *Informal:* bitty. **4. unsettled** disturbed, turbid, turbulent. **5. riotous** agitated, boisterous, bouncing, clamant, clamorous, dishevelled, fidgety, furious, hectic, hurly-burly, insurgent, jittery, jumpy, mad, noisy, obstreperous, obstropolous, open-mouthed, pandemoniac, pandemonic, pell-mell, rackety, rampageous, rebellious, restless, roaring, robust, robustious, rorty, rough, rough-and-tumble, rowdy, rowdyish, rude, rumbustious, stormy, tempestuous, troubled, tumultuary, tumultuous, unquiet, unruly, uproarious, violent, vociferant, vociferous, wild. *Informal:* churned up, harum-scarum, rambunctious *(US)*, rip-roaring.

7.   **1. untidy** beat-up, bedraggled, blowzy, buggy, decrepit, dingy, dishevelled, disorderly, down at heel, draggletailed, en déshabillé, flea-bitten, frowzy, grubby, lousy, mangy, messy, moth-eaten, mothy, out at elbows, out at the elbow, pedicular, ragged, raggle-taggle, raggle-tailed, ramshackle, ratty, scrubby, seedy, shabby, shaggy, slatternly, sleazy, slipshod, slovenly, slummocky, sluttish, sordid, squalid, tatty, the worse for wear, unkempt, verminous, weather-beaten, weevily, wild, windblown, windswept, wretched. *Informal:* chatty, grungy, mussy *(Chiefly US)*, scruffy, sloppy, tacky, warby, wild and woolly.

v.   **8.**   **1. disorder** agitate, box up, derange, disarrange, disjoint, dislocate, disorganise, disorientate, disrupt, disturb, embroil, entangle, mess, mither *(Chiefly British)*, mix up, muddle, muss up, overset, paddle, perturb, puddle, ravel, scamp, shake up, tumble, unsettle, upset. *Informal:* make a box of, muss *(Chiefly US)*. **2. raise cain** rabble, raise the dust, wreak havoc. *Informal:* create, cry blue murder, make a song and dance about, raise hell, scream blue murder, whoop it up, whoop things up. **3. bungle** blunder, mess up. *Informal:* balls something up, balls up, foul up, snafu.

9.   **1. untidy** clutter, convolute, derange, disarrange, disarray, dishevel, disorder, enmesh, entangle, entrammel, foul, immesh, jumble, knot, litter, litter up, ruffle, rumple, shuffle, snarl, tangle, tousle, wind. *Informal:* be all over the place like (or look like) a madwoman's breakfast (or washing) (or custard) (or knitting) (or lunch box). **2. sprawl** knock about, slummock. **3. confuse** anarchise, discompose, embrangle, embroil, fuddle, obfuscate, unfix, unhinge, unsettle. *Informal:* gum up the works, make hay, make the feathers fly, make the fur fly, put the cart before the horse, rock the boat, throw a spanner in the works, upset the applecart.

adv.   **10.**   **1. disorderly** at random, at sixes and sevens, chaotically, confusedly, higgledy-piggledy, irregularly, slapdash, topsy-turvy, willy-nilly. *Informal:* all over the shop, hurry-scurry. **2. helter-skelter** confusedly, hurly-burly, hurry-scurry, pell-mell. **3. confusedly** confusingly, desultorily, discomposedly, immethodically. **4. riotously** harum-scarum, madly, recklessly, rowdily, run amok, tempestuously, tumultuously, uproariously, wildly. **5. untidily** frowzily, seedily, shabbily, sleazily, sloppily.

RELATED KEYWORDS: DISAGREEMENT, ANARCHY, CONFUSION, DISOBEDIENCE

DISPERSION

n.   **1.**   **1. dispersion** deployment, diffusion, dispersal, dissipation, perfusion, scatter, scattering. **2. atomisation** aeration, gaseous diffusion. **3. sprinkle** aspersion, spray, sprinkling. **4. dispersion** decentralisation, diaspora, dispersal, interspersion. **5. dissemination** apportionment, circularisation, circulation, distribution, pervasion, semination. **6. branching** divarication, divergence, flare, radiation, ramification, spread.

7. break-up disintegration, disorganisation, dissolution, karyolysis. **8. break-out** escape, rout, stampede. **9. demobilisation** *Informal:* demob.

  2. **1. diffusiveness** contagiousness, diffusibility, pervasiveness, solubility, solubleness. **2. diffuseness** dissipatedness.

  3. **1. disperser** stampeder, tedder. **2. scatterer** diffuser, disseminator, dotter, duster, sifter. **3. dispeller** nebuliser. **4. distributor** broadcaster, circulariser. **5. sprinkler** aerator, aerosol, aspergillum, aspersorium, atomiser, knapsack spray, scent spray, sparge pipe, sparger, spray.

adj. **4.** **1. dispersive** contagious, diffusive, disseminative, dissipative, dissolutive, flaring, scattering.

  5. **1. dispersed** broadcast, cosmopolitan, countrywide, diffuse, dissipated, far-flung, pervasive, scattered, widespread, widespreading. **2. besprinkled** besprent *(Poetic)*, bestrewed, bestrewn. **3. sparse** isolated, scanty, sporadic, sporadical. **4. diffused** branching, extended, radiate, ramiform.

v. **6.** **1. disperse** diffuse, disject, dismiss, scatter, scatter to the winds, spread. **2. deploy** decentralise, diversify, farm out. **3. demobilise** cast adrift, cast out, disband. **4. dissipate** disintegrate, dispel, dissolve, ionise. **5. fan out** branch, branch out, divaricate, diverge, eradiate, radiate, ramify, ray, spread, spread like wildfire, straggle, unroll. **6. diffuse** circumfuse, effuse, extravasate, interfuse, pervade. **7. strew** bestrew, intersperse, shed, sift, slough, sow, spill, string out. **8. disseminate** broadcast, circularise, circulate, convey, deal, dispense, measure out (or off), pass, pass out, propagate, relay, retail, scatter, seed, sow, spread, transmit. **9. spread** make hay, ted. **10. sprinkle** bespatter, besprinkle, bestud, dot, litter, patter, sow, spot. **11. atomise** aerate, nebulise, spray. **12. dust** powder, sand. **13. spatter** dabble, scintillate, shed, slop, slosh, spat, splash, splatter, squirt. **14. sputter** spit, splutter. *Informal:* slag. **15. stampede** discomfit, put to flight, rout, rout someone out. **16. deal out** apportion, distribute, dole out. **17. broadcast** cable, datacast, satellite, telecast, telemeter, webcast.

adv. **7.** **1. dispersedly** abroad, around, broadcast, diffusely, diffusively, dissipatedly, flaringly, here and there, passim, sporadically. **2. scatteringly** spatteringly. **3. pervasively** contagiously.

RELATED KEYWORDS: EMISSION, FLOOD, EXCLUSION, SEPARATION

DISPLAY

n. **1.** **1. display** demonstration, exhibit, exhibition, exhibitry, exposal, exposure, indictment, manifestation, presentation, presentment, production, re-presentation, rendition, show, showing, unfoldment. **2. show** array, exhibition, expo, exposition, fair, parade. *Informal:* demo. **3. spectacle** fireworks, gala, ostentation, pageantry, phantasmagoria, phantasmagory, pomp and circumstance, pyrotechnics, riot, show, splash, tamasha *(Indian English)*. *Informal:* splurge. **4. preview** sneak preview, view.

  2. **1. ostentation** bravura, eclat, exhibitionism, gaudery, pyrotechnics, show, showiness, showmanship, window-dressing. **2. blatancy** flagrancy, obviousness, openness. **3. demonstrativeness** expressiveness.

  3. **1. displayer** demonstrationist, demonstrator, exhibitor, manifestant, present, presenter, unfolder, window-dresser. **2. showman** blazoner, exhibitionist, limelighter, pyrotechnist.

  4. **1. exhibition area** art gallery, gallery, museum, showroom. **2. display case** display window, shopwindow, show window, showcase, vitrine. *Informal:* goldfish-bowl.

adj. **5.** **1. displayed** arrayed, on display, on show, on view, open, open to the public, public. **2. exhibitive** demonstrational, exhibitory, presentational. **3. demonstrative** expressive, ostensive.

  6. **1. spectacular** gala, panoplied, splendid. *Informal:* all-singing, all-dancing. **2. showy** blazing, dashing, dashy, dramatic, eye-catching, florid, for show, gay, ornate, ostentatious, phantasmagorical, pretentious, pyrotechnic, triumphal. *Informal:* flash, splashy.

  7. **1. obvious** apparent, as plain as a pikestaff, clear, clear as day, evident, evincible, manifest, manifestative, open-and-shut, overt, patent, plain, transparent, unmistakable, visible. **2. in the limelight** conspicuous, in the foreground, pronounced. **3. uncovered** barefaced, flaunted, naked, undisguised. **4. blatant** flagrant, glaring, gross, striking.

v. **8.** **1. display** argue, bear, betray, bring forward, demonstrate, exhibit, make, present, show, wear. *Informal:* demo. **2. expose** betray, bring to light, display, evidence, evince, lay bare, make public, manifest, overexpose, point up, prove, release, reveal, root out (or up), splay, uncloak, uncover, unlock. **3. spotlight** highlight, illuminate.

4. express act out, breathe, indicate, turn on. **5. lay out** display, hang out, hold up, produce, unfold, unroll. *Informal:* trot out. **6. parade** make perform, put through one's paces, show off to its best advantage. **7. flaunt** blazon, brandish, flourish, maintain a high profile, shake. *Informal:* sport. **8. show off** make a spectacle of oneself, parade, promenade, steal the limelight. *Informal:* let it all hang out.

adv. **9. 1. demonstratively** for all to see, from the housetops (or rooftops), in the open, publicly. **2. obviously** blatantly, manifestly, overtly, patently.

RELATED KEYWORDS: COMMUNICATION, REVELATION, PUBLICITY, SHOWINESS, SIGHT

DISPLEASURE

n. **1. 1. displeasure** anger, annoyance, chafe, chagrin, disfavour, dissatisfaction, exasperation, fret, fury, ill temper, indignation, irritation, nuisance, pique, resentment, temper, trouble, umbrage, vehemence, vexation, vexedness. *Informal:* miff. **2. discomposure** agitation, discomfort, disease, embarrassment, inquietude, malaise, mortification, uneasiness. **3. an awkward moment** a bad patch, a moment's uneasiness, a sticky moment, a trouble spot, mauvais quart d'heure.

2. 1. dislike abhorrence, abomination, antipathy, averseness, aversion, detestation, disapprobation, disapproval, discountenance, disfavour, disgust, disrelish, distaste, hate, hatred, loathing, objection, odium, prejudice, repugnance, repulsion, revulsion. *Informal:* allergy, scunner. **2. opposition** animosity, recalcitration, resistance.

adj. **3. 1. displeased** ablaze, aggrieved, angry, annoyed, apoplectic, bilious, black-browed, choleric, crabbed, crabby, cranky, cross, crusty, cut-up, discontent, disgruntled, dissatisfied, hopping, huffish, huffy, indignant, injured, irate, ireful, irritable, irritated, livid, mad, malcontent, offended, on the warpath, pettish, petulant, put out, quarrelsome, querulous, red-hot, resentful, restless, snarly, snuffy, sour, spiteful, spleenful, splenetic, upset, vexed, vinegary, wally, wrathful, wroth. *Informal:* cheesed-off, crooked on, cross as two sticks, cut up, dark, dirty, fed up (to the back teeth), fit to be tied, fraught, full up, hot under the collar, jack of, lemony, mad as a cut snake, mad as a hornet, mad as a maggot, mad as a meataxe, miffed, narked, pippy, ratty, ropeable, scotty, shirty, sore, spiky, steamed-up, tooshie, uptight. **2. hard to please** cantankerous, discontented, fractious, fretful, like a bear with a sore head, moody, on edge, out of humour, peevish, perverse, scratchy, teasy, temperamental, wry. *Informal:* crotchety, grumpy, snaky, snitchy, snotty.

v. **4. 1. dislike** abhor, abominate, despise, detest, disrelish, execrate, hate, have had, have no stomach for, have no use for, loathe, object to, revolt from, take a dislike to. *Informal:* hate someone's guts, have a hate on (or against). **2. frown** curl one's lip, glower, lour, make a face, pout, scowl. **3. fret and fume** be put out, gnash one's teeth, have a bad time of it. **4. put up with** bear, bear with, endure, suffer, take. *Informal:* hack.

RELATED KEYWORDS: DISCONTENTEDNESS, UNFRIENDLINESS, BADNESS, LOW REGARD, HATE

DISREPUTE

n. **1. 1. disrepute** bad odour, contempt, disesteem, disfavour, disgrace, dishonour, disregard, disreputability, disreputation, disrespectability, ignominy, oblivion, resentment. **2. bad reputation** bad name, doubtful character, past, shady reputation. **3. dishonour** affront, contumely, discourtesy, discredit, disrepute, humiliation, ignominy, indignity, insult, mockery, put-down, reproach, slight. *Informal:* a slap in the face. **4. disgrace** contempt, crying shame, dishonour, ignominy, infamy, obloquy, odium, opprobrium, scorn, shame, sharam. **5. scandal** carry-on, commotion, welter. *Informal:* kerfuffle, ruckus, song and dance, stink, watergate. **6. notoriety** ill fame, infamy, notoriousness. **7. anonymity** obscure, obscurity.

2. 1. disreputableness disreputability, doubtfulness, raffishness, seediness, shadiness, wretchedness. **2. disgracefulness** damnableness, degradingness, derogatory, despicability, despicableness, dishonourableness, ignominiousness, reproachfulness. **3. shamefulness** abjection, abjectness, ignobility, ignobleness, ingloriousness, invidiousness, opprobriousness, pitiableness, pitifulness, unworthiness. **4. inexcusableness** exceptionableness, inexcusability, inexpiableness. **5. reproachableness** censurableness. **6. notoriousness** infamousness.

3. 1. denigration attack, calumniation, calumny, defamation, dirt, disparagement, innuendo, insinuation, libel, malediction, personality, racial vilification, scandal, slander, stigmatisation, vilification. *Informal:* defo. **2. reproach** abuse, blame, censure, commination, condemnation, criticism, denunciation, derogation, detraction, disapprobation, headshaking, invective, obloquy, rebuff, reprobation, reproof, vitriol, vituperation. *Informal:* flak. **3. defilement** contamination, corruption, pollution. **4. taint** attaint, blemish, blot, brand, cloud, discredit, slur, smear, smirch, spot, stain, stigma, tarnish.

       5. skeleton in the cupboard badge of infamy, blot on the escutcheon, dirty linen, family skeleton, mark of Cain.

4.   **1. denigrator** stigmatiser. **2. disgracer** defiler, dishonourer, low joint. **3. scandal sheet** gutter press, yellow press. *Informal:* rag.

adj. **5.**   **1. disreputable** abominable, damnable, detestable, discreditable, dishonourable, disrespectable, doubtful, dubious, dubitable, equivocal, odious, problematic, questionable, uncertain. *Informal:* shady. **2. disgraceful** abhorrent, abominable, abysmal, appalling, atrocious, awful, contemptible, contumelious, currish, damnable, deplorable, despicable, detestable, disgusting, dishonourable, disreputable, dreadful, execrable, heinous, illaudable, inglorious, monstrous, nauseous, opprobrious, outrageous, repulsive, revolting, rotten, shameful, shocking, terrible, vile. *Informal:* bastard, damned, ungodly, unholy. **3. discreditable** compromising, damaging, disgraceful, disreputable, inglorious, invidious, opprobrious. **4. degrading** burlesque, debasing, demeaning, lowering. **5. ignoble** base, beneath one's dignity, discreditable, disgraceful, disreputable, humiliating, ignominious, inglorious, low, low-down, mean, opprobrious, scandalous, scurvy, shameful, slavish, sordid, spicy. **6. scandalous** abominable, arrant, flagrant, glaring, grievous, gross, ill-famed, infamous, inglorious, notorious, obscene, opprobrious, outrageous, shameful, shocking. **7. blameworthy** exceptionable, ghastly, hideous, ignominious, ill-favoured, indefensible, inexcusable, inexpiable, nasty, objectionable, obnoxious, repugnant, undesirable, unmentionable, unspeakable, vile. *Informal:* appalling, perishing. **8. reproachable** censurable, criticisable, rebukeable. **9. of doubtful reputation** doubtful, dubious, incalculable, leary, mistrustful, questionable, suspect, suspected, suspicious, uncertain. *Informal:* leery, shady, shonky, sleazy, suss. **10. disgraced** discredited, down, fallen, honourless. **11. humbled** cut down to size, debunked. **12. nameless** characterless, nubilous, obscure, uncertain. **13. unsung**.

v.   **6.**   **1. be of no repute** be at a discount, not be thought much of. *Informal:* stink. **2. be in disgrace** be in bad odour with, be in bad with, be in disfavour with, be in Dutch with, be in someone's black books, be in wrong with, be on somebody's black list, be persona non grata, be under a cloud. *Informal:* be in the doghouse, sleep under the house. **3. fall from grace** blot one's copybook, come down, condescend, deign, demean oneself, drop, fall, go into eclipse, lose ground, stoop.

       7.   **1. disgrace** abase, attaint, bring into disrepute, bring shame upon, declass, defile, degrade, dishonour, foul, imbrute. **2. shame** affront, attaint, bastardise, disgrace, expose, foul, humiliate, mortify, pillory, reproach, show up. *Informal:* dig (the) dirt on. **3. defame** anathematise, asperse, attaint, backbite, badmouth, belie, bespatter, blacken, blaspheme, brand, calumniate, curse, denigrate, discredit, disgrace, disparage, drag through the mire, execrate, fling, libel, malign, pelt, slander, smear, squib, stigmatise, traduce, vilify, vilipend. *Informal:* dis, put the knife into, slag. **4. defile** besmear, besmirch, blot, cloud, contaminate, corrupt, debauch, defame, denigrate, foul, pollute, smear, smirch, soil, stain, sully, taint, tarnish. **5. detract from** cast a slur on, censure, cut down to size, debunk, put to shame, throw dishonour upon. **6. have a low opinion of** find fault, see in a bad light, view unfavourably.

       RELATED KEYWORDS: DISAPPROVAL, SLANDER, LOW REGARD

DISSONANCE

n.   **1.**   **1. dissonance** atonalism, atonality, cacophony, discord, discordance, disharmony, inharmoniousness, preparation, wolf, wolf note. **2. cross-relation** consecutive fifths, false relation, suspension. **3. unmusicalness** tonelessness. **4. harshness** roughness. **5. hoarseness** graininess, gutturalness, raggedness. *Informal:* frog in the throat. **6. raucousness** brassiness, raucity, stridency. **7. clang** clash, jangle. **8. blare** bray, stridor. **9. croak** crack, goose, guttural, hoarseness, huskiness, roop, roup, snore. **10. groan** creak. **11. rasp** grate, gride, grind, jar, scraping, scratch, scroop, skirr.

adj. **2.**   **1. dissonant** cacophonous, discordant, disharmonious, inharmonious, off-key. **2. atonal** ajar, anharmonic, inharmonic, jarring, non-harmonic. **3. out of tune** flat, gruff, guttural, harsh, off key, off pitch, sharp. *Informal:* blue, bum. **4. unmusical** noteless, tuneless, unmelodious. **5. harsh** grating, grinding, inartistic, rasping, rough, rude, rugged. **6. hoarse** cracked, croaky, grainy, gravelly, gritty, husky, ragged, rasping, raucous, roupy, thick, throaty. **7. creaky** squeaking, squeaky. **8. raucous** brassy, grating, hoarse, roupy, strident.

v.   **3.**   **1. be dissonant** clang, clash, jangle. **2. blare** bray. **3. hoarsen** crack, croak, snore. **4. groan** creak. **5. grate** graunch *(Chiefly NZ)*, gride, grind, grit, jar, rasp, scrape, scratch, scroop.

adv. **4.** **1. dissonantly** atonally, discordantly.

RELATED KEYWORDS: HISSING, LOUDNESS, RESONANCE, SHRILLNESS, SOUND

DISTORTION

n. **1.** **1. distortion** abnormality, abnormity, crookedness, deformation, deformity, disfigurement, distortedness, irregularity, malformation, misshapenness. **2. warp** bend, bias, buckle, convolution, kink, knar, screw, set, strain, twist, writhe. **3. geological deformation** anamorphosis, creep, diastrophism, shear strain, upheaval, uplift, upthrust. **4. grimace** grin, mouth, snarl. *Informal:* mug *(British).* **5. contortion** convulsion, fit, rictus, seizure, spasm.

2. **1. distorter** contortionist, deformer, twister, warper, wrester, wrier, writher.

adj. **3.** **1. distorted** anamorphous, axonometric, bent, buckled, contorted, convoluted, convulsed, perverted. **2. deformed** crooked, diastrophic, disfigured, epeirogenic, grotesque, malformed, miscreated, misshapen, monstrous, prodigious. *Informal:* squiffy. **3. warped** kinky, perverted, twisted, wry.

4. **1. distortional** contortional, convulsionary, convulsive.

5. **1. physically malformed** acromegalic, bandy, bandy-legged, bow-legged, clubfooted, crookbacked, gibbous, hare-lipped, humpbacked, humped, hunchbacked, intoed, knock-kneed, pigeon-breasted, pigeon-toed, sway-backed, taliped, valgus.

v. **6.** **1. distort** bend, buckle, cast, contort, convolute, crimple, deform, intort, misshape, overdraw, screw, strain, twist, warp, wrench, wrest, wrick, wring, writhe.

adv. **7.** **1. distortedly** convolutely, crookedly, deformedly, misshapenly, pervertedly. **2. askew** out of shape. *Informal:* skew-whiff.

RELATED KEYWORDS: UGLINESS, STRANGENESS, IMPERFECTION, SHAPELESSNESS, TWIST

DISUSE

n. **1.** **1. disuse** desuetude, dispensation. **2. boycott** cessation, discontinuance, discontinuation, rejection. **3. obsolescence** defunctness, retirement, supersedure, supersession. **4. lack of use** suspension. **5. lack of practice** rustiness. **6. planned obsolescence**. **7. throwaway society**.

2. **1. discard** cast-off, cast-out, jetsam, jettison, slough. **2. rejectamenta** junk, reject, throw-out, throwaway. **3. retired list** scrap heap, slab-heap *(NZ).* **4. leftover** discontinued line, fag end, remnant. **5. hand-me-down** *(Informal)* reach-me-down. **6. has-been** *(Informal)* back number.

3. **1. non-user** boycotter, discarder, rejecter, shepherd, sparer.

adj. **4.** **1. disused** derelict, scrap, waste. **2. obsolete** antiquated, archaic, dead, discredited, extinct, extinguished, obsolescent, out-of-date, outdated, outmoded, outworn, passé, quenched, superannuated. **3. discarded** cast-off, cast-out, obsolete, outcast, outgrown, outworn, rejected. **4. out of use** defunct, in mothballs, laid up, out of commission. **5. superannuated** antediluvian, antiquated, antique, obsolete, on the scrap heap, outworn, retired, written off. *Informal:* on the shelf. **6. rusty** out of practice, out of the habit.

5. **1. unused** maiden, manqué, new, unbeaten, unfired, untapped, untouched, untravelled, untried, unweighed, virgin, virginal. **2. at a loose end** at liberty, free, loose, standing, vacant.

v. **6.** **1. disuse** decommission, lay aside, mothball, retire, set aside, shelve. *Informal:* chuck, dish, junk. **2. discard** condemn, dump, give the sword, have no use for, reject, scrap, throw away, throw out. *Informal:* can, ditch. **3. jettison** throw overboard. **4. dispense with** boycott, break, discontinue, leave off, pension off, superannuate. *Informal:* put out to grass. **5. dismiss** fire. *Informal:* boot, chop, jeff *(Victoria).* **6. outgrow** cast off, doff, outwear, shed, slough. **7. leave unused** do without, hold, hold in abeyance, reserve, save, shepherd, spare.

7. **1. fall into disuse** antiquate, archaise, be superseded, give place, lapse, not catch on, rust. **2. go by the board** dilapidate, go begging, go to waste.

RELATED KEYWORDS: IDLENESS, DAMAGE, DISMISSAL, MISUSE, OLDNESS, REMNANT, USELESSNESS

DIVE

n. **1.** **1. dive** backflip, belly whacker, gainer, jackknife, jackknife dive, pike, pike dive, plunge, swallow dive, tuck. *Informal:* belly buster, belly flop, header. **2. dip** duck, immersion, souse. **3. dive-bomb** *Informal:* honey pot. **4. swoop** pounce, stoop.

      5. nosedive crash dive, power-dive, spin, tailspin. **6. skydiving** freefalling, parachuting. **7. skindiving** diving, scuba diving. **8. stage dive** crowd surfing.

2. 1. diver abalone diver, frogman, skindiver, try diver. **2. dipper** ducker, dunker.

3. 1. diving board springboard.

v. **4. 1. dive** go down like a stone, plummet, plunge, sound, stage dive, submerge. *Informal:* belly flop, dive-bomb, honey-pot, take a header. **2. dip** douse, duck, dunk, immerse, souse, submerge. **3. swoop** pounce, stoop. **4. skydive** bail out, free-fall, jump, parachute. **5. nosedive** crash-dive, power-dive.

RELATED KEYWORDS: DESCENT, FLYING, JUMP

DIVERGENCE

n. **1. 1. divergence** arborisation, bifurcation, branching, divarication, divergency, division, embranchment, flare, forking, furcation, parting, radiation, ramification, separation, trifurcation.

2. 1. branch anabranch, arm, byroad, embranchment, offshoot, ramus, side road. **2. fork** crotch, crutch, elbow. **3. radius** spoke, sprag. **4. diverter** divaricator.

adj. **3. 1. divergent** bifurcate, crotched, divaricate, divided, furcate, oblique, splay, trifurcate. **2. radial** abducent, adverse, averse, centrifugal, radiate. **3. branching** alternate, arterial, brachiate, branchlike, branchy, enate, ramiform, ramose, ramous, ramulose.

v. **4. 1. diverge** bifurcate, branch, divaricate, divide, fork, furcate, gape, move apart, part, ramify, splay, subdivide, trifurcate. **2. divert** avert, detour, fly off, fly off at a tangent, haul off, shunt. **3. radiate** branch out, branch out in all directions, disperse, eradiate, ramify, scatter, spread.

adv. **5. 1. divergently** divaricately. **2. radially** centrifugally.

RELATED KEYWORDS: REMOTENESS, DISPERSION, SEPARATION

DRUG

n. **1. 1. drug** addictive drug, designer drug, drug of abuse, drug of dependence. *Informal:* Bob Hope, bomb, dope, gear. **2. hard drugs** narcotics. *Informal:* hard stuff. **3. deal** *Informal:* deck. **4. drug supply** *Informal:* stash. **5. spiked drink**.

2. 1. marijuana bang, bhang, cannabis, ganga, ganja, hashish, hemp, Indian hemp, keef, kif, yandi *(Aboriginal English)*, yarndi *(Aboriginal English)*. *Informal:* dope, grass, hash, Mary Jane, mull, pot, tea, the herb *(US)*, the weed, weed. **2. hash oil** tetrahydrocannabinol, THC. **3. marijuana cigarette** *Informal:* jay, joint, log, number, reefer, roach, scoob, spliff, stick *(US)*.

3. 1. narcotic *Informal:* junk. **2. type of narcotic** dadah *(Malaysian English)*, datura, henbane, kat, mandragora, mandrake, narcotic, pituri, piturine. **3. heroin** China White, diacetylmorphine, diamorphine. *Informal:* hammer, horse, scag, smack, snow. **4. opium** laudanum, meconium, opiate, poppy, poppyhead, twang. **5. morphine** diacetylmorphine, diamorphine, Morphia. *Informal:* Miss Emma, morph. **6. tranquilliser** anxiolytic, ataractic, stupefacient, stupefier. *Informal:* downer, no-go pill, stopper. **7. type of tranquilliser** amytal, barbiturate, chlordiazepoxide, chlorpromazine, codeine, depressant, librium, mandrax, methylmorphine, nembutal, pentobarbitone, phenobarb, phenobarbitone, potassium bromide, seconal, valium. *Informal:* mandy, nebbie.

4. 1. stimulant dance drug, starter, upper. *Informal:* beans, go pill, goofball, happy pill, jolly bean, pep pill, yippee beans. **2. type of stimulant** amphetamine, benzedrine, caffeine, dexedrine, GHB, MDA, methamphetamine, methedrine, methylamphetamine, purple heart, zedoary. *Informal:* benny, businessman's trip, ice, meth, shabu, speed. **3. cocaine** angel, coca, crack, white lines. *Informal:* angie, coke, ready rock, snow. **4. ecstasy** MDMA, methylenedioxymethamphetamine. *Informal:* disco biscuit, E, eccy, fantasy. **5. speedball** *(Informal)* snowcone.

5. 1. hallucinogen mind-altering drug, psychoactive drug, psychochemical. **2. type of hallucinogen** angel dust, DET, dimethyltryptamine, hallucinogen, ketamine, NTP, phencyclidine, STP. *Informal:* Special K. **3. magic mushroom** blue meanie, gold cap, gold top, psylocibin. **4. mescaline** mescaline buttons, peyote. *Informal:* mesc. **5. LSD** lysergic acid, lysergic acid diethylamide. *Informal:* acid, microdot, mike, ticket, trip.

6. 1. performance-enhancing steroid anabolic steroid, designer steroid, steroid. *Informal:* roid. **2. type of steroid** creatine, DMT, eGH, equine growth hormone, nandrolone, THG, trenbolone.

7. **1. drug equipment** bong, chillum, hookah, hubble-bubble, kalian, narghile, water pipe. *Informal:* billy, cone, mull bowl. **2. hypodermic** hypodermic needle, needle. *Informal:* fit, hype, hypo, outfit, pick, spike, works.

8. **1. safe-injecting room** injecting room, shooting room. **2. opium den** grass castle.

9. **1. drug user** glue-sniffer, IV drug user. *Informal:* acidhead, doper, head, hophead, hound *(US)*, hype, mainliner, mull head, pothead, snowbird *(US)*. **2. addict** *Informal:* cokie, cone-head, dope fiend, drug fiend, druggie, hound *(US)*, junkie, pill popper, smackhead.

10. **1. drug use** *Informal:* fix, hit, session, skinpop, trip. **2. drug-induced state** *Informal:* buzz, high. **3. overdose** narcosis, stupor. *Informal:* OD. **4. doping** blood doping, gene doping.

11. **1. drug addiction** addiction, drug abuse, habit, substance abuse. *Informal:* monkey on one's back. **2. narcotism** cocainism, morphinism, opiumism. **3. withdrawal** detox, drying-out, withdrawal symptom. *Informal:* cold turkey. **4. drug treatment** detox centre, detoxification centre, methadone treatment.

12. **1. drug dealer** dealer, peddler, pusher, trafficker. *Informal:* dope peddler, doper, greengrocer.

13. **1. drug squad** dog squad. **2. drug search** body-search, cavity search. *Informal:* bust.

adj. **14.** **1. drugged** blocked, bombed, kef, off the air, poppied, skagged-out, spaced-out. *Informal:* dopey, freak-out, high, high as a kite, loaded, mandied, off one's face, on a high, ripped, scagged-out, smacked-out, smashed, spacey, stoked, stoned, wigged-out.

v. **15.** **1. take drugs** *Informal:* blow one's mind, bomb out, bong on, cone on, drop, drop acid, fly high, goof, snort, turn on. **2. inject** *Informal:* hit up, mainline, shoot up, skinpop. **3. overdose** *Informal:* OD. **4. look for drugs** *Informal:* cruise.

RELATED KEYWORDS: MEDICATION, TOBACCO

DRYNESS

n. **1.** **1. dryness** aridity, aridness, drought, semiaridity, the dry, torridity, torridness. **2. astringency** stypticity. **3. watertightness**. **4. arid zone** gibber country, gibber plain, salt pan, waste, wasteland. **5. desert** dead centre, dead heart, erg, rain shadow.

2. **1. drying** airing, dehumidification, dehydration, desiccation, evaporation, exsiccation, torrefaction, ustulation. **2. drainage** dereliction. **3. marcescence**.

3. **1. drier** blow-drier, clothes drier, dryer, fugal, hair drier, hair dryer, mangle, spin-drier, tumble-drier, tumble-dryer, tumbler, whizzer, wringer. **2. clothes hoist** clothes horse, clothes line, hoist, line, rotary clothes hoist, rotary hoist. **3. dehumidifier** air-conditioner, evaporator, exsiccator. **4. desiccant** desiccator, siccative. **5. drainer** draining-board. **6. wiper** squeegee, windscreen-wiper. **7. towel** bath sheet, bath towel, beach towel, handtowel, napkin, paper towel, tea cloth, Turkish towel. **8. blotter** pounce. **9. astringent** antiperspirant.

adj. **4.** **1. dry** arid, bone-dry, fair, fine, high and dry, rough-dry, sear *(Chiefly Poetic)*, sere, thirsty, tinder-like. *Informal:* dry as a sunstruck bone, dry as the Nullarbor. **2. desiccated** anhydrous, dehydrated, dried, powdered. **3. arid** aneroid, cloudless, dewless, droughty, dry, floodless, fountainless, rainless, semiarid, subarid, sun-dried, sunbaked, torrid, waterless, xeric. *Informal:* hazed-off. **4. withered** blasted, dried-up, faded, marcescent, sapless, sere, shrivelled, tabescent, wasted, wizened. **5. waterproof** coated, damp-proof, showerproof, staunch, water-repellent, water-resistant, watertight. **6. xerophilous** xerophytic.

5. **1. drying** desiccant, desiccative, evaporative, exsiccative, parching, siccative, sub-astringent. **2. astringent** styptic.

v. **6.** **1. dry** air-dry, blow-dry, drip-dry, kiln-dry, rough-dry, sop up, spin-dry, sponge up, sun, ted, win *(Scottish)*. **2. wipe** absorb, blot, mop, rub, sponge, squeegee, swab, towel. **3. drain** bleed. **4. desiccate** dehumidify, dehydrate, evaporate, exsiccate, mummify, mummy, season, torrefy, torrify, weather. **5. parch** sear, shrivel, wither, wizen.

adv. **7.** **1. drily** aridly, dryly, thirstily.

RELATED KEYWORDS: INFERTILITY, HEAT, HEATING

DULLNESS

n. **1.** **1. dullness** drabness, dreariness, lacklustre, paleness, softness. **2. dimness** darkness, duskiness, faintness, gloom, indistinctness, obscurity. **3. murkiness** dinginess, dirtiness, mugginess. **4. opacity** opaqueness.

adj. **2.** **1. dull** dim, drab, dreary, faded, lacklustre, old, sad, sombre, toneless. **2. pale** muted, soft, washed-out. **3. dingy** dirty, gloomy, muddy, murky. **4. dim** dun, dusky, faint, leaden, obscure. **5. lustreless** dead, flat, glossless, mat, matt, matte *(US)*, matted.

v. **3.** **1. make dull** bedim, dull, soften, take the shine out of. **2. become dull** dull, fade, soften. **3. matt** opaque. **4. tarnish** discolour, muddy.

RELATED KEYWORDS: DARK, INVISIBILITY

DWELLING

n. **1.** **1. dwelling** abode, address, cubby, domicile, dwelling house, dwelling place, establishment, habitat, habitation, hang-out, harbour, hermitage, home, home away from home, manor, manse, mansion, McMansion, palace, pied-à-terre, place, residence, residency, roof, roof over one's head, shelter, squat, tenement. *Informal:* hole in the wall, joint, kipsie, pad, shovel. **2. premises** messuage. **3. fireside** hearth, ingleside. **4. settlement** cabana, colony, commune, housing, plantation, social settlement, village settlement. **5. reservation** reserve. **6. retirement village** community house, halfway house, receiving home, rest home, sheltered housing. **7. foster home** orphanage. **8. safety house** safe house.

2. **1. house** home. **2. terrace house** duplex, semidetached *(Chiefly NSW)*, town house, villa, villa home, villa unit. *Informal:* semi. **3. cottage** bungalow, dower house, project house, tied cottage *(British)*. **4. maisonette** doll's house. **5. cluster house**. **6. housing commission house** council house *(British)*, glebe house, state house *(NZ)*. **7. defence service home** war service home. **8. homestead** grange *(British)*, hacienda, hall, head station, ranch house, rancho *(in Spanish America and the southwestern US)*, station house. *Informal:* Government House, the house. **9. outstation** country camp, outpost. **10. country house** abbey, bow, chateau, dacha, manor house, seat, villa. **11. farmhouse** farm. **12. lodge** gatehouse, schoolhouse, station house, tollhouse. **13. palace** castle, chateau, court, hall, manor, motte and bailey, palazzo, seigneury, seraglio. **14. house of a government official** consulate, government house *(ACT)*, prefecture. *Informal:* ex-guvvie *(ACT)*, govie, guvvie. **15. house of member of clergy** manse, parsonage, presbytery, rectory, vicarage. **16. ethnic house** bure, donga *(Chiefly PNG)*, igloo, rondavel. **17. prehistoric house** beehive house, lake-dwelling, pile-dwelling. **18. miscellaneous types of construction** adobe, blockhouse, split-level, wattle and daub. **19. style of house** Californian bungalow, Cape Cod house, Federation house, Fediterranean house, Georgian terrace, Italo house, Victorian terrace.

3. **1. block of houses** area defined by houses, block, mew, mews, row, terrace. **2. housing estate** allotment, cluster housing, council estate *(British)*, development, estate, housing development, infill development. **3. public housing**.

4. **1. flat** apartment, apartments, bachelor flat, bed-sitter *(Chiefly British)*, bed-sitting room, flatette, flatlet, home unit, lodgings, maisonette, own-your-own, penthouse, quarters, rooms, serviced flat, studio apartment, unit. *Informal:* condo *(Chiefly US)*, diggings, digs, shoebox. **2. garden flat** chalet *(Tasmania, Victoria)*, granny flat. **3. block of flats** block, condominium *(Chiefly US)*, high-rise, tenement, tenement house, walk-up. **4. apartments** apartment house *(US)*, mansion, mansions.

5. **1. cabin** bach *(NZ (North Island))*, beach hut, box, bush house, cabana *(US)*, casino, crannog, crib *(NZ (South Island))*, holiday house, hut, lodge, shack, shooting lodge *(Chiefly British)*, weekender. **2. hut** apple hut, badger box *(Tasmania)*, bark hut, bothy *(Scottish)*, cabane, caboose, chalet, cot, crib, gunyah, hutch, lawn locker, lodge, melon hut, rancho *(in Spanish America and the south-western US)*, slab hut. *Informal:* mustard hut *(Tasmania)*. **3. prefab** donga, quonset hut *(US)*. **4. cubby house** cubby, cubbyhouse. **5. humpy** bush hut, gundy, gunyah, mia-mia, wurley. **6. lean-to** donga, outhouse, skillion, springhouse *(Chiefly US)*. **7. hovel** badger-box, hutch, shack, shanty, whare *(NZ)*. **8. slum** den, doghouse, dugout, hole, squat, sty. *Informal:* dogbox, dump. **9. slums** rabbit warren, warren.

6. **1. caravan** camper, campervan, mobile home, motorhome, relocatable home, trailer *(US)*. **2. caravanserai** serai.

7. **1. camp** bivouac, canvas town, fly-camp *(NZ)*, laager *(South African)*, strike camp, tent city, tentage, transit camp, transit site. *Informal:* bivvy. **2. camp site** campground, camping ground, caravan park, encampment, motor camp *(NZ)*, night camp. **3. tent** bell tent, canvas, fly, marquee, pavilion, pup tent. *Informal:* bivvy. **4. wigwam** teepee, tepee, tipi, whare, yurt.

8. **1. hotel** accommodation house, boatel, convention centre, halfway house, house, inn, lodge, motel, pensione, public house, roadhouse, tavern, YMCA. *Informal:* pub, rub-a-dub-dub. **2. hostel** youth hostel. **3. boarding house** guesthouse, hydro, lodging house, pension, rooming house *(Chiefly US)*, spa. **4. bunkhouse** charnel-house, dosshouse, flophouse. **5. poorhouse** almshouse, beadhouse *(British)*, bedehouse, hospice, hospitium. **6. creche** nursery. *Informal:* baby-farm. **7. accommodation** B & B, bed, bed and board, bed and breakfast, billet, board, full board, house of accommodation, infill development, lodging, migrant hostel, pension, safe house, safety house.

9. **1. barracks** blockhouse, cabin, hut, lines, quarters, station. **2. college** hall, hall of residence, inn *(British)*. **3. sleeping quarters** dormitory *(US)*. *Informal:* dorm. **4. mess** long house, pueblo, roundhouse. **5. selamlik. 6. seraglio** harem.

10. **1. animal dwelling** cattery, doghouse, kennel. **2. cowshed** bullpen, byre, cattlepen, corral, cowhouse, crib, stall. **3. stable** box, livery stable, loosebox, mews, riding stables, stabling. **4. pigsty** piggery, pigpen, sty. **5. coop** birdcage, cage, goldfish-bowl, hencoop, hutch, Shirley Temple, terrarium. **6. beehive** apiary, hive, vespiary. **7. dovecot** columbarium, henhouse, pigeonhole. **8. nest** aerie, aery, aviary, eyrie, hatchery, heronry, nide, nidus, perch, rookery, roost. **9. ant bed** ant hill, termitarium. **10. lair** couch, den, form, foxhole, home, lodge. **11. warren** burrow, crabhole, earth, hole, rabbit warren, sett, tunnel.

11. **1. habitat** domain, element, home ground, home range, medium, microhabitat, province, purlieu, range, sphere, zone.

12. **1. domesticity** domestication, domiciliation, homeliness. **2. domestic life** domesticities, home life.

adj. **13.** **1. domestic** domiciliary, home, house, household. **2. residential** tenementary. **3. homelike** domestic, homely, homey, well-appointed. **4. manorial** seignorial.

v. **14.** **1. house** accommodate, barrack, bed down, billet, domicile, domiciliate, put up, quarter, rehouse, sleep, take in. **2. reside** board, domicile, house, lodge, put up, quarter, room. **3. keep house** run an establishment.

RELATED KEYWORDS: ENCLOSURE, HABITATION, SHELTER

EARLINESS

n. **1.** **1. earliness** seasonableness. **2. prematurity** precocity. **3. early days** early hour. **4. early mark** early minute. **5. false start** break, breakaway *(Chiefly US)*. **6. untimeliness** immaturity, unripeness. **7. early bird** *(Informal)*.

adj. **2.** **1. early** earliest, early-stage, first, premier. **2. earlier** elder, former, lower, youthful. **3. premature** abortive, slink, untimely. *Informal:* premmie, previous. **4. forward** precocious. **5. seasonable**.

v. **3.** **1. be early** be premature, go off at half-cock, go off half-cocked. **2. take an early mark** put the clock forward. **3. antedate. 4. start prematurely** beat the gun, break, break away, jump the gun.

adv. **4.** **1. early** at crack of dawn, at first crack, at sparrow fart, before time, bright and early, early on, first thing, in the wee small hours. **2. earlier** before, early, sooner. **3. beforehand** ahead of time, in advance, up-front. **4. timely** betimes, in good season, in time, seasonably. **5. prematurely** precociously.

phr. **5.** **1. the early bird catches the worm**.

RELATED KEYWORDS: SPEED, UNTIMELINESS

EASINESS

n. **1.** **1. easiness** comfortableness, effortlessness, freedom, freeness, painlessness. **2. life of ease** bed of roses, life of Riley. *Informal:* easy wicket, silk department. **3. facility** amenity, convenience, ease, facileness, fluentness, glibness, handiness, readiness. **4. manageableness** handiness, smoothness.

2. **1. easy thing** armchair ride, child's play, sinecure. *Informal:* a sweet cop, breeze, cinch, gift, loaf, picnic, piece of cake, pushover, sitter, snack, snap, walk-up start, walkaway, walkover. **2. plain sailing** highroad, line of least resistance, primrose path. *Informal:* set-up, soda.

3. **1. facilitation** easement, easer, simplification, stepping stone.

adj. **4.** **1. easy** cinchy, comfortable, effortless, facile, light, painless, sweet, undemanding, unexacting. *Informal:* cruisy, cushy, easy as falling off a log, easy as pie, easy-peasy, like shooting fish in a barrel, like taking candy from a baby. **2. simple** convenient, knotless, no-frills, runaway, smooth. **3. manageable** DIY, do-it-yourself, manoeuvrable, tractable, wieldy. **4. convenient** handy, ready. *Informal:* come-at-able, get-at-able. **5. facile** flowing, fluent, free, glib, light.

v. **5.** **1. ease** allay, alleviate, comfort, console, cushion, facilitate, lighten, mitigate, moderate, mollify, relieve, soften, solace, soothe, spare, sugar the pill, temper.

6. **1. do easily** breeze through, get along, glide through, iron out, make nothing of, make short work of, rest, sail through, step into, walk over. *Informal:* do on one's ear, drive a coach and four through, lope through. **2. win hands down** romp home, walk the course, win at a canter. *Informal:* romp it in. **3. have it easy** live a life of ease. *Informal:* be on a soda, be sitting pretty, cop it sweet, have it made, live the life of Riley.

7. **1. be easy** be no object, be nothing to it. *Informal:* be a breeze, be a piece of cake.

8. **1. facilitate** aid, cater to, disencumber, enable, frank, grease, make way for, speed.

adv. **9.** **1. easily** comfortably, conveniently, effortlessly, facilely, familiarly, flowingly, fluently, freely, hand over fist, light, lightly, like a bird, painlessly, readily, smooth, smoothly, well. *Informal:* a piece of cake, easy, home on the pig's back. **2. in an easy fashion** cheaply, comfortably, glidingly, snugly. *Informal:* on a plate, on a platter, on easy street.

phr. **10.** **1. that's fine** *Informal:* no problem, no sweat, no worries.

RELATED KEYWORDS: REST, GOOD FORTUNE

EDGE

n. **1.** **1. edge** brim, brink, brow, deckle edge, limb, limbus, purfle. **2. outline** contour, lines, profile. **3. border** board, fringe, margin, precincts, rand *(Scottish)*, skirts, verge. **4. circumference** ambit, boundary, bounds, bourn, circuit, circumscription, compass, confines, girdle. **5. true edge** false edge. **6. rim** chime, collar, flange, gunwale, lip, rail. **7. ledge** apron, eaves, mantel, mantelshelf, mantle. **8. hem** basque, falbala, flounce, frill, fringe, furbelow, hemline, orphrey, ruffle, selvage, thrum, valance. **9. borderline** boundary, frontier *(Chiefly British)*, limit, march, outskirts, Rubicon.

2. **1. limit** measure, mete, pale, threshold. **2. demarcation** delimitation, partition, screen. **3. boundary** barrier, behind line, by-line, dead-ball line, ditch, goal line, line *(Sport)*, score, sideline, tramlines. **4. deadline** cut-off, term, time limit, time line. **5. terminus** farthest reaches, term, termination, the ends of the earth, ultima Thule. **6. upper limit** ceiling, high-water mark. **7. lower limit** bottom, dead finish, low-water mark, rock bottom. **8. the end of one's tether** the bounds of one's patience.

3. **1. kerbing** capstone, coaming, coping, curbing *(Chiefly US)*, curbstone *(Chiefly US)*, kerb, kerb blister, kerbstone. **2. roadside** boardwalk, footpath, nature strip, shoulder, street lawn *(Especially WA)*, verge, wayside. **3. building line** alignment, building alignment, linage.

4. **1. horizon** equator, skyline, visible horizon. **2. coastline** bank, coast, littoral, riverside, seaboard, seafront, seashore, seaside, shore, shoreline, strand *(Poetic)*, strandline, tidemark. **3. waterfront** lakefront, oceanfront, riverfront, waterside. **4. continental shelf** embayment.

5. **1. frame** annulet, architrave, archivolt, baseboard *(US)*, bead, beading, cased frame, doorframe, dwang *(NZ Building Trades)*, epistyle, framing, lipping, molding, moulding, ovolo, picture mould *(Chiefly US)*, picture rail, reeding, skirting, skirting board, stile, taenia, washboard *(US)*, window sash. **2. edging** beading, beads, bias binding, binding, gimp, piping. **3. surround** back, doorframe, gutter, mat. **4. perimeter** boundary, cushion, periphery, railings, ropes. **5. end** beam-ends, head.

6. **1. finiteness** definability, definiteness, delimitation, finitude. **2. margination** engrailment.

adj. **7.** **1. boundary** circumferential, circumscriptive, limbic, perimetrical. **2. peripheral** extreme, frontier, outermost, outmost, terminal. **3. marginal** limbate. **4. roadside** wayside. **5. waterside** coastal, lakeside, littoral, maritime, onshore, riverside, seaboard, seaside.

8. **1. edged** bordered, marginate. **2. fringed** fringy, tasselled.

9. **1. limiting** borderline, cut-off, delimitative, limitary, limitative, restrictive, terminational, terminative. **2. limited** definite, finite, narrow, restricted.

v. **10.** **1. edge** fringe, purfle, rim. **2. bind** braid, burr, hem, list, twine. **3. frame** hedge in, margin, marginate, mat. **4. outline** circumscribe, conscribe, contour.

11. **1. limit** circumscribe, circumvallate, conscribe, contain, define, delimit, draw the line, enwreathe, terminate. **2. demarcate** beat the bounds, mark out, peg out, zone. **3. bound** bank, embank, kerb. **4. reach the limit** bottom out, hit the wall.

12. **1. border** abut, adjoin, bound, skirt.

adv. **13.** **1. marginally** perimetrically, peripherally.

14. **1. finitely** at the outside, definably, terminatively.

RELATED KEYWORDS: ENCLOSURE, OUTSIDE, SURROUNDINGS

EFFORT

n. **1.** **1. effort** diligence, exertion, industriousness, labour, lucubration, painstaking, work. **2. drive** conatus, endeavour, nisus, striving. *Informal:* push. **3. strain** overexertion, overwork, travail. **4. muscle** brawn, elbow grease.

2. **1. toil** drudgery, graft, moil, slavery. *Informal:* donkey work, fag, grind, slog, sweat. **2. laboriousness** arduousness, burdensomeness, operoseness, strenuousness, sweatiness, toilsomeness. **3. task** backbreaker, charge, chore, fatigue, load.

3. **1. striver** endeavourer. *Informal:* conchie, doer. **2. battler** lucubrator, old soldier, plodder, plugger. **3. toiler** grafter, labourer, party hack, workhorse. *Informal:* a beggar for punishment, a tiger for punishment (or work).

4. **1. exercise** constitutional, daily dozen, exercitation, pacework, practice, sweat, workout. **2. physical education** acrobatics, aerobics, aquarobics, athletics, body building, callisthenics, circuit training, gym, gymnastics, indoor sports, isometrics, P.E., P.T., parkour, PE, physical training, sport, Swedish movements, weightlifting, yoga. *Informal:* physical jerks. **3. exercises** backflip, cartwheel, flip, forward roll, half lever, handspring, handstand, hang, knee-bend, lunge, neck roll, press-up, push-up, scissors, somersault, splits, summersault.

adj. **5.** **1. effortful** arduous, backbreaking, burdensome, exertive, hard, herculean, laborious, labour-intensive, painful, painstaking, stiff, sweaty, toilful, toilsome, uphill, wearisome, weary. **2. laboured** operose. **3. industrious** energetic, hard at it, hard-working, operose. **4. thorough** diligent, sedulous.

6. **1. athletic** active, agile, limber, long-limbed, nimble, spry. **2. gymnastic** aerobic, callisthenic, isometric.

v. **7.** **1. make an effort** bend the bow, exert oneself, go the whole nine yards *(Chiefly US)*, keep at it, pull one's weight, put one's shoulder to the wheel, roll up one's sleeves, take the labouring oar, tax oneself. **2. spare no effort** bend over backwards, do all in one's power, do all one can, do one's utmost, do or die, do the best one can, fall over backwards to do something, go all out, go out of one's way, go to great lengths, lean over backwards, leave no stone unturned, move heaven and earth, pull out all the stops, sink or swim. *Informal:* burst one's boiler, bust a gut, bust one's boiler, do one's darnedest, give it everything one has got, go eyes out. **3. work at** beaver away at, buckle down to, buckle into, elaborate, grapple with, knuckle down to, pitch into, plough into, put one's back into, stick at, take the bit between one's teeth, take to, till, turn to, wade into. *Informal:* bullock at, get stuck into, hoe into, hop into. **4. toil** be hard at it, burn the midnight oil, do double duty, drudge, graft, grub, keep one's nose to the grindstone, labour, lucubrate, make a meal of, moil, overstrain, plod, slave, tug, work day and night, work like a dog, work like a galley slave, work like a horse, work like a Trojan. *Informal:* footslog, grind, slog, sweat blood, work like Jacky, work one's guts out, work one's slot out. **5. take pains** agonise over. **6. battle** grabble, scrabble, scramble, scrimmage, scuffle, strive, struggle. **7. get moving** bestir oneself, sally forth, set to, strike a blow. *Informal:* get cracking, get weaving, pull one's finger out, pull one's socks up, wade in (or into).

adv. **8.** **1. with effort** agonisingly, arduously, burdensomely, drudgingly, grindingly, heavily, laboriously, labouringly, strenuously, sweatily, toilfully, toilsomely. **2. industriously** ably, energetically, enthusiastically, for all one's worth, for the life of one, hard, hurry-scurry, operosely, with might and main. *Informal:* full bore. **3. athletically** agilely, gymnastically.

RELATED KEYWORDS: BUSYNESS, ACTION, DIFFICULTY, WORK

ELECTRICITY

n. **1.** **1. electricity** charge, power. *Informal:* juice. **2. types of electricity** faradism, geothermal power, hydro-electricity, hydropower, magneto-electricity, nuclear power, piezoelectricity, pyroelectricity, solar power, static electricity, thermoelectricity, thermonuclear energy, tidal power, triboelectricity, voltaism, wave power, wind power. **3. electric current** alternate, alternating current, amperage, commutation, current density, direct current, eddy current, Foucault current, grid current, ripple current, thermionic current. **4. conductance** admittance, conductivity, superconductivity. **5. resistance** impedance, load, ohmage, reactance, resistivity, susceptance. **6. power** power factor, wattage. **7. inductance** induction. **8. capacitance** absolute permittivity, capacity, dielectric strength, elastance, relative permittivity, susceptibility. **9. voltage** electric field strength, electric intensity, electric potential, electromotive force, flux, grid bias, potential, potential difference, tension, voltage drop, Zener voltage. **10. spark** arc, carbon arc. **11. discharge** brush, brush discharge, corona, disruptive discharge, flashover, gas discharge, glow discharge, leakage current, shot noise. **12. static** atmospherics, electrophorus.

2. **1. electric circuit** circuit, circuitry, closed circuit, IC, microcircuit, network, open circuit, printed circuit, resonant circuit, stage, tuned circuit, winding, wiring. **2. short circuit** short. **3. contact** brush, busbar, commutator, slipring. *Informal:* buzz bar. **4. switch** air-switch, button, contact-breaker, contactor, cryotron, dimmer, dip switch, double-throw switch, interrupter, knife switch, make and break, membrane switch, point, push-button, stepping switch, switchgear, tumbler switch. *Informal:* tit. **5. terminal** anode, anodic, anticathode, cathode, electrode, emitter, gate, grid, kathode. **6. conductor** anolyte, electrolyte, superconductor. **7. semiconductor** amorphous semiconductor, extrinsic semiconductor, intrinsic semiconductor, n-type semiconductor, p-type semiconductor, thermistor. **8. insulator** dielectric. **9. thermocouple** thermoelectric couple, thermopile. **10. wire** filament. **11. solenoid** coil, differential, field coil, field winding. **12. armature** rotor, stator. **13. power cable** catenary, conduit, feeder, grid, jumper leads, power wire, transmission line. **14. current collector** pantograph, plough, skate, third rail, trolley. **15. earth** busbar, buzz bar, earth loop, earth return, ground plate, lightning conductor. **16. power point** bayonet holder, double adapter, general-purpose outlet, receptacle *(US Electricity)*, socket, socket outlet, valve base, valve socket. **17. plug** balun, connection, jack, jack plug, star connection. **18. patch board** patch cord, plug board. **19. fuse** breaker, circuit-breaker, fuse link, fuse wire, link, safety fuse. **20. switchboard** fuse box, junction box, switchbox.

3. **1. electric generator** accumulator, battery, cadmium cell, cell, Daniell cell, dry battery, dry cell, Edison accumulator, electric cell, fuel cell, galvanic battery, gravity cell, mercury cell, Ni-Fe accumulator, photovoltaic cell, primary cell, secondary cell, selenium cell, solar battery, solar paddle, standard cell, storage battery, voltaic battery, Weston cell, wet cell. **2. spark generator** ignition coil, plug, spark coil, spark plug, sparker, tesla coil. **3. transformer** booster, induction coil, isolating transformer, step-up transformer. *Informal:* trannie. **4. power station** generating station, hydroelectric plant, nuclear power station, power plant, power reactor, powerhouse, solar power plant, substation, wind farm. **5. generator** aerogenerator, alternator, Faraday disc, homopolar generator, magneto, magneto-generator, turbogenerator, wind generator. **6. dynamo** charger, electrostatic generator, power pack, static machine, Van de Graaff generator, Wimshurst machine.

4. **1. electrician** auto-electrician, electrical engineer. *Informal:* sparks, sparky.

5. **1. electronics** avionics, electrical engineering, electrochemistry, electrodynamics, electrokinetics, electrostatics, mechatronics, optoelectronics, spintronics. **2. microelectronics** microcircuitry, microminiaturisation, microtechnology.

6. **1. electrical device** *Informal:* black box. **2. photoelectric cell** electric eye, photocell, phototube. **3. valve** anode, beam tube, cathode-ray tube, cistern valve, diode, dynatron, electron gun, electron tube *(US Electronics)*, heptode, pentagrid, pentode, picture tube, radio valve, tetrode, thermionic valve, triode, tube, vacuum tube. **4. rectifier** converter, crystal detector, electrolytic rectifier, half-wave rectifier, inverter, junction rectifier, rotary converter, silicon-controlled rectifier, synchronous converter, thyristor. **5. resistor** ballast resistor, bleeder, resistance, rheostat. **6. capacitor** air-condenser, capacitance, condenser, electrolytic capacitor, grid condenser, trimmer, trimmer capacitor, trimmer condenser, tuning capacitor, varactor. **7. solid-state device** acceptor, charge-coupled device, FET, field effect transistor, integrated circuit, junction transistor, metal oxide semiconductor, MOS, p-n junction, phototransistor, semiconductor diode, transistor, tunnel diode, unijunction transistor, Zener diode. **8. klystron** buncher resonator, catcher resonator. **9. crystal** crystal oscillator, liquid crystal display, quartz plate.

7. **1. electric motor** compound-wound motor, dynamotor, electromotor, induction motor, linear motor, motor generator, motor starter, series-wound motor, shunt-wound motor, squirrel-cage motor, synchro unit, synchronous motor, telemotor, universal motor, universal-wound motor. **2. electronic device** attenuator, automatic gain control, band-pass filter, bimorph, bypass, choke, choking coil, coupler, crossover network, delay line, delayer, electron lens, equaliser, finetuner, flip-flop, gate *(British)*, inductor, low-pass filter, noise gate, op amp, operational amplifier, potential divider, potentiometer, push-pull, reactor, relay, scaler, scintillation spectrometer, sensor, shunt, square-law detector, suppressor, swept frequency oscillator, tuning coil, variometer, voltage divider, volume control, warbler, wobulator.

8. **1. measuring devices** ammeter, astatic galvanometer, ballistic galvanometer, coulometer, electrometer, faradmeter, galvanometer, measuring devices: ammeter, ohmmeter, post-office box, potentiometer, radiomicrometer, tangent galvanometer, variometer,

voltameter, voltammeter, voltmeter, wattmeter, Wheatstone bridge. **2. oscilloscope** cathode-ray oscilloscope, CRO, iconoscope, radarscope, rheoscope.

9. 1. electric unit ampere, ampere hour, ampere-turn, ampere-turns, biot, coulomb, electromagnetic unit, farad, giga-electron volt, gilbert, kilowatt, megawatt, ohm, siemens, volt, volt-ampere, watt.

adj. **10. 1. electric** electrical, galvanic, plug-in, power, supply, voltaic. **2. electronic** microelectronic, solid-state, transistor. **3. ac-dc** diphase, quarter-phase, single-phase, split-phase, three-phase, two-phase. **4. live** alive, high-tension, high-voltage, low-tension, low-voltage. **5. electromotive** electrodynamic, electrokinetic. **6. electro-**electrochemical, electromagnetic, electrometallurgical, ferroelectric, hydro, hydro-electric, magneto-electric, photoelectric, piezoelectric, thermoelectric.

v. **11. 1. electrify** charge, electrolyse, excite, galvanise, power, shock. **2. transistorise**. **3. earth** ground, neutralise. **4. spark** arc, discharge, flashover, strike an arc. **5. conduct** commutate. **6. connect** plug in.

RELATED KEYWORDS: FUEL, MACHINE, POWER

ELOQUENCE

n. **1. 1. eloquence** articulateness, fluentness, good speaking, oratory. *Informal:* gift of the gab. **2. rhetoric** demagoguery, floridness, floweriness, grandiloquence, loftiness, magniloquence, orotundity, picturesqueness, word-painting. **3. wit** Atticism, esprit, pungency, repartee. **4. purple prose** purple passage.

2. 1. oration account, address, address-in-reply, allocution, declamation, defence, discourse, effusion, first speech, harangue, homily, inaugural, King's speech, maiden speech, monologue, narration, panegyric, preaching, Queen's speech, sermon, soliloquy, speech. *Informal:* spiel. **2. recitation** reading, recital, set speech. **3. prologue** exordium, peroration. **4. funeral oration** valediction, valedictory. **5. eulogy** encomium. **6. speechifying** homiletics, sermonising.

3. 1. rhetorical device alliteration, anaphora, anastrophe, antithesis, apostrophe, assonance, asyndeton, ellipsis, epigram, euphemism, euphuism, flourish, flower of rhetoric, hypocorism, inversion, parallelism, periods, prolepsis, rhetorical question, syncope. **2. bon mot** aphorism, Atticism, boutade, jeu d'esprit, mot juste, Parthian shot, quip, sally, witticism. **3. repartee** retort, riposte. *Informal:* comeback.

4. 1. orator aphorist, bard, declaimer, demagogue, elocutionist, haranguer, homilist, lecturer, narrator, oratrix, poet, polemicist, rabble-rouser, rabblerouser, ranter, reader, rhapsodist, rhetor, rhetorician, singer, skald, smooth-talker, soapbox orator, speaker, spokesman, spokesperson, spokeswoman, stump orator *(Chiefly US)*, stylist, valedictorian *(US)*, word-spinner. *Informal:* mouthpiece, tub-thumper. **2. spieler** *(Informal)* amster, deipnosophist, smart talker, spruiker. **3. public speaker** after-dinner speaker, toastmaster, toastmistress. **4. preacher** evangelist, gospeller, pulpiteer, sermoniser. *Informal:* Amen snorter, bible-basher, hot-gospeller.

adj. **5. 1. eloquent** articulate, elocution, epideictic, epidictic, magniloquent, persuasive, picturesque, silver, silver-tongued, slick, smooth, smooth-spoken, smooth-tongued. **2. rhetorical** apostrophic, cadenced, controversial, declamatory, florid, flowery, flowing, grand, grandiloquent, grandiose, heroic, high-flown, high-sounding, homiletic, Johnsonian, lofty, magniloquent, oratorical, polemic, polemical, purple, recitative, sermonic, sonorous.

v. **6. 1. speak well** *Informal:* have the gift of the gab. **2. declaim** hold forth, mouth, orate, pour forth, proclaim, read, reel off, smart talk, speak. *Informal:* pull out all the stops, spiel, spout, spruik. **3. address** apostrophise, call. **4. harangue** evangelise, lecture, perorate, preach, preach at, preachify, sermonise. *Informal:* earbash, give someone an earful, trawl. **5. have one's say** have the floor. *Informal:* say a mouthful.

adv. **7. 1. eloquently** articulately, in a nutshell, picturesquely, slickly. **2. rhetorically** loftily, magniloquently, oratorically.

RELATED KEYWORDS: BREVITY, VERBOSITY, FIGURE OF SPEECH, SPEECH, TALKATIVENESS

EMBLEM

n. **1. 1. emblem** badge, ensign, figure, image, sacrament, sign, symbol, totem. **2. emblem worn** armband, badge, brassard, button, chevron, cluster *(US Army)*, cockade, cockle, cockleshell, cognisance, collar, cordon, cordon bleu, decoration, double diamond, facings, favour, flash, hatband, love knot, medal, medallion, mourning band, patch, ribbon, shoulder flash, shoulder patch, star, stripes, truelove knot, weeper. *Informal:* gong, pip.

3. seal on a letter broad seal, bull, bulla, cachet, chop, common seal, crest, great seal, seal, sigil. **4. stamp** seal, sigil, signet, stamper. **5. mark made by a stamp** colophon, hallmark, impress, imprint, plate-mark, rubber-stamp, stamp, steel engraving, trademark. **6. badge of office** coronet, insignia, regalia, wings. **7. badge of honour** George Cross, Iron Cross. **8. badge as prize** bronze medal, gold medal, silver medal.

2. **1. crown** coronal, coronet, diadem, tiara. **2. badge of sovereignty** globe, orb, regalia, sceptre. **3. stick indicating power** baton, caduceus, crosier, crozier, gavel, mace, mark of office, pastoral, rod, sceptre, staff, truncheon, verge, wand, warder. **4. special clothes** guernsey, hood, livery, pontificals, purple, regimentals, trappings, uniform, vestment. **5. special colour** colours, racing stripes.

3. **1. emblem** ankh, asp, bush, caduceus, Christopher medal, corn poppy, cross, dove, encolpion, Flanders poppy, holy picture, horseshoe, laurel, olive branch, palm, paschal candle, scalp, scarab, scarabaeus, tarot card, uraeus, yoke. **2. stick as emblem** barber's pole, fasces, totem pole. **3. symbolic gesture** cross, salute, sign of the cross, V-sign. **4. symbolic dance** dance of death, danse macabre, sun dance. **5. symbolic sign** broad arrow, cross, crossbones, hammer and sickle, mandala, ouroboros, pentagram, Red Crescent, rising sun, scarlet letter, skull and crossbones, Star of David, swastika, triskelion, uroboros, white feather, XP. **6. type of cross** Celtic cross, fiery cross, Greek cross, Jerusalem cross, Latin cross, Maltese cross, papal cross, patriarchal cross, Red Cross, Saint Andrew's Cross, Saint George's Cross, Saint Patrick's Cross, tau cross. **7. national emblems** bear *(Russia)*, Celtic harp *(Ireland)*, Federation Star *(Australia)*, golden wattle *(Australia)*, Iron Cross *(Germany)*, kangaroo *(Australia)*, kiwi *(NZ)*, leek *(Wales)*, lion *(Czech Republic, Denmark, England, Finland, Montenegro, Netherlands, Norway, Sri Lanka, Sweden)*, maple leaf *(Canada)*, merlion *(Singapore)*, red dragon *(Wales)*, rising sun *(Japan)*, Saint Andrew's Cross *(Scotland)*, Saint George's Cross *(England)*, Saint Patrick's Cross *(Ireland)*, Scotch thistle *(Scotland)*, shamrock *(Ireland)*, silver fern *(NZ)*, Southern Cross *(Australia, NZ)*, spread eagle *(US)*, springbok *(South Africa)*, star and crescent *(Turkey)*, Star of David *(Israel)*, Tudor rose *(England)*. **8. Australian state floral emblems** Cooktown orchid *(Qld)*, kangaroo-paw *(WA)*, pink heath *(Victoria)*, royal bluebell *(ACT)*, Sturt's desert pea *(SA)*, Sturt's desert rose *(NT)*, Tasmanian blue gum *(Tasmania)*, waratah *(NSW)*.

4. **1. flag** banderol, banner, banneret, bannerette, bannerol, bunting, burgee, dogvane, ensign, fanion, flying colours, gonfalon, guidon, hoist, jack, labarum, pendant, pendent, pennant, pennon, racing colours, standard, streamer, vexillum. *Informal:* flogger.

5. **1. type of flag** Australian national flag, black flag, blackjack, blue ensign, blue peter, commercial flag, courtesy ensign, dive flag, Eureka flag, false colours, flag, flag of convenience, flag of distress, flag of truce, house flag, Jolly Roger, merchant flag, national flag, Old Glory, oriflamme, pilot flag, recall, red ensign, red flag, Star-Spangled Banner, Stars and Bars, Stars and Stripes, surf flag, tricolour, Union Flag, Union Jack, white ensign, white flag, yellow flag, yellow jack, yellow jacket.

6. **1. heraldry** armory, blazon, blazonry, emblazonry. **2. armorial bearings** arms, blazon, blazonry, coat of arms, crest, hatchment, heraldry, passant. **3. place for device** escutcheon, field, lozenge, scutcheon, shield. **4. device** bearing, charge, ordinary. **5. sphragistics** vexillology.

7. **1. heraldic device** bar, bar sinister, baton, bend, bend sinister, canton, chevron, cotise, cross, crosslet, dancette, diminutive, escallop, fess, fleur-de-lis, fur, fusil, leopard, lily, lion, lioncel, luce, martlet, nombril, orle, pall, pile, saltire, sun, sun in splendour, supporter, tincture, tressure, unicorn.

8. **1. heraldic point** chief, dexter base, dexter chief, fess point, honour point, middle base, middle chief, nombril point, sinister base, sinister chief.

9. **1. emblematist** armorist, blazoner.

adj. **10.** **1. emblematic** armorial, heraldic, sigillary, sphragistic, symbolic. **2. emblazoned** blazoned, crested, escutcheoned. **3. in regalia** cockaded, coronate, liveried, sceptred.

11. **1. heraldic descriptions** compony, couchant, dancetty, dexter, fleury, flory, gardant, guardant, issuant, jessant, nebuly, rampant, regardant, sejant, sinister, vairy, volant.

v. **12.** **1. emblematise** hallmark, imprint, seal, signet. **2. blazon** blaze, charge, emblazon, quarter, unpale.

adv. **13.** **1. emblematically** heraldically, symbolically.

RELATED KEYWORDS: AWARD, SIGN

EMISSION

n. **1.** **1. emission** discharge, emanation, eradiation, radiation. **2. expulsion** dehiscence, disgorgement, ejaculation, elimination, evacuation, extrusion, voidance. **3. eruption** effusion, excretion, extravasation, flux, outpouring, precipitation, suppuration. **4. regurgitation** emesis, hyperemesis, vomiting, vomiturition. **5. deflation** degasification.

    2.   **1. burp** belch, eructation, retch. **2. vomit** pellet, sick, vomitus. *Informal:* barf, berley, chuck, chuck-up, liquid laugh, technicolour yawn, yellow yawn. **3. flatus** gas. *Informal:* air biscuit, braff, fart, fluff, raspberry tart, SBD, smelly. **4. breaking wind** flatulency, wind. *Informal:* farting.

    3.   **1. emitter** eliminator, evacuator, expeller, vomiter. **2. emetic** aperient, cathartic, expellant, vomitory.

adj. **4.**   **1. emissive** deflationary, ejective, eliminatory, eruptive, expellant, expulsive, extrusive. **2. effusive** emissive, suppurative. **3. egestive** anethole, carminative, cathartic, emetic, errhine, evacuant, flatulent, laxative, purgative, vomitive, vomitory.

v. **5.**   **1. emit** eradiate, give off, give out, irradiate, radiate, reek, spit, sputter, steam. **2. discharge** excrete, exude, pour out, suppurate. **3. expel** disgorge, dump, egest, ejaculate, eliminate, evacuate, express, extrude, pump out, spout, vent, void. **4. erupt** burst, bust, effuse, regorge. **5. deflate** degas, degasify.

    6.   **1. vomit** be sick, bring up, cast, dry-retch, heave, keck, regurgitate, reject, retch. *Informal:* barf, bark, chuck, chunder, cry ruth, feed the fishes, fetch up, go for the big spit, have a sale, have the chuck-ups, have the spews, herk, hurl, lose one's lunch, make a sale, perk, perk up, puke, ralph, sick up, spew, spue, throw up, yodel. **2. burp** belch, eruct, eructate, repeat. **3. break wind** expel gas. *Informal:* blow off, braff, drop a bundle, drop one's lunch, fart, fluff, go off, let off, open one's lunch box, pop off, shoot a bunny, shoot a fairy.

RELATED KEYWORDS: BODILY DISCHARGE, FLOOD, EXCLUSION

EMOTION

n. **1.**   **1. emotion** affection, feeling, mood, pulse, sensation, sentiment. *Informal:* sob-story, vibes, vibrations. **2. spirits** cheer, heart, morale, temper. **3. heart** bosom, breast, heart of hearts, heartstrings, inner man, soul, spirit. **4. fervour** ardency, ardour, elan, enthusiasm, fervency, ferventness, fervidness, fieriness, fire, flame, franticness, glow, heat, impassionedness, passion, passionateness, perfervour, rage, torridness, vehemence, warmth, zeal. **5. ecstasy** paroxysm, spasm, transport.

    2.   **1. emotionality** demonstrativeness, effusiveness, emotionalism, emotivity, gushiness, lyricalness, lyricism, moodiness, romanticism. **2. sensitivity** affectivity, delicacy, delicateness, feeling, hypersensitivity, passibility, refinement, sensibility, sensitiveness, sentience, susceptibility, susceptibleness, susceptiveness, touchiness, warmness, warmth. **3. sympathy** empathy, fellow feeling. **4. sentimentality** bathos, drivel, gooiness, hearts-and-flowers *(Chiefly US)*, maudlinness, mawkishness, sentimentalism, slobber, soppiness, soulfulness. *Informal:* mush, schmalz, slush, syrup. **5. histrionics** melodrama. **6. emotional genre** love story, melodrama, Mills and Boon, novelette, romance. *Informal:* chick flick, tear-jerker. **7. sob story** hard luck story, hardship tale. *Informal:* tear-jerker. **8. heart-to-heart** deep-and-meaningful. *Informal:* D and M.

    3.   **1. outburst** access, blaze, burst, ebullition, outbreak, passion, riot, spurt, tornado. **2. flush** swell, wave.

    4.   **1. emotional person** diva, drama queen, dramatiser, emo, emotionalist, tinderbox. *Informal:* prima donna, sob-sister. **2. romantic** cornball *(Chiefly US)*, sentimentalist.

adj. **5.**   **1. emotional** affective, feeling, lyric, moody, passional, temperamental. **2. fervent** ablaze, afire, ardent, athirst, eager, ebullient, enthusiastic, fervid, feverish, fiery, flaming, glowing, hearty, high-pitched, hot, impassioned, intense, keen, on fire, passionate, perfervid, raring, red-hot, sharp, torrid, vehement, violent, warm-blooded. *Informal:* churned up, in a tear, in a willy, psyched, thingy, toey. **3. heartfelt** close to one's heart, deep, devout, earnest, gut, heart-to-heart, heart-whole, hearty, infelt, profound, sincere, single-hearted. **4. effusive** demonstrative, exuberant, gushy. **5. ecstatic** beside oneself, rapt, rapturous, rhapsodical. *Informal:* wrapped. **6. sensitive** delicate, hypersensitive, irritable, moody, oversensitive, passible, prickly, sentient, supersensitive, susceptible, susceptive, thin-skinned, touchy. *Informal:* miffy, quiche-eating. **7. sympathetic** empathetic, empathic, responsive, understanding, warm. **8. sentimental** bathetic, maudlin, mawkish, Mills-and-Boon, misty-eyed, namby-pamby, novelettish, over-emotional, romantic, rosewater, sawney, schmaltzy, schmalzy, sickly, slushy, soft, soulful, soupy. *Informal:* cheesy, corny, gooey, hokey *(US)*, icky, mushy, sloppy, soppy, syrupy. **9. theatrical** histrionic, melodramatic.

    6.   **1. emotive** affecting, affective, cutsie-pie, feelgood, heart-warming, heartbreaking, moving, pathetic, poignant, pungent, rousing, stirring, touching, upsetting.

v.   **7.**   **1. emotionalise** get up a feeling, supercharge. **2. affect** awake, excite, impress, make an impact on, move, stir, touch. *Informal:* grab. **3. impassion** fire, inflame, set fire to, set on fire. **4. ravish** rock, smite, transport.

     8.   **1. feel emotion** be overcome, care, cheer, experience, feel, mind, take to heart. *Informal:* have a thing about. **2. sympathise** commiserate, feel for (or with), know what it is to, respond. **3. sentimentalise** gush, slobber, slop over. **4. theatricalise** melodramatise, overdo. *Informal:* bung it on, emote, ham it up, stack it on. **5. burn** boil, fire, flame, glow, rage, seethe, smoulder, tear one's hair out. **6. thrill** throb, vibrate.

adv.   **9.**   **1. emotionally** affettuoso, animato, con anima, con espressione, demonstratively, effusively, feelingly, sympathetically, sympathisingly, warmly. **2. emotively** affectingly, affectively, movingly, poignantly, pungently, touchingly. **3. fervently** appassionato, ardently, con fuoco, enthusiastically, fervidly, fierily, glowingly, impassionedly, passionately, torridly, vehemently. **4. sensitively** delicately. **5. deeply** earnestly, from the bottom of one's heart, heart and soul, intensely, intimately, sincerely, with all one's heart. **6. sentimentally** languishingly, mawkishly, melodramatically, sloppily, soppily, soulfully. **7. ecstatically** rhapsodically.

RELATED KEYWORDS: ANGER, EXCITEMENT, SURPRISE, HAPPINESS, UNHAPPINESS, HOPE, DESPAIR, JOY, GRIEF, LOVE, HATE, PLEASURE

EMPLOYMENT

n.   **1.**   **1. employment** admission, appointment, assignation, assignment, designation, empanelment, entrustment, nomination, placement, reinstatement, secondment. *Informal:* body hire. **2. state of employment** employ, placement, service, work. **3. overemployment** featherbedding. **4. investiture** coronation, enthronisation, incardination, investment, ordainment, ordination, provision. **5. divine appointment** call, vocation. **6. delegation** deputation, procuration.

     2.   **1. function** commission, duty, office, place. **2. position** appointment, billet, booking, brevet, commission, engagement, hat, incumbency, office, place, post, posting, situation, station, vacancy. *Informal:* berth. **3. task** assignment, business, detail, errand, mission.

     3.   **1. appointed group** committee, delegation, deputation. **2. appointee** administrator, functionary, heir-designate, nominee, office-bearer, officer, official.

     4.   **1. employer** appointer, appointor, assignor, commissioning editor, constitutor, designator, nominator, ordainer.

     5.   **1. promotion** advance, advancement, brevet *(Military)*, preferment. **2. peter principle** glass ceiling. **3. headhunting** *Informal:* body-snatching.

adj.   **6.**   **1. employed** acting, actively employed, appointed, designate, elect, in a job, nominative.

v.   **7.**   **1. employ** appoint, assign, commission, engage, entrust, hire, place, set in place over, take on, underemploy. **2. invest** crown, enact, enthrone, incardinate, inthrone, mitre, ordain. **3. install** consecrate, inaugurate, induct, institute. **4. assign** attach, depute, detail, tell off. **5. dob in for** nobble with. *Informal:* put in. **6. reinstate** headhunt, revest. **7. accredit** empower, give power of attorney. **8. empanel** impanel, panel. **9. nominate** name, postulate, slate.

     8.   **1. be appointed** be promoted, get on. *Informal:* get the nod.

     9.   **1. promote** advance, brevet *(Military)*, prefer, upgrade. *Informal:* kick upstairs. **2. exalt** elevate, lift, raise.

RELATED KEYWORDS: WORK, WORKER

EMPTINESS

n.   **1.**   **1. emptiness** inanition, inanity, vacancy, vacuousness, voidness. **2. emptying** evacuation, vacation. **3. vacuum** blank, hollow, vacancy, vacuity, void.

     2.   **1. tabula rasa** clean slate. **2. null set** empty set. **3. blank** blank space, white, white line, white space. **4. empty bottle** *Informal:* dead marine, empty.

adj.   **3.**   **1. empty** exhausted, inane, vacant, vacuous, vacuum, void. *Informal:* dead. **2. vacant** deserted, empty, uninhabited, unoccupied. **3. blank** white. **4. unladen** clear, empty-handed.

v.   **4.**   **1. empty** evacuate, vacate, void. **2. clean out** strip, turn out. **3. blank out** white. **4. drain** bail out, disembogue, exhaust, leach, start.

RELATED KEYWORDS: DEFICIENCY, ABSENCE

ENCLOSURE

n.   **1.**   **1. enclosure** approvement, circumscription, enceinte, encirclement, encompassment, purpresture *(British)*, subdivision. **2. envelopment** boxing, encapsulation, encasement, enshrinement, enswathement, packaging. **3. incarceration** confinement, immurement, impoundage, imprisonment, mandatory detention, poundage. **4. surround** frame, gobo.

2. 1. pen accommodation paddock, bullpen, byre, cattlepen, compound, corral, cowhouse, crib, fold, holding paddock, kraal *(South African)*, mews, paddock, piggery, pigpen, pigsty, playpen, pound, saddling paddock, shearing paddock, sheepcote *(Chiefly British)*, sheepfold, stable, stall, stockade, stockyard, sty, walk. **2. holding pen** catching pen, counting-out pen, creep feeder, crush, crush-pen *(NZ)*, drafting yard, draining pen, farrowing house, forcing pen. **3. barrier stall** starting box, starting grid, swabbing stall.

adj. **3. 1. enclosed** boxed in, capsulate, circumscribed, cleidoic, cloistered, close, closed-up, confined, encased, enveloped, fenced-in, included, landlocked, shut-in, snowbound. **2. encircled** ringed, surrounded. **3. close** claustrophobic, smothery. *Informal:* without room to swing a cat.

v. **4. 1. enclose** box in, brick up, cabin, close, close in, confine, coop up, cordon off, cramp, fasten in, kernel, pinch, shut, shut in, smother. **2. envelop** enswathe, enwrap. **3. encase** box, cage, case, crate, enshrine, inshrine, pocket, saggar, shrine. **4. sheathe** insheathe, sheath. **5. encircle** begird, belt, cinch, cincture, circle, circumscribe, clip, embay, embrace, encompass, engird, engirdle, enlace, envelop, environ, enwreathe, gird, girdle, girth, hoop, loop, moat, orb *(Poetic)*, ring, round, surround, zone. **6. wall in** bower, chamber, confine, embank, embower, enwall, fence in, hedge, immure, imprison, incarcerate, inwall, lock off, pale, picket, shut up. *Informal:* send up. **7. pen** corral, fold, impound, paddock, pinfold, pound, sty.

RELATED KEYWORDS: DWELLING, EDGE, IMPRISONMENT, SURROUNDINGS

ENCOURAGEMENT

n. **1. 1. encouragement** abetment, exhortation, furtherance, induction, moral support, promotion. **2. motivation** actuation, agenda, drive, impetus, impulse, impulsion, incentive, incitation, incitement, inducement, induction, influence, motive, provocation, push, stimulation. **3. inspiration** afflatus, ambrosia, awakening. **4. enticement** allurement, attraction, bait, bewitchment, enchantment, inducement, seduction, solicitation. **5. agitation** activism, barratry, consciousness raising, fomentation, incendiarism, inflammation, provocativeness, revolutionary activity, sedition, seditiousness, stirring.

2. 1. incentive appetiser, bribe, carrot, carrot and stick, enticement, instigation, prompt, seduction, source of motivation. *Informal:* kickback, spiff, sweetener. **2. stimulus** fillip, goad, hurry-up, impellent, impulse, incentive, inducer, instigation, pep talk, prodder, prompt, prompter, provocative, recommender, spur, stimulative, stimulator, sting, urge. **3. impetus** arrière-pensée, raison d'être, reason, ulterior motive. **4. spur** ankus, battery stick, cattle prod, crop, gad, goad, paroo dog, prod, riding crop, sjambok *(South African)*, sting, stockwhip, whip. *Informal:* gully-raker. **5. shout of encouragement** cheer, encouragement, haka, promotion, war dance. *Informal:* hype. **6. promotion** advertisement, advertising, advertising campaign, blurb, commercial, film clip, loss leader, promo, recommendation, teaser, teaser ad, trailer. *Informal:* ad, advert, hard sell, plug, sell, soft sell. **7. inducement** bribery, compensation, consideration, incentive, inducement allowance, payola, quid pro quo, reward. *Informal:* cigarette money *(Philippine English)*, coffee money *(Singaporean and Malaysian English)*, come-on. **8. cajolery** blandishments, flattery, honeyed words, palaver, soft soap.

3. 1. encourager abetter, cohort, patron, sponsor, supporter. **2. motivator** ampster, lobbyist, promoter, ring leader. *Informal:* urger. **3. inspirer** actuator, animater, animator, impeller, Muse, soul. **4. barracker** cheer squad, cheerer, cheerleader, flagwaver, rooter. **5. agitator** actionist, activist, agent provocateur, barrator, enkindler, firebrand, incendiary, inciter, inflamer, provocateur, provoker, rabble-rouser, seditionary, spurrer. *Informal:* rouser, stirrer. **6. promoter** advertiser, advertising agency, commercial traveller, pig drummer, salesperson, spruiker, tambour. **7. fosterer** kindler, nourisher. **8. enticer** blandisher, coaxer, enchantress, seducer, siren, tempter, wheedler.

4. 1. motive arrière-pensée, cause, drive, impetus, incentive, raison d'être, reason, the why and the wherefore, the whys and wherefores, ulterior motive, what makes one tick.

adj. **5. 1. encouraging** hortative, hortatory, incentive, inductive, motivational, motive, moving, provocative, stimulant, stimulative, tonic, touching. **2. inviting** alluring, appetising, awe-inspiring, captivating, entrancing, exciting, fascinating, inspirational, irresistible, piquant, provocative, provoking, rousing, seductive, stimulating, stirring, taking, tempting, titillative. **3. impellent** impulsive. **4. incendiary** barratrous, inflammatory, seditionary, seditious.

v. **6.** **1. encourage** abet, coax, counsel, entice, excite, impel, incite, induce, inveigle, press, provide an example, put someone up to, set an example, urge, work up. *Informal:* hype up. **2. motivate** actuate, instigate, move, provoke, stimulate. **3. inspire** afflated, animate, awake, inform. **4. influence** affect, convince, impress, inspire, lead by the nose, over-persuade, persuade, play upon another's feelings, prevail upon, sway, talk over, turn someone's head, weigh heavily with, wrangle. **5. seduce** beckon, bewitch, captivate, charm, enchant, ensorcell *(Poetic)*, enthral, entice, entrance, lead astray, lure, tempt. **6. cheer** barrack for, cheer on, egg on, spirit, whoop. **7. promote** advertorialise, ballyhoo, drum up trade, encourage, sell. *Informal:* spiel, spruik. **8. recommend** advocate, suggest, support. **9. nurture** foster, nourish, nurse, promote, suckle. **10. back up** assure, favour, support.

7. **1. arouse** bestir, call forth, evoke, goad, kindle interest, kittle *(Scottish)*, prompt, roust, rout out, stir up. *Informal:* kick up. **2. incite** agitate, enkindle, fan, fire, inflame, inspirit, rouse, set on fire, skitch, sool. **3. stir the possum** cook up a storm, trail a coat. **4. goad** force on, hound, hurry along, hurry up, hustle, needle, prick, prod, push, spur, sting, stockwhip. *Informal:* get on someone's back, scrub.

8. **1. be motivated** become carried away, become fired with enthusiasm, follow another's lead, obey a call, yield to temptation. **2. have an axe to grind** be driven on.

adv. **9.** **1. encouragingly** hortatively, inspirationally. **2. appetisingly** enticingly. **3. incitingly** barratrously, inflamingly, inflammatorily, provocatively, seditiously. **4. movingly** piquantly, provokingly, rousingly, stirringly, touchingly.

RELATED KEYWORDS: ALLURE, BRIBERY, WILLINGNESS

ENERGY

n. **1.** **1. energy** action, conatus, effort, force, impetus, impulse, motive power, motivity, power, stress, thrust, torc, torque. **2. type of energy** atomic energy, atomic power, binding energy, bioenergy, electric power, enthalpy, entropy, fusion energy, hydraulic power, hydro-electric power, internal energy, kinetic energy, linear momentum, momentum, nuclear energy, nuclear power, potential energy, renewable, shear stress, solar energy, sun-power, waterpower, windpower, zero point energy. **3. unit of energy** light quantum, phonon, photon, quantum. **4. force** ampere-turn, centrifugal force, centripetal force, electromotive force, Lorentz force, magnetomotive force. **5. potential energy** electric potential, electrokinetic potential, energy level, ionisation potential, magnetic potential, magnetic scalar potential, Planck's constant, potential, zetapotential. **6. unit of work** British thermal unit, cal, calorie, erg, gigajoule, joule, kilocalorie, kilogram calorie, kilojoule, kilowatt hour, terajoule, therm. **7. unit of force** dyne, kilogram-force, newton, newton metre, pound, pound-force, poundal. **8. unit of power** electrostatic unit, horsepower, kilowatt, manpower, megawatt, watt. **9. science of energy** biodynamics, dynamics, energetics, geodynamics, hydrodynamics, hydromechanics, magnetohydrodynamics, physics, thermodynamics.

2. **1. vitality** alacrity, aliveness, animal spirits, animation, ardour, brilliance, brio, dynamism, ebullience, effervescency, exuberance, libido, life, liveliness, lustiness, spirit, spiritedness, sprightliness, vibrancy, vital force, vitalness, vivaciousness, vivacity. **2. invigoration** energising, enlivenment, innervation, stimulation, vitalisation, vivification. **3. vigour** dash, elan, fire, gusto, nerve, peppiness, pith, pizazz, red-bloodedness, spirit, sthenia, verve, vigorousness, vim, zest. *Informal:* bang *(US)*, kick, pep, snap, zap, zing, zip *(Chiefly US)*. **4. briskness** athleticism, freshness, rompishness, tirelessness, unweariedness. **5. get-up-and-go** bustle, ginger. *Informal:* go, gumption, herbs, oomph, push, spunk, steam. **6. drive** aggressivity, ambition, enterprise.

3. **1. energiser** activator, booster, exhilarator, ginger group, impeller, invigorator, prime mover, stimulator, stimulus, sustainer, vivifier. **2. striver** laster, pusher, self-starter. *Informal:* dynamo, hustler, livewire.

adj. **4.** **1. energetic** aggressive, ambitious, driving, dynamic, forceful, high-powered, high-pressure, intense, motivated, strenuous, strong, vigorous. *Informal:* peppy. **2. tireless** inexhaustible, unwearied, weariless. **3. vigorous** active, athletic, cracking, full-blooded, lively, quick, red-blooded, sinewy, spirited, virile. **4. headlong** helter-skelter, impetuous. **5. lively** bouncing, crisp, ebullient, effervescent, flush, fresh, lusty, pert, proud *(Poetic)*, rompish, sappy, sprightly, spritely, vibrant, vital, vivacious, vivid. *Informal:* bright-eyed and bushy-tailed, live, oomphy, peppy, pumped up, swinging, zippy. **6. alive** *Informal:* alive and kicking, full of beans. **7. spirited** animated, rousing, spanking, stirring, warm. *Informal:* ding-dong. **8. jazzy** jazzed up, racy, souped-up. **9. invigorating** bracing, brisk, crisp, invigorative.

v. **5.** **1. energise** activate, animate, boost, brisk up, enliven, exhilarate, flush, galvanise, innerve, invigorate, quicken, sauce, stimulate, vitalise, vivify, zest. *Informal:* ginger up, jazz up, pep up, soup up.
6. **1. be energetic** brace up, effervesce, feel one's oats, perk up. **2. bustle** hustle, make an effort, overcompensate, strive. **3. get into** plough into, put one's back into, put one's shoulder to the wheel, take the bit between one's teeth, throw oneself into, turn one's hand to, warm to. *Informal:* get cracking, get stuck into, hoe into, hop into.
adv. **7.** **1. energetically** aggressively, briskly, bustlingly, strenuously, tirelessly, unweariedly, vigorously. **2. full pelt** animatedly, forcefully, harum-scarum, headlong, helter-skelter, impetuously, impulsively, madly, violently, wildly, with a vengeance. *Informal:* like billyo. **3. spiritedly** con forza, forzando, sforzando. **4. vibrantly** ebulliently, effervescently, invigoratingly, lively, vivaciously, warmly.
RELATED KEYWORDS: ELECTRICITY, FUEL, POWER, STRENGTH, FOOD

ENTERTAINER

n. **1.** **1. entertainer** busker, geisha, jongleur, minstrel, mountebank, performer, play-actor, player, puppeteer, reciter, showman, song-and-dance man, stroller, strolling player, troubadour. **2. comedian** amuser, blackface, comedienne, comic, farceur, farceuse, humorist, slapstick comedian, stand-up comedian, stand-up comic, straight man, vaudevillist. *Informal:* funnyman. **3. clown** buffoon, fool, jester. **4. announcer** anchor, anchorman, caller, commentator, compere, deejay, disc jockey, diseur, DJ, epilogist, epilogue, front man, frontman, linkboy, linkman, main man, presenter, prologue, quizmaster, race caller, ringmaster, shock jock, veejay, VJ. *Informal:* talking head. **5. impersonator** female impersonator, improvisator, improviser, masker, masquer, mime, mimer, mimic, mummer, mute, pantomime, pantomimist, personator. **6. multimedia personality**.
2. **1. actor** acting, actress, actrine, artist, artiste, character actor, double, method actor, portrayer, quick-change artist, straight man, Thespian, tragedian, tragedienne, trouper. *Informal:* ham, luvvy. **2. star** antihero, co-star, coryphaeus, film star, hero, lead, leading lady, leading man, matinee idol, megastar, premiere, principal, principal boy, scene-stealer, soloist, starlet, superstar. **3. extra** bit-player, chorus member, figurant, figurante, spear-carrier, supernumerary, support, supporting actor, walk-on. **4. chorus girl** showgirl. *Informal:* hoofer *(US)*. **5. understudy** alternate, double, stand-in, stuntman. **6. villain** black hat, heavy. *Informal:* baddie. **7. dame** endman, ingenue, interlocutrix, juvenile, pantomime dame, soubrette. **8. part** bit part, cameo, role. **9. stage name**.
3. **1. Punch** Columbine, Harlequin, Judy, Pantaloon, Pierrette, Pierrot, Pulcinella, Scaramouche.
4. **1. circus performer** acrobat, aerialist, balancer, bareback rider, clown, equilibrist, flier, highwire artist, juggler, lion tamer, magician, rope-walker, slackwire artist, strongman, sword-swallower, tightrope walker, trapeze artist, tumbler. **2. snake-charmer**. **3. fire-eater** fire-swallower, pyrotechnist.
5. **1. puppet** glove puppet, hand puppet, Judy, marionette, penis puppet, Punch, shadow puppet.
6. **1. theatrical company** circus, cirque, ensemble, minstrel show, repertory, stock company, three-ring circus, troupe. *Informal:* rep. **2. cast** characters, dramatis personae. **3. chorus** support. **4. backer** choragus. *Informal:* angel.
RELATED KEYWORDS: ARTIST, DANCING, FINE ARTS, MUSICIAN, POETRY, WRITING

ENTERTAINMENT

n. **1.** **1. entertainment** attraction, divertissement, music theatre, night-life, performing arts, regalement, show business, variety, vaudeville. **2. show** blockbuster, circus, cirque, exhibition, festival, fluxus, ice show, lightshow, pageant, phantasmagoria, son et lumière, spectacle, spectacular, street theatre, three-ring circus, variety show, vaudeville. **3. cinema** bioscope, celluloid, film theatre, films, movie theatre, pitcher-pitcher *(Aboriginal English)*, silver screen, the movies, the pictures, theatre. *Informal:* flicks, piccie, pickies, pikkie. **4. cabaret** floor show, follies, revue. **5. supporting act** sideshow. **6. roadshow** circuit, circus, fair, showboat *(US)*, three-ring circus. **7. benefit** *Informal:* barrel. **8. an evening out** a night on the town. *Informal:* blow-out, rage.
2. **1. acting** mummery, rendering. **2. characterisation** portrayal, representation. **3. Stanislavsky method** Alexander technique, method acting, the Method. **4. dramatics** histrionics, theatricals. **5. showmanship** stagecraft, theatrecraft.
3. **1. drama** closet drama, conversation piece, costume drama, costume piece, epic, experimental theatre, Grand Guignol, history, kitchen-sink drama, mask, masque, maxi-series,

melodrama, miracle play, monodrama, morality play, music drama, mystery play, panto-mime, passion play, piece, play, playlet, poetic drama, problem play, Punch and Judy show, puppet play, shadow play, theatricals. *Informal:* panto. **2. opera** Chinese opera, kabuki, No, tamasha, wayang, wayang kulit. **3. tragedy** buskin, tragicomedy. **4. comedy** bedroom comedy, black comedy, burlesque, comedy of ideas, comedy of manners, com-media dell'arte, farce, high comedy, interlude, low comedy, musical comedy, parody, screwball comedy, sitcom, situation comedy, skit, slapstick, theatre of the absurd, theatresports, tragicomedy.

4. 1. film *Informal:* flick. **2. movie** B-grade film, cinefilm, double bill, double feature, feature, feature film, motion picture, moving picture *(Chiefly US)*, picture, picture show, silent film, telemovie. *Informal:* talkie. **3. shorts** trailer, travelogue. **4. video** clip, film clip, video clip. **5. cinemascope** 3-D, cinematography, cinerama, computer animation, IMAX, sensurround, technicolour, vista-vision. **6. footage** mute negative, mute print, reduction print, rough cut, rushes. **7. cartoon** animate, animated, animated cartoon, animation, cell animation, claymation, manga movie. **8. documentary** actuality, bio-pic, cinéma-vérité, docudrama, hour show, newsreel, rockumentary, semidocumentary. *Informal:* doco. **9. sequel** prequel, tetralogy, trilogy. **10. action movie. 11. buddy film. 12. film noir** noir. **13. heist movie. 14. horror film** splatter film. **15. porno movie** peepshow, snuff movie. *Informal:* blue movie, porno, skin flick, video nasty. **16. road movie. 17. Western** B-grade western, horse opera, meat-pie western, spa-ghetti western. **18. home movie. 19. Hollywood** Bollywood.

5. 1. program chat show, docusoap, game show, live broadcast, magazine, mini-series, quiz show, radio play, radio program, reality TV, serial, series, soap, talent quest, talk-back program, telefilm, telethon. *Informal:* soap opera, soapie, soapy, talk show.

6. 1. performance command performance. **2. premiere** debut, first night, matinee, one-night stand. **3. crowd-pleaser** spine-tingling. *Informal:* potboiler, tear-jerker, weepie. **4. preview** off-Broadway run. *Informal:* tryout. **5. rehearsal** run-through. **6. suc-cess** smash. *Informal:* sell-out, smash-hit. **7. failure** clambake *(US)*.

7. 1. theatrepiece act, afterpiece, catastasis, drop scene, episode, love-scene, scena, scene, sequence. **2. routine** number, show stopper, showpiece. *Informal:* schtick. **3. inter-lude** antimasque, ballet, curtain-raiser, entr'acte, episode, hokum *(US)*, intermezzo, lol-lipop, waits. **4. character sketch** duologue, impersonation, monologue, personation, rendition, representation, sketch, skit. **5. curtain call** curtain speech, epilogue, pro-logue, protasis.

8. 1. performance space amphitheatre, arena, auditorium, circus, coliseum, colosseum, hippodrome, little theatre. **2. building** big top, chamber of horrors, drama theatre, hippodrome, house, lyric theatre, mausoleum, music hall, nickelodeon *(US History)*, odeum, opera house, palace, playhouse, showboat *(US)*, strip club, strip joint, theatre, theatre in the round, top. **3. picture theatre** art house, cinema, drive-in, film theatre, hardtop, movieplex, multiplex, multiplex cinema, pictures, theatre. *Informal:* fleas-'n'-itches, passion pit. **4. seating** balcony, box, box seat, circle, dress circle, front of house, gallery, loge, lounge, parquet *(US)*, parquet circle *(US)*, stalls, the gods, upper circle.

9. 1. stage boards, false stage, pageant, rostrum. **2. parts of stage** apron, coulisses, curtain, downstage, flies, fly gallery, fly-floor, fly-loft, footlights, foots, forestage, gridiron, opposite prompt, parterre *(US)*, prompt box, proscenium, slips, stage door, stage left, stage right, tormentor. **3. scenery** backcloth, backdrop, cyclorama, decor, flat, flown scenery, mise en scène, scene, set, set piece, setting, special effects, stage effect. **4. equipment** machine, machinery, projection room, prop, property. **5. effects** effect, sound effects, special effects. **6. green room** dressing-room.

10. 1. theatre people director, dresser, flyman, producer, projectionist, prompt, property man, propman, scene-shifter, stage manager, stagehand, wardrobe mistress. **2. design-er** choreographer, costume designer, make-up artist, set designer. **3. film people** best boy, camera crew, cameraman, cinematographer, clapper loader, clapper preparer, con-tinuity girl, director, film crew, floor manager, focus puller, gaffer, producer, sound mixer. *Informal:* gofer.

11. 1. audience admass, captive audience, claque, full house, theatre, turnout. **2. play-goer** cineaste, cinemagoer, fan, film freak, first-nighter, groundling.

12. 1. staging adaptation, dramatisation, dramaturgy, improvisation, presentation, pro-duction, recitation, serialisation, stichomythia. **2. revival** *Informal:* blast from the past.

adj. **13. 1. dramatic** dramaturgical, Grand Guignol, heavy, Thespian, tragic, tragicomical. **2. comic** burlesque, Chaplinesque, clownish, custard-pie, farcical, hammy, harlequinesque, macaronic, pantomimic, slapstick, variety. **3. didactic** agitprop. **4. theatrical** histrionic, make-believe, scenic, stagy. **5. choric** stichomythic. **6. solo** lead, monological, one-man, one-woman.

14. 1. filmic celluloid, cinematic, cinematographic, filmable. **2. all-star** star-studded. **3. movie-minded** starstruck. **4. slow-motion. 5. wide-screen** Imax, split-screen.

15. 1. entertaining absorbing, amusing, diverting.

v. **16. 1. perform** act, acting, appear in, clown, mime, mum, outact, play, play-act, role-play, tread the boards, ventriloquise, walk a slackwire, walk a tightrope. **2. portray** impersonate, represent. *Informal:* come. **3. recite** busk, do a number, put across, regale with. **4. support** co-star, compere. **5. go on the stage** go on the road, have one's name in lights, make one's bow, tour. **6. overact** rant, show off. *Informal:* ham it up. **7. improvise** *Informal:* wing.

17. 1. stage acting, direct, mount, premiere, produce, put on, screen, serialise, stage-manage. **2. cast** audition. **3. preview** try out. **4. dramatise** farcify, melodramatise, ring down the curtain, ring up the curtain, theatricalise.

18. 1. cinematise cinematograph, dissolve, film, flashback, freeze-frame, morphing, pan, shoot, slow motion.

adv. **19. 1. dramatically** acrobatically, cinematically, clownishly, farcically, histrionically, scenically, stagily, theatrically, tragically. **2. backstage** behind the scenes, downstage, in the limelight, in the spotlight, in the wings, offstage, on the boards, on the stage, onstage, upstage.

RELATED KEYWORDS: AMUSEMENT, DANCING, HUMOUR, MUSIC, WRITING, TELECOMMUNICATIONS

ENTHUSIASM

n. **1. 1. enthusiasm** anxiety, ardency, ardour, avidity, eagerness, ebullience, ebulliency, fervency, fervour, fire, flame, forwardness, furore, get-up-and-go, glow, greediness, gusto, heart, heartiness, keenness, pizzazz, rage, second wind, sharpness, vehemence, verve, warmness, warmth, zeal, zealousness, zest, zestfulness. *Informal:* zing, zip. **2. devotion** craze, dedication, devotedness, devotement, monomania, passion. **3. fanaticism** chauvinism, rabidness, radicalness, voraciousness, zealotry. *Informal:* desperation. **4. fad** fancy, rage.

2. 1. enthusiast aficionado, boffin, buff, devotee, eager beaver, fan, fancier, high-flier, votary, votress. *Informal:* a beggar for, a glutton for, a great one for, a nut about, freak. **2. fanatic** chauvinist, energumen, enthusiast. *Informal:* mad mullah, tub-thumper. **3. lunatic fringe** mad Left, mad Right, radical, zealot.

adj. **3. 1. enthusiastic** ablaze, afire, aflame, agog, ardent, athirst, avid, eager, ebullient, forward, glowing, greedy, hearty, hot, keen, on fire, raring, red-hot, sharp, sharp-set, vehement, vital, young-eyed, zealous, zestful, zesty, zingy. *Informal:* psyched, toey, wrapped. **2. extravagant** gung-ho, keen as mustard, on edge, voracious. *Informal:* bright-eyed and bushy-tailed, wild. **3. fanatical** chauvinistic, fanatic, overzealous, rabid. *Informal:* mad.

v. **4. 1. enthuse** fanaticise, fire, pique, warm, whet. *Informal:* switch on. **2. be eager** be pie on, be spoiling for, beat the gun, champ at the bit, fall over oneself, take fire, warm to. *Informal:* be sold on, get into. **3. wax lyrical** go overboard, go to town about, hype up. *Informal:* rave.

adv. **5. 1. enthusiastically** ardently, avidly, eagerly, ebulliently, greedily, hard, heartily, keenly, sharply, urgently, vehemently, warmly, with all one's heart, zealously, zestfully. *Informal:* like a rat up a drainpipe.

RELATED KEYWORDS: DESIRE, ENCOURAGEMENT, INTENTION, WILLINGNESS

ENTRANCE

n. **1. 1. entrance** adit, admit, admittance, aperture, avenue, door, doorway, dromos, entry, entryway, gateway, ingress, inlet, introitus, loophole, passage, passageway, porte-cochère, water gate.

2. 1. entrance room antechamber, foyer, hall, hallway, lobby, porch, vestibule. **2. opening** adit, aperture, arch, archway, conning tower, gorge, hatch, hatchway, loading bay, loophole, platform, port, port of entry. **3. door** back door, bulkhead, cat door, doorway, drop, Dutch door, fly door, folding doors, gateway, hatch, jib door, portal, portiere, postern, revolving door, screen door, serving hatch, stable door, stern door, stop door, storm door *(US)*, swing door, tollgate, vampire, wire door. **4. gate** Bogan gate, lichgate, pearly gates, stile, turnstile, wicket. **5. port** hatchway, manhole, trap, trapdoor. **6. access** admission, admittance, embarkation, entrée, entrance, open door, re-entrance, re-entry. **7. encroachment** breaking and entering, inflow, influx, inroads, invasion, trespass. *Informal:* bust.

    3.   **1. enterer** arrival, comer, entrant, immigrant, import, incomer, intrant, invitee. **2. embarking** embussing. **3. invader** encroacher, forcer, gatecrasher, incomer, interloper, intruder, trespasser. **4. doorkeeper** commissionaire, concierge, door bitch, doorman, porter, portress.

adj.   **4.**   **1. entering** immigrant, incoming, ingoing, ingressive, inpouring, invasive, inward.

v.   **5.**   **1. enter** bounce into, come in, get inside, hop in, immigrate, jump in, re-enter, set foot in. **2. board** embark, emplane, enplane, entrain.

    6.   **1. encroach** barge in, break in, break into, gatecrash, infiltrate, invade, push in, trespass. *Informal:* bust, butt in, crash.

RELATED KEYWORDS: ARRIVAL, INSERTION, INSIDE, INTAKE, OPENING

ENTREATY

n.   **1.**   **1. entreaty** adjuration, assailment, canvass, courtship, dilatory plea, impetration, imploration, invocation, obsecration, petition, pleading, request, solicitation, suppliance, urging. **2. intercession** interpellation. **3. plea** address, appeal, epiclesis, importunities, prayer, supplication. **4. petition** application, claim, motion, offer, postulation, proposal, round robin, suggestion, suit. **5. invitation**.

    2.   **1. request** call, claim, demand, requisition, ultimatum. **2. cadge** *Informal:* bite, sting, touch. **3. begging letter** agony column, classified ad, personal column, want ad.

    3.   **1. importunacy** earnestness, imploringness, importunateness, importunity, prayerfulness, suppliance. **2. beggary** mendicancy, mendicity. **3. pressure** campaigning, heavying, lobbying.

    4.   **1. asker** adjurer, beseecher, conjurer, impetrator, implorer, importuner, pleader, postulant, requester, suppliant, supplicant. **2. applicant** appealer, appellant, canvasser, imprecator, invoker, petitioner. **3. interceder** intercessor, interpellant, interpellator, lobbyist. **4. beggar** beggarman, cadger, craver, mendicant, panhandler. *Informal:* bludger, hum.

adj.   **5.**   **1. begging** adjuratory, beseeching, impetrative, imploratory, importunate, imprecatory, invocatory, petitionary, precatory, rogatory, suppliant, supplicating, supplicatory. **2. cap in hand** on bended knee. **3. intercessional** intercessory.

v.   **6.**   **1. entreat** adjure, advocate, assail, beg, beseech, crave for, impetrate, implore, importune, obsecrate, obtest, plead, pray, supplicate, wish. **2. petition** address, appeal to, apply to, go cap in hand to, go on bended knees to, have recourse to, re-petition, recur to, turn to. **3. apply for** bid for, make a bid, make an approach, move for, put in for. **4. desire** crave, cry for, whistle for. **5. request** ask, bid, court, invite, solicit, woo. *Informal:* pop the question. **6. invoke** call on, command, conjure, imprecate, require. **7. intercede** interpellate, interpose, intervene. **8. bespeak** book, commission. **9. lobby** besiege, canvass, dun, entreat, leaguer, ply, press, urge. **10. canvass** ask around, campaign, consult, enquire of, put pressure on. *Informal:* heavy, lean on.

    7.   **1. cadge** accost, blackleg. *Informal:* bite someone for, bite something off, bludge, bot, bum, fang, hum, panhandle *(US)*, put the acid on, put the bite on, put the fangs into, put the hooks into, put the nips into, scab, scunge, snip, sting, touch. **2. take up a collection** hold a barrel, hold a benefit, levy, pass round the hat, whip round.

interj.   **8.**   **1. please** for God's sake(s), for goodness sake, for heaven's sake, I beg of you.

RELATED KEYWORDS: HELP, INSISTENCE, OFFER

EQUALITY

n.   **1.**   **1. equality** balance, commensuration, comparableness, evenness, levelness, parity, sameness. **2. symmetry** bisymmetry, conformation, evenness, parallelism, regularity, symmetricalness. **3. equilibrium** equilibration, equipoise, equiponderance, isostasy, poise. **4. egalitarianism** democracy, equalitarianism, isocracy, isonomy. **5. equalisation** equation. **6. equivalence** closeness, coextension, correspondence, equidistance, equipollency, equivalence relation, isometry, par. **7. coequality** coordinateness, coordination, parity. **8. isomorphism** isodimorphism.

    2.   **1. equal** coequal, compeer, equivalent, fellow, match, parallel, peer. **2. counterweight** balance, balance wheel, counterpoise, tare. **3. dead heat** barrage *(Fencing)*, deuce, draw, tie. *Informal:* Mexican stand-off. **4. break-even** margin.

adj.   **3.**   **1. equal** equational, isopiestic, isothermal, level. **2. even** commeasurable, commensurate, half-and-half, par, proportional, proportionate. **3. equivalent** enharmonic, equipollent, fellow, matchable, one-to-one, proportionable. **4. coequal** assessorial, comparable, concurrent, coordinate. **5. as good as** a match for. **6. symmetrical** actinomorphic, bisymmetrical, isodiametric, isogonic, spheral, symmetric. **7. equidistant** coextensive. **8. equipotent** equimolecular, equinoctial, equiponderant, equipotential. **9. equilateral** equiangular, isosceles, square. **10. isostatic** isenthalpic, isentropic, isoclinal, isodimorphous, isodynamic, isomerous, isotropic. **11. level-pegging** drawn, equalised, level, quits, tied. **12. democratic** egalitarian, equalitarian, isocratic, isonomic. **13. ambidextrous** bimanous, two-handed.

v. **4.** **1. equal** match. **2. be evens** balance, draw, poise, tie. **3. amount to** add up to, aggregate, come up to. **4. match** be up with, get the measure of someone, go all the way with, measure up to, play catch-up, rival, run abreast. **5. compare** amount to the same thing, equal, parallel. **6. correspond** homologise. **7. break even** break square. **8. coextend** commeasure.

5. **1. equalise** balance, bracket, equate, equilibrate, even out, level out, match, symmetrise. **2. counterbalance** counterpoise, counterweigh. **3. democratise** level.

adv. **6.** **1. equally** alike, both, correspondingly, identically, level, levelly, proportionately. **2. democratically. 3. evenly** ana, commensurately, evens, half-and-half, isometrically. *Informal:* fifty-fifty. **4. abreast** even stevens, neck and neck, nip and tuck *(US)*, pari passu, side by side. **5. equivalently** enharmonically. **6. equidistantly** coextensively. **7. equilaterally** bisymmetrically, isostatically, symmetrically. **8. comparably** coequally, comparatively, coordinately.

RELATED KEYWORDS: ACCORD, HOMOGENEITY, SIMILARITY

ERECTNESS

n. **1.** **1. erectness** straightness, uprightness. **2. perpendicularity** orthogonality, plumbness, right-angledness, verticalness. **3. perpendicular position** perpendicular, plumb, upright, vertical. **4. perpendicular line** apothem, vertical. **5. plumbline** plumb-bob, plumb-rule, plummet.

adj. **2.** **1. erect** columnar, columned, horrent, rampant, ramping, stand-up, standing up, steady *(Nautical)*, straight up, tower-like, up, upright, upstanding. **2. vertical** bluff, normal *(Mathematics)*, orthogonal, perpendicular, plumb, square, straight.

v. **3.** **1. erect** pitch, plum, plumb, raise, raise up, right, set up, up-end, upraise, uprear. **2. cock up** prick up, prickle, rear, rear up, sit up. **3. stand up** hold up, keep one's feet. **4. arise** get to one's feet, rise, rise up.

adv. **4.** **1. erectly** bolt upright, erect, on end, on hind legs, topside up, up, upright, uprightly. **2. perpendicularly** at right angles, plumb, vertically.

RELATED KEYWORDS: ASCENT, STRAIGHTNESS, SUPPORT

ERROR

n. **1.** **1. error** baulk, blunder, boss-shot, brain snap, bug, fault, foot-fault, foul-up, glitch, inaccuracy, lapse, miscue, mismove, mistake, parapraxis, slip, stumble, trip, wrong foot. *Informal:* bad, bad idea, balls-up, barry, bloomer, blue, bone, boner, boo-boo, boob, fluff, shocker, slip-up. **2. misjudgement** misapplication, misapprehension, miscalculation, misconception, miscount, mismeasurement, misplacement, oversight. **3. faux pas** blooper, Freudian slip, gaffe, howler, impropriety, malapropism, mispronunciation, slip of the tongue, solecism, stumble. *Informal:* clanger. **4. clerical error** author's error, contamination, corrigendum, erratum, haplography, literal, misprint, offset, printer's error, set-off. *Informal:* typo. **5. probable error** PE. **6. false alarm** false start. **7. comedy of errors** farce. **8. GIGO (garbage in garbage out).**

2. **1. erroneousness** incorrectness, wrongness. **2. falseness** deceit, falsity, untruth. **3. inaccurateness** carelessness, casualness, confusedness, misapprehensiveness. **4. falsity** deceit, fallacy, falsehood, untruth. **5. subjectiveness** personal equation, self-deception. **6. fallibility** fallibleness.

adj. **3.** **1. erroneous** apocryphal, corrupt, fallacious, fallible, false, inaccurate, incorrect, mendacious, misleading, mistakable, mistaken, off the beam, out, unfactual, untrue, wrong. **2. astray** misapprehensive, on the wrong tack. *Informal:* off to billyo, up a gumtree, up the booay, up the pole. **3. deceptive** hallucinatory, illusory. **4. fallible** careless, erring. **5. misguided** perverse, wrongheaded. **6. subjective** arbitrary.

v. **4.** **1. err** back the wrong horse, bark up the wrong tree, blunder, boob, fall in, fault, get the wrong end of the stick, lapse, miscalculate, miscount, mistake, stumble, trip up. *Informal:* get one's lines crossed, goof, make a boo-boo. **2. misdo** blunder, corrupt, misapply, mislay, mismeasure, misplace, mispronounce, misstate, trip up. *Informal:* boob, goof.

3. misconceive get someone wrong, misapprehend, miscalculate, misconstrue, misinterpret, misjudge, misread, misreckon, mistake, misunderstand.

adv. **5. 1. erroneously** amiss, blunderingly, confusedly, fallaciously, fallibly, falsely, inaccurately, incorrectly, misapprehensively, mistakenly, wrong, wrongly.

RELATED KEYWORDS: INCOMPETENCE, FANTASY, DISHONESTY, MISJUDGEMENT, WRONGDOING, UNTRUTHFULNESS

ESCAPE

n. **1. 1. escape** elusion, escapade. *Informal:* lam *(US)*. **2. evasion** elopement, flit, slip, truancy. *Informal:* disappearing trick, moonlight flit. **3. break-out** escape, gaolbreak, getaway, jailbreak. **4. breakaway** bolt, break, escapade, gambado, stampede. **5. narrow escape** near miss, near thing. *Informal:* close call, close shave, close thing, squeak. **6. escapology.**

2. 1. means of escape back door, bolthole, Davis apparatus, escape hatch, escape lock, fire-escape. **2. loophole** let-out, out. *Informal:* cop-out. **3. vent** safety valve.

3. 1. escapee absentee, absentee into the woods, absentee without leave, escaper, fleer, prison-breaker. **2. runaway** break, breakaway *(Chiefly US)*, defector, deserter, fugitive, ladino, stampeder. **3. absconder** bilker, dodger, eloper, eluder, truant. **4. refugee** asylum seeker, boat people, displaced person, fugitive, illegal immigrant. *Informal:* reffo, refo. **5. escapologist** houdini.

adj. **4. 1. escaped** at large, free, fugitive, runaway. *Informal:* off the hook, on the lam *(US)*, on the run. **2. fugitive** truant. **3. elusive** slippery. **4. breakaway** ladino.

v. **5. 1. escape** abscond, bolt, break out, extricate oneself, flee, fly, run away. *Informal:* blow through, cut, cut and run, do a bunk, do a getaway, hit the toe, lam *(US)*, make a getaway, show a clean pair of heels, take it on the lam *(US)*, turn tail. **2. bolt** break away, stampede. **3. abscond** elope, jump. *Informal:* do a moonlight flit, flit, fly the gap, shoot the moon, skip. **4. evade** bilk, elude, get away from, give someone the slip, shake, throw off. *Informal:* shake off. **5. slip through one's fingers** get away, slip the collar. **6. scrape through** get away with it, save one's bacon, save one's skin, survive. **7. get out from under** fade out. *Informal:* do a fade. **8. get off** secure an acquittal.

RELATED KEYWORDS: RETREAT, AVOIDANCE, ABANDONMENT, LIBERATION

ESSAY

n. **1. 1. essay** apercu, composition, descant, discourse, disquisition, dissertation, exposition, lucubration, piece, quodlibet, review, theme, thesis, tract, tractate, treatise. **2. study** analysis, discourse, exercitation, memoirs, monograph, sketch, survey. **3. summary** abstract, compendium, conspectus, digest, epitome, pandect, précis, precis, resumé, rundown, synopsis. **4. dialogue** colloquy. **5. introduction** foreword, preamble, preface, prelims, prolegomenon, prologue, prolusion. *Informal:* intro. **6. criticism** appreciation, commentary, discussion, excursus. **7. almagest** dispensatory, flora, formulary, herbal, pastoral, pharmacopoeia, poetics, zoology. **8. pamphlet** blurb, booklet, broadsheet, brochure, hand-out, handout, prospectus, screed. **9. article** causerie, column, contribution, cover story, editorial, feature, feature story, leader, leading article, write-up. **10. critique** comment, crit, notice, review. **11. paper** address, lecture, speech, symposium. **12. homily** sermon.

2. 1. essayist belletrist, editor, expositor, gnomist, leader writer, monographer, pamphleteer. **2. critic** commentator, editorialist, reviewer, scholiast.

adj. **3. 1. discursive** critical, disquisitional, dissertational, dissertative, expository.

v. **4. 1. discourse** canvass, comment, critique, descant, discant, discuss, dissertate, lucubrate, pamphleteer, review, treat, write about, write up.

RELATED KEYWORDS: BREVITY, NARRATIVE, BOOK, WRITING

ESSENCE

n. **1. 1. essence** deep structure, elements, haecceity, hypostasis, istigkeit, noumenon, point, quick. *Informal:* the name of the game. **2. basis** base, basic *(Chiefly US)*, bottom, foundation, fundamental, groundwork, hypokeimenon, root. **3. rudiments** ABC, accidence, alphabet, constitution, first principle, grammar. **4. skeleton** cage, fabric, frame, framework, matrix, roll cage. **5. grassroots** brass tacks, nuts and bolts. **6. nub** crux, gist, juice, marrow, pith, point. *Informal:* nitty-gritty. **7. substance** content, gist, meaning, spirit, sum. *Informal:* the long and the short of it. **8. meat** hard core, vitals. **9. epitome** abstract, archetype, being, dharma, elixir, entity, form, inscape, pneuma, quiddity, quintessence, soul, substratum, type. **10. nature** aroma, character, flavour, inbeing, inside, noumenon, principle, quality. **11. soul** ambience, anima, animus, dasein, personality. **12. attribute** property, quality. **13. extract** boil-down, decoction, distillate, distillation, distilment, spirit. **14. stereotype** caricature.

   2.   **1. distillery** alembic, distillation column, pot still, smelter, smeltery.

   3.   **1. essentialness** elementariness, essentiality, intrinsicality, inwardness, radicalness, substantiveness, vitalness. **2. fundamentality** immanency, inherence, inherency. **3. innateness** connation, indigenousness, intimateness.

adj. **4.**   **1. essential** constitutional, constitutive, crucial, intimate, intrinsic, noumenous, qualitative, quintessential, resident, substantial, substantival, substantive, true, veritable, very. **2. typical** characteristic, epitomical, stereotypical.

   5.   **1. fundamental** au fond, basal, base, basic *(Chiefly US)*, basilar, bottom, essential, innate, key, material, original, radical, ultimate, underlying, vital. **2. primary** basic *(Chiefly US)*, prime. **3. elementary** elemental, raw, simple, skeleton. **4. substantial** meaty.

   6.   **1. inborn** born, congenital, connate, connatural, inbred, innate, native, unconditioned, untaught. **2. inherent** built-in, constitutional, immanent, in-built, intrinsic, inward, natural, radical. **3. personal** complexional, individual, specific, subjective, subjectivistic.

   7.   **1. distilled** alembicated, distillable, distillatory.

v.   **8.**   **1. distil** boil down, chastise, decoct, isolate, smelt. **2. stereotype** characterise. **3. constitute** comprehend, comprise, consist of, contain, embrace, form, include.

adv. **9.**   **1. essentially** constitutively, in substance, intimately, intrinsically, per se, qualitatively, subjectively, substantially, substantively. **2. veritably** vitally. **3. inherently** congenitally, connately, connaturally, deep down, immanently, innately, radically. **4. naturally** by nature, in rerum natura, indigenously, to the manner born. **5. typically** characteristically. **6. basically** at bottom, at heart, basally, chiefly, fundamentally, in essence, originally, primarily *(Chiefly US)*, ultimately. **7. elementarily** elementally, hypostatically.

RELATED KEYWORDS: ACTUALITY, CHARACTER, STATE

ETERNITY

n.   **1.**   **1. eternity** coeternity, everlasting, perpetuity, sempiternity, the everlasting, time immemorial, time out of mind. **2. immortality** amrita, athanasia, deathlessness. **3. permanence** endlessness, eternalness, everlastingness, lastingness, perpetuality, timelessness. **4. perpetuation** immortalisation, perpetuance.

   2.   **1. immortal** hero *(Antiquity)*, the elect. **2. everlasting** amaranth *(Poetic)*, eternal, immortelle, never-ending. **3. perpetual motion** perpetuo moto.

adj. **3.**   **1. eternal** aeonian, coeternal, everlasting, fadeless. **2. endless** ceaseless, chronic, constant, immortal, incessant, interminable, lasting, lifelong, lifetime, perpetual, unceasing, unending, uninterrupted. **3. permanent** amaranthine, everlasting, imperishable, incorruptible, perdurable, perennial, unfading. **4. immortal** ageless, dateless, deathless, elect, evergreen, timeless, undying.

v.   **4.**   **1. eternalise** eternise, perpetuate. **2. immortalise** eternalise, eternise. **3. last** endure, go on and on, have no end, outlast.

adv. **5.**   **1. eternally** coeternally, everlastingly, immortally, lastingly, perdurably, perennially, perpetually, unfailingly. **2. endlessly** ceaselessly, constantly, interminably, timelessly, undyingly, week in week out, without cease. **3. permanently** all along, always, aye *(Poetic)*, e'er *(Poetic)*, ever, evermore, for ever, for ever and a day, for good, for good and all, for the duration, forever, forevermore, from age to age, in perpetuity, in perpetuum, till the end of time, without term, world without end. *Informal:* till the cows come home.

RELATED KEYWORDS: CONTINUATION, INFINITY, STEADINESS

EVIDENCE

n.   **1.**   **1. evidence** ammunition, circumstantial evidence, corroboration *(Law)*, cumulative evidence, direct evidence, indirect evidence, king's evidence, prima-facie evidence, probable cause, proof, queen's evidence, state's evidence *(Chiefly US)*. **2. piece of evidence** clue, corroborant, indication, mark, show, sign, signal, telltale sign, title *(Law)*, token, trace. **3. testimony** alibi, appearances, attestation, authority, deposition, statement, testimonial, witness. **4. conclusive evidence** apodixis. **5. argument** allegation, case, con, demonstration, explanation, interpretation, presumption, pro, proof, substantiation, the proof of the pudding. **6. swearing on oath** affidavit, affirmation, avouchment, sustainment, sworn statement, testification, verification.

2. **1. authentication** accreditation, certificate, certification, confirmation, jurat, manifestation, probate, testamur, validation, verification, voucher, warrant. **2. identification** exequatur, ID, papers. **3. medical certificate** aegrotat. **4. grounds** corpus delicti, data, exhibit, gist. **5. reference** adduction, authority, chapter and verse, citation, locus classicus, ruling.

3. **1. disproof** confutation, counterevidence, disproval, elenchus, falsification, ignoratio elenchi, invalidation, rebuttal, refutation.

4. **1. testifier** attestor, crown witness, deposer, earwitness, eyewitness, hostile witness, identifier, informant, informer, swearer, voucher, witness, witnesser. *Informal:* gig. **2. verifier** affirmant, affirmer, authenticator, compurgator, confirmer, corroborator, establisher, surrebutter. **3. informer** fizgig, supergrass. *Informal:* chocolate frog, copper's nark, dog, fizzer, grasser, nark, Noah's Ark, shelf, snitch.

5. **1. disprover** confounder, confuter, devil's advocate, falsifier, rebutter, refuter, reprover.

adj. 6. **1. evidential** demonstrable, demonstrational, deposable, documentary, evidentiary, manifestable, probative, substantiative, testimonial. **2. confirmatory** corroboratory, probate, verificative, verifying.

7. **1. disproving** confutative, elenctic. **2. disprovable** rebuttable, refutable, unwarrantable.

v. 8. **1. give evidence** affirm, attest, bear witness, depose, testify, testify against, witness. *Informal:* jump the box. **2. argue** adduce evidence, allege, exhibit, go on, lead evidence.

9. **1. authenticate** accredit, acknowledge, authorise, certify, endorse, indorse, notarise, testify, validate, vouch. **2. prove** bear out, certify, confirm, corroborate, demonstrate, document, establish, make good, make out, manifest, re-prove, show, substantiate, sustain, try, verify, vouch.

10. **1. evidence** certify, evince, go to show, show, speak for itself, speak volumes, tell its own tale.

11. **1. disprove** answer, confound, confute, cut the ground from under someone's feet, falsify, invalidate, knock the bottom out of, make a liar of, prove wrong, rebuke, rebut, refute, reprimand. **2. tell another story** belie, give the lie to.

adv. 12. **1. evidentially** corroboratively, demonstratively, in evidence. **2. for example** for instance.

RELATED KEYWORDS: ASSERTION, DENIAL, COURT OF LAW, JUSTIFICATION, LITIGATION

EVOLUTION

n. 1. **1. evolution** acquired characteristics, adaptive radiation, anagenesis, development, emergent evolution, evolvement, intergradation, natural selection, ontogeny, phylogeny, progress, sexual selection, speciation, survival of the fittest. **2. convergent evolution** adaptation, coevolution, convergence, naturalisation. **3. convergence** affinity. **4. anthropogenesis** cainogenesis, cytogenesis, kainogenesis, monogenesis, palingenesis, phytogenesis. **5. genetics** cladistics, cytogenetics, genomics, phylogenetics, physical anthropology. **6. Darwinism** evolutionary taxonomy, Lamarckism, Neo-Darwinism, Neo-Lamarckism, transformism. *Informal:* evo-devo. **7. adaptiveness** accommodativeness, struggle for existence. **8. accommodation** acculturation.

2. **1. evolutionist** Darwinian, Darwinist, transformist.

adj. 3. **1. evolutional** adaptational. **2. adaptive** accommodative, acculturative, intergradient.

4. **1. evolutionary** anthropogenic, cainogenetic, monogenetic, orthogenetic, palingenetic, phylogenic, phytogenetical. **2. mutant** mutational, mutative. **3. evolutionistic** Darwinian.

v. 5. **1. evolve** coevolve, develop, intergrade. **2. adapt** accord, acculturate, naturalise. **3. naturalise** acculturate.

RELATED KEYWORDS: CHANGE, IMPROVEMENT

EXAGGERATION

n. 1. **1. exaggeration** amplification, embroidery, enlargement, euphuism, extravagance, extravagancy, hyperbole, hyperbolism, overkill, overstatement, puff, purple passage, wiredrawing. **2. much ado about nothing** a storm in a teacup. **3. tall story** exaggeration, flight of fancy, snake yarn, traveller's tale. *Informal:* lulu. **4. caricature** parody. *Informal:* send-up. **5. theatricality** heroics, histrionics, melodrama, melodramatics, play-acting, theatricalism, theatricalness.

2. **1. exaggerator** boomerang bender, embroiderer, romancer, wiredrawer. *Informal:* bilge artist, bull artist, storyteller.

adj. **3.** **1. exaggerated** agonistic, exaggerative, extravagant, high-flown, high-flying, highly coloured, histrionic, hyperbolic, magniloquent, outré, overdone, overstated, strained, vaulting. *Informal:* steep, tall.

v. **4.** **1. exaggerate** boast, distend, embroider, glorify, hyperbolise, magnify, make a mountain out of a molehill, melodramatise, out-Herod Herod, overstate, puff up, theatricalise, wiredraw. *Informal:* amplify *(US)*, bull, bulldust, shoot one's mouth off, sound off, stack it on. **2. overstate** overwrite, turn on the agony. *Informal:* lay it on, lay it on (with a trowel) or (a bit thick), lay it on thick, pile on the agony. **3. make a good story** draw a long bow, exaggerate, imagine, pitch a tale, pull a long bow, romance, spin a yarn, tell stories. **4. overplay** exaggerate, make too much of, overact, overcharge, overdo, overdraw, overkill, overshoot the mark. *Informal:* amplify *(US)*, bull, emote, ham.

RELATED KEYWORDS: ERROR, FANTASY, DISHONESTY, NARRATIVE, UNTRUTHFULNESS

EXCESS

n. **1.** **1. excess** deluge, drug, ebullience, flood, lake, nimiety, overflow, overfullness, overplus *(Chiefly US)*, overprint, overrun, overstock, oversupply, plethora, repletion, superabundance, superfluity, superflux, surfeit, surplus, surplusage. *Informal:* pile-up. **2. surfeit** excess, glut, more than enough, too much of a good thing. *Informal:* bellyful, gutful. **3. overdose** overkill. *Informal:* OD. **4. luxury** enough and to spare, featherbed, fruit on the sideboard, milk and honey, more than enough. **5. overlap** allowance, extra, margin, over. **6. something extra** bonus, bonus issue, fringe benefit. *Informal:* gash. **7. extra person** super, supernumerary.

2. **1. excessiveness** exorbitance, extremism, immoderateness, immoderation, inordinateness, intemperance, lavishness, ultraism, unconscionableness. **2. extravagance** conspicuous consumption, costliness, extravagancy, extravagantness, gross consumption, prodigality, profligacy. **3. overabundance** ebulliency, embarrassment, excess, luxuriousness, overmuchness, overproduction, plethora, superabundance. **4. superfluousness** redundancy. **5. congestion** engorgement, fullness, overcrowding, overpopulation.

adj. **3.** **1. excess** extra, luxury, needless, overabundant, redundant, superabundant, supererogatory, superfluous, supernumerary, surplus, uncalled-for, unnecessary, waste. **2. overfull** bursting, congested, crammed, engorged, flush, inflated, plethoric, smothery. **3. extra** excessive, extreme, over, ultra.

4. **1. excessive** dear, exceeding, exorbitant, extortionate, high, steep, stiff. **2. immoderate** deadly, extravagant, extreme, inordinate, obsessive, overweening, overwhelming, radical, unconscionable, undue, unmoderated. *Informal:* all-fired *(Chiefly US)*, devilish, fearful. **3. too much** de trop, over-the-top, too-too. *Informal:* OTT. **4. cloying** saccharine, satiating. *Informal:* syrupy.

v. **5.** **1. be excessive** be over the top, go too far, overdrive, overshoot the mark, overstep the mark, overwork. *Informal:* gild the lily, lay it on (with a trowel) or (a bit thick), lay it on thick, make a welter of it, push it. **2. burn the candle at both ends** overdo it, overtax oneself.

6. **1. be surplus** exuberate, go begging, go to waste, overabound, run over, superabound. **2. overflow** brim over, overrun, run a banker, well over. **3. burst** burst at the seams, bust.

7. **1. oversupply** cloy, congest, cram, drug, engorge, fill to overflowing, glut, jam, overcrowd, overfill, overpack, pall, sate, satiate, stuff, surfeit. **2. deluge** drown, flood, glut the market, load, overwhelm, plaster, smother, swamp. **3. overproduce** overstock, pile up.

8. **1. consume to excess** congest, cram, engorge, glut, stuff, swill. **2. overdose** *Informal:* OD.

adv. **9.** **1. excessively** beyond measure, consumedly, devilishly, exceedingly, exorbitantly, extravagantly, fearfully, immoderately, inordinately, overly, overweeningly, overwhelmingly, unconscionably, unduly, unnecessarily. *Informal:* deadly, devilish, to the max. **2. superfluously** redundantly, superabundantly. **3. extra** by half, over, over and above. **4. too much** a bit thick, ad nauseam, over the fence, over the odds, overly, overmuch, tanto, to a fault, to the skies, troppo *(Music)*.

RELATED KEYWORDS: OVERINDULGENCE, FLOOD, MANY

EXCHANGE

n. **1.** **1. exchange** barter, commutation, interchange, reciprocation, truck. **2. transposition** metathesis. **3. trade** intermigration, passage, traffic. **4. substitution** grafting, metasomatism, novation, replacement, shift, subrogation, succession, surrogation, transfer, transformation. **5. swap** dicker *(Chiefly US)*, fungible, quid pro quo, trade, trade-in.

2.   **1. substitute** alternate, fill-in, replacement, stand-in, supernumerary, surrogate, understudy. **2. stand-in** locum, pinch-hitter, relay, relief, stopgap, supersub. **3. option** fudge, ossia, second string. **4. changeling** elfchild, oaf. **5. makeshift** a poor excuse for, apology, ersatz. *Informal:* fake, ring-in. **6. prosthesis** artificial limb, artificial skin, hairpiece. **7. toy** blow-up doll, dildo, vibrator.

3.   **1. exchangeability** commutability, interchangeableness, reciprocity, synonymity, synonymy, transponibility.

adj.   4.   **1. exchangeable** commutable, commutative, convertible, fungible, interchangeable, reciprocal, synonymical, trade-in, transponible, transposable.

5.   **1. substitutive** false, makeshift, stopgap, substitutionary, supernumerary. *Informal:* Clayton's. **2. transpositional** metathetical.

v.   6.   **1. exchange** change, counterchange, shift, swap, switch, swop, trade, transpose. **2. interchange** alternate, change places, compare notes, pass, reciprocate. **3. barter** dicker *(Chiefly US)*, exchange, swap, trade, truck.

7.   **1. substitute** dub, replace, ring in, subrogate, supplant, surrogate. **2. relieve** act for, pinch-hit, spell, stand in. **3. graft** allograft, transplant.

adv.   8.   **1. in exchange for** in loco parentis.

          RELATED KEYWORDS: EQUALITY, INTERACTION, COMMERCE

EXCITEMENT

n.   1.   **1. excitement** agitation, ecstasy, excitation, exhilaration, fever, feverishness, tension, thrillingness, wildness. **2. frenzy** agony, delirium, fever pitch, hysteria, hysterics, nympholepsy, orgasm, overexcitement, pink fit, state, stir. *Informal:* conniptions, spin. **3. fluster** ado, dither, flurry, flustration, flutter, fuss, stir, twitter. *Informal:* flap. **4. thrill** frisson. *Informal:* bang *(US)*, buzz, charge, kick. **5. furore** combustion, ferment, scene, sensation, tumult. *Informal:* boil-up, three-day night. **6. much ado about nothing** a storm in a teacup. **7. boiling point** fever pitch, white heat. **8. sensationalism** luridness, sensuism, titillation.

2.   **1. liveliness** animation, ebullience, ebulliency, effervescency, enthusiasm, fervour, friskiness, get-up-and-go, ginger, life, vibrancy, vivacity. *Informal:* zing.

3.   **1. excitability** combustibleness, excitableness, inflammableness.

adj.   4.   **1. excited** above oneself, agog, ebullient, exalted, exhilarated, feverish, feverous, frisky, hectic, keyed up, on tenterhooks, red-hot. *Informal:* gone, hyped, psyched. **2. agitated** dithery, fluttery, jittery, jumpy, overwrought, tremulous, twittery, wrought-up. *Informal:* uncool. **3. frenzied** crazy, delirious, frantic, frenetic, hysterical, mad, maenadic, phrenetic, wild. *Informal:* berko, off one's chump *(Chiefly British)*, off one's head. **4. hot-blooded** passionate, rackety. **5. excitable** combustible, combustive, feisty, frisky, high-spirited, inflammable, nervy, overexcitable. *Informal:* toey.

5.   **1. exciting** action-packed, amazing, awe-inspiring, breathtaking, excitative, excitatory, exhilarating, exhilarative, exhilaratory, heady, intoxicative, lively, mind-bending, nail-biting, spectacular, stirring, thrilling, vibrant. *Informal:* hairy, mind-blowing. **2. sensational** lurid.

v.   6.   **1. excite** agitate, electrify, enliven, exhilarate, invigorate, quicken, sauce, thrill. **2. overexcite** frenzy, whip up, work up. *Informal:* hype up, wind up. **3. intoxicate** send wild. *Informal:* send, turn on. **4. sensationalise** dramatise.

7.   **1. be excited** boil over, galumph, go wild, hot up, rave, run amok, take off, take on, throw a fit, throw a willy. *Informal:* go ape. **2. flutter** tremble, twitter. *Informal:* flap. **3. reach fever pitch** be jumping, take off. *Informal:* go off.

adv.   8.   **1. excitedly** agitatedly, agog with, breathlessly, feverishly, feverously, frenetically, hectically, phrenetically, wildly.

9.   **1. excitingly** ebulliently, exhilaratingly, headily, intoxicatingly, luridly, sensationally, thrillingly, vibrantly.

          RELATED KEYWORDS: ANTICIPATION, DISCONTENTEDNESS, EMOTION, JOY

EXCLUSION

n.   1.   **1. exclusion** elimination, exception, isolation, omission, ostracism, reservation, shutout. **2. segregation** apartheid, colour bar, exclusionism. **3. disbarment** ban, debarment, disenfranchisement, disinheritance, dismissal, dispossession, disqualification, excommunication, preclusion, reprobation. *Informal:* order of the boot. **4. bar** barrier, embargo, interdict, interdiction, prohibition, taboo. **5. banishment** deportation, estrangement, exile, expulsion, extraordinary rendition, riddance, sequestration. **6. ejection** defenestration, displacement, ejectment, eviction. **7. deletion** cancel, cancellation, cut, dele, delenda, elision, ellipsis, excision, nullification.

2. **1. excluder** alienator, banisher, black-baller, forbidder, isolator, ostraciser. **2. segregator** exclusionist, exclusivist, segregationist. **3. ejector** evictor, ouster. *Informal:* bouncer, chucker-out.

3. **1. outcast** fringe dweller, Harijan, Ishmael, Ishmaelite, leper, lost soul, marginal person, outlander, outsider, pariah, stranger, untouchable, wanderer. **2. exile** alien, expatriate, refugee, removee. *Informal:* expat.

adj. **4.** **1. exclusive** exclusory, preclusive, segregate, segregated, segregative. **2. restricted** off limits, out of bounds. **3. taboo** forbidden. **4. omissive** elimination, eliminatory, exceptive, knockout.

5. **1. excluded** apart, autonomous, beyond the pale, fringe, inadmissible, independent, not included, separate. **2. culled** cast for age, out of court, out of the loop. **3. exiled** in exile, ostracised, outcast.

v. **6.** **1. exclude** bar, except, forbid, foreclose, leave off, leave out, omit, overleap, preclude, segregate, shut, skip. *Informal:* include out. **2. eliminate** abolish, cancel, cut, dele *(Printing)*, delete, drop, excise, quash, rule out. *Informal:* scrub. **3. get rid of** cull, cut out, off-load, weed out, winnow. **4. eject** clean out, clear out, defenestrate, fling out, jettison, oust, out, reject, rout, throw out. *Informal:* boot out, bounce, chuck out, ding, kick out, turf out.

7. **1. isolate** alienate, blackball, cold-shoulder, freeze out, give someone the cold shoulder, interdict, ostracise, reject, send to Coventry, shut out, spurn. **2. banish** curse, deport, excommunicate, exile, expatriate, expel, extradite, proscribe, send away, transport, unchurch. *Informal:* send packing. **3. evict** displace, turn out, turn out of house and home. **4. disinherit** cut off without a penny, cut off without a shilling.

8. **1. boycott** bar, blackball, delist, keep out, shut, ward off. **2. disbar** count out, debar, disenfranchise, disfranchise, dismiss, disqualify, drum out, give someone the boot, recuse *(US Law)*, suspend. *Informal:* axe. **3. proscribe** ban, bar, black-list, eject, exclude, forbid, ground, inhibit, interdict, lower the boom on, outlaw, prohibit, send down *(British)*, strike off, taboo. **4. avert**.

prep. **9.** **1. except** apart from, bar, barring, bating, beside, besides, but, ex, excepting, excluding, outside, save, saving, with the exception of.

RELATED KEYWORDS: DISMISSAL, FOREIGNNESS, EXTRACTION, SOLITUDE

EXIT

n. **1.** **1. exit** débouché, debouch, egress, issue, mouth, outfall, outlet, solfatara, way out. **2. emergence** coming out, debouchment, surfacing. **3. outflow** burst, discharge, drainage, effluence, effluent, efflux, effusion, emanation, emission, eruption, exudation, flash, issuance, issue, leak, leakage, outbreak, outburst, outgoing, outpouring, run-off, seep, seepage, spate. **4. vent** air drain, bunghole, channel, chimney, chimneystack, chute, drain, emergency exit, exhaust, exhaust pipe, nozzle, opening, orifice, snout, stovepipe, tap, taphole, venturi, vomitory, waterspout. *Informal:* zoomie. **5. egression** departure, escape, exodus, outgo, outgoing. **6. sally** sortie.

adj. **2.** **1. emergent** effluent, effusive, emanating, emanatory, emerging, excurrent, exoreic, forthcoming, issuing, jessant, outflowing. **2. eruptive** effusive, expulsive.

v. **3.** **1. exit** clear, depart, go forth, issue forth, outfly, sally, sortie, spring forth, spring out. *Informal:* hop it. **2. emerge** come forth, come out, debouch. **3. erupt** break out, burst forth, burst out, escape.

4. **1. discharge** disembogue, drain, draw, empty, exhaust, give off, gush, issue, let out, spill, vent. **2. exude** drip, effuse, emit, froth, leak, ooze, seep, weep, well. **3. flow out** effuse, emanate, issue, outpour, run, spout, stream, teem.

RELATED KEYWORDS: RETREAT, DEPARTURE, CHANNEL, EMISSION, FLOOD, ESCAPE, OUTSIDE, OPENING

EXPECTATION

n. **1.** **1. expectation** anticipation, breathless expectation, clockwatching, contemplation, eager anticipation, expectance, expectancy, forecast, foresight, foretaste, forethought, hope, lookout, prelibation, presumption, prospect, view, wait, waiting. **2. hope** belief, good faith, optimism, prospects, sanguine hope. **3. apprehension** apprehensiveness, curiosity, inquisitiveness, suspense. **4. imminence** prevenance, prevenience.

     2.   **1. expected thing** consummation greatly to be desired, contingency, destiny, expected outcome, fate, fortune, future, karma, kismet, outlook, predestination, presumption, sanguine hope. *Informal:* the goods. **2. dream** anticipation, contemplation, expectations, lookout, prospect, view. **3. foretaste** anticipation, prelibation, thought. **4. time bomb** pregnant situation, ticking bomb. **5. expected person** comer, great white hope, hopeful, Messiah. **6. fancy** favourite.

adj.   **3.**   **1. expectant** anticipant, anticipant of, hopeful, intended, prospective, sanguine, tiptoe, tiptoe with excitement. **2. clockwatching** anticipating, looking forward to, on tiptoe. **3. anticipatory** anticipant, anticipative, expectative, forward-looking, prevenient. **4. apprehensive** fearful, threatened. *Informal:* toey.

     4.   **1. expected** anticipated, expectant, future, imminent, impendent, impending, intended, likely, pendent, pending, potential, prospective. **2. foreseen** long expected, Messianic, prophesised. **3. favourite** deemed most likely to succeed, fancied.

v.   **5.**   **1. expect** anticipate, ask, bargain for, contemplate, count upon, envisage, envision, foreclose, foresee, forestall, foretaste, give thought to, have in store, look ahead, look at, look for, look to, plan against, prepare for, previse, second-guess, take precautions, think, think likely. **2. await** anticipate, cool one's heels, drool, expect, hold one's breath, kick one's heels, lie in wait, listen for, mark time, wait, wait for, watch for, watch out for. **3. anticipate** apprehend, bide one's time, consider, contemplate, forerun, imagine, preempt. *Informal:* sweat on. **4. hope for** look forward to, look to, pitch one's hopes at, promise oneself, watchout.

adv.   **6.**   **1. expectantly** agog, anticipatively, anticipatorily, apprehensively, in expectation of, on tenterhooks, on tiptoe, prospectively. **2. on the horizon** almost upon us, in the pipeline, in view, just around the corner.

     RELATED KEYWORDS: ANTICIPATION, DISENCHANTMENT, HOPE, DESPAIR, THE FUTURE, PATIENCE, PREDICTION

EXPEDIENCE

n.   **1.**   **1. expedience** advantageousness, advisability, advisableness, appropriateness, desirableness, expediency, suitableness. **2. resourcefulness** extemporaneousness, extemporariness, extemporisation, practicality, pragmatism, utilitarianism. **3. propriety** commodiousness, judiciousness, towardness.

     2.   **1. opportunism** craftiness, cunning, gamesmanship, political skill, shiftiness. **2. back scratching** flattery, sycophancy.

     3.   **1. expedient** contrivance, gambit, means to an end, strings to one's bow, wherewithal. **2. convenience** accommodation, advantage. **3. contrivance** artifice, connivance, design, gimmick, knack, loophole, shift, trick, waiting game. *Informal:* caper, dodge, fiddle, wangle, wheeze *(British)*. **4. makeshift** bandaid solution, improvisation, remount, stopgap, substitute, temporary expedience. **5. jury mast** jury rig. **6. bush breakfast** bush champagne, colonial goose. **7. last resort** sheet anchor. *Informal:* insurance.

     4.   **1. opportunist** carpetbagger, self-seeker, soldier of fortune, timeserver, trimmer. **2. flatterer** gamesman, sycophant. *Informal:* back scratcher. **3. wangler** conniver, Machiavellian, wriggler. **4. improviser** adaptor, extemporiser, improvisator.

adj.   **5.**   **1. expedient** advantageous, advisable, conducive to advantage, desirable, expediential, handy, opportune, profitable, timely, worth one's while. **2. appropriate** applicable, befitting, congruous, fit, fitting, opportune, proper, right, ripe, suitable. **3. politic** judicious. **4. workable** executable, feasible, practicable, practical, useful, utilitarian, utility, viable. **5. convenient** commodious, satisfactory. **6. improvised** ad hoc, ad lib, extemporaneous, extemporary, extempore, impromptu, improvisatory, jury, make-do, makeshift, stopgap.

     6.   **1. opportunist** artful, crafty, cunning, devious, resourceful, shifty. **2. self-seeking** selfish, timeserving. **3. scheming** astute, calculating, conniving, Machiavellian, manipulatory, ruthless. **4. practical** pragmatic.

v.   **7.**   **1. be expedient** advantage, befit, beseem, profit, suit one's purpose. **2. serve** answer, produce results, satisfy, suffice. *Informal:* deliver the goods, do, fill the bill, hit the spot.

     8.   **1. make do** adapt, extemporise, improvise, shift, think on one's feet. **2. take advantage of** be in the right place at the right time, benefit, fall back on, find a loophole, fish in troubled waters, get mileage out of, jockey, make a good thing out of, make the best of, make the most of, profit, resort to, seize an opportunity, strike while the iron is hot, turn to one's advantage. *Informal:* clean up. **3. climb on the bandwagon** get with the strength. **4. play a waiting game** bide one's time, have a card up one's sleeve, trim. **5. connive** arrange, contrive, intrigue, plot, wheedle, wriggle. *Informal:* wangle.

adv. **9.** **1. expediently** advantageously, advisably, desirably. **2. by means of** through the means of, with the aid of. **3. conveniently** appropriately, at the last moment, commodiously, in the nick of time. **4. to advantage** all to the good, just as well. **5. extemporarily** extemporaneously, resourcefully. **6. politicly** with an eye to the main chance.

RELATED KEYWORDS: ADEQUACY, HELP, LUCK, METHOD, SUPPLY, USE

EXPENSIVENESS

n. **1.** **1. expensiveness** costliness, dearness. **2. valuableness** preciousness, pricelessness. **3. ritziness** sumptuousness. **4. prohibitiveness** excessiveness. **5. overvaluation** inflatedness. **6. extortion** daylight robbery, exorbitance. *Informal:* highway robbery.

2. **1. inflation** accelerator principle, bracket creep, cost-push inflation, credit squeeze, demand economy, demand-pull inflation, hyperflation, inflationary spiral, inflationism, price spiral, stagflation. **2. appreciation** capital appreciation, revaluation, upvaluation. **3. rise** advance, hike, jump, mark-up. **4. surcharge** extra, overcharge, rip-off. *Informal:* slug.

adj. **3.** **1. expensive** big-ticket, costly, dear, high, high-priced. *Informal:* a bit hot, pricey, top-dollar. **2. prohibitive** beyond one's means. **3. extravagant** excessive, exorbitant, extortionate, high, inflated, inflationary, stiff. *Informal:* over-the-top, steep. **4. valuable** costly, precious, rich. **5. priceless** beyond price, invaluable, unpriced *(Poetic).* **6. sumptuous** plush, plushy. *Informal:* ritzy, swanky.

v. **4.** **1. be expensive** be at a premium, be at a price, cost the earth. *Informal:* cost an arm and a leg.

5. **1. overcharge** anti-gazumping, gazump, overprice, overvalue, surcharge. *Informal:* charge like a wounded bull.

RELATED KEYWORDS: BUYING, EXTRAVAGANCE, PAYMENT, ROBBERY, WEALTH

EXPLOSION

n. **1.** **1. explosion** blast, BLEVE, blow-out, blow-up, destruct, dissiliency, eruption, fulmination, implosion. **2. report** air burst, backfire, burst, drumfire, fire, ground burst, gunfire. **3. discharge** detonation, salvo, volley. **4. outburst** storm, tornado. **5. explosive power** brisance, explosiveness, ground-shock effect, megaton. **6. bang** boom, clap, crack, crash, crump, peal, pop, pound, slam, slap, smash, thump, thunder, whiz-bang.

2. **1. crackle** crackling, crepitation, decrepitation, rattle. **2. sputter** fizz, snort.

3. **1. splash** dash, drip, plash, plop, spatter, splat, squash, squelch, squish, swash, wash.

4. **1. explosive** charge, destruct system, shot. **2. detonator** autodestruct, cap, gunlock, igniter, matchlock, percussion cap, primer, selfdestruct, squib. **3. explosive device** bomb, bombshell, IED, mine, shell, star shell. **4. high explosive** ammonal, cheddite, cordite, cyclonite, dirty bomb, dynamite, fraceur, gelignite, glonoine, glyceryl trinitrate, guncotton, gunpowder, hexogen, lycopodium, lyddite, maximite, melinite, mercuric cyanate, mercury fulminate, mineral jelly, nitroglycerine, picric acid, plastic explosive, RDX, smokeless powder, TNT, tonite, trinitrotoluene. *Informal:* jelly, nitro. **5. low explosive** bipropellant, fulminating compound, fulminating powder, propellant. **6. wick** fuse, proximity fuse, touchpaper, train, trip-wire, variable time fuse.

5. **1. fireworks display** bonfire night, cracker night, fireworks, pyrotechnics. **2. fireworks** bunger, cascade, catherine-wheel, cracker, double bunger, double happy *(NZ)*, firecracker, fizgig, girandole, jumping jack, maroon, petard, pinwheel, ponga, popper, rocket, Roman candle, serpent, skyrocket, squib, star jump, sunburst, tourbillion, wheel, whiz-bang. *Informal:* banger, throwdown. **3. bonbon** cracker, table cracker.

adj. **6.** **1. explosive** dissilient, dynamitic, fulminatory, live, pyrotechnic, selfdestruct.

7. **1. crackly** fizzy, snappy, sputtering.

8. **1. splashy** plashy, squishy.

v. **9.** **1. explode** backfire, burst asunder, burst on the ear, detonate, fly off, fulminate, go off, implode, pop, selfdestruct. **2. set off** blast, blow up, bomb, destruct, detonate, discharge, dynamite, explode, fire, fulminate, let off, shoot, spring, squib, torpedo *(US).* **3. bang** bark, boom, clap, crack, crash, peal, pound, slam, thump, thunder. **4. misfire** be a fizzer.

10. **1. crackle** crepitate, decrepitate, fizz, fizzle, sputter.

11. **1. splash** plash, plop, splatter, sputter, squash, squelch, squish.

RELATED KEYWORDS: FIRE, LOUDNESS, WEAPON

EXTINGUISHING

n. **1.** **1. extinguishing** eclipse, extinction, extinctive, extinguishment. **2. blackout** brownout, darkness, dim-out *(US)*, lights out.

2. **1. nonflammability** athermancy, fire-resistance, fireproofing, incombustibility. **2. fireproof material** asbestos, asbestos suit, fire blanket, fire curtain, firewall, incombustible, safety curtain.

3. **1. extinguisher** douser, quencher. **2. fire-extinguishing device** fire hydrant, fire truck, fire-engine, fireplug *(Chiefly US)*, plug *(US)*, sprinkler system. **3. fire-extinguisher** bcf, carbon dioxide, carbon tetrachloride, carbonic acid gas, foam, retardant, sands, soda-acid, tetrachloromethane, waters.

4. **1. firefighter** bush brigade, bush fire brigade, engineman, fire brigade, fireman. *Informal:* firey. **2. fire station** firehouse *(US)*.

adj. **5.** **1. nonflammable** athermanous, fire-resistant, fireproof, flameproof, incombustible, thermoduric, unflammable.

6. **1. extinguished** dead, extinct, quenched, spent.

v. **7.** **1. extinguish** bank down, blow out, butt, damp down, dowse, puff out, rake out, smother, snuff out. **2. douse** *(Informal)* quench, waterbomb. **3. butt** extinguish, stub out. **4. put out** defuse, switch off, turn out. **5. black out** brown out.

8. **1. burn out** die down, expire.

RELATED KEYWORDS: COLDNESS, COOLING, DARK

EXTRACTION

n. **1.** **1. extraction** abstraction, epilation, eradication, exsection, extrication, remotion, removal, taking out, withdrawal. **2. pull** tug, twist, wrench, wrest. **3. drainage** bleeding, decoction, draught, evulsion, expression, filtration, phlebotomy, sublimation, suction, tapping.

2. **1. extractor** drawer, gouger, sucker. **2. auger** corer, corkscrew, deriver, wimble. **3. forceps** pincers, pinchers, pliers, tweezers. **4. pump** bowser, force-pump, pulsator, pulsometer, stomach pump, vacuum pump, worm pump. **5. drainer** crusher, filter, filterer, juicer, milker, milking machine, mill, squeezer, sweatbox, tapper, trocar. **6. bloodsucker** leech, phlebotomist.

3. **1. extract** core, crush, educt, eduction, essence, extractive. **2. decoction** infusion.

v. **4.** **1. extract** derive, disengage, disentangle, draw, draw out, epilate, exhaust, exterminate, extricate, pluck, pluck out, pull out, remove, shuck, take out, winkle out, withdraw. **2. eradicate** extirpate, root out, weed out. **3. cut out** core, excide, excise, exscind, exsect, rip out, tear out. **4. dig out** dredge, mine, pull up, root up, unroot, uproot. **5. drain** bleed, crush, decoct, empty, exhaust, express, extravasate, filter, filtrate, flow, juice, leech, milk, press, press out, pump, pump out, sluice, squeeze, squeeze out, start, suck, tap, wring from. **6. derive** aspirate, draw, infuse, render, soak, sublimate, sublime.

RELATED KEYWORDS: CUT, DIGGING, EXIT, EMISSION, FLOOD, REMOVAL

EXTRAVAGANCE

n. **1.** **1. extravagance** a taste for luxury, champagne taste, conspicuous consumption, extravagancy, extravagant desire, extravagantness, gross consumption. **2. excess** prodigality, profuseness, profusion, superfluity, superflux. **3. wastefulness** dissipation, profligacy, profligateness, thriftlessness, unthriftiness, wantonness, waste. **4. splurge** jag, midnight feast, spree. *Informal:* beanfeast, beano, bender, binge, blow-out, scatter.

2. **1. big spender** high roller, jetsetter, playboy. *Informal:* two-bob millionaire. **2. squanderer** dissipater, fritterer, misspender, prodigal, profligate, scattergood, spendthrift, waster, wastrel.

adj. **3.** **1. extravagant** dissipative, lavish, magnificent. **2. excessive** supererogatory, superfluous. **3. wasteful** highrolling, improvident, pound-foolish, profligate, spendthrift, thriftless, uneconomical, wanton.

v. **4.** **1. spend freely** be prodigal, burn up one's capital, live in lotus land, overspend, spend money like water, splurge. *Informal:* knock down, lamb down, lash out. **2. squander** consume, dilapidate, dissipate, fritter away, kill the goose that laid the golden eggs, make ducks and drakes of, misspend, riot away, run through, throw away, wanton, waste. *Informal:* blow, blue, bust. **3. gamble away** game away, sport away.

RELATED KEYWORDS: OVERINDULGENCE, BUYING, EXPENSIVENESS, GENEROSITY, JOY, PAYMENT, USELESSNESS

FACTORY

n. **1.** **1. factory** assembly line, establishment, flatted factory *(Singapore, Hong Kong)*, hong *(China)*, industrial estate, industrial park, installation, pilot plant, plant, shop, shop floor, stable, station, trading estate *(British)*, workshop. **2. foundry** grindery, ironworks, machine shop, smelter, smeltery, steelworks, wireworks, works. **3. forge** blacksmith's shop, smithery, smithy, stithy. **4. yard** brickfield, brickyard, dockyard, freight terminal, goods yard, shipyard. **5. saltworks** salina, saltern. **6. refinery** gasworks. **7. meatworks** boiling-down works, freezing works, knackery, rabbitoir, slaughterhouse. **8. mine** colliery, pithead, stall. **9. mill** chip-mill, flour mill, ginnery, rolling mill, sawmill. **10. sheltered workshop. 11. sweatshop** female factory, salt mines, workhouse.

    2. **1. workplace** work station, workshop. **2. workroom** atelier, studio, study. **3. office** agency, bureau, business, chambers, head office. **4. regional office** branch, district office, local office. **5. laboratory** research laboratory. *Informal:* lab.

RELATED KEYWORDS: CREATION, MACHINE, RESULT, SHOP, WORK

FAILURE

n. **1.** **1. failure** abort, abortion, calamity, disaster, fiasco, forlorn hope, misfire. *Informal:* bomb, damp squib, fizzer, fizzle, fizzler, flop, frost, lemon, muck-up, no-hoper, squib, turkey, wash-out, washaway, wipe-out, write-off. **2. failing** fall, lapse, the fall. **3. fail** *Informal:* flunk, plough *(British)*. **4. collapse** bust-up, crash, nosedive, slump, smash. *Informal:* crack-up, gutser. **5. loss** bottom, naught. *Informal:* blue duck, bummer, bust, dead loss. **6. bungle** blunder, botch, error, false step, fault, fiasco, foul-up, fumble, hash, mess, mess-up, miscarriage, mishap, mistake, mix-up, muddle, shambles, slip, stumble, trip. *Informal:* bad, balls-up, barry, blue, boner, boo-boo, clanger, fizzer, flub, fluff, foozle, howler, kettle of fish, muck-up, shemozzle, shocker, slip-up, stuff-up. **7. miss** break, fault, near miss, rabbit, strike. **8. unsuccessfulness** abortiveness.

    2. **1. nonachiever** cipher, failure, low achiever, nonentity. *Informal:* dead loss, disaster area, fizzle, gutless wonder, no-hoper, tanker. **2. dud** dead duck, debacle, disaster, lost cause. *Informal:* crookie. **3. loser** a good loser, also-ran, bad shot, booby, lapser, nonentity, nonstarter. *Informal:* easybeat, ferret, flop, hairy goat, stiff.

adj. **3.** **1. failed** manqué, ruined, unsuccessful. *Informal:* done like a dinner, duff, gone to Gowings *(NSW)*, washed-up. **2. unsuccessful** bootless, empty, feckless, fruitless, futile, idle, impotent, ineffective, ineffectual, inept, inutile, lost, non-effective, null, otiose, unavailing, unfortunate, unplaced, unprofitable, useless, vain, void, weak, wide of the mark. **3. losing** no-win, self-defeating. **4. unaccomplished** abortive, stillborn.

v. **4.** **1. fail** abort, backfire, break down, collapse, crack, crash, crumple, fall down, fall flat, fall short, fall through, fold, fold up, give up the ghost, go (or end) up in smoke, go under, lapse, miscarry, misfire, nosedive, not come up to scratch, not make the grade, not suffice. *Informal:* cark, clap out, come undone (or unstuck) (or unglued), crack up, die in the hole, die standing up, die the death, fizzle out, flop, go belly up, go down like a lead balloon, go down the plughole, go down the tube(s), go phut, gutser, kark, miss the boat (or bus). **2. suffer disaster** come to grief, do no good, draw a blank, get (or go) nowhere, go to the devil, go to the wall, go under, lose, lose out, lose out on, measure one's length, not to have any joy. *Informal:* bomb, bomb out, come a buster, come a cropper, come a gutser, come undone, come undone (or unstuck) (or unglued), fall flat on one's (or its) face, have had one's chips, lay an egg, not get to first base, not to be able to take a trick. **3. miss** go wide. **4. bungle** abort, blunder, boggle, botch, butcher, dig one's own grave, fail, gum up the works, hinder, make a hash of, make a poor fist of, mess, misdo, mull, ruin, scupper *(British)*, trip, wreck. *Informal:* balls something up, bitch, blow, bollocks, bugger up, cook, cruel, dud up, flub, fluff, foozle, foul up, louse up, make a muck of, make a muff of, muck, muck up, muff, queer. **5. make a mistake** make a false step, strike out. *Informal:* flunk, make a blue. **6. underachieve** run dead. **7. lose** be among the also-rans, be bested, come off second best, come off worst, get left behind, go down, lose out, take a beating. *Informal:* bite the dust. **8. give in** admit defeat, cave in, default, give someone (or something) best, give way, give way to, go back on, let someone down, put up the shutters, sag, submit, succumb, surrender. *Informal:* buckle under, cop out, crap out, knuckle under, sky the towel, throw (or toss) in the towel, throw it in.

RELATED KEYWORDS: INCOMPETENCE, DAMAGE, MISFORTUNE, DEFEAT

FAIRNESS

n. **1.** **1. fairness** candidness, candour, dispassionateness, equity, fair-mindedness, impartiality, impartialness, objectiveness, objectivity. **2. justice** equity, justness, natural justice, poetic justice, propriety, rightfulness, rightness. **3. even-handedness** egalitarianism, equableness, equalitarianism, equitableness, measure for measure. **4. just reward** desert, merit. **5. karma** inevitable consequence, retributive justice, scales of justice, sword of justice.

2. **1. fair action** square deal, the right thing. *Informal:* fair buck *(NZ)*, fair do *(NZ)*, fair go. **2. fair play** cricket, good sportsmanship, Marquis of Queensberry rules.

3. **1. fair person** honest broker, nature's gentleman, real sportsman, square-shooter.

adj. **4.** **1. fair** candid, colourless, disinterested, dispassionate, fair-minded, impartial, objective, open-minded, unbiased, uninterested, unprejudiced. **2. egalitarian** democratic, equalitarian. **3. even-handed** equable, equitable, even. **4. sporting** sportsmanlike. **5. just** conscionable, fair and square, honest, morally right, reasonable, right, rightful, square. **6. deserved** as it should be, fit, fitting, justifiable, lawful, legitimate, well-earned. *Informal:* legit.

v. **5.** **1. behave fairly** deal honestly, do justice to, do the right thing by, right, see that justice is done. **2. deal fairly with someone** give a person his due, give the devil his due. *Informal:* give someone a break, give someone a fair go, give someone a go. **3. play fairly** be a sport, play the game.

6. **1. deserve** be entitled to, merit, rate. **2. get one's just deserts** be hoist with one's own petard, have it coming to one, reap the whirlwind, serve one right. **3. be right** be only natural justice.

adv. **7.** **1. fairly** candidly, fair, fair and square, honestly, justly, on the square, sportingly, square. **2. impartially** dispassionately, equably, equitably, even, objectively, without fear or favour, without prejudice, without regard to person. **3. rightfully** by rights, in justice.

phr. **8.** **1. fair's fair** *Informal:* fair buck *(NZ)*, fair crack of the whip, fair do *(NZ)*, fair go, fair shake of the dice, fair suck of the sauce bottle, fair suck of the sav.

RELATED KEYWORDS: HONESTY, LAWFULNESS, MORALITY

FAITHFULNESS

n. **1.** **1. faithfulness** allegiance, constancy, devotedness, fidelity, loyalism, loyalty. **2. integrity** bona fides, dependableness, good faith, honesty, honour, izzat, probity, sincerity, true-heartedness, trustworthiness, truth. **3. dutifulness** devotion, duteousness, sense of responsibility, supererogation. **4. reliableness** adherence, adhesion, constancy, staunchness, steadfastness. **5. authenticity** genuineness.

2. **1. faithful person** trouper, true blue, trusty. *Informal:* a good sort. **2. loyalist** liegeman. **3. the faithful.**

adj. **3.** **1. faithful** liege, loyal, single-hearted, true, true-blue, true-hearted. *Informal:* white *(British)*. **2. honourable** as good as one's word, good, straight, trustworthy, upright. **3. dutiful** allegiant, duteous. **4. reliable** dedicated, dependable, devoted, infallible, sound, true, trustworthy, trusty, unfailing. **5. staunch** certain, constant, firm, fixed, set, stanch, steadfast, steady, strong, sure, unwavering. **6. authentic** genuine.

v. **4.** **1. be faithful to** abide by, adhere to, be true to, go all the way with someone, stand by, stay with, stick by, stick to, stick with, support, uphold. **2. owe loyalty** bear allegiance, render homage. **3. stay together** hang together, stick together.

adv. **5.** **1. faithfully** constantly, devotedly, leally, loyally, staunchly, steadfastly. **2. dutifully** duteously, honourably, reliably, responsibly. **3. authentically** genuinely, straightly.

RELATED KEYWORDS: HONESTY, MORALITY, OBLIGATION

FANTASY

n. **1.** **1. fantasy** fancifulness, fancy, imagery, imagination, imaginativeness, improvisation, ingeniousness, mind's eye. **2. fabulousness** apocryphalness, fictitiousness, idealness, imaginariness, unreality, vaporosity. **3. idealism** absurdism, escapism, romanticism, surrealism, vision, visionariness. **4. stargazing** wool-gathering. **5. introversion** autism, schizophrenia, split personality, withdrawal.

2. **1. image** conceit, conception, crotchet, fiction, flight of fancy, idea, ideation, imago, notion, projection, representation, vagary, vision, whimsy. **2. phantom** apparition, eidolon, idol, phantasm, shape, spectre.

3. **1. dream** chimera, hallucination, mirage, nightmare, phantasm, phantasma, phantasmagoria, phantasmagory, pink elephant. **2. daydream** pipedream, romantics, stardust. **3. fantasy land** castles in the air, cloud-cuckoo-land, dystopia, fairyland, never-never land, pie in the sky, utopia, wonderland.

4. **1. fantasiser** daydreamer, Don Quixote, dreamer, fabler, fabulist, idealist, imaginer, improviser, poet, romancer, stargazer, storyteller, surrealist, Walter Mitty, wool-gatherer.

adj. **5.** **1. fantastic** apocryphal, chimerical, concocted, fabled, fabulous, fancied, fictional, fictitious, ideational, imaginal, imaginary, imaginational, invented, legendary, made-up, mythic, mythical, mythological, pretend, romantic, storybook. **2. surreal** extraordinary, metaphysical, phantasmal, phantom, preternatural, supernatural, surrealistic, transcendental, unearthly. **3. imaginative** daedal *(Chiefly Poetic)*, fancy, improvisatorial, improvisatory, ingenious.

6. **1. unrealistic** escapist, fairytale, fanciful, fantastic, fantasy, idealist, imaginative, moonshiny, notional, quixotic, romantic, starry-eyed, unreal, utopian, vaporous, visionary.

v. **7.** **1. fantasise** build castles in the air, daydream, dream, dream dreams, fancy, have one's head in the clouds, have visions, hear voices, live in a fantasy land, romance, romanticise, stargaze, suppose, tilt at windmills. *Informal:* be away with the fairies, goof off. **2. pretend** make believe. **3. imagine** conjure up, ideate, invent. **4. envision** image, picture, project, visualise. **5. concoct** coin, fabricate, forge, improvise.

adv. **8.** **1. fancifully** fantastically, imaginatively, ingeniously. **2. imaginarily** ideally, ideationally, notionally.

RELATED KEYWORDS: IDEA, THINKING, UNTRUTHFULNESS

FARMING

n. **1.** **1. farming** agrarianism, agribusiness, agriculture, agronomy, cultivation, husbandry, pastoralism, primary industry, ruralism. **2. agronomy** agrobiology, agrology, agronomics, chemurgy, geoponics, pedology, soil mechanics, soil science. **3. stock farming** agistment, animal husbandry, breeding, custom feeding, stock raising, wool-growing. **4. dairy farming** cow-cockying, dairying, herd testing, sharemilking. **5. forestry** afforestation, agroforestry, arboriculture, forestation, reforestation, silviculture, sylviculture, woodcraft *(Chiefly US)*. **6. viticulture** oenology, viniculture, winegrowing. **7. apiculture** sericulture. **8. marine farming** aquaculture, mariculture. **9. organic farming** biological control, companion planting, hydroponics, permaculture, tank farming. **10. miscellaneous types of farming** broadacre farming, bush-farming, market gardening, mixed farming, subsistence farming. **11. ploughing** contour ploughing, culture, tillage. **12. type of cultivation** clean cultivation, crop rotation, dry farming, extensive cultivation, intensive cultivation, ley farming, monoculture, multiple cropping, shifting agriculture, strip cropping, sustainable agriculture. **13. harvesting** cocksfooting *(NZ)*, harvest, harvest home, haymaking, inning, mowing, reaping. **14. grazing** crash-grazing, intensive stocking, rotational grazing, set stocking, strategic grazing, strip grazing, zero grazing. **15. muster** bangtail muster, round-up, yarding. **16. drenching** dipping, Mules operation, mulesing.

2. **1. shearing** barrowing, sheepshearing, throwing the belly wool. **2. wool classing** bulk classing, core testing.

3. **1. horticulture** gardening, landscape gardening, pomiculture, pomology, topiary. **2. market gardening** trucking *(US)*.

4. **1. farm** acreage, bush farm *(NZ)*, chook farm, croft, estate, factory farm, farmlet, free selection, fruit block *(Chiefly SA)*, grange *(British)*, hacienda, hobby farm, homestead selection, organic farm, plantation, property, ranch, rancho *(in Spanish America and the south-western US)*, selection, smallholding, spread *(Chiefly US)*, stud-farm, vinery, vineyard, wood lot. **2. farmhouse** farmstead, grange *(British)*, hacienda, head station, homestead, ranch house. *Informal:* Government House. **3. collective farm** cooperative farm, kibbutz, kolkhoz. **4. station** back-station, cattle run, cattle station, cattle-run, dude ranch *(US)*, estancia, outstation, property, ranch, rancho *(in Spanish America and the south-western US)*, sheep run, sheep station, sheep-run, spread *(Chiefly US)*, stock farm. **5. dairy farm** creamery, dairy, herringbone dairy, milking shed. **6. miscellaneous types of farm** crocodile farm, oyster farm, trout farm, turtle farm.

5. **1. stable** bails, cowshed, offices. **2. shed** boss of the board, depot shed, shearing shed, stand, woolshed. **3. barn** garner, granary, hayshed, hopper, pit silo, silage pit, silo.

6. **1. farmland** baulk, downland, field, glebe, infield, ley, ley line, mead *(Poetic)*, meadow *(Chiefly British)*, paddock, prairie, swidden, turbary. **2. back paddock** back country, back run, outfield. **3. cultivated land** cultivation paddock, tillage, tilth. *Informal:* plough. **4. crop field** cornfield, cotton field, hayfield, paddy, paddy field, wheatfield. **5. crop area** rice bowl, wheatbelt. **6. pasture** artificial grass, grass, improved pasture, mat-grass, pasturage, run-off *(NZ)*. **7. grazing land** long paddock, sheepwalk *(British)*, springer paddock, stock run, walk. **8. farmyard** barnyard, feedlot, home paddock, resting paddock, stockyard.

7. **1. garden** bed, plot. **2. type of garden** alley, Chinese garden, fernery, flower garden, herb garden, Japanese garden, knot garden, parterre, potager, rock garden, roof garden, rooftop garden, rosary, shrubbery, sunken garden, topiary, water garden, wilderness, wintergarden. **3. bed** border, flowerbed, hotbed, rockery, seedbed. **4. plot** patch, plat. **5. market garden** allotment *(British)*, kitchen garden, vegetable garden. **6. nursery** bush house, conservatory, garden centre, glasshouse, grapery, greenery, greenhouse, hothouse, terrarium. **7. green** lawn, nature strip, street lawn, verge. **8. orchard** arbor, arboretum, grove, orangery, pinery, pinetum, plantation. **9. park** botanical gardens.

8. **1. farmer** agriculturalist, husbandman, landsman, primary producer, ruralist, the man on the land. **2. small farmer** agistor, blocker, bush-farmer, crofter, free selector, selector. *Informal:* blockie, cockatoo, cocky, dungaree settler, sheep cocky, stringy-bark cockatoo, wheat-cocky. **3. stockbreeder** breeder, cutter-out, stirpiculturist, stock farmer, stock raiser. **4. dairy farmer** herd tester. *Informal:* cow cocky, cowbanger, cowspanker. **5. grazier** cattleman, rancher, ranchero, ranchman *(US)*, run-holder, sheepholder, sheepman, station-owner, stockholder, stockkeeper, stockman, woolgrower. **6. apiarist** apiculturist, beekeeper, sericulturist. **7. planter** canefarmer, canegrower, sugar farmer, tea-planter. *Informal:* cane-cocky. **8. winegrower** oenologist, vigneron, vinedresser, vineyardist, viniculturist, viticulturer. **9. orchardist** fruit-grower, fruiter, fruitgrower, pomiculturist, pomologist. *Informal:* blockie. **10. hobby farmer** *Informal:* Collins Street cocky, Piccadilly bushman, Pitt Street farmer, Queen Street bushie. **11. tenant farmer** cropper, sharecropper *(Chiefly US)*, sharefarmer, sharemilker *(NZ)*. *Informal:* share-cocky. **12. farm manager** overseer, station manager. *Informal:* boss cocky, cove. **13. stock and station agent** stock agent. **14. agriculturalist** agriculturist, agrobiologist, agronomist, forester. **15. peasant** bucolic, cottager *(British)*, cottar *(Scottish, Irish)*, cottier, ploughman, ryot. *Informal:* bushie, hick, redneck *(US)*.

9. **1. farmhand** green-hand, help, jackaroo, jackeroo, jillaroo, knockabout, rouseabout, roustabout, stablehand, station hand. *Informal:* blue-tongue, leatherneck, loppy, narangy, rouser, rousie, wood-and-water joey. **2. stockman** cow hand, cowboy *(Chiefly US)*, cowgirl, drover, gaucho, herder, musterer, ringer, stockboy, stockrider, stockworker, tailer, tailer-up, vaquero *(US)*. *Informal:* buckaroo, cowpoke *(US)*, cowpuncher *(US)*. **3. boundary rider** *Informal:* jerker, lizard. **4. shepherd** cowherd, dog driver, goatherd, gooseherd, herder, herdsman, hutkeeper, monkey dodger, motherer, shepherdess, swanherd, swineherd, wrangler *(US)*. **5. dairyman** cowman, dairywoman, milkmaid. **6. tiller** ploughboy, plougher, ploughman, plowboy *(US)*, plowman *(US)*. **7. reaper** canecutter, cutter, gleaner, harvester, harvestman, thresher. *Informal:* cocksfooter, daddy-long-legs, emu-bobber, stick-picker. **8. haymaker** crow *(NZ)*, tedder, windrower. **9. picker** hop-picker, nutter, vintager.

10. **1. shearer** bladeshearer, bladesman, sheepshearer. *Informal:* greasy, jingling Johnny, stooper, tiger, woolhawk. **2. expert shearer** gun shearer, ringer, ryebuck shearer, shed-boss. *Informal:* deuce artist, deucer, good iron, squirt. **3. learner** *Informal:* Cunnamulla gun, drummer, snagger. **4. shedhand** bailer, baler, board boy, dag picker, penner, picker, picker-up. *Informal:* broomie, brownie gorger, pony, sheepo, tarboy. **5. dag-picker** dag boy, dagger. **6. fleece-picker** piece-picker, table hand. *Informal:* fleece-oh, fleecy. **7. roller** fleeceroller, skirter, woolroller. **8. wool classer** guesser, wool classing, wool sorter, wool stapler.

11. **1. gardener** arborist, landscape gardener, nurseryman, rosarian, topiarist. **2. market gardener** cabbage-gardener, trucker *(US)*, vegetable gardener. **3. groundsman** greenkeeper, hedger.

12. **1. farm machinery** aerator, chain harrow, chisel-plough, combine, combine harvester, cultivator, dead stock, disc plough, drag, drill, dump rake, gang cultivator, gang plough, harrow, harvester, header, header harvester, pick-up baler, planter, plough, plow *(Chiefly US)*, rotary hoe, rotary plough, scarifier, seed drill, self-binder, side delivery rake, stump-jump plough, tractor.

13. **1. shears** b-bows, blades, bows, daggers, dover, hand shears, snow comb, swords, wool shears. *Informal:* tongs. **2. handpiece** bogghi. *Informal:* lizard, merry widows.

adj. **14.** **1. agrarian** agrestic, bucolic, country, farming, georgic, pastoral, peasant, rural, rustic, villatic. **2. agricultural** agrarian, agrobiologic, agrological, agronomical, geoponic, hydroponic. **3. farmyard** free-range, open-range, organic. **4. arboricultural** silvicultural. **5. vinicultural** oenological, viticultural. **6. apicultural** apiarian, sericultural.

15. **1. farmable** arable, cultivable, cultivatable, improvable, pasturable, tillable. **2. fallow** uncultivated, unseeded.

v. **16.** **1. farm** be on the land, ranch. *Informal:* cocky. **2. dairyfarm** *Informal:* cowbang, cowspank. **3. drove** drift, herd, hunt away, muster, tail, wrangle *(US)*. **4. graze** agist, block-graze, browse, crash-graze, creep-graze, fatten, feed, feedlot, graze back (or down), open-graze, pasture, range, run, soil. **5. feed** graze, run. **6. breed** grow, lamb down. **7. stock** overstock. **8. milk** rest. **9. cultivate** bring in *(NZ)*, farm, grow, husband, improve, subdue. **10. plough** chip, chisel-plough, dibble, dig, disc, grub, loosen, rake, scarify, stub, stump, subsoil, till. **11. fallow** rest. **12. plant** bed, heel in, implant, pot, prick out, slip, transplant, vernalise. **13. sow** broadcast, checkrow *(US Agriculture)*, direct drill, inseminate, seed, sodseed, stratify. **14. afforest** forest.

17. **1. harvest** crop, cut, gather, glean, head, ingather, mow, pick, reap, scythe, strip. **2. thresh** fan, flail, thrash, willow, winnow. **3. bale** bind, ensile, rick, stook, windrow.

18. **1. shear** barrow, channel, crutch, cut, pink, tomahawk. *Informal:* poke off, undress. **2. dag** belly, channel, crutch, ring, wig. **3. ring the board** ring the shed. *Informal:* do a Jimmy Gibbs, swing the gate.

RELATED KEYWORDS: CUT, DIGGING, FERTILITY, PLANTS, ANIMALS, MACHINE

FASHION

n. **1.** **1. fashion** craze, cult, fad, height of fashion, rage, the going thing, the last word, the latest, the new look, vogue. **2. style** cut, guise, tone. **3. haute couture** bon ton, high fashion. **4. fashionability** chic, coolness, dressiness, exclusiveness, faddishness, modishness, smartness, stylishness, trendyism, up-to-dateness. **5. dapperness** jauntiness, nattiness, rakishness, sauciness, snappiness, sportiness, spruceness, swankiness. *Informal:* swank. **6. dandyism** faddism, trendyism. **7. titivation** dandification.

2. **1. fashionable person** faddist, fashionable, trendsetter. **2. beau monde** grand monde, haut monde, the scene. **3. high society** beautiful people, glitterati, jet set, smart set. **4. socialite** jetsetter, man about town. **5. dandy** ball of style, fop, gilded youth, high-stepper, jack-a-dandy, prinker, titivator. *Informal:* swell *(Chiefly US)*. **6. fashion plate** bag hag. *Informal:* fashion victim.

adj. **3.** **1. fashionable** contemporary, in, in vogue, modern, new-fashioned, up-to-date, up-to-the-minute, with-it. *Informal:* all the go, all the rage, cool, now. **2. dressed up** dandy, dandyish, dapper, dressed to the nines, smart, snappy, spiffy *(British)*, sporty, spruce, swanky. *Informal:* all gussied up. **3. chic** dashing, dashy, dressy, exclusive, faddish, faddy, fashion, high-stepping, jaunty, modish, natty, newfangled, rakish, retro, saucy, smart, snazzy, stylish, swishy. *Informal:* cool, hot, mod, supercool, swell *(Chiefly US)*, swish. **4. trendy** ultrafashionable.

v. **4.** **1. be fashionable** be all the rage, catch on. **2. be with the fashion** *Informal:* be in, be in the swim, be U, be with it. **3. dress up** gussy up, spruce up. **4. be all dressed up** look like you've just come (or stepped) out of a bandbox. **5. dandify** caparison, primp, prink. **6. set a trend** be a trendsetter.

adv. **5.** **1. fashionably** à la mode, exclusively, modishly, on the scene, stylishly, stylistically. **2. dapperly** dashingly, jauntily, nattily, rakishly, saucily, snappily, sprucely, swankily.

RELATED KEYWORDS: CLOTHES, CONFORMITY, CUSTOM, NEWNESS

FASTENING

n. **1.** **1. fastening** affixture, attachment, infixion. **2. binding** colligation, coupling, hitching, lashing, seizing, tying. **3. connexion** engagement. **4. fixedness** firmness, fixity, secureness.

2. **1. fastener** bonder, fast, holdfast, locker, securer. **2. binder** bracer, lasher, tier, trusser. **3. nailer** pinner, riveter. **4. grasper** clasper, clincher, gripper, hooker. **5. hitcher** hobbler, shackler.

3. **1. bond** bind, hitch, ligament, ligature, link, tie, vinculum. **2. yoke** fetter. **3. bandage** ligature.

4. **1. belt** band, bands, belting, cestus, cinch, cincture, garter belt *(US)*, girdle, girth, strap, surcingle. **2. ribbon** aglet, aiglet, apron strings, cordon, drawstring, fillet, lacing, streamer, string, stringer, tie. **3. lace** bootlace, latchet. **4. garter** suspender, suspender belt. **5. watch-chain** albert, watch-guard, watchband, watchstrap. **6. elastic band** keylock closure, lacker band, rubber band, rubber ring, twist-tie, wire closure. **7. octopus strap** bungee cord *(US)*, octopus, spider. *Informal:* ockie strap. **8. metal strap** astragal.

5. **1. knot** belay, bend, bow, bowline, carrick bend, cat's-paw, clench, clinch, clove hitch, double-knot, figure of eight, fisherman's bend, half-hitch, hawser bend, hitch, overhand knot, reef knot, rolling hitch, running knot, sheepshank, sheet bend, slipknot, square knot *(US)*, stevedore's knot, surgeon's knot, timber hitch, turle knot, weaver's knot. *Informal:* granny. **2. splice** eye splice, snell, snood.

6.   **1. button**   Anzac button, collar stud, cufflink, dome, hook and eye, link, pearl button, press-stud, snap fastener, stud, tuft. *Informal:* popper. **2. buckle** clasp. **3. toggle** frog. **4. ring** woggle. **5. zipper** slide fastener, zip, zip-fastener. **6. buttonhook**.

7.   **1. nail**   brad, ceiling dog, clasp-nail, clout, clout nail, dog nail, dog spike, doornail, drawing-pin, panel pin, skewnail, sparable, spike, sprig, stub nail, stud, tack, thumbtack, tintack. **2. screw** dowel screw, grubscrew, Phillips screw, screw-eye, self-tapping screw, setscrew, thumbscrew, woodscrew. **3. pin** belaying pin, bodkin, break pin, cotter, dowel, forelock, hatpin, headpin, key, kingpin, linchpin, lug, nog, peg, pintle, safety pin, shear pin, split pin, split pin, stickpin, stud, swivel pin, tap-bolt, tiepin, tongue, treenail, trunnel, wedge, wrist, wristpin. **4. rivet** explosive rivet.

8.   **1. clip**   alligator clip, bicycle clip, binding, bulldog clip, clothes peg, crocodile clip, paperclip, peg, piton, staple. **2. hairclip** bobby pin, butterfly clip, hair slide, hairgrip, hairpin, pin, slide. **3. clamp** agraffe, brace, clam, cramp, cramp iron, lyre, vice.

9.   **1. bolt**   barrel bolt, bow shackle, cap screw, explosive bolt, eye bolt, fishbolt, panic bolt, ringbolt. **2. nut** butterfly nut, castellated nut, locknut, wing nut. **3. lock** ball catch, catch, cylinder lock, dead latch, deadlock, fast, night latch, padlock, safety catch, springlock, steering lock, yale lock. **4. latch** hasp. **5. tumbler** snib, talon.

10.   **1. brace** batten, cleat, stair-rod, stretcher, truss, winding strip. **2. plate** chill, cog, fishplate, gang nail, tang.

11.   **1. anchor** bower, dead man, dogstick, drag-anchor, grapnel, kedge anchor, kellick, killick, sheet anchor, sprag. *Informal:* mudhook, pick. **2. hook** grapnel, grapple, grappler, grappling, grappling hook, grappling iron, tenterhook, ottfur hook. **3. clevis** hame, lunette, ottfur hook.

12.   **1. anchorage** dolphin, makefast *(US)*, moorage, moorings. **2. bollard** bitt, post, timberhead.

adj. **13.**   **1. fastened** adnate, engaged, firm, fixed, iron, secure, sure. **2. bound** bandaged, corded, fasciate, lashed, tied. **3. at anchor** girt.

14.   **1. fixative** ligamentary, ligamentous. **2. lockup** self-locking.

v. **15.**   **1. fasten** affix, anchor, attach, fix, grapple, hitch, hoop, latch, loop, pin, post, rivet, secure, sprig, stick, zip. **2. infix** engage, joggle, seat. **3. hang** hook up, suspend. **4. bind** bight, colligate, garter, knot, ligature, noose, strap, tie, withe, wrap. **5. do up** belt up, button, zip up. **6. lash** bowse, cable, cord, frap, gammon, gripe, lace, reeve, rope, seize. **7. nail** bolt, roove, screw, tack. **8. clamp** clasp, clench, clinch. **9. stitch** side-stitch, staple. **10. make fast** anchor, moor, tie up. **11. tether** enchain, hobble, hopple, iron, leash, picket, shackle, stake. **12. lock** bar, deadlock, double-lock, forelock, hasp, padlock.

16.   **1. be fastened** be fixed, fay.

RELATED KEYWORDS: CORD, HOLD, JOINING, RESTRAINTS, SUPPORT

FAULTY SIGHT

n.   **1.**   **1. faulty sight** ametropia, aniseikonia, anisometropia, astigmatism, cataract, cataracts, cycloplegia, detached retina, diplopia, double image, eye defect, glaucoma, hypopyon, miosis, muscae volitantes, mydriasis, myosis, nebula, nystagmus, presbyopia, pterygium, retinal detachment, scotoma. **2. short-sightedness** myopia, nearsightedness. **3. long-sightedness** hypermetropia, hyperopia. **4. dimness** amblyopia, blear, dimness of vision, purblindness, tunnel vision. **5. night blindness** nyctalopia. **6. ophthalmia** blight, conjunctivitis, ophthalmitis, pinkeye, retinitis, sandy blight, scleritis, sclerotitis, trachoma, xerophthalmia. **7. cross-eye** cast, cockeye, squint, strabismus, walleye. **8. colour blindness** blue-blindness, daltonism, dichromatism, dichromic vision, monochromasia, protanopia, red-blindness, tritanopia.

2.   **1. blindness** amaurosis, blackout, moon blindness, retrolental fibroplasia. **2. temporary blindness** day blindness, dazzle, flash blindness, hemeralopia, snow blindness.

3.   **1. blind person** myope, protanope, squinter, the blind, tritanope. *Informal:* four-eyes. **2. boko** boco. **3. monochromat**.

adj. **4.**   **1. having faulty sight** ametropic, astigmatic, bespectacled, isometropic, miotic, mydriatic, myotic, nystagmic, one-eyed, presbyopic, sclerotitic. **2. near-sighted** myopic, short-sighted. **3. long-sighted** far-seeing, far-sighted, hypermetropic, hyperopic. **4. dim-sighted** amblyopic, blear, bleary, bleary-eyed, dim, gravel-blind, purblind. **5. cross-eyed** boss-eyed, cockeyed, squint, squint-eyed, strabismal, strabismic, strabismical, wall-eyed. **6. colour-blind** dichroic, dichromatic, monochromatic.

5. 1. **blind** amaurotic, blinded, eyeless, moon-blind, sightless, stone-blind, visionless. *Informal:* blind as a bat, blind as a wombat. 2. **temporarily blind** bedazzled, blind drunk, nyctalopic, snow-blind.

v. 6. 1. **blind** bedazzle, blear, blindfold, hoodwink, put someone's eyes out, throw dust in someone's eyes. 2. **be blind** go blind, lose one's sight. 3. **blindfold** cowl, darken, dazzle, hood.

RELATED KEYWORDS: ILL HEALTH, DARK, OPTICS, INVISIBILITY

FAULTY SPEECH

n. 1. 1. **faulty speech** alalia, alogia, anarthria, aphasia, aphonia, denasality, dyslalia, dysphasia, dysphonia, glossolalia, inarticulateness, infantilism, lallation, lambdacism, paralalia, puerilism, rhinolalia, rhotacism, tachyphemia. 2. **logopaedics**. 3. **mutism** dumbness, speechlessness. 4. **speech impediment** speech defect. 5. **stammer** disconnectedness, disjointedness, fumble, fumbling, splutter, sputter, stutter. 6. **mispronunciation** clip, falter, hesitation, ineloquence, lisp, mumble, mutter, quaver, slur, spelling pronunciation. 7. **gibberish** babble, gabble, gibber, jabber. *Informal:* abracadabra, double-dutch.

2. 1. **stammerer** aphasiac, aphasic, fumbler, lisper, mumbler, mutterer, splutterer, sputterer, stutterer. 2. **mute** *Informal:* dummy.

adj. 3. 1. **inarticulate** aphasic, bitty, broken, disconnected, disjointed, disjunct, dysphonic, fumbling, hesitant, incoherent, ineloquent, quavery. 2. **mute** aphonic, dumb, silent, speechless, tongue-tied, voiceless, wordless.

v. 4. 1. **mispronounce** clip, lisp, mumble, murmur, mutter, nasalise, quaver, slur. 2. **falter** fumble, haw, hem, hesitate, hum and haw, stammer, stutter. 3. **splutter** burble, chatter, clutter, gabble, jabber, sputter, swallow one's words.

adv. 5. 1. **inarticulately** disconnectedly, disjointedly, ineloquently, lispingly, mutteringly. 2. **stammeringly** falteringly, fumblingly, hesitantly, hesitatingly, mumblingly, stutteringly. 3. **dumbly** mutely, speechlessly. 4. **stammeringly** falteringly, fumblingly, hesitantly, hesitatingly, mumblingly, stutteringly. 5. **dumbly** mutely, speechlessly.

FEATHER

n. 1. 1. **feather** aftershaft, alula, auriculars, axillaries, bastard wing, coverts, filoplume, flight feather, hackle, lore, penna, pennon *(Poetic)*, pin-feather, pinfeather, pinion, pinna, plume, plumelet, plumule, primary, quill, rectrix, remex, secondary, sickle feather, tertial, tertiary, vibrissa, whisker, winglet. 2. **quill** aftershaft, barb, barbicel, barbule, barrel, calamus, filament, flue, fluff, harl, herl, pinnula, rachis, rhachis, shaft. 3. **marabou** aigrette, osprey, ossifrage, ostrich feather, peacock feather. 4. **plumage** feather, feathering, plume. 5. **contour feathers** aigrette, barb, barbule, crest, crissum, ducktail, egret, flag, hackle, moustache, muff, topknot, torques, web, whiskers, wing-coverts. 6. **down** eiderdown, floccus, swan's-down. 7. **plume** ala, flight, panache, pennon *(Poetic)*, wing.

2. 1. **featheriness** downiness, plumosity.

adj. 3. 1. **feathery** downy, fluffy, pappose. 2. **feather-like** feathery, pinnal, pinnate, plumate, plumelike, plumose, plumy. 3. **feathered** pennate. 4. **crested** cristate, pileated.

v. 4. 1. **feather** fledge, fluff, plume, preen, ruffle. 2. **fletch** flight, tuft.

RELATED KEYWORDS: ANIMALS, HAIR

FERTILITY

n. 1. 1. **fertility** arability, fatness, fecundity, fructuousness, fruitfulness, heartiness, pinguidity, productivity. 2. **lushness** richness, verdancy, verdure. 3. **abundance** cornucopia, luxuriance, milk and honey, opulence, overabundance, plenty, profligacy, prolificness, rampancy, store, superabundance, wealth. 4. **teeming womb** teeming loins.

2. 1. **act of fertilisation** agamic, AI, conception, enrichment, fecundation, fertilisation, impregnation. 2. **state of being fertilised** conception, enrichment, fecundation, fertilisation, impregnation. 3. **fruition** fructification, fruitage, pullulation.

3. 1. **fertile land** arable, farmland, kindly ground, land of milk and honey, oasis, water meadow. 2. **topsoil** humus, leaf mould, litter.

4. 1. **fertiliser** ammonium nitrate, ammonium sulfate (phosphate), apatite, bat guano, blood and bone, bonemeal, Chile saltpetre, compost, copperas, dolomite, dressing, dung, ferrous sulfate, fishmeal, green manure, guano, gypsum, iron sulfate, manure, marl, mulch, muriate, nitrate, nitre, nitrochalk, oilcake, phosphorite, potassium nitrate, saltpetre,

seaware, seaweed, side dressing, sodium nitrate, super, superphosphate, tankage *(British)*, top dressing, urea. **2. crop dusting** aerial spraying, aerial supering, aerial top dressing.

adj. **5.** **1. fertile** arable, eutrophic, farmable, fat, fructuous, fruitful, generous, hearty, pinguid, polycarpic, productive, prolific. **2. lush** exuberant, fecund, luxuriant, rampant, rich, verdant. **3. abundant** ample, bounteous, bountiful, copious, enough and to spare, overabundant, plenteous, plentiful, prodigal, profuse, prolific, superabundant, teeming.

v. **6.** **1. be fertile** burgeon, flourish. **2. produce** bear, birth, crop, fruit, overbear, overcrop, overproduce, spawn, yield. **3. abound** overabound, overrun, proliferate, superabound, swarm, teem.

7. **1. fertilise** enrich, fatten, fecundate, fructify, improve. **2. fertilise by treatment** bone, compost, dress, dung, inoculate, manure, marl, mulch, nitrify, side-dress, super, top, top-dress.

8. **1. impregnate** fecundate, fertilise, inseminate, make pregnant. *Informal:* duff, knock up, pot. **2. pollinate** pollen.

adv. **9.** **1. fertilely** abundantly, copiously, exuberantly, fructuously, fruitfully, luxuriantly, prodigally, productively, profusely, prolifically, rampantly, richly, superabundantly.

RELATED KEYWORDS: CREATION, FARMING, OFFSPRING, RESULT, REPRODUCTION

A FEW

n. **1.** **1. a few** a handful, just one or two, trickle. *Informal:* two men and a dog. **2. the few** minority, remnant, rump. **3. rare person or thing** curiosity, rara avis.

adj. **2.** **1. few** hardly any, infrequent, not many, rare, several, unique, wheen *(Scottish)*. *Informal:* damn-all, rare as hen's teeth, scarce as hen's teeth. **2. scant** bare, exiguous, light, little, low-density, meagre, narrow, scant of, scanty, scattered, scrimp, scrimpy, skimpy, slender, slim, small, sparing, sparse, stingy, thin, tiny. **3. scarce** diminished, flat, reduced, thin on the ground, tight.

v. **3.** **1. be few and far between** be thin on the ground, be weak in numbers. **2. decrease in number** abate, abridge, bate, cut, cut down, decrease, diminish, lessen, lower, minify, reduce, scant. **3. be scant** run short. **4. be in the minority** be too few, be without a quorum.

RELATED KEYWORDS: RARENESS, TWO, THREE, FOUR

FIGHTER

n. **1.** **1. fighter** battler, combatant, combater, contender, contestant, striver, struggler, tussler. **2. aggressor** assailant, belligerent, feudist, fire-eater, fire-swallower, swashbuckler. **3. knight** banneret, chevalier, jouster, knight banneret, knight-errant, man-at-arms, paladin, samurai, shogun, tilter. **4. warrior** Amazon, baresark, berserk, berserker, brave, champion, ghazi, hero, Hun, samurai, Valkyrie. *Informal:* champ. **5. fighting drunk** *Informal:* fighting cock. **6. bullfighter** matador, picador, toreador, torero. **7. swordsman** épéeist, backswordsman, duellist, fencer, foilsman, gladiator, sabreur, swashbuckler. **8. gunman** firelock, firer, franc-tireur, gun, gunfighter *(US)*, gunner, gunslinger *(US)*, marksman, markswoman, sharpshooter, shooter, sniper. **9. militarist** chauvinist, hawk, jingoist, militant, war lord, warmonger. **10. mercenary** auxiliaries, condottiere, foreign legion, freelance, hired gun *(US)*, hireling, landsknecht, lansquenet, legionnaire, professional soldier, soldier of fortune. **11. adventurer** buccaneer, filibuster, freebooter.

2. **1. pugilist** boxer, bruiser, infighter, prize-fighter, sparring partner. *Informal:* ex-pug, fisticuffer, palooka, pug, slugger. **2. class of boxer** bantam, bantamweight, featherweight, flyweight, heavyweight, junior middleweight, light flyweight, light heavyweight, light middleweight, light welterweight, middleweight, welterweight. *Informal:* dreadnought. **3. bludgeoner** buffeter, cudgeller. **4. wrestler** junior. *Informal:* grappler. **5. judoist** ju-jitsuist, judoka.

3. **1. armed forces** armed services, defence forces, defence services. **2. army** artillery, cavalry, general staff, horse, infantry, land forces, light horse, military, soldiery, the rifles. **3. navy** fleet, flotilla, marine, senior service. **4. air force** flying squadron. **5. nation in arms** army of occupation, land power, Sabaoth, standing army. **6. unit** arm, battalion, battery, brigade, century, cohort, column, command, contingent, corps, division, forces, garrison, legion, maniple, phalanx, platoon, regiment, staff section. *Informal:* divvy. **7. squad** cadre, company, element, group, outfit, platoon, squadron, sub-unit, troop. **8. detachment** detail, party. **9. array** air picket, convoy, line, square, wedge. **10. army reserve** armed constabulary *(NZ)*, home guard, militia. *Informal:* Dad's army.

4.   **1. soldier**   Anzac, blue-bonnet, Federal, G.I., galloglass, gallowglass, imperial, infanteer, man-at-arms, Peshmerga, ranker, redcoat, regular, sepoy, trooper, Unknown Soldier. *Informal:* crunchie, desert rat, digger, doughboy *(US)*, GI, Hun, Jerry, Joe *(US)*, pongo *(Chiefly British Military and Nautical)*, rat, tommy, Tommy Atkins, Yankee. **2. legionary** breakaway, centurion, flanker, franc-tireur, manipular, palatine. **3. infantryman** foot soldier, janissary, peon, pioneer. *Informal:* crunchie, doughboy *(US)*, footslogger, grunt. **4. artilleryman** bazookaman, bombardier, bomber, cannoneer, gunner, powder monkey, spotter, strafer. **5. rifleman** carabineer, carbineer, fusilier, grenadier, harquebusier, jaeger, musketeer, pistoleer. **6. swordsman** halberdier, lance, paviser, pikeman, sabre, spear, spearman. **7. archer** anchor point, arbalester, bowman, crossbowman. **8. cavalryman** bashibazouk, cameleer, carabin, carabineer, cuirassier, dragoon, guardsman *(British)*, horse marine *(US History)*, hussar, lancer, lighthorseman, trooper, uhlan. **9. airman** ace, aircraftman, aircraftswoman, fighter pilot. **10. standard-bearer** color guard *(US)*, colour company, colour party, colour sergeant, cornet, ensign, guidon, vexillary. **11. sentinel** sentry. **12. drill sergeant** drillmaster, drum-major, fugleman. **13. engineer** sapper, signalman, specialist *(US Military)*.

5.   **1. serviceman** effective, enlisted man *(US)*, servicewoman. **2. conscript** chocolate soldier, draftee *(US)*, selectee *(US)*. *Informal:* chocko, nasho. **3. recruit** substitute, volunteer. *Informal:* rookie, sprog, vollie. **4. militiaman** minute man *(US)*, reserve, reservist, state trooper *(US)*, territorial. *Informal:* Dad's Army. **5. ex-serviceman** campaigner, ex-servicewoman, old soldier, returned soldier, RSL, veteran, warhorse. *Informal:* vet. **6. non-combatant** tin soldier. *Informal:* base wallah, base walloper *(NZ)*. **7. military policeman** gendarme.

6.   **1. combat troops** field army, firing line, front, front line. *Informal:* cannon fodder. **2. task force** advance *(US)*, advance guard, chasseur, flying column, screen, sortie, spearhead, van, vanguard. **3. outpost** flank, post, rear, rearguard, wing. **4. storm troops** commando, double diamond, paratroops, shock troops, SS. *Informal:* paras.

7.   **1. guerilla** ambusher, freedom fighter, irregular, partisan, skirmisher, terrorist, urban guerrilla. **2. terrorist** bombmaker, suicide bomber.

8.   **1. high command** generalissimo, supreme commander *(US)*. **2. officer** commandant, commissioned officer, constable, duty officer, major, ranker, staff officer, underofficer. *Informal:* brass, brass hat, red hat. **3. non-commissioned officer** NCO. *Informal:* non-com.

9.   **1. army rank** adjutant, adjutant general, aga, aide, aide-de-camp, batman, bombardier, brigade major, brigadier, captain, colonel, colonel-in-chief, commander, commander-in-chief, commanding officer, commissary, corporal, field marshal, field officer, flag lieutenant, general, general officer, gunner, lance bombardier, lance corporal, lance sergeant, lieutenant, lieutenant colonel, lieutenant general, major, major general, marshal, master sergeant, noncommissioned officer, private, quartermaster sergeant, second lieutenant, sergeant, staff sergeant, technical sergeant *(US)*, warrant officer class one, warrant officer class two. *Informal:* lance jack.

10.   **1. naval rank** able seaman, able-bodied seaman, admiral, captain, chief petty officer, commander, commander-in-chief, commodore, ensign, fleet admiral, leading seaman, lieutenant, lieutenant commander, petty officer, rear admiral, seaman, sergeant major, sublieutenant, vice-admiral, warrant officer, Wran, Wren *(British)*.

11.   **1. air force rank** air chief marshal, air commodore, air marshal, air vice-marshal, aircraftman, captain, corporal, flight lieutenant, flight sergeant, flying officer, group captain, leading aircraftman, pilot officer, squadron leader, warrant officer, wing-commander.

adj. **12.**   **1. martial** amazonian, bellicose, belligerent, combatant, combative, filibusterous, militant, pugilistic, pugnacious, warlike. **2. soldierly** military, soldierlike.

v. **13.**   **1. join the armed forces** enlist, enrol, join, join the colours, join up, take the king's shilling, volunteer.

     RELATED KEYWORDS: ATTACK, CONTEST, FLYING, HITTING, KILLING, MARINER, RETALIATION, VIOLENCE, WAR

FIGURE OF SPEECH

n. **1.**   **1. figure of speech** figuration, figure, rhetorical device. **2. type of figure of speech** anacoluthon, anaphora, antithesis, asyndeton, calque, chiasmus, climax, enallage, epistrophe, euphuism, hendiadys, hysteron proteron, inversion, kenning, litotes, metaphor, mixed metaphor, onomatopoeia, oxymoron, polysyndeton, rhetorical question, simile, syllepsis, tmesis, trope, zeugma. **3. allegory** Aesopian, allegorise, anagoge, apologia, apologue, cautionary tale, exemplum, fable, old wives' tale, parable, proverb, satire, sermon. **4. idiom** colloquialism, expression, parlance, phrase, turn of phrase, usage. **5. conceit** catachresis, circumlocution, cliché, crank, malapropism, pleonasm, solecism, tautology. **6. imagery** image, symbolism. **7. irony** antiphrasis, bathos, dramatic irony, Socratic irony. **8. play on words** double entendre, equivoque, paronomasia, pun, quibble, riddle, word play. **9. poetic device** acrostic, alliteration, anadiplosis, assonance, balance, gemination, hypallage, metanalysis, metathesis, metre, palindrome, parallelism, parenthesis, repetition, rhyme, rhythm, spoonerism. **10. metonymy** metonym, synecdoche. **11. personification** antonomasia, apostrophe, prosopopoeia. **12. mot juste.**

2. **1. figurativeness** alliterativeness, allusiveness, idiomaticalness, ironicalness, tropology. **2. classicalism** classicism.

adj. 3. **1. figurative** allegorical, allegoristic, anagogical, archetypal, figural, figured, metaphoric, metaphorical, symbolic, tropical, tropologic. **2. rhetoric** euphuistic, hyperbolic. **3. idiomatic** clichéd, colloquial. **4. ironic** sardonic. **5. punning** paronomastic. **6. antithetic** climactic, inverted. **7. euphemistic** hypocoristic, pantagruelian. **8. alliterative** assonant, metrical, onomatapoeic, rhyming, rhythmic, rhythmical. **9. metonymical** synecdochic.

adv. 4. **1. figuratively** allegorically, allusively, hyperbolically, hypocoristically, idiomatically, ironically, metaphorically, metonymically, tropologically.

RELATED KEYWORDS: ELOQUENCE, POETRY, PROVERB

FINANCE

n. 1. **1. finance** commerce, financial affairs, investment, money management. **2. high finance** big business, capitalisation, funding, overcapitalisation, recapitalisation, wheeling and dealing. **3. banking** clearing, electronic banking, merchant banking, retail banking, wholesale banking. **4. dealings** electronic funds transfer, kerbs, over-the-counter trading. **5. brokerage** brokage, jobbing, stockbroking. **6. speculation** agio, agiotage, arbitrage, bubble, investment. **7. offsetting** hedge, marriage. **8. readjustment** shake-out.

2. **1. bank** acceptance house, building society, central bank, clearing house, community bank, discount house, finance company, investment bank, merchant bank, mutual savings bank, reserve bank, savings bank, terminating building society, trading bank. **2. Stock Exchange** all-industrials, bourse, Change, exchange, kerb, pit. **3. market** aftermarket, bear market, bull market, buy-back market, cash market, commercial bill market, commodities market, contango, futures exchange, futures market, grey market, inter-company market, physical market, seller's market, short-term money market, spot market, stock market. **4. books closing date** ex date, spot month.

3. **1. capital** asset backing, authorised capital, capital expenditure, capital stock, circulating capital, corpus, fixed capital, issued capital, nominal capital, paid-up capital, principal, registered capital, risk capital, shareholders' funds, stock, working capital. **2. funds** loan fund, revolving fund, sinking fund, vulture fund. **3. assets** current assets, goodwill, intangibles, liquid assets. **4. bill** accommodation bill, allonge, bank bill, bill of exchange, bill of sale, demand bill, documentary bill, foreign bill, sight bill, Treasury bill *(British)*, Treasury note. **5. deposit** fixed deposit, statutory reserve deposit, term deposit, time deposit. **6. bank rate** bond rate, differential rate, dividend rate, interest, rediscount rate. **7. credit note** credit, credit slip, credit transfer, letter of credit. **8. credit** credit rating. **9. credit card** account card, cash-card, charge card, debit card. *Informal:* plastic, plastic money. **10. bond** acceptance, certificate of deposit, margin, security, unsecured note.

4. **1. stocks and shares** block, blue chip, bonus issue, capital stock, common share, contributing share, convertible note, cumulative preference share, debenture, deferred delivery share, deferred share, equities, founders' shares, funds, futures, futures contract, joint stock, long-term bond, margin, marketable parcel, ordinary share, per cent, preference share, preference stock, preferred stock *(US)*, scrip, scrip issue, securities, stock unit, trading stock, tranche, vendor's shares. **2. all-ordinaries** all-resources, chemicals, metals, oils, steel, utilities *(US)*. *Informal:* Kangaroos *(British)*. **3. capital issue** bonus, bonus issue, capital distribution, rights issue. **4. option** call, double option, put, put option, right, stop loss order. **5. dividend** accrued interest, active, dividend yield, franked dividend, interest, margin, turn, unearned increment, yield. *Informal:* divvy. **6. share index** All-Ordinaries index, All-Ords index, Dow Jones index, Footsie 100, FTSE 100, Hang Seng index, Nasdaq, Nikkei index.

5. **1. financier** backer, banker, gnome, merchant banker. *Informal:* angel. **2. speculator** arbitrager, arbitrageur, bear, bull, investor, operator, stag. *Informal:* arb, piker,

plunger, wheeler-dealer *(Chiefly US)*. **3. broker** bucket shop, cambist, discount broker, jobber, kerb broker, share-pusher, sharebroker, stockbroker, stockjobber. **4. shareholder** bondholder, holder, stockholder.

v. **6. 1. finance** bankroll, capitalise, cashflow, financier, fund, overcapitalise, put money into, underfund, underwrite. **2. float** afloat, circulate, utter. **3. freeze** tie up.

7. 1. invest accredit, aggressive, average down, average up, bear, bull, buy in, close out, embark, hedge, hive off, job, operate, overbuy, play the market, play the stock market, put, speculate. *Informal:* scalp.

adj. **8. 1. financial** economic, fiscal, monetary, pecuniary. **2. speculative**.

RELATED KEYWORDS: ACCOUNTING, BUYING, SELLING, MONEY, COMMERCE

FINDING

n. **1. 1. finding** detecting, discovering, locating, tracking, unearthing. **2. discovery** detection, uncovering. **3. instinct for finding** nose, sixth sense. **4. find** discovery, strike, treasure-trove, turn-up. **5. accidental discovery** find, happenstance, serendipity.

2. 1. finder descrier, detector, discoverer, diviner, explorer, perceiver.

adj. **3. 1. findable** ascertainable, detectable, discoverable. **2. on the right track** getting warm, on the scent, warm.

v. **4. 1. find** detect, discover, locate, spot, trace, track down. **2. perceive** cognise, descry, recognise, see, see through, spot. **3. light on** come by, come on, come upon, fall on (or upon), hit on, pick up, strike, stumble on (or upon) (or across). *Informal:* lob on (or onto). **4. unearth** bring to light, dig up, dredge up, elicit, ferret out, nose into, rummage out, smell out, turn up. **5. scent** follow one's nose, get wind of, nose about. **6. be able to find** have a nose for.

5. 1. find out get on to (or onto), glean, realise. *Informal:* (take a) tumble to someone. **2. catch** catch out, expose, show up, surprise, take by surprise. *Informal:* rumble, spring.

RELATED KEYWORDS: ANALYSIS, REVELATION, PROFIT, SIGHT, VISIBILITY

FINE ARTS

n. **1. 1. fine arts** arts, graphic arts, plastic arts, visual arts. **2. depiction** abstraction, illustration, representation. **3. artistry** brushwork, craft, craftsmanship, draughtsmanship, feeling, touch. **4. art form** acrylic, calligraphy, ceramics, commercial art, computer art, embroidery, enamelling, engraving, folk art, graphics, illumination, intarsia, loom, marquetry, mosaic, needlepoint, ordonnance, origami, painting, primitive art, printing, quilting, rock art, scenography, sculpture, serigraphy, tapestry, tessellation, weaving. **5. style** breadth, form, idiom, palette, tonality, tone. **6. technography** art history.

2. 1. work of art chef-d'oeuvre, classic, composition, creation, magnum opus, masterpiece, oeuvre, opus, production. **2. objet d'art** antique, collectable, museum piece, old master, virtu. **3. set piece** period piece. **4. found object** objet trouvé, ready-made. **5. collage** assemblage, bark art, combine painting, decoupage, montage, papier collé, pastiche. **6. collection** loan collection.

3. 1. painting all-over painting, aquarelle, bark painting, batik, canvas, cave painting, daubery, drip painting, grisaille, monochrome, pallet, pallette, portraiture, rock painting. **2. picture** diptych, icon, lunette, panel, polyptych, predella, triptych. **3. portrait** figure, half-face, half-length, likeness, nude, portraiture, profile, self-portrait, silhouette, torso. **4. scene** anthemion, landscape, marine, moonscape, nocturne, pastoral, seascape, still life, tableau, townscape, view, waterscape. **5. kakemono** tanka. **6. fresco** aerosol art, frieze, graffiti, mural. **7. technique** aerial perspective, alla prima, chiaroscuro, direct painting, encaustic, gouache, painting technique, perspective, sfumato, sgraffito, stereochrome, stipple. **8. painting medium** acrylic colour, acrylics, body colour, distemper, gouache, oil colour, oils, polymer colour, poster colour, tempera, wash, watercolour. **9. canvas** easel, picture plane, support. **10. palette** oils, paintbox, paints.

4. 1. drawing drafting, mechanical drawing, sketching, technical drawing. **2. sketch** black-and-white art, line drawing, outline. **3. draft** cartoon, drawing, rough, sinopia, sketch, study, thumbnail, thumbnail sketch, vignette, visual. **4. caricature** cartoon, comic strip, strip cartoon. **5. pattern** blot drawing, design. **6. shading** crosshatching, hachure, hatching, shadow. **7. sketchbook** colouring-in book, sketchblock, sketchpad.

5. 1. sculpture ceroplastics, modelling, statuary. **2. carving** direct carving, woodcarving, woodwork. **3. statue** bronze, bust, figurine, glyph, herm, herma, marble, monument, plaster cast, stabile, statuette. **4. relief** alto-rilievo, bas-relief, basso-rilievo, demirelief, glyph, high relief, low relief, mezzo-rilievo, relievo, rilievo, round. **5. petroglyph** rock carving, rock engraving. **6. mobile** kinetic art. **7. cameo** miniature.

6. 1. ceramics agateware, basaltware, belleek, biscuit, bisque, bucchero, cameo ware, celadon, china, crackle, crackleware, delft, Dresden china, earthenware, eggshell china, faïence, graniteware, greenware, ironstone, majolica, Ming, nankeen, porcelain, pottery, raku, scraperboard, semiporcelain, Sevres, terracotta, ware, Wedgwood, willow-ware. **2. clay** glaze, slip.

7. 1. enamelwork champlevé, cloisonné, majolica. **2. glassware** duotone, frostwork, glass sculpture, glasswork, leadlight, murrhine glass, stained glass, Venetian glass. **3. techniques** blowpipe, etching, firing, glassblowing. **4. cut glass** crystal, crystal glass, frost, frosting, lead crystal. **5. coloured glass** cobalt bloom, erythrite, opal glass, ruby glass, smalt, zaffre.

8. 1. engraving cerography, chalcography, glyptography, pyrography, toreutics, woodcutting, xylography. **2. print** aquatint, block print, cerograph, chromo, chromolithograph, collotype, halftone, line engraving, linocut, lithograph, mezzotint, oleograph, photogravure, photolithograph, rubbing, silk-screen print, wood engraving, woodcut, xylograph. **3. printing** collotype, die-sinking, die-stamping, etching, flexography, foil printing, intaglio, letterpress, lithography, matrix, metallography, oleography, photolithography, process printing, relief, zincography. **4. plate** remarque. **5. artist's proof** proof.

9. 1. computer art computer graphics, digital imaging, photoshopping, programmed art.

10. 1. art movement Aborigiana, abstract art, abstract expressionism, abstractionism, action painting, art brut, Art Deco, Art Nouveau, automatism, baroque, Bauhaus, brutalism, Byzantine, Chinoiserie, classicalism, classicism, computer art, conceptual art, concrete art, constructivism, cubism, dadaism, divisionism, earthworks, expressionism, Fauvism, Flemish school, funk art, futurism, genre, Gothic, Gothicism, greenery-yallery, idealism, illusionism, impressionism, informal art, Jugendstil, junk art, kinetic art, land architecture, land art, Mannerism, metaphysical painting, minimal art, neo-impressionism, neoclassicism, new wave, nouvelle vague, op art, orphism, pointillism, pop art, post-impressionism, post-object art, pre-Raphaelite art, programmed art, purism, quattrocento, realism, Renaissance, rococo, romanticism, Rubenism, semantic painting, sensationalism, social realism, suprematism, surrealism, symbolism, synchromism, tachisme, tenebrism, trompe l'oeil, videoart, vorticism.

adj. **11. 1. artistic** aesthetic, painterly, pictorial. **2. pictorial** graphic, illustrated, illustrative, picturesque, vivid. **3. abstract** non-objective, non-representational, surrealistic. **4. naturalistic** impressionist, objective, realist, representational. **5. formal** dry. **6. colouristic**. **7. in perspective** axonometric, cabinet, to scale. **8. stippled** daubed, flown, hard-edge, malerisch.

12. 1. sculptural sculpturesque, statuary. **2. carved** engraved, glyptic, sculptured. **3. in relief** anaglyptic, embossed, repoussé, toreutic.

v. **13. 1. depict** depicture, etch, limn, portray, represent. **2. draw** crayon, delineate, design, draft, illustrate, line, outline, profile, sketch. **3. paint** accidental, airbrush, blot, colour, daub, fresco, illuminate, scumble, spray-paint, stencil, tint, touch up. **4. pencil** charcoal, crayon, crosshatch, hachure, hatch, ink, shade, stipple. **5. glaze** decorate. **6. model** cast, mould. **7. sculpt** carve, chip, sculp, sculpture. **8. fecit** sculpsit.

14. 1. engrave carve, cut, incise, scrimshaw. **2. print** aquatint, lithograph, mezzotint, photolithograph, screen-print, silk-screen, silk-screen print. **3. emboss** boss, snarl. **4. etch** bite. **5. impress** stamp.

RELATED KEYWORDS: ARTIST, PHOTOGRAPHY, PRINTING, REPRESENTATION, TEXTILES

FINISH

n. **1. 1. finish** anticlimax, bitter end, catastrophe, climax, close, completion, conclusion, consummation, dead finish, denouement, end, end point, ending, eventuation, exeunt, expiration, expiry, finale, finals, finis, grandstand finish, omega, termination, terminus. **2. coda** cadence, close, codetta, feminine cadence, fine, half-cadence, stretta, tag. **3. epilogue** afterword, amen, desinence, end, envoy, finis, punch line, ultimatum. **4. coup de grâce** burn out, death knell, death-knock, expiration, expiry, quietus, tag end, the last straw. **5. final** conclusion, cusp, dernier cri, extreme, last words, tail. *Informal:* last. **6. ending** cesser, close, endgame, wind-up. **7. termination** abruption, cessation, closure, closure motion, cut-off, discontinuance, end, extremity, finalisation, winding-up. **8. finality** definitiveness, terminability, terminableness, ultimateness. **9. goal** tape, winning post, wire. **10. home straight** home stretch, run-in. **11. terminus** cul-de-sac, dead-end, railhead. **12. terminal** destination, end, extremity. **13. closing time** afternoon, evening, full-time, knock-off time, muck-up day, no-side *(British Rugby Football)*, period, stumps, sunset, time. *Informal:* curtains. **14. settlement** conclusion, settling, upshot.

2. 1. extremity butt, close, club, coda, conclusion, end, fingertip, finial, finis, foot, heelpiece, neb, pole, tag, tail, tail end, tailpiece, termination, tip, toe.

3. 1. last day Armageddon, crack of doom, day of judgement, day of reckoning, Götterdämmerung, judgement, judgement day.

4. 1. finisher concluder, consummator, destroyer, ender, obturator, terminator.

5. 1. endman lanterne rouge, tail ender. **2. bell sheep** catch, cut-out.

adj. **6. 1. finished** all over, complete, completed, completive, concluded, done, ended, executed, over, wound up. *Informal:* all over bar the shouting, washed up. **2. moribund** ante-mortem, dead-end, dying, extinguishable, extirpative, terminational, terminative.

7. 1. final back-end, climactic, concluding, consequent, eventual, extreme, last, lattermost, net, nth, supreme, terminal, ultimate. **2. latter** afternoon, last-minute.

8. 1. endmost aftermost, backmost, distal, farthest, furthermost, hindermost, hindmost, rearmost.

v. **9. 1. finish** accomplish, be in at the death, be on the home straight, be on the home stretch, cease, close, complete, conclude, consummate, determine, do, end, finalise, fulfil, have done with, muddle through, perfect, play out, polish off, put the lid on, see the back of, settle, sew up, stop, terminate. *Informal:* bang it over, wind up, wrap up. **2. terminate** abolish, annul, break, break off, cease, chop off, destroy, dissolve, draw stumps, drop, lapse, phase out, razor-gang, ring down the curtain on, rule off, stop. **3. be ancient history** be a closed book, be done with. **4. climax** arrive, come, conclude, eventuate. **5. expire** be all over with, be all up with, be curtains for, be gathered to one's fathers, breathe one's last, decease, decline, depart, die, die off, die on someone, exit, go, go to one's account, part, pass away, pass on, perish, predecease, starve, stop, succumb. *Informal:* buy it, buy the farm *(US)*, cark, cark it, cash in one's chips, come to a sticky end, conk out, croak, croak it, do a perish, fall off the perch, flatline, give up the ghost, go west, hop (or fall off) the twig, kark, kick off *(US)*, kick the bucket, pass in one's marble, peg out, pop off, snuff it, throw a seven, turn up one's toes. **6. give out** go out.

adv. **10. 1. finally** at last, at long last, at the end of the day, eventually, in conclusion, in the long run, terminally, ultimately. **2. terminably** definitively, once and for all, terminatively. **3. right through** al fine, to the bitter end. **4. last** lastly, latterly.

interj. **11. 1. finis** that's that. *Informal:* all in the whippy's taken, the jig is up.

RELATED KEYWORDS: COMING AFTER, STOPPAGE, RESULT

FIRE

n. **1. 1. fire** blaze, conflagration, deflagration, flames, flare-up, phlegethon. **2. open fire** bonfire, camp fire, watch-fire. **3. bushfire** burn-back, bush-burn *(NZ)*, grassfire, regeneration burn, spot fire, wildfire. *Informal:* the red steer. **4. volcano** fumarole, hot spot, mantle plume, solfatara. **5. flare** belch, blaze, flame, flash, gleam, glint, glow, sparkle. **6. ember** spark. **7. ash** ashes, char, charcoal, cinder, smut, soot. **8. smoke** smother, smoulder, smudge. **9. fieriness** incandescence.

2. 1. firing auto-ignition, ignition, kindling, lighting. **2. combustion** afterburning, detonation, explosion, flashback, spontaneous combustion. **3. burning** auto-da-fé, cremation, incineration. **4. burning off** back-burning, control burning, controlled burning, hazard burning, prescribed burning. **5. carbonisation. 6. arson** black lightning, fire-raising, incendiarism, pyromania. **7. immolation** self-immolation, the stake.

3. 1. flammability combustibility, combustibleness, ignitability, inflammability, inflammableness.

4. 1. lighter firestick, friction match, fusee, light, lucifer, lucifer match, match, safety match, slow match, vesta. *Informal:* anarchist. **2. flint** steel. **3. taper** fuse, proximity fuse, spill, touchpaper, touchwood, train, variable time fuse, wick. **4. torch** firebrand, firestick, flambeau, flare, glow stick, Hawaiian flare, link, luau light. **5. firebox** tinderbox. **6. tinder** amadou, combustible, firelighter, ignescent, kindling, kindling wood, mornings wood, punk *(Chiefly US)*.

5. 1. firer enkindler, igniter, inflamer, kindler. **2. burner** cremationist, cremator. **3. arsonist** fire-raiser, incendiary, pyromaniac. *Informal:* firebug.

6. 1. fireplace chimney, chimney corner, fireside, grate, hearth. **2. incinerator** crematorium, crematory, furnace, solar furnace.

adj. **7.**   **1. on fire** blazing, conflagrant, fiery, flaming, flamy, flaring. **2. flammable** combustible, combustive, fireable, ignescent, ignitable, inflammable, piceous, touchy. **3. incendiary** calcinatory, caustic, igneous. **4. burnt** ashen, ashy, charred, charry, sooty.

v. **8.**   **1. ignite** enkindle, fire, kindle, light, set fire to, set on fire. **2. incinerate** burn, cremate, sweal. **3. burn** calcinate, carbonise, char, incinerate. **4. roast** scald, scorch, sear, singe, toast. **5. cauterise** brand, burn in. **6. burn off** back-burn. **7. immolate** burn at the stake, self-immolate.

9.   **1. catch fire** blaze, burn ahead, deflagrate, go up in smoke, sweal, take fire. **2. flame** conflagrate, flare up, flash, spark. **3. smoke** smolder *(US)*, smoulder.

RELATED KEYWORDS: EXPLOSION, FUNERAL RITES, HEAT, HEATING, KILLING, LIGHT

FIVE

n. **1.**   **1. five** cinque, fifth, lustrum, pentad, pentameter, pentarchy, quinary, quinquennium, quintet, quintuple, quintuplet, quintuplicate. *Informal:* fiver. **2. pentagon** pentacle, pentagram, pentahedron, pentalpha, pentangle, quincunx. **3. quintuplets** *Informal:* quin.

2.   **1. six** half-a-dozen, half-dozen, hexad, hexagram, hexameter, hexarchy, sestet, sextet, sextuplet, sixth. **2. hexagon** hexagram, hexahedron.

3.   **1. seven** hebdomad, heptad, heptameter, heptarchy, septenary, septet, septuplet, seventh. **2. heptagon** heptahedron.

4.   **1. eight** eighth, octad, octameter, octarchy, octave, octet, octuplet, ogdoad. **2. octagon** octahedron.

5.   **1. nine** ennead, ninth, nonet. **2. nonagon** enneagon.

6.   **1. ten** decade, decimal, decuple, dicker, tenth. **2. decagon** decahedron.

7.   **1. eleven** cricket eleven, eleventh, hendecasyllable. **2. hendecagon** hendecahedron. **3. elevenses** elevener *(Qld)*.

8.   **1. twelve** dozen, duodecimal, gross, twelfth. **2. dodecagon** dodecahedron.

9.   **1. twenty** score, twentieth.

10.   **1. hundred** century, hundredth, ton.

11.   **1. thousand** chiliad, K, millenary, millesimal. *Informal:* thou. **2. millennium** siècle.

12.   **1. million** millionth. **2. billion** billionth. **3. trillion** nonillion, octillion, quadrillion, quintillion, septillion, sextillion, trillionth. **4. milliard. 5. googol** googolplex.

adj. **13.**   **1. five** fifth, fivefold, pentagonal, pentahedral, pentamerous, quinary, quincuncial, quinquennial, quintuple, quintuplicate.

14.   **1. six** half-a-dozen, half-dozen, hexadic, hexagonal, hexahedral, hexamerous, hexangular, senary, sextuple, sixfold, sixth.

15.   **1. seven** heptagonal, heptahedral, heptamerous, heptangular, septenary, septennial, septuple, sevenfold, seventh.

16.   **1. eight** eightfold, eighth, octadic, octagonal, octahedral, octal, octamerous, octan, octangular, octonary, octuple.

17.   **1. nine** enneadic, ninefold, ninth, nonagonal.

18.   **1. ten** decagonal, decennial, decimal, decuman, decuple, denary, tenfold, tenth.

19.   **1. twenty** twentieth, vicenary, vigesimal.

20.   **1. hundred** centesimal, centuple, hundredfold, hundredth.

21.   **1. thousand** millenarian, millenary, millennial, millesimal, thousandfold, thousandth. **2. ten thousand.**

22.   **1. million** billion, billionth, millionth, nonillion, nonillionth, octillion, septillion, septillionth, sextillion, sextillionth, trillion, trillionth. **2. myriad.**

RELATED KEYWORDS: INFINITY, MANY, SHAPE, PART

FLATTERY

n. **1.**   **1. flattery** adulation, blandishments, compliment, flummery. *Informal:* oil. **2. sweet talk** blarney, honeyed words, palaver. *Informal:* flannel *(British)*, soft soap, syrup. **3. ingratiation** cajolement, cajolery, insinuation. **4. sycophancy** fawning, flunkeyism, obsequiousness, puffery, toadyism, unctuousness. *Informal:* oiliness, smarm, smoodging. **5. hero-worship** personality cult.

2.   **1. flatterer** courtier, crawler, fawner, flunkey, lickspittle *(British)*, member of a claque, pickthank, reptile, respecter of persons, satellite, sycophant, toady. *Informal:* bootlicker, creeping Jesus, greaser, greasespot, smoodger, suckhole. **2. wheedler** blandisher, cajoler, carney, smooth talker, soft-soaper, sweet-talker. **3. self-flatterer** mutual-admiration society.

adj. **3.**   **1. flattering** adulatory, candied, complimentary, courtly, ingratiating, obsequious. **2. sycophantical** fawning, flunkeyish, fulsome, reptilean, servile, smooth-faced, smooth-spoken, smooth-tongued. *Informal:* buddy-buddy, smarmy, toadyish. **3. unctuous** buttery, candied, honeyed, ingratiatory, oily, soapy, soft, sugared, sugary.

v. **4.**   **1. flatter** carney, make much of, praise to the skies, puff, speak someone fair, throw a bouquet. *Informal:* buddy-buddy, butter up, flannel up, lay it on thick, oil, smarm, smoodge. **2. behave sycophantically** fawn, jolly along, pander to, play up to, slaver, toady. *Informal:* chum up to, dag, get gravel rash, make up to, slime, smarm, suck up to. **3. cajole** blandish, blarney, coax, get round, jolly, palaver, sweet-talk, wheedle. **4. curry favour** *Informal:* duchess, make one's alley good, soap up. **5. flatter each other** *Informal:* be up each other. **6. hero-worship** adulate.

adv. **5.**   **1. flatteringly** complimentarily, fulsomely. **2. sycophantically** fawningly, ingratiatingly, obsequiously, oilily, oily, servilely, smarmily, subserviently, unctuously.

RELATED KEYWORDS: APPROVAL, HIGH REGARD, DISHONESTY

FLOOD

n. **1.**   **1. flood** deluge, inundation, spate. **2. overflow** overgrowth, overrun, profusion, smother. **3. spread** pervasion, suffusion. **4. pervasiveness** prevalence. **5. epidemic** eruption, outbreak, plague. **6. infestation** invasion.

adj. **2.**   **1. flooding** diluvial, torrential. **2. in flood** bank and bank *(NZ)*, over the banks, over the high-water mark. **3. rambling** sprawling, trailing. **4. diffused** outspread, widespread. **5. pervasive** prevalent, suffusive. **6. epidemic** epidemical, rife.

3.   **1. flooded** afloat, awash, inundated.

v. **4.**   **1. flood** deluge, drown, engulf, float, inundate, overwhelm, run a banker, swamp. **2. overflow** boil over, brim over, burst the banks, overspill, pour out, pour over, run over, spill, spill out, spill over, well over. **3. overrun** cover, overflow, overgrow, overspread, run riot, smother. **4. spread** ramble, sprawl, spread out, swarm, trail. **5. pervade** diffuse, metastasise, perfuse, permeate, spread like wildfire, spread through, suffuse. **6. infest** plague, swarm.

RELATED KEYWORDS: EMISSION, FLOW, LIQUID, EXCESS

FLOW

n. **1.**   **1. flow** current, flowage, fluency, fluentness, flux, pour, stream, turbulent flow, wash. **2. overflow** flow, flowage, run-off. **3. torrent** debacle, eruption, flood, gush, gust, jet, onrush, spate, spout, surge, uprush, upsurge, upsurgeance. **4. effluence** efflux, effusion, emanation, emission, exosmosis, flow, outflow, outpour, outpouring. **5. influx** affluence, afflux, endosmosis, flux, inflow, inrush, inrushing, inset, primary flow, secondary flow. **6. circulation** capillarity, capillary action, convection, osmosis. **7. dribble** drip, dripping, dropping, spray, sprinkle, trickle. **8. bleeding** blood nose, epistaxis, haemorrhage, nosebleed. **9. discharge** ooze, seep.

2.   **1. current** backwash, bombora, countercurrent, cross-current, drift, ebb and flow, flood, flood tide, flux, overfall, rip, stream, tidal current, tide, tide-rip, underset, undertow, wash. **2. tide** dodge tide, ebb tide, flood tide, half-tide, high tide, lee tide, low tide, low water, neap, neap tide, rip-tide, spring tide, tidal wave. **3. flood** deluge, inundation, spring tide. **4. flash flood** freshet, stormwater. **5. surge** disemboguement, ground swell, gurgitation, surf, wash, wave. **6. tidal wave** tsunami. **7. eustatic movement**. **8. race** millrace, millrun, tide-race, tideway. **9. eddy** maelstrom, vortex, whirlpool.

3.   **1. stream** arroyo, branch, creek, englacial stream, fresh, freshet, rivulet, tail. **2. streamlet** beck *(British)*, brook, brooklet, burn *(Scottish)*, millstream, rill, rivulet, run, runlet, runnel. **3. river** trunk, watercourse, waterway. **4. tributary** affluent, anabranch, arm, branch, confluent, distributary, effluent, feeder, influent, wadi. **5. underground river** sub-artesian water, underdrainage, vein. **6. confluence** conflux, estuary, mouth. **7. slack water** backwater, fan delta, marsh, swamp.

4.   **1. spring** fount, fountain, fountainhead, headspring, source, springhead, springlet, well, wellhead, wellspring. **2. headwaters** head, headstream, riverhead. **3. geyser** hot spring, thermae, thermal springs. **4. mineral spring** salina, spa, waters. **5. waterfall** cascade, cataract, chute, falls, rapids. **6. fountain** fount. **7. bubbler** bubble tap, drinking fountain, drinking tap, fountain, water fountain.

5.   **1. haemorrhage** bleed, bleeding, blood nose, discharge, epistaxis, gush, nosebleed. **2. bleeder** haemophiliac.

      6.   **1. ash flow**   coulee, earthflow, lava flow, mudflow.

adj.   **7.**   **1. flowing** affluent, fluent, fluxionary, mobile, osmotic, profluent, streaming, streamy. **2. effluent** emanatory, emissive, exosmic. **3. influent** endoreic, endosmotic, incurrent.

      8.   **1. fluvial** fluviatile, fluvioglacial, potamic, riverine, streamy. **2. tributary** estuarial, estuarine. **3. fountain-like** fontal.

      9.   **1. bleeding** discharging, haemorrhagic, oozing, weeping.

v. **10.**   **1. flow** drain, filter, fleet, flux, gutter, leach, ooze, pour, rill, run, set, strain, stream, transude, trickle. **2. swell** surge, upsurge. **3. rise and fall** ebb, make, rise, tide. **4. wash** lap, lave *(Poetic)*, splash, swash. **5. well up** gurgle, rise, swell, well forth, well out. **6. flood** deluge, inundate, overflow, overspill, run a banker, sluice, swamp. **7. spurt** gush, jet, spout, squirt. **8. swirl** eddy. **9. flush** sluice, wash out. **10. dribble** drip, ooze, trickle. **11. strain** drain, percolate, sluice. **12. pour** decant, dribble, drip, spill, trickle. **13. discharge** flow, outpour, pour forth, pour out. **14. bleed** haemorrhage.

RELATED KEYWORDS: CHANNEL, SEA, LIQUID, RAINFALL, WETNESS

FLYING

n.   **1.**   **1. flying** aeronautics, aviation, volitation. **2. gliding** aerostation, ballooning, free-falling, hang-gliding, parachuting, paraflying, paragliding, parasailing, skydiving, soaring. **3. aerobatics** hedgehopping, skywriting. **4. take-off** lift-off. **5. landing** touchdown. **6. aero tow** auto tow. **7. navigation** area navigation, instrument flying, instrument landing. **8. airmanship** airmindedness. **9. aeronautics** aerodonetics. **10. space travel** moon walk, moonshot, walk in space. **11. astronautics** bio-astronautics, cosmonautics.

      2.   **1. flight** air alert, air cover, air picket, airflight, charter flight, contact flight, fly, joy-flight, overflight, paradrop, solo, sortie. *Informal:* flip, hop, milk run. **2. fly-past** flying circus. **3. formation** escadrille *(US)*, flight, stack. **4. aerobatical manoeuvre** chandelle, fishtail, ground loop, loop, nosedive, power-dive, roll, sideslip, snap-roll, spin, spiral, stall, tailspin, whipstall, wingover.

      3.   **1. pilot** ace, aircrew, airman, airwoman, aviator, aviatress, aviatrix, birdman, bush pilot, captain, copilot, crew, flier, flight engineer, high-flyer, navigator, observer, paraflier, test pilot. *Informal:* fly-boy *(US)*, sky pilot *(US)*, skyman. **2. cabin crew** flight attendant, hostess, steward, stewardess. *Informal:* hostie, trolley dolly. **3. aeronaut** balloonist, parachutist. **4. glider** hang-glider, soarer. **5. astronaut** cosmonaut, spaceman, spacewoman. **6. aeroplane passenger** pax.

      4.   **1. airport** aerodrome, hangar. **2. runway** apron, landing strip, tarmac, threshold. **3. air traffic control** control tower, ground control.

      5.   **1. aircraft** aerodyne, aeroplane, craft, delta wing, plane, ship. *Informal:* bird, goony bird, kite. **2. helicopter** autogiro, autogyro, gyrocopter, gyroplane, helitanker, ornithopter, rotary wing aircraft, rotorcraft. *Informal:* chopper, copter, egg beater, whirlybird *(US)*. **3. flying boat** amphibian, float plane, seaplane. **4. glider** box kite, hang-glider, sailplane, soarer. *Informal:* kite. **5. parachute** canopy, drogue. *Informal:* brolly *(British Military)*, chute. **6. aerostat** airship, balloon, blimp, captive balloon, dirigible, kite balloon, montgolfier, sausage, zeppelin. **7. gondola** car, nacelle. **8. UFO** flying saucer, magic carpet. *Informal:* bogy.

      6.   **1. type of aeroplane** air ambulance, air-taxi, airbus, airliner, biplane, canard, charter plane, convertiplane, fixed-wing aircraft, flying wing, freighter, glider-tug, jet, jetliner, jumbo, jump-jet, monocoque, monoplane, penguin, pilotless plane, propjet, pusher, ski-plane, STOL, stratocruiser, stressed skin, swing-wing, tanker, tractor, transport, triplane, turbojet, turboprop, VTOL. **2. military plane** anti-aircraft, bomber, dive-bomber, fighter, fighter-bomber, helicopter gunship, interceptor, pathfinder, spotter, spotter plane, troop carrier, warplane *(US)*. *Informal:* warbird.

      7.   **1. aircraft body** aerofoil, aileron, air-brake, airframe, astrodome, bay, blister, body, bulkhead, cabin, canopy, cell, chassis, cockpit, cowl, cowling, delta wing, droop, elevator, empennage, fence, fin, flap, flight deck, fuselage, hull, hydroplane, landing gear, leading edge, longeron, main plane, nose, outrigger, panel, plane, rudder, shroud, skid fin, slat, spar, spoiler, surface, tab, tail, tail skid, tailplane, trailing edge, trim tab, undercarriage, vertical stabiliser, wing. **2. means of propulsion** aero-engine, airscrew, athodyd, booster, combustor, flame-holder, gas burner, gas jet, gaslight, oil burner, ottfur hook, prop, propeller, pusher, ramjet, rotor, tail rotor, tractor, tractor engine, vectored thrust. **3. aircraft control** control column, control stick, controls, joystick, stick. **4. aircraft instrumentation** accelerometer, autoland gear, automatic direction finder, automatic flight control system, automatic pilot, inclinometer, instrument landing system, instruments, machmeter, teleran, variometer, VASIS.

    8. **1. spacecraft** ablative, ablator, capsule, earth satellite, fixed satellite, launch vehicle, Luna, lunar module, module, posigrade rocket, probe, re-entry vehicle, satellite, sonde, space probe, space shuttle, space station, spaceship, sputnik, stage, step rocket, thruster, vehicle, vernier rocket.

adj. **9.** **1. flying** aerial, airborne, airworthy, on the wing, volant, volitant, winged *(especially Poetic)*. **2. aeronautic** aero, aeronautical, aviational, volitational. **3. aerobatic. 4. aerostatic** heavier-than-air, lighter-than-air. **5. aeromarine. 6. astronautic** aerospace, cosmonautic.

v. **10.** **1. fly** hover, take wing, wing. **2. glide** balloon, free-fall, hang-glide, parachute, plane, sailplane, sky-dive, soar, volplane. **3. pilot** navigate. **4. take off** lift off. **5. land** touch down. **6. loop** buzz, crab, dive, fishtail, flatten, hedgehop, loop the loop, power-dive, pull out, roll, sideslip, trim, undershoot, whipstall.

adv. **11.** **1. aerially** aeronautically, astronautically, cosmonautically.

RELATED KEYWORDS: ASCENT, DIVE, MOVEMENT, TRANSPORT, TRAVEL, VEHICLE

FOLD

n. **1.** **1. fold** buckle, cockle, crease, crimp, crumple, dog-ear, ruck, ruga, rumple. **2. wrinkle** cockle, crinkle, crow's-foots, laugh-line, laughter line, line, pucker, rugosity. **3. pleat** box pleat, knife pleat, pintuck, plait, tuck. **4. hem** cuff, lap, lapel, lappet, trouser-cuff, turn-up *(British)*. **5. frill** falbala, flounce, furbelow, gathering, gathers, ruche, ruff, ruffle, shirr, shirring, smocking.

    2. **1. ridge** anticline, arris, bank, carina, chenier, costa, embankment, isocline, knurl, razorback, ripple, ripplemark, stop-ridge, stria, striation, strix. **2. corrugation** carination. **3. corrugated material** corrugated board, corrugated iron, corrugated paper.

    3. **1. folding** enfoldment, invagination, plication. **2. paper folding** origami.

adj. **4.** **1. folded** accordion, complicate, conduplicate, dog-eared, double, doubled, replicate, turn-up, turndown. **2. wrinkled** creased, crinkly, rugate, rugged, rugose, wrinkly. **3. frilly** crimpy, puckery, ruffed. **4. pleated** accordion-pleated, box-pleated, kilted, plicate.

    5. **1. corrugated** carinal, carinate, knurled, ribbed, striate, strigose.

v. **6.** **1. fold** crease, crumple, dog-ear, ruck. **2. wrinkle** cockle, crimple, crinkle, furrow, knit, line, pucker, purse, scrumple, shrivel. **3. corrugate** concertina, knurl, ridge, rumple. **4. buckle** double up, jackknife. **5. pleat** kilt, pintuck, tuck. **6. fold over** enfold, hem, interfold, lap, reflex, turn back, turn down, turn up, wrap. **7. frill** crimp, crimple, drape, gather, gauge, goffer, ruck, shirr, smock.

RELATED KEYWORDS: FURROW, OVERTURN

FOOD

n. **1.** **1. food** alimentary, ambrosia, bite, comestible, commons, consumable, esculent, fare, fuel, health food, kai moana *(NZ)*, manna, nourishment, nurture, nutrient, nutriment, nutrition, pabulum, roughage, solids, staple diet, sustenance, table, tack, viand *(Philippine English)*, viands, victuals, wholefood. *Informal:* chow, dodger, grub, kai, kosher, munga, pot luck, scoff, scran, slipslop, tucker. **2. nourishment** alimentary, alimentation, diet, drip-feed, food, nurture, nutriment, nutrition, nutritiveness, sustenance, sustentation. **3. provisions** board, cheer, compo rations, eats, edibles, foodstuff, lazy ration, meat, provender, ration, scouse. **4. goodies** dainty, delicacy, eatables, eats, good cheer, refreshments. *Informal:* num-num, num-nums, nyum-nyum, tuck *(Chiefly British)*. **5. bush tucker** bush food, mai *(Aboriginal English)*, manna, mayi *(Aboriginal English)*, tuck-out *(Aboriginal English)*. **6. convenience food** fast food, frozen food, junk food. **7. stodge** *(Informal)* slops, swill. *Informal:* blotting paper. **8. animal food** beebread, drought-feed, fodder, forage, pig swill, pig-swill, pigwash. *Informal:* pig-tucker *(NZ)*.

    2. **1. drink** amrita, beverage, draught, drinkables, drinking water, nectar, potables, wash. *Informal:* dishwater, eye-opener, heart-starter, pipe-opener. **2. tea** billy tea, black tea, brew, bush tea, Darjeeling, green tea, gunpowder, hyson, Jack the Painter, maté, oolong, orange pekoe, Paraguay tea, pekoe, saloop. *Informal:* chai, char, cuppa, post-and-rail tea. **3. coffee** café au lait, cappuccino, coffee royal, congou, drip coffee, espresso, expresso, flat white, Irish coffee, long black, macchiato, milk coffee, mocha, mokha, mugaccino, percolated coffee, plunger coffee, short black, vienna. *Informal:* cap. **4. soft drink** barley water, breville, chalybeate, cider, cider-cup, coke, cola, cool drink, cooldrink *(Aboriginal*

English), cordial, creaming soda, crush, cyder, fizz *(Chiefly US)*, fizzy cordial, fizzy drink, fruit cup, ginger ale, ginger beer, hydromel, ice-cream soda, julep *(US)*, lemon squash, lemonade, mead *(US)*, mineral water, orangeade, orgeat, pop, ptisan, punch, root beer *(US)*, sarsaparilla, seltzer, soda, soda-water, spa water, spider, squash, sweet cider, tonic water, vichy water. *Informal:* dry, lolly water, tonic. **5. milk** acidophilus milk, beestings, buttermilk, colostrum, malted milk, milkshake, plasma, polymilk, shake, skim milk, the bottle, thick shake, whey, whole milk. *Informal:* cow juice. **6. eggflip** flip. *Informal:* Murrumbidgee oyster, prairie oyster. **7. guarana. 8. cocoa** chocolate. *Informal:* chocky.

3.   1. meal agape, banquet, barbecue, buffet, chop picnic, clambake *(US)*, collation, cookout *(US)*, feast, fete, fry *(US)*, gorge, hangi, junket, love feast, luau, meat and two veg, merrymaking, midnight feast, picnic, refection, repast, short order, smorgasbord, spree, table d'hôte, TV dinner, umu *(NZ)*. *Informal:* barbie, blow-out, chew-'n'-spew, feed, kai, nosh-up, sausage sizzle, spread, tuck-in. **2. snack** afternoon tea, afters, amuse-bouche, bite, cocktail, coffee break, continental breakfast, crib, Devonshire tea, finger food, little lunch, morning piece, morning tea, munchies, nibble, playlunch, refreshments, scroggin, trail mix. *Informal:* elevenses *(British)*, nosh. **3. breakfast** brunch, bush breakfast, déjeuner, wedding breakfast. *Informal:* brekkie. **4. lunch** big lunch, counter lunch, cut lunch, cut-lunch, fork luncheon, luncheon, oslo lunch, packed lunch, ploughman's lunch, pub lunch, tiffin. **5. dinner** fork dinner, high tea, progressive dinner, supper, tea. *Informal:* din-din, din-dins, dinnies. **6. course** à la mode, afters, antipasto, dessert, dish, entree, entremets, fork dish, hors d'oeuvre, pièce de résistance, plat du jour, pudding, savoury, side-dish, soupe du jour, starters, sweets. *Informal:* goodies, pud.

4.   1. meat breast, chine, chop, cut, eye fillet, fillet, flank, flesh, forequarter, gobbet, haunch, hindquarter, joint, knuckle, loin, marrowbone, mid loin, mince, mincemeat, neck, noisette, polymeat, red meat, rib loin, rolled roast, shank, shoulder, specialty cut, tenderloin, undercut. **2. beef and veal** air-beef, aitchbone, baron, baron of beef, beefsteak, blade, bladebone, bobby veal, bolar blade, brisket, butt, chateaubriand, chuck steak, clod, club steak, cube roll, delmonico steak, edgebone, entrecote, escalope, filet, filet mignon, fillet, fricandeau, gravy beef, ground beef *(US)*, oyster blade, polybeef, rib eye, rib steak, rolled beef, round steak, rump, scaloppine, schnitzel, Scotch fillet, set of ribs, shin, silverside, sirloin, skirt steak, spencer roll, staggering bob, steak, steakhouse, stirk veal, surloin, T-bone steak, topside, tournedos, Wiener schnitzel. **3. lamb and mutton** best neck, chump chop, colonial goose, crown roast, cutlet, gigot, hog, hogget, rack of lamb, saddle, scrag, short loin chop, sucker lamb. *Informal:* banjo, concertina. **4. pork** butt, butterfly steak, collar, crackling, cracknels, cushion, foreloin, hock, medallion steak, pork fillet, spare ribs, spring, spring of pork, sucking-pig. **5. miscellaneous meats** chevon, coney, cony, grenouilles, horseflesh, horsemeat, huhu, huhu grub, jugged hare, kangaroo, venison, witchetty grub. *Informal:* bunny, rabbit, underground mutton. **6. offal** bone marrow, brains, chitterlings, cow heel, fancy meat, harslet, haslet, kidney, lamb's fry, liver, marrow, numbles, oxtail, oxtongue, pettitoes, pluck, souse, sweetbread, tongue, tripe, trotter, variety meat. **7. long pig. 8. preserved meat** biltong, bully, charqui, jerk, junk, mahogany beef, pemmican, salt pork. *Informal:* bully beef, tinned dog.

5.   1. meat dishes adobo, beef stroganoff, blanquette, cabob, cannelloni, carbonade, carpetbag steak, casserole, chilli, chilli con carne, chop suey, club steak, cottage pie, couscous, croquette, curry, delmonico steak, dim sim, dim sum, dolmades, doner kebab, faggot, fricassee, galantine, gallimaufry *(US)*, goulash, grill, hash, hotchpotch, hotpot, Irish stew, kebab, korma, lobscouse, mami, meat loaf, meat pie, meatball, mixed grill, moussaka, mulligan stew, nasi goreng, navarin, olla, olla-podrida, osso buco, paella, pancake roll, pastie, paupiette, pepper pot, pilaf, pilau, piperade, pot roast, pot-au-feu, quenelle, réchauffé, ragout, raznici, risotto, rissole, roast, roulade, salmagundi, salmi, saltimbocca, sambal goreng, satay, sauté, Scotch collops, shashlik, shepherd's pie, shish kebab, skilly *(British)*, steak diane, steak tartare, stew, stroganoff, sukiyaki, Swiss steak, tamale, tartar steak, teriyaki, timbale, vindaloo. *Informal:* chew-'n'-spew.

6.   1. fish anthias, barracuda, bloater *(Chiefly British)*, Bombay duck, buckling, bummalo, callop, candlefish, caviar, char, cod, coral trout, eulachon, filefish, fillet, flake, freshwater bream, golden perch, kipper, lax, leatherjacket, mackerel, Murray perch, pilchard, red emperor, red herring, red mullet, rollmop, salmon, sea pike, seafood, silverfish, stockfish, triggerfish, turbot, whitefish, yellow mullet, yellow-belly, yellowfin tuna. *Informal:* barra, barracouta *(NZ)*, Dolly Varden, finnan haddie haddock, pillie. **2. shellfish** abalone, bêche-de-mer, Balmain bug, coral, crab, crabmeat, crawbob, crawchie, crawfish, craybob, craydab, crayfish, ear fish, escargot, koura *(NZ)*, langouste, lobby *(Chiefly Qld)*, lobster, Moreton Bay bug, mutton-fish, oyster, prawn, quahog, rock lobster, scallop, scampi, scollop, sea crayfish, sea ear, seafood, shovel-nosed lobster, shrimp, soft-shelled crab, spiny lobster, Sydney rock oyster, toheroa, yabby. *Informal:* cray. **3. fish dishes** cocktail, fish and chips, fish cocktail, fish finger, fishcake, gefilte fish, kedgeree, lobster Newburg, lobster thermidor, lox, matelote, prawn cocktail, prawn cutlet, sashimi, sea pie, seafood cocktail, spitchcock, tempura. *Informal:* greasies.

7.   **1. smallgoods** charcuterie. **2. ham** bacon, flitch, gammon, ham-de-luxe, pastrami, prosciutto, rasher, speck. **3. sausage** Aberdeen sausage, battered sav, Belgium sausage, black pudding, blood pudding, blood sausage, bologna sausage, bratwurst, brawn, cabana, cabanossi, camp pie, chipolata, chorizo, cocktail frankfurt, continental frankfurt, csabai, dagwood dog, devon, dippy dog, empire sausage, frankfurt, fritz, garlic, garlic sausage, German sausage, haggis, kabana, kabanossi, knackwurst, liver sausage, liverwurst, luncheon meat, luncheon sausage, mortadella, pepperoni, pluto pup, polony, pork fritz, provolone, salami, sausage meat, saveloy, spam, vienna, wiener *(US)*, Windsor sausage, wurst. *Informal:* bag of mystery, banger, boloney, cheerio, footy frank, franger, little boy, mystery bag, rillettes, sav, snag, snagger, snarler, snork, snorker, starver. **4. pâté** foie gras, pâté de foie gras, terrine.

8.   **1. poultry** boiler, broiler, capon, chick, chicken, domestic fowl, drumstick, duck, fowl, goose, griller, poulard, poussin, quail, spatchcock, turkey, white meat. *Informal:* chook, chookie. **2. game** mutton-bird, ortolan, partridge, pheasant, ring-necked pheasant, titi *(NZ)*. **3. chicken dishes** chicken à la king, cock-a-leekie, cocky-leeky, coq au vin, gombo, gumbo *(Chiefly US)*, suprême. **4. pope's nose** giblets, parson's nose.

9.   **1. vegetable** alfalfa *(Chiefly US)*, alligator pear, aloo, alu, artichoke, artichoke heart, asparagus, aubergine, avocado, baby marrow, bean, bean shoot, bean sprout, beech orange, beet, beetroot, Belgian endive, bell pepper, blackfellow's bread, blackfellow's yam, bok choy, brinjal *(Asian English)*, broad bean, broccoli, broccolini, brussels sprout, burdock, burnet, butterbean, butternut, butternut pumpkin, button mushroom, cabbage, capsicum, cardoon, carrot, cassava, cauliflower, celeriac, celery, celery cabbage, champignon, chanterelle, chard, chayote, chicory, Chinese broccoli, choko, collard, cos, costmary, courgette, cress, cucumber, eddo, eggfruit, eggplant, elephant's ear, endive, eschalot, faba bean, fava bean, field mushroom, French bean, frijol, globe artichoke, gram, gramma *(NSW)*, green bean, green corn, green gram, green pepper, green vegetable, greenstuff, Haas avocado, haricot, jack bean, Jerusalem artichoke, kale, kamote *(Philippine English)*, kohlrabi, leek, legume, lettuce, love apple, Maori cabbage *(NZ)*, marrow, marrow squash *(US)*, marrowfat pea, merino, mirrnyong, mung bean, murrnong, mushroom, myrrnong, neep *(Scottish)*, okra, onion, orach, oyster plant, parsnip, pea, pepper, petits pois, pimiento, plantain, potato, pratie *(Irish)*, puha, pumpkin, puwha, radish, rampion, ramsons, rauriki *(NZ)*, red bean, red beet, red cabbage, runner bean, rutabaga *(US)*, samphire, savoy, scallion *(Chiefly US)*, scarlet runner, shallot, shell bean *(US)*, silver beet, silverbeet, snapbean *(US)*, snow pea, sorrel, Spanish onion, spinach, spring onion, sprout, squash *(US)*, strawberry tomato, string bean, succory, sugar pea, swede, sweet corn, sweet pepper, sweet potato, Swiss chard *(US)*, sword bean, taro, tomato, turnip, udo, veg., vegetable marrow, water-chestnut, watercress, wax bean *(US)*, white potato, witlof, witloof chicory *(US)*, yam, yam daisy, zucchini. *Informal:* avo, caulie, chat, cuie, cukie, greens, martie, murphy, mushie, sparrowgrass, spud, tater, veggie. **2. dried vegetables** bean, bean curd, butter bean, chickpea, dal, dhal, French green lentil, lentil, lima bean, pea, pulse, soya bean, split pea, tofu, white bean. **3. vegetable dishes** baked beans, bhaji, bubble-and-squeak, cabbage roll, caesar salad, chip, colcannon, coleslaw, crudité, falafel, felafel, French fried potatoes, French salad, fried rice, hommos, hoummus, hummus, jardinière, julienne, lumpia, macedoine, maya, mirepoix, pancake roll, popiah *(Singaporean and Malaysian English)*, potato cake, potato chip, potato scallop, printanier, ratatouille, Russian salad, salad, sauerkraut, scallop, shoestring potatoes, side salad, slaw, Spanish rice, spring roll, succotash, tabouli, tossed salad, waldorf salad. *Informal:* chippie, rabbit food. **4. nut steak** extruded protein, nut cutlet, spun protein, TVP.

10.   **1. fruit** amarelle *(US)*, apple, apricot, Asian pear, babaco, banana, bilberry, bitter orange, black sapote, blackberry, blackcurrant, blackheart, blaeberry, blood orange, blueberry, boysenberry, breadfruit, calabash nutmeg, caltrop, cantaloupe, Cape gooseberry, ceriman, cherimoya, cherry, cherry-plum, chiku, Chinese gooseberry, chocolate pudding fruit, chucky chucky, citron, clementine, cling peach, clingstone, codling, colane, Cox's orange pippin, crab-apple, cranberry, cumquat, currant, custard apple, damson, date, Delicious, dragon's eye, drupe, eater, elderberry, emu-apple, fig, foxgrape, fruit salad plant, gage, geebung, genipap, Golden Delicious, gooseberry, goosegog, Granny Smith, grape, grapefruit, greengage, greening, grenadine, ground cherry, gruie, guanabana, guava, hackberry, hanepoot, honeydew melon, huckleberry, jackfruit, Japanese loquat, Japanese medlar, jonathan, jostaberry, kiwi berry, kiwifruit, konini, kumquat, lady's finger, ladyfinger, lamyai, lemon, lichee, lichi, lime, litchi, loganberry, longan, loquat, lotus, lungan, lychee, malaga, mamey, mammee, mandarin, mandarine, mango, mangosteen, manzanilla, marasca, Marsanne, May apple, miracle fruit, miraculous fruit, monstera deliciosa, morello, mulberry, muscadel, muscatel, muskmelon, naseberry, nashi pear, navel orange, nectarine, olive, orange, papaw, passionfruit, pawpaw, peach, pear, Pekingese, persimmon, pineapple, pineapple guava, pippin, plum, pomegranate, pomelo, pommelo, prickly custard apple, pumelo, quince, rambutan, raspberry, redcurrant, rhubarb, rockmelon, rose hip, russet, sapodilla, Seville orange, shaddock, sloe, sorb, sour gourd, sour orange, soursop, star-apple, stone fruit, strawberry, sweet orange, sweeting *(Chiefly British)*, tamarillo, tamarind, tangelo, tangerine, teaberry, tree tomato, ugli fruit, warden, water chestnut, watermelon, whiteheart, whortleberry, wine grape, youngberry. *Informal:* blackcap *(US)*, granny, jonnie, nana, pine, pinie. **2. dried fruits** acinus, craisin, currant, lychee nut, plum, prune, raisin, sultana. **3. nut** almond, bauple nut, beechnut, bopple nut, brazil, brazil nut, brazilwood, butternut, cashew, chestnut, cob, cobnut, coconut, cola, desert quandong, filbert, goober *(US)*, groundnut, hazelnut, hickory nut, katunga, kola nut, macadamia, macadamia nut, macapuno, macca, makapuno, marron, monkey nut, nutlet, peanut, pecan, pili, pine nut, pistachio, quandong, Queensland nut, quondong, shagbark *(US)*, shellbark, souari nut, Spanish chestnut, walnut.

11. 1. soup beef tea, bird's-nest soup, bisk, bisque, borsch, bouillabaisse, bouillon, brose *(Scottish)*, broth, brunoise, chowder, cock-a-leekie, cocky-leeky, consommé, cream, French onion soup, gazpacho, gumbo *(Chiefly US)*, kangaroo-tail soup, laksa, long soup, madrilène, minestrone, mock turtle soup, mulligatawny, okra, pea soup, potage, pottage, puree, Scotch broth, short soup, tea, toheroa, vichyssoise, won ton. *Informal:* loop-the-loop. **2. stock** court bouillon, fumet.

12. 1. cheese ambrosia, Appenzeller, Babybel, baker's cheese, Bega, bel paese, bierkäse, Bjelke blue, blue castello, blue cheese, blue vein, Bodalla, Bonbel, brie, burrino, cacio cavallo, Caerphilly, camembert, cheddar, cheedam, cheshire cheese, club, coeur à la crème, colby, cottage cheese, cream cheese, curd cheese, danablu, danbo, Danish blue, dunlop, Dutch cheese, edam, emmenthaler, erbo, feta, fetta, gbejna, Gloucester, goat (chèvre), gorgonzola, gouda, grana, gruyère, haloumi, havarti, jarlsberg, Kameruka, Kashkaval, kasseri, komijne kaas, Leicester, Leyden, Limburger, münster, mascarpone, matured, Mersey Valley cheese, mild, monterey, mozzarella, neufchâtel, New Zealand cheddar, parmesan, pecorino, pepato, pepper, philadelphia, plastic cheese, Port 'l Evêque, port-salut, processed cheese, provolone, ragnit, ricotta, romano, roquefort, Saint-André, samsoe, sapsago, savoury, scarmorze, sharp, smoked cheese, stilton, stracchino, strasbourg, swiss cheese, taffel, tasty cheese, tilsit, unity blue, Velveeta, vintage, wensleydale. *Informal:* bunghole, mouse cheese. **2. cheese dishes** buck rarebit, cauliflower cheese, fondue, macaroni cheese, mornay, rarebit, Welsh rarebit.

13. 1. egg albumen, double-yolker, eggwhite, googy-egg, yellow. *Informal:* cackle berry, cackle fruit, goog, hen fruit. **2. Easter egg. 3. egg dishes** egg roll, eggs Benedict, French toast, fried egg, mami, omelette, Scotch egg, Scotch woodcock, soufflé, Spanish omelette, toad-in-the-hole.

14. 1. pasta agnolotti, cannelloni, farfel, fettuccine, fusilli, gnocchi, lasagne, macaroni, maccaroni, noodle, penne, ravioli, rigatoni, risoni, spaghetti, spaghettini, tagliatelle, tortellini, vermicelli. *Informal:* spag.

15. 1. dessert affogato, apple charlotte, apple crumble, apple sauce, applepie, baba, baked custard, banana split, blancmange, bread and butter pudding, brown betty, cabinet pudding, canary pudding, charlotte, charlotte russe, cheesecake, Christmas pudding, cobbler, compote, condé, congress tart, cottage pudding, crème brûlée, crème caramel, cream caramel, crepe suzette, crumble, custard, flummery, fool, fruit cocktail, fruit salad, jelly *(US)*, junket, mousse, pandowdy *(US)*, pavlova, plum duff, plum pudding, posset, pudding, queen pudding, rice pudding, roly-poly, rum baba, sabayon, savarin, shortcake, sillabub, snow, snow pudding, spotted dick, spotted dog, suet pudding, summer pudding, trifle, zabaglione. *Informal:* frog's eggs, pav, pud. **2. ice-cream** alaska, baked alaska, bat, bombe, bombe Alaska, cassata, choc-ice, cone, coupe, double-header, frappé, fruit-ice, gelato, granita, ice, ice-cream cone, iceblock, icy pole, milk-ice, nesselrode, parfait, peach Melba, sherbet, sorbet, split, spumone, sundae, tutti-fruitti, vacherin, water-ice, whip.

16. 1. pastry apple strudel, baklava, choux pastry, Cornish pastie, cream horn, cream puff, croissant, croquembouche, croustade, custard slice, Danish pastry, daube, filo pastry, flaky pastry, flan-case, frangipane, French pastry, ˈlady's finger, ladyfinger, match, napoleon, neenish tart, pastie, piecrust, puff pastry, rough puff pastry, shortcrust pastry, strudel, tart, tartlet, turnover, vanilla slice, vol-au-vent. *Informal:* pus pie, snot-block. **2. pie** Bakewell tart, burek, cherry pie, custard pie, custard tart, flan, floater, hunza pie, meat pie, mince pie, pasticcio, pasty, patty, pizza, pork-pie, quiche, raised pie, samousa, sausage roll, umble pie. *Informal:* dog's eye, mystery bundle, Nellie Bly. **3. spring roll** chiko roll, dim sim, dim sum, lumpiang Shanghai, pancake roll, popiah *(Singaporean and Malaysian English)*, taco, won ton.

17. **1. cake** éclair, angel food cake, banbury cake, battenburg cake, butter cake, butterfly cake, Christmas cake, coffee cake, cream cake, cupcake, devil's food cake, fairy cake, fancy cake, fruit cake, fruit slice, gateau, Genoa cake, gingerbread, hedgehog cake, jelly cake, jumble, lamington, lardy cake, layer cake, Madeira cake, madeleine, maid of honour, marble cake, meringue, mocha, panettone, pascha, patisserie, patty cake, petit four, poundcake, profiterole, puff, queen cake, rock-cake, sand-cake, sandwich cake, seedcake, simnel cake, sponge, sponge cake, sponge sandwich, Swiss roll, tipsy cake, torte, upside-down cake, victoria sandwich, wedding cake. **2. biscuit** Afghan, amoretto, Anzac biscuit, arrowroot biscuit, brandysnap, cheese straw, chocolate crackle, cookie *(Chiefly US)*, cracker, cracknel, currant luncheon, digestive biscuit, Florentine, fortune cookie, fruit slice, garibaldi, ginger biscuit, ginger nut, gingersnap, hardtack, krupuk, macaroon, pretzel, ratafia biscuit, refrigerator biscuit, rusk, savoiardi biscuit, sea biscuit, ship's biscuit, shortbread, soda biscuit, sponge finger, tea biscuit, wafer, water-biscuit, wine biscuit, zwieback. *Informal:* bickie, bikkie, dead fly biscuit, fly cemetery, fly pie, squashed fly biscuit. **3. pancake** batter, beignet, blini, crepe, crumpet, dosa, drop scone, flapjack, French pancake, fritter, hotcake *(US)*, pikelet, popover, Scotch pancake, slapjack *(US)*, waffle, Yorkshire pudding. **4. doughnut** donut, doughie. *Informal:* hoop, sinker *(US)*, two bob.

18. **1. bread** Arab bread, bagel, baguette, bannock, bap, beygel, black bread, bread stick, brown bread, bun loaf, chapatti, chupardy, chupatti, cottage loaf, crispbread, dough, enzyme, farmhouse loaf, flatbread, French bread, gluten bread, grissini, hot bread, injera, lavash, Lebanese bread, loaf, malt loaf, matzo, milk bread, milk loaf, naan, nut loaf, oatcake, pappadum, pide, pipe loaf, pitta, pocket bread, pone *(US)*, popadum, poppadum, poppyseed loaf, pumpernickel, quick bread, raisin bread, ryebread, sandwich loaf, Scotch bun, soda bread, tank loaf, tortilla, tsoureki, twist, wheaten. *Informal:* husband-beater, long john *(NZ)*, wife-beater. **2. damper** beggars-on-the-coals, brownie, buckjumper, bush bread, bush plum cake, johnnycake. *Informal:* devil-on-the-coals, sod. **3. bun** bath bun, brioche, chelsea bun, cream bun, croissant, date and nut loaf, date loaf, drop scone, gem scone, griddlecake, horseshoe roll, hot cross bun, hot dog, kulich, muffin, puftaloon, roll, scone, teacake, yeast cake. **4. toast** croustade, crouton, fairy toast, French toast, Melba toast, raisin toast, sippet. **5. dumpling** dip, doughboy, gnocchi. **6. milksop** panada, pap, sop.

19. **1. sandwich** American sandwich, bread and butter, club sandwich, dagwood sandwich, Danish sandwich, fairy bread, jaffle, open sandwich, round, submarine. *Informal:* butty *(British)*, doorstep, sambo, sammidge, sammie, sanger, toastie *(NZ)*, toastie pie. **2. hamburger** beefburger, burger, cheeseburger.

20. **1. confectionery** acid drop, all-day sucker, angelica, barley sugar, blackball, blackjack, bonbon, brandyball, brittle, bubblegum, bullseye, butterball, butterscotch, cachou, candy *(US)*, candy floss, caramel, chew *(NZ)*, chewing gum, chocolate, chocolate truffle, coconut ice, confect, confection, confetti, conversation lolly, cotton candy *(US)*, cracker, creams, dolly mixture, drop, Easter egg, fairy floss, fondant, fruit gum, fudge, gobstopper, Grecian delight, gum, gumdrop, halva, hokey-pokey *(Chiefly NZ)*, humbug, hundreds and thousands, jelly baby, jelly bean, jube, jujube, licorice, liquorice, liquorice allsorts, lollipop, lolly, lozenge, marrons glacés, marshmallow, marzipan, milk chocolate, nonpareils, nougat, paddle-pop, panocha *(US)*, pastille, peanut brittle, pear drop, peppermint, praline, rainbow ball, rock, rocky road, rumball, snowball, sugar candy, sugar plum, sweet, sweetmeats, taffy *(US)*, toffee, toffee apple, truffle, Turkish delight. *Informal:* chewie, chewy, chockie, chocky, chokkie, chuddy, chuttie, gunk, jaw-breaker, stickjaw, sweetie.

21. **1. preserves** cheese, chow-chow, confection, conserves, damson cheese, jam, lemon cheese, maraschino cherry, marmalade, mincemeat, raspberry jam.

22. **1. sauce** à la king, ailloli, aioli, Alfredo sauce, allemande sauce, barbecue sauce, bearnaise sauce, bechamel sauce, belacan, beurre noire, black butter sauce, bolognaise sauce, bordelaise, bread sauce, caper sauce, catchup *(Chiefly US)*, chaud froid sauce, cocktail sauce, cream sauce, dressing, French dressing, gipsy sauce, glaze, gravy, gypsy sauce, hard sauce, hollandaise sauce, jus, marinade, matelote, mayonnaise, Melba sauce, mousseline sauce, pepper sauce, pesto, pickle, portugaise sauce, remoulade, Russian dressing, salad dressing, sauce béarnaise, sauce béchamel, sauce noire, soubise, tartare sauce, terasi, thousand island dressing, tomato sauce, topping, velouté, velvet sauce, vinaigrette sauce, white sauce, Worcestershire sauce, zingara sauce. **2. relish** blachan, black sauce, catsup, chilli sauce, French mustard, horseradish, ketchup, kinaki *(NZ)*, mustard, soya sauce, tahina, trasi. *Informal:* cornichon, dead horse. **3. pickles** achar, chutney, cocktail onion, dill cucumber, dill pickle, gherkin, piccalilli. **4. stuffing** farce, farcemeat, forcemeat, seasoning.

23. **1. seasoning** ajinomoto, birdseye chilli, caper, cassareep, Chinese salt, condiment, garlic salt, green ginger, masala *(Indian English)*, miso, monosodium glutamate, MSG, poppy seed, saffron, salt, sambal, sesame, tabasco, taste powder, vetsin *(Philippine English)*. **2. herb** adder's meat, ajowan, basil, bouquet garni, chervil, chive, dill, estragon, faggot, fines herbes, garlic, mint, oregano *(US)*, peppermint, potherb, salsify, tarragon, vegetable oyster, wort. **3. spice** allspice, angelica, anise, aniseed, asafoetida, black pepper, canella, caraway, cardamom, cassia, cayenne, Ceylon cinnamon, cinnamon, cumin, curry powder, fenugreek, galangal, garam masala, ginger, lemongrass, mace, masala *(Indian English)*, nutmeg, paprika, pepper, pimento, red pepper, tamara, turmeric, vanilla, white pepper. **4. vinegar** brine, vanillin, verjuice.

24. **1. sugar** beet sugar, brown sugar, cane sugar, caster sugar, castor sugar, coffee crystals, confectioners' sugar *(US)*, cube sugar, d-glucose, demerara, dextroglucose, dextrose, frosting, glucose, granulated sugar, grape sugar, icing, icing sugar, lactose, laevoglucose, levoglucose *(US)*, loaf sugar, mannose, milk sugar, muscovado, palm sugar, panocha *(US)*, piping, powdered sugar *(US)*, royal icing, saccharose, sorghum, spun sugar, sucrose, sugar loaf, sugar of milk, sweetening. **2. honey** blackstrap, corn syrup *(US)*, flax honey *(NZ)*, golden syrup, honey bee *(Aboriginal English)*, honeybag, honeybee sugar *(Aboriginal English)*, mel, molasses *(US)*, sorghum, sugarbag *(Aboriginal English)*, syrup, treacle. *Informal:* bullocky's joy, Bundaberg honey, cocky's joy, honey pot, Murrumbidgee jam. **3. malt** malt extract. **4. lerp** manna.

25. **1. grain** arrowroot, barley, barleycorn, brown rice, buckwheat, bulgur, burghul, cereal, corn *(US)*, cracked wheat, durra, durum wheat, grist, grits, groats, hard wheat, Indian corn, kaoliang, maize, mealies *(South African)*, millet, oats, paddy, Patna rice, pearl barley, pearl millet, popcorn, rice, rice paddy, rye, sago, spelt, teff, triticale, wheat, whole-wheat. **2. flour** arrowroot, cassava, coontie, corn meal, cornflour, cornstarch *(US)*, custard powder, farina, gluten flour, Indian meal, manioc, meal, nardoo, oatmeal, pinole, plain flour, poi, polenta, salep, self-raising flour, semolina, starches, tapioca, wheatmeal. **3. wheat germ. 4. breakfast foods** cornflake, cornflakes, muesli, rice bubbles, rolled oats. **5. porridge** bergoo, burgoo, fromenty, frumenty, gruel, hominy, loblolly, pease pudding, polenta. *Informal:* moosh, mush.

26. **1. fat** bard, bran, cacao butter, chaff, cocoa butter, coconut butter, copha, dripping, fatback, grease, lard, lardoons, leaf-lard, margarine, oleomargarine, palm butter, shortening, suet, vegetable butter. *Informal:* axle-grease, axlegrease, marg, marge. **2. oil** canola oil, cottonseed oil, nut oil, oleo oil, olio, olive oil, palm oil, safflower oil, salad oil, sesame oil. **3. butter** butterfat, Chantilly, clotted cream, dairy butter *(NZ)*, Devonshire cream, ghee.

27. **1. cream** single cream *(British)*, sour cream. **2. yoghurt** bonnyclabber, clabber, condensed milk, curd *(Indian English)*, evaporated milk, furfur, matzoon. **3. coconut milk** coconut cream, coconut water.

28. **1. spread** dip, fishpaste, marmite, paste, peanut butter, peanut paste *(Qld, WA, SA)*, peanut spread, vegemite. **2. dip** baba ganoush, bagoong, belacan, guacamole, hummus, pate de foie gras, savoury dip, tapenade, taramasalata, tzatziki.

29. **1. appetiser** angel-on-horseback, canapé, crisp, crudité, devil-on-horseback, savoury, whet, yum cha. **2. titbit** bit, breadcrumbs, crumb, morceau, morsel, nibble, potato crisp, prawn crisp, scraps, shred, tidbit *(US)*.

30. **1. raising agent** baking powder, baking soda, bicarb, bicarbonate of soda, cream of tartar, leaven, sodium bicarbonate, sourdough, yeast.

31. **1. fodder** agistment, alfalfa *(Chiefly US)*, artificial grass, beastings, bee-bread, beech mast, beestings, biestings, birdseed, bonemeal, browse, calf starter, canary seed, carob, concentrate, cotton cake, cottonseed meal, crumble feed, deerlick, drought feed, ensilage, feed, feed grain, fishmeal, food grain, forage, good pick, gram, grass, greenfeed, haycock, haymow, hayrick, haystack, herbage, hognut, improved pasture, lap, linseed cake, lotus, lucerne, mash, mast, mineral block, nosebag, oilcake, pasturage, pasture, perennial rye, pigswill, pigwash, pollard, provender, rape-cake, red clover, run-off *(NZ)*, salt-lick, sheep nuts, silage, slop, soilage, St John's bread, stockfeed, stover, swill, trail feeding, yarran, zero grazing. *Informal:* dog-tucker, pig-tucker *(NZ)*.

32. **1. eater** banqueter, breakfaster, crammer, deipnosophist, dietarian, dieter, digester, diner, epicurean, feaster, feeder, freegan, gobbler, gorger, gulper, junketer, masticator, muncher, nibbler, omnivore, swallower, turophile. *Informal:* carboholic. **2. epicure** gastronome, gastronomist, gormand, gourmand, gourmet. **3. vegetarian** fruitarian,

vegan. *Informal:* vegie, vego. **4. carnivore** flesh-eater, meat-eater. **5. cannibal** anthropophagi, anthropophagite, anthropophagus, man-eater. **6. geophagist** omophagist. **7. drinker** swiller. *Informal:* quaffer.

33. 1. eating absorption, assimilation, deglutition, digestion, engorgement, eupepsia, feasting, gastronomy, ingestion, ingurgitation, mastication, monophagia, monophagy, omophagia, polyphagia. **2. cannibalism** anthropophagy. **3. geophagy** geophagism. **4. swallow** bolus, gulp.

34. 1. dietary regime ethical eating, fruitarianism, lacto-ovo-vegetarianism, lacto-vegetarianism, raw food movement, raw-foodism, vegetarianism.

35. 1. hunger edaciousness, edacity, hungriness, pecker, stomach, turophilia, voraciousness, voracity.

36. 1. restaurant B.Y.O., bevery, bistro, brasserie, buffet, buffet car, caf, cafe, cafeteria, canteen, chophouse *(British, US)*, coffee bar, coffee house, coffee shop, diner, dining car, dining hall, dining room, eating house, espresso bar, estaminet, grill, grillroom, inn *(British)*, kiosk, luncheonette, meals on wheels, mess, milk bar, pizzeria, pull-in *(British)*, refectory, restaurant car, roadhouse, saloon car, self-service, snack bar, soda fountain *(US)*, soup kitchen, steakhouse, take-out, takeaway, tavern, tea-garden, tea-house, tearoom, teashop *(British)*, trattatoria, tuckshop, wardroom. *Informal:* caff, eatery, el cheapo, greasy spoon, hash house, joint, noshery, ref, refec.

37. 1. food science dietetics, gastronomy, molecular gastronomy, molecular mixology.

adj. **38. 1. eating** apivorous, baccivorous, carnivorous, carpophagous, coprophagous, coprophilous, entomophagous, flesh-eating, geophagous, graminivorous, granivorous, herbivorous, insectivorous, maigre, monophagous, myrmecophagous, omnivorous, omophagic, omophagous, phytophagous, piscivorous, rhizophagous, vegetarian, vermivorous, xylophagous, zoophilous. **2. cannibal** anthropophagic, anthropophagical, anthropophagous, cannibalistic. **3. dinnertime** lunch, post-prandial, postcibal, prandial, pre-prandial. **4. ingestive** internal.

39. 1. nutritive alible, alimental, alimentative, nourishing, nutrient, nutritional, nutritious, sustentative, trophic. **2. dietetic** cardioprotective, lite, low-fat, polyunsaturated.

v. **40. 1. eat** bolt, consume, cram, degust, devour, down, drink, eat like a horse, engorge, glut, gobble, gollop, gorge, gulp, guzzle, ingest, ingurgitate, kaikai *(Aboriginal English)*, live on, overeat, pick, raven, refresh, refresh oneself with, sate, slurp, snack, stodge, stuff, sup, swallow, swill, take, taste, wash down, weigh into, wolf. *Informal:* bog in, chow down, demolish, dig in, get into, get outside of, get stuck into, grub, hoe in, hoe into, knock back, knock off, nosh, pick at, pig out, put away, scoff, sink, stake up, toss off, tuck in, tuck into (or away). **2. chew** bite, browse, champ, chaw *(US Dialect)*, masticate, mumble, munch, nibble, snap, take. *Informal:* chomp, chumble *(British)*. **3. diet** be on a diet. **4. dine** banquet, break bread, breakfast, dine out, do lunch, eat out, feast, junket, lunch, mess, picnic, put on the feedbag, sup, tiffin, wine and dine. **5. flash one's dover** *(Informal)*. **6. digest** absorb, assimilate, keep down, stomach. **7. predigest** peptonise.

41. 1. feed bottle-feed, breastfeed, drip-feed, eat, nourish, nurse, nurture, regale, spoon-feed, subsist, suckle. *Informal:* grub. **2. keep a good table. 3. serve** dish up.

42. 1. hunger *Informal:* fang, have hollow legs, have the munchies. **2. thirst**.

43. 1. drink absorb, consume, down, drain, imbibe, lap, quaff, refresh oneself with, rehydrate, sip, slurp, suck, swallow, swill. *Informal:* bend one's elbow, chug-a-lug, knock down, raise one's elbow, scull, sink, sock away, swig, toss off, wet one's whistle.

44. 1. pasture agist, depasture. **2. graze** block-graze, browse, crash-graze, creep-graze, graze back (or down), ruminate. **3. feed** fatten, feedlot, fodder, force-feed, handfeed, open-graze, soil, stall-feed, winterfeed. **4. range** run, winter. **5. circumvallate. 6. crumble-feed. 7. flesh**.

adv. **45. 1. nutritionally** alimentally, dietetically, gastronomically, nutritively, trophically.

RELATED KEYWORDS: OVERINDULGENCE, ALCOHOL, COOKERY, PLANTS, ANIMALS, OIL, PLEASANT FLAVOUR, TASTE

FOOL

n. **1. 1. fool** ass, automaton, blockhead, blunderbuss, booby, buffer, bullhead, clod, clodpate, clodpoll *(British)*, cretin, cuckoo, dillpot, dolt, donkey, driveller, drongo, duffer, dullard, dunce, dunderhead, emptyhead, fathead, foolish virgin, gawk, gimp, goose, idiot, imbecile, jackass, jay, knucklehead, lardhead, log of wood, loggerhead, loon, lostie, lowbrow, lubber, meat-head *(Chiefly US)*, moron, muddle-head, nincompoop, nitwit, noddy, noodle, popinjay, sawney, silly, simple, simpleton, spaghetti-for-brains, spastic, tomfool, twaddler, twirp, village idiot, wacker. *Informal:* b.f., berk, bevan *(Especially Qld)*, billy goat, Billy Muggins, bimbette, blob, bonehead, boob, boofhead, bozo *(Chiefly US)*, bullethead, bunny, butthead, charlie, chinless wonder, chucklehead, chump, clot, clown, coot, cough drop *(British)*, der, dick, dickbrain, dickhead, dill, dillberry, dimwit, ding-a-ling, dipstick, ditz, dodo, donk, doofus, dope, dork, doughhead *(Chiefly US)*, doughie, drip, droob, drube, dumb Dora, dumbbell, dumbcluck, dumdum, dummy, eejit *(Chiefly Irish and Scottish)*, egg roll, fart, flathead, Fred Nerk, fruitloop, galah, galloot, galoot, gazob, gig, git *(Chiefly British)*, goat, goober, goof, goon, great ape, gup, half-axe, hen, hoon, idjut, imbo, jerk, joe, juggins, lamebrain *(US)*, lemon, log, loghead, lummox, lump, lunkhead *(US)*, melon, melonhead, minda, mong, moo, mopoke, mug, mug alec, muggins, mule, mutt, mutton-head, nana, nerd, nig-nog, ning-nong, ninny, nit, nong, nuff nuff, numbskull, numskull, nut, nut case, nutter, palooka, pea eater, peabrain, pinhead, poon, prat, pudding, pudding head, rabbit, random *(Chiefly US)*, retard, Richard Cranium, rock ape, sap, saphead, schlub *(US)*, schmo, schmuck, shlemiel, shmo, silly-billy, spaz, spinner, spoony, stem, stumbletum, stupid, thickhead, turkey, twerp, twit, wally, whacker, wild goose, woodenhead. **2. birdbrain** featherbrain, featherhead, flibbertigibbet, rattlebrain, scatterbrain. *Informal:* airhead, bimbo, bit of fluff, himbo *(US)*, whirligig, wooz.

RELATED KEYWORDS: INCOMPETENCE, FOOLISHNESS, STUPIDITY, IGNORANCE

FOOLISHNESS

n. **1.**   **1. foolishness** asininity, childishness, chuckleheadedness, clottishness, daftness, dizziness, fatuity, fatuousness, flightiness, folly, foolhardiness, frivolity, frivolousness, idiocy, imbecility, insipience, juvenileness, light-headedness, looniness, lunacy, madness, puerility, senselessness, silliness, stupidity, stupidness, unreason, unwariness, unwisdom, witlessness. *Informal:* goofiness. **2. ludicrousness** absurdity, absurdness, bathos, imbecility, nonsense, preposterousness, ridiculousness. **3. foolish fondness** dotage, infatuation, uxoriousness.

     2.   **1. folly** absurdity, bêtise, fatuity, foolery, lunacy, nonsense, puerility, stupidity, tomfoolery. *Informal:* brain explosion, midsummer madness. **2. foolery** apery, baboonery, buffoonery, carryings-on, stuff and nonsense, three-ring circus, tomfoolery. *Informal:* chenanigans, fandangle, funny business, shenanigans.

adj. **3.**   **1. foolish** anserine, baboonish, buffoonish, childish, clottish, empty, empty-headed, fatuous, footling, frivolous, idiotic, imbecilic, inane, light-headed, mad, puerile, senseless, shallow, silly, witless. *Informal:* moony, spoony, Uncle Willy. **2. featherbrained** daft, dilly, empty-headed, featherheaded, flighty, giddy, giggly, insipient, knuckleheaded, lamebrained, mad, scatterbrained, scatty. *Informal:* airhead, batty, chuckleheaded, cuckoo, daffy, dillberry, dippy, ditzy, dizzy, goofy, headless, like a chook with its head cut off, loony, mad as a two-bob watch, mental, mug, nitty, nutty, nutty as a fruitcake, off one's chump *(Chiefly British)*, off one's nut, pillock *(British)*, potty, sapheaded, sappy, silly as a two-bob watch, silly as a wet hen, sonky, spaz, spoony, twitty, wacky *(Chiefly US)*, whacky, yampy. **3. ludicrous** absurd, bathetic, crazy, farcical, imbecile, imbecilic, impertinent, inept, laughable, nonsensical, preposterous, rich, ridiculous, senseless, silly, tomfool, unearthly, zany. **4. imprudent** foolhardy, foolish, ill-advised, impolitic, incautious, indiscreet, rash, unadvised, unguarded, unwary, unwise, wild. **5. infatuated** besotted, doting, fond, infatuate, uxorious. *Informal:* sloppy, spoony.

v. **4.**   **1. behave like a fool** fool, fool around (or about), mess around (or about), muck about (or around), tomfool. *Informal:* act the (giddy) goat, act the angora, bugger about (or around), carry on like a pork chop, carry on like a two-bob watch, make a joe of oneself, play silly buggers, ponce about.

adv. **5.**   **1. foolishly** childishly, clottishly, daftly, dotingly, fatuously, idiotically, ill-advisedly, imbecilely, impoliticly, imprudently, inanely, infatuatedly, madly, puerilely, sillily, unguardedly, unwarily, witlessly. **2. ludicrously** absurdly, farcically, madly, nonsensically, preposterously. **3. light-headedly** dizzily, flightily, frivolously, goofily, senselessly, shallowly.

RELATED KEYWORDS: INCOMPETENCE, STUPIDITY, INSANITY, FOOL

FORCE

n. **1.**   **1. force** brute force, muscle, power, the sword, violence. **2. force majeure** juggernaut, steamroller, vis major. *Informal:* bulldozer. **3. threat** blackmail, Hobson's choice, pressure. **4. enforcement** exaction, penalty, sanction.

     2.   **1. forcefulness** powerfulness. **2. compulsion** coaction, coercion, constraint, duress, rape. **3. conscription** draft, impressment, press. **4. tyranny** arbitrariness, despotism,

Nazism, tyrannicalness. **5. intimidation** bullying, terrorisation. **6. forcedness** compulsion, compulsoriness, duress.

3. **1. forcer** coercer, compeller, constrainer, enforcer, exactor, impeller. *Informal:* toecutter. **2. drafter** press-gang. **3. tyrant** Caesar, despot, dictator, dictatrix, oppressor, supremo, tyranniser. **4. bully** bludgeoner, browbeater, bullyboy, hoodlum, hooligan, intimidator, nazi, standover man, swashbuckler, terroriser. *Informal:* bovver boy *(British)*, bruiser, bucko, bulldozer, hood.

adj. 4. **1. forced** coerced, compelled, constrained, hard-pressed. **2. conscript** conscripted, press-ganged. **3. coercible** compellable, constrainable.

5. **1. compulsory** compulsive, enforced, exactable, forced, forcible, mandatory, necessary, obligatory, required.

6. **1. forceful** driving, forcible, high-powered, powerful, strong, strong-willed. *Informal:* punchy, swingeing. **2. compelling** compulsive, constraining. **3. sledgehammer** bulldozing, steamroller. **4. tyrannical** absolute, arbitrary, authoritarian, despotic, dictatorial, hard-handed, Nazi, tyrannous. **5. intimidating** bullyboy, bullying, coactive, coercive, impellent, jack-booted, overbearing, terrorist, threatening. *Informal:* heavy.

v. 7. **1. force** bring someone to their knees, coerce, compel, constrain, dragoon, drive, enforce, juggernaut, lead by the nose, make, press, urge. **2. intimidate** blackmail, cow, give the third degree, menace, put the screws on, stand over, terrorise, threaten, wave a big stick. *Informal:* lean on, put the heat on, squeeze. **3. bully** blackjack, bludgeon, browbeat, bulldoze, bullyrag, steamroll, steamroller, throw one's weight around, tyrannise. *Informal:* railroad. **4. conscript** conscribe, draft, impress, press. **5. enforce** exact. **6. force someone's hand** *Informal:* rush. **7. insist on** demand, not take no for an answer, ram something down someone's throat, require. **8. override** pull rank.

adv. 8. **1. forcefully** forcibly, overpoweringly, powerfully, strong, strongly, vigorously. **2. tyrannically** arbitrarily, despotically, dictatorially, tyrannisingly. **3. coercively** intimidatingly, threateningly.

RELATED KEYWORDS: INSISTENCE, HARSHNESS, REPRESSION, POWER, RESTRAINTS, STRENGTH

FOREIGNNESS

n. 1. **1. foreignness** adventitiousness, alienage, alienism, exoticism, extraneousness, foreignism *(US)*, strangeness. **2. alienation** estrangement, exclusion. **3. migration** chain migration, emigration, immigration, transportation. **4. non-residency** dual citizenship, dual nationality.

2. **1. foreigner** alien, denizen, expatriate, outlander, outsider, stranger, tramontane. *Informal:* expat. **2. gentile** barbarian, tramontane. **3. ethnic** *(Informal)* Arab, continental. *Informal:* gweilo *(Hong Kong English)*, kwai loh *(Singaporean and Malaysian English)*. **4. refugee** asylum seeker, boat people, displaced person, DP. **5. illegal immigrant** deportee, removee. **6. foreign population** minority, out-group. **7. diaspora** exodus. **8. stray** adventive, straggler. **9. curiosity** exotic. **10. intruder** a grape on the business, gatecrasher, interloper, stowaway, trespasser, uninvited guest, unwelcome addition. **11. foreign body** inclusion, xenolith.

adj. 3. **1. foreign** alien, imported, non-resident, unacclimatised, unassimilated. **2. ethnic** exterritorial, extraterritorial. **3. gentile** barbarous, heathen, heathenish, pagan, paganish, profane, uncircumcised. **4. exotic** adventive, unfamiliar. **5. extraneous** adventitious, stray. **6. external** ecdemic, heterogenous, outside. **7. uninvited** excluded, intrusive.

adv. 4. **1. overseas** abroad, afield, in foreign parts, out. *Informal:* o.s. **2. exotically** outlandishly, strange, strangely.

RELATED KEYWORDS: EXCLUSION, STRANGENESS, TRAVEL

FORGETTING

n. 1. **1. forgetting** blackout, memory lapse, mental block, senior moment, total blank. **2. absent-mindedness** absence of mind, absentness, abstraction, forgetfulness, irretentiveness, obliviousness, obliviscence, preoccupation. **3. amnesia** anomia, fugue.

2. **1. forgetfulness** oblivion, silence. **2. Lethe** lotus land. **3. omission** nonfeasance, oversight, slip of the memory, slip of the mind.

3. **1. forgetter** absent-minded professor, amnesiac, lotus-eater. *Informal:* space cadet. **2. nepenthe** lotus.

187

adj.   **4.**   **1. forgetful** absent, absent-minded, abstracted, amnestic, distrait, irretentive, misty, oblivious, preoccupied, vague, woolly-minded. **2. amnesic** amnesiac, forgetful-making, nepenthean. **3. forgotten** forgot, out of mind, sunk in oblivion.

v.   **5.**   **1. forget** clean forget, have no recollection of, misremember. *Informal:* disremember, let in one ear and out the other. **2. consign to oblivion** blot out, bury, constrain, forget, live down, repress, unlearn, unteach. **3. be on the tip of one's tongue** be almost there. **4. go out of one's head** fly out of one's mind, slip one's mind.

    6.   **1. be forgetful** *Informal:* have a head like a sieve.

adv.   **7.**   **1. forgetfully** absent-mindedly, obliviously.

RELATED KEYWORDS: INATTENTION, CONFUSION, IGNORANCE

FORGIVENESS

n.   **1.**   **1. forgiveness** clemency, grace, mercy. **2. absolution** plenary indulgence, remission. **3. pardon** absolute emancipation, absolute pardon, amnesty, conditional pardon, exemption, forgiving, indemnity, remission, reprieve. **4. exoneration** acquittal, condonation, exculpation, excusal, justification, vindication.

    2.   **1. forgivingness** forbearance, forgiveness, leniency, lenity, magnanimity, magnanimousness, placableness.

    3.   **1. forgiver** condoner, excuser, pardoner, redeemer, sparer.

adj.   **4.**   **1. forgivable** absolvable, atonable, excusable, expiable, pardonable, remittable, venial.

    5.   **1. forgiving** absolutory. **2. magnanimous** placable.

v.   **6.**   **1. forgive** condone, discount, dismiss, disregard, extenuate, overlook, pass over, think no more of. **2. put the past behind one** let bygones be bygones. **3. pardon** absolve, amnesty, excuse, justify, shrive. **4. spare** acquit, clear, exculpate, exonerate, remit, reprieve. **5. show mercy** *Informal:* have a heart.

adv.   **7.**   **1. forgivingly** magnanimously, placably.

    8.   **1. forgivably** excusably, venially.

RELATED KEYWORDS: ACQUITTAL, INNOCENCE, JUSTIFICATION, LENIENCE, PITY

FORMALITY

n.   **1.**   **1. formality** ceremoniousness, ceremony, dignity, gravity, heraldry, pomp, pomp and circumstance, solemnities, solemnness, state, stateliness. **2. etiquette** form, protocol. **3. spit and polish** *Informal:* drill. **4. preciseness** correctness, gentility, precision, punctilio, punctiliousness, savoir faire, savoir vivre. **5. refinement** niceness. **6. reservedness** frigidity, ice, iciness, perfunctoriness, reserve. **7. stiffness** starch, starchiness, stiltedness, undemonstrativeness.

    2.   **1. formal occasion** ceremony, formal function, observance, rite, ritual, solemnities. **2. formalisation** solemnification, solemnisation.

    3.   **1. formal dress** academic dress, academicals, ball gown, black tie, class A's, court dress *(British)*, dinner jacket, dinner suit, dress, dress coat, dress suit, evening dress, formals, regalia, Sunday best, tails, uniform, white tie. *Informal:* best bib and tucker, number ones.

adj.   **4.**   **1. formal** ceremonial, ceremonious, courtly, dignified, official, ritual, ritualistic, solemn, state, stately. **2. precise** correct, starchy, stickling. **3. reserved** frigid, icy, perfunctory, stiff, stilted, undemonstrative, uneasy. **4. dress** full-dress. *Informal:* Sunday-go-to-meeting *(US)*.

v.   **5.**   **1. formalise** ceremonialise, officialise, solemnify, solemnise. **2. stand on ceremony** observe protocol.

adv.   **6.**   **1. formally** ceremonially, ceremoniously, courtly, precisely, reservedly, solemnly, starchily, stiffly, stiltedly. **2. perfunctorily** by the book, frigidly, icily, pro forma, undemonstratively.

RELATED KEYWORDS: CONFORMITY, COURTESY, CUSTOM, FASHION

FOUR

n.   **1.**   **1. four** quadruplicate, quartet, quaternary, quaternion, tetrad, tetralogy. **2. quadruplet** *Informal:* quad. **3. quadruple** quadrivalency, quadruplication. **4. quarter** fourth, quartering.

    2.   **1. square** quadrate, quadrum. **2. quadrilateral** diamond, lozenge, oblong, parallelogram, quadrangle, rectangle, rhomb, rhomboid, rhombus, tetragon, trapezium, trapezoid. **3. tetrahedron** triangular pyramid.

adj. **3.** **1. fourfold** foursome, quadruple, quadruplex, quadruplicate, quaternary. **2. quadripartite** quadrifid, quadrinomial, quadrivalent, quadrivial, quadruped, quartered, quaternary, tetramerous, tetravalent. **3. fourth** quarter.
4. **1. square** foursquare, quadrangular, quadrate, quadratic, quadrilateral, rectangular, squarish, tetragonal. **2. tetrahedral.**
RELATED KEYWORDS: SHAPE, PART

FREQUENCY

n. **1.** **1. frequency** commonness, constancy, continuity, frequentness, recurrence, regularity, relative frequency, repetition. **2. hertz** angular frequency, cycle, cycle per second, cycles per second, extremely high frequency, high frequency, kilohertz, low frequency, medium frequency, meg, megahertz, radiofrequency, super high frequency, ultra high frequency, very high frequency, very low frequency.

adj. **2.** **1. frequent** chronic, common, continual, ever-recurring, habitual, horary, hourly, incessant, invariant, perennial, recurrent, recurring, repeated, resumptive, steady. **2. repetitive** cyclic, harping, iterative, nagging, repetitional, repetitious, stuck in a groove, tautological. **3. regular** drumming, periodic, rhythmical. **4. worn-out** banal, cliché-ridden, clichéd, commonplace, dull, flat, hackneyed, mundane, musty, old, overused, pedestrian, stale, threadbare, trite, well-worn. **5. monotonous** singsong, unvarying. **6. multitudinous** a dime a dozen, all over the place, thick on the ground.

adv. **3.** **1. frequently** always, continually, many a time, oft *(Chiefly Poetic)*, often, recurrently, regularly, repeatedly, time after time.
RELATED KEYWORDS: MANY, REGULARITY, REPETITION

FRIENDLINESS

n. **1.** **1. friendliness** affableness, amiableness, amicableness, consociation, fellowship, friendship. **2. cordiality** approachability, approachableness, geniality, genialness, heartiness, hospitality. **3. warmth** warm-heartedness.
2. **1. friendship** backslapping, brotherhood, brotherliness, camaraderie, comradeship, fraternalism, fraternity, mateship, neighbourliness, sodality. *Informal:* mateyness. **2. fellow feeling** fellowship, solidarity, sympathy. **3. goodwill** regard. **4. intimacy** closeness, devotion, familiarity, intimateness, involvement, togetherness. **5. understanding** amity, entente. **6. fraternisation** acquaintance, acquaintanceship, association, companionship, company, consociation, conversation, fellowship, society. **7. greetings** open arms, salutation, welcome. **8. attentions** assiduities, embrace, endearment, handclasp, handshake, hug, kiss, squeeze.
3. **1. friend** amigo, bedfellow, chum, comate, companion, comrade, crony, cuz *(Aboriginal English),* ehoa *(NZ),* familiar, main man, mate, partner, playmate, schoolfriend, sparring partner, yokefellow. *Informal:* bud, buddy, buddy-buddy, china, cobber, digger, mucker *(British),* old fellow, pal, pard *(US),* pardner *(US),* sidekick. **2. well-wisher** ally, bunji *(Chiefly Qld and NT Aboriginal English),* supporter. **3. acquaintance** associate, contact, contact man, fraterniser, penfriend, penpal. **4. intimate** best friend, blood brother, bosom buddy, bosom friend, close friend, confidant. **5. inseparables** alter ego, birds of a feather, shadow, soul mate. **6. sweetheart** darl, darling, deary, love, lover, swain *(Chiefly Poetic),* truelove. *Informal:* ducky, sweetie. **7. girlfriend** nuba *(Aboriginal English). Informal:* bird, floozy, gf, girl, moll, potato peeler, sheila, squeeze. **8. boyfriend** beau. *Informal:* babester, bf, boy, fellow, guy, man, squeeze. **9. favourite** darling, pet. *Informal:* fave.
4. **1. forms of address** comrade, mate. *Informal:* kiddo. **2. brother** *Informal:* bro, cobber, cock *(British, Tasmania),* digger, sport. **3. sister** *(Aboriginal English)* auntie, aunty. *Informal:* girl.

adj. **5.** **1. friendly** affable, amiable, amicable, companionable, neighbourly, polite, sociable, social. *Informal:* matey, palsy-walsy. **2. chummy** brotherly, comradely, fraternal, on good terms, well in with. *Informal:* matey, pally. **3. warm-hearted** approachable, hearty, open-hearted, outgoing. *Informal:* folksy *(US),* homey. **4. welcoming** cordial, genial, hospitable, warm. **5. hail-fellow-well-met** backslapping, bluff, cordial, hearty, warm. **6. intimate** bosom, close, familiar, inseparable, thick as thieves. *Informal:* thick. **7. devoted** assiduous, staunch. **8. compatible** after one's own heart, of one mind, platonic, simpatico, sympathetic.

v. **6.** **1. be friends** associate with, be hand in glove with, be mates with, fraternise, get along with, get on with, hobnob, neighbour with, stick together. *Informal:* go around with, go with, knock around with, pal. **2. befriend** brother, chum up with, fall in with, make friends with. *Informal:* pal up with. **3. warm to** cotton on to, take to. *Informal:* click.

7. **1. welcome** be sociable, entertain, greet, receive. **2. keep in with** cultivate, ingratiate oneself. *Informal:* be all over, make one's marble good with, make up to.

adv. **8.** **1. friendlily** affably, amiably, amicably, cordially, friendly, heartily, warm-heartedly, warmly, with open arms. **2. devotedly** assiduously, devoutly. **3. intimately** familiarly, fraternally, hetaeristically.

RELATED KEYWORDS: KINDNESS, LOVE, PITY, SOCIABILITY

FRIGHT

n. **1.** **1. fright** alarm, awe, boggle, consternation, dismay, fear, horror, jumpiness, panic, phobia, scare, superstition, terror, the creeps. *Informal:* blue funk, funk, heebie-jeebies, the jitters, willies. **2. apprehension** alarm, angst, anxiety, anxiousness, apprehensiveness, care, concern, concernment, disquiet, disquietude, dread, misgiving, nervousness, performance anxiety, qualm, solicitude, trepidation, unease, uneasiness, worry. *Informal:* jimjams, worriment. **3. timidity** diffidence, shyness, timidness, timorousness, tremulousness. **4. tremble** cold shivers, cold sweat, horripilation, shudder, start, tremor.

2. **1. frightener** *(Informal)* affright, alarmist, bogey, bogeyman, bogle, bogy, bogyman, boogieman, bugaboo, bugbear, chamber of horrors, demoraliser, discourager, ghost, gorgon, hair-raiser, hobgoblin, holy terror, horror, intimidator, kehua *(NZ)*, phantasm, phantom, poltergeist, presence, scarecrow, scaremonger, scarer, shade, shadow, spectre, spinechiller, startler, taipo *(NZ)*, terrifier, terroriser, visitant. *Informal:* spook.

3. **1. frightfulness** awesomeness, awfulness, creepiness, direfulness, dreadfulness, eeriness, fearfulness, fearsomeness, forbiddingness, formidability, grimness, grisliness, horribleness, horridness, terribleness, uncanniness. **2. terrorisation** alarmism, demoralisation, discouragement, disheartenment, horrification, intimidation, terrorism.

4. **1. frightened person** blencher, milquetoast *(US)*, panic merchant, shyer.

adj. **5.** **1. frightened** abhorrent of, afraid, aghast, alarmed, awe-struck, horror-stricken, horror-struck, out of one's wits, panic-stricken, panicky, pavid, petrified, scared, shocked, terrified, terror-stricken, terror-struck, trembly, tremulant, tremulous, white. *Informal:* green at the gills, scared stiff, shit-scared, spooked, white at the gills. **2. timorous** anxious, apprehensive, cowardly, dispirited, faint-hearted, fear for, fearful, gun-shy, haunted, jittery, jumpy, nervous, nervy, on pins and needles, pavid, phobic, pigeon-hearted, shy, superstitious, timid, white-livered, worrisome. *Informal:* toey, windy.

6. **1. frightening** appalling, awe-inspiring, awesome, awful, bloodcurdling, chilling, creepy, Dantean, Dantesque, dire, direful, dread, dreadful, eerie, fearful, fearsome, forbidding, formidable, frightful, ghastly, grim, grisly, gruesome, hair-raising, horrendous, horrible, horrid, horrific, nerve-racking, nightmarish, redoubtable, redoubted, spinechilling, terrible, terrific, terrifying, uncanny, unnerving. *Informal:* crawly, creepy-crawly, hairy, scary, spooky.

v. **7.** **1. frighten** affright, alarm, appal, awe, blanch, consternate, curdle the blood, fear, freak, fright *(Poetic)*, horrify, make one's flesh creep, make someone's hair stand on end, panic, petrify, scare, strike fear into, terrify, terrorise, turn one's bowels to water. *Informal:* funk, put the breeze up, put the wind up, scare (or frighten) the (living) daylights out of someone, spook. **2. daunt** chill, dash, demoralise, discourage, dishearten, dismay, dispirit.

8. **1. be frightened** be at panic stations, get cold feet, have one's heart in one's boots, have one's heart in one's mouth (or throat), jump out of one's skin, lose one's nerve, press (or hit) the panic button, turn to jelly. *Informal:* freak out, get the wind up, go off the deep end, have (or take) a willy, have kittens, have the breeze up, pack death (or it). **2. fear** dread, misgive. **3. squib** *Informal:* funk. **4. tremble** blanch, blench, boggle, cower, quail, shake, shudder, shy, start, turn pale, waver.

adv. **9.** **1. frighteningly** alarmingly, appallingly, awesomely, awfully, chillingly, direfully, dreadfully, eerily, fearsomely, forbiddingly, formidably, grimly, hauntingly, horrendously, horribly, horridly, redoubtably, scaringly, terribly, terrifically.

10. **1. fearfully** affrightedly, anxiously, apprehensively, shyly, timidly, timorously, tremblingly, tremulously, with knees knocking.

RELATED KEYWORDS: ANXIETY, COWARDICE

FRONT

n. **1.** **1. front** A-side, face, fore edge, obverse. **2. head** heading, top. **3. forefront** firing line, fore, foreside. **4. front line** front *(Military)*. **5. anteriority** forwardness.

2. **1. facade** elevation, facing, front, frontage, frontispiece. **2. bow** bowsprit, cutwater, focsle, forecastle, hawse, head, nose, prow.

adj. **3.** **1. front** anterior, frontal. **2. forward** fore. **3. head** headmost. **4. obverse** facing-out, right.

v. **4.** **1. front** affront, face.

adv. **5.** **1. frontally** anteriorly, forwardly. **2. forward** ahead, before, fore, forwards, frontwards, in advance, onwards, to the fore. **3. headfirst** down by the head, head-on, headlong.

RELATED KEYWORDS: COMING BEFORE, EDGE, OUTSIDE, START, TOP

FUEL

n. **1.** **1. fuel** combustible, feed, firing, primer, priming. *Informal:* juice. **2. fuelling** bunkering, firing, fuel-injection, priming. **3. woodheap** pyre, woodpile. **4. firewood** billet, brushwood, faggot, greasebush, greasewood, log, matchstick, ovenwood, torchwood, wood. **5. kindling** firelighter, morning sticks *(Tasmania)*, tinder. **6. wick** gas mantle, mantle, touchpaper. **7. coal** anthracite, boghead coal, briquette, brown coal, coking coal, culm, hard coal, lignite, slack, wood coal. **8. coke** char, charcoal. **9. peat** turf. **10. gas** bottled gas, CNG, coal gas, liquefied petroleum gas, LPG, producer gas, town gas. **11. fossil fuel** benzine *(Chiefly US)*, carburant, derv *(British)*, diesel, diesel oil, dieseline, distillate, fuel oil, gas oil, gasoline *(Chiefly US)*, motor spirit, naphtha, oil, petranol, petrodiesel, petrol, petroleum, standard, super, unleaded, unleaded petrol. *Informal:* gas *(Chiefly US)*. **12. kerosene** alkane, avgas, paraffin, paraffin oil *(British)*. *Informal:* kero. **13. propellant** acetylene, borane, butane, carbinol, ethine, ethyl, ethyne, grain, heptane, isobutane, lead tetraethyl, liquid oxygen, methylpropane, pentaborane, propane, solid propellant, tetraethyl lead. *Informal:* lox. **14. incendiary** fireball, Greek fire, napalm, wildfire. **15. nuclear fuel** fuel element, pile, rod, uranium. **16. renewable fuel** biodiesel, biofuel, biogas, methane.

v. **2.** **1. fuel** bunker, coal, refuel, tank up. **2. fire** feed, feed the flames, lay a fire, prime, stoke, underfeed.

RELATED KEYWORDS: ATOM, ENERGY, FIRE, GAS, HEATING, OIL, THROW

FULLNESS

n. **1.** **1. fullness** capacity, impletion, maximum, one's fill, plenitude, satiety, saturation. **2. plenty** abundance, amplitude, copiousness, full and plenty, plentifulness. **3. tightness** completion, cram, engorgement, saturation point. **4. replenishment** fill-up, refill. **5. occupancy** possession, tenure.

2. **1. full amount** armful, bagful, barrelful, basinful, boatful, capful, dishful, eyeful, fistful, glassful, handful, houseful, kettleful, lapful, mouthful, pipeful, plateful, pocketful, potful, quiverful, sackful, shovelful. *Informal:* bellyful, earful, gutful, hatful, neckful, skinful. **2. full glass** bumper.

3. **1. filler** packager, packer, padder. **2. filling** backfill, grout, packing, padding, sandfill, shim, washer. **3. occupant** occupier, preoccupier.

adj. **4.** **1. full** chock-full, choke-full, chuck-full, cram-full, crammed, jammed, overcrowded, stopped. *Informal:* chock-a-block, chocka, chocker, full up, jam-packed. **2. brimful** brimming, topped up, well filled. **3. plentiful** ample, copious. **4. loaded** charged, heavy-laden, laden. **5. bulging** big with, pregnant with. **6. occupied** ensconced, in possession. **7. overfull** at saturation point, drowned, overflowing, rolling in, saturate *(Chiefly Poetic)*, saturated, slopping, swamped. **8. crowded** overfull, packed, plethoric, tight. **9. replete** *Informal:* full as a boot (or goog) (or tick) (or fart), full as a state school, full up. **10. bursting at the seams** gorged, sated.

v. **5.** **1. fill** brim, bumper, charge, fill up. **2. refill** replenish, top up. **3. pack** freight, lade, load. **4. occupy** ensconce oneself in, take possession of. **5. fill in** backfill, calk, caulk, chink *(US)*, chinse, grout, loam, pad, plaster, point, pug, shim, silt. **6. overfill** drown, saturate, swamp. **7. cram** choke, engorge, glut, jam, line, overpack, pack, ram, stuff. **8. overrun** crowd, throng.

adv. **6.** **1. fully** absolutely, completely, quite, wholly. *Informal:* plenty. **2. plentifully** amply, copiously. **3. tightly** solidly.

RELATED KEYWORDS: EXCESS, SATISFACTION, WHOLE

FUNERAL RITES

n. **1.** **1. funeral rites** exequies, funeral, obsequies, office of the dead, smoking ceremony, sorry business *(Aboriginal English)*. **2. burial** committal, entombment, immurement, inhumation, interment, intombment, inurnment, sati, sepulture. **3. cremation** incineration. **4. embalmment** mummification. **5. requiem** coronach, dead march, dirge, epicedium, knell, lament, last post, requiescat, requiescat in pace, taps *(US Military),* threnode, threnody. **6. obituary** elegy, epitaph, funeral oration, in memoriam, necrology, RIP. **7. lamentation** hartal *(Indian English),* vigil, wake. **8. mourning** black armband, crepe, half-mourning, kopi, sables, weed, weeds, widow's weeds. **9. funeral pyre** pile, pyre. **10. shroud** breasting, cerecloth, cerements, graveclothes, winding sheet. **11. death bell** minute gun, passing bell. **12. floral tribute** wreath. **13. funeral pole** pukamani pole. **14. mark of respect** half-mast, lowering of the flag, tolling of the bell.

  2. **1. coffin** casket, cist, columbarium, ossuary, sarcophagus, urn. **2. bier** hearse, pall. **3. corpse** mummy.

  3. **1. grave** resting place. **2. tomb** burial chamber, catacombs, cist, confession, cromlech, crypt, cubiculum, dolmen, grave, hypogeum, mastaba, mausoleum, samadhi *(Indian English),* sepulchre, undercroft, vault, yin house *(Asian English).* **3. burial mound** barrow, kurgan, tumulus. **4. headstone** alignment, cairn, central cylinder, gravestone, ledger, menhir, orthostat, stela, stele, stone, tombstone. **5. cenotaph** commemoration, memorial, monument, pantheon, war memorial. **6. watery grave** Davy Jones's locker, locker.

  4. **1. cemetery** burial ground, churchyard, field of Mars, garden of remembrance, God's acre, graveyard, necropolis, potter's field. *Informal:* boneyard, marble orchard. **2. crematorium** burning ghat, cinerarium, crematory. **3. mortuary** charnel, charnel-house, funeral parlour, morgue. *Informal:* deadhouse.

  5. **1. exhumation** disentombment, disinterment. **2. body-snatching**.

  6. **1. undertaker** burier, cremationist, ecclesiarch, embalmer, funeral director, gravedigger, mortician, sexton. **2. pallbearer** bearer, mourner, mute, weeper. **3. firing party**. **4. exhumer. 5. body-snatcher.**

adj. **7.** **1. funereal** funerary. **2. obituary** elegiac, obsequial, threnodic. **3. sepulchral** cinerary, crematory, cryptal, funereal, mausolean, mortuary, tomblike.

v. **8.** **1. mourn** pay one's last respects, salute, toll the bell. **2. bury** coffin, entomb, immure, inhume, inter, intomb, inurn, lay, lay to rest, pit, sepulchre, tomb, vault. **3. embalm** cere *(Poetic),* lay out, mummify, mummy, shroud. **4. lie buried** lie, lie six feet under. *Informal:* push up daisies.

  9. **1. exhume** disentomb, disinter, unearth.

RELATED KEYWORDS: GRIEF, DEATH

FURNITURE

n. **1.** **1. furniture** accoutrements, appointments, appurtenances, chattels, fittings, furnishings, furnishments, trappings. **2. movable** built-in. **3. types of furniture** bush furniture, domestic furniture, lawn furniture, office furniture, outdoor furniture, pool furniture. **4. timber furniture** teak furniture, whitewood furniture.

  2. **1. chair** banquette, basket chair, bentwood chair, butterfly chair, camp chair, camp stool, cane chair, captain's chair, carver, deckchair, dining chair, director's chair, dos-à-dos, fan-back chair, fiddleback, folding chair, garden chair, garden seat, highchair, kitchen chair, ladder-back chair, love seat, Morris chair, occasional chair, pull-up chair, seat, stacking chair, straight-backed chair, swivel chair, tete-a-tete, throne, tubchair, upholstered chair, vis-a-vis, window seat, Windsor chair, wing chair. **2. easychair** armchair, club chair, hanging chair, lounge chair, recliner, rocker, rocking chair, squatter's chair, squatter's delight, steamer chair, swing chair, TV chair, veranda chair. **3. stool** bar stool, bedroom stool, dressing stool, footrest, footstool, hassock, kitchen stool, milking stool, music stool, ottoman, piano stool, pouf, taboret, tripod, tuffet, vanity stool. **4. highchair** baby bouncer, bouncer, bouncinette, cuddle seat, high seat. **5. bench** form, ingle seat, pulvinar, settle, window seat. **6. toilet seat** lavatory seat. *Informal:* the throne.

  3. **1. couch** banana bed, banana chair, canapé, chaise longue, chaise lounge, chesterfield, conversation pit, cuddle seat, divan, fauteuil, lounge, lounge suite, settee, sofa. **2. sofa bed** davenport, day bed, night-and-day, studio couch. **3. cushion** bolster, ottoman, scatter cushion.

  4. **1. bed** bed base, bedhead, bedstead, berth, box bed, brass bed, bunk, charpoy, couch, couchette, divan, double bed, double-bunk, ensemble, featherbed, foldaway bed, folding bed, four-poster, four-poster bed, headboard, king-size bed, pallet, queen-size bed, roll-away bed, shakedown, sickbed, single bed, tester bed, three-quarter bed, twin bed, waterbed. *Informal:* doss, pad. **2. stretcher** air bed, air mattress, camp bed, camp stretcher, cot, hammock, li-lo, sleeping-bag, trestle bed, truckle, truckle bed, trundle bed. **3. cot** baby basket, bassinette, bosun's chair, carry basket, carrycot, child's bed, cradle, cradle scythe, creeper, crib, humidicrib, rocker. **4. mattress** bolster, Dutch wife, foam mattress, futon, inner-spring mattress, paillasse, pallet, palliasse, rubber mattress.

5. **1. table** bedside table, bench, butterfly table, card table, coffee table, counter, credence, draw table, dresser, dressing table, drop leaf, drop-end table, duchesse, dumb waiter *(British)*, extension table, folding table, gate-leg table, gate-legged table, kitchen table, nest of tables, occasional table, pedestal table, Pembroke table, refectory table, tea table, teapoy, telephone table, trestle table. **2. dining table** breakfast table, dining nook, dining suite, dinner table, refectory table. **3. side-table** bar top, console, console table, pier table, tabletop, working top. **4. bar** bench, benchtop, buffet, cocktail bar, counter, kitchen bench. **5. work table** skirting table, workbench.

6. **1. tray** autotray *(Chiefly Victoria)*, dumb waiter, lapboard, tea tray, tea trolley, tray-mobile, wheeling tray. **2. lazy Susan** dumb waiter *(British)*.

7. **1. desk** bureau, cash desk, credenza, davenport, desktop, escritoire, reading desk, roll-top desk, secretaire, secretary, writing desk, writing table. *Informal:* workstation.

8. **1. cupboard** almery, ambry, armoire, aumbry, base unit, bookcase, buttery, cabinet, cellaret, chandlery, chiffonier, china cabinet, closet, clothes press, cocktail cabinet, commode, corner cabinet, display cabinet, filing cabinet, glory hole, hot-water cupboard, hutch, kitchen cupboard, larder, linen cupboard, linen press, locker, meat safe, medicine cabinet, pantry, press, safe, storeroom, wall unit. **2. sideboard** ambry, buffet, credenza, dresser, Welsh dresser. **3. wardrobe** aparador *(Philippine English)*, armoire, built-in wardrobe, clothes cupboard, clothes press, lowboy, robe, walk-in wardrobe. **4. chest of drawers** bottom drawer, bureau, chiffonier, drawer, dressing table, glory box, hope chest, lowboy, tallboy.

9. **1. shelving** bookshelf, compactus, kitchen shelf, overmantel, pigeonhole, retable, revolving shelf, vegetable racks, vegetable trays, whatnot.

RELATED KEYWORDS: CONTAINER, SUPPORT

FURROW

n. **1.** **1. furrow** bowling crease, cannelure, channel, chase, check, croze, dap, drill, fillister, fissure, flute, glyph, gouge, groove, nick, notch, rabbet, rebate, recess, return crease, rifle, ruck, rut, scarf, seam, stria, strias, striation, sulcus, vallecula, wrinkle. **2. ditch** canal, channel, costean, coulisse, cut, dike, dyke, entrenchments, fire trench, fosse, foxhole, gutter, keyway, lateral, moat, rill, riverbed, rubble drain, runnel, sap, ship canal, slit trench, slot, sondage, table drain, tideway, trench, trough. **3. crease** corrugation, crinkle, fold, pucker, rumple, seam. **4. ripple** eddy, purl. **5. scratch** microgroove, run-in groove, scarification, score. **6. milling** broom finish, broomed finish, chatter marks, fluting, rifling, ruttiness, striation, sulcation. **7. guttering** spouting.

2. **1. furrower** chisel-plough, ditcher, gang plough, plough, plow *(Chiefly US)*, rotary plough, stump-jump plough, trencher. **2. gouge** bezel, boaster, bolster, burin, chisel, cold chisel, crosscut chisel, drove, firmer chisel, fuller, graver, hardy, osteotome, pitching tool, pressing board, router, set chisel, spud, trepan. **3. engraver** chaser, etcher, fluter.

adj. **3.** **1. furrowed** fluted, glyphic, grooved, milled, quirk, ripple, ripply, rugged, rutty, scrobiculate, seamed, striate, sulcate, sulcated, vallecular, valleculate, wrinkly.

v. **4.** **1. furrow** channel, flute, groove, gutter, mill, nick, rabbet, rebate, rifle, rout, rut, striate, trepan. **2. crease** cockle, corrugate, crimple, crinkle, crumple, knit, pucker, purl, purse, ripple, rumple, scrumple, seam, shrivel, wimple, wrinkle. **3. ditch** costean, dig in, dike, dyke, entrench, intrench, sap, trench. **4. engrave** chase, etch, incise, indent, nick, notch, whittle. **5. plough** garden, harrow, scarify, till. **6. scratch** overscore, scarify, score.

RELATED KEYWORDS: CUT, FARMING, FOLD

THE FUTURE

n. **1.** **1. the future** coming ages, futurity, hereafter, time to come. **2. tomorrow** tonight. **3. mañana** the by and by. *Informal:* Pancake Day, the sweet by and by. **4. doomsday** judgement day. **5. imminence** impendency.

adj. **2.** **1. future** eventual, unborn. **2. forward** long-range, prospective. **3. futuristic** space-age, twenty-first century. **4. imminent** close at hand, impendent, impending, in the offing, in view, near, nearly upon one, pendent, pending.

v. **3.** **1. impend** approach, be imminent, be near at hand, draw near.

adv. **4.** **1. in the future** at length, eventually, finally, in the fullness of time, sooner or later, ultimately. **2. imminently** at any moment, before long, by and by, momentarily *(Chiefly US)*, pendently, presently, shortly, soon. **3. onwards** afterwards, ahead, forth, forwards, from this time on, henceforth, off, onward, onwards in time, thence, thenceforth, thenceforward, thereafter. **4. some day** mañana, one day, sometime, tomorrow, tonight. **5. next** near. **6. in waiting** a day off, a week off, in store, in the offing, in the wind, some time off. **7. yet** still. **8. then** since, thereon, thereupon, therewith.

RELATED KEYWORDS: EXPECTATION, NEWNESS, PREDICTION

GAMBLING

n. **1.**   **1. gambling** betting, bookmaking, gaming, hippomania. **2. type of betting** betting on the dogs, betting on the horses, betting on the races, football pools, footy TAB, SP betting, the pools. **3. odds** even money, evens, fixed odds, long odds, long shot, quotation, short odds, SP, starting price. *Informal:* pot, roughie, toss-up.

2.   **1. gamble** adventure, bid, leap in the dark, speculation, throw, venture. *Informal:* a pig in a poke, act of faith, burl, flutter, Russian roulette, spec. **2. bet** aleatory contract, punt, wager. **3. type of bet** all-in bet, all-up, bet, box trifecta, collect, daily double, double, double or quits, doubles, each-way bet, exacta, feature double, forecast quinella, jackpot tote, lay, martingale, over-round system, parimutuel *(Chiefly US)*, parlay *(Chiefly US)*, quadrella, quinella, saver, side bet, skinner, spread betting, stake, stand-out bet, straight-out bet, superfecta, tote, triella, trifecta. **4. record of bets** book. **5. bid** abundance, call, calling, contract, declaration, jump bid, misère, no-trump, psychic bid. **6. the luck of the draw** toss of the coin.

3.   **1. gambling games** fan-tan, pea and thimble trick, thimblerig, toodle-em-buck *(Victoria)*. **2. lottery** art union, Calcutta, football pools, Golden Casket, grab bag, lot, lucky dip, pakapoo, policy *(US)*, raffle, scratch ticket, sweep, sweepstake, sweepstakes, Tambaroora muster, the pools. *Informal:* consultation. **3. bingo** cow pat lotto, housie, housie-housie, hoy, lotto, tombola. **4. chocolate wheel** roulette. **5. card game** écarté, all-fours, ante-up, baccarat, banker, blackjack, bridge, canasta, chemin de fer, conquian, contract bridge, cooncan, cribbage, faro, five hundred, gin, gin rummy, happy families, hearts, lansquenet, loo, monte, poker, pontoon, quadrille, rouge et noir, skat, solo, stud, stud game, stud poker, trente et quarante, twenty-one, vingt-et-un, whist. *Informal:* chemmy. **6. two-up** the national game, toss, toss-up, two-up school. *Informal:* swy. **7. dice** ace, craps, dicing, hazard, poker dice.

4.   **1. gambler** better, bettor, bidder, crapshooter *(US)*, dicer, gamester, hazarder, hippomaniac, player, punt, punter, side-better, wagerer. *Informal:* emu, sport. **2. bookmaker** commission agent *(British)*, geno, rails bookmaker, SP bookmaker, tick-tack man, tout, turf accountant *(British)*. *Informal:* bagman, bagswinger, balancer, bester, book, bookie, fielder, SP bookie. **3. bookie's runner** *Informal:* bagboy, crusher. **4. banker** ombre. *Informal:* monte. **5. backer** turfman. *Informal:* plunger. **6. alley loafer** welsher. **7. stakeholder** boxer, croupier, ringkeeper. **8. two-up player** alley, alley clerk, alley loafer, boxer, centre, centreman, headie, ringie, ringkeeper, spinner, swy school, tailie, tosser, two-up ring. *Informal:* cockatoo. **9. adventurer** adventuress, gentleman of fortune, land shark, land-jobber, speculator.

5.   **1. gambling equipment** parimutuel *(Chiefly US)*, totalisator. **2. dice** astragals, bones, die, poker dice, snake's-eyes, trey. *Informal:* ivories. **3. poker machine** fruit machine *(Chiefly British and US)*, gaming machine, slot machine, video poker machine. *Informal:* bandit, cardie, one-armed bandit, pokey, pokies. **4. kip** bat, kiley, kylie, stick. **5. chip** blue chip, marker, prize money. *Informal:* razoo, velvet. **6. stake** ante, kitty, pool, pot, stakes. *Informal:* dibs, guts.

6.   **1. gambling hall** casino, disorderly house, gaming house, hell *(British)*, poolroom. **2. betting ring** ring. *Informal:* outer. **3. betting shop** pub TAB, TAB, the machine *(NZ)*, totalisator, Totalisator Agency Board. *Informal:* lucky shop *(Victoria)*, SP joint, tote shop.

7.   **1. gambling terms – miscellaneous** ambs-ace, ames-ace, butterfly, crabs, doublets, floater, ones, showdown, sixer, tern *(US)*, two ones.

adj. **8.**   **1. gambling** hippomanic, sporting, turfy.

v. **9.**   **1. gamble** ballot, chance it, dice, false-card, game, one them, overtrump, play, play the market, speculate, take risks, throw dice, trump, try one's luck. *Informal:* chance one's arm, flutter, take a punt on. **2. bet** get set, have a bet both ways, hazard, lay, punt, put, roll, stake, wager. **3. bet heavily** *Informal:* go for broke, plunge, put one's shirt on. **4. make a bet** bet all up, bet double or quits, bet each way, bet evens, crush the price, parlay *(Chiefly US)*, play for dibs, stay. *Informal:* go for the doctor. **5. take bets** field a book, frame a book, make a book, run the track of, tout. **6. raise** fatten, jump, up. *Informal:* sweeten. **7. bid** call, false card, go, make, outbid, overbid. **8. bid on** back. **9. hedge** lay off. **10. stake** ante, jackpot, wager. **11. play two-up** head 'em up, tail 'em up. **12. toss up** call, toss. *Informal:* head them, mick, ned them, nut them, skull them, tail them. **13. win** be in the black, be on a good thing, romp home (or in), whipsaw *(US)*. *Informal:* be on a winning streak. **14. be at stake** be in hazard.

RELATED KEYWORDS: AMUSEMENT, LUCK, POSSIBILITY

GAP

n. **1.** **1. gap** aperture, areola, blank, breach, break, clearance, four foot, gape, hiatus, infill, interspace, interstice, interval, lacuna, opening, space, vacancy, void. **2. split** avulsion, fissure, parting, rent, rip, slit, tear, vent. **3. opening** air gap, crenel, crenelle, headroom, intercolumniation, oculus, spiracle. **4. crack** breach, chap, chimney, chink, cleavage, cleft, craze, crevice, cut, fissure, flaw, fracture, gash, leak, mofette, rift, sandcrack, spring. **5. chasm** abysm *(Poetic)*, abyss, breakaway, canyon, channel, chine, clearance, clearing, coomb, crevasse, dale, defile, dell, depth, dingle *(Chiefly Poetic)*, flume *(US)*, gap, gate, glen, gorge, graben, grike, gulch *(Chiefly US)*, gulf, gully, gut, hanging valley, opening *(US)*, pass, profundity, ravine, rift valley, strath, vale *(Chiefly Poetic)*, valley, water gap, wind gap, yawn. **6. diastema** cleft lip, earhole, sand-crack, toe-crack.

adj. **2.** **1. gaping** agape, ajar, avulsed, broken, dehiscent, open, oscitant, patulous, wide-open, yawning. **2. spaced** areolate, effuse, gap-toothed, gappy, hiatal. **3. cleft** bilobate, cloven, cloven-hoofed, cracked, dipartite, dissected, fissile, fissirostral, multifid, parted, partible, partite, pedatifid, rent, riven, segmental, slit, split. **4. interspatial** interstitial.

v. **3.** **1. gape** open, tent, unclench, yawn. **2. separate** decollate, dichotomise, disaggregate, disjoin, gap, interspace, pair, set apart, space, space out, spread, subdivide. **3. split** bisect, canton, chap, cleave, compartment, crack, delaminate, departmentalise, divide, factionalise, fissure, fraction, fragment, part, phlebotomise, pip, regionalise, rend, rive, rupture, section, shiver, slice, spall, splinter, sunder, unseam.

RELATED KEYWORDS: CUT, FURROW, INTERRUPTION, INTERVAL, OPENING, ABSENCE

GAS

n. **1.** **1. gas** atmosphere, fluid, plasma. **2. type of gas** acetylene, ammonia, arsine, biogas, boron trifluoride, butane, carbon dioxide, carbon monoxide, chlorofluorocarbon, chloromethane, cyanogen, detonating gas, diazomethane, dichlorodifluoromethane, ethane, ethene, ethylene, ethyne, fluorine, formaldehyde, greenhouse gas, hydrogen, hydrogen bromide, hydrogen chloride, hydrogen cyanide, hydrogen fluoride, hydrogen iodide, iodine, isobutene, isobutylene, ketene, methanal, methane, methyl chloride, methylpropene, monosilane, nitrogen, nitrogen dioxide, nitrous oxide, oxygen, oxyhydrogen, ozone, phosphine, Pintsch gas, propane, stibine, sulfuretted hydrogen, tetrafluoroethylene, vinyl chloride. **3. vapour** fumes, live steam, reek, saturated vapour, steam, water vapour. **4. smoke. 5. bubble** air-bell, bead. **6. afterdamp** blackdamp, carbon monoxide, chokedamp, firedamp, flue gas, ignis fatuus, whitedamp. **7. effluvium** eduction, emanon, exhaust, malaria, marsh gas, mephitis, miasma, mofette. **8. sewer gas** sewage gas. **9. chemical agent** adamsite, blister gas, capsicum spray, CS gas, diphosgene, hydrogen sulfide, lachrymator, laughing gas, Mace gas, mustard gas, nerve gas, phosgene, poison gas, sarin, tear gas, yperite. *Informal:* rotten egg gas. **10. breath** exhalation, flatus, gas, steam, wind. **11. puff** *Informal:* toke. **12. atmosphere** air, chromosphere, fireball, photosphere, planetary nebula, plasmapause, prominence. **13. vapour trail** chemtrail, condensation trail, tail. **14. ideal gas** perfect gas, permanent gas. **15. bottled gas** aerosol, propellant. **16. coolant** electrolytic gas. **17. rare gas** actinon, argon, helium, inert gas, krypton, neon, noble gas, radium emanation, radon, xenon. **18. fuel gas** CNG, coal gas, liquefied petroleum gas, LNG, LPG, natural gas, producer gas, town gas, water gas.

2. **1. gaseousness** fluidity, gaseity, gassiness, steaminess, vaporosity. **2. vaporisation** atomisation, evaporation, evolution, fluidisation, gasification, vaporescence, volatilisation. **3. gassing** aeration, fumigation, sulfurisation. **4. evaporability** vapourability. **5. volatileness** volatility. **6. pneumatics** aerodynamics, aerography, aerology, aeromechanics, aerometry, aerostatics, eudiometry, pneumodynamics. **7. gas laws** Boyle's law, Charles's law, ideal gas law.

3. **1. vaporiser** atomiser, evaporator, fluidiser, generator, inhaler, rebreathing apparatus, steamer, vaporimeter, volatiliser. **2. gasworks** gas holder, gas tank, gasometer. **3. gas field** gas well, geothermal field.

adj. **4.** **1. gaseous** effluvial, flatulent, fluidic, gasiform, pneumatic. **2. evaporative** volatile. **3. vaporescent** vaporific. **4. gassy** fumelike, gas, steamy, vapourish, vapoury.

v. **5.** **1. vaporise** ablate, atomise, fluidise, gasify, sublime, volatilise. **2. steam** fume, gas, smoke, vapour. **3. evaporate** boil. **4. smoke** reek. **5. breathe** inspire, puff, respire, vapour. **6. fumigate** fume, gas, smoke, sulfur.

RELATED KEYWORDS: AIR, BUBBLINESS, CLOUD, MATTER, INTANGIBILITY

GATHERING

n. **1.** **1. gathering** assemblage, assembly, bee, busy bee, ceilidh, corroboree, count-muster, ecclesia, flash mob, jamboree, meet, muster, rally, re-collection, roll-up, runanga, stand-to, turnout, unlawful assembly. *Informal:* drinkies, get-together. **2. association** body, college, company, conflux, congregation, convocation. **3. meeting** hui, indaba, witan, witenagemot. **4. group** aggrupation *(Philippine English)*, band, company, crew, outfit, pack, party, troop. **5. gang** chain gang, colour gang, crew, mob, ruck, squad. *Informal:* emu parade. **6. crowd** cloud, confluence, crew, crush, droves, flock, galaxy, herd, horde, host, huddle, legion, mob, multitude, press, ruck, sea of faces, shoal, swarm, throng, troop. **7. jam** squeeze. *Informal:* bunfight. **8. mob** gaggle, lynch mob, rabble. **9. grouping** caste, class, league, school of thought, social subset. **10. stable** string. **11. pack** clowder, pride. **12. flock** bevy, clutch, covey, flight, gaggle, murmuration, wisp. **13. herd** drove, flock, hordes, troop, troupe. **14. school** shoal. **15. community** aggregation, biome, climax community, colony, society. **16. congregativeness** gregariousness, herd instinct, sociality. **17. centralisation** centralism.

2. **1. accumulation** agglomerate, agglomeration, aggregate, aggregation, collective, conglomerate, conglomeration, cumulation, deposit, glomeration, group. **2. hoard** budget, stock. *Informal:* stash. **3. backlog** bank-up, stockpile. *Informal:* pile-up. **4. heap** congeries, cumulus, drift, haymow, hayrick, haystack, hill, mound, pile, pyre, stack, stockpile. **5. batch** battery, crop. **6. lot** nest, set. *Informal:* the whole (kit and) caboodle. **7. package** bundle, pack, packet, parcel, shiralee, truss. **8. mass** forest, sea, wilderness. **9. accumulativeness** amassment, cumulativeness. **10. crowdedness** denseness, multitudinousness.

3. **1. gatherer** bundler, gleaner, heaper, ingatherer, stacker. **2. drover** herd, herder, herdsman, mobber, musterer. **3. collector** bibliophile, bibliophilist, discophil, discophile, epidopterist, ex-librist, lepidopterist, numismatist, philatelist, phillumenist, stamp-collector.

adj. **4.** **1. collective** congregate, congregative, gregarious. **2. clustered** aciniform, acinose, acinous, agminate, agminated. **3. cumulate** aggregate. **4. clustery** clumpy.

v. **5.** **1. gather** bramble, clam *(US)*, dry-shell, glean, harvest, hive, ingather, nut, pick, rake up, sheaf, sheave, vintage. **2. accumulate** agglomerate, aggregate, amalgamate, amass, ball, bank up, collect, conglomerate, cumulate, gather, heap, jackpot, pile up, run, snowball, stack up, summate. **3. hoard** amass, garner, heap, scavenge, stack away, stockpile, store. *Informal:* sock away. **4. cluster** bale, bunch, bundle, bundle up, clump, constellate, pack, steeve. **5. heap** lumber, pile, stack. **6. congregate** assemble, band, band together, collect, concentrate, convene, echelon, foregather, forgather, formate, gam, gather, group, league, mass, meet, regroup, rendezvous, sit, squadron, syndicate, throw together, turn out. *Informal:* turn up.

adv. **6.** **1. accumulatively** aggregately, collectively, cumulatively, in the aggregate. **2. together** crowdedly, en masse, tout ensemble.

RELATED KEYWORDS: COMBINATION, INCLUSION, JOINING, MANY, SOCIETY

GENERALITY

n. **1.** **1. generality** catholicity, commonness, generalness, omnifariousness, prevailingness, prevalence, regnancy, ubiquitousness, ubiquity, universalism, universality, universalness. **2. cosmopolitanism** broad-mindedness, cosmopolitism.

2. **1. impersonality** anonymity, depersonalisation, facelessness.

3. **1. generalisation** abstraction, generality, universalisation. **2. conspectus** bird's-eye view, broad spectrum, helicopter view, overview, panorama.

4. **1. generalist** all-rounder, jack-of-all-trades, one-man band, Renaissance man. **2. globalist** cosmopolite, internationalist, universalist.

5. **1. any** and what not, anybody, anyone, anything, some, somebody, someone, something, suchlike, whatever, whichever, whichsoever, whoever, whomever. *Informal:* whatnot. **2. everybody** all, every manjack, everyman, everyone. **3. all and sundry** one and all. *Informal:* every man and his dog, every man jack, Tom, Dick, and Harry. **4. everything** *Informal:* everything but the kitchen sink, full monty, the whole kit and caboodle, the whole shebang. **5. sundries** thing, what-d'ye-call-it, what-d'ye-m'-call-it. *Informal:* do-hickey *(Chiefly US)*, doodackie *(NZ)*, doodad, doodah, doofer, doohickie, doover, dooverlackie, thang, thingo, thingummyjig, whatnot, whatsit, whosie-whatsit.

adj. **6.** **1. general** all, all-round, any, broad, broadbrush, broadscale, catholic, ecumenical, universal, universalistic. **2. comprehensive** all-embracing, blanket, broad-spectrum, broadbrush, collective, extensive, far-reaching, global, inclusive, indiscriminate, multifaceted, omnibus, panoptic, panoptical, panoramic, plenary, sweeping, umbrella, wide-ranging. **3. cosmopolitan** azonic, global, intercontinental, international, multinational, multiracial, worldwide. **4. exoteric** broadcast, encyclic, encyclical. **5. prevalent** common, countrywide, current, diffuse, general, omnipresent, pandemic, prevailing, regnant, rife, ruling, ubiquitary, ubiquitous, universal, widespread, widespreading.

* * **7. 1. impersonal** anonymous, cryptonymous, faceless, general, indefinite, indeterminate, innominate, miscellaneous, nameless, of sorts, omnifarious, open, overhead, unmarked, unnamed, unspecified.

v. **8. 1. generalise** abstract, catholicise, universalise. **2. broadcast** spread. **3. depersonalise** impersonalise. **4. prevail** be everywhere, obtain, predominate, rule.

adv. **9. 1. generally** across the board, all over, commonly, everywhere, globally, high and low, popularly, sweepingly, ubiquitously, universally. **2. in general** altogether, broadly, by and large, catholically, ecumenically, in the abstract, largely, on (or upon) the whole, prevailingly, prevalently.

RELATED KEYWORDS: CONFORMITY, INCLUSION, ORDINARINESS

GENEROSITY

n. **1. 1. generosity** bounteousness, bountifulness, bounty, charitableness, charity, free-handedness, freeness, generousness, goodness, handsomeness, kindness, large-heartedness, largesse, lavishness, liberality, liberalness, magnanimity, munificence, open-handedness, open-heartedness, princeliness, prodigality, soft-heartedness, unsparingness. **2. benefaction** almsgiving, beneficence, bounty, cent sale, charity, hospitality, philanthropy, voluntaryism. **3. contribution** a good turn, act of charity, baksheesh, benefit, charity, Christmas box *(British)*, donation, favour, gift, good deed, koha *(NZ)*, widow's mite. **4. open house** drop-in centre, liberty hall, soup kitchen. **5. shout** treat.

2. 1. philanthropist altruist, benefactor, lady bountiful, soft touch. **2. charity** benevolent institution.

adj. **3. 1. generous** beneficent, benevolent, big, big-hearted, bounteous, bountiful, charitable, chivalric, eleemosynary, free, free-handed, gallant, generous-spirited, good-hearted, gracious, great-hearted, grudgeless, handsome, hospitable, kind, kind-hearted, kindly, large-hearted, lavish, liberal, magnanimous, magnificent, munificent, open, open-handed, open-hearted, philanthropic, princely, prodigal, prodigal of, profuse in, propitious, ungrudging, unsparing, unstinting. **2. touchable** impressible, impressionable, soft-hearted, susceptible, susceptive, tender-hearted.

v. **4. 1. be generous** bestow, do someone proud, do the right (or handsome) thing by, give carte blanche, give one's all, lavish, shower, spare no expense.

adv. **5. 1. generously** a (fair) treat, beneficently, bounteously, bountifully, charitably, freely, handsomely, lavishly, liberally, magnanimously, magnificently, munificently, open-handedly, open-heartedly, prodigally, profusely, unsparingly, with open hand, without stint.

RELATED KEYWORDS: EXTRAVAGANCE, GIVING, KINDNESS, SHARING

GIVING

n. **1. 1. giving** accommodation, bequeathal, bestowment, commitment, committal, conferment, conferral, consignment, dedication, dispensation, disposal, distribution, grant, impartment, investiture, offering, presentation, presentment, provision, testation, vouchsafement.

2. 1. gift compliment, contribution, donative, eulogia, favour, handsel, keepsake, offering, present, presentation, remembrance. *Informal:* pressie, pressy, prezzie. **2. grant** endowment, foundation, legacy, subsidy, subvention. **3. offering** burnt offering, donary, immolation, oblation, offertory, peace-offering, sacrifice, thank-offering. **4. alms** donation, handout. **5. tip** baksheesh, consideration, cumshaw, douceur, gratuity, pourboire. *Informal:* beer money. **6. prize** award, reward. **7. bursary** scholarship, studentship. **8. bequest** mortuary. **9. dowry** devise, dot, dower, marriage portion, portion. **10. free sample** handout. *Informal:* freebie, giveaway. **11. bonus issue** bonus, capital distribution, capital issue, premium, scrip issue. **12. largesse** bounty, manna from heaven. **13. Christmas stocking** Christmas box *(British)*, Christmas hamper.

3. 1. giver almoner, benefactor, benefactress, bestower, conferrer, contributor, dedicator, deviser, dispenser, donator, donor, endower, fairy godmother, granter, grantor, humanitarian, imparter, lady bountiful, legator, patron, philanthropist, presenter, testator, testatrix, tipper. *Informal:* angel, Santa Claus.

v. **4.** **1. give** accord, allot, assign, award, bestow, confer, dedicate, dish out, dole out, donate, extend, gift, grant, hand out, heap on, lot, make a present of, oblige with, portion out, present, provide, shower, tender. *Informal:* cough up. **2. contribute** dob in, subscribe. *Informal:* chip in, fork over, kick in. **3. tip** baksheesh, remember, reward. **4. consign** commit, delegate, deliver, dispense, dispose of, distribute, entrust, give into someone's keeping, hand in, hand over, make over, part with, pass into someone's charge, put into someone's hands, sign away, surrender, turn over. **5. grant** accord, afford, agree, allow, concede, seise, vouchsafe, yield. **6. bequeath** assign, devise, endow, leave, settle, vest, will. **7. sacrifice** give up, immolate, offer, spend.

RELATED KEYWORDS: COMPENSATION, GENEROSITY, LOAN, SHARING

GOD

n. **1.** **1. god** daemon, demigod, demigoddess, demon, divinity, goddess, godhead, godling, Olympian, omnipotent, presence. **2. deity** ancestral being, atua *(NZ)*, earthmother, manes, numen, snake-god, sun-god, zombie. **3. household god** kitchen god, lares and penates. **4. incarnation** avatar, embodiment. **5. false god** Baal, idol. **6. pantheon** powers, thearchy. **7. godship** blessedness, divineness, divinity, glory, godhead, godhood, godliness, grace, sacredness, sacrosanctity, saintliness, sanctity, theomorphism. **8. thearchy**. **9. theomachy**. **10. ambrosia** ichor, nectar.

2. **1. God** Atman, Being, deity, Providence, Spirit, the Eternal, the Everlasting, the Infinite, the Invisible. **2. demiurge**. **3. Almighty** Allah, Creator, Father, Jehovah, Lord, Saviour, Supreme Being, the Infinite Being, the Omnipotent, the Omniscient, Yahweh. **4. Messiah** Redeemer.

adj. **3.** **1. godlike** ambrosial, ambrosian, Capitoline, Cyllenian, deific, deiform, divine, Jovian, Martial, numinous, Olympian, Pandean, theandric, theanthropic, theomorphic. **2. holy** all-knowing, all-powerful, all-seeing, almighty, celestial, divine, ethereal, hallowed, heavenly, omnipotent, omnipresent, omniscient, pious, sacred, sacrosanct, sanctified, supernal. **3. demiurgic**. **4. tripersonal** hypostatic, triune. **5. Messianic**.

RELATED KEYWORDS: AFTERWORLD, RELIGION, SUPERNATURAL BEING

GOOD FORTUNE

n. **1.** **1. good fortune** fortune, happiness, luck, propitiousness, prosperity, rosiness, the devil's own luck. **2. bonanza** blessing, godsend, piece of good luck, stroke, stroke of fortune, treasure-trove, trove. *Informal:* snap. **3. prosperousness** auspiciousness, blessedness, boom times, flowering, fortunateness, luckiness, run of luck, serendipity, thriving, thrivingness, winning streak. **4. wellbeing** welfare. **5. break** lucky streak.

2. **1. luxury** a good living, a place in the sun, bed of roses, easy street, featherbed, life of Riley, milk and honey, plenty, the fat of the land, the good life. **2. heyday** golden age, good old days, good times, halcyon days, happy days, high day, salad days, summer, sunshine.

adj. **3.** **1. fortunate** auspicious, happy, heaven-sent, in luck's way, lucky, providential, white. *Informal:* tinny. **2. prosperous** blooming, booming, flourishing, golden, palmy, promising, roseate, rosy, Saturnian, thriving, up-and-coming, well-to-do. **3. auspicious** benign, benignant, blessed, blest, bright, favonian, fortunate, happy, promising, propitious, prosperous.

v. **4.** **1. prosper** be made, be on to a good thing, do a roaring trade, go from rags to riches, have never had it so good, have the Midas touch, live high, live on milk and honey, make good, soar, strike it lucky, strike it rich, strike oil, succeed, thrive. *Informal:* make a rise. **2. boom** be on the crest of a wave, be on the make, be on the up and up, bloom, blossom, flourish, rise in the world, thrive. **3. be in luck** be born under a lucky star, be born with a silver spoon in one's mouth, be in clover, be in the silk, be in velvet, bear a charmed life, fall (or land) on one's feet, have the ball at one's feet, land on one's feet, live off the fat of the land, one's luck is in. *Informal:* be on a good wicket, be sitting pretty, cop it sweet, have (got) it made.

adv. **5.** **1. fortunately** auspiciously, beneficially, blessedly, for the best, happily, luckily, propitiously, providentially, rosily. **2. prosperously** flourishingly, swimmingly, thrivingly.

RELATED KEYWORDS: ACCOMPLISHMENT, LUCK, WEALTH, WINNING

GOODNESS

n. **1.** **1. goodness** choiceness, desirableness, fineness, niceness. **2. excellence** exceptionalness, exquisiteness, fabulousness, ideality, idealness, marvellousness, peerlessness, perfection, rareness, splendidness, superbness, supremeness, tremendousness, wonderfulness. **3. refinement** class, culture, elegance, finesse, finish, gentility, polish, preciosity, selectness, taste. **4. quality** merit, preciousness, value, virtue, worth. **5. wholesomeness** healthiness. **6. rareness** rarity, remarkableness, uncommonness.

2. **1. good** advantage, benefit, boon, virtue. *Informal:* silver lining. **2. blessing** benediction, benefaction, favour, manna from heaven, mercy. **3. the common good** commonweal, summum bonum, the public good, welfare.

3. **1. good thing** front-ranker, marvel, miracle, plum, sensation, swan, topnotcher, treasure. *Informal:* a bit of all right, beaut, beauty, bobby-dazzler, bottler, clinker, clipper, corker, cracker, crackerjack, daisy, dandy, dilly, dinkum, dinky, dinnyhayser, dynamite, gas, gasser, honey, hot stuff, humdinger, hummer, just what the doctor ordered, knockout, one out of the box, peach, purler, ripsnorter, rube *(NZ)*, ruby-dazzler, sollicker, topper, trimmer. **2. showpiece** aristocrat, bijou, centrepiece, chef-d'oeuvre, flower, gem, jewel, magnum opus, masterpiece, masterwork, pearl, pièce de résistance, pride, the Rolls Royce of. *Informal:* a (little) beauty. **3. beau ideal** idea, ideal, picture, top *(Poetic)*. **4. bijou** tidbit *(US)*, titbit. **5. better** betters, superior. **6. the best** acme, cap, climax, culmination, first water, high point, high spot, ne plus ultra, the ultimate. *Informal:* (the) tops, mostest, the full two bob, the most (or mostest), tiptop. **7. one in a million** one in a thousand, the icing on the cake. *Informal:* the ant's pants, the bee's knees, the cat's pyjamas (or whiskers), the glassy, the greatest, the oil *(NZ)*.

4. **1. good person** angel, cherub, cynosure of all eyes, dove, goddess, impeccable, jewel, lion, one in a thousand, one of the best, perfection, saint, the pick of the bunch. *Informal:* (the) tops, a good sort, beaut, beaut bloke, beaut sheila, Christian, dinky-di Aussie, good egg, good Joe, goodie, goody, honey, ripsnorter. **2. goody-goody** *(Informal)* moraliser, stick-in-the-mud, Victorian. *Informal:* fuddy-duddy, old maid. **3. salt of the earth** one of nature's gentlemen, rough diamond, sportsman. *Informal:* a good sport. **4. stalwart** just man, just woman, pillar of society. **5. model** ambassador, poster child. *Informal:* pin-up. **6. benefactor** benefactress. *Informal:* great. **7. hero** folk hero, heroine, knight in shining armour, saviour. **8. champion** demigod, Galahad, Robin Hood, Superman, Tarzan.

adj. **5.** **1. good** amazing, bonny *(Scottish)*, bosker, braw *(Scottish)*, brilliant, capital, desirable, excellent, extra grouse, extraordinaire, extraordinary, fantastical, fine, gorgeous, grand, heavenly, incredible, mad, magnificent, marvellous, nice, phenomenal, prodigious, royal, shining, splendid, sumptuous, super, superb, superfine, well, wonderful, wondrous. *Informal:* bang-up, bitchin', bonzer, copasetic *(US)*, corker, crack, crackerjack, cracking, crash-hot, daisy, dandy, deadly, dope, extra, fab, fabbo, fabuloso, fabulous, famous, fantabulous, fantastic, fazzo, gas, gnarly, good-o, great, grouse, hunky, immense, kapai *(NZ)*, nobby, not bad, peachy, plum, radical, ripping, ruby-dazzler, sensational, slap-up, slashing, smashing, snifter, sollicking, spiffing *(British)*, splendiferous, super-duper, swell *(Chiefly US)*, swinging, terrif, terrific, tickety-boo *(British)*, top, topping *(Chiefly British)*, tops, wizard *(Chiefly British)*, you-beaut. **2. rare** exotic, freak, one-off, recherché, select, uncommon, unexampled, unique, unprecedented, unusual. **3. first-class** A-one, best, extraordinaire, extreme, first, first-rate, five-star, front rank, giant, greatest, high-class, high-grade, in the first flight, in the front rank, maximal, monumental, of the first water, optimal, optimum, superfine, superior, superlative, suprême, top, top-flight, topmost, unbeatable, up to par, up to scratch, up to the knocker, uttermost, world-class. *Informal:* A-1, ace, champion *(British)*, filthy, great, mickey mouse, purler, tiptop, top-hole *(Chiefly British)*, topnotch, whizzbang. **4. better** extraordinary, super, superior. **5. ideal** faultless, perfect. **6. premium** bijou, blue-chip, blue-ribbon, choice, classic, deluxe, elect, elegant, exquisite, finished, gilt-edged, goodly, hand-picked, polished, prime, quality, select, superior. **7. matchless** especial, exceptional, extra-special, incomparable, irreplaceable, nonpareil, outstanding, peerless, prize, special, stellar, unequalled, unmatched, unparalleled, unrivalled. **8. sound** fine, healthful, healthy, robust, salutary, trim, well. *Informal:* A-OK *(US)*, fit as a fiddle, in the pink. **9. beneficial** aidful, salutary, salutiferous. **10. satisfactory** all right, alright, fine and dandy, good enough, right. *Informal:* all serene, all Sir Garnet (or cigarnette) (or segarnio) (or sogarnio), cush-n-andy, hunky, hunky-dory, jake, jakeloo, OK, okay. **11. sublime** divine, heavenly, out of this world. *Informal:* dreamy, insane, unreal. **12. classy** *(Informal)* golden, sterling, vintage. *Informal:* class, plummy, silk department. **13. helluva** *Informal:* beaut, hell of a, hella. **14. polished** slick. *Informal:* cool, neat, nifty. **15. benevolent** favourable.

adv. **6.** **1. well** amazingly, bonnily, capitally, excellently, fabulously, famously, finely, grandly, magnificently, marvellously, sensationally, soundly, splendidly, superbly, swingingly, tremendously, unreally, wonderfully. *Informal:* wicked, wizardly *(Chiefly British)*. **2. exquisitely** choicely, divinely, elegantly. **3. uncommonly** exceptionally, extremely, peerlessly, remarkably, supremely, unco *(Scottish)*, uncommon. **4. fine** *(Informal)* okay, right. *Informal:* cush-n-andy, OK. **5. beneficially** advantageously.

interj.   **7.**   **1. excellent**   capital *(Chiefly British)*, classic, great, super, sweet, tops. *Informal:* beaut, bewdy, cool, good iron, goody, goody (goody) gumdrops, groovy, kapai *(NZ)*, solid, you beauty, you bloody bewdy, you little beauty. **2. all's well**   *Informal:* she'll be sweet, she's apples.

RELATED KEYWORDS: EXPEDIENCE, IMPROVEMENT, MORALITY, PERFECTION, SUPERIORITY

GOOD TASTE

n.   **1.**   **1. good taste**   breeding, civilisation, class, cultivation, culture, finesse, finish, genteelness, gentility, gentleness, politeness, refinement, seemliness, sensitivity. **2. taste** appreciation, fancy, likes, liking, palate, penchant, virtu. **3. style** bon ton, chic, dapperness, dressiness, elegance, manners, poshness, savoir faire, smartness, sophistication, tastefulness, tone, urbaneness, urbanities, urbanity. *Informal:* swank. **4. daintiness** delicateness, fineness, rarefaction. **5. fastidiousness** preciosity. **6. artistry** virtuosity. **7. delicacy** choiceness, discretion, discrimination, judgement. **8. aesthetics** sensibility.

   2.   **1. aesthete** artist, cognoscente, connoisseur, critic, culturist, epicure, gastronome, gentleman, gourmet, highbrow, judge, lady, sophisticate. *Informal:* culture-vulture, fusspot, toff. **2. cognoscenti** the discerning.

adj.   **3.**   **1. tasteful** exquisite, fancy, fine. **2. chic** dapper, dressy, elegant. *Informal:* nifty, nobby. **3. stylish** smart, sophisticated, urbane. *Informal:* cool, fly, hot, mod, snazzy, swish. **4. up-market** aristocratic, blue-chip, champagne, classy, deluxe, elegant, first-class, high, highbrow, luxurious, rich, silken, toffy. *Informal:* A-1, posh, swanky, swell *(Chiefly US)*.

   4.   **1. refined** appreciative, attic, civilised, cultivated, cultured, discerning, discriminating, educated, fine, mannerly, polished, polite, seemly, well-bred, well-educated, well-spoken, well-tried. *Informal:* a cut above. **2. fastidious** precious. **3. aesthetic** aesthetical, rarefactive, sensitive. **4. delicate** exquisite.

v.   **5.**   **1. have good taste** have a discerning eye, have a nose for, have an ear for, have an eye for.

adv.   **6.**   **1. aesthetically** civilly, delicately, esthetically, genteelly, in good taste, politely, seemly, tastefully. **2. elegantly** dapperly, dressily, urbanely. **3. daintily** delicately, fussily, squeamishly. **4. fastidiously** preciously. **5. aristocratically** poshly, richly.

RELATED KEYWORDS: BEAUTY, DISCERNMENT, SUPERIORITY

GOVERNMENT

n.   **1.**   **1. government** administration, authority, dominion, executive authority, executive power, governance, polity, power, rule. **2. administration** bureaucracy, civil service, officialism, public service. **3. regime** administration, government of the day, regimen, rule, the government. **4. legislation** law-making, lawgiving.

   2.   **1. system of government** adhocracy, aristocracy, autocracy, bureaucracy, cabinet government, coalition government, democracy, direct democracy, federal government, gerontocracy, grand coalition, hagiocracy, hierocracy, isocracy, local government, meritocracy, minority government, monocracy, ochlocracy, open government, parliamentary democracy, plutocracy, presidential system, representative democracy, representative government, responsible government, state government, stratocracy, theocracy, timocracy, two-party system, Westminster system.

   3.   **1. executive body** administrative committee, agora, annual general meeting, board, cabinet, caucus, comitia, commissariat, commission, conclave, convocation, curia, divan, duma, executive, executive council, joint committee, junta, management, meeting, ministry, politburo, presidium, senate, standing committee, steering committee, sub-committee, synod. **2. statutory authority** government agency, quango, semi-government authority. **3. legislative body** assembly, chamber, congress, gemot, house, legislature, moot, parliament, senate, soviet. *Informal:* cowards castle, talking shop. **4. lower house** lower chamber, second chamber. **5. upper house** upper chamber. **6. municipal council** borough council, Corporation *(British)*, county council, district, local authority *(Chiefly British)*, local government, municipality, shire, shire council, town council. **7. place of assembly** chamber, chambers, house, moot hall, parliament house, statehouse *(US)*.

   4.   **1. legislative bodies** Althing, Chamber of Deputies, Congress, Cortes, Diet, Duma, Eduskunta, Federal Assembly, Federal Parliament, Folketing, Grand National Assembly, Knesset, Legislative Assembly, National Assembly, National Congress, National People's Congress, Oireachtas, Parliament, People's Assembly, People's Consultative Congress, Riksdag, Sejm, State Parliament, States-General, Storting, Supreme Soviet, Volkskammer. **2. lower houses (chambers)** Bundestag, Chamber of Deputies, Chamber of

Representatives, Chamber of the People, Commons, Council of the Union, Dáil Eireann, House of Assembly, House of Commons, House of Keys, House of Representatives, Legislative Assembly, Lok Sabha, National Council, Reichstag. *Informal:* the Reps. **3. upper houses (chambers)** Bundesrat, Council of Nationalities, First Chamber, House of Councillors, House of Lords, Legislative Assembly, Legislative Council, Lords, Rajya Sabha, Reichsrat, Senate.

5. 1. administrative area arrondissement, barrio, borough, canton, city, commonwealth, constituency, council, county, deme, department, district, division, electorate, eparchy, federal district, hundred, local government area, municipal district, municipality, nomarchy, nome, oblast, parish *(British)*, precinct *(US)*, province, region, riding, satrapy, shire, state, subdivision, town, township, ward.

6. 1. head of government chancellor, doge, PM, premier, president, prime minister. **2. bureaucrat** administrator, civil servant, commissar, commissary, commissioner, director-general, femocrat, functionary, kiap, mandarin, official, palatine, public servant, shire president. **3. legislator** lawmaker. **4. member of parliament** MP, parliamentarian, representative.

adj. **7. 1. governmental** county, federal, government, municipal, state. **2. bureaucratic** administrative, executive. **3. legislative** cabinet, comitial, congressional, curial, lawmaking, legislatorial, nomothetic, parliamentary. **4. unicameral** bicameral.

v. **8. 1. govern** administer, be in power, hold office, hold power, rule. **2. legislate** codify, enact, make laws, pass laws.

RELATED KEYWORDS: COUNCIL, AUTHORITY, LAWFULNESS, REPRESSION, MANAGEMENT, POLITICIAN, POLITICS

GRADATION

n. **1. 1. gradation** gradations, shading. **2. step** degree, notch, peg, pitch, point, remove, stage. **3. graduation** calibration, scale. **4. measurements** accent, apothecaries' weight, Celsius, centimetre-gram-second system, f.p.s., Fahrenheit, foot-pound-second system, imperial system, International System of Units, measure, metre-kilogram-second system, metric system, scale, SI, wine measure. **5. unit** degree, denomination, fundamental unit, indication. **6. measure** size.

2. 1. grade class, level, order, rank, year. **2. level** plane. **3. rating** class, footing, grading, position, rate, standing, station, status. **4. ranking** A grade, B grade, front rank, reserve grade. **5. alpha** beta, gamma, omega.

adj. **3. 1. gradational** calibrated, graduated, hierarchical. **2. gradual** absolute, fading, shading. **3. graded** first-degree, second-degree, third-degree.

v. **4. 1. graduate** calibrate, divide, scale. **2. grade** class, rank, rate.

adv. **5. 1. gradually** a little at a time, bit by bit, by degrees, by inches, inchmeal, little by little, piecemeal, poco a poco, step by step. **2. somewhat** a bit, in some measure, to some extent. *Informal:* some. **3. at one remove** a step away, one step up from.

RELATED KEYWORDS: MEASUREMENT, QUANTITY, REGULARITY

GRAMMATICAL ERROR

n. **1. 1. grammatical error** abusage, barbarism, error, impropriety, infelicity, lapsus linguae, malapropism, misusage, mixed metaphor, slip, slip of the tongue, solecism. **2. faulty language** anacoluthia, anacoluthon, bad grammar, lack of concord, mispunctuation, misspelling, tautology. *Informal:* slipslop.

adj. **2. 1. ungrammatical** anacoluthic, incorrect, slipshod, solecistic, unidiomatic, wrong.

v. **3. 1. use faulty language** mispronounce, mispunctuate, misspeak, misspell, misword, miswrite.

RELATED KEYWORDS: OBSCURITY, BOMBAST, NONSENSE, WRONGDOING

GRATEFULNESS

n. **1. 1. gratefulness** appreciation, appreciativeness, gratitude, hearty thanks, sense of obligation, thankfulness, thanks. **2. thanksgiving** celebration. **3. acknowledgement** bow, credit, recognition, thank-offering, thanksgiving, thankyou, tribute, vote of thanks. **4. requital** gratuity, recognition, recognition of one's services, return, return favour, reward, thankyou present, tip, token of one's gratitude. **5. thankyou letter** bread-and-butter letter. **6. grace** eucharist, grace before meals, praise.

adj.   **2.**   **1. grateful** appreciative, appreciatory, thankful. **2. thankyou** recognitory. **3. obliged** beholden, indebted, much obliged. **4. thankworthy**.

v.   **3.**   **1. be grateful** be overwhelmed by someone's generosity, be thankful, say thankyou, thank. *Informal:* say ta. **2. appreciate** bless. **3. be full of gratitude**. **4. acknowledge** acknowledge one's debt to, give credit where credit is due, give someone their due. **5. thank God** give praise to the Lord, give thanks, thank one's lucky stars. **6. be grateful for small mercies** be grateful for what you can get. **7. accept gratefully** not look a gift horse in the mouth, receive with open arms.

adv.   **4.**   **1. gratefully** appreciatively, appreciatorily, thankfully.

interj.   **5.**   **1. thank you** merci, merci beaucoup, thanks. *Informal:* ta, thanks a bunch, thanks a million. **2. Deo gratias** praise be to God, thank the Lord, thanks be to God.

RELATED KEYWORDS: KINDNESS

GREATNESS

n.   **1.**   **1. greatness** ampleness, amplitude, bigness, bulk, bulkiness, enormity, enormousness, extremeness, fullness, giganticness, hugeness, immenseness, immensity, largeness, magnitude, mass, massiness, massiveness, mightiness, size, spaciousness, substantialness, tremendousness, vastitude, vastness. **2. intensity** blaze, deep, deepness, denseness, depth, extremity, fierceness, force, grievousness, heat, intenseness, intension, keenness, perfervour, poignancy, rigour, severeness, severity, sharpness, violence, vividness. **3. stupendousness** awesomeness, awfulness, fabulousness, fearfulness, frightfulness, ineffableness, portentousness, prodigiousness, terribleness.

  2.   **1. much** a good (or great) many, a lot, abundance, affluence, copiousness, flood, horn of plenty, host, lot, mass, mountain, muchness, multitude, ocean, peck, plenitude, plenty, prodigality, profusion, quantity, quiverful, raft, rain, river, sea, store, torrent, volume, wealth, world. *Informal:* a sight, bucketload, heap, pile, power. **2. a good deal** a mint. *Informal:* a big mob, acres, any amount, bags, biggest mobs, lashings, lots, neckful, no end, oodles, reams, scads, stacks, tons, whips of. **3. most** best part, bulk, majority, the lion's share. *Informal:* mostest. **4. maximum** maxima, the lot. *Informal:* the full bore. **5. extreme** utmost, uttermost. **6. cornucopia** land of milk and honey, the groaning board.

adj.   **3.**   **1. large** appreciable, big, decuman, extended, family-size, full-scale, good, good-sized, great, hearty, high, horse, jumbo, king, king-size, large-scale, mickle *(Scottish)*, much, myriad, sizable, spacious, XL. *Informal:* ginormous, mega, old-man. **2. sizeable** biggish, largish, respectable. *Informal:* pretty, tidy. **3. abundant** aplenty, bounteous, bountiful, copious, exuberant, fecund, luxuriant, plenteous, plentiful, profuse, prolific, rich in (or with), rife, superabundant, teeming, vast. *Informal:* bags of. **4. ample** affluent, colossal, considerable, goodly, handsome, luxuriant, mighty, numerous, opulent, princely, rich, round, substantial, tall, thick, wealthy.

  4.   **1. enormous** astronomic, astronomical, cyclopean, elephantine, gargantuan, giant, gigantean, gigantesque, gigantic, herculean, huge, immense, mammoth, monster, monstrous, monumental, mountain, mountainous, overblown, overgrown, prodigious, titanic, towering, tremendous, vast, vasty *(Poetic)*. *Informal:* massive, whopping. **2. bulky** ample, full, gross, massive, massy, monumental, portly, solid, voluminous. **3. awesome** astonishing, astounding, awe-inspiring, awful, dreadful, fabulous, immense, ineffable, intimidating, mind-boggling, oracular, overwhelming, phenomenal, portentous, stupendous.

  5.   **1. most** all, best, consummate, extreme, maximal, maximum, maximus, supreme, top, utmost, uttermost, veriest. **2. major** dominant, main, most, ruling. **3. all-time** absolute, arrant, blank, bumper, downright, fantastic, fantastical, out-and-out, passing, positive, resounding, surpassing, tearing, thoroughgoing, uncommon, unmistakable, unmitigated, unqualified, utter. *Informal:* almighty, awful, bally, bleeding *(Chiefly British)*, bloody, blooming, flaming, flat, flipping, flopping, frigging, hang of a, helluva, howling, humming, mother of a, plumb, rattling, smacking, sollicking, some, spanking, stinking, swingeing, the father of a ..., thumping, thundering, walloping, whacking.

  6.   **1. intense** bad, dense, exquisite, frightful, grievous, heavy, high, keen, particular, perfervid, poignant, profound, severe, sharp, special, terrible, terrific, towering, violent, vivid.

adv.   **7.**   **1. greatly** appreciably, big, considerably, in a big way, mightily, on a large scale, widely. **2. mostly** chiefly, especially, for the most part, generally, in the main, largely, mainly, maximally, most, principally, substantially. **3. much** a lot, by far, far, far and away, lots. **4. galore** *Informal:* as ... as all get-out, like anything, like hell, like the devil, till it hurts, to the skies. **5. abundantly** amply, by far, by half, considerably, copiously, far and away, handsomely, in bulk, largely, luxuriantly, opulently, richly, substantially, substantively, thickly, widely. *Informal:* by a long chalk, hand over fist, no end. **6. in full measure** *Informal:* and a half and then some, and how, some *(US)*. **7. absolutely** dead, downright, entirely, exceedingly, extremely, hundred-per-cent, ineffably, insuperably, invincibly, monumentally, out, out and away, out and out, outright, overwhelmingly, perfectly, plain, simply, spaciously, stark, supremely, surpassingly, totally, toweringly, unutterably, utterly. *Informal:* hugely, plumb. **8. awesomely** devastatingly, extra-specially, fabulously, fantastically, frighteningly, frightfully, horribly, impossibly, phenomenally, portentously, prodigiously, shockingly, stupendously. **9. grandiosely** big, grandly, regally. **10. massively** bulkily, solidly.

8. 1. intensely dearly, deeply, extremely, grievously, highly, intensively, keenly, perfervidly, poignantly, resoundingly, severely, sharply, violently, vividly, with a vengeance.

9. 1. very almightily, almighty, awfully, bad, badly, decidedly, devilishly, extra, great, how, molto, not a little, particularly, perishingly, precious, pretty, remarkably, signally, terribly, terrifically, thumpingly, thunderingly, too, uncommon, uncommonly. *Informal:* and how, bally, bleeding, bloody, blooming, damned, darned, deuced, devilish, ever so, frigging, jolly, mega, not half, perishing, plenty, rattling, real, ruddy, stinking.

10. 1. enormously astronomically, colossally, gigantically, hugely, immensely, mountainously, tremendously, vastly.

RELATED KEYWORDS: SIZE, LENGTH

GREEN

n. **1. 1. green** emerald, jade, jade green, leek green, vert. **2. sea green** aqua, aquamarine, beryl, blue-green, Nile blue, Nile green, saxe blue, turquoise. **3. yellow-green** chartreuse, grass-green, lime-green, pea green, pistachio, sulphur. **4. apple green** almond green, celadon. **5. khaki** bottle green, jungle green, olivaceous, olive, olive green. **6. grey-green** mignonette, reseda, sage-green.

2. 1. greenness verdancy, verdure, verdurousness, virescence, viridescence, viridity. **2. greenery** greenness, verdure, viridity. **3. verdigris. 4. green pigment** bice, chlorophyll, chrome green, Paris green, terre-verte, verditer, viridian.

adj. **3. 1. green** aquamarine, celadon, chartreuse, emerald, glaucous, greenish, greeny, olive, prasine, reseda, sage-green, verdant, vert, virescent, viridescent. **2. verdant** grass-like, grassy, green, leafy, turfy, verdurous.

RELATED KEYWORDS: BLUE, COLOUR, PLANTS, ORANGE

GREY

n. **1. 1. grey** ash colour, ash-grey, battleship grey, iron-grey. **2. charcoal grey** gunmetal, slate. **3. dove colour** dove grey. **4. drab** beige, dun, fuscous, isabel, mouse-dun, putty, stone, taupe. **5. merle. 6. pearl** off-white, oyster, oyster white, pearl blue, pearl grey. **7. French grey** sage-green. **8. blue-grey** Copenhagen blue, steel blue, steel grey. **9. grizzle** grey hair, pepper and salt. **10. grisaille. 11. greyness** hoariness, leadenness, lividness. **12. silver** frostiness, silveriness.

adj. **2. 1. grey** ash-coloured, ash-grey, ashen, ashy, cinereal, cinereous, gray *(US)*, greyish, grizzled, grizzly, hoary, iron-grey. **2. blue-grey** livid, slaty. **3. dove-coloured** columbine, dove-grey. **4. dapple-grey** merle. **5. leaden** dusty, frosty, leady. **6. smoky** fuliginous. **7. drab** beige, dun, fulvous, isabel, isabelline, putty. **8. pearlgrey** griseous, off-white, pearl, pearly. **9. sage-green. 10. silver** argent, iron, penumbral, silvery, steel.

3. 1. grey-haired canescent, grey, grey-headed, greying, grizzled, grizzly, hoary, pepper-and-salt, silver-haired, white-haired.

v. **4. 1. grey** grizzle, silver.

RELATED KEYWORDS: BLACK, WHITE, MATURITY, COLOURLESSNESS

GRIEF

n. **1. 1. grief** dolour, grieving, heartbreak, lamentation, misery, moan, mournfulness, mourning, sadness, sorrow, woe. **2. lament** cri de coeur. **3. song of lament** coronach, dead march, dirge, elegy, epicedium, jeremiad, knell, last post, monody, requiem, threnode, threnody. **4. wake** exequies, tangi. **5. mourning clothes** armband, black, half-mourning, hatband, mourning, mourning band, sables, weeds, weeper.

2. 1. cry crying, howl, sob, wail, whimper, whine. *Informal:* bawl, blubber, boohoo, snivel, weep. **2. keen** croon, ululation. **3. groan** sigh.

3. **1. griever** lamenter, mourner, sorrower. **2. weeper** snuffler, wailer. *Informal:* bawler, blubberer, sniveller. **3. keener** crooner, monodist, threnodist. **4. groaner** sigher. **5. pietà**.

adj. 4. **1. grieving** broken-hearted, cut up, desolate, desolated, grief-stricken, heart-stricken, heartbroken, heartsick, heartsore, in mourning, inconsolable, lamenting, mourning, pining, sorrowful, sorrowing. **2. mournful** doleful, dolorous, grievous, lugubrious, plaintive, sorry, tragic, woebegone, woeful. **3. crying** sobbing, tearful, wailing, waterish, watery, weeping. *Informal:* blubbering, snivelly. **4. groaning** howling, ululant, ululating, wailful, wailsome. **5. elegiac** epicedian, exequial, threnodic.

v. 5. **1. grieve** anguish, be in mourning, bewail, bleed for, grieve over, have a broken heart, mourn, pine, pine away, pine for, regret. **2. bemoan** bewail, elegise, lament, moan, threnodise, wail, weep over. **3. cry** cry one's eyes out, cry one's heart out, shed tears, snuffle, sob, weep, weep one's eyes out. *Informal:* bawl, blub, blubber, boohoo, snivel, tune one's pipes. **4. moan** croon *(Scottish, Irish)*, groan, keen, sigh, ululate, wail. **5. whine** howl, whimper. **6. hold a wake for** give someone a good send-off, tangi *(NZ)*. **7. wear black** be in black, don widow's weeds, go into mourning, wear sackcloth and ashes. **8. wring one's hands** beat one's breast, go berserk, rend one's garments. **9. lower the flag** half-mast the flag.

RELATED KEYWORDS: EMOTION, FUNERAL RITES, UNHAPPINESS, DEATH, SOMBRENESS

GROWTH

n. 1. **1. growth** anabolism, concrescence, development, evolution, evolvement, increase, intergrowth, upgrowth. **2. accumulation** accretion, accrual, accruement, build-up, increment. **3. distension** aggrandisement, amplification, enlargement, expansion, spread, swell. **4. proliferation** reproduction. **5. advance** outreach, outspread, progress. **6. rebirth** palingenesis, regeneration, revegetation. **7. overgrowth** hypertrophy, overdevelopment. **8. ripeness** vigour. **9. teething problems** growing pains, teething troubles.

2. **1. flower** blossom, bud, fruit, shoot, tiller. **2. excrescence** bubo, bump, bunion, callosity, callus, chondroma, desmoid, excrescency, fungus, fusee, gall, growth, hernia, neoplasm, neurofibroma, neuroma, node, outgrowth, scirrhus, swelling, tragus, tubercle, tumour. **3. intumescence** ingrowth.

3. **1. breeding ground** hatchabator, incubator, womb. **2. cradle** nursery. **3. hotbed** fertile soil, good soil, seedbed. **4. hothouse** conservatory, garden, glasshouse, grapery, greenery, greenhouse, terrarium. **5. auxanometer** crescograph.

adj. 4. **1. growing** anabolic, crescent, developing, going, proliferous, regenerative, rising. **2. accumulative** accretive, cumulative. **3. developmental** evolutional, evolutionary. **4. excrescent** fungoid, gallic, intumescent, scirrhoid. **5. distensible** distensile, enlargeable. **6. flourishing** fulminant, hypertrophic, luxuriant, mushroom, overgrown, rank, sturdy, wanton *(Poetic)*. **7. germinant** gemmate, germinative.

5. **1. ingrowing** accrete, ingrown. **2. geophilous** epigeal, epigenous, epigeous.

v. 6. **1. grow** bloom, bud, develop, germinate, grow together, pullulate, rise, sprout, unfold. **2. branch** branch out, bush, extend, mallee. **3. climb** creep, ramble, run, twine. **4. outgrow** extend, outreach. **5. overgrow** deluge, mushroom, outspread, outstretch, overflow, overreach, overrun, overspread, run wild. *Informal:* grow like Topsy. **6. distend** aggrandise, amplify, bag, balloon, belly, bilge, billow, bloat, bulge, enlarge, expand, fill, fill out, heave, hypertrophy, inflate, intumesce, puff up, swell, tumefy. **7. accumulate** accrete, accrue, multiply. **8. advance** burgeon, progress.

7. **1. flower** anisocarpic, anthesis, bloom, blossom, blow, bud, burgeon, foliate, fungate, gemmate, ratoon, rise, tassel. **2. bear** fruit. **3. germinate** pullulate, root, shoot, spear, spring, sprout, stool, strike, take, take (or strike) root, tiller. **4. breed** multiply, proliferate, propagate, pullulate, reproduce, teem. **5. cultivate** cross-fertilise, cross-pollinate, culture, fertilise, force, impregnate, inoculate, pollen, pollinate, revegetate, scarify. **6. ripen** bloom, blossom, flourish, hay off, run riot, thrive, wax.

RELATED KEYWORDS: INCREASE, CREATION, SIZE, REPRODUCTION

GUIDANCE

n. 1. **1. guidance** direction, drilling, education, instruction, leadership, pedagogy, suasion, teaching, tuition, tutelage, tutorage. **2. consultation** conference, reference, referral. **3. advice** briefing, counsel, counsel of perfection, guidance, instruction, marriage guidance, words of wisdom. **4. hint** clue, cue, lead, piece of advice, pointer, points, suggestion, tip, word of advice. *Informal:* heads-up. **5. exhortation** behest, charge, direction, injunction, instruction, instructions, moralising, solicitation.

6. criticism constructive criticism, correction, emendation. **7. admonition** admonishment, caution, execration, expostulation, monition, object lesson, protestation, tip-off, warning. *Informal:* earful. **8. guidelines** instruction, recommendation.

2. **1. guide** assessor, consulter, director, exhorter, mentor, role model, teacher. **2. adviser** advocate, advocator, amicus curiae, consigliore, consultant, councillor, counsellor, guidance officer, school counsellor. **3. authority** advisory body, advisory council, oracle, sage. **4. careers adviser** extension worker *(NZ)*, family doctor, farm consultant, marriage guidance counsellor. **5. confidant** confessor, confident, father confessor. **6. admonisher** corrector, expostulator, monitor, warner. **7. back-seat driver** *Informal:* kibitzer *(US)*. **8. think tank** brains trust, council of war.

adj.   3. **1. advisory** assessorial, consultative, consultatory, consulting, deliberative. **2. exhortative** exhortatory, hortative, hortatory, recommendatory, suasory. **3. admonitory** correctional, corrective, directive, expostulative, expostulatory, moralising, remonstrant, warning.

v.   4. **1. guide** advise, advocate, commend, counsel, give advice, lead, prescribe, recommend. *Informal:* kibitz *(US)*. **2. suggest** advance, moot, move, offer, propose, propound, put forward, submit. **3. exhort** charge, urge. **4. admonish** advise against, advise someone of something, caution, expostulate, forewarn, obtest, premonish, remonstrate, remonstrate with, set (or put) someone straight, warn. *Informal:* put wise, tip off.

5. **1. seek guidance** confer, confide, consult, deliberate, refer, seek advice. **2. be advised** take advice, take one's cue from.

RELATED KEYWORDS: COUNCIL, HELP, INFLUENCE, TEACHING

GUILT

n.   1. **1. guilt** blood guilt, blood-guiltiness, complicity, fault, guilt by association, guiltiness. **2. blameworthiness** censurableness, criminality, damnableness, delinquency. **3. shame** ashamedness, contriteness, contrition, embarrassment, pang of guilt, peccavi, qualm.

adj.   2. **1. guilty** at fault, blood-guilty, bloodstained, culpable, double-dyed, faulty, in fault, in the wrong, nocent, to blame. **2. damned** impure, unchaste. **3. damnable** blameworthy, condemnable, criminal, delinquent, punishable, reprehensible.

3. **1. ashamed** conscience-smitten, conscience-stricken, contrite, embarrassed, guilt-stricken, penitent, penitential, remorseful, repentant, repenting, self-accusing, sorry.

v.   4. **1. be guilty** have something to hide. *Informal:* have a skeleton in the cupboard. **2. be ashamed** blush, feel guilty, feel small, have qualms. *Informal:* hang one's head, hide one's head. **3. confess** admit, admit one's guilt, avow, own, own up. *Informal:* come clean, go to press.

adv.   5. **1. guiltily** damningly, in flagrante delicto, red-handed. **2. ashamedly** contritely, repentantly.

RELATED KEYWORDS: ACCUSATION, BADNESS, UNLAWFULNESS, IMMORALITY, PENITENCE

HABITATION

n.   1. **1. habitation** abode, domicile, dwelling, dwelling house, dwelling place, habitat, home, lodgings, place, residence, residency, tenement. *Informal:* joint, kipsie, pad. **2. inhabitancy** abidance, cohabitation, inhabitance, inhabitation. **3. quartering** accommodation, baching, billet, boarding, harbourage, hostelling, lodging, lodgings, stabling. **4. lodgement** encampment, establishment, installation, location. **5. occupancy** cotenancy, occupation, possession, tenancy.

2. **1. inhabitant** abider, citizen, denizen, dweller, habitant, indweller, inhabiter, resident, residentiary. **2. neighbour** local. **3. frontiersman** borderer, marcher, outlier. **4. inlander** highlander, lowlander, mainlander, marsh dweller, mountaineer, sylvan, ultra-montane, woodlander. *Informal:* bogtrotter *(Chiefly British)*. **5. caveman** cave-dweller, troglodyte. *Informal:* trog. **6. terrestrial** earthling, earthman, mortal, tellurian. **7. isthmian** islander.

3. **1. occupant** cotenant, homesteader, householder, landholder, leaseholder, occupier, ratepayer, tenant. **2. homemaker** *Informal:* homebody. **3. household** family, house, ménage. *Informal:* brood. **4. cohabiter** flatmate, housemate, inmate. **5. lodger** boarder, hosteller, paying guest, roomer *(Chiefly US)*. **6. guest** commensal, company, house guest, sojourner, visitant, visitor.

4. **1. population** citizenry, city. **2. towndweller** burgess, burgher, citizen, city dweller, fringe dweller, metropolitan, slummer, townsman, townswoman, urbanite. *Informal:* townie. **3. suburbanite** commuter, exurbanite. *Informal:* straphanger. **4. townspeople**

suburbia, town, townsfolk, township *(Chiefly British History)*, village. **5. countrydweller** back-countryman, backblocker, backwoodsman, bushman, bushy, cottager, cottar, cottier, countryman, countryside, countrywoman, hatter, hillbilly *(Chiefly US)*, peasant, provincial, ryot *(Indian English)*, villager, yeoman *(British)*. *Informal:* bushie, bushwhacker *(US)*. **6. settler** colonist, currency lad, currency lass, illegitimate, old settler, overstraiter, soldier settler, squatter. **7. immigrant** alien, black hat, boat people, foreigner, illegal immigrant, incomer, migrant, new arrival, newcomer, nominated migrant, outlander, refugee, tramontane. *Informal:* ethnic, ethno, reffo, ten pound Pom. **8. new chum** chum. *Informal:* sterling. **9. native** aborigine, autochthon, indigene. **10. native-born** *Informal:* Apple Islander, banana-bender, cabbage gardener, cockroach *(Chiefly Qld)*, currency, gumsucker, mappie, top-ender.

adj. **5. 1. demography** demographics, ekistics. **2. demographist** town-planner.

6. 1. inhabited lived-in, occupied, populated. **2. well-populated** populous.

7. 1. inhabitable habitable, livable, liveable, tenantable.

8. 1. resident indwelling, quartered, residentiary, residing. **2. native** aboriginal, autochthonous, endemic, indigenous. **3. first-generation** native-born. **4. home** domestic, local. **5. migrant** alien, ethnic. **6. parasitic** entophytic, entozoan, entozoic, epizoic, inquiline, inquilinous. **7. commensal** symbiotical. **8. aerial** arboreal, arenicolous, epigeal, fenny *(British)*, geophilous, marine, riparian, terrestrial, terricolous.

v. **9. 1. inhabit** affect, domicile, dwell, indwell, live in, occupy, populate, reside, squat, tenant. **2. dwell** house, live, reside, stay, subsist in. *Informal:* hang out. **3. stay** sojourn, stop, tarry, visit. **4. lodge** board, put up, quarter, room. **5. flat** bachelorise. *Informal:* bach, batch, pad down. **6. move in** settle in. **7. live together** live with. *Informal:* muck in, shack up (with). **8. live out** sleep out. **9. camp out** bivouac, camp, encamp, pitch a tent, tent. *Informal:* bivvy. **10. kennel** nest, stable, stall, sty. **11. cabin** barrack, hut. **12. caravan** campervan.

10. 1. come from belong to, hail from. **2. colonise** people, plant, populate. **3. settle** anchor, take up residence. *Informal:* swallow the anchor.

RELATED KEYWORDS: CITY, THE BUSH, DWELLING, NATION

HAIR

n. **1. 1. hair** down, flue, fluff, lanugo, pile, shag. *Informal:* fuzz. **2. filament** penicil, vibrissa, whisker, wire. **3. bristle** arista, awn, beard, chaeta, cilia, down, gare, seta, setula, vibrissa, villus. **4. hair of the head** bush, combings, dreadlocks, dreads, frizz, head, locks, mane, mat, mop, thatch, towhead. **5. grizzle** snow. **6. curl** kiss-curl, lock, pin-curl, quiff, ringlet, strand, tag, tresses. **7. elflock** cowlick, feather, forelock, lovelock, topknot, tourbillion, widow's peak. **8. bangs** bob, bun, chignon, cue, French roll, fringe, lovelock *(British History)*, mullet, pompadour, puff, topknot. **9. eyebrow** cilia, eyelash. *Informal:* falsies. **10. pubes** pubic hair. *Informal:* fur. **11. tail** braid, bunches, ducktail, horse tail, horsy tail, pigtail, plait, ponytail, queue, rat's tail.

2. 1. animal's coat coat, fleece, jacket, pelage. **2. fur** badger, beaver, blue fox, broadtail, buckskin, caracul, chinchilla, cony, deerskin, ermine, fisher, fitch, fox, galyak, hamster, karakul, kolinsky, lapin, miniver, mink, monkey, muskrat, musquash, nutria, peltry, pointed fox, puma, sable, seal, sealskin, skunk, squirrel, vair, wig, wolf, zibeline. **3. wool** alpaca, angora, astrakhan, camelhair, cashmere, grogram, horsehair, kashmir, mohair, mother hair, Persian lamb, pile. **4. horsehair** coat. **5. crest** coma, foretop. **6. bellies** belly-wool, locks, underfur. **7. dag** abb, dagging, daglock, dagwool, tag. **8. tuft** fetlock, fetterlock, floccus, flock, switch. **9. mane** collar, frill, hackles, torques. **10. eyeclip** eyewool, moustache, topknot, wig.

3. 1. hairpiece crepe hair, fall, merkin, postiche, switch, toupee. *Informal:* rug. **2. wig** bobwig, buzzwig, periwig, peruke, spencer.

4. 1. beard beaver, burnsides *(US)*, down, five o'clock shadow, goatee, imperial, neck, Vandyke beard. *Informal:* bumfluff, face fungus, ziff. **2. moustache** handlebar moustache, mustache *(US)*, mustachio, walrus moustache, whiskers, Zapata moustache. *Informal:* face fungus, lice ladders, mo, moey. **3. sideburns** dundrearies, mutton-chop whiskers, mutton-chops, side-whiskers, sideboards, sidelevers.

5. 1. hairiness curliness, fuzziness, hirsuteness, hispidity, stubbiness. **2. fluffiness** downiness, pilosity, pubescence, tomentum. **3. fleeciness** furriness. **4. penicillation** fimbriation, villosity. **5. hairy person** gorilla. *Informal:* fungus face, hairy-legs. **6. long-hair** *(Informal)* curlyhead.

6. 1. hair colour. 2. blonde ash-blond, fair head, goldilocks, peroxide blonde, platinum blonde, strawberry blonde, towhead. *Informal:* bottle blonde, bushfire blonde, lemonhead.

3. redhead coppernob, Ginger. *Informal:* carrot top, coppertop. **4. brunette** brunet. *Informal:* bitumen blonde. **5. whitebeard** greybeard.

7. **1. hairdressing** setting. **2. haircut** afro, blunt cut, bob, buzz cut, clip, crew cut, crop, cut, dreadlocks, Eton crop, flat-top, frizz, mop top, pageboy, razor cut, shingle, short back and sides, trim. *Informal:* convict cut, nana. **3. hairstyle** coiffure, cornrow braiding, cornrows, hairdo, mullet, pouf, quiff, rat's tail, tonsure. *Informal:* big hair, do. **4. wave** blow-wave, cold wave, finger-wave, perm, permanent wave, root perm, water-wave.

8. **1. hairdresser** barber, coiffeur, comber, hairstylist, stylist, wigmaker. *Informal:* Sydney Harbour. **2. hairdresser's salon** barber shop, beauty shop, wiggery.

adj. **9.** **1. hairy** bristly, brushy, chaetophorous, comate, comose, crinite, fur, furred, furry, hirsute, hispid, maned, pileous, piliferous, pilose, rough, setaceous, setiferous, setigerous, setose, setulose, setulous, shaggy, stubby, ulotrichous, whiskery, wire-haired. **2. fleecy** downy, fluey, fluffy, fuzzy, lanuginose, lanuginous, tomentose. **3. flocculent** bunchy, floccose, flocky, lanate, lanigerous, tufted, tufty, woolly. **4. arachnoid** fimbrial, fimbriate, fimbriated, fimbrillate, pubescent, silky, villiform, villose, villous. **5. long-haired** bewigged, ringleted, shockheaded, tressed, wigged. **6. bearded** barbate, barbed, black-browed, side-whiskered, whiskery.

10. **1. coloured (of hair).** **2. ash-blond** blonde, fair-haired, peroxide, strawberry, tow-headed. **3. red-headed** carroty. **4. brunette.** **5. grey** grey-headed, grizzled, grizzly, hoary, white-haired, white-headed.

11. **1. hairlike** capillaceous, capillary, pileous, piliform, pilous, setaceous, trichoid. **2. bristlelike** barbellate, bristle-shaped, penicillate, setaceous, setiform. **3. wiglike**. **4. beardlike**.

v. **12.** **1. do one's hair** brush, comb, dress, fix. **2. curl** coil, crimp, frizz, kink, wave.

RELATED KEYWORDS: FEATHER, TEXTILES

HANGING

n. **1.** **1. hanging** impendency, pendency, pendulousness, pensility, suspense, suspension, suspensiveness. **2. bagginess** flabbiness, flaccidness, slouchiness. **3. hang** dangle, drape, droop, fall, pend, sag, set, slouch, sweep.

2. **1. pendant** drop, hanging ornament, pendent. **2. chandelier** corona. **3. swing** cuddle seat, flying trapeze, hammock, trapeze. **4. pendulum** bob, bobber, lead, plumb-bob, plummet. **5. tassel** bobble, dangle. *Informal:* fandangle. **6. hangings** arras, curtain, dossal, dosser, drapery, drapes, frontlet, swag, tapestry, valance, wall-hanging. **7. skirt** tail, tails, tippet, train. **8. flap** flapper, lappet.

3. **1. hanger** billyhook, hook, peg, piton, suspender.

adj. **4.** **1. hanging** dangling, dependent, hovering, overhung, pendent, pending, pendulous, pensile, poised, suspended, suspensive. **2. overhanging** imminent, impendent, impending, projecting. **3. drooping** cernuous, deflexed, epinastic, flagging, flaggy, nodding, nutant, sagging. **4. baggy** droopy, flabby, flaccid, flaggy, limp, saggy, slouchy. **5. flowing** floating, flying, streaming.

v. **5.** **1. hang** dangle, depend, pend, poise, swing. **2. overhang** hang over. **3. flow** float, fly, stream. **4. hang** bag, blouse, droop, fall, flag, hang down, loll, lop, nod, sag, slouch. **5. drag** draggle, sweep, trail. **6. suspend** append, hang, hang out, hang up, sling, string, string up, suspercollate.

RELATED KEYWORDS: DESCENT, BULGE, SUPPORT

HAPPINESS

n. **1.** **1. happiness** blithesomeness, cheer, cheerfulness, cheeriness, delight, enlivenment, exhilaration, felicity, festiveness, gladness, gladsomeness, glee, gleefulness, gleesomeness, good cheer, good humour, good nature, good-humouredness, good-naturedness, jolliness, joy, joyfulness, joyousness, lightsomeness, merriness, mirthfulness, rejoicing, sunniness, sunny side, sunshine, wellness. **2. rapture** ecstasy, ravishment. **3. liveliness** airiness, animal spirits, animation, ardour, boyishness, breeziness, brightness, brilliance, brio, debonairness, dynamism, ebullience, enthusiasm, exuberance, fervour, frolic, frolicsomeness, gaieties, gaiety, get-up-and-go, good spirits, high spirits, hilariousness, hilarity, insouciance, jauntiness, jocundity, joie de vivre, jollities, jollity, merriment, merrymaking, mirth, playfulness, spirit, sportfulness, sportiveness, sprightliness, vitality, vivaciousness, vivacity. **4. joviality** cordiality, cordialness, geniality, genialness, goodwill, jovialness, mellowness, pleasantness. **5. buoyancy** resilience, resiliency. **6. levity** flippantness, frivolousness, kittenishness, light-heartedness, light-mindedness, lightness, tricksiness.

2. **1. smile** beaming smile, broad smile, grin, radiant smile. **2. smiley face** happy face.

adj. 3. **1. happy** beaming, blithe, blithesome, bright, buoyant, carefree, cheerful, cheery, delighted, elate, elated, enchanted, eudemonic, gay, glad, gladsome, good, hilarious, insouciant, jocund *(Poetic)*, joyful, joyous, light, light-hearted, lightsome, merry, mirthful, pleasant, riant, rident. *Informal:* chuffed, full of beans, happy as a sandboy, happy as Larry, pleased as Punch, slaphappy. **2. genial** amiable, Anacreontic, backslapping, benign, boon, bully, cheerful, convivial, cordial, festive, forward, gleeful, gleesome, good-humoured, good-natured, good-tempered, hail-fellow-well-met, high, jolly, jovial, kind-hearted, kindly, mellow, merry, merrymaking, rollicking, sociable, sweet-tempered. **3. lively** airy, animated, boyish, breezy, bright, brilliant, carefree, cheerful, chirrupy, dapper, debonair, effervescent, exuberant, frisky, giocoso, jaunty, kittenish, pacy, peart, perky, pert, quick, racy, radiant, sappy, spirited, spiritoso, sprightly, vital, vivacious, vivid, warm. *Informal:* bright-eyed and bushy-tailed, chipper, chirpy, live, peppy, swinging, zippy. **4. hilarious** bouncy, frolic, frolicsome, gamesome, tricksy, wanton *(Poetic)*. **5. sanguine** bullish, confident, happy-go-lucky, hopeful, irrepressible, optimistic, positive, rosaceous, rose-coloured, rosy, sanguineous, starry-eyed, sunny, sunshine, up-beat. **6. frivolous** blithesome, flippant, giggly, idle, jesting, jocose, light, light-hearted, light-minded, lightsome, playful, rompish, scherzando, sportive, trifling. *Informal:* flip. **7. exhilarating** exhilarant, exhilarative, exhilaratory.

v. 4. **1. be happy** be in good spirits, be in high spirits, gladden, sparkle, walk (or tread) on air. *Informal:* be full of beans, feel like all one's Christmases have come at once, feel one's oats, grin (or smile) like a Cheshire cat. **2. cheer up** brighten, brighten up, gladden, keep one's chin up, lighten, liven up, look on the bright side, perk oneself up, rise, take heart. *Informal:* buck up, ginger up, keep one's pecker up, lighten up. **3. be optimistic** be of good cheer, look at through rose-coloured glasses, look on the bright side. **4. make merry** frolic, joke, kick up one's heels, racket, rollick. *Informal:* frivol. **5. gladden** delight, elate, exhilarate, gratify, please, uplift.

5. **1. make happy** beatify, brighten, cheer, delectate, delight, elate, elevate, enliven, exhilarate, gladden, hearten, imparadise, liven up, revive, thrill to bits. *Informal:* buck up, jollify.

adv. 6. **1. happily** beamingly, breezily, brightly, buoyantly, cheerfully, cheerily, chirpily, effervescently, giocoso, gladly, gladsomely, gleefully, gleesomely, good-humouredly, good-naturedly, jocundly, jollily, joyfully, joyously, merrily, mirthfully, riantly, smilingly, spiritoso, sunnily. **2. debonairly** airily, blithely, blithesomely, exhilaratingly, gaily, jauntily, lightly, lightsomely, sprightly, vivaciously. **3. frivolously** airily, flippantly, kittenishly, light-heartedly, light-mindedly, lightly. **4. genially** convivially, heartily, jovially, mellowly, merrily, pleasantly. **5. hilariously** boyishly, exuberantly, frolicsomely, playfully, sportively, tricksily.

RELATED KEYWORDS: CONTENTEDNESS, EMOTION, HOPE, JOY

HARDNESS

n. 1. **1. hardness** boniness, flintiness, horniness, infusibleness, microhardness, rockiness, solidity, solidness, steeliness, stoniness, stubbornness, temper, toughness, vitreosity, woodenness, woodiness. **2. rigidness** erectility, firmness, inflexibleness, rigidity, rigor, solid, stiffness, tautness, unbendingness. **3. Mohs scale** Brinell number, Knoop hardness. **4. sclerometer** indentor.

2. **1. hardening** burning, calcification, carburisation, concretion, crystallisation, cyanide hardening, ectostosis, encrustation, incrustation, induration, lignification, nitriding, ossification, ostosis, petrifaction, petrification, rigor mortis, sclerosis, setting, solidification, strain-hardening, vitrifaction, vitrification, work-hardening. **2. hardener** carburiser, clear-starcher, fixer, stiffener, toughener. **3. starch** amylum.

adj. 3. **1. hard** adamant, adamantine, bricklike, concrete, concretionary, crystalline, flinty, glass, glasslike, glassy, granitic, gritty, iron, ironbound, marble, marbly, pebbly, petrosal, petrous, rocklike, rocky, semivitreous, steel, steely, stone, stonelike, stony, vitreous, vitriform, wooden, woody. **2. bony** bonelike, ceratoid, chitinous, corneous, horny, osseous, ossiferous, osteal, osteoid, scalelike, scaly, scleritic, sclerodermatous, scleroid, sclerosal, sclerotic, sclerous, spongy, testaceous. **3. rigid** cast-iron, erect, erectile, indurate, inflexible, ironbound, springless, starched, starchy, stark, stiff, stiff as a poker, taut, unbending, uncrushable, wiry. **4. tough** chewy, leathery. **5. weathered** weather-beaten. **6. solid** compacted, dense, firm, impassable, impermeable, impervious, infusible, stout, stubborn, sturdy. **7. hardened** high-speed, ironbound, prestressed, sealed, set, strain-hardened, tempered, weathered, weatherworn. **8. hardening** calcifying, indurative, ossifying, petrifactive, sclerosed.

v. **4.** **1. become hard** calcify, chill, congeal, consolidate, cornify, crust, crystallise, curd, encrust, fix, fossilise, freeze, harden, ice, lignify, ossify, petrify, season, set, solidify, stiffen, tauten, temper, tense, toughen, vitrify. **2. consolidate** bind, compact, concrete, condense, firm. **3. make hard** bake, callus, carburise, case-harden, chill, compact, consolidate, freeze, harden, incrust, indurate, lignify, ossify, petrify, season, set, solidify, steel, stiffen, strengthen, tauten, temper, toughen, vitrify. **4. starch** clear-starch.

adv. **5.** **1. hard** inflexibly, rigidly, starkly, stiff, tautly, tight, tightly, unbendingly, woodenly. **2. solidly** sturdily. **3. stonily** flintily. **4. glassily** vitreously.

RELATED KEYWORDS: SOLIDITY

HARSHNESS

n. **1.** **1. harshness** grimness, rigor, rigour, ruggedness, severity, sternness. **2. strictness** despotism, firmness, infrangibleness, iron fist, iron fist (or hand) in a velvet glove, iron hand, martinetism, rigidness, tender mercies, tight hand, tight rein, tyranny, zero tolerance. **3. exactingness** closeness, formalism, rigor, rigorism, rigorousness, rigour, severeness, severity, strictness, stringency. **4. intransigency** inclemency, iron will, mercilessness, obdurateness, relentlessness, unmercifulness, unrelentingness. **5. astringency** acerbity, asperity, sharpness, stringency. **6. puritanicalness** asceticism, austereness, austerity, dourness, orthodoxy, puritanism.

2. **1. strict person** Caesar, despot, disciplinarian, Dutch uncle, formalist, hanging judge, hard master, hard taskmaster, kaiser, martinet, slavedriver, tyrant. **2. intransigent** diehard, rigorist. **3. puritan** ascetic, Calvinist, Hole and Corner man *(Australian History)*, spartan.

adj. **3.** **1. harsh** firm, grim, hard, iron, rugged, stern. **2. strict** determined, dour, martinetish, no-nonsense, relentless, rigid, uncompromising, unrelenting. **3. exacting** demanding, draconian, draconic, exhausting, exigent, fierce, gruelling, rigoristic, rigorous, severe. **4. inflexible** binding, hard and fast, hardline, infrangible, ironbound, ironclad, irrefrangible, rigid, set, strict, strictly enforced, stringent, tight, unbreakable. **5. intransigent** adamant, cast-iron, determinate, hard as nails, hard core, hard-baked, hardheaded, hard-hearted, hard-hitting, hardened, heavy-handed, inexorable, inflexible, iron, iron-fisted, iron-handed, merciless, obdurate, pitiless, relentless, remorseless, resolute, ruthless, steadfast, steely, stiff, stony, stony-hearted, unbending, uncompromising, unfeeling, unmerciful, unrelenting, unsparing, unswayed, unwavering, unyielding. **6. oppressive** discriminatory, down on, persecutory, punitive, rough on. **7. astringent** cruel, cutting, merciless, sharp. **8. puritanical** ascetic, ascetical, austere, Calvinistic, dour, hard on oneself, prudish, puritan, severe, spartan, straight-arrow, straitlaced, strict.

v. **4.** **1. be strict** bear down on, clamp down on, crack down on, give no quarter, rule with a rod of iron, stand no nonsense. *Informal:* come down on like a ton of bricks. **2. discipline** castigate, chasten, chastise, gruel, punish, scourge, take in hand, use severely. *Informal:* chew out, tear (or take) strips off, tear strips off, throw the book at. **3. harden** harden one's heart, indurate, put one's foot down, stiffen.

adv. **5.** **1. harshly** cruelly, grimly, hard, intransigently, mercilessly, relentlessly, roundly, ruggedly, severely, unmercifully, unrelentingly, unsparingly, with a heavy hand. **2. strictly** rigidly, severely, sharply, starkly, sternly, stringently. **3. exactingly** draconically, rigorously, straitly. **4. firmly** infrangibly, irrefrangibly, stiffly, unbendingly. **5. puritanically** ascetically, astringently, austerely, dourly.

RELATED KEYWORDS: FORCE, INSISTENCE, REPRESSION, RULE

HATE

n. **1.** **1. hate** abhorrence, antipathy, aversion, disgust, dislike, hatred, loathing, nausea, odium, repugnance, revulsion. *Informal:* allergy. **2. detestation** abhorrence, abomination, animosity, execration, hatred, nauseation, repugnance. **3. malice** bitterness, despite, embitterment, malevolence, rancorousness, rancour, spite, venom, virulence. **4. enmity** alienation, antagonism, bad blood, bad feeling, estrangement, hostility, ill feeling, ill will, implacableness, opposition. **5. misanthropy** Islamophobia, misandry, misogyny, race-hatred, racism, xenophobia.

2. **1. hatefulness** abominableness, accursedness, contemptibleness, damnableness, heinousness, invidiousness, loathsomeness, nauseousness, odiousness.

3. **1. hater** abhorrer, despiser, detester, execrator. **2. embitterer** activist. *Informal:* stirrer. **3. enemy** foe. **4. misanthrope** misogynist, racist, witch-hunter, xenophobe.

4. **1. something hated** abhorrence, abomination, anathema, aversion, detestation, execration, hate, hate figure, pet hate.

5. **1. expression of hate** flame mail, hate mail, hate session.

adj. **6.** **1. hating** antipathetic, bitter, embittered, execrative, hostile, inimical, misanthropic. **2. spiteful** cattish, malevolent, malicious, malignant, nasty, poisonous, rancorous, snaky, ugly, venomous, vicious, viperish, viperous, virulent. **3. misanthropic** misogynous, xenophobic. **4. love-hate** ambivalent.

7. **1. hateful** abhorrent, abominable, accursed, atrocious, contemptible, cursed, curst, damnable, damned, deplorable, despicable, detestable, disgusting, dislikeable, execrable, foul, hateable, hated, heinous, invidious, loathsome, loveless, nauseous, objectionable, obnoxious, odious, offensive, outrageous, putrid, rank, repugnant, repulsive, revolting, unspeakable, vile. *Informal:* cussed.

v. **8.** **1. hate** abhor, abominate, be disgusted by, be nauseated by, be unable to abide, despise, detest, dislike, execrate, loathe, recoil from, revolt from, shrink from, view with horror, view with loathing. *Informal:* hate someone's guts, have a hate on (or against). **2. burn in effigy** hang in effigy, stick pins into.

9. **1. provoke hatred** alienate, cause bad blood, disaffect, embitter, estrange, incur enmity, incur wrath, make another see red, raise someone's ire, set by the ears, sow dissension, stir up bad blood. **2. be anathema to** disgust, go against the grain, make someone's flesh creep, nauseate, revolt, stink in one's nostrils, turn someone's stomach.

adv. **10.** **1. malevolently** bitterly, hostilely, inimically, maliciously, spitefully. **2. hatefully** abhorrently, abominably, accursedly, damnably, disgustfully, disgustingly, invidiously, nauseously, odiously, revoltingly.

RELATED KEYWORDS: EMOTION, UNFRIENDLINESS, LOW REGARD, UNKINDNESS, DISPLEASURE

HEALING

n. **1.** **1. healing** folk medicine, internal medicine, medical science, medicine, preventive medicine, therapeutics. **2. diagnostics** aetiology, clinical pathology, pathology, symptomatology. **3. alternative medicine** acupressure, acupuncture, Alexander technique, chiropractic, herbalism, homoeopathy, iridology, laser acupuncture, naprapathy, naturopathy, osteopathy, radionics, shiatsu. **4. allopathy** iatrochemistry, pharmaceutics, pharmacology, pharmacy, posology, radiopharmacology. **5. psychosomatic medicine** absent healing, faith cure, faith-healing, mental healing.

2. **1. medical treatment** combination therapy, intervention, therapy, treatment. **2. nursing** after-care, care, intensive care, rest cure. **3. physiotherapy** manipulation, massage, massotherapy, materia medica, mechanotherapy, occupational therapy, orthoptic exercises, orthotics, physical therapy *(US)*, physio, prosthetics, reflexology. **4. occupational therapy** diversionary therapy, OT. **5. speech therapy** speech pathology. **6. heat therapy** diathermy, electrodesiccation, heliotherapy, insolaton, phototherapy, radiothermy, thermotherapy. **7. hydrotherapy** hydropathy, pneumatotherapy, water cure. **8. hormone replacement therapy** HRT. **9. lavage** irrigation, toilet, wash-out. **10. artificial respiration** kiss of life, mouth-to-mouth resuscitation, resuscitation. **11. surgery** ablation, excision. **12. radiotherapy** irradiation, X-ray therapy. **13. immunisation** auto-immunisation, auto-inoculation, immunotherapy, inoculation, mithridatism, pasteurism, prophylaxis, tuberculisation, vaccination, vaccinisation, variolation. **14. transfusion** blood transfusion, exchange. **15. blood-letting** bleeding, cupping, phlebotomy, venesection, venipuncture. **16. transplantation** grafting, implantation, plastic surgery, tissue engineering. **17. dialysis** haemodialysis. **18. chemotherapy** chemotherapeutics. *Informal:* chemo. **19. electrotherapy** cardioversion, cataphoresis, defibrillation, electrotherapeutics, faradism, fulguration. **20. hypnotherapy.** **21. gynaecology** gyniatrics, midwifery, obstetrics, tocology. **22. dentistry** bridgework, exodontia, exodontics, odontology, orthodontia, orthodontics, periodontics, prosthodontia, prosthodontics. **23. veterinary science** veterinary medicine.

3. **1. surgery** ablation, adenoidectomy, adrenalectomy, anaplasty, appendectomy, autoplasty, blepharoplasty, bypass, bypass operation, bypass surgery, caesarean section, castration, chiloplasty, cholecystectomy, cholecystostomy, colectomy, colostomy, cosmetic surgery, craniotomy, cryosurgery, cystectomy, cystotomy, debridement, decerebration, dermatoplasty, embolectomy, embryotomy, embryulcia, encephalotomy, enterostomy, fenestration, forceps delivery, gastrectomy, gastrostomy, gastrotomy, glossectomy, gonadectomy, haemorrhoidectomy, herniorrhaphy, heteroplasty, hysterectomy, ileostomy, laparotomy, laryngectomy, laryngotomy, Lempert operation, leucotomy, lipectomy, lobectomy, lobotomy, lumpectomy, mammaplasty, mammoplasty, mastectomy, mastoidectomy, meatotomy, microsurgery, neoplasty, nephrectomy, oesophagectomy, oophorectomy, open-heart surgery, orchidectomy, osteoplasty, osteotomy, ovariotomy, plastic surgery, pneumonectomy, prostatectomy, psychosurgery, pylorectomy, rhinoplasty, rhizotomy, sclerotomy, sequestrectomy, sex change, shunt, silactic prosthesis, skin grafting, splenectomy, staphyloplasty, staphylorrhaphy, stomach stapling, stomatoplasty, strabotomy, sympathectomy, symphysiotomy, tenorrhaphy, tenotomy, thoracoplasty, thyroidectomy, tonsillectomy, tracheotomy, vaginectomy, vagotomy, valvotomy, valvulotomy, varicotomy, vasectomy, xenotransplantation. *Informal:* caesar, encore surgery, short circuiting, spare parts surgery. **2. plastic surgery** autoplasty, chiloplasty, dermatoplasty, heteroplasty, osteoplasty, rhinoplasty, silactic prosthesis, skin grafting, staphyloplasty, staphylorrhaphy, stomatoplasty. **3. modality** acupuncture, catharsis, drainage, haemostasis, intubation, jugulation, levitation, lumbar puncture, osteoclasis, purgation, stypsis, tamponade, taxis. **4. graft** adhesion, CABG, heart transplant, heart-lung transplant, heterotransplant, homotransplantation, kidney transplant, punch graft, transplant, zooplasty. **5. curettage** curette, D and C, hysterotomy, scrope.

4.   **1. hospital** base hospital, clinic, community hospital, cottage hospital, district hospital, general hospital, infirmary, institution, maternity hospital, pavilion, polyclinic *(British)*, private hospital, public hospital, teaching hospital. **2. field hospital** clearing hospital, clearing station, dressing station. **3. clinic** baby health centre, fertility clinic, health centre, prenatal clinic, STD clinic, V.D. clinic. *Informal:* the house that Jack built. **4. nursing home** convalescent home, hospice, hospitium. **5. sanatorium** health camp *(NZ)*, health farm, hydro, isolation hospital, lazaretto, leprosarium, quarantine, spa, watering-place. *Informal:* fat farm. **6. sick room** sanatorium, sick bay, solarium. *Informal:* san. **7. ward** casualty, intensive care unit, labour ward, outpatients' department, private ward, public ward. **8. psychiatric hospital** asylum, lunatic asylum, madhouse, mental home, mental hospital, retreat. *Informal:* booby hatch *(US)*, funny farm, giggle factory, loony bin, nut factory, nuthouse, rat factory *(NZ)*, rathouse.

5.   **1. medicine** medicament, medication. **2. prescription** scrip, script. **3. dispensary** all-night chemist, chemist, drugstore *(US)*, night chemist, pharmaceutics, pharmacy. **4. pharmacopoeia** materia medica, open list. **5. medicine chest** first-aid kit, medicine box.

6.   **1. healer** curer, orthoptist, orthotist, treater. **2. therapist** therapeutist. **3. doctor** barefoot doctor, clinician, doctress, family doctor, flying doctor, general practitioner, GP, hakim, paramedic *(US)*, physician, radio doctor. *Informal:* doc, medic, medico, quack. **4. specialist** Collins Street doctor, consultant, Harley Street doctor, Macquarie Street doctor, visiting medical officer, VMO. **5. bacteriologist** biotechnologist, cardiologist, chemotherapist, ENT, ENT specialist, epidemiologist, foetologist, gastroenterologist, gastrologer, geriatrist, gerontologist, immunologist, laryngologist, neonatologist, neurologist, osteologist, otolaryngologist, paediatrician, paediatrist, pediatrician, proctologist, psychotherapeutist, radiologist, rhinologist, syphilologist, urologist, venereologist, virologist. **6. resident medical officer** intern *(Chiefly US)*, interne, registrar, RMO. **7. surgeon** plastic surgeon. *Informal:* orthopod, sawbones. **8. diagnostician** aetiologist, pathologist. **9. gynaecologist** accoucheur, accoucheuse, midwife, obstetrician. *Informal:* gyno. **10. anaesthetist** anesthetist. **11. sexologist** **12. physiotherapist** massageuse, massagist, masseur, occupational therapist. *Informal:* physio. **13. podiatrist** chiropodist.   **14. chiropractor** chiropractic.   *Informal:* osteo. **15. audiologist**. **16. psychiatrist** analyst, psychoanalyst, therapist. **17. paramedic** ambulanceman, hospital orderly, medical orderly, nursing aide, orderly, stretcherbearer. *Informal:* ambo, zambuck. **18. nurse** amah, bush nurse, charge nurse *(Chiefly British)*, district nurse, dresser, health visitor *(British)*, hospitaller, Karitane nurse, matron, nursing unit manager, Plunket nurse, registered nurse, sister, Tresillian nurse, wardsman. **19. medical orderly**. **20. pharmacologist** chemist, druggist *(US)*, pharmaceutist, pharmacist. **21. dentist** dental technician, endodontist, exodontist, orthodontist, prosthodontist. *Informal:* gum-digger. **22. faith-healer**. **23. balneologist** cupper, phlebotomist. **24. mountebank** snake-out merchant. **25. veterinary surgeon** farrier, vet, veterinarian.

7.   **1. specialisation** aerotherapeutics, aerotherapy, anaesthetics, angiology, audiology, aviation medicine, bacteriology, balneology, cardiology, cauter, cautery, chemotherapeutics, chemotherapy, chiropody, cupping, electrotherapeutics, epidemiology, fetology, foetology, gastroenterology, gastrology, geriatrics, gerontology, hydrotherapeutics, immunology, laryngology, neonatology, neurology, neurosurgery, oncology, ophthalmology, optometry, orthopaedics, orthoptics, osteology, otolaryngology, otology, otorhinolaryngology, paediatrics, paedology, pathology, pediatrics, pedicure, pedology *(US)*, pharyngology, phlebotomy, phototherapeutics, podiatry, proctology, prosthetics, psychiatry, psychoanalysis, psychotherapeutics, psychotherapy, pyretology, radiology, radiotherapy, regenerative medicine, rheumatology, rhinology, roentgenology, semeiology,

serology, sexology, sports medicine, stoechiology, stoicheiology, stoichiology, stomatology, syphilology, tonometry, tropical medicine, typhlology, urology, venereology, venesection, virology.

8. **1. diagnostic processes** auscultation, barium meal, biopsy, endoscopy, gastroscopy, laparoscopy, ophthalmoscopy, percussion, rhinoscopy, scatology, succussion, tracheoscopy, urethroscopy, uroscopy. **2. electrocardiography** angiography, electroencephalography, electromyography, EMG, encephalography, mammography, placentography, pyelography, radiography, tomography, ultrasound. **3. cardiogram** angiogram, brainwaves, ECG, EEG, electrocardiogram, electroencephalogram, encephalogram, encephalograph, mammogram, myocardiogram, pyelogram, radiogram, radiograph, roentgen ray, roentgenogram, shadowgraph, tomogram, tomograph, X-radiation, X-ray. **4. test** blood test, cancer smear, cervical smear, Pap smear, Papanicolaou smear, Schick test, smear test, Wassermann reaction, Wassermann test.

9. **1. medical equipment** cardiograph, ECG, EEG, electrocardiograph, electroencephalograph, encephalograph, optometer, polygraph, pulsimeter, pulsometer, tonometer. **2. probe** compressor, cystoscope, dilatant, dilatator, dilator, diploscope, endoscope, hysteroscope, laparoscope, laryngoscope, myoscope, ophthalmoscope, pharyngoscope, proctoscope, rhinoscope, urethroscope. **3. catheter** airway, bougie, cannula, drain, drip, drip transfusion, seton. **4. inhaler** inhalator, insufflator. **5. surgical and medical tools** écraseur, argon laser photocoagulator, bistoury, blowpipe, bronchoscope, cautery, crotchet, curette, dermatome, enema, forceps, gag, gastroscope, guillotine, knife, lance, lancet, laser, probang, scalpel, scarificator, sigmoidoscope, snare, sound, stapler, stethoscope, stomach pump, syringe, tenaculum, trocar, xyster.

10. **1. life-support system** artificial kidney, artificial organ, defibrillator, dialyser, dialysis machine, heart-lung machine, humidicrib, iron lung, kidney machine, oxygen tent, pacemaker, respirator, resuscitator, ventilator.

adj. **11.** **1. medical** alterant, biomedical, clinical, doctoral, iatric, iatrical, medicative, medicinal, paramedic, paramedical, premedical, prosthetic, remedial, therapeutic. **2. Aesculapian** Galenic, Hippocratic. **3. allopathic** homeopathic. **4. diagnostic** diacritic. **5. surgical** chirurgical, ENT, operating, operative, post-operative. **6. dental** orthodontic. **7. medicable** curable, operable. **8. medicinal** curing, healing, sanative.

v. **12.** **1. practise medicine** cure, doctor, heal, irradiate, medicine, rehabilitate, remedy, restore, scar, treat. **2. nurse** special. **3. diagnose** auscultate, sound, succuss.

RELATED KEYWORDS: HEALTH, ILL HEALTH, IMPROVEMENT, DETERIORATION, MEDICATION

HEALTH

n. **1.** **1. health** affection, bloom, clean bill of health, good health, haleness, healthiness, normality, soundness, welfare, wellbeing. **2. robustness** bonniness, buckishness, buxomness, freshness, get up and go, hardiness, heartiness, lustiness, red-bloodedness, strength, vigour, vim. *Informal:* go. **3. condition** constitution, form, tone, tonicity. **4. wholesomeness** healthfulness, hygiene, salubrity, salutariness, sanitariness. **5. resilience** recuperativeness, resiliency.

2. **1. recovery** convalescence, cure, rally, recruitment, recuperation, rehabilitation, sanation.

3. **1. healthy person** flourisher, thriver. *Informal:* a ball of muscle (or strength).

4. **1. health centre** baby health centre, health camp *(NZ)*, health farm, hydro, lazaretto, leprosarium, maternal and child health centre, quarantine, sanatorium, spa, wateringplace. *Informal:* fat farm, san.

adj. **5.** **1. healthy** A-OK *(US)*, abled, better, fine, hale, hale and hearty, healthful, normal, resilient, right, sound, sound as a bell, trim, uninjured, well, whole. *Informal:* alive and kicking, fit as a fiddle, good, right as rain. **2. flourishing** blooming, bonny, bouncing, buxom, fresh, glowing, thriving. *Informal:* bright-eyed and bushy-tailed, full of beans. **3. fit** full-blooded, hardy, hearty, in high feather, in training, lusty, red-blooded, robust, rude, sound, stalwart, strong, sturdy, vigorous, well. *Informal:* buckish, fighting fit, fit as a mallee bull. **4. all right** so-so. *Informal:* middling, tolerable. **5. convalescent** better, on the mend, up and about. *Informal:* on the improve.

6. **1. wholesome** clean, healthful, hygienic, macrobiotic, salubrious, salutary, salutiferous, sanatory, sanitarian, sanitary. **2. tonic** analeptic, recuperative, restorative, restoring.

v. **7.** **1. be healthy** feel good. *Informal:* be a box of birds. **2. thrive** bloom, blossom, flourish. **3. keep fit** condition, tone up. **4. recover** convalesce, feel oneself, lick one's wounds, pick up, pull round, pull through, rally, recruit, recuperate, rehabilitate, rejuvenise, renew, restore, turn the corner.

adv. **8.** **1. healthily** buckishly, buxomly, lustily, robustly, soundly. **2. flourishingly** freshly, glowingly, thrivingly. **3. wholesomely** healthfully, hygienically, salubriously, salutarily, sanitarily.

RELATED KEYWORDS: HEALING, IMPROVEMENT, MEDICATION

HEARING

n. **1.** **1. hearing** audience, audition, auscultation, listening. **2. audibleness** earshot. **3. perception** diplacusis, hyperacusis. **4. audiology** acoustic, acoustics, audiometry. **5. auscultation** stethoscopy. **6. monophony** discrete system quadrophony, matrix system quadrophony, quadraphonics, quadrophony, stereophonics, stereophony.

2. **1. hearer** audience, audient, audile, auditor, hearkener, listener. **2. eavesdropper** overhearer. *Informal:* earwig. **3. audiologist** acoustician.

3. **1. hearing device** headphones, headpiece, headset, hearing aid. **2. stethoscope** audiometer, otoscope. **3. tap** phone tap, telephone tap, wire tap.

adj. **4.** **1. hearing** attentive, audient, listening. **2. auditory** acoustic, audile, audiovisual, aural, auricular, otic. **3. audible** heard. **4. audiological** audiometric. **5. monophonic** audio, heterodyne, hi-fi, high-fidelity, lo-fi, mono, quadraphonic, quadrasonic, stereo, stereophonic.

v. **5.** **1. hear** catch, get. **2. listen** hark, harken, hear out, listen for, listen in. *Informal:* be all ears, prick up one's ears. **3. sound** auscultate. **4. give ear** give audience, interview. **5. overhear** bug, earwig, eavesdrop, listen in. **6. mishear.**

adv. **6.** **1. audibly** within earshot, within hail, within hearing.

RELATED KEYWORDS: PERCEPTION, SOUND

HEAT

n. **1.** **1. heat** caloric, caloricity, enthalpy, heat content, temperature, total heat. *Informal:* temp. **2. warmth** lukewarmness, tepidness, warmness. **3. intense heat** ardour, burning heat, causticity, ferventness, fervidness, fervour, fever heat, swelter, torridness. **4. red heat** afterheat, overheat, shutdown heat, steam heat, superheat, white heat. **5. incandescence** calefaction, decalescence, recalescence. **6. incubation** insulation.

2. **1. temperature** absolute temperature, critical temperature, curie point, fixed point, melting point, strike, sulfur point, transition temperature, triple point. *Informal:* temp. **2. boiling point** fire point, firing point, flashover, flashpoint, ignition temperature, steam point. **3. body temperature** blood heat, glow. **4. heat capacity** calorific value, latent heat, thermal capacity, water equivalent.

3. **1. thermometer** Beckmann thermometer, calorimeter, clinical thermometer, differential thermometer, gas thermometer, maximum and minimum thermometer, mercury thermometer, micropyrometer, platinum thermometer, pyrheliometer, pyrometer, pyrophotometer, radiomicrometer, resistance thermometer, telethermometer, thermobarograph, thermobarometer, thermoelectric thermometer, thermograph, thermoscope. **2. cryometer** cryoscope. **3. thermostat** pyrostat. **4. calorie** British thermal unit, Btu, cal, Cal, Calorie, gram calorie, kilocalorie, kilogram calorie, large calorie, small calorie, therm. **5. temperature scale** Celsius, Fahrenheit, international practical temperature scale, Kelvin scale, Rankine, Reaumur. **6. thermometry** calorimetry, telethermometry. **7. thermodynamics** thermionics, thermochemistry, thermoelectricity, thermostatics.

4. **1. heat transfer** advection, conduction, convection, radiation. **2. thermogenesis** thermaesthesia, thermanaesthesia, thermolysis. **3. thermotropism** thermotaxis, xerophily.

adj. **5.** **1. hot** baking, blazing, blistering, furnace-like, roasting, scalding, scorching, searing, sultry, sweltering, torrid, warm. *Informal:* hot as Hades, hot as Hay, Hell, and Booligal. **2. fervent** ablaze, afire, aflame, alight, ardent, fervid, fiery, flaming, lurid, sulphurous. **3. incandescent** ardent, candent, candescent, glowing, ignescent, recalescent. **4. burning** glowing, live, living. **5. heated** caustic, overheated, piping hot, red-hot, superheated, white-hot. **6. fiery** aflame, angry, ardent, fervent, fervid, glowing, hot, inflamed, inflammatory, sulphurous, sultry, torrid. **7. fevered** febriferous, febrific, febrile, feverish, feverous, hectic, pyrexic, subfebrile. **8. warm** lukewarm, tepid, warmish. **9. summery** summer, summer-like, sun-drenched. **10. fine** balmy, fair, fair-weather, genial, mild, sunny, sunshiny, temperate. **11. humid** close, muggy, oppressive, stifling, suffocating, sultry, sweltering. **12. tropical** equatorial, semitropical, subtropical, torrid, tropic, ultratropical.

    6. **1. thermal** caloric, calorific, thermic. **2. thermometrical** calorimetrical, pyrometrical, thermoscopical. **3. thermodynamical** geothermal, geothermic, photothermic, thermostatic. **4. adiabatic** diathermanous, diathermic, isenthalpic, isocheimal, isotheral, isothermal, recalescent. **5. radiant** actinism, convectional, decalescent, endothermic, exothermic. **6. thermophilic** thermotaxic, thermotropic.

v.   **7.** **1. be hot** blaze, boil, broil, burn, conflagrate, inflame, overheat, sweal, swelter, warm up. **2. flush** blush, glow, redden, run a temperature. **3. heat** boil, broil, burn, overheat, roast, stew, superheat, swelter, warm, warm up.

adv. **8.** **1. hotly** burningly, fervently, fervidly, fierily, hot. **2. scorchingly** sultrily, sunnily, torridly, tropically. **3. warmly** lukewarmly, tepidly. **4. incandescently**.

        RELATED KEYWORDS: COOKERY, FIRE, HEATING, LIGHT, WEATHER, DRYNESS

HEATING

n.   **1.** **1. heating** calefaction, incubation, insulation, tepefaction, thaw, warming. **2. decalescence** calescence, incalescence. **3. boiling** decoction, sterilisation. **4. incubation** aluminothermics, eddy current heating, greenhouse effect, open-hearth process, radio-frequency heating, reverberation. **5. fomentation** torrefaction. **6. pyrolysis** cupellation, destructive distillation, dry distillation, fractional distillation, thermal cracking. **7. case-hardening** cyanide hardening, vulcaniser. **8. sunbaking** insolation, sunbathing.

    2. **1. burning** baking, calcination, carbonation, carbonisation, decrepitation, firing, flashing, roasting, singeing, ustulation. **2. combustion** afterburning, ignition, kindling. **3. pyrography** branding, cauterisation, cautery, galvanocautery.

    3. **1. heater** convector, gas fire, heat reservoir, hypocaust, open fire, radiator, room-heater, space heater, storage heater, strip heater. **2. fireplace** chimney, grate, hearth, hearthstone, ingle. **3. forge** furnace, hearth, stove, wood stove. **4. incubator** hatchabator, heat reservoir, superheater, warmer. **5. direct heating** central heating, dielectric heating, ducted heating, panel heating. **6. boiler** califont *(NZ)*, chip heater, fire-tube boiler, geyser, hot-water system, immersion heater, solar water heater, steam-boiler, water-back, water-tube boiler. **7. heat exchanger** heat pipe, heat pump, heat sink, intercooler, recuperator. **8. demister** de-icer. **9. water bath** bain-marie, bath. **10. furnace** afterburner, Bessemer converter, blast furnace, bosh, cockle, combustion chamber, combustion tube, converter, cupola, dry kiln, electric furnace, glass tank, muffle, regenerative furnace, regenerator, reverberatory, tank furnace. **11. kiln** brick-kiln, lehr, oast, oast-house, roaster. **12. brazier** chauffer, cockle, devil. **13. blowtorch** acetylene lamp, blowlamp, Bunsen burner, fantail, loggerhead, oxyacetylene torch, oxyhydrogen burner, soldering-iron, Welsbach burner. **14. burning-glass** argon laser photocoagulator, sunglass.

    4. **1. melting pot** crucible, cupel, retort.

    5. **1. pyrogen** calefacient, febrifacient, inflamer, rubefacient.

adj. **6.** **1. heating** calefacient, calefactory, febrifacient, inflammatory, pyretic, pyrogenic, rubefacient, sudatory, warming. **2. incubatory** incubational, slow. **3. burning** calcinatory, caustic, pyrographic, pyrolytic. **4. calescent** incalescent.

    7. **1. heated** pyrogenous, roast, roasted. **2. gas-fired** external-combustion, oil-fired, open-hearth.

v.   **8.** **1. heat** cook, flame, hot up, incubate, irradiate, preheat, reverberate, tepefy, warm, warm up. **2. thaw** de-ice, defreeze, defrost, deliquesce, liquefy, melt, sweal, unfreeze. **3. overheat** boil, stew, superheat, sweat. **4. bake** blind-bake, broil, cook, decrepitate, grill, heat, parch, plank *(US)*, roast, rub, shirr. **5. parch** burn, calcine, carbonise, scorch, sweal, torrefy, torrify. **6. heat-treat** anneal, cupel, cure, normalise, recalesce, reverberate, temper, vulcanise. **7. stove** fire, kiln, kiln-dry, slump, underburn. **8. cast** found, smelt, sweat. **9. steam** sterilise. **10. boil** coddle, decoct, hard-boil, kier, parboil, poach, seethe, simmer.

    9. **1. sunbake** bake, bask, insolate, sun, sunbathe.

        RELATED KEYWORDS: COOKERY, FIRE, FUEL, HEAT

HEAVINESS

n.   **1.** **1. heaviness** displacement, gravity, mass, poundage, solidity, solidness, tare, weight. *Informal:* avoirdupois. **2. cumbrousness** burdensomeness, cumbersomeness, leadenness, ponderability, ponderosity, preponderance, preponderation, weightiness. **3. heftiness** beefiness, lumpiness, stodginess. *Informal:* beef. **4. avoirdupois weight** avoirdupois, troy weight. **5. gravimetry**.

2. **1. weight** burden, charge, dead weight, lift, load, log, tod. **2. burden** cumbrance, dead weight, encumbrance, impedimenta, incumbrance, load, overburden, overcharge, overload, overweight, surcharge. **3. ballast** burden, cargo, loading, span-loading. **4. counterweight** balance, balance wheel, balancer, counterbalance, counterpoise, equilibrant, makeweight, offset, tare. **5. bias** overbalance. **6. pack** bluey, drum, frame pack, haversack, knapsack, musette bag *(US)*, packsack *(US)*, pikau *(NZ)*, rucksack, satchel, shiralee, swag. *Informal:* matilda, tote. **7. paperweight** dumbbell, plumb-bob, plummet, sandbag, sinker. **8. weigh-in**.

3. **1. unit of weight** amu, arroba, atomic mass unit, carat, catty, cental, dalton, displacement ton, drachm, dram, freight ton, grain, gram, gross ton, hundredweight, kantar, karat, kilo, kilogram, kiloton, long ton, megaton, metric carat, metric ton, milligram, ounce, pikul, pound, pound troy, quarter, quintal, scruple, shekel, short ton, stone, tael, tahil, talent, tod, ton, tonne, troy ounce, Twaddell degree. **2. gross weight** cargo deadweight mass, chilled weight, dead load, deadweight mass, deadweight tonnage, dressed weight, live load, loaded displacement mass, loaded displacement tonnage, ultimate load, ultimate stress, working load. **3. atomic weight** atomic mass, mass defect, relative atomic mass.

4. **1. scales** balance, jockey scales, microbalance, spring balance, steelyard, ultra-microbalance, weighbridge.

adj. **5.** **1. heavy** heavier-than-air, leaden, leady, massive, ponderable, ponderous, preponderant, preponderating, weighty. **2. hefty** *(Informal)* beefy, elephantine, hulking, lumbering, lumpy, overweight, solid. **3. burdensome** cumbersome, cumbrous, heavy, leaden, onerous, oppressive, overburdensome, weighty. **4. heavy-laden** burdened, loaded. **5. counterweighted** counterpoised, equiponderant.

v. **6.** **1. weigh** bulk, scale, tip the scales at, weigh a ton, weigh in at. **2. outweigh** outbalance, overbalance, overweigh, preponderate. **3. balance** scale, tare, weigh.

7. **1. burden** break the back of, charge, cumber, encumber, incumber, load, lumber, overbear, overburden, overcharge, overlade, overload, overweight, overwhelm, pack, surcharge, tax the strength of, weight.

adv. **8.** **1. heavily** leadenly, ponderously. **2. weightily** heftily, solidly. **3. burdensomely** cumbersomely, cumbrously, overwhelmingly.

RELATED KEYWORDS: SIZE, SOLIDITY, THICKNESS

HEIGHT

n. **1.** **1. height** dizzy height, elevation. **2. loftiness** domination, elevation, eminence, grandness, height, hilliness, sublimity. **3. steepness** precipitousness. **4. altitude** absolute altitude, almacantar, almucantar, elevation. **5. stature** hand, tallness. **6. rise** height, loft, pitch.

2. **1. altimeter** almacantar, almucantar, cathetometer, ceilometer, hypsometer, orometer, radio altimeter, water-gauge. **2. altimetry** hypsography, hypsometry, isometry.

3. **1. apex** acme, apogee, apolune, cap, ceiling, climax, critical altitude, culmination, height, ne plus ultra, pinnacle, roof, tip, tiptop, upper, vertex, zenith. **2. summit** brow, crest, crown, head, top. **3. edge** border, brink, verge. **4. high-water mark** benchmark, bush line, floodmark, timber line, tree line, water level, waterline, watermark.

4. **1. mound** ant bed, ant heap, ant hill, barrow, burial mound, dene, effigy-mound, embankment, hillock, hornito, hummock, hump, kurgan, midden, mogul, molehill, monticule, moraine, niggerhead, salt dome, seif-dune, stage, tell, tope, tuffet, tumulus, upthrow. **2. rampart** bulwark, dike, mole.

5. **1. mountain** alp, alps, altitude, ascent, ben *(Scottish)*, bluff, cliff, cone, crag, crag-and-tail, escarpment, fjeld, massif, mount, nunatak, peak, pinnacle, plateau, precipice, prominence, table, tableland, volcano, wall. *Informal:* hen-cackle *(NZ)*. **2. mountain range** alps, chain, continental divide, cordillera, ghats, interfluve, palisades, sierra, slopes, the tops, tiers. **3. ridge** esker, horseback *(US)*, offset, os, rand *(South African)*, scarp, sideling, spur, watershed. **4. high country** highland, paramo, plateau, table, the heights, upland, uplands, wold. **5. hill** barchan, bill, brae *(Scottish)*, butte, drumlin, dune, escarp, foothill, gentle Annie *(NZ)*, headland, hill site, hillock, hillside, hilltop, holt *(Chiefly Poetic)*, island, knob, knoll, kop *(South African)*, kopje *(South African)*, mesa, monadnock, outcrop, pitch, promontory, rise, sand dune, sand-dune, sandhill, skillion, slope, swell, talus, tor, versant. **6. incline** acclivity, bank.

6. **1. tower** acropolis, beacon, belfry, belltower, belvedere, broach spire, campanile, column, conning tower, cooling tower, cupola, dome, elevator, helter-skelter, louvre, Martello tower, minaret, pagoda, peel, pile, pillar, pylon, pyramid, roof turret, shot tower, silo, skyscraper, spire, steeple, transmission tower, turret, watchtower. **2. perch** aerie, aery, coign of vantage, crows-nest, eyrie, lookdown, lookout, vantage point. **3. loft** attic, garret, hayloft, mansard roof, upstairs.

7. 1. tall person colossus, giant, tall *(Australian Rules)*. *Informal:* beanpole, beanstalk, giraffe, lofty, lolly legs, long streak of misery, longshanks, six-footer, slab, strapper, streak, yard of drink water.

8. 1. elevator cable lift, dumb waiter, escalator, goods lift, grain elevator, heightener, hoist, ladder lift, lift, moving staircase, noria, service lift, ski lift. **2. forklift** fork hoist *(NZ)*.

adj. **9. 1. high** aerial, aery *(Poetic)*, airy, aloft, apogeal, apogean, elevated, ethereal, high-flying, high-level, lofty, midair, sky-high, skyey *(Chiefly Poetic)*. **2. altitudinal** hypsometric. **3. elevated** highblocked, highset *(Chiefly Qld)*, hilly, winged *(especially Poetic)*. **4. top** apical, climactic, culminant, tiptop, topmost, upmost, upper, uppermost. **5. overhead** hanging. **6. uphill** upstairs.

10. 1. mountainous alpine, cordilleran, elevated, high-country, highland, huge, montane, mountain, rangy, subalpine, upland, volcanic, vulcanian. **2. precipitous** cliffy, cragged, craggy, hilly, ridgy, rugged, steep. **3. hilly** hillocky, hummocky, steep.

11. 1. tall lanky, long-waisted, rangy, strapping, tallish. **2. towering** all-highest, beetling, colossal, dominating, dominative, eminent, exalted, giant, gigantic, grand, high, high-rise, huge, immense, large, lofty, majestic, mammoth, monstrous, multistorey, overhanging, soaring, sublime, superb, supernal, tall *(Australian Rules)*, topless, towery, uplifted, vast, vasty *(Poetic)*. **3. spired** spirelike, spiry, tower-like, towery, turrical, turriculate.

v. **12. 1. tower** bestride, command, crest, crown, dominate, domineer, head, overhang, overlie, overlook, overshadow, overstride, overtop, rise above, scale, stand over, surmount, top, tower above. **2. soar** ascend, climb, mount, rise. **3. have a bird's-eye view** be suspended, hang, hover, perch.

13. 1. raise up elevate, erect, heighten, hoist, lever up, lift, prise, raise, rear, upheave, uplift, upraise, uprear.

adv. **14. 1. high** aerially, midair, overhead, sky-high, uppishly, upwards. **2. on high** aloft, o'er, on tiptoe. **3. loftily** eminently, grandly, majestically. **4. mountainously** precipitously, toweringly.

RELATED KEYWORDS: DEPTH, ERECTNESS, TOP

HELP

n. **1. 1. help** aid, assistance, relief, succour, support. **2. backing** advocacy, boost, championship, encouragement, furtherance, promotion. **3. patronage** auspices, favour, recourse, sponsorship. **4. support** aegis, alimentation, endorsement, fosterage, nurture, protection, sustainment, sustenance, sustention. **5. benevolence** almsgiving, charity, cheer, favourableness, helping hand, moral support, succour. **6. relief** aid, deliverance, help, helping hand, succour, visitation. **7. service** good turn, yeoman service. **8. altruism** almsgiving, benefaction, beneficence, charity, mercy, philanthropy, subvention, voluntaryism. **9. solicitude** attendance, attention, care, ministration, ministry, obligingness, service, tendance. *Informal:* TLC. **10. facilitation** accommodation, obligingness. **11. helpfulness** cooperativeness, responsiveness. **12. favouritism** abetment, complicity, partisanship, preferential treatment. **13. resource** facility. **14. helping hand** a leg up, aid, assistance, boost, crutch, lift, springboard, stepping stone.

2. 1. charity aid, alms, almsgiving, auxiliary, benevolence, helping hand, relief, succour. **2. subsidy** advance, allowance, bounty, bursary, expense account, grant, hand-out, handout, pension, pocket money, scholarship, studentship, subsidisation. **3. foreign aid** economic aid. **4. social welfare** social bandaid, social security, state aid. **5. benefit** allocated pension, allowance, annuity, child allowance, dole, family allowance, pension, rehabilitation *(NZ)*, repatriation, unemployment benefit. *Informal:* repat. **6. relief work** casework, legal aid, meals on wheels, social service, social work, welfare, welfare work. **7. appeal** bottle drive, button day, door knock, drive, flag day, fundraiser, strawberry fete *(SA)*, tarpaulin muster, telethon, war effort, whip-around. **8. fund** collection plate, community chest *(Chiefly US, Canadian)*, kitty, poor box, the tin. **9. maintenance** alimony *(US)*, keep, keeping, palimony *(US)*, subsistence, supplies, support.

3. 1. almshouse refuge, settlement, shelter, social settlement.

4. 1. helper abetter, adjuvant, aid, aider, ally, ancillary, facilitator, help, obliger, supporter. **2. assistant** accessory, adjutant, aid *(US)*, aide, aide-de-camp, ally, assessor, assister, assistor, associate, best boy, bottle-holder, coadjutress, coadjutrix, copartner, deputy, handler, helper, mate, offsider, PDA, research assistant, right hand, right-hand man, second. *Informal:* jaffa, sidekick. **3. auxiliary** paraprofessional, reinforcement, stand-by. **4. attendant** acolyte, pursuivant. **5. servant** domestic, domestic help, girl Friday, help, helper, home aid, home help, man Friday, server, yardman, yardsman. *Informal:* yardie. **6. secretary** private secretary, receptionist. **7. paranymph** best man, bridesmaid, flower girl, groomsman, maid of honour, matron of honour, pageboy, trainbearer. **8. benefactor** breadwinner, deliverer, donor, easy touch, fairy godmother, favourer, intercessor, Lady Bountiful, paraclete, patron, patroness, provider, ready giver, Robin Hood, soft touch, subsidiser. *Informal:* angel, softie, sugar daddy. **9. supporter** actionist, activist, advocate, backer, champion, fan, promoter, rooter. **10. nurturer** administrant, carer, fosterer, ministrant, nurse, succourer. *Informal:* fuzzy wuzzy angel. **11. helpmate** booster, companion, comrade, friend, friend in need, vade mecum. *Informal:* pal. **12. tower of strength** Atlas, bastion, cheerer, comforter, moral support, pillar, prop, soldier, strengthener, support. **13. counsellor** adviser, almoner, almsgiver, altruist, case worker, guidance officer, humanitarian, philanthropist, probation officer, school counsellor, settlement worker, social worker, voluntaryist. *Informal:* do-gooder. **14. help desk** information office.

adj. **5.** **1. helpful** accommodating, cooperative, helping, obliging, responsive, useful, well-disposed. **2. altruistic** big-hearted, generous, patronal. **3. charitable** eleemosynary, subventionary. **4. ministrative** ministrant, visitational. **5. sustaining** alimental, comfortable, nutrient, supporting. **6. auxiliary** adjuvant, ancillary, assistant, helpful, subsidiary, supernumerary. **7. useful** handy, necessary, of service. **8. favourable** advantageous, auspicial, beneficial, conducive to, helpful, propitious, useful. **9. subsidised** aided, backed. **10. contributary** contributory, facilitatory, tributary.

v. **6.** **1. help** accommodate, aid, assist, favour, oblige, offer a helping hand, serve, succour. **2. sustain** aid, assist, carry through, comfort, help, succour, support, tide over. **3. administer to** attend, care for, fix someone up, minister, nurse, spoon-feed, visit. **4. strengthen** buoy, carry, prop up, stay, sustain. **5. nurture** provide for, support, sustain. **6. further** accelerate, advance, boost, cultivate, encourage, feed, foment, forward, foster, pilot, promote, prompt. **7. favour** oblige, patronise, shine on, shine upon, smile on, smile upon. **8. champion** aid, befriend, defend, go all the way for, side with, support, take sides, take someone's part, throw in one's lot with. *Informal:* push someone's barrow, root for *(US)*, stick up for. **9. serve** be at someone's service, be of service, be useful, make oneself useful, promote, stand by, stand with. *Informal:* hold someone's hand. **10. abet** collaborate. **11. assist** bear a hand, come forward, give a hand, help out, lend a hand, rally, second. **12. cheer** encourage, give someone heart. **13. sponsor** back, back up, bankroll, finance, put someone on his feet, set someone on his feet, subsidise. **14. pass round the hat** come to the party, put money in the tin, whip round. *Informal:* chip in. **15. endow** back, fund, support. *Informal:* play Santa Claus.

adv. **7.** **1. helpfully** altruistically, comfortingly, constructively, cooperatively, helpingly, obligingly, responsively. **2. favourably** favouringly.

prep. **8.** **1. by the aid of** on the strength of, thanks to. **2. on behalf of** for the sake of, on someone's account, on someone's behalf.

RELATED KEYWORDS: COOPERATION, GIVING, KINDNESS, PARTNER

HIDING

n. **1.** **1. hiding** adumbration, concealment, covering, coverture, delitescence, effacement, retirement, screening, shelter. **2. anonymity** pseudonymity. **3. secrecy** concealment, cover, covertness, coverture, privacy, retirement, retreat, seclusion, secretness, sequestration. **4. cover-up** double blind, mystification, smokescreen, white lie, whitewash. **5. smokescreen** blackout, brownout, dim-out *(US)*, white-out.

2. **1. disguise** cloak, incognito, veil. **2. camouflage** countershading. **3. dissimulation** acting, double bluff, doubleness, feigning, hypocrisy, plea, pretence, simulation. **4. pretext** excuse, stalking-horse, stall. **5. deception** camouflage, humbuggery, pretence, pretension. *Informal:* alibi, put-on. **6. alias** alter ego, codename, cover, cryptonym, nom de guerre, nom de plume, pen-name, persona, pseudonym, sobriquet. *Informal:* bodgie. **7. mask** domino, false face, loup, veil, visor. **8. masquerade** fancy-dress party, masked ball. **9. cache-sex** figleaf, G-string. **10. protective colouring** camouflage, ink. **11. enigma** conundrum, riddle. **12. cryptography** cipher, code, cryptochannel, cryptogram, cryptograph, cryptology, invisible ink, microdot, palimpsest, steganography, sympathetic ink.

3. **1. hiding place** asylum, bolthole, burrow, den, harbour, hide, hide-out, hideaway, hidey-hole, home, mai mai *(NZ)*, mew, priest-hole, refuge, retreat, sanctum, shelter.

Informal: lurk. **2. cache** *Informal:* plant, stash. **3. concealed drawer** false bottom. **4. ambush** ambuscade, blind, decoy, lure, pitfall, surprise attack, trap. *Informal:* set-up.

4. **1. hider** concealer, disguiser, effacer, enveloper, harbourer, masquerader, secretor. **2. spy** beagle, counterspy, detective, dissembler, dissimulator, double agent, front, hoodwinker, incognita, incognito, intelligencer, mole, operative *(US)*, secret agent, sleeper, snake in the grass. *Informal:* crypto, plant, spook. **3. secret organisation** underground. **4. cryptographer** cryptographist.

adj. **5.** **1. hidden** backdoor, blind, clandestine, concealed, covert, cryptic, dark, dead, delitescent, esoteric, latent, obscure, perdu, secret. *Informal:* hush-hush. **2. camouflaged** apatetic, gilded, sugar-coated. **3. covered over** blacked out, covert, disguised, veiled. **4. private** backstage, confidential, offstage, privy. **5. unadmitted** ulterior. **6. unnoticed** unmarked, unremarked, unseen, unwitnessed. **7. undercover** backdoor, clandestine, deep-laid, gone to ground, hidden away, latent, obscured, out-of-the-way, perdu, retired, secluded, secret, sequestered, submerged, subterranean, underground. **8. covert** anonymous, concealed, disguised, feigned, incognita, incognito, nameless, pseudonymous, secret. *Informal:* incog. **9. obscure** abstruse, arcane, esoteric, hidden, mysterious, occult, recondite, runic, secret, unilluminating. **10. cryptic** cryptogrammic, cryptographic, enigmatic, shrouded in mystery, veiled in mystery.

v. **6.** **1. hide** blind, blot, bosom, cloud, conceal, cover, darken, eclipse, hush up, mask, mew up, obfuscate, obscure, occult. **2. keep secret** give nothing away, hold back, keep back, keep dark, keep one's own counsel, keep to oneself, let go no further, not breathe a syllable, not breathe a word. **3. envelop** adumbrate, becloud, befog, blanket, cloak, clothe, conceal, disguise, draw the veil, enshroud, harbour, hide, mantle, mask, obscure, secrete, shade, shroud, smother, swallow up, veil. **4. cache** bury, conceal, harbour, hide, lock up, put out of sight, salt away, salt down, seclude, secrete, shut away, sink, stow away, suppress. *Informal:* plant, stash. **5. cover** conceal, curtain, cushion, disguise, ensconce, mask, screen, screen off, shelter. **6. erase** annihilate, blot out, cancel, efface, expunge, obliterate, undo. *Informal:* scrub. **7. disguise** camouflage, cloak, conceal, guise *(Scottish)*, mask, masquerade. **8. cover up** black out, cover one's tracks, gild, paper over, whitewash. *Informal:* watergate. **9. bamboozle** hoodwink, hugger-mugger, snow. *Informal:* snooker. **10. dissemble** dissimulate. **11. interiorise** internalise, self-censor. **12. censor** suppress.

7. **1. lie low** burrow, go bush, go to ground, hide, hole up, lie doggo, retire, retreat. *Informal:* make oneself scarce, take to the hills. **2. ambush** ambuscade, lie in wait, lurk.

adv. **8.** **1. secretly** by (or through) the back door, cryptically, on the sly, under the counter. *Informal:* on the side. **2. privately** behind closed doors, behind the scenes, between ourselves, between you and me, confidentially, entre nous, in camera, in confidence, in secret, in the background, sub rosa, under the rose. *Informal:* on the q.t., under one's hat. **3. stealthily** behind someone's back, like a thief in the night.

phr. **9.** **1. mum's the word** *(Informal)* it must go no further, keep it under your hat, no-one will be the wiser.

RELATED KEYWORDS: COVERING, SECRECY, RETICENCE

HIGH REGARD

n. **1.** **1. high regard** devotion, esteem, estimation, honour, regard, respect, reverence, veneration. **2. respectfulness** civility, comity, consideration, courtesy, deference, good manners, regardfulness. **3. adoration** hero-worship, homage, idolatry, idolisation, idolism, obsequiousness, piety, piousness, whoredom, worshipfulness. **4. awe** dread, fear, reverence.

2. **1. respectability** admirableness, respectableness, venerableness. **2. awesomeness** dreadfulness, fearfulness, redoubtableness. **3. estimableness** value, worth, worthiness.

3. **1. admiration** approbation, commendation, laudation, praise. **2. tribute** accolade, attentions, commendations, compliment, congratulation, toast. **3. respects** court, deference, devoirs, duty, fealty, homage, loyalty, obedience, respect. **4. bow** bob, congé, curtsey, curtsy, genuflection, kneeling, kowtow, obeisance, prostration, reverence, salaam, salutation, salute. **5. expression of praise** encomium, eulogy, panegyric. **6. miscellaneous forms of tribute** award, crown, decoration, festschrift, floral tribute, garland, herogram, laurels, medal, palm, plume, ribbon, tickertape parade.

4. **1. commemoration** ceremonial parade, fly-past, honour board, honour book, honour guard, honour roll, march-past, procession, roll of honour. **2. commemorative** ex post facto, memorial, retrospective, roll of honour, war memorial. **3. honour** decoration, honourable mention, honours list, knighthood, medal, wreath.

5. **1. respecter** commemorator, honourer, saluter, tributary, tributer, valuer, venerator. **2. idoliser** adorer, fan club, genuflector, hero-worshipper, kowtower.

adj. 6. **1. highly regarded** dear, esteemed, good, honourable, in high esteem, in high regard, respected, revered, reverend. **2. respectable** decent, decorous, estimable, honest, time-honoured, venerable, worthy. **3. commendable** laudable. **4. awesome** awe-inspiring, awe-struck, awful, compelling, dread, dreadful, fearful, impressive, redoubtable, redoubted, revered.

7. **1. respectful** bareheaded, cap in hand, deferent, deferential, humble, obeisant, obsequious, pious, regardful, reverent, reverential, tributary. **2. awe-struck** adoring, worshipful.

v. 8. **1. hold in high regard** consider highly, esteem, have a high opinion of, hold in high esteem, honour, regard, respect, revere, reverence, think highly of, think much of, think well of, venerate. **2. idolise** adore, hallow, idolatrise, look up to, venerate, worship. **3. cherish** embosom, love, prize, take to one's bosom, treasure. **4. fear** hold in awe.

9. **1. honour** celebrate, pay respect to, pay tribute to, salute. **2. pay homage** abase oneself, bend the knee, bob, bow, bow and scrape, cross, curtsy, fall down before, fire a twenty-one gun salute, genuflect, hail, humble oneself, kiss the hem of another's garment, kneel, kotow, kowtow, prostrate oneself, pull one's forelock, remove one's hat, salaam, salute, touch one's forelock, tug one's forelock, uncap, uncover. *Informal:* dip one's lid. **3. commemorate** celebrate, do honour to, observe, remember. **4. enshrine** consecrate, inshrine, shrine. **5. defer to** keep one's distance, make way for, stand aside for, stand back for.

10. **1. command respect** awe, dazzle, impress, inspire respect, overawe. **2. stand on one's dignity** observe due decorum, stand on ceremony.

adv. 11. **1. respectfully** deferentially, regardfully. **2. in deference to** with all respect, with respect. **3. adoringly** piously, worshipfully.

12. **1. respectably** venerably. **2. awesomely** awfully, dreadfully, fearfully, impressively, redoubtably.

interj. 13. **1. here's to** all hail, hail *(Poetic)*, l'haim, long life to, long live, viva. *Informal:* good on you.

RELATED KEYWORDS: APPROVAL, FLATTERY, LOVE, PLEASURE

HINDRANCE

n. 1. **1. hindrance** blockage, difficulty, drawback, hitch, impedient, impediment, let, obstruction. **2. encumbrance** clog, cumbrance, dead weight, deadwood, hamper, impedimenta, incubus, lumber, weight. **3. burden** dead hand, drag, penalty. **4. preventive** counter measure, countercheck. **5. barrier** bar, barricade, blockade, dam, hitch, obstacle, roadblock. **6. estoppel** bar, conclusion, head. **7. handicap** embarrassment, inconvenience, inconveniency. **8. hitch** snag. *Informal:* embuggerance, fly in the ointment, glitch, nigger in the woodpile, Spaniard in the works, spanner in the works. **9. setback** check, damp, dash, discouragement, rebuff, repulse, throwback. *Informal:* facer. **10. delaying tactic** stall. **11. impasse** brick wall, catch 22, deadlock, stalemate, sticking point, stumbling block, stymie, vicious circle. **12. bottleneck** blockage, congestion, shackle, trammels. *Informal:* jam. **13. blind alley** cul-de-sac, dead end. **14. bodycheck** coathanger, hand-off, intercept, sliding tackle, smother tackle, spear tackle, stiff-arm, stiff-arm tackle, tackle. **15. occupational hazard** inconvenience.

2. **1. obstructiveness** bloody-mindedness, obstructionism. **2. interference** forestalment, intercept, interception, interposal, interposition, interruption, mental block. **3. prevention** limitation, preclusion, restriction. **4. discouragement** crossing, frustration, oppilation, thwarting. **5. cumbrousness** awkwardness, unwieldiness.

3. **1. obstacle** barrier, baulk, block, hurdle, impediment, stop, traverse. **2. barricade** abatis, balloon barrage, barbed wire, barrage, booby trap, caltrop, cheval-de-frises, concertina wire, fence, gabionade, razor wire, trou-de-loup, wire entanglement. **3. gate** cattle ramp, cattlegrid, cattlestop, portcullis, turnpike, turnstile. **4. roadblock** boom gate, humps, judder bar *(NZ)*, speed bumps, speed-trap, tollbar. **5. crash barrier** bannister, bollard, buffer, bumper, bumper bar, cowcatcher, fender, guardrail, handrail, kangaroo bar, roo bar, stone shield. **6. dam** boom, breakwater, dike, embankment, sandbank, sandbar, sudd, weir. **7. chock** doorstop, doorstopper, floor stop, skid, stop, trig. **8. deflector** baffle, baffle plate, breakweather, breakwind, stopping, windbreak. **9. airlock** air-trap, P trap, vapour lock. **10. bunker** hazard, sand-trap. **11. jump** camel jump, crossbar, fence, hurdle, oxer, water-jump. **12. obstacle race** obstacle course. **13. debil-debil country** no man's land.

    4.   **1. hinderer** backstop, baffler, impeder, interceptor, interferer, interposer. **2. obstructor** blocker, defeater, dog in the manger, filibusterer, obstructionist, stonewaller. **3. handicapper** cumberer, lumberer. **4. preventer** counterworker, forbidder, forestaller, opposer, thwarter. **5. discourager** damper, heckler, killjoy, spoilsport, wet blanket, wowser.

adj. **5.**   **1. obstructed** air-bound, choked, clogged, congested, fitchered, icebound, impassable, insurmountable, snowbound. **2. blocked off** barricaded, dead-end. **3. frustrated** stopped. *Informal:* dished.

    6.   **1. hindering** cumbersome, cumbrous, impedient, impedimentary, impeditive, obstruent, retardatory. **2. obstructive** difficult, filibusterous. *Informal:* bloody-minded. **3. interceptive** counteractive, interferential, preclusive, preventive, prohibitive. **4. in the way** discouraging, inconvenient.

v. **7.**   **1. hinder** block, forestall, hold up, impede, incommode, inconvenience, interrupt, obstruct, put a spanner in the works, put a spoke in someone's wheel, retard, set back, spike someone's guns, stonewall. *Informal:* drag the chain, mozz. **2. hamper** backfoot, clog, cumber, embarrass, encumber, hinder, impede, lumber, retard. **3. handicap** cramp, penalise, pinch. **4. thwart** baffle, baulk, bilk, counterwork, cross, dash, defeat, foil, frustrate, nullify, put paid to, spite, stymie, stymy, traverse. *Informal:* dish, snooker. **5. hinder** ban, bar, debar, exclude, forbid, foreclose, inhibit, interdict, lower the boom on, oppose, outlaw, preclude, prevent, prohibit, stop. **6. trip** booby trap, cripple, disenable, hogtie *(Chiefly US)*, mask, snag, tie down, tie someone's hands, trip up. **7. discourage** damp, take the wind out of one's sails. **8. cramp someone's style** discomfit, embarrass. *Informal:* faze. **9. be difficult** filibuster, hedge about (or around).

    8.   **1. obstruct** intercept, interpose, intrude, obtrude. **2. block** arrest, bar, dam, embank, hedge in, snow in, stop. *Informal:* sprag. **3. occlude** choke, clog, congest, foul, gorge, gum up, jam, oppilate, shut. **4. chock** trig, wedge. **5. bunker** trap. **6. bodycheck** box in, hem in.

    9.   **1. meet an obstacle** baulk at, come up against, refuse, seize up, stick at, stop at.

adv. **10.**   **1. hinderingly** discouragingly, impedingly, insurmountably, interferingly, obstructively, preclusively, prohibitively. **2. with difficulty** against the flow, against the odds, three steps forward, two steps back.

      RELATED KEYWORDS: CONTROLLING DEVICE, DIFFICULTY, DISCOURAGEMENT, RESTRAINTS

HISSING

n. **1.**   **1. hissing** affrication, affricative, assibilation, audible friction, frication, sibilancy. **2. fizzing** carbonation, effervescence.

    2.   **1. hiss** sigh, sough, surface hiss, whisper. **2. rush of air** swish, whish, whistle, whiz, whoosh. *Informal:* zip. **3. sibilant** affricate, aspirate, fricative. **4. puff** chug. **5. fizz** bubble, bubbling, fizzing, fizzle, hubble-bubble. **6. rustle** crinkle, froufrou. **7. snuffle** sneeze, sniffle, snore, snort, sob, souffle. **8. sizzle** fizzle, spatter, sputter. **9. suck** slurp.

    3.   **1. hisser** fizzler, sizzler, sputterer. **2. snuffler** sneezer, snorer, snorter.

adj. **4.**   **1. hissing** affricated, aspirated, crinkly, fricative, rustling, sibilant, wheezy. **2. fizzy** effervescent, effervescible.

v. **5.**   **1. hiss** affricate, aspirate, assibilate, blow, sibilate, whistle. **2. rustle** crinkle, sigh, sough, swish, whisper. **3. whoosh** whish, whiz. **4. sniffle** sneeze, sniff, snivel, snore, snuffle. **5. fizz** effervesce, fizzle, frizzle, sizzle. **6. spit** spatter, splutter, sputter.

      RELATED KEYWORDS: DISSONANCE, SHRILLNESS, SOUND

HITTING

n. **1.**   **1. hitting** bashing, buffeting, pounding. **2. beating** bashing, bastinado, belting, dressing-down, drubbing, hiding, lacing *(British)*, larruping, plastering, spanking, thrashing. *Informal:* doing, dusting, hammering, licking, milling, pasting, shellacking, strapping, tanning, towelling, trimming *(British)*, walloping, workover. **3. assault** battery, corporal punishment. *Informal:* once-over, the works. **4. whipping** flagellation, flogging, fustigation, lashing. **5. stoning** lapidation.

    2.   **1. hit** bash, bat, blow, clap, crack, drub, knock, slap, stroke. *Informal:* bong, bonk, conk, konk, swipe, swipes *(British)*. **2. punch** blow, box, buff, buffet, clip, clock, clout, clump, cuff, fisticuff, floorer. *Informal:* biff, clonk, conk, dong, dook, duke, facer, flea in someone's ear, job, knuckle sandwich, plug. **3. pound** slog. *Informal:* packet, pile-driver, slosh, smacker, smasher, sock, wallop, wham, whop. **4. body blow** backhander, bolo punch, combination, cross, flick, haymaker, hook, left, pivot punch, rally, right, sideswipe, uppercut. *Informal:* combo, rabbit-killer, sidewinder *(US)*, sucker punch. **5. king hit** chop, coup de grâce, deathblow, flattener, knockout, stunner. *Informal:* kayo, KO, woodener. **6. smack** flap, slap, spank, spanking, spat, swack *(Chiefly Scottish)*, thwack. *Informal:* paddywhack, swat, whack. **7. whip** cut, flagellum, lash, pandy *(Chiefly Scottish)*, slash, stripe, swish, switch, thrash, welt. **8. turkey slap** *(Informal)*.

3. 1. stroke ace, backhand, backstroke, bricole, bunt, chip, chop, cover drive, drive, drop shot, flyer, forehand, ground stroke, half-volley, kill, lob, loft, outstroke, passing shot, pelt, power serve, rush, serve, slash, smash, smasher, stop volley, strike, swash, volley. *Informal:* agricultural, swipe, swipes *(British)*. **2. slice** back cut, chip shot, chop, chop stroke, cross-shot, cut, glance, late cut, leg glance, pitch shot, sweep. **3. hook** edge, nick, snick, top. **4. shot** break, bricole, cannon, carom, follow, massé, plant, string, Whitechapel. **5. thrust** bind, botte, home thrust, joust, lunge, tilt.

4. 1. pat bob, brush, chuck, dab, fillip, flick, flip, peck, rap, tap, tip, touch. **2. stamp** appel. **3. prod** bunt, butt, dig, dub, goose, jab, jerk, poke, stab, thrust. **4. push** jog, jolt, jostle, nudge, stir. **5. accolade** dubbing.

5. 1. kick balloon, banana kick, bicycle kick, bomb, checkside kick, corner, crosskick, drop kick, foot, garryowen, hack, header, line-kick, placekick, punt, scissors kick, spiral punt, stab, stab kick, tap-kick, torpedo, torpedo punt, up-and-under. *Informal:* boot, rainmaker, torp.

6. 1. impact concussion, impingement, impulse, jar, percussion, shock. **2. collision** bang, bump, clash, conflict, confliction, crash, ding, elastic collision, foul, hurtle *(Poetic)*, knock, slam, smash, thud, thump, whang. *Informal:* crack-up, prang, stack. **3. smash-up** concertina crash, head-on. *Informal:* pile-up, stack-up. **4. tackle** flying tackle, headhigh tackle, smother tackle. *Informal:* bonecrusher, bootlace tackle. **5. bounce. 6. rebound** croquet, ricochet, roquet.

7. 1. club bastinado, bat, blackjack, bludgeon, cosh, cudgel, knobkerrie, leangle, lifepreserver *(British)*, mace, mere, nightstick *(US)*, nilla-nilla, nulla-nulla, patu, shillelagh, staff, stave, stick, swagger stick, truncheon, waddy. *Informal:* donger. **2. staff** club, prodder, quarterstaff, rod, shakuhachi, singlestick, stick, taiaha. **3. whip** birch, bullock whip, cane, cat, cat-o'-nine-tails, crop, flagellum, horsewhip, knout, lash, quirt *(US)*, rawhide, rope's end, scorpion, scourge, sjambok *(South African)*, stockwhip, strap, switch, tawse *(Chiefly Scottish)*, whiplash. **4. flail** swingle, swipple, thresher. **5. flyswat** flapper, swatter. **6. bat** battledore, bumble puppy, crosse, mallet, racket, racquet. *Informal:* willow, willower. **7. golf club** blaster, brassy, broomstick putter, bulger, cleek, driver, iron, jigger, lofting iron, mashie, mid-iron, niblick, pitcher, putter, sand wedge, spoon, wedge, wood. **8. hammer** ballpein hammer, claw hammer, club hammer, drop hammer, flatter, fuller, gavel, jackhammer, knapping hammer, lump hammer, mallet, maul, plessor, plexor, sledge, sledgehammer, steam hammer, tilt hammer, triphammer. **9. ram** battering ram, beetle, pile-driver, pounder, rammer.

8. 1. hitter bat, batsman, batter, pinch-hitter, striker. *Informal:* whacker. **2. beater** larruper, smacker, smiter, striker, thrasher, thresher. *Informal:* walloper. **3. bludgeoner** cudgeller, fustigator, hammerer, pounder, slogger, smasher, thumper. **4. flogger** flagellant, lasher. **5. puncher** boxer, fighter, fisticuffer, plugger, pugilist, pusher, shover, stroller. *Informal:* slugger.

adj. **9. 1. battered** beaten, hammered, hit, smitten, stricken. *Informal:* creamed. **2. knocked over** floored. *Informal:* unloaded.

v. **10. 1. hit** bat, chop, connect with, knock, ping, punch, sideswipe, sledge, smite, strike, sweep, swing at. *Informal:* bean, bong, bonk, bop, clock, crease, crown, ding, dob, dot, job, swat, swipe, zot. **2. tap** bob, dab, dub, fillip, flap, flick, pat, peck, rap, spat, tip, touch. **3. drum** percuss, thrum. **4. bang** boom, clank, clonk, knock, pound, rap, slam, thud, thump, wham, whang. **5. smack** clap, slap, slipper, snap, spank, thwack. *Informal:* paddle *(US)*, whack. **6. bash** belt, dash, pound, ram, thump. *Informal:* slog, sock, wallop, whop. **7. punch** bludgeon, box, buffet, clip, clout, cuff, fist, fisticuff, strike, uppercut. *Informal:* biff, bop, clock, clonk, clump, conk, dong, dot, duke, give someone the old one-two, hang one on someone, job, mug, plug, roof, scone, slog, slug, take a poke at, thump. **8. hammer** beetle, gavel, knap, tamp.

11. 1. beat batter, belabour, best, cob, curry, flog, hammer, lambaste, maul, pelt, pommel *(Chiefly US)*, pound, pummel, thrash, trounce. *Informal:* beat (or belt) the (living) daylights out of someone, beat to a pulp, clobber, cream, fib, knock the bejesus out of, lace *(British)*, lam, larrup, lather, paste, plaster, pulverise, quilt, tan, wallop, whale. **2. beat up** bash, bash up, tan someone's hide. *Informal:* beat (the) hell out of, beat the tripe out of, do for, give someone Bondi, give someone Larry Dooley, lam into, whale into.

12. **1. flog** baste, bastinado, cudgel, drub, flagellate, pistol-whip. **2. bludgeon** blackjack, club, cosh, sledgehammer, truncheon, waddy. **3. belt** cane, ferule, pandy *(Chiefly Scottish)*, strap, welt. **4. whip** beat, birch, bullock-whip, cat, cowhide *(US)*, cut, flagellate, flail, flog, horsewhip, knout, lash, scourge, slash, swish, switch, thresh. **5. pelt** catapult, pebble, pellet, pepper. *Informal:* pip.

13. **1. kick** crosskick, foot, hack, knee, toe. *Informal:* put in the boot, put the boot into. **2. stamp** stamp on. *Informal:* stomp.

14. **1. collide** barge into, cannon into, clash, connect *(Baseball, Tennis)*, crash, fall foul of each other, impact, impinge, smash together. **2. bump** foul, hustle, jostle, knock, push, shoulder, shove, thrust. **3. crash** lose it, smash, stack. *Informal:* crack up, pile up, prang.

15. **1. bowl over** bottle, bowl down, lay low, skittle. *Informal:* barrel, deck. **2. fell** down, drop, floor, grass, iron out, knock down, knock endways, knock endwise, lay, level, run down, tackle, topple, tumble. *Informal:* flatten, spread-eagle. **3. knock out** concuss, king-hit, lay out, wooden. **4. overturn** roll, tip over, tip up, upset.

RELATED KEYWORDS: ATTACK, MACHINE, SPORT, THROW, VIOLENCE

HOLD

n. **1.** **1. hold** clench, clinch, grab, grapple, grasp, wrestle. **2. wrestling hold** aeroplane spin, arm lock, body scissors, buttock, chip, collar-and-elbow, full nelson, grapevine, half-nelson, hammer lock, headlock, knee drop, lock, maginnis, nelson, octopus clamp, scissors, stranglehold, toehold, wristlock. **3. Christmas hold** *Informal:* squirrel grip. **4. grip** bite, clutch, grasp, gripe, handhold, purchase. **5. eastern grip** handshake grip. **6. hug** bear hug, clasp, cuddle, embrace, snuggle, squeeze.

2. **1. holdings** deforcement, retention, retentiveness, retentivity, tenaciousness, tenacity, tenure, withholding. **2. prehension** prehensility, retainment.

3. **1. hold** handgrip, handhold, helve, starting handle, winch, withe. **2. handlebars** *Informal:* ape hangers. **3. haft** grip, gripe, handgrip, handle, hilt, pistol-grip, snath, stock, whipstock. **4. dead man's handle.**

4. **1. holder** billy tongs, clams, forceps, lazy tongs, nippers, pincers, pinchers, pliers, spondonicles, spongs, sugar tongs, tongs, tweezers. **2. clamp** bitstock, bootjack, brace, clam, cramp, face-plate, footstock, holdfast, jig, oarlock, rowlock, tailstock, vice. **3. clasp** catch, clip, split ring, tiepin, woggle. **4. clipboard** copyholder, folder. **5. hook** anchor, grapnel, grapple, grappling iron, holdfast, jaw. **6. climbing irons** chock-stone, clinker, piton.

adj. **5.** **1. holding** cheliform, grasping, griping, prehensile, raptorial. **2. tenacious** adhesive, clingy, retentive, tacky, viscid, viscous.

6. **1. holdable** graspable, retainable. **2. handled** ansate, hilted. **3. held** hand-held.

v. **7.** **1. hold** clench, grasp, grip, gripe. **2. hold down** guy. **3. grasp** catch, catch at, clasp, clutch, clutch at, fist, gobble, grab, grip, gripe, hook, lay hold of, seize, snatch, take. *Informal:* collar, snaffle. **4. clinch** grapple, hang on, pin. **5. cling** cleave, hold fast. **6. clamp** clip, cramp, vice. **7. detain** buttonhole, collar, withhold. **8. keep** have, retain. **9. hug** bosom, cuddle, embosom, embrace, enfold, fold, fondle, nestle, nuzzle, press, snuggle. **10. nurse** cradle, inarm.

adv. **8.** **1. graspingly** clingingly, tenaciously.

RELATED KEYWORDS: FASTENING, TAKING, MACHINE

HOLLOW

n. **1.** **1. hollow** calyx, cavity, cup, depression, funnel, pit. **2. hole** crater, cup, kettle, kettle hole, pit, pitfall, pot *(Scottish)*, pothole, tomo *(NZ)*. **3. pocket** amygdale, amygdule, druse, geode, pouch, vugh. **4. dish** concave, depression, hollow, pan, scoop. **5. crater** amphitheatre, basin, bolson, bunker, caldera, cirque, comb, combe, coomb, corrie, cwm, devil's punchbowl, dolina, doline, lap, pan, polje, punchbowl, retarding basin, saddle, salt flat, salt pan, shott, volcanic neck, walled plain. **6. valley** canyon, dale, dell, dingle *(Chiefly Poetic)*, dip, glen, gully, hollow, inclination, ravine, strath, vale *(Chiefly Poetic)*. **7. waterhole** artesian basin, claypan, gnamma hole, hole, melon hole, namma hole, rock hole, soak, wallow, watering hole. **8. sinkhole** pothole, sink, soakage pit, soakaway, sump, well. **9. hollowness** cavity, concaveness, concavity, curvature, depression, dish, hollow, sag.

2. **1. niche** alcove, almery, ambry, angle, apse, apsis, aumbry, bay window, columbarium, conch, concha, cove, fenestella, inglenook, lacunar, nook, pigeonhole, pit, recess, setback, tabernacle. **2. socket** caisson, gouge, groove, mortice, rebate, saddle.

222

    3.   **1. indentation** cranny, dent, depression, dink, dint, furrow, indent, indention, indenture, puncture. *Informal:* bingle, ding. **2. dimple** pock. **3. pore** chink, crypt, domatium, fossa, fovea, foveola, interstice. **4. impression** footprint, impress, imprint, incision, notch, pockmark, print, toehold, variole. **5. intaglio** champlevé, cloisonné.

    4.   **1. cave** cavern, cove, dugout, grot *(Poetic)*, grotto. **2. chamber** catacombs, columbarium, crypt, grave, hypogeum, mastaba, samadhi *(Indian English)*, tomb, undercroft. **3. burrow** cubbyhole, den, hole, wormhole.

    5.   **1. excavation** bal, chalkpit, coal pit, cutting, ditch, foxhole, goaf, gob, gullet, gum-hole *(NZ)*, gunny, mine, mineshaft, open cut, pit, quarry, salt mine, saltpit, sawpit, stope, trench, wheal. *Informal:* show. **2. mine shaft** drive, moulin, shaft, winze. **3. well** oilwell, step-out, step-out well.

    6.   **1. organic cavity** alveolus, antrum, atrium, bladder, caecum, cell, cellule, coelenteron, conceptacle, cul-de-sac, follicle, hair follicle, lacuna, lumen, myelocoele, reservoir, sac, sinus, vacuole, venter, ventricle, vesicle, vestibule, womb. **2. bodily hollow** armpit, axilla, fontanelle, infundibulum. *Informal:* saltcellar. **3. navel** omphalos, umbilication, umbilicus. *Informal:* bellybutton, innie.

    7.   **1. tunneller** burrower, miner, quarrier, quarryman, sapper. **2. potholer** caver, speleologist.

adj. **8.**   **1. hollow** cavernous, cryptal, spelean, tomblike. **2. sunken** basined, dished. **3. concave** amphicoelous, biconcave, concavo-concave, concavo-convex, convexo-concave, convexo-plane, plano-concave. **4. pitted** bore, craterous, dented, dimpled, dimply, foveal, foveate, foveolate, foveolated, perforate, pockmarked, rimose, rout, variolar, variolous. **5. crannied** nooky. **6. cup-shaped** arytenoid, cotyloid, cotyloidal, cuplike, cupped, cyathiform, glenoid, infundibulate. **7. bottle-shaped** ampullaceal, ampullaceous. **8. pouchy** bladdery, vesicular, vesiculate. **9. navel-like** umbilicate, umbiliform.

    9.   **1. cellular** alveolate, amydaloidal, amygdaloidal, cellulous, faveolate, geodic, honeycombed, lacunal, lacunar, lacunary, lacunose, vacuolate, vacuolated. **2. porous** bibulous, cancellate, leachy, open, poriferous, spongy. **3. chambered** ventricular.

v. **10.**   **1. hollow** cave, concave, dig, dig up, dish, gouge, hollow out, scoop. **2. excavate** burrow, channel, dig, drive, mine, open-cut, sink, tunnel, undermine. **3. pit** crater, dibble, dimple, drill, perforate. **4. indent** dent, impress, matchmark, press in, stamp.

    RELATED KEYWORDS: BODY, CURVE, DIGGING, OPENING, SHAPE, SHARPNESS

HOMOGENEITY

n. **1.**   **1. homogeneity** homogeneousness. **2. uniformity** agreement, conformation, uniformness, unity. **3. sameness** identicalness, identity, indistinguishableness, selfsameness. **4. constancy** evenness, monotony, steadiness.

adj. **2.**   **1. homogeneous** constant, diffused, even, homogenous, invariant, monotonous, uniform, unvarying. **2. solid** monolithic, monomorphic, of a piece, unstratified. **3. constant** continual, endless, enduring, eternal, everlasting, everyday, frequent, incessant, interminable, invariant, monotonous, perdurable, perennial, perpetual, persistent, recurrent, regular, standing, steady, uniform, unvarying. *Informal:* 24/7, round the clock. **4. monotone** fleckless, immaculate, orthotropous, self-coloured. **5. identical** indistinguishable, selfsame.

v. **3.**   **1. homogenise** gauge.

adv. **4.**   **1. homogeneously** indistinguishably, solidly, uniformly. **2. constantly** perennially, steadily, steady. **3. alike** ibid, ibidem, identically.

    RELATED KEYWORDS: ACCORD, IMITATION, REGULARITY, SIMILARITY

HONESTY

n. **1.**   **1. honesty** incorruptness, integrity, plain dealing, plainness, probity, rightness, scrupulosity, scrupulousness, straightness, truthfulness, uprightness. **2. straightforwardness** candidness, candour, fairness, frankness, free-spokenness, openness, outspokenness, plain dealing, sincereness, sincerity, single-mindedness, unreserve, unreservedness. **3. genuineness** integrity, probity, unfeignedness, uprightness, veraciousness, veracity, veridicality, verity. **4. fairness** honour, impartiality, manliness, virtuousness. **5. reliability** bona fides, credit, reliableness, soundness, trueness, trustiness, trustworthiness, validity. **6. point of honour** matter of principle. **7. good faith** uberrima fidei. **8. the genuine article** the real thing. *Informal:* the dinkum article, the drum, the full two bob, the good guts, the good oil, the griff, the straight wire. **9. fact** reality, truth.

2. **1. honest person** man of his word, man of honour, woman of her word, woman of honour. **2. straight talker** plain-dealer. *Informal:* square-shooter, straight shooter.

adj. **3.** **1. honest** above suspicion, aboveboard, all-right, candid, clean, creditable, decent, direct, downright, flat, frank, just, legitimate, open, right, righteous, round, scrupulous, square, straight, straight as a die, true, true-hearted, trustworthy, truthful, upright. *Informal:* dinkum, legit, on the up and up, ridgy-didge, straight-out, straight-up, white *(British).* **2. straightforward** aboveboard, blunt, candid, earnest, forthright, frank, free-spoken, guileless, manly, open, outspoken, plain-spoken, round, single-minded, unreserved, up-front, warts-and-all. **3. genuine** authentic, bona fide, good, legitimate, real, right, simple-hearted, sincere, sound, square, true, true-hearted, truth-telling, unfeigned, veracious, veridical. *Informal:* dinkum, dinky, dinky-di, fair dinkum, kosher, ridgy-didge, straight-up. **4. reliable** as good as one's word, faithful, honourable, indefectible, independent, jonick, loyal, open, pure, steadfast, true, trustworthy, trusty, upright, upstanding, valid. **5. fair** candid, disinterested, dispassionate, equitable, even-handed, fair-minded, impartial, neutral, objective, unbiased, unprejudiced.

v. **4.** **1. be honest** go straight, have clean hands, keep faith, keep one's promise, play fair, play the game, play with a straight bat, turn an honest penny. **2. be straightforward** call a spade a spade, lay it on the line, make no bones, nail one's colours to the mast, plump out *(British),* speak one's mind, speak out. **3. confess** admit, make a clean breast of, own, own up, put (or lay) one's cards on the table, put one's cards on the table, reveal all, shrive, tell the truth. *Informal:* come clean, come one's guts, go to press.

adv. **5.** **1. honestly** aboveboard, by fair means, deservedly, fair, fair and square, fairly, impartially, justly, on the level, on the square, openly, plainly, rightly, square, straight from the shoulder, unfeignedly, uprightly. **2. straightforwardly** candidly, frankly, from the bottom of one's heart, heart-to-heart, openly, outspokenly, sincerely, single-mindedly, straightly. **3. genuinely** actually, certainly, in all conscience, in fact, in reality, indeed, quite, really, true, truly, truthfully, veraciously, veridically. *Informal:* fair dinkum. **4. reliably** honest, trustily, trustworthily. **5. honourably** virtuously, without fear or favour.

interj. **6.** **1. honestly** blood oath, dicken, honest, honest to God, honour bright, in truth, on my word, really, right, true, true dinks. *Informal:* dinkum, dinky, dinky-di, fair dinkum, honest Injun, ridgy-didge.

RELATED KEYWORDS: FAIRNESS, MORALITY, PROPRIETY, TRUTH

HOPE

n. **1.** **1. hope** aspiration, belief, confidence, credence, faith, hopefulness, trust. **2. optimism** assurance, buoyancy, definiteness, enterprise, insouciance, overconfidence, positivism. **3. anticipation** contemplation, expectation, forecast, foresight, foretaste, future, hope, musing, prelibation, prospect, thought. **4. wishful thinking** false optimism, micawberism. **5. dream** pie in the sky, pious hope, pipedream, velleity, vision. **6. favourite** conceit, fancy, hope, white hope. *Informal:* comer.

2. **1. favourableness** rosiness, towardliness, towardness. **2. promise** favourable auspices, good omen, likelihood. **3. prospects** expectations.

3. **1. optimist** bull, positivist, truster. **2. aspirant** aspirer, young hopeful.

adj. **4.** **1. hopeful** bullish, buoyant, optimistic, overconfident, positive, positivistic, rose-coloured, roseate, rosy, starry-eyed, up-beat. **2. confident** beaming, carefree, debonair, happy-go-lucky, insouciant, invigorating, promising, provident, radiant, sanguine, sanguineous, sure. **3. aspiring** would-be.

5. **1. favourable** auspicious, bright, encouraging, fair, favonian, golden, hopeful, likely, opportune, promising, propitious, prospective, prosperous, rose-coloured, roseate, rosy, sanguine, white.

v. **6.** **1. hope** aspire after, aspire to, believe, have faith, reckon on, trust. **2. be hopeful** catch at straws, gamble, hope against hope, keep one's fingers crossed, look on the bright side, look through rose-coloured glasses. **3. expect** anticipate, believe in, come true, contemplate, count on, count one's chickens before they are hatched, count upon, envision, hope for, lick one's chops, lick one's lips, look for, pin one's hopes on, place one's trust in, pre-empt, put confidence in, repose, think, trust in. **4. dream** blue-sky, build castles in the air, fancy, fantasise, live in a fool's paradise, wish.

adv. **7.** **1. hopefully** hopingly, optimistically.

RELATED KEYWORDS: DELUSION, EMOTION, ENCOURAGEMENT, EXPECTATION, FANTASY, GOOD FORTUNE, HAPPINESS

HUMANITY

n. **1.** **1. humanity** generations of man, human family, human race, human society, human species, humankind, lords of creation, man, mankind, microcosm, mortals, the living. **2. the world** the earth, the universe. **3. people** brothers, fellow creatures, fellow man, folk, neighbours, tribe. **4. race** ethnic group. **5. master race** ubermensch. **6. earthling** earthman, mortal, postdiluvian, tellurian, terrestrial. **7. humanness** blood, carnality, flesh, flesh and blood, human nature, manhood.

2. **1. person** individual, man, party, personage, woman. **2. human being** Adamite, being, hominoid, Homo, Homo sapiens, human, mortal. **3. head** hand. **4. character** body, creature, fellow, persona, type. *Informal:* bird, bleeder, blighter, bod, boy, card, cookie, cove, cuss *(Chiefly US)*, customer, kiddo, stick. **5. worthy** soul. *Informal:* Christian.

3. **1. indigine** autochthon, native, tribesman. **2. black person** black, coloured, maroon, Negro. **3. Aboriginal** Aborigine, blackfella *(Chiefly Aboriginal English)*, blackfellow, boori, coori, koori, myall, myrnonger, warrigal. *Informal:* binghi. **4. Aboriginal group** Anangu, Koori, Murri, Noongar, Nunga, Nyungar, Yamatji. **5. black woman** Mary *(Aboriginal English)*, Negress, Wahini. **6. Pacific islander** Islander, Kanaka, Maori. *Informal:* Henare *(NZ)*, hori *(NZ)*. **7. semite** Jew, rabbinist. *Informal:* yiddisher. **8. Romani** Gypsy. **9. Asian** Asiatic. **10. gaucho 11. person of mixed race** full blood, half-blood, half-breed, half-caste, hybrid, kuri *(NZ)*, ladino, métis *(US)*, mestee, mestizo, mulatto. **12. white person** Anglo, Anglo Celt, buckra, European, gub, gubba *(Aboriginal English)*, matsalleh, memsahib *(Indian English)*, pakeha *(NZ)*, palagi, paleface, wanda, wandoo, WASP, white Mary *(Aboriginal English)*. *Informal:* honky *(US)*, wonk.

4. **1. prehistoric man** Australopithecine, Cro-Magnon man, Heidelberg man, Java man, Neanderthal man, Neanderthaloid, Palaeolithic man, Peking man, Pithecanthropus. **2. primitive man** cave-dweller, caveman.

5. **1. humanisation** anthropomorphosis. **2. personification** anthropomorphism, pathetic fallacy, prosopopoeia. **3. humanism** anthropocentricism, personalism.

6. **1. anthropology** anthropogenesis, anthropogeography, anthropography, anthropometrics, anthropometry, anthroponomy, ethnogeny, ethnography, ethnology, palaeethnology, somatology. **2. social studies** demography, social anthropology, social science.

7. **1. races** Australoid, Caucasian, Malayan, Mongoloid, Negroid. **2. Polynesian** Melanesian.

adj. **8.** **1. human** carnal, earthborn, fleshly, mortal. **2. incarnate** impersonate. **3. humanoid** anthropoid, anthropomorphous, australopithecine, hominoid, pithecanthropoid. **4. racial** ethnic, interracial, intertribal, phyletic, phylogenic.

9. **1. anthropological** anthropogenic, anthropologic, palae-ethnologic, somatological. **2. ethnologic** ethnographic, ethnographical, ethnological. **3. humanistic** anthropocentric, anthropomorphic.

v. **10.** **1. humanise** anthropomorphise, incarnate, personalise, personify.

RELATED KEYWORDS: YOUTH, MATURITY, LIFE, NATION, PARENTAGE

HUMOUR

n. **1.** **1. humour** amusement, comedy, drollery, enjoyment, fun, jest, whimsy. **2. humorousness** amusingness, drollness, funniness, hilariousness, jesting, jocoseness, jocosity, jocularity, jokiness, joking, laughter, risibility, uproariousness. **3. merriness** clownishness, impishness, jape, jest, jocosity, mirthfulness, playfulness, scintillation, sense of humour, sportfulness, waggery, waggishness. **4. wit** Attic salt, Attic wit, salt. **5. wittiness** dryness, epigrammatism, facetiousness, saltiness, wryness. **6. absurdity** absurdness, comicality, comicalness, ludicrousness, nonsense, whimsicality, whimsicalness, zanyism.

2. **1. comedy** bedroom comedy, comic opera, farce, high comedy, humoresque, interlude, musical comedy, opéra comique, sitcom, situation comedy, sketch, skit. **2. burlesque** antimasque, buffoonery, caricature, clownery, commedia dell'arte, harlequinade, low comedy, mime, parody, screwball comedy, slapstick. **3. practical joking** prankery. **4. black comedy** gallows humour, graveyard humour, sly humour, tragicomedy. **5. sarcasm** irony, lampoon, lampoonery, pasquil, pasquinade, satire. *Informal:* send-up, take-off.

3. **1. joke** drollery, gag, gibe, jape, jest, jocosity, jocularism, laugh, one-liner, punch line, punchline, shaggy dog story, sight gag, visual gag, wheeze. *Informal:* crack, funny.

2. prank apery, caper, capriccio, caprice, escapade, hoax, hotfoot *(US)*, lark, leg-pulling, monkey tricks, play, sport. *Informal:* berley, monkeyshine *(US)*, sell. **3. practical joke** apple-pie bed, short sheet. **4. pun** double entendre, equivoque, paronomasia, play on words, quibble, word play. **5. witticism** bon mot, boutade, epigram, facetiae, gag, gibe, hit, in-joke, jape, jeu d'esprit, jocosity, jocularism, joke, quip, sally. *Informal:* crack, nifty *(Chiefly US)*, wisecrack. **6. malapropism** blooper, spoonerism. **7. banter** badinage, chaff, gibe, jape, jest, jibe, persiflage, pleasantry, raillery, repartee, riposte. *Informal:* josh *(US)*. **8. dirty joke** blue story, double entendre. **9. stale joke** *Informal:* chestnut. **10. comics** comic strip, strip cartoon. *Informal:* funnies.

4. 1. mirth hilarity, jollities, laughing, laughter, merriment, risibility. **2. smile** grin. **3. giggle** nicker *(Scottish)*, snicker, snigger, teehee, the giggles, titter. **4. laugh** belly laugh, cachinnation, chuckle, convulsion, guffaw, horse laugh, nicker *(Scottish)*, roar. *Informal:* haw-haw. **5. shriek** cackle, chortle, gaggle, hoot, howl, shout.

5. 1. humorist amuser, cap and bells, clown, comedian, comedienne, comic, farceur, funnyman, gag-man, jester, joker, mime, pantomime, stand-up comedian, stand-up comic, wag. **2. joker** hard case, hard doer, monkey, scream, wag. *Informal:* card, dag. **3. practical joker** buffoon, gagger, gagster, imp, japer, Pantagruelist, prankster, Rabelaisian. **4. banterer** josher, kidder, sporter. **5. wit** punster, quipster, wisecracker. **6. satirist** ironist, lampooner, lampoonist.

6. 1. smiler grinner. **2. giggler** cackler, chortler, chuckler, shouter, shrieker, titterer. *Informal:* screamer.

adj. **7. 1. humorous** absurd, amusing, Chaplinesque, comedic, comic, comical, droll, fun, funny, humoristic, imbecile, jokey, jolly, laughable, ludicrous, pleasant, risible, silly, waggish. **2. amused** in stitches, mirthful, tickled. **3. Rabelaisian** Pantagruelian. **4. seriocomic** tragicomical. **5. farcical** absurd, comical, Gilbertian, laughable, ludicrous, ridiculous, zany. **6. slapstick** custard-pie, prankish. **7. witty** amusing, attic, bright, clever, salty, scintillating. **8. ironic** caustic, dry, facetious, mordant, salty, sarcastic, scintillating, tongue-in-cheek, witty, wry. *Informal:* sarky. **9. quizzical** daggish, whimsical. **10. bantering** ironic, playful, sly, sportful, tongue-in-cheek. **11. jesting** amusing, jocose, jocular, merry, mirthful, playful, pleasant, waggish. **12. hilarious** uproarious. *Informal:* killing, priceless, screaming, side-splitting.

v. **8. 1. joke** fun, gag, gibe, jest, jibe, lark, pun, quip, sport. *Informal:* poke fun at, wisecrack. **2. play the wag** fool, play. **3. amuse** make someone laugh, make someone weak *(Aboriginal English)*. *Informal:* slay. **4. banter** backcomb, chaff, get (or take) a rise out of, pull someone's leg, tease. *Informal:* bag, have a lend of someone, have a loan of someone, josh *(US)*, kid, rag, rib, take the micky. **5. satirise** epigrammatise, lampoon. *Informal:* poke borak.

9. 1. laugh chortle, chuckle, guffaw, hoot. *Informal:* haw-haw. **2. giggle** laugh in one's sleeve, laugh up one's sleeve, snicker, snigger, teehee, titter, twitter. **3. shriek** cackle, gabble, gaggle, hoot, laugh, roar, scream, shout, snort. **4. laugh uncontrollably** cack oneself (laughing). **5. fall about** *(Informal)* cachinnate, convulse. *Informal:* break up, kill oneself, laugh fit to kill, laugh like a drain, laugh one's socks off, split one's sides. **6. smile** fleer, grin.

adv. **10. 1. humorously** amusingly, comicality, comically. **2. hilariously** killingly, screamingly, side-splittingly, uproariously. **3. wittily** caustically, dryly, ironically, mordantly, saltily, sarcastically, satirically, with one's tongue in one's cheek, wryly. **4. quizzically** amusedly, funnily, whimsically. **5. farcically** absurdly, ludicrously.

11. 1. laughingly gaily, jollification, jollity, merrily, mirthfully. **2. banteringly** playfully, sportfully. **3. jocularly** facetiously, jestingly, jocosely, jokingly, pleasantly.

RELATED KEYWORDS: AMUSEMENT, ENTERTAINER, ENTERTAINMENT, HAPPINESS, JOY

IDEA

n. **1. 1. idea** abstract, abstraction, apprehension, conceit, concept, conception, construct, form, generalisation, image, intellection, notion, noumenon, recept, theory, thought, visualisation. **2. fixed idea** conceit, idée fixe, kink, vagary. **3. brainwave** brainstorm, suggestion, tip. *Informal:* wrinkle. **4. intuition** feeling, gut feeling, gut reaction, hunch, inspiration, instinct, premonition, presentiment, sixth sense, suspicion. **5. inkling** glimmer, glimmering, glimpse, impression, notion.

adj. **2. 1. notional** conceptual, ideal, ideate, ideational, inspirational, intellective.

v. **3. 1. devise** cogitate, conceive, conceive of, concoct, ideate, image, imagine, suppose, think, visualise. *Informal:* dream up, reckon. **2. occur to one** come to one, cross one's mind, dawn on, dawn upon, pop into one's mind.

adv. **4.** **1. notionally** conceptually, ideally, ideationally.
    RELATED KEYWORDS: IMPULSIVENESS, CONJECTURE, FANTASY, MIND, THINKING

IDLENESS

n. **1.** **1. idleness** accidie, acedia, effortlessness, faineance, indolence, inexertion, laziness, oscitancy, otiosity, shiftlessness, slackness, sloth, slothfulness, vacuousness. *Informal:* Mondayitis. **2. lethargy** anergy, apathy, languish, languishment, languor, listlessness, sleepiness, sluggishness, spiritlessness, torpidness, torpor.

2. **1. inaction** cataplexy, idleness, inactivation, inactivity, inertia, inertness, inoperativeness, motionlessness, quiescency, repose, rest, stagnancy, stagnation, stoniness, supineness, unemployment. **2. abstention** arrest, default, delay, forbearance, procrastination. **3. sedentariness** vegetation. **4. quietness** calmness, depression, drowsiness, languidness, languor, quietude, stillness. **5. dawdling** dalliance, delay, tarrying. **6. recumbency** disengagement, idleness, inactivity, inoccupation. **7. passivity** inactivity, laissez faire. **8. paralysis** atropism, catatonia, cerebral palsy, diplegia, hemiplegia, infantile paralysis, monoplegia, palsy, panplegia, paralysation, paraplegia.

3. **1. period of inaction** abeyance, general strike, latent period, laying-off season, low season, off-season, sit-down, sit-down strike, stop-work meeting, strike, vacation, waiting, walkout. **2. calm** peace, quiet, repose, slack, slumber, slump. *Informal:* Irishman's hurricane. **3. dormancy** aestivation, cold storage, coma, diapause, estivation, hibernation, inactivity, sleep, sopor, suspended animation, torpidity, torpor. **4. loaf** laze, lounge, skulk, slack, wait. **5. resting place**.

4. **1. idler** beachcomber, crawler, drone, good-for-nothing, hobo, layabout, loafer, lotus-eater, shirk, shirker, skulk, skulker, sluggard, sponger, trifler, unemployed, vagrant, waster, wastrel. *Informal:* beat, bludger, bum, deadbeat, dole bludger, droog, passenger, poler, slacker, vag. **2. sluggard** log, loller, recumbent, snail. *Informal:* couch potato, lazybones, sleepyhead, sooner. **3. dawdler** dallier, delayer, loiterer, lounger, tarrier. *Informal:* lizard. **4. paralytic** catatonic. *Informal:* cot case.

adj. **5.** **1. idle** bone-idle, indolent, lazy, oscitant, recumbent, remiss, shiftless, slack, slothful, sluggardly, vacuous. **2. sluggardly** dronish, effortless, idle, inactive, indolent, inert, languid, lazy, leaden, leisured, leisurely, lymphatic, otiose, remiss, slack, slothful, slow, sluggard, sluggish, snail-like, work-shy.

6. **1. inactive** abeyant, actionless, at a loose end, at rest, idle, in abeyance, indolent, inert, inoperative, noble, passive, quiescent, recumbent, silent, sluggish, supine. **2. sedentary** *Informal:* chairborne. **3. lethargic** catatonic, coasty, dozy, indolent, listless, musty, palsied, paralytic, phlegmatic, phlegmatical, phlegmy, poppied, remiss, sleepy, slow, somnolent, thick. *Informal:* stonkered. **4. dormant** asleep, comatose, dormient, hibernating, torpid. **5. off-peak** closed, dead, dead-and-alive, drowsy, dull, dullish, flat, inanimate, inertial, languid, languishing, languorous, lifeless, off-season, quiet, slack, sleepy, slow, sluggish, slumberous, slumbrous, stagnant. *Informal:* q.t. **6. out of action** hors de combat, laid low, on the back burner, on the sidelines, run-down, u/s, unserviceable. **7. calm** airless, breathless, down, motionless, stationary, still, stock-still, stony, unmoving. **8. fogbound** becalmed, icebound.

v. **7.** **1. idle** coast along, couch, drowse, laze, lie, lie in, lie up, loaf, loaf away, loll, lounge, lounge (a)round, not pull one's weight, rest, shirk, skulk, slack. *Informal:* bludge, bum, donga, moon, moon about, spinebash, swing the lead. **2. dawdle** dally, dally away, delay, dillydally, linger, loiter, play for time, procrastinate, tarry, trail, wait. *Informal:* drag the chain, mooch. **3. kill time** daydream, idle, trifle, trifle away, twiddle. *Informal:* boondoggle, fiddle around, goof off.

8. **1. be inactive** bide one's time, not lift a finger, rest on one's laurels, rest on one's oars, sit, sit tight, sleep, slumber, stagnate, tick over, vegetate, while away, wile away. *Informal:* warm a seat. **2. become inactive** desist, flag, give up, languish, rest, retire, slacken, slake, stand by, stop, wind down. *Informal:* cop out, corpse, throw in the towel (or sponge), throw it in. **3. hibernate** aestivate, estivate, hole up, let up. **4. sit out** leave someone to it, let sleeping dogs lie, let someone alone (or be), sit on the fence. **5. hold off** default, forbear, hold one's peace, pocket *(US)*, refrain, refuse, resist, strike.

9. **1. inactivate** assuage, backburner, becalm, calm, calm down, defuse, easy, lull, pacificate, pacify, placate, put on the backburner, quell, quiet, quieten, sedate, smooth, stay, still, tranquillise. **2. paralyse** palsy, petrify.

adv. **10.** **1. idly** at a loose end, dallyingly, loiteringly, recumbently. **2. lazily** indolently, languorously, otiosely, shiftlessly, slack, slackly, slothfully. **3. lethargically** listlessly, mustily, passively, phlegmatically, vacuously.

11. **1. inactively** down, inertly, on the back burner, quiescently, sedentarily, supinely. **2. sluggishly** at a snail's pace, drowsily, languidly, languishingly, on ice, quietly, sleepily, torpidly. **3. at rest** motionlessly, stagnantly, still, stonily.

RELATED KEYWORDS: REST, SLEEP, DISUSE

IGNORANCE

n. **1.** **1. ignorance** blindness, darkness, illiteracy, illiterateness, innocence, nescience, simpleness. **2. unknowingness** incognisance, obliviousness, unconsciousness, unwittingness. **3. illiteracy** illiterateness, innumeracy. **4. paralexia** dyslexia. **5. inexperience** artlessness, callowness, greenness, innocence, naivety, unadvisedness, unfamiliarity, unworldliness, verdancy, viridity. **6. boorishness** barbarianism, barbarism, barbarity, illiberalness, loutishness, ockerdom, rudeness.

2. **1. unknown person or thing** stranger, unknown. **2. closed book** dark horse. **3. blind spot**. **4. gamble** *Informal:* pig in a poke.

3. **1. ignoramus** dogberry, illiterate, lowbrow, simple, simpleton. *Informal:* doob, dope. **2. boor** backwoodsman *(Chiefly US)*, barbarian, bumpkin, clod, clodhopper, country bumpkin, country cousin, lout, philistine, rustic, yokel. *Informal:* alf, bushie, bushwhacker, hayseed, hick, ocker, ockerina, peasant, redneck *(US)*, rube *(US)*, troglodyte. **3. novice** a babe in the woods, abecedarian, abecedary, amateur, apprentice, beginner, cub, fledgling, fresher, freshette, greenhorn, infant, innocent, learner, naif, neophyte, new chum, novitiate, raw material, raw recruit, shlemiel, tabula rasa, tenderfoot, tiro, tyro, youngling. *Informal:* Jacky Raw, Johnny Raw, kook, parcel-post man, rookie. **4. outsider** *Informal:* mushroom.

adj. **4.** **1. ignorant** backward, benighted, dark, illiberal, illiterate, naive, natural, nescient, simple, uneducated, unenlightened, unformed, uninformed, unknowing, unlearned, unlettered, unread, unscholarly, unschooled, untaught, untrained, untutored. *Informal:* bog-Irish, clueless, dooby. **2. unknowing** blind to, ignorant, incognisant, insensible, unaware, uncomprehending, unconscious, unwitting. **3. illiterate** analphabetic, dyslectic, innumerate, paralexic. **4. boorish** backwoods, barbarian, barbarous, crude, illiberal, illiterate, philistine, rough, rustic, troglodytical, uncivil, uncivilised, uncultivated. *Informal:* hick, ocker, ockerish, redneck, rude. **5. inexperienced** amateur, armchair, artless, callow, fresh, freshwater, green, green-hand, guiltless, home-town, inexpert, innocent, naive, raw, semiskilled, unexperienced, uninitiated, unseasoned, unsophisticated, unstudied, untravelled, unversed, unworldly, verdant, wide-eyed, young. *Informal:* clueless, half-baked, new-laid, wet behind the ears.

5. **1. unknown** strange, trackless, unbeaten, uncharted, unco *(Scottish)*, unexplored, unfamiliar, unfathomed, unheard, unheard-of, unplumbed, unrecognised, unsounded, unsuspected, untrodden. **2. unnamed** anonym, anonymous, cryptonymous, innominate, nameless, unbranded, unlisted.

v. **6.** **1. be ignorant** be none the wiser, be out of the loop, lose the plot, not have a clue, not know someone from Adam. *Informal:* have come down in the last shower, have come up by parcel-post, not have an earthly, not have the faintest, not have the foggiest, not know B from a bull's foot. **2. become ignorant** lose track. **3. keep in ignorance** keep in the dark.

adv. **7.** **1. ignorantly** artlessly, illiterately, inexpertly, simple-mindedly, unlearnedly. **2. boorishly** barbarically, illiberally, rudely. **3. unknowingly** blindly, inadvertently, unawares, uncomprehendingly, unconsciously, unsuspectedly, unwittingly.

RELATED KEYWORDS: INCOMPETENCE, FOOLISHNESS, STUPIDITY, STUDENT, FOOL

ILL HEALTH

n. **1.** **1. ill health** delicacy, infirmity, infirmness, invalidism, poor health, senility, sickliness, unhealthiness, unsoundness. **2. weakness** adynamia, asthenia, atrophy, cachexia, carphology, consumption, debility, feebleness, floccillation, languor, marasmus, myasthenia, phthisis, tabes, tabescence.

2. **1. illness** affection *(Pathology)*, affliction, ailment, complaint, discomfort, disease, disorder, distemper, evil, idiopathy, ill, indisposition, malady, malaise, morbidity, sickness, trouble, upset. **2. symptom** syndrome. **3. attack** convulsion, dose, fit, onset, paroxysm, seizure, touch, turn. **4. complication** epiphenomenon, sequela. **5. infection** auto-infection, contagion, death, endemic, epidemic, exogenesis, pandemic, pest, pestilence, plague, zoonosis. **6. infectiousness** contagiousness, deleteriousness, infection, unwholesomeness. **7. infectious disease** sepsis, superbug, virus, zymosis. *Informal:* bug, lurgy, the dreaded lurgy, wog.

3. **1. patient** ambulatory, case, day patient, in-patient, invalid, outpatient, private patient, public patient, reactor, subject, sufferer, TPI, valetudinarian, victim. **2. sufferer from specific complaint** arthritic, asthmatic, bleeder, consumptive, diabetic, haemophiliac, hectic, leper, neuropath, neurotic, paraplegic, quadriplegic, rheumatic, spastic, syphilitic. **3. convalescent** recuperator.

4. **1. infectious ailments** acquired immune deficiency syndrome, actinomycosis, African sleeping sickness, AIDS, alastrim, amoebic meningitis, angina, ankylostomiasis, anthrax, Asiatic cholera, black measles, brucellosis, candidiasis, cellulitis, cerebrospinal fever, cerebrospinal meningitis, chickenpox, cholera, coccidioidomycosis, coccidiosis, diphtheria, dysentery, echinococcosis, encephalitis, erysipelas, erysipeloid, foot-and-mouth disease, framboesia, German measles, glandular fever, Hansen's disease, hepatitis, herpes, herpes facialis, herpes labialis, herpes simplex, herpes zoster, hydrophobia, impetigo, infantile paralysis, infectious mononucleosis, influenza, jail fever, king's evil, legionnaire's disease, leprosy, leptospirosis, lockjaw, lupus, lyssavirus, madness, malaria, mastitis, measles, melioidosis, monilia, monocytosis, mononucleosis, morbilli, mumps, mycetoma, mycosis, ornithosis, osteomyelitis, paludism, paratyphoid fever, parotitis, parrot disease, parrot fever, pertussis, pestilence, phthisic, phthisis, polio, poliomyelitis, pox, pseudoglanders, psittacosis, puerperal fever, quinsy, rabies, ringworm, Rocky Mountain spotted fever, rubella, rubeola, sandy blight, sarcosporidiosis, scarlatina, scarlet fever, schizomycosis, scrofula, scrub typhus, shingles, sleeping sickness, smallpox, sporadic cholera, sporotrichosis, struma, swamp fever *(US)*, sweating sickness, swine flu *(US)*, swine pox, TB, tetanus, thrush, tinea, toxic shock syndrome, toxoplasmosis, trachoma, trench mouth, trichomoniasis, trismus, TSS, tuberculosis, tularaemia, typhoid fever, typhus, typhus fever, vaccinia, varicella, variola, varioloid, Vincent's angina, Vincent's infection, viral hepatitis, viral meningitis, waterpox, Weil's disease, white plague, whooping cough, wool-sorters' disease, yaws, yellow fever, yellow jack, zoster, zymotic disease. *Informal:* jock itch, lurgy, midsummer disease, sarco. **2. plague** Black Death, bubonic plague, pneumonic plague, septicaemic plague.

5. **1. cold** bott, chill, coryza, cough, flu, grippe, influenza, rheum, URTI. *Informal:* the bot, the dog's disease, the sniffles, the snuffles. **2. septic throat** adenoids, laryngitis, pharyngitis, quinsy, relaxed throat, tonsillitis, tracheitis, uvulitis. *Informal:* strep throat. **3. ear infection** glue ear, labyrinthitis, Ménière's syndrome, otalgia, otitis, tinnitus, tympanitis, utriculitis.

6. **1. respiratory ailments** adenovirus, anoxia, anthracosis, asthma, bott, bronchiolitis, bronchitis, bronchopneumonia, consumption, croup, cyanopathy, cyanosis, diphtheria, dyspnoea, emphysema, empyema, flu, grippe, haemoptysis, hydrothorax, hyperpnoea, hyperventilation, hypopnoea, hypoventilation, hypoxia, influenza, legionnaire's disease, LRTI, MDR-TB, miner's disease, pertussis, pleurisy, pleuropneumonia, pneumoconiosis, pneumonia, rhinitis, siderosis, SIDS, silicosis, sinusitis, stridor, sudden infant death syndrome, tachypnoea, TB, thrill, tracheitis, tuberculosis, vomica, white plague, whooping cough, wool-sorters' disease. *Informal:* pleuro.

7. **1. fever** ague, calenture, febricity, febricula, feverishness, fire, flush, hectic, hyperpyrexia, inflammation, pyrexia. **2. shaking** ague, algor, chill, rigor, trembles.

8. **1. fevers** adenovirus, Bang's disease, blackwater fever, brain fever, breakbone fever, brucellosis, cerebrospinal fever, cerebrospinal meningitis, childbed fever, dengue, dumb ague, enteric fever, gaol fever, glandular fever, infectious mononucleosis, intermittent fever, jail fever, Japanese river fever, jungle fever, Lassa fever, malaria, Malta fever, Mediterranean fever, mononucleosis, paratyphoid fever, puerperal fever, Q fever, quartan, quotidian, rabbit fever, ratbite disease, ratbite fever, redwater fever, relapsing fever, remittent fever, rheumatic fever, rheumatism, Rock fever, Rocky Mountain spotted fever, Ross River fever, scarlatina, scarlet fever, sextan, spotted fever, spring fever, swamp fever *(US)*, sweating sickness, tertian, tick fever, trench fever, tularaemia, typhoid, typhoid fever, typhus, typhus fever, undulant fever, yellow fever, yellow jack.

9. **1. nausea** airsickness, altitude sickness, Barcoo spews, biliousness, carsickness, jet lag, mal de mer, mawkishness, morning sickness, mountain sickness, nauseousness, regurgitation, seasickness, the Barcoo, trainsickness. **2. indigestion** dyspepsia, dyspepsy, dysphagia, heartburn, hyperacidity, hypoacidity, waterbrash. **3. stomach-ache** colic, gastralgia, gripes, painter's colic. *Informal:* collywobbles. **4. diarrhoea** amoebic dysentery, dysentery, flux, food poisoning, gastroenteritis, scouring, scours. *Informal:* Bali belly, collywobbles, gastro, Jimmy Brits, Montezuma's revenge, squitters, the runs, the shits, the trots, tomtits. **5. haemorrhoid** piles. *Informal:* grapes.

10. **1. gastrointestinal ailments** adhesion, aerophagia, ankylostomiasis, appendicitis, ascites, black vomit, bubonocele, cholera, coeliac disease, colitis, constipation, cramps, Crohn's disease, cryptosporidiosis, diverticulitis, duodenitis, dysentery, endamoeba, enteritis, enterovirus, gastralgia, gastric ulcer, gastritis, gastroenteritis, hernia, hiatus hernia, hookworm, hookworm disease, hyperemesis, ileitis, ileus, intussusception, invagination, norovirus, peptic ulcer, peritonitis, proctitis, psilosis, rectocele, regional enteritis, rupture, sprue, steatorrhoea, tenesmus, tympanites, typhlitis, ulcer, volvulus.

11. 1. heart disease cardiac arrest, cardiomyopathy, coronary, coronary occlusion, coronary thrombosis, fibrillation, heart attack, heart block, heart failure, hole in the heart, myocardial infarct. **2. arrhythmia** arhythmia, bradycardia, flutter heart, tachycardia, ventricular fibrillation. **3. thrombosis** arteriosclerosis, atheroma, atherosclerosis, phlebitis, phlebosclerosis, varices, varicosis, varicosity, varix. **4. embolus** embolism, plaque, thrombus. **5. oedema** dropsy, hypostasis, white leg.

12. 1. cardiovascular ailments acrotism, anaphylactic shock, anasarca, aneurysm, angina, angina pectoris, arteritis, cardialgia, cardiogenic shock, carditis, coronary heart disease, cyanopathy, endocarditis, endotoxin shock syndrome, heart murmur, hydrothorax, murmur, myocarditis, palpitation, pericarditis, pyaemia, pyemia, Raynaud's disease, tamponade, telangiectasis, tobacco heart, valvulitis.

13. 1. venereal disease French pox, genital herpes, gonorrhoea, great pox, herpes, herpes simplex, locomotor ataxia, lues, nonspecific urethritis, pox, Saigon rose, sexually transmitted disease, STD, syphilis, tabes, tabes dorsalis, trichomoniasis, urethritis, VD. *Informal:* load, social disease, the clap, the jack. **2. syphilitic lesion** chancre, gumma.

14. 1. genital and reproductive organ ailments amenorrhoea, balanitis, candidiasis, cervicitis, colpitis, dysmenorrhoea, dyspareunia, dystocia, eclampsia, endometriosis, endometritis, herpes simplex, hot flush, hydrocele, leiomyoma, menorrhagia, metritis, metrorrhagia, monilia, oophoritis, ovaritis, pelvic inflammatory disease, PID, placenta praevia, PMT, premenstrual tension, priapism, prostatitis, puerperal fever, rectocele, retroflexion, retroversion, salpingitis, spermatorrhoea, thrush, toxic shock syndrome, undescended testicle, vaginitis, varicocele, vulvitis, whites.

15. 1. urinary ailments albuminuria, bed-wetting, Bright's disease, chlamydia, cystitis, cystocoele, diuresis, dysuria, enuresis, frequency, gravel, nebula, nephralgia, nephrism, nephritis, nephrosis, oedema, oliguresis, oliguria, phosphaturia, polyuria, proteinuria, pyelitis, pyelonephritis, strangury, tenesmus, uraemia, uremia, urethritis, urinary calculus, urolith, wet bottom. *Informal:* strain.

16. 1. sore abscess, anthracoid, anthrax, blain, boil, canker, carbuncle, cold sore, felon, fester, furuncle, gathering, gumboil, herpes facialis, herpes labialis, scab, sinus, stigma, ulcer, wale, weal, welt, whitlow. **2. pustule** blackhead, bulla, comedo, eruption, head, milium, papilla, papule, pimple, pock, wen, whelk, whitehead. *Informal:* crunchie, zit. **3. contusion** bruise, haematoma. **4. rash** barber's itch, barber's rash, efflorescence, eruption, exanthema, gravel rash, prickly heat, shaving rash. **5. acne** herpes, impetigo, pimple, whelk. *Informal:* crunchie, school sores, zit, zits. **6. dermatitis** brigalow itch, cradle cap, eczema, hives, uredo, urticaria.

17. 1. skin ailments acariasis, athlete's foot, black measles, blackhead, chickenpox, chloracne, comedo, cowpox, dermatographia, dermatomyositis, dermatophyte, dermatosis, dermographism, dermoid, desquamation, empyema, erysipelas, exanthema, German measles, grog blossom, herpes, herpes zoster, hidrosis, hyperkeratosis, ichthyosis, icterus, jaundice, keratosis, lichen, lupus, Lyme disease, mange, measles, melanoma, melanosis, miliaria, mole, morbilli, mycosis, naevus, nappy rash, nettle rash, phagedaena, phlyctena, pinta, pityriasis, plaque, prurigo, pruritus, psoriasis, purpura, pustulation, pyaemia, pyogenesis, pyosis, ringworm, roseola, rubella, rubeola, scabies, scleroderma, sclerodermia, seborrhoea, serpigo, shingles, skin cancer, strophulus, sun cancer, sunburn, sunspot, sycosis, telangiectasis, tetter, the itch, thelitis, tinea, trench foot, trichosis, vaccinia, varicella, vitiligo, waterpox, windburn, xeroderma, xerodermia, zoster.

18. 1. toothache cavity, decay, dry socket, gingivitis, gumboil, malocclusion, odontalgia, odontoblast, periodontitis, plaque, pyorrhoea, Riggs' disease. **2. oral ailments** candidiasis, canker, glossitis, herpes simplex, monilia, noma, ptyalism, stomatitis, thrush, tongue-tie, trench mouth, Vincent's angina, Vincent's infection.

19. 1. eye ailments ametropia, aniseikonia, astigmatism, black eye, blennorrhoea, blepharitis, blight, cast, cataract, cockeye, colour blindness, conjunctivitis, cross-eye, cycloplegia, detached retina, diplopia, double image, exophthalmia, exophthalmos, eyestrain, floater, glaucoma, hippus, hypermetropia, hyperopia, hypopyon, iritis, klieg eyes, longsightedness, miosis, muscae volitantes, mydriasis, myopia, myosis, nebula, nystagmus, ophthalmia, ophthalmitis, opthalmitis, pinkeye, presbyopia, proptosis, pterygium, retinal detachment, retinitis, retrolental fibroplasia, sandy blight, scleritis, sclerotitis, scotoma, squint, staphyloma, strabismus, sty, trachoma, trichiasis, uveitis, xerophthalmia. *Informal:* mouse, shiner.

20. **1. allergy** allergen, allergenic, anaphylaxis, hay fever, hypersensitivity, idiosyncrasy, MCS, photoallergy, pollenosis, pollinosis.

21. **1. tumour** growth. *Informal:* Jimmy dancer, the big C. **2. carcinogenesis** oncogenesis, sarcomatosis. **3. cancer form** adenoma, cancroid, carcinoma, carcinomatosis, encephaloma, enchondroma, endothelioma, epithelioma, fibroid, fibroma, glioma, granuloma, haemangioma, Kaposi's sarcoma, KS, leiomyoma, leucaemia, leukaemia, lymphoma, melanoma, molluscum, myoma, osteoma, Paget's disease, radiation sickness, rhabdomyoma, sarcoma, scirrhus, scleroma, sun cancer.

22. **1. malnutrition** avitaminosis, beri-beri, chlorosis, deficiency disease, hypocalcaemia, kwashiorkor, malassimilation, marasmus, milk fever, pellagra, rachitis, rickets, scurvy.

23. **1. neurological ailments** agnosia, agraphia, alalia, alexia, alienation, alogia, Alzheimer's disease, anarthria, anomia, aphasia, apraxia, ataxia, Australian arbo-encephalitis, Australian X disease, brain fever, causalgia, cerebrospinal fever, cerebrospinal meningitis, CJD, Creutzfeldt-Jakob disease, dementia, demyelination, demyelisation, disseminated sclerosis, dysarthria, dysgraphia, dyslalia, dyslexia, dysphagia, dysphasia, dysphemia, echolalia, echopraxia, encephalitis, encephalitis lethargica, encephaloma, encephalomyelitis, encephalopathy, encephalosis, epilepsy, festination, footdrop, general paralysis of the insane, general paresis, glossolalia, hemiplegia, Huntington's chorea, hydrocephalus, hydrocephaly, insanity, locomotor ataxia, maladjustment, ME, melancholia, meningitis, MND, motor neuron disease, motor neurone disease, MS, multiple neuritis, multiple sclerosis, Murray Valley encephalitis, myelitis, myoclonus, neuralgia, neuritis, neuropathy, neuropsychosis, neurosis, paralexia, paralysis agitans, Parkinson's disease, Parkinsonism, perineuritis, phenylketonuria, psychoneurosis, psychopathy, psychosis, sciatica, sleeping sickness, specific learning difficulty, St Vitus dance, strephosymbolia, Sydenham's chorea, syringomyelia, the big A, tic, tic douloureux, titubation, word blindness, wrist drop. **2. paralysis** atropism, catatonia, cerebral palsy, clonus, diplegia, hemiplegia, infantile paralysis, monoplegia, palsy, panplegia, paraplegia, poliomyelitis, quadraplegia, quadriplegia, shaking palsy, tetany, tetraplegia, trepidation.

24. **1. cramp** cork leg, coxalgia, graphospasm, sprain, stiffness, stitch, strain, subluxation, tic, tic douloureux, writer's cramp. *Informal:* charley horse *(US).* **2. slipped disc** spondylitis, spondylolisthesis. **3. rheumatism** ankylosis, arthritis, bursitis, gout, housemaid's knee, lumbago, osteoarthritis, podagra, rheumatics, rheumatoid arthritis, synovitis, tennis elbow, tenosynovitis, tophus. *Informal:* teno. **4. fibrositis** tenonitis. **5. RSI** carpal tunnel syndrome, repetition strain injury, repetitive strain injury.

25. **1. muscular ailments** ataxia, dermatomyositis, hyperkinesia, hypokinesia, hypokinesis, leiomyoma, locomotor ataxia, muscular dystrophy, myalgia, myasthenia, myelitis, myoclonus, myoma, rhabdomyoma, tabes dorsalis, tetanus.

26. **1. bone ailments** achondroplasia, brittle bone disease, brittle-bones syndrome, eburnation, enchondroma, hyperostosis, mastoiditis, myelitis, non-union, osteitis, osteoma, osteomalacia, osteomyelitis, Paget's disease, periostitis, Perthes' disease, Pott's disease, rachitis, rickets, sarcoma, sarcomatosis.

27. **1. blood ailments** agranulocytosis, aplastic anaemia, bacteraemia, bilharzia, bilharziasis, blood-poisoning, caisson disease, erythraemia, glandular fever, haemangioma, haematocele, haemophilia, haemorrhage, Hodgkin's disease, hyperaemia, hyperemia *(Chiefly US),* hyperglycaemia, hypertension, hypocalcaemia, hypoglycaemia, jaundice, leukaemia, lymphadenitis, lymphangiitis, lymphangitis, macrocytic anaemia, malaria, milk fever, monocytosis, mononucleosis, oligocythaemia, pernicious anaemia, plaque, pyaemia, sapraemia, schistosomiasis, septicaemia, sickle-cell anaemia, thalassaemia, the bends, thrombophilia, thrombosis, toxaemia.

28. **1. liver ailments** cirrhosis, hepatitis, icterus, jaundice, kernicterus, pemphigus. **2. glandular ailments** hyperpituitarism, hyperthyroidism, hypopituitarism, hypothyroidism, myxoedema, pancreatitis, splenitis, splenomegaly, thyroiditis, thyrotoxicosis.

29. **1. secretion ailments** acidosis, Addison's disease, adult onset diabetes, alkalosis, alkaptonuria, cystic fibrosis, diabetes, glucosuria, glycosuria, goitre, Graves' disease, hyperglycaemia, hyperpituitarism, hyperthyroidism, hypoactivity, hypocalcaemia, hypoglycaemia, hypopituitarism, hypothyroidism, ketonuria, ketosis, myxoedema, phenylketonuria, porphyria, struma, thyrotoxicosis.

30. **1. congenital ailments** achondroplasia, acromegaly, aplasia, birthmark, blue baby, cleft palate, coeliac disease, dermoid, dwarfism, giantism, gigantism, hydrocephalus, hydrocephaly, ichthyosis, lentigo, mole, Mongolian spot, naevus, nevus *(US),* spina bifida, stork mark, strawberry mark, tongue-tie, uranoschisis, webfoot.

31. **1. worms** anchylostomiasis, ancylostomiasis, ankylostomiasis, ascarid, bilharziasis, echinococcosis, elephantiasis, filaria, filariasis, gapeworm, guinea worm, heartworm, hookworm, hookworm disease, hydatid, kidney worm, lungworm, nematode, pinworm, ringworm, roundworm, schistosomiasis, stomach worm, taenia, taeniasis, tapeworm, threadworm, trichina, trypanosomiasis, uncinariasis, wheatworm, whipworm, wireworm.

32. 1. animal ailments actinomycosis, Akabane virus, anaplasmosis, anthrax, aspergillosis, Bang's disease, barbs, bighead, black disease, blackhead, blackleg, blind staggers, bloat, blowfly strike, blue comb, botryomycosis, bots, braxy, broken wind, brooder pneumonia, brucellosis, bull burn, bull nose, bumble foot, bush sickness, canary sassafras, canine parvovirus, canker, capped hock, cattle sickness, chlamydia, cholera, circling disease, coast disease, coast sickness, coccidiosis, coenurus, coital exanthema, coryza, cowpox, cuckoo scab, curb, devil's grip, dewclaw, distemper, dourine, ecthyma, enterotoxaemia, enzootic, epizootic, epizooty, erethism, exanthema, facial eczema, farcy, farcy bud, farcy button, feline agranulocytosis, feline enteritis, fistula, fly strike, flystrike, foot-and-mouth disease, footrot, fouls, founder, fowl cholera, fowlpox, French moult, gall, gapes, garget, gid, glanders, grapes, grass sickness, grass staggers, grass tetany, grease, haemorrhagic septicaemia, hardpad, heaves, hexamitiasis, hypomagnesaemia, influenza, Johne's disease, joint ill, keel, kennel cough, kidney worm, Kimberley disease, laminitis, leucosis, listeriosis, liver fluke, loco disease, lump jaw, lumpy jaw, lumpy wool, lupinosis, mad cow disease, malanders, mallenders, mange, mastitis, measles, megrims, melon blindness, meningitis, mineral block, moon blindness, mooneye, murrain, mycotic dermatitis, myxomatosis, necrobacillus, necrotic enteritis, Newcastle disease, ornithosis, pants, parrot disease, parrot fever, parvo, parvovirus, pasteurellosis, peg leg *(Chiefly NT)*, perosis, pigeonpox, pinkeye, pityriasis, pizzle rot, pleuropneumonia, plica, psittacosis, pullorum disease, quittor, rabies, redwater fever, rickets, rinderpest, ringbone, roaring, roop, roup, scab, scabby mouth, scabies, scratches, seteriasis, sheath rot, sheep measles, sheep strike, shipping fever, sore mouth, spavin, spirochaetosis, splint, sporotrichosis, spraddle legs, springhalt, staggers, stigma, strangle, stringhalt, strongyle, sturdy, swamp cancer, swamp fever, sway-back, sweeny, swine fever, swine flu *(US)*, swine pox, tapeworm, the pip, the puffs, thoroughpin, thrush, tick fever, toxoplasmosis, trembles, trombidiasis, tularaemia, Turkish towel, vaccinia, vesicular exanthema, walkabout, walkabout disease, warble, waterbrain, whistler, whistling, wilt, wilt disease, windgall, windsucker, wry-tail, yellow sassafras, yellows. *Informal:* fink, myxo, pleuro, ploorer, wobbles.

33. 1. plant ailments allyl sulfide, ambury, anbury, anthracnose, black rot, black rust, black spot, blackheart, blackleg, blast, blight, brown patch, brown rot, bunchy top, bunt, canker, crown gall, curl, curly leaf, damping-off, dieback, dollar spot, dry rot, Dutch elm disease, ergot, greening, grey mould, late blight, leaf curl, mildew, oak-apple, oak-gall, oidium, phytophthora, rootrot, rot, rust, scab, scald, sigatoka, smut, soft rot, spring dead spot, stinking smut, take-all, verticillium, wilt, wilt disease, yellows.

adj. **34. 1. ill** ailing, bad, disabled, down, indisposed, off, out of sorts, poorly, sick, unwell. *Informal:* cronk, crook, dicky, in the miseries, lousy, not so (or too) hot, off-colour, sick as a dog, wonky. **2. invalid** bedridden, doddered, feeble, helpless, infirm, laid up, senile. **3. sickly** adynamic, ailing, asthenic, debilitated, frail, languorous, malnourished, pale, pallid, peaky, pimping, sickish, wan, weakly, weedy, white-livered. *Informal:* washed-out.

35. 1. feverish aguish, febriferous, febrific, febrile, feverous, subfebrile. **2. delirious**. **3. faint** dizzy, giddy, gone, light-headed, swimming. **4. unconscious** comatose, out, senseless.

36. 1. lame hipshot. *Informal:* game, gammy. **2. arthritic** gouty, rheumatic, rheumatoid, rheumatoidal, stiff. **3. paralysed** paraplegic, quadraplegic, quadriplegic. **4. dislocated** out of joint.

37. 1. short-winded asthmatic, wheezy, wind-broken. *Informal:* chesty, out of puff. **2. catarrhal** allergic, stuffy. *Informal:* stuffed up. **3. consumptive** hectic, tubercular, tuberculate, wasting. **4. pneumonic** pleuritic, pulmonary, pulmonic.

38. 1. nauseous airsick, bilious, carsick, green, mawkish, qualmish, queasy, seasick, sick, squeamish, trainsick, upset. *Informal:* warby, white (or green) at the gills. **2. constipated** bound, costive. **3. venereal** jacked up, syphilitic.

39. 1. unwholesome insalubrious, morbid, morbific, morbifical, unhealthy, unsound. **2. infective**. **3. septic** abscessed, cankerous, mature, purulent, scorbutic, scorbutical, ulcerative, ulcerous, watery. *Informal:* bung. **4. cancerous** aggressive, carcinogenic, carcinomatous, tumorous. **5. wasted** atrophied, degenerate, emaciated, retrograde, tabescent, waxy. **6. anaemic** exsanguine. **7. dropsical** hydropic, hydropical. **8. subclinical**. **9. chronic** confirmed. **10. incurable** immedicable, remediless. **11. infectious** catching, endemic, epidemic, pandemic. **12. deleterious**. **13. pathogenetic** bacterial, germinal, viral.

v. **40.**   **1. be ill** ail, sicken. *Informal:* have one foot in the grave. **2. present with** complain of, suffer. **3. relapse. 4. faint** collapse, crumple, lose consciousness, swoon. **5. waste** decay, dwindle, fall away, invalid, languish, lyse, macerate, peak, pine.

41.   **1. disease** canker, disorder, distemper, fever, infect, inflame. **2. blast** atrophy, blight, dwindle, shrivel, smut, wither, wizen. **3. paralyse** founder, palsy, petrify.

RELATED KEYWORDS: HEALING, DETERIORATION, MEDICATION

ILLOGICALITY

n. **1.**   **1. illogicality** ad hoc argument, false dilemma, false reasoning, illogicalness, inconsistency, irrationalism, irrationality, irrationalness, misjudgment, misology, reasonlessness, repugnance, unreason, unreasonableness. **2. fallaciousness** error, groundlessness, illegitimacy, inconsequence, sophisticalness, ungroundedness, unsoundness. **3. arbitrariness** blindness, capriciousness, randomness, speciousness, unaccountability, unaccountableness. **4. absurdity** absurdness, balderdash, boloney, falderal, farmyard confetti, fudge, hogwash, imbecility, ineptitude, ineptness, mere words, nonsense, solecism, the ridiculous, trumpery. *Informal:* a load of old cobblers, apple sauce, balls, bilge, bosh, bulldust, bunk, claptrap, codswallop, crock, eyewash, fandangle, fiddle-faddle, flapdoodle, flim-flam, garbage, gunk, heifer dust, hokum *(US)*, hoo-ha, kibosh, kybosh, macaroni, poppycock, rot, rubbish, todge, tommyrot, tosh, tripe. **5. inconsistency** antilogy, contradiction, contradiction in terms, contradictoriness, incompatibility, incompatibles, paradox, repugnance, self-contradiction. **6. fallacy** chicanery, elenchus, equivocation, false premise, flaw, ignoratio elenchi, non sequitur, paralogism, quibble, quirk, sophism, sophistication, sophistry, weak argument, weak case. **7. begging the question** hysteron proteron, petitio principii. **8. casuistry** chicanery, equivocation, fencing, hairsplitting, jesuitism, mystification, quibble, quibbling, quiddity, runround, sophistry, special pleading, subterfuge. *Informal:* run-around.

adj. **2.**   **1. illogical** alogical, arbitrary, blind, discretional, discretionary, fanciful, random, unreasonable, without rhyme or reason. **2. irrational** apocryphal, erroneous, fallacious, fallible, false, flimsy, gratuitous, groundless, idle, ill-founded, inaccurate, incorrect, loose, mendacious, mistaken, out, post hoc, subreptitious, unaccountable, unreasonable, unreasoned, unscientific, unsound, untrue, weak, wrong. **3. groundless** causeless, implausible, reasonless, untenable. **4. contradictory** antilogous, paradoxical, self-contradictory. **5. incompatible** inconsistent, mutually exclusive, self-contradictory. **6. absurd** extravagant, fantastic, farcical, frivolous, harebrained, inept, laughable, lightsome, ludicrous, nonsensical, preposterous, ridiculous, scatterbrained, senseless, silly. *Informal:* rich, unearthly. **7. fanciful** emotional, fantastic, imaginary, unreasoning. **8. incoherent** bitty, broken, disconnected, disjointed, disjunct, lacking cohesion, rambling, unconnected, uncoordinated, wandering.

3.   **1. casuistic** deceptive, elenctic, fallacious, illegitimate, jesuitical, misleading, paralogistic, perverse, sophistic. **2. quibbling** fine-spun, inconsequent, inconsequential, over subtle, paltry, pettifogging, petty. *Informal:* piffling, potty *(British)*.

adv. **4.**   **1. illogically** illegitimately, inconsequently, inconsistently, irrationally, reasonlessly, unreasonably, unreasoningly, unsoundly. **2. intuitively** brutally, brutishly, by intuition. **3. arbitrarily** alogically, blindly, groundlessly. **4. casuistically** fallaciously, jesuitically, sophistically. **5. fancifully** emotionally, fantastically. **6. absurdly** ineptly, ridiculously, senselessly. **7. on the wrong tack** awry.

RELATED KEYWORDS: ERROR, MISJUDGEMENT, NONSENSE, INSANITY

IMITATION

n. **1.**   **1. imitation** apery, apishness, duplication, echo, emulation, emulousness, foreignism *(US)*, imitativeness, impersonation, impression, mimesis, mimicry, representation, simulacrum, simulation. **2. plagiarism** plagiary. **3. onomatopoeia** echoism. **4. copy** autotype, clone, counterpart, double, duplicate, duplication, ectype, effigy, facsimile, likeness, match, photocopy, record, recording, replica, replication, representation, reproduction, semblance, simulacrum, transcript, transcription, xerox. *Informal:* ditto. **5. forgery** counterfeit, sham. *Informal:* fake. **6. caricature** burlesque, cartoon, mockery, mockumentary, parody, pastiche, postiche, skit, travesty. *Informal:* send-up, spoof, take-off.

2.   **1. imitator** ape, copier, copycat, echoer, emulator, epigone, follower, reproducer. *Informal:* kook. **2. plagiariser** magpie, plagiarist. **3. mimer** caricaturist, impersonator, mimic, monkey, parodist. **4. feigner** affecter, counterfeiter, simulant, simulator. **5. forger** *Informal:* short-story writer.

adj. **3.** **1. imitative** apish, clone, copycat, derivative, echoic, echolike, emulative, emulous, imitational, plagiaristic, simulative. **2. artificial** counterfeit, ersatz, faux, imitation, man-made, mock, simulant. *Informal:* Clayton's. **3. mimic** mimetic, pantomimic.

v. **4.** **1. imitate** ape, copy, duplicate, echo, emulate, follow, mirror, sham, take a leaf out of someone's book. *Informal:* make like. **2. plagiarise** counterfeit, forge. **3. mimic** impersonate. **4. caricature** burlesque, mock, monkey, parody, take off, travesty. *Informal:* spoof. **5. feign** act, affect, counterfeit, pretend, profess. *Informal:* fake. **6. simulate** represent.

adv. **5.** **1. imitatively** apishly, emulously, literally, reproductively.

phr. **6.** **1. in the manner of** à la.

RELATED KEYWORDS: COPY, REPETITION, REPRESENTATION, SIMILARITY, UNTRUTHFULNESS

IMMORALITY

n. **1.** **1. immorality** corruption, debauch, debauchery, degeneracy, degeneration, degradedness, depravity, loose morals, moral turpitude, perversion, Satanism, transgression, turpitude, vice, wickedness. **2. foulness** filthiness, nastiness, odiousness, rottenness, scrofulousness, uncleanliness, unhealthiness, vileness. **3. human frailty** failing, feet of clay, infirmity, looseness, the old Adam, wantonness, weakness, weakness of the flesh. **4. wickedness** atrociousness, belial, blackness, corruptness, darkness, devilry, enormity, enormousness, evil, evilness, heinousness, iniquitousness, iniquity, maleficence, nefariousness, perniciousness, sinfulness, sinisterness, ungodliness, unholiness, unrighteousness, viciousness. **5. damnation** depths, perdition.

2. **1. evildoing** abomination, atrocity, crime, debauch, depravity, devilry, evil, ill, immorality, infamous conduct, malefaction, seduction, sin, turpitude, vice, villainy. **2. sin** cardinal sin, deadly sin, debt, mortal sin, original sin, seven deadly sins, trespass, wrongdoing. **3. fault** demerit, faible, foible, misdeed, peccadillo, venial sin. **4. fall** lapse. **5. debauchment** depravation.

3. **1. immoral person** blackguard, decadent, profligate, reprobate, wretch. *Informal:* sick puppy. **2. backslider** recidivist. **3. wrongdoer** evildoer, malefactor, malefactress, Mr Sin, sinner. **4. devil** archenemy, Beelzebub, bugeen, cloven foot, cloven hoof, demon, fiend, Mammon, Satan, the evil one. *Informal:* divil. **5. corrupter** depraver, pander, polluter, seducer.

4. **1. den of vice** cesspool, cloaca, den of iniquity, sink, underworld. **2. Babylon** cities of the plain, Gomorrah, Sodom. *Informal:* sin city.

adj. **5.** **1. immoral** corrupt, corrupted, debased, debauched, decadent, degenerate, degraded, depraved, evil, fallen, ruined, spoiled, unprincipled, vitiated, wicked. **2. disreputable** devious, knavish, louche, miscreant, scoundrelly, scrofulous, sinister, villainous. **3. indecent** base, gross, loose, profligate, unbecoming, unchaste, unseemly, wanton. **4. frail** only human, slight, weak. **5. reprobate** abandoned, deserted, forlorn, forsaken, incorrigible, irredeemable, lost, recidivous, wicked. **6. sinful** Babylonian, base, black, black-hearted, dark, depraved, erring, evil, evil-minded, flagitious, malevolent, malicious, malignant, mean, nasty, naughty, nefarious, peccant, pernicious, profligate, sinister, ungodly, vicious, villainous, wicked. **7. godless** heathen, impious, infidel, irreligious, pagan, profane, unblessed, ungodly, unhallowed, unholy, unreligious, unrighteous. **8. devilish** accursed, cloven-footed, cloven-hoofed, demoniac, demonian, demonic, diabolic, diabolical, fiendish, hellish, infernal, satanic. **9. foul** abominable, beastly, corruptive, deplorable, filthy, hideous, nasty, obscene, polluted, putrid, rank, rotten, ulcerous, unclean, unhealthy, vile. **10. atrocious** enormous, heinous, inexpiable, iniquitous, unpardonable. **11. corruptive** seductive.

v. **6.** **1. be immoral** contravene, err, infract, infringe, sin, stray, transgress, trespass, violate. **2. backslide** fall, fall from grace, go to the bad, go to the devil, lapse, spoil one's record.

adv. **7.** **1. immorally** corruptly, decadently, degradedly, vilely, wantonly. **2. filthily** nastily, rottenly, unhealthily. **3. evilly** enormously, iniquitously, malignly, nefariously, perniciously, viciously, villainously, wickedly. **4. sinfully** erringly, unrighteously. **5. diabolically** hellishly, satanically.

RELATED KEYWORDS: MISBEHAVIOUR, BADNESS, DISHONESTY, GUILT, UNLAWFULNESS, WRONGDOING

IMPENITENCE

n. **1.** **1. impenitence** brassiness, brazenness, impenitency, impenitentness, obduracy, obdurateness, obstinacy, recusancy, shamelessness, unblushingness.

    2.   **1. impenitent person** constant offender, habitual criminal, hardened criminal, recidivist, recusant, self-confessed sinner.

adj.   **3.**   **1. impenitent** barefaced, bold-faced, brazen, brazen-faced, immodest, impudent, indecent, remorseless, revealing, scarlet, shameless, sinful, unashamed, unblushing, unreformed, unregenerate, unrepentant, unshriven, vulgar, wicked. *Informal:* brassy. **2. obstinate** callous, cold-blooded, cruel, hard, hard-hearted, hard-nosed, hardened, heartless, indurate, indurated, inured, obdurate, recusant, rocky, scleroid, shameless, steely, stony, stony-hearted, tough, unfeeling. **3. incorrigible** irreclaimable, irredeemable.

v.   **4.**   **1. be impenitent** be fixed in one's ways, be seared, brazen it out, die game, harden one's heart, have no shame, not give a damn.

adv.   **5.**   **1. impenitently** brassily, brazenly, obdurately, shamelessly, unashamedly, unblushingly, unrepentantly.

      RELATED KEYWORDS: IMMORALITY

IMPERFECTION

n.   **1.**   **1. imperfection** defectiveness, faultiness, imperfectness, sketchiness, weakness. **2. underdevelopment** immatureness, immaturity, unripeness. **3. contamination** adulteration, impureness, impurity. **4. defect** failing, fault, foible, shortcoming, spot, vice. *Informal:* bugs, fly in the ointment. **5. weak point** Achilles heel, chink in one's armour, faultiness, feet of clay, weak link in the chain, weak spot, weakness. **6. impurity** blemish, flaw.

adj.   **2.**   **1. imperfect** incomplete, unideal. **2. defective** bad, deficient, faulty, maladaptive, sketchy, unsound, vicious. **3. underdone** immature, underdeveloped, unripe. **4. impure** adulterated.

v.   **3.**   **1. be imperfect** fall short of perfection, have a fault.

adv.   **4.**   **1. imperfectly** defectively, faultily, ill, sketchily.

      RELATED KEYWORDS: BLEMISH, BADNESS, WRONGDOING, WEAKNESS, UNTIMELINESS

IMPORTANCE

n.   **1.**   **1. importance** account, concern, concernment, consequence, consequentiality, consideration, greatness, import, interest, magnitude, matter, moment, notability, notableness, note, noteworthiness, pith, significance, significancy, signification, size, substance. **2. seriousness** depth, earnestness, eventfulness, fatefulness, graveness, gravity, momentousness, portentousness, severity, sobriety, solemnity, weight, weightiness. **3. essentiality** essentialness, vitalness. **4. urgency** acuity, acuteness, criticality, criticalness, imperativeness, precedence, pressure, primacy, priority. **5. profoundness** deepness, profundities, profundity. **6. emphasis** accent, accentuation, force, import, matter, meaning, significance, signification, stress, value. **7. value** force, good, importance, worth. **8. eminence** altitude, conspicuousness, credit, distinction, egregiousness, elevation, grandeur, grandiosity, grandness, mark, nobility, note, preeminence, prominence, report, reputation, repute, standing, stature, stock, supremeness.

    2.   **1. important thing** cardinal point, crux, heart of the matter, issue, point, sixty-four dollar question, the thing. **2. climax** climacteric, conjuncture, crisis, great divide, head, juncture, moment of truth, red-letter day, turning point. **3. key word** punch line. **4. a matter of life and death** a big deal, be-all and end-all, everything, no joke, no laughing matter, significance, vital concern. **5. gist** core, heart, substance, vitals, yolk. **6. basics** bedrock, essential, essentials, fundamentals, sine qua non. *Informal:* nitty-gritty. **7. cornerstone** headpin, keynote, kingpin, linchpin. **8. pride of place** face, front, head and front, spearhead. **9. notabilia** rubric, something, unco *(Scottish)*. **10. masterpiece** centrepiece, chef-d'oeuvre, magnum opus, masterwork, pièce de résistance.

    3.   **1. important person** boss, chief, dignitary, foremost, giant, great, high-up, leading, lord, luminary, magnate, magnifico, mogul, notable, number one, personage, pontiff, prince, principal, somebody, top, V.I.P., who's who. *Informal:* big gun, big noise, big pot, big shot, big wheel, bigwig, boss man *(Aboriginal English)*, brass, buzzwig, everybody who is anybody, his nibs, honcho, Mr Big, numero uno, tall poppy, top brass, top dog, topliner, visiting fireman, wheel. **2. star** first fiddle, lead, leading light, prima donna. **3. key person** anchor, anchorman, anchorperson, anchorwoman, mainstay. **4. pompous person** panjandrum. *Informal:* boiled shirt, stuffed shirt.

adj.   **4.**   **1. important** acute, all-important, clamant, consequential, considerable, essential, imperative, imperious, indispensable, insistent, insisting, landmark, pressing, prominent, significant, urgent. **2. notable** bodacious, extraordinary, famous, great, impressive, memorable, noted, noteworthy, remarkable, signal, unforgettable, unimaginable, unique. *Informal:* raving, tremendous. **3. momentous** climacteric, critical, eventful, fatal, fateful, grave, oracular, portentous. **4. prominent** big, celebrated, conspicuous, distingué, distinguished, eminent, famous, grand, great, illustrious, important, marked, noble, pre-eminent, renowned, signal, significant, well-known. **5. essential** all-important, basal, basic *(Chiefly US)*, basilar, crucial, fundamental, indispensable, irreplaceable, key, material, necessary, obbligato, pivotal, primary, to the point, vital. **6. earth-shattering** breathtaking, colossal, earth-shaking, epoch-making, shattering, stirring, world-shaking. **7. newsworthy** front-page. *Informal:* big-time. **8. serious** earnest, fateful, grave, heavy, important, prominent, weighty. **9. major** arch, boss, broad, capital, cardinal, chief, dominant, first, foremost, fundamental, high, key, leading, main, master, paramount, pet, premier, primal, prime, principal, staple, supreme, top. **10. exalted** august, grand, grandiose, high, high-level, high-up, lofty, lordly, maestoso, majestic, noble, princely, regal, senior, stately, supernal, top-level. **11. dominant** chief, culminant, foremost, front-line, highest, number one, paramount, predominant, prepotent, regnant, supreme, top, top-line, topmost, upmost, upper, uppermost. **12. top-priority** high-priority.

v. **5. 1. emphasise** accent *(Chiefly US)*, accentuate, boot home, elaborate, labour, make a point of, make a thing of, press, stress, underline, underscore. **2. bring to the fore** enhance, give weight to, highlight, intensify, magnify, put on the map. **3. magnify** adore, aggrandise, bless, deify, dignify, elevate, ennoble, enthrone, exalt, extol, fete, glorify, hallow, honour, inthrone, laud, lift, lionise, praise, revere, reverence, transfigure, venerate, worship.

6. 1. be important carry, conduct, drive, impel, import, lead, matter, report, signify, tell, weigh. *Informal:* be a big deal, be something else again, be the biggie. **2. carry weight** bulk large. *Informal:* be in big on. **3. concern** affect, interest, involve.

adv. **7. 1. importantly** above all, uppermost. **2. significantly** materially, notably, notedly, noteworthily, signally. **3. seriously** earnestly, for dear life, gravely. **4. momentously** eventfully, fatefully, portentously, weightily. **5. vitally** acutely, critically, pressingly, urgently. **6. basically** fundamentally. **7. eminently** dominantly, egregiously, par excellence, pre-eminently, prominently, supremely.

RELATED KEYWORDS: HIGH REGARD, SUPERIORITY

IMPOSITION

n. **1. 1. imposition** distrainment, distraint, enactment, enforcement, exaction, infliction. **2. demand** call, charge, commandment, decree, dictum, edict, fiat, order, order of the day, ordination, requirement, requisite, requisition, ukase. **3. impost** burden, load, millstone, obligation, onus, tax.

2. 1. imposer agistor, distrainer, enforcer, exactor, inflictor, tasker, wreaker.

adj. **3. 1. imposing** domineering, exacting, high-handed, imperial, imperious, magisterial, overbearing, peremptory.

v. **4. 1. impose** administer, agist, assign, constitute, dispense, distrain, enact, encroach, enjoin, entail, exact, inflict, lay a burden on, ordain, overtask, prescribe, put a responsibility on, require, task, wreak. **2. foist on** land with, lumber, palm off on, saddle with, wish on. **3. requisition** commandeer. **4. domineer** command, demand, force, instruct, rule, tyrannise. **5. tax** levy.

5. 1. take advantage of abuse, exploit, put upon. *Informal:* bludge on, come it a bit much, let in for, pole on, put in the fangs, put in the hooks, put in the nips, put in the screws, put the acid on. **2. leave in the lurch** not play the game. *Informal:* die on someone, leave someone holding the baby.

RELATED KEYWORDS: COMMAND, FORCE, INDEBTEDNESS, REPRESSION, OBLIGATION

IMPOSSIBILITY

n. **1. 1. impossibility** hopelessness, inconceivability, insuperability, unimaginableness. **2. preclusion** exclusion, incompatibleness. **3. paradox** paradoxicalness. **4. impasse** deadlock. *Informal:* no go, no-no. **5. infeasibility** impassability, impracticability, impracticalness, inaccessibility, unworkability.

adj. **2. 1. impossible** beyond the bounds of reason, beyond the realm(s) of possibility, contrary to reason, hopeless, lost to, no-go, not to be thought of, out of the question, unattainable, uncome-at-able. *Informal:* out of court. **2. infeasible** absurd, impracticable, inexecutable, out of reach, quixotic, unaccomplishable, unachievable, unattainable, unfeasible, unobtainable, unworkable. **3. inconceivable** incogitable, incredible,

unimaginable, unthinkable. **4. insuperable** impassable, inextricable, insurmountable, invincible.
3. **1. incompatible** incongruous, inconsistent, insolvable, irresolvable, mutually exclusive, paradoxical, preclusive, self-contradictory.
4. **1. unavailable** elusive, inaccessible, irretraceable, not to be had, unobtainable, unrealisable. **2. vain** fruitless, futile, futilitarian, idle, improbable, ineffective, ineffectual, inept, non-effective, otiose, Sisyphean, unavailing, unlikely, unpractical, unprofitable, useless, void.

RELATED KEYWORDS: UNLIKELIHOOD, POWERLESSNESS

IMPRECISION

n. **1.** **1. imprecision** approximation, impreciseness, inaccuracy, inaccurateness, inexactitude, inexactness, inexplicitness, looseness, rule of thumb. *Informal:* bush reckoning. **2. vagueness** grey area, indefinableness, indefiniteness, indeterminancy, indeterminateness, indetermination, intangibility, intangibleness, tenuousness, uncertainty. **3. shapelessness** amorphism, amorphousness. **4. indistinctness** bleariness, blur, blurriness, dimness, faintness, fog, haze, haziness, macule, mistiness, nebulousness, obscurity, shadow, vaporousness. **5. uncertainty** ambiguity, ambiguousness, incomprehensibility, indefiniteness, indistinctness, moot point, mystery, obscureness, obscurity, open question, pig in a poke, query. **6. obscurantism** equivocalness, woolliness. *Informal:* waffle.

adj. **2.** **1. imprecise** approximate, inaccurate, inexact, proximate, wide of the mark. **2. vague** ambiguous, amphibolous, aoristic, bleary, blurred, blurry, borderline, dim, doubtful, dreamy, equivocal, faint, faraway, hazy, indefinable, indefinite, indeterminate, indistinct, inexplicable, inscrutable, intangible, loose, misty, muddy, mysterious, nebulose, nebulous, nondescript, nubilous, obscure, oracular, puzzling, shady, tenuous, uncertain, vaporous, vapoury, veiled. **3. shadowy** airy, bleary, blurry, cloudy, fuzzy, ghostlike, ill-defined, indistinct, misty, phantom, uncertain, wraithlike. **4. inexplicit** ambiguous, confused, cryptic, enigmatic, equivocal, woolly. **5. shapeless** amorphous, undefined, unformed, unshapen.

adv. **3.** **1. imprecisely** dreamily, inaccurately, indefinitely, indeterminately, inexactly, loosely, tenuously, vaguely. **2. ambiguously** inexplicitly, woollily. **3. indistinctly** faintly, hazily, mistily, nebulously, obscurely, vaporously. **4. approximately** about, in some sort, more or less, or so, proximately, roughly, sort of. *Informal:* like. **5. upwards of** *Informal:* off the ballpark.

RELATED KEYWORDS: CONJECTURE, JUDGEMENT, INTANGIBILITY, WRONGDOING

IMPRISONMENT

n. **1.** **1. imprisonment** false imprisonment, immurement, incarceration, internment, wrongful imprisonment. **2. arrest** apprehension, arrestment, attachment, capture, detention. *Informal:* cop, pinch. **3. order** capias, capias ad satisfaciendum, commitment, mittimus, warrant, writ. **4. captivity** confinement, constraint, custody, durance, durance vile, duress, imprisonment, solitary. **5. custody** confinement, constraint, detainment, detention, house arrest, keeping, protective custody, remand, restraint, surveillance, ward. **6. commitment** committal. **7. time** *Informal:* bed and breakfast, bird, brick, clock, drag, dream, Kath, lag, lagging, lost weekend, porridge, rest, sleep, snooze, spin, stretch, swy, zack. **8. life imprisonment** *Informal:* the lot, the twist.

2. **1. prison** bagnio, cage, dungeon, factory, female factory, gaol, jail, jailhouse *(Chiefly US)*, limbo, penitentiary *(US)*, salt mines, state prison *(Chiefly US)*, tower. *Informal:* bin, bird, boob, booby hatch *(US)*, caboose, calaboose *(US)*, choky, clink, college, cooler, coop, hole, hoosegow *(US)*, jug, nick, pen, pokey, quad, quod, rock college, slammer, stir, the can. **2. compound** concentration camp, internment camp, labour camp, penal settlement, presidio, prison farm, prison-camp, rules, stalag, stockade *(US)*. **3. Botany Bay** Alcatraz, Bastille, Devil's Island, Fort Denison, Moreton Bay, Norfolk Island, Pinchgut, Port Arthur, the Establishment, the Ocean Hell, the Tench, the Tower. **4. lockup** brig, detention centre, dock, watch-house. *Informal:* bullpen *(US)*. **5. reform school** borstal *(British)*, reformatory, training school. **6. prison ship** hulks.

3. **1. cell** black hole, circle, condemned cell, death cell, death row, dungeon, oubliette, pound, solitary confinement, sweatbox. *Informal:* black peter, calaboose *(US)*, chokey, digger *(NZ Prison)*, dummy *(NZ Prison)*, glasshouse *(British Military)*, go-slow, peter, slot, slough. **2. penalty box** *Informal:* sin-bin. **3. pen** crib, pound, stabling. **4. cage** coop, kennel, Skinner box. *Informal:* clink, nick, quod. **5. stocks** pillory. **6. paddy**

wagon paddy-wagon, patrol wagon, wagon. *Informal:* black maria, bull wagon, bun wagon, divvy van *(Chiefly Victoria)*.

4. 1. jailer Cerberus, deathwatch, gaoler, guard, guarder, guardsman, prison officer, turnkey, warden, warder, wardress. *Informal:* four-by-two, kangaroo, screw, trump. **2. incarcerator** confiner, detainer, securer. **3. trusty** farm constable. **4. apprehender** captor, capturer. **5. penology** convictism, prison reform.

5. 1. prisoner captive, convict, criminal, felon, inmate, probation pass-holder, state prisoner *(Chiefly US)*. *Informal:* boobhead, con, crim, gaolbird, gaolie, graduate, jailbird, jailie, keyman, lag, lifer, trusty, yellow jacket. **2. detainee** intern, internee, remandee. **3. periodic detainee** weekender. *Informal:* short-timer, toe-ragger. **4. convict** Cockatoo Islander, croppy, Derwent duck, emancipist, expiree, felon, Hawkesbury duck, legitimate, old chum, old hand, prisoner of the crown, prisoner servant, sevener, ticket of leaver, transportee, Vandemonian, yellow jacket. *Informal:* canary, canary bird, cockatoo, con. **5. chain gang** gaol gang, iron gang, jail gang. **6. prisoner of war** POW.

adj. **6. 1. imprisoned** captive, incarcerate. **2. secured** bonded, confined, fast, pent, pent-up, restrained. **3. cramped** claustrophobic, close, confined, constrained, gated, limitative, limited, pent-up, pokey, poky, restricted. **4. penal** custodial, institutional, non-parole, nonparole, penitentiary. **5. maximum-security** minimum-security.

v. **7. 1. imprison** arrest, confine, gaol, immure, incarcerate, jail, lock away, pound, shut in, shut up. *Informal:* jug, lag, nab, nick, put away, send down *(British)*, send up, tuck away. **2. detain** guard, hold, intern, keep, reconsign, remand. **3. confine** cabin, cloister, coop, cordon off, cramp, immure, imprison, lock in, lock up, pocket, restrain, restrict, secure, shut away, shut in, shut up. **4. lock in** *Informal:* slot, slough up. **5. limit** circumscribe, conscribe. **6. cage** corner, encage, hedge in, hem in, immure, pound. **7. pen** kraal, paddock, stall. **8. fetter** chain, enchain, enfetter, gyve, handcuff, iron, manacle, shackle. **9. ground** gate *(British)*. *Informal:* keep in.

8. 1. arrest apprehend, capture, catch, do, give in charge, recapture, seize, trap. *Informal:* bag, bounce, chuck, collar, knock off, lumber, nab, nick, pick up, pinch, pull in.

RELATED KEYWORDS: COURT OF LAW, UNLAWFULNESS, PUNISHMENT, RESTRAINTS

IMPROVEMENT

n. **1. 1. improvement** amelioration, amendment, betterment, enhancement, melioration. **2. reform** advancement, development, enrichment, preferment, promotion, reformation, regeneration, self-improvement. **3. progress** development, enrichment, preferment, transfiguration, transformation. **4. regeneracy** rebirth, reformation, regeneration, renaissance, renascence. **5. recovery** rally, upswing. *Informal:* pick-up.

2. 1. change for the better amelioration, amendment, betterments, improvement. **2. advance** a leap forward, gain, refinement. **3. reform** counter-reformation. **4. repair** mend, renovation, retouch.

3. 1. improver ameliorator, developer, meliorator, meliorist, perfecter, refiner, uplifter. **2. mender** detailer, repairer, retoucher. **3. reformer** amender, progressionist, progressive, redressor, reformist. **4. conditioner** civilising influence. **5. social climber** advancer. *Informal:* wannabe.

4. 1. progressivism Fabianism, meliorism, progressionism, progressiveness, reformism.

adj. **5. 1. improving** ameliorative, amendatory *(US)*, beneficial, civilising, corrective, edificatory, edifying, meliorative, reformational, reformative, reforming, remedial. **2. progressive** Fabian, forward-looking, go-ahead, reformist. **3. improvable** ameliorable, amendable, developable, mendable, perfectible, reformable.

6. 1. improved better, enhanced, enriched, reformed, regenerate, up-and-coming, upwardly mobile. *Informal:* on the improve, on the mend, on the up and up, on the upgrade.

v. **7. 1. improve** advance, ameliorate, gain, get better, meliorate, mend, upskill. *Informal:* clean up one's act, lift one's game. **2. advance** be none the worse for, better oneself, climb, develop, evolve, gain ground, leapfrog, make headway, make progress, make strides, move forward, press, progress, pull ahead, pull up. **3. reform** go straight, mend one's ways, turn over a new leaf. **4. come good** brighten, rally, recover, regenerate, take a turn for the better. *Informal:* look up, pick up. **5. mellow** develop, ripen.

8. 1. make better ameliorate, amend, better, enrich, improve, meliorate, perfect, refine, reform, transfigure, upgrade, uplift. **2. smarten** brush up, detail, elaborate, enhance, refurbish, touch up. *Informal:* polish up. **3. mend** remodel, repair, retouch. **4. civilise** cultivate, culture, edify, enlighten, refine. **5. benefit** assist, facilitate, help.

adv. **9. 1. improvingly** beneficially, edifyingly, progressively.
RELATED KEYWORDS: REPAIR, GOODNESS, HEALTH

IMPULSIVENESS

n. **1. 1. impulsiveness** arbitrariness, capriciousness, giddiness, impetuousness, impulsivity, promiscuousness, spontaneities, spontaneity, whimsicality, whimsicalness. **2. waywardness** self-will. **3. extemporaneousness** adhocery, adhockery, extemporariness.

2. 1. impulse capriccio, caprice, conceit, crotchet, fancy, fantasy, humour, inspiration, knee-jerk reaction, notion, spurt of imagination, sudden thought, vagary, whim, whimsy. **2. caprice** caper, capriccio, capriciousness, dash, fancy, prank, vagary, whim, whimsicality. **3. extemporisation** ad lib, fantasia, impromptu, improvisation.

3. 1. impulsive person creature of impulse. *Informal:* tearaway.

adj. **4. 1. impulsive** artistic, artistical, capricious, dashing, errant, fanciful, flighty, freakish, giddy, harebrained, hasty, impetuous, maggoty, notional *(Chiefly US)*, precipitate, rash, reckless, skittish, slapdash, spirited, undisciplined, vagarious, wanton, whimsical. **2. wayward** arbitrary, flighty, fly-away, frivolous, uncertain, volatile. **3. extemporaneous** ad hoc, ad lib, extemporary, extempore, impromptu, improvised, jury, off-the-cuff, spontaneous, stopgap, unpremeditated.

v. **5. 1. be impulsive** lose one's head, not think twice, rush headlong into. *Informal:* go at something baldheaded, leap in feet first. **2. extemporise** adlib, improvise. **3. talk off the top of one's head** say the first thing that comes into one's mind.

adv. **6. 1. impulsively** arbitrarily, capriccioso, capriciously, giddily, lightly, like an artist, notionally, on the spur of the moment, promiscuously, waywardly, whimsically, without a second thought, without arriére-pensée, without rhyme or reason, without thinking. **2. impetuously** at the drop of a hat, dashingly. **3. extemporaneously** ad lib, ad libitum, extemporarily, extempore, off the cuff, offhand. *Informal:* by the seat of one's pants, off the top of one's head.

RELATED KEYWORDS: RASHNESS, EXPEDIENCE, FANTASY, INDECISION, INTENTION

IMPUTATION

n. **1. 1. imputation** accreditation, adscription, arrogation, ascription, assignation, assignment, attribution, buck-passing, projection, witch-hunting. **2. blame** censure, censure motion, head-hunting, headshaking, reproach, reprobation. *Informal:* flak, rap.

2. 1. accountability accountableness, answerableness, avouchment, responsibility. **2. assignability** attributiveness, imputativeness. **3. blameworthiness** blamefulness, culpableness, guilt.

adj. **3. 1. imputable** ascribable, assignable, attributable, due, explainable. **2. blamable** accountable, answerable, answerable for, blameful, blameworthy, censurable, chargeable, culpable, guilty, in fault, indictable, liable, nocent, responsible, to blame.

v. **4. 1. impute** affix, arrogate, ascribe, assign, assume, attach, attribute, chalk up to, lay at the door of, make out, object, put down, put down to, put on, put to, sheet home, source. **2. charge** accredit with, accuse, attack, blame, bring to account, call to account, challenge, criminate, impeach, implicate, inculpate, question. *Informal:* pick on. **3. avoid censure** *Informal:* pass the buck, sling the hook.

adv. **5. 1. imputatively** assignably, attributably. **2. blamefully** blamably, culpably. **3. accordingly** and so, because of, by reason of, consequently, considering, ergo, hence, in as much as, in consequence, in that, in the light of, in view of, now that, on account of, owing to, seeing that, since, thanks to, then, thence, therefore, thus.

RELATED KEYWORDS: ACCUSATION, DISAPPROVAL, CAUSE, GUILT

INADEQUACY

n. **1. 1. inadequacy** inadequateness, incommensurateness, jejuneness. **2. insufficiency** dearth, defect, deficiency, half-measure, inadequateness, incompleteness, lack, meagreness, pitifulness, scantiness, scarceness, scarcity, scrimpiness, shortage, underage, want. **3. deficit** default, deficiency, lack, missing link, shortage, shortfall, ullage, underage, wantage *(US)*. **4. scarcity** privation. **5. need** destitution, distress, indigence, misery, necessity, neediness, pauperism, penury, poorness, poverty, starvation, want.

adj. **2. 1. inadequate** chary of, deficient, incommensurate, insufficient, jejune, lacking, lacking in, lean, meagre, poor, scant, scant of, scanty, scrimp, scrimpy, short, short of, short on, shy, slim, sparse, strapped, threadbare, unequal to, wanting, weak. *Informal:* airy-fairy. **2. insufficient** light on, poor, scarce, short. **3. substandard** inadequate, ineffectual, meagre, mean, poor, scraggy, short, weak. *Informal:*

measly. **4. ineffectual** anile, hopeless, inept, powerless, weak. *Informal:* not able to fight one's way out of a (wet) (or brown) paper bag.

v. **3.** **1. fall short** fail, fall flat, fall through, run short, ullage. **2. lack** need, require, want. **3. be lacking** be badly off for, be out of, be short of.

adv. **4.** **1. inadequately** incommensurately, jejunely, meagrely, poorly, scraggily. **2. insufficiently** deficiently, leanly, scantily, scantly, scrimpily.

RELATED KEYWORDS: DEFICIENCY, BADNESS, A FEW

INATTENTION

n. **1.** **1. inattention** absence of mind, absent-mindedness, disregard, heedlessness, inadvertence, inadvertency, inattentiveness, inobservance, mindlessness, oversight, thoughtlessness, unmindfulness, unthinkingness. **2. abstractedness** absent-mindedness, abstraction, brown study, daydreaming, doodling, dreaminess, oscitancy, reverie, woolgathering. **3. carelessness** disregard, neglect, neglectfulness, oversight, remissness.

2. **1. daydreamer** doodler, stargazer, wool-gatherer.

adj. **3.** **1. inattentive** half asleep, incurious, inobservant, oscitant. **2. abstracted** absent, absent-minded, bemused, distracted, distrait, dreamy, lost in thought, preoccupied, woolgathering. *Informal:* moony, on auto, spacey. **3. unheeding** disregardful, inadvertent, regardless of. **4. thoughtless** careless, disregardful, dizzy, heedless, mindless, not switched on, scatterbrained, scatty, unmindful, unthinking. *Informal:* ditsy, ditzy. **5. careless** casual, cursory, disregardful, lackadaisical, lax, neglectful, remiss, slipshod.

v. **4.** **1. be inattentive** be lost in, contemplate one's navel, daydream, dream, have one's head in the clouds, let one's thoughts wander, lose oneself in, nod, sleep, stargaze, wander. *Informal:* goof off, switch off. **2. be distracted** lose the thread, lose track of, pay no attention. **3. disregard** blink at, forget, ignore, let pass, let slide, miss, overlook, pretermit. *Informal:* give someone (or something) the go-by, treat with ignore. **4. skim over** pass over, slip, slur over.

adv. **5.** **1. inattentively** absent-mindedly, absently, abstractedly, cursorily, distractedly, in a dream. **2. unheedingly** inadvertently, mindlessly, thoughtlessly, unmindfully, unthinkingly.

RELATED KEYWORDS: NEGLECT, NEUTRALITY, IMPRECISION

INCLUSION

n. **1.** **1. inclusion** comprehension, comprisal, coverage, embracement, entailment, incorporation. **2. inclusiveness** comprehension, comprehensiveness, generality.

adj. **2.** **1. inclusive** across-the-board, all-embracing, all-in, comprehensive, entire, fulsome, general, global, grand, incorporative, omnibus, outright, overall, panoptic, round, sweeping, total, tutto, umbrella, universal, wall-to-wall, whole, wholesale. **2. all told** all found, all-included, all-inclusive, all-up, in all.

v. **3.** **1. include** add in, assimilate, comprehend, contain, count in, cover, embody, embrace, entail, incorporate, join, number, subsume, take in. **2. comprise** consist of, contain, have, hold. **3. be included** be in it. *Informal:* have a finger in the pie.

prep. **4.** **1. inclusive of** cum, including, through *(US)*. **2. amongst** among, mongst *(Poetic)*, throughout, together with.

INCOMPETENCE

n. **1.** **1. incompetence** fumbling, ignorance, incompetency, ineffectualness, inefficiency, ineptitude, inexperience, inexpertness, maladministration, mismanagement. **2. Peter principle**. **3. incapacity** apraxia, developmental disability, disability, disablement, dyspraxia, impotence, impotency, inaptitude, incapability, incapableness, incapacitation, unfitness. **4. artlessness** amateurishness, amateurism, cubbishness, gaucheness, gaucherie, lubberliness, naivety, otherworldliness. **5. awkwardness** angularness, bearishness, clumsiness, flat-footedness, gawkiness, heavy-handedness, ineptness, left-handedness, lumpiness, lumpishness, maladdress, maladroitness, stiffness, ungainliness, ungracefulness, unhandiness, unskilfulness. **6. unprofessionalism** lack of expertise, quackery. **7. hopelessness** badness, poorness. **8. foolishness** clownishness, folly, goofiness, imbecility. **9. uncouthness** slovenliness, ungraciousness.

2. **1. bungle** botch, error, fault, flub, fumble, gaffe, grope, howler, mistake, trip. *Informal:* bad, balls-up, barry, blue, boner, boob, clambake *(US)*, foul-up, slip-up. **2. blunder** blooper, fluff, Freudian slip, malapropism, slip, slip of the tongue, stumble. *Informal:* foot-in-mouth disease. **3. botchery** piece of incompetence, slopwork.

Informal: a fat lot of use. **4. bad shot** foozle, mis-hit, miscue, misfield, shank. *Informal:* cow shot.

3. 1. incompetent boggler, botcher, bungler, fumbler, incapable, misdoer, mismanager, mucker-up, muddler, tinker. **2. duffer** bad shot, dillpot, dolt, dunce, fool, galloot, idiot, imbecile, incompetent, lame dog, nincompoop. *Informal:* billy goat, boob, boofhead, chucklehead, clown, deadhead, dickhead, dill, dipstick, dork, dumbbell, dumbcluck, ferret, galoot, great ape, klutz, knucklehead, lame duck, melonhead, nong, numbskull, palooka, rabbit, spastic. **3. clumsy person** blunderbuss, blunderer, bull in a china shop, bumpkin, clodhopper, gawk, hobbledehoy, hulk, lubber, mullocker. *Informal:* butterfingers, gazob, lolly legs, lummox, lump, schlub *(US)*, slab, unco. **4. bunch of idiots** *Informal:* a pack of galahs, the awkward squad. **5. bad workman** bush carpenter, cobbler, cub, quack. *Informal:* backyarder, blackjack merchant, snagger, wood butcher. **6. sloven** slouch. *Informal:* slob. **7. hopeless case** hopeless lot, the (living) end. *Informal:* dead loss, no-hoper, write-off. **8. dogberry** bureaucrat, flunkey, lackey, seatwarmer.

4. 1. novice beginner, fresher, greenhorn, neophyte, novitiate, raw material, raw recruit, tenderfoot, tiro, tyro. *Informal:* rookie. **2. amateur** anorak, dabbler, dilettante, landlubber, landsman, lilywhite, lubber, potterer, tinkerer. *Informal:* calf, dilutee.

adj. **5. 1. incompetent** helpless, hopeless, ineffective, ineffectual, inefficient, inept, powerless, useless. *Informal:* not able to fight one's way out of a (wet) (or brown) paper bag. **2. incapable** impotent, inapt, incompetent, inept, infelicitous, unfit, unhappy, unplanned, unqualified. **3. unpractised** backyard, fumbling, inexpert, new-chum, ungifted, unskilful, unskilled, untalented. **4. amateurish** amateur, artless, cubbish, home-made, landlubberly, lubberly, unprofessional. *Informal:* cut-lunch, half-baked. **5. untrained** callow, fresh, green, ignorant, inexperienced, raw, semiskilled, unexperienced, wet behind the ears, young. **6. slovenly** bearish, gauche, offhand, uncouth, unhandy, unmechanical. **7. foolish** clownish, goofy, imbecile, imbecilic. *Informal:* nitty, spastic, uncool. **8. clumsy** accident-prone, all thumbs, awkward, bumble-footed, bungling, cacky-handed, clodhopping, elephantine, gawky, green-hand, ham-fisted, ham-handed, heavy, heavy-handed, hipshot, hulking, hulky, kack-handed, left-handed, lumbering, lumpish, lumpy, maladroit, ungainly, ungraceful, unwieldy. *Informal:* cack-handed, flat-footed, footless *(US)*, unco.

6. 1. badly-done angular, bad, bad at, botched, botchy, faulty, poor. *Informal:* crappy, not much chop. **2. ill-contrived** ill-chosen, ill-conceived, ill-devised.

v. **7. 1. bungle** blow it, blunder, boggle, botch, botch up, butcher, flub, fluff, foozle, make a hash of, make a mess of, make a poor fist of, maladminister, mess, misconduct, misdo, mishandle, mismanage. *Informal:* balls something up, bollocks, bugger up, make a muff of, muck, muck up, muff. **2. blunder** be slipping, bumble, bumble one's way through, bungle, flounder, fumble, get in the road, grope, muddle, stumble. *Informal:* be a blob at, goof, goof up, put one's (big) foot in it. **3. fool around** clown, clown around, tomfool. *Informal:* bugger about (or around), gammon around, mess around (or about), muck about (or around), play silly buggers. **4. dabble** dawdle, dawdle away, potter, tinker. *Informal:* piddle along (or about). **5. be incapacitated** *Informal:* have two left feet. **6. jerry-build** cobble, slum. **7. charge at** charge at like a bull at a gate, go bull-headed at. **8. fumble** catch a crab, duff, mis-hit, miscue, misfield, misthrow, pull, shank, slice, top.

adv. **8. 1. incompetently** amateurishly, artlessly, inaptly, incapably, ineptly, lubberly, unfitly, unhandily, unprofessionally, unskilfully. **2. awkwardly** angularly, bearishly, clumsily, flat-footedly, fumblingly, gawkily, left-handedly, lumpishly, maladroitly, uncouthly, ungainly, ungracefully, unwieldily. **3. imbecilely** clownishly. **4. inefficiently** blunderingly, bunglingly, ill, ineptly, poorly, slovenly.

RELATED KEYWORDS: FOOLISHNESS, STUPIDITY, IGNORANCE, POWERLESSNESS, FOOL

INCREASE

n. **1. 1. increase** accession, accretion, accumulation, add-on, added value, addition, amplification, appreciation, augmentation, bank-up, blow-out, build-up, cumulation, enhancement, exacerbation, expansion, extension, gain, heterosis, increment, inflation, overfall, ramp-up, reinforcements, surge. **2. intensification** aggravation, concentration, crescendo, enrichment, escalation, exaggeration, intension, magnification, maximisation, regeneration, rise, swell. **3. proliferation** elaboration, escalation, multiplication, propagation, pullulation, rash. **4. acceleration** speed-up. **5. boom** rally, revaluation, rise, upswing, upturn.

2. **1. enlargement** dilation, elongation, erection, excrescence, growth, hypertrophy, stretch, swell, swelling, tumidity. **2. inflatedness** dilatancy, erectility, excrescency, pulse, swollenness.

3. **1. breast enlargement** boob job, breast augmentation.

4. **1. increaser** accumulator, augmenter, concentrator, enhancer, expander, grower, maximiser. **2. amplifier** enlarger, exaggerator, heightener, magnifier. **3. inflator** dilatant, dilator. **4. multiplier** propagator. **5. expansionist** inflationist. **6. accelerator** accelerant, booster.

adj. 5. **1. increasing** crescent, dilatant, dilative, expansive, growing, increscent, multiplying, waxing. **2. enhancive** concentrative, exaggeratory, intensifying. **3. accelerative** acceleratory, progressive. **4. augmentative** accretive, accumulative, cumulative, exponential, multiplicative.

6. **1. increased** bloated, blown, blubber, blubbered, blubbery, enlarged, erect, expanded, inflated, puffy, swelling, swollen, tumescent, tumid, turgid, tympanitic. **2. intensified** concentrate, concentrated, intensive. **3. more** above, additional, further, other, plus.

v. 7. **1. increase** accumulate, aggrandise, amplify, augment, beef up, blow up, boost, broach, broaden, build up, build up to, bump up, clap on, cumulate, deepen, develop, double, elongate, enhance, enlarge, enrich, escalate, expand, extend, flash, flesh out, gross up, heighten, hot up, increment, inflate, lengthen, let out, magnify, maximalise, maximise, multiply, pad, piece out, propagate, redouble, reinforce, space out, spin out, step up, surge, thicken, turn up, up, upsize, widen, work up. **2. exaggerate** add fuel to the fire, exacerbate. *Informal:* lay it on (with a trowel) or (a bit thick). **3. accelerate** gather, pick up, speed, speed up. *Informal:* plant the (or one's) foot. **4. revalue** approve, bull, enhance, hike up, jump, load, mark up, pyramid, raise, raise (or up) the ante, rise.

8. **1. accumulate** add up, bank up, gain, gather, grow, regenerate, snowball, stack up, thrive. **2. proliferate** advance, appreciate, blow out, boom, branch out, develop, gain, harden, increase, jump, lengthen, mount, multiply, pullulate, rise, rocket, shoot up, take off, upswing, wax. **3. intensify** concentrate, escalate, fade in (or up), gain strength, rise. **4. swell** bag, balloon, belly, bilge, bloat, blouse out, bulge, dilate, distend, fill, fill out, hypertrophy, inflate, intumesce, puff up, stretch, tumefy. **5. double** quadruple, quintuple, sextuple, triple.

adv. 9. **1. increasingly** accumulatively, cumulatively, exponentially, multiplicatively. **2. more** out of all proportion.

RELATED KEYWORDS: ADDITION, SIZE, GROWTH, MANY

INDEBTEDNESS

n. 1. **1. indebtedness** obligation. **2. arrears** arrearage, default, non-payment. **3. bankruptcy** commercial failure, failure, financial collapse, financial crash, insolvency, receivership. *Informal:* bust, bust-up.

2. **1. debt** amortisation, bad debt, debit, debt of honour, deficit, funded debt, interminable debt, national debt, offset, outstanding account, set-off. *Informal:* a dead horse, a dog tied up. **2. liability** charge, current liabilities, dues, fixed liability, insury, interest, tribute. **3. credit** advance, charge account, creditor, equitable mortgage, first mortgage, gain, house loan, mortgage, overdraft, personal loan, second mortgage. *Informal:* poultice. **4. hire-purchase** H.P., HP, lay-away *(US)*, lay-by. *Informal:* the never-never.

3. **1. bill** demand, dun, final notice, invoice, tax invoice. *Informal:* blister, Jack-n'-Jill. **2. account** reckoning, score, tab, tally. **3. IOU** acknowledgement, marker. **4. promissory note** bill, bond, calabash, certificate of deposit, debenture, debenture stock, mortgage debenture.

4. **1. debtor** arrestee *(Scottish Law)*, arrestment *(Scottish Law)*, bankrupt, borrower, contributory, defaulter, garnishee, mortgagee, undischarged bankrupt.

adj. 5. **1. in debt** amenable, encumbered, in arrears, in difficulties, in financial difficulties, indebted, liable, responsible. *Informal:* head over heels in debt, in beyond one's depth, in the red. **2. overdrawn** behindhand, embarrassed, out of pocket. **3. bankrupt** broken, insolvent, ruined. *Informal:* bust, stumered.

6. **1. owing** chargeable, due, floating, outstanding, payable, undischarged, unpaid.

v. 7. **1. be in debt** be indebted, be under obligation to pay, have insufficient funds, owe. *Informal:* take the knock. **2. go bankrupt** collapse, crash, fail. *Informal:* be gazetted, go bung, go bust, go to the wall. **3. get into debt** borrow, dishonour a cheque, incur a debt, overdraw, refinance, run up a bill.

adv. **8.** **1. on credit** on account, on H.P., on hire-purchase, on lay-by. *Informal:* on the never-never, on the nod, on tick.

RELATED KEYWORDS: ACCOUNTING, MISFORTUNE, FINANCE, LOAN, NON-PAYMENT

INDECISION

n. **1.** **1. indecision** aboulia, ambivalence, double-mindedness, doubtfulness, dubiety, incertitude, indecisiveness, tentativeness, uncertainness, undecidedness. **2. irresoluteness** haltingness, inconsistency, infirmness, limpness, shakiness, unstableness, unsteadiness. **3. aimlessness** unsettledness, unsettlement. **4. second thoughts** hesitancy, hesitation, misgiving, pause, pendency, poise, quandary, shillyshally, suspense, vacillation. **5. procrastination** pause, temporisation. **6. evasion** chicanery, equivocation, excuse, prevarication, quirk, subterfuge. *Informal:* run-around. **7. capriciousness** capriccio, caprice, fancy, fantasy, flightiness, skittishness, whimsicality.

2. **1. equivocator** prevaricator, procrastinator, temporiser. **2. waverer** wobbler. *Informal:* weathercock. **3. abstainer** fence-sitter, trimmer.

adj. **3.** **1. indecisive** aboulic, ambivalent, cautious, changeable, changeful, discrepant, double-minded, doubtful, dubious, dubitative, fickle, halting, hesitant, hesitating, inconsistent, inconstant, irresolute, pendulous, shaky, shillyshally, suspensive, tentative, undecided, vacillating, vacillatory, variable, wavering, willy-nilly. **2. unsure** amphibolic, arbitrary, capricious, changeful, hesitant, irresolute, open, shillyshally, stop-start, uncertain, uncommitted, undecided, unsettled, variable, wayward. **3. perplexed** at a loss, at one's wit's end, bewildered, dizzy, on the horns of a dilemma, puzzled. *Informal:* in a sweat. **4. irresolute** aimless, arbitrary, capricious, doubtful, errant, fickle, flighty, fluctuating, fly-away, mercurial, mutable, objectless, purposeless, shillyshally, skittish, uncertain, undecided, unstable, unsteadfast, unsteady, vacillating, volatile, wavering, whimsical, willy-nilly. **5. evasive** middle-of-the-road, non-committal. **6. weak-willed** cowardly, weak.

4. **1. undetermined** arbitrary, borderline, capricious, in the air, inconclusive, open, pendent, pending, uncertain, undecided, variable. *Informal:* lineball. **2. perplexing** debatable, doubtful, paradoxical, problematical, questionable, ticklish.

v. **5.** **1. agonise over** be torn between, be up in the air, dicker *(Chiefly US)*, dither, flirt, fluctuate, flutter, halt, hang, have a bit both ways, hesitate, hover, librate, oscillate, pause, sway, swing, tergiversate, vacillate, vibrate, wait, waver, weigh up the options, whiffle, wobble. *Informal:* back and fill, blow hot and cold, boggle, change one's tune, chop and change, um and ah. **2. shillyshally** dally, dicker *(Chiefly US)*, dillydally, loiter, niggle, pussyfoot, pussyfoot around, tarry, trifle, vacillate, wobble. *Informal:* buggerise about, buggerise around, fiddle, give someone the run-around. **3. prevaricate** bide one's time, equivocate, evade, pettifog, quibble, temporise. *Informal:* boggle, leg-rope. **4. delay** defer, postpone, procrastinate.

adv. **6.** **1. irresolutely** indecisively, shakily, shillyshally, unstably, unsteadily, vacillatingly, waveringly. **2. uncertainly** doubtfully, dubiously, haltingly, hesitatingly, hoveringly, pausingly, pendently, pendulously, uncommittedly, undecidedly. **3. aimlessly** at random, errantly, flightily, skittishly. **4. evasively** non-committally. **5. inconclusively** by chance, p'raps, possibly, potentially. *Informal:* happen *(British)*. **6. perhaps** by chance, maybe.

RELATED KEYWORDS: IMPULSIVENESS, UNCERTAINTY, CHANGE OF ALLEGIANCE

INDEPENDENCE

n. **1.** **1. independence** autarchy, autocephaly, autonomy, freedom, home rule, republicanism, self-determination, self-government, self-regulation, self-rule, self-sufficiency, separatism. **2. freedom** discretion, free will, freedom of action, freedom of choice, liberty, volition. **3. anarchy** anarchism, libertarianism. **4. individualism** individuality, self-expression. **5. self-sufficiency** autarky, autonomy, confidence, independence, independency, inner-direction, self-reliance, toughness. **6. self-support** independent means, private means, private practice, self-employment, self-help.

2. **1. independent person** autarkist, crossbencher, feme sole, free agent, free spirit, independent, individualist, lone hand, loner, mugwump *(US)*, one's own person, rugged individualist, self-made man, separatist. **2. breakaway** ginger group, separatist, splinter group. **3. anarchist** libertarian. **4. independent contractor** freelance, freelancer, private practitioner, self-starter.

adj. **3.** **1. independent** acephalous, autocephalous, autonomic, autonomous, free, free-wheeling, hermetic, incoercible, indomitable, loose, self-contained, self-governing, self-sufficient, substantive. **2. self-determining** autonomous, independent, self-governed, self-governing, self-regulating, self-ruling. **3. separatist** individual, isolationist, separate. **4. non-partisan** detached, independent, insular, unattached, uncommitted, unconcerned, uninvolved. **5. anarchic** anarchistic, libertarian. **6. single-handed** individual, removed, separate, sole, unconnected, undirected, unsupported.

4. **1. self-sufficient** autarkical, autonomous, independent, individualistic, inner-directed, self-adaptive, self-contained, self-made, self-reliant, self-supported, self-supporting. **2. freelance** self-employed. **3. self-supported** self-supporting, self-sustaining.

v. **5.** **1. be independent** be one's own boss, be one's own master, be one's own person, call no man master, do one's own thing, fend for oneself, go it alone, go one's own way, kick over the traces, paddle one's own canoe, pull oneself up by the bootstraps, shift for oneself.

adv. **6.** **1. independently** autonomically, autonomously, separately. **2. by oneself** off one's own bat, on one's own, on one's own initiative, on one's own responsibility, on one's own undertaking, single-handedly, singly. **3. anarchically**.

RELATED KEYWORDS: LIBERATION, DISOBEDIENCE

INEQUALITY

n. **1.** **1. inequality** disequilibrium, disparity, disproportion, disproportionateness, imbalance, imparity, irregularity, unequalness, unevenness. **2. lopsidedness** asymmetry, bias, dissymmetry, list, unbalance. **3. mismatch** misfit.

adj. **2.** **1. unequal** aeolotropic, anisotropic, disparate, irregular, patchy, unequals, uneven. **2. disproportional** disproportionate, out of proportion. **3. lopsided** anisometric, asymmetrical, dissymetric, dissymmetrical, free-form, oblique, one-sided, secund, unbalanced, unilateral. **4. mismatched** at odds, ill-fitting, ill-suited. **5. perissodactyl** perissodactylous. **6. scalene**. **7. orthorhombic** triclinic.

adv. **3.** **1. unequally** irregularly, unevenly. **2. lopsidedly** askew, awry, disproportionately.

RELATED KEYWORDS: DISCORD, IRREGULARITY, DIFFERENCE

INEVITABILITY

n. **1.** **1. inevitability** fatality, ineluctability, inevitableness, sureness, unavoidability, unavoidableness. **2. predestination** foreordainment, foreordination, predetermination, preordainment, preordination. **3. fatalism** karma, predestinarianism. **4. fatefulness** doom, feyness.

2. **1. fate** appanage, chance, destiny, doom, fatality, fortune, fortunes, karma, kismet, lot, luck, predestination, providence, star, the inevitable. **2. the Fates** (Three) Weird Sisters. **3. wheel of Fortune**.

adj. **3.** **1. inevitable** bound to, certain, fatal, fated, fateful, ineluctable, ineludible, inescapable, irresistible, predestinate, predeterminate, predetermined, sure, unavoidable. **2. doomed** fatal, fateful, fey, starred.

4. **1. fateful** fatal, karmic, providential, weird. **2. fatalistic** predestinarian, predeterminative.

v. **5.** **1. preordain** destine, fate, foreordain, ordain, order, predestinate, predestine, predetermine. **2. doom** foredoom.

adv. **6.** **1. inevitably** fatally, fatefully, for sure, ineluctably, ineludibly, providentially, surely, unavoidably.

RELATED KEYWORDS: CERTAINTY, NECESSITY, LUCK

INEXPEDIENCE

n. **1.** **1. inexpedience** disadvantageousness, incommodiousness, incommodity, inconveniency, inexpediency, unprofitability, unprofitableness, untowardness. **2. disadvantage** disutility, handicap, ill fortune, injuriousness, misfortune. **3. drawback** disadvantage, disbenefit, hindrance, ill effect, infelicity, liability, misfortune, penalty. *Informal:* slug. **4. awkwardness** clumsiness, ineptitude, ineptness, infelicity. **5. unhelpfulness** disobligingness, impertinence, inimicality, uncooperativeness.

2. **1. inappropriateness** impropriety, inadvisability, inappositeness, inaptitude, inaptness, unfitness, unqualifiedness, unsatisfactoriness. **2. inapplicability** futility, impracticableness, inapplicableness, infeasibility, unpracticalness, vainness. **3. uselessness** needlessness, unsuitableness. **4. unwiseness** craziness, impoliticness.

adj. **3.** **1. inexpedient** impolitic, incommodious, inconvenient. **2. disadvantageous** infelicitous, needless, nugatory, undesirable, unfavourable, unfortunate, unprofitable, unsatisfactory, useless, worthless. **3. untoward** improper, objectionable, unseemly. **4. inapplicable** futile, impossible, impracticable, ineffective, infeasible, unpractical, vain.

    4.   **1. inappropriate** de trop, impertinent, inadmissible, inapposite, inapt, ineligible, inopportune, malapropos, out of place, unapt, unfit, unfortunate, unqualified, unsuitable, unsuited, wrong. **2. unwise** crazy, foolish, ill-advised, impolitic, inadvisable. **3. awkward** clumsy, inept, infelicitous, unmanageable. **4. unhelpful** disobliging, impertinent, inimical, uncooperative.

v.   **5.**   **1. be inexpedient** be a dead end, be a waste of time, have no future. *Informal:* be a dead loss, gum up the works. **2. disadvantage** discommode, embarrass, forestall, have someone on (or upon) the hip, hinder, incommode, inconvenience, indispose, put out, set back. *Informal:* mozz. **3. shoot oneself in the foot** be a fool to oneself. **4. encounter difficulties** hit a brick wall, run into trouble, run up against. **5. run afoul of** incur a penalty.

adv.   **6.**   **1. inexpediently** disadvantageously, inappositely, incommodiously, inconveniently, ineptly, unprofitably. **2. unhelpfully** disobligingly, inimically, uncooperatively.

    7.   **1. inappropriately** awkwardly, impoliticly, inadvisably, inaptly, infelicitously, unqualifiedly, unsatisfactorily, unsuitably, untowardly. **2. inapplicably** impossibly, impracticably, in the clouds, unpractically. **3. unwisely** crazily, impoliticly, needlessly, uselessly.

      RELATED KEYWORDS: INADEQUACY, MISFORTUNE, HINDRANCE, USELESSNESS

INFERIORITY

n.   **1.**   **1. inferiority** baseness, coarseness, ignobility, ignobleness, imperfection, lowness, meanness, mediocrity, poshlost, vileness. **2. debasement** adulteration, minimisation, subordination. **3. lowliness** lack of position, lack of rank, lack of standing, poorness. **4. ordinariness** scrubbiness, shoddiness. **5. subnormality** bottom, low tide. **6. minimum** least, less, lesser, worse, worst. **7. inferiority complex** cultural cringe, feeling of inadequacy, sense of inadequacy.

    2.   **1. inferior** adjunct, adjutant, aid *(US)*, aide, aide-de-camp, assessor, assistant, best boy, busboy *(Originally US)*, cog, delegate, deputy, helper, junior, minor, number two, offsider, poor relation, representative, satellite, second, second class, second tenor, secondary, subaltern, subeditor, subordinate, subsidiary, underling, underservant. *Informal:* crud, delo, dep, pig swill, sidekick, sub, subbie. **2. supporting artist** backing group, ensemble, session musician, sessionman, studio musician. **3. stand-in** alternate, ersatz, fill-in, locum, relief, replacement, substitute, surrogate, understudy.

adj.   **3.**   **1. inferior** auxiliary, colonial, junior, minor, of lesser importance, partial, puisne, second-class, second-rate, secondary, side, subordinate, subsequent, subsidiary, thrown in the shade, under, young, younger. *Informal:* mongrel, naff. **2. subordinate** assistant, associate, attendant, auxiliary, subaltern, subordinative, subservient, subsidiary. **3. lowly** abject, base, baseborn, below the salt, common, debasing, degrading, humble, ignoble, low, mean, mundane, non-u, of low caste, ordinary, peasant, poor, simple, small, the bakya crowd *(Philippine English)*, vassal, vile, vulgar, worse off. *Informal:* crap, infra dig, pov, scuzz, scuzzy. **4. less** last, lesser, littler, minimal, smaller, worse, worst. **5. second-class** bog-standard, down-market, inadequate, inferior, mediocre, middlebrow, of sorts, run-of-the-mill, second-best, second-rate, secondary, sub, subnormal, subordinate, substandard, third-rate. *Informal:* half-pie, low-rent, middling, nothing out of the box. **6. adulterated** adulterate, broken-down, cut, watery. **7. of less height** inferior, lower, subjacent.

v.   **4.**   **1. be inferior** be below standard, fall short, not hold a candle to, not measure up, not pass muster, not shape up. **2. play second fiddle** bow before, depend, take a back seat.

adv.   **5.**   **1. inferiorly** lowly, secondarily, subordinately. **2. on the wrong side of the tracks** in a humble station, in a low station, in lowly circumstances, in poor circumstances.

      RELATED KEYWORDS: WORKING CLASS, BADNESS, UNIMPORTANCE, MEDIOCRITY, IMPERFECTION, SERVANT, FOOL

INFERTILITY

n.   **1.**   **1. infertility** aridity, aridness, barrenness, desolateness, dryness, sterility. **2. unproductiveness** fruitlessness, impotence, malfunction, non-productiveness, non-productivity, unprofitability, uselessness, vainness. **3. unfruitfulness** childlessness. **4. menopause** anovulation, change of life, climacteric.

    2.   **1. wasteland** barrens *(US)*, desert, desolation, dust bowl, gumland *(NZ)*, no-man's-land, scabland, waste, wilderness, wilds.

    3.   **1. contraception** birth control, family planning. **2. rhythm method** Billings method, contraception method, mucus method, ovulation method, safe period, safe period method. *Informal:* Vatican roulette. **3. coitus interruptus** onanism. **4. contraceptive**

device cap, combination pill, contraceptive, copper 7, curette, Depo-Provera, diaphragm, Dutch cap, intra-uterine device, IUCD, IUD, loop, low dose pill, minipill, once a month pill, pessary, preventive, prophylactic, sequential pill, spermicide, the pill. **5. condom** contraceptive sheath, durex *(British)*, sheath. *Informal:* franger, French letter, frenchy, frog, preservative, raincoat, rubber *(Chiefly US)*, skin. **6. sterilisation** castration, ligation, tubal ligation, vasectomy. **7. abortion** D and C, dilatation, dilation and curettage, embryectomy, termination, vacuum aspiration. **8. abortifacient** aborticide, abortion pill, morning-after pill.

4. 1. childless female nullipara. **2. castrated male** castrato, eunuch, hijra *(Indian English)*, spado. **3. unproductive animal** gilt. **4. sterilised animal** barrow, eunuch, mule, neuter, poulard, steer.

adj. **5. 1. infertile** barren, dead, fruitless, sterile, unfruitful, unproductive. **2. arid** dead, desert, desolate, dried up, dry, exhausted, hungry, poor *(Aboriginal English)*, sheep-sick, sick, stony, submarginal, waste. **3. uncultivated** fallow, unseeded, untilled, unused, virgin. **4. not reproducing** acarpous, anovulatory, arid, barren, celibate, dead, farrow, seedless, shy, sterile, unjoined, untouched, untried, unused, virgin, virginal. **5. childless** non-parous, nulliparous, without issue. **6. impotent** castrated, neuter, sexless, spayed, unmanned. **7. contraceptive** abortifacient.

6. 1. unprofitable abortive, academic, dead, dead-end, effete, futile, ineffective, ineffectual, infertile, non-productive, sisyphean, unavailing, useless, vain. **2. counterproductive** inefficient, uneconomic.

v. **7. 1. be infertile** go to waste, lie fallow, shrivel, stagnate, wither. **2. abort** miscarry, spike.

8. 1. make infertile exhaust, impoverish, overcrop. **2. sterilise** castrate, cut, desex, do, emasculate, fix, geld, mark, mutilate, neuter, spay, unsex. *Informal:* alter, deknacker, doctor.

adv. **9. 1. barrenly** aridly, desolately, sterilely. **2. unproductively** fruitlessly, in vain, ineffectively, non-productively, unfruitfully, unprofitably, vainly.

RELATED KEYWORDS: POWERLESSNESS, USELESSNESS

INFINITY

n. **1. 1. infinity** endlessness, eternity, immenseness, immensity, infiniteness, infinitude, perpetuity. **2. boundlessness** illimitableness, illimitabless, immeasurableness, unboundedness, unlimitedness. **3. the infinite** the eternal. **4. abyss** bottomless deep, bottomless pit.

adj. **2. 1. infinite** immense, transfinite. **2. boundless** endless, exhaustless, illimitable, indefinite, inexhaustible, infinite, interminable, limitless, measureless, never-ending, perpetual, shoreless, spaceless, termless, unbounded, uncounted, unfathomable, unlimited, unmeasured, without end. **3. immeasurable** countless, immensurable, incalculable, incomputable, inestimable, innumerable, interminable, myriad, numberless, umpteen, uncountable, unmeasurable, unnumbered, untold, without measure, without number.

adv. **3. 1. infinitely** immeasurably, immensely, incalculably, inestimably, till the end of time, unmeasurably. **2. boundlessly** endlessly, illimitably, unboundedly, unlimitedly.

RELATED KEYWORDS: ETERNITY, SIZE, MANY

INFLUENCE

n. **1. 1. influence** affection, atmosphere, hidden hand, impression, imprint, inspiration, operation, penetration. **2. power of influence** authority, becharm, charisma, dominion, fascination, force, hold, imposingness, influence, leverage, magic, mana, potency, potentness, power, powerfulness, pressure, prestige, pull, push, spell, sway, weight. *Informal:* mojo *(Chiefly US)*, whammy. **3. predominance** ascendancy, dominance, domination, dominion, predomination, prevailingness, regnancy. **4. patronage** auspices, control, dominion, good offices, influence.

2. 1. persuasion agitation, agitprop, blarney, brainwashing, cajolery, coaxing, convincement, emotional blackmail, hypnosis, hypnotisation, lobbyism, manipulation, mesmerisation, mesmerism, palaver, propaganda, psychological warfare, salesmanship, suggestion, wheedling. **2. sales talk** argument, patter, persuasive, pitch, propaganda. *Informal:* hard sell, sell, soft sell, spiel.

3. 1. susceptibleness exorability, impressibility, impressionability, impressionableness, persuasibility, pliability, pliancy, pliantness, sensibility, sensitiveness, sensitivity, suggestibility, suggestiveness, susceptibility, susceptiveness, susceptivity, tractability, tractableness. **2. amenability** amenableness, other-directedness, other-direction, perviousness.

4. **1. persuader** affecter, arguer, assurer, blandisher, cajoler, coaxer, convincer, pleader, reasoner, swayer, sweet-talker, urger, wheedler. **2. catalyst** activator. **3. brainwasher** conditioner, hypnotiser, manipulator, mesmeriser, mesmerist, svengali. **4. lobbyist** string-puller, wire-puller. *Informal:* operator. **5. lobby** connections, pressure group. **6. determinative** determinant, organiser.

5. **1. influential person** éminence grise, a friend at court, authority, backer, backroom boy, big wheel, genius, high priest, in, influence, patron, power, power behind the throne.

adj. **6.** **1. influential** active, decisive, far-reaching, impingent, imposing, intervenient, seminal, strong, weighty. *Informal:* well-in. **2. predominant** ascendant, chief, dominant, foremost, master, overriding, pre-eminent, preponderant, preponderating, prepotent, prevailing, regnant, sovereign, superior, supreme, uppermost. **3. charismatic** infectious, manipular, manipulative, manipulatory, mesmeric. **4. convincing** coaxing, eloquent, luculent, persuasive, silver, silver-tongued.

7. **1. influenced** affected, biased, coloured, interested. **2. susceptible** exorable, impressible, impressionable, other-directed, pervious, plastic, pliable, responsive, sensitive, soft, susceptive. **3. amenable** adaptable, agreeable, complaisant, compliable, compliant, complying, conformable, convincible, easy, facile, flexible, malleable, obliging, open, persuadable, persuasible, pliable, pliant, suggestible, tractable, yielding.

v. **8.** **1. influence** act on (or upon), affect, bear on, decide, determine, impinge on, impress, inspire, militate, move, move to, operate on, sway, touch, work on. *Informal:* grab. **2. predominate** hold the balance of power, hold the reins, preponderate, prevail, surmount. **3. pull rank** pull strings, throw one's weight about, throw one's weight around. *Informal:* pull the braid, pull wires *(Chiefly US)*. **4. be influential** carry weight, impress, make an impact on, strike, tell with, tip the scales, touch. *Informal:* grab, have a drag with *(US)*, have an in, have pull.

9. **1. persuade** convince, handrush, induce, influence, inspire, lead, lobby, overpersuade, put up to, talk around, talk into, wrangle. **2. urge** blandish, blarney, cajole, carry away, coax, drive, impel, importune, ingratiate, inspire, jolly, palaver, ply, press, push, solicit, sweet-talk, wheedle. **3. manipulate** angle for, bias, brainwash, charm, coax, condition, impose on, manage, manoeuvre, mesmerise, pervert, prejudice, prepossess, seed, sway, swing, tamper, tamper with, twist round one's little finger, warp. *Informal:* psych. **4. argue** assure, debate, plead, ratiocinate, reason, talk.

adv. **10.** **1. influentially** catalytically, inspiringly, seminally. **2. predominantly** decisively, imposingly, predominatingly, preponderantly, preponderatingly, prepotently, prevailingly, tellingly. **3. persuasively** coaxingly, convincingly, luculently, mesmerically, tendentiously.

11. **1. susceptibly** amenably, plastically, pliably, pliantly, sensitively.

RELATED KEYWORDS: CAUSE, ENCOURAGEMENT, FORCE, LOGICALITY

INFORMALITY

n. **1.** **1. informality** intimateness, lack of ceremony. **2. casualness** carelessness, colloquialism, ease, easiness, offhandedness, permissiveness, unaffectedness. **3. approachability** approachableness. **4. anomie** social vacuum. **5. casual dress** dishabille, en déshabillé, fatigues, mufti, undress. **6. unconventionality** bohemianism, lack of inhibition.

adj. **2.** **1. informal** familiar, offhand, rude, unceremonious, unofficial. *Informal:* folksy *(US)*. **2. casual** airy, cavalier, easy, easygoing, familiar, free, free and easy, laid-back, offhand, offhanded, relaxed, unbuttoned, unconcerned, unembarrassed. **3. unconventional** bohemian, broad, nonconformist, permissive, uninhibited. **4. colloquial** conversational. **5. casually dressed** déshabillé, in dishabille.

v. **3.** **1. be informal** let one's hair down, not stand on ceremony, relax, unbutton, underdress, unwind.

adv. **4.** **1. informally** casually, unceremoniously, unembarrassedly, unofficially.

RELATED KEYWORDS: ANARCHY, NONCONFORMITY

INFORMATION

n. **1.** **1. information** advice, change, communication, HUMINT, inside information, intelligence, intelligence product, knowledge, news, notice, notification, the facts, the latest, tidings, word. *Informal:* dope, drum, gen, good guts, info, intel, lowdown, run-down, the dinkum oil, the good oil, the goods. **2. data** facts, facts and figures, figures, statistics. **3. advice** caution, clue, counsel, lead, notice, notification, object lesson, suggestion, tip, tip-off, warning, word, word in the ear. *Informal:* heads-up. **4. hint** cue, hot tip, inkling, intimation, sidelight, suggestion. **5. report** account, backgrounder, brief, case history, document, follow-up, hyperlink, newsletter, praecipe, statement, story, summary, white paper. **6. bulletin** circular, communiqué, memo, memorandum, newsletter, notice, notification. *Informal:* bung. **7. message** dispatch, line, note. **8. propaganda** advertising, agitprop, disinformation. **9. reference collection** bibliotheca, card file, card index, catalogue, clipping service, databank, database, dossier, file, index, library, material, reference library, source material, tickle box.

2. 1. digital information data, databank, database, relational database, teletext, term bank. **2. the internet** infobahn, information superhighway, World Wide Web. **3. information technology** information theory, IT. **4. search mechanism** Boolean search, search engine. **5. datum** binary code, block, data, quantum bit. **6. bit** byte, field, word. **7. baud.**

3. 1. dissemination circularisation, communication, conveyance, notification, propagation, transmission. **2. briefing** direction, exposition, guidance, instruction, showing, summa. **3. debriefing** debrief, feedback, interrogation, questioning. **4. propagandism** indoctrination, proselytism.

4. 1. informant conveyor, informer, narrator, notifier, scout, teller. *Informal:* a little bird. **2. messenger** channel, courier, runner. **3. source** adviser, authority, consultant, referral. **4. guide** cicerone, pole star. **5. information network** *Informal:* grapevine. **6. tipster** *Informal:* urger. **7. telltale** informer, pimp, sneak, tale-bearer, tattler, tattletale, welsher. *Informal:* blabber, chocolate frog, copper's nark, deep throat, dobber, dobber-in, dog, golliwog, grass, grasser, nark, Noah's Ark, shelf, silvertail, snitch, squealer, stool pigeon *(Chiefly US)*, supergrass. **8. spy** eavesdropper, intelligencer, mole, scout, secret agent, security police, spier, wire-tapper. *Informal:* plant, sleeper, spook.

5. 1. information agency bureau, clearing house, credit agency, mercantile agency, office, trade reference.

adj. **6. 1. informed** advised, au courant, enlightened, in on, in the know, savvy, up on, up-to-date, well-informed. *Informal:* clued-up, cluey, in the picture. **2. advised** briefed, instructed, posted, primed.

7. 1. informative communicative, directive, directory, documentary, encyclopedic, informational, instructional, instructive, intelligential. **2. communicative** chatty, communicatory. *Informal:* newsy.

v. **8. 1. inform** acquaint someone of, acquaint with, address, apprise, brief, circumstance, direct, enlighten, fill someone in, give to understand, impart information to, instruct. *Informal:* drum up, oil up, put in the picture, put wise. **2. warn** tip off. **3. notify** advise, circularise, keep posted, notice *(Chiefly US)*, warn. **4. communicate** announce, convey, elaborate on, enunciate, impart, keynote *(US)*, make known, notify, project, show, tell. **5. advertise** circularise, propagandise, publicise. **6. hint** drop, infer, insinuate, intimate. *Informal:* let drop.

9. 1. consult look up, refer to. **2. get information** reconnoitre, scout, scout out (or around for), sit (or be) across. *Informal:* gen up on, get a line on, get the good guts on, recce, wise up on.

10. 1. report on delate, give up, inform, shelve, tell on, welsh on. *Informal:* blow the whistle on, dingo on someone, dob, dob in, dob on, drop someone in, finger, grass on, nark, put in, put someone's weights up, put the finger on, rat on, shelf, shop *(Chiefly British)*, sing, squeak, squeal. **2. expose** divulge. *Informal:* blow, drop a bundle.

adv. **11. 1. informingly** communicatively, instructively.

interj. **12. 1. what's the latest?** *Informal:* what's the biz?.

RELATED KEYWORDS: COMMUNICATION, KNOWLEDGE, MESSAGE, NEWS, PUBLICITY, TEACHING

INNOCENCE

n. **1. 1. innocence** blamelessness, guiltlessness. **2. purity** chastity, immaculateness, maidenhead, maidenhood, maidenliness, pureness, sinlessness, state of grace, virginity, virtue, whiteness. **3. artlessness** dupability, guilelessness, inexperience, simpleness, simplicity.

2. 1. innocent person child of nature, cleanskin, dove, innocent, lamb, newborn babe. *Informal:* the meat in the sandwich.

adj. **3. 1. innocent** blameless, clean, clean-handed, clear, guiltless, inculpable, irreproachable, offenceless, reproachless, unsullied, white-handed. **2. pure** dovelike, immaculate, impeccant, incorruptible, innocent, lamblike, lily, lilywhite, maidenly, sinless, unsullied, untouched, virginal, virtuous, white. **3. artless** dupable, fresh, green, inexperienced, ingenuous, naive, open-faced, simple, uncalculating, unsophisticated, unworldly.

v. **4. 1. be innocent** have a clear conscience, have clean hands, have nothing to hide.

adv. **5.** **1. innocently** blamelessly, inculpably. **2. purely** immaculately, incorruptibly, virtuously.

RELATED KEYWORDS: ACQUITTAL, YOUTH, GOODNESS, JUSTIFICATION, LAWFULNESS, MORALITY

INSANITY

n. **1.** **1. insanity** craze, craziness, daftness, derangement, franticness, insaneness, looniness, lunacy, madness, neuropsychosis, psychopathy, psychosis, queerness, strangeness, theomania, unbalance, unreason, unsoundness of mind, wildness. **2. nervous breakdown** mental illness, mental instability. **3. delirium** deliration, deliriousness, fantasy, hallucination, morbidity, morbidness, subdelirium. **4. mental flaw** aberration, crack. **5. brainstorm** delirium, distraction, fit, frenzy, hysteria, hysterics, ictus, madness. *Informal:* conniptions, pink fit. **6. craze** mania, obsession.

2. **1. insane person** cyclothymiac, demoniac, energumen, hypochondriac, lunatic, luny, lycanthrope, madman, madwoman, maenad, maniac, mattoid, melancholiac, paranoiac, phrenetic, psychopath, psychotic, schizoid, schizophrenic. *Informal:* basket case, crackbrain, crackpot, crazy, cyberchondriac, dingbat, fruit cake, kook, loco (US), loony, nut, nutter, odd bod, psycho, schizo, wacko, whacko.

adj. **3.** **1. insane** balmy (US), bizarre, brainsick, certifiable, certified, crackbrained, cranky, crazed, crazy, delirious, demented, deranged, disordered, eccentric, erratic, flighty, frantic, frenetic, giddy, giggly, headless, hysterical, irrational, lunatic, luny, mad, maggoty, maniac, maniacal, manic, mentally ill, moonstruck, obsessional, odd, off-centre, offbeat, over the edge, peculiar, phrenetic, pixilated, queer, scatty, screwed up, singular, strange, unbalanced, unusual, weak-minded, whacky, wild. *Informal:* barmy, barmy as a bandicoot, bats, batty, bonkers, cockamamie, cracked, crackers, crackpot, crank, cuckoo, daffy, daft, daggy, dilly, dingbats, dippy, ditzy, dizzy, dotty, far gone, gaga, gonzo, hoity-toity, kinky, kooky, like a chook with its head cut off, loco, loony, loopy, mad as a (cut) snake, mad as a gumtree full of galahs, mad as a hatter, mad as a March hare, mad as a meataxe, magnoon, mental, mug, nitty, non compos, nuts, nutty, nutty as a fruitcake, oddball, off one's block, off one's chump (Chiefly British), off one's face, off one's head, off one's nut, off one's onion, off one's rocker, off one's saucer, off one's scone, off one's tile, off one's trolley, off the air, off the beam, off the rails, off the wall, original, out of one's head, out of one's mind, out of one's tree, porangi (NZ), potty, psycho, ratty, round the bend, round the twist, sapheaded, sappy, schizo, screwball, screwy, silly as a wet hen, soft in the head, sonky, spaz, spoony, starkers, troppo, unhinged, up the pole, wacko, wacky (Chiefly US), way-out, womba, wrong in the head, yampy, yarra. **2. frenzied** berserk, beside oneself, distraught, frenetic, mad, maddened, maddening, phrenetic, possessed, rabid, uncontrollable, violent, wild. *Informal:* beresk, berko.

v. **4.** **1. be insane** *Informal:* act the (giddy) goat, be a few cans short of a six pack, be a sausage short of a barbecue, be a shingle short, be out of one's tree, carry on like a pork chop, have bats in the belfry, have kangaroos in the top paddock, have the ha-has, have white ants upstairs (or in the attic), need one's head read, not play with a full deck. **2. take a fit** have a turn, run amuck. *Informal:* chuck a mental. **3. go insane** go haywire. *Informal:* crack, get the Darling pea, lose one's marbles.

5. **1. madden** craze, dement, derange, frenzy, loco, turn someone's mind, unbalance.

RELATED KEYWORDS: FOOLISHNESS, STUPIDITY, ILLOGICALITY, PSYCHE, FOOL

INSERTION

n. **1.** **1. insertion** embolism, epenthesis, grafting, infixion, insinuation, intercalation, interpolation, introduction, intromission, putting in. **2. implantation** embedding, embedment, emboly, engraftation, engraftment, graft, grafting, heterograft, implant. **3. inoculation** vaccination, variolation. **4. impregnation** insemination.

2. **1. perforation** impalement, irruption, penetration, prick, stab, sting, transfixion.

3. **1. insert** Dutchman, enclosure, fold-out, gatefold, gusset, infiltrate, inlay, inlay graft, input, inset, interlining, peg, stuffing, suppository, tibby. *Informal:* noddy. **2. injection** enema, fuel-injection, infiltration, infusion, instillation, instilment, intrusion. *Informal:* jab, shot, skinpop.

4. **1. inserter** bottler, canner, enroller, grafter, implanter, infuser, inoculator, introducer, packer, stinger, vaccinator. **2. injector** fuel-injector, hypodermic, hypodermic needle, infiltrator, needle, vaccine gun. *Informal:* hype, hypo, pick, spike. **3. drill** diamond drill, perforator.

adj. **5.** **1. inserted** embolismic, epenthetic, immersed, inlaid, interlineal, interlinear. **2. intercalative** introducible, intrusive, intussusceptive, irruptive. **3. penetrating** infiltrative, intercalary, interpenetrative, interpolated, intervenient, penetrative. **4. infiltrative** infusive, inoculative.

v. **6.** **1. insert** catheterise, ease in, implant, infix, inlet, inset, intercalate, interline, interlineate, introduce, intromit, intubate, invaginate, put in, slip in, slot in, stuff, tip in, work in. *Informal:* whack in. **2. interpolate** insinuate, intercalate, interject, interlay, interleaf, interleave, interpose, interstratify, sandwich, slot in. **3. enclose** bag, barrel, bottle, box, encapsulate, incapsulate. **4. embed** bury, engulf, imbed, immerse, ingulf, mire. **5. enter** file, fill in, inscribe. **6. implant** bed, embed, engraft, enroot, fecundate, graft, heel in, imbed, imbue, immerse, infix, ingraft, inlay, plant, root, tincture, tub. **7. inject** implant, infuse into, insinuate, instil, intrude, syringe. *Informal:* mainline, shoot, skinpop. **8. impregnate** imbrue with, infect, inoculate, inseminate, vaccinate, variolate.

7. **1. perforate** bite, bore, cleave through, crack, dub, gore, gride, honeycomb, horn, impale, interpenetrate, jab, javelin, lancinate, penetrate, pierce, pike, pink, plunge, poke, prick, prickle, prong, puncture, reach, riddle, rowel, run through, spear, spit, spur, stab, stick, sting, thorn, thrust, transfix, tusk.

RELATED KEYWORDS: ENTRANCE, INSIDE, INTAKE, OPENING, PLACEMENT

INSIDE

n. **1.** **1. inside** bottom, interior, pith, within. **2. innards** belly, bowels, contents, entrails, insides, internal organs, internals, interns, intestines, inwards, viscera, vitals. *Informal:* comic cuts, guts. **3. innermost** core, endocrine, heart, intima, kernel, marrow, penetralia, yolk. **4. inland** dead centre, dead heart, heartland, outback, red centre, upcountry. **5. inwardness** innerness, inscape, interiority, internality. **6. inset** chine, concavity, fissure, insert, interstice, recesses.

adj. **2.** **1. inside** deep-seated, enclosed, enteric, included, inmost, inner, innermost, interior, intern, internal, interstitial, intestine. **2. inland** domestic, interior, inward, up-country. **3. inward** endoreic, incurrent, ingrowing, re-entrant. **4. indoor** domestic, in-house, inboard, ingrown, inmost, interior, intimate, intramural. **5. inlying** endogenous, intratelluric. **6. visceral** intestinal, splanchnic, subcutaneous.

v. **3.** **1. interiorise** embed, imbed, immerse, internalise, put inside. **2. introvert** withdraw into oneself.

adv. **4.** **1. inside** aboard, herein, in, inboard, indoors, inwardly, therein, within. **2. inward** centripetally, hereinto, inwards. **3. internally** endogenously, interiorly, inwardly. **4. inland** up-country. **5. at home** en famille, home, in the bosom of one's family, in the family.

RELATED KEYWORDS: CENTRE, INSERTION

INSIPIDITY

n. **1.** **1. insipidity** blandness, insipidness, mildness, plainness, tastelessness, vapidity, washiness, weak flavour. **2. milk and water** pap, sop.

adj. **2.** **1. insipid** diluted, flat, flavourless, floury, milk-and-water, savourless, tasteless, undistinguished, unseasoned, vapid, washy, waterish, watery, weak, wishy-washy. **2. flat** dead, plastic, stale. **3. mild** bland, plain, unflavoured, unseasoned, unspiced, vanilla.

RELATED KEYWORDS: UNPLEASANT FLAVOUR, TASTE

INSISTENCE

n. **1.** **1. insistence** clamour, hue and cry, importunacy, importunate, insistency, outcry, public outcry, urgency. **2. demand** call, claim, counterclaim, encore, exaction, request, requisite, requisition, summons, ultimatum. **3. order** behest, charge, command, commandment, countermand, decree, dictate, directive, edict, exhortation, fiat, imperative, injunction, mandate, ordinance, stipulation, ukase. *Informal:* say-so. **4. type of order** affiliation order, charging order, closing order, community service order, fatwa, interim conservation order, permanent conservation order, prohibition order *(NZ)*, restraining order, standing order, stop loss order, stop order. **5. writ of right** breve, fierifacias, prerogative order, prerogative writ, quo warranto, warrant, writ, writ of execution, writ of prohibition. **6. levy** burden, imposition, imposture, requirement, requisition, strain, tax. **7. bill** dun, invoice. *Informal:* blister, Jack-'n'-Jill.

2. **1. insister** a stickler for something, asker, demander, exactor, stipulator. **2. claimant** claimer, counterclaimant.

adj. **3.** **1. insistent** clamorous, commanding, demanding, exacting, exigent, exigible, imperative, stipulatory, urgent. *Informal:* me-too.

v. **4.** **1. insist on** ask, be tough on, call, call for, challenge, clamour, deliver an ultimatum, demand, order, order about, press, propound, rack-rent, require, stipulate, summon. **2. claim** arrogate, boast of, counterclaim, postulate, prescribe, re-claim. *Informal:* bags. **3. exact** estreat, impose on, levy, make heavy demands on, overtax, requisition, task, tax, tithe. **4. bill** bulk-bill, call *(US)*, direct bill, dun, exact payment, foreclose, invoice. *Informal:* hold the hand out.

RELATED KEYWORDS: COMMAND, DESIRE, QUESTION, STUBBORNNESS

INTAKE

n. **1.** **1. intake** drag, draw, drawback, gasp, gulp, in-draught, inhalation, inrush, inrushing, inspiration, pant, puff, pull, suck, suction, whiff. *Informal:* toke. **2. assimilation** digestion, embracement, osmosis. **3. absorption** absorptance, consumption, engorgement, imbibition, ingestion, ingurgitation, occlusion, persorption, sorption. **4. absorbency** absorptiveness, absorptivity, receptivity, recipience, recipiency.

2. **1. absorber** absorbent, consumer, devourer, digester, embracer, imbiber, inhaler, recipient, swallower. **2. absorbent material or item** activated charcoal, active carbon, bentonite, Bentonitic clay, blotter, blotting paper, cadmium, cushion, disposable nappy, dope, India paper, mop, nappy, nappy liner, pounce, root hair, sanitary napkin, sanitary pad, sponge, squeegee mop, sweatband, tampon, wettex. **3. aspirator** haustellum, sucker, suction pump, vacuum aspiration, vacuum cleaner.

adj. **3.** **1. absorbent** absorbefacient, absorptive, bibulous, humectant, hygroscopic, leachy, leaky, permeable, pervious, porous, radiolucent, receptive, recipient, semipermeable, spongelike, suctorial. **2. ingestive** aspiratory, assimilative, assimilatory, diathermanous, diathermic, digestive, edacious, inhalant, inspiratory. **3. assimilable** digestible. **4. breathable** respirable.

v. **4.** **1. absorb** assimilate, chemisorb, digest, merge, merge into, occlude, poison, resorb, soak up. **2. sponge up** blot, sop, sponge, sponge off (or away), swab. **3. consume** bolt, choke down, devour, down, drain, drink, eat, engorge, get into, go through, gobble, gollop, gorge, gulp, guzzle, imbibe, ingest, ingurgitate, kaikai *(Aboriginal English)*, keep down, lap up, overdose, quaff, rehydrate, scull, sip, skol, slurp, snack, suckle, sup, swallow, swallow up, swill, take, taste, tipple, tuck into (or away), wassail, weigh into, wolf. *Informal:* be heavy on, bog in, booze, carb up, carbo-load, chow down, chug-a-lug, demolish, dig in, get outside of, get stuck into, goof, grog, grub, hoe in, hoe into, knock back, knock down *(NZ)*, knock off, lush, nosh, OD, put away, scoff, shicker, sink, soak it up, sock away, stodge, stoke up, stop one, swig, toss off, tuck in, wet one's whistle. **4. respire** aspirate, breathe, breathe hard, breathe heavily, breathe in, draw breath, gasp, inbreathe, inhale, inspire, insufflate, pull, smoke, sniff, snuff, suck, whiff.

RELATED KEYWORDS: INSERTION, FOOD

INTANGIBILITY

n. **1.** **1. intangibility** abstractness, disembodiment, immateriality, immaterialness, impalpability, imponderability, imponderableness, incorporeity, inessentiality, intangibleness, invisibility, unreality. **2. ethereality** airiness, etherealness, vaporosity, vaporousness. **3. evanescence** fugitiveness, transience. **4. insubstantiality** flimsiness, tenuousness, thinness.

2. **1. the intangible** the abstract, the imponderable, the unknowable. **2. abstraction** concept, conception, idea, ideal, notion, supposition. **3. figment** bubble, fantasy, idol, imagining, mirage, smoke. **4. straw company** kite.

3. **1. soul** anima, atman, inner being, inner nature, mind, monad, psyche, self, spirit, spiritual self, wairua. **2. life force** breath of life, ectoplasm, etheric body, etheric force, mauri, vital force. **3. phantom** apparition, astral body, astral spirit, eidolon, ghost, kehua *(NZ)*, phantasm, shade, shadow, spectre, spirit, umbra, vapour, visitant, wraith. *Informal:* spook.

4. **1. idealism** ideology, platonism. **2. metaphysics** metempirics. **3. subjectivity** internality. **4. spirituality** immaterialism, spiritualisation, spiritualism, spiritualness, transcendentalism, transcendentness, unworldliness.

5. **1. idealist** ideologist, ideologue, platonist. **2. metaphysician** immaterialist, metempiricist.

adj. **6.** **1. intangible** bodiless, disembodied, ectoplasmic, imaginary, immaterial, impalpable, imperceptible, inappreciable, incorporate, incorporeal, insubstantial, invisible, spiritual, unreal, untouchable. **2. supersensory** imponderable, inconceivable, incredible, inessential, insubstantial, supersensible, supersensual, unessential, unimaginable, unknowable, unthinkable. **3. internal** mental, noetic, subjective. **4. abstract** conceptual,

ideological, metaphysical, metempiric, metempirical, speculative, theoretical, transcendental.
7. **1. ethereal** aerial, aery *(Poetic)*, airy, astral, fanciful, nebulous, shadowy, shady, vaporous, whimsical. *Informal:* airy-fairy. **2. evanescent** ephemeral, fleeting, fugacious, fugitive, transient, transitory, volatile. **3. ghostly** phantasmal, spectral, unearthly, wraithlike. **4. flimsy** cardboard, insubstantial, slight, tenuous, thin, vague, weak. **5. delicate** gossamer, subtle.
8. **1. spiritual** extramundane, ghostly, hyperphysical, inner, interior, inward, otherworldly, preternatural, spectral, supernatural, superphysical, transcendent, transcendental, transcending, translunary, transmundane, unearthly, unworldly.
9. **1. ideal** fantasy, notional, platonic, platonist, speculative, supposed, visionary.
v. 10. **1. etherealise** dematerialise, immaterialise, spiritualise, thin, vaporise. **2. idealise** abstract, internalise, transcend.
adv. 11. **1. intangibly** impalpably, imponderably, unreally. **2. abstractly** metaphysically, supersensibly, transcendentally, transcendently. **3. incorporeally** immaterially, unsubstantially. **4. flimsily** airily, delicately, tenuously, thin, thinly. **5. ethereally** aerially, fugitively, vaporously.
12. **1. spiritually** preternaturally, transcendentally. **2. mentally** notionally, platonically.
RELATED KEYWORDS: NON-EXISTENCE, CHANGE, CHANGEABLENESS, FANTASY, IDEA, THINKING

INTELLECTUAL

n. **1. 1. intellectual** academic, blue, bluestocking, bookman, bookworm, brahman, classicalist, classicist, diplomate, doctor, don, dux, fellow, humanist, intellect, intellectualist, knowledge worker, pandit, postgraduate, professor, pundit, rabbi, rabbin, reader, researcher, sage, scholar, scholastic, schoolman, scribe, sophist, swami, teacher. *Informal:* acca, brain, egghead, pointy-head *(Chiefly US)*. **2. highbrow** academician, cognoscente, connoisseur, critic, don, philosophe, polyhistor, polymath, virtuoso. **3. pedant** Dryasdust, scholastic. **4. graduate** diplomate, licentiate, matriculate, postgraduate. **5. bohemian** *Informal:* long-hair.
2. 1. intellectualism bohemianism, bookishness, classicalism, eruditeness, erudition, intellectuality, intellectualness, neo-scholasticism, scholarliness, scholarship, scholasticism. **2. pedantry** donnishness, scholasticism. **3. academia** Academe *(Poetic)*, academy, ivory tower, the academy. **4. intelligentsia** clerisy, cognoscenti, literati.
adj. **3. 1. intellectual** academic, cerebral, educated, erudite, intellectualistic, learned, literate, mental, scholarly, scholastic, sophisticated, well-informed. **2. cerebral** bluestocking, bohemian, bookish, heavy, highbrow, literary, long-haired. **3. highbrow** bluestocking, long-haired. **4. bohemian** *Informal:* boho. **5. pedantic** bookish, donnish, pedantical.
adv. **4. 1. intellectually** academically, bookishly, eruditely, learnedly, scholarly, scholastically.
RELATED KEYWORDS: INTELLIGENCE, KNOWLEDGE, TEACHER, WISE PERSON

INTELLIGENCE

n. **1. 1. intelligence** ambidexterity, aptitude, aptness, braininess, brainpower, brains, brightness, brilliance, brilliantness, capableness, capacity, cleverness, conceitedness, faculty, luminousness, understanding, uptake. *Informal:* grey matter, the smarts. **2. intellect** discernment, genius, insight, penetration, penetrativeness, reason, subtlety. **3. sharp-wittedness** acumen, acuteness, aptitude, esprit, flair, keenness, knowingness, perspicacity, perspicuity, perspicuousness, sharp-sightedness, sharpness, skill. **4. quick-wittedness** nimbleness, precocity, quickness.
2. 1. wisdom far-sightedness, judiciousness, long-headedness, policy, prudence, sageness, sapiency. **2. shrewdness** astuteness, canniness, policy, sagaciousness, sagacity, subtleness, subtlety, supersubtlety. **3. common sense** commonsensicality, levelheadedness, mother wit, nous, reason, reasonableness, savvy, sense, sensibleness. *Informal:* gumption, horse sense. **4. profundity** deepness, profoundness.
adj. **3. 1. intelligent** able, brainy, bright, brilliant, capable, clever, cleverish, ingenious, intellective, intellectual, intelligential, knowing, knowledgeable, luminous, smart, strongminded, thinking, understanding. **2. quick-witted** apprehensive, apt, attic, nimble, precocious, quick, quick on the uptake, ready, ready-witted, receptive. **3. sharp-witted** acuminous, acute, attic, clear-eyed, clear-sighted, discerning, discriminate, discriminating, discriminative, gnomic, keen, knowing, penetrating, penetrative, perspicacious, perspicuous, sharp, sharp-sighted, wide-awake.
4. 1. wise far-seeing, far-sighted, judicious, long-headed, old, Palladian, politic, prudent, sagacious, sage, sapient, sapiential. **2. shrewd** astute, canny, foxy, judicious, politic,

savvy, sharp, smart, statesmanly, subtle, supersubtle. *Informal:* all there. **3. sensible** commonsensical, level-headed, realistic, reasonable. **4. judicious** circumspect, deep, intense, politic, profound, prudent. **5. profound** deep.

v. **5. 1. be wise** have a (good) head on one's shoulders, have a lot of nous, have one's head screwed on (the right way).

adv. **6. 1. intelligently** aptly, brightly, brilliantly, capably, cleverly, conceitedly, ingeniously, intellectively, luminously, neatly, smartly. **2. shrewdly** acutely, astutely, cannily, canny, keenly, knowingly, nimbly, parlously, penetratingly, penetratively, perspicaciously, politicly, precociously, quick-wittedly, sharply, subtly.

7. 1. wisely deeply, far-sightedly, judiciously, profoundly, sagaciously, sagely, sapientially, sapiently, understandingly. **2. commonsensically** judiciously, prudently, realistically, reasonably, sensibly. **3. profoundly** deep, deeply.

RELATED KEYWORDS: CUNNING, KNOWLEDGE, LOGICALITY, WISE PERSON

INTENTION

n. **1. 1. intention** aim, animus, counsel, determination, end, frame of mind, gleam in one's eye, intent, purpose, resolve, view. **2. will** choice, craving, desire, hankering, inclination, leaning, liking, mind, penchant, pick, pleasure, preference, selection, velleity, volition, want, wish, yen. **3. voluntarism** conation, free will, pleasure principle.

2. 1. decisiveness decidedness, decision, deliberateness, determinateness, determination, determinedness, earnestness, firmness, heart of oak, immovability, immovableness, intension, intentness, killer instinct, premeditation, purposefulness, purposiveness, seriousness, seriousness of purpose, stability, stableness, steadfastness, steadiness. **2. resoluteness** an iron hand, iron will, resolution, single-mindedness, strength of purpose, strength of will, willpower. **3. wilfulness** a mind of one's own, a will of one's own, headstrongness.

3. 1. intender premeditator, voluntarist, voluntary.

adj. **4. 1. intended** accidentally on purpose, calculated, conative, concerted, conscious, deliberate, designed, intentional, intentioned, planned, premeditated, premeditative, prepense, purposed, purposeful, purposive, studied, wilful. *Informal:* put-up. **2. voluntary** freewill, self-determined, volitional, volitionary, volitive.

5. 1. intent bent on, earnest, intent on, serious, set on. **2. decisive** constant, dauntless, determined, faithful, firm, fixed, hard-set, indomitable, purposeful, resolved, set, stable, staunch, steadfast, steady, steady of purpose, stout, stout-hearted, stubborn, sturdy, unflagging, unwavering. *Informal:* deadset. **3. resolute** decided, definite, determinate, determined, firm, pronounced, resolved, set, settled. **4. uncompromising** cast-iron, closed shop, confirmed, hell-bent, immovable, inexorable, inflexible, insistent, intransigent, iron-fisted, rigid, single-minded, stiff, strong-willed, unbending, unrelenting, vocal. **5. wilful** contumacious, headstrong, insisting, obstinate, persistent, refractory, self-willed, stiff-necked, stubborn, wanton.

v. **6. 1. intend** choose, design, destine, mean, mean to, plan, vow. *Informal:* calculate *(US)*. **2. have a good mind to** have a great mind to, have half a mind to, think fit. **3. consider** consult, contemplate, deliberate, envisage, meditate, ponder, premeditate, ruminate, take, think, think about, think out, think through. **4. desire** choose, covet, long for, want, will, wish, yearn for.

adv. **7. 1. voluntarily** by choice, by one's own free will, volitionally. **2. at will** as you like, when ready. **3. intentionally** by design, consciously, deliberately, designingly, in cold blood, on purpose, premeditatedly, purposefully, purposely, purposively.

8. 1. wilfully wantonly. **2. resolutely** immovably, risoluto, single-mindedly, unbendingly, uncompromisingly. **3. decisively** earnestly, in earnest, resolvedly, seriously, stably, steadfastly, steadily.

conj. **9. 1. with a view to** in order to, so that.

RELATED KEYWORDS: DESIRE, PERSISTENCE, STUBBORNNESS, WILLINGNESS

INTERACTION

n. **1. 1. interaction** alternation, bilateralness, connection, correlation, dynamic, exchange, give and take, interchange, interconnection, intercourse, interdependency, interplay, interrelation, mutuality, reciprocality, reciprocation, reciprocity, relationship, tete-a-tete. **2. mutualism** biocenology, endosymbiosis, symbiosis. **3. fundamental interaction of nature** electromagnetic interaction, fundamental force, gravitational interaction, strong interaction, weak interaction. **4. ratio** correlation, correlation ratio, correspondence, direct ratio, direct relation, functional relationship, inverse ratio, inverse relation.

          5. **barter** exchange, trade, traffic. **6. toing and froing** coming and going, commutation, commuting. **7. exchange of ideas** cross-fertilisation, cultural exchange. **8. globalisation**.

adj.   **2.**   **1. interactive** bilateral, commutative, interfacial, mutual, reciprocal, reciprocative. **2. interdependent** alternate, interchangeable, interconnected. **3. international** interdominion, inter-island, intercolonial, intercontinental, intermundane, interoceanic, interstate, intertropical. **4. interracial** intertribal. **5. interdepartmental** intercollegiate. **6. interpersonal** intergenerational.

v.   **3.**   **1. interact** alternate, be a function of, be proportional to, come together, correlate, correspond, cut across one another, interchange, intercross, interface, interflow, interlace, interlock, intermarry, intermingle, interplay, interrelate, intersect, intertwine, intervolve, interweave, mingle, mutualise *(Chiefly US)*, reciprocate, reticulate. **2. exchange** come and go between, commute, interchange, intercommunicate, interconnect, swap. **3. cause to interact** correlate, enweave, intercross, interface, interlock, intertwine, interweave, mutualise *(Chiefly US)*, reciprocate, twine.

adv.   **4.**   **1. interactively** bilaterally, inter vivos, mutually, reciprocally, together.

          RELATED KEYWORDS: COMMUNICATION, EQUALITY, EXCHANGE, RELATION

INTERPRETATION

n.   **1.**   **1. interpretation** anagoge, clarification, eisegesis, elucidation, exegesis, explanation, explication, illumination. **2. illustration** exemplification. **3. exegetics** deconstruction, deconstructionism, deconstructionist theory, diagnostics, euhemerism, hermeneutics, higher criticism, oneirocriticism, oneirology, semiotics, solarism, symbology. **4. key** clue, crib, solution.

        2.   **1. translation** transcript, transcription, transliteration, vernacularisation. **2. paraphrase** abridgement, epitome, metaphrase, rewording, simplification. **3. version** lection, reading, remix, rendering, rendition, varia lectio, variant. **4. construction** angle, construe, sense, slant.

        3.   **1. commentary** comment, crit, criticism, critique, discussion, editorial, review. **2. caption** closed captioning, inscription, legend, supertext. **3. annotation** adversaria, apostil, appendix, casenotes, comment, critical apparatus, end note, excursus, footnote, gloss, glossary, marginalia, note, notes, protocol, schedule, scholium, sidenote.

        4.   **1. interpreter** constructionist, construer, deconstructionist, exegete, explainer, expounder, glossator. **2. semiotician** hermeneutist, hierophant, oneirocritic, solarist, symbolist. **3. paraphrast** paraphraser, renderer. **4. commentator** critic, editorialist, reviewer, scholiast. **5. annotator** glosser, scholiast.

        5.   **1. translator** dragoman, lip-reader, transcriber, vernacularist. **2. decoder** decipherer.

adj.   **6.**   **1. interpretive** declaratory, explanatory, explicative, exponential, expository, illustrative, interpretational, interpretative. **2. paraphrastic** transcriptive. **3. exegetic** anagogical, hermeneutic, hierophantic. **4. commentarial** annotative, glossarial.

        7.   **1. interpretable** construable. **2. translatable** decipherable, paraphrasable, renderable.

v.   **8.**   **1. interpret** construe, deconstruct, make of, read, read between the lines, take, understand. **2. explain** clarify, clear up, define, elucidate, explicate, expound, illuminate, illumine, parabolise, shed (or throw) light on, shed light on, spell out, throw light on, translate, unfold. **3. solve** decipher, decode, decrypt, puzzle out, unravel, unscramble. **4. comment** commentate, editorialise. **5. illustrate** exemplify. **6. annotate** edit, gloss, margin, pave.

        9.   **1. translate** jargonise, mistranslate, render, transcribe, transliterate, turn, vernacularise. **2. decipher** decode. **3. rephrase** metaphrase, paraphrase, reword, simplify. **4. lipread**.

adv.   **10.**   **1. interpretatively** editorially, explanatorily, interpretively.

        RELATED KEYWORDS: SUGGESTION, CLARITY, MEANING

INTERRUPTION

n.   **1.**   **1. interruption** discontinuation, discontinuity, disjunction, disturbance, interference, interposition, intervention, intrusion. *Informal:* embuggerance, embuggery. **2. pause** abeyance, anacoluthon, anoestrus, bracket, break, caesura, cessation, cesura, chasm, entr'acte, gap, hiatus, interlude, intermission, interregnum, interruption, interval, let-up, lull, parenthesis, rest, spell, stay. **3. digression** bracket, episode, parenthesis. **4. interjection** exclamation, interposal, show stopper. **5. commercial break** station break.

    2. **1. interrupter** disturber, embuggerist, interjector, interposer, intruder.

adj.   **3.** **1. interrupted** broken, catchy, disconnected, discontinuous, discrete, episodic, few and far between, fitful, intermittent, spasmodic. **2. in abeyance** abeyant, on hold.

    4. **1. interfering** busy, curious, inquisitive, intrusive, meddlesome, obstructive, officious, prying. *Informal:* nosy, rubberneck, squizzy, stickybeaking. **2. interruptive** caesural, disjunctive, interjectional, interjectory, intrusive, parenthetic, parenthetical.

v.   **5.** **1. interrupt** break into, cut, disconnect, disturb, punctuate, stop. *Informal:* bust up. **2. pause** put on hold. *Informal:* put in cold storage. **3. interfere** break in, burst in, cut in, intermeddle, interpose, interrupt, intervene, intrude, irrupt, meddle. *Informal:* barge in, bib in, butt in, have a finger in the pie, horn in, mess in, nose about, nose into, poke one's nose into, put one's bib in, put one's oar in, stick one's nose in, stickybeak. **4. interject** chime in, cut someone short, interpose, put in. *Informal:* chip in, weigh in with.

adv.   **6.** **1. interruptedly** at intervals, by (or in) fits (and starts), by snatches, discontinuously, falteringly, fitfully, spasmodically.

        RELATED KEYWORDS: INTERVAL, IRREGULARITY

INTERVAL

n.   **1.** **1. interval** bracket, break, chasm, gap, hiatus, interregnum, interruption, interspace, parenthesis, pause, rest, space. *Informal:* spell. **2. interim** interspace, interval, meantime. **3. interlude** antimasque, entr'acte, episode, intermezzo, intermission, interval, wait. **4. suspension** abeyance, armistice, ceasefire, moratorium, prorogation, rainout, remission, respite, truce. **5. lull** break, breather, breathing space, coffee break, dwell, half-time, interlude, let-up, lunchbreak, pause, recess, spell, tea-break, time-out. *Informal:* boil-up, orange time, pit stop, smoko. **6. lag** dead time, headway, hysteresis, lead, response time, time-lag.

adj.   **2.** **1. interim** intercurrent, intermediate, intermissive, interregnal, interspatial, intervenient, intervening.

adv.   **3.** **1. meanwhile** between, betweenwhiles, meantime.

        RELATED KEYWORDS: REST, GAP, INTERRUPTION

INTOLERANCE

n.   **1.** **1. intolerance** blindness, bumbledom, darkness, impenetrability, impenetrableness, misanthropy, narrow-mindedness, opinionativeness, vigilantism. **2. bigotry** anti-Semitism, apartheid, colour prejudice, colour-bar, heterophobia, heterosexism, homophobia, Jim Crowism, McCarthyism, racialism, racism, segregation. *Informal:* commie bashing, jew-baiting, poofter-bashing, union bashing. **3. chauvinism** ageism, fascism, jingoism, misandry, misogyny, misoneism, sexism. **4. pettiness** illiberality, illiberalness, littleness, micrology, small-mindedness, smallness. **5. parochialism** clannishness, insularism, insularity, provincialism, sectionalism. **6. puritanism** bowdlerism, Grundyism. **7. prejudice** angle, bias, fixed idea, idée fixe, jaundiced view, obsession, partiality, partisanship, ply, preconception, predilection, predisposition, preference, prenotion, prepossession, set, slant, warp. **8. Deep North** cracker-barrel *(Chiefly US)*, Deep South, parish pump.

    2. **1. intolerant person** anti-Semite, bigot, closed mind, fascist, heterophobe, homophobe, misanthrope, racialist, racist, redneck, sectarian, segregationist. *Informal:* jew-baiter, poofter-basher. **2. chauvinist** jingoist, male chauvinist, misandrist, misogynist, sexist. *Informal:* alf, caveman, male chauvinist pig, MCP, Neanderthal, ocker. **3. wowser** bowdleriser, jeremiah, killjoy, puritan. *Informal:* bible-basher, party pooper, snufflebuster. **4. fogy** blimp *(British)*, diehard, doctrinaire, fogey, fogram, ramrod, stick-in-the-mud. *Informal:* fuddy-duddy, mossback *(US)*. **5. provincial** Lilliputian, suburban, suburbanite.

adj.   **3.** **1. intolerant** blind, blinkered, impenetrable, narrow, narrow-minded, unenlightened. **2. small-minded** black-and-white, doctrinaire, dogmatic, hidebound, illiberal, little, mean, one-track, opinionated, opinionative, petty, picky, small. **3. puritanical** ascetic, austere, blue-rinse, conservative, fogram, fusty, mealy-mouthed, moss-grown, old-fashioned, old-line *(US)*, prudish, puritan, spartan, straight, straight-arrow, straitlaced, stuffy, uptight, whitebread *(Chiefly US)*. **4. insular** clannish, home-town, jingoistic, parish-pump, parochial, provincial. **5. suburban** Lilliputian, pokey, poky. **6. bigoted** anti-Semitic, blimpish, chauvinist, chauvinistic, fascist, heterosexist, homosexist, male chauvinist, misoneist, sexist. **7. biased** coloured, discriminatory, distorted, ex parte, factional, hometown, loaded, one-eyed, one-sided, partial, partisan, predisposed, prejudiced, selective, tendencious, tendentious, unbalanced, unfair, unilateral, unjust, unreasonable, warped.

v. **4.** **1. be prejudiced against** have a bias against, see one side only. *Informal:* have a derry on, have a down on. **2. ossify** become set in one's ways, congeal *(US)*, fossilise.

adv. **5.** **1. intolerantly** blindly, ex parte, illiberally, impenetrably, narrow-mindedly, pettily. **2. parochially** clannishly, insularly, provincially. **3. bigotedly** anti-Semitically, chauvinistically.

RELATED KEYWORDS: MISJUDGEMENT, UNKINDNESS, HARSHNESS, ILLOGICALITY

INVISIBILITY

n. **1.** **1. invisibility** imperceptibleness, inconspicuousness, latency, latescence, obscureness, obscurity, smoke. **2. indistinctness** blur, blurriness, dimness, fogginess, obscurity, shadowiness. **3. obscuration** eclipse, immergence, immersion. **4. invisible ink** sympathetic ink.

adj. **2.** **1. invisible** concealed, hidden, imperceptible, inconspicuous, insidious, latent, latescent, low, obscure, out of sight, perdu, sightless, unnoticeable, viewless. **2. unseen** invisible, unbeknown to, unobserved, unperceived, unsighted, unwitnessed. **3. obscured** dead, fogbound. **4. indistinct** bleary, blurry, cloudy, darkling *(Poetic)*, dim, dreamy, faint, foggy, fuzzy, hazy, misty, murky, nebulose, nebulous, nubilous, obscure, shadowy, shady, thick, uncertain, vague. **5. asymptomatic** latent, symptomless.

v. **3.** **1. obscure** black out, blanket out, blot, cloud, cover, darken, darkle, dim, eclipse, envelop, fog, hide, overcloud.

adv. **4.** **1. invisibly** behind the scenes, imperceptibly, inconspicuously, latently, viewlessly. **2. indistinctly** blurrily, darkly, dimly, foggily, obscurely. **3. asymptomatically**.

RELATED KEYWORDS: DISAPPEARANCE, HIDING, DARK, IMPRECISION, OPACITY

IRREGULARITY

n. **1.** **1. irregularity** abruptness, aperiodicity, arrhythmia, casualness, desultoriness, fitfulness, fluctuation, inconstancy, jerkiness, patchiness, raggedness, randomness, uncertainness, unequalness, unevenness, unsteadiness, variableness. **2. intermittency** intermission, interruption, remittency. **3. fluctuation** jump, surge.

adj. **2.** **1. irregular** acyclic, agogic, aperiodic, arrhythmic, broken, catchy, deciduous, desultory, disconnected, discontinuous, episodic, few and far between, fitful, fluttery, impermanent, inordinate, intermittent, labile, movable, occasional, on-off, semipermanent, spotty, stop-go, transitory, uncertain, unequal, uneven, unsteady, variable. **2. sporadic** casual, erratic, flickering, fulgurating, infrequent, intermissive, intermittent, irregular, occasional, odd, periodic, remittent, snatchy, spasmodic, sporadical, unsystematic. **3. jerky** abrupt, jolty, rickety, rough, unequal. **4. ragged** patchy, scraggly, scraggy.

v. **3.** **1. fluctuate** beat, break, flap, flick, flicker, flitter, flutter, intermit, quiver, skitter, stutter, twitch, vibrate, waver. **2. jerk** break step, flick, jog, joggle, jolt, snatch. *Informal:* yank.

adv. **4.** **1. irregularly** brokenly, by (or in) fits (and starts), desultorily, fitfully, flutteringly, infrequently, patchily, raggedly, uncertainly, unequally, unevenly, unsteadily. **2. intermittently** at intervals, intermittingly, now and again, now and then, on and off, periodically, remittently, spasmodically, sporadically. **3. jerkily** abruptly, roughly, unequally.

RELATED KEYWORDS: CHANGE, STOPPAGE, TEMPORARINESS

IRREVERENCE

n. **1.** **1. irreverence** impiety, impiousness, irreligion. **2. profanity** blasphemousness, blasphemy, debasement, defilement, desecration, iconoclasm, irreverence, oath, pollution, profanation, profaneness, sacrilege, simony, violation. *Informal:* French. **3. godlessness** fall from grace, unblessedness, ungodliness, unholiness. **4. faithlessness** agnosticism, atheism, doubt, dubitation, free thought, impiety, indifferentism, irreligion, lack of faith, nescience, nihilism, pyrrhonism, scepticism, secularisation. **5. paganism** heathendom, heathenism, heathenry, infidelity, pagandom. **6. secularism** secularity, worldliness.

2. **1. irreverent person** blasphemer, desecrater, freethinker, iconoclast, libertine, polluter, profaner, renegade, simoniac, simonist, the ungodly, the unrighteous, violator. **2. unbeliever** agnostic, atheist, doubting Thomas, infidel, irreligionist, kafir, materialist, nescient, nullifidian, sceptic, secular humanist, seculariser, secularist, skeptic *(US)*. **3. pagan** heathen, infidel. **4. antichristian** antichrist.

adj. **3.** **1. irreverent** Babylonian, blasphemous, iconoclastic, impious, natural, profanatory, profaning, sacrilegious, sinful, unblessed, ungodly, unhallowed, unholy, unregenerate, unrighteous, violative *(Chiefly US)*. **2. profane** dark, evil, heathen, ill, impious, irreligious, pernicious, sinful, sinister, unblessed, ungodly, unhallowed, unholy, unsanctified, wicked. **3. apostate** accursed, churchless, creedless, faithless, godforsaken, godless, unredeemed. **4. unreligious** agnostic, anti-church, anti-religious, antichristian, anti-clerical, atheist, distrustful, doubtful, freethinking, heathen, impious, inconvincible, incredulous, irreligious, mistrustful, nescient, profane, sceptic, sceptical, suspicious, unbelieving, unchristian, uncircumcised, undevout, ungodly, unholy. **5. heathen** barbarous, gentile, heathenish, infidel, irreligious, pagan, paganish, profane, uncircumcised. **6. secular** carnal, earthbound, earthly, earthy, mundane, planetary, secularistic, subcelestial, sublunary, tellurian, telluric, temporal, terrene, terrestrial, unspiritual, worldly.

v. **4.** **1. profane** befoul, contaminate, corrupt, debase, debauch, defile, deflower, degrade, demean, deprave, desecrate, dishallow, foul, infract, pervert, pollute, prostitute, violate, vitiate. **2. blaspheme** anathematise, blacken, blackguard, curse, damn, execrate, imprecate, swear. *Informal:* cuss *(Chiefly US)*, darn, let rip, swear like a trooper. **3. deconsecrate** banish, curse, excommunicate, exile, expatriate, proscribe, secularise, send away, unchurch.

adv. **5.** **1. irreverently** blasphemously, iconoclastically, irreligiously, profanely, sacrilegiously, unholily, unregenerately. **2. faithlessly** heathenishly, sceptically, secularly, unbelievingly, unchristianly, worldly.

RELATED KEYWORDS: DISBELIEF

IRRITABLENESS

n. **1.** **1. irritableness** atrabiliousness, bile, biliousness, cantankerousness, crabbiness, crankiness, crossness, crotchetiness, crustiness, distemper, edginess, exasperation, fractiousness, fretfulness, hyperirritability, ill humour, ill nature, ill temper, ill-naturedness, ill-temperedness, impatience, irritability, moodiness, moroseness, peevishness, perverseness, perversity, pettishness, petulance, petulancy, querulousness, sourness, spleen, sulkiness, sullenness, surliness, terseness, vexedness, vinegar, vixenishness. *Informal:* grouchiness, grumpiness, huffiness. **2. irascibleness** fieriness, hastiness, pepperiness, prickliness, snappishness, testiness, tetchiness, touchiness, waspishness.

2. **1. irritation** aggravation, annoyance, chafe, fret, nuisance, provocation, rub, trouble, vexation. *Informal:* peeve. **2. fit of pique** pet, pout, sulk, tantrum, temper. *Informal:* act, blow-up, cob *(NZ, British)*, the hump, tiff. **3. scowl** flounce, frown, glower, lour, pout, snarl. *Informal:* dirty look, grouch.

3. **1. irritable person** curmudgeon, scowler, shrew, spitfire, termagant, virago, vixen, wasp, xanthippe. *Informal:* bat, cow, crabstick, crosspatch, grouch, sourpuss.

4. **1. irritator** aggravator, provoker, teaser, vexer.

adj. **5.** **1. irritable** apoplectic, atrabilious, bad-tempered, bilious, brittle, cantankerous, crabbed, crabby, cranky, cross, crotchety, crusty, cursed, fractious, fretful, hot-tempered, ill-humoured, ill-natured, ill-tempered, impatient, on edge, out of humour, peevish, pettish, petulant, quarrelsome, querulous, scratchy, sour, spleenful, spleeny, splenetic, temperamental, verjuice, vexed, vinegary. *Informal:* grumpy, huffish, huffy, lemony, like a bear with a sore head, narked, pippy, ratty, scotty, shirty, snarly, snitchy, snuffy, sore, spiky, teasy, uptight. **2. irascible** choleric, fiery, hasty, peppery, prickly, quick-tempered, short-tempered, snappish, snappy, techy, testy, tetchy, touchy, virago-like, vixenly, waspish, waspy. *Informal:* ornery *(US)*. **3. moody** bearish, broody, churlish, farouche, glowering, gruff, ill-conditioned, lowering, morose, saturnine, sulky, sullen, surly. *Informal:* grouchy, huffy.

6. **1. irritating** abrasive, aggravating, annoying, exasperating, infuriating, irritant, irritative, offensive, provoking, tiresome, trying, vexatious. *Informal:* pesky *(Chiefly US)*, pestiferous.

v. **7.** **1. irritate** acerbate, aggravate, annoy, chafe, chagrin, exacerbate, exasperate, fray, fret, gall, get on someone's nerves, get to, get under someone's skin, goad, irk, jangle, nettle, niggle, offend, peeve, pip, pique, provoke, put out, put someone out, rankle, rasp, rile, roil, rub (up) the wrong way, ruffle, sting, tease, vex. *Informal:* bug, drive someone up the wall, get (on) someone's goat, get (or take) a rise out of, get across, get in someone's hair, get on someone's quince, get on someone's wick, get up someone's nose, give someone the irrits, give someone the pip, nark, put someone's back up, rag, stick in someone's craw. **2. nag** chide, scold, tongue. *Informal:* air-raid, go on at, grouch, nark, peck at, rag.

8. **1. become irritated** frown, get up on the wrong side of bed, glower, look black, lour, pout, scowl. *Informal:* arc up, bung on an act, burr up, chuck a mental, go spare, go to market, pop one's cork, throw (or chuck) a micky.

adv. **9.** **1. irritably** apoplectically, biliously, cantankerously, crossly, exasperatedly, fierily, fractiously, fretfully, hastily, huffily, huffishly, ill-humouredly, ill-naturedly, ill-temperedly, impatiently, peevishly, pettishly, petulantly, snappishly, splenetically, testily, tetchily, touchily, vexedly, vixenishly, waspishly. **2. moodily** loweringly, morosely, scowlingly, sourly, surlily.

10. **1. irritatingly** aggravatingly, annoyingly, exasperatingly, provokingly, vexingly.

RELATED KEYWORDS: ANGER, DISCONTENTEDNESS, UNKINDNESS, DISPLEASURE

JEALOUSY

n. **1.** **1. jealousy** covetousness, emulation, enviousness, envy, grudgingness, heartburn, heartburning, jaundice, jealousness, rivalry. *Informal:* green-eyed monster, sour grapes.

2. **1. apple of discord** bone of contention. **2. the other woman** love triangle, the competition.

adj. **3.** **1. jealous** covetous, envious, green, green with envy, green-eyed.

v. **4.** **1. be jealous of** envy. **2. covet** crave, crave for (or after), desire, hunger, long for, lust after. *Informal:* eat one's heart out. **3. begrudge** be put out, grudge, take a jaundiced view, view with a jaundiced eye. *Informal:* have one's nose out of joint.

adv. **5.** **1. jealously** enviously, envyingly.

RELATED KEYWORDS: DISCONTENTEDNESS, DESIRE

JOB

n. **1.** **1. job** avocation, calling, career, craft, employment, service, trade, vocation, work. *Informal:* gig. **2. position** appointment, billet, commission, consultancy, engagement, incumbency, office, opening, place, post, posting, province, rank, role, situation, station, vacancy. *Informal:* berth. **3. occupation** business, enterprise, follow-the-job occupation, industry, metier, practice, private practice, profession, pursuit. *Informal:* walk of life. **4. game** *Informal:* lurk, racket, ready. **5. field** area, area of expertise, bailiwick, beat, department, domain, line of work, orbit, province, realm, speciality, specialty, sphere, sphere of activity. **7. sinecure** cushy job, soft job. *Informal:* a sweet cop, bludge. **8. duty** affair, assignment, business, care, charge, chore, commission, concern, concernment, detail, errand, function, interest, job, mission, obligation, office, onus, part, place, responsibility, task, undertaking, work. *Informal:* indaba. **9. the press of business** the demands of one's job.

v. **2.** **1. have a job** fill a position, hold a chair, hold a portfolio, hold an office, hold down a job, join the workforce, occupy a position, take up a position. *Informal:* carry a cut-lunch. **2. earn a living** make a living, produce, support oneself. *Informal:* bring home the bacon, keep body and soul together, keep the wolf from the door, turn an honest penny. **3. practise** be in, carry on, concern oneself with, do, engage in, follow, have to do with, occupy oneself with, ply, profess, pursue, serve time as, spend one's time on, work as. **4. be self-employed** have a practice, work for oneself.

RELATED KEYWORDS: EMPLOYMENT, FACTORY, WORK, WORKER

JOINING

n. **1.** **1. joining** conjunction, join, joinder, juncture. **2. union** conjugation, copulation, coupling. **3. linkage** attachment, catenation, concatenation, linkwork. **4. annexation** affixture, appendence. **5. contact** communication, connection, contingence, hook-up, intercommunication, interconnection, networking, rete, tie-up. **6. fusion** combination, merging, polymerisation. **7. splicing** grafting, inarching, inosculation. **8. connectedness** connectivity, inseparableness, unitedness.

2. **1. join** close, connection, coupling, junction, juncture, knot, link, loop, nexus, tie. **2. link** attachment, bond, copula, hitch, interlink, ligament, ligature, tie. **3. confluence** abutment, meeting point. **4. intersection** cloverleaf, cusp, four-leaf clover, spinode. **5. attachment** adjunct, affix, appendage, appendant, appendicle, appurtenance, appurtenant. **6. chemical bond** closed chain, conjugated bond, coordinate bond, coordinate covalent bond, covalent bond, dative bond, donor bond, double bond, electrovalent bond, ionic bond, polar bond, semipolar bond, triple bond, valency bond.

3. **1. joint** articulation, connector, syndesmosis. **2. type of joint** ball-and-socket joint, butt joint, dovetail, knuckle joint, lap joint, mitre joint, mortice and tenon joint, mortise, pin, rebate, scarf-joint, straight joint, tongue-and-groove joint, uni-joint, universal coupling, universal joint. **3. hinge** butt, scarf, swivel. **4. fishplate** fishjoint, gang nail. **5. tie** bar, bride, faggoting, nexus. **6. sleeve** con rod, connecting rod, cross, nipple, reducer, turnbuckle. **7. plug** crocodile clip, jack. **8. splice** carabiner, graft, karabiner.

9. sprocket cog, tooth. **10. weld** capillary fitting, cold shut, shut, spot-weld. **11. seam** commissure, nasion, suture. **12. mortaring** bond, jointing, perpend, pointing, tuck pointing. **13. cornerstone** key, keystone.

4. 1. joiner affixer, carpenter *(US)*, conjoiner, connecter, jointer, scarfer, seamer, uniter, welder.

5. 1. welding arc welding, argon welding, electric welding, gas welding, high-frequency welding, radio-frequency welding, resistance welding, seam welding, spot welding, ultrasonic welding. **2. welder** arc welder, plastic welder, soldering-iron, torch.

adj. **6. 1. joined** conjoined, conjoint, conjugate, conjunct, conjunctive, coordinate, copular, coupled, joint. **2. allied** associated, married, partnered, wedded. **3. united** adhesion, banded together, combined, incorporated, inseparable, osculant, rolled into one. **4. cohesive** adhesive, loose-knit, tenacious, well-knit. **5. adjacent** adjoining, bordering, conterminous, contiguous, coterminous, neighbouring, se-tenant, semidetached, tangent, tangential, touching. **6. connected** hooked up, on-line. **7. seamed** commissural, connectional, seamy, sutural. **8. linked** concatenate. **9. attached** appendant, sessile. **10. inextricable** jammed, wedged.

7. 1. connecting conjugative, conjunctional, conjunctive, connective, copulative, integrative, intercommunicative, syndetic.

v. **8. 1. join** bracket, catenate, compact, concatenate, conjoin, connect, contact, couple, hook up, hyphenate, intercommunicate, interconnect, interlink, link, make, marry, match, mate, osculate, partner, reunite, splice, suture, tie, unite. **2. span** bridge. **3. interlock** engage, mesh. **4. fuse** anchylose, ankylose, interknit, knit. **5. merge** ally, federalise, incorporate, integrate, lump together, meld, roll into one. **6. attach** affix, annex, fasten, fix, glue, pin, post, tack on. **7. append** add, affix, annex, attach, postfix, subjoin, suffix, tag. **8. tie** hoop, knot, lace, seam, sew. **9. splice** graft, hook up with, inarch, inosculate. **10. hinge** articulate. **11. butt** fay, joint, tenon. **12. weld** braze, cement, solder, spot-weld. **13. hyperlink** hot-link.

adv. **9. 1. jointly** conjointly, conjunctively, conjunctly, connectedly, connectively, syndetically. **2. closely** inseparably, unitedly. **3. arm in arm** hand in hand.

RELATED KEYWORDS: ADDITION, COMBINATION, FASTENING, STICKINESS

JOY

n. **1. 1. joy** bliss, delight, exaltation, felicity, festiveness, gaiety, gladness, glee, gleefulness, gleesomeness, happiness, joyfulness, joyousness, jubilation, jubilee, mirth, paradise, pleasure, rapture, ravishment, rejoicing, seventh heaven, transport. **2. festivity** frolic, gaieties, jollity, jubilee, merriment. **3. joie de vivre** charivari, excess of spirits, exuberance, high spirits, jubilancy. **4. elation** ecstasy, elatedness, rapture, rapturousness, ravishment. **5. paradise** seventh heaven. **6. triumph** exultation. **7. revelry** carnival, carousing, celebration, frolic, gala, good cheer, jollification, lark, merrymaking, revel, revels, shindy. *Informal:* whoopee.

2. 1. celebration festivities, jollities, revels, silly season. **2. party** après-ski, asalto *(Philippine English)*, bienvenida *(Philippine English)*, bottle party, bowl, carousal, carouse, cocktail party, corroboree, despedida *(Philippine English)*, festivity, hen party, hootenanny *(US)*, house-warming, jamboree, love-in, merrymaking, potlatch, preparty, recovery party, revels, riot, social, soiree, spree, the turn, twenty-first, wassail, wayzgoose. *Informal:* bash, beer-up, bender, booze-up, boozeroo *(NZ)*, bust, do, drunk, grog-on, grog-up, rage, rave, rort, scatter, send-off, shindig, shindy, shivaree *(US)*, shivoo, show, wing-ding. **3. function** garden party, levee, reception. **4. feasting** annual picnic, banquet, feast, feast day, fete, hangi, junket, love feast, luau, midnight feast, spree, umu *(NZ)*. *Informal:* beanfeast, beano, blow-out, bunfight, prawn night, spread. **5. spree** bacchanal, bacchanalia, happy hour, jag, orgy, saturnalia, stag party. *Informal:* a night on the tiles, a night on the town, barney, bash, bat, binge, blind, blinder, booze, drinkies, lush, pub crawl, six o'clock swill, soak.

3. 1. festival bangtail muster, carnival, fair, feast, festa, festivity, fete, fete day, fiesta, holiday, jubilee, kermis, kirmess, mardi gras, pageant, show. **2. jubilee** anniversary, birthday, centenary, commemoration, commemorative, encaenia, feast, wedding anniversary. **3. centenary** bicentenary, bicentennial, centennial *(US, NZ)*, quadricentennial *(US)*, quatercentenary, quincentenary, quincentennial, sesquicentenary, sesquicentennial, sexcentenary, sexennial *(US)*, tercentenary, tercentennial *(US)*, tricentennial. **4. religious festival** feast day *(Philippine English)*, feast-day, festal day, fiesta, high day, holiday, holy day, moveable feast, name-day, saint's day, ticket day. **5. harvest festival** harvest home.

4.   **1. rejoicer** caroller, celebrant, celebrator, exalter, mafficker, merrymaker, party-goer, partygoer, reveller. *Informal:* rager. **2. roisterer** bacchanal, bacchant, banqueter, feaster, junketer, wassailer. *Informal:* party animal.

adj.   5.   **1. joyful** beatific, blissful, blithe, cock-a-hoop, delighted, ecstatic, elate, elated, elevated, enrapt, enraptured, exuberant, festive, gleeful, gleesome, glowing, happy, high, hilarious, in high spirits, in raptures, joyous, merry, mirthful, on top of the world, overjoyed, rapt, rapturous. *Informal:* high as a kite, stoked. **2. triumphant** exultant, jubilant, jubilatory, triumphal.

6.   **1. celebratory** commemorational, commemorative, commemoratory. **2. congratulatory** gratulatory. **3. convivial** backslapping, boon, cheery, festive, gay, gladsome, jocund *(Poetic)*, jolly, jovial, joyful, merry, merrymaking, sunny. **4. revelling** bacchanal, bacchanalian, bacchic, mad, roisterous, rollicking, saturnalian. *Informal:* on the loose, on the town.

7.   **1. festive** carnie, festal, festival, gala, holiday.

v.   8.   **1. rejoice** clap hands, delight, exult, fling one's cap in the air, have one's heart leap for joy, hug oneself, joy, jubilate, jump for joy, make merry, thank one's lucky stars, tread on air, walk on air. *Informal:* jollify. **2. triumph** crow, gloat, glory. **3. celebrate** commemorate, jubilate, maffick *(Chiefly British)*. **4. fete** shivaree. **5. carol** hail, sing for joy. **6. congratulate** give, pledge, toast. **7. make merry** carouse, dance the night away, go wild, racket, revel, riot, roister, wassail. *Informal:* be on the tiles, go on the town, go to town, paint the town red, whoop it up. **8. banquet** feast, junket, kill the fatted calf.

adv.   9.   **1. joyfully** blithely, elatedly, exuberantly, gleefully, gleesomely, glowingly, happily, joyously, jubilantly, rapturously, rejoicingly. **2. festively** commemoratively, festally. **3. triumphantly** exultantly, exultingly, gloatingly.

interj.   10.   **1. hooray** aha, alleluia, alley oop, booya, eureka, Glory be, hallelujah, heaven be praised, hip hip hooray (or hurrah), hosanna, hurrah, hurray, huzza, pie on *(NZ)*, saints be praised. *Informal:* boy, cowabunga, goody (goody) gumdrops, groovy, kapai *(NZ)*, ooh, rah, sweet, whoopee, woo hoo, yahoo, yippee, you bloody bewdy.

RELATED KEYWORDS: OVERINDULGENCE, ALCOHOL, REST, EMOTION, HAPPINESS, SOCIABILITY, FOOD

JUDGE

n.   1.   **1. judge** adjudicator, arbiter, arbitrator, arbitress, awarder, hakim, judicator, justice, sentencer. *Informal:* beak. **2. judiciary** court, judicature, syndicate, the bench. **3. wise judge** a Daniel come to judgement, a Solomon, Portia. **4. type of judge** alcalde *(Spanish)*, archon *(Ancient Greek)*, bailie *(Scottish)*, burgomaster *(Germanic)*, cadi *(Muslim)*, chancellor, Chief Justice, circuit judge, coroner, deemster *(Isle of Man)*, gymnasiarch *(Ancient Greek)*, JP, judge advocate, judge advocate general, justice of the peace, law lord *(British)*, magistrate, master, prefect, puisne judge, recorder *(English, Welsh)*, reeve, registrar, seneschal, sheriff *(Scottish)*, sheriff-depute *(Scottish)*, squire *(US)*, stipendiary magistrate, syndic. **5. umpire** referee.

2.   **1. judgeship** archonship, chair, chancellorship, coronership, justiceship, magistracy, umpirage. **2. wig** black cap. **3. jurisdiction** summary jurisdiction.

3.   **1. jury** grand jury *(US)*, hung jury, inquest, panel, petit jury, petty jury, quest, tales. **2. juror** foreman, jurat, juryman, petty juror, talesman.

RELATED KEYWORDS: COURT OF LAW, LAWYER, LITIGATION

JUDGEMENT

n.   1.   **1. judgement** adjudgement, adjudication, arbitrament, arbitration, decision, decision-making, determination, diagnosis, discrimination, reckoning, resolution, umpirage. **2. ruling** adjudication, arbitrament, class resolution, decision, determination, judgement, opinion, order, pronouncement, resolution. **3. verdict** award, conclusion, declaration, decree, decretal, doom, finding, judgement, non prosequitur, nonsuit, ratio decidendi, sentence. **4. justice** arbitrament, arbitration, judicature, jurisprudence.

2.   **1. assessment** account, appraisal, appraisement, appreciation, consideration, estimation, evaluation, revaluation, reviewal, stocktaking, valorisation, valuation. **2. appraisal** diagnosis, estimate, evaluation, judgement, opinion, revaluation, valuation, value. **3. review** comment, crit, criticism, critique, notice, report, textual criticism.

3. **1. adjudicator** arbiter, arbitrator, arbitress, concluder, condemner, decider, determiner, disposer, judge, judger, judicator, juror, jury, referee, umpire. *Informal:* beak. **2. referee** central umpire, field umpire, goal umpire, touch judge, umpire. *Informal:* ref, third man, ump, umpie, white maggot.

4. **1. assessor** appraiser, appreciator, estimator, gauger, judge, valuator, valuer, valuer general. **2. reviewer** commentator, critic.

adj. **5.** **1. adjudicative** arbitral, arbitrational, arbitrative, decretal, decretive, decretory, determinant, determinative, determining, judging, judicative, judicatory, judicial, judiciary. **2. assessorial** estimative, judicial, valuational. **3. judgemental** moralising, moralistic, sententious. **4. critical** commentative, evaluative.

6. **1. assessable** appraisable, arbitrable, decidable, determinable, estimable, gaugeable, judicable, judiciable.

v. **7.** **1. judge** adjudicate, arbitrate, hear, pass *(US)*, sit in judgement on, try. **2. assess** appraise, assay, call, criticise, critique, diagnose, esteem, estimate, evaluate, examine, figure, gauge, grade, judge, measure, prize, rank, rate, reckon, size up, sum up, survey, try, valorise, valuate, value. **3. take stock** consider, deliberate, ponder, reckon, ruminate, weigh. **4. review** comment on, criticise, give an opinion on.

8. **1. determine** adjudge, adjudicate, appoint, arbitrate, award, conclude, decide, decree, dispose, find, judge, pass *(US)*, pronounce on, resolve, rule. **2. pass sentence on** bring in a verdict, condemn, doom, judge, pass judgement on, sentence.

RELATED KEYWORDS: CONJECTURE, JUDGE, LITIGATION, TEST

JUMP

n. **1.** **1. jump** bounce, bound, flying jump, hop, leap, pounce, spring, take-off, vault. *Informal:* flyer. **2. type of jump** BASE-jump, bungee jump, hop skip and jump, jumping jack, safety jump, star jump. **3. caper** capriole, frisk, gambol, leap, prance, skip. **4. buck** buckjump, capriole, croupade, curvet, gambado, tittup. **5. long jump** broad jump, Eastern roll, Fosbury flop, high jump, hop, step, and jump, jump, pole vault, polevault, straddle, triple jump, vault, Western roll. **6. ski-jump** axel, ski jump. **7. volte** demivolt, volt.

2. **1. jumping** buckjumping, leaping, saltation, skipping. **2. type of jumping** BASE-jumping, bungee jumping, hurdling, leapfrogging, showjumping.

3. **1. leaper** bouncer, caperer, frisker, hopper, hurdler, jumper, prancer, skipper, springer, tumbler, vaulter. **2. bucker** buckjumper.

adj. **4.** **1. jumping** leaping, salient, saltant, saltatorial, saltatory, saltigrade, vaulting. **2. buckish** bounding, capering, coltish, curvetting, frisky, leaping.

v. **5.** **1. jump** bound, bungee-jump, hop, leap, start, tumble, vault. *Informal:* galumph, lollop. **2. caper** bob around, bob up and down, cavort, curvet, dance, frisk, gambol, hop, leap, prance, pronk, skip. **3. pounce** spring. **4. buck** buckjump, capriole, jackknife, rear, tittup. *Informal:* kangaroo. **5. trampoline** bounce. **6. jump over** clear, fence, hop, hurdle, jump, leap, leap over, leapfrog, overleap, skip, top, vault.

RELATED KEYWORDS: DIVE, FLYING, SPORT

JUSTIFICATION

n. **1.** **1. justification** apologia, apology, reason, self-justification, vindication, warrant. **2. vindication** defence, exculpation. **3. excuse** cover-up, extenuating circumstance, extenuation, plea, pretence, pretension, pretext. *Informal:* alibi, put-on, sob-story. **4. defence** allegation, autrefois convict, plea, pleading, self-defence. **5. extenuation** mitigation, palliation. *Informal:* snow job.

2. **1. justifiableness** defensibleness. **2. excusableness** venialness. **3. deniability** plausible deniability.

3. **1. justifier** apologiser, apologist, defender, excuser, extenuator, vindicator.

adj. **4.** **1. justificatory** self-justifying, valid, vindicative, vindicatory, well-founded, well-grounded. **2. extenuative** exculpatory, excusatory.

5. **1. defensible** justifiable, pleadable, warrantable. **2. excusable** exculpable, pardonable, venial.

v. **6.** **1. justify** defend, explain, maintain, substantiate, validate, vindicate. **2. vindicate** authorise, be a reason for, be an excuse for, excuse, explain, justify, warrant. **3. excuse** acquit, clear, exculpate, exonerate, justify, let out, purge. **4. make excuses** explain, plead, plead ignorance, rationalise. **5. extenuate** gloss over, gloze, gloze over, make allowances, palliate, smooth over, varnish over, whitewash.

RELATED KEYWORDS: ACQUITTAL, LAWFULNESS

KILLING

n. **1.** **1. killing** blood-letting, bloodshed, kill. *Informal:* rubout *(Chiefly US).* **2. murder** assassination, chance-medley, death, first-degree murder, foul play, homicide, manslaughter, manslaying, multicide, murder-suicide, second-degree murder *(US),* slaughter, violent death. *Informal:* hit. **3. homicide** aborticide, deicide, exposure of infants, filicide, foeticide, fratricide, infanticide, matricide, parricide, patricide, regicide, sororicide, tyrannicide, uxoricide. **4. suicide** Bushido, felo-de-se, harakiri, harikari, Russian roulette, self-destruction, self-murder, self-poisoning, seppuku. **5. sacrifice** hecatomb, immolation, ritual killing, sati, supreme sacrifice. **6. execution** beheading, capital punishment, chair, crucifixion, decapitation, decollation, electric chair, electrocution, garrote, hanging, lapidation, lynching, stoning to death. **7. euthanasia** active euthanasia, mercy killing, passive euthanasia.

2. **1. massacre** battue, blood, bloodbath, butchery, carnage, hecatomb, holocaust, slaughter, sword. **2. genocide** ethnic cleansing, ethnocide, extermination, race murder. **3. purge** decimation, depopulation, pogrom. **4. butchery** slaughter.

3. **1. murderousness** bloodthirstiness, perniciousness, sanguinariness.

4. **1. deathblow** coup de grâce, dispatch, quietus. **2. death warrant** auto-da-fé, death penalty. **3. gallows** drop, gibbet, halter, rope, rope's end, tree. **4. strangulation** asphyxiation, garrotte, jugulation, suffocation, thuggee. **5. guillotine** beheading. **6. gas chamber** Auschwitz, Belsen, Dachau, gas oven. **7. electric chair** chair. *Informal:* hot seat. **8. poison** arsenic, cyanide, hemlock, poison cart, strychnine. **9. pesticide** germicide, insecticide, rodenticide, vermicide. **10. defenestration.**

5. **1. place of killing** abattoir, abattoirs, butchery, knackery, shambles, slaughterhouse. **2. arena** bearpit, bullring. **3. death cell** death row. **4. battlefield** afield, battleground, field, killing field.

6. **1. killer** assassin, assassinator, bravo, butcher, Cain, cutthroat, decapitator, decimator, decollator, depopulator, dispatcher, gangster, gunman, hatchet man, headhunter, hired killer, hit squad, homicide, manslaughterer, manslayer, massacrer, murderer, murderess, poisoner, purger, scalper, slaughterer, slayer, strangler, thrill killer, thug. *Informal:* hit man. **2. executioner** firing party, firing squad, garrotter, guillotiner, hangman, headsman. **3. sacrificer** immolator. **4. suicide bomber. 5. butcher** chainman, gun-chain, harpooner, knacker, slaughterman. **6. toreador** bullfighter, matador, torero.

adj. **7.** **1. killing** deadly, death-dealing, deathly, fatal, lethal, mortal, mortiferous, murderous, pernicious, slaughterous, suffocative. **2. asphyxiant. 3. poisonous** alloy, toxic, toxicant. **4. germicidal** bactericidal, insecticidal.

8. **1. murderous** bloodthirsty, bloody, butcherly, cutthroat, destructive, homicidal, sanguinary, sanguine, slaughterous, thuggish, tigerish, tigrish. **2. sanguinary** blood-guilty, bloodstained, bloody, crimson, internecine. **3. fratricidal** deicidal, filicidal, foeticidal, genocidal, matricidal, parricidal, patricidal, regicidal, sororicidal, tyrannicidal, uxoricidal. **4. suicidal** banzai, kamikaze, self-destructive. **5. sacrificial** immolatory.

v. **9.** **1. kill** account for, decimate, destroy, dispatch, do away with, do for, do to death, finish off, frag, ice, make away with, remove, shed blood, slay, smite, stiff *(Aboriginal English),* victimise. *Informal:* croak, get, perish, snuff, spiflicate, zot. **2. murder** assassinate, butcher, execute, ice, kill, liquidate, remove, slaughter. *Informal:* blow away, bump off, croak, do in, get, knock off, off, rub out, take for a ride, waste. **3. execute** bone *(Aboriginal English),* condemn to death, electrocute, point the bone at, put to death, sign the death warrant of, sing. **4. slay** asphyxiate, axe to death, bayonet, behead, blow the brains out, bowstring, brain, burke, burn, choke, club to death, cut the throat of, decapitate, decollate, drown, garrotte, gibbet, guillotine, hang, jugulate, knife to death, lynch, neck, necklace, overlie, pick off, poison, poleaxe, sabre, scalp, shoot, shoot down, smother, spear to death, stab to death, stick, stifle, stiletto, stone, strangle, strangulate, suffocate, suspercollate, throttle, tomahawk, wring the neck of. *Informal:* scrag, string up. **5. suicide** blow one's brains out, commit harakiri, do oneself in, fall on one's sword, jump overboard, kill oneself, overdose, put one's head in the oven, self-immolate, slit one's wrists, take poison. *Informal:* go off the bars, go off the tub, jump the Gap, OD. **6. sacrifice** immolate.

10. **1. butcher** halal, pith, slaughter. **2. hunt to death** bag, be in for the kill, harpoon. **3. put down** put away, put out of misery, put to sleep.

11. **1. massacre** butcher, mow down, put to the sword, slaughter. **2. purge** annihilate, commit genocide, decimate, depopulate, expurgate, exterminate, extirpate, kill off, liquidate, wipe out.

12. **1. be killed** hang. *Informal:* dangle, get hers, get his, go for a burton *(Chiefly British).*

adv. **13.** **1. murderously** bloodthirstily, homicidally, sanguinarily. **2. sacrificially** capitally, suicidally.

RELATED KEYWORDS: VICTIM, DEATH, POISON, PUNISHMENT, WAR

KINDNESS

n. **1.** **1. kindness** considerateness, consideration, goodness, kind-heartedness, loving-kindness, niceness, regardfulness, solicitousness, solicitude, sweetness, thoughtfulness, warmheartedness. **2. benevolence** charitableness, goodwill, grace, graciosity, kindliness. **3. altruism** charitableness, generosity, humanitarianism, philanthropy, unselfishness, volunteerism. **4. friendliness** amiableness, geniality, good-heartedness, warmness. **5. gentleness** benignancy, benignity, humaneness, humanity, leniency, mildness, propitiousness, softness, tender-heartedness. **6. paternalism** grace, patronage.

2. **1. kind act** a good deed, a good turn, favour, service.

adj. **3.** **1. kind** amiable, big-hearted, considerate, good-hearted, good-tempered, kindly, nice, regardful, sweet, sweet-tempered, tactful, thoughtful, warm-hearted. *Informal:* decent. **2. benevolent** amiable, beneficent, big-hearted, gracious, grandfatherly, hospitable, kind-hearted, kindly, open-hearted, propitious, well-disposed, well-wishing. **3. sympathetic** caring, compassionate, concerned, consolatory, consoling, involved, softhearted, solicitous. **4. gentle** benign, charitable, clement, easy, forgiving, gracious, humane, indulgent, kindly, lenient, mild, soft, sparing, tender-hearted. **5. friendly** amiable, genial, good-hearted, good-humoured, good-natured, hearty. **6. altruistic** active, benevolent, charitable, Christianly, civic-minded, generous, great-hearted, humanitarian, large-hearted, philanthropic, public-spirited, self-forgetful, selfless, unselfish. **7. paternalistic** benignant, gracious. **8. overkind** smothery, well-meaning, well-meant.

adv. **4.** **1. kindly** considerately, gently, humanely, mildly, nicely, sweetly, thoughtfully. **2. benevolently** beneficently, graciously, kind-heartedly. **3. sympathetically** comfortingly, compassionately, solicitously, warm-heartedly. **4. amiably** decently, good-heartedly, warmly. **5. altruistically** philanthropically. **6. paternalistically** benignantly.

RELATED KEYWORDS: FRIENDLINESS, GOODNESS, HELP, PITY, UNSELFISHNESS

KNOWLEDGE

n. **1.** **1. knowledge** cognisance, enlightenment, illumination, information, ken, knowingness, light, lore, science, wisdom. **2. omniscience** encyclopedism, pansophy. **3. mastery** experience, expertise, expertness, grasp, mastership. **4. rudimentary knowledge** equipment, grounding, propaedeutics, rudiments. **5. smattering** sciolism, smatter, tincture. **6. esotery** privity. **7. common knowledge** a household word, general knowledge, open secret. *Informal:* ancient history. **8. folklore** folk memory, lore, tradition. **9. sophistication** savoir-faire, savoir-vivre, urbaneness, urbanity, worldliness. **10. familiarity** acquaintance, conversancy, intimateness. **11. study of knowledge** architectonics, epistemology, pantology.

2. **1. knowledgeableness** book-learning, clerkliness, education, eruditeness, erudition, knowledge, learnedness, learning, lore, reading, scholarship. **2. wisdom** anthroposophy.

3. **1. understanding** comprehension, discernment, insight. **2. awareness** apperception, apprehension, cognisance, consciousness, initiation, insight, knowledge, perception, prehension, realisation, recognisance, recognition, self-awareness, self-consciousness, self-knowledge, sense. **3. perception** apperception, cognition, introspection, noesis, observation, perceptiveness, percipiency, sensibility.

4. **1. specialist** adept, authority, consultant, expert, judge, master, master hand, old hand, past master, professional, sophisticate, technician, veteran, virtuoso, wizard. *Informal:* boffin, crack, hot dog *(US)*, king, old stager, stager, tech-head, vet, whiz. **2. expert** appreciator, apprehender, cognoscente, connoisseur, perceiver, percipient, polyhistor, recogniser. *Informal:* buff, maven *(US)*. **3. scholar** humanist. **4. illuminati** clerisy, literati. **5. generalist** illuminist, pansophist, pantologist, Renaissance man, scientist.

adj. **5.** **1. knowledgeable** advised, big on, cultivated, cultured, educated, enlightened, erudite, informed, knowing, learned, lettered, literate, read, sciential, self-educated, well-informed, well-read. **2. omniscient** all-knowing, pansophical. **3. experienced** able, expert, practised, proficient, savvy, seasoned, skilful, skilled, versed in, veteran. *Informal:* salted. **4. scholarly** Alexandrian, classical, humanistic, wise. **5. worldly-wise** knowing, not born yesterday, sophisticated, urbane. **6. awake up to** privy to. *Informal:* in the loop, on to. **7. familiar** abreast of (or with), acquainted, at home, au fait, conversant, intimate with, no stranger to, up in, well-acquainted.

6. 1. perceptive apperceptive, cognitive, insightful, knowing, percipient, understanding. **2. in the know** au courant, not born yesterday, on the ball, well-informed. *Informal:* clued-up, cluey, hep *(Chiefly US)*, hip *(Chiefly US)*, in the loop, on the beam, switched-on, with-it. **3. aware** apprised, cognisant. **4. self-aware** self-conscious.

7. 1. known given, understood, unspoken. **2. well-known** arrant, celebrated, distinguished, famed, familiar, famous, front-line, historic, household name, ill-famed, infamous, notable, noted, notorious, old, prominent, proverbial, renowned. **3. perceptible** appreciable, cognisable, cognoscible, identifiable, knowable, objective, perceivable, perceptional, perceptual, sensible, supraliminal, vivid. **4. esoteric** gnostic.

8. 1. epistemological epistemic, pantological, philosophical, polyhistoric. **2. scientific** clinical, polytechnic, technic, technical, technological.

v. **9. 1. know** cognise, discern, intuit, perceive, recognise. *Informal:* savvy. **2. understand** accept, apperceive, appreciate, apprehend, bottom, comprehend, conceive, digest, fathom, follow, grasp, observe, penetrate, perceive, read, receive, recognise, see, sense, take, take in. *Informal:* get, jerry. **3. be familiar with** acquainted with, assimilate, get, have at one's finger tips, know, understand, unpack. *Informal:* dig *(Chiefly US)*, get inside, twig. **4. know the score** be awake to, be well informed, have an ear to the ground. *Informal:* be in the picture, have been (a)round the ridges, have someone taped, know how many beans make five, not have come down in the last shower, the ropes. **5. hear of** be informed, get wind of, get word of. **6. catch on** assimilate, cotton on, get, hear *(Aboriginal English)*, make head or tail of, see the light, take a tumble to, take a wake-up, trick to, tumble to, understand, unpack. *Informal:* click, dig *(Chiefly US)*, get the message, get the picture, jerry to, join (all) the dots, savvy, the penny drops, twig.

10. 1. become known circulate, get about, get around, get out, percolate. **2. dawn on** dawn upon, sink in, soak in. *Informal:* click.

adv. **11. 1. knowingly** comprehendingly, consciously, perceptively, with one's eyes open, wittingly. **2. omnisciently. 3. eruditely** learnedly, philosophically, scientifically, technically, technologically, wisely. **4. urbanely** knowingly, sophisticatedly.

RELATED KEYWORDS: COMPETENCE, INFORMATION, INTELLECTUAL, INTELLIGENCE, LEARNING, WISE PERSON

LAKE

n. **1. 1. lake** basin, broad, inland sea, lagoon, landlocked water, loch *(Scottish)*, lough, mere, meromictic lake, overflow lake, pond, salt lagoon, sea, sea loch. **2. salt lake** drowned valley, playa, shott. **3. dam** arched dam, backwater, basin, gravity dam, lock, milldam, reservoir, sluice, tank, turkey nest dam, weir. **4. watering hole** water point. **5. billabong** backwater, bayou, lunette. **6. rock hole** bogie, claypan, gnamma hole, hole, melon hole, namma hole, soak. **7. waterhole** bogeyhole, wallow. **8. pool** cut-off, lagoon, linn, mere, millpond, oxbow, pond, tarn, tidal pool. **9. swimming pool** bath, baths, natatorium *(US)*, ocean baths, plunge *(US)*, pool, thermae. **10. fish pond** fish ladder. **11. puddle** plash, pool, puddling. **12. standing water** dead water, stagnant water, still water.

adj. **2. 1. laky** lacustrine, lagoonal, pondlike, pondy.

RELATED KEYWORDS: SEA, SWAMP

LAND

n. **1. 1. land** earth, real estate, terra, terra firma. **2. landmass** continent, country, land, main, mainland, nation, soil, state. **3. terrain** country. **4. ground** earth, soil. *Informal:* floor. **5. inland** heartland, hinterland, interior, midland. **6. delta** bird's-foot delta, fan delta. **7. flood plain** cove, doab, holm *(British)*, warpland. **8. lowland** coastal plain, innings, polder. **9. lithosphere** asthenosphere, barysphere, centrosphere, crust, sial. **10. centrosphere** barysphere.

2. 1. headland cape, foreland, head, mull *(Scottish)*, naze, point, promontory. **2. isthmus** landbridge, neck, tombolo. **3. peninsula** chersonese, hook, key, spit, tied island, tongue.

3. 1. coast coastline, foreshore, littoral, seaboard, seacoast, seafront, seaside, tidewater *(US)*, waterfront, waterfrontage. **2. shore** bank, beach, dene, dunes, foreshore, riverside, sands, sea bank, seashore, shingle, shoreline, strand *(Poetic)*, strandline, wash, wavecut platform. **3. seabed** bed, bottom, sea floor, sea-floor, wavecut platform.

4. **1. island** ait, atoll, cay, coral island, high island, holm *(British)*, inch *(Scottish)*, isle, islet, key, street island. **2. archipelago** chain, group. **3. reef** barrier reef, bombora, coral reef. **4. sandbank** bar, barrier, sandbar, shelf, shoal, spit, swash.

5. **1. soil** adobe, clay, dirt, duplex soil, earth, loam, mould *(Poetic)*, red soil, rhizosphere, topsoil, zonal soil. **2. ochre** bole, chestnut soil, red earth, terra rossa, umber. **3. subsoil** bind, hardpan, horizon, pan, substrate, substratum, underclay, undersoil, understratum. **4. clay** adobe, argil, bole, brick clay, china clay, fireclay, frit, fuller's earth, kaolin, lithomarge, malm, pâte, paste, petuntse, pipeclay, potter's clay, puddle, slip, terra alba, till. **5. marl** black cotton soil, black earth, chernozem, malm, regur, rendzina, tropical black earth. **6. sand** diatomaceous earth, kieselguhr, mineral sand. **7. deposit** alluvial, alluvion, alluvium, caliche, eluvium, geest, loess, sediment, warp, wash. **8. humus** black cotton soil, black earth, black soil, brown forest soil, chernozem, duff, marl, mould, muck, muck soil, peat, regur, rendzina, tropical black earth, wad. *Informal:* cack. **9. podsol** gleisoil, gombo, gumbo *(Chiefly US)*. **10. drift** apron, boulder clay, diluvium, moraine, till. **11. calcrete** caliche, capstone. **12. acid soil** alkali soil. **13. azonal soil** intrazonal soil.

6. **1. land-dweller** landlubber, landsman, mainlander. **2. islander** island dweller, isthmian.

adj. **7.** **1. land** earthy, geophilous, lowland, telluric, terraqueous, terrene, terrestrial. **2. ground** shore, surface. **3. continental** inland, insular, inward, landlocked, midland. **4. coastal** littoral, longshore, low, maritime, onshore, seaboard, seaside. **5. insular** archipelagic. **6. peninsular** isthmian. **7. riverside** deltaic, riparian, riverine. **8. land-dwelling** geophilous, landlubberly.

adv. **8.** **1. landwards** to shore. **2. aground** ashore, on shore.

RELATED KEYWORDS: THE BUSH, PLANTS, NATION, REGION, ROCK

LANGUAGE

n. **1.** **1. language** accents *(Poetic)*, acrolect, anaptotic, basilect, code, competence, creole, decreolisation, dialect, idiolect, idiom, langue, lect, lingua franca, LOTE, matrilect, mother tongue, paralanguage, parlance, parole, patois, performance, pidgin, pigeon, regional dialect, register, social dialect, sociolect, speech, speech variety, talk, tongue. *Informal:* lingo. **2. Standard English** formal English, good English, good grammar, King's English, literary language, plain English, prestige dialect, prestige form, Queen's English, Received Pronunciation, RP. **3. jargon** argot, baby talk, back slang, cant, colloquialism, flash, foreignism *(US)*, hobson-jobson, informal language, jive, patter, pidgin, rechtub kelat, rhyming slang, slang, talk, vernacular, vernacularism. *Informal:* gobbledegook, jabberwocky, lingo. **4. technical language** cablese, commercialese, euphuism, journalese, legalese, officialese, telegraphese. **5. terminology** brand name, nomenclature, technology, trade description, trade name. **6. code** cipher, clear, cypher, microdot, scrambled message. **7. bad language** bullocky, colourful language, expletive, foul language, swearing, swearword, taboo term. **8. language type** agglutinating language, analytic language, artificial language, interlanguage, isolating language, metalanguage, object language, protolanguage, synthetic language, target language, tonal language, tone language, universal language. **9. language family** family, group of languages, stock, subfamily.

2. **1. linguistics** analogy, applied linguistics, articulatory phonetics, comparative linguistics, comparative philology, computational linguistics, contrastive linguistics, descriptive grammar, dialectology, etymology, generative grammar, generative semantics, grammar, language acquisition studies, lexicography, lexicology, metalinguistics, morphemics, morphology, morphophonemics, natural language processing, NLP, onomastics, orthography, paralinguistics, perceptual phonetics, philology, phonemics, phonetics, phonology, phonotype, pragmatics, prescriptive grammar, psycholinguistics, semantics, semasiology, sentential calculus, sociolinguistics, structuralism, stylistics, syntax, tagmemics, transformational grammar. **2. grammaticality** acceptability, correctness, grammaticism, rightness, well-formedness. **3. deep structure** base component, generation, rewrite rules, surface structure, transform, transformation, word order. **4. linguistic geography** dialect geography.

3. **1. linguist** dialectician, dialectologist, etymologist, field linguist, generativist, glottologist, grammarian, lexicographer, morphologist, parser, philologer, philologist, phonetician, phonologist, psycholinguist, psychologist, semanticist, semasiologist, sociolinguist, vernacularist. **2. archaist** archaiser, euphuist.

adj. **4.** **1. linguistic** etymological, glottologic, grammatical, morphemic, morphological, paralinguistic, philological, phonemic, phonetic, psycholinguistic, semantic, sociolinguistic,

syntactic, syntactical. **2. agglutinate** agglutinative, analytic, centum, inflective, isolating, satem, synthetic.
RELATED KEYWORDS: ALPHABET, MEANING, WRITING, SPEECH, WORD

LATENESS

n. **1.**   **1. lateness** backwardness, belatedness, tardiness. **2. last minute** eleventh hour. **3. act of delaying** delay, detainment, procrastination, retardation. **4. instance of delaying** cunctation, delay, demurrage, hold-up, wait.

     2.   **1. deferment** abeyance, adjournment, continuance, deferral, postponement, prorogation, respite, suspension. *Informal:* raincheck.

     3.   **1. deferrer** delayer, postponer, procrastinator, tarrier. **2. detainer** retarder.

     4.   **1. latecomer** Johnny-come-lately. **2. night owl** stopout.

adj. **5.**   **1. late** belated, latish, serotinous, tardy. **2. dilatory** backward, behindhand, slow, tardy. **3. delaying** retardant. **4. overdue** belated. **5. last-minute** eleventh-hour. **6. last** latest, lattermost, the latter. **7. later** latter.

     6.   **1. deferred** abeyant, adjourned, carried over, delayed, in abeyance, in cold storage, on the backburner, postponed, prorogued, suspended.

v. **7.**   **1. be late** miss the boat, miss the bus. **2. sleep in** lie over. **3. delay** be slow off the mark, dally, defer, dillydally, fiddle, gain time, hang fire, linger, loiter, lose time, play for time, procrastinate, slow, stall for time, tarry, trifle.

     8.   **1. defer** adjourn, carry over, charge, continue, count out *(British Parliamentary Procedure)*, delay, hold over, postpone, put in cold storage, put in the too-hard basket, put off, put on the backburner, put over *(US)*, remit, retard, sleep on it, suspend, wait, waive. *Informal:* take a raincheck. **2. retard** delay, halt, hold up. *Informal:* leg-rope.

adv. **9.**   **1. late** belatedly, tardily. **2. slowly** at a snail's pace, in slow motion. **3. latterly. 4. last.**

RELATED KEYWORDS: UNTIMELINESS

LAWFULNESS

n. **1.**   **1. lawfulness** allowableness, constitutionality, legality, legitimacy, legitimateness, validity, validness. **2. legalisation** legitimation, legitimisation, validation.

     2.   **1. law** appointment, by-law, caption, charter *(British)*, code, consolidation, dead letter, decree, edict, enactment, ex post facto law, institution, legal code, ordinance, prescript, regulation, rescript, rule, rule of law, statute. **2. type of law** Aboriginal customary law, Aboriginal law, administrative law, anti-hooning law, case law, civil law, commercial law, common law, consumer protection, criminal law, crown law, equity, family law, international law, Islamic law, jungle law, jurisprudence, law *(Aboriginal English)*, law merchant, law of nations, law of the jungle, legislation, lex, maritime law, martial law, military law, natural law, organic law, penal code, prohibition order, Roman law, statute law, sumptuary law, unwritten law. **3. code** canon, capitularies, Code Napoléon, corpus juris, Decalogue, judicature system, novel, pandects, Ten Commandments, the Digest. **4. Act** act of Parliament, adjournment of debate, bill, measure, ordonnance, private act, private bill, private member's bill, public bill, rider, standing order, statutory instrument, ways and means. **5. amendment** novel *(Civil Law)*. **6. precedent** authority, nice point, precept, ruling. **7. jurisprudence** codification, jurimetrics, legislation, nomography, nomology.

     3.   **1. capacity** competence, jus, majority, power, right. **2. entitlement** claim, colour, droit, right, title.

     4.   **1. legal centre** community justice centre.

adj. **5.**   **1. lawful** according to the law, admissible, allowable, authorised, chartered, constitutional, just, kosher, legal, legitimate, licit, major, permissible, permissive, permitted, rightful, statutory, true, unalienable, valid. *Informal:* legit. **2. paralegal** quasi-judicial. **3. judicial** adjective, forensic, jural, juridical, juristic, justiciary, legal. **4. jurisprudential** jurisprudent, nomographical, nomological.

v. **6.**   **1. legalise** approve, authorise, clear, decriminalise, enact, legitimate, legitimatise, legitimise, ordain, sanction, validate, warrant. **2. formulate** codify.

adv. **7.**   **1. lawfully** legally, legitimately, validly. **2. in the eye of the law** de jure, jurally, juristically.

RELATED KEYWORDS: COURT OF LAW, JUDGE, LAWYER, LITIGATION, MORALITY, PROPRIETY

LAWYER

n. **1.**   **1. lawyer** articled clerk, attorney *(Chiefly US)*, jurisconsult, jurisprudent, jurist, legal adviser, legist, limb of the law, nomographer, nomologist, proctor, procurator, publicist, trial lawyer. *Informal:* legal eagle. **2. crooked lawyer** pettifogger. *Informal:* shicer, shyster. **3. barrister** adviser, advocate *(Chiefly Scottish)*, barrister-at-law, bencher *(British)*, counsel, counsellor *(US)*, junior, KC, King's Counsel, leader, pleader, QC, Queen's Counsel, senior, Senior Counsel, silk, utter barrister. *Informal:* brief, mouthpiece. **4. prosecutor** crown prosecutor, Crown prosecutor, DA *(US)*, district attorney *(Chiefly US)*, fiscal, police prosecutor, public prosecutor, state's attorney *(US)*. **5. solicitor** ambulance chaser, attorney *(Chiefly US)*, attorney at law *(Chiefly US)*, chamber magistrate, clerk of the peace, commissioner for oaths, conveyancer, counsellor *(US)*, duty solicitor, lawyer, notary, notary public, shopfront lawyer. **6. attorney-general** prothonotary, solicitor-general.

     2.   **1. legal profession** bar, inner bar, law, outer bar. **2. legal advice** legal aid.

v. **3.**   **1. practise law** advise, assist, brief, defend, do conveyancing, do the lawyering, plead cases, prepare briefs, prosecute, represent. **2. take silk** be called to the bar.

RELATED KEYWORDS: COURT OF LAW, JUDGE, LITIGATION

LAYER

n. **1.**   **1. layer** flake, folium, interleaf, lamella, lamina, molecular film, slice, stratum, thickness, tier. **2. band** course, cross reef, flookan, frieze, friezing, line, lode, panel, reef, rib, schlieren, seam, stage, stratum, streak, string, string-course, vein. **3. stratum** band, bar, basement, basement complex, bed, bind, bone bed, cap rock, colluvium, counter, disconformity, flake, floor, footwall, hardpan, horizon, killas, lamella, ledge, lithosphere, litter, mantle, mantle rock, mantua, pallium, pan, regolith, roadbed, shelf, sial, sill, sima, stratification, stripe, subsoil, substrate, substratum, superstratum, unconformity, underclay, underlay, undersoil, understratum, varve, vein, watertable. **4. strata** coal measures, cross-course, measures, series.

     2.   **1. coating** armour, backing, cladding, collodion, colouring, covering, deposit, frost, glaze ice, impasto, lorica, petrifying liquid, plating, pricking coat, respray, sheet, silver frost, skin, stucco, veneering, wash, washing. **2. coat** bark, capsule, carapace, epicarp, epidermis, exocarp, hull, husk, integument, investment, mother-of-pearl, nacre, rind, shell, skin, test, tunic. **3. cladding** armour plate, double glazing, housing, sheathing, skin. **4. tile** roofboard, shingle, slate. **5. top dressing** macadamisation. **6. facing** chemise, crib, cribbing, cribs, fireback, lamina, layer, leaf, liner, lining, overlay, revetment, veneer. *Informal:* shimmy. **7. panel** backboard, board, flag, foil, lath, louvre-board, plank, plate, shale, shavings, slab, slat, strip, wafer. **8. sheeting** aponeurosis, carpet, dustsheet, endoperidium, endopleura, endothelium, epidermis, epithelium, exoperidium, hypodermis, membrane, mesothelium, peridium, squama, tissue. **9. stripe** section, vitta, zone. **10. shoe lining** heeltap, innersole, insole, lift, rand, sole, welt. **11. underlay** underfelt.

     3.   **1. stratification** bedding, delamination, flake, interlamination, interstratification, lamina, lamination, leaf, stratum. **2. scaliness** flakiness, foliation, imbrication, squamation, squamousness, superimposition, superincumbence, superincumbency, superposition.

     4.   **1. glaze** bloom, crust, finish, glost, laitance, lamella, patina, rust, salt glaze, scale, verdigris. **2. film** filminess.

     5.   **1. storey** basement, belvedere, cellar, clerestory, entresol, floor, ground floor, hayloft, mezzanine, piano nobile, roof garden, rooftop garden, story *(Chiefly US)*, upstairs.

     6.   **1. liner** colourer, sheather, stuccoer, surfacer, waxer.

adj. **7.**   **1. split-level** decked, double-deck, double-decker, storeyed, storied *(Chiefly US)*. **2. stratal** crustal, crusty, desmoid, substrative, superincumbent, superjacent, supernatant. **3. laminate** clinker, clinker-built, flaggy, laminar, laminose, lapstrake. **4. striped** barred, sliced, vittate. **5. filmy** membranous. **6. layered** cross-bedded, laminated, multilaminate, multiseriate, stratiform, tegular, three-ply.

     8.   **1. flaky** exfoliative, flocculent, foliaceous, foliated, imbricate, imbricated, imbricative, lamellar, lamellate, lamellose, laminable, laminar, laminose, scalelike, scutellate.

v. **9.**   **1. layer** flake, laminate, slice, stratify. **2. coat** clad, cover, crust, encrust, face, film, glaze, laminate, line, sheet, veneer. **3. stratify** strata.

RELATED KEYWORDS: COVERING, SKIN

LEARNING

n. **1.** **1. learning** book-learning, culture, education, erudition, knowledge, lore, scholarship, schooling, wisdom. **2. comprehension** absorptance, absorption, assimilation, digestion, infixion, ingestion, mastery, taking-in, understanding. **3. study** brainwork, conning, conning up, homework, learning, lucubration, memorisation, overstudy, preparation, training. *Informal:* boning up, cramming, grind, prep, swotting. **4. studiousness** bookishness, culture, scholarliness. **5. learning curve**.

2. **1. lesson** activity, class, colloquium, lecture, object lesson, practical, practicum, school, section *(NZ)*, seminar, sermon, session, teach-in, tutorial, webinar. *Informal:* prac, tute. **2. drill** boat drill, discipline, dismounted drill, dress rehearsal, exercise, exercitation, fire drill, full-dress rehearsal, manoeuvre, pack drill, practice, rehearsal, rifle drill, rote learning, run-through, skeleton exercise, square bashing, walk-through. **3. exercise** assignment, homework, task.

3. **1. course** correspondence course, extension course, external course, in-service course, internship, novitiate, postgraduate course, refresher course, sandwich course, seminar. **2. introductory course** ABC's, elementary course, elements, initiation, isagogics, propaedeutics, rudiments, three R's. **3. curriculum** KLA, program, syllabus. **4. subject** area, credit, elective, major, minor *(US)*, module, unit. **5. discipline** field, major, speciality, specialty, study. **6. branch of learning** arts, classics, humanities, industrial arts, liberal arts, manual arts, quadrivium, the sciences, trivium.

adj. **4.** **1. learned** academic, antiquarian, book-learned, bookish, cultivated, cultured, educated, enlightened, erudite, informed, lettered, literate, owlish, pedantical, scholarly, scholastic, self-educated, self-taught, studious, well-educated, well-informed, well-read. **2. practised** experienced, expert, full-fledged, proficient, schooled, trained, versed in, well-grounded, well-versed. **3. up-to-date** au courant, briefed, informed, posted, primed, up on, well-informed.

5. **1. educational** edifying, educative, educatory, instructive.

v. **6.** **1. learn** absorb, acquaint oneself with, announce, assimilate, compass, consume, digest, get into, imbibe, infix, ingrain, take in. **2. master** pick up. *Informal:* get the hang of, get the knack of. **3. learn by rote** commit to memory, get down pat, know by heart, learn, learn by heart, memorise, study. **4. gain experience** cut one's eyeteeth, cut one's teeth, experience, learn the ropes, pick someone's brains, serve one's apprenticeship. *Informal:* get one's feet wet, get wise, live and learn.

7. **1. study** apply one's mind to, brush up on, con, do, overstudy, read, restudy, review. *Informal:* gen up. **2. revise** con, grind away at, learn, lucubrate, overstudy, study. *Informal:* bone up on, burn the midnight oil, cram, grub, mug up, swot, swot up. **3. practise** drill, familiarise oneself, rehearse, run through, train, tutor.

8. **1. specialise in** do honours in, major in, minor in *(US)*, research, study, take as a subject.

RELATED KEYWORDS: COMPETENCE, GUIDANCE, KNOWLEDGE, SCHOOL, TEACHER, STUDENT, TEACHING, WISE PERSON

LEFT

n. **1.** **1. left** left wing, verso. **2. port** nearside, prompt side. **3. left-handedness** cackhandedness. **4. left-hander** left-footer. *Informal:* cackie, leftie, mollydooker, southpaw.

adj. **2.** **1. left-hand** left, leftward, sinister, sinistral, sinistrous. **2. port** near, nearside. **3. left-handed** *Informal:* cack-handed, cacky-handed, southpaw.

adv. **3.** **1. left** aport, leftward, leftwards, on the left, sinisterwise, sinistrally.

RELATED KEYWORDS: SIDE

LENGTH

n. **1.** **1. length** distance, expanse, extent, fetch, piece *(US)*, range, reach, scope, space, spacing, span, straddle, tract. **2. extension** coextension, elongation, expanse, expansion, extent, lankiness, lankness, lengthiness, linearity. **3. linear measure** altazimuth, altitude, angular distance, chainage, easting, footage, latitude, long measure, longitude, milage, mileage, northing, southing, surveyor's measure, westing. **4. trajectory** arrowshot, bowshot, cannon shot, carry, cast, flight, gunshot, outreach, shot, throw. **5. hand's-breadth** canvas, digit, finger, fingerbreadth, footstep, handbreadth, hank, head, march, neck, nose, pace, palm, span, step, stride. **6. yarn length** bundle *(British Textiles)*, hank, lea, spindle. **7. calibre** bore, gauge. **8. miscellaneous length** clearance, draw, drift, drop, epoch, focal length, focus, freeboard, frontage, gap, headway, lap, overhang, overlap, pitch, projection, recoil, setback, slippage, travel, traverse, wheelbase. **9. unit of length** angstrom, astronomical unit, cable length, centimetre, chain, cubit, degree, ell, em, fathom, foot, furlong, inch, international nautical mile, kilometre, league, light-year, line, link, meridional part, meter *(US)*, metre, microinch, micrometre, micron, mil, mile, millimetre, minute, module, nail, nautical mile, parsec, perch, point, pole, rod, verst, yard. *Informal:* kay, thou.

2. **1. line** axis, band, bar, canal, crossbar, dash, guideline, hatch, outline, ray, ribbon, rule, straight, streak, stria, strip, stripe, stroke, swath, tail, thread, track, trail, vein, veinlet, vitta. **2. row** chain, column, file, hedgerow, Indian file, line, orthostichy, procession, queue, rank, single file, string, train, windrow. **3. geometric line** asymptote, chord, circumference, curve, diameter, directrix, median, perimeter, radius, secant, tangent. **4. equator** girth, great circle, magnetic meridian, meridian, parallel, thermal equator. **5. lineation** crosshatching, grain, hatching, ruling, striation, veining. **6. specific line** baseline, buttock line, condensation trail, contour, contour line, em rule, fall line, international date line, load line, magistral, magistral line, pinstripe, pitch line, plimsoll line, ridge, service line, sidelines, taw, thalweg, touchline, vapour trail, waterline.

3. **1. length-measurer** cathetometer, chain, chain measure, cyclometer, echo sounder, engineer's chain, erythrocytometer, fathomer, fathometer, feeler gauge, foot rule, gunter's chain, interferometer, log, micrometer, mileometer, odograph, odometer, pedometer, rangefinder, ranger, rule, ruler, scale, stadiometer, surveyor's chain, tachometer, tachymeter, tape measure, tripmeter, ultramicrometer, yardstick. *Informal:* tacho.

adj. **4.** **1. long** annexe, elongate, elongated, expanded, expansive, extended, farthest, lengthy, longish. **2. lengthwise** axial, endlong, fore-and-aft, full-length, longitudinal, overall, whole-length. **3. extendable** expansible, expansile, extensible, extensile. **4. metric** kilometric, kilometrical, milliary, sesquipedalian, uncial. **5. lanky** gangling, gangly, lank, rangy, stalky.

5. **1. linear** bilinear, collinear, lineal, one-dimensional, rectilinear, running, straight-line. **2. meridian** diametral, diametrical, meridional, perimetric, perimetrical, tangential. **3. line-like** flagelliform, stringlike, threadlike, vermiform, vinelike, wiredrawn. **4. lined** barred, lineate, lineolate, liney, liny, streaky, striate, striped, veined.

v. **6.** **1. extend** coextend, continue, cross, go, lengthen, reach, run, span, spread, stretch, track. **2. stretch out** crane, extend, outstretch, protract. **3. lengthen** draw out, drop the hem of, elongate, extend, stretch, wiredraw.

7. **1. line** band, crosshatch, hatch, ray, rule, rule off, streak, striate, strip, stripe, vein. **2. align** collimate, lay out, range, rank, rectify, windrow. **3. line up** defile, queue, string, string out, trail.

adv. **8.** **1. lengthways** along, amidships, at length, axially, fore-and-aft, from end to end, from stem to stem, in extenso, lengthwise, longitudinally, longways, meridionally, out, tandem.

9. **1. lengthily** extendedly, lankily, lankly, long.

10. **1. lineally** collinearly, linearly, rectilinearly.

RELATED KEYWORDS: DEPTH, HEIGHT, MEASUREMENT, THICKNESS

LENIENCE

n. **1.** **1. lenience** forbearance, forbearing, gentleness, leniency, lenity, mildness, moderation, temperance, toleration. **2. charitableness** benevolence, clemency, compassion, fellow feeling, forbearance, grace, mercifulness, mercy, misericordia, quarter, sympathies. **3. relaxation** unbending. **4. laxness** elasticity, indiscipline, indulgence, laxity, liberalness, looseness, permissive society, rafferty's rules. **5. dispensation** days of grace, moratorium, reprieve.

2. **1. lenient person** indulger, liberaliser, loosener, mollycoddler. *Informal:* a good sport.

adj. **3.** **1. lenient** agreeable, amiable, benign, charitable, clement, compassionate, complaisant, compliant, easy, easygoing, forgiving, gentle, gracious, humane, indulgent, kindly, liberal, merciful, mild, obliging, soft, soft-hearted, sparing, tender-hearted, tolerant, uncritical, unexacting. **2. lax** accommodating, bohemian, casual, elastic, familiar, flexible, free and easy, informal, laid-back, loose, permissive, relaxed, slack, unbuttoned, unconventional, uninhibited, wide-open.

v. **4.** **1. be lenient** baby, bear with, coddle, featherbed, handle with kid gloves, humour, indulge, mollycoddle, spare. *Informal:* cut someone some slack, go easy on. **2. relent** come round, give quarter, go soft, yield. *Informal:* take the acid off, take the heat off. **3. relax** liberalise, loosen, slacken, stretch a point, unbend, unbutton. **4. dispense** exempt, indulgence, remit, reprieve.

adv. **5.** **1. leniently** charitably, clemently, liberally, mercifully. **2. laxly** elastically, indulgently, loose, loosely.

RELATED KEYWORDS: FORGIVENESS, KINDNESS, PITY, TOLERANCE

LEVEL

n. **1.** **1. level** flat, plane, stratum, table. **2. horizontal** artificial horizon, false horizon, geoid, horizon, mean sea-level, sea-level, true level.

2. **1. levelness** evenness, flatness, planeness, straightness. **2. recumbency** accumbency, proneness, prostration, reclination, recumbent, supineness.

3. **1. leveller** evener, flattener, flatter, float, garden roller, grader, heavy roller, mallee roller, plane, planer, planisher, road-roller, roll, roller, steamroller. **2. surveyor's level** alidade bubble, chalk-line, gimbals, level, plumb-rule, plumbline, plummet, stringline, wye level.

adj. **4.** **1. level** equal, even, fair, flat, flattish, flush, horizontal, invariable, lamellar, lamellate, plain, planar, plane, regular, smooth, square, straight, table-top, tabular, uniplanar. **2. levelled** compressed, flattened, pitch-faced. **3. recumbent** accumbent, decumbent, fallen, horizontal, leaning, lolling, lying down, procumbent, prone, prostrate, reclining, resupine, sprawling, supine.

v. **5.** **1. level** bed, cut, cut down, fell, flatten, floor, hew down, knock endways, knock end-wise, landplane, laser, laser-level, lay, lay down, mow down, raze. *Informal:* barrel, bush-bash, shake down. **2. even** face, float, flush, garden *(Cricket)*, grade, level, pat, plane, planish, plaster, pumice, roll, smooth, smoothen, square, strike.

6. **1. recline** couch, lie, lie down, loll, lounge, measure one's length, prostrate, prostrate oneself, repose, sprawl, stretch out. *Informal:* spinebash.

adv. **7.** **1. levelly** even, evenly, flat, flush, horizontally, level. **2. recumbently** asprawl, on one's back, pronely, supinely. *Informal:* flat out, flat out like a lizard drinking.

RELATED KEYWORDS: LAYER, POSE, PRESSURE, SMOOTHNESS

LIBERATION

n. **1.** **1. liberation** affranchisement, deliverance, delivery, emancipation, enfranchisement, manumission, ransom, redemption, release. *Informal:* lib. **2. acquittal** absolution, acquittance, deliverance, discharge, exoneration, quittance, redemption. **3. discharge** bail, bailment, dismissal, pardon, parole, remission, remittal, reprieve. **4. disengagement** decontrol, extrication. **5. immunity** act of indemnity, disentailment, exemption. **6. unboundedness** unaccountability, unconditionality, unconditionalness, unlimitedness.

2. **1. liberty** autonomy, freedom, freeness, independence, manumission, self-determination, self-regulation, self-sufficiency. **2. right to freedom** academic freedom, free speech, freedom of the seas. **3. unrestraint** abandon, anarchism, anarchy, incontinence, incontinency, indiscipline, inordinacy, intemperateness, irrepressibility, irrepressibleness, libertarianism, looseness, open-handedness, spontaneity, spontaneousness, wantonness, wildness. **4. latitude** breadth, elbow-room, leg room, licence, margin, option, play, poetic licence, sufferance, tolerance. **5. leave** exequatur, permission. **6. free hand** blank cheque, carte blanche, free rein, free swing *(US)*. *Informal:* open go, open slather. **7. sanctuary** asylum, diplomatic immunity. **8. open door** admission, egress, entrance, entree, entry. **9. parole** bail, cartel, force majeure, out, ransom, remission, ticket-of-leave, vis major. **10. world outside prison** rules *(British)*, the outer, the outside.

3. **1. liberalism** broad-mindedness, existentialism, forbearance, informality, laissez faire, liberality, liberalness, non-intervention, non-restraint, toleration, tolerationism, unbiasedness.

4. **1. liberator** emancipationist, emancipator, emancipist, liberationist. **2. deliverer** absolutist, acquitter, discharger, exonerator, manumitter, messiah, ransomer, redeemer, saviour.

5. **1. freed person** emancipated convict, emancipist, expiree, freedman, freedwoman, old hand, parolee, ticket-of-leaver. *Informal:* clean potato. **2. free settler** franklin, free agent, freeman, pure merino.

6. **1. libertarian** civil libertarian, existentialist, liberal, liberaliser, liberalist, non-interventionist, tolerationist. *Informal:* libber.

adj. **7.** **1. liberated** emancipated, exonerated, free, free of the country, free on the ground, freeborn, independent, released, scot-free. **2. liberal** free-handed, liberalist, liberalistic, non-restrictive, open-handed. **3. unbridled** abandoned, all-in, anarchic, anarchistic, facile, incoercible, incontinent, inordinate, intemperate, irrepressible, laissez-faire, loose, outspoken, unbent, unbidden, unbitted, unbowed, unbroken, unconfined, uncontrolled, uncrossed, unfettered, unregulated, unrestrained, untrammelled, wanton, wild. *Informal:*

tearaway. **4. uninhibited** expansive, fancy-free, footloose, forthright, frank, free, free-hearted, free-spoken, independent, open, outspoken, spontaneous, unashamed, unconventional, unembarrassed, unfettered, unreserved. **5. unlimited** arbitrary, boundless, broad, common, open, rampant, unbounded, unchartered, unclassified, unconditional, undetermined, unhampered, unmeasured, unrestricted, unstructured, upstanding.

v. **8. 1. liberate** deliver, disengage, emancipate, extricate, free, manumit, rescue. **2. acquit** absolve, affranchise, clear, discharge, disengage, disentail, dispense with, exculpate, exempt, exonerate, forgive, frank, free, justify, let off, let out, loosen, pardon, parole, purge, ransom, release, remit, reprieve, unburden, vindicate. **3. release** let go, loose. *Informal:* spring. **4. unleash** decontrol, free, give someone his head, loose, release, unbind, unbridle, uncage, unchain, unfetter, unloose, unmuzzle, unscrew, unshackle, untie. **5. decolonise** grant self-government to.

9. 1. unfasten cast off, disyoke, loose, slip, unbind, unbrace, unbuckle, unbutton, unclasp, unfetter, unfix, unfreeze, unglue, unharness, unhasp, unhinge, unhitch, unhook, unlatch, unmoor, unpeg, unpen, unpin, unscrew, unsling, unsnap, unstick, untie, unyoke.

10. 1. let oneself go do as one pleases, do what one likes, have one's own way, play, run about, run riot, run wild, wanton. *Informal:* freewheel, have one's fling, let it all hang out, let off steam, let one's hair down. **2. deliver oneself from** break free, break loose, cast off the trammels, get rid of, shake off the yoke, slip, slip the collar, throw off.

adv. **11. 1. at liberty** at large, loose, on the loose, out of the wood. **2. freely** free, imprescriptibly, liberally, open-handedly. **3. unconditionally** unboundedly, unlimitedly. **4. unrestrainedly** anarchically, hundred-per-cent, incontinently, inordinately, intemperately, out, outspokenly, perfectly, quite, spontaneously, unashamedly, unconventionally, unreservedly, utterly, wantonly, wildly.

RELATED KEYWORDS: ACQUITTAL, ESCAPE, INDEPENDENCE, RIGHTS

LIFE

n. **1. 1. life** being, existence, living, modus vivendi, subsistence, survival, sustentation. **2. existence** being, creation, nature. **3. course of life** days, expectation of life, life cycle, life-expectancy. **4. longevity** long life, survivorship, viability. **5. animation** a new lease of life, quickening, reanimation, resurgence, resurrection, revival, reviviscence, vitalisation, vivification. **6. vital force** anima, animus, atman, eros, essence, inner nature, libido, life force, pneuma, prana, psyche, soul, spirit, vital fluid, vital spark, wairua. **7. lifeblood** blood, breath, heart, heart's blood, heartblood, life's blood, marrow, pith, pulse, vitality.

adj. **2. 1. living** alive, alive and kicking, animate, breathing, existent, existing, in the flesh, in the land of the living, live, quick, surviving, to the fore. *Informal:* above ground, on deck. **2. long-lived** longeval, longevous. **3. viable** capable of life. **4. resurgent** renascent, resurrectional, resurrectionary, reviviscent. **5. vital** alive, animated, bright, full of life, lively, pert, proud *(Poetic)*, red-blooded, spirited, sprightly, vigorous, vivacious, vivid, zingy. *Informal:* chipper, chirpy, jazzy, live, peppy, snappy, swinging, zippy. **6. green** blooming, blossoming, fresh, juicy, sappy, verdant. **7. life-giving** animating, animative, invigorating, quickening, vivifying.

v. **3. 1. live** be, be alive and well, breathe, endure, exist, keep body and soul together, outlive, persist, subsist, survive. **2. come back to life** awaken, come to, quicken, resurge, revive, rise, waken.

4. 1. bring back to life animate, breathe life into, bring to, quicken, reanimate, recall *(Poetic)*, recreate, resurrect, resuscitate, revitalise, revive, revivify.

RELATED KEYWORDS: ACTUALITY, ENERGY, PLANTS, ANIMALS, HUMANITY, REPRODUCTION

LIGHT

n. **1. 1. light** illuminance, illumination, luminance, luminous energy. **2. type of lighting** candlelight, electric light, firelight, gaslight, lamplight, torchlight. **3. type of light** arc light, Bengal light, calcium light, floodlight, follow spot, limelight, magnesium light, red fire, spot, spotlight. **4. beam** irradiation, moonbeam, pencil, phlegethon, ray, shaft, sunbeam, sunray. **5. glow** candescence, fluorescence, gleam, incandescence, lustre, phosphorescence, radiance, refulgence. **6. flash** arc, belch, blaze, flare, flare-up, fulguration. **7. sparkle** blink, coruscation, flicker, glance, gleam, glimmer, glimmering, glint, glister, glitter, light, lustre, scintillation, shimmer, spark, twinkle, twinkling, wink. **8. daylight** day, daytime, light, sun, sunburst, sunlight, sunniness, sunshine. **9. dawn** break of day, daybreak, daylight, dayspring *(Poetic)*, false dawn, first light, light, piccaninny daylight, sun-up, sunrise. **10. aurora** aurora australis, aurora borealis, northern lights, polar lights, southern lights. **11. airglow** afterglow, alpenglow, blink, gegenschein, green flash, iceblink, rainbow, snowblink, sunbow, sundog, white-out. **12. moonlight** earthlight, earthshine, moonshine, starlight, zodiacal light. **13. earthshine** earthlight. **14. will-o'-the-wisp** friar's lantern, ignis fatuus, jack-o'-lantern, marsh light, wildfire. **15. parhelion** mock moon, mock sun, paraselene, photosphere. **16. corona** aureole, circle, gloriole, halo.

2. **1. brightness** brilliance, brilliantness, dazzle, effulgence, fieriness, fire, flame, flashiness, garishness, glare, glaringness, irradiancy, lambency, liveliness, lucency, luridness, resplendence, sheen, silveriness, splendour, starriness, vividness. **2. luminescence** asterism, bioluminescence, chemiluminescence, electroluminescence, fluorescence, luminosity, luminousness, noctilucence, phosphorescence, photoluminescence, radioluminescence, thermoluminescence, triboluminescence. **3. polish** burnish, glint, gloss, glossiness, lustre, lustrousness, sheen, shine, shininess, sleekness, slickness, varnish. **4. iridescence** highlights, opalescence, orient, reflet, schiller.

3. **1. lightning** ball lightning, bolt, chain lightning, fireball, heat lightning, sheet lightning, summer lightning, thunderbolt, wildfire. **2. St Elmo's fire** corposant.

4. **1. radiation** actinic rays, actinometer, alpha radiation, alpha wave, beta radiation, black light, cosmic rays, infra-red, light, luminous energy, near infra-red, photon, radio wave, roentgen ray, sunrays, thermal radiation, travelling wave, ultra violet, ultraviolet B, wave, wave train, white light, X-rays.

5. **1. lighting** illumination, irradiation. **2. electric light** arc lamp, arc light, bulb, city lights, fluorescent tube, gas lamp, gaslight, glow lamp, harbour lights, incandescent lamp, light bulb, light globe, mercury-vapour lamp, neon lamp, port light, port lights, quartz-iodine lamp, security light, sensor light, starboard light, tungsten lamp, uplighter. **3. chandelier** cresset, lustre, pendant, pennant. **4. concealed lighting** indirect lighting, panel lighting, strip lighting, strobe lighting. **5. sidelight. 6. lamp** Aldis lamp, dark lantern, droplight, flashlight, hurricane, hurricane lamp, jacklight *(US)*, Japanese lantern, lampion, lantern, night-light, slush lamp, standard lamp, storm lantern *(British)*, Tilley lamp, torch, wall-washer. **7. safety lamp** Davy lamp. **8. Chinese lantern** fairy lights, jack-o'-lantern. **9. streetlight** lamp standard, lamppost, pavement light, vault light. **10. footlights** floats, floodlight, foots, klieg light, spot, spotlight. **11. sunlamp. 12. vehicle light** blinker, brakelight, clicker, courtesy light, flasher *(Chiefly British)*, flickers, fog lamp, hazard lights, headlamp, headlight, indicator light, light, parker, sidelight, stoplight, tail-light, trafficator, turning-indicator. *Informal:* winker. **13. searchlight** star shell, Very light. **14. lighthouse** pharos. **15. flashbulb** electronic flash, flash, flashcube, flashgun, flashlight, photoflash lamp, photoflood lamp, strobe. **16. safelight. 17. floodlight projector** sun gun, up-lighter.

6. **1. candle** bougie, dip, taper, tea light. **2. candlestick** candelabra, candelabrum, flambeau, girandole, menorah, pricket. **3. torch** flambeau, flare, Hawaiian flare, link, luau light.

7. **1. illuminator** brightener, illuminant, inflamer, irradiator, kindler, lightener, lighter, luminary, scintillator. **2. torchbearer** lamplighter, linkboy, linkman.

adj. 8. **1. light** illuminative, photic. **2. bright** aureate, beaming, brilliant, clear, effulgent, fulgent, gleaming, irradiate, lambent, lightsome, live, lively, lucid, luminous, radiant, refulgent, relucent, resplendent, shimmering, shimmery, shining, splendent, splendorous, vivid. **3. glowing** aglow, ardent, candent, candescent, incandescent. **4. sparkling** agleam, aglimmer, aglitter, asteriated, aventurine, chatoyant, clinquant, diamanté, glittering, glittery, scintillant, scintillating, twinkling. **5. glaring** blinding, dazzling, garish, glary, lurid. **6. flashing** fulgurant, fulgurous, fulminous. **7. shiny** ganoid, glacé, glare, glassy, glossy, lustrous, polished, satin, satin-like, satiny, sheeny, silky, silvery, sleek, slick, waxlike, waxy, wet look. **8. lustrous** iridescent, lustred, nacreous, opalescent, opaline, orient, oriental, pearl, pearly. **9. clear** crystal, empyreal, empyrean. **10. luminous** fluorescent, irradiant, irradiative, luciferous, luminescent, luminiferous, noctilucent, phosphorescent, radiative. **11. cloudless** clear, shadeless, shadowless, unshadowed. **12. sunny** sun-drenched, sunlit, sunshine, sunshiny. **13. moonlit** moonlight, moonshiny, moony, star-studded, starlight, starlit, starry. **14. lamplit** torchlit. **15. backlit.**

9. **1. photoactive** heliotactic, heliotropic, photophilous, photosensitive, phototonic, phototropic.

v. 10. **1. shine** beam, beat, blind, effulge, flare, glare, outshine, overshine. **2. glow** incandesce. **3. sparkle** blink, coruscate, flash, flicker, glance, gleam, glimmer, glint, glisten, glister, glitter, scintillate, scintillation, shimmer, shiner, spangle, spark, twinkle, wink. **4. flash** fulgurate, lighten. **5. radiate** diffract, ray, reflect, refract. **6. luminesce** fluoresce, phosphoresce. **7. burn** blaze, flame, flare, glow, shine.

11. **1. lighten** brighten. **2. illuminate** floodlight, illume *(Poetic)*, illumine, kindle, light, lighten, relume, spotlight. **3. irradiate** illuminate, insolate, solarise, sun. **4. gloss** burnish, lustre, polish, schillerise, shine, varnish, wax.

adv. **12.** **1. brightly** bright, brilliantly, clear, clearly, illuminatingly, lucidly, resplendently, vividly. **2. glowingly** candescently, effulgently, fulgently, incandescently, lambently, lustrously, radiantly, refulgently. **3. glitteringly** flickeringly, glimmeringly, glisteningly, starrily. **4. glossily** silkily, sleekly, slickly. **5. fierily** flamingly. **6. glaringly** blindingly, dazzlingly. **7. garishly** luridly.

RELATED KEYWORDS: COLOUR, OPTICS, SIGHT, VISIBILITY

LIGHTNESS

n. **1.** **1. lightness** filminess, fineness, flimsiness, fluffiness, fuzziness, gauziness. **2. airiness** etherealness, rarefaction, rareness, rarity, tenuousness, thinness. **3. weightlessness** imponderableness, levity, zero gravity. **4. buoyancy** floatability, flotage, flotation, hover, poise, wafture. **5. agility** lambency, light-footedness, lightsomeness, nimbleness.

2. **1. float** bob, bobber, buoy, buoyage, floater, torpedo tube. **2. raft** float, floating island, flotsam, landing stage, mooring buoy, pontoon, spar buoy. **3. lifebuoy** air jacket, float, floaties, life jacket, life-preserver *(US)*, lifebelt, Mae West, rubber ring.

3. **1. fluff** film, floss, foam, fuzz, gauze, thistledown.

adj. **4.** **1. light** airy, delicate, feathery, filmy, fine, flimsy, floaty, flossy, fluffy, frivolous, fuzzy, gauzy, gossamer, lightsome, papery, papyraceous, subtle. *Informal:* airy-fairy. **2. airy** aerial, aery *(Poetic)*, astral, rare, rarefied, spiritual, spirituel, spirituelle, tenuous, thin, weightless. **3. lightweight** microlight, ultralight.

5. **1. light-footed** agile, alacritous, alert, flitting, lambent, lightsome, nimble, tripping, volant *(Poetic)*, volante. *Informal:* slippy.

6. **1. buoyant** afloat, floatable, floating, floaty, natant.

v. **7.** **1. float** bob, buoy, hover, levitate, swim, waft. **2. have a light touch** feather.

adv. **8.** **1. lightly** airily, filmily, flimsily, fluffily, fuzzily, light. **2. airily** buoyantly, ethereally, lightly, tenuously, thinly. **3. agilely** lambently, light-footedly, lightly, lightsomely, volante.

RELATED KEYWORDS: SMALLNESS, INTANGIBILITY, THINNESS

LIKELIHOOD

n. **1.** **1. likelihood** every chance, good chance, good prospect, likeliness, probability, promise, reason to hope, reasonable chance, well-founded view. **2. credibility** credit, plausibility, verisimilitude. **3. expectation** conditional probability, normal curve, presumption, probability curve, reasonable hope. **4. favourite** best bet, the one most likely to succeed. *Informal:* fave, goer, great white hope.

adj. **2.** **1. likely** favourable, feasible, odds-on, on the cards, presumable, probable, promising, to be expected. **2. liable to** apt to, in line, incident to, incidental to, like to, likely to, ready to. **3. credible** believable, easy to believe, ostensible, ostensive, plausible, verisimilar.

v. **3.** **1. be likely** be odds-on favourite, be sure to win, seem probable. *Informal:* be London to a brick (on). **2. think likely** believe, count on, dare say, expect, guess, have reason to believe, imagine, presume, suppose, suspect, take for granted. **3. seem likely** bid fair, have a strong probability, imply, lend colour to, point to, promise. **4. stand a good chance** be favoured to win, be the favourite, have every chance of winning, run a good chance.

adv. **4.** **1. likely** doubtless, doubtlessly, easily, evidently, in all likelihood, in all probability, like as not, no doubt, ostensibly, presumably, probably, professedly, seemingly, to all appearances.

RELATED KEYWORDS: CERTAINTY, INEVITABILITY, LUCK, POSSIBILITY

LIQUID

n. **1.** **1. liquid** ablution, aqua, condensate, dew, effusion, emulsion, fluid, grume, juice, liquor, moisture, sap, water. **2. solution** colloidal solution, decoction, distillate, emulsion, emulsoid, hydrosol, infusion, lixivium, lye, standard solution. **3. bath** dip, soak, souse, steep, wash. **4. drop** bead, blob, dewdrop, drip, droplet, gutta. **5. melt** thaw. **6. spillage** plash, spill, splash. **7. soakage** leachate, percolate, seepage. **8. waterdivining** dowsing, rhabdomancy.

2.   **1. water** Adam's ale, aqua, drinking water, tap-water. **2. groundwater** artesian water, bore water, connate water, englacial stream, floodwater, gravitational water, melt-water, mickery, pondage, rainwater, soakage, subartesian water, underground water, watertable. **3. town water** recycled water, scheme water. **4. salt water** brine, sea water. **5. coordinated water** deuterium oxide, heavy water, vadose circulation, water of crystallisation, water of hydration. **6. bilge** dishwater, slops, sullage, swill. **7. waterworks** water board.

3.   **1. liquidity** fluidity, fluidness, flux, liquidness, serosity, wateriness. **2. solubility** dissolubility, dissolubleness, dissolvableness, solubleness, solvability, solvableness. **3. fusibility**
fusibleness, thixotropy. **4. hydrology** fluid mechanics, hydraulics, hydrodynamics, hydrokinetics, hydromechanics, hydrostatics.

4.   **1. liquefaction** biolysis, deliquescence, dispersal, dispersion, dissolution, distillation, emulsification, fluidisation, fusion. **2. leaching** lixiviation, percolation, washing away.

5.   **1. liquefier** fluidiser, liquefacient, watermaker. **2. solvent** alcahest, alkahest, amyl acetate, anticoagulant, antifreeze, dispersion medium, dissolvent, dissolver, emulsifier, menstruum, thinner.

adj. 6.   **1. liquid** emulsive, fluctuant, fluid, fluidal, fluidic, molten, run, running, runny. **2. watery** aqueous, dewy, hydrogenous, hydrous, hygric, juicy, sappy, serous, sloppy, succulent, water, waterish, waterlike, wishy-washy. **3. dissolved** in solution, liquefied, solute, uncongealed. **4. hydraulic** hydrodynamic, hydrokinetic, hydrologic, hydro-mechanical, hydrostatic.

7.   **1. liquefiable** eutectic, eutectoid, fusible, thixotropic. **2. soluble** dissoluble, dis-solvable, dissolvent, solvable, water-soluble. **3. deliquescent** liquescent. **4. hydro-philic** hydrophobic, hydrotropic. **5. solvent** anticoagulant, dissolvent.

v. 8.   **1. liquefy** caramelise, defrost, deliquesce, dissolve, melt, run, sweal, thaw, unfreeze. **2. dissolve** degrade, disintegrate, disperse. **3. liquidise** fluidise, flux, fuse, malt, melt, render, smelt, try. **4. soak** draw, infuse, leach, lixiviate, percolate, steep, water-soak.

adv. 9.   **1. liquidly** fluidly.

RELATED KEYWORDS: FLOW, SEA, LAKE, RAINFALL, SLUDGE, SWAMP, WETNESS

LIST

n. 1.   **1. list** backlist, beadroll, catalogue, enumeration, file, headcount, inventory, listing, log, manifest, record, register, scroll, syllabus, tally. *Informal:* cattle dog. **2. table** charts, scale. **3. calendar** almanac, atlas, gazette, gazetteer, yearbook. **4. word list** con-cordance, dictionary, gloss, glossary, lexicon, syllabary, synonymy, thesaurus, vocabulary. **5. contents** bibliography, bibliotheca, corrigenda, errata, sigla, syllabus, synposis. **6. account** docket, invoice, ledger, receipt, stock book. *Informal:* kill list. **7. com-mercial list** basket, bill of lading, bill of quantities, check list, manifest, price list, stocktaking, waybill. **8. roll** accession list, active list, army list, beadroll, cartulary, census, chartulary, class list, class roll, electoral roll, empanelment, enrolment, law list, mailing list, muster roll, necrology, panel, payroll, peerage, poll, roster, rota, sick list, studbook, transfer list, waiting list, waitlist. **9. telephone directory** phone book, tele-dex, white pages, yellow pages. **10. mailing list** address book. *Informal:* block list, bozo list, kill list. **11. short list** slate, ticket. **12. betting list** book, race-card. **13. cred-its** directory, list of contributors. **14. roll of honour** honour board, honour roll, hon-our scroll. **15. list of saints** canon, hagiology, martyrology. **16. black list** black book, index. *Informal:* hit list, kill list. **17. conduct sheet** charge sheet, crime sheet. **18. wish list** birthday list, Christmas list.

2.   **1. agenda** docket *(US)*, notice paper, program, range of options, set of alternatives. **2. schedule** timetable. **3. repertoire** repertory, stock. **4. program** bill, playlist, TV program. **5. menu** à la carte, bill of fare, carte, diet chart, table d'hôte, tariff. **6. bath menu** pillow menu. **7. questionnaire** questionary, survey. **8. ballot paper** unity ticket.

3.   **1. listing** analysis, assay, breakdown, citation, enumeration, itemisation, recountal, tabularisation, tabulation.

4.   **1. itemiser** bibliographer, cataloguer, cataloguist, enroller, indexer, tabulator.

v. 5.   **1. list** accession, book, catalogue, index, inventory, table, tabularise, tabulate, take stock. **2. enumerate** docket, itemise, recite, recount, run through. **3. schedule** bill, calendar, gazette, register. **4. enrol** empanel, enter, impanel, inscribe, matriculate, poll, register, short-list, waitlist. **5. black-list** proscribe.

RELATED KEYWORDS: ACCOUNTING, CLASSIFICATION, ORDER

LITIGATION

n. **1.**   **1. litigation** action, case, cause, dispute, hearing, instance, law, lawsuit, legal proceeding, lis pendens, petition, plea, proceeding, process, reference, suit. **2. legal action** assumpsit, cattle trespass, class action, commercial cause, cross-action, interpleader, praemunire *(British Law)*, remanet, repetition, test case, trover, wager of law. *Informal:* fender case. **3. summons** arraignment, breve, citation, compurgation, detainer, duces tecum, habeas corpus, impeachment *(US)*, monition, subpoena, writ. *Informal:* blister, blue, bluey.

     2.   **1. litigant** alleger, appellant, complainant, libellant, maker, party, plaintiff, privy, suer, suitor. **2. accused** appellee, co-respondent, codefendant, defendant, libellee, remand, respondent. **3. witness** crown witness, defence witness, interested party. **4. process-server.**

adj. **3.**   **1. litigious** adversarial, adversary, litigant. **2. summonsed to appear** due in court, subpoenaed.

     4.   **1. actionable** appealable, committable, issuable, judicable, justiciable, litigable, reviewable, suable, triable.

v. **5.**   **1. litigate** bring an action against, bring to justice, bring to trial, file a suit against, go to law, interplead, proceed against, process, prosecute, pursue, put on trial, settle out of court, sue, take action, take to court. *Informal:* fit. **2. arraign** account to, accuse, cite, convene, court-martial, give in charge, impeach, impute, indict, name, plead, serve with a writ, subpoena, summon, summons. *Informal:* have up.

RELATED KEYWORDS: ACCUSATION, ACQUITTAL, COURT OF LAW, JUDGE, LAWYER, PUNISHMENT

LOAN

n. **1.**   **1. loan** accommodation, advance, imprest. *Informal:* boomerang, touch. **2. type of loan** bridging finance, defence service loan, low-doc loan, permanent loan, soft loan, terminating loan, war service loan. *Informal:* lo-doc loan, no-doc loan. **3. lease** agricultural holding, headlease, lease-back, let, leveraged lease, location, oyster lease, sublease, under-lease, wet lease. **4. rent** bond, bond money, dead rent, fair rent, farm, ground rent, hire, peppercorn rent, quit rent, rack-rent. *Informal:* Duke of Kent. **5. mortgage** encumbrance, equitable mortgage, first mortgage, home loan, incumbrance. *Informal:* monkey, poultice. **6. tenancy** lessee-ship, undertenancy. **7. charter** hire. **8. hire-purchase** credit foncier, h.p., never. *Informal:* the never-never. **9. usury** pawnbroking.

     2.   **1. borrower** debtor, mortgagor. **2. lessee** hirer, renter, sublessee, subtenant, tenant, under-lessee, under-lessor, undertenant. **3. leaser** underletter. **4. cadger** leech, parasite, scrounger, sponge, sponger, trencherman, vampire. *Informal:* bastard from the bush, bloodsucker, bludger, bot, ten-per-center.

     3.   **1. lender** advancer, creditor, discounter, loaner, moneylender, mortgagee. **2. lessor** host, landlady, landlord, rack-renter, sublessor, zamindar. **3. credit union** building society, permanent building society. **4. usurer** kulak, pawnbroker. *Informal:* Ikey Mo, loan shark, uncle. **5. pawnshop** mont-de-piété. *Informal:* hockshop *(US)*, Moscow, pop-shop.

adj. **4.**   **1. on loan** rented out. **2. pawned** in pawn. *Informal:* gone to (or in) Moscow, in hock.

v. **5.**   **1. lend** loan. *Informal:* spot. **2. rent** demise, farm, hire out, lease, lease out, let, release, rent out, sublease, sublet, underlet, wet-lease. **3. mortgage** bond. **4. fund** accommodate, finance, refinance, refund. **5. pawn** impawn, pledge. *Informal:* hock, Moscow, pop.

     6.   **1. borrow** charter, gear, hire, lease, rent. **2. cadge** beg, bite someone for, bite something off, blackleg. *Informal:* bludge, bludge on, bot, bum, fang, hum, panhandle *(US)*, put in the screws, put the acid on, put the bite on, put the fangs into, put the hooks into, put the nips into, scab, scrounge, scunge, snip, sting, touch.

RELATED KEYWORDS: FINANCE, INDEBTEDNESS, COMMERCE

LOGICALITY

n. **1.**   **1. logicality** cogency, coherence, equipollence, equipollency, legitimacy, legitimateness, logic, modality, rationalisation, rationality, reasonableness, syllogisation, unanswerableness, undeniability, validation, validity, validness. **2. sense** commonsense, enlightenment, pragmatism, reason.

     2.   **1. reasoning** argument, argumentation, assumption, consecution, debate, dialectic, dialogism, discursion, discursiveness, discussion, disputation, exercise, illation, philosophism, polemic, proof, ratiocination, rationale, reason, refinement, subtilisation, syllogism, synthesis. **2. logic** apologetics, Aristotelian logic, dialectics, formal logic, mathematical logic, methodology, polemics, propositional calculus, symbolic logic, syntax.

3. 1. logical argument abduction, analogy, antecedent, apagoge, argumentum ad hominem, argumentum ad rem, categorical syllogism, category, colligation, comprehension, conclusion, condition, connotation, consequent, contradiction, dilemma, disjunction, enthymeme, epagoge, figure, form, hypothesis, hypothetical syllogism, implication, law of contradiction, lemma, major premise, major term, middle term, minor premise, minor term, mode, mood, obverse, obversion, polysyllogism, predicament, premise, reason, sorites, species, subaltern, subcontrary, subsistence, substance, subsumption, superordinate, superordination, syllogism, synthesis, tautology, theorem, topic, undistributed middle, universal, universal class, universe, universe of discourse.

4. 1. logician analogist, arguer, debater, dialectician, philosophiser, polemicist, ratiocinator, reasoner, refiner, syllogiser, synthesist.

adj. **5. 1. logical** analytic, cogent, coherent, consequent, consequential, deductive, dianoetic, discursive, illative, inferential, legitimate, potent, ratiocinative, rational, reasonable, reasoned, sensible, sound, tenable, valid. **2. deducible** extractable, inferable.

v. **6. 1. reason** analogise, argue, chop logic, construe, contend, controvert, debate, discuss, dispute, infer, judge, ratiocinate, refine on, refine upon, subtilise, syllogise, thrash out. **2. deduce** conclude, derive, figure, gather, induce.

7. 1. stand to reason add up, cohere, make sense.

adv. **8. 1. logically** cogently, coherently, deductively, discursively, illatively, legitimately, rationally, reasonably, validly.

RELATED KEYWORDS: CLARITY, MEANING, SANITY, THINKING, TRUTH

LOSING

n. **1. 1. losing** loss, mislaying, misplacement. **2. loss** forfeit, forfeiture, penalty, sacrifice, write-off. **3. total loss** dead loss. **4. dispossession** bereavement, deprivation. **5. losses** casualties, death toll, fatalities. **6. wastage** drain, leakage.

adj. **2. 1. lost** mislaid, misplaced. **2. absent** disappeared, lacking, missing. **3. irrecoverable** cast, forfeited, irreclaimable, irredeemable. *Informal:* down the gurgler. **4. astray** disorientated, lost, off-track. *Informal:* bushed, bushwhacked, slewed. **5. dispossessed** bereft, deprived of.

v. **3. 1. lose possession of** lose, mislay, misplace. **2. forfeit** sink one's money. *Informal:* do one's dough, lose one's shirt. **3. be misplaced** be lost, disappear, go astray, go missing. *Informal:* go west.

4. 1. lose one's way get lost, stray off course, wander off course.

RELATED KEYWORDS: TAKING, MISPLACEMENT, REMOVAL, ROBBERY

LOUDNESS

n. **1. 1. loudness** audibleness, distinctness, volume. **2. crescendo** forte, intension, magnification, rise, swell. **3. noisiness** boisterousness, clamorousness, obstreperousness, riotousness, tumultuousness, unquietness, uproariousness, vociferousness.

2. 1. noise affray, babel, bedlam, blare, bluster, brawl, broil, call, carry-on, clamour, clangour, clatter, commotion, cry, din, disturbance, furore, fuss, hubbub, hue, hurly, hurly-burly, melee, outcry, pandemonium, pother, racket, roar, rout, screech, shindy, shivaree *(US)*, tempest, tumult, turbulence, turmoil, uproar. *Informal:* ballyhoo, ballyhooly, bovver *(British)*, brouhaha, bust-up, hoo-ha, hullabaloo, kafuffle, kerfuffle, rhubarb, rough-house, row, ruckus, rumpus, shemozzle, shindig, song and dance. **2. bang** blast, clap, clash, crash, explosion, report. **3. clang** beep, blare, clarion call, peal. **4. thunder** roar, roaring, roll, sonic boom, thunderclap, thunderpeal. **5. rattle** volley. **6. slurp** snore, snort, stridor. **7. shout** bellow, bray, hoot, scream, yell. **8. howl** shriek, ululation. **9. vociferance** vociferation. *Informal:* yammer, yap, yawp. **10. cachinnation** belly laugh. **11. noisy place** bear garden.

3. 1. siren air horn, alarm clock, beeper, bell, burglar alarm, curfew, foghorn, hooter, horn, klaxon, shark siren, tocsin, whistle. **2. bell** alarum, cowbell, death bell, passing bell, sacring bell, sanctuary bell, Sanctus bell, shark bell, sleighbell.

4. 1. noisy person blusterer, boyo, clamourer, loudmouth, noise maker, raver, roarer, roisterer, stentor, vociferant, vociferator, yammerer, yawper.

adj. **5. 1. loud** big, deafening, deep, forte, fortissimo, full, full-throated, heavy, loudish, obstropolous, plangent, resonant, rotund, sonorous, strong, voiceful. **2. audible** clear, distinct, evident, noticeable, obvious, plain, unmistakable. **3. crescendo** rising.

4. resounding echoing, reboant, resonant. **5. shrill** clarion, ear-piercing, ear-splitting, piercing, piping, pipy, strident, ululant. **6. powerful** deep-throated, stentorian. **7. vociferous** clamant, clamorous, loud, loudmouthed, open-mouthed, vociferant. **8. howling** roaring. **9. thunderous** clamorous, clangorous, fulminant, fulminatory, fulminous, strepitous, thundering, thundery.

6. **1. noisy** blusterous, boisterous, bouncing, clamorous, disorderly, hurly-burly, obstreperous, pandemonic, pell-mell, rackety, riotous, roaring, roisterous, rorty, rowdy, rumbustious, tumultuary, tumultuous, unquiet, uproarious. *Informal:* rambunctious *(US)*, rip-roaring.

v. **7.** **1. be loud** be enough to wake the dead, deafen, hoot. **2. be noisy** brawl, broil, clamour, crow, go hammer and tongs, racket, roister, shatter the silence. *Informal:* row. **3. shout** bawl, bellow, call, holler, hoot, noise, raise the roof, roar, scream, scream blue murder, yell. **4. vociferate** bluster, cry, give tongue, hawk, loudmouth, rave, shout down, speak up, stress, talk down. *Informal:* ballyhoo, yammer, yap. **5. bang** beat, boom, clang, clangour, crack, crash, fulminate, peal, pound, rumble, slam, thud, thump, thunder. **6. resound** pierce, rattle, resonate, ring, volley. **7. clang** bell, blare, bray, honk, hoot, peal, trumpet. **8. howl** caterwaul, hoot, shriek, skirl *(Chiefly Scottish)*, ululate, wail.

8. **1. louden** lift, raise. **2. rise** louden, swell.

adv. **9.** **1. loudly** deafeningly, loud, resonantly, sonorously. **2. aloud** audibly. **3. forte** crescendo, fortissimo, rinforzando. **4. noisily** clamorously, riotously, tumultuously, uproariously.

RELATED KEYWORDS: EXPLOSION, DISSONANCE, SHRILLNESS, SOUND

LOVE

n. **1.** **1. love** adoration, affection, after, attachment, devotion, fondness, love at first sight. **2. infatuation** calf love, dotage, puppy love. *Informal:* crush. **3. sexual love** desire, eros, eroticism, libido, lust, passion. **4. spiritual love** agape, caritas, charity, courtly love, love, platonic love, platonism. **5. representation of love** Cupid, Eros, Venus. **6. cupid statue** amoretto, amorino, cupid, putto.

2. **1. love affair** affair, affaire de coeur, amour, eternal triangle, flirtation, intrigue, involvement, liaison, romance. **2. date** assignation, tryst.

3. **1. lovingness** affectionateness, amorousness, lovesickness, passionateness, tenderness. **2. dearness** adorability.

4. **1. lover** admirer, adorer, beloved, captive, darling, doter, idoliser, light-o'-love, love, paramour, sweetheart, truelove, valentine. *Informal:* easy rider *(US)*, flame, steady. **2. lovebirds** couple, lovers, pair. **3. boyfriend** beau, cicisbeo, darling, inamorato, paramour, sleeping partner, spark, suitor, swain *(Chiefly Poetic, British)*, sweetheart. *Informal:* babester, boy, fellow, guy, man, squeeze. **4. girlfriend** dulcinea, hetaira, inamorata, ladylove, lass, nuba *(Aboriginal English)*, sultana, sweetheart. *Informal:* babe, bird, floozy, girl, missus, mole, moll, potato peeler, sheila, squeeze, tom-tart. **5. ladies' man** amorist, Casanova, Don Juan, gay Lothario, gigolo, Lothario, lover, rake, Romeo, roué, swain *(Chiefly Poetic)*. *Informal:* fancy man, lady-killer. **6. catamite** *Informal:* cat, punk, second-hand Sue. **7. mistress** chatelaine, concubine, courtesan, demimondaine, gun-moll, hetaera, kept woman, number two *(Philippine English)*, paramour. *Informal:* kulasisi *(Philippine English)*, moll, woman. **8. de facto** partner, tallywoman. *Informal:* tallyman. **9. ex** lost love, old flame. **10. love object** goddess, heart-throb, idol. *Informal:* dreamboat.

5. **1. terms of affection** chérie, chookie, cutie-pie *(Chiefly US)*, darl, darling, dear, deary, dovey *(British)*, duck *(British)*, ducky, honey, honey bee *(Aboriginal English)*, honey bun, honey bunch *(Chiefly US)*, honey pot, luv, luvvy, mavourneen, pet, possum, precious, snooks, snookums, sugar, sweet, sweetheart, sweetie, tootsy.

adj. **6.** **1. loving** adoring, affectionate, amatory, amoroso, devoted, fond, smoodgy, tender. **2. amorous** amatory, erotic, passionate, romantic, tender. **3. infatuated** at someone's feet, besotted, captivated, captive, doting, in love, lovelorn, lovesick, uxorious. *Informal:* gaga, gone, gone on, lovey-dovey, mad, shook on, smitten, spoony, struck on, stuck on, sweet on. **4. love-hate** ambivalent.

7. **1. beloved** cherished, darling, dear, honey, loved, precious, sweet, well-beloved. **2. favourite** blue-eyed, darling, fair-haired *(US)*, pet, special, white-haired, white-headed.

v. **8.** **1. love** be enamoured of, be smitten with, care for. *Informal:* be soft on someone, burn a candle for, carry a torch for. **2. fall in love with** adore, fall for, idolise, lose one's heart to. *Informal:* have got it bad for. **3. lust after** desire. *Informal:* do one's nuts over.

4. embrace bosom, caress, cuddle, embosom, enfold, fold, fondle, hug, nuzzle, press, snuggle, squeeze. *Informal:* raunch. **5. infatuate** besot, smite. **6. matchmake** play Cupid.

adv. **9. 1. lovingly** adoringly, affectionately, amoroso, con amore, dear, dearly, devotedly, fondly, tenderly. **2. amorously** passionately.

RELATED KEYWORDS: EMOTION, ROMANCE, FRIENDLINESS, HIGH REGARD, PLEASURE, SEX, MARRIAGE

LOW REGARD

n. **1. 1. low regard** disesteem, disregard, disrespect. **2. disdain** contempt, contumely, derision, disparagement, misprision, mockery, ridicule, scorn. **3. disrespectfulness** contemptuousness, contumeliousness, derisiveness, flippantness, impiety, impiousness, irreverence, superciliousness. **4. insolence** assurance, audacity, cheekiness, effrontery, gall, impertinence, impudence, presumption. *Informal:* cheek, chutzpah, crust, face, hide, nerve, sauce. **5. impoliteness** discourtesy, rudeness, unceremoniousness, uncivilness.

2. 1. disrespectful act or treatment affront, contumely, discourtesy, dishonour, humiliation, hurt, impertinence, impiety, impudence, indignity, insult, mock, mockery, putdown, revilement, slight, snub, spurn. *Informal:* a slap in the face, smack in the eye. **2. gibe** crack, dig, hit, jeer, joke, knock, mock, rub, scoff, sneer, taunt, witticism. **3. hiss** boo, Bronx cheer *(Chiefly US)*, catcall, slow handclap. *Informal:* bird, raspberry. **4. disrespectful gesture** air quotes, the finger, thumbs up, V-sign. **5. leer** giggle, nicker *(Scottish)*, smirk, sneer, snicker, snigger, teehee, titter.

3. 1. disgrace contempt, dishonour, humiliation, ignominy, mortification, put-down, shame.

4. 1. disdainer contemnor, despiser, scorner, sneerer, snubber, spurner. **2. dishonourer** profaner, violator. **3. insolent person** insolent, minx, missy. *Informal:* baggage.

adj. **5. 1. disdainful** cavalier, contemptuous, contumelious, scornful, sneering, supercilious. **2. derogatory** belittling, derogative, disparaging, slighting, snide. **3. pejorative** deprecatory, depreciative. **4. disrespectful** blasphemous, impious, irreligious, irreverent, profanatory, profane, sacrilegious. **5. flippant** airy, cavalier, offhand. *Informal:* cheeky, flip.

6. 1. insulting abusive, injurious, scurrile. **2. impolite** discourteous, familiar, rude, unceremonious, uncivil, uncourteous, unhandsome. **3. insolent** assumptive, audacious, bold, bold-faced, brash, brazen, brazen-faced, flash *(Aboriginal English)*, forward, fresh, impertinent, impudent, pert, precocious, presumptuous, saucy. *Informal:* brassy, sassy.

v. **7. 1. hold in low regard** belittle, depreciate, despise, disesteem, extenuate, misesteem, misprise, slight, underestimate, underrate, undervalue, vilipend. **2. disrespect** befoul, debase, defile, demean, desecrate, dishallow, disregard, flout, foul, make free with, pollute, profane, take liberties, violate. **3. despise** disdain, look down on, look down one's nose, look down one's nose at, scorn, sneer at, spurn.

8. 1. be scornful curl one's lip, snap one's fingers at, sniff at, turn one's nose up. *Informal:* give someone the glassy eye, give someone the greasy eyeball. **2. ridicule** deride, fleer, flout, gibe, gird at, heckle, jeer, jeer at, jest, jibe, laugh at, laugh out of court, make fun of, mock, monkey, needle, poke fun at, scoff, scorn, sledge, sport, taunt. *Informal:* burl, chiack, gig, guy, have a shot at, poke borak, poke mullock at, rag, rib, rubbish, slag, take the micky, twit. **3. insult** abuse, affront, blister, call names, put down, revile, slang, trample on. *Informal:* slag off. **4. snub** cut dead, give someone the cold shoulder, set down, slight, turn one's back on. *Informal:* give someone (or something) the go-by. **5. affront** disoblige, humiliate, mortify, offend. *Informal:* miff. **6. be rude** be lacking in courtesy, show disrespect. *Informal:* backchat, cheek, sauce. **7. snigger** gibe, laugh, leer, sneer, snort. **8. gesture rudely** cock a snoot at, look cross-eyed at, make a face at, poke out one's tongue at, thumb one's nose. *Informal:* give someone the finger.

adv. **9. 1. disrespectfully** contemptuously, derisively, disdainfully, disparagingly, insultingly, irreverently, scornfully. **2. insolently** boldly, familiarly, impertinently, impolitely, impudently, rudely.

RELATED KEYWORDS: DISAPPROVAL, SLANDER, HATE, MOCKERY, DISPLEASURE

LUCK

n. **1. 1. luck** accident, cess *(Irish)*, chance, destiny, fate, fortuity, fortune, karma, kismet, lot, plight, star. **2. fortuity** accident, act of God, coincidence, fluke, haphazard, happenstance, lucky dip, pot luck, stroke of fortune, the luck of the draw. **3. chance** break, half a chance, opportunity, pot shot. *Informal:* Buckley's. **4. good luck** Chinaman's luck, fortune, good fortune, the luck of the Irish. **5. a run of good luck** lucky streak.

Informal: a good trot. **6. bonanza** pianola, windfall. **7. bad luck** ambs-ace, doom, ill fortune, misadventure, mischance, misfortune, mozzle. *Informal:* hard lines. **8. a run of bad luck** *Informal:* a bad trot. **9. jinx** hex, jonah, mozzle. *Informal:* hoodoo, mozz, schlemiel *(US)*.

2. **1. luckiness** fortuitism, fortuitousness, fortuity, fortunateness, serendipity. **2. haphazardness** accidentalness, adventitiousness, arbitrariness, casualness, flukiness, hazardousness, indeterminateness, promiscuousness, ticklishness.

3. **1. lucky person** child of fortune. *Informal:* lucky dog, tin bum. **2. unlucky person** *Informal:* schlemiel *(US)*.

4. **1. lucky charm** birthstone, four-leaf clover, good luck charm, good omen, handsel, horseshoe, lucky stone, mascot, merrythought, rabbit's foot, talisman, wishbone.

adj. **5.** **1. lucky** fortunate, happy. *Informal:* tinny. **2. happy-go-lucky** adventurous, careless, devil-may-care, sporting. **3. providential** opportune. **4. chance** accidental, adventitious, aleatory, arbitrary, casual, chanceful, circumstantial, fortuitous, incidental, indeterminate, unmeant. *Informal:* scratch. **5. haphazard** arbitrary, coincidental, desultory, fluky, hit-and-miss, hit-or-miss, random.

6. **1. unlucky** crossed, down on one's luck, hapless, ill-fated, ill-starred, luckless, out of luck, sinistrous, star-crossed, starred, unfortunate, unhappy. *Informal:* stiff.

v. **7.** **1. take a chance** be in the running, chance, chance one's arm, do on the off-chance, gamble, push one's luck, risk, run a risk, sail close to the wind, take a pot shot, venture. *Informal:* give it a buck, give it a go, give it a whirl, have a crack at, have a go, have a smack at, take (or have) a punt. **2. be lucky** be born under a lucky star, be one's lucky day, fall on one's feet, hit the jackpot, land on one's feet, live a charmed life, strike it lucky. *Informal:* be on a roll, have all one's Christmases come at once, luck out. **3. be unlucky** be jinxed, be jonahed. *Informal:* have killed a Chinaman. **4. jinx** hex, jonah, put the mozz on someone. *Informal:* hoodoo, mozz, put the mocker(s) on.

8. **1. chance on** fluke, happen on (or upon), hit on, light on (or upon), stumble on. **2. happen** bechance, chance, fall to one's lot.

adv. **9.** **1. by chance** accidentally, adventitiously, arbitrarily, at a venture, at hazard, bechance, casually, coincidentally, desultorily, haphazard, haphazardly, happy-go-lucky, unexpectedly, without rhyme or reason. *Informal:* happen *(British)*. **2. whatever happens** in any event. **3. luckily** fortuitously, fortunately, providentially. **4. unluckily** haplessly, sadly, unfortunately, unhappily.

RELATED KEYWORDS: GAMBLING, GOOD FORTUNE, MISFORTUNE, INEVITABILITY

MACHINE

n. **1.** **1. machine** apparatus, appliance, contraption, contrivance, device, engine, equipment, machinery, mechanical device, mechanism, rig, unit. **2. mechanism** action, appurtenances, assembly, clockwork, movement, parts, rig, subassembly, works. **3. motor** motor drive, prime mover, servomechanism, servomotor. **4. plant** assembly line, enginery, equipment, machinery, tooling. **5. simple machine** inclined plane, sand wedge, screw, wedge, wheel and axle. **6. lever** crow, crowbar, handspike, jemmy, jimmy *(US)*, pinch, pinch-bar, sweep, swipe, throttle lever. **7. winch** block and tackle, breech, burton, capstan, cat, cheek, coffee grinder, coffee-grinder winch, crab, davit, deadeye, differential windlass, garnet, grinder, halliard, halyard, headgear, jeers, luff tackle, parbuckle, pulley, sheave, sheave-block, snatch block, truckle, wharve, whim, whip, winder, windlass. **8. waterwheel** water-motor, watermill, windmill, windpump. **9. automaton** aerobot, android, automatic, golem, humanoid, robot. *Informal:* auto.

2. **1. tool** artefact, artifact, implement, instrument, utensil. **2. gadget** appliance, contraption, contrivance, device. *Informal:* gismo, gizmo, widget.

3. **1. engine** air turbine, compressed air motor, compressor, diesel, diesel engine, diesel-electric engine, donkey engine, four-stroke, gas engine, heat engine, inboard, inboard motor, internal-combustion engine, multicylinder engine, orbital engine, outboard motor, overhead valve engine, radial engine, reciprocating engine, rotary engine, sarich engine, Sarich orbital engine, side-valve engine, stationary engine, steam engine, traction engine, traction motor, two-cycle engine *(US)*, two-stroke, v8, Wankel engine, wankel engine. *Informal:* donk. **2. reaction engine** air turbine, air-breathing, athodyd, gas turbine, impulse turbine, ion engine, jet engine, pulse-jet, ramjet, reaction turbine, rocket engine, steam turbine, turbine. **3. motor** dynamotor, electric motor, electromotor, induction motor, squirrel-cage motor, synchronous motor, telemotor, thermomotor, universal motor, water motor.

4. **1. machine part** arbor, axle, beam, cam, camshaft, connecting rod, crank, crosshead, crown wheel, detent, dial, escapement, feed, finger, fixture, flywheel, gate, jigger, mandrel, overhead camshaft, pawl, piston, quadrant, ratch, ratchet, ratchet wheel, small end, spline, tappet, tongue, traveller, universal joint, valve gear, wicket, yoke.

5. **1. transmission**   automatic transmission, clutch, column shift, crash gearbox, differential, drive, drive shaft, driver, driving wheel, fluid drive, gearbox, gearing, gearstick, gut, hydraulic torque converter, low, preselector, propeller shaft, reverse, selective transmission, shift, synchromesh, tail shaft, torque converter, trace. *Informal:* diff, diffy *(NZ)*, four-on-the-floor, slush box, three-on-the-tree.

6. **1. gear**   bevel gear, chain gear, chain-gear, cog, cogwheel, derailleur, differential, differential gear, double helical gear, epicyclic gear (train), escape wheel, escapement, face gear, fly, flywheel, gearwheel, gipsy, helical gear, herringbone gear, idler, idler pulley, idler wheel, lantern pinion, mitre wheel, pinion, rack and pinion, scapewheel, spur gear, trundle, tumbler, tumbler gear, wheelwork, worm gear, worm wheel.

7. **1. earth-moving machinery**   backhoe, bobcat, bucket conveyor (excavator), bulldozer, calfdozer, caterpillar, continuous miner, crawler, dipper, doze, dozer, dragline, dredge, dredger, dredging machine, drott, earthmover, front-end loader, grader, landplane, load, loader, longwall miner, road plant, road-roller, scraper, shovel, steam-shovel, steamroller, tractor shovel, water ouzel.

8. **1. mill**   ball mill, colloid mill, cone crusher, gristmill, gyratory crusher, hammer mill, jaw crusher, muller, pin mill, rod mill, roller, stamping mill, steamroller. **2. strip mill**   bloom mill, rolling mill, slab mill.

9. **1. materials handling equipment**   auger, belt, borer, conveyor (belt), conveyor belt, dumb waiter, elevator, fork hoist *(NZ)*, fork lift (hoist), forklift, goods lift, grain elevator, hoist, ladder lift, lift, noria, pallet, palletiser, post-hole digger, screw, service lift.

10. **1. agricultural implement**   aerator, binder, boom spray, buck rake, canecutter, chain harrow, chain-harrow, chisel-plough, colter, combine, combine harvester, coulter, cradle, cultivator, dead stock, disc harrow, drag, drill, dump rake, fanning mill *(US)*, flail, fodder roller, gang cultivator, gang plough, grub hoe, harrow, harvester, hayfork, header harvester, hoe, hop-picker, hopper, mallee roller, milking machine, moldboard *(US)*, mouldboard, pick-up baler, pitchfork, planter, plough, plow *(Chiefly US)*, rotary hoe, rotary plough, scrub roller, seed drill, seeder, self-binder, side delivery rake, sod-seeder, sodseeder, stock, stump-jump plough, tedder, threshing machine, winnowing machine. *Informal:* header.

11. **1. garden tool**   bill, billhook, broom, cangkul, dibbler, edger, fork, grass-catcher, grass-clipper, grubber, hose, lawn-mower, mattock, mower, pick, pickaxe, pooper scooper, pruning hook, pruning knife, pruning shears, rake, scuffle *(US)*, scythe, secateurs, shovel, sickle, sit-on mower, spade, sprinkler, spud, trowel, watering-can. *Informal:* banjo.

12. **1. bearing**   ball-bearing, bowl, needle-bearing, roller-bearing, slipper bearing, thrust-bearing.

13. **1. building tool**   auger, axe, ballpein hammer, bevel, bevel square, bit, bitstock, bolt-cutter, brace, brace and bit, bradawl, buzz-saw, centre-bit, circular saw, clamp, docking saw, dog, Douglas, dresser, drill, drill press, drill string, file, findings, framesaw, gigue, hacksaw, hammer, handsaw, impact driver, jig, mallet, multigrips, nail punch, nail set, nippers, Phillips screwdriver, pincers, plane, planer saw, pliers, power drill, ripsaw, saw, screwdriver, swage, vice, wire-cutter.

14. **1. spanner**   allen key, box spanner, crescent spanner, hex key, monkey-wrench, pipe wrench, shifter, shifting spanner, Stillson wrench, twist, wrest.

15. **1. technical drawing equipment**   arcograph, bow compass, bow pen, curve, cyclograph, dividers, french curve, French curve, geometry set, pen, pencil, radioactive tracer, railway curve, square, straightedge, t square, tracer, trammel.

16. **1. artist's equipment**   aerograph, aerogun, airbrush, brush, mahlstick, maulstick, pallet, roller, spray-gun.

17. **1. office machinery and gadgets**   computer, dictaphone, fax, fax machine, hole punch, photocopier, shredder, staple remover, stapling machine, typewriter.

18. **1. household appliance**   agitator, answerphone, breadmaker, carpet-sweeper, dishwasher, drier, dryer, floor polisher, garbage disposal unit, hair dryer, hoover, knitting machine, rice cooker, sewing machine, telephone answering machine, top-loader, vacuum, vacuum cleaner, washing machine.

19. **1. kitchen gadget**   beater, blender, can-opener, cookware, corer, corkscrew, egg beater, egglifter, eggslice, eggwhisk, fishslice, food processor, grater, grinder, juicer, ladle, liquidiser, mandolin, melon baller, mincer, mixer, mortar and pestle, nutcrackers, opener, peeler, pepper-mill, pop-up toaster, potato masher, potato peeler, pothook, ricer, rolling pin, rotary beater, salad servers, scoop, sieve, sifter, slice, spider, steel, tin-opener, toaster, toasting fork, trivet, vitamiser, whisk.

20. **1. cutlery** apostle spoon, breadknife, butterknife, canteen, carver, carving knife, case-knife, chopsticks, coffee spoon, corer, dessertspoon, dinner service, dinner set, dover, eggspoon, fish knife, flatware *(Chiefly US, Canadian)*, fondue fork, fork, French knife, fruit knife, gold plate, knife, pair of carvers, parfait spoon, runcible spoon, server, service, silver, silver plate, silverware, soup-spoon, splayd, spoon, spork, tablespoon, tableware, teaspoon, wooden spoon. *Informal:* eating irons.

21. **1. stone age tool** burin, celt, elouera, eolith, grattoir, leilira, neolith, palaeolith, pirri point, tula-adze flake, turtleback.

22. **1. mechanisation** automation, automatism, industrialisation, motorisation, robotism.

adj. 23. **1. mechanical** mechanistic, motor, motored, powered. **2. robotic** bionic, robotistic. **3. automatic** autokinetic, mechanical, self-acting, self-adjusting, self-moving, self-regulating, semiautomatic, servo-assisted, servomechanical.

v. 24. **1. mechanise** automate, motorise. **2. tool up** gear up.

RELATED KEYWORDS: CONTROLLING DEVICE, CUT, FACTORY

MAGIC

n. 1. **1. magic** alchemy, bewitchery, bewitchment, conjuration, devilry, enchantment, glamourie *(Poetic)*, incantation, sorcery, sortilege, the black art, witchcraft, witchery, witching, wizardry. **2. type of magic** black art, black magic, diablerie, diabolism, fetishism, goditcha magic, hoodoo, incantation, kadaicha magic, kadaitja magic, kurdaitcha magic, necromancy, obi, santeria, sciomancy, sympathetic magic, thaumaturgy, theurgy, voodoo, voodooism, white magic. **3. prestidigitation** conjuring, legerdemain, magic, pass, sleight of hand.

2. **1. magic spell** hex, spell. *Informal:* mozz. **2. incantation** abracadabra, charm, conjuration, enchantment, invocation, mumbo jumbo. **3. magic trick** hocus-pocus, hokey-pokey. **4. charm** amulet, fetish, grigri, juju, obeah, obi, palladium, periapt, talisman, voodoo. *Informal:* mojo *(Chiefly US)*. **5. magical paraphernalia** Aladdin's lamp, black cat, broomstick, kadaitja shoes, kurdaitcha shoes, magic carpet, philosopher's stone, wand, witch's cauldron, witch's hat. **6. magic potion** philtre, potion. **7. crystal ball. 8. pentagram** magic circle, magic square.

3. **1. bewitcher** black witch, carline *(Chiefly Scottish)*, charmer, diviner, enchanter, enchantress, hag, hellcat, illusionist, magician, magus, pythoness, shaman, sibyl, sorcerer, sorceress, warlock, white witch, witch, wizard. **2. alchemist. 3. witchdoctor** bone-pointer, fetishist, gulli-gulli man, kadaicha man, koradji, medicine man, sorcerer, voodooist. **4. conjurer** enchanter, illusionist, magician, prestidigitator. **5. esbat** coven.

adj. 4. **1. magic** magical, mystic, sorcerous, theurgic, theurgical, witching, wizard, wizardly. **2. alchemical** alchemic, alchemistic, alchemistical. **3. voodooistic** fetishistic, talismanic.

5. **1. bewitched** enchanted, entranced, fascinated, fey, hypnotised, mesmerised, spellbound, under a spell.

v. 6. **1. bewitch** becharm, charm, enchant, ensorcell *(Poetic)*, hypnotise, mesmerise, spellbind, witch. **2. cast a spell on** bedevil, bewitch, charm, conjure, curse, ensorcell *(Poetic)*, execrate, hex, jinx, overlook, transmogrify, voodoo, witch. *Informal:* mozz, point the bone at, put the maginnis on someone, put the mozz on someone.

RELATED KEYWORDS: THE SUPERNATURAL

MAN

n. 1. **1. man** agnate, brave, he, male, the man of the house. *Informal:* boy. **2. mankind** menfolk. **3. bloke** *(Informal)* a real man, chap, hombre *(Chiefly US)*, jack, man of the world, olmen *(Aboriginal English)*, spark, tomcat, wallah *(Indian English)*, wild colonial boy. *Informal:* bastard, buck, bugger, chappie, codger, coot, cove, dog, feller, fellow, geezer, guy, Joe *(US)*, johnny, joker, old man, scout, skate *(US)*. **4. gentleman** cavalier, chevalier, rye, señor, squire. *Informal:* gent. **5. husband** lord and master. *Informal:* hubby, old man. **6. boy** colt, cub, gossoon *(Irish)*, hobbledehoy, jackanapes, lad, laddie *(Chiefly Scottish)*, pup, puppy, spalpeen, sprig, stripling, urchin, weei, whelp, youngster, youth. *Informal:* bucko, nipper, shaver. **7. sissy** *(Informal)* asthenic, cissy, coward, cowardly custard, craven, dingo, eunuch, lily, Little Lord Fauntleroy, milksop, paper tiger, poltroon, poove, recreant, sheep, squib, weakling, wimp. *Informal:* a nervous Nellie, aunty, cat, chicken, cream puff, creamer, cry-baby, fraidy-cat, gussie, gutless wonder, nancy boy, old woman, pansy, ponce, poofter, quiche-eater, ringtail, scaredy-cat, sis, softie, sook, sop, weakie, yellow-belly. **8. he-man** *(Informal)* alf, behemoth, boor, bronzed Aussie, bull, churl, clown, giant, goliath, iron man, jock, lion, lout, macho, macho man, male chauvinist, Neanderthal, stalwart, strongman, superman, urban cowboy.

Informal: apeman, bruiser, butch, caveman, gangster *(NZ)*, husky *(US)*, lager lout *(British)*, male chauvinist pig, MCP, muscle man, ocker, rugger-bugger, strapper, yobbo. **9. buck** blade, blood, stag, stud. *Informal:* bodgie, lair, lout, son of a gun *(Chiefly US)*, teddy bear. **10. pretty boy** adonis, beau, dandy, fop, hunk. *Informal:* a good sort. **11. metrosexual** rural sexual, ubersexual. **12. homosexual** camp, catamite, effeminate, fascine, gay, paederast, queer. *Informal:* fairy, homo, pansy, poof, poofter, poonce, queen.

  2. **1. manliness** animus, gentlemanliness, lingam, machismo, maleness, manhood, mannishness, masculineness, masculinity, unfeminineness. **2. virility** manhood, manly vigour, potency, virileness. **3. male chauvinism** male supremacy, masculism, paternalism. **4. boyishness** coltishness.

adj. **3.** **1. male** buck, he, yang. **2. masculine** brave, full-blooded, hot-blooded, macho, manful, manlike, manly, mannish, potent, red-blooded, virile. **3. bull** buck, stag. *Informal:* hunky. **4. gentlemanly** chivalrous. **5. boyish** coltish. **6. effeminate** anile, emasculate, feminine, petticoat, poncy, sawney, sorney, unmanly, womanish, womanlike. *Informal:* pooncey, trissy. **7. homosexual** camp, gay, high-camp, queer.

adv. **4.** **1. masculinely** mannishly. **2. boyishly** coltishly.

RELATED KEYWORDS: OFFSPRING, RELATIVE, REPRODUCTION, SEX, MARRIAGE

MANAGEMENT

n. **1.** **1. management** administration, agency, direction, dispensation, economy, government, organisation, polity, regulation. *Informal:* admin. **2. type of management** crisis management, economic management, environmental management, financial management, flattened management, knowledge management, risk management, waste management. **3. supervision** conduct, deportment, directing, direction, handling, intendance, intendancy, management, managing, oversight, running, superintendence, superintendency, surveillance. **4. managership** chairmanship, chairpersonship, commission, management, superintendentship, supervisorship. **5. housekeeping** economy, frugality, housewifery, husbandry, ménage, thrift. **6. bureaucracy** apparatus, board, body corporate, bureau, directorate, owners' corporation *(NSW)*, umbrella organisation. **7. officialdom** administrivia, bureaucracy, officialism, overmanagement, red tape, regulations.

adj. **2.** **1. managerial** administrative, bureaucratic, directorial, dispensational, entrepreneurial, executive, governmental, hegemonic, organisational, superintendent, supervisory, surveillant.

v. **3.** **1. manage** administer, administrate, be in charge of, carry on, conduct, control, direct, handle, keep in order, make out, monitor, overlook, oversee, oversight, police, regulate, run, see to, steward, superintend, supervise. **2. control** be in the chair, command, dominate, govern, guide, head, head a team, induce, influence, instruct, lead, pilot, preside over, steer, take over, take the reins. **3. domineer** boss, boss it over. **4. sweat** drive. **5. organise** get up, mastermind, package. **6. manage one's resources** economise, husband, retrench.

adv. **4.** **1. managerially** administratively, bureaucratically, executively, governmentally.

RELATED KEYWORDS: AUTHORITY, COMMAND, GOVERNMENT, MANAGER, POLITICS

MANAGER

n. **1.** **1. manager** administrator, administratrix, adminstratrix, agent, bureaucrat, burgrave, captain, chief, commissar, commissary, commissioner, comptroller, controller, curator, director, director-general, directress, directrix, dispensator, engineer, entrepreneur, eparch, executive, executor, functionary, governor, governor-general, grand master, head, inspector, inspector-general, intendant, leader, legislator, manageress, mandarin, marshal, master, monitor, office-bearer, official, overseer, padrone *(US)*, palatine, president, principal, proconsul, procurator, receiver, satrap, secretary-general, shipmaster, slavedriver, stadtholder, state governor, super, superintendent, supervisor, surveillant, taskmaster, taskmistress. *Informal:* commish. **2. boss** baas *(South African)*, boss man *(Aboriginal English)*, boss of the board, boss woman *(Aboriginal English)*, bossboy, bwana, curator, employer, foreperson, ganger, maluka, manager, number one, serang, shed boss, sherang, skipper, slavedriver, straw boss *(Chiefly US)*, sweater. *Informal:* bloke, boss cocky, chief, gaffer *(Chiefly British)*, governor, head serang, joss, pannikin boss, the man, top banana, two-bob boss. **3. overseer** charge hand, chief, forelady, foreman, foreperson, forewoman, grass captain, headman, leader, marshal, overlooker, sardar, superintendent, supervisor, surveyor. *Informal:* cove. **4. official** agent, dignitary, functionary, mace, representative, vizier. *Informal:* silvertail. **5. head of household** chatelaine, lady, lord, master, matriarch, mistress, padrone *(US)*, patriarch. *Informal:* missis, missus. **6. housekeeper** bailiff, butler, castellan, cellarman, chamberlain, chatelaine, factor, housewife, maître d', maître d'hôtel, major-domo, manciple, matron, reeve, seneschal, sewer, steward. **7. hotelier** hostess, innkeeper, motelier, padrone *(US)*, publican, restaurateur. **8. ranger** park ranger.

2. 1. leader captain, chief. **2. mastermind** éminence grise, brains, father, power behind the throne. *Informal:* wheeler-dealer. **3. leading light** cock, leader, prime mover, protagonist, ringleader, ruling spirit. *Informal:* top dog. **4. chairperson** chair, chairman, chairwoman, master of ceremonies, moderator, prolocutor, symposiarch, toastmaster, toastmistress, whip. **5. principal** chancellor *(US)*, dean, headmaster, headmistress, provost, rector, rectorate, regent, scholarch, vice-chancellor, warden. **6. orchestra leader** bandmaster, capellmeister, choirmaster, concertmaster, conductor, coryphaeus, first violin, Kapellmeister, leader, maestro. **7. guide** cockswain, cox, coxswain, driver, helmsman, leader, pilot, steersman, wheelman *(US)*. **8. standard-bearer** cheerleader, ensign. **9. pioneer** pathfinder, scout, trailblazer. **10. bellwether** judas goat, judas sheep. **11. scout leader** akela, brown owl, group leader, guider, scouter, scoutmaster, tawny owl, troop leader.

RELATED KEYWORDS: POLITICIAN, RULER

MANY

n. **1. 1. many** a good few, a good many, a great many, a heap, a respectable number, cumulation, loads, lot, lots, magnitude, mass, myriad, pile, quite a few, size, some few, stacks, tons. *Informal:* a big mob, a hatful, more than one can poke a stick at, more than one can shake a stick at. **2. crowd** army, array, battalion, bevy, cloud, confluence, crew, crush, droves, fleet, flock, forest, gathering, herd, hive, horde, host, legion, mob, multiplicity, multitude, press, rabble, ruck, shoal, swarm, throng, tribe, troop. *Informal:* power. **3. large numbers** billions, dozens, hundreds, millions, quintillions, scores, thousands, zillions.

2. 1. numerousness infinity, innumerability, innumerableness, multiplicity, pluralism, plurality. **2. abundance** a lot, affluence, ampleness, amplitude, copiousness, cornucopia, flood, horn of plenty, milk and honey, mountain, much, opulence, overabundance, plenitude, plenteousness, plentifulness, plenty, profligacy, profusion, store, wealth. *Informal:* heap, lashings. **3. multitudinousness** manifoldness, many-sidedness, multifariousness.

adj. **3. 1. many** any number of, considerable, countless, divers, immeasurable, immense, immensurable, incalculable, incomputable, inestimable, infinite, innumerable, limitless, manifold, measureless, much, multiple, multiplex, multiplicate, myriad, numberless, plural, rife, several, substantial, sundry, umpteen, uncounted, unfathomable, unmeasured, unnumbered, untold, various, without number. *Informal:* biggest mobs of. **2. multifarious** all-round, manifold, many-sided, multilateral, multiplex, multiplicate. **3. abounding** abundant, abundant in, affluent, ample, aplenty, bounteous, bountiful, copious, exuberant, fat, fruitful, galore, handsome, luxuriant, opulent, plenteous, plentiful, profuse, prolific, rich, rife, superabound in (or with), superabundant, thick, thick on the ground, wealthy. **4. teeming** abounding with, aswarm, big, crowded, legion, multitudinous *(Poetic)*, packed, populous, swarming, thick with, thronged, wall to wall with *(Colloquial)*. *Informal:* alive with, crawling with, stiff with.

v. **4. 1. abound** crowd, deluge, flock, formicate, mass, overcrowd, overrun, pack, press, serry, shoal, stuff, swarm, teem, throng, troop. **2. oversupply** congest, deluge, drown, fill, flood, glut the market, load, overman, overpack, overwhelm, plaster, snow under, swamp. **3. increase in number** mount, multiply, proliferate.

adv. **5. 1. abundantly** affluently, amply, copiously, innumerably, multitudinously, numerously, plenteously, plentifully, sufficiently, thickly. **2. manyfold** manifoldly, variously.

RELATED KEYWORDS: FREQUENCY, GATHERING, INFINITY, EXCESS, NUMBER, FIVE AND OVER

MARINER

n. **1. 1. mariner** bluejacket, jack, matelot, navigator, raftsman, sailor, seafarer, shellback, shipmate, submariner. *Informal:* boatie, Jack Tar *(British)*, salt, sea-dog, tar. **2. ship's crew** company, complement, crew, ship. **3. navy** mercantile marine, merchant marine, merchant navy, senior service. **4. yachtsman** sailboarder, sailor, windsurfer, yachtswoman, yachty. *Informal:* rock-hopper, yottie. **5. windjammer** reefer, sheethand. **6. ferryman** bargee, boatman, bumboatman, gondolier, lighterman, wherryman. **7. oarsman** bow, bow oar, bowhand, bowman, canoeist, galley slave, oar, paddler, rower, sculler, stroke, waterman. **8. rowing crew** bank, eight, four.

2. 1. seaman able seaman, able-bodied seaman, artisan, bluejacket, bunting tosser, deckhand, lower deck, marine, ordinary seaman, rating, topman. *Informal:* deckie, leatherneck *(US)*, limey. **2. ship's officer** admiral, air commodore, captain, commander, commodore, coxswain, deck officer, engine-room artificer, engineer officer, ensign *(US Navy)*, first officer, flag captain, flag officer, lieutenant, lieutenant commander, master, master mariner, mister, officer of the watch, privateer, rear admiral, sea-captain, second mate, shipmaster, skipper, sublieutenant, vice-admiral, wardroom. *Informal:* number one. **3. petty officer** bo's'n, boatswain, bosun, master-at-arms, steward *(US Navy)*, yeoman. *Informal:* jaunty. **4. steersman** cockswain, cox, coxswain, helmsman, leadsman, navigator, pilot, wheelman *(US)*. **5. midshipman** *Informal:* middy, snotty. **6. cabin boy** midshipman, powder monkey. **7. purser** supercargo.

3. 1. pirate buccaneer, corsair, freebooter, picaroon, sea robber, sea rover, sea-robber, searover, Viking.

RELATED KEYWORDS: SEA, LAKE, TRANSPORT, TRAVEL, VEHICLE, WATERCRAFT

MARRIAGE

n. **1. 1. marriage** conjugal bliss, conjugality, connubiality, matrimony, nuptials, unitedness, wedded bliss, wedlock. **2. wifehood** matronage, wifedom, wifeliness. **3. match** alliance, union. **4. mismatch** mésalliance, misalliance, mismarriage. **5. type of marriage** endogamy, exogamy, group marriage, levirate, mariage blanc, sororate, white marriage. **6. arranged marriage** mariage de convenance, marriage of convenience, morganatic marriage. **7. de facto marriage** cohabitation, common-law marriage, companionate marriage, concubinage, living in sin, trial marriage. **8. mixed marriage** intermarriage, miscegenation. **9. remarriage** deuterogamy. **10. love match. 11. bigamy** digamy, monandry, monogamy, monogyny, polyandry, polygamy, polygyny.

2. 1. wedding bridal, espousal, marriage, nuptials, spousals. **2. church wedding** civil marriage, double wedding, elopement, shotgun wedding, white wedding. **3. marriage rites** covenant marriage *(US)*, nuptial mass, solemnisation, tea ceremony, wedding service. **4. marriage celebrant** celebrant, solemniser, uniter. **5. bridal party** best man, bridesmaid, flower girl, groomsman, maid of honour, matron of honour, pageboy, paranymph, trainbearer, wedding party. **6. banns** lines, marriage certificate. **7. reception** wedding breakfast. **8. bucks party** hens' night, stag night, stag party. **9. wedding march** charivari, epithalamion, epithalamium, hymeneal, nuptial song, prothalamion, wedding song. **10. honeymoon. 11. proposal** motion, offer, proffer. **12. engagement** affiance, betrothal, contract, precontract. **13. hand** promise. **14. dowry** bride price, dot, dower, marriage portion, marriage settlement, portion. **15. matchmaker** go-between, marriage broker.

3. 1. betrothed affianced, bride-to-be, fiancé, fiancée, intended.

4. 1. spouse affinity, better half, companion, consort, designated spouse equivalent, helpmate, match, mate, nuba, partner, yokefellow. *Informal:* significant other. **2. wife** concubine, feme, feme covert, feme sole, first lady, lady, maharani, mail-order bride, queen, queen consort. *Informal:* little woman, missis, missus, old Dutch, old girl *(Chiefly British)*, old lady, old woman, rib, the little woman, the old ball and chain, trouble and strife, woman. **3. husband** lord, lord and master, man, the lord of the manor. *Informal:* his lordship, hubby, old boy *(Chiefly British)*, old fellow, old man. **4. newlywed** benedick, blushing bride, eloper, honeymooner, war bride. **5. de facto** concubine, courtesan, de facto husband, de facto wife, demimondaine, hetaera, kept woman, mistress, number two *(Philippine English)*, paramour. *Informal:* gun-moll, kulasisi *(Philippine English)*, moll. **6. marrier** bigamist, deuterogamist, monogamist, polygamist. **7. couple** couplet, husband and wife, man and wife, pair. *Informal:* Darby and Joan. **8. bridal pair** bride, bridegroom, groom.

5. 1. marriageability eligibility, marriageableness, nubility.

adj. **6. 1. marital** concubinary, conjugal, connubial, matrimonial, nuptial, spousal. **2. premarital. 3. nuptial** bridal, epithalamic, hymeneal, matrimonial, postnuptial, spousal. **4. wifely** matronly, uxorial. **5. bigamous** digamous, endogamous, exogamic, exogamous, leviratic, leviratical, monandrous, monogamistic, monogamous, polyandrous, polygamous, polygynous.

7. 1. married married up, one, united, wedded. *Informal:* hitched, hooked, spliced. **2. engaged** betrothed.

v. **8. 1. marry** espouse, make an honest woman of, make someone an honest woman, mate, take to wife, wed. **2. get married** become one, settle down. *Informal:* go off. **3. elope** run away. *Informal:* flit. **4. pair off** ally with, cohabit, match, mate. *Informal:* set up housekeeping. **5. intermarry** miscegenate. **6. remarry** commit bigamy.

7. **propose** offer. *Informal:* pop the question. 8. **betroth** affiance, contract matrimony, engage, lead to the altar, offer, plight, precontract, promise, win. *Informal:* hook. 9. **join in marriage** consolidate, couple, declare man and wife, hitch, intermarry, join, marry, merge, splice, unite, wed. *Informal:* tie the knot. 10. **give in marriage** give away, marry off.

adv.   9.   1. **maritally** conjugally, connubially, matrimonially. 2. **bigamously** polygamously.

RELATED KEYWORDS: COMPANIONSHIP, ROMANCE, LOVE, RELATIVE

MATTER

n.   1.   1. **matter** antimatter, material, stuff, substance. 2. **grain** crystal, granule, micron, mikron, particle, sand, seed crystal. 3. **thing** anything, article, matter, object, phenomenon, something. *Informal:* do-hickey *(Chiefly US)*, doodackie *(NZ)*, doodad, doodah, doofer, doohickie, doover, dooverlackie, thingo, thingummybob, thingummyjig, whosiewhatsit, wigwam for a goose's bridle. 4. **mass** block, body, concrete. 5. **material world** cosmos, creation, macrocosm, nature, plenum, universe, world.

2.   1. **materialisation** being, corporeity, embodiment, existence, materiality, precipitation. 2. **tangibility** concreteness, corporality, corporeality, corporealness, earthliness, fleshliness, materialness, naturalness, palpability, substantiality, substantiation.

3.   1. **chemical element** actinide, actinon, allotrope, cerium metals, dyad, element, halogen, isotope, metal, non-metal, radioelement, rare-earth elements, terbium metals, transition element, transuranic element. 2. **atom** monas, nucleide, nuclide. 3. **chemical compound** binary compound, clathrate compound, earth, epimer, gas hydrate, isomer, saccharate, salt, tautomer. 4. **isomerism** cis-trans isomerism, dimorphism, enantiomorphism, enantiotropy, epimerisation, geometric isomerism, isotopy, racemism, tautomerism.

4.   1. **chemical agent** activator, agent, anticatalyst, biocatalyst, carrier, catalyst, inhibitor, metabolite, negative catalyst, precursor, promoter, reactant, reagent, sequestrating agent. 2. **chemical component** fraction, reaction product. 3. **oxidant** oxidiser, oxidising agent, oxygenation. 4. **deoxidiser** reducing agent. 5. **precipitate** condensate, flocculent precipitate, sediment, settlings, solute, sublimate. 6. **crystal** anisometric, dimorph, tree, trimorph. 7. **solution** colloidal solution, saturated solution, sol, spirit. 8. **chemical reaction** biosynthesis, degradation, double decomposition, metathesis, nucleosynthesis, synthesis. 9. **valency** bivalency, covalency, quadrivalency, trivalency, valence *(Chiefly US)*.

5.   1. **chemistry** alchemy, analysis, biochemistry, biophysics, chemurgy, electrochemistry, enzymology, gravimetry, inorganic chemistry, magneto-chemistry, microchemistry, molecular biology, organic chemistry, oxidimetry, photochemistry, physical chemistry, stereochemistry, stoechiometry, stoichiometry, surface chemistry, thermochemistry, topochemistry, zymurgy.

6.   1. **physics** astrophysics, classical physics, helioseismology, macrophysics, natural philosophy, physical science, quantum electrodynamics, quantum mechanics.

7.   1. **the elements** 1. hydrogen (h), 10. neon (ne), 100. fermium (fm), 101. mendelevium (md), 102. nobelium (no), 103. lawrencium (lw), 104. rutherfordium (rf), 105. hahnium (ha), 11. sodium (na - natrium), 12. magnesium (mg), 13. aluminium (al), 14. silicon (si), 15. phosphorus (p), 16. sulfur (s), 17. chlorine (cl), 18. argon (ar), 19. potassium (k - kalium), 2. helium (he), 20. calcium (ca), 21. scandium (sc), 22. titanium (ti), 23. vanadium (v), 24. chromium (cr), 25. manganese (mn), 26. iron (fe - ferrum), 27. cobalt (co), 28. nickel (ni), 29. copper (cu - cuprum), 3. lithium (li), 30. zinc (zn), 31. gallium (ga), 32. germanium (ge), 33. arsenic (as), 34. selenium (se), 35. bromine (br), 36. krypton (kr), 37. rubidium (rb), 38. strontium (sr), 39. yttrium (y), 4. beryllium (be), 40. zirconium (zr), 41. niobium (nb), 42. molybdenum (mo), 43. technetium (tc), 44. ruthenium (ru), 45. rhodium (rh), 46. palladium (pd), 47. silver (ag - argentum), 48. cadmium (cd), 49. indium (in), 5. boron (b), 50. tin (sn - stannum), 51. antimony (sb - stibium), 52. tellurium (te), 53. iodine (i), 54. xenon (xe), 55. caesium (cs), 56. barium (ba), 57. lanthanum (la), 58. cerium (ce), 59. praseodymium (pr), 6. carbon (c), 60. neodymium (nd), 61. promethium (pm), 62. samarium (sm), 63. europium (eu), 64. gadolinium (gd), 65. terbium (tb), 66. dysprosium (dy), 67. holmium (ho), 68. erbium (er), 69. thulium (tm), 7. nitrogen (n), 70. ytterbium (tb), 71. lutetium (lu), 72. hafnium (hf), 73. tantalum (ta), 74. tungsten (w - wolfram), 75. rhenium (re), 76. osmium (os), 77. iridium (ir), 78. platinum (pt), 79. gold (au - aurum), 8. oxygen (o), 80. mercury (hg - hydrargyrum), 81. thallium (tl), 82. lead (pb - plumbum), 83. bismuth (bi), 84. polonium (po), 85. astatine (at), 86. radon (rn), 87. francium (fr), 88. radium (ra), 89. actinium (ac), 9. fluorine (f), 90. thorium (th), 91. protactinium (pa), 92. uranium (u), 93. neptunium (np), 94. plutonium (pu), 95. americium (am), 96. curium

(cm), 97. berkelium (bk), 98. californium (cf), 99. einsteinium (es), astatine, berkelium, bohrium, boron, bromine, californium, einsteinium, erbium, europium, fermium, gadolinium, holmium, illinium, lanthanum, meitnerium, mendelevium, neodymium, nobelium, praseodymium, promethium, protactinium, rutherfordium, samarium, tantalum, tellurium, terbium. **2. obsolete names for elements** brimstone, columbium, venus.

8. **1. acids** acetic acid, alkali, alkalimeter, alkaline earth, alkaloid, alkene, alkyl group, alkyne, aqua fortis, aqua regia, boric acid, butanoic acid, butenedioic acid, carbolic acid, carbonic acid, carboxylic acid, Caro's acid, chloracetic acid, chloric acid, chromic acid, citric acid, cyanuric acid, disulfuric acid, dithionic acid, dithionous acid, ethanoic acid, fatty acid, fluorophosphoric acid, fluorosilicic acid, formic acid, fulminic acid, glacial acetic acid, hydriodic acid, hydrochloric acid, hydrofluoboric acid, hydrosulfurous acid, hydroxybenzene, hyponitrous acid, hyposulfurous acid, levulinic acid *(US)*, maleic acid, malic acid, malonic acid, malonyl urea, manganic acid, margaric acid, meconic acid, methanoic acid, methyl benzoic acid, n-nonoic acid, n-nonylic acid, niacin, nicotinic acid, nitric acid, nonanoic acid, oxaloacetic acid, per-acid, perboric acid, perchloric acid, perchromic acid, perdisulfuric acid, permonosulfuric acid, peroxyacid, peroxydisulfuric acid, peroxymonosulfuric acid, phenol, phenyl acetate, propanoic acid, pyrosulfuric acid, salicylic acid, selenous acid, silicic acid, spirits of salt, suberic acid, sulfonic acid, sulfonyl chloride, sulfuric acid, sulfurous acid, sylvic acid, tartaric acid, tetracyanoplatinic acid, thiocyanic acid, tricyanic acid, xylic acid. **2. alkalis** ammonia, aqua ammoniae, aqueous ammonia, calcium hydroxide, caustic, caustic potash, caustic soda, methylamine, sodium hydroxide, spirits of hartshorn.

9. **1. common compounds** acetaldehyde, acetone, acetylene, alcohol, alkali, alkyl halide, allyl alcohol, allylthiourea, alum, alumina, amide, ammine, ammonia, ammonium carbonate, amyl alcohol, amyl nitrite, arsenic, arsenide, benzene, benzine, benzoline, borax, calcium carbonate, calcium chloride, camphane, camphor, carbamide, carbohydrate, carbon dioxide, carbon monoxide, carbon silicide, carbon tetrachloride, carbonic acid gas, carborundum, cellulose, cellulose nitrate, chlorobenzene, chloroform, creosote, cresol, cyclohexane, dextrose, dichlorodifluoromethane, dichlorodiphenyltrichloroethane (ddt), dichloromethane, dicyandiamide, dinitrobenzene, diphenylamine, disulphuric acid, dripstone, epoxy, ethanal, ethanol, ethanolamine, ethene, ether, ethine, ethyl acetate, ethyl alcohol, ethyl ether, ethylene, ethylene glycol, ferric oxide, ferrite, fluorescein, fluorocarbon, formaldehyde, formalin, freon, gas black, gas carbon, gelatine, glucoprotein, glycol, grape sugar, guanidine, hexose, hydroxide, imide, ketone, lime, malonic ester, manganese dioxide, menthene, mesitylene, methane, methionine, methylene, methylene chloride, monosaccharide, naphtha, naphthalene, nitrous oxide, nordhausen acid, oil of vitriol, oxalate, oxalic acid, paraffin, peroxide, potash, propanone, radiocarbon, radium B, saccharide, sal soda, sal volatile, silicon carbide, silicone, silver bromide, silver chloride, silver iodide, soda ash, sulphuric acid, sulphuric ether, tartrazine, terpene, thiophen, tincal, tolan, toluene, toluic acid, toluol, trichloroacetic acid, tungsten carbide, urea, urea formaldehyde, vinylidene, vitriol, washing soda, xylene, zein, zinc chloride, zinc oxide.

10. **1. biochemicals** ACTH, adenosine triphosphate (atp), adenyl cyclase, adrenaline, albumen, albumin, aldolase, aldosterone, aleurone, alpha-amino acid, alpha-foetoprotein, alpha-helix, amide, amino acid, amylase, andrase, animal starch, antibody, arginine, asparagine, bilirubin, carbohydrase, carbohydrate, catecholamine, cellulase, chlorophyll, cholesterol, cholic acid, collagen, creatine, cysteine, cystine, cytidine, cytochrome, cytosine, decarboxylase, dehydrogenase, deoxyribonuclease, deoxyribonucleic acid (dna), diethylstilboestrol, dihydroxyphenylalanine, dopa, ecdysone, endorphin, enzyme, enzymogen, epinephrine, flavin adenine dinucleotide, flavin mononucleotide, flavoprotein, gestrinone, globin, glucosidase, glycogen, glycoprotein, glycosidase, guanosine, guanylic acid, haem, haemoglobin, histaminase, hormone, insulin, isoenzyme, lactase, lactate dehydrogenase, legumin, lipid, luciferin, maltase, messenger RNA, methaemoglobin, myoglobin, neuropeptide, noradrenaline, norepinephrine, nuclease, nucleoprotein, nucleoside, opioid, ornithine, oxyhaemoglobin, pectase, peptide, peptone, phenylalanine, phosphagen, phosphatide, phospholipid, phosphoprotein, polypeptide, prolactin, protease, ptyalin, pyruvic acid, reductase, renin, ribonuclease, ribonucleic acid (rna), ribose, ricin, squalene, steroid, sterol, succinate dehydrogenase, thymidine, thymine, tyrosinase, tyrosine, urease, valine, zymogen.

11. **1. salts** amine, aniline, arsenate, benzoate, bichromate, borate, borosilicate, bromate, bromide, butyrate, carbamate, carbide, carbonate, carbonyl, carboxyl group, chlorate, chloride, chlorite, chromate, citrate, corrosive sublimate, cyanate, deoxyribonucleotide, diazonium salts, dichromate, diethylmalonate, dioxide, disulfate, disulfide, double salt, ester, ether, ethyl nitrate, ethyl nitrite, ethylate, fluoride, fluoroborate, fluorophosphate, fluorosilicate, formate, glutamate, hydnocarpate, hypochlorite, hyponitrite,

hypophosphate, hypophosphite, lactate, malate, maleate, manganate, manganepidote, manganese epidote, manganite, mercaptide, mercuric chloride, methacrylate, molybdate, molybdite, niobate, nitrous acid, oleate, oxide, palmitate, pectate, perchlorate, periodate, permanganate, peroxide, persulfate, phenetidine, phenetole, phenolate, phosphite, picrate, piperidine, platinocyanide, propionate, psilocybin, putrescine, pyrogallate, pyrosulfate, pyrrolidine, quinoxaline, saccharate, salicylate, selenate, silicide, stannate, stearate, sulfate, sulfide, sulfite, sulfonate, tannate, tantalate, tartrate, tellurate, thiocyanate, thiosulfate, toluate, triethylamine, triphosphopyridine nucleotide, tungstate, urate, urethane, vanadate, xanthate, zincate.

12. **1. imaginary substances** elixir, ether, kryptonite, philosopher's stone, phlogiston.

13. **1. chemical processes** anorthic, aromatisation, carbonation, condensation, crystallisation, dehydrogenisation, deionisation, deoxidisation, deoxygenation, distillation, esterification, etherification, fixation, glycolysis, inversion, neutralisation, oxidation, oxidisation, precipitation, reduction, sedimentation, vitriolisation, zymogenesis.

14. **1. biological cycle** citric acid cycle, gluconeogenesis, Krebs cycle, oxidative phosphorylation, pentose phosphate pathway, tricarboxylic acid cycle, urea cycle.

adj. **15.** **1. tangible** actual, bodily, concrete, concretive, corporeal, cosmic, external, fleshly, material, mechanical, natural, objective, palpable, phenomenal, physical, real, spatiotemporal, substantial.

16. **1. chemical** alchemic, alchemical, aliphatic, biochemic, biochemical, biophysical, chemurgic, chemurgical, electrochemical, enzymological, inorganic, microchemical, organic, stoichiometric, thermochemical.

v. **17.** **1. materialise** body forth, embody, incarnate, objectify, objectivise, reify, substantialise. **2. crystallise** degrade, fix, fractionate, neutralise.

adv. **18.** **1. tangibly** animally, concretely, concretively, corporally, corporeally, materially, physically, substantially.

RELATED KEYWORDS: ATOM, ACTUALITY, SKY, GAS, LIQUID, METAL, OIL, RAW MATERIALS, ROCK

MATURITY

n. **1.** **1. maturity** matureness, ripeness. **2. adulthood** achievement age, adultness, affirmance, age of consent, age of discretion, drinking age, driving age, full age, legal age, legal majority, majority, manhood, matronage, maturity, prime, prime of life, summer, voting age, womanhood. **3. marriageableness** nubility. **4. age** age bracket, chronological age, life expectancy, life span, longevity, mental age. **5. age group** generation, peer group.

2. **1. middle age** andropause, certain age, change of life, climacteric, fifties, forties, menopause. **2. autumn of life** autumn, seniority, sixties. **3. old age** antiquity, eighties, elderliness, Indian summer, mellowness, nineties, one's declining years, seventies, three score years and ten, twilight years. **4. agedness** ancientness, oldness, senescence. **5. senility** dotage, second childhood. *Informal:* anecdotage. **6. geratology** geriatrics, gerontology, nostology. **7. geriatrician** gerontologist.

3. **1. adult** grown-up. **2. old person** ancient, antediluvian, dotard, geriatric, methuselah, museum piece, old identity, old thing, senior, senior citizen, veteran. *Informal:* fossil, geri, has-been, old bird, old crock, old fogy, old stager, oldie, oldster, wrinkly. **3. old man** blimp *(British)*, father, grampus, grandfather, grandpapa, greybeard, nonno, whitebeard. *Informal:* dadda, daddy-o *(Chiefly US)*, gaffer *(British)*, grampers, gramps, grandad, grandpa, old boy *(Chiefly British)*, old codger, old-timer. **4. old woman** carline *(Chiefly Scottish)*, crone, grandam, grande dame, grandmamma, grandmother, grimalkin, hag, harpy, Mother, mother, mother of vinegar, nana, nanny, nonna, old maid. *Informal:* biddy, gran, grandma, granny, nanna, old boiler, old chook, old girl. **5. old people** Darby and Joan, grey nomads, grey power, old guard, older generation, the aged, the ageing, the elderly, the old. *Informal:* Dad's Army, olds. **6. elder** doyen, elder statesman, grand old ..., kaumatua, matriarch, Nestor, olgomen *(Aboriginal English)*, olmen *(Aboriginal English)*, patriarch, senior, tjamu *(Aboriginal English)*, tjilbi *(Aboriginal English)*. **7. centenarian** nonagenarian, octogenarian, quinquagenarian, septuagenarian, septuagenary, sexagenarian, sexagenary.

adj. **4.** **1. mature** adult, full-grown, fully-fledged, fully-grown, grown, grown-up, of age, ripe, ripe and ready. **2. marriageable** nubile. **3. middle-aged** menopausal. **4. senior** mellowed. **5. ageing** declining, elderly, failing, getting on, in one's declining years, in the autumn of life, oldish, senescent, with one foot in the grave. **6. retired** pensioned off, superannuated. **7. old-aged** advanced in years, age-old, aged, ancient, autumnal, elderly, frosty, grey, grey-headed, hoary, in the sere and sallow, long-lived, longeval, old,

old as Methuselah, white-haired, white-headed. *Informal:* as old as the hills, long in the tooth, out of the ark. **8. senile** decrepit, doddering, doting, feeble, infirm, past one's prime, tottering. *Informal:* gaga, geriatric, over the hill, past it. **9. anile** haggish. **10. venerable** august, hoary, matriarchic, patriarchal. **11. centenarian** nonagenarian, nonagenary, octogenarian, octogenary, quinquagenarian, quinquagenary, septuagenarian, septuagenary, sexagenarian, sexagenary. **12. geriatric** nostologic. **13. elder** aîné, older. **14. eldest** firstborn, major *(British)*, maximus, oldest, senior.

v. **5. 1. mature** bloom, blossom, come of age, develop, flower, grow up, reach adulthood, ripen. **2. grow old** age, decline, deteriorate, go (or run) to seed, mellow, wane. **3. be old** live to a ripe old age. *Informal:* be over the hill, be past it, have had a good innings, have one foot in the grave. **4. outlive** outwear.

adv. **6. 1. maturely** autumnally, mellowly, ripely. **2. agedly. 3. upwards of** upwards. *Informal:* on the shady side of.

RELATED KEYWORDS: KNOWLEDGE, OLDNESS, WISE PERSON

MEANING

n. **1. 1. meaning** content, drift, effect, force, gist, import, intendment, intent, intention, matter, message, point, purport, purpose, sense, significance, signification, substance, tenor, value. *Informal:* the strong of it. **2. connotation** implication, nuance, polysemy. **3. denotation** acceptation, application, definition, designation, extension, indication, significance, signification, usage. **4. synonymousness** equivalence, synonymity, synonymy. **5. ambiguity** double meaning, equivoque.

adj. **2. 1. meaningful** indicative, pithy, pointed, portentous, pregnant, profound, significant, succinct, terse. **2. connotative** allusive, evocative, suggestive. **3. denotative** designative, explicit, expressive, indicative, meaning, notional, significant, significative, suggestive, unambiguous, unequivocal, univocal. **4. synonymous** equivalent, synonymic, synonymical. **5. ambiguous** amphibolous, equivocal, inexplicit, polysemous. **6. semantic** semasiological.

v. **3. 1. mean** betoken, connote, convey, denote, designate, express, imply, import, indicate, purport, signify, specify. **2. represent** stand for, symbolise.

adv. **4. 1. meaningfully** pointedly, portentously, pregnantly, profoundly, significantly.

RELATED KEYWORDS: SUGGESTION, CLARITY, FIGURE OF SPEECH, INFORMATION, INTERPRETATION

MEANNESS

n. **1. 1. meanness** cheeseparing, churlishness, closeness, manginess, miserliness, niggardliness, parsimony, penuriousness, stinginess, tightness. **2. avarice** avariciousness, greediness, hungriness, sordidness. **3. ungenerosity** illiberalness, shabbiness, smallness, uncharitableness, ungenerousness, unhandsomeness.

2. 1. miser curmudgeon, death adder, dog in the manger, penny pincher, pinchpenny, Scrooge, Shylock, skinflint. *Informal:* codger, meanie, money-grubber, screw, tightwad. **2. cheapskate** last of the big spenders. *Informal:* piker.

adj. **3. 1. mean** careful, cheeseparing, churlish, close, mangy, miserly, near, niggardly, parsimonious, penny-ante, penny-pinching, penurious, petty, pinchpenny, skimp, skimpy, small, stingy, tight-fisted. *Informal:* cheap, mingy, tight. **2. avaricious** close-fisted, covetous, greedy, hard-fisted, hungry, iron-fisted, money-grubbing, niggardly, rapacious, sordid. **3. ungenerous** grudging, mean-minded, mean-spirited, shabby, uncharitable, unhandsome.

v. **4. 1. be miserly** begrudge, dole out, hold back, pinch, scrimp, skimp, stint, withhold. *Informal:* have a death adder in one's pocket, have short arms and long pockets, stay at home on button day, throw money around like a man with no hands.

adv. **5. 1. meanly** churlishly, mangily, parsimoniously, penuriously, poorly, stingily, tightly. **2. avariciously** hungrily. **3. ungenerously** shabbily, uncharitably, unhandsomely, with a sparing hand.

RELATED KEYWORDS: THRIFT, SELFISHNESS

MEASUREMENT

n. **1. 1. measurement** admeasurement, measure, mensuration, quantification. **2. exact science** metrology, micrometry. **3. evaluation** analysis, rating. **4. calibration. 5. dimensions** measure, size, vital statistics. **6. gauge** dial, dial gauge, digital readout, instrument, LCD, measure, meter, recording instrument, standard gauge, VU meter.

2. **1. method of measurement – volumetry** cubature, cubic measure, spirometry, stereometry, titration, volumetrics. **2. depth-sounding** altimetry, bathometry, cast, hydrography, plumbing, soundings. **3. chemical methods** alkalimetry, colorimetry, cryoscopy, ebullioscopy, photometry, radiometry, spectrophotometry, stoechiometry, stoichiometry, thermometry.

3. **1. system of measurement** apothecaries' measure, apothecaries' weight, centimetre-gram-second system, Douglas Scale, f.p.s., foot-pound-second system, FPS system, imperial system, International System of Units, liquid measure, metre-kilogram-second system, metric system, Rankine scale, Reaumur scale, Richter scale, Scoville scale, SI, wine measure.

4. **1. unit of measurement** derived unit, SI unit. **2. metric length** centimetre, kilometre, metre, micrometre, micron, millimetre. *Informal:* k, kay. **3. imperial length** chain, digit, finger, foot, furlong, inch, line, link, microinch, mil, mile, perch, point, pole, rod, rood, yard. **4. metric weight** gram, kilogram, tonne. **5. imperial weight** drachm, dram, ounce, pound, ton. **6. metric area** are, hectare, square centimetre, square kilometre, square metre. **7. imperial area** acre, hide, pole, rod, square, square foot, square inch, square mile, square yard, virgate. **8. metric volume** cubic centimetre, cubic metre. **9. imperial volume** board foot, bushel, cubic foot, cubic inch, cubic yard, quarter, stack, super foot, superficial foot, tun. **10. metric liquid volume** arroba, liter *(US)*, litre, mil, millilitre, Sydharb. **11. imperial liquid volume** butt, cup, dram, fluid drachm, fluid ounce, gallon, gill, hogshead, kilderkin, minim, pint, quart, terce, tierce. **12. pace** cubit, digit, finger, footstep, palm, span, step, stride. **13. circular measure** circular mil, degree, grade, radian, steradian. **14. illumination** candela, candela per square metre, candlepower, international candle, lambert, luces, lumen, luminous efficiency, lux, nit. **15. chemistry** mole. **16. astronomical unit** digit, light-year. **17. paper size** A0, A1, A2, A3, A4, A5, A6, A7, A8, B0, B1, B2, B3, B4, B5, B6, B7, B8, C0, C1, C2, C3, C4, C5, C6, C7, C8, crown, demy, foolscap, imperial, ISO RA1, ISO RA2, ISO SRA1, ISO SRA2, quarto, royal. **18. miscellaneous measures** langley, pH, tesla.

5. **1. measuring instrument – length or distance** calliper (rule), cathetometer, chain, chain measure, dividers, echo sounder, engineer's chain, erythrocytometer, feeler gauge, feelers, hodometer, log, micrometer, mileometer, odograph, odometer, pedometer, rule, ruler, scale, stadiometer, surveyor's chain, tape (measure), tape measure, telemeter, tripmeter, ultramicrometer, vernier, yardstick. **2. height or depth** altimeter, asdic, ceilometer, depth finder, depth sounder, dip stick, fathometer, hypsometer, orometer, plumb-bob, plumbline, plummet, radio altimeter, sonar, sounder, sounding line, water-gauge. **3. weight** balance, jockey scales, microbalance, scales, spring balance, steelyard, ultramicrobalance, weighbridge. **4. volume** board rule, burette, drosometer, gas meter, measuring cup, measuring cylinder, pipette, pycnometer, spirometer, vaporimeter, volumeter. **5. surveying** alidade, alidade bubble, astrocompass, astrolabe, clinometer, declinometer, director, gradiograph, gradiometer, heliometer, octant, telemeter, theodolite, transit *(US)*, transit theodolite, trigonometer, vertical circle. **6. colour** barrel, bolometer, colorimeter, photometer, radiometer, solarimeter, spectrobolometer, spectrometer, spectrophotometer, spectroscope, tintometer. **7. electricity** ammeter, astatic galvanometer, ballistic galvanometer, coulometer, electrometer, galvanometer, multimeter, tangent galvanometer, voltameter, voltammeter, voltmeter, wattmeter. **8. temperature** Beckmann thermometer, clinical thermometer, cryometer, cryoscope, differential thermometer, gas thermometer, maximum and minimum thermometer, micropyrometer, platinum thermometer, pyrometer, pyrophotometer, radiomicrometer, telethermometer, thermobarometer, thermograph, thermometer. **9. wind speed** airsock, anemometer, rheometer, wind cone, wind gauge, wind sleeve, windsock, wind-vane. **10. miscellaneous** aerial magnetometer, aerometer, airborne magnetometer, algometer, amphometer, aneroid, barometer, cephalometer, dilatometer, dip circle, dip needle, dipping needle, dynamometer, ergograph, ergometer, flight indicator, Fortin's barometer, gravimeter, hyetograph, hygrometer, magnetometer, manometer, marigraph, meteorograph, microbarograph, nephelometer, ombrometer, osmometer, penetrometer, piezometer, pinch test, planimeter, pluviometer, pneumatometer, pressure gauge, psychrometer, radiosclerometer, rain gauge, scintillometer, sclerometer, snow gauge, spherometer, spygmomanometer, static-pressure tube, statoscope, step counter, tensimeter, tensiometer, thermobarometer, tide gauge, udometer, vacuum gauge, viscometer, visibility meter, wet-and-dry bulb hygrometer, wire-gauge.

adj. **6.** **1. measurable** assessable, gaugeable, mensurable, quantifiable, rateable, surveyable.

7. **1. measuring** admeasurement, dimensional, mensural, mensurative, metrical, quantitative.

v. **8.** **1. measure** dial, gauge, meter, quantify. **2. rate** appraise, assess, evaluate, grade, measure, revalue, score. **3. calibrate.** **4. pace** caliper, cube, fathom, sound, span, step, tape, titrate, walk. **5. survey** shoot, triangulate. **6. scale** plot, prick off.

RELATED KEYWORDS: ANALYSIS, CALCULATION, COMPARISON, JUDGEMENT, TEST

MEDIATION

n. **1.** **1. mediation** arbitrament, arbitration, conciliation, diplomacy, good offices, healing, intercession, intermediacy, intermediation, interposal, interposition, intervention, negotiation, pacification, propitiation, reconcilement, temporisation, troubleshooting. **2. peace conference** parley. **3. peace settlement** armistice, compromise, concord, makarrata, treaty, truce. **4. peace token** calumet, flag of truce, olive branch, peace pipe, pipe of peace, white flag.

2. **1. mediator** adjudicator, arbiter, arbitrator, arbitress, conciliation committee, conciliator, diplomat, diplomatist, interceder, intercessor, intermediator, intervener, interventionist, judge, judicator, negotiator, propitiator, referee, troubleshooter, umpire, video referee. *Informal:* firefighter, ump, umpie. **2. reconciler** advocate, healer, intercessor, paraclete. **3. compromiser** temporiser. **4. intermediary** go-between, mouthpiece, next friend, proxy.

adj. **3.** **1. mediatory** arbitral, arbitrational, arbitrative, conciliatory, diplomatic, intercessional, intercessory, intervenient, interventional, mediate, mediating, mediative, pacific, propitiative, propitiatory, reconciliatory.

v. **4.** **1. mediate** arbitrate, conciliate, decide, determine, go between, intercede, intermediate, interpose, intervene, negotiate, placate, umpire. **2. appease** placate, propitiate, temporise. **3. settle** allay, amend, answer, appease, arrange, assuage, bring together, bury the hatchet, compose, compromise, heal, make up, pacificate, pacify, patch things up, pour oil on troubled waters, smooth things over.

RELATED KEYWORDS: AGENT, JUDGE, PARTICIPATION, PEACE

MEDICATION

n. **1.** **1. medication** alterant, bush medicine, curative, drug, folk medicine, magic bullet, medicament, medicine, physic, premedication, prescription, prescription drug, remedy, scrip, script, specific. **2. dose** administration, dosage, draught, drench. **3. botanical** herb *(US)*, wort. **4. adjuvant** synergist. **5. materia medica** pharmacopoeia. **6. pharmacy** pharmaceutics, pharmacognosy, pharmacology, posology, radiopharmacology. **7. dispensary** chemist, drug store, drugstore *(US)*, night chemist, pharmacy. **8. cure** arcanum, catholicon, cup, cure-all, panacea, proprietary, remedy, vulnerary. **9. faith-healing** faith cure, nostrum. **10. folk remedy** bush cure. **11. placebo** sugar pill. **12. prophylactic** antiserum, antivenene, bacterin, blood serum, prevention, preventive, remedy, serum, vaccine. **13. antidote** alexipharmic, antivenom, counterpoison, theriac. **14. application** bath, cold pack, compress, corn plaster, eyewash, fomentation, hot pack, icebag, icepack, mud bath, mustard plaster, poultice, stupe, wash, wet pack. **15. dressing** bandage, bandaid, blister plaster, compression bandage, court plaster, diachylon, dossil, elastoplast, frog plaster, lint, plaster, pledget, sticking plaster, swab, swob, tent. **16. suture** stitch. **17. ointment** abirritant, aftershave, antifungal, balm, balsam, cerate, cold cream, counterirritant, demulcent, emollient, hand cream, inunction, liniment, lotion, magma, salve, unction, unguent. **18. powder** Dover's powder, fuller's earth, pomander, triturate. **19. pessary** bougie, implantation, suppository. **20. pill** bolus, caplet, capsule, durule, pilule, tablet, tabloid, tabsule, time-release capsule, troche, wafer. *Informal:* cap, football, tab. **21. leptogenic** slimming pill. **22. obesogenic.** **23. absorbefacient.** **24. lozenge** cachou, confection, excipient, masticatory, pastille. **25. vitamin** megavitamin. **26. vaccine** bacterin, MMR vaccine, Sabin vaccine, TAB, triple antigen. **27. elixir** cure-all, decoction, drops, electuary, panacea, philtre, potion, ptisan, tincture. **28. inhalation** errhine, vaporisation. **29. injection** booster, hypodermic, launch vehicle, needle. *Informal:* hype, jab, shot. **30. sling** cast, plaster, plaster cast, spica, suspensor, tourniquet. **31. surgical appliance** caliper, crutch, orthosis, peg leg, prosthesis, truss, wooden leg. **32. filling** bridge, cap, crown, inlay.

2. **1. balm** calamine, camphor ice, carron oil, lanolin, lemon balm, oil of cade, petrolatum, petroleum jelly, tiger balm, vaseline, wool fat.

3. **1. tonic** invigorant, koumis, kumis, roborant. **2. stimulant** adrenaline, belladonna, caffeine, cardiac glycoside, deadly nightshade, dexamphetamine, dexedrine, dextroamphetamine, digitalis, digitoxin, ephedrine, hydrastinine, methaqualone, nikethamide,

oil of turpentine, ouabain, purple heart, spirits of turpentine, theobromine, turpentine.
3. smelling salts sal vital (volatile).

4. **1. sedative** amytal, antipsychotic, barbital, barbitone, barbiturate, bromureide, chlordiazepoxide, chlorpromazine, depressant, dimethoxymethane, librium, lupulin, mandrax, methyal, methylal, narcotic, nembutal, opiate, pentobarbitone, phenobarbitone, potassium bromide, rauwolfia, reserpine, soporific, thalidomide, valerian, valium, veronal. *Informal:* bromide, downer.

5. **1. anaesthetic** alpha-eucaine, anaesthesin, atropine, benzamine, benzocaine, beta-eucaine, chalybeate, chloral, cocaine, cyclopropane, diethyl ether, epidural, ether, ethyl ether, eucaine, fluothane, general anaesthetic, halothane, hyoscine, hyoscyamine, lignocaine, local, local anaesthetic, morphine, novocaine, orthocaine, phenacaine, phencyclidine, procaine, scopolamine, scopoline, sodium pentothal, sulfuric ether, tribromoethanol, trichlorethylene, trilene.

6. **1. analgesic** acetylsalicylic acid, anodyne, APC, aspirin, bromal, codeine, disprin, etorphine, hydromorphone, laudanum, methylmorphine, morphine, oil of cloves, painkiller, palfium, paracetamol, pethidine, phenazocine hydrobromide, stramonium. *Informal:* palf, peth. **2. antifebrin** acetanilide, aminobenzene, antipyrine, cinchonine, hydroquinone, quinol.

7. **1. decongestant** amphetamine, guaiacol, phenylephrine, PSE, pseudoephedrine, sympathomimetic. **2. dilator** alupent, aminophylline, amyl nitrite, banana oil, benzedrine, dilatant, disodium cromoglycate, hyoscine, intal, mydriatic, neo-synephrine, salbutamol, scopolamine, sympathomimetic, trinitrine, ventolin. *Informal:* amyl.

8. **1. antibiotic** acriflavine, allicin, antigen, arsphenamine, aureomycin, chloramphenicol, chloromycetin, doxycycline, erythromycin, gantrisin, gramicidin, hapten, isoniazid, kaomycin, neomycin, novobiocin, penicillin, procaine penicillin, salvarsan, streptomycin, streptothricin, sulfa drugs, sulfadiazine, sulfafurazole, sulfanilamide, sulfapyridine, sulfathiazole, sulfonamide, terramycin. **2. antiseptic** argyrol, chloramine, dakin's solution, Dakin's solution, dettol, eusol, hexachlorophene, hexylresorcinol, hydrogen peroxide, hydroxybenzene, ichthammol, ichthyol, iodoform, Javel water, lysol, mercuric oxide, orthoboric acid, white vitriol, zinc ointment, zinc oxide. **3. non-steroidal anti-inflammatory** acetylsalicylic acid, aspirin, guaiacum, menthol, phenylbutazone, veratrine. **4. antimalarial** atabrine, Atebrin, chloroquine, mepacrine, plasmoquin, quinacrine, quinidine, quinine. **5. antihistamine** benadryl, chlorpromazine, dramamine. **6. antipyretic** hydroquinone, phenacetin, quassia. **7. antidepressant** psychostimulant, tricyclic, tricyclic antidepressant, tryptanol. **8. anticonvulsant** antidiphtheritic, convulsant, haematic, KS-7, miotic, nervine, oxytocic. **9. anti-cancer medication** antiangiogenic, cytotoxic drug, endostatin, MSTR, radiopharmaceutical, raloxifene, SERM, tamoxifen.

9. **1. steroid – anti-inflammatory** corticosteroid, cortisone, fludrocortisone, hydrocortisone, prednisone. **2. steroid – performace-enhancing** anabolic steroid, DMT, nandrolone, THG, trenbolone. **3. steroid – abortifacient** mifepristone, RU 486.

10. **1. digestive tract medication** aloes, aloin, apomorphine, caffeine, calomel, castor oil, emetine, Epsom salts, Glauber salt, kamala, kaomagma, lign-aloes, liquid paraffin, magnesia, magnesium oxide, magnesium sulfate, magnesium sulphate, mercury chloride, milk of magnesia, oil of turpentine, paraffin, paraffin oil, phenolphthalein, pilocarpine, pinkroot, podophyllin, Rochelle powder, Rochelle salt, Seidlitz powder, squill, sweet spirit of nitre, taeniafuge, tartar emetic, theobromine, turpentine.

11. **1. herbal laxative** cambogia, cascara sagrada, cassia, copaiba, corn silk, cow-itch, cowage, culver's root, elaterium, ipecacuanha, ipomoea, jalap, jequirity beans, Leichhardt bean, licorice, manna, nux-vomica, pareira, rhubarb, sanguinaria, santonica, scammony, senega, senna, taraxacum, tolu, turpeth, wormseed. *Informal:* fluid tablet.

12. **1. vitamins** aneurin, paba, vitamin A, vitamin B1 (thiamine), vitamin B12 (cyanocobalamine), vitamin B2 (riboflavin), vitamin B3 (niacin), vitamin B6 (pyridoxine), vitamin B9 (folic acid), vitamin C (ascorbic acid), vitamin D (cholecalciferol), vitamin E (tocopherol), vitamin K, vitamin P (bioflavinoids).

13. **1. herbal medicine** aconite, alumroot, ammoniac, angelica, angostura bark, anise, aniseed, arnica, asafoetida, asthma-plant, belladonna, benzoin, cajuput, calendula, calisaya, camomile, canella, capsicum, caraway, cardamom, cardamon, cardamum, carminative, cascarilla, cashew, caterpillar weed, centaury, cevadilla, chamomile, china bark, cinchona, coca, colchicum, contrayerva, cubeb, cumin, deadly nightshade, digitalis, dill water, foxglove, friar's balsam, galangal, gentian, ginger, gingerroot, ginseng, goldenseal, goldthread, grindelia, guaco, guaiacum, gum ammoniac, gum benzoin, heliotrope, hops, horseradish, kidney vetch, kino gum, ladies' fingers, laos, liquidambar, madder, milfoil, nard, Peruvian bark, podophyllum, race ginger, rhatany, sabadilla, safflower, salep, sarsaparilla, sassafras, savin, selfheal, slippery elm, snakeroot, sweet gum, turmeric, valerian, viburnum, witch-hazel, wych-hazel, yarrow, zanthoxlyum.

14.   **1. aphrodisiac**   cantharides, ginseng, ground pearl, horny goat weed, mandrake root, oysters, rhinoceros horn, snake bile, Spanish fly.

adj. **15.**   **1. medicinal** active, alterant, curative, healing, medical, medicative, panacean, remedial, sanative, sanatory, therapeutic. **2. antidotal** alexipharmic, antitoxic, preservative, preventive, prophylactic, theriacal. **3. adjuvant** synergetic, synergic, synergistic. **4. nervine** tetanic. **5. tonic** roborant. **6. calmative** sedative, tranquillising. **7. endermic** hypodermic, intravenous, IV, parenteral, topical. **8. ethical** magistral, officinal. **9. over the counter**.

v. **16.**   **1. medicate** cure, dispense, dose, medicine, physic, prescribe, remedy, treat. **2. cure** doctor, heal, nurse, rehabilitate, remedy, restore. **3. resuscitate** recall *(Poetic)*, revive, revivify. **4. inoculate** mithridatise, pasteurise, tubercularise, tuberculinise, tuberculise, vaccinate, variolate. **5. drench** fog, footrot, spray. **6. massage** manipulate, percuss.

RELATED KEYWORDS: DRUG, HEALTH, ILL HEALTH, HEALING, IMPROVEMENT

MEDIOCRITY

n. **1.**   **1. mediocrity** averageness, mundaneness, ordinariness, pedestrianism, triteness. **2. passableness** fairness, indifference, tolerableness.

adj. **2.**   **1. mediocre** common, indifferent, mean, middling, mundane, nothing to boast of, ordinary, plain, simple, trivial, undistinguished. *Informal:* half-pie, nothing to write home about. **2. tolerable** acceptable, decent, fair, fair to middling, middling, moderate, moderato, not bad, passable, unobjectionable. *Informal:* fair enough, not so dusty. **3. second-rate** inferior, minor *(US)*, moderate, not so hot, not too hot, of sorts, run-of-the-mill, second-best, second-class. *Informal:* low-rent, no great shakes, nothing out of the box. **4. commonplace** bog-standard, common-or-garden, conventional, multi-run, moderate, mundane, nondescript, ordinary, pedestrian, plebeian, prosaic, run-of-the-mill, stock, unexceptional. *Informal:* blah. **5. hackneyed** banal, clichéd, common, commonplace, deja vu, hack, stale, stereotyped, threadbare, tired, trite, unoriginal. **6. middlebrow** bourgeois, common, conventional, middle-of-the-road, middling, moderate, run-of-the-mill, second-rate. *Informal:* straight-up. **7. so-so** average, fifty-fifty, much of a muchness.

adv. **3.**   **1. passably** after a fashion, averagely, fairly, in a fashion, indifferently, middling, moderately, mundanely, so-so, tolerably.

RELATED KEYWORDS: CONFORMITY, BADNESS, UNIMPORTANCE, ORDINARINESS, INFERIORITY

MEEKNESS

n. **1.**   **1. meekness** abasement, humbleness, lowliness, resignation, self-abasement, self-effacement, sense of shame. *Informal:* a worm's eye view. **2. humility** abashment, abjectness, chagrin, cheapness, confusion, crestfallenness, embarrassment, modesty, prudery, pudency. **3. obsequiousness** flattery, flunkeyism, palaver, servileness, suppleness, sycophancy, toadyism.

2.   **1. crawler** courtier, encomiast, eulogist, fawner, flunkey, grease, groveller, lackey, lickspittle *(British)*, pickthank, reptile, respecter of persons, satellite, spaniel, sponger, sycophant, toady. *Informal:* bootlicker, creeping Jesus, greaser, greasespot. **2. groveller** earthworm, the muck of the earth, worm. *Informal:* doormat.

adj. **3.**   **1. meek** abashed, ashamed, bashful, browbeaten, coy, crestfallen, diffident, guidable, humbled, lowly, mean, modest, out of countenance, self-deprecating, shamefaced, sheepish, skittish, small, struck all of a heap, timid. **2. humble** abject, chagrined, intropunitive, meek, milky, pigeon-hearted, pigeon-livered, self-critical, self-effacing, small, submissive. **3. obsequious** flunkeyish, servile, subservient, supple, sycophantic, toadyish, wormlike.

v. **4.**   **1. be meek** bow and scrape, creep, eat humble pie, eat one's words, eat out of someone's hand, get off one's high horse, grovel, know one's place, lose face, not dare to show one's face again, sing small, submit, submit to. *Informal:* eat crow, eat dirt, hide one's head, kiss the dust, lick the dust, smarm. **2. grovel** chum up to, crawl, fawn, kotow, kowtow, lick someone's boots, prostrate, pull one's forelock, slaver, toady, touch (or tug) (or pull) one's forelock, truckle to. *Informal:* get gravel rash, smarm. **3. humble oneself** condescend, deign, demean oneself, stoop, vouchsafe. **4. be humbled** be made to look foolish, receive a snub.

5.   **1. humble** abase, abash, bastardise, bring down, bring someone to their knees, chagrin, confuse, crush, cut down to size, dash, embarrass, humiliate, lower, make someone look foolish, mortify, put down, put out of countenance, put someone in their place, send away with a flea in one's ear, snub, take down, take down a peg. *Informal:* flatten, wipe the floor with.

adv. **6.** **1. meekly** abjectly, cap in hand, crawlingly, humbly, low, on bended knee, servilely. **2. crestfallenly** ashamedly, ignominiously, shamefacedly, sheepishly, with one's tail between one's legs.

RELATED KEYWORDS: ARTLESSNESS, REPRESSION, MODESTY

MENACE

n. **1.** **1. menace** commination, sword of Damocles, threat. **2. menaces** intimidation, scare tactics, standover tactics, strongarm methods. **3. bluster** defiance, fulmination. **4. stalking** cyberstalking, prowling. **5. blackmail** embracery. **6. death threat**. **7. gunboat diplomacy** mailed fist, sabre-rattling. **8. war cloud** dark clouds, gathering clouds. **9. fearsomeness** minaciousness, minacity, ominousness, sinisterness, ugliness.

2. **1. menacer** bludgeoner, blusterer, bully, standover man, standover merchant, threatener. *Informal:* bovver boy *(British)*, bucko, bulldozer, goon, hood, hoodlum, hooligan, larrikin, yobbo. **2. blackmailer** embraceor. **3. stalker** cyberstalker, prowler.

adj. **3.** **1. menacing** baleful, comminatory, intimidating, minacious, minatory, pernicious, pestilent, tammany-hall, threatening, ugly, wicked. **2. foreboding** boding, boding ill, illboding, looming, ominous, portentous, threatening. **3. sinister** ominous, slinky.

v. **4.** **1. menace** abuse, cow, harass, hassle, haze, intimidate, look daggers at, mandamus, monster, overhang, shake the fist at, tease, threaten, torment. **2. bully** badger, blackjack, blackmail, bludgeon, browbeat, bulldoze, bullyrag, hector, put pressure on, stand over. *Informal:* do a heavy, heavy. **3. stalk** cyberstalk, prowl. **4. bark** growl, snarl. **5. bluster** fulminate, tell someone what for, thunder. **6. overawe** cow, have under threat, intimidate, threaten. **7. forebode** have hanging over one, loom large.

adv. **5.** **1. menacingly** darkly, minaciously, minatorily, threateningly. **2. sinisterly** balefully, uglily. **3. forebodingly** bodingly, ominously. **4. at gunpoint**.

RELATED KEYWORDS: ATTACK, FRIGHT

MESSAGE

n. **1.** **1. message** communications, notification, piece of information, word. **2. correspondence** exchange of letters. **3. letter** aerogram, air letter, communication, covering letter, dead letter, dispatch, encyclical, epistle, express letter, missive, note, writing. **4. love letter** billet-doux, Dear John letter. **5. bread-and-butter letter** follow-up, reply. **6. card** lettercard, notelet, postal card *(US)*, postcard, valentine. *Informal:* postal *(US)*. **7. circular** advertisement, bulletin, dodger, form letter, junk mail, open letter, pamphlet, petition, round robin. **8. telegram** cable, cablegram, dispatch, heliogram, phonogram, radiotelegram, radiotelegraph, telex, wire *(US)*. **9. bush telegram** *Informal:* bush wire, mulga wire. **10. strippergram** fatogram, gorillagram. **11. SMS message** SMS, text message. **12. postal order** bank draft, banker's draft, money order, postal note. **13. postal chess** correspondence chess, postal shoot, postal vote.

2. **1. messenger** forerunner, herald, mercury, officer at arms, orderly, peon, pursuivant, runner. **2. envoy** ambassador, legate. **3. bellboy** bellhop *(US)*, buttons, callboy, devil, errand boy, gopher, leg man, messenger boy, pageboy *(British)*, printer's devil. **4. doorman** commissionaire. **5. courier** dispatch bearer, dispatch rider, express, herald, peon, runner. **6. carrier pigeon** carrier, homing pigeon. **7. postman** mail driver, mail sorter, mailman, postboy, postmaster, postmaster general, postmaster-general, postmistress, postrider, telegraph boy. *Informal:* postie. **8. telegraphist** telegrapher, wirer.

3. **1. correspondent** addressee, consignee, epistler, letter writer, penfriend, penpal.

4. **1. mail** airmail, certified mail, consignment, express, mail-out, par avion, parcel post, post, priority-paid mail, registered mail, registered post, registered publications post, S.A.L., snail mail, surface mail. **2. fan mail** herogram, junk mail. **3. electronic mail** email, webmail. **4. delivery** first post, last post. **5. mailbag** post bag. **6. post office** Australia Post, dead-letter office, G.P.O., letterbox, locked bag, mail change, mailbox, pillar-box, post, post-box, post-office box, postbox, poste restante, rural delivery. **7. telegraph** multiplex telegraphy.

5. **1. address** accommodation address, box number, direction, postcode, redirection, superscription, zipcode *(US)*.

v. **6.** **1. send a message** leave word, pass information, send word. **2. correspond** communicate with, correspond with, drop a line to, respond to, write *(US)*.

3. circularise advise, file a report, notify. **4. mail** consign, courier, drop, letterbox, post. **5. telegraph** cable, telephone, telex, wire *(US)*, wireless. **6. email. 7. SMS** text. **8. address** direct, redirect.

RELATED KEYWORDS: COMMUNICATION, NEWS, TELECOMMUNICATIONS

METAL

n. **1. 1. metal** alloy, amalgam. **2. iron** alpha iron, cast iron, delta iron, ferrite, galvanised iron, gamma iron, grey cast iron, grey iron, hot metal, ingot iron, iron pyrites, malleable cast iron, malleable iron, mitis, mundic, pig-iron, spiegeleisen, white cast iron, wrought iron. *Informal:* gal, galvo. **3. fusible metal** cast iron, eutectic, eutectoid, malleable iron. **4. ingot** bar, bead, billet, bullion, cast, pig, sinter, sow. **5. bell metal** gunmetal, mischmetal, pot metal, silvering, speculum metal, tinwork, tool steel, type metal. **6. foil** black plate, expanded metal, latten, leaf, nickel plate, plate, rolled steel, taggers, tin plate, tinfoil. **7. gold foil** Dutch foil, Dutch gold, Dutch leaf, Dutch metal, gilding, gilt, gold leaf, gold plate, mosaic gold, ormolu, rolled gold. **8. dross** matte, regulus, scoria, slag, speiss, sprue, sullage. **9. mould** flan, ingot, ingot mould, pig, sow. **10. steel** carbon steel, cast steel, chrome steel, chromium steel, Damascus steel, damask, hard steel, heat-resisting steel, high steel, killed steel, low steel, martensite, medium steel, mild steel, soft steel, stainless steel, tool steel, tungsten steel, vanadium steel. **11. zinc** spelter. **12. blank** burr, coin, compact, faggot, planchet. **13. lodestone** loadstone, magnet, permanent magnet. **14. metalwork** hammered work, ironwork, metal goods, metal-ware, tinsel, tole, trifles, vermeil.

2. 1. mineral ore. **2. reef** bushoo, deep ground, deposit, ledge, lens, lode, mother lode, ore body, ore shoot, outcrop, pipe, placer, pocket, quartz-reef, surface reef, underset, vein, winning. *Informal:* jeweller's shop. **3. gold-bearing soil** alluvial, alluvial cone, alluvial fan, alluvial ground, bar, pay-dirt, placer, wash, washing. **4. colour** glance, opacite. **5. metal dust** dust, gold dust, platinum black, sponge. **6. nugget** floater, slug. **7. gold** fool's gold, iron pyrites, mundic, yellow metal.

3. 1. metals alumina, aluminium, aluminum *(US)*, americium, antimony, arsenic, arsenite, barium, baryta, beryllium, bismuth, cadmium, caesium, calcium, cerium, cesium, chromium, cobalt, copper (cuprum), dysprosium, francium, germanium, glucinum, gold (aurum), hafnium, hahnium, iridium, iron, lead, lithium, magnesium, manganese, manganese steel, masurium, mercury (quicksilver), molybdenum, nickel, niobium, platinum, potash, potassium, radium, rhenium, rhodium, rubidium, scandium, silver (argentum), sodium, stibium, strontium, technetium, thulium, tin, tin (stannum), titanium, tungsten, uranium, vanadium, wolfram, wolframium, ytterbium, yttrium, zinc, zirconium. **2. alloys** amalgam, babbitt, babbitt metal, billon, brass, britannia metal, bronze, constantan, cupronickel, duralumin, electrum, ferrochromium, ferromanganese, ferro-molybdenum, ferronickel, ferrosilicon, ferrotitanium, ferrotungsten, ferrovanadium, fer-rozirconium, German silver, invar, iridosmine, latten, magnalium, manganese bronze, manganin, Monel metal, Muntz metal, nichrome, nickel silver, oroide, osmiridium, perm-alloy, pewter, phosphor bronze, pinchbeck, plastic bronze, platina, platiniridium, plati-noid, red brass, Rose's metal, steel, superalloy, trifle, white gold, white metal, yellow metal. **3. alkali metal** alkaline-earth metal, earth metal, noble metal, precious metal, rare earth.

4. 1. metallurgy alchemy, amalgamation, cyanide process, electrometallurgy, electrowin-ning, hydrometallurgy, metallography, metallurgical engineering, Mond process, pyro-metallurgy. **2. mineralogy** petrology. **3. smithing** drop-forging, flame-hardening, heat treatment, metallurgy. **4. pouring** die-casting, metal spinning, metal spraying, rolling. **5. welding**.

5. 1. metalworks forge, foundry, ironworks, rolling mill, smelter, smeltery, smithery, smithy, stannary, steelworks, stithy, strip mill, tinworks, wireworks. **2. furnace** blast furnace, finery, hearth.

6. 1. metalworker coiner, gilder, metal fabricator, pewterer. **2. smith** arc welder, blacksmith, coppersmith, founder, galvaniser, gold-beater, goldsmith, ironmaster, iron-smith, ironworker, plumber, silversmith, smelter, steelworker, tinman, tinner, tinsmith, welder, whitesmith. **3. metallurgist** alchemist, mineralogist.

adj. **7. 1. metallic** bimetallic, metalline, mineral. **2. golden** aureate, auric, aurous, gilded, gilt, gold. **3. brass** brassy, brazen. **4. bronzy. 5. copper** coppery, cupreous, cupro-nickel. **6. iron** ferritic, ferruginous. **7. lead** leaden, plumbeous, plumbic. **8. silver** argent, argental, argentine, lunar, lunarian, silvery. **9. platinum** platinoid. **10. steel** steely. **11. tinny** stannic, stannous, tin. **12. zinc** zincic, zincky, zincous.

8. **1. metalliferous** aluminiferous, aluminium, argentiferous, auriferous, cupriferous, ferriferous, ferruginous, manganic, manganous, nickeliferous, plumbiferous, quick, stanniferous, titanous, yttriferous, zinciferous.

9. **1. metallurgic** metallurgical, mineralogical, vulcanian. **2. ductile** eutectic, eutectoid, forgeable, mitis, self-annealing, self-hardened, self-hardening, weldable.

v. **10.** **1. work metal** cold-work, work. **2. plate** braze, copper, electroplate, foil, galvanise, gild, metal, nickel, nickel-plate, platinise, sherardise, silver-plate, sputter, steel, tin, zinc, zincify. **3. forge** cast, drop-forge, found, heat-treat, sinter. **4. amalgamate** alchemise, alloy, meld. **5. smelt** reduce, scorify, slag. **6. weld** braze. **7. coin** mint.

RELATED KEYWORDS: HARDNESS, MATTER, RAW MATERIALS, ROCK

METHOD

n. **1.** **1. method** course, fashion, manner, mode, procedure, sort, technic, technique, way. **2. line** approach, tack. **3. avenue** channel, course, highroad, path, road, stepping stone, track, way. **4. means** agency, agent, implement, instrument, instrumentality, medium, the how, tool, vehicle, way, ways and means, wherewithal. **5. process** mechanics, mechanism, modus operandi, operation, working. **6. expedient** contraption, device, gimmick, nostrum. **7. routine** custom, practice, usual way.

adv. **2.** **1. how** what, whereto. **2. however** howsomever. **3. any way** anyways, by hook or by crook. **4. so** thus. **5. hereby** herewith. **6. in a manner** in a manner of speaking.

RELATED KEYWORDS: ACTION, EXPEDIENCE, USE

MIDDLE CLASS

n. **1.** **1. middle class** bourgeoisie, equites, lower middle class, petite bourgeoisie, professional class, upper middle class. **2. member of the middle class** bourgeois, businessman, capitalist, employer, petit bourgeois, professional, rentier, yeoman. **3. social climber** new-rich, nouveau riche, parvenu, upstart.

adj. **2.** **1. middle-class** bourgeois, comfortably well-off, mobile, petit-bourgeois, risen from the ranks, untitled, upwardly mobile. *Informal:* non-U.

RELATED KEYWORDS: OWNERSHIP

MIND

n. **1.** **1. mind** breast, consciousness, head, headpiece, psyche, sentient. *Informal:* loaf, melon, skull, upper storey. **2. intellect** brains, capacity, faculties, genius, intellectuality, intelligence, judgement, lights, mentality, mind, normality, percipience, powers, psychology, rationality, reason, saneness, sanity, senses, thought, understanding, wits. *Informal:* brainpower, grey matter, the smarts. **3. intellection** cerebration, thinking. **4. psychogenesis** psychology.

adj. **2.** **1. mental** cerebral, intellectual, intelligential, noetic, phrenic, psychic, psychobiological, psychological, psychophysiological. **2. conscious** apprehensive, aware, cognitive, perceptional, perceptive, percipient, sensible, sentient. **3. intelligent** able, clever, intellective, lucid, rational, reasonable, sane, thinking, understanding.

v. **3.** **1. think** be in a brown study, be lost in thought, cerebrate, cogitate, concentrate, consider, contemplate, cudgel one's brain, meditate, muse, ponder, put on one's thinking cap, rack one's brains, reflect, ruminate. *Informal:* sleep on it. **2. think about** chew over, consider, contemplate, deliberate about, entertain the idea of, give thought to, mull over, muse on, reflect on, ruminate about, think on, turn over in one's mind, weigh up. **3. play mind games** mess with someone's mind.

adv. **4.** **1. mentally** intellectively, intellectually, psychically, psychologically. **2. consciously** perceptively. **3. intelligently** reasonably, sanely.

RELATED KEYWORDS: IDEA, INTELLIGENCE, STUPIDITY, LOGICALITY, PERCEPTION, PSYCHE, THINKING

MISBEHAVIOUR

n. **1.** **1. misbehaviour** bad behaviour, bad manners, delinquency, dereliction, improperness, impropriety, malfeasance, malpractice, malversation, misconduct, misdoing, naughtiness. **2. rascality** bastardry, caddishness, cruelty, devilment, doggery, knavishness, malefaction, mischief, obstreperousness, waywardness. **3. disrespect** discourtesy, disesteem, impudence, incivility, insolence, lese-majesty, pertness, rudeness, tactlessness. **4. mischievousness** devilment, elfishness, impishness, mischief, mischief-making, rascality, roguery, roguishness. **5. slyness** archness, kittenishness, tricksiness. **6. acerbity** acrimony, asperity, bad language, harsh words, tartness, unparliamentary language, virulence. **7. hooliganism** coarseness, criminality, irresponsibleness, juvenile delinquency, larrikinism, restiveness, rowdiness, rowdyism, rudeness, ruffianism, vulgarity. **8. brutality** bestiality, blackguardism, brutishness, infamy. **9. infamous conduct** conduct unbecoming, infamy.

2. **1. misdemeanour** fault, indiscretion, misbehaviour, misdeed, misstep, offence, peccadillo, slip, transgression, trip, venial sin, wrong, wrongdoing. **2. sin** cardinal sin, deadly sin, evil deeds. **3. escapade** apery, caper, capriccio, practical joke, prank, trick, trickery. *Informal:* berley, monkey tricks (or business), monkeyshine *(US)*. **4. disorder** disorderliness, disorderly conduct, riot, tumult. *Informal:* rough-house, rumble.

3. **1. mischief-maker** elf, gremlin, imp, jackanapes, jester, monkey, prankster, rogue, scalawag, scallawag, scallywag, scamp. *Informal:* muck-up, pickle. **2. enfant terrible** brat, problem child. *Informal:* perisher, tyke, Young Turk. **3. gamin** gamine, guttersnipe, urchin. *Informal:* mudlark *(British)*. **4. bastard** *(Informal)* blackguard, blaggard. *Informal:* bugger. **5. hooligan** barbarian, disorderly person, hoodlum, irresponsible, juvenile delinquent, larrikin, raskol *(PNG English)*, scourer *(British)*, yahoo. *Informal:* bovver boy *(British)*, goon, hellion, hood, hoon, lout, rugger-bugger, yobbo. **6. wrongdoer** delinquent, duckshover, hard case, incorrigible, recidivist. *Informal:* wrong 'un. **7. rat pack** *Informal:* brat pack.

adj. 4. **1. badly-behaved** cantankerous, disobedient, ill-behaved, ill-mannered, improper, insubordinate, naughty, pert, perverse, rude, uncivilised, uncooperative, wayward. **2. rascally** blackguardly, furtive, knavish, pestilent, ratbaggy, roguish, sly. **3. mischievous** arch, elfin, elfish, elvish, gamin, impish, knavish, puckish, roguish, scampish, tricksy. **4. disorderly** boisterous, destructive, furious, hooligan, larrikinish, mad, rampageous, riotous, robust, robustious, rorty, rough, rough-and-tumble, rude, tumultuous, undisciplined, uproarious, violent, wild. *Informal:* rip-roaring. **5. irresponsible** improper, wayward, wrong. *Informal:* fly-by-night. **6. uncontrollable** hyperactive, incorrigible, obstreperous, overactive, restive, restless, unruly. *Informal:* rambunctious *(US)*.

v. 5. **1. misbehave** blackguard, carry on, commit transgressions, corrupt others, deviate from the straight and narrow, forget, forget oneself, go astray, lapse, lose one's temper, misconduct oneself, play up, rogue, sow one's wild oats, throw a tantrum, trespass. *Informal:* act up, be up to no good, cut up rough (or nasty), muck up, sell oneself short. **2. cheat** bilk, clip, cozen, defraud, hoodwink, indulge in sharp practice, jockey, rogue, rook, swindle. *Informal:* brass, chisel, diddle, do in the eye, duckshove, gyp, nick. **3. make mischief** be up to monkey tricks, make trouble, mess around (or about), play hob. **4. riot** run riot, vandalise. *Informal:* rough-house. **5. brutalise. 6. overstep the mark** go too far. *Informal:* ask for it (or trouble).

RELATED KEYWORDS: ANARCHY, DISCOURTESY, BADNESS, UNLAWFULNESS, IMMORALITY, DISOBEDIENCE, WRONGDOING, PSYCHE

MISFORTUNE

n. 1. **1. misfortune** accident, ambs-ace, casualty, contretemps, cumbrance, difficulty, evil, evil chance, hard luck story, ill, misadventure, mischance, raw deal, setback, trouble. *Informal:* hard lines, the whole disaster. **2. adversity** asperity, hard life, hardship, sorrow, trouble. *Informal:* rough end of the pineapple, rough end of the stick, worriment. **3. ruination** kiss of death, worst. **4. disaster** blight, calamity, catastrophe, debacle, fatality, plague, tragedy, visitation. *Informal:* basinful. **5. blow** body blow, peripeteia, reversal, reverse, slump, turnabout, turnaround. *Informal:* king hit, packet, smack in the eye. **6. mishap** mess-up, slip. **7. bad luck** just one's luck, stiff luck, the devil, tough luck. *Informal:* deuce, hard (or tough) cheddar, hard cheese (or luck), hard lines, stiff cheese (or cheddar) (or luck). **8. run of bad luck** a rainy day, chapter of accidents, hard times, night. *Informal:* bad trot. **9. evil star** bad fairy, cross, curse, hex, lightning rod, scourge. *Informal:* bad news, fate worse than death, hoodoo, jinx, mozz. **10. black-letter day** black Friday. **11. mixed blessing** good news and bad news. **12. disaster area** Bermuda Triangle, black spot. **13. Pandora's box**.

2. **1. unfortunateness** inauspiciousness, unfavourableness, unluckiness. **2. calamitousness** disastrousness, ruggedness, ruinousness, tragicalness. **3. agony** affliction, anguish, distress, hell, misery, torment, torture, unhappiness, woe, wretchedness. **4. lucklessness** haplessness.

3. **1. victim** Job, loser, miser, scapegoat, underdog, unfortunate, wreck, wretch. *Informal:* cow, lame duck, schlemiel *(US)*. **2. derelict** beachcomber, drummer, hobo, outcast, swagger, swagman, tramp, vagabond, vagrant. *Informal:* bagman, bum, deadbeat, dero, down-and-out, swaggie, toe-ragger, vag.

adj. **4.** **1. unfortunate** badly off, down on one's luck, hapless, lamentable, miserable, out of luck, pitiful, poor, stricken, underprivileged, unhappy, wretched. **2. luckless** hapless, ill-fated, star-crossed, starred, unfortunate, unlucky. *Informal:* for it. **3. ill-fated** accident-prone, accursed, cursed, curst. **4. hard-hit** in a bad way, in dire straits, in trouble, on one's beam-ends, on the hook, on the spot, over a barrel, with one's back to the wall. *Informal:* behind the eight ball, in deep water, in hot water, in the cactus, in the cart, in the poo, in the soup, in the wars, up against it, up the pole. **5. down-and-out** down on one's luck. *Informal:* deadbeat.

5. **1. calamitous** catastrophic, dire, disastrous, dreadful, evil, ruinous, tragic. **2. adverse** difficult, hard, ill, rough, rugged, stiff, thwart, troublesome, unfavourable. **3. inauspicious** boding, foreboding, ill-boding, ill-fated, ill-omened, ill-starred, ominous, sinister, sinistrous, unfavourable. **4. agonising** distressful, distressing.

v. **6.** **1. be out of luck** feel the pinch, go downhill, go through the mill, hit a bad patch, hit bad times. *Informal:* be downhill all the way, be for it, be in the wars, be up against it, draw the short straw, lead a dog's life, stew in one's own juice. **2. come to grief** come unstuck, go to the wall, go under, slump, take a knock. *Informal:* bomb, bomb out, come a buster, come a cropper, come a stumer, cruel one's pitch, feel the draught, go for a sixer, go for six, go to the devil. **3. bear the brunt of misfortune** *Informal:* catch a packet, cop a basinful, cop the lot. **4. ail** distress. **5. hex** cross, put the mozz on. *Informal:* jinx, mozz. **6. be the ruin of** bring down, ruin. *Informal:* be bad news for.

adv. **7.** **1. calamitously** disastrously, ruinously. **2. inauspiciously** evilly. **3. distressingly** agonisedly, distressfully.

8. **1. unfortunately** from bad to worse, haplessly, ill, lucklessly, tragically, unfavourably, unhappily, unluckily.

RELATED KEYWORDS: FAILURE, LUCK, POVERTY, DEFEAT

MISGUIDANCE

n. **1.** **1. misguidance** misdirection, rumour, wrong advice. *Informal:* a bum steer. **2. rumour** furphy. **3. perversion** seduction.

2. **1. misleader** false prophet, ignis fatuus, will-o'-the-wisp. **2. perverter** corrupter, deceiver, seducer, svengali.

adj. **3.** **1. misleading** fallacious, false, illusory. **2. misguided** deluded, misdirected, misled, pseudolearned. **3. perverted** corrupted, deceived, seduced.

v. **4.** **1. misguide** be economical with the truth, bluff, distort, give a false impression, give someone a bum steer, lead astray, lead into error, misadvise, miscolour, miscounsel, misdirect, misinform, mislead, misrepresent, misteach, pervert. **2. confuse** baffle, bamboozle, bemuse, bewilder, confound, fog, fox, fuddle, mither *(Chiefly British),* muddle, mystify, nonplus, perplex, puddle, puzzle, stick, stump, throw off the scent. *Informal:* discombobulate, flummox. **3. fool** give the wrong idea. *Informal:* lead someone a merry dance, lead up the garden path. **4. pervert** corrupt, deceive, lead astray, seduce, subvert.

RELATED KEYWORDS: DECEPTION, MISREPRESENTATION

MISJUDGEMENT

n. **1.** **1. misjudgement** error, fault, miscalculation, miscue, misestimate, misestimation, mistake, overestimate, overestimation, underestimate, underestimation. *Informal:* barry. **2. misconception** hasty conclusion, jaundiced view, misapprehension, misunderstanding, warped judgement. **3. rough calculation** bush mile, country mile, rule of thumb. *Informal:* bush reckoning, guesstimate.

2. **1. preconception** assumption, predilection, prejudgement, prenotion, presumption, presupposal, presupposition, presurmise. **2. wrongheadedness** blind spot, doublethink, injudiciousness, jaundice, self-deception.

3. **1. misjudger** extenuator, misconceiver, perverter, prejudger.

adj. **4.** **1. misjudged** ill-advised, ill-judged, imprudent, indiscreet, injudicious, unsound, unwise, wrongheaded. **2. misconceived** based on false premises, exaggerated, fallacious, misunderstood, wrong. **3. overestimated** overrated, overvalued. **4. underestimated** underrated, undervalued.

v. **5.** **1. misjudge** fly in the face of facts, get someone wrong, miscalculate, misdiagnose, misestimate, misread, misreckon, mistake, misvalue, prejudge, reckon without, show warped judgement. *Informal:* be unable to see the wood for the trees, go off half-cocked, not see beyond one's nose. **2. misconceive** be wrong about, get the wrong idea about, have a bias, have a blind spot, jump to the wrong conclusion, misapprehend, misconstrue, misinterpret, misperceive, misunderstand. **3. overestimate** overplay one's hand, over-rate, overvalue. **4. underestimate** underrate.

RELATED KEYWORDS: DELUSION, ERROR, WRONGDOING, INTOLERANCE

MISPLACEMENT

n. **1.** **1. misplacement** disturbance, ectopia, epeirogenesis, epeirogeny, epirogeny, heave, heterotopia, malposition, prolapse, spill, spillage, version. **2. displacement** adventitiousness, dislocation, dislodgement, driftage, eluviation, luxation, transference. **3. homelessness** statelessness, vagrancy. **4. no-man's-land** limbo.

2. **1. misfit** erratic, fish out of water, horse marine *(US)*, square peg in a round hole.

adj. **3.** **1. misplaced** ectopic, erratic, heterotopous, parallactic. *Informal:* like a fish out of water. **2. displaced** adventitious, dislocated, unbalanced. **3. homeless** houseless, stateless, vagrant. **4. eccentric** askew, awry, off-centre, screwed, splay, wonky.

v. **4.** **1. misplace** misarrange, misdeliver, misfile. **2. displace** antevert, buck, dislodge, disseat, heave, spill, unbalance, unhorse, unsaddle, unseat. **3. dislocate** disjoint, luxate, splay, subluxate, translocate. **4. decentre** unbalance.

adv. **5.** **1. out of place** adventitiously, astray, in no-man's-land, on the streets, out, out of joint.

RELATED KEYWORDS: CHANGEABLENESS, LOSING, OVERTURN, ABSENCE

MISREPRESENTATION

n. **1.** **1. misrepresentation** corruption, cover-up, disinformation, distortedness, distortion, equivocation, exaggeration, fabrication, false portrayal, falsification, falsity, mendacity, misdescription, misinterpretation, perversion, sophistry, violence. *Informal:* bricking. **2. parody** bad likeness, burlesque, caricature, cartoon, iambic, lampoon, mockery, pasquil, pasquinade, postiche, satire, skit, travesty. *Informal:* send-up, spoof, take-off. **3. lie** canard, falsehood, garble, half-truth, invention, misquotation, misquote, misreport, tale, untruth. *Informal:* fib, porky, whopper. **4. optical illusion** anamorphosis, circus mirror, curved mirror, funhouse mirror.

2. **1. misrepresenter** belier, distorter, falsifier, garbler, misreporter.

adj. **3.** **1. misrepresented** distorted, misrepresentative.

v. **4.** **1. misrepresent** belie, contort, distort, falsify, garble, manipulate, miscolour, misde-scribe, misinterpret, misquote, misread, misrelate, misreport, oversimplify, pervert, por-tray falsely, put a false construction on, rig, skew, slant, sophisticate, trump up, twist. *Informal:* brick, cook, doctor, fake, fiddle, wangle. **2. parody** caricature, travesty. **3. bluff** delude, misadvise, miscounsel, misdirect, misguide, misinform, mislead, mis-teach. **4. libel** slander.

RELATED KEYWORDS: DELUSION, ERROR, DISHONESTY

MISUSE

n. **1.** **1. misuse** abusage, abuse, improper use, maladministration, misapplication, mis-appropriation, misdirection, misemployment, mismanagement, misusage, overuse, waste. **2. malpractice** barbarism, breach, corruption, depravity, infraction, malversation, perversion, prostitution, simony, violation. **3. maltreatment** elder abuse, ill usage, ill use, ill-treatment, misapplication, mishandling, mistreatment, misuse.

2. **1. misuser** abuser, lurk man, mauler. **2. perverter** corrupter, pervert, subverter.

v. **3.** **1. misuse** abuse, fool around with, infract, misapply, misappropriate, misemploy, overuse, overwear, tamper with, violate, waste. **2. ill-treat** abuse, ill-use, kick about, kick around, knock about, knock around, maltreat, maul, mishandle, mistreat, misuse, put the boot into, rough up. **3. pervert** contaminate, corrupt, debase, debauch, defile, degrade, deprave, desecrate, dishallow, foul, profane, prostitute, vitiate. **4. misman-age** maladminister, misconduct, misgovern, mishandle, misrule.

RELATED KEYWORDS: DAMAGE, MISGUIDANCE, USE, USELESSNESS

MIXTURE

n. **1.** **1. mixture** amalgam, assortment, medley, melange, miscellanies, mix. **2. jum-ble** catch-all, fantasia, farrago, flotsam and jetsam, gallimaufry, hodgepodge, hotch-potch, macedoine, medley, mishmash, motley, olio, omnium gatherum, paraphernalia, patchwork, pell-mell, polyglot, remnants, rummage, salmagundi, scraps, smorgasbord. *Informal:* bag of tricks, grab bag, mixed bag, odds and ends. **3. assemblage** album, assembly, box, bundle, cluster, collection, congeries, group, motley, muster. **4. pas-tiche** collage, infusion, pasticcio, patchwork, tincture. **5. musical medley** macaronic verse, potpourri. **6. mingling** accretion, admixture, amalgam, amalgamation, blending, combination, commixture, conglomeration, diffusion, fusion, immixture, integration, interfusion, interlarding, interpolation, junction, marriage, merger, mixing, mixture, stirring, synthesis, transfusion. **7. intermixture** entanglement, interlacement, interminglement, interspersion, lacing. **8. synaeresis** crasis, synaesthesia, synaloepha. **9. adulteration** admixture, contamination, corruption, debasement, sophistication, vitiation. **10. hybridisation** hybridism, interbreeding, miscegenation, mongrelisation, mongrelism, mosaicism.

2. 1. diversity biodiversity, difference, dissimilarity, diverseness, diversification, miscellaneousness, variation, variety. **2. heterogeneity** disparateness, eclecticism, heterogeneousness, many-sidedness, multifariousness, pluralism, promiscuity, promiscuousness. **3. miscibility**.

3. 1. hybrid cross, crossbred, crossbreed, half-breed, heterozygote, mosaic, mule. **2. mongrel** kuri *(NZ)*. *Informal:* bitser, bitzer, Heinz, melting pot, mong, ten best breeds in town. **3. half-blood** Eurasian, half-breed, half-caste, ladino, métis, mestee, mestizo, mulatto.

4. 1. mixer amalgamator, blender, food processor, jumbler, mingler, shuffler, vitamiser. **2. mixing tool** blunger, egg whisk, egg-beater, larry, liquidiser, paddle, palette knife, puddling machine, rabble, whisk. **3. adulterator** adulterant, vitiator. **4. cement mixer** concrete mixer.

adj. **5. 1. mixed** assorted, kaleidoscopic, medley, mingled, miscellaneous, motley, multifarious, varicoloured. **2. jumbled** diversiform, farraginous, hotch-potch, macaronic, medley, mingled, motley, muddled, scrappy, unclassified, unsorted. **3. diverse** biodiverse, daedal *(Chiefly Poetic)*, diversified, manifold, many-sided, multi-racial, multicultural, multiform, pluralist, pluralistic, polytypic, varied, variegated, various. **4. heterogeneous** eclectic, heterogenous, heteromerous, multilingual, polyglot, promiscuous. **5. fifty-fifty** half-and-half, Jekyll-and-Hyde, pepper-and-salt. **6. conglomerate** complex, composite, compound, conglomeritic. **7. adulterated** commercial, cut, sophisticated. **8. impure** foul, spoiled, tainted, vitiated.

6. 1. hybrid cross, crossbred, half-blooded, half-breed, heterozygous, interbred, miscegenetic, multi-racial.

v. **7. 1. mix** adulterate, blunge, dash, mash, mingle, muddle *(US)*, paddle, puddle, remix, roil, shake, shake up, stir. **2. blend** admix, emulsify, fold, fold in, fuse, homogenise, impregnate, interblend, interfuse, interlard, meld, mingle. **3. compound** brew, prepare. **4. amalgamate** alloy, combine, conglomerate, fuse, merge, unite. **5. diversify** assort, variegate. **6. shuffle** jumble, make, scramble. **7. mingle** blend, combine, commingle, commix, confound, enlace, immingle, immix, interfile, interfuse, interlace, interlard, intermingle, intermix, intersperse, meld, mix, pleach. **8. adulterate** contaminate, debase, empoison, sophisticate, spoil, taint, vitiate. **9. temper** season, tincture, water, water down. *Informal:* doctor.

8. 1. hybridise backcross, cross, crossbreed, interbreed, intercross, mix, mongrelise.

adv. **9. 1. diversely** diffusely, heterogeneously, miscellaneously, multifariously. **2. indiscriminately** every which way.

RELATED KEYWORDS: COMBINATION, INTERACTION, DISORDER, DIFFERENCE, COMPLEXITY

MOCKERY

n. **1. 1. mockery** derision, derisiveness, name-calling, ridicule, scorn. *Informal:* bagging, borac, razz, sledging. **2. sarcasm** irony, satiricalness. **3. taunting** heckling, ribaldry, scurrility. **4. chaff** chiack, chiacking, jeering, leg-pull, raillery, teasing, wind-up. **5. banter** badinage, jest, persiflage, pleasantry, raillery. **6. satire** burlesque, caricature, cartoon, iambic, lampoon, parody, pasquil, pasquinade, skit, squib, travesty. *Informal:* send-up, spoof, take-off. **7. rogue's march. 8. mock** dig, flout, gibe, hit, jeer, joke, scoff, sneer, taunt, witticism. *Informal:* knock, rub. **9. taunt** fleer, gibe, jeer, twit. **10. jest** jape, joke. *Informal:* crack, josh *(US)*, wisecrack. **11. howl of derision** hoot.

2. 1. mocker cynic, derider, flouter, jeerer, ridiculer, scoffer, sneerer. **2. taunter** barracker, giber, heckler, twitter. **3. banterer** chaffer, leg-puller, teaser. **4. satirist** caricaturist, lampooner, parodist, pasquinader, satiriser.

adj. **3. 1. mocking** chaffing, deriding, derisive, derisory, fleering, hudibrastic, jeering, quizzical, ridiculing, sarcastic, sardonic, scoffing, sneering. *Informal:* nipping, sarky. **2. bantering** sportful, teasing. **3. satiric** burlesque, satirical.

v. **4. 1. mock** badger, chuck off at, debunk, deride, fleer at, flout, gibe, heckle, jeer at, jest, jibe, needle, provoke, scoff, scorn, scout. *Informal:* gig, have a shot at, monkey, rib, sledge. **2. ridicule** laugh at, make a fool of, make a monkey of, make fun of, sport. *Informal:* have a lend of someone, have a loan of someone, poke borak, poke borak at, poke fun at, poke mullock at, rib, take the micky, take the micky out of. **3. taunt** gird at, howl down, knock. *Informal:* burl, guy, joe, laugh out of court, rubbish, slag, sledge. **4. banter** backcomb, chaff, chiack, get (or take) a rise out of, get a rise out of, jest *(Chiefly British),* kid, pull someone's leg, rag, rally, rib, tease, torment, twit, vex. *Informal:* bag, chyack, gig, josh *(US),* joss *(NZ),* razz. **5. hoot** howl. **6. satirise** befool, burlesque, lampoon, squib, travesty. *Informal:* send up. **7. pillory** blister, deride, gibbet, pasquinade. *Informal:* roast.

RELATED KEYWORDS: DISAPPROVAL, SLANDER, LOW REGARD, HUMOUR

MODEL

n. **1.** **1. model** copy, dummy, exemplar, lay figure, maquette, mock-up, mount, pattern, pilot, sample, working model. **2. template** exemplum, form, guide, matrix, mitre box, shape, templet. **3. mould** cast, casting, core, dariole, deckle, die, matrix, roughcast. **4. stamp** engraving, pig, pig-bed, plate, seal, stamper, woodblock, woodcut. **5. design** cartoon, sinopia. **6. block** last. **7. original** archetype, exemplar, manuscript, master, parent, protocol, protoplast, prototype, stock, the copy.

    2. **1. example** case, etymon, exemplification, exemplum, instance, paradigm, pattern, praxis, precedent. **2. specimen** pattern, piece, sample, sort, type, type genus, type specimen. **3. pacesetter** fugleman, pacemaker, pacer. **4. paragon** archetype, classic, exemplar, mirror, original. **5. ideal** beau ideal, dream, ego ideal, idea, picture, the abstract, top *(Poetic).* **6. standard** canon, classic, mark, measure, norm, pattern.

adj. **3.** **1. model** classic, classical, ideal. **2. standard** conventional, formulaic, normal, normative, ordinary, regular, sample, stock, typical. **3. original** archetypal, archetypical, prototypal. **4. exemplary** citatory, copybook, exemplificative, illustrative, paradigmatic, paradigmatical, precedential.

v. **4.** **1. set an example** lead the way, provide a model, set the pace, show the way. **2. pattern by (or after)** copy, model on, set in the same model, use as a guide.

RELATED KEYWORDS: GOODNESS, IMITATION, SHAPE, START

MODERATION

n. **1.** **1. moderation** moderateness, restraint, self-command, self-control, temperance, temperateness. **2. mildness** balminess, gentleness. **3. calmness** coolness, quietness, subduedness. **4. dullness** innocuousness, insipidity, tameness.

    2. **1. abatement** alleviation, assuagement, attenuation, easement, mitigation, palliation, relaxation, relief, remission, remittal, remittance, remittency, wane. **2. pacification** mollification, tranquillisation.

    3. **1. moderator** temperer. **2. assuager** allayer, damper, mitigator, modulator, mollifier, palliative, palliator, queller, quieter, relaxer, soother, tranquilliser. **3. middle-of-the-roader** Centrist, Menshevik, moderate, non-extremist. **4. neutraliser** buffer, cushion, dashpot, deadener.

adj. **4.** **1. moderate** middle-of-the-road, non-extreme, reasonable, temperate. **2. mild** affable, balmy, clement, gentle, kindly, lenient, soft. **3. calm** clear, composed, cool, cool-headed, disimpassioned, even, halcyon, impassive, imperturbable, level-headed, peaceful, placid, possessed, quiet, reposeful, sedate, self-composed, self-contained, self-possessed, serene, sleepy, sober, steady, still, stormless, tranquil, tranquillo, unflappable, unfussed, unmoved, unruffled, untouched. **4. soothing** alleviative, assuasive, attenuant, demulcent, lenitive, mitigative, mitigatory, palliative. **5. dull** dullish, harmless, innocuous, insipid, tame.

v. **5.** **1. moderate** mitigate, modify, modulate, mollify, palliate, qualify. **2. restrain** abate, allay, appease, assuage, bate, chasten, check, lay, mollify, pacify, relieve, subdue. **3. calm** assuage, becalm, calm down, cool down, cool off, defuse, lull, pacificate, pacify, placate, quell, quiet, quieten, smooth, soothe, stay, still, tranquillise. **4. abate** allay, alleviate, attenuate, bate, check, lessen, lighten, lower, milden, reduce, relax, relent, remit, season, slack, slacken, soften, soothe, tame, temper, tone down, turn down, wane. **5. dull** blunt, buff, cushion, dampen, deaden, obtund, opiate, tame.

    6. **1. exercise restraint** back-pedal, be moderate, soft-pedal. *Informal:* mince one's words, take the middle road.

adv. **7.** **1. moderately** in moderation, modestly, restrainedly, temperately, to a degree. **2. calmly** coolly, evenly, quietly. **3. mildly** balmily, gently, leniently. **4. dully** innocuously, tamely.

RELATED KEYWORDS: ABSTINENCE, ALLEVIATION, COMPOSURE, NEUTRALITY, PEACE

MODESTY

n. **1.**   **1. modesty** backwardness, bashfulness, constraint, coyness, demureness, diffidence, humility, prudery, pudency, reserve, reticence, shamefacedness, sheepishness, shyness, timidity. **2. self-effacement** effacement, self-deprecation, unassumingness, unobtrusiveness, unpretentiousness. **3. decency** chastity, continence, decorum, greenness, honour, innocence, piety, purity.

     2.   **1. modest person** blusher, effacer. *Informal:* shrinking violet, wallflower.

adj. **3.**   **1. modest** backward, bashful, blushful, blushing, coy, decent, demure, diffident, doe-eyed, hesitating, humble, meek, reluctant, reserved, restrained, reticent, retiring, shamefaced, sheepish, shy, skittish, timid, withdrawn. **2. self-effacing** discreet, self-deprecating, small, unassuming, unobtrusive, unostentatious, unpretending, unpretentious. **3. decent** chaste, comme il faut, genteel, honest, just, missish, moral, pious, prim, prim and proper, proper, prudish, pure, righteous, scrupulous, upright, upstanding, virtuous. *Informal:* prissy.

v. **4.**   **1. be modest** draw in one's horns, hide one's light under a bushel, keep in the background, keep one's distance, not big-note oneself, not give oneself airs, not put on side, sell oneself short, undersell oneself. **2. blush** crimson, flame up, flush, redden, resile, shrink, withdraw.

adv. **5.**   **1. modestly** backwardly, bashfully, blushingly, coyly, demurely, sheepishly, shyly. **2. self-effacingly** self-deprecatingly, unassumingly, unostentatiously, unpretendingly, unpretentiously, with no fuss or bother, without ceremony.

RELATED KEYWORDS: ARTLESSNESS, MEEKNESS, SOLITUDE

MOMENT

n. **1.**   **1. moment** breath, flash, instant, minute, second, split second, trice, twinkle, twinkling, wink. *Informal:* a brace of shakes, crack, jiffy, mo, sec, shake, tick, whipstitch *(US)*. **2. point of time** epoch, juncture, moment, particular, point, second, time. *Informal:* crack.

     2.   **1. momentariness** abruptness, suddenness, transience. **2. instantaneity** immediacy, immediateness, instantaneousness, quickness.

adj. **3.**   **1. momentary** passing, transient, transitory. **2. instantaneous** elapsing, immediate, instant, overnight, quick, split-second. **3. minute** ready-made. **4. sudden** abrupt, ad hoc, impromptu, impulsive, on-the-spot, snap.

adv. **4.**   **1. momentarily** for a moment, momently. **2. soon** after a bit, awhile, before long, in a bit, readily. **3. in a moment** all at once, asap, fast, in less than no time, in no time, in no time at all, in short order, presto, promptly, quick smart, quickly, rapidly, readily, soon. *Informal:* at warp speed, in a brace of shakes, in half a mo, in two shakes of a dog's tail, in two ticks, lickety-split *(Chiefly US)*, pronto. **4. instantly** at once, at sight, away, directly, forthwith, here and now, immediately, instantaneously, momentarily *(Chiefly US)*, on sight, on the spot, right, right away, shortly, straightaway, with this. **5. suddenly** abruptly, ad hoc, all at once, at the drop of a hat, extempore, impromptu, impulsively, offhand, on the spot, on the spur of the moment, out of hand, overnight, sharp, without notice.

interj. **5.**   **1. wait on** just a sec, just a second, wait up. *Informal:* half a mo, hang on, hang on a bit, just a tick, wait a sec.

RELATED KEYWORDS: SPEED, TEMPORARINESS, TIME MEASUREMENT

MONEY

n. **1.**   **1. money** cash, chips, circulating medium, coinage, currency, dibs, e-money, earnings, gold, hard cash, ill-gotten gains, legal tender, mintage, pelf, purse, riches, shekels, slush money, tender, wealth. *Informal:* big bickies, big bucks, big dollars, brass, bread, chaff, dosh, dough, fast buck, gelt, hard-earned, hay, kale *(US)*, l.s.d., lolly, loot, mazuma, moolah, oscar, readies, splosh, spon, spondulicks, stuff, tin, wampum *(US)*. **2. banknote** bill *(US)*, money order, note, order, paper, paper money. *Informal:* greenback *(US)*, lettuce, shin plaster. **3. pound** *Informal:* fiddley, iron man, jim, quid, seine. **4. dollar** *Informal:* buck, Oxford, Oxford scholar, plunk *(US)*, seine, smacker. **5. wad** bankroll. *Informal:* folding money, roll, scoop. **6. dirty money** narcodollar.

     2.   **1. coinage** change, coin, kembla, loose change, money, rouleau, silver, small change. *Informal:* cobar, shrapnel, specie. **2. coin** billon, copper, mite, picayune *(US)*, piece. *Informal:* bean, bit *(US)*, loonie. **3. counterfeit coin** double-header, grey, jack, nob, rap, slug. **4. numismatics** coin collector, numismatologist, numismatology.

3. **1. cheque** bank cheque, bank draft, bank-draft, banker's draft, bearer cheque, blank cheque, certified cheque, check *(US)*, counter cheque. *Informal:* stumer. **2. voucher** coupon, gift token. *Informal:* IOU. **3. credit card** account card, charge card, debit card. *Informal:* plastic, plastic money.

4. **1. funds** assets, capital, credit, eurodollars, finances, float, fund, gold, hedge fund, income, liquid assets, liquidity, money, money in hand, pelf, petrodollars, petty cash, pocket, quick assets, resources, revenue, royalty, savings, slush fund, supply, war chest, wealth. *Informal:* bread, bread and butter, cunning kick, dibs, exchequer. **2. kitty** jackpot, pool, stakes. **3. bond** bond money. **4. funny money** *(Informal)* mickey mouse money *(Colloquial)*. *Informal:* Monopoly money.

5. **1. allowance** expenses, housekeeping, maintenance, pin money, pocket money, spending money, viaticum. *Informal:* beer money. **2. subsidy** deficiency payment. **3. scholarship** bursary, exhibition. **4. alms** charity, collection, maundy *(British)*, maundy money, offering. **5. expenditure** consumption, disbursement.

6. **1. treasury** bank, bursary, coffers, exchequer, finances, fisc, funds, gold reserve, mint. **2. cash desk** cash register, checkout, p.o.s. terminal, point-of-sale terminal, till. *Informal:* peter. **3. strongroom** strongbox, treasure-house, vault. **4. moneybox** piggy bank. **5. money market** foreign exchange market. **6. treasurer** bursar, cashier, collector. **7. fundholder** investor. **8. moneychanger**.

7. **1. currency** agio, decimal currency, eurocurrency, floating currency, foreign currency, fractional currency, managed currency. **2. standard** bimetallism, gold bullion standard, gold standard, gold-exchange standard, monometallism, silver standard, symmetallism. **3. mintage** coinage, monetisation. **4. exchange** foreign exchange, forward exchange.

8. **1. coins** angel, carolus, caser, cent, colonial dollar, copper, crown, crownpiece, deaner, denarius, dime, doit, dollar, double eagle, dump, farthing, florin, george, government dollar, groat, guinea, ha'pence, ha'penny, half-crown, halfpenny, holey dollar, holy dollar, lepton, mark, moidore, new penny, nickel *(US)*, penny, quarter, queen's shilling, ring dollar, royal, shilling, sixpence, son, sovereign, the king's shilling, threepence, threepenny (bit), thruppence *(Chiefly British)*. *Informal:* bit *(US)*, bob, jitney *(US)*, kick, swy, tanner, toonie *(Canadian)*, trey (bit), two bob, zack. **2. notes** *Informal:* brick, fiver, grand, guinea, half spot, monkey, pony, slice, spin, spot, sum, tenner.

9. **1. monetary unit** afghani, anna, bezant, copeck, cowry, crown, deutschmark, dinar, dollar, doubloon, drachma, ducat, eagle, escudo, euro, eurodollar, franc, guilder, gulden, kina, kopeck, króna, krone, lepton, lira, mark, Mark der Deutschen Notenbank, markka, peag, peseta, peso, pfennig, piastre, piece of eight, pound, rand, real, renminbi, rial, riel, ringgit, riyal, rouble, ruble, rupee, rupiah, sen, sesterce, shekel, solidus, sou, stater, stiver, sycee, tael, talent, taler, thaler, toea, wampum, yen, yuan, zloty. *Informal:* rupe.

adj. 10. **1. monetary** cash, financial, fiscal, hip-pocket, pecuniary. **2. convertible** liquid, realisable, utterable. **3. numismatic** numismatical, nummary, nummular. **4. money-minded**.

v. 11. **1. cash** amortise, change, collect, draw, draw on, float a loan, liquidate, overdraw, realise, run, tap, withdraw from. *Informal:* go liquid, raise the wind.

12. **1. monetise** circulate, coin, counterfeit, forge, issue, mint, utter. **2. revalue** demonetise, devaluate, devalue, down-value, fall, rise, transvalue, upvalue.

adv. 13. **1. monetarily** fiscally, in kind, in specie, pecuniarily.

RELATED KEYWORDS: GIVING, FINANCE, PROPERTY, SIGN, WEALTH

MORALITY

n. 1. **1. morality** moralism, morals, principles, standards. **2. ethics** bioethics, moral philosophy, professional ethics. **3. ethic** dictate, ideal, maxim, moral, moralism, motto, precept, principle, work ethic.

2. **1. moral sense** categorical imperative, conscience, mens rea, superego.

3. **1. moral theories** aestheticism, altruism, axiology, Benthamism, casuistry, Confucianism, deontology, egoism, eudemonics, eudemonism, hedonism, intuitionalism, intuitionism, intuitivism, nihilism, pragmatism, probabilism, relativism, sensationalism, sensualism, subjectivism, teleology, utilitarianism. **2. moral philosopher** altruist, casuist, deontologist, egoist, egotist, ethicist, eudemonist, hedonist, intuitionist, intuitivist, nihilist, relativist, teleologist, utilitarian.

4. **1. moraliser** moralist, puritan. *Informal:* wowser.

adj. 5. **1. moral** axiological, casuistic, ethic, ethical. **2. moralistic** carping, conscience-stricken, puritan, sermonising. *Informal:* wowseristic. **3. decent** clean, principled, well-behaved.

adv. **6. 1. morally** ethically, on principle.

RELATED KEYWORDS: BEHAVIOUR, GOODNESS, HONESTY, PROPRIETY, RULE

MOVEMENT

n. **1. 1. movement** action, Brownian motion, locomotion, motion. **2. perpetual motion** evolution, perpetuo moto. **3. mobility** activity, agility, degree of freedom, manoeuvrability, motility, movability, nimbleness. **4. tropism** galvanotropism, geotropism, heliotaxis, heliotropism, negative geotropism, nyctitropism, photokinesis, phototaxis, phototropism, positive geotropism, sleep-movement, thermotaxis, thigmotaxis. **5. mobilisation** dislocation. **6. dynamics** hydrokinetics, kinematics, kinesiology, kinetics, mechanics. **7. laws of motion** Einstein's general theory of relativity, Einstein's special theory of relativity, Newton's laws. **8. kineme.**

2. 1. move action, business, gesticulation, gesture, motion, movement. **2. rhythm** tempo, time. **3. gait** foot, footfall, footstep, footwork, pace, step, stride, walk. **4. bounce** bob, gurgitation, nod, nutation, prance, shrug. **5. jerk** cant, jolt, snatch, stamp, start, stroke, whip. **6. slide** fishtail, flap, glide, skid, slip, slither, stroke, swim. **7. wriggle** squirm, writhe. **8. course** advance, drift, make one's way, march, path, run, sweep, tack, trajectory. **9. circuit** circle, circulation, meander, orbit. **10. to-and-fro** oscillation.

adj. **3. 1. moving** automobile, automotive, locomotive, locomotor, motile, self-moving. **2. in motion** ambulant, animated, astir, away, live, moving, off, running, shifting, volitant. **3. motor** psychomotor, sensorimotor. **4. circulatory** ambient, circulative. **5. tropic** geotropic, heliotactic, heliotropic, nutational, photokinetic, phototropic, thermotaxic, thigmotactic. **6. mobile** dynamic, kinematic, kinematical, kinetic, manoeuvrable, motive. **7. oscillating** swinging.

v. **4. 1. move** go, heave, make one's way, run, stir, surge, walk. **2. barrel along** bat along, bowl along, coast along, roll along, spank along, thrash along. **3. ply** plough. **4. bounce** bob, bobble, dap, hop, jounce, jump, nod, noddle, prance, surge. **5. jerk** beat, bob, flick, flicker, flitter, flutter, play, quiver, shake, skitter, squib, twitch, waver, winnow. **6. slide** aquaplane, glide, hydroplane, plane, skate, skid, skim, slip, slither. **7. glide** bowl, coast, cruise, ride, roll, sail, skim, sweep. *Informal:* kite. **8. wriggle** contort, intort, snake, squirm, twist, wrench, writhe. **9. oscillate** move to and fro, swing. **10. mobilise** agitate, animate. **11. budge** give way, shift, work. **12. start** commence, launch, let rip. **13. clutch-start** jump-start, push-start, rev up, turn over.

adv. **5. 1. on the move** under way, under weigh, up and about. *Informal:* on the go, on the wing. **2. to-and-fro** back and forth, hither and thither.

interj. **6. 1. let's start** avanti, banzai, let 'er rip, let's go, take it away. *Informal:* let's do it, tally-ho, up and at'em.

RELATED KEYWORDS: DANCING, FLYING, ROUTE, SPEED, SPIN, TRAVEL, TURBULENCE, VIBRATION

MULTICOLOUR

n. **1. 1. multicolour** dichroism, dichromaticism, dichromatism, opalescence, polychromatism, polychromy, trichroism, trichromatism, variedness, variegation. **2. rainbow** bow, prism, spectrum. **3. mosaic** kaleidoscope, motley, patchwork, tessellation. **4. veining** cloudiness, dicing, fasciation, imbrication, maculation, marble, marbling, marking, ocellation, streakiness. **5. blotch** blaze, blemish, fleck, freak, maculation, ocellus, smutch, speck, splash, spot, stain. **6. mottle** dapple, speckle. **7. brindle** merle *(Chiefly Scottish or Poetic).* **8. stripe** band, bar, candy stripe, fascia, pinstripe, streak, vein, vitta. **9. plaid** argyle, mixture, tartan, tattersall. **10. check** checker, hound's-tooth check, shepherd's check. **11. dot** flock dot, polka dot.

adj. **2. 1. multicoloured** bicolour, dichroic, dichromatic, dichromic, motley, particoloured, party-coloured, pavonine, polychromatic, polychrome, prismatic, rainbow, trichroic, trichromatic, tricolour, tricoloured, two-tone, varicoloured, varied, variegated. *Informal:* psychedelic. **2. versicolour** changeable, chatoyant, cloudy, moiré, mother-of-pearl, nacreous, opalescent, opaline, shot, watered. **3. motley** farinaceous, harlequin, heather-mixture, heterochromatic, heterochromous, marble, mealy, pepper-and-salt. **4. dappled** black-and-blue, brindle, brindled, calico *(Chiefly US),* dapple, dapple-bay, dapple-grey, flea-bitten, merle, mottled, piebald, pied, pinto *(US),* roan, skewbald, tabby, tortoiseshell. **5. spotted** blotchy, dotted, speckled, splashy, spotty, stippled, variolitic. **6. barred** banded, candy-striped, fasciate, ring-streaked, ringed, stripe, striped. **7. veined** marble-washed, marbled, streaky. **8. check** checked, checkered *(US),* chequered, compony, tessellate. **9. ocellated** bird's-eye, eyed. **10. plaid** argyle, plaided, tartan, tattersall.

RELATED KEYWORDS: CLOTHES, COLOUR, LAYER

MUSIC

n. **1.** **1. music** accord, consonance, ensemble, harmony, unison. **2. melody** air, aria, chime, klangfarbenmelodie, lilt, measure *(Poetic)*, music, strain, theme, tune. **3. musical subject** countersubject, idea, principal, subsidiary. **4. musicality** canorousness, harmoniousness, lyricalness, lyricism, mellifluousness, melodiousness, sweetness, tunefulness. **5. accompaniment** alberti bass, backing, bass, basso continuo, basso ostinato, boogie bass, bourdon, burden, continuo, drone, figured bass, ground, ground bass, obbligato, stride piano, thoroughbass, tutti, vamp, walking bass.

2. **1. musical piece** composition, cycle, morceau, movement, opus, opuscule, standard, work. *Informal:* potboiler. **2. study** étude, five-finger exercise, gradus. **3. arrangements** preparation, realisation, rifacimento, setting, transcription, transposition. **4. fanfare** bravura, fanfaron, flourish. **5. overture** concert-overture, praeludium, prelude, voluntary. **6. interlude** entr'acte, intermezzo, ritornello. **7. finale** postlude. **8. refrain** chorus, coda, derry, falderal, ritornello, tag. **9. character piece** arabesque, bagatelle, ballade, capriccio, caprice, fantasia, humoresque, idyll, impromptu, invention, legende, nocturne, pastorale, perpetual motion, perpetuo moto, pibroch, potpourri, quodlibet, reverie, rhapsody, romance, scherzo, sketch, toccata.

3. **1. singing** Ambrosian chant, balladry, Bayreuth bark, bel canto, chant, charm, minstrelsy, monotone, vocalisation, vocalism, vocality, vocalness, vocals. **2. part-singing** close harmony, faburden, fauxbourdon, organum. **3. recitative** recitativo secco, scena, Sprechgesang, Sprechstimme.

4. **1. song** anthem, ballad, barcarolle, calypso, cantata, cantilena, canto, cantus, canzone, canzonet, chanson, chant, comeallyers, descant, ditty, folk song, frottola, hit song, hymn, lay, lied, lyrics, melody, national anthem, nursery rhyme, patter song, penillion, pennillion, shanty, song cycle, tabi song, torch song, vocal, vocalise, Volkslied, waiata, warble. **2. part-song** canon, glee, madrigal, villanella. **3. round** catch, roundelay. **4. aria** arietta, cabaletta, cavatina, concert aria. **5. yodel** styrienne. **6. lullaby** berceuse, cradlesong. **7. drinking song** brindisi. **8. marriage song** epithalamion, epithalamium, hymeneal, prothalamion. **9. dirge** coronach, elegy, epicedium, lament, lamentation, last post, monody, taps *(US Military)*, threnode, threnody. **10. theme song** jingle, leitmotiv, signature, signature tune, theme tune. **11. music part** canto, canto fermo, cantus firmus, chart, descant, fundamental bass, line, organum, second, secondo, vocals, voice part.

5. **1. pitch** absolute pitch, concert A, concert pitch, perfect pitch, relative pitch. **2. key** home key, key signature, major, major key, minor, minor key. **3. register** chest register, compass, diapason, head register, head voice, range, tessitura. **4. intonation** sharpness, temperament, tuning. **5. tonality** bitonality, key, polytonality. **6. timbre** brilliance, croon, intensity, note, quality, tone, tone colour, voice. **7. dynamics** swell. **8. modulation** transition. **9. glissando** portamento, slide.

6. **1. musical phrase** figure, phrase, repetend, riff. **2. passage** break, episode, fill, middle eight, period. **3. cadence** buzz bar, close, feminine cadence, half-cadence, imperfect cadence, interrupted cadence, perfect cadence, plagal cadence, rhythm. **4. tone row** note row, retrograde inversion, row, series. **5. coda** codetta, stretta, tag. **6. slur** ligature, melisma.

7. **1. musical score** charts, chord chart, full score, gradual, head, music, part, sheet music, short score, top lines, vocal score. **2. libretto** book, wordbook. **3. stave** air, bar, double bar, ledger line, leger line, line, measure *(Poetic)*, melody, space, staff. **4. note** bind, dot, hook, ligature, stem, tail, tie. **5. direction** expression mark, fermata, ligature, pause, presa, rest, segno, signature, slur, tenuto, time signature. **6. notation** neumes, solfège, solfa, solfeggio, solmisation, staff notation, tablature, tonic sol-fa.

8. **1. concert** chamber concert, festival, prom concert, promenade concert, recital, soirée, subscription concert. **2. eisteddfod. 3. musicale** blow, community singing, jam, jam session, rockfest, sing-sing, singsong. **4. serenade** shivaree *(US)*. **5. item** bracket.

9. **1. opera** ballad opera, comic opera, extravaganza, grand opera, light opera, music drama, music theatre, musical, musical comedy, opéra bouffe, opéra comique, opera seria, operetta, oratorio, pastoral, pastorale, rock opera, singspiel, zarzuela. **2. Chinese opera** Beijing opera, bugaku, gagaku, No drama, Peking opera, wayang, wayang kulit.

10. **1. musicianship** articulation, ensemble, execution, feeling, music appreciation, musicality, touch, virtuosity. **2. musicology** doctrine of affection, ethnomusicology, harmonics, hymnology, melodics, rhythmics.

11. **1. music-lover** concert-goer, emo, listener. **2. audience.**

12. **1. music** absolute music, abstract music, art music, classical music, concrete music, dodecaphony, folk, folk music, gagaku, homophony, incidental music, indeterminate music, musique concrète, muzak, piped music, programme music, serial music, sound piece. **2. symphonic music** ballet music, cassation, concertante, concertino, concerto, concerto grosso, divertimento, divertissement, double concerto, serenata, sinfonia, suite, symphonic poem, symphony, tone poem. **3. chamber music** duet, duo, instrumental, nonet, octet, partita, quartet, quintet, septet, serenade, serenata, sextet, solo, sonata, sonatina, trio. **4. contemporary music genres** acid rock, afro-rock, beat music, bubblegum music, cajun music, commercial music, country and western, country music, country rock, cradle rock, disco, disco music, electronic music, electrophonic music, emo, folk, folk music, folk-rock, funk, goodtime, hard rock, head music, heavy metal, heavy rock, hi-NRG, hip-hop, house, light music, motown, new wave, pop, pop music, punk, punk rock, R'n'B, rap music, reggae, rock, rock (music), rock'n'roll, rock-and-roll, rockabilly, ska, skiffle, soft rock, speed metal, swamp rock. **5. jazz** barrel-house, bebop, blue grass, blues, boogie-woogie, bop, delta blues, dixieland, gospel music, gutbucket, jazz/rock, kwela, latin, mainstream, modern jazz, new orleans, progressive jazz, R & B, R'n'B, ragtime, rebop, rhythm and blues, soul (music), stomp, swing (music), tailboard, tailgate, third stream, traditional, twelve-bar blues. *Informal:* jug, nitty-gritty, rag, razzamatazz, trad. **6. dance music** écossaise, allemande, beguine, bergamasque, bolero, bossa nova, bourrée, cachucha, carioca, carmagnole, chaconne, contredanse, courante, fandango, farandole, flamenco, folk dance, galliard, gallopade, galop, gavotte, gigue, hoedown, hornpipe, jig, ländler, lancers, mazurka, minuet, onestep, passacaglia, pavan, pavin, polka, polonaise, quadrille, reel, rhumba, rigadoon, roundelay, rumba, salsa, saltarello, samba, saraband, schottische, seguidilla, strathspey, tambourin, tango, tarantella, twostep, tyrolienne, waltz. **7. march** cakewalk, dead march, quickstep, rogue's march. **8. religious music** alleluia, anthem, antiphon, antiphony, canticle, canto fermo, cantus, cantus firmus, carol, chant, choral, chorale *(US)*, credo, dithyramb, gradual, Gregorian chant, hallelujah, hymn, hymnody, hymnology, introit, mass, metrical psalm, motet, oratorio, paean, pean, plainchant, plainsong, processional, prose, psalm, psalmody, recessional, recessional (hymn), recessional hymn, requiem, respond, responsory, sequence, service, services, shout song, spiritual, tract, versicle. **9. Agnus Dei** Ave Maria, Crux Fidelis, Jubilate, Kyrie eleison, Magnificat, Miserere, Nunc Dimittis, Sanctus, Tantum Ergo, Te Deum, Tersanctus.

13.   **1. harmony** anticipation, change, fauxbourdon, inversion, preparation, progression, quartal harmony, suspension. **2. discord** cross-relation, false relation, false-relation, preparation, suspension.

14.   **1. rhythm** accent, anacrusis, arsis, back beat, beat, common measure, common time, down-beat, duple time, four-four time, groove, measure *(Poetic)*, movement, numbers, off-beat, polyrhythm, quadruple time, simple time, syncopation, tala, thesis, time, time value, triple measure, triple time, triplex, up-beat, up-tempo. **2. value** duration, length.

15.   **1. musical ornamentation** acciaccatura, agogic accent, appoggiatura, crush note, embellishment, figuration, flourish, flutter-tongue, glide, glissando, grace, grace-note, hammer, hot licks, inverted mordent, lick, mordent, ornament, ornamentation, passage, pralltriller, quaver, roulade, shake, slide, slur, tremolo, trill, turn, vibrato.

16.   **1. musical form** binary form, modulation, rondo, ternary form. **2. mode** Aeolian mode, Dorian mode, Ionian mode, Lydian mode, Mixolydian mode, Phrygian mode. **3. sonata form** bridge passage, coda, development, exposition, recapitulation, transition.

17.   **1. musical note quantity** breve, crotchet, demisemiquaver, eighth note *(US)*, hemidemisemiquaver, large, longa, minim, quarter note, quaver, semibreve, semidemisemiquaver, semiquaver, sixteenth note *(US)*, sixty-fourth note *(US)*, thirty-second note *(US)*, tone, whole note *(US)*. **2. degrees of scale** dominant, final, fundamental (note) (tone), keynote, leading note, mediant, prime, root, subdominant, submediant, subtonic, supertonic, tonal centre, tonic, ut. **3. numbers** duplet, octuplet, quadruplet, quintuplet, septuplet, sextolet, tercet, triplet. *Informal:* quad. **4. interval** bent note, complement, diesis, eighth, fifth, fourth, half-tone *(US)*, harmonic interval, leap, major third, melodic interval, microtone, minor third, ninth, octave, quarter tone, second, semitone, seventh, sixth, step, third, tone, tritone, whole step, whole tone. **5. accidental** auxiliary note, chromatic notes, double flat, double sharp, flat, natural, sharp. **6. harmonics** combination tone, fundamental, fundamental frequency, harmonic, harmonic series, overtone, resultant note, resultant tone.

18.   **1. chord** altered chord, arpeggio, bar chord, barré chord, blue chord, broken chord, chord of the sixth, chording, close position, common chord, diminished seventh chord, dominant seventh chord, hexachord, ninth chord, open position, seventh chord, sixth chord, tetrachord, triad.

19. **1. scale** chromatic scale, diatonic scale, gamut, harmonic minor, hexatone, major scale, minor scale, octave, pentatonic scale, raga, relative major, relative minor, shard, whole-tone scale.

20. **1. clef** alto clef, bass clef, C clef, F clef, G clef, soprano clef, tenor clef, treble clef.

21. **1. voice** alto, baritone, barytone, bass, basso, basso profundo, castrato, coloratura, contralto, countertenor, falsetto, mezzo, mezzosoprano, second, soprano, tenor, treble.

adj. **22.** **1. musical** canorous, consonant, harmonic, perfect. **2. melodious** canorous, harmonious, Lydian, lyrical, mellifluous, mellow, Orphean, rich, songful, sweet, symphonious, tuneable, tuneful. **3. melodic** diapasonic, homophonic, mono, monodic, monophonic. **4. instrumental** grand, orchestral, symphonic. **5. unaccompanied** lead, secco, solo. **6. vocal** choral, choric, lyric, melic, operatic. **7. treble** falsetto, reedy. **8. bass** basso continuo, continuo. **9. classical** baroque, romantic. **10. jazz** bottleneck, cool, honky-tonk. *Informal:* hep *(Chiefly US)*, hip *(Chiefly US)*. **11. pop** calypso. **12. threnodic** epicedial, epicedian, threnodial. **13. rhapsodical** quodlibetical. **14. figurate** florid. **15. through-composed** strophic.

v. **23.** **1. make music** busk, execute, interpret, melodise, perform, play, render, sound. **2. strike up** begin to play. **3. accompany** vamp. **4. trill** flourish, shake. **5. slur** glide. **6. jazz** jam, swing, swing music, syncopate. **7. sight-read** . **8. play by ear** adlib. *Informal:* lug. **9. bow** double-stop, scrape, stop. *Informal:* fiddle. **10. pluck** lute, pick, plunk, strum, thrum, twang. **11. sweep the strings 12. strike** beat, drum, roll, tabor, trill. **13. play the piano** touch the keyboard. *Informal:* soft-pedal, tickle the ivories. **14. play the organ** register, unstop. **15. ring** carillon, chime, knell, knoll, toll. **16. blow** break, bugle, fife, flute, overblow, pipe, skirl *(Chiefly Scottish)*, trump, trumpet, whistle. **17. tongue** double-tongue. **18. conduct** beat time, guide, keep time, lead. **19. compose** arrange, double, harmonise, improvise, note, orchestrate, realise, score, set, transpose. **20. figure** finger.

24. **1. sing** anthem, cantillate, carol, chant, croon *(Scottish, Irish)*, descant, discourse, hum, hymn, intonate, intone, lilt, outsing, precent, psalm, quaver, solfa, vocalise, warble, yodel. **2. chorus** chime in, choir, consort, harmonise. **3. intone** cantillate, chant, descant, intonate, sing. **4. serenade** shivaree.

adv. **25.** **1. musically** canorously, harmoniously, lyrically, mellifluously, melodiously, rhapsodically, rhythmically, sweetly, tunefully. **2. polyphonically** contrapuntally, fugally. **3. vocally** chorally, operatically. **4. tonally** achromatically, diatonically, harmonically. **5. atonally** chromatically, enharmonically.

26. **1. musical directions** a cappella, al fine, all' ottava, arco, col legno, con sordino, da capo, dal segno, down-bow, in altissimo, oppure, pizzicato, senza, sul ponticello, sul tasto, tacet, tasto solo, tre corde, tutti, una (due) (prima) volta, una corda, up-bow, volti. **2. expression marks** a capriccio, affetuoso, agitato, alla marcia, alla tedesca, alla turca, amoroso, animato, appassionato, arioso, assai, attacca, bravura, brillante, cantabile, cantando, capriccioso, con amore, con anima, con brio, con espressione, con forza, con fuoco, con grazia, con moto, con spirito, dolce, dolente, doloroso, fugato, grandioso, grave, gravemente, grazioso, legato, leggiero, maestoso, marcato, martellato, molto, mosso, non troppo, parlando, pesante, più, poco, poco a poco, risoluto, scherzando, semplice, sempre, sostenuto, spiccato, spiritoso, staccato, subito, tanto, tenuto, tranquillo, troppo, vigoroso, vivo. **3. a tempo** accelerando, alla breve, allargando, allegretto, allegro, andante, andantino, calando, doppio movimento, l'istesso tempo, largamente, larghetto, largo, lentamente, lentando, lentissimo, lento, moderato, prestissimo, presto, rallentando, ritardando, rubato, stringendo, tardo, tempo giusto, veloce. **4. forte** crescendo, fortissimo, forzando, mezzoforte, rinforzando, sforzando. **5. piano** decrescendo, diminuendo, mezzopiano, pianissimo.

RELATED KEYWORDS: ENTERTAINMENT, MUSICAL INSTRUMENT, MUSICIAN, SOUND

MUSICAL INSTRUMENT

n. **1.** **1. musical instrument** piece, stick. **2. tuning device** diapason, fork, monochord, phonoscope, pitchpipe, tonometer, tuning fork. **3. rhythm section**.

2. **1. wind instrument** aeolipile, aerophone, reed, wind, wood, woodwind. **2. flute** comb and paper, didge, didgeridoo, didj, didjeribone, didjeridu, drone pipe, fife, fipple flute, flageolet, gumleaf, ocarina, panpipe, penny whistle, piccolo, pipes, quill, recorder, shakuhachi, tin whistle, transverse flute, whistle. **3. clarinet** basset horn, chalumeau, clarionet, hornpipe, saxophone, tarogato. *Informal:* horn, sax. **4. oboe** aulos, bassoon, contrabassoon, cor anglais, crumhorn, double bassoon, English horn, fagotto, hautboy, heckelphone, krummhorn, shawm. **5. bagpipes** cornemuse, drone, musette, pipes.

6. harmonica melodica, mouth organ, mouth-harp, sho. *Informal:* harp. **7. kazoo** gazoo, mirliton, swanee whistle, Tommy talker.

3. 1. brass instrument brass, brass wind. **2. trumpet** Bach trumpet, balance horn, bugle, clarino, clarion, cornet, exponential horn, flugelhorn, horn, shofar. **3. trombone** sackbut, slush pump. **4. French horn** mellophone, wagner tuba. **5. tuba** baritone, barytone, bass horn, bombardon, euphonium, helicon, saxtuba, sousaphone, Wagner tuba. **6. cornet** bass horn, ophicleide, serpent, tuba. **7. saxhorn** althorn, alto, alto horn, tenor horn, tenor saxhorn. **8. hand-horn** alpenhorn, alphorn, coach-horn, post-horn, shophar. **9. conch** concha, murex.

4. 1. string instrument – bowed chest of viols, strings. **2. violin** fiddle, kit, pouchette, rebec, sourdine. **3. viola** alto, second, tenor. **4. cello** violoncello. **5. double bass** baritone, barytone, contrabass, string bass, tea-chest bass. *Informal:* bull fiddle. **6. viol** bass viol, chordophone, double-bass viol, gamba, viola d'amore, viola da braccio, viola da gamba, violone. **7. bow** fiddle bow, fiddlestick. **8. mute** sordino, sourdine. **9. nail violin** nail harmonica, singing saw.

5. 1. string instrument – plucked. 2. guitar air guitar, balalaika, banjo, banjolele, bass guitar, bottleneck guitar, chitarra, citole, cittern, classical guitar, dobro, electric guitar, gittern, Hawaiian guitar, lead guitar, pedal steel guitar, resonator guitar, rhythm guitar, samisen, slide guitar, steel guitar, twelve-string guitar, ukulele, V-box, zithern, zittern. *Informal:* axe, easy rider *(US)*, uke. **3. lute** archlute, bandore, biwa, bouzouki, charango, chitarrone, domra, mandolin, pandora, ramkie, sarod, sitar, sittar, tamboura, theorbo, ud, vina. **4. harp** cithara, citole, crowd, crwth, Irish harp, kithara, lyre, rote, sackbut, sambuca. **5. zither** autoharp, cembalo, cither, citole, cittern, cymbalo, dulcimer, gittern, koto, psaltery, zithern, zittern. **6. dulcimer** cembalo, cimbalom, cymbalo, santir. **7. plectrum** fingerpick, pick. **8. capo** bottleneck, slide. **9. aeolian harp** aeolian lyre, wind harp.

6. 1. piano aliquot scaling, concert grand piano, cottage piano, digitorium, dumb piano, fortepiano, grand, grand piano, mbira, pianoforte, prepared piano, spinet *(US)*, square piano, upright, upright piano. *Informal:* goanna, pianna. **2. clavier** cembalo, clavecina, clavicembalo, clavichord, harpsichord, spinet, virginal. **3. organ** American organ, calliope, choir organ, electric organ, electronic organ, great organ, harmonium, melodeon, pipe organ, portative, portative organ, positive organ, reed organ, regal, sensillum, seraphine, unit organ, wurlitzer. **4. accordion** concertina, piano accordion. *Informal:* squeezebox.

7. 1. percussion instrument agogo, idiophone, membranophone, metallophone, percussion. **2. percussion section** battery. *Informal:* kitchen section. **3. drum** atabal, bass drum, baya, bodhran, bongo, conga, cuica, friction drum, gran cassa, kettle, kettledrum, quica, side-drum, snare-drum, tabla, tabla bayan, tabor, taboret, taborin, tabret, taiko, tam-tam, tambour, tambourine, timbal, timbales, timbrel, timpani, tom-tom, tymbal, tympan, tympanum. **4. drum kit** . *Informal:* skins. **5. cymbal** crash cymbal, high hat, ride cymbal, splash cymbal. **6. maraca** calabash, castanet, cowbell, guiro, jew's-harp, sistrum, washboard, woodblock. **7. rhythm sticks** Chinese block, clap sticks, clapping sticks, claves, music sticks, songsticks. **8. triangle** anvil. **9. lagerphone** crescent *(US)*. **10. bullroarer** churinga, churunga, tchurunga, thunder stick, tjuringa, turinga. **11. noisemaker** bones, clapper, rattle, whip, whistle, wobble board. *Informal:* hooter. **12. gong** tam-tam, tom-tom. **13. bell** carillon, handbell, tintinnabulum. **14. glockenspiel** carillon, celesta, chime, harmonica, mouth organ, mouth-harp, peal, tubular bells, wind chimes. *Informal:* harp. **15. xylophone** gamelan, gender, marimba, vibes, vibraharp *(US)*, vibraphone. **16. glass harmonica** . **17. percussion group** gamelan.

8. 1. electronic instrument beat box, clavinet, drum machine, fairlight, moog, music synthesiser, rhythm machine, synthesiser, theremin, timbron.

9. 1. musical machine barrel organ, hand organ, harmonicon, hurdy-gurdy, musical box, nyckelharpa, orchestrion. **2. pianola** player piano. **3. effects pedal** chorus, phaser, phlanger, wah wah pedal.

10. 1. wind instrument parts bell, chanter, crook, drone, embouchure, fipple, ligature, mouthpiece, pipe, reed, shank, slide, tongue, valve, ventage, wind cap, windbag. **2. string instrument parts** belly, bridge, catgut, chinrest, chord, end pin, f-hole, finetuner, fingerboard, fret, neck, nut, peg, snare, sound board, sound hole, soundbox, soundingboard, soundpost, string, sympathetic string, table, tailpiece, tasto, wire. **3. organ stop** bank, bassoon, bombardon, bourdon, cancel, carillon, chalumeau, chime, choir organ, clarabella, clarino, clarion, console, cornet, cornopean, coupler, diapason, dolce, dulcet, dulciana, flue, fluepipe, fluestop, flute, gamba, great organ, languette, manual, mixture, mouth, oboe, octave, organ pipe, principal, quint, rank, reed pipes, reedstop, register, stop, sub-bass, subprincipal, swell, swell box, swell organ, tremolant, tremolo, tremulant, trumpet, tuba, viola, viola da gamba, violone, voix céleste, vox angelica, vox humana, windchest. **4. keyboard parts** clavier, digital, fingerboard, hammer, ivories, jack, key, keyboard, loud pedal, note, overdamper, pedal, pedal board, quill, short octave, soft pedal, sustaining pedal, tangent, underdamper. **5. drum parts** brace, drumhead, drumstick, head, tympan, tympanum.

RELATED KEYWORDS: MUSIC, MUSICIAN, RESONANCE, SOUND

MUSICIAN

n. **1.** **1. musician** artiste, concert artist, duettist, executant, klezmer, mariachi, performer, soloist, studio musician, virtuoso. *Informal:* muso, sessionman. **2. jazz player** be-bopper. *Informal:* cat, hepcat, swinger. **3. rhythmist** syncopator. **4. accompanist** répétiteur, vamper. **5. tuner** temperer. **6. composer** arranger, contrapuntist, dodecaphonist, harmonist, lyricist, madrigalist, melodiser, melodist, monodist, scorer, singer-songwriter, songwriter, symphonist, transposer, writer. **7. hymnologist** hymnist, hymnodist, psalmist, psalmodist, threnodist. **8. musicologist. 9. tin-pan alley.**

2. **1. instrumentalist** bandsman, first violinist, player, sideman. **2. fiddler** bower, cellist, contrabassist, fiddle, first string, violin, violinist, violist, violoncellist. **3. strummer** banjoist, bass guitar, bassist, guitarist, harper, harpist, lutenist, lyrist, mandolinist, plucker, sitarist, theorbist, thrummer, zitherist. **4. piper** bagpiper, clarinettist, fagottist, fifer, flautist, flute, flutist *(Chiefly US),* oboist. **5. blower** bugler, cornet, horn-player, saxophonist, tailgater, tooter, trombonist, trumpet, trumpeter. **6. percussionist** cymbalist, drummer, kettledrummer, taborer, tambour, tambourinist, timpanist, tympanist. **7. keyboardist** accordionist, cembalist, harpsichordist, keyboarder, organist, pianist, virginalist. **8. vibist** vibrophonist, xylophonist. **9. organ-grinder** hurdy-gurdy man. **10. bellringer** carillonist, carillonneur, ringer.

3. **1. singer** cantatrice, chanter, chanteuse, choirboy, chorister, crooner, descanter, hazan, hummer, precentor, serenader, singer-songwriter, solfaist, songbird, songster, torch-singer, troller, vicar choral *(British),* vocaliser, vocalist, voice, warbler. **2. folk singer** balladeer, carol-singer, caroller, jongleur, minnesinger, minstrel *(Poetic),* troubadour, trouvère, yodeller. *Informal:* folkie. **3. soprano** coloratura, diva, dramatic soprano, prima donna. **4. contralto** alto, mezzo, mezzosoprano, second. **5. tenor** heldentenor, heroic tenor. **6. countertenor** castrato, falsetto. **7. bass** baritone, barytone, bass-baritone, basso, basso profundo. **8. cantor** chanter, chazzan, coryphaeus, hazzan, precentor. **9. choir** aisle, cantoris, choral, chorale *(US),* chorus, consort, liedertafel, waits.

4. **1. conductor** bandmaster, capellmeister, choirmaster, choragus, chronometer, coryphaeus, Kapellmeister, maestro, timekeeper. **2. band leader** concertmaster, first string, first violinist, leader, principal. **3. pipe major** drum-major, trumpet-major.

5. **1. musical band** band, big band, brass band, bush band, concert band, cover band, dance band, gumleaf band, jazz band, jug band, mariachi, military band, one-man band, pub band, steel band, string band, troupe, wind band. *Informal:* combo. **2. group** beat group, pop group, rock group, supergroup. **3. orchestra** chamber orchestra, palm court orchestra, string orchestra, symphony orchestra. **4. musical ensemble** concertino, duo, nonet, octet, quartet, quintet, septet, sestet, sextet, string quartet, trio. **5. music section** back line, brass, front line, lead guitar, percussion, rhythm guitar, strings, woodwind. *Informal:* kitchen section. **6. tutti** ripieno.

RELATED KEYWORDS: ENTERTAINER, MUSIC, MUSICAL INSTRUMENT

NAME

n. **1.** **1. name** aka, appellation, bush name, byname, compellation, courtesy title, honorific, hypocorism, style, title. *Informal:* handle, moniker. **2. common name** binomial, namesake, polynomial, synonym, tautonym, vernacular, vox barbara. **3. denomination** designation, homonym, mark, name, proper name, tag, tag-name. **4. given name** Christian name, family name, first name, forename, middle name, namesake, pet name, praenomen. **5. surname** byname, cognomen, family name, maiden name, metronymic, patronymic. **6. eponym** patrial, titular. **7. nickname** agnomen, byname, cognomen, epithet, sobriquet, soubriquet, surname. **8. alias** anonym. *Informal:* bodgie. **9. pseudonym** allonym, codename, cryptonym, nom de guerre, nom de plume, pen-name, stage-name. **10. brand name** brand, business name, label, style, trade name, trademark. **11. placename** toponym. **12. byword** household word, synonym. **13. misnomer.**

2. **1. title** bastard title, caption, half-title, heading, masthead, rubric, running title, sub-heading, subtitle. **2. signature** autograph, by-line, e-signature, endorsement, mark, subscription. *Informal:* dhobi mark *(South Asian English)*, henry, John Hancock *(US)*, John Henry *(US)*.

3. 1. naming appellation, baptism, designation. **2. eponymy** antonomasia. **3. onomastics** toponymy. **4. nomenclature** terminology. **5. taxonomy** Geneva System, Linnaean System.

4. 1. namer baptiser, denominator, designator, nomenclator. **2. signer** endorser.

5. 1. female form of address Donna, Frau, Fraulein, Gentlewoman, Lady, Ma'am, Madam, Madame, Mademoiselle, Memsahib *(Indian English)*, Miss, Mrs, Ms, Señora, Señorita, Signora, Signorina, Sister, Tengku, Your Ladyship. *Informal:* Missis, Missus.

6. 1. male form of address Bung, Esquire, Herr, M'sieur, Mister, Monsieur, Mr, Sahib *(Indian English)*, Señor, Signor. *Informal:* San. **2. Sir** Aga, Agha, Alhaji, Ameer, Amir, Baas *(South African)*, Bwana, Doctor, Dom, Don, Effendi, Emir, Grace, Honour, Imperator, Lord, Maestro, Maharaja, Maluka, Milord, Mirza, Monseigneur, Mynheer, Nawab, Pacha, Pasha, Prince, Serenity, Signore, Swami, Tunku, Tycoon, Worship, Your Lordship. **3. Grace** Dom, Holiness, Lord, Mahatma, Monsignor, Reverence, Tuan. **4. mate** blue, bluey, bro *(NZ)*, brother, bunji *(Aboriginal English)*, chum, comate, comrade, cuz *(Aboriginal English)*, ehoa *(NZ)*, fella, fellah, fellow, friend, mack, old fruit, pfella, snow, snowy, son, sonny, uncle. *Informal:* boss, bud, buddy, china, cobber, dig, digger, man, matey, mucker *(British)*, pal, pard *(US)*, pardner *(US)*, sidekick, skeeter. **5. so-and-so** what's-his-name. *Informal:* what's-his-face.

adj. **7. 1. named** nee, nominate.

v. **8. 1. name** baptise, call, christen, designate, entitle, nickname, surname, title. **2. designate** call, codename, denominate, denote, dub, entitle, hail, mention, name, style, tag, term. **3. sign** autograph, endorse, indorse, subscribe. **4. misname** miscall.

adv. **9. 1. by name** baptismally, nominally, pseudonymously, titularly. **2. generically** terminologically.

RELATED KEYWORDS: HUMANITY, SIGN, WOMAN, MAN, WORD

NARRATIVE

n. **1. 1. narrative** account, annals, case history, chronicle, Commentaries, history, lore, record, report, statement, summary. **2. plot** action, continuity, counterplot, intrigue, machinery, scenario, story-line, subplot, synopsis, underplot. **3. theme** action, argument, article, burden, counterplot, motif, subject, substance, text, thesis, topic. *Informal:* flute. **4. narration** account, characterisation, delineation, depiction, description, picture, portrayal, profile, recital, relation, representations, sketch, voice-over, word-painting.

2. 1. story anecdote, episode, fit, idyll, narration, novelle, novelette, novella, romance, short story, tale. *Informal:* chestnut, dit, yarn. **2. novel** antinovel, chiller, cyberpunk, fiction, roman, roman à clef, romance, science fiction, stream-of-consciousness novel, thriller, Western. *Informal:* chick lit, fanfic, sci-fi, shocker, whodunnit. **3. allegory** apologue, bestiary, exemplum, fable, parable. **4. legend** fairytale, folk story, folktale, myth, old wives' tale. **5. saga** epic, romance. **6. cycle** legendry. **7. biography** autobiography, life writing.

3. 1. storyteller anecdotist, annalist, chronicler, fabler, fabulist, jongleur, narrator, raconteur, relater, reporter, romancer, teller. *Informal:* magsman. **2. fictionist** mythologist, novelist, short-story writer.

adj. **4. 1. narrative** appellative, delineative, depictive, descriptive. **2. fictional** anecdotal, anecdotic, legendary, myth-making, mythical, mythopoeic, romantic.

v. **5. 1. narrate** account for, chronicle, fable, recite, recount, relate, report, say, set forth, tell. *Informal:* pyalla. **2. describe** character, delineate, depict, depicture, draw, etch, feature, outline, paint, picture, represent, sketch, state. **3. fictionalise** mythologise, novelise, romance. *Informal:* spin a yarn, yarn.

RELATED KEYWORDS: FANTASY, POETRY, BOOK, WRITING, REPRESENTATION

NATION

n. **1. 1. nation** buffer state, city, city-state, commonwealth, country, nation-state, polity, republic, respublica, sovereign state, state. **2. democracy** direct democracy, liberal democracy, parliamentary democracy. **3. monarchy** absolute monarchy, princedom, principality, queendom, sovereignty. **4. diarchy** ethnarchy, gynarchy, heptarchy, matriarchy, oligarchy, patriarchy, triarchy. **5. dictatorship** autocracy, despotism, lordship, monocracy, police state, tsarism, tyranny. **6. plutocracy** pentarchy, tetrarchy, theocracy. **7. superpower** ascendancy, atomic power, authority, dominance, hierarch, influence, land power, nuclear power, power, sea-power, superstate, suzerain, world power. **8. third world country** banana republic, developing country. *Informal:* Absurdistan. **9. confederation** bloc, commonwealth, federation.

2. **1. country** land, nation, shore, soil, state. **2. realm** bourn, domain, kingdom, royalty. **3. empire** colony, demesne, dominion, empery *(Poetic)*, lebensraum, plantation. **4. territory** condominium, Independency, mandate, protectorate, trust territory. **5. homeland** fatherland, home, home country, mother country, motherland, native land, old country.

3. **1. nationalism** love of country, nationality, patriotism, public spirit, supernationalism. **2. regionalism** parochialism, provincialism. **3. symbol of nationhood** Anzac, Australia Day, digger's hat, national flag, national song, slouch hat. **4. Australian values**. **5. jingoism** chauvinism, flag-wagging, flag-waving. **6. imperialism** colonialism, expansionism.

4. **1. nationality** aboriginality, citizenship, compatriotism, dual citizenship, dual nationality, nationalism. **2. nationhood** statehood, territoriality.

5. **1. national** citizen, compatriot, countryman, nationalist, patrial, patriot, stalwart. **2. jingoist** chauvinist, mafficker, minute man *(US)*, supernationalist.

6. **1. Australian** antipodean, Aussielander, dinkum Aussie. *Informal:* Aussie, balt, clog wog, cloggie, dinkydi Aussie, ocker, ockerina, Oz, skip, skippy. **2. migrant** black hat, chum, immigrant, incomer, new arrival, new chum, newcomer, nominated migrant. *Informal:* reffo. **3. New South Welshman** *Informal:* cornstalk, Mexican. **4. Territorian** Top-Ender. **5. Queenslander** *Informal:* banana bender, sugarlander. **6. South Australian** *Informal:* croweater, magpie, wheatlander. **7. Tasmanian** Apple Islander, Derwent duck, Tasmaniac, Taswegian. *Informal:* Derwenter, mutton-bird, mutton-bird eater, Tassie, Tassielander. **8. Victorian** *Informal:* Cabbage-Gardener, Cabbage-Lander, Cabbage-Patcher, gumsucker, Mexican. **9. Western Australian** Westralian. *Informal:* groper, groperlander, sand groper. **10. Eastern Stater** mainlander. *Informal:* othersider *(WA)*, t'othersider.

7. **1. Australia** the Lucky Country. *Informal:* Down Under, god's own country, godzone, Oz.

adj. 8. **1. national** country, patrial, state, territorial. **2. supranational** imperial, metropolitan, supernational. **3. domestic** civil, home, inland, interior, internal, intestine. **4. nationwide** transnational.

9. **1. nationalist** patriotic, public-spirited. **2. jingoistic** chauvinist, chauvinistic, flag-wagging, flag-waving.

adv. 10. **1. nationally** chauvinistically, domestically, internally, nationalistically, patriotically, pro patria, territorially.

RELATED KEYWORDS: CITY, THE BUSH, REGION

NATURE

n. 1. **1. nature** the great outdoors, the wild, tiger country, waste, wilderness, wilderness area. **2. balance of nature** ecosystem. **3. ecology** alternative technology, autecology, bionomics, natural history, natural science, nature study, oecology, physiography, synecology, vermicology.

2. **1. naturalist** allopath, bionomist, ecologist, physiographer, systematist. **2. nature lover** conservationist, environmentalist. *Informal:* greenie, tree hugger.

adj. 3. **1. natural** congenital, crude, fundamental, in a state of nature, inborn, innate, instinctive, native, normal, primitive, savage, uncivilised, unformed, unlearned, unschooled. **2. wild** feral, ferine, ladino, tameless, untameable, untamed, warrigal, wildish. **3. undeveloped** bush, rough, trackless, unimproved, untouched, waste, wild.

adv. 4. **1. naturally** by birth, innately, instinctively. **2. primitively** savagely, savagery, wildly.

RELATED KEYWORDS: THE BUSH, PLANTS, ANIMALS

NECESSITY

n. 1. **1. necessity** (a matter of) life and death, compulsion, indispensableness, needfulness, requisiteness, urgency.

2. **1. necessities** bare necessities, estovers, necessaries. **2. need** call, lack, market, necessity, requirement, use, want. **3. requirement** a must, essential, exigency, hinge, imperative, necessary, need, obbligato, postulate, prerequisite, requisite, requisition, sine qua non, turn, want.

adj. 3. **1. necessary** indispensable, necessitative, needful, requisite. **2. essential** all-important, apodictic, crucial, exigent, imperative, indispensable, mandatory, necessary, obbligato, obligate *(US)*, obligato, pressing, unavoidable, urgent, vital. **3. obligatory** de rigueur, prerequisite.

v.   **4.   1. necessitate** ask, call for, claim, demand, need, oblige, require, take, want, want for. **2. must** have to, maun, need, needs must. **3. need** can (or could) do with, crave.

adv.   **5.   1. necessarily** crucially, indispensably, obligatorily, perforce, requisitely.

RELATED KEYWORDS: DESIRE, INEVITABILITY, OBLIGATION

NEGLECT

n.   **1.   1. neglect** default, dereliction, lapse, laxity, negligence. **2. omission** non-inclusion, nonfeasance, oversight. *Informal:* miss. **3. neglectfulness** carelessness, casualness, forgetfulness, hastiness, heedlessness, irresponsibleness, laxness, mindlessness, recklessness, remissness, slackness, thoughtlessness. **4. negligence** delinquency, disregard, mismothering, neglect, preterition, pretermission, waste. **5. legal negligence** conduct conducing, laches, negligence, res ipsa loquitur. **6. benign neglect**.

2.   1. neglected person cinderella, gamin, grass widow, guttersnipe, latchkey child, street urchin, urchin. *Informal:* mudlark *(British)*.

adj.   **3.   1. neglectful** careless, casual, disregardful, dizzy, forgetful of, glaikit *(Scottish)*, hasty, heedless, lackadaisical, lax, mindless, neglecting, negligent, omissive, slack, slapdash, slipshod, thoughtless, unconsidered, unthinking. **2. irresponsible** delinquent, reckless, remiss.

4.   1. neglected beat-up, derelict, dilapidated, in limbo, ragged, run-down, the worse for wear, tumbledown. *Informal:* grungy.

v.   **5.   1. neglect** default, disregard, evade, forget, ignore, leave out, let slide, not do, omit, overlook, pass over, pigeonhole, pretermit, scamp, shut one's eyes to, slip, waste. *Informal:* treat with ignore. **2. treat neglectfully** mismother, neglect, turn one's back on.

6.   1. be neglected go by the board, go to rack and ruin, go to waste, lapse. **2. neglect oneself** let oneself go, not care how one looks, not take care of oneself, waste.

adv.   **7.   1. neglectfully** delinquently, forgetfully, heedlessly, laxly, mindlessly, negligently, thoughtlessly. **2. carelessly** any way, anyhow, casually, haphazardly, happy-go-lucky, hastily, raggedly, recklessly, slack, slackly, slapdash.

RELATED KEYWORDS: INATTENTION, ABANDONMENT

NEUTRALITY

n.   **1.   1. neutrality** abstention, apathy, detachment, disinterestedness, equity, even-handedness, fairness, impartiality, indifference, isolation, isolationism, lack of involvement, neutralism, objectivity. **2. non-alignment** non-aggression, non-intervention, non-involvement. **3. neutral person** abstainer, civilian, fence-sitter, isolationist, moderate, mugwump *(US)*, neutral, neutralist, non-belligerent, non-combatant. **4. neutral country** neutral territory, no-man's-land, open city.

adj.   **2.   1. neutral** apolitical, candid, colourless, detached, disinterested, equable, equitable, even, even-handed, fair, fair-minded, impartial, just, liberal, non-committal, nonpartisan, objective, open-minded, unbiased, uncommitted, unprejudiced. *Informal:* fair and square. **2. non-aligned** non-affiliated, non-involved, unaligned, uninvolved.

v.   **3.   1. be neutral** abstain, abstain from voting, defuse, depoliticise, have no hand in, have nothing to do with, keep the peace, not take sides, sit on the fence, stand aloof, steer a middle course, take no part, trim one's course. *Informal:* pull one's head in. **2. neutralise** counteract, counterbalance, negate, nullify, offset.

adv.   **4.   1. neutrally** disinterestedly, fairly, impartially.

RELATED KEYWORDS: IDLENESS, APATHY

NEWNESS

n.   **1.   1. newness** change, curiousness, freshness, innovativeness, new look, novelty, originality, speciality. **2. modernity** modernism, modernness, recentness, up-to-dateness.

2.   1. innovation bright idea, modernity, neologism, neology, novelty. *Informal:* newie, note, wrinkle. **2. renovation** re-creation, reanimation, rebirth, recast, renaissance, renewal, republication, resurrection, revival, reviviscence. **3. modernisation** aggiornamento, revivification, update. **4. latest fashion** the last word, the latest. *Informal:* the in thing. **5. cutting edge** bleeding edge, leading edge.

3.   1. innovator innovationist, neologist, original, original thinker, originator, trailblazer, trend-setter. **2. moderniser** freshener, refurbisher, restorer, reviver, revolutionary, Young Turk. **3. modern** bright young thing, modernist. *Informal:* swinger, trendy. **4. nouveau riche** arriviste, parvenu, upstart. *Informal:* trendoid. **5. new wave** a breath of fresh air, avant-garde, ginger group, nouvelle vague, young blood. **6. youth** infancy, spring, springtime.

adj. **4.** **1. new** brand-new, fresh, green, hot, hot off the press, new-laid, novel, original, piping hot, red-hot, spick-and-span, untouched, untried, unused, unworn, virgin, virginal. **2. emergent** nascent, newly-formed, promising, renascent, reviviscent, up-and-coming. **3. first** fledgling, initial, maiden, pioneer, primordial. **4. young** newish, youngish. **5. initiatory** creative, enactory.

5. **1. innovative** creative, fresh, generative, groundbreaking, ingenious, innovational, innovatory, inventive, new, newfangled, novel, original, originative, Promethean, state-of-the-art, unconventional, unprecedented. **2. futuristic** avant-garde, high-tech, space-age, sunrise, trend-setting, ultra-modern. **3. modern** contemporary, cotemporary, current, fashionable, fresh as a daisy, immediate, just out, late-model, latest, live, modernist, modernistic, neological, neoteric, new-fashioned, newschool, passing, recent, redbrick *(Chiefly British)*, running, ultrafashionable, up-to-date, up-to-the-minute, with-it. *Informal:* cool, mod, now, swinging, trendy, wired.

v. **6.** **1. innovate** break new ground, initiate, inspirit, originate, turn over a new leaf. **2. swing** be with it. **3. modernise** bring up to date, do over, do up, fix up, freshen, furbish up, lift, make over, reface, refresh, refurbish, renew, renovate, repair, revamp, revive, update, vamp up.

adv. **7.** **1. newly** emergently, fresh, freshly, new, virginally. **2. modernly** neoterically, not long ago, recently, swingingly. **3. innovatively** for the first time, inspiritingly, novelly, originally, unprecedentedly.

RELATED KEYWORDS: YOUTH, CREATION, EARLINESS, FASHION, OFFSPRING, THE PRESENT, START

NEWS

n. **1.** **1. news** information, intelligence, tidings, word. *Informal:* dope, drum, info, lowdown, the goods. **2. rumour** ana, blue duck *(NZ)*, dirt, furphy, gossip, hearsay, scandal, tale, talk, tattle, tittle-tattle, whisper, word. *Informal:* buzz, goss, scuttlebutt. **3. bulletin** announcement, communiqué, dispatch, hand-out, handout, press conference, press release, report. **4. the latest** stop press, the score. **5. gossiping** tale-bearing, tale-telling.

2. **1. newscast** announcement, article, column, contribution, cover story, exclusive, feature, feature story, flash, item, leader, leading article, news item, newsfeed, newsflash, newsreel, personal *(US)*, report, scoop, sensation, sound bite, spread, story, telecast, write-up. *Informal:* a good spread, beat-up. **2. column** editorial, gossip column, leader. **3. advertisement** ad, advertorial, blurb, classified ad, commercial, promo, promotion, recommendation, soft sell, teaser, teaser ad, trailer, want ad. *Informal:* advert, plug, sell. **4. headlines** banner, caption, head, headline, side heading, strapline, streamer. *Informal:* cap.

3. **1. journalist** correspondent, cub reporter, editorship, foreign correspondent, news-hound, newsman, newspaperman, paparazzo, photojournalist, pressman, reporter, roundsman, roving reporter, special correspondent, stringer, war correspondent. *Informal:* journo, newshawk. **2. newsreader** newscaster. **3. columnist** agony aunt, editor, feature writer, finance editor, gossip columnist, sob-sister. **4. newsagent** news-dealer *(US)*, newsstand, newsvendor, paper shop, paperstand. **5. news desk** city desk *(British)*, newsroom. **6. press agent** p.r.o., press officer, press secretary, public relations officer, publicity agent. *Informal:* flack, spin doctor.

4. **1. the media** electronic media, fleet street, fourth estate, press, print journalism, print media, print press, printed press, the press, yellow press. *Informal:* the daily blatts. **2. press gallery** press-box. **3. journalism** coverage, investigative journalism, photojournalism, reportage. **4. publication** publishment, syndication. **5. news agency** news syndicate, press agency, press office. **6. newsiness** news, newsworthiness.

5. **1. gossip** chitchat, gossipmonger, hearsay, newsmonger, quidnunc, scandalmonger, talk, tittle-tattle, whisperer. *Informal:* scuttlebutt. **2. tale-bearer** babbler, blabber, conveyor, gossip, informer, scout, sneak, stool pigeon *(Chiefly US)*, taleteller, tattler, tattletale, teller, telltale, tittle-tattle, tittle-tattler. *Informal:* blabbermouth, scuttlebutt, shelf, sieve, snitch, tabby. **3. informer** dogvane, informant, intelligencer, pimp, super-grass. *Informal:* chocolate frog, copper's nark, dobber, dobber-in, dog, golliwog, grass, grasser, nark, Noah's Ark, silvertail.

v. **6.** **1. publish** carry, feature, issue, lay before the public, print, run. **2. report** cover, reveal, write up. **3. broadcast** colourcast, newscast, radio, relay, satellite, telecast, tele-vise, webcast. **4. scoop. 5. edit** prepare copy, put to bed, subedit. *Informal:* sub.

7. 1. noise abroad bruit, herald, noise, retail. **2. gossip** rumour, talk. *Informal:* chew the fat, fly a kite, natter. **3. tattle** inform on, pimp, tell tales. *Informal:* ponce.
RELATED KEYWORDS: COMMUNICATION, INFORMATION, BOOK, TALKATIVENESS, TELE-COMMUNICATIONS

NIGHT

n. **1.** **1. night** moonrise, night-time. **2. night shift** dogwatch, graveyard shift, night patrol, night school. **3. weeknight** *Informal:* three-day night, three-dog night.
2. **1. evening** curfew, e'en *(Poetic)*, vesper. **2. sunset** dark, decline, fall of evening, night, nightfall, sundown. **3. twilight** candlelight, crepuscule, dusk, gloaming *(Poetic)*, night, shades, shadows. **4. dinnertime** bedtime, suppertime, teatime. **5. Evensong** Evening Prayer, vespers, vigil, vigils. **6. midnight** the dead of night, witching hour. **7. the small hours** the wee (small) hours.
3. **1. night person** all-nighter, night-bird, nightwalker, owl. **2. night watchman** night-porter. *Informal:* night owl, nighthawk.
adj. **4.** **1. nightly** all-night, nightlong, noctivagant, nocturnal, overnight, owl-like, owlish. **2. midnight** midnightly. **3. evening** goodnight, vesper, vespertinal, vespertine. **4. twilight** acronychal, crepuscular, duskish, moonlight.
adv. **5.** **1. nightly** all night, midnightly, nightlong, nocturnally, overnight, under the stars. *Informal:* nights.
RELATED KEYWORDS: LATENESS, DARK, PERIOD

NONCONFORMITY

n. **1.** **1. nonconformity** disconformity, inconformity, irregularity, nonconformance, unfashionableness. **2. informality** bohemianism, licence, unconventionality. **3. eccentricity** craziness, oddness, originality, peculiarity, queerness, singularity, singularness. *Informal:* high strikes. **4. aberrancy** abnormality, abnormity, deviancy, deviation, kinkiness, unnaturalness. **5. radicalness** boldness, dissent, heresy, heterodoxy, iconoclasm, nonconformity, progressiveness, rebellion, unorthodoxy. **6. exceptionalness** extraordinariness, tremendousness, uniqueness.
2. **1. nonconformist** beatnik, bohemian, conscientious objector, dropout, flowerchild, hippie, hippy, intellectual, Promethean, sharpie. *Informal:* beat, long-hair. **2. eccentric** character, enfant terrible, erratic, freak, lunatic, original. *Informal:* a one, a queer fish, bird, card, case, caution, crackpot, crank, crazy, dag, ding-a-ling, dingbat, fruitcake, geek, geezer, hangman *(NZ)*, kook, loco *(US)*, nut, nut case, nutter, odd bod, oddball, old bat, poon, ratbag, screwball, trick, wack, weirdo, whacker. **3. deviant** deviate *(Chiefly US)*, pervert. *Informal:* bent, perv. **4. radical** angry young man, Bolshevik, bolshevist, dissenter, extremist, iconoclast, leftist, Pink, Radical, rebel, Red, reformist, troublemaker. *Informal:* bolshie, leftie. **5. misfit** fish out of water, square peg in a round hole. *Informal:* gaylord, neville, nigel *(Especially Qld and NSW)*, no-hoper, spock. **6. exception** curiosity, freak, heteroclite, irregular, odd one out, oddity, rarity. **7. bohemia** alternative lifestyle, beat generation, cafe society, counterculture, demimonde, hip-hop culture. **8. Push** the beautiful people.
adj. **3.** **1. nonconformist** abnormal, anomalous, heteroclite, heterodox, informal, irregular, non-standard, nonconforming, unconformable, uncustomary, unorthodox, unusual. **2. informal** irregular, not by the book, not by the rule, relaxed. **3. exceptional** extraordinary, notable, rare, remarkable, stand alone, uncommon, unexampled, unheard-of, unimaginable, unique, unparalleled, unprecedented, unusual. *Informal:* raving, tremendous. **4. aberrant** aberrational, abnormal, deviant, deviate *(Chiefly US)*, freakish, freaky, improper, perverted, quirky, unnatural. *Informal:* bent, kinky. **5. eccentric** bizarre, cranky, crazy, curious, dilly, erratic, fey, lunatic, mad, mad as a hatter, odd, odd-bod, offbeat, peculiar, pixilated, queer, singular. *Informal:* barmy as a bandicoot, bats, bonkers, crackpot, crank, daggish, daggy, dingbats, dotty, gaga, gonzo, kinky, kooky, loco, loony, loopy, mad as a (cut) snake, mad as a meataxe, maggoty, magnoon, nuts, nutty as a fruitcake, oddball, off one's nut, off the wall, ratbaggy, ratty, rummy, screwball, screwy, strange, up the pole, wacko, wacky *(Chiefly US)*, way-out, whacky, wrong in the head, yarra. **6. unconventional** alternative, beat, bohemian, unfashionable. *Informal:* boho, left-field, uncool. **7. radical** bold, forward, iconoclastic, leftist, Radical, reformist.
adv. **4.** **1. unconventionally** informally, irregularly, unfashionably. **2. eccentrically** erratically, out of step, singularly, uniquely, unnaturally.
RELATED KEYWORDS: STRANGENESS, INSANITY

NON-EXISTENCE

n. **1.** **1. non-existence** inexistency, nihilism, non-being, nonentity, nullity. **2. nothingness** absence, blank, blankness, negation, nihilism, nihility, non-existence, nowhere, vacuum, void, voidness. **3. insubstantiality** abstractness, intangibleness, the intangible. **4. annihilation** abolition, abrogation, annulment, death, defeasance, dematerialisation, destruction, elimination, erasure, expunction, extermination, extinction, genocide, removal.

2. **1. nothing** neither hide nor hair, nihil, nil, nocht *(Scottish),* none, nought, zero. *Informal:* damn-all, jack, nix, not a sausage, nowt, zilch *(Chiefly US),* zip *(Chiefly US).* **2. zero** duck, duck's egg, love, nought.

adj. **3.** **1. nonexistent** absent, blank, extinct, inexistent, missing, unhistorical. *Informal:* napoo. **2. intangible** abstract, insubstantial, metempirical, speculative, theoretical, unessential, virtual. **3. no** nane *(Scottish),* null.

v. **4.** **1. annihilate** abrogate, annul, disannul, exterminate, extinguish, extirpate, nullify, wipe out. *Informal:* spiflicate. **2. expunge** blank out, blot out, efface, wipe off the map. *Informal:* nuke.

RELATED KEYWORDS: DESTRUCTION, KILLING, DEATH, INTANGIBILITY, REMOVAL

NON-PAYMENT

n. **1.** **1. non-payment** avoidance, default, dishonour, evasion, repudiation. *Informal:* moonlight flit. **2. tax avoidance** bottom-of-the-harbour scheme, dry Slutzkin, tax dodge, tax evasion, tax evasion scheme, tax haven, tax shelter, underground economy, wet Slutzkin. *Informal:* tax lurk. **3. bankruptcy** failure, insolvency, insufficiency of funds, overdrawn account, receivership. *Informal:* bust, bust-up.

2. **1. debt** bad debt, book debt, debit, debt of honour, deficit, funded debt, interminable debt, national debt, set-off. *Informal:* a dog tied up, dead horse. **2. dishonoured cheque** bad cheque, bogus cheque, bouncing cheque. *Informal:* boomerang, floater, rubber cheque. **3. stop order** abatement, days of grace, moratorium, protest, stop, stop payment, suspension.

3. **1. defaulter** absconder, bankrupt, bilker, dishonourer, insolvent, scaler, stag, undischarged bankrupt, welsher. *Informal:* fly-by-night, wife starver.

adj. **4.** **1. non-paying** bankrupt, behind, behindhand, bereft, blank, broken, dry, dumb, empty-handed, gazetted, in arrears, insolvent, ruined, unable to make both ends meet, unable to pay, unprovided for, vacant, wanting. *Informal:* broke, bust, minus, stumered.

5. **1. unpaid** chargeable, due, due to, floating, moratory, outstanding, owing, payable, undischarged. **2. complimentary** free, gratis, gratuitous, honorary, interest-free, tax-deductible, tax-free, untaxed. *Informal:* buckshee. **3. honorary** uncustomed, unpaid, unremunerated, unrewarded, voluntary.

v. **6.** **1. fail to pay** brass, break an agreement, default, dishonour a cheque, nullify an agreement. *Informal:* do a moonlight flit, freeload, scarper, shoot through, welsh. **2. defraud** beat *(US),* bilk, bite, cheat, clip, cog, cozen, fudge, hoozle, jockey, mountebank, overreach, palm, point, rogue, rook, smuggle, swindle, take down, trick out of, victimise. *Informal:* brass, chisel, con, diddle, do, do down, do in the eye, do out of, finagle, flim-flam, gyp, hotpoint, nick, quack, ringbolt *(NZ),* short-change, sting, suck in, swizzle, take the palm, work a slanter.

7. **1. be unable to pay** charge, collapse, crash, fail, go bankrupt, go bung, go to the wall. *Informal:* go bust. **2. defer payment** postpone payment, put on account, put on the slate. **3. stop payment** protest, refuse payment, repudiate, scale down, suspend.

RELATED KEYWORDS: INDEBTEDNESS, LOAN, POVERTY

NONSENSE

n. **1.** **1. nonsense** babble, blather, blither, chatter, drivel, fable, falderal, fudge, fustian, garbage, gibberish, givor, imbecility, jabber, jargon, kid-stakes, lie, mere words, palaver, pap, patter, persiflage, prattle, rant, rigmarole, rubbish, silliness, sound and fury, stuff and nonsense, tarradiddle, tomfoolery, trash, trumpery, verbiage. *Informal:* a load of old cobblers, abracadabra, apple sauce *(US, Canadian),* balderdash, baloney, bilge, bizzo, blah, boloney, bosh, bull, bulldust, bullo, bullswool, bumf, bunk, bunkum, claptrap, cock and bull story, cock-and-bull, codswallop, cowyard confetti, crock, double-dutch, doubletalk, eyewash, fandangle, farmyard confetti, fiddle-faddle, fiddlesticks, flamdoodle *(Chiefly US),* flapdoodle, Flemington confetti, flim-flam, flummery, footle, fribble, froth and bubble, gammon, gammon and spinach, gas, guff, guiver, guivo, gunk, guyver, gyver, gyvo, heifer dust, hocus-pocus, hogwash, hokum *(US),* hoo-ha, hooey *(Chiefly US),* jabberwocky, kibosh, kybosh, macaroni, malarky, moonshine, mumbo jumbo, pack of nonsense, piffle, poppycock, rave, rhubarb, rot, slipslop, story, taradiddle, todge, tommyrot, tosh, tripe, twaddle, waffle, yak, yawp. **2. absurdity** amphigory, bagatelle, contradiction, exaggeration, imbecility, impertinence, inanity, inconsistency, paradox, platitude, quibble, sophism, triviality, vagueness, verbalism. **3. nonsense verse** derry, doggerel. **4. tomfoolery** monkey tricks, mummery, practical joke, trickery. *Informal:* jiggery-pokery, shenanigans.

    2. **1. meaninglessness** absurdness, gassiness, inconsequence, inconsequentiality, pointlessness, ridiculousness, senselessness, trashiness, unmeaningness.

    3. **1. talker of nonsense** babbler, jabberer, joker, maunderer, patterer, prankster. *Informal:* bilge artist, magger, magpie, piffler, raver, storyteller, twaddler, yawper.

adj. **4.** **1. nonsensical** absurd, extravagant, fantastic, inconsistent, insignificant, jumbled, paltry, paradoxical, petty, preposterous, puerile, ridiculous, self-contradictory, silly, sophistical, too-too. *Informal:* cock and bull, cockeyed, crappy, footling, meatball, nitty, piffling, rich. **2. meaningless** amphigoric, artificial, chimerical, fictitious, flat, insignificant, moonshiny, pointless, senseless, signifying little, unmeaning, visionary, without rhyme or reason. **3. inconsequential** absurd, babbly, blithering, disjointed, farcical, futile, illogical, incoherent, inconsequent, irrelevant, nonsensical, quibbling, raving, rubbishy, voluble, windy. *Informal:* flim-flam, gassy, piffling, potty *(British)*, rich.

v. **5.** **1. talk nonsense** babble, blather, blether *(British)*, burble, chatter, fluff, fudge, gabble, garble, gibber, jabber, jargon, jargonise, lie, maunder, patter, prattle, quibble, rant, rave, talk, talk rubbish, yaffle. *Informal:* gammon, gas, mag, natter, piffle, rabbit on, talk through one's hat, talk through the back of one's neck, twaddle, waffle, yak, yakety-yak, yawp.

adv. **6.** **1. nonsensically** absurdly, incoherently, inconsequentially, inconsequently, jabberingly, meaninglessly, paradoxically, pointlessly, ridiculously, senselessly, unmeaningly.

    RELATED KEYWORDS: OBSCURITY, BOMBAST, ERROR, FOOLISHNESS

NUMBER

n. **1.** **1. number** digit, figure, integer, value. **2. numeral** cipher, lining figure, modern figure, number. **3. integer** binary digit, binary number, natural number, number, perfect number, rational number, whole number. **4. cardinal number** ordinal, ordinal number. **5. decimal number** compound number, decimal fraction, floating point number, half-integer, mixed number, real number, recurring decimal, repeating decimal, transcendental. **6. imaginary number** complex number, composite number. **7. prime number** square number. **8. surd** irrational number. **9. variable** dependent variable, independent variable, unknown, x. **10. constant** invariable, invariant. **11. absolute value** magnitude, modulus. **12. factor** common factor, dividend, divisor, greatest common divisor, Stirling's formula, submultiple. **13. coefficient** modulus, regression coefficient. **14. square** cube, exponential, factorial, root mean square. **15. square root** cube root, root. **16. mathematical function** binomial, expression, form, formula, integral, polynomial, potential, quadratic, quadrinomial, quantic, quintic, step function, trinomial. **17. mathematical series** arithmetic progression, geometric progression, harmonic progression, time series. **18. continuum** domain, field, four-dimensional continuum. **19. number element** characteristic, decimal place, decimal point, exponent, mantissa, repetend, significant figures. **20. fraction** common fraction, complex fraction, compound fraction, continued fraction, improper fraction, proper fraction, ratio, recurring fraction, simple fraction, vulgar fraction. **21. denominator** common denominator, lowest common denominator. **22. numerator**.

    2. **1. trigonometrical function** arc sine, arc tangent, cos., cosec, cosecant, cosine, cotangent, haversine, inverse sine, inverse tangent, secant, sin, sin., sine, tan., tangent, vers., versed sine. **2. hyperbolic function** cosech, cosh, cotan, cotanh, coth, hyperbolic functions, sech, sinh, tanh. **3. logarithm** common logarithm, Napierian logarithm, natural logarithm. **4. antilog** antilogarithm. **5. pi** e.

    3. **1. score** aggregate, circulation, count, head, raw score, strength, sum, tally, total. **2. attendance** enrolment. **3. majority** quorum, quota.

    4. **1. numbering** foliation, numeration, pagination.

    5. **1. number system** binary notation, binary number system, binary scale, decimal system, duodecimal system, hexadecimal system, octal system. **2. arabic numerals** aleph-nought, aleph-null, aleph-zero, algorism, cipher, roman numerals. **3. numerical set** network, sequence, subordinate set, subsequence, subset, system, tree. **4. arithmetic scale** reflexive relation, relation, sliding scale. **5. numerology. 6. numeracy.**

6. **1. numbers – miscellaneous** aspect ratio, atomic number, Avogadro's number, box number, call number, chromosome number, combination, coordination number, correlation coefficient, f number, f-stop, flight number, folio, index number, licence number, ligancy, mach number, magic number, oxidation number, page number, postcode, quantum number, serial number, tax file number, telephone number, zipcode *(US)*.

adj. 7. **1. numerical** alphanumeric, numeral, numerary, numeric. **2. integral** digital, prime, round, whole. **3. real**. **4. fractional** half-integral, rational. **5. imaginary** even, odd, uneven. **6. negative** plus, positive, subtractive. **7. exponential** differential, irrational, logarithmic, logometric. **8. cardinal** ordinal. **9. decimal** binary, binomial, digital, duodecimal, duodenary, hexadecimal, octal, quinary, sexagesimal, uncial, undecimal. **10. submultiple**. **11. reciprocal** complementary. **12. plus** positive.

8. **1. numerate** good at figure-work.

v. 9. **1. number** enumerate, numerate. **2. paginate** foliate, folio, page.

adv. 10. **1. numerically** alphanumerically, by numbers, in numbers, in numbers and letters.

RELATED KEYWORDS: CALCULATION, MANY, A FEW

OBEDIENCE

n. 1. **1. obedience** acquiescing, compliance, deference, non-resistance, passiveness, passivity, subjection, submission, yielding. **2. dutifulness** ductility, duteousness, duty, fealty, homage, loyalty, obeisance, obsequiousness, orderliness, respect, servility, submissiveness, towardliness, tractability, yieldingness. **3. compulsion** domination, enforcement.

2. **1. obeyer** adherent, child, complier, disciple, follower, fulfiller, nonresistant, observant. *Informal:* clean potato, yes-man. **2. sycophant** lackey, puppet, slave, teacher's pet, toady. *Informal:* stooge, yes-man.

adj. 3. **1. obedient** compliable, compliant, complying, conformable, law-abiding, obliging, observant, subordinate, willing. **2. submissive** at someone's beck and call, corrigible, deferential, flexible, henpecked, obsequious, passive, resigned, servile, subservient, under control, weak-kneed, yielding. **3. dutiful** devoted, duteous, faithful, loyal, orderly. **4. acquiescent** agreeable, complacent, complaisant, concessive. **5. tractable** amenable, biddable, controllable, docile, easy, flexile, guidable, nonresistant, persuasible, pliable, pliant, suggestible, tame.

v. 4. **1. obey** carry out orders, do someone's bidding, do what one is told, serve, submit, submit to, toe the line, yield. **2. comply** accommodate, answer the helm, carry out, clear, come (or fall) into line, comply with, conform, follow, fulfil, heed, keep, mind, observe, quadrate, shape up. **3. grovel** bow and scrape, defer to, follow someone's lead, jump through hoops, play second fiddle.

adv. 5. **1. obediently** compliantly, duteously, dutifully, loyally, observantly. **2. tractably** yieldingly. **3. in compliance with** at one's beck and call.

RELATED KEYWORDS: AGREEMENT, COOPERATION, LAWFULNESS, SERVANT

OBLIGATION

n. 1. **1. obligation** band, bounden duty, burden, charge, demand, duty, impost, load, millstone, onus, requirement, responsibility, weight. **2. bond** accord, agreement, astriction, band, call of duty, categorical imperative, compact, concordat, contract, covenant, deal, engagement, faith, indenture, obligation, pact, personal responsibility, tie. **3. liability** agistment, cess, imposition, judgement, levy, service due, tax, tithe, tithes, tribute, vassalage. **4. job** assignment, calling, career, chore, duty, employment, errand, function, guild, mission, occupation, part, piece of work, plan, profession, project, pursuit, role, task, tenancy, trade, undertaking, vocation, work. *Informal:* gig, racket, yakka. **5. quota** darg, production target.

2. **1. dutifulness** conscientiousness, moralism, religiousness, responsibleness. **2. conscience** clean hands, conscientiousness, morality, morals, sense of fitness, sense of right and wrong, still small voice within, voice of conscience. **3. loyalty** allegiance, constancy, fidelity. **4. propriety** completion, conduct becoming, decorum, discharge, fitness, fulfilment, observance, proper behaviour, rectitude, rightness, seemliness, the proper thing, the right thing. **5. observance** discharge.

adj. 3. **1. obligatory** binding, bounden, de rigueur, imperative, incumbent, irremissible, mandatory, necessary, obbligato, obligatory on (or upon), obliging, peremptory, required.

4. **1. obligated** beholden, bound, constrained, duty-bound, in duty bound, indebted, obligate *(US)*, obliged, tied, under a compliment to someone, under an obligation to someone. **2. liable** accountable, amenable, answerable, answerable for, blamable,

blameful, censurable, chargeable, culpable, guilty, indictable, nocent, responsible, saddled with.

5. **1. dutiful** biddable, civic-minded, conscientious, duteous, faithful, law-abiding, loyal, obedient, observant, orderly, public-spirited, submissive, supererogatory, yielding. **2. conscientious** pious, principled, religious, scrupulous, squeamish.

v. **6.** **1. obligate** astrict, bind, oblige, tie. **2. be one's duty to** be incumbent on, be up to, befit, behove, devolve, fall to one's lot, import, oblige, rest in, rest on, rest upon, rest with. **3. be obligated** had better, have got to, ought, should.

7. **1. do one's duty** acquit oneself well, act honourably, answer the call of duty, avenge someone's honour, be at one's post, comport oneself well, discharge a duty, fulfil an obligation, man, pay off a score, perform a duty, satisfy, serve, settle a score, supererogate. **2. be responsible** have broad shoulders, have the ball in one's court, have the matter rest on one's shoulders, take it upon oneself. *Informal:* carry the can.

adv. **8.** **1. obligatorily** at one's own risk, bindingly, incumbently, irremissibly, upon one's own head. **2. on one's own responsibility** at one's own risk, on one's hands, upon one's own head.

9. **1. dutifully** conscientiously, observantly, responsibly. **2. on duty** on the spot. **3. by reason of obligation** of necessity, perforce.

RELATED KEYWORDS: BEHAVIOUR, CONTRACT, IMPOSITION, OBEDIENCE, RULE, SURETY

OBSCENITY

n. **1.** **1. obscenity** bawdiness, dirt, filthiness, foulness, irreverence, lasciviousness, lewdness, lubricity, obsceneness, profanity, rankness, salaciousness, scabrousness, vileness. **2. indecency** bawdry, bawdy, coarseness, dirtiness, impropriety, ribaldry, scurrility, vulgarity, vulgarness, wantonness. **3. foul-mindedness** prurience, scopophilia, skeptophilia, voyeurism. **4. suggestiveness** earthiness, raciness, raffishness, smuttiness. **5. immodesty** impudicity, indecorousness, shamelessness. **6. impureness** impurity, unchasteness. **7. dirty word** four-letter word, vulgarism.

2. **1. pornography** child pornography, dirty postcard, hard-core pornography, snuff movie, soft-core pornography, yellow culture *(Singaporean and Malaysian English)*. *Informal:* beefcake, blue movie, cheesecake, cyberporn, hard porn, pin-up, porn, porno, skin flick, soft porn, video nasty. **2. pornographic writing** banned book, curiosa, erotica, ithyphallic, yellowback. **3. bawdy yarn** *(Informal)* double entendre. **4. indecent exposure** lap dance, strip, strip joint. *Informal:* full monty, poppy show. **5. stripper** artiste, male stripper, striptease.

adj. **3.** **1. obscene** adult, beastly, bedroom, Corinthian, Cyprian, dissipated, dissolute, filthy, foul, free, immoral, ithyphallic, lewd, libertine, licentious, light, lubricious, nasty, pornographic, raunchy, riotous, salacious, scatalogical, sensual, vicious, vile, wanton. *Informal:* anatomical, blue, green *(Philippine English)*, on the tiles, porno, ripe. **2. vulgar** bawdy, broad, cacky, dirty, earthy, evil-minded, Fescennine, lecherous, mucky, profane, profligate, rabelaisian, raffish, rampant, ribald, smutty, unchaste. *Informal:* buaya *(Singaporean and Malaysian English)*, French, grotty. **3. suggestive** borderline, close to the bone, close to the knuckle, daring, fruity, juicy, naughty, near the bone, near the knuckle, racy, risky, risqué, scabrous, spicy, titillating. **4. erotic** concupiscent, hot, lascivious, lewd, libidinous, lustful, phallic, priapic, salacious, sexy. **5. indecent** base, coarse, coarse-grained, common, crude, gross, heavy, indelicate, inelegant, low, profane, rank, rorty, rough, rude, uncivil, uncivilised, unmannerly, unpolished, unrefined, unseemly. *Informal:* lairy. **6. unprintable** unparliamentary, unrepeatable, unspeakable. **7. foul-minded** foul-mouthed, prurient, thersitical, voyeuristic. **8. immodest** audacious, barefaced, bold-faced, brazen, bumptious, flaunting, forward, impenitent, pert, presumptuous, shameless, unashamed, unblushing. *Informal:* brassy.

adv. **4.** **1. obscenely** bawdily, coarsely, filthily, foully, immodestly, indecently, lustfully, profanely, racily, salaciously, smuttily, vilely, vulgarly.

RELATED KEYWORDS: VULGARITY, WRONGDOING, SEX, SWEARING, VOLUPTUOUSNESS

OBSCURITY

n. **1.** **1. obscurity** abstruseness, ambiguity, ambiguousness, deepness, double meaning, encryption, obscureness, opacity, reconditeness. **2. mysteriousness** anagrammatism, elusiveness, inscrutableness, vagueness. **3. incomprehensibleness** impalpability, impenetrability, impenetrableness, inexplicableness, unaccountableness, unfathomableness, unintelligibleness. **4. insolubleness** indecipherability, insolvability. **5. illegibleness** crabbedness, unreadableness. **6. incoherence** incoherency, incomprehensiveness.

> 2. **1. incomprehension** inapprehension. **2. puzzlement** bafflement, bamboozlement, bewilderment, confusion, mystification, nonplus, perplexity.
>
> 3. **1. code** arcanums, argot, cant, cipher, cryptogram, cryptograph, cypher, digital signature, enigma, morse code, riddle, secret. **2. gabble** abracadabra, babble, double-dutch, gibber, gibberish, jabber, nonsense, splutter.
>
> 4. **1. puzzle** conundrum, koan, mystery, paradox, pons asinorum, poser, problem, puzzler, quodlibet, sealed book, stumper, teaser. *Informal:* brainteaser, headache, sticker, tickler. **2. puzzle game** acrostic, anagram, anagrammatic, crossword, cryptic crossword, logogram, logogriph, rebus, Rubik's cube, sudoku, tangram, x-word.

adj. 5. **1. obscure** abstract, abstruse, confusing, dark, deep, dim, equivocatory, esoteric, hazy, misty, opaque, oracular, rarefied, recondite, uncertain, unclear, vague. **2. puzzling** baffling, bewildering, beyond comprehension, challenging, difficult, elusive, paradoxical, past comprehension, perplexing. **3. mysterious** arcane, cryptic, enigmatic, inscrutable, mystical. **4. Delphic** ambiguous, enigmatic, oracular. **5. incomprehensible** all Greek, fathomless, impalpable, impenetrable, inapprehensible, over someone's head, unfathomable, unintelligible. *Informal:* clear as mud. **6. insoluble** impenetrable, incalculable, incomprehensible, indeterminable, inexplicable, inscrutable, insolvable, mysterious, unaccountable, unexplainable, unfathomable, unknowable, unsearchable. **7. illegible** crabbed, cramped, hieroglyphic, ill-defined, indecipherable, undecipherable, unreadable.

v. 6. **1. puzzle** addle, anagrammatise, baffle, bamboozle, be (all) Greek to someone, bemuse, bewilder, confound, confuse, elude, fox, mystify, perplex, riddle, stick, throw off the scent.

> 7. **1. misunderstand** be all at sea, be at cross-purposes, be beyond (or out of) one's depth, make little of, make neither head nor tail of, make nothing of, misinterpret, misperceive, miss the point, see through a glass darkly. *Informal:* have (or get) one's wires crossed.

adv. 8. **1. obscurely** abstrusely, ambiguously, bafflingly, bewilderingly, darkly, deeply, equivocatingly, puzzlingly, reconditely, unclearly. **2. mysteriously** cryptically, elusively, enigmatically, incomprehensively, inscrutably, puzzlingly. **3. unintelligibly** fathomlessly, impalpably, impenetrably, incomprehensibly, inexplicably, unaccountably, unfathomably. **4. insolubly** insolvably. **5. illegibly** crabbedly, unreadably.

RELATED KEYWORDS: SUGGESTION, FIGURE OF SPEECH, NONSENSE, SECRECY

OBVIOUSNESS

n. 1. **1. obviousness** apparentness, clearness, conspicuousness, distinctness, manifestness, notability, palpability, plainness, prominence. **2. truism** axiom, self-evidence, tautology.

adj. 2. **1. obvious** clear, definite, distinct, evident, manifest, patent, plain, transparent. *Informal:* as plain as a pikestaff, plain as the nose on your face. **2. unmistakable** black-and-white, broad, clean-cut, clear as day, clear-cut, explicit, limpid, lucid, luculent, pellucid, perspicuous, specific, straightforward, unambiguous, unequivocal, univocal. **3. apparent** appreciable, audible, in the foreground, notable, noticeable, palpable, tangible, visible, vivid. **4. conspicuous** distinguished, exposed, eye-catching, in view, marked, on view, open, outstanding, pointed, prominent, pronounced, salient, splendent, striking, uncovered, under one's nose. **5. glaring** blatant, flagrant, gross, notorious, shroudless, striking, unshaded. **6. self-evident** axiomatic, incontestable, incontrovertible, open-and-shut, self-explanatory, truistic.

v. 3. **1. be obvious** go without saying, speak for itself, stand to reason, tell its own tale. **2. be prominent** be right under one's nose, loom large, stand out, stand out a mile, stare one in the face, stick out. *Informal:* stick out like a sore toe, stick out like dogs' balls. **3. show up** keep a high profile, maintain a high profile, shine.

adv. 4. **1. obviously** appreciably, clear, clearly, distinctly, evidently, in evidence, manifestly, noticeably, palpably, plain, plainly. **2. conspicuously** prominently, pronouncedly. **3. self-evidently** axiomatically.

RELATED KEYWORDS: CLARITY, DISPLAY, SHOWINESS, VISIBILITY

OCCURRENCE

n. 1. **1. occurrence** circumstance, contingency, contingent, episode, event, experience, happening, incident, occasion, phenomenon. **2. incidence** advent, incurrence, occasion.

> 2. **1. affair** business, concern, concernment, interest, job, matter. *Informal:* indaba, piece, shebang, spin, thing.
>
> 3. **1. circumstances** conjuncture, matter, scenario, scene, show, situation, state of affairs. *Informal:* kettle of fish, set-up.

adj. **4.** **1. occurrent** actual, afoot, astir, current, emergent, going, happening, in progress, incidental, occasional, occurring, on, ongoing, passing, present, running, up. **2. phenomenal** empirical, experiential, experimental, practical.

v. **5.** **1. occur** arise, arrive, be, bechance, befall, break, break out, brew, come about, come one's way, come over, come to pass, come up, fall, fare, give, happen, offer, recur, rise, take place, transpire, turn up. *Informal:* pop up, see the light of day. **2. turn out** come off, fall out, fare, go off, go on, happen, pass off.

6. **1. undergo** come upon, encounter, endure, experience, fare, incur, meet, meet with, run across, run into, run up against, stumble on, stumble upon, suffer, sustain, walk into.

RELATED KEYWORDS: ACTUALITY

ODOURLESSNESS

n. **1.** **1. odourlessness** freshness, inodorousness, scentlessness. **2. deodorisation**. **3. deodoriser** activated charcoal, active carbon, deodorant, room freshener. **4. anosmia** inability to smell.

adj. **2.** **1. odourless** inodorous, scentless. **2. unscented** deodorised, fragrance-free, unperfumed. **3. deodorant** roll-on. **4. anosmatic**.

v. **3.** **1. deodorise**. **2. ventilate** air.

OFFER

n. **1.** **1. offer** ante, bid, bidding, call, overbid, proffer, proposition, tender, underbid. **2. recommendation** motion, suggestion. **3. approach** feeler, opener, overture. **4. proposal** application, bill, claim, formal proposal, motion, petition, round robin, suit. **5. last offer** final word, ultimatum.

2. **1. offering** candidateship, candidature, presentation, presentment. **2. launching** sponsorship. **3. calling** bidding. **4. oblation** immolation, offering, offertory, peace-offering, propitiation, sacrifice.

3. **1. offerer** bidder, presenter, tenderer. **2. proposer** advocate, proponent, propounder, sponsor. **3. bargainer** underbidder.

adj. **4.** **1. offered** proffered, tendered. **2. proposed** advocated. **3. recommendatory** advocatory.

v. **5.** **1. offer** bargain, bid, call, extend, give, hold out, outbid, overbid, tender, underbid. **2. propose** advance, give, initiate, institute, lay a plan before, make a suggestion, move, move a motion, offer, pose, present, project, proposition, propound, put forward, put up, raise a matter, sponsor, submit, suggest. *Informal:* give an airing to, hawk an idea. **3. make an overture** approach, launch, offer, overture, sound out. **4. proposition** *Informal:* crack onto, put the hard word on. **5. volunteer** make oneself available, offer oneself, put oneself at another's disposal. **6. advocate** recommend, stand for, support. **7. toast**.

RELATED KEYWORDS: ATTEMPT, CONTRACT, ENTREATY

OFFSPRING

n. **1.** **1. offspring** blood, family, flesh and blood, fruit of the womb, generation, increase, issue, posterity, progeny, seed, strain, young. **2. scion** cadet, child, clone, cross, daughter, descendant, favourite son, firstborn, firstling, offshoot, offspring, pigeon pair, son, sprig, sprout. *Informal:* kid. **3. twins** quadruplets, quintuplets, sextuplet, triplets. **4. illegitimate** bastard, by-blow, love child. *Informal:* basket, git *(Chiefly British)*. **5. orphan** foundling. **6. baby** bairn *(Chiefly Scottish)*, blue baby, bottle baby, child, cooboo *(WA)*, infant, neonate, nursling, papoose, test-tube baby, war baby. *Informal:* babe, bambino, bub, bubba, bubby, little stranger, prem, premmie. **7. toddler** mite, tot.

2. **1. children** grandchildren, small fry, the young. *Informal:* kiddiewinks. **2. child** baby, brat, chiel *(Scottish)*, innocent, junior, youngster. *Informal:* ankle biter, bambino, billy, elf, joey, kid, kiddie, Little Johnny, little tacker, little vegemite, littlie, nipper, piccaninny, sprog, subteen, tiddler, tin lid, weeny-bopper, youngie. **3. kindergartener** preschooler. **4. prodigy** child wonder, hopeful, wunderkind. **5. changeling** devilkin, elfchild, oaf. **6. brat** enfant terrible, jackanapes. *Informal:* little bugger, perisher, pickle, tyke, Young Turk. **7. minx** chit, hussy, missy. **8. urchin** gamin, latchkey child, ragamuffin, street urchin, waif. **9. boy** laddie *(Chiefly Scottish)*, master, sonny. *Informal:* buster *(Chiefly US)*, smacker. **10. girl** demoiselle, lass, mademoiselle, maid, maiden, miss, moppet, nymph *(Chiefly Poetic)*. *Informal:* baby, bint, chicken, chook, colleen, filly, gal, girlie, lassie, popsy, puss. **11. tomboy** gamine, hoyden.

3. **1. adolescent** adolesce, juvenile, teenager, teeny-bopper, whelp, youngling, youngster, youth. *Informal:* grommet, spring chicken. **2. lad** colt, cub, debutant, fledgling, gossoon *(Irish)*, hobbledehoy, jackanapes, pup, puppy, sapling, spalpeen, sprig, stripling, weei, whelp, youth. *Informal:* bucko, nipper, shaver. **3. hoodlum** bully, bullyboy, hooligan, juvenile delinquent, larrikin, oaf, yob. *Informal:* bovver boy *(British)*, bucko, hood, hoon, lout, yobbo. **4. bodgie** *Informal:* boardie, mod, punk, rocker, seaweed, skinhead, surfie, ted *(British)*, teddy boy *(British)*, waxhead, waxie. **5. widgie** *Informal:* bobbysoxer *(Chiefly US)*, bud. **6. nymphette** Lolita. **7. debutante** *Informal:* deb. **8. virgin** nullipara. **9. youthful person** evergreen, Peter Pan, young blood.

4. **1. animal offspring** cub, juvenile, pup, puppy, suckling, whelp, wolf cub. **2. kitten** kitty. **3. colt** fawn, filly, foal, yearling. **4. calf** bobby calf, maverick *(US)*, poddy, slink, staggering bob, weaner, weanling. *Informal:* sheep vanner. **5. lamb** baa-lamb, kid, lambkin, Persian lamb, yeanling. **6. piglet** piggie, pigling, shoat, sucker, sucking-pig. **7. joey**. **8. chicken** cygnet, duckling, eaglet, fledgling, gosling, green duck, juvenal, juvenile, nestling, owlet, poult. **9. tiddler** alevin, cercaria, codling, fingerling, fry, poddy mullet. **10. larva** caseworm, maggot, measles, miracidium, planula, polliwog, pollywog, tadpole. *Informal:* taddie. **11. pupa** chrysalid, chrysalis, nymph. **12. spiderling** money spider. **13. dragonet**. **14. litter** drop, farrow. **15. brood** clutch, hatch, nide. **16. spawn** culch, cultch, spat.

RELATED KEYWORDS: YOUTH, PARENTAGE, RELATIVE, REPRODUCTION, WOMAN, MAN

OIL

n. **1.** **1. oil** aromatic oil, balsam, fixed oil, oleoresin, volatile oil. **2. miscellaneous oil** drying oil, furniture polish, neat's-foot oil, oil of turpentine, stand oil, tung-oil, turpentine, vegetable tallow, wood pitch, wood tar.

2. **1. animal fat** adipocere, blubber, bone oil, butter, butterfat, cellulite, dripping, fat, ghee, grease, lard, sebum, shortening, suet, tallow, train oil, yolk. *Informal:* axlegrease. **2. fish oil** cod-liver oil, sperm, sperm oil. **3. wax** beeswax, carnauba, ceresin, ceroplastics, cerumen, earth wax, earwax, lignite wax, paraffin, paraffin wax, sperm, spermaceti, vegetable wax, white wax.

3. **1. vegetable oil** bard, blown oil, bran, cacao butter, chaff, cocoa butter, coconut butter, cooking oil, copha, edible oil, fatback, leaf-lard, margarine, oleo oil, oleomargarine, palm butter, salad oil, sweet oil *(Chiefly US)*, vegetable butter. *Informal:* marg, marge. **2. pressed oil** almond oil, canola oil, colza oil, cottonseed oil, gingeli, gingili, jojoba oil, linseed oil, mustard oil, nut oil, olio, olive oil, palm oil, rapeseed oil, safflower oil, sesame oil, soya bean oil, soya oil. **3. essential oil** balsam, bergamot, cajuput oil, cineol, eucalyptol, eucalyptus oil, eugenol, ilang-ilang, neroli oil, peppermint, sassafras oil, turpentine, wintergreen, ylang-ylang. *Informal:* euky oil, turps.

4. **1. ointment** anointment, balm, balsam, calamine, camphor ice, cerate, chrism, chrisom, lanolin, lemon balm, liniment, retinol, salve, unction, unguent, vaseline, wool fat. **2. sunscreen** blockout, sunblock, suncream. **3. cosmetic oil** almond oil, brilliantine, coconut oil, face cream, hair oil, hand cream, hand lotion, lotion, Macassar oil, zinc ointment. **4. medicinal oil** almond oil, carron oil, castor oil, emu oil, goanna oil, oil of cloves, tea-tree oil.

5. **1. fuel oil** benzine *(Chiefly US)*, black gold, butter, carburant, crude, derv *(British)*, diesel, diesel oil, dieseline, distillate, fossil fuel, gas oil, gasoline *(Chiefly US)*, mineral oil, motor spirit, naphtha, oil, petranol, petrodiesel, petrol, petroleum, rock oil, shale oil, standard, super, train oil, unleaded, unleaded petrol. *Informal:* gas *(Chiefly US)*.

6. **1. lubricant** antifriction, axlegrease, cyclopentane, grease. **2. lubrication** force-feed, lube. **3. lubricator** grease gun, oilcan, oiler.

7. **1. oilwell** gusher, step-out, step-out well. **2. grasspay sandstone. 3. oilman** *Informal:* spudder.

8. **1. oiliness** greasiness, lubricity, oleaginousness, pinguidity, unctuousness. **2. fattiness** adiposity, fatness.

adj. **9.** **1. oily** greasy, lubricous, oil, oleaginous, slick. **2. unctuous** balsamic, chrismal, unguinous. **3. lubricant** antifriction, lubricative. **4. fatty** adipose, buttery, butyraceous, fat, lardaceous, lardlike, lardy, lipoid, pinguescent, pinguid, stearic. **5. mono-unsaturated** polyunsaturated. **6. adipose** blubbery. **7. sebaceous** ceraceous, waxy.

v. **10.** **1. oil** anoint, grease, lubricate. **2. butter. 3. anoint** baste.

adv. **11. oilily** greasily, oily, soapily.

RELATED KEYWORDS: ENERGY, FUEL, LIQUID, FOOD

OLDNESS

n. **1.** **1. oldness** agedness, antiqueness, elderliness, hoariness, old age. **2. great age** ancient, ancientness, antiquarianism, antiquity, archaism, classicality, classicism, medievalism. **3. ageing** fossilisation, photo-ageing. **4. decrepitude** obsolescence, primitiveness, ruin. **5. staleness** fustiness, mouldiness, mucidness, must, mustiness, rancidity, rancidness. **6. old thing** antique, hand-me-down. *Informal:* relic. **7. antiquities** relics.

adj. **2.** **1. old** age-old, aged, ancient, antediluvian, antiquated, antique, autumnal, dulled, elderly, fossil, fossil-like, grey, hoary, ole, original, preadamite, prehistoric, primal, pristine. *Informal:* as old as Adam, as old as Methuselah, as old as the hills, long in the tooth, out of the ark, white-headed. **2. immemorial** ancient, long-gone, of yore. **3. outmoded** antiquarian, antiquated, archaic, archaistic, backward, behind the times, dated, dead, dead-and-alive, demoded, dinosaur, discontinued, extinct, fogram, low-tech, moss-grown, obsolescent, obsolete, old hat, old-fashioned, old-line *(US)*, out of fashion, out-of-date, outdated, outworn, passé, slow, steam, superannuated. **4. vintage** anachronistic, anachronous, antediluvian, antiquated, antique, classic, classical, dateless, former, fusty, old hat, old-fashioned, old-time, olde-worlde, rancio, ripe, traditional, veteran. *Informal:* trad. **5. prehistoric** antediluvian, antemundane, azoic, eolithic, preglacial, prehuman, primeval, primigenial, primitive, primordial, protolithic. **6. timeworn** crumbling, decayed, decrepit, feeble, moth-eaten, mothy, threadbare. **7. burnt out** beat-up, dilapidated. *Informal:* clapped-out. **8. stale** fusty, mouldy, mucid, musty, rancid, stuffy. **9. second-hand** hand-me-down, pre-owned, third-hand, used. *Informal:* preloved.

v. **3.** **1. be old** be ancient, have seen its day. *Informal:* have whiskers on it. **2. age** fossilise, get on, get on in years, go to seed. **3. stale** crumble, fade, wither.

RELATED KEYWORDS: MATURITY, LATENESS, THE PAST, UNTIMELINESS

ONE

n. **1.** **1. one** ace, ane. **2. single item** monad, monas, odd one, singleton, solo, the one and only, unit. **3. individual** one, one-man band, one-man show, soloist. **4. loner** Crusoe, hermit, lone wolf, odd man out, solitary. *Informal:* Jimmy Woodser.

2. **1. oneness** conjugation, identicalness, indivisibility, indivisibleness, solidarity, unification, union, unity. **2. singleness** aloneness, exclusiveness, individuality, oddness, oneness, solitariness, unicity, uniqueness. **3. loneliness** isolation, purdah, retirement, seclusion, solitude.

adj. **3.** **1. a** an, ane, any, one, unit, unitarian, unitary. **2. single** individual, only, separate, singular, sole, solo. **3. unique** exclusive, one-off, only-begotten. **4. unilateral** azygous, haploid, unipolar. **5. unifying** unific. **6. lone** insular, lonely, single-handed, solitary, solo, unaccompanied, unaided, unattended.

adv. **4.** **1. each** apart, apiece, individually, one at a time, one by one, per capita, respectively, severally, singly. *Informal:* a pop.

5. **1. alone** on one's own, single-handed, single-handedly, solitarily, solo, solus. *Informal:* like a bandicoot on a burnt ridge, like a country dunny, like a lily on a dirt box, like a lily on a dustbin, like a petunia in an onion patch, like a shag on a rock, on one's ace, on one's pat, on one's Pat Malone.

6. **1. only** alone, exclusively, solely, solo. **2. once** for the nonce.

RELATED KEYWORDS: COMBINATION, PARTICULARITY, SOLITUDE, WHOLE

OPACITY

n. **1.** **1. opacity** density, solidity, thickness. **2. turbidity** cloudiness, muddiness. **3. haziness** blurredness, dinginess, mistiness. **4. non-transparency** denseness, opaqueness.

adj. **2.** **1. opaque** dense, intense, thick. **2. turbid** cloudy, muddy, roily. **3. hazy** blurry, dingy, misty.

RELATED KEYWORDS: DARK, MATTER, SOLIDITY

OPENING

n. **1.** **1. opening** aperture, breach, cranny, crevice, cut, gap, gash, hole, incision, interstice, laceration, nick, ostiole, perforation, pinhole, pinprick, pit, prick, scotch, slit, slot, snick, snip, yawn. **2. orifice** blastopore, blowhole, fistula, foramen, foramen magnum, jaws, meatus, micropyle, mouth, os, osculum, pore, stoma, vent. **3. breach** break, chasm, chink, cleft, crack, fissure, flaw, gape, leak, puncture, rent, rift, slit, tear, wash-out. **4. bore** blowhole, borehole, mofette, mohole, quarry, winning. **5. manhole** bulkhead, deadlight, drop, hatch, hatchway, trap, trapdoor, vampire. **6. scupper** hawse, hawsehole, lubber's hole, scuttle. **7. escape lock** Davis apparatus. **8. peephole** hagioscope, judas hole, peep, spy-hole, squint. **9. aperture** airbrick, airhole, core, core hole, embrasure, grille, gunport, hazard, loophole, machicolation, port, service hatch, serving hatch, sleeve, weephole.

2. 1. window ancient light, bay, bay window, bow window, bullseye, casement, catherine-wheel, dormer window, drop window, fanlight, fenestella, fenestra, French window, gable window, hopper window, Jesse window, lancet window, light, louvre window, lunette, luthern, picture window, quarter-vent window, rose, rose window, sash-window, sidelight, skylight, transom *(Chiefly US)*. *Informal:* flipper window. **2. porthole** port.

3. 1. gateway arch, archway, débouché, door, doorway, French door, torii.

4. 1. openness gape, oscitance, oscitancy, patulousness, rictus.

5. 1. opener borer, broach, can-opener, cardpunch, drill, driller, hole puncher, key, key punch, latchkey, latchstring, pass key, perforator, piercer, ripcord, skeleton key, tin-opener, trepan, undoer, wimble.

adj. **6. 1. open** agape, ajar, blown, dehiscent, expanded, gaping, patulous, rictal, ringent, unsealed, wide-open. **2. perforated** bibulous, cancellate, holey, leachy, perforate, poriferous, porous, spongy.

v. **7. 1. open** loosen, reopen, throw open, unbar, unbolt, unbuckle, unclench, unclose, uncork, undo, unfasten, unglue, unhook, unlatch, unlock, unloosen, unplug, unseal, untie, unwrap, unzip. **2. pierce** bore, breach, broach, buttonhole, drawbore, drill, eat into, eye, eyelet, gimlet, gride, hole, lancinate, loophole, peck, perforate, pin-prick, pink, prick, prickle, prong, puncture, rebore, roulette, scuttle, search, stab, stave, tap, tunnel, wimble, window. **3. tear** gap, gash, shred, slash, slit. **4. force** jemmy, pick.

8. 1. open up become open, bilge, break, crevasse, dehisce, fissure, leak, open, pop, reopen, rift. **2. gape** expand, loosen, open out, run, slacken, spread, uncurl, undouble, unfold, unfurl, yawn.

adv. **9. 1. open** ajar, gapingly, patulously, wide.

RELATED KEYWORDS: HOLLOW, CUT, ENTRANCE, EXIT, GAP, SHARPNESS

OPERATION

n. **1. 1. operation** action, activity, affair, application. **2. function** cycle, exercise, machinery, procedure, process. **3. actuation** effectuation, implementation, making. **4. governance** administration, command, conduct, control, direction, government, handling, jurisdiction, management, mastership, polity, regulation, treatment. *Informal:* admin.

2. 1. administrator actuator, administrant, agent, applier, commission, effecter, force, operant, operator, representative. **2. headquarters** command, management, operations branch.

adj. **3. 1. operating** adequate, effectual, in effect, operant, operational. **2. going** acting, afloat, agent, alive, at work, effective, efficacious, efficient, functioning, go, in force, in motion, in play, in the pipeline, in the system, live, on, on stream, operational, operative, ready, up, working. *Informal:* on deck. **3. running** good. *Informal:* A-OK *(US)*, A-okay, going strong, good to go. **4. functional** applied, economic, expedient, expediential, handy, no-nonsense, practical, profitable, useful.

v. **4. 1. operate** act, be operative, function, go, move, play, run, serve, work. **2. work** act, be in operation, be in working order, be under way, take effect, tell. **3. actuate** act on, erect, float, functionalise, gear up, ignite, make work, move, ply, run in, summon up, switch on. *Informal:* wind up. **4. administer** administrate, command, drive, hold, manage, minister. **5. drive** force, power. **6. apply** exercise. **7. institute** action, bring to bear.

RELATED KEYWORDS: ACTION, POWER, WORK

OPPOSITENESS

n. **1. 1. oppositeness** antagonism, antipathy, antithesis, contrariety, contrariness, contrast, opposability, opposition, paradoxicalness. **2. antithesis** antipode *(Chiefly US)*, inverse, reverse. **3. ambivalence** ambitendency, bisexuality, hermaphroditism, virilism. *Informal:* bi.

2. 1. opposite meaning antithesis, contraposition, contrary, contrast, converse, the contrary, the other extreme. **2. inverse** contrary, counter, reverse. **3. antonym** opposite. **4. enantiosis** a contradiction in terms, adversative, irony, paradox, sarcasm.

adj. **3. 1. opposing** antagonistic, antithetic, antithetical, conflicting, contradictory, contrary, contrasted, counter, cross, foul, inconsistent, mutually exclusive, opposed, opposite, oppositional, oppugnant, paradoxical, the other, tother. *Informal:* like chalk and cheese.

2. antonymic opposite in meaning. **3. inverse** back-to-front, backward, converse, inversive, retrograde, reverse, reversed. **4. on opposite sides** antipodean, at cross purposes, at opposite poles. *Informal:* like oil and water. **5. ambivalent** ambisexual, bisexual, hermaphrodite, hermaphroditic, hermaphroditical, two-edged. *Informal:* ac-dc, bi.

v. **4. 1. oppose** contradict, invert, negate, run counter to, turn upside down.

adv. **5. 1. oppositely** adversatively, antithetically, conversely, opposite, paradoxically, poles apart, vice versa. **2. contrarily** au contraire, but then again, contrariwise, contrary, counter, on the contrary, on the other hand, rather, to the contrary. **3. inversely** conversely, reversely, vice versa. *Informal:* topsy-turvy. **4. ambivalently**.

RELATED KEYWORDS: DISAGREEMENT, DENIAL, DISCORD, COMPARISON, OVERTURN

OPPOSITE POSITION

n. **1. 1. opposite position** adverseness, confrontation, contraposition, contrariness, opposition. **2. polarity** bilateralism, bilateralness, bipolarity, dissymetry, polarisation. **3. pole** antipodes. **4. opposite side** opposite number, verso, vis-a-vis. *Informal:* flip side.

adj. **2. 1. face to face** across, diametrically opposite, vis-a-vis. **2. opposed** antagonistic, antithetic, conflicting, contradictory, contrary, cross, foul, opposable, opposite, oppugnant, polarised. **3. adverse** contrapositive, opponent, opposing. **4. polar** bipolar. **5. antipodal** antipodean.

3. 1. dissymetric dissymmetrical. **2. pinnate** distichous, imparipinnate, pinnatifid, pinnatilobate, pinnatisect.

v. **4. 1. invert** contrapose, oppose, polarise. **2. confront** face, subtend.

adv. **5. 1. opposite** contrary, dos-à-dos, oppositely, overleaf, vis-a-vis. **2. contrarily** adversely, au contraire, contrariwise, counter, on the contrary, per contra, to the contrary. **3. bilaterally** distichously.

prep **6. 1. opposite** face to face with, facing, vis-a-vis. **2. against** over against.

RELATED KEYWORDS: FRONT, REAR, OVERTURN

OPTICS

n. **1. 1. optics** dioptrics, geometrical optics. **2. fibre optics** catoptrics.

2. 1. lens burning-glass, eyepiece, hand glass, magnifier, magnifying glass, meniscus, prism, sunglass, Wollaston prism. **2. lens system** amplifier, collimator, eyeglass, eyepiece, field lens, fish-eye lens, Huygens eyepiece, immersion objective, magnetic lens, object glass, objective, ocular, optical zoom, telephoto lens, wide-angle lens, zoom, zoom lens.

3. 1. glasses bifocals, eyeglasses, goggles, half-frames, John Lennon glasses, lorgnette, pince-nez, specs, spectacles. *Informal:* Coke bottle glasses. **2. contact lenses** hydrophilic contact lenses. **3. sunglasses** dark glasses. *Informal:* polaroids, shades, sunnies. **4. goggles** safety glasses. *Informal:* gogs. **5. monocle** lorgnon.

4. 1. scopes bioscope, fluoroscope, kaleidoscope, monochromator, ophthalmoscope, prismatic instrument, stauroscope, stereoscope, tachistoscope, telespectroscope. **2. microscope** compound microscope, dark microscope, dark-field microscope, electron microscope, phase contrast microscope, polarising microscope, simple microscope, ultramicroscope, ultraviolet microscope. **3. telescope** Cassegrainian telescope, cometfinder, Gregorian telescope, Newtonian telescope, reflecting telescope, refracting telescope, refractor, spyglass, zenith tube. **4. binoculars** field glasses, field-glasses, lorgnette, lorgnon, opera glasses, telestereoscope. **5. periscope** camera lucida, camera obscura. **6. hydroscope** waterglass. **7. gastroscope** cystoscope, diploscope, endoscope, hysteroscope, laryngoscope, myoscope, pharyngoscope, proctoscope, rhinoscope, urethroscope.

5. 1. mirror anamorphoscope, cheval glass, distorting mirror, glass, hand glass, looking glass, magic mirror, pier glass, rear-vision mirror, reflector, speculum, wing mirror.

6. 1. reflection reflexion, total internal reflection. **2. image** mirror image. **3. refraction** birefringence, diffraction, fringe, interference, refringence. **4. polarisation** analyser. **5. aberration** achromatism, aplanatism, chromatic aberration, coma, spherical aberration, stigmatism. **6. angle of incidence** angle, angle of reflection, angle of refraction. **7. focus** cardinal points, centre of curvature, focal plane, focal point, nodal point, principal axis, principal focus, principal points. **8. focal length** critical angle, depth of field, depth of focus, dioptre, magnification, numerical aperture, power, resolution, resolving power.

7.   **1. projector** magic lantern, planetarium, stereopticon, wheel of life, zoetrope.

8.   **1. measuring instruments** dioptometer, etalon, mass spectrograph, perimeter, polarimeter, polariscope, retinoscope, skiascope, spectrometer, spectrophotometer, spectroscope.

9.   **1. optical techniques** exaggerated stereo, fluoroscopy, hyperstereoscopy, microscopy, ophthalmoscopy, retinoscopy, screening, spectroscopy, stereoscopy, stereovision, telescopy, ultramicroscopy.

adj. 10.   **1. optic** catoptric, dioptric, fibre-optic, optical. **2. reflecting** reflectional, reflective.

11.   **1. lens-type** aplanatic, apochromatic, biconcave, biconvex, bifocal, concave, concavo-convex, confocal, convex, convexo-concave, convexo-convex, convexo-plane, lenticular, plano-concave, plano-convex, prismatic, stigmatic, toric.

RELATED KEYWORDS: LIGHT, SIGHT, VISIBILITY

ORANGE

n. 1.   **1. orange** amber, cadmium orange, tangerine. **2. orange-red** carmine, carnation, Chinese red, chrome red, flame colour, ginger, henna, incarnadine, mehndi, Pompeian red, poppy, red lead, rust, scarlet. *Informal:* orangey-red. **3. orange-brown** terracotta, titian. **4. peach** apricot, coral, yellow-pink. **5. brass** copper, old gold.

2.   **1. yellow** butter, buttercup, cadmium yellow, canary-yellow, citrine, daffodil, gamboge, lemon, lemon-yellow, ochre, primrose, straw colour. **2. yellow-brown** buff, isabel, maize, nankeen, sand, tan, tawny, wheat. **3. mustard** cambogia, crocus, gamboge, saffron, saffron yellow, yellow-orange. **4. yellow-green** chartreuse, grass-green, lime-green, pea green, pistachio, sulphur. **5. cream** champagne, eggshell, honey. **6. blond** blonde. **7. gold**.

3.   **1. yellowness** blondness, creaminess, goldenness, sandiness, tawniness. **2. jaundice** chlorosis, sallowness, yellows.

4.   **1. yellow pigment** brazilin, cadmium orange, cadmium yellow, cambogia, flavin, flavone, flavopurpurina, gamboge, gold, henna, indian red, kamala, luteolin, mehndi, naples yellow, ochre, or, orange-brown, quercetin, quercitron, saffron, tartrazine, tropaeolin, turmeric, urochrome, weld, xanthein, xanthin, yellow, yellow-orange, zinc chromate, zinc chrome, zinc yellow.

adj. 5.   **1. orange** amber, auburn, bronze, carroty, copper, cupreous, ferruginous, foxy, ginger, gingery, hazel, hepatic, liver, rubiginous, russet, rust-coloured, rusty, tangerine, terracotta, testaceous. **2. peach** apricot, coral-coloured, coralline, luteous.

6.   **1. yellow** canary, canary-coloured, chartreuse, citreous, citrine, citron, lemon, lemon-coloured, quercetic, stramineous, sulphurous, sulphury, xanthic, xanthous, yellowish. **2. ochre** ochreous, ochroid, ochrous, ochry. **3. ash-blond** blond, blonde. **4. buff** cervine, corn-coloured, fallow, flaxen, flaxy, fulvous, isabel, sandy, stramineous, straw-coloured, tawny, tow. **5. creamy** champagne, cream, cream-coloured, eggshell. **6. yellowing** flavescent, xanthous, yellowish, yellowy. **7. sallow** chlorotic, jaundiced, sallowish. **8. gold** aureate, auric, brass, brazen, coppery, gilded, gilt, golden.

v. 7.   **1. yellow** gild. **2. turn yellow** jaundice, sallow.

RELATED KEYWORDS: BROWN, COLOUR, GREEN, RED

ORDER

n. 1.   **1. order** combination, conformation, form, geometry, Gestalt, matrix, organisation, shape, structure, system, taxis. **2. arrangement** architecture, array, arrayal, calibre, cast, collation, collocation, composition, configuration, constitution, contexture, dispensation, disposal, distribution, emplacement, layout, line-up, make-up, ordination, ordonnance, permutation, placement, plan, structure. **3. battle formation** battleline, close-order, echelon, flight formation. **4. brick arrangement** bond, colonial bond, English bond, Flemish bond, garden-wall bond, half bond, hit-and-miss brickwork, indenting, stack bond, stretcher bond, toothing. *Informal:* four-and-a-half bond. **5. floral formation** aestivation, anthotaxy, inflorescence, phyllotaxis, vernation.

2.   **1. tidiness** accord, apple-pie order, consistency, eutaxy, harmony, methodicalness, neatness, orderliness, regularity, snugness, systematism, tautness, trim, trimness, unison.

3.   **1. ordering** alphabetisation, orchestration, organisation, rationalisation, recomposition, redeployment, schematisation, systematisation, systemisation. **2. coordination** imposition, regimentation, regularisation, subjunction. **3. systematics** architectonics, economy, methodology, systematology, teleology, typology.

    4. **1. orderer** aligner, alphabetiser, collator, composer, disposer, distributor, filer, marshaller, methodiser, organiser, rationaliser, schematiser, systematiser, systematist, systemiser.

adj.   **5.** **1. ordered** architectonic, structured. **2. orderly** businesslike, methodical, regular, scientific, streamlined, systematic, tight-knit, well-regulated. **3. harmonious** concordant, cosmic, harmonic, organic, symphonious, unisonous. **4. sequential** chronological, datal, seriate, synchronistic, tabular.

    6. **1. tidy** dapper, just so, neat, proper, shipshape, smug, snug, spick-and-span, taut, tiddly, trim, well-groomed. **2. well-ordered** orderly, regular, steady, uniform. **3. disciplined** couth, good, good-mannered, law-abiding, obedient, polite, pukka, respectable, seemly, well-behaved, well-mannered. *Informal:* straight-arrow.

v.   **7.** **1. order** adjust, compose, fix, form, format, gather, make up, permute, position, range, set, settle. **2. arrange** code, coordinate, orchestrate, permutate, program, rotate, seed, set to rights, structure, tabularise, tabulate, timetable. *Informal:* jack *(NZ)*. **3. systematise** adjust, alphabetise, codify, digest, methodise, organise, rationalise, regularise, schematise, systemise. **4. sort** assort, categorise, class, classify, coordinate, distinguish, gradate, grade, identify, label, lemmatise, mark, pigeonhole, rank, rate, size, staple. **5. divide** compartment, departmentalise, distribute, factionalise, parcel out (or up), stratify, stream, zone. **6. rearrange** re-form, re-format, re-sort, readjust, recast, reclassify, recompose, reconstitute, reconstruct, redeploy, reorder, reorganise. *Informal:* rejig.

    8. **1. tidy** do up, dress, fettle, groom, neaten, put one's house in order, set (or put) to rights, set one's house in order, straighten, tidy up, trig. **2. array** file, interfile, lay out, place, set, set out. **3. dispose** align, aline, collate, collocate, justify, right. **4. marshal** alert, draw up, dress, form up, rally, regiment, troop.

adv.   **9.** **1. orderly** harmoniously, harmonistically, regularly, systematically, systemically. **2. sequentially** in order, just so, seriately, step by step, stepwise.

    10. **1. tidily** neatly, shipshape, snug, snugly, straight, to rights, trim.

    RELATED KEYWORDS: CLASSIFICATION, CLEANLINESS, LIST, SHAPE

ORDINARINESS

n.   **1.** **1. ordinariness** commonness, normality, standardness, typicalness, usualness. **2. mediocrity** indifference, moderateness. **3. triteness** commonplaceness, pedestrianism, platitudinousness, poshlost, prosaicness, prosaism, triviality, trivialness. **4. standardisation** normalisation.

    2. **1. average** common run, mean, measure, medium, middle, norm, normal, par, standard. **2. arithmetic mean** centroid, geometric mean, harmonic mean, indifference point, mean deviation, mean distance, mean free path, median, moment, root mean square. **3. middlings** intergrade. **4. golden mean** compromise, happy medium, middle course.

    3. **1. platitude** bêtise, banality, cliché, commonplace, prosaism, trivialism, triviality, truism. *Informal:* bromide.

    4. **1. ordinary person** John Citizen, the man in the street. *Informal:* Joe *(US)*, Joe Bloggs, Joe Blow, little Aussie battler. **2. middle-of-the-roader** middlebrow, moderate.

adj.   **5.** **1. ordinary** accepted, accustomed, average, bog-standard, bread-and-butter, conventional, customary, expected, familiar, formulaic, general, matter-of-fact, normal, normative, par for the course, plebeian, regular, run-of-the-mill, simple, standard, stock, typical, unremarkable, usual. *Informal:* straight-up, vanilla. **2. commonplace** boring, clichéd, colourless, common, common-or-garden, day-to-day, everyday, ho-hum, homespun, household, humdrum, jejune, mill-run, mundane, nondescript, pedestrian, plain, practical, prosaic, prosy, ready-made, slow, stale, stupid, tasteless, unexceptional, uninspired, uninspiring, unreadable, vapid, workaday, world-weary. *Informal:* blah, random *(Chiefly US)*. **3. average** fair to middling, mediocre, medium, middling, moderate, much of a muchness, nothing to write home about, par, second-class, secondrate, so-so, tolerable, undistinguished. *Informal:* fifty-fifty, half-pie. **4. mean** average, medial. **5. indifferent** apathetic. **6. trite** banal, deja vu, dull, flat, gormless, hack, hackneyed, musty, old, stereotyped, threadbare, tired, trivial, vulgar, well-worn, wornout. **7. middle-of-the-road** bourgeois, middlebrow, moderate, MOR.

v.   **6.** **1. average** compromise, equalise, even up, iron out differences, split the difference, standardise. **2. normalise**.

adv.   **7.** **1. ordinarily** averagely, commonly, indifferently, medially, middlingly, moderately, on the average, usually. *Informal:* middling. **2. commonly** mundanely, prosaically, tritely.

    RELATED KEYWORDS: CONFORMITY, CUSTOM, MEDIOCRITY

ORGANISM

n. **1.** **1. organism** haploid, individual, organisation, zooid. **2. micro-organism** aerobe, amoeboid, anaerobe, anaerobiont, anaerobium, animalcule, animalculum, coenocyte, extremophile, infusorian, microbe, microparasite, monad, monas, nanoplankton, protist, protistan, protozoan. **3. pathogen** amphitricha, bacteria, bacteriophage, bacterium, germ, microbe, rickettsia, virus. *Informal:* bug, wog. **4. culture** plate, pure culture, subculture. **5. colony** clump, coenobium, plasmodium, zoogloea. **6. microfauna** intestinal flora. **7. gemmule** gemma.

2. **1. living thing** biota, organic matter, protoplast. **2. chromatin** aneuploidy, chromosome, dna, gene, genetic material, plasmagene, spireme. **3. biotype** genotype, haplotype, phenotype.

3. **1. cell** amitochondriate, anaplastic, basidiospore, corpuscle, cyst, endospore, erythrocyte, fibroblast, gamete, gametocyte, gemmule, germ cell, germen, gonocyte, haemocyte, haemoleucocyte, heterogamete, isogamete, leucocyte, lymph cell, lymphocyte, macrocyte, macrogamete, microcyte, monocyte, muscle cell, nerve cell, neuroblast, neuron, neurone, neutrophil, oocyte, ovocyte, ovum, phagocyte, planogamete, red blood cell, sperm, spermatid, spermatocyte, spermatozoon, spore, sporule, swarm spore, swarmer, tetraspore, white blood cell.

4. **1. protoplasm** alloplasm, archiplasm, archoplasm, bioplasm, coenosarc, cytoplasm, ectoplasm, ectosarc, endoplasm, endosarc, karyoplasm, nucleoplasm, plasma, stroma, trophoplasm. **2. organelle** air vesicle, astrosphere, cell membrane, cell wall, centriole, centrosome, chloroplast, chondriosome, chromoplast, endoplasmic reticulum, Golgi Complex, karyosome, lysosome, mitochondrion, nucleolus, nucleus, plasmosome, plastid, ribosome, vacuole, vesicle. **3. blastula** anlage, blastema, blastocoel, blastodisc, blastomere, blastosphere, germinal disc, segmentation cavity. **4. cilium** filament, flagellum, microvillus, villosity, villus.

5. **1. protozoan** actinopod, ameba, amoeba, endamoeba, euglena, foraminifer, heliozoan, nummulite, plasmodium, radiolarian, rhizopod, rotifer, sun animalcule, trypanosome, wheel animalcule.

6. **1. bacillus** acetobacter, amphitricha, botulinus, chlorella, coccidia, comma bacillus, golden staph, gonococcus, Klebs-Löffler bacillus, Koch's bacillus, leptospira, MAC, micrococcus, monotricha, mycobacterium, peritricha, pneumobacillus, pneumococcus, rhizobium, rod, spirillum, spirochaete, staphylococcus, streptococcus, tetanus bacillus, tubercle bacillus, typhoid bacillus, vibrio.

7. **1. virus** adenovirus, arbovirus, Barmah Forest virus, calicivirus, coronavirus, Coxsackie virus, cytomegalovirus, Ebola virus, Epstein-Barr virus, equine morbilivirus, norovirus, parvo, parvovirus, phage, prion, retrovirus, Ross River virus, slow virus, tobacco mosaic virus, tobacco necrosis virus.

8. **1. mould** actinomycete, fungus, myxomycete, phycomycete, schizomycete, slime mould, yeast.

9. **1. biology** agrobiology, astrobiology, autoecology, bacteriology, biochemistry, biodynamics, biogeny, bionics, bionomics, biophysics, cryobiology, cytology, ecology, electrobiology, geobiology, histology, histopathology, karyology, marine biology, microbiology, molecular biology, neurobiology, oecology, organic chemistry, palaeobiology, photobiology, psychobiology, radiobiology, sociobiology, synecology. **2. biologist** agrobiologist, astrobiologist, bacteriologist, biochemist, biogenist, bionomist, biophysicist, cryobiologist, cytologist, ecologist, electrobiologist, geobiologist, histologist, histopathologist, marine biologist, microbiologist, neurobiologist, organic chemist, palaeobiologist, photobiologist, psychobiologist, radiobiologist, sociobiologist.

RELATED KEYWORDS: BODY, PLANTS, ANIMALS, ILL HEALTH, LIFE, REPRODUCTION

OUTSIDE

n. **1.** **1. outside** exterior, external, outward, superficies, surface, top. **2. face** facade, facia, fascia, front. **3. covering** casing, coverture, crust, epidermis, integument, rind, shell, skin, superstratum. **4. outline** boundary, circumference, outer limits, periphery, profile, silhouette.

2. **1. outwardness** exteriority, externality, extrinsicality, superficiality, superficialness.

adj. **3.** **1. outside** exoteric, exterior, external, extrinsic, out, outer, outward. **2. surface** crustal, crusty, epidermal, epidermic, epigene, epigenic, external, out, outward, superficial, top, upper. **3. out-of-doors** alfresco, extramural, field, open-air, outdoor. **4. peripheral** boundary, circumambient, circumjacent, surrounding. **5. extraneous** external, extrinsic, out, outlying.

adv. **4.** **1. outside** out, outward, outwards, without. **2. on the outside** externally, extrinsically, on the face of it, on the surface, outwardly, superficially. **3. out of doors** abroad, afield, alfresco, en plein air, in the open air, out-of-doors, outdoors. *Informal:* out the back.

prep. **5.** **1. outside** beyond, round.

RELATED KEYWORDS: COVERING, EDGE, FOREIGNNESS, FRONT, EXTRACTION, SKIN, SURROUNDINGS

OVERINDULGENCE

n. **1.** **1. overindulgence** bacchanalianism, crapulousness, debauchery, dissipatedness, dissipation, dissoluteness, excess, glut, immoderateness, intemperance, intemperateness, overflow, profligacy, profligateness, rakishness, riotousness, self-indulgence, surfeit, unrestraint, wantonness, wildness.

2. **1. binge** bacchanal, bacchanalia, carousal, debauch, gorge, jag, orgy, saturnalia, spree, wallow. *Informal:* barney, bash, bat, beanfeast, beano, bender, blinder, blow-out, bust, drunk, grog-up, high jinks, lost weekend, rave, rort, scatter, shivoo, splurge.

3. **1. indulger** bacchanal, bacchant, Corinthian, dissipater, goliard, good timer, profligate, rioter, surfeiter, wallower. *Informal:* rip, swinger. **2. rake** boudoir bandicoot, debauchee, debaucher, Don Juan, libertine, Lothario, roué, satyr.

4. **1. greed** avarice, avidity, concupiscence, cupidity, desire, fire, greediness, lust, rapacity. **2. greediness** esuriency, gluttonousness, gluttony, hoggishness, overeating, piggery, piggishness, swinishness. **3. voraciousness** insatiableness, ravenousness, wolfishness. **4. epicureanism** gormandising.

5. **1. glutton** beast, gorger, gormandiser, gulper, gutzer, guzzler, trencherman. *Informal:* garbage guts, greedy-guts, guts, gutser, guzzle-guts, hog, pig. **2. epicure** bon vivant, bon viveur, epicurean, gastronome, gastronomer, gormand, gormandiser, gourmand, gourmet, sensualist, sybarite, voluptuary.

adj. **6.** **1. overindulgent** abandoned, crapulous, dionysian, excessive, immoderate, incontinent, intemperate, irrepressible, orgiastic, profligate, saturnalian, unbounded, unbridled, uncontrolled, unfettered, unmeasured, unrestrained, wild. *Informal:* wild and woolly. **2. dissipated** Corinthian, Cyprian, debauched, dissolute, fast, free, goliardic, intemperate, lascivious, libertine, licentious, light, loose, luxurious, rakish, riotous, salacious, unchaste, wanton. **3. intemperate** compulsive, indulgent, self-indulgent.

7. **1. greedy** avaricious, devouring, edacious, extortionate, gluttonous, insatiable, insatiate, rapacious, ravening, ravenous, voracious. **2. gluttonous** esurient, greedy, hoggish, hoglike, open-mouthed, piggish, rapacious, ravenous, swinish, voracious. *Informal:* gutsy. **3. epicurean** gastronomic, gormandising, sybaritic.

v. **8.** **1. overindulge** burn the candle at both ends, carouse, debauch, dissipate, give oneself up to, go overboard, go to town, go wild, indulge, live fast, live hard, luxuriate, philander, racket, revel, riot, roister, run riot, sow one's wild oats, wallow, wanton, wassail. *Informal:* be out on the tiles, live high on the hog, paint the town red.

9. **1. gluttonise** be like vultures, cram, eat like a horse, gorge, gormandise, make a pig of oneself, overeat, stuff, surfeit. *Informal:* bog in, eat fit to bust, guts, have hollow legs, like (or enjoy) one's food, pig out, stodge. **2. devour** bolt, engorge, glut, gobble, gollop, gorge, gulp, guzzle, ingurgitate, raven, sate, swill, weigh into, wolf. *Informal:* demolish, dig in, get stuck into, hoe in, hoe into, knock back, put away, scoff, stodge, tuck in.

RELATED KEYWORDS: ALCOHOL, JOY, EXCESS, PROMISCUITY, SEX, FOOD

OVERTAKING

n. **1.** **1. overtaking** overlap, overlapping, overstepping, passing. **2. passing lane** fast lane, outside lane.

v. **2.** **1. overtake** beat, catch up with, drop, dust *(Aboriginal English)*, forereach, gain upon, lap, leave behind, leave standing, outdistance, outgo, outpace, outride, outrun, outstrip, overhaul, pass, pull ahead, ride down, shoot ahead, street. **2. pass** go beyond, go past, move past, overtake, shoot by, shoot past, whistle by, whistle past, whizz by, whizz past. **3. skirt** slide past, slip past. **4. overshoot** go further, move ahead, override, overrun, overshoot the mark, overstand, overstep, overstride.

RELATED KEYWORDS: CROSSING, SPEED

OVERTURN

n. **1.** **1. overturn** bouleversement, careen, eskimo roll, inversion, overset, overthrow, reversion, tip, turnover, upset. **2. somersault** backflip, cartwheel, flick-roll, flip, forward roll, neck roll, roll, snap-roll. **3. topsy-turviness** topsy-turvydom.

 2. **1. inversion** anastrophe, chiasmus, hysteron proteron, palindrome. **2. inverse** mirror image.

 3. **1. turning inside-out** evagination, eversion, extraversion, extroversion.

adj. **4.** **1. overturned** back-to-front, inverted, reversed, topsy-turvy, upset, upside down, upturned, wrong side up. **2. inverted** backward, inversive, reversionary. **3. converse** inverse.

v. **5.** **1. overturn** capsize, keel, overthrow, skittle, tip, tip over, tip up, turn over, upset, upturn. **2. invert** put the cart before the horse. **3. overbalance** careen, keel over, loop, pitch pole, stand on one's head, turn turtle. **4. somersault** cartwheel, roll, troll, trundle, tumble.

 6. **1. turn inside out** evaginate, evert.

adv. **7.** **1. head over heels** backwards, base over apex, on one's head, topsy-turvily, topsy-turvy. **2. inside out** inversely, reversely. **3. contrariwise** vice versa.

 RELATED KEYWORDS: DESCENT, OPPOSITE POSITION, REVOLUTION, SPIN

OWNERSHIP

n. **1.** **1. ownership** allodium, demesne, domain, easement, estate, grasp, holdings, interest, occupancy, possession, property, proprietary, proprietorship, stake, tenure, vested interest. **2. freehold** coparcenary, copyhold, dead hand *(Law)*, exclusive right, impropriation, interest, leasehold, mortmain *(Law)*, seigniorage, seisin *(Law)*, seizin *(Law)*, severance, socage, tenancy, tenure, vacant possession, villeinage. **3. lordship** lairdship, landownership, landowning, seigniory, signory. **4. title** company title, copyright, escheat, fee, fee simple, fee tail, feoff, feud, fief, free grant, patency, patent, reversion, title deed, Torrens title, trust instrument. **5. monopoly** corner, monopolisation, monopolism.

 2. **1. owner** capitalist, franklin, homesteader, householder, joint owner, lady, laird, landholder, lord, master, mistress, monopolist, occupant, possessor, proprietary, proprietor, proprietress, ratepayer, riparian, señora, squatter, tenant in common, traditional owner *(Law)*. **2. holder** claimholder, coparcener, copyholder, freeholder, impropriator, owner, parcener, proprietary, proprietor. **3. landlord** absentee landlord, body corporate, landlady, landowner, owners' corporation. **4. alienee** cestui que vie.

adj. **3.** **1. own** ain *(Scottish)*, appropriative, belonging, inalienable. **2. of one's own** exclusive, individual, private, privy. **3. claimed** bespoke, previously claimed, spoken for. **4. of the house** maison. **5. pre-owned** second-hand, third-hand, used. *Informal:* preloved.

 4. **1. propertied** adverse possession, land-holding, landed, landowning, tenurial. **2. possessed of** long, possessory, proprietary, proprietorial.

v. **5.** **1. own** be worth, bear, command, enfeoff, enjoy, enjoy the use of, have, have all to oneself, have in hand, hold, hold in fee, possess. **2. monopolise** buy out, buy up, collar, corner, engross, privatise. *Informal:* gridiron, peacock. **3. gain possession of** get one's hands on, occupy, overrun, squat in, take over.

 6. **1. belong** appertain.

phr. **7.** **1. in one's possession** at call, in hand, in one's clutches, in one's own hands, on hand, to hand, to one's credit, to one's name, to the good.

 RELATED KEYWORDS: BUYING, TAKING, PROFIT, PROPERTY, ROBBERY

PAIN

n. **1.** **1. pain** affliction, damage, discomfort, harm, hurt, ill, injury, malaise. *Informal:* gip. **2. irritation** annoyance, chafe, exacerbation, exasperation, fret, nuisance, thorn in one's flesh, trouble, vexation. *Informal:* peeve. **3. suffering** travail. **4. agony** affliction, anguish, distress, excruciation, hell, misery, slow death, torment, torture, tortures, wrack. **5. ordeal** affliction, baptism of fire, gethsemane, golgotha, trial. **6. martyrdom** crucifixion. **7. algolagnia** bondage, discipline, masochism, sadism, sadomasochism. *Informal:* B & D. **8. algometry** algometer.

 2. **1. ache** beating, pain, pang, qualm, throb, throe, twinge, twitch. **2. headache** cluster headache, migraine, sick headache, splitting headache. **3. earache** otalgia, toothache. **4. backache**. **5. stomach-ache** colic, gastralgia, gripes, hunger pain, stomach migraine. *Informal:* collywobbles, pain in the gut. **6. afterpains** growing pains, phantom limb pains, referred pain, teething pains. **7. cardialgia** angina, angina pectoris, heartburn, waterbrash. **8. hyperalgesia** arthralgia, brachialgia, causalgia, face-ache, hemialgia, neuralgia, neuritis.

 3. **1. painfulness** bitterness, distressfulness, hurtfulness, malignancy, poignancy, severeness, severity. **2. soreness** displeasure, grief, irritancy, sensitiveness, tenderness, trouble. *Informal:* dander. **3. qualmishness** queasiness, queerness, seediness, wooziness. **4. pain threshold.**

4.   **1. tormentor** afflicter, crucifier, harmer, sadomasochist, torturer.

adj. **5.**   **1. painful** afflictive, distressful, distressing, harrowing, heart-rending, piquant, poignant, upsetting. **2. excruciating** agonising, torturous. **3. biting** bitter, brutal, burning, cruel, keen, nipping, piercing, shooting, smarting, stabbing, stinging, throbbing. **4. griping** colicky, fulgurating. **5. sore** exposed, raw, tender, vulnerable. **6. achy** footsore, footworn, headachy, saddle-sore. **7. suffering** aching, racked with pain.

v. **6.**   **1. pain** ache, beat, gripe, hurt, inflame, palpitate, pound, pulse, smart, throb, tingle, trouble, twinge. *Informal:* give one gip, jump, play hell, play merry hell. **2. sting** urticate. **3. chafe** fret, gall, pinch, rub. **4. fester** rankle. **5. cause pain** afflict, agonise, anguish, bother, distress, excruciate, grill, harrow, hurt, lacerate, pain, plague, rack, torment, torture, vex, worry, wring. *Informal:* cut up. **6. wound** bite, break, lacerate, lancinate, nip, prick, prickle, stab, sting, tear. **7. torture** crucify, excruciate. **8. prolong the agony** kill by inches.

7.   **1. feel pain** agonise, anguish, bear, brook, burn one's fingers, receive, suffer, take, undergo, wring. **2. flinch** nip, start, twitch, wince. **3. writhe** squirm, twist, wrench, wriggle. **4. travail** be on the rack, have a bad time of it. *Informal:* do a perish.

RELATED KEYWORDS: DISCONTENTEDNESS, ILL HEALTH, PUNISHMENT

PARENTAGE

n. **1.**   **1. parentage** family, parenthood, parenting. **2. maternity** mothercraft, motherhood, mothering, motherliness. **3. paternity** fatherhood, fatherliness.

2.   **1. ancestry** birth, descent, extraction, lineage, origin, roots, strain. **2. genealogy** family tree, genealogical tree, stemma, tree. **3. herd-book** studbook. **4. pedigree** ancestry, blood, family, line. **5. pure line** straight line. **6. breed** brood, strain, type. **7. stock** root, rootstock, stem, stirps. **8. branch** lop, moiety, offshoot, rod, side, sprig. **9. matriline** distaff side, matriarchy, spear side. **10. patriline** patriarchy. **11. clan** blood, breed, family, flesh and blood, gens, house, ilk, issue, kin, kindred, kinsfolk, kith and kin, lineage, nation, nationality, phratry, primary group, progeny, race, sept, stock, strain, tribe. *Informal:* brood. **12. legitimacy. 13. illegitimacy** bastard, bastardy, by-blow, illegitimate, love child. *Informal:* basket, git *(Chiefly British)*. **14. polygenesis** difference.

3.   **1. genetics** hereditarianism, Mendel's laws, Mendelism. **2. eugenics** AI, AID, allogamy, artificial insemination, artificial selection, autogamy, crossbreeding, crossing, fancy, genetic engineering, homogamy, hybridism, in-vitro fertilisation, inbreeding, intercross, miscegenation, mongrelism, outcrossing, selection, stirpiculture, thremmatology, xenogamy. **3. heritability** hereditability. **4. reversion** atavism, recapitulation. *Informal:* recap. **5. gene** allele, allelomorph, ancient code, dna, factor, gemma, gemmule, genetic code, genome, genotype, germ plasm, idioplasm, unit, unit factor.

4.   **1. descendant** coheir, distaff, heir, heir apparent, heir presumptive, heiress, heritress, inheritress, inheritrix, offspring. *Informal:* chip off the old block. **2. offshoot** root, scion. **3. full blood** bloodstock, purebred. **4. half-blood** cross, half-breed, half-caste, heterozygote, kuri *(NZ)*, ladino, métis *(US)*, métisse, mestiza, mestizo, mulatto, quartercaste. *Informal:* bitzer, bronze-wing, creamy, mongrel, mule-skinner *(US)*, muleteer. **5. hybrid** cross, crossbreed, crossbreed, crossover, grade, mule, second cross, top cross. *Informal:* bitzer, mong, mongrel. **6. throwback** atavist, reversion, reverter.

adj. **5.**   **1. matriarchal** distaff, matriclinous, matrilineal, spindle *(US)*. **2. patriarchal** patriclinous, patrilineal. **3. legitimate** lawful, true, well-born. **4. illegitimate** base, baseborn, bastard, misbegotten, on the wrong side of the blanket, unfathered, unlawful.

6.   **1. genetic** genic, genotypic, idioplasmic, mendelian. **2. hereditary** ancestral, descendible, hereditable, heritable, inheritable, inherited, receivable. **3. phyletic** monophyletic, phylogenic, polyphyletic, racial. **4. lineal** direct, secund, unilateral. **5. collateral** indirect. **6. pedigreed** blooded, well-bred. **7. purebred** blood, full blood, full-blooded, inbred, legitimate, thoroughbred, true, true-born, true-bred. **8. half-blooded** half-breed, half-caste, miscegenetic. **9. hybrid** cross, crossbred, half-blooded, interbred. *Informal:* mongrel. **10. atavistic** reversionary.

adv. **7.**   **1. ancestrally** genealogically. **2. hereditarily** biological, lineally. **3. genetically** hereditably, heritably, inheritably.

RELATED KEYWORDS: OFFSPRING, RELATIVE, REPRODUCTION

PART

n.   **1.**   **1. part** bit, canton, fraction, fragment, lot, moiety, per cent, percentage, portion, proportion, share, slice. **2. constituent** component, detail, element, ingredient, integral, integrant, item, material, member, module, particular, tessera. **3. section** branch, compartment, department, desk, division, panel, partition, segment, side, subdivision, subsection, unit. **4. cross-section** example. **5. allotment** allocation, allowance, contingent, dividend, helping, length, lot, parcel, percentage, portion, quantum, quota, ration, share, slice. *Informal:* a slice of the cake, chop, cut, divvy, rake-off, whack. **6. chunk** gobbet, hunk, lump, nugget. *Informal:* dollop, glob. **7. slice** cantle, finger, lop, part, piece, shive, wedge. **8. greater part** absolute majority, body, bulk, majority, mass, plurality. **9. particle** bit, bite, chip, crumb, driblet, morceau, morsel, nibble, nubbin *(US)*, nubble, scrap, shred. *Informal:* droob. **10. fragment** bit, chip, end, flake, flinders, frazzle, fritter, piece, potsherd, scrap, shard, shiver, shrapnel, shred, sliver, snatch, spill, splinter, split, whittlings. **11. bits and pieces** fragmentation, fragments, leftovers, odds and ends, relicts, remains, remnants, scraps, smithereens.

adj.   **2.**   **1. partial** fractional, half, halfway, imperfect, incomplete, part, truncated. **2. fragmentary** bitty, broken, disconnected, disjointed, fragmental, imperfect, incomplete, piecemeal, scrap, scrappy, splintery. **3. partite** bipartite, compartmentalised, departmentalised, disjunct, disunited, dividable, divided, divisible, divisional, divisionary, fractional, multipartite, partial, polytomous, quinquepartite, sectional, segmental, segmentary, segmented, separate, separated, shared, split, volumed. **4. articulated** modular.

     3.   **1. constituent** cantonal, component, composing, elemental, elementary, fractional, integral, integrant, partial, uncompounded.

adv.   **4.**   **1. partially** fractionally, half, in part, part, partly. **2. piecemeal** bit by bit, gradually, part by part, piece by piece, scrappily.

     RELATED KEYWORDS: INADEQUACY, DEFICIENCY, SEPARATION, IMPERFECTION, QUANTITY, REMNANT

PARTICIPATION

n.   **1.**   **1. participation** affiliation, association, collaboration, commitment, company, consociation, contribution, engagement, entanglement, immixture, interestedness, involution, sympathy. *Informal:* stake. **2. involvement** complicity, concernment, connection, implication, interest.

     2.   **1. participant** accessory, collaborator, contributor, member, partaker, participator, party, sympathiser.

adj.   **3.**   **1. participating** concerned with, in the same boat, in the thick of, involute. **2. involved** concerned, implicated. **3. interested** busy *(Chiefly US)*, engaged, for, full of, occupied, participating, rapt in, wrapped up in.

v.   **4.**   **1. participate** be a party to, become committed, buy in, buy into, enter, enter into, get into, get involved, get up to, have a hand in, have an interest in, join, join in, make a stand, mix up in, partake in, play a part, share, take part. *Informal:* be up to one's neck in, go the whole hog.

     5.   **1. involve** catch up, compromise, concern, concern oneself, condemn, enmesh, ensnare, entangle, entrap, immesh, implicate, incur, inmesh, intervolve, overcommit, put up to, tangle. *Informal:* rope in. **2. interest**.

     RELATED KEYWORDS: ACTION, ENTHUSIASM

PARTICULARITY

n.   **1.**   **1. particularity** categoricalness, circumscription, circumstantiality, definability, definiteness, definitiveness, distinctness, individuality, separateness, specificity, specificness. **2. uniqueness** inimitableness.

     2.   **1. characteristic** attribute, character, difference, differentia, distinction, distinctive feature, distinguishing feature, essence, flavour, form, genius, idiom, idiosyncrasy, lineament, mannerism, mark, marking, parts, personality, predicable, property, speciality, specific, trait. **2. peculiarity** individualism, particularity, quirk, singularity.

     3.   **1. particular** article, circumstance, detail, elements, fine print, individuality, item, minutiae, minutias, note, parameter, part, piece, point, portion, property, small print, specialty, specification. *Informal:* nitty-gritty. **2. way** manner, mode, style. *Informal:* schtick.

adj.   **4.**   **1. particular** certain, circumstantial, definite, deictic, diacritical, especial, exact, exclusive, given, niche, noteworthy, peculiar, precise, special, specific, unusual. **2. respective** appropriate, different, distributive, individual, itemised, proper, separate, several. **3. specifiable** assignable, circumscriptive, definable, differentiable, identifiable, isolable. **4. for a particular occasion** ad hoc, magistral. **5. of one's own** exclusive, one's, personal, private, privy, unipersonal. **6. bespoke** custom-built, custom-made, customised, made-to-measure, made-to-order, ready-rolled, specially made, tailor-made. **7. purpose-built** personalised, site-specific. **8. each** every one, ilk *(Scottish)*, ilka *(Scottish)*, that, this.

v. **5. 1. particularise** asterisk, characterise, customise, define, determine, discriminate, distinguish, identify, individualise, individuate, mark, predefine, specialise. *Informal:* ID, peg. **2. circumstantiate** circumstance, detail, differentiate, elaborate, elaborate on, expand. **3. specify** assign, designate, indicate, mark, note, predesignate, refer, type. *Informal:* have someone tabbed.

adv. **6. 1. particularly** ad hoc, ad hominem, circumstantially, especially, in detail, in particular, namely, peculiar to, peculiarly, specially, specifically. **2. for my (his, her, etc.) part** as far as I am concerned, in my opinion, on all counts, speaking for myself. **3. locally** here, hereat, there, thereto. **4. respectively** apart, apiece, bit by bit, each, individually, separately, severally, singly. **5. differentially** diacritically, dividually. **6. for example** e.g., such as, to wit, videlicet, viz.

RELATED KEYWORDS: NONCONFORMITY, ONE

PARTNER

n. **1. 1. partner** accomplice, ally, associate, bedfellow, bunji *(Aboriginal English, Aboriginal English)*, chum, coequal, comate, companion, compeer, comrade, confrère, copartner, duumvir, fellow, friend, intimate, match, mate, offsider, peer, running mate, sparring partner. *Informal:* buddy-buddy, pard *(US)*, pardner *(US)*. **2. silent partner** partner, sleeping partner. **3. assistant** acolyte, adjunct, adjutant, aide, aide-de-camp, assessor, attaché, attendant, backer, chaperone, coadjutress, coadjutrix, deputy, helper, junior, offsider, representative, satellite, second, secondary, subaltern. *Informal:* dep, sidekick. **4. helpmate** aid, companion, helping hand. **5. comrade** associate, brother, commensal, fellow, frère, mate, sister, track mate. *Informal:* buddy, pal. **6. co-worker** associate, colleague, fellow worker, messmate, shipmate, team-mate, workfellow, workmate, yokefellow. **7. compatriot** countryman, countrywoman, townsman, townswoman.

2. 1. accomplice abettor, accessary, accessory, camorrist, colluder, confederate, conspirator, particeps criminis, partner in crime, plotter. *Informal:* pal. **2. ally** affiliate, aligner, associate, auxiliary, cobelligerent, confederate, friend at court, supporter, trusty. **3. collaborator** fellow traveller, fifth columnist, quisling, sympathiser. **4. factionary** champion, cultist, factionist, partisan, votary. **5. follower** adherent, camp follower, disciple, hanger-on, henchman, parasite, protégé, satellite, shadow, trencherman. *Informal:* stooge, yes-man.

3. 1. member charter member, clubman, clubwoman, committeeman, committeewoman, communitarian. **2. new member** entrant, initiate. **3. federator** federalist, internationalist, leaguer, uniter.

v. **4. 1. partner** accompany, associate, chaperone, companion, consociate, consort, join with, mate, mingle, run (around) with, see, take out. *Informal:* wax. **2. ally with** go into business with, keep company with, take up with. *Informal:* hang around with, hang with, latch on to, mess with, pal up with, string along with, tie up with. **3. haunt** follow, shadow. **4. assist** accompany, aid, attend, have a hand in, help, participate, take a hand in.

RELATED KEYWORDS: COMPANIONSHIP, COOPERATION, FRIENDLINESS, HELP, MARRIAGE, SOCIETY

THE PAST

n. **1. 1. the past** antiquity, auld lang syne, days of old, days of yore, dreamtime, foretime, horse-and-buggy age, langsyne *(Scottish)*, the bygone, time immemorial, time out of mind, yesterday, yore. *Informal:* the good old days. **2. earliness** antiqueness, historicity.

2. 1. retrospectivity anamnesis, hindsight, mind, nostalgia, recollection, remembrance, reminiscence, retrospect, retrospection, review. **2. flashback** repeat, replay. **3. time machine** time travel.

3. 1. history ancient history, annals, chronicles, modern history. **2. archaeology** coprology, egyptology, etruscology, industrial archaeology, palaeogeography, palaeogeology, palaeontology, prehistory, protohistory, scatology. **3. antiquarianism** medievalism.

4. **1. historian** annalist, chronicler. **2. archaeologist** egyptologist, etruscologist. **3. antiquarian** antiquary.

5. **1. fossil** eolith, neolith, petrified forest, relics, reliquiae, remains, remnant, ruins, stone-lily, vestige.

adj. **6.** **1. past** agone, back, bygone, dead-and-buried, departed, earlier, erstwhile, foregone, former, historical, late, lost, of yore, old-fashioned, old-time, one-time, other, over, prior, quondam, sometime, whilom, yesterday. **2. nostalgic** evocative, implicative, recollective, redolent of, remindful, reminiscent of. **3. retrospective** ex post facto, memorial, retroactive. **4. perfect** historic tense, past perfect, perfective, pluperfect, preterite. **5. primeval** atavistic, early, early-stage, inchoate, original, primal, primigenial, primitive, primordial, pristine, protomorphic, protopathic. **6. early** ancient, mythical, Old. **7. ancient** anciently, antiquity, classical, immemorial, preadamite, premillennial, venerable. **8. prehistoric** aboriginal, age-old, aged, ancient, antediluvian, antemundane, archaean, archaeological, archaeozoic, archeological, azoic, eolithic, grey, neanderthal, old, ole, palaeogeographical, palaeogeological, palaeolithic, preglacial, prehuman, primal, primeval, primitive, primordial, protolithic. *Informal:* as old as the hills, out of the ark. **9. fossil** fossil-like, fossiliferous. **10. postdiluvian** postclassical, postwar. **11. recent** latter-day, low, of late.

7. **1. antique** anachronistic, anachronous, ancient, antediluvian, antiquarian, antiquated, archaic, classic, classical, dateless, dead, demoded, dinosaur, extinct, former, fusty, moss-grown, obsolescent, obsolete, old-fashioned, old-world, olde-worlde, outmoded, period, slow, steam *(humorous)*, trad, veteran, vintage. **2. outdated** antiquated, archaic, backward, behind the times, dated, dead-and-alive, fogram, old hat, old-fashioned, old-line *(US)*, oldschool, out-of-date, outworn, passé, primitive, superannuated. **3. expired** elapsed, extinct, lapsed, run out.

adv. **8.** **1. in the past** ago, agone, already, back, before now, by, formerly, heretofore, hitherto, since, sometime, then. **2. before that time** theretofore. **3. yesterday** last century, last week, last year, lately, latterly, new, newly, recently, the other day, the other night, yesteryear *(Chiefly Poetic)*. **4. long ago** at one time, early, formerly, historically, immemorially, in the olden days, in the year dot, langsyne *(Scottish)*, late, low, once, once upon a time, onetime *(Aboriginal English)*.

RELATED KEYWORDS: EARLINESS, OLDNESS, UNTIMELINESS

PATIENCE

n. **1.** **1. patience** allowance, endurance, enduringness, forbearance, forbearing, fortitude, lenity, long-suffering, longanimity, meekness, resignation, stoicalness, submission, sufferance, sustainment, tolerance, toleration.

2. **1. patient person** Griselda, Job, long-sufferer, stoic.

3. **1. perseverance** assiduity, diligence, doggedness, obstinacy, persistence, sedulousness, single-mindedness, stalwartness, stamina, staying power, steadfastness, tenacity, uncompromisingness, unwaveringness.

adj. **4.** **1. patient** enduring, forbearing, liberal-minded, long-suffering, meek, stoical, tolerant. **2. persevering** assiduous, diligent, dogged, hardworking, obstinate, persistent, sedulous, single-minded, stalwart, steadfast, strong-willed, tenacious, uncompromising, unwavering.

5. **1. bearable** endurable, liveable, maintainable, passable, sufferable, supportable, sustainable, swallowable, tolerable.

v. **6.** **1. be patient** bide one's time, play a waiting game, sit tight, stand by, wait. *Informal:* sweat it out.

7. **1. persevere** bear with, crack hardy, crack hearty, endure, have patience with, hold the line, last the distance, persist, ride out, see through, sit tight, stay with, stick at, stick it out, stick to one's guns, sustain, weather the storm. *Informal:* hang in. **2. bear up** bite one's lip, cool one's heels, grin and bear it, grit one's teeth, hold one's tongue, keep one's cool, keep one's temper, kick one's heels, put on a brave front, roll with the punches, stand one's ground, take it on the chin, take the rough with the smooth. **3. bear** abide, abide by, accept, brook, digest, endure, hack it, lump it, put up with, stomach, stomach it, suffer, support, swallow, take, tolerate, undergo. *Informal:* cop, hack, sit pat, take it.

phr. **8.** **1. be patient** hold on, just a minute, slow down, steady on, wait a minute. *Informal:* don't get your knickers in a knot, don't get your knickers in a twist, half a mo, hang on, hold your horses, hold your water, just a tick, simmer down.

RELATED KEYWORDS: ABSTINENCE, FORGIVENESS, KINDNESS, PITY

PAYMENT

n. **1.** **1. payment** aid, alimony *(US)*, amortisation, amortisement, claim, commission, composition, defrayal, disbursement, discharge, down payment, drawback, foregift, handsel, imprest, key money, maintenance, overpayment, perpetuity, prepayment, quarterage, redundancy, remittance, satisfaction, spot cash, time payment, token payment, valuable consideration. *Informal:* cop. **2. expenditure** abnormal item, capital expenditure, charge, cost, current expenses, expense, expenses, incidentals, outgo, outgoings, outlay, price, rate, score. *Informal:* damage. **3. outlay** anticipation *(Law)*, disbursement, expenditure, pump priming. **4. contribution** benevolence, indemnity, Peter's pence, subscription, subsidy. **5. impost** custom, imposition, levy, toll, tribute. **6. settlement** extinguishment, recoup, recoupment, redemption, requital, return. **7. payoff** backsheesh, blackmail, bribe, sop, tong *(Philippine English)*. *Informal:* backhander, baksheesh, bonus, boodle *(Chiefly US)*, fix, kickback, sling, spiff, sweetener, touch, you'lldo. **8. refund** drawback, recompense.

2. **1. income** above-award, annuity, disposable income, dole, earnings, emolument, hire, independent means, lurks and perks, money wages, nominal wages, pay, pay-packet, real wages, remuneration, revenue, salary, stipend, sturt, take-home pay, tontine, total wage, unearned income, wages. *Informal:* screw. **2. livelihood** bread and butter, living. *Informal:* crust, meal ticket. **3. living** benefice, fellowship, scholarship. **4. stipend** allocated pension, allowance, annuity, baksheesh, bounty system, Christmas box *(British)*, consideration, cumshaw, gratuity, pension, pourboire, prebend, recompense, reward, salary, tip. *Informal:* beer money. **5. basic wage** award wage, industry award, living wage, minimum wage, ordinary pay. **6. penalty rate** back pay, double time, half-pay, margin, overtime, piece rate, severance pay, sick pay, strike pay, time-and-a-half, triple time, weekend penalty rate. **7. blood money** danger money. **8. allowance** attraction money, climatic allowance, dirt money, district allowance, field allowance, heat money, height money, industry allowance, isolation allowance, living allowance, loading, locality allowance, lost time allowance, meal allowance, mess allowance, mileage, per diem, percentage, separation allowance, shift allowance, subsistence allowance, tea money, time allowance, tool allowance, war loading, weighting, workers compensation, zone allowance. *Informal:* compo. **9. bonus** baby bonus, bounty, cost-of-living bonus, gratuity, perquisite, premium. *Informal:* perk. **10. advance** *Informal:* sub. **11. royalty** douceur, enfeoffment, fee, public lending right, retainer, retaining fee, retainment. **12. rent** bond, bond money, fair rent, farm, ground rent, hire, peppercorn rent, quit rent, rack-rent, rental. *Informal:* Duke of Kent. **13. pension** age pension, child allowance, disability allowance, old age pension, super, superannuation. **14. benefit** dole, sickness benefit, sit-down money *(Aboriginal English)*, sustenance, unemployment benefit. *Informal:* gate money.

3. **1. charge** corkage, cover charge, fixed charge, flag fall, floating charge. **2. service charge** breakage, brokage, brokerage, cranage, drayage, ferriage, footage, lockage, quayage. **3. admission** admission fee, doormoney, entrance, fare, fee. **4. gate money** appearance money, attendance money.

4. **1. payer** defrayer, disburser, discharger, expender, ratepayer, remitter, subscriber. **2. contributor** contributory, tributary, tributer. **3. taxpayer** taxables *(US)*. **4. pay officer** paymaster, paymistress.

adj. **5.** **1. payable** collect, defrayable, disbursable, dischargeable, due, expendable, penal, prepayable, redeemable, remittable, renderable. **2. taxable** customable, declarable, dutiable, excisable, leviable.

v. **6.** **1. pay** advance, defray, disburse, expend, invest, outlay, overpay, prepay, refund, remit, render payment, spend. *Informal:* lay out. **2. pay up** alley up, dip into one's pocket, loosen the purse strings, pay one's way, subscribe, untie the purse strings. *Informal:* ante up, cash up, fork over, part up, pony up, shell out, stump up. **3. settle** acquit, adjust, amortise, clear, compound, discharge, extinguish, liquidate, pay off, redeem, satisfy, square up. **4. pay the bill** bear the costs, make out, pay the costs, pay the piper, stand the costs, stand treat. *Informal:* foot the bill, pick up the tab. **5. contribute** club in, tithe. *Informal:* go Dutch. **6. make payable** declare. **7. remunerate** cross someone's palm with silver, guerdon *(Poetic)*, recompense, recoup, refund, reimburse, reward. *Informal:* grease someone's palm, tickle someone's palm. **8. yield** return. **9. deposit** put down. *Informal:* plank down.

7. **1. charge** levy, reverse charges, tax, tithe.

RELATED KEYWORDS: BUYING, COST, FINANCE, INDEBTEDNESS, LOAN

PEACE

n. **1.** **1. peace** accord, agreement, amity, amnesty, bloodlessness, chime, compromise, concord, consonance, flower power, harmony, neutrality, non-aggression, non-belligerency, non-resistance, non-violence, oneness, pax, peaceful coexistence, quiet, repose, unity. **2. peacefulness** calmness, composure, quiet, quietism, quietness, repose, rest, sereneness, serenity, tranquillity, tranquilness. **3. peacetime** halcyon days, nirvana. **4. armistice** ceasefire, moratorium, pullout, respite, rest, retirement, retreat, suspension of hostilities, truce, withdrawal. **5. demilitarised zone** limbo, no-man's-land.

2. 1. pacification appeasement, assuagement, conciliation, détente, expiation, frank and free discussion, meaningful exchange, mediation, mollification, negotiation, peacekeeping, reconciliation, tranquillisation. **2. peace-offering** bird of peace, calumet, compromise, dove, olive branch, overtures, peace-pipe, pipe of peace. **3. white flag** flag of truce. **4. demilitarisation** non-proliferation.

3. 1. pacifism ahimsa *(Indian English)*, disarmament, peace march, peace movement. **2. peaceableness** amicability, amicableness, amity, anti-militarism, friendship.

4. 1. peacemaker appeaser, arbitrator, assuager, compromiser, concha, conciliator, conscientious objector, dove, flowerchild, hippie, hippy, mediator, mollifier, non-belligerent, non-combatant, non-resistant, pacificator, pacifier, pacifist, quieter. *Informal:* conch, conchie, long-hair, peacenik *(Chiefly US)*.

adj. **5. 1. peaceful** amicable, bloodless, calm, composed, congruous, eirenic, friendly, gentle, halcyon, harmonious, irenic, lazy, non-aggression, nonviolent, pacific, peaceable, peacetime, placid, quiet, reposeful, retired, sedate, sequestered, serene, subdued, symphonious, tranquil, withdrawn. **2. anti-war** anti-militarist, dovish, neutral, non-combatant, non-proliferation, pacifist. **3. peacekeeping** pacificatory. **4. appeaseable** mollifiable, subduable.

6. 1. peacetime post-bellum, postwar, prewar.

v. **7. 1. make peace** bury the hatchet, come to terms with, hold out the olive branch, make it up, make up, negotiate terms, offer the hand of peace, patch up a quarrel, shake hands, turn swords into ploughshares. **2. pacify** assuage, becalm, bring peace, bring to terms, bring to the table, calm, compose, demilitarise, denuclearise, disarm, lull, pacificate, placate, quell, quiet, quieten, reconcile, restore harmony, stay, still, unarm. **3. appease** assuage, becalm, chasten, crucify, defuse, mollify, pacificate, pacify, placate, pour oil on troubled waters, quiet, smooth, subdue, tranquillise. **4. retreat** back out, retire, retract, turn the other cheek, withdraw. **5. be at peace** keep the peace, live in harmony.

adv. **8. 1. peacefully** amicably, mollifyingly, pacifically, peaceably, quietly, serenely, subduedly, tranquilly. **2. non-violently** bloodlessly.

RELATED KEYWORDS: COMPOSURE, REST, MEDIATION

PENITENCE

n. **1. 1. penitence** attrition, contriteness, contrition, guilt, mortification, repentance, self-reproach, soul-searching. **2. remorse** abashment, compunction, grief, remorsefulness, shame, sorrow, sorrowfulness. **3. regret** compunction, regretfulness, remorse, repentance, sorriness, sorrow. **4. apology** beg-pardon, by-your-leave. **5. regrets** apologies, excuse.

2. 1. penitent a sadder and a wiser man, Magdalene, penitential, prodigal son.

adj. **3. 1. penitent** abashed, ashamed, contrite, penitential, repentant, repenting, self-accusing, shamefaced. **2. regretful** afraid, bad, compunctious, conscience-stricken, contrite, deplorable, guilty, remorseful, rueful, sorry. **3. apologetic** deprecatory.

v. **4. 1. be penitent** admit, avow, confess, have learnt one's lesson, mend one's ways, reform, repent, turn over a new leaf. **2. apologise** make up, say one is sorry, shake hands. **3. regret** cry over spilt milk, deplore, mourn, rue, rue the day. *Informal:* kick oneself.

RELATED KEYWORDS: GUILT

PERCEPTION

n. **1. 1. perception** apperception, appreciation, experience, feeling, idea, impression, mental impulse, observation, percept, sensation, sense, sense datum, undersense. **2. perceptiveness** aesthesia, aesthesis, anabiosis, awareness, consciousness, mind, passibility, perceptibility, sentience, wits. **3. excitement** aura, feel, flutter, fremitus, frisson, hot flush, irritation, quiver, quivering, shiver, stir, thrill, tingle, tingling, tremble, tremor, vibration. **4. five senses** five wits, sensorium.

2. 1. perceptivity coenaesthesia, delicacy, feeling, immediacy, impressibility, impressionability, irritability, paraesthesia, percipience, refinement, sensibilities, sensibility, sensitisation, sensitiveness, sensitivity, susceptibility, synaesthesia, telaesthesia, tone. **2. hypersensitivity** acuteness, hyperaesthesia, keenness, supersensitiveness, touchiness.

3. 1. sentient observer, receptor, sensor.

adj. **4.** **1. perceptive** affected, alive to, anabiotic, apperceptive, aware, cognisant, conscious, feeling, knowing, passible, protopathic, sensate, sensible, sentient, touched. **2. percipient** observant, paraesthetic, sensitive. **3. supersensitive** delicate, hyperaesthetic, hypersensitive, ill-tempered, irritable, moody, oversensitive, prickly, sensitive, susceptible, susceptive, temperamental, thin-skinned, ticklish, touchy. *Informal:* miffy, quiche-eating.

    5. **1. perceived** appreciated, sensed. **2. acute** exquisite, intense, keen, poignant.

    6. **1. perceptional** observational, perceptual, sensate. **2. perceptible** appreciable, cognisable, considerable, knowable, noticeable, objective, phenomenal, sensible, vivid. **3. sensory** organoleptic, sensorial, sensorimotor, sensual, sensuous.

v. **7.** **1. perceive** apperceive, appreciate, become aware of, cognise, comprehend, drink in, experience, feel, mind, notice, observe, savour, sense, suffer, understand. **2. regain consciousness** come back to one's senses, come to.

adv. **8.** **1. perceptively** consciously, observantly, observingly, sensitively, sentiently. **2. acutely** on the raw, to the quick, vividly.

RELATED KEYWORDS: ATTENTION, EMOTION, HEARING, PAIN, SIGHT, SMELL, TASTE, TOUCH

PERFECTION

n. **1.** **1. perfection** absoluteness, completeness, entireness, ideality, idealness, infiniteness, infinitude. **2. prime** bloom, matureness, maturity. **3. consummation** completion, fulfilment, redintegration. **4. purity** chastity, cleanness, faultlessness, flawlessness, immaculacy, immaculateness, impeccability, incorruptness, innocence, pureness. **5. infallibility** indefectibility, inerrability, inerrableness, infallibleness, watertightness.

    2. **1. perfect thing** acme, apogee, apotheosis, beau ideal, best-case scenario, culmination, elixir, idea, ideal, ideal type, quintessence, summit, the absolute, the abstract, the tops. **2. classic** model, standard. **3. utopia** a perfect world.

    3. **1. perfectionist** purist. **2. perfecter** finisher, polisher, purifier.

adj. **4.** **1. perfect** absolute, complete, consummate, entire, faultless, finished, hundred-per-cent, infinite, intact, quintessential, rounded, thoroughpaced, unbroken, whole. **2. sublime** beatific, beautiful, best, blissful, celestial, divine, Elysian, empyreal, empyrean, ethereal, fair, heavenly, ideal, optimal, paradisaical, paradisiacal, perfect, superb, supernal, superterrestrial, supreme, transcendent. **3. unparalleled** inaccessible, inapproachable, incomparable, inimitable, matchless, nonpareil, out of this world, peerless, supereminent, superordinate, unapproachable, unbeatable, unequalled, unmatched, unrivalled, untouchable. **4. flawless** blameless, blotless, candid, chaste, clean, clear, fair, faultless, fine, fresh, good, immaculate, impeccable, innocent, irreproachable, lily, perfect, polished, pristine, pure, spotless, stainless, sublime, virgin, virginal. *Informal:* copperplate. **5. infallible** faultless, flawless, impeccable, indefectible, inerrable, sound, unfailing, watertight. **6. unblemished** incorrupt, inviolate, unimpaired, unscratched, unspoilt, unsullied, unworn.

    5. **1. perfectionist** idealist, idealistic, puristic, transcendental, utopian.

    6. **1. perfective** purificatory, redintegrative.

v. **7.** **1. perfect** bring to perfection, complete, consummate, leave nothing to be desired, mature, redintegrate, round off. **2. purify** polish. **3. ripen** mature. **4. idealise** put (or place) (or set) someone on a pedestal.

adv. **8.** **1. perfectly** consummately, superbly. **2. flawlessly** faultlessly, immaculately, impeccably. **3. infallibly** indefectibly, inerrably. **4. to a turn** to perfection. **5. in a perfect world** ideally.

RELATED KEYWORDS: CLEANLINESS, GOODNESS, WHOLE

PERIOD

n. **1.** **1. period** season, space, span, term, tract. **2. reign** diaconate, dictatorship, papacy, regency, sitting, tenancy, tenure, tsarism. **3. period of duty** hours, session, shift, stint, stretch, time. *Informal:* hitch *(US)*. **4. sitting** session. **5. bout** innings, patch, round, run, shift, spell, stretch, turn. *Informal:* go, streak. **6. era** age, culture, cycle, day, days, epoch, generation, lost generation, siècle, times, Yuga. **7. episode** page, stage. **8. academic year** Lent term, Michaelmas term, semester, term, trimester, Trinity term. **9. prison term** accumulative sentence, life, time. *Informal:* a brick, a clock, a drag, a sleep, a spin, a swy, a zack, air and exercise, bed and breakfast, bird, brick, clock, drag, dream, hitch *(US)*, jolt, Kath, lag, lagging, lost weekend, porridge, rest, sleep, snooze, spin, stretch, swy, the lot, zack.

    2. **1. duration** length, standing. **2. life span** anno Domini, generation, life, lifetime, one's born days, run time, shelf life, short life, time, time limit, time line. **3. aeon** age, ages, eon, eternity. *Informal:* donkey's years, yonks.

    3. **1. century** decade, fin de siècle. **2. centuries** cinquecento, duecento, dugento, novecento, ottocento, quattrocentro, seicento, settecento, trecento. **3. famous decades** Age of Marvellous Melbourne, Hungry Thirties, Jazz Age, Naughty Nineties, Prohibition Era, Roaring Twenties, Swinging Sixties, The Depression. **4. twenty-first century** *Informal:* the noughties. **5. golden age** silver age. **6. ages** Bronze Age, Iron Age, Medieval Age, Middle Age, Modern Times, Stone Age. **7. atomic age** nuclear age, space age. **8. cultural periods** Antiquity, baroque, Christian Era, Dark Ages, Edwardian period, Elizabethan period, Georgian period, Industrial Revolution, Jacobean period, Middle Ages, pre-industrial age, preclassical era, Regency period, Renaissance, the Enlightenment, the Restoration, Tudor period, Victorian age. **9. the Dreaming. 10. generation** baby boomers, beat generation, C generation, gen X, gen Y, generation X, generation Y, Me generation, Net generation, Pokémon generation, X generation.

    4. **1. Palaeozoic era** Algonkian, Cambrian, Carboniferous, Devonian, Ordovician, Permian, Pre-Cambrian, Silurian. **2. Mesozoic era** Cretaceous, Jurassic, Triassic. **3. Cainozoic era Tertiary** Eocene, Miocene, Neocene, Neogene, Oligocene, Palaeocene, Pleistocene, Pliocene. **4. Quaternary** Holocene, Recent.

    5. **1. Ice Age** Bondaian period, Bronze Age, Eloueran period, Glacial epoch, Iron age, Neolithic, New Stone Age, Old Stone Age, Palaeolithic, Stone Age.

    RELATED KEYWORDS: INTERVAL, THE PAST, TIME, TIME MEASUREMENT

PERMISSION

n. **1.** **1. permission** accession, approbation, approval, assent, authorisation, consent, dispensation, endorsement, go-ahead, green light, imprimatur, leave, licence, planning permission, ratification, release, royal assent, sanction, support, the call, thumbs up, vouchsafement. **2. licence** approval, authorisation, clearance, empowerment, faculty, imprimatur, indult, nihil obstat, passport, permit, pratique, sanction, warrant. **3. free hand** blank cheque, carte blanche, liberty. **4. consent** acceptance, accordance, acquiescence, agreement, appro, approbation, approval, assent, compliance, conformance, conformity, correspondence, courtesy, obedience, permission, permit, resignation, submission, subscription.

    2. **1. permissibility** admissibility, admissibleness, allowableness, sufferableness.

    3. **1. permitter** approver, authoriser, consenter, licenser.

adj. **4.** **1. permitted** allowed, authorised, granted, permissive, sanctioned. **2. permissible** admissible, allowable, constitutional, just, justifiable, lawful, legal, legitimate, licit, rightful, statutory, true, unalienable, valid. *Informal:* legit.

v. **5.** **1. permit** accept, accredit, admit, adopt, advocate, affirm, allow, amen, approbate *(Chiefly US, Scottish Law)*, approve, attest, authorise, bear out, certify, clear, confirm, consent to, corroborate, countersign, empower, enable, encourage, endorse, fortify, give one's permission, give the green light to, give the nod to, have, hold a brief for, hold with, homologate, indorse, legitimate, legitimise, let, license, pass, privilege, ratify, recognise, sanction, seal, set one's seal on (or to), sign, subscribe, suffer, support, sympathise, tolerate, uphold, verify, vouchsafe, warrant.

    6. **1. be permitted to** be allowed to, can, clear with, get the nod, may, mayst. *Informal:* get the murray cod.

adv. **7.** **1. permissibly** admissibly, allowably, allowedly.

    RELATED KEYWORDS: AGREEMENT, ASSERTION, LAWFULNESS

PERSISTENCE

n. **1.** **1. persistence** determination, doggedness, firmness, grit, inexorability, inexorableness, perseverance, pertinaciousness, pertinacity, resoluteness, resolve, stubbornness. **2. assiduity** application, assiduousness, diligence, enterprise, get-up-and-go, industry, sedulity, sedulousness, single-mindedness, tenaciousness, tenacity. *Informal:* push. **3. steadfastness** endurance, indefatigability, indefatigableness, intestinal fortitude, stability, stamina, staying power, stoutness, tirelessness. *Informal:* stay *(US)*.

    2. **1. battler** heart of oak, ironside, plodder, stayer, sticker, the walking wounded. *Informal:* grind.

adj. **3.** **1. persistent** decided, determinate, determined, persevering, pertinacious, purposeful, resolved, risoluto, set, settled, unflagging, unremitting. **2. assiduous** consistent, determined, diehard, diligent, dogged, hard-set, hardworking, hell-bent, obstinate, perseverant, persevering, resolute, sedulous, self-willed, single-minded, strong-willed, stubborn, tenacious, uncompromising, unflinching, unswayed, unwavering. **3. steadfast** adamant, adamantine, constant, dauntless, decisive, doughty, enduring, faithful, firm, hard-bitten, indefatigable, indomitable, inexorable, stalwart, staunch, steady, steely, stern, sthenic, stout-hearted, sturdy, tireless, unalterable, unbending, unwearied, unyielding. *Informal:* deadset. **4. durable** cast-iron, hard-wearing, hardy, heavy-duty, indissoluble, industrial-strength, iron, ironbound, knockabout, serviceable, steel, stout, tough.

v. **4.** **1. persist** continue, endure, go on, hang in there, keep at it, keep on, keep the ball rolling, keep up, last, persevere, plod on, proceed, push on, rub through, see through, soldier on, stay, stick it out, wear, weather. *Informal:* box on, hang in, kick on, plug on. **2. apply oneself** plough through, toil, work at. *Informal:* dig in, grind, peg away at, slog. **3. endure** bear, bear up, hold on, not take no for an answer, stand one's ground, stomach, suffer, undergo, weather the storm, worry along, worry through. *Informal:* hang on, sit pat, stick to one's guns.

adv. **5.** **1. perseveringly** firm, firmly, like grim death, manfully, pertinaciously, sedulously, staunchly, stout-heartedly, stoutly, tenaciously, through thick and thin, uncompromisingly. **2. assiduously** diligently. **3. persistently** doggedly, inexorably.

RELATED KEYWORDS: CAREFULNESS, STUBBORNNESS, INTENTION

PHOTOGRAPHY

n. **1.** **1. photography** aerial photography, astrophotography, colour photography, digital photography, flash, flash photography, four-colour photography, halftone photography, heliography, infra-red photography, macrophotography, microphotography, nephography, photochromy, schlieren photography, spark photography, spectroheliography, subtractive photography, synchroflash photography, telephotography, thermography, three-colour photography, time-lapse photography. **2. photogravure** photo-offset, photolithography.

2. **1. photograph** aerial photograph, dropout, facsimile, flash picture, frame, orthophotograph, Penry picture, photo, photogravure, photomaton *(US)*, picture, positive, rotogravure, screenie, screenshot, shot, snap, snapshot, still, visual, wirephoto. *Informal:* pickie. **2. print** bromide, contact print, proof. **3. slide** fiche, lantern slide, microfiche, mount, negative, transparency. *Informal:* trannie. **4. black-and-white** monochrome, sepia, vignette. **5. composite photograph** double exposure. **6. portrait** mug shot. **7. close-up** blow-up, enlargement, long shot, reduction. **8. photomural** panel, photomontage. **9. ambrotype** anaglyph, autoradiograph, autotype, blueprint, calotype, cyanotype, daguerreotype, ferrotype, gravure, heliotype, hologram, macrograph, microdot, microform, micrograph, microphotograph, photochronograph, photogram, photomicrograph, platinotype, radioautograph, radiograph, roentgenogram, schlieren photograph, shadowgraph, stereophotograph, telephotograph, tintype, tomogram, X-ray photograph. **10. photojournalism** photoresearch.

3. **1. photographer** cameraman, cinematographer, daguerreotypist, snapshotter. *Informal:* shooter, shutterbug. **2. photojournalist** photoresearcher.

4. **1. camera** box brownie, box camera, camera obscura, car cam, cinematograph, continuous strip camera, digital camera, instamatic, kinematograph, magic eye, miniature camera, polaroid camera, reflex camera, stop-action camera, web camera. **2. heliograph** nephograph, photochronograph, spectroheliograph. **3. optical printer** sensitometer, vignetter. **4. projector** bioscope, magic lantern, viewer.

5. **1. camera part** cable release, gate, lens turret, magazine. **2. lens** amplifier, anastigmatic, collimator, eyeglass, eyepiece, field lens, fish-eye lens, immersion objective, magnetic lens, object glass, objective, ocular, optical zoom, telephoto lens, wide-angle lens, zoom, zoom lens. **3. light meter** exposure meter, extinction meter, photoelectric meter. **4. viewfinder** finder, focuser, rangefinder, telemeter. **5. shutter** focal plane shutter. **6. filter** blur filter, colour-filter, diffuser, UV filter. **7. flash** electronic flash, flashbulb, flashcube, flashgun, flashlight, photoflash lamp, photoflood lamp, strobe. **8. aperture** depth of field, depth of focus, f number, hyperfocal distance, stop. **9. shutter speed** acutance, ASA/BS, density, DIN, intensity, latitude, opacity.

6. **1. photographic processing** carbon paper, carbon process, contact paper, dry plate, emulsion, plate. **2. film strip** reel, roll film. **3. microfilm** biblio film, fast film, fine-grain film, high-speed film, infra-red film, isochromatic film, microphotograph, orthochromatic film, slow film, X-ray film. **4. darkroom. 5. photographic**

chemical amidol, cyanine, developer, metol, reducer, restrainer, stop bath. **6. resolution** dpi, megapixel, pixel.

adj. **7.** **1. photographic** photogenic. **2. overexposed** contrasty, developing, foggy, grainy, in focus, out of focus, underdeveloped, underexposed.

v. **8.** **1. photograph** film, screen, shoot, snap. *Informal:* mug *(US).* **2. develop** cut, enlarge, fix, print, reduce. **3. tone** exalt, fog, intensify, sensitise, solarise, tint. **4. expose** overexpose, underdevelop, underexpose.

RELATED KEYWORDS: FINE ARTS, OPTICS, PRINTING, REPRESENTATION

PITY

n. **1.** **1. pity** feeling, fellow feeling, graciosity, heart, humaneness, humanity, ruefulness, ruthfulness, soft-heartedness, sorriness, tender-heartedness, tenderness. **2. compassion** benevolence, bowels of compassion, charity, clemency, compassionateness, forbearance, forgiveness, grace, mercifulness, mercy, misericordia, quarter, sympathies, sympathy. **3. sympathy** commiserations, condolence, consolation, empathy. **4. compassionate leave**.

2. **1. pitifulness** miserableness, piteousness, pitiableness, wretchedness. **2. pathos** touchingness.

3. **1. pitier** condoler, sympathiser. *Informal:* bleeding heart, softie. **2. humanitarian** good Samaritan, philanthropist.

adj. **4.** **1. pitying** bleeding, feeling, humane, humanitarian, rueful, sorry. **2. compassionate** clement, gracious, lenient, merciful, sparing. **3. sympathising** commiserative, condolatory. **4. soft-hearted** lenient, sympathetic, tender-hearted.

5. **1. pitiable** hapless, harrowing, heartbreaking, lamentable, miserable, pathetic, piteous, pitiful, poor, rueful, sorry, unhappy, upsetting, wretched. **2. unfortunate** badly off, underprivileged.

v. **6.** **1. pity** be moved, commiserate, compassion, compassionate, enter into, feel for (or with), have a heart, soften, sympathise, take pity on. **2. bleed for** bemoan, feel sorry for. **3. condole** commiserate, pity, send one's condolences.

adv. **7.** **1. pityingly** humanely, ruthfully. **2. compassionately** clemently, graciously, mercifully. **3. sympathisingly** commiseratively, condolingly, sympathetically.

8. **1. pitiably** pathetically, piteously, pitifully, ruefully, ruthfully, wretchedly.

RELATED KEYWORDS: FAIRNESS, FRIENDLINESS, KINDNESS

PLACEMENT

n. **1.** **1. placement** emplacement, location, lodgement, placing, positioning, posting, postposition, reposition, setting, settlement, settling, stationing. **2. putting down** deposit, deposition. **3. tabling** preferment, presentation. **4. putting on** application, superposition. **5. storage** bestowal, bestowment, cargo, charge, content, contents, freight, lading, load, loading, pack, packing, payload, stowage, wealth.

adj. **2.** **1. placed** positioned, settled, situated, stationed.

v. **3.** **1. place** allocate, arrange, determine, draw, emplace, establish, install, instate, lay, localise, locate, lodge, park, perch, pinpoint, pitch, plant, posit, position, post, put, reposition, set, site, situate, stage, station, stick. *Informal:* bung, camp, plank down. **2. deposit** bank, margin, place, put, put down, set down. **3. table** prefer, present, put forward. **4. put on** apply, paint, slap on, slather, slosh, superpose, trowel. **5. store** bestow, freight, load, pigeonhole, stack, stow, truck.

RELATED KEYWORDS: INSERTION, POSITION

PLACE OF WORSHIP

n. **1.** **1. place of worship** bora, high place, holy, sacrarium, sacred place, sacred site, sanctuary, stupa. **2. Holy City** Holy Land, Jerusalem, Lourdes, Mecca, Medina, Varanasi, Vatican City.

2. **1. church** basilica, cathedral, House of God, kirk *(Scottish)*, minster, procathedral, temple, title. **2. temple** conventicle, joss house, mosque, naos, pagoda, pantheon, synagogue, tabernacle, wat, ziggurat. **3. meeting house** bethel *(Chiefly US)*, chapel, chapter, chapterhouse, oratory. **4. vicarage** manse, parsonage, presbytery, rectory. **5. parts of church** aisle, ambulatory, antechoir, apse, apsis, blindstorey, choir, choir screen, clerestory, cloister, confessional, decanal, decani, epistle side, gospel side, nave, precinct, pulpit, retrochoir, rood loft, rostrum, transept, tribune, triforium. **6. corona** jesse window, tambour. **7. pulpit** ambo, lectern, minbar, reading desk, rostrum, tribune. **8. pew** faldstool, propitiary, sedile, tribune. **9. crypt** easter sepulchre, sepulchre, undercroft. **10. steeple** minaret, spire.

3. **1. abbey** cell, chartreuse, cloister, closet, convent, hermitage, mew, monastery, monkery, nunnery, priorate, priory. **2. ashram** Buddhist monastery.

4. **1. shrine** adytum, aedicule, ark of the covenant, cella, chantry, chapel, edicule, feretory, holy of holies, Lady Chapel, martyry, naos, oracle, oratory, reliquary, sacrarium, sanctuary, sanctum, sanctum sanctorum, tabernacle. **2. altar** bema, chancel, high altar, Lord's table, predella, prothesis. **3. altarpiece** antependium, baldachin, ciborium, reredos. **4. ambry** almery, aumbry, conch, credence, fenestella, niche, tabernacle. **5. reliquary** phylactery. **6. font** baptistery, lavabo, laver, stoup. **7. grail** ark, burse, calix, chalice, chrismatory, cist, cup, lune, lunette, monstrance, phylactery, pix, pyx, shrine, tabernacle. **8. thurible** censer. **9. sacring bell** bell, death bell, passing bell, sanctuary bell, Sanctus bell. **10. purificator**. **11. menorah** paschal candle. **12. mihrab**.

adj. **5.** **1. church** basilic, synagogical, tabernacular.

RELATED KEYWORDS: GOD, RELIGION, RELIGIOUS CEREMONY

PLAN

n. **1.** **1. plan** conception, contrivance, counsel, design, device, idea, intent, intention, itinerary, layout, project, proposal, proposition, scheme. **2. suggestion** cogitation, conception, contemplation, contrivance, intention, motion, notion, proposal, thought. **3. program** agenda, arrangements, budget, démarche, format, nostrum, outline, regime, regimen, schedule, schema, schematism, syllabus, system, timetable. **4. policy** ideology, lines, platform. **5. tactics** card, commander's concept, concept of operations, healy prison, pitch, ploy, stratagem, strategic plan, strategy, tactic. *Informal:* dart.

2. **1. conspiracy** cabal, cobweb, collusion, complot, contrivance, countermine, counterplot, intrigue, machinations, plot, scheme. *Informal:* frame, frame-up, lurk, plant, racket, ready, set-up.

3. **1. aim** address, all in all, ambition, be-all and end-all, design, end, errand, ideal, intention, mission, motivation, object, purpose, target, view. **2. goal** aim, bourn, destination, end, mecca, view. **3. target** bird, bull, bullseye, butts, carton, chase, checkpoint, clay pigeon, dartboard, inner, magpie, mark, outer, pin, popinjay, red, rover, tee. **4. purpose** aim, be (of) about, determination, end, end use, intention, object, purport, sake.

4. **1. systematisation** architectonics, economy, systematics, systematism, systematology, systemisation, teleology. **2. town planning** Radburn planning. **3. imagineering** brainstorming.

5. **1. schemer** complotter, conspirator, conspiratress, contriver, designer, framer, hatcher, intriguer, machinator, plotter. **2. planner** arranger, deviser, strategist, systematiser, systematist, systemiser, tactician, teleologist.

adj. **6.** **1. planned** concerted, destined, devised, intended, prearranged, projected, studied. *Informal:* put-up. **2. systematic** schedular, schematic. **3. strategic** tactic, tactical. **4. teleological** destined, telic.

v. **7.** **1. plan** arrange, concert, engineer, forecast, format, frame, get up, lead up to, manage, mastermind, organise, prepare, reorganise. *Informal:* calculate (US), jack (NZ), tee up. **2. schedule** bill, budget, slate, timetable. **3. map out** arrange, chalk out (British), chart, lay out, phase, plan, set out. *Informal:* calculate (US). **4. devise** brainstorm, brew, cast, cast about for, cogitate, compass, concert, concoct, contrive, design, hatch, make up, project, propose, scheme. *Informal:* cook up. **5. systemise** adjust, alphabetise, categorise, class, classify, codify, coordinate, digest, distinguish, distribute, divide, firerate, gradate, grade, identify, label, lemmatise, mark, order, organise, pigeonhole, range, rank, rate, reclassify, schematise, size, sort, systematise.

8. **1. aim at** aim, aspire to, design, intend, mean, premeditate, pretend to, purpose.

9. **1. conspire** cabal, collaborate, collude, complot, concoct, connive, connive at, contrive, counterplot, intrigue, lay heads together, lay plans, machinate, manoeuvre, plot, put heads together, scheme, tick-tack with. *Informal:* work one's nut.

conj. **10.** **1. so that** in order that, in order to, to.

RELATED KEYWORDS: ATTEMPT, DESIRE, UNDERTAKING, INTENTION

PLANTS

n. **1.** **1. plants** botany, flora, greenery, herbage, plant kingdom, plant life, vegetable kingdom, vegetation, verdure.

2.   **1. plant** bush, cactus, carnivore, climber, creeper, ephemeral, epiphyll, evergreen, forb, grass, herb *(US)*, legume, liana, mallee, monocarp, palm, parasite, rambler, runner, sandbinder, sapling, sedge, shrub, succulent, tiller, tree, twiner, vine, weed, winder. **2. annual** biennial, perennial. **3. seed plant** acotyledon, angiosperm, dicot, dicotyledon, gymnosperm, monocot, monocotyledon. **4. -phyte** bryophyte, cormophyte, cryophyte, cyanophyte, dermatophyte, endophyte, entophyte, epiphyte, gametophyte, geophyte, halophyte, helophyte, hydrophyte, hygrophyte, lithophyte, mesophyte, microphyte, myrmecophyte, oophyte, pteridophyte, rhodophyte, saprophyte, schizophyte, spermatophyte, spermophyte, sporophyte, thallophyte, tropophyte, xerophyte, zygophyte.

3.   **1. forest** bush, greenwood, jungle, taiga, woodland, woods. **2. rainforest** cloud forest, dry rainforest, subtropical rainforest, tropical rainforest. **3. sclerophyll forest** dry sclerophyll forest, wet sclerophyll forest. **4. scrub** boscage, bosket, brush, brushwood, canebrake *(US)*, chaparral *(US)*, coppice, copse, grove, spinney *(British)*, thicket, vine thicket, wallum, whipstick, woods. **5. undergrowth** underbrush, understorey, underwood. **6. miscellaneous areas of vegetation** bog, fen *(British)*, Fjaeldmark, herbfield, plantation.

4.   **1. grassland** downs, heath, mead *(Poetic)*, meadow *(US)*, moor, pampas, prairie, savanna, steppe, tundra.

5.   **1. root** buttress root, monopode, monopodium, prop root, radicel, radicle, rootlet, taproot, tuberous root. **2. root organ** calyptra, pneumatophore, rhizoid, root hair, root nodule, rootlet, tuber, velamen.

6.   **1. stem** axis, bine, caudex, cladode, cladophyll, culm, floccose stem, haulm, phylloclade, pseudaxis, rhizome, runner, stock, stolon, sympodium, vimen, vine, whipstick. **2. stem part** aculeus, ala, articulation, bark, bole, bough, branch, branchlet, bud, bulb, bulbil, caulicle, caulis, cirrus, cladode, cladophyll, corm, crown, gemma, gemmule, internode, leaf-scar, lenticel, limb, node, phylloclade, phyllotaxy, prickle, rootstock, scar, shoot, sprout, stolon, sucker, tendril, thorn, tiller, tomentum, trunk, tuber, turion, twig. **3. shoot** sprout. **4. slip** cutting, scion, set, stock.

7.   **1. leaf** blade, cataphyll, compound leaf, leaflet, palea, phyllome, pine needle, quatrefoil, scale, simple leaf. **2. leaf organ** arista, auricle, awn, axil, blade, bulbil, costa, footstalk, gemma, hair, lamina, lamination, leaf bud, leaflet, leafstalk, lobe, lobule, midrib, ocrea, petiole, phyllode, pinna, pinnule, pulvinus, rachilla, rachis, rhachilla, rhachis, rib, sheath, stem, stipel, stipule, stoma, tomentum, tooth, vagina, vein. **3. foliage** crown, foliation, gum tips, head, leaf, leafage.

8.   **1. flower** blossom, bud, floret, flower bud, floweret, posy, ray. **2. flower organ** androecium, anther, anthophore, brush, bulbil, calycle, calyptra, calyx, carpel, carpogonium, carpophore, claw, connective, corolla, corona, disc, endothecium, farina, filament, floral envelope, footstalk, foramen, galea, gynaecium, gynoecium, gynophore, hypanthium, labellum, labium, leaf, limb, lip, loculus, lodicule, nectary, ovary, pedicel, peduncle, perianth, petal, phalanx, pistil, pistillode, placenta, podium, pollen, pollen tube, rachis, ray, receptacle, rictus, rostellum, sepal, spur, stamen, staminode, standard, stem, stigma, stipe, style, stylopodium, tepal, torus, tube, unguis, vexillum, wing. **3. inflorescence** amentum, anthodium, bract, capitulum, catkin, cincinnus, corymb, cupule, dichasium, glume, head, involucre, Job's tears, locusta, monochasium, panicle, raceme, rosette, spike, thyrsus, umbel, umbellule. **4. floral ornament** bouquet, boutonniere, buttonhole, chaplet, coronal, corsage, garland, nosegay, posy, spray, wreath.

9.   **1. fruit** apocarp, berry, boll, burr, capsule, caryopsis, cob, cone, corncob, cypsela, drupe, ear, follicle, fructification, hesperidium, key fruit, legume, loment, lomentum, mutt-eye, mutti, nut, nutlet, pepo, pod, pome, pseudocarp, pyxidium, pyxis, regma, samara, sarcocarp, schizocarp, simple fruit, sorosis, strobilus, syncarp, tryma, xylocarp. **2. fruit part** achene, acinus, acorn, awn, beak, beard, calyptra, capsule, coccus, down, drupelet, endocarp, epicarp, exocarp, gumnut, husk, kernel, lacuna, loculus, mericarp, operculum, pericarp, pit, pulp, putamen, pyrene, rag, sarcocarp, seed capsule, seed vessel, shell, stone, suture, syconium, valve, wing.

10.   **1. seed and seed part** albumen, aril, arillode, caruncle, collar, coma, cotyledon, down, egret, endopleura, endosperm, funicle, funiculus, hilum, husk, integument, kernel, ovule, pappus, perisperm, pippin, plumule, radicle, raphe, seed, suspensor, testa, tunic, umbilicus. **2. seedling** coleoptile, coleorhiza, cotyledon, epicotyl, hypocotyl, radicle, seed and seed part, seed leaf.

11.   **1. trees – eucalypts** alpine ash, apple box, apple gum, Argyle apple, ash, bangalay, bimble box, black gum, black sally, blackbutt, blue gum, blue mallee, box, brittle gum, brown barrel, brown mallet, bundy, but but, candle bark, coolibah, Darwin stringybark, Darwin woollybutt, eucalypt, eucalyptus, eurabbie, flame gum, flooded gum, forest red gum, giant mallee, gimlet, green mallee, grey box, grey gum, grey ironbark, gum, gum coolibah, gum tree, gungurru, iron gum, ironbark, jarrah, karri, mahogany, mallee, mallet, manna gum, marble gum, marlock, messmate, moort, morrell, mountain ash, mugga, muttlegar, narrow-leaf ironbark, native apple, peppermint, peppermint gum, red gum, red stringybark, redwood, ribbon gum, river red gum, rivergum, sally, salmon gum, scribbly gum, silver box, silver-leaf ironbark, slaty gum, snappy gum, snow gum, stinking gum, stringy-bark, sugar gum, swamp gum, swamp mahogany, Sydney blue gum, tallowwood, Tasmanian blue gum, tingle tingle, tuart, wandoo, weeping box, white box, white gum, white mahogany, white sally, woolly butt, yapunyah, yate, yellow box, yellow gum, yertchuk, yorrell. **2. corymbia** bloodwood, cabbage gum, cadagi, carbeen, ghost gum, lemon-scented gum, marri, Moreton Bay ash, red bloodwood, spotted gum, white bloodwood, yellow jacket. **3. angophora** apple, coolabah apple, rough-barked apple, rusty gum, Sydney red gum.

12. **1. trees – wattles (acacia)** acacia, babul, bastard myall, belalie, bendee, berrigan, bitterbush, black gidgee, black wattle, blackwood, blue skin, boree, bowyakka bendee, brigalow, Broughton willow, cedar wattle, cinnamon wattle, cooba, Cootamundra wattle, curracabah, dune wattle, eumung, fever-tree, Georgina gidgee, gidgee, golden wattle, green wattle, gundabluey, hickory, ironwood, jam tree, kangaroo-thorn, karri, kurara, lancewood, Maitland's wattle, miljee, mimosa bush, minni-ritchi, motherumbah, mountain cedar wattle, mudgerabah, mulga, myall, myall-gidgee, native apricot, native willow, nealie, nelia, pin bush, prickly Moses, prickly wattle, purplewood, Queensland silver wattle, ranji bush, raspberry-jam tree, red mulga, river cooba, sandhill wattle, silver wattle, stinking wattle, sunshine wattle, Sydney golden wattle, turpentine, turpentine tree, umbrella bush, umbrella mulga, umbrella wattle, waddy-wood, wait-a-while, wattle, weeping myall, wirewood, wirilda, witchetty bush, wyrilda, yarran.

13. **1. trees – rainforest** Antarctic beech, axe-handle wood, azedarach, banyalla, basswood, beech, beechwood, birch, birdlime tree, black apple, black bean, bleeding-heart, bolly gum, booyong, bopple nut *(Qld)*, Brisbane box, brush bloodwood, brush box, bumpy ash, Burdekin plum, canary sassafras, caper berry, carabeen, carrol, cedar, celerywood, cheese-tree, cheesewood, coachwood, corkwood, crow's ash, crowsfoot elm, cudgerie, cudjerie, deep yellowwood, durobby, featherwood, fig, finger cherry, firewheel tree, flame-tree, ghittoe, gympie nettle, Herbert River cherry, hickory, horizontal, horizontal scrub, Illawarra flame-tree, ironwood, Kerosene wood, lacebark, lancewood, leatherwood, lignum-vitae, lilly pilly, macadamia nut, mahogany, maiden's blush, milk-wood, milky pine, mira mahogany, Moreton Bay chestnut, Moreton Bay fig, mutton-wood, myrtle, myrtle beech, native elm, native mulberry, native teak, nettle tree, nigger-head beech, Oliver's sassafras, onionwood, penda, pigeonberry ash, prickly ash, quandong, Queensland ebony, Queensland maple, Queensland nut *(Chiefly Qld and Northern NSW)*, Queensland walnut, red bean, red cedar, robby, rose mahogany, rose satinash, rosewood, saffron heart, sassafras, satinwood, scrub beefwood, scrub caper berry, scrub stringybark, silky oak, socketwood, southern sassafras, stinging tree, tallowwood, Tasmanian myrtle, thorny yellowwood, tulip oak, tulipwood, umbrella tree, Western red cedar, whalebone tree, white bean, white beech, white cedar, yellow boxwood, yellow carrabeen, yellow sassafras, yellowwood, yiel-yiel.

14. **1. trees – legumes – Australian** albizia, bats-wing coral-tree, bauhinia, bean tree, black bean, Cape wattle, cassia, Cooktown ironwood, corkwood, crested wattle, ironwood, Leichhardt bean, Moreton Bay chestnut, Queensland bean, white dragon tree, yalbah. **2. legumes – other** acacia, algarroba, babul, bauhinia, bean tree, camwood, Cape teak, carob, cassia, coral tree, divi-divi, fever-tree, flamboyant, golden chain, golden rain, honey locust, honey-locust, Judas tree, laburnum, locust, marble wood, mesquite, pagoda tree, poinciana, redbud, rose acacia, sappanwood, sassy, sassy bark, tagasaste, tamarind, tonka bean, tree lucerne.

15. **1. trees – conifers – Australian** araucaria, black cypress pine, black pine, brown pine, bunya-bunya, celery pine, celery-top pine, cypress, cypress pine, hoop pine, Huon pine, Illawarra pine, kauri, King Billy pine, King William pine, pine, plum pine, Port Jackson pine, Queensland kauri, she pine, white pine, Wollemi pine. **2. conifers – NZ** arbor vitae *(NZ)*, black pine, celery pine, celery-top pine, kahikatea, kauri, kawaka, matai, miro, mountain pine, red pine, ricker *(NZ)*, rika *(NZ)*, rimu, silver pine, tanekaha *(NZ)*, toatoa, totara, white pine. **3. conifers – other** araucaria, arbor vitae, azedarach, balsam, balsam fir, balsam spruce, black spruce, blue spruce, cade, cedar, cluster pine, cypress, deodar, Douglas fir, Douglas pine, Douglas spruce, fir, hemlock, hemlock spruce, insignis pine, Irish yew, jack pine, Japanese cedar, juniper, kawaka, klinki pine, larch, loblolly, longleaf pine, macrocarpa, maritime pine, monkey-puzzle tree, Monterey cypress, Monterey pine, Norfolk Island pine, Norway spruce, nut pine, Oregon pine, pine, pitch pine, radiata pine, red cedar, red fir, redwood, sandarac, savin, Scotch fir, Scots pine, sequoia, sequoiadendron, silver fir, slash pine, spruce, tamarack, thuja, western hemlock, Western red cedar, white cedar *(US)*, white pine, white spruce, yellowwood, yew.

16. **1. trees – palms – Australian** bangalow palm, cabbage palm, cabbage tree, kentia palm, piccabeen *(Chiefly Qld)*, walking-stick palm. **2. palms – other** areca, betel nut, betel palm, coco, coconut palm, cohune, coquilla nut, coquito, date palm, doum-palm, fan palm, gomuti, grugru, ivory palm, lady palm, nipa, oil palm, oil-palm, palmetto, palmyra, parlour palm, piassava, raffia, raphis palm, royal palm, sago, talipot, Washington palm, wax palm, wine palm.

17. **1. trees – other Australian** ballart, ballee, banksia, baobab, barringtonia, beefwood, belah, bell-fruit tree, bitterbark, black oak, black tea-tree, blanket-leaf, blind-your-eyes, blueberry ash, boab, boonery, bottle tree, budda, bull oak, cajuput, casuarina, cherry ballart, Christmas bush, Christmas tree, cockatoo apple, colane, cottontree, cow-itch tree, desert kurrajong, desert lemon, desert oak, desert poplar, desert walnut, durin, emu-apple, forest oak, grey mangrove, gruie, he-oak, jack-in-the-box, kanooka, kurrajong, Leichhardt tree, leopard tree, mangrove, melaleuca, milkwood, mock-olive, moonah, native mulberry, needlewood, nonda, Norfolk Island hibiscus, pandanus, paperbark, pittosporum, poison peach, poison tree, Port Jackson fig, quinine bush, red ash, red satinay, river mangrove, river oak, rusty fig, sandal, sandalwood, santal, screw-pine, she-oak, silkcotton tree, sugarwood, supplejack, swamp box, swamp oak, tea-tree, warrior bush, watergum, whitewood, willow myrtle, woody pear.

18. **1. trees – NZ** aka, Antarctic beech, beech, birch *(NZ)*, black beech, broadleaf *(NZ)*, bucket-of-water-wood, cabbage tree, clinker beech, cracker *(NZ)*, hard beech, hinau, honeysuckle *(NZ)*, horopito *(NZ)*, houhere, ironwood, kamahi, kapuka, karaka, karo, kawakawa *(NZ)*, kohekohe, kotukutuku, kowhai, lace-wood, lacebark, lancewood *(NZ)*, lemonwood, maire, makomako, mapou, matipo, milk tree, New Zealand beech, ngaio, nikau, pigeonwood, pohutukawa, porokaiwhiri, pukatea, puriri, rata, red beech, rewarewa, ribbonwood, silver beech, silver birch *(NZ)*, taraire, tarata *(NZ)*, tawa, tawhai, tawine *(NZ)*, tea-tree, thousand-jacket, ti, ti-palm, ti-tree, titoki, towai, turepo, whau, whiteywood *(NZ)*, wineberry.

19. **1. trees – miscellaneous** abele, abi, abiu, acajou, ailanthus, alamo *(US)*, alder, almond, amarelle *(US)*, anchovy pear, antiar, apricot, aspen, assegai, athel tree, babaco, balata, balm of Gilead, balsam poplar, bamboo, banyan, bay, bayberry, bebeeru, ben, benzoin, bergamot, bird-cherry, bitterwood, black elder, black walnut, blanket bush, bo tree, Bodhi tree, box elder, buckeye, bully tree, button tree, buttonwood, caimo, calabash, camphor laurel, camphorwood, candleberry, candlenut, candletree, Cape ash, Cape chestnut, catalpa, champak, cherry laurel, cherry-plum, chincapin, Chinese elm, chinquapin, chokecherry, copper beech, cork oak, cornel, cottonwood, crepe myrtle, cucumber tree, dita, dogwood, dracaena, dragon tree, durmast, elder, elderberry, elm, English elm, fiddlewood, frangipanni, fringe tree, gingerbread tree, gum benzoin, gum tree, hackberry, hawthorn, Hercules'-club, hognut, holly, holly oak, holm, holm oak, hornbeam, horse chestnut, horseradish tree, ilex, jacaranda, Joshua tree, Juneberry, karee, Kiwi star, lagerstroemia, laurel, lime tree, lime tree, linden, liquidambar, liriodendron, live oak, Lombardy poplar, madroña, magnolia, mahoe, mahonia, mammee, maple, may, maytree, mazard, monkey-bread, morello, mountain ash *(US)*, mountain laurel, oak, Osage orange, papaw, paper birch, paulownia, pawpaw *(US)*, pepperina, peppertree, pignut, pimento, pipal, plane, plane tree, platan, poplar, port wine magnolia, prunus, pussy willow, quercitron, quillai bark, red oak, rhus tree, roble, rowan, rubber plant, sacred fig tree, saguaro, sallow, sally *(British)*, sandbox tree, saskatoon, sassafras, seringa, service tree, serviceberry, silver maple, silver tree, silverbell, simarouba, sloe, snowdrop tree, soapbark, soapberry, sorrel tree, sour gourd, sour gum, spindle tree, spotted laurel, star-anise, stinkwood, storax, strawberry tree, sugar maple, sumac, sweet bay, sweet gum, sycamore, tacamahac, tamarisk, terebinth, thorn, toothache tree, traveller's tree, tree of heaven, trifoliata, trifoliate orange, tulip tree, tupelo, turkey oak, turpentine tree, ule, umbrella tree, vitex, water-oak, watergum *(US)*, wax tree, wedding bush, weeping willow, western catalpa, white beam, white birch, white poplar, whitethorn, wicopy *(US)*, wild cherry, willow, willower, witch-elm, wych-elm, yellow poplar.

20. **1. shrubs – Australian** abutilon, agonis, alpine celery, alpine cider gum, alpine heath, amulla, Australian bindweed, Australian boxthorn, ballart, banksia, bauera, Baw-Baw berry, beach naupatea, beard-heath, berry saltbush, biddy bush, black boy, black gin, black wattle, black-eyed Susan, blackfellow's hemp, bladder saltbush, blanket bush, blue halgania, bluebush, bolwarra, boobialla, bootlace bush, boronia, bottlebrush, boy, buck bush, bush pea, bush tomato, callistemon, cherry ballart, Chinese lantern, chucky chucky, coast rosemary, coastal saltbush, conebush, conker berry, conkle berry, copper burr, correa, cottonbush, cottonwood, cough-bush, crowea, daisy bush, desert jasmine, desert lantern, desert lime, desert rose, digger's speedwell, dillon bush, djelwuck, dogrose, drumsticks, dryandra, Ellangowan poison bush, emu bush, epacris, eriostemon, Esperance wax, feather flower, five-corners, fringe-myrtle, fuchsia, gaultheria, geebung, Geraldton wax, giant saltbush, goathead burr, goodenia, granny's bonnet, grass tree, green bush, grevillea, grey saltbush, guinea flower, gunyang, hakea, heath, heath-myrtle, helichrysum, hibbertia, hibiscus, honey flower, honeysuckle, hopbush, hoya, jam tarts, Japanese lantern, jerry-jerry, jockey's cap, kangaroo apple, kangaroo tail, kerrawang, leptospermum, leschenaultia, lignum, mallee saltbush, manatoka, manuka, marsh saltbush, mealy saltbush, melaleuca, midyim, minnerichi, mint-bush, mock-olive, Mondurup bell, moonah, moort, morrison, mountain devil, mountain pepper, muntry, mustard bush, narrawa burr, native elder, native ginger, native rose, native rosella, native sorrel, needlewood, nepine, nitre bush, old-man saltbush, olearia, oondoroo, pearl bluebush, philotheca, pink bells, pink heath, pituri, plum bush, Port Jackson rose, potato bush, poverty bush, prickly Moses, qualup bell, Queensland bluebush, rewarewa, rice-flower, ruby saltbush, saltbush, sand spurge, slender rice-flower, sloe, smoke-bush, snake vine, snowberry, solanum, spider flower, Sturt's desert rose, styphelia, sunshine wattle, Sydney golden wattle, Sydney rose, tea-tree, tickbush, turkey bush, turpentine bush, waratah, wax, waxberry, waxflower, waxplant, wedding bush, westringia, white elder, wild lime, wild parsnip, woody pear, yacca *(Chiefly SA)*.

21.   1. shrubs – NZ akeake, bull-a-bull, coffee bush, coprosma, dracaena, hebe, horopito *(NZ)*, Irishman *(NZ)*, kahikatoa, kaka beak, kanuka, karamu, karo, kawakawa *(NZ)*, koromiko, leptospermum, looking-glass plant, manuka, matagouri, mirror plant, missionary *(NZ)*, neinei, New Zealand lilac, ngaio, parrot's beak, peppertree, pohutukawa, poroporo, ramarama, rangiora, snowberry, tauhinu *(NZ)*, taupata, tawine *(NZ)*, tea-tree, ti, ti-palm, ti-tree, toot, tumatakuru, tutu, vegetable sheep *(NZ)*, veronica, whau, wild Irishman.

22.   1. shrubs – legumes – Australian bacon-and-eggs, bitter-pea, bossiaea, box poison, broom brush, brother-brother, bush-pea, chorizema, cockroach bush, false sarsaparilla, fire bush, flame pea, flat-pea, Flinders River poison, globe-pea, golden-tip, gompholobium, green birdflower, heart-leaf poison, hop, hovea, indigo, karalla, mountain beauty, native indigo, native senna, oxylobium, parrot pea, poison sage, poison-bush, prickly poison, punty bush, sarsaparilla, senna, shaggy pea, silver cassia, Sturt's pea, wattleflower poison, wedge-pea, wild indigo, yellow pea, york-road poison. **2. legumes – other** bird flower, broom, camel's-thorn, cassia, dillwynia, dyer's greenwood, furze, genista, gorse, ground plum, gunga, mimosa, psoralea, rattlepod, rhatany, scurf-pea, sensitive plant, Spanish broom, tragacanth, whin, wisteria.

23.   1. shrubs – other abelia, absinthe, acalypha, alder, althaea, ambary, anil, aralia, arbutus, azalea, balm of Gilead, barberry, bauhinia, bayberry, bell heather, birch, bitou bush, blackcurrant, blackthorn, bog myrtle, boneseed, bougainvillea, box, boxthorn, boxwood, bramble, Brazilian cherry, briar, buckthorn, buddleia, button tree, camellia, candleberry, candlenut, candletree, caper, capriole, cascarilla, centipede plant, cestrum, chaste tree, cherry laurel, China rose, chinquapin, chokeberry, Christ's-thorn, cocoplum, common sallow, cornel, cotoneaster, creosote bush, crepe myrtle, croton, crowberry, currant, damask rose, daphne, deutzia, diosma, dita, divi-divi, dogberry, dogwood, eglantine, elder, elderberry, erica, euonymus, euphorbia, evonymus, feijoa, fig, filbert, firethorn, floribunda, flowering dogwood, flowering quince, fly honeysuckle, forsythia, frangipani, fringe tree, fustic, gale, gardenia, gaultheria, geranium, germander, goldfussia, gooseberry, greasebush, greasewood, groundsel bush, guelder-rose, gum plant, hardhack, hazel, heath, heather, heliotrope, henna, Hercules'-club, hibiscus, huckleberry, hydrangea, ilex, inkweed, jade plant, Japan laurel, Japanese lantern, japonica, jasmine, Jerusalem cherry, Jerusalem sage, jojoba, Juneberry, Kaffir orange, kalmia, kat, kava, kenaf, lad's love, lantana, lasiandra, laurel, laurustinus, lavender, lemon geranium, lemon verbena, lilac, ling, luculia, madroña, manchineel, marula, matrimony vine, may, mezereon, mickey mouse plant, milk-bush, milkwort, mistletoe, mock orange, moss rose, mountain laurel, musk rose, myrtle, nandina, nightshade, num-num, oak, ochna, old man, oleander, oleaster, orange jessamine, osier, pelargonium, pepino, philadelphus, photinia, pittosporum, plumbago, poinciana, poinsettia, poison oak, poison sumach, polygala, pomegranate, port wine magnolia, prickly ash, privet, protea, prunus, pussy willow, pyracantha, ramie, rauwolfia, redcurrant, rewarewa, rhododendron, rhodora, rhus, rockrose, rose, rose mallow, rose of Sharon, rosella, rosemary, rubber tree, sage, sagebrush, sallow, sally *(British)*, saltbush, saltwort, salvia, Scotch heather, serviceberry, smoke tree, snowdrop tree, solanum, southernwood, Spanish bayonet, spicebush, spider flower, spike lavender, spindle tree, spiraea, spirea, spotted laurel, spurge, spurge laurel, stagger-bush, star-anise, stephanotis, stinkwood, storax, strawberry tree, strophanthus, sugar bush, sumac, sumach, sunn, sweet bay, sweet gale, sweetbriar, syringa, tagasaste, tamarillo, tay berry, tea, tea-rose, thyme, titi, trailing arbutus, tree heath, trumpet flower, viburnum, vitex, wax myrtle, wax-myrtle, wayfaring tree, weigela, whortleberry, wicopy *(US)*, wild ginger, wild rose, wild thyme, wintergreen, wintersweet, witch-hazel, withy, wormwood, wych-hazel, yaupon, yesterday, today and tomorrow.

24. **1. herbaceous legumes – Australian** Broughton pea, clianthus, Cooper's clover, coral-pea, crotalaria, Darling clover, Darling pea, dwarf swainsona, kidney vetch, ladies' fingers, Menindie clover, psoralea, rattlepod, running postman, scurf-pea, Sturt's desert pea, swainson pea.

25. **1. herbaceous legumes – other** alfalfa *(Chiefly US)*, alsike, alsike clover, barrel medic, bird flower, bird's-foot, bird's-foot trefoil, black-eyed pea, blue lupin, Bokhara clover, burr medic, chickpea, clianthus, clover, cowpea, crotalaria, cut-leaf medic, Dutch clover, field pea, five-finger, glory pea, Hexham scent, hop-clover, horseshoe vetch, Indian licorice, King Island melilot, ladies' fingers, lespedeza, liquorice, loco *(US)*, locoweed, loment, lotus, lucerne, lupin, melilot, milk vetch, mimosa, nelumbo, psoralea, rattlepod, rest-harrow, sainfoin, scurf-pea, serradella, shamrock, sola, stylo, subterranean clover, sweet clover, sweet lupin, sweet pea, tare, telegraph plant, Townsville stylo, trefoil, trifolium, vetch, white clover, wild indigo.

26. **1. bulbs/corms/tubers – Australian** blackfellow's yam, blackman's potatoes, bloodroot, bluebell, crinum, cunje, cunjevoi, curcuma, Darling lily, early Nancy, garland lily, milkmaids, murnong, Murray lily, myrrnong, native dandelion, sanguinaria, sourgrass *(Chiefly WA and Victoria)*, vanilla flower, yam, yam daisy, yelka.

27. **1. bulbs/corms/tubers – other** African lily, agapanthus, allium, amaryllis, arum, asphodel, autumn crocus, belladonna lily, calla, camass, Cape tulip, chincherinchee, clivia, colchicum, crinum, crocus, crow garlic, cyclamen, daffodil, daffodilly *(Poetic)*, daffodowndilly, daffydowndilly, dogtooth violet, earthnut, eucharis, flame lily, freesia, fritillary, gladiola, gladiolus, grape hyacinth, hippeastrum, hyacinth, ixia, jacinth, Jerusalem artichoke, jonquil, Madonna lily, martagon lily, meadow saffron, naked ladies, narcissus, nerine, onion grass, onion weed, oxalis, pheasant's-eye, pignut, polyanthus, potato, saffron, scilla, sea-onion, sea-squill, snowdrop, snowflake, soursob *(Chiefly SA)*, sowbread, sparaxis, spider lily, squill, star-of-Bethlehem, sword lily, tiger lily, tuberose, tulip, Turk's-cap lily, wake-robin, watsonia, wood hyacinth. *Informal:* daff, glad, gladdie.

28. **1. grasses – Australian** aristida, astrebla, Balcarra grass, bamboo grass, bandicoot grass, barbwire grass, bayonet grass, beard grass, beetle grass, blady grass, blown grass, blue couch, blue grass, bottlewashers, bunch spear grass, button grass, canary grass, cane, cane grass, comet grass, common reed, corkscrew grass, cotton panic grass, danthonia, eight-day grass, fairy grass, fescue, festuca, five minute grass, Flinders grass, hare's-foot grass, hare's-tail, kangaroo grass, kerosene grass, kunai, Landsborough grass, lovegrass, Mitchell grass, Mossman River grass, mulga grass, mulka grass, native millet, neverfail grass, oatgrass, panic, para grass, Parramatta grass, pepper grass, pigeon grass, plains grass, porcupine grass, Queensland blue, Queensland blue couch, rats tail couch, river grass, sago grass, salt couch, salt grass, sand brome, sandhill cane-grass, satin top, scented grass, shot grass, silky browntop, silky-heads, small burr grass, snowgrass, spaniard *(NZ)*, spear grass, spider grass, spike grass, spinifex, spiny mud-grass, stink grass, sugar grass, swamp grass, three-awn grass, tropical reed, tussocky poa, umbrella cane-grass, umbrella grass, variable spear grass, wallaby grass, Warrego grass, water couch, wheat grass, wild rubber, windmill grass, wire grass, woolly butt, yakka grass.

29. **1. grasses – other** barb-grass, barley grass, barnyard grass, bent, bent grass, bermuda grass, birdwood grass, blowfly grass, bristlegrass, brome, browntop, buffalo grass, buffel grass, burr grass, carpet grass, cat's tail, Chewings fescue, cocksfoot, cockspur, cogon, cord grass, couch, crabgrass, creeping bent grass, creeping red fescue, crowsfoot, darnel, dog's-tail, dog's-tooth grass, dropseed, English couch grass, esparto, false brome, feathergrass, fingergrass, flote-grass, fog, foxtail, giant panic, grama grass, guinea grass, hairgrass, heath grass, holy-grass, Italian rye, job's-tears, Johnson grass, kikuyu, lyme grass, marram grass, mat-grass, meadow grass, nasella tussock, Natal red-grass, nitgrass, oats, pampas grass, panic, paspalum, perennial rye, phalaris, pigeon grass, quack grass, quaking grass, quick grass, quitch grass, rat's-tail fescue, reed, reed grass, Rhodes grass, ribbon grass, rye-grass, scutch, serrated tussock, sheep's fescue, shivery grass, snowgrass *(NZ)*, softgrass, spaniard, sweet vernal grass, teosinte, timothy, tussock, twitch, velvet grass, vetiver, water meadow grass, whitlow grass, wild oat, Wimmera rye, Yass river tussock, Yorkshire fog.

30. **1. sedges/rushes – Australian** arrow-grass, Bergalia tussock, bog-rush, bulrush, button grass, cat's-tail, club rush, cumbungi, cutting-grass, drooping sedge, finger rush,

flag, hook grass, Mullumbimby couch, nalgoo, razor grass, reed mace, rush, sag *(Chiefly Tasmania)*, saw sedge, sawgrass, sea rush, spike-rush, toad-rush. **2. sedges/rushes – NZ** cooper's flag *(NZ)*, cutty-grass *(NZ)*, Maori-head *(NZ)*, pingao, raupo, toetoe *(NZ)*. **3. sedges/rushed – other** bulrush, chufa, club rush, deergrass, flag, galingale, hammer sedge, hard-rush, hook grass, papyrus, reed mace, rush, sawgrass, spike-rush, toad-rush, woodrush.

31. 1. orchids – Australian ant orchid, babe-in-a-cradle, beardy, bee orchid, beech orchid, bird orchid, bush orchid, caladenia, Cooktown orchid, cowslip orchid, cucumber orchid, cymbidium, dagger orchid, dendrobium, diuris, donkey orchid, double tails, elbow orchid, enamel orchid, flying-duck orchid, golden moths, green bird orchid, greenhood, helmet orchid, hyacinth orchid, ironbark orchid, king-in-his-carriage, leek orchid, midge orchid, mignonette orchid, mosquito orchid, onion orchid, orange-blossom orchid, orchis, parson's bands, pencil orchid, potato orchid, praying virgin, raspy-root, rat's-tail orchid, rock lily, rock orchid, spider-orchid, sugar orchid, sun orchid, tangle orchid, white feather orchid.

32. 1. orchids – other bee orchid, calypso, crucifix orchid, cymbidium, cypripedium, dead men's fingers, dendrobium, odontoglossum, vanilla.

33. 1. succulents – Australian ant-house plant, bottletree caustic, caustic bush, caustic vine, desert spurge, galvanised burr, Gascoyne spurge, karkalla, milk bush, parakeelya, pigface, prickly saltwort, purslane, roly-poly, spinach.

34. 1. succulents – other agave, aloe, aloe vera, American aloe, amole, artillery-plant, barilla, cactus, carrion flower, century plant, cereus, euphorbia, glasswort, halfmens, hen-and-chicken fern, hen-and-chickens, Hottentot fig, houseleek, ice plant, kali, livelong, Livingstone daisy, maguey, milk-bush, navelwort, New Zealand spinach, nopal, opuntia, pear, pest pear, portulaca, prickly pear, quiver tree, samphire, sansevieria, sedum, sisal, sour fig, spurge, stapelia, stonecrop, tuna, wall pepper.

35. 1. insectivores bladderwort, flytrap, huntsman's-cup, pitcher plant, sarracenia, sundew, Venus flytrap.

36. 1. herbaceous plants – Australian apple bush, Australian centaury, Australian edelweiss, bachelor's button, baldoo, billy button, bindi-eye, bittercress, blue parsnip, blue rod, blue tinsel lily, bogan flea, boggabri, bottle-washers, Brown's dock, bulbine lily, burr-daisy, buttons, caltrop, Caraweena clover, caterpillar-flower, cattle bush, caustic weed, chocolate lily, Christmas bell, claytonia, cotton fireweed, cranesbill, crowfoot, cudweed, cunjevoi, daisy burr, Darling clover, dianella, digger's speedwell, dog's-tongue, duckweed, euphrasy, everlasting daisy, eyebright, fairy lanterns, fairy spectacles, fan-flower, feather heads, fireweed, flannel flower, flax, flax-lily, forget-me-not, fringed lily, fruit-salad plant, fuzz weed, giant lily, giant pigweed, globe amaranth, goodenia, Gymea lily, hairy bitter-cress, helichrysum, helipterum, hogweed, hop lily, hound's-tongue, incense plant, jersey cudweed, kangaroo-paw, kidney weed, knawel, Koonamore daisy, lagoon spurge, lamb's-tail, leek lily, life-saver burr, mat-rush, minnie-daisy, mud-mat, mudwort, mulga cabbage, mulga nettle, mulga spinach, mulla-mulla, myosotis, native crowfoot, native hollyhock, paperdaisy, pelargonium, poached-egg daisy, pop saltbush, potato bush, prickly poppy, prickly saltwort, Prince of Wales' feather, purslane, pussycat's tails, pussytails, quena, roly-poly, sand lily, selfheal, settler's flax, settler's twine, silver bush, silver tails, sneeze-weed, snow daisy, snow flower, solanum, spear lily, speedwell, squash bush, stinging nettle, stork's-bill, Swan River daisy, tar-vine, tassel top, tomato bush, trigger flower, trigger plant, vanilla lily, vernonia, Ward's weed, Warrigal cabbage, waterbuttons, waterweed, white foxtail, white-root, wild carrot, wild gooseberry, wild parsnip, woolly buttons, woolly mat-rush, yellow tails.

37. 1. herbaceous plants – NZ aniseed, bayonet grass, biddy-biddy *(NZ)*, brachycome, Chatham Island lily, cotton plant, flax, glory pea, kaka beak, korari, Mount Cook lily, mountain daisy, New Zealand flax, parrot's beak, penwiper plant *(NZ)*, piripiri, snow daisy, spaniard *(NZ)*, spear grass.

38. 1. herbaceous plants – other abelmosk, acanthus, aconite, Adam's needle, adder's-meat, African lily, African violet, ageratum, agrimony, alexanders, alkanet, allseed, althaea, alumroot, alyssum, amaranth, ambrosia, anchusin, anemone, angelica, anti-rrhinum, apple of Peru, apple of Sodom, aquilegia, archangel, arnica, arrow-grass, arrowhead, arrowroot, artichoke thistle, aspidistra, aster, astilbe, aubrietia, auricula, babies'-breath, baby's tears, baldmoney, balsam, baneberry, bear's-breech, bedstraw, begonia, bellflower, bells-of-Ireland, bennet, bergamot, billbergia, bird of paradise, bishop's weed, bistort, bittercress, bladder campion, bleeding-heart, blinks, bloodroot, blue borage, blue weed, bluebell, borage, bouncing Bess, bouncing Bett, brooklime, brookweed, broomrape, bugle, bugloss, buttercup, caladium, calamus, calceolaria, calendula, calibrachoa, Californian poppy, calliopsis, camomile, campanula, campion, candytuft, canna, Canterbury bell, cardinal flower, cardoon, carline, carnation, catchfly, caterpillar weed, catmint, catnip, celandine, celosia, centaury, chamomile, Christmas rose, chrysanthemum, cicely, cineraria, cinquefoil, clarkia, claytonia, cleavers, cleome, clockweed, clove pink, cockscomb, cockspur, coleus, columbine, coneflower, coreopsis, corn poppy, cornflower, corydalis, cosmos, cow-parsley, cow-parsnip, cow-wheat, cowslip, coxcomb, cranesbill, crowfoot, cuckooflower, cuckoopint, curly pondweed, cytaster, dahlia, dame's violet, day lily, deadnettle, delphinium, Deptford pink, dianthus, dimorphotheca, dittander, dittany, dog fennel, dog's mercury, dog's-tongue, dogbane, dumb cane, dwarf mallow, earthnut, edelweiss, elecampane, enchanter's nightshade, erigeron, eringo, eryngo, eupatorium, euphorbia, euphrasy, evening primrose, eyebright, fennelflower, ferula, feverfew, figwort, five-finger, flag, flamingo-flower, Flanders poppy, flax, fleabane, fleawort, fleur-de-lis, Florida moss, flower of Jove, flower-de-luce, fool's parsley, fool's watercress, four-o'clock, foxglove, fraxinella, gaillardia, garlic mustard, gazania, gentian, geranium, gerbera, German ivy, germander, geum, gillyflower, ginger, gladdon, globe amaranth, globe thistle, globeflower, gloxinia, goat's-rue, godetia, gold-of-pleasure, golden aster, golden saxifrage, goldenrod, goldenseal, goldilocks, goldthread, goosegrass, granny's bonnet, grass of Parnassus, green dragon, grindelia, gromwell, ground cherry, ground ivy, groundsel, guayule, gypsophila, gypsywort, harebell, hawk's-beard, hawkbit, hawkweed, heart's-ease, hedge parsley, hedge-hyssop, helianthus, heliotrope, hellebore, hemp agrimony, hen-and-chicken fern, hen-and-chickens, hepatica, herb bennet, herb Christopher, herb Paris, herb Peter, herb Robert, hog's-fennel, hognut, hollyhock, honesty, horned poppy, horse nettle, horsemint, hound's-tongue, hydrargyrum, hypericum, Iceland poppy, immortelle, impatiens, Indian pipe, Indian shot, Indian tobacco, iris, Jacob's-ladder, keck, kingcup, knapweed, knawel, kniphofia, lad's-love, lamb's ear, lamb's tongue, larkspur, lily, lily-of-the-valley, lobelia, London pride, loosestrife, lousewort, love-in-a-mist, love-in-idleness, love-lies-bleeding, lungwort, lychnis, maiden pink, mallow, marguerite, marigold, marsh mallow, marsh marigold, marvel-of-Peru, May apple, May blobs, May lily, meadow rue, meadowsweet, mercury, Michaelmas daisy, mignonette, milfoil, military fern, milk bush, milkweed, milkwort, mind-your-ownbusiness, Molucca balm, monkey-flower, monkshood, moon daisy, moonwort, motherof-thousands, mousetail, mudsill, mugwort, musk, myosotis, nasturtium, nemesia, nipplewort, orpine, ox-eye, ox-eye daisy, oxlip, oxtongue, paeony, paigle, pansy, paradise, paschal flower, pasqueflower, pearlwort, pennywort, pentstemon, peony, periwinkle, petunia, pheasant's-eye, phlox, picotee, pignut, pimpernel, pipewort, ploughman's spikenard, poison creeper, polyanthus, polygala, polygonum, poor-man's orchid, poppy, poppyhead, portulaca, pot marigold, potentilla, primrose, primula, prince's-feather, pulsatilla, pyrethrum, Queen Anne's lace, rafflesia, ragged robin, ragweed, ragwort, rampion, ranunculus, red valerian, red-hot poker, reseda, ribbon-weed, rock-cress, rocket, Roman nettle, rose campion, rose mallow, rose of Jericho, rose of Sharon, rosebay willowherb, rudbeckia, salad burnet, saltwort, salvia, samphire, sand spurry, sandwort, santonica, saxifrage, scabious, scammony, scarlet pimpernel, schizanthus, Scotch bluebell, Scotch thistle, sea holly, sea tassel, sea-campion, sea-heath, sea-holly, sea-kale, sealavender, sea-rocket, seablite, selfheal, shamrock, shasta daisy, sheep's bit, shepherd's cress, shooting star, Siberian wallflower, silkweed, silver grass, silverweed, skullcap, smartweed, snakeroot, snapdragon, sneezeweed, sneezewort, snow-in-summer, soapwort, solanum, solidago, Solomon's-seal, Spanish moss, speedwell, spider flower, spiderwort, spignel, spurge, spurry, St John's wort, St Peters wort, starwort, statice, stinging nettle, stitchwort, stork's-bill, strelitzia, subterranean clover, sun spurge, sunflower, swallowwort, swamp lily, sweet alyssum, sweet cicely, sweet flag, sweet william, tansy, tape vine, tar-vine, taraxacum, teasel, teazel, teazle, thistle, tillandsia, toadflax, tormentil, touch-menot, tradescantia, trillium, tropaeolum, truelove, truth, tutsan, twinflower, valerian, verbena, veronica, viola, violet, viper's bugloss, Virginia stock, wait-a-bit, wake-robin, wall rocket, wallflower, wandering jew, water primrose, water-betony, water-chickweed, waterdropwort, water-hemlock, water-mat, water-parsnip, waterpepper, Welsh poppy, wicopy *(US)*, wild carrot, wild parsley, wild parsnip, wild sorghum, willowherb, windflower, winter aconite, winter cress, winter heliotrope, winter rose, wolf's-bane, wood sorrel, woodruff, woundwort, yarrow, zinnia. *Informal:* chrysie.

39. **1. aquatic plants – Australian** bladderwort, duckweed, eelgrass, floating heart, fringed waterlily, grass-wrack, lotus, milfoil, nelumbo, pondweed, seagrass, starwort, water blinks, water nymph, water ribbons, water thyme, waterbuttons, waterlily, waterweed, yarrow.

40. **1. aquatic plants – other** azolla, bopple nut *(Qld)*, Canadian pondweed, Cape pondweed, elodea, flote-grass, flowering rush, horned pondweed, hornwort, mare's tail, naiad, papyrus, pickerelweed, sea pink, seagrass, spatterdock, star fruit, tape-grass, thrift, victoria, water hyacinth, water milfoil, water plantain, water shield, water soldier, water speedwell, water starwort, water thyme, yellow waterlily.

41. **1. climbing plants – Australian** apple-berry, barrister, bluebell creeper, bridal creeper, burny bean, bush-lawyer, button orchid, calamus, caustic vine, clematis, coral-pea, derris, devil's guts, devil's twine, dodder laurel, doubah, dumplings, false sarsaparilla, hoya, ipomoea, kangaroo vine, lawyer-cane, matchbox bean, monkey rope, passionflower, Queensland bean, sarsaparilla, scimitar pod, smilax, watervine, waxplant, wombat berry, wonga-wonga.

42. **1. climbing plants – other** ampelopsis, Argentine trumpet-vine, balloon vine, banana passionfruit, Banksia rose, bell-vine, bignonia, bindweed, bine, birthwort, bittersweet, black bindweed, black bryony, black-eyed Susan, bryony, butterfly pea, calabash, canary creeper, Cape ivy, Carolina jasmine, ceriman, clematis, convolvulus, cow-itch, cowage, cross vine, cucurbit, dodder, Dutchman's-pipe, five-finger, fruit salad plant, giegie, gourd, guaco, heartseed, hog peanut, honeysuckle, ipomoea, ivy, jalap, Japanese ivy, jasmine, jequirity, kiekie, lamb's-tail, madder, Madeira vine, mignonette vine, monstera deliciosa, moonflower, moonseed, morning glory, Mysore thorn, philodendron, poison ivy, poison oak, rata, rattan, squirting cucumber, stephanotis, sweet pea, thunbergia, traveller's joy, trumpet flower, trumpet honeysuckle, virgin's-bower, Virginia creeper, white bryony, wisteria, woodbine, woody nightshade, yellow jasmine.

43. **1. fungi/bacteria/lichens** agaric, amanita, ambrosia, ascomycete, aspergillus, awheto *(NZ)*, basket fungus, beech orange, blackfellow's bread, blewits, boletus, botrytis cinerea, breadmould, chanterelle, coral fungus, death cap, death cup, downy mildew, earthstar, ergot, fairies' closet, field mushroom, fly agaric, gill fungus, gold cap, gold top, grey mould, hairy jew's ear, horse mushroom, Iceland moss, ink-cap, jew's ear, magic mushroom, metarhizium, microphyte, mildew, morel, mould, mushroom, myxomycete, net fungus, orchil, penicillium, phytophthora, puffball, reindeer moss, rust, slime mould, sooty blotch, sooty mould, stinkhorn, toadstool, truffle, tuckahoe, vegetable caterpillar, yeast, yeast plant. *Informal:* mushie. **2. mosses and liverworts** bog moss, club moss, hepatic, sphagnum.

44. **1. algae** anabaena, black scum, blackfish-weed, bladderwrack, blue-green algae, brown algae, carrageen, Ceylon moss, coralline, desmid, diatom, dulse, frogspawn, frogspit, fucoid, fucus, green algae, green weed, gulfweed, Irish moss, jelly plant, kelp, laver, Neptune's necklace, nullipore, phytoplankton, pond scum, red algae, rock weed, sargasso, sargassum, sea lettuce, sea-wrack, seaware, seaweed, spirogyra, stonewort, wrack.

45. **1. ferns and fern allies** adder's tongue, azolla, bird's-nest fern, bladder fern, bracken, brake, club moss, Dutch rush, elkhorn fern, equisetum, fishbone fern, hare's foot, hare's-foot, hart's-tongue, hen-and-chicken fern, holly fern, horseshoe fern, horsetail, king-fern, lace-fern, lycopodium, maidenhair, male fern, marsh fern, marsh horsetail, moonwort, nardoo, osmund, pillwort, polypody, quillwort, rasp fern, rock fern, rock-fern, royal fern, scouring rush, selaginella, shield-fern, sickle fern, spleenwort, stag's-horn moss, staghorn fern, tender brake, tree fern, umbrella fern, Venus's hair, walking fern, wall rue, waterfern, woolly cloak-fern. **2. NZ ferns** bunger, crape fern *(NZ)*, filmy fern, gully fern, kidney fern, king-fern, mamaku, mangemange, necklace fern, pig fern *(NZ)*, ponga, Prince of Wales feather, silver fern.

46. **1. cycads and minor gymnosperm** burrawang, coontie, gingko, ginkgo, macrozamia, maidenhair tree, sago, welwitschia, zamia, zamia palm.

47. **1. grains/cereals/pulses/oilseeds** algarroba, arborio rice, arrowroot, barley, barleycorn, basmati rice, bean, bean curd, benne, black gram, black rice, bourghul, brown rice, buckwheat, bulgur, burghul, butter bean, camellia, canary grass, carob, cereal, chickpea, cohune, colza, corn, cowpea, cracked wheat, dal, dhal, doura, durra, durum wheat, einkorn, emmer, French bean, French green lentil, frijol, gingili, grain, gram, green gram, grist, groundnut, guinea corn, hard wheat, haricot, helianthus, Indian corn, Indian millet, Indian rice, kaffir, kaffir corn, kaoliang, kidney bean, lentil, lima bean, lupin, maize, mealies *(South African)*, millet, milo, mung bean, oats, oil-palm, olive, palm sugar, panic, pea, pearl barley, pearl millet, pigeon pea, popcorn, pulse, ragi, rape, rapeseed, rice, rye, safflower, sago, semolina, sesame, shea, shell bean *(US)*, sorghum, sorgo, soya bean, spelt, St John's bread, sunflower, teff, til, triticale, urad dal, wheat, white bean, wild rice. *Informal:* tilly *(Especially Qld and Rural Northern NSW)*.

48. **1. vegetable/root crops** artichoke, artichoke heart, artichoke thistle, asparagus, aubergine, avocado, baby marrow, bean, bean shoot, bean sprout, beansprout, beet, beetroot, Belgian endive, bell pepper, bhindi *(Indian English)*, bitter melon, black gram, bok choy, brassicas, brinjal *(Asian English)*, broad bean, broccoli, broccolini, brussels sprout, burdock, burnet, butternut, butternut pumpkin, cabbage, calabash, capsicum, cardoon, carrot, casaba, cassava, cauliflower, celeriac, celery, celery cabbage, chard, chayote, chicory, Chinese broccoli, Chinese cabbage, Chinese kale, choko, chufa, chye sim, cole, collard, coontie, cos, cos lettuce, courgette, cress, cucumber, dasheen, day lily, dolichos, earthnut, eddo, eggfruit, eggplant, elephant's ear, endive, English spinach, eschalot, faba bean, fava bean, French bean, frijol, garden orach, garlic, gherkin, globe artichoke, gobo, gram, gramma *(NSW)*, green bean, green corn, green pepper, green vegetable, gumbo *(Chiefly US)*, Haas avocado, hairy jew's ear, haricot, hognut, jack bean, Jerusalem artichoke, kai lan, kale, kamote *(Philippine English)*, kangkong, kidney bean, kohlrabi, lablab, leek, lettuce, lima bean, love apple, manioc, Maori cabbage *(NZ)*, marrow, marrow squash *(US)*, merino, mirrnyong, mung bean, neep *(Scottish)*, New Zealand spinach, okra, onion, orach, oyster plant, palm-cabbage, parsley, parsnip, pea, pepper, petits pois, pigeon pea, pimiento, plantain, poor man's bean, potato, pratie *(Irish)*, puha, pumpkin, purslane, puwha, radish, rampion, ramsons, rauriki *(NZ)*, red bean, red beet, red cabbage, rhubarb, rocambole, rosella bush, runner, runner bean, rutabaga *(US)*, salad burnet, salsify, samphire, savoy, scallion *(Chiefly US)*, scarlet runner, sea-kale, shallot, shell bean *(US)*, silverbeet, skirret, snapbean *(US)*, snow pea, sorrel, Spanish onion, spinach, spring onion, sprout, squash *(US)*, strawberry tomato, string bean, succory, sugar beet, sugar pea, swede, sweet corn, sweet pepper, sweet potato, Swiss chard *(US)*, sword bean, taro, tomato, trombone *(Especially SA)*, turnip, udo, vegetable, vegetable marrow, vegetable oyster, water-chestnut, watercress, wax bean *(US)*, wax-bean, white potato, winged bean, winter melon, witlof, witloof chicory *(US)*, yam, yam bean, zucchini. *Informal:* caulie, chat, cuie, cukie, greens, greenstuff, horse bean, martie, murphy, sparrowgrass, spud, tater.

49.   **1. fruits** abiu, alligator pear, amarelle *(US)*, anchovy pear, apple, apricot, Asian pear, avocado, babaco, banana, banana passionfruit, barberry, bilberry, bird-cherry, bitter orange, black cherry, black sapote, blackberry, blackcurrant, blackerry, blackheart, blaeberry, blood orange, blueberry, boysenberry, bramble, breadfruit, bush lemon, but but, cainite, calabash nutmeg, caltrop, cantaloupe, Cape gooseberry, caper berry, ceriman, cherimoya, cherry, cherry guava, cherry-plum, chiku, Chinese apple *(Especially Qld and WA)*, Chinese gooseberry, Chinese orange, chocolate pudding fruit, chokeberry, chokecherry, choko, chucky chucky, citron, citronelle, citrus, clementine, cling peach, clingstone, codling, crab-apple, cranberry, cumquat, currant, custard-apple, damson, date, date plum, Delicious, dewberry, dogberry, dragon's eye, durian, elderberry, emuapple, feijoa, fig, foxgrape, gage, gean, geebung, genipap, gooseberry, goosegog, granadilla, Granny Smith, grape, grapefruit, grapevine, greengage, greening, grenadilla, ground cherry, guanabana, guava, hackberry, hanepoot, honeydew melon, Hottentot fig, huckleberry, jaboticaba, jackfruit, jam melon, Japanese loquat, Japanese medlar, jonathan, jostaberry, jujube, Kaffir lime, Kaffir orange, kaki, kalamansi, katunga, kiwano, Kiwi fruit, konini, ladyfinger, lamyai, lemon, lime, loganberry, longan, loquat, lotus, lungan, lychee, malaga, mammee, mandarin, mango, mangosteen, May apple, medlar, miracle fruit, miraculous fruit, monstera deliciosa, morello, mulberry, muscadel, muscat, muskmelon, naranjilla, naseberry, nashi pear, navel orange, nectarine, nopal, olive, opuntia, orange, Osage orange, passionfruit, pawpaw, peach, pear, Pekingese, persimmon, pie melon, pineapple, pineapple guava, pippin, plum, pomegranate, pomelo, prickly custard apple, prune, quandong, quince, rambutan, raspberry, redcurrant, rennet, rhubarb, rockmelon, rose-apple, rosella, rough lemon, russet, sapodilla, sapote, satsuma mandarin, Seville orange, shaddock, sloe, sorb apple, sour fig, sour gourd, sour orange, soursop, star apple, stone fruit, strawberry, sweet cherry, sweet orange, sweeting *(Chiefly British)*, sweetsop, table grape, tamarillo, tamarind, tangelo, tangerine, tay berry, teaberry, thornapple, tree tomato, tuna, ugli fruit, warden, water chestnut, watermelon, wax jambu, white currant, white sapote, whiteheart, whortleberry, wild cherry, youngberry. *Informal:* avo, blackcap *(US)*, eater, granny, jonnie, nana, pine, pinie, strawb.

50.   **1. nuts** almond, Barcelona nut, bauple nut *(Chiefly South-Eastern Qld)*, beech mast, beechnut, betel nut, black walnut, bopple nut *(Qld)*, brazil, brazil nut, butternut, cashew, chestnut, chinquapin, cob, cobnut, coconut, cola, coquilla nut, desert quandong, filbert, goober *(US)*, groundnut, hazel, hazelnut, hickory, hickory nut, Japanese chestnut, Jordan almond, macadamia nut, marron, monkey nut, nut pine, oyster nut, peanut, pecan, pignut, pili, pine nut, pinyon, pistache, pistachio, Queensland nut *(Chiefly Qld and Northern NSW)*, quondong, shagbark *(US)*, shellbark, souari nut, Spanish chestnut, walnut.

51.   **1. herbs and spices** acanthus, allspice, angelica, anise, aniseed, aspidistra, Australian edelweiss, bachelor's button, balm, basil, bay, bay tree, bear's breech, bishop's weed, black pepper, bluebell, borage, bugle, calabash nutmeg, canella, caper, caraway, cardamom, cassia, caterpillar-flower, catmint, catnip, cayenne, Ceylon cinnamon, chervil, chilli, chive, cicely, cinnamon, clary, clove, costmary, cow-parsley, cumin, cunjevoi, curcuma, curry powder, dianella, dill, dittander, dwarf mallow, estragon, fennel, fennelflower, fenugreek, fool's parsley, fool's watercress, galangal, garam masala, garlic mustard, gazania, gerbera, gherkin, ginger, gingerroot, goodenia, grains of paradise, ground ivy, hawkweed, heliotrope, hellebore, honesty, hop, horsemint, horseradish, hyssop, lad's-love, laos, laurel, lemon balm, lemongrass, lily-of-the-valley, liquorice, lovage, mace, marasca, marjoram, masala *(Indian English)*, mint, nasturtium, nutmeg, opium poppy, oregano *(US)*, origan, paprika, parsley, pennyroyal, penwiper plant *(NZ)*, pepper, peppermint, pimento, pimpernel, pot marigold, race ginger, ragwort, ramson, red pepper, rosemary, saffron, sage, salad burnet, samphire, shasta daisy, shepherd's cress, spear lily, spearmint, spice, staranise, sweet basil, sweet bay, sweet cicely, tamara, tamarind, tansy, tarragon, thyme, toadflax, turmeric, vanilla, white pepper, wild carrot, winter cress, winter heliotrope.

52. **1. beverage plants** absinthe, black elder, burdock, cacao, chamomile, chicory, cocoa bean, coffee, coffee tree, cola, coquito, dandelion, elder, elderberry, gomuti, grape, hop, horehound, hyson, juniper, kat, kava, maté, mint, sarsaparilla, smilax, souchong, tea, wormwood, yaupon, yeast, yerba.

53. **1. drug and medicinal plants** aconite, alkaloid, aloe, aloe vera, alumroot, ammoniac, angelica, angostura bark, aniseed, arnica, asafoetida, asthma-plant, atropine, bayberry, bebeeru, belladonna, benzoin, betel nut, betel palm, betel pepper, betony, bhang, bitterbark, bitterwood, bloodroot, bryony, buckthorn, bull-a-bull, cade, cajuput, calendula, calisaya, canella, cannabis, capsicum, cardinal flower, carrageen, cascara, cascara sagrada, cascarilla, cascarilla bark, cashew, cassia, castor bean *(US)*, castor seed, castor-oil plant, cevadilla, chamomile, chaulmoogra, china bark, cinchona, citronella, coca, cocaine, cola, colchicum, colocynth, coltsfoot, comfrey, contrayerva, copaiba, corkwood, corn silk, croton, cubeb, Culver's root, curare, dagga *(South African)*, datura, deadly nightshade, digitalis, dill, dogbane, ephedra, ergot, eucalypt, fennel, fennelflower, fenugreek, ferula, fever-root, fever-tree, feverfew, fimble, fleawort, foxglove, friar's balsam, fumitory, gagroot, galbanum, ganga, gentian, ginseng, gold cap, gold top, goldenseal, goldthread, gotu kola, grains of paradise, greenheart, grindelia, guaco, guaiacum, gum ammoniac, gunga, gunyang, hedge-hyssop, heliotrope, hemp, henbane, herb Paris, herbal medicine, hop, horehound, horseradish, Hottentot fig, Iceland moss, Indian hemp, ipecacuanha, jaborandi, jalap, jequirity, jimson weed, kangaroo apple, kat, kino gum, lavender, lignum vitae, liquorice, madder, mandragora, mandrake, marijuana, May apple, mescal, milfoil, morphine, moxa, nard, nicotine, nightshade, nux-vomica, opium poppy, pagoda tree, pan, pareira, pellitory, penicillium, pennyroyal, peppermint, Peruvian bark, pimento, pinkroot, pituri, podophyllum, poke, pokeweed, poppy, poppyhead, pyrethrum, quebracho, quinine bush, rauwolfia, rhatany, rhubarb, rue, sabadilla, safflower, Saigon cinnamon, salep, sanguinaria, sarsaparilla, sassafras, savin, scammony, sea-onion, sea-squill, senega, senna, simarouba, slippery elm, smilax, snakeroot, solanum, spikenard, squill, sticky weed, stramonium, strophanthus, strychnine, swallow-wort, taraxacum, thornapple, thuja, tobacco, tonka bean, toothache tree, tormentil, tragacanth, turpeth, valerian, viburnum, wall pellitory, waria-waria, wattle, witch-hazel, wormseed, wormwood, woundwort, yarrow, zanthoxylum.

54. **1. perfumery plants and materials** abelmosk, allspice, aspic, bay, bdellium, bergamot, boronia, cassie-flower, champak, citronella, damask rose, eaglewood, frangipanni, gardenia, ilang-ilang, iris, jasmine, labdanum, ladanum, lavender, lemon geranium, lemongrass, lily-of-the-valley, marigold, mignonette, mimosa, myrrh, orange blossom, orris, orrisroot, patchouli, pennyroyal, peppermint, pimento, rose, sandalwood, spike lavender, spikenard, stinking roger, tonka bean, tuberose, vetiver, ylang-ylang.

55. **1. dye plants** alkanet, anatto, anchusin, anil, annatto, betony, bloodroot, brazil, camwood, dyer's greenweed, dyer's rocket, fustic, haemotoxylin, henna, indigo, logwood, madder, mehndi, orchil, pastel, puccoon, quebracho, quercetin, quercitron, redwood, safflower, sappanwood, valonia, weld, woad, yellowwood.

56. **1. fibre plants** abaca tree, ambari, bast, bhang, bowstring hemp, broom millet, broomcorn, bullswool, calamus, coco, coconut palm, cogon, coir, cottontree, dishcloth gourd, esparto, fimble, flax, ganga, gomuti, hemp, Indian Hemp, jute, kapok, kenaf, korari, loofah, maguey, millet, New Zealand flax, osier, palmiet, papyrus, pita, sansevieria, silk-cotton tree, sunn, tapa, teasel, vetiver. *Informal:* flaxie *(NZ)*.

57. **1. timber plants** acajou, alamo *(US)*, alpine ash, araucaria, arbor vitae, ash, balsa, balsam fir, balsawood, bamboo, bangalay, banyalla, basswood, bebeeru, beech, birch, black bean, black pine, black walnut, blackbutt, blackwood, blue gum, bolly gum, box, boxwood, brazil, briar, brush box, brushwood, buttonwood, camphor laurel, camphorwood, canary sassafras, candle bark, cane, Cape ash, cedar, celery-top pine, clinker beech, coachwood, cork, cottonwood, cudgerie, cypress pine, Douglas fir, Douglas pine, Douglas spruce, durmast, durobby, ebon *(Poetic)*, ebony, eucalyptus, fiddlewood, flooded gum, greenheart, guaiacum, haematoxylin, hemlock spruce, hickory, honey locust, hoop pine,

Huon pine, insignis pine, jacaranda, Japanese cedar, jarrah, kahikatea, karri, kauri, King William pine, kingwood, klinki pine, larch, laurel, lignum vitae, loblolly, locust, longleaf pine, Mackay cedar, mahogany, marmalade tree, miro, Monterey pine, Moreton bay chestnut, mountain ash, Norway spruce, oak, Oregon pine, padauk, partridge-wood, penda, pine, poon, poplar, prickly ash, pulpwood, puriri, Queensland kauri, Queensland maple, radiata pine, red cedar, red fir, red pine, redwood, rimu, river red gum, robby, rosewood, sandalwood, satinwood, Scots pine, sequoia, settler's matches, shagbark *(US)*, silky oak, silver fir, slash pine, sneezewood, Spanish chestnut, spotted gum, spruce, sugar maple, sweetbriar, Sydney blue gum, tallowwood, Tasmanian blue gum, Tasmanian myrtle, Tasmanian oak, tawa, teak, thuja, toon, turpentine, turpentine tree, violet wood, walnut, western hemlock, Western red cedar, white beech, white pine, white spruce, yellow sassafras, yew.

58. 1. timbers/barks balsawood, bamboo, boxwood, brazil, brushwood, bullswool, camphorwood, candle bark, cane, cork, fiddlewood, jacaranda, kingwood, pulpwood, rattan, rosewood, sandalwood, settler's matches, sola *(India)*, violet wood, whangee, withe, withy, zebrawood.

59. 1. fodder and pasture plants alfalfa *(Chiefly US)*, algarroba, alsike, alsike clover, baldoo, barley grass, beech mast, beet, bird's-foot trefoil, birdwood grass, black pine, bladder saltbush, blue grass, blue lupin, Bokhara clover, brome, browntop, buffel grass, burr medic, canary grass, chou moellier, clover, coastal saltbush, cocksfoot, cole, comfrey, Cooper's clover, cottonbush, cowpea, Darling clover, dolichos, Dutch clover, fenugreek, field pea, Flinders grass, giant panic, giant saltbush, grey saltbush, guinea grass, herbage, kikuyu, King Island melilot, lablab, Lachlan lilac *(Rural NSW)*, Landsborough grass, lespedeza, lucerne, lupin, Mackay cedar, maize, mangel-wurzel, mangold, mealy saltbush, melilot, Menindie clover, mesquite, millet, Mitchell grass, Murrumbidgee sweet pea *(Rural NSW)*, mustard bush, oats, old-man saltbush, panic, paspalum, Paterson's curse, pearl millet, perennial rye, phalaris, Queensland blue, rape, red clover, rhodes grass, Riverina bluebell *(Rural NSW)*, rutabaga *(US)*, rye-grass, sago grass, sainfoin, saltbush, salvation Jane, Salvation Jane *(Especially SA)*, serradella, shot grass, small burr grass, sorghum, sorgo, soya bean, stylo, subterranean clover, sugar cane, sugar grass, sugarcane, swede, sweet clover, sweet lupin, Tasmanian myrtle, teosinte, timothy, Townsville lucerne, Townsville stylo, trifolium, turnip, veldt grass, vetch, water meadow grass, wheat grass, white cedar, white clover, wild sorghum, wilga, Wimmera rye, windmill grass. *Informal:* chow *(NZ)*.

60. 1. oils/resins/chemicals agar, agar-agar, Aleppo gall, babul, balata, balm, balm of Gilead, balsam, barilla, bdellium, benzoin, black gram, buttongrass, camphor, candleberry, candlenut, candlewood, carnauba, carrageen, cashew, castor bean *(US)*, castor seed, castor-oil, catechu, cutch, dragon's blood, galbanum, galipot, gallipot, gibberellin, guar gum, guayule, gum, gum benzoin, gutta balata, kangaroo grass, latex, linseed, mastic, palm oil, papain, quillai bark, rubber, sandarac, soapbark, soapberry, storax, tacamahac, tannin, tragacanth, turpentine, ule, varnish, wallaby grass, wattlebark, wintergreen. *Informal:* turps.

61. 1. weeds Aaron's rod, African boxthorn, alexanders, allseed, amaranth, anabaena, apple of Peru, apple of Sodom, asphodel, asthma plant, azolla, balloon vine, barley grass, barnyard grass, Bathurst burr, bearded oat, beggar's tick, Bergalia tussock, billygoat weed, bindi-eye *(Eastern Mainland and South-Western WA)*, bindweed, bitou bush, bitter melon, bittercress, black bindweed, black nightshade, black oat, black thistle, blackberry, blue borage, blue couch, blue devil, blue thistle, blue top, blue weed, boneseed, boxthorn, bracken, bramble, briar, brome, Brown's dock, buffalo burr, burdock, burr grass, burrmarigold, calliopsis, caltrop, camel melon *(Chiefly NSW)*, camphor laurel, Cape gooseberry, Cape ivy, capeweed, carpet grass, castor-oil plant, cat's head, cat's-ear, caterpillar weed, charlock, chickweed, chinee apple, cleavers, cockspur, cogon, colocynth, coltsfoot, compass plant, conium, convolvulus, coreopsis, corn poppy, corn spurry, corncockle, cornflower, cottonbush, couch, crabgrass, cracker *(NZ)*, creeping oxalis, creeping thistle, crofton weed, crowfoot, crown beard, crowsfoot grass, cudweed, dandelion, darnel, datura, deadly nightshade, devil's claw, dock, dodder, dog fennel, double gee, drooping sedge, duckweed, dwarf mallow, elodea, English couch grass, eryngo, eupatorium, evening primrose, fat-hen, fennel, field madder, fierce thornapple, fireweed, Flanders poppy, flat weed, flatweed, fleabane, flixweed, fluellen, fumitory, furze, gallant soldier, galvanised burr, Good-King-Henry, goose grass, goosefoot, gorse, gromwell, ground elder, groundsel, groundsel bush, Guildford grass, hairy bittercress, hardheads, hare's-ear, hare's-foot, hawk's-beard, hawkweed, hedgemustard, heliotrope, hemlock, hemp agrimony, henbit, herb Gerard, Hexham scent, hoary cress, hogweed, horehound, horned poppy, Indian hedge-mustard, Indian weed, inkweed, jalap, Japanese honeysuckle, jelly-leaf, Jerusalem cherry, jimson weed, Johnson grass, joy-weed, khaki weed, King Island melilot, knapweed, knotweed, lamb's ear, lamb's tongue, lamb's-tail, land cress, lantana, London rocket, Madeira vine, mallow, Maltese cockspur, mayweed, mesquite, Mexican poppy, Mexican tea, milk thistle, milk vetch, milkweed, mimosa, mintweed, missionary *(NZ)*, mist flower, moon daisy, mouse-ear, mullein, Mullumbimby couch, Mysore thorn, nassella tussock, native hops, needle burr, nettle, Noogoora burr, nopal, nutgrass, oatgrass, oats, onion grass, onion weed, opuntia, ox-eye daisy, oxalis, Paddy's lucerne, paddymelon, pampas grass, pampas lily-of-the-valley, Parramatta grass, parsley piert, pascalia weed, Paterson's curse, pear, pearlwort, pellitory, penny-cress, pennywort, peppercress, pest pear, petty spurge, pheasant's-eye, pig melon *(WA)*, pimpernel, plantain, polygonum, portulaca, prairie grass, prickly lettuce, prickly pear, prickly pear melon, prickly poppy, privet, purple top, purslane, quaking grass, Queensland hemp, ragweed, ragwort, rat's-tail fescue, Rhodes grass, ribwort, rocket, rubber vine, saffron thistle, Saint Barnaby's thistle, salvation Jane, sand spurry, scarlet pimpernel, Scotch thistle, sensitive plant, serrated tussock, sheep's sorrel, shepherd's needle, shepherd's-purse, shivery grass, sida weed, silkweed, skeleton weed, slender celery, small crofton weed, smartweed, smilax, snakeweed, sorrel, soursob, sow-thistle, sowbane, spear thistle, spiny burr grass, spiny emex, spurge, spurry, St John's wort, stagger-weed, star thistle, star-of-Bethlehem, star-wort, stemless thistle, sticktight, sticky agrimony, stinging nettle, stink grass, stinking roger, stinkweed, stinkwort, summer grass, sun spurge, swamp dock, sweetbriar, swine-cress, taraxacum, tare, thistle, thornapple, three-cornered jack, tiger pear, tobacco tree, tradescantia, treacle mustard, tree of heaven, tulip, turnip weed, tutsan, twitch, variegated thistle, verbena, vetch, viper's bugloss, wall pellitory, wandering jew, wartcress, water hyacinth, waterpepper, whin, whitlow grass, wild carrot, wild lettuce, wild mustard, wild oat, wild onion, willowherb, winter grass, wireweed, witchweed, wood sorrel, xanthium, Yass river tussock, yellow sorrel, yellow wood sorrel, yellow-flowered oxalis.

62. **1. poisonous and irritant plants** aconite, amanita, antiar, autumn crocus, baneberry, barringtonia, belladonna, blind-your-eyes, blue rod, bottletree caustic, box poison, brother-brother, buttercup, Calabar bean, Cape tulip, castor-oil plant, caustic weed, cestrum, cherry laurel, cockatoo apple, colchicum, conium, Cooktown ironwood, cot-tonbush, cow-itch, cow-parsnip, cowage, cowbane, curare, Darling pea, datura, deadly nightshade, death cup, delphinium, derris, dumb cane, dwale, Ellangowan poison bush, ergot, euphorbia, finger cherry, flame lily, fly agaric, fool's parsley, foxglove, Gascoyne spurge, giant stinging tree, gidgee, gympie nettle, heart-leaf poison, hellebore, hemlock, henbane, herb Christopher, jequirity, jimson weed, Johnson grass, kalmia, karaka, lark-spur, laurel, loco *(US)*, locoweed, macrozamia, Madeira vine, manchineel, mignonette vine, mintweed, monkshood, mountain laurel, narcissus, nettle, nettle tree, nightshade, oleander, poison ivy, poison oak, poison sumach, poison-bush, prickly poison, ragweed, ranunculus, rhus tree, rock-fern, sassy, sassy bark, smartweed, stagger-bush, stavesacre, stinging nettle, stinging tree, strophanthus, sugar gum, thornapple, toadstool, toot, tutu, upas, wallflower poison, wax tree, weir vine, winter rose, wolf's bane, yew, york-road poison.

63. **1. plants used by Aborigines** amulla, apple-berry, ballart, bats-wing coral-tree, bau-hinia, beech orange, berrigan, black bean, black boy, blackfellow's bread, blackfellow's hemp, blackfellow's yam, blackman's potatoes, bloodroot, bolwarra, boobialla, bottle tree, bunya-bunya, Burdekin plum, burrawang, cabbage palm, cabbage tree, calamus, caterpillar-flower, cherry ballart, chucky chucky, colane, condoroo, cunjevoi, desert lemon, desert lime, doubah, early Nancy, Ellangowan poison bush, emu bush, emu-apple, gunyang, kangaroo apple, kurrajong, lilly pilly, manatoka, mat-rush, Mitchell grass, murrnong, myrrnong, nalgoo, nardoo, native cherry, native dandelion, native millet, native mulberry, native rosella, native sorrel, native willow, nelumbo, nonda, panic, pigface, pitcheri, pituri, potato bush, quandong, quena, settler's flax, settler's twine, snowberry, tomato bush, warrigal cabbage, waterlily, waxberry, wild goosebery, wild lime, wild orange, wild tomato, yam, yam daisy.

64. **1. botany** biosystematics, dendrochronology, floristics, mycology, paleobotany, paly-nology, phycology, phytocoenology, plant taxonomy.

adj. **65.** **1. floral** flowery. **2. abloom** blooming, bloomy, blossoming, blossomy, efflorescent, efflorescing, florescent, flowered, full-blown. **3. green** grassy, lush, turfy, verdant, ver-durous. **4. leafy** foliaceous, foliaged, foliate, foliated, foliose, frondescent, in leaf, leaved. **5. leaf-like** foliaceous, foliar, foliate, foliated, leafy. **6. viny** ivied, twining. **7. tufty** caespitose, cespitose *(US)*, stubbly. **8. herbaceous** herbal, herby. **9. shrub-by** broomy, bushy, scrubby, shrublike. **10. ferny** rushy. **11. brambly** branchy, brushy, furzy. **12. frutescent** fruticose.

66. **1. arboreal** arboreous, arborescent, silvan, sylvan, woody. **2. bushy** arboreous, bosky, forested, silvan, sylvan, wooded, woodsy *(US)*, woody. **3. beechen** cedarn *(Poetic)*, citrus, olive, palmy, piney, piny, willowy.

67. **1. botanical** vegetable, vegetal, vegetational, vegetative. **2. botanical family description** acanthaceous, amaryllidaceous, ambrosiaceous, aroid, asclepiad, bignoniaceous, boraginaceous, caprifoliaceous, caryophyllaceous, chenopodiaceous, composite, crassulaceous, cucurbitaceous, dipsacaceous, ericaceous, euphorbiaceous, gramineous, iridaceous, juncaceous, lauraceous, liliaceous, lythraceous, magnoliaceous, malvaceous, moraceous, musaceous, myrtaceous, oleaceous, papaveraceous, polygonaceous, portulacaceous, primulaceous, ranunculaceous, rhamnaceous, rosaceous, rubiaceous, rutaceous, santalaceous, sapindaceous, sapotaceous, saxifragaceous, scrophulariaceous, solanaceous, umbelliferous, verbenaceous, violaceous, vitaceous.

68. **1. horticultural** arboricultural, floricultural.

RELATED KEYWORDS: FARMING

PLEASANT FLAVOUR

n.   **1.**   **1. pleasant flavour** deliciousness, lusciousness, mellowness, niceness, palatability, palatableness, sapidity, savour, savouriness, tastiness, toothsomeness. **2. relish** life, tang, zest.

adj.   **2.**   **1. delicious** ambrosial, ambrosian, delectable, epicurean, fit for the gods, flavorous, lipsmacking, luscious, mouth-watering, nectareous, nice, succulent, sweet, tasty, yum. *Informal:* delish, goluptious, more-ish, nummy, scrummy, scrumptious, yummy. **2. delicate** dainty, minikin, nice. **3. savoury** appetising, enticing, flavourful, flavoursome, mouth-watering, palatable, piquant, sapid, savorous *(Chiefly US)*, savory, tangy, tasty, toothsome, zestful, zesty.

v.   **3.**   **1. savour** lap up, lick one's fingers, smack the lips. **2. taste good** tickle the palate.

interj.   **4.**   **1. yummy** *Informal:* delish, mmm, scrummy, scrumptious, what a feast, yum, yum-o.

RELATED KEYWORDS: PUNGENCY, FOOD, SWEETNESS, TASTE

PLEASANTNESS

n.   **1.**   **1. pleasantness** acceptableness, agreeableness, amenity, blandness, inoffensiveness, niceness, palatableness, pleasingness. **2. amiability** amiableness, douceur, good-naturedness, likeability, likeableness, lovableness, sweetness. **3. charm** allure, allurement, animal magnetism, attraction, attractiveness, charisma, comeliness, cuteness, enchant, enticement, fascination, glamour, grace, gracefulness, loveliness, zest. *Informal:* glam. **4. cheerfulness** cosiness. **5. delightfulness** delectability, deliciousness, delightsomeness, gloriousness, gorgeousness, heavenliness, lusciousness, luxuriousness, mellifluousness. **6. pleasant place** Eden, Elysium, heaven, millennium, paradise.

adj.   **2.**   **1. pleasant** acceptable, agreeable, enjoyable, good, likeable, nice, palatable, piacevole, pleasing, pleasurable, pretty, sapid, simpatico, to one's taste, toothsome. *Informal:* easy-to-take. **2. amiable** benign, big-hearted, considerate, cordial, courteous, friendly, genial, gentle, good-hearted, good-humoured, good-natured, good-tempered, hearty, kind, kind-hearted, kindly, lovable, mellow, mild, nice, sweet-tempered, thoughtful, warm-hearted. *Informal:* decent. **3. charming** alluring, attractive, beautiful, becoming, catching, charismatic, desirable, enchanting, engaging, fair, fascinating, fetching, glamorous, graceful, impressive, interesting, piquant, taking, tempting, winning, winsome, witching. *Informal:* glam. **4. cheerful** cosy, jolly, merry. *Informal:* slaphappy. **5. delightful** delectable, delicious, fragrant, gladsome, glorious, heavenly, lipsmacking, lovely. *Informal:* goluptious, gorgeous. **6. sweet** dulcet, honeyed, luscious, mellifluent, mellifluous, sugary. **7. bittersweet** piquant.

v.   **3.**   **1. make pleasant** appease, candy, dulcify, mollify, sauce, sweeten, zest.

4.   **1. be pleasant** appeal to, attract, charm, delight, endear oneself to, please. *Informal:* charm the pants off.

adv.   **5.**   **1. pleasantly** acceptably, agreeably, amiably, inoffensively, nicely, piacevole, pleasingly. **2. charmingly** attractively, becomingly, delectably, deliciously, delightfully, delightsomely, engagingly, piquantly, sweetly.

RELATED KEYWORDS: BEAUTY, CONTENTEDNESS, EMOTION, GOODNESS, PLEASURE

PLEASURE

n.   **1.**   **1. pleasure** delight, delightedness, felicity, gladness, gladsomeness, happiness, joy, joyfulness, joyousness, rapture, sunshine. **2. enjoyment** delectation, delight, fun, recreation, refreshment, sport. **3. gratification** fulfilment, satisfaction, sensuality, voluptuosity, voluptuousness. **4. indulgence** delicacy, epicureanism, feasting, festivity, hedonics, hedonism, indulgency, luxuriation, luxuriousness, luxury, pleasure principle. **5. pleasurableness** enjoyableness, pleasantness, thrillingness. **6. creature comforts** cakes and ale, comfort, comfort food, cosiness, ease, snugness, well-being. **7. liking** affinity, aptitude, fancy, favour, fondness, inclination, palate, partiality, penchant, predilection, preference, proclivity, propensity, relish, stomach, taste. **8. appreciation** admiration, gratitude, love, pleasure. **9. joie de vivre** gusto, zest, zestfulness. **10. rapture** abandonment, bliss, blitheness, cheer, ecstasy, elation, exaltation, gladness, rapturousness, ravishment, transport. **11. seventh heaven** beatification, beatitude, blessedness, blissfulness, heaven. **12. enchantment** beguilement, bewitchment, ecstasy, rapture, ravishment, titillation. **13. euphoria** bliss, ecstatics, raptures, transports. **14. thrill** *Informal:* bang, buzz, charge, kick. **15. high** *(Informal)* trip, upper.

2. **1. good time** ball, feast, field day, idyll, time of one's life. *Informal:* high time, picnic. **2. pastime** amusement, dissipation, distraction, diversion, entertainment, fun, game, hobby, play, recreation, sport. **3. red-letter day** special occasion. **4. dolce vita** gracious living, high life, life of Riley. **5. paradise** Eden, Elysium, heaven, land of milk and honey, lucky country. **6. a place in the sun** a bed of roses, a good living, bed of roses, featherbed, in clover, lap of luxury, luxury, milk and honey, the fat of the land, the good life, the primrose path. *Informal:* a good scene.

3. **1. enjoyer** delighter, reveller. **2. indulger** feaster, voluptuary. **3. bon vivant** bon viveur, epicure, epicurean, gastronome, gormand, gourmand, hedonist, high-stepper, jetsetter, sensualist, worldling. **4. jet set** beau monde, beautiful people. **5. admirer** amorist, appreciator, fancier, lover, spark, suitor, swain *(Chiefly Poetic, British)*. *Informal:* fellow.

adj. 4. **1. pleasurable** appealing, bland, delectable, enjoyable, fragrant, funky, mild-mannered, pleasant. *Informal:* groovy. **2. pleasing** agreeable, charming, good, gratifying, jolly, likeable, nice, piacevole, satisfying, sweet. *Informal:* easy-to-take. **3. idyllic** blithesome, carefree, debonair, edenic, elysian, halcyon, insouciant, joyous, light-hearted, paradisiacal.

5. **1. pleased** blithe, cheerful, delighted, glad, happy, happy as Larry, joyful, joyous, on top of the world, rapt. *Informal:* chuffed, high as a kite. **2. enchanted** charmed. **3. delighted** enchanted, enrapt, enraptured, glad, overjoyed, pleased, pleased as punch, rapt, thrilled, tickled to death. *Informal:* chuffed, stoked, tickled pink, tickled to bits. **4. euphoric** beatific, blissful, delirious, ecstatic, enraptured, frenzied, high, in raptures, rapturous, raving. *Informal:* high as a kite, on a high. **5. enjoying oneself** turned on. *Informal:* in the groove.

6. **1. pleasure-loving** high-stepping, indulgent, luxurious, pleasure-seeking, sybaritic, voluptuary, voluptuous. **2. hedonistic** epicurean, hedonic.

v. 7. **1. enjoy** admire, adore, appreciate, care for, delight in, fancy, have a soft spot for something, like, love, relish, savour, take a fancy to, take pleasure in, take to, welcome. *Informal:* dig *(Chiefly US)*, get a kick out of. **2. revel in** feast on. *Informal:* groove on. **3. go into ecstasies** swoon. *Informal:* be crazy about, be mad about, blow one's mind, drool over, rave, trip.

8. **1. please** appease, content, delectate, divert, elicit a positive response, engage, feed, fulfil oneself, gratify, grow on, indulge, satisfy, tickle. *Informal:* chuff, rub up the right way. **2. enchant** allure, be (much) in demand, becharm, beguile, bewitch, captivate, charm, delectate, enrapture, ensorcell *(Poetic)*, enthral, entrance, intrigue into. *Informal:* fetch, vamp. **3. gladden** beatify, cheer, delight, elevate, enliven, exhilarate, imparadise, lighten, liven up, thrill to bits, transport. *Informal:* buck up, jollify.

9. **1. be pleased** congratulate oneself, gladden, laugh, purr, rejoice, smile. **2. have a good time** enjoy oneself, jet set. *Informal:* bliss out, kick up one's heels, let one's hair down, live, live it up, rage. **3. luxuriate** bask, indulge, wallow.

adv. 10. **1. pleasurably** enjoyably. **2. gratifyingly** satisfyingly. **3. hedonistically** hedonically, indulgently, sybaritically, voluptuously. **4. delightedly** happily, zestfully. **5. ecstatically** blissfully, exalted, idyllically, paradisiacally, rapturously.

RELATED KEYWORDS: CONTENTEDNESS, FRIENDLINESS, KINDNESS, LOVE, PLEASANTNESS

PLIABILITY

n. 1. **1. pliability** flexibility, flexibleness, limberness, lissomness, litheness, pliableness, pliancy, pliantness, suppleness, tone, twistability. **2. resilience** body, bounce, bounciness, buoyancy, elasticity, rebound, renitency, spring, springiness, temper, tension, tonicity, torsibility. **3. elasticity** aero-elasticity, give, plasticity, snapback, sponginess.

4. stretchability ductility, stretchiness, tensility, tractility. **5. elasticisation** jellification, plasticisation, Young's modulus.

2. 1. elastic elastic band, rubber band, rubber ring. *Informal:* lacker band *(Chiefly Victoria),* lacky band. **2. spring** C-spring, cee-spring, jiggerboard, leaf spring, mainspring, spring-loading, springboard, torsion bar, valve spring.

3. 1. rubber amadou, buna, butyl rubber, caoutchouc, crepe rubber, elastic bitumen, elastomer, elaterite, foam rubber, gum, gutta-percha, indiarubber, jelly, mineral caoutchouc, nitrile rubber, pará rubber, quayule, sponge rubber, stereo-regular rubber, two-way stretch.

adj. **4. 1. pliable** bendable, bendy, double-jointed, ductile, elastic, flexible, flexile, floppy, lax, light, limber, lissom, lithe, malleable, nimble, plastic, pliant, pulvinar, springy, supple, tractable, twistable, twisty, whippy, willowish, willowy, wristy. **2. resilient** bouncy, buoyant, inflated, renitent, spring, spring-loaded, spring-loading, tonic. **3. elastic** aeroelastic, elastomeric, rubbery, stretchy. **4. jelly-like** gelatinous, indiarubber, jellied. **5. mouldable** fictile, plastic, thermoplastic. **6. stretchable** ductile, elastic, plastic, stretch, stretchy, tensible, tensile, tractile.

v. **5. 1. bounce** rebound, resile, spring.

6. 1. elasticise plasticise, stretch. **2. jellify**.

7. 1. limber flex, limber up, stretch, tenter.

adv. **8. 1. pliantly** flexibly, limberly, lithely, pliably, springily, supply. **2. resiliently** elastically, plastically.

RELATED KEYWORDS: SOFTNESS, PULP, RAW MATERIALS, SLUDGE

POETRY

n. **1. 1. poetry** verse. **2. balladry** concrete poetry, goliardery, hymnody, hymnology, minstrelsy, namby-pamby, nonsense verse, satire. **3. poetic art** ars poetica, poetics, prosody, the muse. **4. poem** Anacreontic, lines, lyric, monostrophe, piece, prose poem, rhyme, rime, song, strain. **5. lyric** ballade, canzone, cento, Cowleyan ode, dithyramb, ditty, eclogue, Elizabethan sonnet, epode, erotic, ghazal, Horatian ode, idyll, irregular ode, ithyphallic, lyricism, madrigal, monody, ode, pantun, pindaric ode, pseudo-pindaric ode, regular ode, rondeau, rondel, roundel, rune *(Poetic),* Sapphic ode, sestina, sextain, sonnet, tanka, villanelle, virelay. **6. ballad** broadsheet, bush ballad, doggerel, fit, jingle, macaronics, nursery rhyme, singsong. **7. epic** épopée, chanson de geste, epopoeia, epos, heroic verse, heroics, Homeric, rhapsody. **8. romance** fabliau, lay, roman. **9. georgic** bucolic, pastoral. **10. elegy** coronach, dead march, dirge, epicedium, jeremiad, lament, lamentation, last post, monody, post, threnode, threnody. **11. epithalamium** charivari, epithalamion, hymeneal, prothalamion. **12. hymn** psalm, recessional. **13. epigram** acrostic, clerihew, gnomic verse, haiku, limerick, monostich. **14. book of poetry** anthology, chapbook, parnassus. **15. sonnet** Italian sonnet, Petrarchan sonnet, Shakespearean sonnet.

2. 1. stanza Alcaic, Alexandrine, ballad stanza, bob, canto, couplet, distich, envoy, epode, heptastich, heroic couplet, hexastich, monostich, octave, octet, octonary, passus, pentastich, quatrain, refrain, seguidilla, sestet, Spenserian stanza, stave, strophe, tag, tercet, tetrastich, triolet, triplet, versicle, wheel. **2. blank verse** free verse.

3. 1. rhyme clink, crambo, eye rhyme, female rhyme, feminine rhyme, half rhyme, internal rhyme, masculine rhyme, perfect rhyme, rhyme scheme. **2. alliteration** assonance, echoism, onomatopoeia, rhyme, staff, stave.

4. 1. poetic rhythm accent, measure, metre, metrics, movement, numbers, rhythmics, scansion, sprung rhythm, versification. **2. stress** accent, beat, ictus. **3. systole**. **4. enjambment**.

5. 1. rhyme scheme Alcaics, decasyllabics, elegiac, free verse, heroic couplets, iambics, logoedic, ottava rima, rhyme royal, Spenserian, terza rima, vers libre. **2. anacrusis** arsis, caesura, dieresis, feminine ending, outride, position, rove-over, slack, stave, thesis, time, weak ending. **3. foot** amphibrach, amphimacer, anapaest, choriamb, choriambus, dactyl, dactylic, iamb, iambus, Ionic, paeon, proceleusmatic, pyrrhic, spondee, tribrach, trochaic, trochee. **4. line** acatalectic, Adonic, Alexandrine, Asclepiadean, decasyllable, dimeter, dipody, hemistich, heptameter, hexameter, hexapody, hypermeter, Ionic, monometer, monostich, octameter, octosyllable, pentameter, Sapphic, septenary, stich, syzygy, tetrabrach, tetrameter, tetrapody, trimeter, tripody.

6. 1. poet ballad-monger, balladeer, bard, dithyrambist, elegist, hymnist, hymnodist, idyllist, imagist, jongleur, laureate, lyricist, lyrist, metrician, metrifier, metrist, minnesinger, minstrel *(Poetic),* monodist, poet laureate, poetaster, poetess, prosodist, rhapsodist, rhymer, rhymester, rimester, scop, singer, skald, songster, songwriter, sonneteer, troubadour, trouvère, vers librist, versifier.

adj. **7.** **1. poetic** bardic, Parnassian. **2. lyric** elegiac, idyllic, lyrical, melic, odic. **3. heroic** Dantesque, epic, homeric. **4. bucolic** pastoral. **5. satiric** mock-heroic. **6. metric** isosyllabic, measured, metrical, prosodic, prosodical, quantitative, rhythmical, scannable. **7. versicular** stanzaic, stichic, strophic, systolic.

v. **8.** **1. versify** berhyme, metrify, poetise, sing. **2. rhyme** clink, jingle. **3. scan.**

adv. **9.** **1. poetically** epically, lyrically, prosodically. **2. rhythmically** metrically.

RELATED KEYWORDS: MUSIC, NARRATIVE, WRITING

POISON

n. **1.** **1. poison** autotoxin, bait, bane, endotoxin, exotoxin, intoxicant, pizen, potion, toxicant, toxin, toxoid. **2. venom** snakebite, venin, zootoxin. **3. germ** infection, virus. **4. chemical agent** biological weapon, BW, nerve agent, phosgene, sternutator, yellow rain. **5. biocide** Agent Blue, Agent Orange, Agent Purple, Agent White, anticrop agent, defoliant, fungicide, herbicide, knockdown herbicide, picloran, weedicide, weed-killer. **6. radiation** annihilation radiation, fallout, strontium-90. **7. poison gas** adamsite, arsine, asphyxiant, blister gas, diphosgene, effluvium, emanon, gas, lewisite, mephitis, miasma, mofette, mustard gas, nerve gas, vapours, vesicant, yperite. **8. pesticide** acaricide, aerosol bomb, arsenicals, chlordane, chlorinated camphene, DDT, dichlorodiphenyltrichloroethane, dieldrin, insecticide, malathion, metaldehyde, miticide, organophosphate, Paris green, pyrethrum, rotenone, toxaphene. **9. dioxin** 2,4,5-T, 2,4-D, dichlorophenoxyacetic acid, trichlorophenoxyacetic acid. **10. poisonousness** nocuousness, noisomeness, noxiousness, toxicity, venomousness, virulence. **11. sting** bite, urtication.

2. **1. poisoning** alcoholism, auto-intoxication, autotoxaemia, bromism, ciguatera, cinchonism, gassing, intoxication, lead poisoning, urtication. **2. contamination** biomagnification, denaturation, toxication. **3. biological warfare** aerial spraying, BW, chemical warfare, germ warfare.

3. **1. poisoner** baiter, contaminator, stinger. **2. poison cart** gas chamber, gas oven.

4. **1. poisons** arsenite, arsine, atropine, botulin, brucine, carbon monoxide, carcinogen, coniine, CS gas, cyanic acid, cyanide, cyanogen, delphinine, diazomethane, hydrazoic acid, hydrochloric acid, hydrocyanic acid, hydrofluoric acid, hydrogen bromide, hydrogen chloride, hydrogen cyanide, hydrogen fluoride, hydrogen iodide, hydrogen sulfide, hyoscyamine, muriatic acid, nitrogen dioxide, ozone, phosphine, prussic acid, ptomaine, ratsbane, rotten egg gas, sarin, stibine, strophanthin, strychnine, sulfuretted hydrogen, thebaine, urushiol, water gas, whitedamp.

5. **1. poisonous plants** aconite, amanita, antiar, autumn crocus, baneberry, barringtonia, belladonna, blind-your-eyes, box poison, brother-brother, buttercup, Calabar bean, Cape tulip, castor-oil plant, caustic weed, cestrum, cherry laurel, cockatoo apple, colchicum, conium, cottonbush, cow-itch, cow-parsnip, cowage, cowbane, curare, Darling pea, datura, deadly nightshade, death cup, delphinium, derris, dwale, Ellangowan poison bush, ergot, euphorbia, finger cherry, flame lily, fly agaric, fool's parsley, foxglove, gidgee, gympie nettle, heart-leaf poison, heliotrope, hellebore, hemlock, henbane, herb Christopher, jequirity, jimson weed, Johnson grass, kalmia, karaka, lantana, larkspur, loco *(US)*, locoweed, macrozamia, manchineel, mintweed, monkshood, narcissus, nettle, nettle tree, nightshade, oleander, ourari, poison ivy, poison oak, poison sumach, poison-bush, poison-tree, ranunculus, rhus tree, sassy, sassy bark, sowbane, stagger-bush, stavesacre, stinging nettle, stinging tree, strophanthus, sugar gum, thornapple, toadstool, toot, tutu, upas, upas tree, water-hemlock, wax tree, winter rose, wolf's bane, yew, york-road poison.

adj. **6.** **1. poisonous** autotoxic, baited, baneful, carcinogenic, caustic, cyanic, deadly, epipastic, escharotic, mephitic, miasmal, miasmatic, miasmatical, miasmic, nocuous, noisome, noxious, pernicious, pestilent, pestilential, poison, strychnic, toxic, toxicant, toxicogenic, venomous, virulent, zootoxic.

v. **7.** **1. poison** bait, cyanide *(NZ)*, drug, empoison, envenom, loco. **2. sting** urticate. **3. contaminate** denature, denaturise, infect. **4. biomagnify.**

adv. **8.** **1. poisonously** banefully, nocuously, noisomely, venomously. **2. noxiously** mephitically, pestilently.

RELATED KEYWORDS: BADNESS, ILL HEALTH, KILLING

POLE

n. **1.** **1. pole** barber's pole, beanpole, caber, flagpole, hydro pole *(Tasmania)*, jackstaff, maypole, meat-pole, snow pole, totem pole. **2. telegraph pole** breakaway, frangible, Stobie pole *(SA)*, utility pole. **3. barge pole** catching pole, roping pole. **4. mast** fore, fore-topgallant mast, fore-topmast, foremast, jigger, jiggermast, jury mast, main-topgallant mast, main-topmast, mainmast, mizzen, mizzenmast, royal mast, samson post, stick, topgallant, topmast. **5. boom** bowsprit, bumpkin, dolphin striker, foreyard, gaff, jackyard, jib boom, jockey pole, mainyard, martingale, sailyard, spar, sprit, steeve, traveller, yard.

2. 1. post bedpost. **2. pile** block, piling, stilt. **3. gatepost** gradient post, heelpost, hitching post, quintain, strainer, strainer post, winning post. **4. bollard** barrel, bitt, loggerhead. **5. column** anta, atlantes, caryatid, clustered column, gnomon, monolith, obelisk, pilaster, pillar, piloti, pylon, shaft, stele, verge. **6. dado** die, scape, trunk.

3. 1. shaft lath, pale, paling, palisade, picket, shim, slat, slip, spline, staff, stake, stave. **2. board** baseboard *(US)*, dwang *(NZ Building Trades)*, floorboard, skirt, skirting, skirting board, stile, washboard *(US)*, window sash. **3. plank** deal, gangplank, gangway, logway, skid *(US)*, wale. **4. beam** bar, baulk, bellcast batten, binder, box girder, couple, crossbar, crosstree, dead shore, fascine, fish, flitch beam, flying shore, gallows top, girder, hammerbeam, I-beam, joist, lintel, manteltree, noggin, nogging, open web joist, principal, purlin, rafter, rolled steel joist, rood beam, RSJ, shore, shoring, sill, sleeper, splat, stanchion, straining beam, stretcher, stringer, strut, subprincipal, supporter, tie beam, timber, transom, tree, trestletree, trimmer, trussed beam, trussing. **5. crossbeam** buttock, collar tie, crossbar, crosscut, crosspiece, fess, summer, thwart, tie beam, transom, transversal, transverse, traverse.

4. 1. bar arch bar, bail, capstan bar, crossbar, drawbar, flat, jack, manrope, rail, sliprail. **2. metal bar** angle, angle iron, channel iron, roll bar, T-bar, U-bolt. **3. crowbar** crow, handspike, heaver, jemmy, jimmy *(US)*, lever, pinch, pinch-bar, sweep, swipe, tiller, tommy bar.

5. 1. rod con rod, connecting rod, piston rod, pitman *(Chiefly US Machinery)*, reach, tie rod. **2. shafting** countershaft, crankshaft, jackshaft, prop shaft, propeller shaft, quill, quill shaft, rockshaft, tail shaft. **3. axle** arbor, axis, axletree, mandrel, pinion, pintle, spindle. **4. pin** belaying pin, bodkin, break pin, broach, cottar *(Scottish)*, cotter, dowel, fid, forelock, hatpin, headpin, hob, key, kingpin, linchpin, nog, peg, pintle, pivot, shear pin, spill, split pin, stem, stickpin, stud, swivel pin, tap-bolt, tiepin, toggle, tongue, treenail, trunnel, wrist, wristpin. **5. skewer** brochette.

6. 1. stick broomstick, crabstick, hickory, rattan. **2. birch** ferula, ferule, swish, switch. **3. stave** cue, divining rod, dowsing rod, perch. **4. walking-stick** alpenstock, cane, crutch, Malacca cane, ski-pole, stick, stilts, supplejack, sword cane, swordstick. **5. dolly** copper stick, posser, washing dolly. **6. digging stick** yam stick. **7. slapstick** bauble. **8. bullroarer** churinga, churunga, tchurunga, thunder stick, tjuringa, turinga. **9. yardstick** tally. **10. staff** caduceus, crosier, crozier, distaff, gavel, mace, mere, pastoral, pikestaff, quarterstaff, rod, shaft, taiaha, tipstaff. **11. ramrod** pontil, probang, punty, toby. **12. cudgel** bastinado, bat, baton, bludgeon, club, cosh, knobkerrie, leangle, loom, nightstick *(US)*, nilla-nilla, nulla-nulla, patu, shakuhachi, shillelagh, singlestick, stick, swagger stick, trolley pole, truncheon, verge, wand. *Informal:* donger. **13. totem pole**

adj. **7. 1. shafted** beamed, trabeated, transomed. **2. columned** dipteral, hypostyle, peristylar.

RELATED KEYWORDS: MACHINE, SUPPORT

POLITICIAN

n. **1. 1. politician** candidate, canvasser, favourite son, man of the people, politico *(Chiefly US)*, statesman, stateswoman. *Informal:* pollie. **2. political activist** agitprop, agropolitician, barnstormer, crusader, demagogue, fellow traveller, kingmaker, lobbyist, polemicist, political enthusiast, rabblerouser, soapbox orator, strategist, stump orator *(Chiefly US)*. *Informal:* crypto, tub-thumper.

2. 1. member of parliament backbencher, Congressman, Congresswoman, deputy, honourable member, law-maker, legislator, legislatress, magnate, member of the house of representatives, MHR, MP, oncer, parliamentarian, representative, senator. **2. alderman** bailie, burgess, burgomaster, city father, councillor, lord mayor, mayor, mayoress, provost, town councillor. **3. independent** crossbencher, freelance, mugwump *(US)*. **4. minister** administrator, agent-general, attorney-general, cabinet minister, foreign secretary *(British)*, frontbencher, member of cabinet, minister without portfolio *(British)*, postmaster general, secretary, secretary of state *(British)*, shadow minister, speaker, state secretary, treasurer. **5. prime minister** PM, premier. **6. power behind the throne** éminence grise, grey eminence, machine. **7. party whip** numbers man.

3. 1. political ideologist centrist, coalitionist, democrat, federalist, fusionist, liberal, liberalist, moderate, ochlocrat, reformist, small-l liberal, technocrat, unicameralist.

2. left-winger alternative culture, Bolshevik, bolshevist, collectivist, communalist, communist, comrade, leftist, Leninist, Maoist, Marxist, nationaliser, progressive, radical, Red, republican, socialist, sovietist, syndicalist, Trotskyite. *Informal:* bolshie, com, comm, commie, commo, leftie, loony left, Pink, pinkie, pinko, red-ragger. **3. revolutionary** Jacobin, street fighter, terrorist, urban guerilla. *Informal:* cut-lunch revolutionary, weekend revolutionary. **4. nationalist** free-stater, home-ruler, Little Englander, separatist. **5. feminist** femocrat, radical feminist, suffragette, suffragist, women's libber. *Informal:* feminazi, femmo. **6. conservationist** environmentalist, nature lover. *Informal:* greenie, tree hugger. **7. right-winger** anti-communist, Babbitt, capitalist, capitalist roader, conservative, counter-revolutionary, fundamentalist, grouper, legitimist, reactionary, revisionist, rightist, suburban, suburbanite, Tory, true blue, WASP. *Informal:* mossback *(US)*, right-to-lifer. **8. Fascist** absolutist, elitist, feudalist, imperialist, monarchist, monocrat, neo-fascist, royalist, stratocrat, territorialist, theocrat, totalitarian. **9. hawk** cold warrior.

RELATED KEYWORDS: AUTHORITY, GOVERNMENT, POLITICS

POLITICS

n. **1.** **1. politics** agripolitics, class warfare, lobbyism, mugwumpery, party politics, power structure, statecraft, statesmanship, statism. *Informal:* political football. **2. diplomacy** balance of power, brinkmanship, cold war, domino theory, escalation, gunboat diplomacy, irredentism, megaphone diplomacy, power politics, realpolitik, shuttle diplomacy, summitry, ultimatum. **3. political science** geopolitics.

2. **1. political spectrum** arm, caucus, centre, faction, left wing, party, right wing, the left, the right, wing. **2. pressure group** big business, business, labour, lobbyist, management, the bosses.

3. **1. electioneering** agitprop, canvass *(Chiefly US)*, crusade, party political broadcast, party political speech, stump oratory, television debate, whistlestop. **2. dirty tricks** gerrymander, pork-barrelling, smear campaign. **3. redistribution**

4. **1. electorate** borough *(British)*, congressional district, constituency, country seat, marginal seat, rotten borough, seat, swinging seat. **2. voter** abstainer, aspirational voter, caster, constituent, elector, electoral college *(US)*, floating vote, floating voter, mandator, quorum, swinging voter. **3. right to vote** franchise, isonomy, manhood suffrage, suffrage, universal suffrage, women's suffrage. **4. vote** absence vote, absentee vote, alternative vote, declaration vote, donkey vote, informal vote, postal vote, primary vote.

5. **1. parliamentary procedure** standing orders. **2. motion** ay, no, urgency motion, urgent bill, vote of confidence, vote of no confidence. **3. division** absolute majority, majority, minority, plurality *(US)*, simple majority. **4. question time** budget speech, dorothy dixer, first speech, maiden, maiden speech, reply. **5. sitting** assembly, opening, recall, recall of parliament. **6. dissolution** dismissal, double dissolution, prorogation.

6. **1. political ideology** centralism, constitutionalism, democracy, direct democracy, federalism, liberalism, parliamentarianism, reformism. **2. radicalism** bolshevism, collectivism, communalism, communism, Eurocommunism, guild socialism *(British)*, Jacobinism, Maoism, Marxism, Marxist-Leninism, Menshevism, progressivism, republicanism, Schweikism, socialism, syndicalism, Trotskyism. **3. feminism** affirmative action, equal opportunity, suffragettism, votes for women, women's lib, women's liberation, women's rights. **4. liberationism** black power, gay lib, grey power. **5. conservatism** capitalism, legitimism, revisionism. **6. Fascism** absolutism, aristocratism, Caesarism, colonialism, czarism, elitism, hierarchism, imperialism, monarchism, neocolonialism, neo-fascism, royalism, territorialism, totalitarianism, tsarism.

adj. **7.** **1. political** all-party, party, sociopolitical. **2. electioneering** agitprop, barnstorming, whistlestop.

v. **8.** **1. run for parliament** barnstorm, campaign, canvass, crusade, electioneer, meet the people, stand for. *Informal:* go on the stump, press flesh, stump *(Chiefly US)*. **2. hold an election** dissolve parliament, go to the country, go to the people, go to the polls, prorogue parliament.

9. **1. politicise** agitate, propagandise, raise consciousness. **2. lobby** pressure. **3. redistribute** gerrymander.

RELATED KEYWORDS: AUTHORITY, GOVERNMENT, POLITICIAN, REVOLUTION

POSE

n. **1.** **1. pose** attitude, position, posture, stance. **2. bearing** air, carriage, comportment, conduct, demeanour, deportment, manner, mien, outward, port, set. **3. recumbency** accumbency, couching, decumbence, decumbency, prostration. **4. sitting** seat, seating, sedentariness, straddle. **5. genuflection** bending, bob, bow, congé, curtsey, curtsy, kneeling, kowtow, salaam, squat, stoop. **6. slouch** droop, sprawl.

2. **1. poser** attitudinarian, croucher, kneeler, posturer, saluter, sitter, sprawler, squatter, straddler.

adj. **3.** **1. postural** attitudinal. **2. reclining** accumbent, decumbent, face downwards, fallen, lying down, procumbent, prone, prostrate, recumbent, resupine, sprawl, spread-eagled, supine. *Informal:* flat out. **3. kneeling** crouching, drooping, stooped. **4. standing** erect, upright.

v. **4.** **1. pose** imitate, position oneself, posture, posturise, square off, square one's shoulders, strike a pose. **2. bear oneself** carry oneself. **3. stand erect** be upstanding, draw oneself up, stand up, stand up properly, stand up straight.

5. **1. repose** couch, lie, lie down, loll, lounge, lying, prostrate, recline, shake, spread-eagle, stretch out. *Informal:* spinebash. **2. sit** sit up. **3. straddle** sit astride, spraddle. **4. genuflect** bend, bow, bow and scrape, cross, curtsy, dip one's lid, hail, have one's knees fold beneath one, kneel, kotow, kowtow, salaam, salute, sink, stoop, uncap, uncover. **5. squat** crouch. *Informal:* kangaroo. **6. slouch** stoop.

adv. **6.** **1. on bended knee** on all fours, on hands and knees, on one's haunches.

RELATED KEYWORDS: ERECTNESS, LEVEL

POSITION

n. **1.** **1. position** line, locality, locus, pitch, place, plot, point, set, set-up, site, situation, situs, spot, station. *Informal:* possie. **2. location** address, whereabouts. **3. locale** haunts, locality, post, setting. *Informal:* stamping ground, stomping ground. **4. rendezvous** collocate, tryst, trysting place, venue.

2. **1. positioning** collocation, composition, configuration, constitution, deployment, deposition, distribution, emplacement, establishment, installation, instatement, layout, localisation, orientation, pitch, placement. **2. echolocation** echo ranging, fix, radiolocation. **3. radar** asdic, Doppler radar, loran, magnetron, minitrack, racon, radar scanner, radio beacon, radio-compass, radiolocation, sonobuoy.

adj. **3.** **1. positioned** disposed, in situ, located, placed, sited, situated.

v. **4.** **1. position** allocate, arrange, bung, determine, draw, emplace, establish, install, instate, localise, locate, lodge, park, perch, pinpoint, pitch, place, plant, posit, post, put, re-position, set, site, situate, stage, station, stick. *Informal:* camp. **2. deploy** collocate, dispose, line, range. **3. lie** rest, sit, stand, take one's place. **4. lay** *Informal:* plank down, plonk down, whack down.

adv. **5.** **1. here** herein, inside, out here. **2. there** ad loc, o'er, over there, thereabouts, thereat, thereby, thither, yonder. **3. at hand** herein, in, on board, on hand, on the scene, on the spot, round, to hand. **4. locally** in loc. cit., in loco, in one's tracks, in situ, on the spot. **5. op. cit.** opere citato. **6. suo loco**.

6. **1. where** where'er, whereabout, whereabouts, whereat, wherein, whereinto, wheresoever, wherever. **2. wherefrom**.

conj. **7.** **1. where** where'er *(Poetic)*, wherein, wherever. **2. whence** whencesoever, wherefrom. **3. whereto** whither. **4. whereabouts** where.

RELATED KEYWORDS: PLACEMENT, PRESENCE

POSSIBILITY

n. **1.** **1. possibility** chance, contingency, eventuality, fighting chance, gamble, half chance, happenstance, liability, likelihood, off-chance, potential, potentiality. **2. feasibility** conceivability, conceivableness, feasibleness, practicability, practicalness, viability, workability, workableness. **3. accessibility** attainability.

2. **1. opportunity** chance, happenstance, occasion, open, open go, opening, possibility, potentiality, resource, room, scope. *Informal:* crack, show. **2. psychological moment** high time, right moment, right time.

adj. **3.** **1. possible** believable, conceivable, contingent, credible, earthly, imaginable, liable, on the cards, open, open-ended, potential, uncertain. *Informal:* chancy. **2. feasible** accessible, accomplishable, achievable, actable, executable, performable, practicable, superable, surmountable, sustainable, viable, within reach, within the bounds of possibility, workable.

v. **4.** **1. be possible** admit of, bear, brook, can, have a chance, may, stand a chance, stand the strain.

5. **1. make possible** admit, afford, allow, bear, capacitate, enable, let, permit.

adv. **6.** **1. possibly** bechance, by chance, maybe, p'raps, perhaps, potentially, practicably. *Informal:* happen *(British)*.

RELATED KEYWORDS: LIKELIHOOD, LUCK

POVERTY

n. **1.** **1. poverty** destitution, distress, impecuniosity, impecuniousness, indigence, miserableness, misery, necessity, need, neediness, pauperism, penuriousness, penury, poorness, privation, starvation, want, wretchedness. **2. impoverishment** deprivation, destitution, pauperisation, privation. **3. beggardom** beggarhood, beggarliness, beggary, hoboism, mendicancy, mendicity. **4. poverty line**.

2. **1. poor person** beadsman, beadswoman, bedesman, cracker *(US)*, derelict, garreteer, have-not, needer, pauper, poor white *(US)*. *Informal:* deadbeat, dero, derro, down-and-out, toe-ragger. **2. beggar** almsman, almswoman, battler, beachcomber, beggarman, mendicant, rogue, starveling, tatterdemalion, tramp, vagabond, vagrant. *Informal:* beat, bum, hobo, swaggie, vag. **3. ragamuffin** cinderella, gamin, guttersnipe, tatterdemalion. *Informal:* mudlark *(British)*. **4. the poor** poor white trash, the have-nots, the other half. *Informal:* trash *(US)*, white trash *(US)*.

3. **1. poorhouse** almshouse, doghouse. **2. slums** shantytown. *Informal:* dump. **3. depressed area** distressed area, ghetto.

adj. **4.** **1. poor** badly off, depressed, destitute, disadvantaged, distressed, dowerless, down at heel, down on one's luck, down to the bottom dollar, down to the last crust, downcast, fortuneless, gone to Gowings, indigent, landless, miserable, needy, on one's beam-ends, on one's uppers, out at elbows, poor as a church mouse, slim, threadbare, underprivileged, without, wretched. *Informal:* hard up, miserable as a bandicoot, poor as a bandicoot, pov. **2. destitute** beggarly, done for, down-and-out, hopeless, impoverished, living on queer street, miserable, naked, on skid row, on the streets, penurious, pitiable, poverty-stricken, slummy, starving, vagrant, wretched. **3. impecunious** bankrupt, bled white, hard-up, out of pocket, penniless, poor, strapped. *Informal:* broke, broke to the wide, bust, dead motherless broke, flat broke, flyblown, on the beach, on the outer, on the strap, skint, skun, stiff, stiff as a crutch, stone-broke, stony, stony-broke, stumped up. **4. bankrupt** broken, ruined. *Informal:* bust.

v. **5.** **1. impoverish** bankrupt, beggar, bleed white, pauperise, ruin, take to the cleaners. *Informal:* bust, clean out, skin. **2. be poor** have empty pockets. *Informal:* be on one's uppers, be short of a quid, not have a bean, not have a dime.

adv. **6.** **1. poorly** comfortlessly, impecuniously, indigently, miserably, on the wrong side of the tracks, penuriously, wretchedly. **2. from hand to mouth** at subsistence level, on a shoestring, on the breadline, on the downgrade.

RELATED KEYWORDS: WORKING CLASS, MISFORTUNE, INDEBTEDNESS

POWDER

n. **1.** **1. powder** dust, grit, pounce. **2. ash** ash fall, ashes, calx, cinders, fly-ash, volcanic ash. **3. sand** black sand *(NZ)*, greensand, shingle. **4. flour** bran, grist, grits, meal. **5. plaster** cement, flock, petuntse, terra alba. **6. ochre** kamala, kohl, mascara, rouge. **7. talcum powder** face powder, sachet, talc. **8. bloom** efflorescence. **9. speck** corn, detritus, filing, fines, grain, mote, particle, seed, spore, sporule. **10. miscellaneous powders** coaldust, confectioners' sugar *(US)*, cosmic dust, crocus, diamond dust, flowers of sulfur, glacial meal, ground glass, gum, icing sugar, platinum black, powdered chalk, powdered charcoal, powdered sugar *(US)*, pumice, rock-flour, sawdust, slack, streak, triturate. *Informal:* bulldust.

2. **1. powderiness** friability, friableness, mealiness. **2. grittiness** sabulosity, sandiness.

3. **1. powdering** abrasion, comminution, detrition, filing, granulation, grind, grinding, levigation, pulverisation, triturate, trituration. **2. milling** dollying, quartz-crushing, rock-crushing.

4. **1. powderer** file, grater, grinder, pouncer, pulveriser, rasp. **2. pestle** dolly, posser. **3. millstone** ball mill, grindstone, mortar, muller, puddling box, puddling tub, spider, stone. **4. mill** colloid mill, flour mill, gristmill, hammermill, hand mill, pestle, quern, roller-mill, stamp mill. **5. konometer**.

adj. **5.** **1. powdery** branlike, efflorescent, flocculent, furfuraceous, grainy, granular, pruinose, pulverulent. **2. floury** farinaceous, flourlike, mealy. **3. ashy** ashen. **4. sandy** arenaceous, dusty, gritty, sabulous, sand-like.

6. **1. powdered** desiccated, ground, kibble, milled, pulverised, sifted, stoneground. **2. fine** crumby, impalpable, light, pulverable, pulverisable.

v. **7.** **1. powder** abrade, bray, bruise, comminute, crumble, crunch, crush, levigate, mash, pestle, pound, pulverise, rasp, stamp, triturate. **2. pestle** dolly, puddle. **3. grind** file, grate, gride, kibble, mill, rasp, razor, sand, sandblast. **4. granulate** corn, grain. **5. effloresce** come to dust, crumble, disintegrate, fall to dust, moulder, reduce to powder, tetter.

RELATED KEYWORDS: SMALLNESS, LIGHTNESS, RUBBING

POWER

n. **1.** **1. power** authority, force, forcefulness, manpower, marrow, might, mightiness, pith, potence, potency, potentness, powerfulness, strength. **2. dominion** control, domain, dominance, domination, empire, generalship, governance, government, jurisdiction, lordship, rule, sovereignty, supremacy. **3. influence** charisma, clout, energy, hidden hand, hold, impression, leverage, mana, operation, pressure, sway, vigour, vim, virtue, weight. *Informal:* mojo *(Chiefly US)*, push, wallop.

2. **1. predominance** advantage, almightiness, ascendancy, ascendant, dominance, hegemony, pre-eminence, predomination, preponderance, preponderation, superhumanity, supremeness. **2. supremacy** absolute power, dominion, empire, omnipotence. **3. autocracy** despotism, dictatorship, lordship, monocracy, police state, tsarism, tyranny.

3. **1. capability** ability, capableness, capacity, faculty, power. **2. effectiveness** cogency, effectualness, efficaciousness, efficacy, forcefulness, forcibility, operativeness, strength, virtuousness.

4. **1. powerful person** éminence grise, Big Brother, boss of the board, bwana, cock of the walk, grey eminence, high priest, high-flyer, maluka, Mr Big, omnipotent, oppressor, plenipotentiary, predominator, strongman, tycoon. *Informal:* boss, boss cocky, head serang, the old man, top banana, top dog. **2. autocrat** absolute ruler, ayatollah, Caesar, despot, dictator, oligarch, overlord, paramount, robber baron, shogun, supremo, tyrant, war lord. **3. power behind the throne** crowner of kings, kingmaker. **4. the Establishment** vested interests. **5. effective person** prime mover. *Informal:* dynamo, operator.

adj. **5.** **1. powerful** almighty, armipotent, elemental, indomitable, mighty, omnipotent, overpowering, plenipotent, potent, staunch, strong. **2. all-powerful** almighty, minister plenipotentiary, omnipotent, plenipotentiary. **3. authoritative** commanding, dictatorial, magisterial, masterful. **4. domineering** authoritarian, autocratic, dictatorial, doctrinaire, dogmatic, exacting, fascist, feudal, high-handed, imperial, imperious, imposing, lordly, magisterial, officious, opinionated, opinionative, overbearing, overruling, peremptory, pushy, totalitarian, tsarist, tyrannical. *Informal:* bossy.

6. **1. predominant** ascendant, authoritative, chief, competent, culminant, dominant, dominating, eminent, high-flying, imperial, master, paramount, pre-eminent, preponderant, preponderating, prepotent, prevailing, regnant, sovereign, superior, supreme, top, top-line, topmost, upmost, upper, uppermost.

7. **1. capable** able. **2. effective** cogent, effectual, efficacious, emphatic, energetic, forcible, operative, potent, telling, vigorous. *Informal:* mean, punchy. **3. energetic** cracking, exertive, high-performance, high-powered, jazzy, lively, overwhelming, pushing, red-blooded, sledge-hammer, spirited, spirítoso, vigoroso, vigorous, vivacious.

v. **8.** **1. have power** control, dictate, dominate, have carte blanche, hold in fee *(Poetic)*, hold sway over, hold the balance of power, reign, ride, rule. *Informal:* put the maginnis on. **2. predominate** in the saddle, outbalance, outvote, outweigh, overbalance, preponderate, prevail, surmount. **3. surmount** be in the ascendant, have one's day, triumph. **4. be effective** have clout, have teeth.

adv. **9.** **1. powerfully** almightily, omnipotently, potently, puissantly. **2. authoritatively** commandingly, masterfully. **3. forcefully** forcibly, mightily, powerfully, strong, strongly, vigorously, with might and main. **4. domineeringly** autocratically, dictatorially, imperiously, tyrannically. **5. energetically** emphatically, raunchily, spunkily, vigorously.

10. **1. predominantly** eminently, pre-eminently, predominatingly, preponderantly, preponderatingly, prepotently, sovereignly, supremely.

11. **1. capably** ably. **2. effectively** cogently, effectually, efficaciously, forcefully, forcibly, operatively, tellingly, virtuously.

RELATED KEYWORDS: AUTHORITY, COMPETENCE, FORCE, INSISTENCE, REPRESSION, STRENGTH, SUPERIORITY

POWERLESSNESS

n. **1.** **1. powerlessness** debility, decrepitude, dotage, exhaustion, feebleness, floccillation, helplessness, impuissance, inability, inanition, incapability, incapableness, incapacity, incompetence, ineptitude, languor, lassitude, marasmus, milkiness, prostration, senility, tabes, weakness. **2. enervation** ataxia, caducity, debilitation, decay, enfeeblement, impalement, impoverishment, incapacitation, paralysis, senility, slough, wane. **3. asthenia** adynamia, anergy, atony, atrophy, consumption, infirmity, malaise, myasthenia, phthisis. **4. impotence** *Informal:* brewer's droop.

  2. **1. ineffectualness** futility, ineffectiveness, ineffectuality, inefficaciousness, inefficacity, inefficacy, inefficiency, inutility, nullity, uselessness, voidness.

  3. **1. ineffectual person** asthenic, dead duck, dingo, dotard, eunuch, lily, milksop, paper tiger, poltroon, recreant, sheep, skulk, spado, squib, weakling, wheyface, wreck. *Informal:* alf, aunty, cream puff, creamer, cry-baby, deadhead, funk, gussie, nancy boy, nine day wonder, old woman, pansy, ponce, poof, poofter, quiche-eater, ringtail, sis, sissy, softie, sook, sop, weakie, wimp. **2. dud** *Informal:* brummy, fizzer. **3. has-been** *Informal:* disso, retread.

adj. **4.** **1. powerless** dependent, doddered, effete, emptied, expugnable, feeble, helpless, hopeless, impotent, impuissant, incapable, ineffectual, inept, inutile, invalid, nerveless, on one's last legs, otiose, unable, unavailing, useless, vain, void, weak, weakling. *Informal:* limp-wristed, pooncey, sawney, wimpy. **2. incapacitated** castrated, crippled, debilitated, enervate, enervated, irreparable, neutralised, paralysed, screwed up. *Informal:* buggered, scrammy, shot, washed-out, washed-up. **3. ataxic** adynamic, asthenic, atactic, atrophied, avirulent, non-virulent. **4. decrepit** doddering, doting, feeble, gone (or run) to seed, infirm, obsolete, past one's prime, senile. *Informal:* gaga, geriatric, over the hill, past it, superannuated. **5. good-for-nothing** inept, milky, milquetoast, pathetic, prostrate, useless, vagabond. *Informal:* sissy.

  5. **1. ineffectual** adiaphorous, bootless, cardboard cutout, empty, futilitarian, helpless, idle, imperfect, in chancery, ineffective, inefficacious, inefficient, inept, non-effective, nugatory, null, null and void, Sisyphean, useless, vain, void. *Informal:* brummy, not able to fight one's way out of a (wet) (or brown) paper bag.

  6. **1. enervating** castrating, enervative, exhausting, exhaustive, gorgonian.

adv. **7.** **1. powerlessly** impotently, ineffectually.

  8. **1. ineffectually** helplessly, incapably, ineffectively, inefficaciously.

   RELATED KEYWORDS: FAILURE, INCOMPETENCE, WEAKNESS

PRECISION

n. **1.** **1. precision** accuracy, accurateness, correctness, exactness, niceness, nicety, preciseness, squareness, unerringness. **2. exactness** accuracy, definitude, exactitude, fidelity, preciseness, precision, punctiliousness, rightness, veracity. **3. alignment** face edge, face side, register, tram, true, trueness, working edge, working face. **4. sharpness** acuity, definition. **5. regulation** adjustment, calibration, ensendation. **6. formulation** formularisation, formulisation. **7. literality** explicitness, literalism, literalness, the letter of the law. **8. strictness** pedantry, scrupulosity, severeness, severity. **9. punctilio** technicality.

  2. **1. precisionist** elaborator, formulator, formuliser, literaliser, literalist, paedagogue, pedant, perfectionist, refiner.

adj. **3.** **1. precise** accurate, exact, in focus, pat, perfect, pinpoint, right on, sharp, strict, very. *Informal:* bang-on, on the beam, spot-on. **2. unambiguous** apparent, articulate, as plain as a pikestaff, audible, candid, clean-cut, clear, clear-cut, definite, distinct, evident, obvious, plain, sharp-cut, specific, unequivocal, univocal, unmistakable. **3. minute** detailed, fine, particular, specific. **4. measured** calculated, definite, determinate, exact, mathematical, nicely calculated, precise, strict, unerring, well-defined. **5. explicit** elaborate, elaborative, express, identical. **6. true** even, flush, level, uniform. **7. made-to-measure** made-to-order, precut, ready-made. **8. punctilious** fastidious, meticulous, punctual, rigorous, scrupulous, severe. *Informal:* pernickety. **9. pedantic** donnish, pedantical. **10. refined** correct, exact, nice, proper, pukka, right, rigid, strict, tight. **11. literal** matter-of-fact, practical, technical. **12. letter-perfect** verbal, verbatim, word perfect.

v. **4.** **1. be precise** take care. *Informal:* dot one's i's and cross one's t's, mind one's p's and q's. **2. get it right** hit the nail on the head. **3. elaborate** emendate, quote chapter and verse, refine. **4. literalise.** **5. formulate** abstract, boil down, digest, encapsulate, formularise, formulise, outline, precis, sum up, summarise. **6. regulate** emend, tram. *Informal:* get technical. **7. pinpoint** bring into focus, define, true. *Informal:* register.

adv. **5.** **1. precisely** accurately, directly, just, minutely, squarely, strictly, to a nicety, to a t, truly, unerringly, with clockwork precision. **2. exactly** dead, dead-centre, directly, flat, full, just, plumb. *Informal:* slap-bang, square. **3. measuredly** mathematically, scientifically. **4. flush** true. **5. punctiliously** punctually, scrupulously. **6. pedantically** donnishly. **7. verbatim** ad litteram, ad verbum, explicitly, literally, literatim, off pat, pat, sic, to the letter, word for word.

RELATED KEYWORDS: DISCERNMENT, MEASUREMENT, PROPRIETY

PREDICTION

n. **1.** **1. prediction** bodement, forecast, prognostic, prognostication, prophecy, self-fulfilling prophecy, soothsaying, vaticination. **2. forecast** cast, presage, prognosis, prognostic, prognostication. **3. estimate** approximation, cost estimate, cost-benefit analysis, predicted cost, quantity survey. *Informal:* guesstimate. **4. tip** nap *(Horseracing)*. **5. promise** reason to hope, something to look forward to.

2. **1. omen** augury, auspice, boding, foreboding, forerunner, forewarning, harbinger, herald, portent, premonition, presage, presentiment, prognostic, sign, signifier, type, writing on the wall. **2. harbinger of evil** death knell, premonition of death, time bomb. **3. destiny** doom, fatality, fate, fortune, karma, kismet, lot, predestination, star.

3. **1. fortune-telling** alomancy, astrology, augurship, augury, ballgazing, cartomancy, chirognomy, chiromancy, clairvoyance, crystal-gazing, divination, divining, ESP, extrasensory perception, extrasensory perception, foretelling, futurology, hand-reading, metagnomy, onomancy, palmistry, prefiguration, prefigurement, prognostication, second sight, soothsaying, tephramancy, vaticination. **2. crystal ball** crystal, fortune cookie. **3. horoscope** ascendant, aspect, constellation, house, midheaven, nativity, planet, sign, star. **4. signs of the zodiac** Aquarius, Aries, Cancer, Capricorn, Gemini, Leo, Libra, Pisces, Sagittarius, Scorpio, Taurus, Virgo. **5. palmistry** chirognomy, hand-reading. **6. palmistry terms** fate line, headline, heart line, lifeline, line of happiness, line of health, line of wealth, mount, mount (or mound) of Venus, mount of the moon, rascette, simian line. **7. tarot cards** Judgement, lesser arcanum, major arcanum, minor arcanum, the Fool, the Hanged Man, the Moon, the wheel of Fortune, triumph card, trump. **8. tarot suits** cups, pentacles, swords, wands.

4. **1. predictor** augur, clairvoyant, diviner, foreboder, foreteller, geomancer, haruspex, oneiromancer, oracle, presager, prognosticator, prophesier, prophet, seer, soothsayer, vaticinator. **2. prophet of doom** cassandra, jeremiah.

5. **1. fortune teller** astrologist, ballgazer, chiromancer, crystal-gazer, futurologist, numerologist, palmist, rhabdomantist, stargazer, water diviner, water witch *(US)*, waterfinder.

6. **1. divination methods** aeromancy, alectryomancy, aleuromancy, alphitomancy, anthropomancy, anthroposcopy, apantomancy, arithmomancy, austromancy, belomancy, bibliomancy, bletonism, botanomancy, capnomancy, catoptromancy, causimomancy, cephaleonomancy, ceraunoscopy, ceromancy, chaomancy, chiromancy, cleromancy, clidomancy, coscinomancy, crithomancy, crystallomancy, dactyliomancy, geomancy, gyromancy, halomancy, hand-reading, haruspicy, hieromancy, hydromancy, ichthyomancy, libanomancy, lithomancy, meteoromancy, myomancy, necromancy, numerology, oenomancy, oneiromancy, onomancy, ophiomancy, ornithomancy, palmistry, pegomancy, pessomancy, psephomancy, pyromancy, rhabdomancy, sciomancy, sortilege, stichomancy, sycomancy, tasseography, tephramancy, theomancy, xylomancy.

adj. **7.** **1. predictive** oracular, portentous, prefigurative, prognosticative, significative. **2. prophetic** all-seeing, augural, auspicial, clairvoyant, divinatory, fateful, fatidic, mantic, oracular, prognostic, vatic, vaticinal, weatherwise, zodiacal. **3. auspicious** promising. **4. ominous** boding, fateful, foreboding, ill-boding, ill-fated, ill-omened, ill-starred, inauspicious, portentous, prophetic, sinister, sinistrous.

v. **8.** **1. predict** augur, bode, divine, forebode, forecast, foresee, foretell, forewarn, harbinger, herald, presage, presignify, previse, prognosticate, prophesy, read, see, shadow forth, soothsay, vaticinate. **2. promise** bid fair to, point to, raise expectations, raise hopes. **3. signify** imply, indicate, portend, spell, suggest. **4. tell someone's fortune** cast a horoscope. **5. cross someone's palm with silver** have one's fortune told. **6. warn** bode, forebode, omen, portend, presage. **7. prefigure** adumbrate, foreshadow, foreshow, foretell, foretoken, pretypify. **8. tip** nap *(Horseracing)*. **9. estimate** conjecture, cost, guess, judge, take a stab at.

adv. **9.** **1. predictively** mantically, oracularly, prophetically. **2. ominously** bodingly, forebodingly, sinisterly.

RELATED KEYWORDS: ANTICIPATION, EXPECTATION, THE FUTURE, THE SUPERNATURAL

PREPAREDNESS

n.   **1.**   **1. preparedness** alertness, anticipation, preparation, readiness. **2. preparations** arrangements, hedge, make-ready, plan, precaution, preparative, provision, scramble. **3. groundwork** foundation, training. **4. rehearsal** boat drill, discipline, dismounted drill, dress rehearsal, drill, dry run, dummy run, exercise, exercitation, field trial, fire drill, full-dress rehearsal, haute école, hit-up, knock-up *(Chiefly British)*, pilot study, practice, road test, run-through, skeleton exercise, trial, trial run, tryout, walk-through, war game, warm-up, work-out. **5. stand-by** red alert. **6. countdown** lead time.

adj.   **2.**   **1. prepared** fit, in readiness, in working order, on tap, operational, ready, set. *Informal:* on one's toes, raring to go. **2. forearmed** in battle array, in battle-readiness, sword in hand. **3. in one's best bib and tucker** *Informal:* dressed to kill, dressed to the nines, with one's warpaint on. **4. previously prepared** already prepared, prerecorded, ready-made. *Informal:* canned *(Chiefly US)*.

    3.   **1. preparatory** introductory, isagogic, precursory, prefatory, preliminary, prelusive, preparative, prolegomenous, prolusory, propaedeutic. *Informal:* prep.

v.   **4.**   **1. prepare** accoutre, address, appoint, arm, arrange, equip, fit, fit out, furbish, furnish, gear, gear up, get into working order, get ready, kit, make ready, make up, prime, refit, set someone up, turn out, win. *Informal:* prep. **2. prime** cock, unlimber. **3. dress** curry, forward, gather, lick into shape, taw. **4. bring to readiness** arrange, brew, cogitate, concert, concoct, contrive, design, devise, gestate, hatch, incubate, mature, prepare, project, propose, ripen. **5. train** apprentice, bring up to form, bring up to scratch, coach, cultivate, drill, educate, familiarise, groom, ground in, implant, inculcate, indoctrinate, instil, instruct, mark, practise, rehearse, run through, school, teach, tutor. **6. make preparations** address oneself to, arrange, chalk out *(British)*, chart, close ranks, cook up a plan, draw up, engineer, gather together, get one's act together, lay out, lead up to, make, make provision, map out, organise, plan, prepare, take steps. *Informal:* calculate *(US)*, do one's homework, jack *(NZ)*, tee up. **7. prepare oneself** buckle down, clear the decks, get into harness, gird (up) one's loins, gird oneself (up) for, go into training, roll up one's sleeves, set one's house in order. **8. anticipate** expect, foreknow, forerun, foresee, look ahead, pre-empt, preconceive, predict, prediction, presage, prophecy, provide against a rainy day, provide for the future, see.

adv.   **5.**   **1. preparedly** at hand, at the ready, in hand, in the wings, on call, on ice, on stand-by, on the qui vive. **2. ready and waiting** in the pipeline, in the press, under consideration, up one's sleeve. **3. in preparation** afoot, in embryo, in train, on the drawing board, on the stocks.

interj.   **6.**   **1. get ready** get set, on your block(s), on your mark(s), take your places.

    RELATED KEYWORDS: ANTICIPATION, COMPETENCE, SUPPLY

PRESENCE

n.   **1.**   **1. presence** appearance, company, immanence, immanency, occupancy, occupation. **2. attendance** audience, durbar, presence, turn-up. **3. omnipresence** incidence, ubiquitousness, ubiquity.

adj.   **2.**   **1. present** as large as life, attendant. **2. immanent** essential, ingrained, inherent, innate, intrinsic. **3. omnipresent** ubiquitous.

v.   **3.**   **1. be present** attend, gatecrash, lie at, lie in, occupy, sit in on, take one's place. *Informal:* front, hang, hang on. **2. habituate** frequent, hang around, haunt. *Informal:* hang about, mooch, stick around. **3. stay** sojourn, stick on, stop, stop over, tarry, visit.

prep.   **4.**   **1. at** chez.

    RELATED KEYWORDS: ARRIVAL, ACTUALITY, ENTRANCE, POSITION

THE PRESENT

n.   **1.**   **1. the present** now, nowadays, the here and now, the instant, the present juncture, the present moment, the present time, the times, today, tonight. **2. immediacy** immediateness.

adj.   **2.**   **1. current** immediate, instant, live, now happening, passing, running. **2. immediate** current, instant, last, latest. **3. existing** actual, present. **4. contemporary** cotemporary, current, living, modern-day, present-day, rife, up-to-date. **5. modern** fashionable, in, in fashion, modernist, modernistic, neoteric, new-fashioned, recent, ultrafashionable, up-to-date, up-to-the-minute, up-to-the-moment, with-it. *Informal:* cool, mod, now, swinging, trendy, wired.

adv.   **3.**   **1. now** as of now, at present, at the present moment, at this point in time, before one's very eyes, currently, for the nonce, for the time being, here and now, in the short run, just now, nowadays, presently, still. **2. directly** outright, right, straight. **3. today** nowadays, tonight. **4. to date** as yet. **5. already** even, still, yet. **6. immediately** at once, away, directly, forthwith, instantly, momentarily *(Chiefly US)*, on the spot, on the spur of the moment, quick smart, right, right away, straightaway. *Informal:* asap, pronto.

RELATED KEYWORDS: FASHION, NEWNESS, SIMULTANEITY

PRESERVATION

n.   **1.**   **1. preservation** bottling, canning, cold storage, cryopreservation, dehydration, desiccation, ensilage, freeze-drying, hydro-cooling, pickling, refrigeration. **2. insulation** insulator, lagging, mineral wool, rock-wool. **3. proofing** fireproofing, resist, waterproofing. **4. embalmment** mummification, taxidermy. **5. conservation** conservancy, environmentalism. **6. green ban**.

    2.   **1. preserver** embalmer, salter, taxidermist. **2. caretaker** aquarist, archivist, conservator, curator, custodian, gamekeeper, guard, guardian, janitor, keeper, nightwatchman, warden, watchman. **3. conservationist** environmentalist, nature lover, preservationist. *Informal:* greenie, tree hugger.

    3.   **1. nature reserve** chase, flora and fauna reserve, game reserve, marine sanctuary, national park, native reserve, reserve, sanctuary. **2. national estate** heritage item.

    4.   **1. environmental management** biobank, biodiversity credit, environmental impact assessment, environmental impact statement, environmental impact study, interim conservation order.

adj.   **5.**   **1. preserved** alcoholic, canned *(Chiefly US)*, corned, cryovac, cured, frozen, pickled, potted, salt, salted, smoked, sun-cured, tinned, vacuum-packed, vacuum-sealed. **2. conserved** preserved, protected, safeguarded. **3. coated** rainproof, showerproof, waterproof. **4. fireproof** fire-resistant, flame-resistant, flameproof. **5. stuffed** taxidermic.

v.   **6.**   **1. preserve** bottle, brine, can, conserve, corn, cure, dehydrate, desiccate, dry, ensilage, ensile, freeze-dry, ice, jerk, keep, kipper, lyophilise, pickle, pot, put up, refrigerate, salt, salt away (or down), silo, smoke, souse, tin. **2. conserve** husband, keep, preserve, protect, safeguard, save. **3. proof** all-weather, fireproof, prove, rainproof, showerproof, waterproof. **4. plate** cellulose, underseal. **5. embalm** fix, lay out, mummify, mummy, stuff.

RELATED KEYWORDS: REPAIR, PROTECTION, SAFETY, SHELTER

PRESSURE

n.   **1.**   **1. pressure** air-pressure, critical pressure, fluid pressure, gauge pressure, nip, osmotic pressure, pressure head, shock wave, superdensity, trigger pressure, vapour pressure. **2. strain** stress, tension.

    2.   **1. pressing** constriction, detrusion, expression, extrusion, impaction, ironing, jam, milling, nip, pinch, press, scrunch, squash, squeeze, strangulation, trample, vellication.

    3.   **1. imprint** die, impression, print, stamp, touch.

    4.   **1. press** ball mill, box iron, calender, colloid mill, cramp, cramp iron, cylinder, cylinder press, garbage compactor, hammermill, mill, monkey, oil-press, pestle, pug mill, ram, road-roller, roll, roller-mill, rolling mill, rolling pin, stamp mill, stamp-head, steamroller, supercalender, wine press, wool press. **2. iron** clothes press, flatiron, fluting iron, hot-press, mangle, smoothing-iron, steam iron. **3. stamp** clicking press, imprinter, puncheon, stamper. **4. presser** ironer, trampler, treader. **5. compressor** booster, pump, supercharger. **6. extruder** crush, crusher, mangle, squasher, squeezer, squelcher, wringer. **7. tourniquet**. **8. clamp** clench, clip, nippers, pincers, pinchcock, pinchers, vice.

    5.   **1. pressure unit** bar, barye, foot, foot of water, inch, inch of mercury, inch of water, kilopascal, millibar, millimetre of mercury, pascal, standard atmosphere, torr. **2. isobar** isopiestic. **3. piezometry** hydrostatics.

    6.   **1. pressure gauge** altimeter, aneroid, aneroid barometer, barometer, Bourdon gauge, dynamometer, Fortin's barometer, gravimeter, indicator, manometer, mercury barometer, meteorograph, microbarograph, osmometer, piezometer, static-pressure tube, statoscope, thermobarometer, vacuum gauge.

adj.   **7.**   **1. pressed** adpressed, compact, compressed, condensed, dense, extrusive, impacted, incuse, milled, superdense.

v.   **8.**   **1. press** beat out, calender, iron, iron out, mangle, mill, pestle, steamroller, supercalender. **2. pressurise** squelch, supercharge, trample, tread. **3. compress** affix, astringe, clamp, clench, clip, constrict, depress, detrude, impact, jam, knead, nip, pack, pinch, pug, scrunch, squash, squeeze, strangulate, vice. **4. squeeze out** crush, express, extrude, pump out, wring off, wring out. **5. impress** hallmark, imprint, incuse, print, seal, stamp, touch, trace.

RELATED KEYWORDS: HEAVINESS, HOLD, RUBBING

PRINTING

n. **1.** **1. printing** engraving, letterpress, lithography, screen-printing, silk-screening, typography. **2. typesetting** composition, computer typesetting, filmsetting, photocomposition, phototypesetting.

2. **1. publication** edition, impression, offprint, preprint, revision. **2. print run** edition, final, impression, issue, overprint, overrun, printing, vanity edition. **3. imprint** colophon. **4. page** bleed, column, crosshead, crossheading, fold-out, fore edge, gatefold, guard, insert, lift-out, measure, overmatter, overset, run-around, run-in, sheet, spill, tibby. **5. folio** duodecimo, quarto, sexto, sextodecimo, signature, sixteenmo, thirty-twomo, trigesimo-secundo, twelvemo. **6. copy** artwork, body matter, counterpart, fudge, letterpress, matter, transcription, typescript. **7. presswork** backup, imposition, makeready, overlay, register. **8. format** dummy, mock-up, paste-up.

3. **1. printing press** addressograph, composing machine, cylinder press, electrograph, flat-bed cylinder press, intertype, line printer, linotype, perfector, platen, rotary press, stop-cylinder press, typesetter. **2. typeface** face, fixed type, font, form, fount, matrix, movable type, pie, type.

4. **1. printing person** bookbinder, chromolithographer, compositor, copyeditor, copyholder, copytaker, devil, engraver, filmsetter, lithographer, photoengraver, pressman, printer, printer's devil, proofreader, reader, stereotyper, stonehand, typefounder, typesetter, typographer, zincographer. *Informal:* clicker. **2. printing machine** bubble-jet printer, daisy-wheel printer, dot-matrix printer, dye-sub printer, dye-sublimation printer, inkjet printer, jet printer, laser printer, line printer, phase-change printer, photocopier, teleprinter, thermal image transfer printer, thermal printer, typewriter. **3. printery** composing room, press, printers.

5. **1. printing** cerotype, chromolithography, collotype, copperplate, die-stamping, driography, duotone printing, electrography, engraving, etching, flexography, foil printing, four-colour printing, gravure, halftone, halftone printing, intaglio, letterpress, linotype, lithography, logography, metallography, monotype, offset, oleography, photo-offset, photoengraving, photogravure, photolithography, phototypy, planography, process printing, relief, rotogravure, steel engraving, stereotype, stereotypy, web-offset, zincography.

6. **1. block** copperplate, cut, electro, electrotype, engraving, founders' type, halfstone, logo, logotype, metal, mortice, mould, photoelectrotype, photoengraving, photogravure, plate, standing matter, stereotype, wood, woodblock, woodcut, zincograph. **2. forme** bed, bray, brayer, case, chase, composing stick, copyholder, cylinder, dabber, frisket, furniture, galley, hairspace, imposing stone, ink table, lead, leading, lower case, mat, overlay, quad, quadrat, quoin, rocker, rule, scaleboard, sidestick, slab, slug, space, stick, stone, table, transfer-paper, tympan, underlay, upper case, white, white line. **3. ink** colour, ribbon, weight.

7. **1. typeface** antique, arbitrary, black-letter, blackface, block letter, bold face, church text, condensed type, cursive, extrabold, feint, Gothic, hairline, italics, modern, Old English, old style, peculiar, phonotype, ronde, script, sorts, special sort. **2. type size** agate *(US)*, brilliant, canon, diamond, elite, gem, ruby, two-line brevier. **3. case** capitals, caps, lower case, majuscule, minuscule, small letters, upper case. **4. body** ascender, beard, counter, descender, foot, neck, serif, shank, shoulder. **5. type measure** cicero, em, en, nut, pica, point.

8. **1. proof** dyeline, foundry proof, galley proof, ozalid, page proof, press proof, proof sheet, reproduction proof, slip. **2. print** chromo, chromolithograph, halftone, lithograph, oleograph, photolithograph, printout.

v. **9.** **1. print** print out, run off, type. **2. go to press** put to bed. **3. lithograph** engrave, linotype, offset, overlay, photoengrave, photolithograph. **4. set** compose, filmset, handset, typeset. **5. justify** overrun, overset, white. **6. italicise** bold, capitalise, underline.

RELATED KEYWORDS: IMITATION, BOOK, WRITING

PROFIT

n. **1.** **1. profit** advantage, benefit, fruit of one's labours, gain, remuneration, reward. **2. financial profit** bonus, capital gains, clearings, commission, dividend, dividend rate, earnings, earnings per share, earnings yield, franked dividend, gains, graft, gross profits, income, increase, interest, issue, money, net profit, percentage, plus, proceeds, return, returns, revenue, share, take, takings, the main chance, windfall profits, yield. *Informal:* bunce *(British)*, clean-up, dibs, divvies, divvy, gravy, rake-off, velvet. **3. spoils** booty, filthy lucre, haul, loot, lucre, pillage, plunder, prize, proceeds, spoil, takings, theft, unjust enrichment. *Informal:* a fast (or quick) buck, something that fell off the back of a truck. **4. money-spinner** a sprat to catch a mackerel, cash cow, goldmine. **5. advantage** grist to the mill, leverage.

adj. **2. 1. profitable** advantageous, beneficial, engrossing, gainful, lucrative, monopolising, productive, remunerative, worthwhile. **2. making a profit** ahead, better off, in pocket, running at a profit, showing a profit, to the good.

v. **3. 1. profit** advantage, avail, benefit, cash in on, exploit, make capital of, make money, profiteer, reap great reward. *Informal:* clean up, strike (or hit) paydirt.

4. 1. gain accrue, accumulate, acquire, acquisition, annex, attain, bring home, catch, clear, collect, come by, come into, earn, fetch, gather, get, get hold of, have, lay one's hands on, obtain, pocket, procure, realise, receive, recover, secure, take out, take over, take possession, win, wrest. *Informal:* cop, git, land, scrounge, sub. **2. earn** gross, net. **3. reach** accede to, attain to, get to, reach to.

RELATED KEYWORDS: BUYING, FINDING, ACQUIREMENT, FINANCE, HOLD, OWNERSHIP, WEALTH

PROHIBITION

n. **1. 1. prohibition** ban, charging order, enjoiner, enjoinment, injunction, interdict *(Scottish Law)*, interdiction, writ of prohibition. **2. debarment** bar, inhibition, injunction, interdict *(Scottish Law)*, veto. **3. black ban** black list, boycott, embargo, Expurgatory Index, Index of Prohibited Books. **4. prohibited item** contraband. **5. taboo** juju, no-go. *Informal:* no-no. **6. disqualification** disability, impediment, impedimenta, impediments, incapability, incapableness, incapacity. **7. censorship** bowdlerisation, bowdlerism, comstockery *(Chiefly US)*. **8. repression** containment, control, extinction, hindrance, limitation, proscription, restraint, restriction, suppression. **9. disablement** exclusiveness, inadmissibility, incapacitation, ineligibility. **10. impermissibility** no-go.

2. 1. prohibiter bowdleriser, censor, censorship, forbidder, inhibiter, Lord Chamberlain, proscriber, vetoer. **2. killjoy** jeremiah. *Informal:* snufflebuster, wowserdom. **3. prohibitionist** teetotaller. *Informal:* dry *(US)*.

adj. **3. 1. prohibited** black, forbidden, haram, impermissible, inadmissible, ineffable, not to be countenanced, not to be thought of, off-limits, out of bounds, verboten. **2. contraband** backstreet, banned, black, bootleg *(Chiefly US)*, illegal, illicit, sly, unauthorised, unlawful. **3. taboo** forbidden fruit, unclean. **4. ineligible** incapable, incompetent, unfit. **5. closed** close. **6. unlicensed** backyard, colorum *(Philippine English)*, unregistered.

4. 1. prohibitive censorial, exclusive, injunctive, interdictory, proscriptive.

v. **5. 1. prohibit** ban, be not on, be out, blue-pencil, bowdlerise, censor, clip someone's wings, enjoin, forbid, inhibit, interdict, lower the boom on, outlaw, proclaim, proscribe, taboo. **2. debar** banish, bar, disbar, dismiss, disqualify, drum out, exclude, expel, forbid, interdict, outlaw, preclude, rule out, send down *(British)*, shut, shut out, strike off, unchurch, unfrock, warn off. **3. disallow** ban, black-list, forbid the banns, inhibit, kill, make taboo, outlaw, overrule, repress, veto. **4. disqualify** disable, incapacitate, unfit. **5. blackban** blackball, boycott, declare black, embargo, ostracise, send to coventry, unfit.

adv. **6. 1. prohibitively** proscriptively. **2. in no way** on no account. **3. inadmissibly** exclusively, ineligibly.

RELATED KEYWORDS: CANCELLATION, COMMAND, EXCLUSION, UNLAWFULNESS, REFUSAL

PROMISCUITY

n. **1. 1. promiscuity** bawdry, licence, looseness, promiscuousness, unchastity. **2. profligacy** profligateness, raffishness, rakishness. **3. lechery** goatishness, lecherousness, libertinage, libertinism, licentiousness.

2. 1. promiscuous person alley cat, callboy, callgirl, cocotte, courtesan, drab, harlot, hospitality girl *(Philippine English)*, hussy, jezebel, light-o'-love *(British, US)*, man-eater, nightwalker, painted woman, prostitute, quean, scarlet woman, sex worker, slut, streetwalker, taxi girl, trollop, wanton, white slave, whore. *Informal:* aspro, bagswinger, battler, bike, chromo, crow, floozy, goodtime girl, gunnie, ho *(US)*, hooer, hooker, kelly, kewpie, lowheel, moll, nympho, office bike, player, pro, prossie, rent boy, scrubber *(Chiefly British)*, second-hand Sue, skank, slack, slag, slapper *(Chiefly British)*, slurry, tart, tom

(British), town bike, tramp, worker, working boy, working girl. **2. lecher** Casanova, debauchee, Don Juan, ladies' man, libertine, Lothario, philanderer, profligate, rake, roué, satyr, stud, wencher, womaniser. *Informal:* boudoir bandicoot, buaya *(Singaporean and Malaysian English)*, d.o.m., daddy, dirty old man, goat, lad, lady-killer, lech, pants man, slut, sugar daddy, wolf.

adj. **3. 1. promiscuous** concupiscent, Cyprian, dissolute, fast, free, free-living, fruity, hircine, immoral, indecent, intemperate, lascivious, lewd, libertine, licentious, light, loose, permissive, salacious, scabrous, sensual, swinging, trashy, unchaste, unvirtuous, vicious, wanton. *Informal:* cheap, easy, ripe, slack, toey. **2. on the street** on the streets. **3. harlot** lewd, sluttish, whorish. **4. lecherous** bawdy, concupiscent, earthy, erotic, Fescennine, goatish, hot, lascivious, libidinous, lubricious, lustful, lusty, on heat, oversexed, phallic, priapic, profligate, racy, raffish, rakish, rampant, raunchy, ribald, salacious, satyric. *Informal:* buaya *(Singaporean and Malaysian English)*, on the make, randy.

v. **4. 1. be promiscuous** prostitute, put out, run around, sleep around, swing the bag, whore. *Informal:* lech onto someone, swing. **2. philander** debauch, fornicate, sow one's wild oats, wench, whore, womanise. **3. seduce** debauch, deflower, ruin. *Informal:* make. **4. rape** force, gang rape, ravish, violate.

RELATED KEYWORDS: OVERINDULGENCE, SEX, VOLUPTUOUSNESS

PROPERTY

n. **1. 1. property** appanage, assets, capital, endowment, holdings, one's all, peculium, possessions, principal, proprietary, resources, salvage, settlement, substance, temporalities, temporals, thirds, wealth, worth. **2. dowry** bride price, dot, dower, dower house, jointure, marriage portion, marriage settlement, portion. **3. estate** bequest, coinheritance, deceased estate, first estate, heirdom, heirloom, hereditament, heritage, inheritance, legacy, patrimony, reversion, second estate, taluk. **4. after-acquired property** escheat. **5. fixed assets** capital assets, capital goods. **6. liquid assets** current assets, floating assets, liquidity. **7. stocks and shares** blue chip, capital stock, gilt-edged investment, stock.

2. 1. personal property belongings, collectibles, effects, equipment, gear, goods, goods and chattels, household goods, lares and penates, moveables, paraphernalia, personal effects, personalty, stock-in-trade, tangibles, things. **2. article of personal property** chattel, chattel personal, chose, fixture, moveables, taonga *(NZ)*.

3. 1. real estate airspace, country seat, demesne, domain, dominant estate, dominant tenement, entail, estate, fee, fee simple, fee tail, feoff, fief, freehold, immoveables, land, lordship, manor, mesnalty, real property, realty, seigneury, seigniory, servient tenement, tenements, thanage.

RELATED KEYWORDS: FINANCE, OWNERSHIP, PROFIT, WEALTH

PROPRIETY

n. **1. 1. propriety** appropriateness, becomingness, correctness, decency, decentness, decorousness, decorum, ijma, irreproachability, irreproachableness, right-mindedness, savouriness, seemliness, the conventionalities, the conventions. *Informal:* the thing. **2. right** ethicalness, justness, morality, principles, probity, propriety, rectitude, righteousness, rightness, the straight and narrow, uprightness, virtue, virtuousness, welldoing. **3. straightness** a step in the right direction, lawfulness, orthodoxy, rightness, scrupulosity, the right track, the ticket, trueness, unerringness.

2. 1. correction emendation, proofreading, redaction, revision. **2. rectification** amendment, edification, reform, reformation.

3. 1. corrector amender, book editor, checker *(US)*, copyeditor, edifier, emendator, proofreader, reader, rectifier, redactor, reviser, revisionist, righter of wrongs, subeditor. *Informal:* sub, subbie.

adj. **4. 1. proper** appropriate, becoming, comme il faut, correct, decent, decorous, fair and above board, family, fitting, honest, honourable, incorrupt, irreproachable, just, moral, principled, reproachless, right, right-minded, right-thinking, righteous, rightful, scrupulous, seemly, straight, unspotted, up to the mark, upright, upstanding, viceless, virtuous. *Informal:* Christian, kosher, squeaky-clean, straight-up. **2. correct** exact, just, lawful, licit, right as rain, sure, unerring, unimpeachable. **3. authorised** authoritative, canonical, orthodox, recognised. **4. true** authentic, bona fide, correct, factual, fiducial, genuine, historical, infallible, legitimate, literal, real, truthful, veracious, veridical, veritable, very. *Informal:* dinkum, dinky, dinky-di, fair dinkum, legit, ridge, ridgy-didge.

5. 1. corrective amendatory *(US)*, rectifying, reformational, reformative, reformatory. **6. 1. rectifiable** amendable, emendable, reformable.

v. **7.** **1. correct** amend, blue-pencil, copyedit, crosscheck, double-check, edit, edit in, emend, proofread, recheck, red-pencil, redact, revise, subedit. **2. rectify** amend, disabuse, edify, expurgate, redress, set to rights, straighten. **3. check** authenticate. **4. speak bluntly** *Informal:* call a spade a spade, play (with) a straight bat.

adv. **8.** **1. properly** appropriately, decently, decorously, fairly, in reason, seemly, within bounds, within reason. **2. rightly** by right, correctly, duly, fairly, honestly, honourably, incorruptly, irreproachably, lawfully, legitimately, morally, righteously, straight, truly, unimpeachably, uprightly, virtuously. *Informal:* dinkum. **3. correctly** aright, by the book, exactly, orthodoxly, properly, scrupulously, unerringly.

RELATED KEYWORDS: BEHAVIOUR, MORALITY, OBEDIENCE, TRUTH

PROTECTION

n. **1.** **1. protection** cover, defence, immunity. **2. defence** backstop, bulwark, fender, protection, screen, umbrella. **3. custody** aegis, auspices, care, charge, coverture, fatherly eye, fosterage, guardianship, keeping, ministry, providence, safekeeping, trust, ward. **4. guardianship** custodianship, tutelage, wardenry, wardenship, wardship. **5. safe-conduct** air cover, bodyguard, convoy, escort, protective custody, safeguard.

2. **1. insurance** assurance, bond, burial society, coinsurance, comprehensive insurance, cover, coverage, guarantee, mortality table, pledge, protection, protective trust, reinsurance, surety, tontine. **2. type of insurance** consequential loss insurance, credit insurance, credit life insurance, CTP insurance, disability insurance, endowment insurance, fire insurance, liability insurance, life assurance, life insurance, marine insurance, mutual insurance, public liability insurance, third-party insurance, valued policy, whole-life insurance. **3. indemnity** back bond, compensation, counterindemnity, guarantee, indemnification, invalid pension, security, surety. **4. policy** cover note, floating policy, open policy. **5. superannuation** allocated pension, annuity, deferred annuity, eligible termination payment, employee contribution, employer contribution, provident fund, salary sacrifice, SMSF, super fund, superannuation fund.

3. **1. protector** babysitter, carer, committee, duenna, father, genius loci, guardian, housefather, housemother, keeper, minder, mother, nurse, patron, patroness, protectress, provider, provost, tutelary. **2. guard** air-raid warden, bodyguard, caretaker, coast-watcher, coastguard, coastwatcher, concierge, conductor *(US)*, conservator, curator, custodian, doorkeeper, fire warden, firewatcher, guard commander, hired gun, janitor, keeper, lifeguard, night watch, nightwatchman, patrolman, porter, portress, safeguard, security guard, security officer, sentinel, sentry, sky marshal, warden. **3. body-guard** convoy, escort, gentleman-at-arms, guard, patrol, safeguard. **4. defender** harbourer, keeper, shelterer, shielder.

adj. **4.** **1. protected** guarded, immune, secure, under one's wing. **2. insured** covered. **3. indemnified** compensated, guaranteed.

5. **1. protective** alimentary, custodial, guardian, tutelary.

v. **6.** **1. protect** bulwark, buy insurance, cocoon, cover, defend, fence, fend, forefend, guard, keep, overshadow, pad, patrol, safeguard, save, screen, secure, shade, shadow, shelter, shield, snug, stand up for, take someone's part, watch over, wrap. **2. patrol** picket. **3. immunise** inoculate, vaccinate. **4. bless** charm.

RELATED KEYWORDS: DEFENCE, PRESERVATION, HELP, SAFETY

PROVERB

n. **1.** **1. proverb** adage, byword, dictum, household word, motto, saying, truth. **2. maxim** aphorism, apophthegm, apothegm, dictum, epigram, gnome, logion, notabilia, saw. **3. axiom** Logos, noumenon, postulate, principle, theorem. **4. apologue** moralism, parable. **5. device** adspeak, catchphrase, catchword, motto, slogan, tag. **6. plati-tude** banality, cliché, commonplace, poshlost, prosaism, trivialism, triviality, truism. *Informal:* bromide.

adj. **2.** **1. proverbial** aphorismatic, aphorismic, aphoristic, axiomatic, epigrammatic, gnomic, parabolic, sententious. **2. platitudinous** moralising, stock, trite.

v. **3.** **1. proverb** aphorise, apophthegmatise, epigrammatise.

adv. **4.** **1. proverbially** aphoristically, parabolically.

RELATED KEYWORDS: BREVITY, WRITING, TRUTH

PSYCHE

n. **1.** **1. psyche** pneuma, psychogenesis, self, soul. **2. ego** I, id, superego. **3. the unconscious** collective unconscious, inner space, preconscious, subconscious.

4. preconsciousness coconsciousness, subconsciousness. **5. engram** memory, trace. **6. motivation** drive, praxiology, purpose. **7. motive force** libido, vital impulse. **8. ambiversion** extroversion, introversion.

2. 1. psychic disturbance complex, factitious disorder by proxy, fetish, fixation, fixed idea, obsession, phobia. *Informal:* a monkey on one's back, hang-up. **2. mania** cacoethes, compulsion, craze, insanity. **3. hallucination** delusion, illusion. *Informal:* pink elephant. **4. inhibition** censor, censorship, repression, suppression. **5. Freudian slip** parapraxis. **6. regression** reversion. **7. schizophrenia** culture shock, identity crisis, multiple personality, paranoid schizophrenia, split personality. **8. shock** repressed memory, trauma. **9. hysteria** agony, delirium, frenzy, hysterics, nympholepsy, state, stir. *Informal:* conniptions, pink fit, spin. **10. shell shock** battle fatigue. **11. future shock. 12. syndrome** Down syndrome, factitious disorder by proxy, housewife's syndrome, Munchausen syndrome, Stockholm syndrome, sudden wealth syndrome, Tourette syndrome.

3. 1. psychic disorder acute confusional state, alienation, anomie, craze, deliration, delirium, dementia, derangement, echolalia, echopraxia, insanity, lunacy, madness, maladjustment, mania, neuropsychosis, neurosis, psychoneurosis, psychopathy, psychosis, schizothymia, subdelirium. *Informal:* imaginitis. **2. dementia praecox** hebephrenia. **3. nervous breakdown** breakdown, collapse. **4. paranoia** hallucinosis. **5. dissimulation** simulation. **6. amnesia** fugue. **7. masochism** sadism, sadomasochism. **8. psychosomatic disorder** hysterical fever, hysterical pregnancy, phantom pregnancy. **9. specific learning difficulty** agnosia, agraphia, alexia, alogia, aphasia, dysarthria, dysgraphia, dyslalia, dyslexia, dysphasia, dysphemia, dysphonia, glossolalia, lallation, paralexia, rhotacism, strephosymbolia, stuttering, tachyphemia, word blindness. **10. mental deficiency** anility, dotage, idiotism, imbecility, mental retardation, moronity, retardation, senility.

4. 1. mental disorder Alzheimer's disease, anorexia, anorexia nervosa, Asperger's syndrome, autism, bipolar disorder, coprophilia, cyclothymia, G.P.I., general paralysis of the insane, hysteria, infantilism, lethologica, logorrhea, lycanthropy, manic depression, multiple personality disorder, post-traumatic stress disorder, puerilism, senile dementia, shell shock, tarantism. **2. depression** atrabiliousness, hypochondria, melancholia, morbidity, morbidness, psychasthenia. **3. phobia** acrophobia, agoraphobia, agoraphobia, algophobia, Anglophobia, aquaphobia, arachnophobia, astraphobia, cancerophobia, claustrophobia, coprophobia, erythrophobia, gynophobia, hydrophobia, Islamophobia, lyssophobia, monophobia, nosophobia, ochlophobia, panophobia, photophobia, sitophobia, toxiphobia, triskaidekaphobia, zoophobia. **4. mania** cleptomania, kleptomania, megalomania, monomania, pyromania, sitomania, theomania. **5. eroticism** bestiality, erotomania, exhibitionism, fetishism, narcissism, nymphomania, paedophilia, pedophilia, satyriasis, scopophilia, sodomy, voyeurism.

5. 1. psychotic basket case, cyclothymiac, demoniac, energumen, hypochondriac, lunatic, lycanthrope, madwoman, maenad, manic-depressive, mattoid, melancholiac, paranoiac, phrenetic, psychopath, schizoid, schizophrenic, whacko. *Informal:* crackbrain, crackpot, crazy, cyberchondriac, loco *(US)*, loony, nut, psycho, schizo, wacko. **2. neurotic** hysteric, neuropath, wreck. **3. ambivert** extravert, extrovert, introvert. **4. masochist** sadist, sadomasochist. **5. erotomaniac** exhibitionist, fetishist, kink, narcissist, nymphomaniac, peeping Tom, pervert, satyr, secco, sex maniac, voyeur. *Informal:* birdwatcher, cheesecake, d.o.m., dirty old man, flasher, nympho, perv, secko. **6. maniac** madman. *Informal:* nutter. **7. mental deficient** amentum, cretin, defective, halfwit, idiot, imbecile, mental defective, oaf, subnormal. *Informal:* b.f., dubbo *(Chiefly NSW)*, eejit *(Chiefly Irish and Scottish)*, grommet, spacbrain. **8. analysand**.

6. 1. psychology nomology, psychogenesis, psychometry. **2. psychology discipline** abnormal psychology, aesthetics, analysis, behavioural psychology, behaviourism, clinical psychology, existential psychology, Gestalt psychology, hedonics, introspection, metapsychology, occupational psychology, parapsychology, psychoanalysis, psychophysics, sensationism. **3. psychologism. 4. psychiatry** alienism, orthopsychiatry, psychopathology, psychopathy, thanatology.

7. 1. psychotherapy aversion therapy, behaviour therapy, catharsis, deep-sleep therapy, E.C.T., electroconvulsive therapy, narcosynthesis, occupational therapy, OT, primal scream therapy, psychotherapeutics, sex therapy, shock therapy, shock treatment, therapy, token economy, transactional analysis, treatment. **2. counselling** child guidance, exit counselling, readjustment. **3. group therapy** encounter group, T-group. **4. psychodrama** acting out. **5. psychoanalysis** analysis, hypnoanalysis, hypnosis, psychognosis. **6. psychograph** psychometer. **7. personality test** Binet test, free association test, ink-blot test, Rorschach test. **8. hypnosis** abreaction, hypnology, hypnotisation, hypnotism. **9. certification** stultification. **10. mental hospital** asylum, lunatic asylum, madhouse, psychiatric hospital, retreat. *Informal:* booby hatch *(US)*, funny farm, giggle factory, loony bin, nut factory, nuthouse, rat factory *(NZ)*, rathouse.

8. 1. psychologist analyst, behaviourist, Freudian, Jungian, nomologist, psychoanalyser, psychoanalyst, psychobiologist, psychopathologist, sensationist. **2. third force**. **3. hypnotist** hypnotiser. **4. psychiatrist** orthopsychiatrist, psychotherapist. *Informal:* headshrinker, shrink, trick cyclist.

9. 1. Freudian terminology cathexis, condensation, consciousness, defence mechanism, displacement, dissociation, dream, introjection, penis envy, primitive, projection, rationalisation, sublimation, suggestion, transference, wish fulfilment. **2. complex** castration complex, Electra complex, guilt complex, inferiority complex, martyr complex, Oedipus complex, overcompensation, persecution complex.

adj. **10. 1. psychological** idiographic, nomological, nomothetic, psychobiological, psychogenetic, psychophysical, psychophysiological. **2. psychoanalytic** Freudian, Jungian, psychoanalytical, psychographic, psychometric. **3. psychiatric** mental, neuropsychiatric, noetic, psychiatrical, psychopathological, psychosexual, psychotherapeutic.

11. 1. psychologically disturbed fixated, maladjusted. **2. insane** balmy *(US)*, brainsick, certifiable, certified, crazed, crazy, daft, delirious, demented, deranged, dilly, disordered, eccentric, frenetic, irrational, lunatic, mad, mad as a hatter, maniac, maniacal, manic, mentally ill, moonstruck, odd, off the rails, off-centre, out of one's head, out of one's mind, over the edge, peculiar, phrenetic, screwed up, strange, suspicional, unbalanced, unusual, weak-minded. *Informal:* barmy, barmy as a bandicoot, bats, batty, be out of one's tree, bonkers, cockamamie, cracked, crackers, crackpot, cuckoo, daffy, dingbats, dotty, far gone, gaga, get the Darling pea, gonzo, kinky, loco, loony, loopy, mad as a meataxe, mental, non compos, nuts, nutty, nutty as a fruitcake, oddball, off one's block, off one's chump *(Chiefly British)*, off one's face, off one's head, off one's nut, off one's onion, off one's rocker, off one's scone, off one's trolley, off the air, off the wall, original, porangi *(NZ)*, potty, queer, round the bend, round the twist, screwball, soft in the head, starkers, troppo, unhinged, up the pole, wacko, womba, wrong in the head, yarra. **3. compulsive** manic. *Informal:* fixated on, obsessed with, yampy. **4. obsessed** obsessional. *Informal:* fixated, hipped on *(US)*. **5. manic-depressive** cycloid, cycloidal, cyclothymic. **6. depressive** atrabilious, hypochondriac, melancholiac, melancholic, morbid, phobic. **7. neurotic** hysteric, hysterical, hysteroid, neuropathic, psychasthenic. *Informal:* freaked-out, hung-up. **8. psychotic** paranoid, psychopathic, schizo, schizoid, schizophrenic. *Informal:* psycho. **9. delusional** expansive. **10. shell-shocked**. **11. boob happy** *Informal:* stir-crazy. **12. mentally deficient** anile, autistic, be a shingle short, cretinous, defective, doddering, doting, feeble-minded, impolitic, ineducable, insensate, mentally handicapped, mindless, mongoloid, retarded, senile, simple, simple-minded, subnormal, unintelligent, unteachable. *Informal:* gaga.

v. **12. 1. psychoanalyse** abreact, analyse, condition, depersonalise, hypnotise. **2. fixate** introspect, overcompensate, rationalise, repress, sublimate, subtilise. **3. psychologise** be an amateur psychologist. **4. certify** stultify.

adv. **13. 1. psychiatrically** psychoanalytically, psychogenetically, psychologically, psychotherapeutically.

RELATED KEYWORDS: HEALING, STUPIDITY, MIND, INSANITY

PUBLICITY

n. **1. 1. publicity** build-up, daylight, notice, promotion. **2. advertising** advertisements, ambient advertising, ambush marketing, ballyhoo, billing. **3. publication** broadcast, divulgation, gazettal, issue, notification, promulgation, propagation, publishment, republication.

2. 1. public notice announcement, banns, call, declaration, enouncement, enunciation, hue and cry, intimation, proclamation, promise, pronunciamento, protest, report. **2. notice** bill, bulletin, green paper *(Chiefly British)*, notice paper. **3. advertisement** advertorial, blurb, classified ad, classifieds, commercial, film clip, hard sell, loss leader, promo, promotion, recommendation, soft sell, teaser, teaser ad, trailer, want ad. *Informal:* ad, advert, plug, sell. **4. personal column** obit, obituary. **5. poster** banner, newsposter, placard, wanted poster. **6. handbill** booklet, broadsheet, broadside, brochure, circular, dodger, flier, flyer, handout, leaflet, literature, pamphlet, placard, playbill, prospectus, screed, showbill, throwaway. **7. sticker** bumper sticker, car sticker. **8. noticeboard** billboard, bulletin board *(US)*, corkboard, hoarding, Ritchie board, sandwich board. **9. edict** act, appointment, ban, brevet, bull, commandment, declaration, decree, decretal, deliverance, dictate, dictum, diktat, directive, dispensation, fiat, instruction, instructions, law, letters of credence, mandate, manifest, manifesto, mitzvah, ordinance, platform, precept, proclamation, pronouncement, pronunciamento, regulation, rescript, rule, ukase.

3. **1. publicist** adman, advertiser, billposter, bullsticker, copywriter, pamphleteer, placarder, plugger, poster. **2. announcer** declarer, divulgator, enunciator, notifier, proclaimer, promulgator, warner. **3. herald** bawler, crier, muezzin, officer at arms, sandwich man, town crier, trumpet, trumpeter. *Informal:* barker, spieler.

v. **4.** **1. publicise** advertise, ballyhoo, bawl, bill, build up, cry up, pamphleteer, puff, tout. *Informal:* bark. **2. announce** acclaim, annunciate, assert, asseverate, aver, call, claim, communicate, convey, declare, elaborate on, enounce, enunciate, impart, intimate, keynote *(US)*, preconise, predicate, proclaim, pronounce, pronounce on, report, show, state, tell, trumpet. **3. decree** adjudge, expedite, gazette, pronounce. **4. publish** advertise, blaze, blazon, broadcast, circulate, divulgate, gazette, give out, go the rounds, hawk about, herald, issue, promulgate, propagandise, propagate, voice. **5. trumpet** blare. **6. toll** ring in, ring out. **7. tell** confide, dictate, emit, enounce, enunciate, express, iterate, narrate, out with, outspeak, pronounce, rap out, relate, report, say, speak, state, utter, vent, vocalise, voice. **8. notify** apprise of, post.

RELATED KEYWORDS: ASSERTION, COMMUNICATION, DISPLAY, REVELATION, BOOK

PULLING

n. **1.** **1. pulling** draught, drawing, haul, haulage, pull, stress, towage, traction, tractive power.

2. **1. pull** drag, draw, haul, heave, lug, manhaul, tow, tug. *Informal:* yank. **2. wrench** tear, twist, wrest. **3. hitch** jerk, pluck, pull, tug, tweak, twitch. *Informal:* yank.

3. **1. puller** haler, hauler, tugger. **2. towrope** hawser, messenger, towline. **3. winch** capstan, coffee-grinder winch, davit, differential windlass, parbuckle, whim, windlass. **4. pulley** block and tackle, breech, burton, cat, crab, garnet, halliard, halyard, jeers, luff tackle, shearlegs, sheave, sheave-block, snatch block, truckle, wharve, whip. **5. prime mover** bank engine, caterpillar, locomotive, tow truck, towboat, traction engine, tractor, tug, tugboat. *Informal:* towie. **6. tractor beam**.

adj. **4.** **1. tractive** draught, tractional.

v. **5.** **1. pull** bowse, brail, clew, drag, draw, hale, haul, heave, lug, rouse away, snig, trice, tug. **2. tow** kedge, tug, warp. **3. trail** draggle. **4. wrench** tear, wrest. **5. strain at** tear at. **6. jerk** pluck, twitch. *Informal:* yank. **7. hitch** hike up. **8. winch** purchase, windlass.

interj. **6.** **1. heave ho** yo-heave-ho.

RELATED KEYWORDS: TRANSPORT

PULP

n. **1.** **1. pulp** chyme, mash, pap, pomace, slops, sop, squash, squelch. **2. dough** clag, magma, paste, sponge.

2. **1. pulpiness** pastiness, soddenness, sogginess, sponginess, squashiness. **2. pulping** mashing, mastication.

adj. **3.** **1. pulpy** doughy, mushy, pappy, pasty, sodden, soggy, sopping, spongy, squashy, squishy.

v. **4.** **1. pulp** crush, knead, mash, masticate, sodden, squash. *Informal:* squish. **2. sodden** sop.

RELATED KEYWORDS: SOFTNESS, SLUDGE, WETNESS

PUNGENCY

n. **1.** **1. pungency** acridity, acridness, gaminess, piquancy, poignancy, raciness, saltiness, spicery, spiciness. **2. bite** edge, salt, strength, tang. **3. pepperiness** fieriness, sharpness. **4. roughness** harshness.

adj. **2.** **1. pungent** acrid, sharp, spicy, strong. **2. piquant** fiery, hot, poignant, racy, savoury. **3. spicy** alliaceous, garlicky, ginger-like, gingery, peppery, piquant, pungent, saltish, salty, sharp, tangy. **4. gamy** earthy, fetid, foetid, gamey, high, rank.

adv. **3.** **1. pungently** acridly, fierily, piquantly, poignantly, saltily, spicily.

RELATED KEYWORDS: PLEASANT FLAVOUR, UNPLEASANT FLAVOUR, FOOD, SOURNESS, TASTE

PUNISHMENT

n. **1.** **1. punishment** condemnation, disciplinary action, penalisation, penalty. **2. forfeiture** amercement, attainder, attaint, praemunire *(British Law)*. **3. chastisement** a piece of one's mind, castigation, chastening, correction, curtain lecture, dressing-down, lashing, mockery, rating, roasting, rod, scolding, scorn, tongue-lashing, what-for. *Informal:* a kick in the pants, bagging, blast, chip, earful, flea in someone's ear, jaw, payout, razz, roast, rocket, serve, slam, talking-to, the rough side of one's tongue, the rounds of the kitchen, the treatment, trimming *(British)*, wigging *(British)*. **4. retribution** nemesis, poetic justice. **5. retaliation** blood feud, compensation, quid pro quo, reciprocity, reprisal, requital, revenge, satisfaction, utu *(NZ)*, vendetta, vengeance, wrath. *Informal:* comeuppance. **6. Day of Judgement** day of reckoning, doom, judgement, visitation. **7. banishment** anathema, commination, excommunication, exile, interdict, interdiction, monition, outlawing, proscription, sequestration, transportation. **8. hellfire** Gehenna, purgatory. **9. persecution** victimisation. **10. fine** forfeit, lesson, mulct, penalty, sanctions. **11. imposition** contribution, custom, impost, infliction, lines, toll, tribute.

2. 1. corporal punishment flagellation, flogging, lashing, scourging, whipping. *Informal:* the cuts. **2. beating** bastinado, dressing-down, drubbing, fustigation, hiding, lacing *(British)*, running the gauntlet, spanking, thrashing, trouncing. *Informal:* bashing, belting, doing, dusting, going-over, hammering, licking, milling, pasting, shellacking, strapping, tanning, towelling, walloping, workover. **3. Botany Bay dozen** *(Convict Obsolete)* bob, bull, canary, tester. **4. blow** box, buff, buffet, clip, clock, clonk, clout, clump, cuff, dong, dook, fisticuff, punch, stroke. *Informal:* biff, conk, duke, facer, flea in someone's ear, job, knuckle sandwich, plug. **5. smack** box on the ear, flap, paddle, rap over the knuckles, slap, spank, spat, swack *(Chiefly Scottish)*, thwack. *Informal:* paddywhack, swat, wallop, whack.

3. 1. torture breaking on the wheel, excruciation, strappado, third degree. **2. solitary confinement** isolation, marooning, sensory deprivation. **3. instrument of torture** Chinese water torture, iron maiden, rack, snake pit, thumbscrew, triangle, wheel.

4. 1. capital punishment death penalty, execution, lynching. **2. method of execution** auto-da-fé, beheading, burning at the stake, crucifixion, decapitation, electrocution, flaying, fusillade, garrotte, hanging, hanging drawing and quartering, impalement, lethal injection, strangulation. **3. instrument of execution** bowstring, cross, electric chair, fire, firing party, firing squad, guillotine, halter, the gallows, the stake.

5. 1. punisher amercer, condemner, sentencer. **2. discipliner** castigator, chastener, chastiser, corrector, excommunicator, persecutor. **3. caner** flogger, fustigator, lasher, scourger, swinger, thrasher, whipper. *Informal:* walloper. **4. executioner** bow-stringer, crucifier, firing party, firing squad, garrotter, hangman, headsman, lynch mob, lyncher, lynching party. **5. torturer** inquisitor. **6. avenger** vindicator.

6. 1. disciplinant flagellant.

adj. **7. 1. punishing** castigatory, corrective, disciplinary, penal, penitentiary, penological, punitive. **2. correctional** baculine, fire-and-brimstone, flagellant. **3. amercing** confiscatory, expropriatory, mulctuary. **4. retributive** persecutional, persecutive, persecutory, retaliatory, revengeful, vengeful, vindicatory, vindictive. **5. comminatory** damning, interdictory.

8. 1. punished disenfranchised, excommunicate, infamous, penalised. **2. convicted** damned. *Informal:* for it, for the high jump, in for it, off tap.

9. 1. punishable statutable, statutory. **2. visitational** amerceable, excommunicable, excommunicative, excommunicatory.

v. **10. 1. punish** afflict, condemn, gruel, penalise, visit. **2. discipline** admonish, attack, baste, berate, blast, bring to book, carpet, castigate, censure, chasten, chastise, chide, come down on, correct, denounce, denunciate, flay, give someone a bad mark, give someone a lesson, haul over the coals, keelhaul, lambaste, lash, mat, objurgate, pelt, put on the mat, rate, rebuke, reprehend, reprimand, reproach, reprobate, reprove, rouse on (or at), sally up *(NZ)*, scold, scourge, take in hand, take to task, tongue, tongue-lash, twit, upbraid, whip. *Informal:* be on at, blast (the) hell out of, blow up, bore it up someone, chew out, dress down, give someone beans, give someone gip, give someone heaps, give someone hell, give someone Larry Dooley, give someone what for, go crook at (or on), go on at, go to town on, hoe into, lay it on, paste, ping, play hell with, put the boot into someone, rag, rap someone over (or on) the knuckles, roust hell out of, strafe, take a piece out of, tear (or take) strips off, tear strips off, throw the book at, tick off, wig *(British)*. **3. sentence** blanket, immure, imprison, incarcerate, jail, pillory, pound, shut in, shut up. *Informal:* jug, lag, put away, send down *(British)*, send up. **4. fine** amerce, estreat, mulct. **5. keelhaul** aloft, duck, masthead. **6. persecute** have heads over, have someone's head, make an example of, tar and feather, victimise. **7. excommunicate** attaint, damn, interdict, rusticate *(British)*. **8. torture** anguish, break on the wheel, distress, excruciate, give the third degree, grill, harrow, hurt, pain, rack, thumbscrew, torment, worry, wring. **9. beat** thrash. *Informal:* beat (or belt) the (living) daylights out of someone, beat to a pulp.

11. **1. execute** lynch, point the bone at. **2. electrocute** gas. **3. hang** gibbet, string up, suspercollate. **4. garrotte** asphyxiate, bow-string, choke, neck, overlie, smother, stifle, strangle, strangulate, suffocate. *Informal:* scrag. **5. crucify** empale, impale. **6. behead** decapitate, decollate, guillotine, neck, send to the scaffold. **7. hang draw and quarter** flay, quarter.

12. **1. be punished** answer for, face the music, get one's just deserts, get what is coming, take one's medicine. *Informal:* catch it, cop it, get it in the neck, take the rap. **2. take one's punishment** run the gauntlet. *Informal:* swing, take the high jump.

RELATED KEYWORDS: VICTIM, HITTING, IMPRISONMENT, KILLING, LITIGATION, PAIN, RETALIATION

PURPLE

n. **1.** **1. purple** burgundy, magenta, murrey, orchid, petunia, plum, purpure, raspberry. **2. lilac** lavender, mauve, violet. **3. amethyst** heliotrope. **4. cerise** carmine, grape, solferino. **5. indigo** indigo blue, raisin, royal purple.

2. **1. purple dye** amaranth *(US)*, carmine, crystal violet, cudbear, gentian violet, indigoid, mauve, orchil, purple of Cassius, solferino, Tyrian purple.

adj. **3.** **1. purple** aubergine, magenta, purpure. **2. purplish** amaranthine, amethystine, vinaceous, violescent. **3. lilac** lavender, lilaceous, mauve, violet. **4. cerise** carmine, vinous. **5. indigo** perse.

RELATED KEYWORDS: BLUE, COLOUR, RED

PURSUIT

n. **1.** **1. pursuit** chasings, derry, hide-and-seek, hidings, hue and cry, man-hunt, prowl, quest, stern chase, tiggy touchwood, wild-goose chase. **2. hunt** battue, chase, chivvy *(British)*, drag hunt, fox hunt, kangaroo drive, pursuit, safari, still hunt *(US)*.

2. **1. pursuer** blacktracker, bounty hunter *(Chiefly US)*, chaser, hunter, police boy, police tracker, prowler, shikari, spoorer, tracer, tracker. **2. searcher** fossicker, noodler, pearler, prospector, rummager, seeker.

3. **1. hunting** blood sport, course, coursing, deerstalking, dogging, falconry, flight shooting, fowling, fox-hunting, gunning, hawking, mutton-birding, pigsticking, sport, spotlighting, stalk, wildfowling, woodcraft *(Chiefly US)*.

4. **1. hunter** batfowler, bird dog *(US)*, birder, bounty hunter *(Chiefly US)*, chaser, chasseur, deerculler *(NZ)*, deerstalker, dog catcher, falconer, ferreter, field, fowler, fox-hunter, hawker, huntress, huntsman, huntswoman, jaeger, kangarooer, mutton-birder, Nimrod, pigsticker, pothunter, rabbiter, ranger, shikari, snarer, stalker, trapper, trepanner, wildfowler, wirer, wolfer, wolver, woodcraftsman, woodsman. *Informal:* dingo stiffener. **2. courser** beagle, bloodhound, cry, gun dog, kangaroo dog, otterhound, pig-dog, preyer, retriever, sleuth, sleuthhound, tracker dog. *Informal:* roo dog.

5. **1. fishing** angling, bay whaling, fly-fishing, ledger-baiting, ledgering, legering, shark meshing, shore whaling, spinning, whaling.

6. **1. fisherman** angler, crabber, fisher, fisho, fly-fisher, gillnetter, prawner, rock-hopper, sealer, shrimper, spearfisherman, striker, surfcaster, trammeller, trawler, troller, whaleman, whaler. *Informal:* prawnie.

7. **1. fishing tackle** bob, boulter, bunt, coop, creel, dropline, fish spear, fishing line, fishing rod, fizgig, float, flue, gaff, ganghook, gig, grains, handline, herl, lance, ledger line, ledger tackle, leger tackle, leister, long-line, net, purse seine, rod, roping pole, scoop net, seine, sinker, spin rod, striker, trammel net, trawl line, trawl net, witch's hat. **2. fishing lure** bait, craypot, ground bait, hackle fly, pot, pound net, spinner, spoon, spoonbait, trap, troll, wet fly, wobbler. **3. fishhook** Aberdeen hook, barbless hook, Carlisle, Carlisle hook, ganghook, hook, Kendal sneck bent hook, kirby hook, Limerick hook, sproat hook. **4. catching equipment** booby trap, butterfly net, catching pole, clapnet, fowling net, lasso, mouse trap, rat-trap, roping pole.

adj. **8.** **1. pursuing** confiscating, hunting, piscatorial, piscatory, predacious, predatory, prehensile, preying, privative, pursuant, raptorial, ravening, venatic.

v. **9.** **1. pursue** chase after, chivvy *(British)*, course, dog, follow up, halloo, hallow, hound, hunt, hunt down, lie in wait, run to earth, shadow, stalk, take after *(US)*, tree. **2. track** dog, hound, lodge, nose after, nose out, pug, sleuth, spoor, trail, wind.

3. search forage, foray, fossick, look, mouse, noodle, pearl, prospect, prowl, quest, quest for (or after), rake, rummage, scout, scrimmage, seek. *Informal:* snoop.

10. **1. hunt** course, dog, drive, follow the hounds, gun, possum, prey, ride to hounds, seek, stalk, still-hunt *(US)*. **2. ferret** flight, hark back, hawk, run, scent. **3. trap** catch, entrap, run to ground, springe, tree, wire. **4. net** enmesh, ensnare, entangle, immesh, inmesh, insnare, snare, trammel. **5. rabbit** bird, fowl, frog, mouse, pigstick, rat, roo, snipe, wolf.

11. **1. fish** angle, bob, cast, chum, dap, dib, fly-fish, gaff, gig, guddle, land, leister, marron, net, play, rock-hop, seine, skitter, spin, spoon, strike, trawl, troll, whale, whip. **2. crab** prawn, seal, shrimp, turtle.

adv. **12.** **1. in pursuit** hot on the trail, in full cry, on the scent.

interj. **13.** **1. tally-ho** halloo, hallow, hoicks, hulloo, yo-ho, yoicks.

RELATED KEYWORDS: ALLURE

QUANTITY

n. **1.** **1. quantity** amount, complement, matter, measure, number, part, portion, proportion, quantum, sum. **2. batch** brew, cast, churning, lot, make, making, measure, output, pour, shear, shower. **3. haul** catch, draught, take. **4. load** boatload, cargo, cartload, freight, keel, lading, lift, pack, payload, pitch, shipload, shipment, truckload, wagonload. **5. supply** flow, output, yield. **6. dose** dosage, overdose. **7. bagful** armful, barrelful, basinful, boatful, boxful, bumper, capful, dipperful, dishful, fistful, forkful, glassful, handful, houseful, kettleful, lapful, mouthful, pipeful, plateful, pocketful, potful, spoonful, sackful, shovelful, spadeful. *Informal:* bellyful, hatful, neckful, skinful. **8. large quantity** infinity, plethora, scads, slather, wad. *Informal:* stack. **9. miscellaneous quantities** biomass, butt, cordage, escort return *(Australian History)*, frail, great gross, gross, haymow, hogshead, mole, reel. *Informal:* bucketload, job lot, shedload *(Chiefly British)*.

2. **1. bit** chip, cut, dab, fraction, fragment, grain, inch, iota, jot, minim, modicum, ounce, particle, patch, pea, peck, pennyworth, peppercorn, piece, pinch, portion, rag, scantling, scrap, section, share, skerrick, smidgin, snip, snippet, soupçon, stint, stiver, tad, tap, tittle, tot, trifle, whit. *Informal:* chop. **2. drop** draught, dreg, dribble, dribs and drabs, drink, pottle, sup, thimbleful. *Informal:* droob. **3. mouthful** bite, chew, gulp. **4. block** cube, nugget, slab. **5. clod** chump, chunk, clot, clump, divot *(Scottish)*, gob, lump, mass, nub, nubbin *(US)*, sod, turf, wad. *Informal:* dollop.

v. **3.** **1. quantify** amass, measure, number, preponderate, reach, take stock.

adv. **4.** **1. quantitatively** volumetrically. **2. so much** a bit of, as far as, better than, upwards of.

RELATED KEYWORDS: CONTAINER, DEPTH, SIZE, SMALLNESS, GREATNESS, HEAVINESS, MEASUREMENT, NUMBER

QUESTION

n. **1.** **1. question** a good question, awkward question, call, challenge, demand, Dorothy Dixer, FAQ, feeler, inquiry, interrogation, interrogatory, leading question, mondo, multiple-choice question, poser, query, question on notice, question without notice.

2. **1. questioning** catechisation, catechism, debrief, debriefing, examination, interrogation, interview, quiz. **2. cross-examination** cross-question, cross-questioning, questioning, re-examination, trial. **3. inquisition** dialectic, dialogue, discussion, post-mortem, Socratic method.

3. **1. investigation** check, enquiry, inquiry, query, review, study. **2. examination** lookaround, probe *(US)*, review, reviewal, scan, scrutiny, survey. **3. research** experiment, R and D, research and development, trial. **4. analysis** anatomisation, appraisal, appraisement, assay, assessment, breakdown, criticism, critique, diagnosis, diagnostic, dissection, evaluation, examination, opinion poll, overhaul, qualitative analysis, quantitative analysis, summated rating. **5. mass observation** airing, gallup poll, market research, opinion poll, poll, questionnaire, random sampling, straw poll, straw vote. **6. field study** case study, field work, sampling. **7. cost-benefit analysis** environmental impact assessment, environmental impact study, feasibility study, systems analysis, time and motion study. **8. spot check** countercheck, fatigue test, inspection, look, lookover, quality control, reconnaissance, reconnoitre, rummage, survey, trip-check, view. *Informal:* going-over, looksee, once-over, shakedown *(US)*. **9. self-examination** soulsearching. **10. identification parade** police line-up. **11. spying** cloak-and-dagger stuff, counterespionage, counterintelligence, espionage, intelligence, wire-tapping.

4. **1. inspection** field day, field trip, reconnaissance, review, visit, visitation. *Informal:* recce, snoop. **2. search** dig, digging, exploration, house-search, hunt, potholing, pursuit, quest, ramp, treasure hunt. **3. body-search** cavity search, strip search. **4. legal search** requisitions on title.

5. **1. examination** audition, exam, examen, finals, open-book examination, oral examination, paper, post, supplementary, test, test paper, viva voce. *Informal:* viva. **2. final school examination** Certificate of Education *(NT, SA, Tasmania, Victoria, WA)*, eleven-plus *(British)*, Higher School Certficate *(NSW)*, HSC, NTCE, SACE, SC, Senior Certificate *(Qld)*, TCE, VCE, WACE, Year 12 Certificate *(ACT)*. **3. university examination** baccalaureate, tripos. **4. trial** test, tryout. **5. driving test** road test. **6. audit** affluence test, matriculation, means test.

6. **1. physical examination** amniocentesis, antenatal, Apgar score, auscultation, Binet test, biopsy, bioscopy, blood cholesterol test, blood test, brain scan, cancer smear, cervical smear, checkup, colonoscopy, electrocardiograph, endoscopy, fluoroscopy, follow-up, gastroscopy, Guthrie test, laparoscopy, magnetic resonance imaging, medical, palpation, Pap smear, Papanicolaou smear, PKU test, postnatal, PSA test, radiology, radioscopy, rhinoscopy, roentgenology, Rorschach test, scatology, Schick test, screening, smear test, spinal tap, tracheoscopy, urethroscopy, Wassermann reaction, X-ray. *Informal:* short-arm parade. **2. post-mortem examination** autopsy, forensic examination, inquest, necropsy, necrotomy, post-mortem.

7. **1. investigator** asker, catechiser, demander, enquirer, field officer, field worker, inquirer, inquisitionist, inquisitor, interrogator, interviewer, querist, question-master, questioner, quizzer, re-examiner, researcher, scout, seeker. **2. pollster** canvasser, sampler. **3. examiner** analyst, appraiser, assayer, checker *(US)*, critic, dissector, examinant, observer, prober, scanner, scrutiniser, surveyor. **4. auditor** datary, head-hunter, health inspector, inspector, reviewer, scrutator, scrutineer, systems analyst, talent scout. **5. committee** court of inquiry, royal commission, standing committee, working party. **6. examinee** catechumen, interviewee.

8. **1. searcher** ransacker, rummager. **2. detective** private investigator, sleuth. *Informal:* bloodhound, dick, frisker, gumshoe *(US)*, private eye, shamus, tec. **3. explorer** fossicker, hunter, potholer, prospector, search party, sourdough *(US)*, spelunker. *Informal:* wildcatter *(US)*.

9. **1. spy** beagle, counterspy, double agent, front, incognito, informer, intelligencer, masker, masquer, mole, operative *(US)*, secret agent, security police, sleeper, snake in the grass, snooper, spier, spyer, undercover agent, wire-tapper. *Informal:* crypto, plant, snoop, spook. **2. secret service** intelligence organisation. **3. secret service organisations** ASIO, ASIS, CIA, JIO, KGB, MI5, SAS.

adj. **10.** **1. inquiring** curious, inquisitional, inquisitive, inquisitorial, interrogational, interrogative, interrogatory, nosey, questioning, searching, snoopy. *Informal:* nosy. **2. investigative** analytic, appraising, diagnostic, exploratory, fact-finding, heuristic, laboratorial, observational, research, scientific, scrutinising. **3. inspectional** check, inspective.

v. **11.** **1. question** ask, challenge, demand, enquire, inquire, interrogate, press, query, seek an answer, survey. **2. interview** audition, examine. **3. interrogate** catechise, cross-examine, cross-question, debrief, give the third degree, hammer, pick someone's brains, probe, pump, put to the question, question, quiz, re-examine, sift the evidence, sound someone out. *Informal:* grill, sweat.

12. **1. examine** analyse, canvass, explore, introspect, investigate, probe, review, scrutinise, search, study. **2. test** ascertain, assay, condition, determine, prove, put to the proof, re-examine, revisit, show, take, try out, verify. **3. study** audit, monitor, scan, scrutineer, scrutinise, vet. **4. inspect** appraise, evaluate, overhaul, review. **5. diagnose** auscultate, palpate, sound, X-ray.

13. **1. investigate** analyse, anatomise, appraise, arrange, assay, assess, break down, catalogue, classify, codify, delve into, derive, digest, dissect, examine, experiment, explore, file, fossick out, group, hunt up, list, look into, look up, plumb, pull apart, pull to pieces, rank, reconnoitre, research, scrutinise, see how the land lies, see into, sift, sort, sound, unravel, winnow. *Informal:* dig, go and (or have a) look-see. **2. check** countercheck, go over, go through, road-test, sample, screen, snuff, swab, vet. **3. survey** have a good look around, hunt about, hunt around, inspect, look, look over, nose around, observe, overlook, rake, reconnoitre, review, scout, see over, shop around, sweep, traverse, view. *Informal:* case, eyeball, squiz.

14. **1. search** comb, leave no stone unturned, ransack, rummage. *Informal:* rat through. **2. cast about** seek a clue. **3. look for** cherchez la femme, keep an eye out for, nose after, nose for, seek. *Informal:* suss out. **4. body-search** cavity-search, strip-search. *Informal:* frisk. **5. spy** drag out, draw out, fish out, make inquiry (or inquiries), nose about, nose after (or for), nose into, poke about, poke about (or around), poke around, pry, smell out, sniff out, sound out, wonder. *Informal:* dig into, fly a kite, poke one's nose into, root around, rubberneck, snoop, stickybeak. **6. explore** fossick, geologise. *Informal:* wildcat.

RELATED KEYWORDS: CURIOSITY, FINDING, PURSUIT, TEST

QUIETNESS

n.   **1.**   **1. quietness** faintness, inaudibility, indistinctness, softness. **2. gentleness** dimness, dreaminess, sedateness. **3. dullness** deadness. **4. huskiness** frog, gruffness, guttural, hoarseness, hollowness, lowness, roup, throatiness. **5. devocalisation** ecthlipsis.

   2.   **1. murmur** burble, burr, croon, hum, murmuration, whispering. **2. whisper** aside, breath, susurration, susurrus, undertone. **3. sigh** ahem, breath, hiss, sniff, swish, waft, whisper. **4. moan** groan, grumbles, grunt, whine. **5. babble** chatter, prattle, twitter. **6. lap** gurgle, plash, purl, ripple, splash. **7. rustle** ruffle, scroop, stir. **8. scratch** scuff, squeak. **9. click** tick. **10. tinkle** clink, tinkling. **11. pitter-patter** pat, patter, pitapat.

   3.   **1. damper** deadener, muffle, mute, overdamper, silencer, soft pedal, softener, sordino, sourdine, temperer. **2. deadening** acoustic tile, insulation.

   4.   **1. quiet person** clam, mouse, oyster. **2. whisperer** murmurer.

adj.   **5.**   **1. quiet** calm, dreamy, gentle, indistinct, low, murmuring, placid, sedate, serene, sober, soft, soft-spoken, still, stilly *(Poetic)*, subdued, tranquil, tranquillo. *Informal:* q.t. **2. whispering** murmuring, murmurous, susurrant, susurrous. **3. husky** cracked, croaky, deep, grainy, gravelly, gritty, groaning, gruff, guttural, hoarse, hollow, ragged, rasping, roupy, thick, throaty. **4. tinkling** humming, ripply, twittery. **5. soft** calm, composed, dim, easeful, faint, gentle, low, low-pitched, pacific, peaceful, piano, quiet, sedate, sleepy, small, still, stilly *(Poetic)*, subdued, tranquil. **6. faint** bleary, blurry, dim, distant, foggy, fuzzy, inaudible, indistinct, inward, misty, muffled, muted, nubilous, obscure, uncertain, vague. **7. unstressed** unaccented, unemphasised, weak. **8. whispered** sotto voce. **9. dull** dead, dim, tinny, tubby. **10. deadening** dulling, tempering.

v.   **6.**   **1. quieten** lower, lull, mute, quiet, shush, soften. **2. temper** damp, dampen, deaden, drown, dull, muffle, mute, obtund, opiate, overdamp, pug, soft-pedal. **3. devocalise** devoice. **4. whisper** breathe, murmur. **5. tinkle** hum, twitter. **6. become quieter** die away, drop, fade.

adv.   **7.**   **1. quietly** dimly, inwardly, low, small, soft, softly, stilly. **2. sotto voce** under one's breath. **3. piano** calando, decrescendo, diminuendo, pianissimo. **4. gently** dreamily, sedately. **5. murmuringly** cooingly, groaningly, moaningly, murmurously. **6. huskily** gruffly, hollowly, thickly, throatily.

RELATED KEYWORDS: HISSING, SOUND

RAINFALL

n.   **1.**   **1. rainfall** precipitation, water cycle. **2. rain** acid rain, blood rain, convectional rain, drizzle, precipitate, serein, virga, water, wet. **3. shower** drizzle, flurry, mizzle, spit, sprinkle, sunshower. **4. downpour** cloudburst, cockeye bob, electrical storm, equinoctial, inundation, pour, rain, rainstorm, spate, storm, thundershower, thunderstorm, torrent, waterspout. *Informal:* knock-em-down rain. **5. inundation** banker, deluge, flood, the deluge. **6. raindrop. 7. hail** ice crystal. **8. rainy season** monsoon, the wet. *Informal:* bogaduck weather. **9. hydrometeor.**

   2.   **1. rainfall measurement** hydrometeorology, udometry. **2. rain gauge** hyetograph, ombrometer, pluviometer, udometer. **3. unit of rainfall** inch, inch of water, millimetre, point.

adj.   **3.**   **1. rainy** drizzly, pluvial, pluvious, showery, wet. **2. teeming** soppy, torrential.

v.   **4.**   **1. rain** precipitate. **2. drizzle** mizzle, shower, spit, sprinkle. **3. pour** pelt, storm, teem. *Informal:* bucket down, rain cats and dogs. **4. inundate** bank and bank *(NZ)*, deluge, drown, float, flood, overflow, run a banker.

RELATED KEYWORDS: FLOW, WEATHER, WETNESS

RARENESS

n.   **1.**   **1. rareness** fewness, rarity, scarceness, scarcity, uncommonness. **2. rarefaction. 3. infrequency** scarcity, seldomness. **4. rarity** bibelot, collector's item, rara avis, rare bird, rare book. **5. intermittency** discontinuity.

adj. **2.** **1. rare** esoteric, exotic, few and far between, rarefied, scarce, uncommon. *Informal:* scarce (or rare) as hen's teeth. **2. rarefactive**. **3. infrequent**. **4. sporadic** casual, intermissive, intermittent, irregular, occasional, odd. **5. unusual** unexampled, unheard-of, unprecedented.

v. **3.** **1. happen infrequently** bob up now and then, come in fits and starts. *Informal:* happen once in a blue moon.

adv. **4.** **1. rarely** hardly ever, infrequently, little, once, once in a month of Sundays, scarcely, scarcely ever, seldom, uncommonly. **2. at times** ever and anon, every now and again, every now and then, every once in a while, every so often, from time to time, now and again, now and then, occasionally, on occasion, once in a while, sometimes.

RELATED KEYWORDS: A FEW, STRANGENESS, IRREGULARITY

RASHNESS

n. **1.** **1. rashness** carelessness, foolhardiness, headiness, heedlessness, hot-headedness, improvidence, imprudence, incaution, incautiousness, indiscreetness, indiscretion, lack of caution, thoughtlessness, unadvisedness. **2. impetuosity** haste, hastiness, hurry, hurry-scurry, impetuousness, impulsivity, precipitance, precipitancies, precipitancy, precipitate-ness, precipitation, precipitousness, prematurity, rush. **3. recklessness** adventurism, adventurousness, audaciousness, audacity, boldness, daredevilry, harum-scarum, over-confidence, presumption, rashness, temerariousness, temerity, wildcatting. **4. desperateness** blindness, craziness, desperation, madness, unreason, unreasonableness, wantonness, wildness. **5. rash act** leap in the dark.

2. **1. rash person** bull at a gate, harum-scarum, hothead, hotspur, madcap, rusher. **2. daredevil** adventurer, adventuress, fire-eater, gambler, Icarus, Promethean, scape-grace. **3. desperado** bravo. *Informal:* destructo.

adj. **3.** **1. rash** brash, devil-may-care, foolhardy, foolish, hardy, harum-scarum, hasty, head-less, headlong, ill-advised, ill-considered, ill-judged, impetuous, imprudent, indiscreet, injudicious, irrational, precipitate, reckless, unadvised, unconsidered, unguarded, unre-flecting, unthinking, unwary, unwise. **2. impetuous** adventurous, ardent, careless, dashing, devil-may-care, harebrained, headstrong, heady, heedless, hot-blooded, hot-headed, impassioned, impatient, mad, madcap, mindless, passionate, rash, reckless, self-willed, thoughtless, unmindful, warm-blooded, wilful. *Informal:* tearaway. **3. over-confident** confident, overbold, presumptuous. **4. hasty** headlong, hurried, hurry-scurry, impetuous, improvident, impulsive, incautious, indiscreet, overhasty, precipitant, precipitate, precipitative, precipitous, premature, quick, rash, rush, slapdash. *Informal:* go-go-go. **5. reckless** adventurous, audacious, bold, careless, daredevil, daring, des-perate, devil-may-care, free and easy, happy-go-lucky, hot-blooded, rash, temerarious, wildcat. **6. wild** blind, blindfold, crazy, unrealistic, unreasonable, wanton. *Informal:* trigger-happy. **7. suicidal** banzai, kamikaze.

v. **4.** **1. act rashly** bulldoze through, buy a pig in a poke, count one's chickens before they are hatched, go off half-cocked, rush in, rush in where angels fear to tread, rush one's fences. *Informal:* go at something baldheaded, go off the deep end, have bats in the belfry. **2. live dangerously** adventure, buy into trouble, chance, chance one's arm, give a hostage to fortune, hazard, play a dangerous game, play with fire, put all one's eggs in one basket, ride for a fall, risk, run the gauntlet, stick one's neck out, take a risk, tempt fate, tempt providence, venture. **3. stop at nothing** be extreme, go to any length(s), stop (or stick) at nothing. **4. burn one's fingers** get out of one's depth.

adv. **5.** **1. rashly** foolhardily, harum-scarum, heedlessly, ill-advisedly, improvidently, impru-dently, incautiously, indiscreetly, recklessly, temerariously, unadvisedly, wildly. **2. headstrongly** head over heels, headfirst, headily, headlong, hot-headedly. **3. over-confidently** adventurously, audaciously, boldly, confidently. **4. hastily** impetuously, impulsively, precipitantly, precipitately, precipitously, prematurely. **5. wildly** blind, blindly, crazily, desperately, unreasonably, wantonly. **6. pell-mell** (at) full fling, neck or nothing.

RELATED KEYWORDS: INATTENTION, IMPULSIVENESS, COURAGE, UNPREPAREDNESS, INSANITY

RAW MATERIALS

n. **1.** **1. raw materials** material, producer goods, raw stock, resources, staple, stuff, sub-stance. **2. raw material** bone, clay, fibre, glass, metal, mineral, ore, paper, plastics, rock, stone, timber, wax.

2. **1. timber** bentwood, cabinet wood, driftwood, hardwood, lumber, Mackay cedar, matchwood, millwork, softwood, stumpage *(US)*, veneer, wood, wood flour, wood pulp, woodchips, woodwool, wrought timber. **2. lumber** clog, faggot, fascine, flitch, four-by-two, log, nog, plank, rollway *(US)*, sawlog, scantling, shake, splint, stay, stick, stock, stud, two-by-four, yule log. **3. chipboard** beaverboard *(US)*, boxboard, cane-ite, corkboard, drywall *(US)*, gib board *(NZ)*, gibraltar board *(NZ)*, gyprock, particle board, pegboard, plasterboard, strawboard. **4. type of wood** amboyna, bamboo, basswood, beech, beechwood, birch *(NZ)*, black cypress pine, black locust, black pine, box, briarroot, briarwood, brushwood, calabash, calamander, calamus, camphorwood, candlewood, cedar, cypress, durmast, ebony, elm, fir, gopherwood, greenheart, guaiacum, gum, hazel, hickory, huon pine, ironwood, kingwood, lancewood, larch, lignum vitae, loblolly, logwood, longleaf pine, mahogany, mallet, maple, monterey pine, mulga, myall, narra, oak, padauk, partridge-wood, Philippine mahogany, pine, poon, poplar, red bean, red beech, red cedar, red fir, red oak, redwood, rosewood, saffronheart, sandalwood, santal, satinwood, shagbark *(US)*, shittim wood, spruce, sumach, tamarack, teak, tupelo, wainscot, walnut, white birch, white cedar, white pine, white poplar, whitewood, wicopy *(US)*, willow, yew, yiel-yiel, zebrawood. **5. wood pulp** mechanical wood pulp.

3. **1. paper** acid-free paper, art paper, blotting paper, bond paper, bristol board, broadsheet, brown paper, calender, carbon paper, cartridge paper, drawing paper, duplicating paper, flong, glassine, graph paper, india paper, kraft paper, laid paper, linen paper, newsprint, oil-paper, papier-mâché, papyrus, plotting paper, supercalendered paper, tape, vellum, wax-paper, white paper, wood-free paper, wove paper. **2. stationery** continuous roll stationery, fanfold, notepaper, parchment, scroll, writing paper. **3. tissue paper** crepe, filter paper, flimsy, kleenex, rice paper, tissue, toilet paper, tracing paper. **4. cardboard** Bristol board, card, corrugated paper, manila, manila paper, millboard, pasteboard, scaleboard. **5. confetti** ticker tape.

4. **1. base course material** asphalt, bitumen, blacktop, blue metal, chipping, cobble, cobblestone, coronus, hardcore, macadam, maltha, metal, mineral pitch, mineral tar, road metal, roadbed, rumble strip, seal, surface dressing, tar, tarmac, tarmacadam, tarseal *(NZ)*, the bitumen.

5. **1. plant material** abaca, abb, acaroid, acetate fibre, acrilan, agalloch, alaska, aloe, ambary, amber, animé, balsam, berlin, berlin wool, bouclé, brazil, byssus, cachou, cane, caoutchouc, carpet wool, catechu, clothing wool, coir, colophony, combed yarn, combing wool, cotton, cottonwool, crewel, esparto, factice, fibre, filasse, fingering, flax, floss, gomuti, gossamer, grease, gum, gum resin, gutta-percha, haulm, hemp, henequen, homespun, istle, ixtle, jute, kapok, kauri gum, kenaf, lac, latex, linen, lint cotton, lisle thread, lurex, maguey, manila, manila hemp, manila rope, merino, mungo, oil of turpentine, organzine, osier, palm butter, palm oil, piassava, pita, plucked wool, raffia, ramie, rattan, raw silk, rayon, resin, rope yarn, rosin, rubber, rush, scoured wool, shellac, shoddy, silk, sisal, skin wool, sleave, slipe, slub, sola, spinner's type, staple, storax, straw, sunn, tanbark, thrown silk, tolu, top maker's type, tow, triacetate fibre, turpentine, tussah, tusser, tussore, ule, vegetable silk, vegetable tallow, vetiver, whangee, wicker, wild rubber, wool, worsted, yarn, zein, zephyr yarn.

6. **1. metal** alloy, aluminium foil, angle iron, barbed wire, barbwire, cellophane, ceramal, cermet, ceruse, chain mesh, chain wire, cheese cutter, chicken wire, crosshair, crosswire, faggot, fascine, fencing panel, fencing wire, fettling, galvanised iron, haywire, iron, latten, mesh, mu-metal, netting wire, niello, piano wire, pig iron, pile, platinised asbestos, pot metal, pressed steel, pyrophoric alloy, scrap iron, scrap metal, sheet iron, sheet metal, silver foil, silver paper, smoothing-iron, solder, stainless steel, steelwork, string, terneplate, tie-wire, tin, tinfoil, weldmesh, wire, wire gauze, wire netting, wire rope. *Informal:* alfoil.

7. **1. plastic** acetate fibre, acrylate resin, acrylic, acrylic resin, araldite, bakelite, celluloid, copolymer, ebonite, erinoid, ethenoid plastics, fibreglass, fluon, foam (rubber), formica, Kevlar, laminated plastic, lurex, lycra, monofil, neoprene, nylon, perspex, phenolic resin, plasticine, plexiglas, poly-cotton, polyester, polyethylene, polymethyl methacrylate, polypropylene, polystyrene, polytetrafluoroethylene, polythene, polyurethane, polyvinyl acetate, polyvinyl chloride, PVC, rayon, spun glass, styrene, styrofoam, teflon, thermoplastics, tinsel, urea formaldehyde, vinyl, vulcanised fibre, vulcanite, xylonite.

8. **1. wax** beeswax, carnauba, ceresin, ceroplastics, cerumen, earth wax, earwax, japan wax, lignite wax, maltha, paraffin, paraffin wax, sperm, spermaceti, tallow, vegetable wax, white wax.

9. **1. bone or shell material** baleen, bone, buck's horn, buckhorn, cuttlebone, horn, ivory, mother-of-pearl, nacre, tortoiseshell, whalebone.

10. **1. building materials** bricks and mortar, lath and plaster, wattle and daub. **2. brick** adobe, ashlar, building block, cement, concrete, plaster, stone. **3. mortar** binder, mastic. **4. roofing** cladding, sheathing, shingle, slate, stucco, thatch, tile, veneering. **5. flooring** boarding, decking, duckboard, floor, lino, linoleum, linotile, malthoid, panelling, paving, planking, stringboard, studding, vinyl tile. **6. insulation**

aerogel, asbestos, batt, batting, fibreglass, fireproofing, glass fibre, rockwool. **7. rubble** backfill, ballast, bedding, fill, filler, riprap.

11. **1. type of building material** acoustic tile, aggregate, airbrick, bauxite cement, besser block, breezeblock, brownstone *(US)*, calc-sinter, callow, cavity block, cement render, chamferboard, clapboard, clinker, cob, common brick, corrugated iron, deal, dimension stone, dressings, drummy, drywall *(US)*, face brick, facia board, facing, ferroconcrete, fibreboard, fibro, fibrocement, fibrous plaster, firebrick, firestone, flagstone, full brick, furring, galvanised iron, gibraltar board *(NZ)*, glass brick, granite, granolith, grout, gyprock, hardboard, lath, loam, marble, masonite, mastic, matchboard, pantile, parget, pargeting, parquet, pavement, paving stone, pisé, plaster, plasterboard, plywood, Portland cement, prestressed concrete, pricking coat, putty, quicklime, quoin, rag *(British)*, rammed earth, ready-mix, refractories, reinforced concrete, render, rendering, revetment, ridge tile, roofing felt, roughcast, rumbled brick, sandstock brick, sandstone, sett, setting coat, siding, skimming coat, staff, stucco, terrazzo, three-ply, travertine, wainscoting, wallboard, wattle and daub, weather-stripping, weatherboard, weatherboarding. *Informal:* galvo. **2. paint** clobber, colourwash, daub, distemper, dope, duco, estapol, gesso, glazing, kalsomine, lacquer, overglaze, poster paint, primer, sealant, sealer, undercoating *(US)*, underseal, varnish, whitewash.

12. **1. clay** adobe, angel stone, argil, bole, brick clay, china clay, china stone, fireclay, frit, fuller's earth, kaolin, lithomarge, malm, paste, petuntse, pipeclay, puddle, slip, terra alba, till.

13. **1. carbon** activated charcoal, active carbon, alicyclic, black lead, carbon black, carbon fibre, char, charcoal, coal, coke, colloidal graphite, fusain, graphite, kish, lampblack, plumbago, retinite, soft coal.

14. **1. glass** bottle-glass, crown glass, cullet, fibreglass, flint glass, fused silica, georgian glass, glass fibre, glass wool, laminated glass, looking glass, murrhine glass, opal glass, optical flint glass, pot glass, pot metal, pyrex, quartz glass, ruby glass, safety glass, shatterproof glass, silica glass, smalt, spun glass, tank glass, toughened glass, vitreous silica, vitrolite.

RELATED KEYWORDS: CREATION, MATTER, METAL, OIL, ROCK, SUPPLY, TEXTILES

REACTION

n. **1.** **1. reaction** answer, echo, feedback, redoublement, rejoinder, reply, respond, respondence, response, return. **2. reflex** knee jerk, kneejerk, shy, start, wince. **3. recoil** backlash, boomerang, kick, rebound, repercussion, reverberation. *Informal:* kickback. **4. backstroke** cannon, carom, ricochet.

adj. **2.** **1. reactive** correspondence, responsive, sensitive, tropistic. **2. reflex** boomerang, feedback, repercussive. **3. hyperreactive** supersensitive.

v. **3.** **1. react** answer, answer to, reply, respond, take it. **2. shy** curl, flinch, jerk, jog, prop, recoil, start, wince. **3. overreact** *Informal:* arc up, freak out, pop one's cork. **4. recoil** cannon, flinch, kick, ricochet. **5. rebound** boomerang, come home to roost, redound, spring back.

RELATED KEYWORDS: ATTRACTION, REPULSION, HITTING, MOVEMENT, ANSWER

READING

n. **1.** **1. reading** intelligibility, map-reading, perusal, read. **2. literacy** reading ability. **3. readableness** decipherability, legibility, legibleness, readability. **4. machine reading** bar coding, e-book reader, electronic scanning, MICR encoding, OCR, optical character reading. **5. reading room** reading desk.

2. **1. reader** bibliophile, bookworm, browser, peruser. **2. readership** readers, subscribers. **3. proofreader** copyreader, proofer, reader. *Informal:* taster.

adj. **3.** **1. readable** decipherable, intelligible, legible, machine-readable, perusable, written.

v. **4.** **1. read** bury oneself in, dip into, go over, peruse, pore over, study, wade through. **2. scan** browse, leaf through, look at, run one's eye over, run through, skim, speed read, taste, thumb through.

RELATED KEYWORDS: KNOWLEDGE, BOOK, SPEECH

REALISM

n. **1.** **1. realism** common sense, earthiness, factualism, factuality, sense, soberness. **2. reality** hardpan, the facts of life, the harsh reality, the truth of the matter. **3. worldliness** hardheadedness, practicality, pragmatism, worldly-mindedness. **4. naturalism** mimesis, social realism, verism.

2. **1. realist** factualist, hardhead, pragmatist, utilitarian, verist. *Informal:* nuts-and-bolts man.

adj. 3. **1. realistic** banausic, bread-and-butter, businesslike, commonsensical, down-to-earth, fanciless, hard-headed, level-headed, matter-of-fact, no-nonsense, practical, pragmatic, sober, unsentimental, utilitarian, worldly, worldly-minded. **2. naturalistic** 3-D, factual, lifelike, living, mimetic, photographic, real, three-dimensional, true-to-life, truthful. **3. earthy** kitchen-sink, veristic, warts-and-all.

v. 4. **1. be realistic** come down (or back) to earth, face facts, get down to tintacks, get wise, have one's feet on the ground, keep one's feet on the ground, know which side one's bread is buttered. **2. make realistic** bring to the light of day, deglamourise, demystify, make come true, realise.

adv. 5. **1. realistically** factually, soberly.

phr. 6. **1. such is life** that's the way it goes. *Informal:* that's the way the cookie crumbles, them's the breaks.

RELATED KEYWORDS: HONESTY, REPRESENTATION, TRUTH

REAR

n. 1. **1. rear** background, backside, gorge, stern. **2. back** reverse, tail. **3. reverse** B-side, smooth, verso. **4. tail end** stern. **5. posterior** behind, bottom, breech, buttock, dorsum, hindquarters, rear, rump. *Informal:* acre, backside, bot, bum, butt, chuff, clacker, ding, dinger, jacksy *(NZ)*, slats, tail. **6. posteriority** postposition. **7. rearguard**. **8. retroflexion** resupination, retroversion.

adj. 2. **1. rear** aft, after, epaxial, hind, hinder, posterior, posticous, tail. **2. hindmost** aftermost, backmost, hindermost, rearmost, sternmost. **3. background** distance, middle distance. **4. backstage**. **5. back** reverse, tail. **6. backward** hindward, rearward. **7. retroflex** resupinate, retrorse, retroussé, revolute.

adv. 3. **1. behind** abaft, adrift of, after. **2. backwards** back, hindwards, rearwards, sternwards. **3. aback** abaft, aft, astern. **4. posteriorly** epaxially, retrorsely. **5. backstage** upstage.

RELATED KEYWORDS: BODY, COMING AFTER, BOTTOM

RECORD

n. 1. **1. record** account, anamnesis, anecdotage, autobiography, backlist, biodata, biography, chronicle, Commentaries, curriculum vitae, CV, document, enumeration, history, life, lifetime, lore, memoir, narration, narrative, prosopography, résumé, register, report, statement, story, tally, track record, travels. *Informal:* bio. **2. annals** archives, commentaries, descant, oral history, reminiscences, transactions. **3. notes** adversaria, brief, briefing, cahier, case history, case record, detail, dictation, item, minutes, particular. **4. note** billet, bulletin, chit, chitty, circular, communiqué, entry, memorandum, newsletter, notation, notice, notification, observation, registration, sidenote, tone *(Chiefly US)*. *Informal:* bung, memo, snarler. **5. file** card catalogue, card file, card index, fiche, field book, filing card, form, jotter, medallion, microfiche, notebook, notepad, notepaper, onion skin, pad, papyrus, parchment, pocket-book, pocketbook, scratchpad *(US)*, scribble block, scribble pad, scroll, slip, stationery, stub, table-book, tablet, vellum, work sheet, writing pad, writing paper. **6. parish register** family bible, vestry book. **7. register** cartulary, chartulary, daybook, journal, logbook, manifest, plod, service record, visitors' book. **8. scorebook** scoreboard, scorecard, scoresheet. **9. score** crenellation, line, lineation, notch, return, scratch, stroke. **10. quipu** glyph, pictograph. **11. legal record** charter *(US)*, court roll, guarantee, specialty, transcript, transcription, transumpt. **12. Act** enactment, statute, statute book. **13. government gazette** gazette, Hansard, law report. **14. articles** articles of association, memorandum, memorandum of association. **15. deed** cadastre, provenance, terrar, terrier, title deed, will. **16. electoral register** census, electoral roll, roll.

2. **1. diary** black book, casebook, commonplace book, daybook, exercise book, flight log, flightlog, journal, log, logbook, personal organiser, ringbinder, tickler *(US)*, workbook. *Informal:* dole diary. **2. album** scrapbook. *Informal:* skitebook.

3. **1. certificate** birth certificate, certificate of title, death certificate, group certificate, land certificate, lines, marriage certificate, master's certificate, navicert, ticket. **2. casebook** bill of health. **3. licence** driving licence, learner's licence, learner's permit, miner's right, pass, passport, trading certificate, visa. *Informal:* learner's. **4. ship's papers** clearance papers, papers, sea letter, working papers.

4. **1. computer record** file, record. **2. database** corpus, memory bank.

5. 1. **recorder** amanuensis, annalist, archivist, biographer, chronicler, clerk *(Chiefly US)*, diarist, filer, hagiographer, hagiologist, historian, historiographer, jerquer, rapporteur, registrar, scorer, secretary, tallyclerk, tallyman. *Informal:* chaser, girl Friday. **2. personnel** office, secretariat. **3. recording instrument** cassette recorder, dvd recorder, oscillograph, seismograph, tape recorder, VCR, video recorder. **4. flight recorder** black box.

adj. 6. 1. **historical** annalistic, archival, biographical, cadastral, hierogrammatic, philologic.

v. 7. 1. **record** book, brief, calendar, card, catalogue, chronicle, diarise, enrol, enter, inscribe, interline, item, journalise, keep track of, log, manifest, minute, notate, note, protocol, put down, register, score, videorecord. *Informal:* keep tabs on. **2. file** archive. **3. tally** mark up, nick, notch, notch up, rack, reckon, record, score. *Informal:* put on the slate.

RELATED KEYWORDS: ACCOUNTING, LIST, WRITING, REMEMBERING

RED

n. 1. 1. **red** blood red, carmine, carnation, Chinese red, chrome red, cinnabar, Congo red, crimson, flame colour, ginger, incarnadine, Indian red, orangey-red, pink, pompadour, Pompeian red, poppy, ruby, rust, scarlet, titian, Turkey red, Venetian red, vermeil, vermilion. **2. maroon** grape, murex, murrey. **3. pink** alsinaceous, carnation, flesh, flesh colour, hot pink, lolly pink, old rose, peachblow, rose, shocking pink.

2. 1. **red dye** alkanet, anatto, anchusin, annatto, bloodroot, brazil, camwood, carmine, cochineal, henna, keel *(British)*, kermes, lake, madder, mehndi, orcein, puccoon, purpurin, raddle, red ochre, reddish, reddle, redwood, rhodamine, rosaniline, ruddle, safranine, sappanwood, solferino, Turkey red, Venetian red, vermilion. **2. make-up** blusher, lip gloss, lipstick, rouge. *Informal:* lippie, lippy.

3. 1. **redness** blush, colour, floridity, floridness, flush, gules, reddishness, rubicundity, ruddiness. **2. rosiness** pinkness. **3. bloodiness** angriness, erythema, erythrism, erythroderma, erythrophobia, flush, hectic flush, inflammation, sanguineness.

4. 1. **reddening** blushing, erubescence, rubefaction, rubescence, rubrication, rufescence. **2. rubricator**.

5. 1. **redhead** strawberry blonde. *Informal:* blood nut, blue, bushfire blonde, carrot top, coppertop, Ginger.

adj. 6. 1. **red** cardinal, cherry, gules, high-coloured, laky, rubicund, ruddy, sanguine. **2. crimson** carmine, cerise, claret, garnet, incarnadine, incarnate, rubious *(Poetic)*, ruby. **3. scarlet** Chinese red, vermeil, vermilion. **4. blood-red** bloodied, bloodlike, bloodstained, bloody, ensanguined, gory, plurry, sanguinary, sanguine, sanguineous, sanguinolent. **5. magenta** murex, port, vinous, wine, wine-coloured, wine-red. **6. pink** blush, carnation, damask. **7. rose** coloured, rosaceous, rose-coloured, roseate, roselike, rosy, rubicund. **8. salmon** apricot, coral, coral-coloured, coralline, peach, peachy, salmon pink, sandy. **9. pinkish** flamingo, flesh-coloured, incarnadine, incarnate. **10. carroty** flame-coloured, gingery, orange. **11. russet** auburn, brick red, bronze, copper, coppery, cupreous, ferruginous, foxy, ginger, hazel, hepatic, lateritious, liver, mahogany, maroon, rubiginous, rust-coloured, rusty, terracotta, testaceous.

7. 1. **reddish** erubescent, rubicund, ruddy, rufescent, rufous, sanguine, strawberry, warm. **2. inflamed** angry, bloodshot, erythematous, erythrismal, hyperaemic, inflammatory, injected, reddened, rubefacient. **3. red-faced** blowzy, blushing, florid, flushed, high-coloured, raddled, red, reddish, rosy-cheeked, rouged, rubescent, rubicund. **4. red-headed** carroty, sandy.

v. 8. 1. **redden** bloody, blush, colour, crimson, ensanguine, flush, inflame, mantle, raddle, rubricate, vermilion. **2. rouge** henna. **3. flush** blush, change colour, colour, colour up, flame up, have the blood rush to one's cheeks, inflame, mantle, redden, rose.

adv. 9. 1. **redly** bloodily, sanguinely. **2. rosily** roseately. **3. red-facedly** floridly.

RELATED KEYWORDS: BROWN, COLOUR, ORANGE, PURPLE

REFUSAL

n. 1. 1. **refusal** declension, declinature, denial, negation, no, non-compliance, point-blank refusal, rebuff. **2. negativity** disapproval, discountenance, negativeness, negativism. **3. veto** disallowance, thumbs down.

2. 1. **rejection** dismissal, knock-back, repudiation, repulse. *Informal:* the (old) heave-ho, the big A. **2. renunciation** abnegation, forswearing, self-denial.

3. 1. **discard** cast-off, reject, throw-out, throwaway.

4. **1. refuser** abnegator, denier, depriver, rejecter, repeller, repulser, spurner. **2. decliner** anti, baulker, demurrer, disclaimer, dissenter, dissentient, dissident, maverick, negativist, protestant, rebel, remonstrant.

v. **5.** **1. refuse** begrudge, deny, not come at, not hear of. **2. baulk at** beg off, chicken out, jack up, kick, kick against. **3. draw the line at** have nothing to do with, have second thoughts, not be in it, set one's face against, turn a deaf ear. **4. veto** decline, disallow, negative, send back, withhold consent from.

6. **1. reject** discountenance, knock back, rebuff, repulse, send away with a flea in the ear, slam the door in someone's face, spurn, turn down, turn one's back on, wash one's hands of. **2. discard** cast away, cast off, disown, reject. *Informal:* junk. **3. renounce** abnegate, forswear, give up, kick the habit, pass up.

RELATED KEYWORDS: DISAGREEMENT, DENIAL, CANCELLATION, PROHIBITION

REGION

n. **1.** **1. region** airspace, area, block, bourn, corner, country, demesne, distance, district, domain, energy field, eparchy, expanse, extent, federal territory, fetch, land, length, limit, limits, locale, locality, location, nation, natural region, neighbourhood, pale, parts, piece *(US)*, place, precinct, precincts, province, purlieu, quarter, range, reach, realm, redevelopment area, restricted area, scope, space, spacing, span, state, straddle, stretch, swath, swathe, terrene, time zone, tract, tract of land, vicinage, zone, zonule. *Informal:* neck of the woods. **2. subdistrict** subregion. **3. neighbourhood** precincts, presence, propinquity, proximity, purlieus, terrain, territory, vicinage, vicinity. *Informal:* backyard. **4. territory** beat, block *(NZ)*, demesne, district, geography, range, region, terrain, terrene. **5. quarter** barrio *(US)*, colony, enclave, exclave, ghetto, plantation, pocket. **6. corridor** air corridor, confines, hook, march, purlieu. **7. lowland** mickery country, surge area, surge line, tideland *(US)*, warpland. **8. top end** *(Informal)* upstate *(US)*. **9. eastern states** northland, southland, the west, west. **10. hinterland** heartland, inland, interior, midland, up-country. **11. frontier** bamboo curtain, border, borderland, boundary, bounds, fringe, margin, outskirts, rand *(Scottish)*, Rubicon, skirts, terminus, verge. **12. no-man's-land** limbo. **13. terra incognita** parts unknown.

2. **1. domain** bourn, demesne, estate, fee, feoff, fief, grounds, kingdom, land, lordship, manor, mesnalty, princedom, principality, queendom, realm, seigneury, seigniory, thanage. **2. kingdom** archduchy, archdukedom, baronage, barony, demesne, duchy, dukedom, earldom, empery *(Poetic)*, grand duchy, margravate, marquisate, palatinate, princedom, realm, regency, territory, thanage. **3. emirate** khanate, sheikhdom, sultanate. **4. district** arrondissement, barrio, borough, built-up area, canton, city, constituency *(British)*, council, country, county, deme, demesne, department, division, dormitory, eparchy, faubourg, federal district, hundred, local government area, lot *(Chiefly US)*, municipal district, municipality, nation, nomarchy, nome, oblast, parish *(British)*, precinct *(US)*, prefecture, province, region, riding, satrapy, shire, state, subdivision, suburb, territory, township, ward. **5. electorate** borough *(British)*, constituency, country seat, seat, ward. **6. jurisdiction** area, compass, free (or full) rein, gauge, judicature, magistracy, room, scope, verge. **7. church land** glebe, glebe land, prebend. **8. parish** mission, vicarate, vicariate. **9. diocese** archbishopric, archdeaconry, archdiocese, bishopric, eparchy, see.

3. **1. field** acre, approvement, back run, baulk, close, common, cornfield, downland, downs, enclosure, farmland, glebe *(Poetic)*, granary, grassland, gumfield, heath, infield, ley, ley line, long paddock, mead *(Poetic)*, meadow *(Chiefly British, US)*, moor, outfield, paddock, pampas, prairie, saddling paddock, savanna, sheepwalk, springer paddock, steppe, stock run, swidden, town common, tundra, turbary, walk, water meadow. **2. paddock** birdcage, enclosure, home paddock, hospital paddock, lunging paddock, police paddock, saddling paddock, spelling paddock. **3. farmyard** barnyard, yard. **4. park** deer park, garden, native reserve, parkland, pleasance, preserve, reserve, rest area.

4. **1. yard** backyard, garden. **2. courtyard** atrium, auricle, backyard, cloister, cloistergarth, close, cortile, court, court shoe, cul-de-sac, forecourt, frontage, garden, garth, lawn, parvis, patio, yard. **3. patio** terrace. **4. schoolyard** campus, playground, quadrangle. *Informal:* quad.

5. **1. building block** acreage, allotment, battleaxe block, block, bush block, curtilage, lot, mark, plat, plot, section, vacant allotment, yard.

6. **1. square** banquette *(Southern US)*, esplanade, footway, kerb, path, pathway, pavement, paving, piazza, place, plaza, roadside, sidewalk *(US)*, walk, walkway. **2. meeting place** agora, forum, marae.

7.   **1. industrial estate** industrial park, trading estate *(British)*. **2. goods yard** brickfield, brickyard, caryard, dockyard, freight terminal, lumberyard, shipyard, stockyard, timber yard, yard. **3. car park** parking area, parking lot *(Chiefly US)*. **4. airfield** field, flying field, pad. **5. gas field** goldfield, oilfield.

adj. 8.   **1. regional** archducal, areal, baronial, local, sectional, subregional, territorial, topographic, topographical, zonal. **2. local** civic, municipal, parochial, territorial, topical. **3. provincial** cantonal, county, departmental, diocesan, divisional, divisionary, eparchial, local, municipal, parochial, prefectural, suburbicarian. **4. interstate** intrastate, upstate *(US)*. **5. neighbouring** adjacent, adjoining, approximal, circumlittoral, connivent, conterminous, contiguous, coterminous, immediate, nearby, neighbour *(US)*, next door, next-door, proximate, surrounding, vicinal.

adv. 9.   **1. regionally** topographically. **2. locally** provincially, territorially, topically.

RELATED KEYWORDS: CITY, THE BUSH, FARMING, PLANTS, LAND, NATION

REGULARITY

n. 1.   **1. regularity** even timing, frequency, isochronism, natural frequency, periodicity, rhythm, rhythmics, rotation, sequacity. **2. biorhythms** alternation of generations, catamenia, circadian rhythms, courses, life cycle, menses, menstrual cycle, menstruation, oestrus cycle, period. *Informal:* girl's week, monthlies, the curse.

2.   **1. anniversary** bicentenary, bicentennial, biennial, centenary, centennial *(US, NZ)*, decennial, jubilee, millennium, quatercentenary, quincentenary, quindecennial, quinquennial, sesquicentenary, sexcentenary, tercentenary, triennial. **2. birthday** feast day *(Philippine English)*, name-day. **3. wedding anniversary** diamond wedding, golden wedding, silver wedding, tin wedding, wooden wedding. **4. Australia Day** Anzac Day, Remembrance Day.

adj. 3.   **1. regular** centennial, constant, equinoctial, even, habitual, horary, hourly, isochronal, isochronous, iterative, measured, momentary, periodic, periodical, recurrent, repeated, repetitious, repetitive, return, rhythmic, rhythmical, seasonal, serial, steady, systolic, tercentennial. **2. alternate** alternant, bicyclic, bimestrial, bimonthly, biweekly, cyclic, every other, peristaltic, reciprocal, revolving, rotary, rotatable, rotational, rotative, rotatory, sequential, successive.

v. 4.   **1. alternate** interchange, reciprocate, recur, take turns, vary. **2. cycle** circulate, revolve, roll round, rotate, turn, wheel.

adv. 5.   **1. regularly** in phase, isochronally, isochronously, like clockwork, measuredly, periodically, rhythmically, sequaciously, serially, steadily, steady. **2. alternately** about, at intervals, by rote, by turns, cyclically, every other day, in rotation, in turn, seasonally, to-and-fro, turn and turn about.

RELATED KEYWORDS: FREQUENCY, PERIOD, RHYTHM, TIME MEASUREMENT

RELATION

n. 1.   **1. relation** affinity, alliance, apposition, association, cognation, coherence, cohesion, combination, communality, confederation, connation, connection, consonance, correlation, correspondence, homomorphism, kinship, nearness, propinquity, proportionality, rapport, relationship, relativity, respondence. **2. compatibility** analogousness, appositeness, compatibleness, correlativeness, relativeness. **3. interrelation** correlation, intercommunion, interrelationship, reciprocality, reciprocation, reciprocity, return.

2.   **1. relationship** affiliation, affinity, alliance, ascription, association, combination, confederation, connection, filiation, knot, liaison, ligature, marriage, relation, tie, tie-up, wedlock. **2. transitive relation** class inclusion. **3. something in common** common denominator, commonage, universal. **4. ratio** correlation, per cent, perspective, proportion, scale. **5. commensuration** per cent, percentage.

adj. 3.   **1. related** affined, affinitive, agnate, akin, allied, analogous, appendant, associated, cognate, connectional, consanguineous, correspondent, corresponding, enate, incident, interdependent, interrelated, relational, relative. **2. proportional** commensurate, correlative, pro rata, proportionate, proportioned. **3. common** collective, communal, conjunctive, cooperative, joint, mutual, shared, social, societal, syndetic, united. **4. correlative** correlated, interrelated, mutual, mutually related, reciprocal, reciprocative. **5. relevant** agreeable, appertaining, applicable, apposite, appropriate, appurtenant, apropos, apt, becoming, befitting, belonging, congruous, decent, due, fit, fitting, generic, germane, in point, opportune, perfect, pertinent, proper, ready-made, relating, relative, right, suitable, to the point, topical, universal, well-adapted.

v. 4.   **1. relate** ally, associate, attach, connect, consort, couple, double, mutualise *(Chiefly US)*, tie in. **2. concern** appertain to, apply to, be in respect of, have regard to, have to do with, pertain to, refer to, touch. **3. interrelate** cohere, correlate, knit, match. **4. reciprocate** return.

adv. **5. 1. relatively** according as, commensurately, comparatively, in proportion, pro rata, proportionally. **2. reciprocally** answerably, appositely, correlatively, in common, jointly, mutually, together.

6. 1. appositively appositionally, associatively, coherently, connately, connectedly, intimately, near, nearly, relatedly. **2. analogously** analogically, correspondently.

prep. **7. 1. concerning** about, after, apropos, apropos of, as for, as regards, as to, association, between, in point of, in respect, of, on, regarding, respecting, touching on, towards, vis-a-vis, with reference to, with regard to, with respect to.

RELATED KEYWORDS: ACCORD, COMPARISON, EQUALITY, INTERACTION

RELATIVE

n. **1. 1. relative** ancestor, clansman, clanswoman, cousin, enate, in-law, kin, kinsman, kinswoman, lation *(Aboriginal English)*, next of kin, relation, sib, tribesman. *Informal:* rellie. **2. kin** ancestry, birth, blood, breed, clan, descent, extraction, family, flesh, flesh and blood, generation, gens, heredity, house, ilk, increase, issue, kindred, kinsfolk, kith and kin, line, lineage, name, nation, nationality, offspring, origin, parentage, pedigree, people, posterity, progenitor, progeny, race, relation, relatives, seed, sept, strain, tribe. *Informal:* brood. **3. family** biological family, blended family, extended family, family circle, folks, nuclear family, single-parent family. **4. tribalist** nepotist. **5. blood relation** agnate, anastomosis, cognate, collateral, connection. **6. aunt** aunty, grand-aunt, great-aunt. **7. uncle** grand-uncle, great-uncle. **8. niece** grand-niece, great-niece. **9. nephew** grand-nephew, great-nephew. **10. cousin** brother *(Aboriginal English)*, country cousin, cousin brother *(Aboriginal English)*, cousin sister *(Aboriginal English)*, cousin-german, coz, first cousin, first cousin once removed, full cousin, kin, kinsman, kinswoman, parallel cousin, second cousin. *Informal:* cuz.

2. 1. parent biological parent, olds, parent-in-law, parents, sole parent. *Informal:* oldie, rent, the olds. **2. foster-parent** father-in-law, foster-father, foster-mother, godfather, godmother, godparent, step-parent, stepfather, stepmother. **3. mother** biological mother, birth mother, ibu *(Malaysian English)*, mama, mamma, mammy, mater, mater dolorosa, materfamilias, nursing mother, surrogate mother. *Informal:* ma, mom *(US)*, mum, mummy, old girl *(Chiefly British)*, old lady, old woman. **4. foster-mother** foster-parent, godmother, godparent, mother-in-law, step-parent, stepmother. **5. father** begetter, biological father, ecumenical patriarch, genitor, père, papa, pappy *(Chiefly Southern US)*, pater, paterfamilias, patriarch, sire *(Poetic)*. *Informal:* dad, dadda, daddy, daddy-o *(Chiefly US)*, gaffer *(British)*, governor, old boy *(Chiefly British)*, old man, pa, pop, poppa. **6. foster-father** father-in-law, foster-parent, godfather, godparent, step-parent, stepfather. **7. grandparent** great-grandfather, great-grandmother, great-grandparent, tipuna *(NZ)*. **8. grandmother** grandam, grande dame, grandmamma. *Informal:* gran, grandma, granny, nan, nanna, nanny, nonna. **9. grandfather** grampus, grandpapa. *Informal:* grampers, gramps, grandad, grandpa, nonno, pop, poppa.

3. 1. child affiliate, baby, bairn *(Chiefly Scottish)*, bambino, boy, chiel *(Scottish)*, cooboo *(WA)*, daughter, descendant, favourite son, innocent, laddie *(Chiefly Scottish)*, little ones, moppet, offshoot, offspring, scion, son, sonny, sprig, sprout, young, youngster. *Informal:* ankle-biter, billy, brat, chick, diddums, joey, kid, kiddie, little tacker *(Especially WA, SA, Victoria and Tasmania)*, littlie, nipper, piccaninny, rug rat, smacker, sprog, subteen, tiddler, tin lid, tweeny, young'un, youngie. **2. grandchild** grand-daughter, granddaughter, grandson, great-grandchild, great-granddaughter, great-grandson, mokopuna *(NZ)*. **3. foster-child** daughter-in-law, foster, foster-daughter, foster-son, fosterling, godchild, goddaughter, godson, son, son-in-law, stepchild, stepdaughter, stepson, ward.

4. 1. sibling brother, brudda *(Aboriginal English)*, fraternal twin, half-blood, hemitrope, identical twin, macle, Siamese twins, sib, sister, thitha *(Aboriginal English)*, tidda *(Aboriginal English)*, titja *(Aboriginal English)*, twins. *Informal:* bro *(Aboriginal English)*. **2. sister** foster-sister, full sister, half-sister, sibling, sister-german, sister-in-law, stepsister, thitha *(Aboriginal English)*, tidda *(Aboriginal English)*, titja *(Aboriginal English)*, whole sister. *Informal:* blister, sis, skin and blister. **3. brother** blood brother, brother-german, brother-in-law, brudda *(Aboriginal English)*, foster-brother, frère, frater, full brother, half-brother, sibling, stepbrother, whole brother. *Informal:* binghi, brer *(Southern US)*, bro *(Aboriginal English)*, bud.

5. 1. kinship agnation, clanship, cognation, consanguinity, cosinage, filiation, nick, relation, relative. **2. familial relationship** brotherhood, fatherhood, fraternalism, fraternity, maternity, motherhood, parenthood, paternity, sisterhood. **3. cousinhood** consanguinity, cosinage, cousinship, kindredship. **4. kinship system** matriarchate, matriarchy, patriarchate, patriarchy. **5. tribalism** clannishness, nepotism. **6. littermate**.

adj. **6.** **1. kindred** akin, kin, near, of kin, once removed, related, sib, twice removed, uterine. **2. consanguine** adoptive, agnate, agnatic, akin, allied, analogous, cognate, connected, consanguineous, correspondent, enate, german, related, relational, relative. **3. familial** family, near. **4. nepotic** clannish, incestuous. **5. tribal** tribalist, tribalistic.

7. **1. parental** parent, parent-like. **2. maternal** grandmotherly, maternity, mother, novercal. **3. paternal** grandfatherly, patriarchal. **4. avuncular**. **5. daughterly** filial.

RELATED KEYWORDS: OFFSPRING, PARENTAGE, MARRIAGE

RELIGION

n. **1.** **1. religion** belief, covenant, denomination, discipleship, faith, persuasion. **2. sect** cult. **3. state religion** established church, establishment. **4. theology** angelology, Christology, covenant theology, divinity, ecclesiology, eschatology, federal theology, hagiology, moral theology, ontology, soteriology, theodicy.

2. **1. heresy** anathema, false doctrine, misbelief, nonconformity. **2. unorthodoxy** dissent, heterodoxy, schism, superstition, unconformity. **3. excommunication**.

3. **1. religious person** adherent, believer, born-again, churchgoer, congregant, co-religionist, deist, disciple, kirkman *(Scottish)*. **2. dogmatist** apologist, dogmatiser. **3. evangelist** apostle, Biblicist, Bibliolater, Biblist, crusader, enthusiast, evangelical, fanatic, fundamentalist, gospeller, missionary, missioner, preacher, revivalist, salvationist, zealot. *Informal:* Amen snorter, bible-banger, bible-basher, hot-gospeller, Jesus-freak. **4. neophyte** catechumen. **5. congregation** church, ecclesia, flock, fold. **6. layperson** brother, churchman, churchwarden, churchwoman, civilian, elder, laic, layman, laywoman, papal knight, parishioner, secular, sidesman. **7. the elect** the faithful. **8. diocesan** regular tertiary, secular tertiary, tertiary. **9. lay preacher** acolyte, lay reader. **10. server** acolyte, altar boy, parish clerk *(British)*, sacristan. **11. laity** brotherhood, confraternity, frère, fraternity, sodality. **12. Bible Belt**.

4. **1. theism** deism, ditheism, divinity, dualism, henotheism, monolatry, monotheism, polytheism, theanthropism, theogony, therianthropism. **2. pantheism** ahimsa, animism, dharma, jnana-yoga, karma, naturalism, palingenesis, reincarnation, vedaism, vedanta.

5. **1. evangelicalism** ecclesiasticism, Pentecostalism. **2. fundamentalism**. **3. creationism** intelligent design.

6. **1. heretic** heresiarch. **2. dissenter** nonconformist. *Informal:* Callithumpian.

adj. **7.** **1. religious** churchgoing, devotional, god-fearing, holy, monkish, monolatrous, spiritual, spiritualist, theocentric. **2. theistic** deistic, deistical, ditheistic, monotheistic, pantheistic, polytheistic, theandric, theanthropic, theist, tritheistic. **3. evangelical** born-again, charismatic, evangelistic, exegetic, gospel, kerugmatik, missionary, Pentecostal, redemptive, redemptory, revivalistic, vatic. **4. fundamentalist** fanatical, fire-and-brimstone. **5. theological** Aaronic, churchly, cleric, clerical, ecclesiastic, ecclesiastical, eschatological, hieratic, ministerial, ontological, priestly, rabbinical, sacerdotal, vicarial, vicarly. **6. canonical** credal, creedal, ecclesiologic, ecclesiological, orthodox, patristic. **7. denominational** sectarian. **8. interdenominational** catholic, ecumenical, interfaith, reunionistic, subjectivistic. **9. esoteric** cabbalistic, kabbalistic, qabalistic. **10. mystic** cryptic, mysterious, mystical, occult, orphic.

8. **1. laic** churchmanly, impropriate, laical, lay, secular, temporal, tertiary.

9. **1. heretical** excommunicable, excommunicate, heretic, misbelieving, perverted, profane, unblessed, unhallowed, warped. **2. unorthodox** heterodox, schismatic.

RELATED KEYWORDS: AFTERWORLD, GOD, PLACE OF WORSHIP, RELIGIOUS LEADER, REVERENCE, SCRIPTURE, THE SUPERNATURAL, TEACHER

RELIGIOUS CEREMONY

n. **1.** **1. religious ceremony** ceremonial, ceremony, common, exercises *(US)*, liturgy, maundy, observance, procession, recession, rite, rite of passage, ritual, smoking ceremony, solemnities, thanksgiving. **2. consecration** epiclesis, lustrum, oblation, preface, sacrifice, sanctification, secret. **3. initiation** anabaptism, aspersion, baptism, christening, circumcision, confirmation, dedication, immersion, initiation ceremony, man making, paedobaptism, palingenesis, simple vow, vow. **4. offering** burnt offering, donary, flagellation, holocaust, immolation, libation, oblation, prothesis, sacrifice, thank-offering, victim. **5. benediction** blessing, devotement, devotions, love, peace-offering, praise, worship. **6. last sacraments** anointment, extreme unction, viaticum. **7. meal of**

fellowship agape, Chaburah, communion, love feast *(Chiefly US)*. **8. corroboree** bora, ceremony, tabi song.

2. 1. prayer alleluia, ceremony, commination, devotions, entreaty, glory, invocation, mission, ordinance, orison, pater, paternoster, petition, pleading, praise, requiescat, requiescat in pace, suffrage, suppliance. **2. liturgy** antiphonal, antiphonary, breviary, catechism, common prayer, diurnal, hours, hymnal, hymnbook, lectionary, mahzor, missal, ordinal, ordo, passional, passionary, pontificals, prayer book, processional, psalmody, psalter, rite, ritual, rubric, service book, siddhur, tantra, vesperal. **3. liturgics** ordinance, rite, sacramentality. **4. creed** credo. **5. mantra** aum, om, omphaloskepsis. **6. church service** chapel *(British)*, church, complin, conventicle, folk mass, kerugma, lection, meeting, prayer meeting, preaching, ritual, sacrifice, thanksgiving, vespers, worship. **7. hymn** alleluia, anthem, antiphon, antiphony, ascription, blessing, cantata, canticle, canto fermo, cantus, carol, chant, choral, chorale *(US)*, creed, devotions, dithyramb, doxology, gradual, greater doxology, hallelujah, henotheism, hymnody, hymnology, introit, lesser doxology, mass, matin, melody, metrical psalm, motet, offertory, oratorio, paean, pean, plainchant, plainsong, praise, processional, prose, psalm, psalmody, recessional, recessional hymn, respond, response, responsory, service, shout song, spiritual, tersanctus, tract, versicle, worship. **8. pageant** mystery play, passion play. **9. canonical hours** complin, compline, laudes, lauds, little hours, matins, nones, prime, sext, terce, tierce, vespers.

3. 1. worship adoration, adore, ancestor worship, blessing, celebration, ceremonial, ceremony, devotion, devotions, extolment, love, manism, praise, prayer, rite, worshipfulness. **2. veneration** adoration, apotheosis, canonisation, ennoblement, enshrinement, enthronement, faith, glorification, iconolatry, idolatry, idolism, piety, reverence, transfigurement. **3. prostration** bow, genuflection, homage, obeisance, reverence, sacramental, sign of the cross.

4. 1. idol graven image, icon, joss, tin god. **2. zombie** entellus, hanuman, uraeus. **3. fetish** fertility symbol, fetich, juju, sun-disc, voodoo. **4. betyl** circle, henge. **5. churinga** bullroarer, tchuringa, thunder stick, tiki, totem.

5. 1. worshipper adorer, consecrator, devotee, enthusiast, extoller, fanatic, genuflector, glorifier, idolater, kowtower, palmer, petitionary, pilgrim, praiser, votaress, votarist, votary, votress, zealot. **2. psalmist** cantor, caroller, lauder, muezzin, psalmodist, reader. **3. churchgoer** celebrant, communicant, congregation, ecclesia, invoker, kirkman *(Scottish)*, watcher. **4. hierolater** hagiolater, iconolater. **5. sacrificer** flagellant, flagellator, immolator. **6. mystic. 7. cultist** alchemist, black witch, carline *(Chiefly Scottish)*, charmer, conjurer, coven, deifier, demonist, demonolater, diabolist, diviner, druidess, enchanter, enchantress, firewalker, heliolater, illusionist, magician, pagan, phallicist, Rastafarian, Satanist, shaman, shamanist, sibyl, sorcerer, spiritualist, sunworshipper, votary, warlock.

adj. **6. 1. worshipful** adoring, reverend, reverent, reverential. **2. prayerful** churchgoing, credent, dedicated, devoted, devotional, devout, god-fearing, godly, hierodulic, holy, pious, practising, religious, sainted, true-hearted, venerable. **3. hagiolatrous** hierolatrous, mariolatrous. **4. idolatrous** barbarous, fetishistic, gentile, heathen, heathenish, infidel, irreligious, pagan, profane, uncircumcised. **5. heliolatrous** druidic, druidical, heliolithic, ophiolatrous.

7. 1. ritualistic canonical, cruciferous, ember, formalistic, haggadic, haggadical, lenten, liturgical, paschal, ritual, rubrical, sabbatic, sabbatical, vesper. **2. benedictional** benedictory, dedicative, dedicatory. **3. sacramental** eucharistic, eucharistical, oblatory. **4. hymnal** doxological. **5. sacrificial** flagellant, holocaustic.

v. **8. 1. worship** adore, celebrate, elevate, emblazon, eulogise, exalt, extol, fete, glorify, honour, hymn, idolatrise, illumine, laud, lift, lionise, magnify, panegyrise, praise, proclaim, translate, uplift. **2. pray** commend, count one's beads, exalt, extol, laud, make a novena, praise, psalm, say one's beads, supplicate, tell one's beads. **3. meditate** contemplate, go on retreat, ruminate, watch. **4. humble oneself** bow, cross, fall on one's knees, genuflect, go down on one's knees, kneel, prostrate oneself. **5. exalt** beatify, bless, canonise, dignify, ennoble, enshrine, enthrone, extol, glorify, hallow, honour, inshrine, inthrone, laud, mysticise, panegyrise, praise, revere, reverence, saint, shrine, transfigure, venerate, worship. **6. deify** apotheosise, divinise.

RELATED KEYWORDS: PLACE OF WORSHIP, RELIGION, RELIGIOUS LEADER, REVERENCE

RELIGIOUS LEADER

n. **1. 1. religious leader** abbé, beneficiary, bush brother, chaplain, churchman, clergyman, cleric, clerical, clerk *(Chiefly US)*, confessor, curé, curate, deacon, dominie, ecclesiastic, elder, father confessor, high priest, incumbent, kirkman *(Scottish)*, magus, man of God, man of the cloth, minister, monsignor, padre, parish priest, parson, pastor, prebend, prebendary, presbyter, priest, priestess, rector, residentiary, shepherd, vicar, vicar-general. *Informal:* Amen snorter, josser, reverend, sin-shifter, sky pilot. **2. divine** doctor of the church, evangel, evangelist, Father, lawyer, rabbin, rabbinate, revivalist, seminarian, seminarist. **3. sanctifier** anointer, baptiser, celebrancy, celebrant, consecrator, insufflator, mystagogue, officiant, officiator, ordainer, seculariser. **4. dean** archpriest, canon, capitular, capitulary, prebend, prebendary, subdean, vicar forane. **5. bishop** diocesan, pontiff, prelate, suffragan *(British)*. **6. rabbi** high priest, rabbinate. **7. ayatollah** high priest, imam, mullah, ulema. **8. archbishop** Abba, archdeacon, eparch, evangel, exarch, ordinary, patriarch, primate, provincial, vicar apostolic. **9. cardinal** cardinalate, ecclesiarch, metropolitan, prince, red hat. **10. Pope** Holy Father, Patriarch of Rome, pontiff. **11. Curia** Curia Romana. **12. the clergy** clergy, the cloth, the pulpit.

2. 1. preacher apostle, Biblicist, biblist, evangel, evangelical, evangelist, gospeller, missionary, missioner, prophet, pulpiteer, revivalist, salvationist, vicar apostolic. *Informal:* Amen snorter, bible-basher, hot-gospeller. **2. acolyte** deacon, deaconess, diaconate, subdeacon. **3. catechist** catechiser.

3. 1. religious dignitary beadle, church commissioner, churchwarden, ecclesiarch, elder, moderator, presbyter, proctor, red band *(Aboriginal English)*, sexton, sidesman, verger, vestryman, warden. **2. elders** classis, colloquy, parish council, presbytery. **3. deputy** acolyte, altar boy, curate, impropriator, lector, oblate, ostiary, porter, surrogate. **4. papal envoy** ablegate, apostolic delegate, friary, internuncio, legate, nuncio, papal nuncio. **5. cantor** chanter, chazzan, choirboy, chorister, coryphaeus, hazzan, precentor, succentor, vicar choral *(British)*. **6. pardoner** simoniac, simonist.

4. 1. monk anchoress, anchoret, anchorite, ascetic, bodhisattva, bonze, caloyer, eremite, exorcist, fakir, frère, fra, friar, hermit, incluse, Jacobin, lama, lay brother, mendicant, monastic, mystic, recluse, seclusionist, solitary, stylite, votary. **2. priest** brother, canon regular, clergyman, flagellant, regular. *Informal:* holy joe. **3. nun** canoness, coenobite, religious, sister, votaress, votress, vower. *Informal:* penguin. **4. novice** canon, canonist, catechumen, chela, convert, disciple, follower, neophyte, novitiate, ordinand, postulant, proselyte, ritualist, scholastic, seminarian, seminarist. *Informal:* theolog. **5. tertiary** regular tertiary, secular tertiary. **6. provost** abbé, abbess, abbot, archimandrite, hegumen, monk, mother, mother superior, prior, prioress, rector, sadhu, superior, vicar. **7. dervish** dancing dervish, fakir, howling dervish, spinning dervish, whirling dervish.

5. 1. monasticism coenobitism, monachism. **2. religious order** congregation, discipline, lamasery, major orders, minor order, monkery, monkhood, observance, order, rule, veil.

6. 1. religious ministry canonicate, canonry, canonship, chapter, clerkship, cloth, curacy, cure, deaconate, deaconry, deaconship, diaconate, eldership, officiation, orders, presbyterate, priestcraft, priesthood, priestliness, rabbinate, rectorate, sacerdotalism, subdiaconate, vicarate, vicariate, vicarship. **2. benefice** cure, incumbency, living, parish, pastorate, pastorship, sinecure, title. **3. abbotship** abbacy, deanship, priorate, priorship, rectorate, subdeanery. **4. archdeaconate** archdeaconry, archidiaconate, archpriesthood. **5. bishopric** episcopacy, episcopate, episcope, lawn sleeves, patriarchate, pontificate, prelacy, prelateship, primatiate, prelatist, prelature, see, suffragan *(British)*, surrogateship, throne. **6. archbishopric** archiepiscopacy, archiepiscopate, bench, eparchy, primacy, primateship. **7. cardinalship** cardinalate, purple, red hat. **8. papacy** apostolate, apostolic succession, patriarchate, pontifical college, pontificate, popedom, primacy, primateship, tiara.

adj. **7. 1. ecclesiastic** Aaronic, Aaronical, churchly, ecclesiastical, hierarchal, theological. **2. missionary** born-again, charismatic, evangelical, evangelistic, revivalist. **3. clerical** churchmanly, cleric, hieratic, Josephite, laic, ministerial, pastoral, presbyteral, priestly, rabbinical, rectorial, reverend, sacerdotal, secular, vicarial, vicarly. **4. synodal** capitular, capitulary, consistorial, consistorian. **5. diaconal** archidiaconal, decanal, neophytic, proctorial, subdiaconal. **6. episcopal** archiepiscopal, metropolitan, prelatic, primatial, suffragan *(British)*. **7. papal** apostolic, curial, legatine, pontifical, primatial, suburbicarian.

8. 1. monastic ascetic, ascetical, churchy, claustral, cloister-like, cloistered, cloistral, holy, institutionary, monachal, monasterial, monkish, professed, religious, secluded, sequestered, tonsured. **2. conventual** abbatial, coenobitic, coenobitical, monkish, rectorial, succursal.

v. **9.** **1. take the cloth** frock, mitre, serve, simple vow, take the veil, take vows, vow. **2. ordain** cloister, consecrate, cowl, episcopise, incardinate, institute, mitre, order, profess, secularise, tonsure.

adv. **10.** **1. ecclesiastically** clerically, clerkly, decanally, hieratically, ministerially, monastically, monkishly, sacerdotally. **2. evangelically** evangelistically. **3. pontifically** apostolically, ex cathedra, ministerially.

RELATED KEYWORDS: PLACE OF WORSHIP, RELIGION, RELIGIOUS CEREMONY, REVERENCE

REMEMBERING

n. **1.** **1. remembering** anamnesis, hindsight, mind, nostalgia, recognition, recollection, remembrance, reminiscence, retrospect, retrospection, retrospectivity, review. **2. memorisation** learning, mnemonics, mnemotechnics, rote learning.

2. **1. remembrance** engram, false memory, feeling, impression, memory, recollection, recovered memory, retention, retentivity, souvenir, trace. **2. flashback** association of ideas, cutback *(US)*, recapture, recurrence. **3. memoirs** anecdotage, anecdotes, annal, autobiography, biography, chronicle, Commentaries, history, life, memoir, memorabilia, oral history, prosopography, record, reminiscences, story. *Informal:* bio. **4. memory** collective memory, long-term memory, memory span, photographic memory, recall, retainment, retentiveness, short-term memory.

3. **1. reminder** admonishment, admonition, monition. **2. prompt** autocue, cue card, idiot board, prompt book, prompter, teleprompter. **3. cue** advice, arrow, catchword, caution, clue, cock, Dorothy Dixer, fingerpost, guide, guidepost, hand, hint, intimation, lead, leading question, message, notice, notification, object lesson, pointer, signal, signpost, suggestion, tip, tip-off, warning, wind, word. *Informal:* heads-up, the office. **4. aide-mémoire** chit, hurry-up, jotting, memo, memorandum, memory-jogger, minute, mnemonic, monitor, note, record, reminder, round robin, tickler *(US)*. *Informal:* bung.

4. **1. memento** commemoration, keepsake, relic, remembrance, remembrancer, reminder, souvenir, token, trophy. **2. commemoration** Auld Lang Syne, commemorative, memorial, testimonial. **3. memorial** cenotaph, chantry, commemoration, cornerstone, epitaph, foundation stone, in memoriam, monument, pantheon, stone, Tomb of the Unknown Soldier, tombstone, tope, war memorial.

adj. **5.** **1. memorable** catchy, eidetic, famous, great, haunting, impressive, notable, noted, noteworthy, recallable, recognisable, remarkable, retainable, signal, unimaginable. **2. unforgotten** fresh, graven, green, remarkable, unforgettable, unique.

6. **1. reminiscent** anecdotal, anecdotic, narrative, nostalgic. **2. recollective** mnemonic, recognitive, recognitory. **3. evocative** redolent of, remindful.

7. **1. commemorative** commemorational, commemoratory, epitaphic, memorial.

v. **8.** **1. remember** be mindful of, bethink oneself of, conjure up, live in the past, relive, retrace, review, think of. **2. retain** hold in mind, keep in mind. **3. recollect** place, recall, recognise, remember. **4. reminisce** flashback, hark back to, rake up the past, recollect, remember. **5. haunt** obsess, possess. **6. have a good memory** *Informal:* have a memory like an elephant.

9. **1. memorise** commit to memory, embalm, etch in one's memory, fix in one's mind, learn. **2. revise** refresh one's memory, rub up on. **3. note** book, brief, calendar, card, catalogue, chronicle, diarise, enrol, enter, inscribe, interline, item, jot, journalise, keep track of, log, manifest, minute, notate, protocol, put down, record, register, remark, score, videorecord. *Informal:* keep tabs on. **4. know by ear** know by heart, know by rote.

10. **1. remind** admonish, jog someone's memory, refresh someone's memory. **2. prompt** cue, hint, infer, jog, nudge. *Informal:* give someone the office. **3. be on the tip of one's tongue** come back, recur. **4. evoke** be reminiscent of, breathe of, bring back, call to mind, call up, put in mind of, recall, recollect, remind of, ring a bell, strike a chord.

11. **1. commemorate** eternalise, eternise, immortalise, memorialise, monumentalise, preserve, retain.

adv. **12.** **1. memorably** unforgettably. **2. reminiscently** nostalgically. **3. in memoriam** commemoratively, memorially, memoriam, pro memoria.

RELATED KEYWORDS: KNOWLEDGE, LEARNING, THE PAST

REMNANT

n. **1.** **1. remnant** crust, end, fag, fag end, fragment, frazzle, oddment, rump, scrap, shard, stump, tag end. **2. remains** dottle, flotsam and jetsam, fragments, leavings, odds and ends, relics, relicts, reliquiae, remnants, residuum, scraps. **3. remainder** balance, bob, carryover, hangover, holdover, leaving, leftover, relicts, residual, rest, surplus, surplusage. **4. vestige** contrail, drag, footmark, footprint, footstep, hint, relic, show, sign, skeleton, toeprint, trace, track, trail, vestigium. **5. cheque butt** butt, counterfoil, stub. **6. leftovers** orts, scraps. *Informal:* scrag end. **7. leavings** draff, dregs, dross, foot, foots, grounds, heeltap, marc, relicts, residue, sediment, settlings, sludge, snuff, waste. **8. debris** ash flow, ashes, flotage, flotsam, jetsam, jettison, lagan, rack, rubbish, ruins, shipwreck, slash *(NZ)*, wrack, wreck, wreckage. *Informal:* smithereens. **9. deposit** alluviation, alluvion, alluvium, eluvium, foot, fur, geest, grounds, heeltap, lees, marc, remains, scum, sediment, settlings, spent grains, sullage, warp, wash. **10. clippings** borings, filings, grass clippings, paring, peelings, sawdust, scrapings, scraps, swarf. **11. tailings** dump, muck, mullock, slime dump, slum, spoil. *Informal:* cack. **12. tartar** wine stone. **13. off-cut** clipping, cutting, docking, off-cuts, offcut, trimmings. **14. pomace** chum, rape, trash. **15. ash** bone ash, bone earth, boneblack, calx, cinders, dust. **16. scruff** salamander, scale, scoria, sow, sprue, sullage, tap-cinder. **17. weapon debris. 18. cotton waste** lint, strass. **19. tree stump** stool, stub, stump. **20. refuse** culch, dross, effluent, filth, garbage, ordure, scum, sewage, sewerage, sullage, truck, wash, waste, waste product. *Informal:* gunk. **21. bombsite** rubble, ruins, waste. **22. earthly remains** ashes, clay, dust, earth, mortal remains.

adj. **2.** **1. remnant** last, left, left behind, left over, net, odd, other, remainder, remaining, surviving. **2. vestigial** remainder, remaining, residual, residuary, rudimentary, scrap, sedimentary, surplus.

RELATED KEYWORDS: SUBTRACTION, DISUSE, USELESSNESS, PART

REMOTENESS

n. **1.** **1. remoteness** aloofness, deviousness, farness, loneliness, outlandishness. **2. distance** length, mileage, range, way. **3. a long way** a fair way, a far cry, a long chalk, a long haul, light-years, miles. *Informal:* a good way. **4. remotest point** aphelion, apocynthion, apogee, apolune, solstice.

2. **1. remote place** hinterland, jumping-off place *(US)*, out beyond, the black stump, the inland, wayback, wilderness. *Informal:* back of beyond, back of Bourke, Bandywallop, Bullabakanka, Bullamakanka, Oodnagalahbi, Outer Mongolia, the back of Bourke, the never-never, Timbuktu, Woop Woop, wop-wops. **2. uttermost** antipodes, end, ends of the earth, infinity, limits, outer limits, Thule, ultima Thule, utmost. **3. back country** backblocks, backwoods, goat country, hinterland, outback, outbush, outside country, Snake Gully, Speewah, the wayback *(NZ)*, tiger country. *Informal:* booay, boohai, boondocks *(Chiefly US)*, cactus, the donga *(Chiefly SA)*, the mallee, the sticks. **4. outpost** back-station, country camp, outstation. **5. back run** back paddock, outrun, runoff *(NZ)*. **6. offing** outing.

adj. **3.** **1. remote** deserted, devious, far-back, far-off, godforsaken, lonely, out, out-of-the-way, outland, outlandish, outlying, secluded, sequestered, wayback. **2. outback** back-country, backblock, backwoods. **3. inaccessible** unapproachable, uncome-at-able, unget-at-able, unreachable, untouchable. **4. overseas** tramontane, transalpine, transmontane, transoceanic, transpacific, ultramarine, ultramontane. *Informal:* o.s., o.t. **5. ultramundane** out of this world.

4. **1. distant** advanced, deep, far, far-off, faraway, farther, further, high, long, offshore, outside. **2. away** cold, distal, removed, terminal, wide. **3. off course** cold. **4. furthermost** apogean, endmost, extreme, farthermost, farthest, final, furthest, hindmost, outermost, rearmost, solstitial, ultimate, utmost, uttermost. **5. long-distance** cross-country, langlauf, long-range, marathon. **6. yonder** thither.

adv. **5.** **1. remotely** deviously, outlandishly. **2. far** a long way off, afar, afield, deeply, distantly, far and near, far and wide, farther, farthest, from afar, further, longway, offshore. *Informal:* off to billyo, off to buggery. **3. away** awa *(Scottish)*, distally, forth, off, out, outward, recessively. **4. outback** *Informal:* back of beyond, up (in) the mulga, up the booay. **5. aloof** aloofly, at arm's length. **6. yonder** over there, there, thither.

RELATED KEYWORDS: THE BUSH, DIVERGENCE, SEPARATION

REMOVAL

n. **1.** **1. removal** abstraction, avulsion, deracination, dislodgement, eradication, exsection, extirpation, extraction, purge, remotion, remove, ripping out, sequestration, shift, stripping, uprooting, withdrawal. **2. disinterment** disentombment, exhumation. **3. obliteration** erasure, rubbing out, wiping out. **4. clearance** clean sweep, clearing, sweep. **5. brushing away** *Informal:* Australian salute, Barcoo salute. **6. emptying** drainage, unfouling, venting. **7. unloading** deconsolidation, offloading, unpacking. **8. clear-felling** back-burning, burning-off, bush bashing, bush-burning, bush-falling, chaining-off, clear-cutting, double-logging, logging, lumbering *(Chiefly US, Canadian)*, ringbarking, scrub bashing, scrub-cutting, scrub-rolling, sucker-bashing, timber-getting.

adj. **2.** **1. removed** disconnected, distant, remote. **2. alien** foreign, unconnected, unrelated. **3. extractive** abstractive, aspiratory, efferent. **4. obliterative** erasing.

v. **3.** **1. remove** grub out, scrub, strike, strip, take away, take down, take off, thin out. *Informal:* pull. **2. take out** abstract, aspirate, bail out, prescind, withdraw. **3. disinter** disentomb, exhume, unearth. **4. obliterate** annihilate, blank, blank out, destroy, erase, extinguish, kill, rub off, rub off, rub out, wipe off, wipe out. **5. cut out** excide, excise, exterminate, extirpate. **6. pull off** nip, pick, pick out, prise. **7. unload** debark, deconsolidate, off-load, ship, unlade, unpack. **8. get rid of** brush aside, clear, clear away, make a clean sweep, make away with, make off, see the back of, shuffle off, shunt, sweep away, swish off, swoop up, whisk away. *Informal:* get shot of, ship out. **9. clear of** free from, purge of, rid of. **10. clear-fell** back-burn, chain off, clear-cut, cut, dock, fell, frill, hew, knock down *(NZ)*, log, ringbark. **11. root out** eradicate, pull up, unroot, uproot. **12. poll** pollard.

RELATED KEYWORDS: EXTRACTION, ABSENCE

REPAIR

n. **1.** **1. repair** darn, mend, patch. **2. overhaul** careenage, check-up, drop test, refit, service. **3. restoration** cannibalisation, facelift, instauration, renovation, reparation, vamp. **4. reclamation** innings, land reclamation, reafforestation, reclaim, reforestation, rescue, retrieval, revegetation, salvage. **5. replenishment** recruitment, reinforcement, replacement. **6. restitution** postliminy, ransom, redemption.

2. **1. rehabilitation** re-establishment, recovery, regression, reinstatement, return to normal. **2. revival** re-creation, reanimation, rebirth, renaissance, republication, resurgence, resurrection, resuscitation, reviviscence. **3. renewal** Indian summer, instauration, redintegration, refreshment, regeneracy, regeneration, urban renewal. **4. rejuvenation** rejuvenescence, second youth.

3. **1. repairer** fix-it man, fixer, handyman, renovator, repairman, restorer, service man. **2. mender** artificer, careener, cobbler, cooper, darner, jerker, master mechanic, mechanic, patcher, piecer, shipwright, spiderman, steeplejack, tailor, tinker, vamper, watchmaker, wheelwright. *Informal:* grease monkey. **3. rejuvenator** reclaimer, recoverer, resurrectionist, salvager. **4. restorative** freshener, invigorant, lifesaver, refresher, roborant, tonic. *Informal:* pick-me-up, pick-up, shot in the arm.

4. **1. workshop** bushhouse, garage, garden shed, shed. **2. service centre** service station, smash repairers.

adj. **5.** **1. restorative** recreational, redintegrative, refreshing, regenerative, rejuvenescent, reparative, reparatory. **2. plastic** anaplastic.

v. **6.** **1. repair** careen, cicatrise, fix, make whole, mend, overhaul, reassemble, recondition, redintegrate, refit, remould, restore, service, tinker. *Informal:* doctor. **2. cobble** fox, half-sole, patch, resole, vamp. **3. renovate** do over, do up, fix up, freshen up, lift, make over, modernise, reface, refresh, refurbish, repair, revamp, touch up, vamp up. *Informal:* bodgie, jack up *(NZ)*. **4. mend** darn, patch, piece together, piece up, reduce, sew. **5. reclaim** reafforest, reforest, retrieve. **6. replenish** recruit, renew, restock. **7. redeem** ransom. **8. rehabilitate** put (or set) someone on their feet, regenerate, reinstate. **9. revive** animate, bring to, bring to life, reanimate, recall *(Poetic)*, recreate, resurrect, resuscitate, revitalise, revivify.

7. **1. revive** be restored, bounce back, come to life, get one's second wind, pick up, rally, recover, rejuvenate, rejuvenise, renew, return to life, return to normal.

RELATED KEYWORDS: GOODNESS, HEALTH, HEALING, IMPROVEMENT, MEDICATION

REPETITION

n. **1.** **1. repetition** cycle, frequency, ingemination, iterance, iteration, recurrence, reiteration, renewal, reprise, resumption, return, rhythm. **2. repeat** action replay, ditto, encore, instant replay, re-enactment, re-run, reappearance, reconstruction, redraft, reduplication, remake, repeat performance, retake, return season. **3. recapitulation** summing-up. *Informal:* recap. **4. reprise** answer, burden, canon, chorus, fugue, imitation, ostinato, passacaglia, recapitulation, refrain, repeat, repetend, repetition, ritornello, rondo, round. **5. twin** autotype, blind copy, carbon copy, clone, copy, counterpart, double, dubbing, dummy, duplicate, duplication, ectype, effigy, facsimile, gemination, image, imitation, like, likeness, look-alike, match, mate, mirror image, photocopy, recording, repetition, replica, replicar, replication, representation, reproduction, semblance, transcript, transcription, xerox. *Informal:* chip off the old block, ditto. **6. anaphora** anadiplosis, dittography, emphasis. **7. repetitiousness** periodicity. **8. series** catena, concatenation, consecution, continuation, cycle, progression, round, sequence, succession. **9. practice** drill, rehearsal, rote learning. **10. tautology** pleonasm, redundancy. **11. repetend** recurring decimal, repeating decimal. **12. ditto** ditto marks, quotation, quote.

2. **1. repeated sounds** *Informal:* ding-dong, flip-flop, tick-tock. **2. reduplicative words** beri-beri, boogie-woogie, devil-devil, dillydally, gee-gee, go-go, hoity-toity, hurry-scurry, knick-knack, mishmash, ping-pong, rickrack, rip rap, roly-poly, seesaw, tittle-tattle, wishy-washy, yakety-yak, zigzag. *Informal:* easy-peasy, fiddle-faddle, okey-doke, slipslop, super-duper, tiptop.

adj. **3.** **1. repetitive** dittographic, iterant, iterative, monotonous, reiterant, reiterative, repetitious, resumptive. **2. repeated** chronic, constant, continual, continuing, eternal, everlasting, frequent, habitual, haunting, incessant, invariable, invariant, perennial, perpetual, reconstructive, recurrent, recurring, recursive, reduplicate, reduplicative, reiterated, return, serial, steady, twice-told, uninterrupted, unvarying, usual. **3. periodic** annual, bicentennial, centennial, cyclic, daily, equinoctial, everyday, horary, hourly, isochronal, isochronous, measured, menstrual, monthly, periodical, regular, rhythmic, rhythmical, seasonal, semiannual, tercentennial, tidal, uniform, weekly, yearly. **4. echolike** echoic, recapitulative, recapitulatory, repercussive, resonant, resounding, reverberant, reverberating, reverberative, reverberatory, sounding. **5. tautological** pleonastic, redundant. **6. abovementioned** above, aforementioned, aforesaid, foregoing, foresaid, said, which. **7. anaphoric** cataphoric, exophoric.

v. **4.** **1. repeat** double, encore, ingeminate, make up, redouble, reduplicate, reiterate, replay, run through again. **2. iterate** come back to, recur, return to, revert to, run. **3. repeat monotonously** beat into the ground, cuckoo, hammer, harp upon, thrash out. *Informal:* ding, do to death. **4. practise** re-act, re-enact, recapture, recite, reconstruct, redraft, rehearse, relive, remake, repeat. **5. ding** drum. **6. echo** re-echo, re-sound, redouble, reply, resonate, resound, reverberate, revoice, ring, ring out. **7. come again** *(Informal)* go over, go over the same ground, parrot, quote, recapitulate, reiterate, repeat, report, reword, tautologise. *Informal:* ditto. **8. duplicate** copy, dub, facsimile, imitate, reduplicate, replicate, reproduce, twin. **9. renew** re-cover, re-create, re-present, reappear, recommence, reconstruct, reface, remodel, reopen, reorientate, repair, restore, resume.

adv. **5.** **1. repeatedly** again and again, cyclically, day by day, day in day out, in-and-in, over and over, perennially, time and time again, without end, year after year, yearly. *Informal:* morning noon and night, till doomsday. **2. afresh** again, anew, bis, da capo, dal segno, ditto, once more, over *(US)*, over again. *Informal:* agin. **3. repetitiously** constantly, pleonastically, tautologically.

RELATED KEYWORDS: FREQUENCY, REGULARITY, RHYTHM, VIBRATION

REPRESENTATION

n. **1.** **1. representation** heraldry, simulacrum, symbolisation, symbolism, symbology. **2. impersonation** characterisation, enactment, mimesis, personation, personification. **3. allegory** apologue, exemplum, fable, imagery, parable, proverb. **4. typification** prefiguration, prefigurement. **5. portrayal** iconography, iconology, imagery, portraiture. **6. cartography** hypsography, hypsometry.

2. **1. portrait** delineation, depiction, drawing, figure, half-face, half-length, identikit, image, indictment, likeness, nude, photograph, picture, portraiture, portrayal, presentment, profile, representation, self-portrait, semblance, silhouette, sketch, speaking likeness. **2. caricature** cartoon. **3. statue** acrolith, bas-relief, bronze, bust, effigy, gargoyle, glyph, herm, herma, marble, plaster cast, sculpture, sculptured figure, statuette, torso. **4. effigy** automaton, doll, dummy, figurine, jackstraw, manikin, mannequin, marionette, model, puppet, robot, waxwork. *Informal:* guy *(British)*, moppet. **5. totem** churinga, churunga, graven image, idol, tchurunga, tiki, tjuringa, totem pole, turinga. **6. mask** disguise, false face, loup, masque, veil. **7. persona** character.

3. **1. tableau** diorama, model, pageant, panorama, tableau vivant. **2. planetarium** georama, globe.

adj. **4.** **1. representational** iconic, iconographic, iconological. **2. symbolical** allegorical, allegoristic, emblematic, figural, figurative, figured, illustrative, symbolic, tropical. **3. representative** prefigurative, symbolic, typical, typological.

      5. **1. depictive** delineative, descriptive, imitative, pictorial. **2. graphic** diagrammatic. **3. cartographical** cosmographical.

v. **6.** **1. represent** allegorise, alphabetise, emblematise, emblemise, express, figure, illustrate, image, incarnate, prefigure, stand for, symbol, symbolise, type, typify. **2. personify** characterise, imitate, impersonate, incarnate, mime, mimic, stereotype. **3. pose** assume a character.

      7. **1. portray** catch a likeness, character, delineate, depict, depicture, describe, draw, etch, feature, hold the mirror up to nature, limn, line, outline, paint, picture, profile, render, represent, sketch. **2. caricature** cartoon. **3. carve** cast, sculpt.

      RELATED KEYWORDS: ARTIST, FINE ARTS, IMITATION, PHOTOGRAPHY, SIGN

REPRESSION

n. **1.** **1. repression** subjection, subjugation. **2. oppression** harassment, persecution, pressure. **3. subdual** colonisation, conquest, defeat, quelling, vanquishment. **4. subjugation** dependence, repression, servitude, slavery, subjection, vassalage. **5. slavery** bondage, chains, enslavement, enthralment, helotism, helotry, heteronomy, serfhood, servitude, thraldom, thrall, tyranny, vassalage. **6. slave trade** blackbirding, slave-trading, white slavery, white-slaving. **7. slave labour** corvée, forced labour, servitude, vassalage. **8. feudal system** assignment system, bondage, colonialism, feudalisation, helotry, peonage, servitude, slavery, villeinage.

      2. **1. repressiveness** authoritarianism, burdensomeness, oppressiveness, tyranny.

      3. **1. represser** authoritarian, Big Brother, Caesar, despot, dictator, oppressor, overrider, persecutor, queller, subjugator, trampler, tyranniser, tyrant. **2. conqueror** coloniser, vanquisher. **3. slaveholder** enslaver, slave-trader, slavedriver, slaver.

      4. **1. slave** blackbird, bondmaid, bondman, bondservant, bondsman, bondwoman, captive, chattel, galley slave, hierodule, thrall. **2. serf** carl, helot, liegeman, peon, vassal, villein. **3. subject** liege, liegeman, man, samurai, vassal. **4. servant** assigned servant, assignee, attendant, bondservant, dependant, flunkey, flunky, follower, footman, forced labourer, kanaka, lackey, maidservant, manservant, menial, peon, servitor, underservant. *Informal:* dogsbody, skivvy. **5. servile follower** creature, flunkey, lackey, liegeman, man, puppet, satellite, stooge, subject.

adj. **5.** **1. repressive** domineering, intimidating, overbearing, overpowering, overwhelming, possessive. **2. oppressive** burdensome, dictatorial, draconian, harsh, heavy-handed, iron, persecutional, persecutory, severe, sledgehammer, stern. **3. despotic** absolute, arbitrary, authoritarian, hard-handed, tyrannic, tyrannical, tyrannous.

      6. **1. repressed** downtrodden, oppressed, subjugated, tyrannised. **2. enslaved** aggrieved *(Law)*, servile, subjected. **3. slavish** abject, controllable, hierodulic, obsequious, prostrate, servile, subduable, submissive, supple, wormlike. **4. downtrodden** at one's beck and call, at one's feet, henpecked. *Informal:* under the thumb.

v. **7.** **1. repress** beat down, crush, destroy, extinguish, oppress, put down, quash, quell, quench, smother, squash, stifle, strangle, suppress. **2. oppress** burden, domineer, grind, grind down, grind under, persecute, trample on, tyrannise. *Informal:* flatten, kneel on. **3. enslave** conquer, enthral, master, quell, slave, subdue, subjugate. **4. colonise** enfeoff, feudalise, imperialise, mediatise. **5. subdue** beat, best, bring someone to their knees, bring to heel, bring to terms, bring under, coerce, compel, conquer, defeat, domesticate, down, force, master, overcome, overmaster, overpower, overwhelm, prostrate, quell, reduce, repress, tame, vanquish. *Informal:* bust *(US)*, floor, roll. **6. keep down** have at one's beck and call, keep on a string, keep under, put the maginnis on. **7. domineer** browbeat, bully, hector, henpeck, lord it over someone, overbear, overlord, override, tread on, treat like dirt, walk all over.

adv. **8.** **1. repressively** burdensomely, despotically, oppressively, overpoweringly, tyrannically, tyrannisingly, with a heavy hand.

      RELATED KEYWORDS: FORCE, IMPRISONMENT, HARSHNESS, SERVANT

REPRODUCTION

n. **1.** **1. reproduction** bearing, engenderment, generation, increase, procreation, propagation, pullulation. **2. sexual reproduction** allogamy, amphimixis, autogamy, cleistogamy, entomophily, exogamy, gamogenesis, hydrophily, isogamy, karyogamy, oogamy, sporogenesis, syngamy, syngenesis, xenogamy, zoogamy. **3. asexual reproduction** agamogenesis, apogamy, apomixis, blastogenesis, duplication, fission, gemination, gemmation, parthenogenesis, schizogenesis, sporogenesis, vegetativeness, virgin birth.

4. biogenesis cainogenesis, palingenesis. **5. maturation** abstriction, anoestrus, gametogenesis, heterospory, oogenesis, ovulation, spermatogenesis, sporogenesis, sporogony. **6. neoteny** paedogenesis. **7. digenesis** metagenesis. **8. epigenesis** germ theory, pangenesis, preformation. **9. cell division** amitosis, anaphase, crossing over, cytogenesis, cytogenetics, cytokinesis, diakinesis, haplosis, karyokinesis, meiosis, metaphase, mitosis, phase, prophase, synapsis, telophase. **10. oestrous cycle** heat, rut. **11. urge to reproduce** baby hunger, biological clock.

2. 1. conception fecundation, impregnation. **2. polyembryony** superfecundation, superfetation, twinning. **3. fertilisation** allogamy, artificial insemination, cross-fertilisation, crosspollination, in-vitro fertilisation, insemination, pollination, self-fertilisation, self-pollination, xenogamy. **4. breeding** allogamy, artificial selection, autogamy, cacogenics, crossing, dysgenics, engraftment, eugenics, fancy, genetic engineering, grafting, homogamy, hybridisation, hybridism, inbreeding, interbreeding, intercross, layering, miscegenation, mosaicism, natural selection, outbreeding, outcrossing, propagation, selection, stirpiculture, thremmatology, xenogamy. **5. birthrate** hatchability, natality.

3. 1. pregnancy cyesis, foetation, gestation, gravidity, interesting condition, sitting. **2. parity** multiparity, oviparity, ovoviviparousness, polycyesis, primiparity, viviparousness. **3. unwanted pregnancy** unplanned pregnancy. *Informal:* accident, mistake.

4. 1. birth accouchement, childbed, childbirth, confinement, delivery, labour, lying-in, parturiency, parturition, time. **2. child-bearing** pregnancy. **3. Leboyer birth** breech birth, breech delivery, caesarean section, homebirth, natural childbirth. *Informal:* caesar. **4. labour** afterpains, pains, throes, travail. **5. false labour** couvade, pre-labour. **6. stages of childbirth** crowning, first stage, presentation, puerperium, second stage, third stage. **7. abortion** medical abortion, miscarriage, stillbirth. **8. delivery room** birth centre, labour ward, maternity hospital, maternity ward. **9. farrowing house** aerie, aery, eyrie, hatchabator, hatchery, heronry, nest, nide, nidus, rookery, springer paddock, stud farm. **10. seedbed**

5. 1. reproductive organs genitalia, genitals, glans, loin *(Bible and Poetic)*, perineum, phallus, private parts, pudendum. **2. female sex organs** Bartholin's glands, cervix, clitoris, fallopian tubes, G spot, hymen, labia, labium, maidenhead, nymphas, ovary, oviduct, tubes, uterus, vagina, vulva, womb, yoni. **3. male sex organs** epididymis, foreskin, lingam, manhood, mesonephros, penis, prepuce, prostate, prostate gland, scrotum, spermatic cord, testicle, testis, vas deferens. **4. sex gland** gonad. **5. hormones** androgen, androsterone, chorionic gonadotropin, follicle stimulating hormone, folliculin, FSH, HPL, human placental lactogen, LH, luteinising hormone, oestradiol, oestriol, oestrogen, oestrone, oxytocin, pheromone, progesterone, progestin, progestogen, stilboestrol, testosterone. **6. amniotic fluid** afterbirth, amnion, amniotic, amniotic membrane, caul, chorion, cotyledon, Graafian follicle, indusium, placenta, umbilical cord, waters. **7. ascogonium** archicarp.

6. 1. reproductive agent ejaculation, emission, seed, semen, seminal fluid, sperm, spermatic fluid. **2. seed** antherozoid, archegonium, basidiospore, cyst, endospore, gamete, gametocyte, gametophyte, gemma, gemmule, germ, germ cell, germen, gonocyte, grain, heterogamete, isogamete, oosperm, oospore, ovule, ovum, planogamete, prothallium, sperm, spermatid, spermatocyte, spermatozoon, spore, sporule, swarm spore, swarmer, tetraspore. **3. egg** egg cell, oocyte, oogonium, oosphere, ovocyte, ovule, ovum, seed. **4. spawn** berry, coral, milt, roe. *Informal:* hen fruit. **5. pollen** pollinium. **6. chromosome** chromatid, chromatin, deoxyribonucleic acid, DNA, heterochromatin, ribonucleic acid, RNA, X chromosome, Y chromosome. **7. gametophore** antheridium, basidium, gametangium, hymenium, ovisac, sporophore. **8. blastocyst** archiblast, barysphere, blastoderm, blastodisc, blastosphere, centromere, centrosome, centrosphere, chalaza, egg cell, endoblast, endoderm, endosperm, endothecium, entoblast, entoderm, gastrula, germ layer, germ plasm, germinal disc, germinal vesicle, hypoblast, idioplasm, mesoderm, morula, parablast, proembryo, pronucleus, trophoblast, yolk.

7. 1. procreator breeder, engenderer, fertiliser, generator, impregnator, propagator. **2. mother** mother-to-be, multipara, primigravida, primipara, venter. **3. stallion** stud, studhorse. **4. mare** springer. **5. bitch** broodbitch. **6. brooder** sitter.

8. 1. breeder eugenicist, eugenist, grower, hybridiser, propagator, stirpiculturist, stockbreeder.

9. 1. midwife accoucheur, accoucheuse, deliverer, gynaecologist, obstetrician. *Informal:* gyno.

adj. **10. 1. reproductive** conceptive, fecund, fertile, fertilisable, generative, procreant, procreative, progenitive, propagable, propagative, virile. **2. genital** genito-urinary, sexual. **3. seminal** embryo, embryonic, germinal, seminiferous, spermatic. **4. sporiferous** sporogenous.

5. eugenic dysgenic, stirpicultural. **6. inbred** heterozygous. **7. amitotic** meiotic, mitotic. **8. allopolyploid** aneuploid, diploid, euploid, haploid, polyploid, triploid.

11. **1. pregnant** enceinte, expectant, full, gone, gravid, heavy, impregnate, with child, with young. *Informal:* expecting, in pod, in the family way, in the pudding club, knocked-up, preggers. **2. brood** at stud. **3. natal** antenatal, congenital, parturient, peri-natal, post-partum, postnatal, prenatal, puerperal. **4. lying-in** maternity, obstetric. **5. broody** clucky, in season, oestrous, on heat, philoprogenitive. **6. biparous** fissiparous, live-bearing, multiparous, oviparous, ovoviviparous, primiparous, pupiparous, uniparous, viviparous. **7. ecbolic** oxytocic.

v. **12.** **1. reproduce** breed, procreate, propagate. **2. procreate** breed, engender, father, generate, germinate, get, mother, produce, sire. **3. lay** oviposit, ovulate, spawn, spore, sporulate. **4. fertilise** cross-fertilise, cross-pollinate, crosspollinate, fecundate, impregnate, pollen, pollinate, superfetate. **5. breed** backcross, clone, cross, crossbreed, duplicate, grade, grow, hybridise, inbreed, interbreed, intercross, mate, milt, mix, mongrelise, multiply, nick, outbreed, propagate. **6. graft** engraft, inarch, ingraft, layer. **7. implant** nidate.

13. **1. conceive** fall pregnant. **2. be pregnant** be with child, bear, carry, gestate. *Informal:* have a bun in the oven. **3. make pregnant** fecundate, imbrue with, impregnate, inseminate. **4. be at stud** service, stand on. **5. rut** be in season, be on heat.

14. **1. give birth** bear, birth, bring into the world, deliver, have, produce, pullulate. *Informal:* drop a bundle. **2. lie in** be confined. **3. labour** travail. **4. abort** cast, miscarry. **5. fruit** berry, germinate, set. **6. drop** calve, farrow, fawn, foal, kid, kitten, lamb, litter, pig, pup, spawn, throw, twin, whelp, yean. **7. slink** slip. **8. brood** clutch, hatch, incubate, nest.

RELATED KEYWORDS: BODY, FERTILITY, OFFSPRING, PARENTAGE, RELATIVE, SEX

REPULSION

n. **1.** **1. repulsion** antipathy, aversion, chemotaxis, dislike, distaste, repellence, repugnance. **2. dismissal** rebuff, repulse, snub, spurning. *Informal:* brush-off, cut, the cold shoulder.

adj. **2.** **1. repellent** disconcerting, dismissive, dismissory, off-putting, repelling, repulsive.

v. **3.** **1. repel** avert, beat off, chase away, dispel, drive away, drive back, drive off, fight off, force, force off, parry, repulse, scare away (or off), send away, stave off, ward off. *Informal:* put the frighteners on, stink out. **2. rebuff** cut, keep at a distance, keep someone at arm's length, scorn, see someone about his business, snub, spurn, turn away, turn down, turn one's back on. *Informal:* give someone the big A, give someone the bum's rush. **3. dismiss** bundle off (or out), cast away, cast off, cast out, exile, fling aside, give someone the red card, hunt, pack off, put off, reject. **4. get rid of** shed, wipe. *Informal:* burke, ditch, doff, give someone (or something) the flick.

RELATED KEYWORDS: DISAPPROVAL, UGLINESS, DIVERGENCE, DISPLEASURE

REPUTE

n. **1.** **1. repute** account, character, estimation, fame, importance, memory, merit, name, note, regard, report, reputation, stamp, store, value, worth. **2. rank** character, class, credit, footing, grade, mark, position, ranking, rate, rating, standing, station, status, stock, terms. *Informal:* form. **3. good reputation** celebrity, credit, distinction, eminence, fame, first class, glory, good name, good report, good repute, high repute, honour, meliority, note, prominence, reputation, stature, worship. **4. renown** celebrity, distinction, eminence, fame, famousness, mark, note, notedness, noteworthiness, reputation. **5. importance** account, altitude, concern, concernment, consequence, consideration, distinction, eminence, import, mark, matter, might, moment, notability, note, pith, pre-eminence, significance, superiority. **6. prestige** cachet, eclat, face, kudos, renown. **7. glory** exaltation, lustre, stardom.

2. **1. reputability** creditableness, respectability, respectableness, worthiness. **2. exaltedness** augustness, distinction, illustriousness, note, venerability, venerableness. **3. majesty** dignity, elevation, gloriousness, glory, grandeur, gravity, impressiveness, magnificence, resplendence, splendidness, splendour, stateliness. **4. brilliance** dazzle, halo, lustre, radiance, sheen, splendour.

3. **1. glorification** celebration, emblazonment, extolment, immortalisation. **2. exaltation** aggrandisement, lionisation, uplift.

4. **1. famous person** A-list, buzzwig, celebrity, character, chief, dignitary, face, figure, first fiddle, giant, hero, high-up, household name, identity, leading light, lion, luminary, magnate, magnifico, mogul, Mr Big, notable, number one, personage, personality, prince, principal, public figure, renown, somebody, star, supermodel, talk of the town, toast of the town, who's who, worthy. *Informal:* big gun, big noise, big shot, bigwig, boss, brass, celeb, everybody who is anybody, great, heavy, heavyweight, his nibs, numero uno, pot, tall poppy, the man outside Hoyts, top dog, VIP, visiting fireman, wheel.

adj. **5.** **1. reputable** admirable, all right, alright, big, conspicuous, decent, decorous, eminent, estimable, excellent, great, honest, honourable, important, in good odour, noble, notable, of good reputation, prominent, respectable, respected, signal, significant, valued, well-thought-of, worthy. **2. eminent** arrant, aureate, bodacious, brilliant, celebrated, chief, distingué, distinguished, elevated, exalted, famed, familiar, famous, foremost, grand, great, illustrious, important, large, leading, lustrous, memorable, noted, noteworthy, old, pre-eminent, prestigious, prominent, proverbial, remarkable, renowned, splendid, splendorous, star, storied, unforgettable, unimaginable, unique, venerable, well-known, worthy. **3. special** especial, premium, prestige. **4. noble** august, brilliant, dashing, dignified, distinguished, elevated, eminent, exalted, flamboyant, glorious, gorgeous, grand, grandiose, great, high, high-level, high-up, Homeric, imperial, impressive, junoesque, lofty, lordly, maestoso, magnificent, majestic, marvellous, Olympian, palmy, princely, proud, regal, resplendent, royal, senior, splendid, stately, sublime *(Poetic)*, sumptuous, superb, supernal, uplifted.

6. **1. famous** celebrated, distinguished, eminent, epic, front-line, imposing, impressive, mentionable, notable, noted, noteworthy, of note, outstanding, prominent, renowned, striking. **2. well-known** celebrated, fashionable, hit, popular, prominent, successful, well-established. **3. legendary** amaranthine, apocryphal, deathless, enduring, eternal, everlasting, fabled, fabulous, heroic, immortal, imperishable, incorruptible, indestructible, indomitable, inextinguishable, inviolable, mythical, never-fading, perdurable, perennial, permanent, proverbial, romantic, undying, unfading. **4. classic** classical, historic, historical, time-honoured.

v. **7.** **1. glorify** acclaim, adore, aggrandise, applaud, beatify, bless, canonise, carol, celebrate, chair, commend, cry up, deify, dignify, distinguish, elevate, emblazon, ennoble, enshrine, enthrone, eulogise, exalt, extol, fame, fete, hail, hallow, honour, hymn, illuminate, illumine, inshrine, inthrone, laud, lift, lionise, magnify, mysticise, panegyrise, praise, proclaim, raise, revere, reverence, saint, shrine, supplicate, transfigure, translate, uplift, upraise, venerate, worship. *Informal:* big-mouth, plug, polish, put on the map, rap up. **2. immortalise** classicise, put (or place) (or set) someone on a pedestal.

8. **1. make history** go down in history, hit the headlines, make a noise in the world, make one's mark, raise one's head, set the world on fire. **2. star** blaze, resound, shine.

adv. **9.** **1. reputably** admirably, creditably, exaltedly, illustriously, respectably, worthily. **2. famously** eminently, in the public eye, notedly, notoriously, pre-eminently, prominently. **3. splendidly** augustly, gloriously, impressively, stately.

RELATED KEYWORDS: APPROVAL, HIGH REGARD, SUPERIORITY

RESONANCE

n. **1.** **1. resonance** fullness, fullness of tone, hollowness, mesomerism, repercussion, replication, resonation, reverberation, rotundity, rotundness. **2. echo** re-echo, repercussion, replication, reverb, reverberation. **3. plangency** sonority, sonorousness, vibrancy.

2. **1. ringing** clang, clangour, ding, ding-dong, knell, peal, ring, stroke, ting, tintinnabulation, toll, tolling, whang. **2. jingle** clink, ting-a-ling, tinkle, tinkling, trill. **3. bellringing** campanology, change-ringing. **4. peal** bob, changes, dodge, hunt, ring, rounds, touch.

3. **1. click** chink, clink, crack, flick, snap, snick, snip, tick, tick-tock. **2. clatter** brattle, chatter, clackety-clack, clip-clop, clop, clutter, death-rattle, disturbance, pitapat, pitter-patter, prattle, rattle, trot-trot. *Informal:* shindig. **3. buzz** bray, buzzing, drone, hem, hum, humming, purr, skirr, stertor, whine, whirr, whiz, woof, zoom. **4. twang** ping, plink-plonk, plonk, plunk, thrum, zing. **5. clap** flap, flip-flop, flop, flutter, thud. *Informal:* flump. **6. footfall** crunch, footstep, pad, plod, step, tramp, tread.

4. **1. boom** bang, bump, clank, clonk, clump, knock, thud, thump, wham. *Informal:* whop. **2. rumble** borborygmus, growl, grumble, gurgle, murmur, thunder. *Informal:* moan. **3. drumbeat** beat, drumming, dub, groove, rap, rappel, rataplan, roll, rub-a-dub, ruffle, tam-tam, tap, tapping, tom-tom. **4. tantara** blare, honk.

5. **1. resonator** cavity resonator, echo chamber, echo unit, resonant cavity, reverb, reverberation unit, reverberator, rhumbatron, soundboard, sounding-board. **2. clacker** chimer, clicker, honker, hummer, rattler, thrummer. **3. bell** carillon, chime, cowbell, death bell, passing bell, sacring bell, sanctuary bell, Sanctus bell, shark bell, sleighbell, tenor, treble. **4. clapper** tongue. **5. alarum** buzzer. **6. siren** shark siren, wail.

6. **1. ringer** bellringer, campanologer, campanologist.

adj. **7.** **1. resonant** echoic, echolike, re-echoing, repercussive, resounding, reverberant, reverberating, reverberative, reverberatory, sounding. **2. sonorous** fruity, full-toned, gonglike, resounding, rotund, round, sonant, sounding, vibrant, voiceful. *Informal:* plummy. **3. plangent** big, forte, fortissimo, full, full-throated, heavy, loud, obstropolous, reboant, resonant, sonorous, strong, wiry. **4. hollow** cavernous, deep, drummy, dull, inward, muffled, sepulchral. **5. rumbly** rolling, stertorous, thundering, thunderous, thundery.

8. **1. ringing** amphoric, bell-like, jingly, silvery, tinkling, tintinnabular. **2. twangy** clangorous, zingy. **3. rattly** abuzz. **4. clumpy** clumpish, wooden.

v. **9.** **1. resonate** resound, reverberate, ring, ring out. **2. echo** answer, re-echo, re-sound, recite, redouble, repeat, reply, resonate, resound, revoice.

10. **1. ring** carillon, chime, ding, dong, knell, knoll, ping, ring the changes, toll. **2. jingle** chink, clank, clink, jangle, rhyme, tinkle. **3. clang** clangour, ding. **4. twang** ping, plunk, sing, thrum. **5. trumpet** blare, blast, honk. **6. trill** peal, resonate, resound, vibrate.

11. **1. boom** bang, beat, clank, clonk, growl, knock, pound, rap, slam, thud, thump, wham, whang. **2. rumble** roll, thunder.

12. **1. click** clip-clop, crackle, craunch, crunch, nick, smack, snap, snick, tick. **2. rattle** brattle, chatter, clack, clatter, clutter, drum, gabble, jabber, mag, rataplan, splutter, sputter, talk. *Informal:* natter. **3. ping** knock, pink. **4. flap** flop. **5. buzz** drone, hum, pur, purr, ring, wail, whir, whirr, whiz, zoom.

adv. **13.** **1. resonantly** forte, fortissimo, loud, loudly, out, resoundingly, sonorously, soundingly, vibrantly.

RELATED KEYWORDS: EXPLOSION, LOUDNESS, QUIETNESS, MUSIC, SHRILLNESS, SOUND

REST

n. **1.** **1. rest** leisure, lie-down, loaf, relaxation. *Informal:* bange, camp, Maori PT *(NZ)*, spinebash. **2. break** a free moment, breath, breather, breathing space, half-time, sit-down, time-out. *Informal:* blow, boil-up, nick, pit stop. **3. meal break** coffee break, dinnertime, lemons, lunch hour, lunchbreak, lunchtime, morning piece, playtime, smoke concert, tea-break. *Informal:* brew-up, orange time, smoko. **4. lull** abeyance, cessation, dwell, interlude, interval, let-up, pause, recess, respite, spell. **5. calm** equilibrium, peace, quiet, quietude, reposal, repose, rest, tranquillity. **6. restfulness** calmness, composedness, composure, downiness, easefulness, heart's ease, leisureliness, poise, quietness, reposefulness. **7. resting** relaxing, reposing. *Informal:* having a break, spinebashing.

2. **1. holiday** bank holiday, break, day of rest, dies non, festa, fete, fete day, half-day, half-holiday, half-term *(Chiefly British)*, long weekend, Lord's day, Picnic Day, pink-eye *(Chiefly WA)*, public holiday, Sabbath, weekend. *Informal:* leavers week *(Perth Region, Chiefly NSW and Qld)*, schoolies week *(Chiefly NSW and Qld)*. **2. leave** Christmas holidays, Easter holidays, furlough, holidays, leave of absence, leavers *(Perth Region)*, long service leave, long vacation, maternity leave, R and R, rec leave, shore leave, time off, vacation. *Informal:* bush week, hollies, hols, vac. **3. study leave** sabbatical, stuvac *(Especially NSW)*, swat vac, swot vac. **4. sick leave** doona day, mental health day. *Informal:* MDO *(NZ)*, sickie. **5. day off** accrued day off, accumulated day off, ADO, flex-day, flexi, flexiday, lay day.

3. **1. rester** camper, holiday-maker, lady of leisure, lingerer, loller, lotus-eater, relaxer. *Informal:* spinebasher.

adj. **4.** **1. resting** still. **2. fallow** off. **3. restful** at ease, at rest, leisure, leisured, leisurely. **4. calm** composed, cool-headed, level-headed, poised, possessed, self-composed, self-contained, self-possessed. **5. sabbatical** ferial, holiday, sabbatic.

v. **5.** **1. rest** hush, lull, quiet, quieten, settle, sit, still. **2. quieten** breathe, lull, unbrace. **3. have a rest** have a break, have a spell, lie down, lie fallow, take a seat. *Informal:* bange, camp, curl up, put one's feet up. **4. relax** mung, unbend, wind down. *Informal:* bange, chill out, mellow, mong, veg out. **5. become quiet** compose oneself, die down, settle down. **6. take it easy** coast along, lie at ease, linger, live on one's fat, rest on one's laurels, rest on one's oars. *Informal:* hang loose. **7. lie at rest** couch, lair, loaf, loll, perch, recline, repose, rest, roost, sit, stretch out. *Informal:* spinebash. **8. pause** take a break. *Informal:* boil the billy, take five. **9. holiday** camp, flex, flex off, get away from it all, pink-eye *(Chiefly WA)*, shut up shop, vacation.

adv. **6.** **1. restfully** easefully, reposefully. **2. calmly** composedly, leisurely, quietly, soothingly. **3. at leisure** off, off duty. **4. at one's leisure** on (or at) the weekend.

RELATED KEYWORDS: IDLENESS, COMPOSURE, SLEEP, TIREDNESS

RESTRAINTS

n. **1.** **1. restraints** ball and chain, bands, bonds, chain stopper, chains, cuff, D-shackle, fetter, gyves, handcuff, hobble, hobblechain, leg-iron, manacle, shackle, tether, trammels. *Informal:* bracelet, darbies, nippers. **2. pillory** bail, cangue, crib, stocks, trave. **3. bond** bind, chain, constraint, curb, hitch, ligament, ligature, link, rein, restraint, tie, vinculum. **4. keeper** cramp, keeping, key, sprig. **5. doorstop** brake, check, chock, dead hand, doorstopper, floor stop, skid, sprag, stop, trig. **6. roofguard** snowguard. **7. rail** fiddle.

2. **1. saddlery** choke chain, harness, tack, tug. **2. bridle** barnacles, bearing rein, bellyband, bit, cannon bit, cavesson, check rein, curb, drop noseband, girth, hackamore *(US)*, halter, headgear, headstall, kerb, martingale, noseband, nosepiece, overcheck, rein, snaffle, surcingle, throatlatch, trace, tug, twitch, withy. *Informal:* ribbons. **3. yoke** oxbow. **4. tether** breeching, creance, dog run, jess, lariat *(US)*, lashing, lasso, lead, leading rein, leash, leg-rope, lune, lunge, lunging rein, muzzle, rope *(US)*, slip. *Informal:* leggy.

3. **1. restrainer** binder, inhibiter, retainer. **2. controller** constrainer, limiter, obstructionist, stinter, withholder.

4. **1. restraining order** ADVO, covenant, D-notice, embargo, injunction, patent, prohibition, tail, writ. **2. gag** guillotine.

5. **1. restraint** astriction, censorship, comstockery *(Chiefly US)*, containment, control, hindrance, inhibition, interdiction, limitation, proscription, repression, restriction, salary cap, suppression. **2. limitation** clampdown, rationing, squeeze, stint, stranglehold. **3. self-control** golden mean, moderation, modesty, self-command, temperance. **4. bondage** binding, enchainment. **5. curfew** custody, detainment, detention, remand, surveillance, ward.

adj. **6.** **1. restraining** binding, inhibitory, limitative, restrictive. **2. repressive** inhibiting, suppressive.

7. **1. restricted** close, constrained, cramped, gated, limited, pokey, poky. **2. repressed** constrained, hidebound, pent-up, restrained. **3. bound** confined, corded, detained, earthbound, fast, fenced-in, housebound, icebound, imprisoned, ironbound, jessed, stormbound, trapped. **4. restrained** discreet, low-key, low-profile, measured, reserved.

v. **8.** **1. restrain** bate, button down, chasten, chastise, check, circumscribe, clip someone's wings, constrain, control, curb, damp, detain, diminish, enjoin, govern, handle, hinder, hobble, hold back, hopple, internalise, keep, keep back, leash, manage, moderate, monitor, picket, regulate, rein, reserve, secrete, shackle, smother, stake, stem, stop, subdue, suppress, temper, tether. **2. hold back** choke, contain, hold in, keep down, rein back, rein in, restrain. **3. silence** burke, choke back, crush, gag, guillotine, jugulate, muzzle, play down, quell, quench, quiet, smother, soft-pedal, soften, stifle, subdue, suppress. *Informal:* squash, squelch. **4. chain** collar, enchain, enfetter, fetter, gyve, handcuff, iron, jess, leg-rope, manacle, put in irons, shackle, trammel. **5. bail** bail up, crib. **6. bit** bridle, curb, halter. **7. tie up** astrict, bind, cord, hogtie *(Chiefly US)*, pinion, rope, secure, string, swaddle, truss, wire. *Informal:* collar. **8. anchor** cast anchor, skid, stay.

9. **1. restrict** confine, constrict, contain, cramp, embargo, ground, inhibit, limit, narrow, stop, withhold. **2. limit** allowance, peg, ration, stint, straiten.

10. **1. restrain oneself** bite one's lip, pull one's punches, refrain. *Informal:* get a hold on oneself, hold one's horses. **2. repress** bite back, bottle up, keep back, keep one's own counsel, laugh up one's sleeve, put down, sit on, stifle, strangle, suppress. *Informal:* clam up, keep one's mouth shut. **3. play gooseberry**.

adv. **11.** **1. restrainedly** discreetly, measuredly. **2. restrictedly** constrainedly, in check, on the bit.

> **RELATED KEYWORDS:** CONTROLLING DEVICE, FASTENING, FORCE, IMPRISONMENT, REPRESSION, MODERATION

RESULT

n. **1.** **1. result** effect, end result, ensemble, output, purport, resultant, turnout. **2. consequence** after-effect, apodosis, attendant, bottom line, butterfly effect, consequent, corollary, effect, flow-on, flowthrough, fruitage, issue, legacy, matter of course, outcome, outgrowth, repercussion, result, secondary, sequel, upshot. *Informal:* pay-off. **3. conclusion** crystallisation, determination, end, event, foregone conclusion, parti pris, realisation, redound, termination. **4. sequel** after-effect, aftermath, aftertaste, result, sequence, sequent, train. **5. development** elaboration, evolution, progress. **6. side effect** adverse event, collateral damage, fallout.

     2.   **1. finished product** construct, construction, contrivance, creation, fabrication, facture, form, formation, handiwork, invention, job, making, manufacture, output, outturn, production, stuff, throughput, works. **2. creation** brainchild. *Informal:* baby. **3. by-product** breakdown product, catabolite, daughter product, end product, spin-off. **4. yield** crop, culture, first fruits, fruit, fruitage, growth, harvest, produce, product. **5. derivate** derivation, derivative. **6. discharge** emanation, emission.

     3.   **1. artefact** basketry, basketwork, carpentry, coopery, handwork, ironmongery, ironwork, metalwork, tinwork, wicker, wickerwork, woodwork. **2. goods** dry goods, durables, fixtures, hard goods, hardware, merchandise, perishables, soft goods, sundries, tableware, toiletries, whitegoods. **3. wares** basaltware, brassware, chinaware, copperware, dinnerware, earthenware, enamelware, glassware, kitchenware, leatherware, metalware, silverware, stoneware, tinware, whitegoods, woodenware.

adj. 4.   **1. resultant** attendant, consecutive, consequent, consequential, flowthrough, following, sequent, sequential, subsequent, successive, terminational, terminative. **2. derivative** derivate, secondary. **3. emanative** emanatory.

v. 5.   **1. result** end, terminate in, turn out. *Informal:* pan out. **2. follow** arise from, attend, ensue, proceed from. **3. emanate** issue from.

adv. 6.   **1. ultimately** ex post facto, in due course.

        RELATED KEYWORDS: CAUSE, COMING AFTER, CREATION, FACTORY, METAL, SHAPE

RETALIATION

n. 1.   **1. retaliation** avengement, blood feud, compensation, payback, quid pro quo, reciprocation, reciprocity, reprisal, requital, retorsion *(International Law)*, retortion, retribution, return, revenge, satisfaction, utu *(NZ)*, vendetta, vengeance. *Informal:* comeuppance. **2. vengefulness** choler, ire, revanchism, revengefulness, vengeance, vindictiveness, wrath. **3. counter-terrorism** counterblast. **4. reply** answer, bite, redoublement, rejoinder, repartee, replication, response, retort, return, riposte. *Informal:* comeback. **5. tit for tat** a dose of one's own medicine, a game that two can play, a Roland for an Oliver, a taste of one's own medicine, an eye for an eye, blow for blow, give-and-take, talion, tat, the biter bit. **6. unwritten law** lex talionis. **7. law of the jungle.**

     2.   **1. avenger** kadaicha man, nemesis, requiter, revenger, vendettist.

adj. 3.   **1. retaliatory** reciprocal, recriminatory, retributive, revengeful, vengeful, vindicatory, vindictive. **2. returnable** requitable.

v. 4.   **1. retaliate** avenge, back-answer, confute, contradict, countercharge, counterclaim, fight back, give as good as one gets, make payment, pay off, pay out, rebut, reciprocate, reply, requite, retort, return, return enemy fire, return the compliment, riposte, take the law into one's own hands, turn on. *Informal:* bite back. **2. get even with** call it quits, fix someone, get back at, get one's own back, pay back, pay back in the same coin, pay off a score, pay off old scores, settle a debt, settle a score, square off with, turn the tables on. *Informal:* have someone's guts for garters. **3. revenge** avenge, exculpate, have revenge, pay a debt.

adv. 5.   **1. in retaliation** in return, revengefully, vengefully, vindictively.

        RELATED KEYWORDS: COMPENSATION, IMPOSITION, PUNISHMENT

RETICENCE

n. 1.   **1. reticence** aloofness, low profile, reserve, undemonstrativeness, understatement. **2. speechlessness** dumbness, muteness, peace, reserve, silence, still *(Poetic)*, stillness, taciturnity, unexpressiveness. **3. reserve** backwardness, bashfulness, distance, shyness. **4. secrecy** closeness, incommunicativeness, omerta, secretiveness.

adj. 2.   **1. reticent** aloof, antisocial, dégagé, dark, disinterested, distant, inexpressive, low-key, low-profile, quiet, reserved, restrained, self-contained, silent, stand-offish, strange, tacit, uncommunicative, undemonstrative, underplayed, unexpressive, withdrawn. *Informal:* offish. **2. shy** backward, bashful, coy, diffident, farouche, hesitating, reluctant, retiring, shamefaced, sheepish, withdrawn. **3. tight-lipped** close, close-lipped, dark, esoteric, incommunicative, non-committal, reserved, reticent, secret, secretive, silent, tacit, taciturn. **4. taciturn** concise, incommunicable, incommunicative, laconic, monosyllabic, of few words, reserved, short-spoken, silent, undemonstrative. **5. silent** dumb, inarticulate, mum, mute, speechless, tongue-tied, unvoiced, voiceless, wordless.

v. 3.   **1. be reticent** hold aloof, hold off, interiorise, internalise. *Informal:* clam up. **2. underplay** not give anything away, underact. **3. suffer in silence** pocket one's pride, swallow one's pride, swallow one's words. **4. withhold** bite back, button down, check, choke, choke back, constrain, control, curb, damp, detain, gulp down, hold back, internalise, keep, keep back, keep close, keep dark, keep one's mouth shut, keep one's own counsel, keep under one's hat, laugh in one's sleeve, laugh up one's sleeve, rein, reserve, restrain, stem, subdue. **5. suppress** burke, repress, smother.

adv. **4.** **1. reticently** aloofly, undemonstratively, unexpressively. **2. shyly** backwardly, bashfully. **3. incommunicatively** dumbly, speechlessly. **4. secretively** close, closely, secretly.

RELATED KEYWORDS: BREVITY, SECRECY, FAULTY SPEECH

RETREAT

n. **1.** **1. retreat** pullout, reaction, recession, regress, regression, rein back, retirement, retrocession, retrogradation, retrogression, retroversion, return, reversal, sternway, withdrawal. **2. return** centre turn, countermarch, homecoming, round trip, U-turn. *Informal:* U-ey. **3. reflux** ebb, ebb tide, refluence. **4. flashback** cutback *(US)*. **5. retraction** back-pedalling, retractation. **6. flinch** shrink.

2. **1. reversion** atavism, backsliding, degeneration, devolution, involution, relapse.

3. **1. retractor** flincher, reverser, shrinker. **2. relapser** atavist, backslider, degenerate.

adj. **4.** **1. retreating** backward, recessional, recurrent, refluent, regressive, retroactive, retrograde, retrogressive, retrospective, reverse. **2. reversionary** atavistic, retrospective.

v. **5.** **1. retreat** back down, back off, back out, back up, back-pedal, beat a retreat, evacuate, flinch, pull one's head in, recall, remove, retire, retract, retrograde, shrink, stand down, vacate, withdraw. *Informal:* draw (or pull) one's horns in, pull out. **2. go back** back, back water, back-pedal, backtrack, countermarch, hark back, recede, regress, retrace, retrocede, retrogress, return, reverse, track out. **3. reflux** ebb, regorge, regurgitate. **4. return** boomerang, do a Melba, get back, make a comeback, make back, return to the fold, turn back. *Informal:* chuck a U-ey. **5. retract** abjure, annul, avoid, back-pedal, backtrack, climb down, countermand, disaffirm, disanoint, eat one's words, renege, renounce, repeal, repudiate, rescind, resile from, reverse, revoke, unsay, unspeak, unswear. **6. relapse** backslide, degenerate, revert.

RELATED KEYWORDS: DEVIATION, MOVEMENT, REACTION

REVELATION

n. **1.** **1. revelation** communication, disclosure, divulgence, enucleation, exposure, impartment, intimation. **2. exposure** disinterment, exposal, overexposure, unfoldment, unveiling. **3. epiphany** apocalypse, discovery, enlightenment, revelation. **4. confession** admission. **5. revealment** daylight, publicity. **6. exposedness** bareness, openness.

2. **1. disclosure** communication, revelation. **2. exposure** exposal. **3. giveaway** a foot in the mouth, betrayal, Freudian slip, indiscretion, telltale sign. **4. eye-opener** exposé, startling disclosure. **5. leak** blab, kiss-and-tell, tattle, verbal. **6. whole truth** clean breast.

3. **1. revealer** discloser, displayer, divulger, enlightener, expresser, imparter, oracle, revelationist, revelator, undeceiver, unmasker. **2. confessor** admitter, unbosomer. **3. telltale** betrayer, blunderer, dogvane, sneak, tale-bearer, taleteller, tattler, tattletale, tittle-tattle, tittle-tattler. *Informal:* blabber, blabbermouth, dobber, grass, sieve, stool pigeon, supergrass.

adj. **4.** **1. revealing** indicative, tattletale, telltale. **2. revelatory** apocalyptic, explanatory, oracular. **3. confessional** confessionary. **4. indiscreet** gossipy, tattletale. *Informal:* leaky.

5. **1. revealed** bare, exposed, full-frontal, unconcealed. **2. professed** confessed, ostensible, ostensive, self-confessed. **3. public** current, open, reported, semipublic.

v. **6.** **1. reveal** come out with, disclose, display, divulge, enucleate, expose, impart, show, splay, uncloak, unfold, unroll. **2. expose** bring out, bring to light, disinter, flush out, give air to, make public, mark, open, overexpose, publish, rake up, root out (or up), show up, smoke out, take the lid off, turn up, unbrick, uncloak, unclothe, uncover, unlock. **3. release** declassify. **4. enlighten** undeceive. **5. unmask** give the lie to, reveal, reveal in true colours, strip off a disguise, uncase, uncloak, unveil. *Informal:* nail. **6. blurt out** blunder, declare one's hand, give oneself away, give the game away, give the show away, lay one's cards on the table, let on, let out, let slip, show one's true colours, tell, wear one's heart on one's sleeve. *Informal:* babble, blab, blabber, blow the gaff, drop a bundle, have egg on one's face, let the cat out of the bag, noise off, put one's foot in one's mouth, shoot off one's mouth, spill, spill the beans. **7. tell on** betray, give away, sneak, tattle, tell tales, tell tales out of school, tittle-tattle. *Informal:* dob, split on.

7. **1. confess** acknowledge, admissive, admit, betray oneself, break cover, confess to, get something off one's chest, make a clean breast of, out with, own up, shrive, unbosom, unbosom oneself, unburden oneself. *Informal:* come clean, come one's guts, spit it out, wash (or air) one's dirty linen in public. **2. express** come out on, declare, indicate, intimate, speak.

8. **1. be revealed** become public knowledge, come to light, leak out, see the light of day, transpire. *Informal:* come out in the wash.

RELATED KEYWORDS: DISPLAY, PUBLICITY, SIGN

REVERENCE

n. 1. **1. reverence** adoration, bhakti, devotedness, devotement, devotion, devotions, devoutness, faith, glorification, honour, honours, hyperdulia, latria, love, praise, respect, trust, veneration, worship. **2. piety** cardinal virtues, dharma, godliness, good, good life, goodness, pietism, piousness, religiousness, righteousness, sanctity, services, virtue. **3. prayerfulness** communion, consideration, contemplation, devoutness, dhyana, meditation, mysticism, ordinance, reflection, religion, religiosity, thanatopsis. **4. religious frenzy** beatitude, ecstasy, enthusiasm, fanaticism, gift of tongues, glossolalia, jerks, theopathy, zealotry. **5. pilgrimage** haj, hajj. **6. ecclesiasticism** bibliolatry, churchmanship, fundamentalism, orthodoxy. **7. crusading spirit** fanaticism, missionary zeal. **8. spirituality** earnestness, inwardness, otherworldliness, spiritism, spiritualism. **9. consecration** apotheosis, blessing, dedication. **10. rite** ceremonial, ceremony, liturgy, prayer, ritual.

2. **1. holiness** godliness, sacredness, sacrosanctity, saintliness, sanctification, sanctity, state of grace. **2. enlightenment** bodhi, conversion, initiation, palingenesis, regeneration. **3. sainthood** beatification, canonisation, hallowedness, mahatmaism, martyrdom, saintliness, saintship, sanctity.

3. **1. holy person** arhat, bodhisattva, hafiz, maharishi, mahatma, man of God, saint, tirthankar. **2. martyr** patron saint, stigmatic. **3. icon** Madonna, Mater Dolorosa, nolime-tangere, pietà. **4. halo** aureole, gloria, gloriole, glory, nimbus, stigmata.

4. **1. believer** convert, devotee, fan, good liver, idolater, initiate, marian, pietist, puritan, the faithful, votary. **2. zealot** bible belt, bibliolater, born-again Christian, enthusiast, fanatic, gospeller, jihadist, salvationist. *Informal:* bible-banger, bible-basher, bush Baptist, hot-gospeller, Jesus-freak. **3. ecstatic** penitent, penitential, spiritualist. **4. ascetic** anchoress, anchoret, anchorite, ancient, archimandrite, bonze, caloyer, coenobite, contemplative, eremite, fakir, flagellant, frère, friar, hermit, incluse, Jacobin, lama, mendicant, monastic, monk, mystic, nun, penitent, recluse, sadhu, seclusionist, sister, solitary, stylite, sufi. **5. pilgrim** alhaji, hadji, haji, hajji.

adj. 5. **1. reverent** believing, credent, dedicated, devoted, devotional, devout, god-fearing, godly, holy, pious, practising, prayerful, religious, sainted, true-hearted, venerable. **2. spiritual** contemplative, devotional, fanatical, holy, meditative, monkish, religious, reverential, ruminant, spiritualist, spiritualistic, supermundane, supersensual, theandric, theanthropic, theocentric, vatic.

6. **1. holy** blessed, blest, celestial, Christly, consecrated, devout, divine, ethereal, god-fearing, hallowed, heaven-born, heavenly, inviolable, pious, sacred, sainted, saintly, sanctified, supernal. **2. sacred** sacrosanct, taboo, tabu, tapu *(Chiefly NZ)*.

v. 7. **1. revere** adore, bless, canonise, dignify, ennoble, enshrine, enthrone, exalt, extol, glorify, hallow, honour, idolatrise, idolise, inshrine, inthrone, laud, look up to, mysticise, praise, respect, reverence, saint, shrine, transfigure, venerate, worship. **2. fear god** keep the faith.

8. **1. consecrate** anoint, christen, dedicate, devote, hallow, halo, martyr, sanctify. **2. saint** beatify, canonise.

RELATED KEYWORDS: PLACE OF WORSHIP, RELIGION, RELIGIOUS CEREMONY

REVOLUTION

n. 1. **1. revolution** blood in the streets, cataclysm, counter-revolution, counterinsurgency, coup, coup d'état, incident, insurgence, insurgency, insurrection, mutiny, outbreak, overthrow, palace revolution, putsch, rebellion, revolt, riot, rising, sedition, subversion, upheaval, uprising, upthrow.

2. **1. revolutionary** abolitionist, agent provocateur, agitator, counter-revolutionary, insurrectionary, insurrectionist, provocateur, rabble-rouser, rebel, revolutionist *(US)*, rioter, seditionary, subversive, subverter. *Informal:* cut-lunch revolutionary, rouser, stirrer. **2. activist** actionist, malcontent. **3. incendiary** dynamiter, firebrand.

adj. **3.** **1. revolutionary** counter-revolutionary, subversive. **2. rebellious** insubordinate, insurgent, insurrectional, insurrectionary, malcontent, rebel, revolting.

v. **4.** **1. revolt** agitate, move, mutiny, rebel, riot, rise up, rise up in arms, storm the barricades.

RELATED KEYWORDS: LIBERATION, POLITICS, WAR

RHYTHM

n. **1.** **1. rhythm** accent, beat, cadence, groove, lilt, movement, swing, tempo, time. **2. type of rhythm** accent, back beat, black beat, cross rhythm, hemiola, ictus, isorhythm, march rhythm, polyrhythm, rock beat, singsong, syncopation, tala, waltz rhythm. **3. time** common measure, common time, duple rhythm, duple time, four-four time, quadruple time, simple time, triple measure, triple rhythm, triple time, triplex. **4. up-beat** anacrusis, arsis. **5. down-beat** thesis. **6. timekeeper** chronometer, clocker, metronome, syncopator.

2. **1. poetic metre** anapaest, dactyl, iamb, spondee, tribrach, trochee.

adj. **3.** **1. rhythmical** eurhythmic, eurythmic, measured, rhythmic, up-tempo. **2. up-tempo** driving, presto. **3. metronomic. 4. metrical** anapaestic, dactylic, iambic, ithyphallic, spondaic, tribrachic, trochaic.

v. **4.** **1. beat time** keep time. **2. syncopate** beat.

RELATED KEYWORDS: DANCING, MUSIC, REGULARITY

RIGHT

n. **1.** **1. right** recto. **2. starboard** bowside. **3. off** side off. **4. righthandedness** dexterity, dextrality, right-handedness. **5. right-hander** righthander.

adj. **2.** **1. right-hand** dexter, dextral, right. **2. starboard** offside, rightward. **3. off** right. **4. right-handed** dexterous, dextral, dextrous.

adv. **3.** **1. right** dextrally, on the right, on the starboard bow, rightward, rightwards, starboard.

RELATED KEYWORDS: SIDE

RIGHTS

n. **1.** **1. rights** abstract of title, claim, colour, droit, duty, entitlement, jus, law, lien, life interest, organic law, prescription, right, scrip, title, toll. **2. authority** carte blanche, jurisdiction, last word, mana, mandamus, parliamentary privilege, power, power of appointment, precedence, prerogative, privilege, rod and sceptre, royalty, yoke. *Informal:* say. **3. charter** bill of rights, muniments, share certificate. **4. civil rights** civil liberty, freedom, human rights, individualism. **5. female suffrage** suffragetism, votes for women, women's emancipation, women's suffrage. **6. franchise** ballot, secret ballot, universal suffrage. **7. birthright** bequest, coinheritance, heirdom, heirship, heritage, inheritance, legacy, primogeniture, ultimogeniture. **8. royal prerogative** droit de seigneur, escheatage, preference, regalia, regality. **9. state rights** Aboriginal land rights, reserve powers, sea rights, states' rights. **10. specific claim** ancient light, angary, beach claim, cabotage, crop lien, fishery, naming rights, profit a prendre, reef claim, right of run, right of search, servitude, trackage *(US)*, turbary *(British Law)*, uti possidetis, veranda rights, water right. **11. title deed** strata title, Torrens title, user *(Law)*, usufruct.

2. **1. intellectual property** copyright, patent, patent right, petty patent, public lending right, trademark.

3. **1. right of way** access, adit, admittance, appurtenance, appurtenant, easement, ingress, ingression, privilege.

adj. **4.** **1. rightful** authorised, entitled, just, lawful, legal, legitimate, precedential, prerogative, statutory, titled, true, valid. *Informal:* legit. **2. jural** prescriptible, prescriptive, usufructuary.

v. **5.** **1. have the right** be authorised, have the last say, stand on one's rights. **2. demand one's rights** call for, claim, insist on. **3. authorise** approbate *(Chiefly US)*, approve, decree, enact, endorse, pass. **4. confer a right** entitle, ordain, sanction.

RELATED KEYWORDS: LAWFULNESS, LIBERATION, POLITICS

ROBBERY

n. **1.** **1. robbery** appropriation, bag snatching, heist, identity theft, rapaciousness, rapacity, subreption, theft, thievery, thieving, thievishness. **2. larceny** cleptomania, fingering, grand larceny, kleptomania, petit larceny, petty larceny, pilferage, pilfering, shoplifting, stealing. *Informal:* crib, five-finger discount, nonch, pinch. **3. burglary** heist, housebreaking. *Informal:* bust, crack, hoist, job. **4. cattle stealing** cattleduffing, horse-duffing, poddy-dodging, rustling. **5. body-snatching** resurrectionism. **6. banditry** bushranging, dacoity *(Indian*

English), hold-up, raven, smash-and-grab, snatch, stick-on, thuggee, thuggery. *Informal:* highway robbery, stick-up. **7. piracy** buccaneering, kidnapping, privateering, skyjack. **8. pillage** brigandage, brigandry, depredation, despoilment, despoliation, maraud, moss-trooping, plunder, plunderage, rapine, raven, sack, spoliation.

2.   **1. embezzlement** defalcation, misappropriation, peculation. **2. fraud** bilk, bubble, cheat, clip, con, confidence trick, cozenage, false pretences, fraudulent speculation, rip-off, swindle. *Informal:* con trick, do, gyp, licence to print money, racket, ramp, set-up, skin game. **3. plagiarism** plagiary.

3.   **1. loot** booty, catch, grab, haul, pickings, pillage, plunder, prize, proceeds, spoil, spoils, stolen goods, take, takings. *Informal:* boodle *(Chiefly US)*, earn.

adj.   4.   **1. thieving** larcenous. **2. crooked** *Informal:* bent. **3. piratical** predatory, rapacious, thuggish.

v.   5.   **1. rob** bail up, hold up, waylay. *Informal:* clean out, mug, roll, strongarm *(US)*. **2. burgle** blind-stab, burglarise *(US)*. **3. steal** annex, appropriate, arrogate, bag, clout on, filch, ginger, grab, heist, loot, make away with, make off with, misappropriate, palm, pick, pick pockets, pickpocket, pilfer, purloin, rifle, rob, ruk *(Aboriginal English)*, run off with, shoplift, snaffle, snatch, spirit away, thieve, tickle the peter, walk off with, whip off. *Informal:* abstract, acquire, cop, finger, flog, frisk, get down on, half-inch, hoist, hook, knock off, liberate, lift, milk the till, mooch, mouch, nick, nip, nonch, oozle, pinch, race off with, rat, reef off, shake, shanghai, sneak, snitch, snowdrop, souvenir, swipe, tax, tea-leaf, thump. **4. plunder** burn, depredate, despoil, fleece, forage, foray, gut, lay waste, loot, maraud, pillage, pirate, prey, prey upon, put to the sword, raid, ransack, ravage, rifle, rob, sack, spoil, spoliate, strip, strip bare. *Informal:* pluck. **5. freeboot** buccaneer, picaroon, pirate, run, smuggle. **6. kidnap** abduct, carjack, highjack, hijack, shanghai, skyjack. **7. impress** crimp, press. **8. duff** lift cattle, poach, rustle. *Informal:* gully-rake.

RELATED KEYWORDS: DECEPTION, TAKING, UNLAWFULNESS, IMMORALITY, THIEF

ROCK

n.   1.   **1. rock** anorthosite, bush stone, igneous rock, metamorphic rock, mylonite, sedimentary rock, siliceous rock, stone, ultrabasic rock, ultramafic rock, volcanic rock. **2. boulder** bomb, erratic, eruptive, floater, gibber, gibber stone. **3. stone** billy boulder, boondy, brinnie *(Chiefly Victoria)*, chinaman *(Mining)*, cobble, cobblestone, drake stone, gonnie *(Chiefly Qld)*, goolie *(Especially Qld, NSW)*, niggerhead, pebble, ronnie *(SA)*, yonnie *(Especially Victoria)*. **4. standing stone** betyl, cairn, central cylinder, cromlech, dolmen, gravestone, headstone, ledger, menhir, orthostat, stela, stele, stone, tombstone. **5. fossil** belemnite, henge, thunder egg, thunderbolt, thunderstone. **6. meteorite** aerolite. **7. gravel** aerolite, brash, debris, lapilli, rubble, scree, shingle. **8. gravel** brash, debris, lapilli, rubble, scree, shingle.

2.   **1. rock outcrop** basset, blow, boss, inlier, roche moutonnée. **2. concretion** dogger, septarian, spherulite. **3. rock stack** aiguille, dyke, needle, yardang, zeuge. **4. stalactite** column, stalagmite, stylolite. **5. megalith** monolith. **6. batholith** bathylith, laccolith, xenolith. **7. stratum** alluvial, aquafer, aquifer, basement, basement complex, bed, bedding, bedrock, berm, bone bed, bushoo, cap rock, colluvium, confined aquifer, counter, cross reef, deep ground, footwall, horizon, horse, killas, lead, ledge, lens, lithosphere, lode, mantle, mantle rock, mantua, mullocky reef, ore body, ore shoot, pipe, quartz-reef, reef, regolith, seam, shelf, sial, sill, sima, substrate, surface reef, underset, vein, wall rock. **8. moraine** glacial meal, rock-flour, till. **9. rock formation** series, shield.

3.   **1. jewel** bijou, brilliant, cameo, double, doublet, gem, gemstone, girandole, precious stone, stone, toadstone. *Informal:* rock. **2. cut jewel** baguette, brilliant, briolette, cabochon, chip, crystal, rose, star, table, tercet, triplet. **3. diamond** adamant, brilliant, diamonds, rough diamond, solitaire. *Informal:* ice, sparkler. **4. mother-of-opal** Andamooka matrix, matrix.

4.   **1. rockiness** chalkiness, schistosity, stoniness. **2. petrifaction** petrogenesis, silicification.

5.   **1. geology** astrogeology, crystallography, gemmology, gemology, geomorphology, lithology, mineralogy, palaeomagnetism, petrography, petrology, photogeology, tectonics, X-ray crystallography.

6.   **1. geologist** geoscientist. *Informal:* geo, rock doctor, rock-hound.

7.   **1. sedimentary rocks** argil, argillite, arkose, basalt, bind, bluestone, breccia, buhrstone, burr, burrstone, burstone, calc-sinter, calc-tufa, chalk, chert, china stone, clay, claystone, conglomerate, coquina, cornbrash, cuckoo sandstone, dolerite, flint, flookan, geyserite, greensand, greywacke, grit, ironstone, itacolumite, kaolin, limestone, malm, marl, mottled sandstone, mudstone, niggerhead, novaculite, oil shale, oolite, papa *(NZ)*,

pelite, phosphate rock, pipestone, pisolite, portland stone, psammite, psephite, pudding stone, Purbeck marble, quartzite, rottenstone, sandstone, scaglia, shale, silex, silicified wood, siltstone, sinter, skarn, stinkstone, touchstone, travertine, tufa, wacke. *Informal:* speckled hen. **2. igneous rocks** agglomerate, andesite, basalt, block lava, blue ground, bluestone, breccia, clinkstone, diabase, dolerite, dunite, elvan, elvanite, felsite, gabbro, glass, granite, granitite, granophyre, greenstone, ignimbrite, lava, margarite, monzonite, nephelinite, obsidian, ophite, pearlite, pegmatite, peridotite, perlite, phonolite, pitchstone, porphyroid, porphyry, pounamu, pozzuolana, propylite, pumice, rhyolite, scoria, slag, syenite, tachylyte, taxite, tephrite, theralite, trachyte, trap, traprock, trass, tuff, volcanic glass, volcanic tuff, whin, whinstone. **3. metamorphic rocks** amphibolite, billy, biotite schist, eclogite, gneiss, granulite, groundmass, hornblende schist, marble, metasediment, metavolcanic, potstone, schist, serpentinite, slate.

8. **1. gemstones** agate, alexandrite, almandine, amethyst, aquamarine, asteria, azurite, beryl, bloodstone, cairngorm, carnelian, cat's-eye, chessylite, chrysoberyl, cinnamon stone, cornelian, cymophane, emerald, essonite, garnet, greenstone, heliodor, heliotrope, hessonite, hiddenite, hyacinth, iron pyrites, jacinth, jargon, Killiecrankie diamond, kunzite, marcasite, moonstone, oriental amethyst, peridot, phenacite, pounamu, pyrites, pyrope, rhodolite, rubellite, ruby, sapphire, sard, sardius, scarab, scarabaeus, schorl, star sapphire, star stone, topaz, tourmaline, turmaline, turquoise, water-sapphire, white sapphire, zircon. *Informal:* aggie. **2. opal** agaty, black opal, cleanskin, cleanskin nobby, clearskin, colours, fire opal, flash, girasol, harlequin, hue, hydrophane, knobby, pineapple, solid, streak, trace, white opal. *Informal:* nobby, stone. **3. ornamental stones** alabaster, amazon-stone, amazonite, calc-sinter, cipolin, crystal, hawk's-eye, jade, jasper, lapis lazuli, marble, murrhine, onyx, porphyry, rhodonite, rock-crystal, sardonyx, serpentine, tiger's-eye, travertine, verd antique.

9. **1. minerals and ores** acmite, adularia, aegerite, albite, alkali, allanite, allophane, alumina, aluminate, aluminosilicate, alunite, amalgam, amber potch, amblygonite, amianthus, amphibole, analcite, anatase, andalusite, andesine, andradite, anglesite, anhydrite, ankerite, annabergite, anorthite, antimonite, antimony glance, apophyllite, apron, aragonite, argentite, arsenopyrite, asbestos, australite, azurite, balas, bandstone, barite, barytes, bauxite, bay salt, biotite, black diamond, black lead, blackfellow's button, blackjack, blende, blue asbestos, boart, boracite, bornite, bort, bortz, bournonite, braunite, brocatelle, button stone, calamine, calaverite, calces, calcine, calcite, calcspar, calx, carbonado, carnallite, cassiterite, celestite, cerargyrite, chabazite, chalcedony, chalcopyrite, chalybite, chessylite, chiastolite, chloanthite, chlorargyrite, chlorite, choline, chromite, chrysoberyl, chrysolite, chrysoprase, chrysotile, cinnabar, citrine, cleveite, cloanthite, cobalt bloom, cobaltite, columbite, copper pyrites, cordierite, corundum, covellite, crocidolite, crocoisite, crocoite, cryolite, cuprite, cymophane, diopside, dioptase, diorite, dolomite, dripstone, earth, emerald copper, emery, enargite, endomorph, enstatite, epidote, erythrite, euclasite, euxenite, fayalite, feldspar, felspar, felspathoid, ferberite, ferric oxide, ferromagnesian, fibrolite, flos feri, fluor, fluorite, fluorspar, fool's gold, forsterite, fracture filling, franklinite, fuchsite, fused silica, gadolinite, gahnite, galena, garnierite, gehlenite, gibbsite, glass, glauberite, glauconite, gossan, graphite, greenland spar, Greenland spar, grossularite, gummite, gypsum, haematite, halite, hauerite, heavy spar, hedenbergite, hematite, hemitrope, horn silver, hornblende, hornstone, idocrase, ilmenite, indianite, iolite, iron glance, iron olivine, iron ore, iron pyrites, ironstone, kamacite, kaolinite, labradorite, laterite, lazulite, lazurite, lead crystal, linarite, loadstone, lodestone, macle, magnesite, magnet, magnetite, malachite, manganite, marcasite, matrix, mawsonite, meerschaum, mica, microcline, minette, mispickel, molybdenite, morion, mundic, murrhine glass, muscovite, nepheline, nephrite, octahederite, octahedrite, oligoclase, olivenite, olivine, oolite, opacite, orpiment, orthite, orthoclase, peacock ore, pentlandite, periclase, perimorph, phacolite, phenacite, phlogopite, pitchblende, plasma, plaster, platinised asbestos, plumbago, potch, prase, prasine, proustite, pyrargyrite, pyrope, pyrrhotite, quartz, realgar, red-lead ore, rhodochrosite, rhyacolite, rock salt, rocksalt, roscoelite, ruby silver, salt, sand, scandium, scapolite, scheelite, scolecite, sea foam, selenite, sepiolite, sericite, shoad, siderite, silex, silica, silicate, sillimanite, silver glance, sinhalite, smaltite, smithsonite, soapstone, sperrylite, sphalerite, sphene, spinel, spodumene, stannite, steatite, steelband, stibnite, sunstone, sylvanite, sylvinite, sylvite, taconite *(US)*, talc, tantalite, tarbuttite, tennantite, tenorite, tetradymite, tetrahedrite, thenardite, thorianite, thorite, thulium, tin pyrites, tinstone, titanate, titanite, torbanite, tremolite, trichite, trona, troostite, tungsten, tungstite, twin, ulexite, uraninite, vermiculite, vesuvianite, vivianite, water sapphire, wavellite, wernerite, wheel ore, white mundic, white nickel, willemite, witherite, wolfram, wolframite, wolframium, wulfenite, wurtzite, xenotime, yellow quartz, yellowcake, ytterbite, yttria, yttrotantalite, zeolite, zinc blende, zinc-spinel, zincite, zinckenite, zinkenite, zirconia, zoisite.

adj. **10.** **1. rocky** amygdaloidal, chalky, crystalloid, felspathose, flinty, lithic, lithoid, marble, marmoreal, petrosal, petrous, pudding stone, quartziferous, semivitreous, shingly, stone, stone-like, stony. **2. crystalloid** clastic, conglomerate, crystalloidal, fragmental, pyroclastic, secondary. **3. crystalline** adamantine, asteriated, clear, crystal, crystalliferous, diaphanous, glassy, hyaline, hyaloid, idiomorphic, lucid, microcrystalline, semitranslucent, semitransparent, translucid, transparent, vitreous. **4. volcanic** tuffaceous. **5. stratiform** stratigraphic, stratigraphical. **6. sedimentary** aqueous, arenaceous. **7. intrusive** hypabyssal, irruptive. **8. acid** acidic, alkali, alkaline, basic *(Chiefly US)*, felsic, intermediate, mafic. **9. precious** diamantine, rich, sapphirine, semiprecious, valuable.

RELATED KEYWORDS: LAND, MATTER, METAL, RAW MATERIALS

ROMANCE

n. **1.** **1. romance** passion, romantic love. **2. wooing** address, courting, courtly attention, courtly love, courtship, gallantry, serenading, suit. **3. dating** going out, keeping company. **4. blind dating** internet dating. **5. flirtation** amour, coquetry, dalliance, seduction. **6. affair** affair of the heart, affaire de coeur, flirtation, love affair, romance. *Informal:* fling.

2. **1. endearments** addresses, assiduities, attentions, blandishments, compliments. **2. amorous glances** ogle, sheep's eyes, the glad eye. **3. kiss** French kiss, osculation, peck. *Informal:* smack, smacker. **4. embrace** caress, clasp, cuddle, hug, snuggle, squeeze, stroke. *Informal:* clinch. **5. petting** billing and cooing, fondling, necking, smooching, smoodging, spooning. *Informal:* pash, snog *(Chiefly British)*. **6. hankypanky** slap-and-tickle. *Informal:* fun and games, funny business, sexploits.

3. **1. tryst** assignation, date, lovers' meeting. **2. love letter** billet-doux, love knot, valentine. **3. love potion** aphrodisiac, cantharides, horny goat weed, love juice, philtre, Spanish fly.

4. **1. lover** amorist, beau, beloved, light-o'-love, love, nuba *(Aboriginal English)*, paramour, sweetheart, truelove, valentine. *Informal:* flame, squeeze, steady. **2. boyfriend** male friend, young man. *Informal:* babester, boy, fellow, guy, man. **3. girlfriend** female friend, inamorata, ladylove, lass. *Informal:* bird, floozy, girl, potato peeler, sheila, woman. **4. date** blind date, coffee date. **5. wooer** admirer, amorist, inamorato, serenader, spark, suer, suitor, swain *(Chiefly Poetic, British)*. **6. caresser** dandler, fondler, kisser, smoocher, smoodger. **7. ladies' man** beau, Casanova, dallier, Don Juan, flirt, flirter, Lothario, ogler, philanderer, rake, Romeo, roué, seducer. *Informal:* lady-killer, wolf. **8. coquette** charmer, flirt, flirter, light-o'-love *(British, US)*, minx, seductress, tease, teaser. *Informal:* sex kitten, vamp. **9. mistress** concubine, courtesan, kept woman, number two *(Philippine English)*. *Informal:* kulasisi *(Philippine English)*, moll. **10. toy** plaything.

adj. **5.** **1. romantic** amatory, amorous, erotic, loving, passionate, sexy. *Informal:* lovey-dovey. **2. in love** amorous, besotted, captivated, enamoured, infatuated, shook on, smitten, smitten by another's charms, uxorious. *Informal:* gaga, gone, gone on, mad, spoony, struck on, stuck on, sweet on. **3. lovelorn** lovesick, sighing. *Informal:* sighing like a furnace. **4. courtly** gallant, swainish. **5. flirtatious** coquet, coquettish. *Informal:* cheeky *(Singaporean and Malaysian English)*, itchy *(Singaporean and Malaysian English)*. **6. kissable** amiable, embraceable, lovable, loveable.

v. **6.** **1. love** be in love with, care for, cherish, die for, fall down, have a crush on, look sweetly on, only have eyes for. **2. fall in love** conceive a passion for, develop feelings for, fall head over heels in love. **3. woo** address, court, make love (to) (or with), pay court to, set one's cap at. *Informal:* spark *(US)*. **4. go out with** be an item, date, go steady, see, take out, walk out with. **5. have an understanding with** get engaged, plight one's troth to. **6. flirt** carry on, coquet, dally, fool around with, galavant, gallivant, make time, play the field, tease. *Informal:* play footsies, play tootsy. **7. flirt with** do a mash with, lead on, throw oneself at, toy with. *Informal:* do a line with, vamp. **8. make eyes at** bat one's eyelids at, ogle. *Informal:* give someone the glad eye. **9. proposition** make a pass at, make up to. *Informal:* chat up, crack onto, do a line for, get off with, put the hard word on, sleaze onto. **10. have an affair** philander. *Informal:* play around, play up.

7. **1. make love** bill and coo, bundle, pet. *Informal:* canoodle, neck, smooch, smoodge, snog *(Chiefly British)*, spoon. **2. caress** chuck, chuck under the chin, dandle, fondle, make out, pat, pet, stroke. *Informal:* raunch. **3. embrace** bosom, clasp, cuddle, embosom, enfold, fold, fold in one's arms, hug, nestle, nuzzle, press, snuggle, squeeze. *Informal:* raunch. **4. kiss** air kiss, blow a kiss, French-kiss, make out, osculate, peck, smack, tongue-kiss.

Informal: bill, mug, pash, pash off, smooch, smoodge, suck face, swap saliva, swap spit. **5. coo** murmur sweet nothings.

adv. **8. 1. romantically** adoringly, amorously, lovingly. **2. flirtatiously** coquettishly, dallyingly, flirtingly.

RELATED KEYWORDS: LOVE, SEX, MARRIAGE

ROOMS

n. **1. 1. rooms** apartments, atrium, attic, basement, chambers, cockloft, compartment, garret, room, solar, suite. *Informal:* pad, shovel. **2. veranda** piazza *(US)*, porch *(US)*, sleep-out, sunporch. **3. gallery** box, choir loft, dedans, floor, gazebo, jube, lantern, loft, loge, loggia, parvis, public gallery, strangers' gallery, traverse, tribune. **4. bathroom** amenities, bagnio, bath, bathhouse, baths, caldarium, closet, comfort station, convenience, en suite, ensuite, facilities, head, ladies, laundry, lavatory, mens, powder room, public convenience, rest room, roundhouse, sauna, shower room, steam room, sudatorium, sudatory, thermae, toilet, urinal, urinary, washroom, water closet. *Informal:* dyke, gents, jerry, lav, lavvy, smallest room, the smallest room, toot. **5. hospital ward** birthing suite, casualty, casualty ward, clinic, emergency room, intensive care, sick room, solarium, surgery, theatre, ward. *Informal:* cas. **6. dressing-room** change room, changing room, cloakroom, fitting room. **7. darkroom** bio-box, booth, projection room. **8. cell** black hole, black peter, condemned cell, death cell, dungeon, guardhouse, guardroom, oubliette, pound, solitary confinement, sweatbox. *Informal:* calaboose *(US)*, chokey, digger *(NZ Prison)*, dummy *(NZ Prison)*, fleapit, glasshouse *(British Military)*, go-slow, peter, slot, slough. **9. booth** bower *(Poetic)*, cabin, carport, carrel, crib, den, lean-to, loosebox, skillion, stall. **10. capsule** airlock, caisson, cockpit, cofferdam, command module, cuddy, engine-room, recompression chamber, stank *(British)*. **11. compartment** anteroom, booth, carrel, cubicle, paperstand, phone box, polling booth, signal box, stall, telephone booth, telephone box, waiting room, well. **12. cellar** basement, coal cellar, coal hole, crypt, sub-basement, subcellar, undercroft, vault. **13. attic** garret. **14. strongroom** vault. **15. gunroom** casemate. **16. schoolroom** classroom, study. **17. crypt** catacombs, cist, cubiculum, hypogeum, mastaba, mausoleum, morgue, samadhi *(Indian English)*, sepulchre, tomb, undercroft, vault. *Informal:* deadhouse. **18. chapel** ante choir, antechapel, antechoir, athenaeum, bema, cella, chancel, choir, naos, prothesis, sacristy, vestry.

2. 1. living room calefactory, club, clubroom, common room, drawing room, family room, front room, green room, hall *(Singaporean and Malaysian English)*, lounge, lounge room, megaron, mess, misericord, parlour, rest room, salon, sitting room, solar, staffroom. **2. sunroom** snuggery, solarium, sunlounge. **3. smoking room** divan, smokeroom. **4. nursery** cubbyhouse, playhouse, playroom, rumpus room, Wendy house. **5. conservatory** gallery, saloon.

3. 1. kitchen bakehouse, bakery, butlery, caboose, cook-shop *(NZ)*, cookhouse, cuisine, dairy, dirty kitchen *(Philippine English)*, gallery, galley, grill, grillroom, kitchenette, scullery, servery. **2. coldroom**. **3. dining room** breakfast room, cenacle, dinette, frater, hall, morning room. **4. dining hall** bar, bistro, bodega, brasserie, butlery, cafe, cafeteria, canteen, chophouse *(British, US)*, cocktail bar, cocktail lounge, coffee bar, coffee house, diner, dining car, eating house, estaminet, grillroom, inn, ladies' lounge, lounge, luncheonette, mess, nightclub, pizzeria, private bar, public, public bar, pull-in *(British)*, refectory, restaurant, saloon, saloon bar, soup kitchen, steakhouse, taproom *(British)*, tavern, tearoom, teashop, wardroom, wine bar, wineshop. *Informal:* caff, clipjoint, dive, eatery, greasy spoon, groggery, hash house, joint, nineteenth hole, ref, swill.

4. 1. bedroom boudoir, bower *(Poetic)*, camera, chamber, closet, cubicle, den, dormitory *(US)*. *Informal:* dorm, pad, passion pit. **2. cabin** berth, billet, double room, guestroom, roomette *(US)*, single room, sleep-out, sleeper, stateroom, twin room. **3. guardroom** billet, guardhouse, quarters, rooms, tollbooth.

5. 1. hall antechamber, anteroom, concert hall, corridor, foyer, galilee, hallway, lobby, loggia, narthex, parvis, porch, propylaeums, propylon, vestibule. **2. auditorium** ballroom, chamber, concert-hall, council chamber, dance hall, divan, durbar, hall, lecture theatre, playhouse, reception room, rotunda, saloon, stateroom, theatre, theatrette.

6. 1. office boardroom, chamber, chancellery, command post, composing room, confined space, consulting room, counting room, headquarters, mailroom, operations room, orderly room, registry, registry office, saleroom, salesroom, studio, surgery, tally-room.

7. 1. heroin injecting room injecting room, safe injecting room, shooting gallery.

RELATED KEYWORDS: CONTAINER, DWELLING, SHAPE

ROUGHNESS

n. **1.** **1. roughness** asperity, brokenness, rudeness, rugosity, unevenness. **2. bumpiness** abnormity, inequality, irregularity, key, lumpiness, nodosity, spottiness, stubbedness, unevenness. **3. cragginess** jaggedness, ruggedness, savageness, scragginess. **4. crenulation** corrugation, crinkle, dentation, denticulation, ripple, serration, serrulation. **5. coarseness** bite, earthiness, grain, graininess, granulation, harshness, scratchiness, texture. **6. shagginess** hispidity, raggedness, scabrousness, scaliness.

2. **1. rough ground** tiger country. *Informal:* sumpbuster. **2. white water** chop, overfall, roughage, turbulence. *Informal:* haystack. **3. crag** peak.

adj. **3.** **1. rough** broken, bullate, cross-grained, gnarled, knaggy, knotted, knotty, knuckly, lumpish, lumpy, nodular, pebbly, ridged, roughish, rubbly, ruckled, rugged, rugose, scratchy, shaggy, stubbed, uneven, wrinkled. **2. jagged** broken, chopping, choppy, hackly, irregular, jaggy, muricate, notched, ragged, scraggly, scraggy, squarrose, tattered. **3. craggy** cragged, ironbound, rock-bound, rocky. **4. jolty** broken, bumpy, rough, uneven. **5. coarse** caespitose, coarse-grained, cross-grained, grainy, rough-hewn, rude, unfinished, unpolished. **6. scaly** furfuraceous, lepidote, scabrous, scurfy, squamate. **7. bristly** acanthaceous, acanthoid, acanthous, burry, bushy, calcarate, ciliate, echinate, fimbriate, fringed, hispid, horrent, prickly, snaggy, spiculate, spiky, spinescent, spiniferous, spinose, spinous, spiny, spurred, thorny, tufted.

4. **1. notched** biserrate, crenate, crenulated, deckle-edged, dentate, denticulate, double serrate, fringed, gnarled, gnarly, jaggy, knurled, pointed, ridged, saw-toothed, scalloped, serrate, serrated, serriform, serrulate, toothed, warded. **2. indented** broken, erose, etched, gnawed away, gorgy, grooved, gullied, incised, scratchy, uneven, unsteady, valleyed.

v. **5.** **1. roughen** carbonado, coarsen, grain, hack, rasp, rough, rough up, scapple, serrate, shag. **2. key** knurl, scabble, stab. **3. rumple** rub the wrong way, ruffle, tousle. **4. chap** rub.

adv. **6.** **1. roughly** irregularly, rough, rudely, unevenly. **2. bumpily** spottily. **3. craggily** ruggedly. **4. jaggedly** raggedly, scraggily. **5. dentately** crenately, denticulately. **6. coarsely** harshly, scabrously, shaggily.

RELATED KEYWORDS: BULGE, CUT, FOLD, FURROW, SHARPNESS

ROUNDNESS

n. **1.** **1. roundness** globosity, globularity, granularity, orbicularity, ovalness, sphericality, sphericity, spheroidicity. **2. conglobation** lobation. **3. circularity** annularity.

2. **1. ball** bomb, circle, crystal ball, full moon, globe, globoid, moon, orb, sphere, spheroid, tore, toroid, torus. **2. celestial globe** celestial sphere, sphere. **3. playing ball** agate, baseball, basketball, beach ball, billiard ball, bowl, bowling ball, cricket ball, cue ball, eight ball, football, golf ball, handball, medicine ball, ping-pong ball, pioneer ball, pushball, rubber ball, shot, soccer ball, softball, spot-ball, squash, squash ball, tennis ball, volleyball, wood. *Informal:* footy, pill, six-stitcher. **4. balloon**.

3. **1. marble** acker, agate, alley, American, bottler, bottley, connie, glassie, peewee, taw, tombola, tombowler. *Informal:* aggie, bottle-oh, doog, fat, mivvy *(British)*.

4. **1. bead** ball-bearing, bubble, bullet, button, gibber, gibber stone, globule, grain, granule, pearl, pellet, pill, pilule, spherule, stone. **2. nut** acinus, berry, boll, corn. **3. bobble** poi, pompom. **4. clew** clue. **5. drop** bead, blob, dewdrop, droplet, gutta. **6. bubble** air-bell, bead, blob, seed.

5. **1. oval** ellipse, ellipsoid, geoid. **2. ovoid** almond, cartouche, egg, mango, ovum. *Informal:* bum nut, cackle berry, goog, googy-egg.

6. **1. circle** circumference, cirque *(Poetic)*, epicycle, great circle, gyre, orbit, radius, roundel, roundlet, small circle, spiral. **2. round** circuit, gyre, lap, loop. **3. rim** felloe, felly, tread. **4. annual ring** annulation. **5. cromlech** fairy ring. **6. equator** celestial equator, ecliptic, equinoctial, equinoctial line, galactic circle, galactic equator, meridian. **7. disc** bezant, button, coin, pearl button, piece, slug, specie. **8. discus** puck. **9. bullseye** bull. **10. moonface**.

7. **1. ring** annulet, annulus, areola, areole, circle, circlet, cirque, sphere. **2. band** bands, belt, belting, cestus, cinch, cincture, collar, fascia, fillet, girdle, girth, headband, ruff, surcingle, torque. **3. garland** chaplet, coronal, crown, daisy-chain, wreath. **4. crown** circle, circlet, coronal, coronet, crownpiece, diadem, frontlet, tiara. **5. bracelet** anklet, armlet, bangle, ringlet, wristlet. **6. hoop** coit, quoit, rubber ring. **7. loop** folium, noose, O ring, piston ring, terry, washer. **8. grummet** gudgeon, terret, traveller. **9. corona** aureole, gloria, halo, nimbus, photosphere, sunglow. **10. napkin ring**.

8. **1. wheel** cartwheel, driving wheel. **2. waterwheel** millwheel, paddle, paddlewheel, windmill. **3. spinning wheel** charka, potter's wheel. **4. roulette** chocolate wheel, wheel of fortune. **5. cogwheel** cog, epicycloidal wheel, escape wheel, face gear, fly, flywheel, gearwheel, gipsy, gypsy, helical gear, idler wheel, lantern pinion, pennon *(Poetic)*, pinion, pinwheel, planet wheel, ratchet wheel, rowel, scapewheel, sheave, sprocket wheel, spur wheel, trundle, tumbler, wharve, worm gear, worm wheel. **6. castor** rundle, truck, trundle. **7. tyre** inner tube, pneumatic tyre, radial, radial-ply tyre, tubeless tyre, whitewall. *Informal:* slick, widey. **8. catherine-wheel** pinwheel. **9. gyroscope** gyro, gyrostat, peg top, teetotum, top.

adj. **9.** **1. round** circular, conglobate, conglomerate, conglomeratic, coniform, cylindric, cylindrical, global, globate, globelike, globoid, globose, globular, moony, orbicular, orbiculate, ringlike, rounded, spheral, spherelike, spheric, spherical, spheroid, spheroidal, spherular, sphery. **2. capitate** clavate, claviform, club-shaped, mooned. **3. beady** beadlike, granular, granulose, pea-like, pilular, pisiform.

10. **1. oval** ecliptic, egg-shaped, ellipsoid, ellipsoidal, elliptical, obovate, obovoid, olivary, ovate, oviform, ovoid, pear-shaped, pineal, piriform, spatulate, testiculate, vesical.

11. **1. circular** clypeate, cycloid, full, orbiculate, revolving, round, rounded, spiral, spirelike, spiriferous. **2. ringed** annular, annulate, annulated, annulose, armillary, circinate, hooped, ringleted, torquate. **3. ringlike** annular, areolar, areolate, circinate, coronary, coronate, cricoid, ring-shaped, round. **4. cyclic** bicyclic, tricyclic. **5. buttony** discal, disclike, discoid, discoidal, placoid, platelike, scutate.

v. **12.** **1. round** ball, conglobate, conglobe, globe, orb, sphere. **2. coil up** clew, clue. *Informal:* roll up. **3. granulate** pellet, pelletise, pill.

RELATED KEYWORDS: BULGE, CURVE, SHAPE, SPIN, TWIST

ROUTE

n. **1.** **1. route** beat, channel, course, highway, lane, laneway, line, march, path, pathway, tack, track, wake. **2. itinerary** travel plan. **3. short cut** crosscut, cut-off, direttissimo. **4. trade route** lifeline. **5. air-route** air route, air structure, air-corridor, airlane, airline, airway, flight path, glide path, great circle route. *Informal:* kangaroo route. **6. trajectory** orbit. **7. sea lane** shipping lane.

2. **1. access** corridor, fairway, gate, pass, passage, thoroughfare, vista, way. **2. right of way** dedication of way. **3. way in** adit, avenue, door, doorway, dromos, entrance, entry, gateway, ingress, inlet, introitus, water gate. **4. way through** cluse, defile, ghat, notch *(US)*. **5. way out** débouché, debouch, egress, exit, issue, outlet. **6. driveway** approach, avenue *(British)*, drive, forecourt *(British)*. **7. runway** airstrip, flare path, strip, tarmac, taxiway.

3. **1. path** bikeway, bridle-track, bridlepath, cyclepath, cycleway, pack-track *(NZ)*, pathway, ride, towpath. **2. footpath** banquette *(Southern US)*, causeway, crazy paving, dyke, flagging, flags, flagstones, footway, kerb, mall, path, pathway, pavement, paving, piazza, side path, sidewalk *(US)*, square, walk, walkway, wayside. **3. travelator** escalator. **4. lane** alley, alleyway, gangway, hutong, laneway, pall-mall, passage, passageway, slow vehicle turnout. **5. aisle** ambulatory, bay, corridor, hall, lobby, passage. **6. arcade** cloister, colonnade, gallery, loggia, ropewalk, slype, walk. **7. arch** archway. **8. subway** tunnel, underpass. **9. manway** catwalk, duckboard, gangboard, gangway, logway, ridgeway, runway. **10. bridge** aerobridge, airbridge, Bailey bridge, bateau, boardwalk, box-girder bridge, caisson, clapper bridge, drawbridge, floating bridge, footbridge, gangplank, gangway, humpback bridge, pivot bridge, pontlevis, pontoon, pontoon bridge, suspension bridge, swing bridge, toll bridge, transporter bridge, traversing bridge, trestle bridge, truss bridge, viaduct. **11. track** bush track, fire trail, nature trail, snig-track, snigging track, trail, walking track. **12. course** cinder track, dirt track, drag strip, dromos, home straight, home stretch, racecourse, racetrack, sandtrack, speedway, straight, straightaway *(US)*, straightway, track. *Informal:* the turf. **13. ramp** cattle ramp, cattlepit, cattlestop. **14. chute** crush, drafting race, race. **15. walk** pad, sheepwalk.

4. **1. road** boulevard, carriageway, roadway, street, thoroughfare. *Informal:* drag, frog and toad. **2. the bitumen** blacktop, macadam, metal road, tarmac. *Informal:* sumpbuster. **3. highway** arterial road, distributor, divided road, dual carriageway, highroad, pike *(US)*, postroad, priority road, ring-road, trunk road, turnpike. **4. expressway** autobahn, autoroute, autostrada, fast road, freeway, motorway. **5. beefroad** beef road. **6. avenue** boulevard, mall, parkway, pedestrian mall, place, row, terrace. **7. promenade** alameda *(Chiefly US)*, broadwalk, esplanade, front, parade, seafront. **8. back**

road backtrack, bypass, byroad, crossroad, detour, diversion, line, side road, sidetrack. **9. backstreet** alley, bypath, bystreet, byway, side street, sideway. **10. dead end** blind alley, cul-de-sac. **11. dirt road** dirt track, gravel road, unmade road, unsealed road, unsurfaced road. **12. access road** feeder, service road, turn-off. **13. cross-street** crossroad, crossway, slip-road *(British)*. **14. junction** bottleneck, intersection, roundabout, traffic circle *(US)*. **15. crossover** flyover, overbridge, overpass. **16. causeway** dyke, embankment, stepping stones. **17. zigzag** switchback. **18. tollway** pike *(US)*, turnpike. **19. stock-route** drove, lane, long paddock, stock route. **20. lane** fast lane, laneway, overtaking lane, pole, traffic lane, transit lane, turnout.

    5.   **1. railway** branch line, cog railway *(Chiefly US)*, feeder, hump, light rail, line, loop, main line, permanent way, plate, plate rail, rack-railway, rail, railroad *(US)*, railway line, road *(US)*, scenic railway, section, shunt, sidetrack *(US)*, siding, switchback, third rail, trackage *(US)*, tramroad, trunk, trunk line, wood line, zigzag. **2. tramline** pinch, tram, tram pinch, tramway. **3. underground** metro, subway, tube, tube train *(British)*, underground railway. **4. cableway** teleferic. **5. cable railway** cable tramway, funicular, funicular railway. **6. points** gauntlet, switch *(Chiefly US)*.

   v. **6.**   **1. beat a path** pave a way, trail *(US)*, tunnel. **2. leave a trail** lay down a track, track. **3. chart** navigate, plot, track.

    RELATED KEYWORDS: CHANNEL, ENTRANCE, EXIT, TRAVEL

RUBBING

   n. **1.**   **1. rubbing** effleurage, embrocation, frottage, massage, rub, rub-down, wipe. *Informal:* noogie. **2. rubbing away** ablation, abrasion, attrition, corrosion, denudation, erosion, fret, gnawing, scraping, wearing away. **3. graze** abrasion, score, scrape, scratch, scuff.

     2.   **1. friction** bite, traction. **2. drag** driftage, head resistance, pressure drag, profile drag, skin friction drag, windage. **3. tribology**.

     3.   **1. abrasive** abradant, abrader, bastard file, bath brick, block plane, compass plane, crosscut file, emery board, emery cloth, emery paper, emery wheel, facer, facing tool, file, floatstone, glasspaper, grinder, grinding wheel, grindstone, hone, jack plane, nailfile, oilstone, plane, riffler, rubber, sandblast, sander, sanding machine, sandpaper, smoothing plane, steel wool, stone, strop, trimmer, wet and dry, whetstone, wire wool. **2. rasp** broach, grattoir, rasper, scraper. **3. scratcher** back scratcher, strigil.

  adj. **4.**   **1. abrasive** abradant, erodent, eroding, erosive, grating, scratchy. **2. frictional** non-skid, non-slip, tractional.

   v. **5.**   **1. rub** currycomb, embrocate, flannel, massage, rub down, stroke, towel, wisp. **2. abrade** arris, file, fray, glasspaper, grate, graze, gride, grind, kibble, mill, paper, rasp, razor, rub, sand, sandblast, sandpaper, scrape, scuff, shave, stone, strop, whet. **3. chafe** rub, rub together. **4. scrabble** claw, crab, rake, rasp, scrape, scratch. **5. erode** abrade, degrade, fret, rub away, scrape.

    RELATED KEYWORDS: POWDER, SMOOTHNESS

RULE

   n. **1.**   **1. rule** axiom, by-law, canon, commandment, convention, criterion, custom, dictate, edict, fiat, first principle, formula, generality, golden rule, ground rules, hard and fast rule, hinge, institute, institution, law, maxim, model, motto, natural order, norm, observance, order, ordinance, pattern, precept, prescript, principle, procrustean bed, regulation, routine, rule of thumb, standard, standing order, sutra, theorem, topic, unwritten law. **2. discipline** bushido, ethics, moral philosophy, protocol, ritual. *Informal:* dos and don'ts. **3. tenets** articles, articles of association, code, constitution, dharma, doctrine, dogma, elements, lore, organon, organum, precept, ruling, teaching. **4. standard** canon, criterion, determinant, determinative, double standard, gage, gauge, key performance indicator, touchstone, yardstick.

   v. **2.**   **1. codify** code, conventionalise, institutionalise, prescribe, ritualise, stylise, subsume.

 adv. **3.**   **1. according to rule** according to Hoyle, bureaucratically, constitutionally, preceptively, prescriptively.

    RELATED KEYWORDS: COMMAND, CONFORMITY, CUSTOM, FORMALITY, LAWFULNESS, OBEDIENCE

RULER

   n. **1.**   **1. ruler** administrator, archduke, archon, ataman, baron, begum, bey, cacique, calif, caliph, caudillo, chancellor *(US)*, chief, chieftain, cock, count, count palatine, dato, demagogue, duke, earl, ecclesiarch, elder, elector, emeer, emir, emperor, eponym, ethnarch, Führer, gerent, grand duke, headman, hero, jarl, judge, kaliph, khalif, king, kinglet, lady, laird, landgrave, leader, liege, lord, lord leiutenant, lord of the manor, lord temporal, maharana, marchese, margrave, marquess, marquis, matriarch, mesne lord, mirza, monarch, monseigneur, overlord, padishah, paramount, pendragon, plutocrat, potentate, prince, principal, queen, queen regent, queen regnant, rajah, rani, regent, regina, rex, shah, sheikh, sovereign, sovran *(Poetic)*, sultan, suzerain, thane *(Scottish History)*, thegn, tribal elder, tsar. *Informal:* plute. **2. bureaucrat** apparatchik, aristocrat, hierocrat, panjandrum, patrician, pooh-bah, technocrat. **3. civilian official** alcalde, alderman, director, marshal, mayor, politician, politico *(Chiefly US)*, provost, syndic. *Informal:* pollie, polly. **4. governor** area commander, bashaw, bey, captain, chief, chief minister, commissar, commissary, commodore, constable, department head, eparch, exarch, gauleiter, governor-general, grand vizier, leader, legate, magistrate, mandarin, minister, pacha, pasha, permanent head, praefect, proconsul, rajah, regent, regulator, satrap, skipper, stadtholder, state governor, tetrarch. **5. military commander** admiral, aga, captain, chief of staff *(US)*, commodore, general, leader. **6. church ruler** archbishop, bishop, imam, lama, lord, patriarch, pope, sherif, vicar apostolic. **7. the authorities** officialdom, the government, the powers that be. **8. head of government** éminence grise, chancellor, consul, doge, duumvir, head of state, P.M., premier, president, president-elect, prime minister, protector, triumvir. **9. emperor** Caesar, czar, czarina, czaritza, empress, imperator, imperial, kaiser, king, mikado, negus, padishah, pharaoh, rajah, sovereign, tsar, tsarevitch, tsarina, tsaritsa, tzar, tzarina. **10. autocrat** absolute monarch, ayatollah, Big Brother, Caesar, despot, dictator, dictatress, dictatrix, führer, feudal lord, oligarch, overlord, paramount, robber baron, shogun, supremo, tyrant, war lord. **11. prefect** head boy, head girl.

2. 1. boss baas *(South African)*, bailiff, boss man *(Aboriginal English)*, boss of the board, boss woman *(Aboriginal English)*, bossboy, bwana, captain, chatelaine, chief, concertmaster, curator, director, directrix, employer, foreman, foreperson, forewoman, ganger, grass captain, head, intendant, leader, maluka, manager, manageress, mandore, master, mistress, overlooker, overseer, padrone *(US)*, sahib *(Indian English)*, sardar, senior, serang, shed boss, sherang, shipmaster, sir, slavedriver, straw boss *(Chiefly US)*, super, superintendent, supervisor, surveyor, sweater, taskmaster, tycoon. *Informal:* big gun, big shot, bigwig, bloke, boss cocky, brass, buzzwig, cock of the walk, cove, gaffer *(Chiefly British)*, Gov., governor, Guv, head serang, joss, missis, missus, Mr Big, number one, numero uno, old man, pannikin boss, skip, skipper, the man, the old man, top banana, top dog, twobob boss. **2. gang boss** capo, don, gang leader, Godfather.

RELATED KEYWORDS: AUTHORITY, FIGHTER, GOVERNMENT, MANAGER, POLITICIAN, RELIGIOUS LEADER

SAFETY

n. **1. 1. safety** safeness, secureness, security. **2. harmlessness** innocence, innocuousness, innoxiousness. **3. safety margin** factor of safety. **4. safeguard** cover, guard, precaution, protection, safekeeping, shelter. **5. immunity** active immunity, freedom. **6. safety first.**

2. 1. armour armature, brigandine, cataphract, chain mail, mail, panoply. **2. shield** aegis, buckler, escutcheon, hielamon, mulga, pavis, scutcheon, scutellum, scutum, target. **3. testudo** tortoise. **4. bard** chamfrain, chanfron. **5. breastplate** byrnie, coat of mail, corslet, cuirass, culet, gorget, habergeon, hauberk, jack, lorica, pectoral, plastron. **6. codpiece** box, cup. **7. helmet** basinet, beaver, burgonet, casque *(Poetic)*, crash hat, crash helmet, crest, hard hat, headpiece, morion, safety helmet, sallet. *Informal:* bash hat, bump cap, skid lid, stackhat, tin hat. **8. faceguard** beaver, eyeshade, goggles, gumshield, mask, mouthguard, mouthpiece, nasal, nosepiece, visard, visor, vizor. **9. gauntlet** basket hilt, coquille, glove, guard, palm. **10. armguard** bracer, brassard, palette, pauldron, rerebrace, vambrace. **11. greave** chausses, cuisse, jambeau, kneepad, kneepiece, pad, tasse, tasset.

3. 1. protective clothing burberry, flak jacket, greatcoat, hazmat suit, mackintosh, overcoat, parka, pressure suit, puffer jacket, raincoat, spacesuit, trench coat. *Informal:* beer coat.

4. 1. condom contraceptive sheath, durex *(British)*, French tickler, prophylactic. *Informal:* connie, dinger, dunlop overcoat, franger, French letter, frenchy, frog, jimmy hat, johnny, love glove, preservative, raincoat, rubber *(Chiefly US)*, rubber johnny, rubber straitjacket, skin.

5. 1. screen baffle, baffle plate, breakweather, breakwind, mantelet, stopping, windbreak. **2. awning** brise-soleil, dodger, heat shield, shade, sunblind, sunbreak, sunscreen, tilt. **3. fireguard** bonnet, cowl, fire-curtain, firebreak, firescreen, firewall, safety curtain. **4. bar** banister, banisters, bollard, buffer, bull-bar, bumper, bumper bar, cowcatcher, crash barrier, fender, grate, grating, guardrail, handrail, kerb, sponson, stone shield. *Informal:* kangaroo bar, roo bar.

6. **1. cocoon** pod, shell.

7. **1. safety harness** booster seat, inertia reel seatbelt, lunger belt, monkey rope, safety belt, seat belt, seatbelt. **2. lifeline** breeches buoy. **3. lifebelt** air jacket, buoy, float, floating island, flotsam, life jacket, life vest, life-preserver *(US)*, lifebuoy, Mae West, mooring buoy, pontoon, raft, spar buoy. **4. safety binding** release binding. **5. safety house** safe house.

8. **1. amulet** charm, Christopher medal, conjuration, fetish, force-field, frontlet, juju, palladium, periapt, scarab, scarabaeus, talisman, voodoo. *Informal:* mojo *(Chiefly US)*.

9. **1. vaccination** antiserum, immunotherapy, inoculant, inoculate, inoculation, inoculum, mithridatism, vaccinisation.

10. **1. rescuer** knight in shining armour, lifesaver, saviour. **2. surf-lifesaver** beach inspector, beltman, lifeguard, lifesaver, reelman. **3. lifesaving** surf-lifesaving.

adj. **11.** **1. safe** all clear, all right, alright, fail-safe, inviolate, safe and sound, secure, shockproof, unhurt. *Informal:* jake, right as rain, safe as houses. **2. harmless** innocuous, innoxious. **3. low-toxicity** hypo-allergenic. **4. protective** alimentary, childproof, flameproof, precautious, prophylactic, shark-proof, waterproof. **5. armoured** armour-plated, bulletproof, heavy-armed, ironclad, loricate, mailed, panoplied, panzer, shellproof.

v. **12.** **1. secure** bulwark, cocoon, cover, defend, guard, keep, overshadow, pad, patrol, protect, safeguard, screen, shade, shadow, shelter, shield, snug, watch over, wrap. **2. armour** bard, cuirass, mail, shield, visor. **3. defilade** sconce.

13. **1. rescue** preserve, safeguard, salvage, salve, save, save someone's life. *Informal:* bail out, get someone out of a tight spot, save someone's bacon (or skin) (or neck). **2. save one's bacon** bear a charmed life.

adv. **14.** **1. safely** in good hands, in safe hands, out of harm's way, securely.

RELATED KEYWORDS: DEFENCE, PRESERVATION, PROTECTION, SHELTER

SANITY

n. **1.** **1. sanity** lucidity, lucidness, mind, normalcy, normality, perspicuity, rationality, reason, saneness, soundness of mind. **2. soberness** responsibleness, sobriety.

adj. **2.** **1. sane** clear-headed, collected, compos mentis, in one's right mind, in possession of one's faculties, lucid, luculent, normal, phlegmatic, rational, reasonable, sensible, sound of mind. *Informal:* all there. **2. sober** responsible, self-contained, self-possessed, well-balanced.

v. **3.** **1. come to one's senses** be of right mind, get into gear. *Informal:* click, have all one's marbles.

adv. **4.** **1. sanely** lucidly, rationally. **2. responsibly** soberly.

RELATED KEYWORDS: LOGICALITY, MIND, THINKING

SATISFACTION

n. **1.** **1. satisfaction** fulfilment, gratification, implementation, realisation. **2. satisfactoriness** suitability, suitableness. **3. contentment** comfort, content, contentedness, satisfaction. **4. appeasement** assuagement. **5. fullness** impletion, repleteness, repletion. **6. satiation** jadedness, satiety. **7. sufficiency** adequacy, competence, enough, fill, glut. *Informal:* bellyful, roomful.

2. **1. satisfier** a natural, fulfiller, gratifier, sufficer. **2. quencher** thirst-quencher. **3. appeaser** assuager.

adj. **3.** **1. satisfactory** acceptable, all right, decent, fair, good-enough, goodish, nominal *(US)*, passable, right, satisfactorily, tolerable, win-win. *Informal:* 10-4, all serene, cool, ducky, fair enough, good enough, hunky, hunky-dory, jake, jakerloo, not bad, OK, okay. **2. up to scratch** all right, excellent, good, well-done. *Informal:* good-o, right. **3. satisfying** gratifying, pleasing, rewarding. **4. square** hearty, satisfying.

4. **1. satisfied** comfortable, content, contented, thirstless. *Informal:* comfy. **2. satiated** replete, sated. *Informal:* chocker, full as a butcher's pup, full as a goog, full up. **3. jaded** blasé.

5. **1. satiable** appeaseable, quenchable.

v. **6.** **1. satisfy** assuage, do the job, fulfil, gratify, please, rise to the occasion, serve, suffice, suit. *Informal:* deliver the goods, do, fill the bill, hit the nail on the head, hit the spot. **2. appease** allay, assuage, content, gratify, indulge, lay, mollify, pacificate, pacify, placate, sate, satisfy. **3. pander to** mollycoddle, pamper, please. **4. satiate** appease, assuage, feast, feed, fill, fulfil oneself, glut, gratify, pall, quench, sate, satisfy, slake, stay, surfeit. **5. pall** cloy, satiate.

adv.   **7.   1. satisfactorily** ably, acceptably, adequately, all right, alright, duly, effectively, sufficiently, very well, well. *Informal:* all cush, good-o, okay. **2. satisfyingly** gratifyingly. **3. comfortably** contentedly.

RELATED KEYWORDS: ADEQUACY, CONTENTEDNESS, FULLNESS, GOODNESS

SCHOOL

n.   **1.   1. school** area school *(Chiefly SA and Tasmania)*, bush school, central school *(Chiefly NSW, also Qld, ACT and Victoria)*, comprehensive school, consolidated school *(Victoria)*, cyberschool, dame school, demonstration school, district school *(Tasmania)*, educational institution, feeder school, government school, hospital school, madrasah, one-teacher school, public school, rural school, secondary modern school *(British)*, state school. *Informal:* blackboard jungle. **2. independent school** charity school *(British)*, G.P.S., non-government school, non-state school, parish school, prep school, preparatory school, private school, public school, ragged school *(British History)*. **3. opportunity school** special school. **4. boarding school** day school. **5. open school** alternative school, open classroom, open planning, progressive school. **6. correspondence school** school of the air. **7. summer school** finishing school. **8. girls' school** *Informal:* heifer paddock. **9. alma mater** old school. **10. convent** seminary. **11. Sunday school** Sabbath school. **12. kindergarten** childcare centre, creche, day care, day nursery, infants' school, kohanga reo, nursery, nursery school, playgroup, preschool. *Informal:* kinder *(Chiefly NSW)*, kindie, kindy. **13. primary school** grade school *(US)*, junior school, preparatory school. *Informal:* prep. **14. secondary school** grammar school *(British)*, high school, junior college, junior high school, junior school, lycée, matriculation college, secondary college, selective high school, technical school. *Informal:* high.

2.   1. college Academe *(Poetic)*, academy, athenaeum, college of advanced education, institute, institution, juniorate, lyceum, madrasah, polytechnic *(British, US)*, seminary, teacher's college, theologate, university college *(British)*. *Informal:* poly *(British, US)*. **2. university** campus, gumtree university, Ivy League, open university, state university *(US)*, university college, university of technology. *Informal:* the shop, uni, varsity. **3. technical college** trade school, training college, training school, vocational school, W.E.A. *Informal:* tech, techie. **4. evening college** institute, literary institute, mechanics' hall, mechanics' institute, night school, school of arts. **5. business college** commercial college. **6. agricultural college** agricultural high school. **7. naval college** arsenal, military college, school ship, training ship. **8. conservatorium** conservatoire, conservatory *(US)*. *Informal:* con. **9. teaching hospital** medical school.

RELATED KEYWORDS: KNOWLEDGE, LEARNING, TEACHER, STUDENT, TEACHING

SCRIPTURE

n.   **1.   1. scripture** canon, dharma, Holy Scripture, Holy Writ, oracles, patrology, revealed religion, revelation, sacred text, the Word of God, Word. **2. the Bible** Authorised Version, Douay Bible, family Bible, Good Book, Holy Bible, the Book, Vulgate. **3. apocrypha** legend, pseudepigrapha, tradition. **4. commandment** bull, decretal, dictate, edict, mitzvah, precept. **5. verse** chapter, harmony, lesson, versicle. **6. psalm** anthem, antiphon, antiphony, canticle, chant, doxology, hymn, introit, metrical psalm, offertory, sequence. **7. psalmody** hymnody. **8. tract** logion.

2.   1. scripturalism bibliolatry, evangelicalism, fundamentalism, patristics, patrology, textualism. **2. exegesis** exegetics, form criticism, hermeneutics, higher criticism, isagogics, kerugma.

3.   1. scripturalist Biblicist, Biblist, exegete, fundamentalist, futurist, textualist, textuary. **2. Talmudist** evangel, haggadist, hierogrammat, hierogrammatist, the Seventy.

adj.   **4.   1. scriptural** biblical, canonical, evangelical, gospel, legal, oracular, orphic, pythonic, synoptic, textual, textuary. **2. apocryphal** pseudepigraphic, pseudepigraphous.

5.   1. scripturalist bibliolatrous, born-again, evangelical, evangelistic, exegetic, fundamentalist, kerugmatik. **2. haggadistic** hierogrammatic.

RELATED KEYWORDS: RELIGION, RELIGIOUS CEREMONY

SEA

n.   **1.   1. sea** brine, deep, Neptune *(Poetic)*, ocean, profound *(Poetic)*, the blue, the deep *(Poetic)*, waters. *Informal:* Davy Jones's locker, ditch, the briny, the drink. **2. open**

411

sea blue water, high sea, main *(Poetic)*, seaway, seven seas, the high seas, the open. **3. waters** territorial waters. **4. offing** outing, outside. **5. shallows** low water, tide-water. **6. archipelago**. **7. sea-floor** ooze, seabed. **8. marine habitat** euphotic zone, water column.

2.   **1. bay** bight, embayment, gulf, harbour, hole *(US)*, ria. **2. inlet** arm, arroyo, canal, cove, creek, estuary, firth *(Chiefly Scottish)*, fjord, flow *(Scottish)*, frith *(Chiefly Scottish)*, loch *(Scottish)*, lough, rivulet, run, sound, tidal inlet. **3. passage** lagoon, sound, strait. **4. tidal basin** tide-lock.

3.   **1. surf** choppy water, head sea. *Informal:* slop. **2. wave** billow, bore, eagre, floodwave, ripple, surge, tidal wave, tsunami. **3. crest** lip, shoulder, tube, tunnel. **4. breaker** beachcomber, beacher, close-out, comber, set, shore break. *Informal:* greenback, greenie, hump. **5. whitecap** white horse. *Informal:* haystack. **6. water spout**. **7. ripple** beach break. **8. wake** backwash.

4.   **1. oceanography** aquaculture, bathometry, hydrography, marine biology, oceanics, thalassography.

5.   **1. oceanographer** aquarist, hydrographer, oceanaut, thalassographer.

6.   **1. sea nymph** Lorelei, mermaid, nereid, nix, ondine, sea witch, seamaid, selkie, siren, undine, water nymph, water sprite. **2. Neptune** merman, the old man of the sea, Triton.

adj.   7.   **1. sea** aquatic, halophilous, marine, Neptunian, oceanic, pelagic, seaborn, seawater, thalassic. **2. maritime** deepwater, ocean-going, seaborne, seafaring, seagoing. **3. deep-sea** abyssal, benthic, deepwater, demersal. **4. underwater** subaquatic, subaqueous, submarine, suboceanic, undersea. **5. surfy** insurgent, surgy. **6. tidal** lunitidal, neap. **7. neritic**. **8. littoral** circumlittoral, inlying, inshore, seagirt. **9. offshore** off, out-ward-bound, seaward. **10. overseas** surface, transmarine, transoceanic, transpacific, ultramarine.

8.   **1. oceanographical** thalassographic.

adv.   9.   **1. at sea** afloat, overseas, undersea. **2. offshore** inshore, outward, seaward, seawards.

     RELATED KEYWORDS: FLOW, LAKE, MARINER, SWAMP, WATERCRAFT

SEASON

n.   1.   **1. season** tide, time of the year. **2. equinox** first quarter. **3. spring** blossom time, Maytide, Maytime, springtime, vernal point. **4. summer** dog days, heat, heatwave, height of summer, Indian summer, midsummer, summer solstice, summertime. **5. autumn** autumnal equinox, autumnal point, equinox, fall *(Chiefly US)*, harvest, harvest home. **6. winter** depth of winter, freeze, freeze-up, midwinter, seedtime, wintertime. **7. the wet** mango season, monsoon season, wet season. **8. the dry** dry season. **9. seasonableness** summeriness, wintriness.

adj.   2.   **1. seasonal** equinoctial, solstitial. **2. seasonable** in, in season. **3. spring** vernal. **4. summer** aestival, estival, midsummer, summer-like, summery. **5. autumn** autumnal. **6. winter** brumal, hibernal, midwinter, wintry.

adv.   3.   **1. seasonally** seasonably. **2. autumnally** summerly, vernally, wintrily.

     RELATED KEYWORDS: PERIOD, TIME, WEATHER

SECRECY

n.   1.   **1. secrecy** caginess, closeness, covertness, dark, privacy, privateness, retirement, retreat, seclusion, secret, secretness, segregation, sequestration, shade, silence. **2. confidentiality** confidence, confidentialness. **3. clandestineness** collusiveness, furtiveness, slyness, sneakiness, stealth, stealthiness, surreptitiousness. **4. conspiracy** cabal, cobweb, collusion, complot, intrigue, plot, scheme. **5. code** argot, cant, cipher, cryptochannel, cryptogram, cryptograph, cypher, enigma, riddle, tick-tack. **6. cryptography** cryptology, steganography.

2.   **1. secret** arcanum, classified information, confidence, dark secret, mystery, official secrets. *Informal:* the skinny. **2. skeleton in the cupboard** dirty linen, family skeleton. **3. silent number.**

3.   **1. arcanums** esotericism, esotery, invisibility, mystery, mystique, occult, secret.

4.   **1. secret society** cabal, inner circle, inside, Mafia. *Informal:* backroom boys. **2. resistance** maquis, underground.

5.   **1. secret place** asylum, bolthole, conclave, conventicle, corner, harbour, hide-out, hideaway, hidey-hole, recesses, refuge, sanctum. *Informal:* funk-hole, lurk. **2. closed court** camera.

adj.   6.   **1. secret** classified, close, confidential, cryptic, dark, esoteric, intimate, personal, private, privy, top-secret, underground. **2. backroom** cabinet, cameral, closet, in camera, inner, interior. *Informal:* hush-hush. **3. unlisted** clandestine, concealed, covert, ex-directory, hidden, invisible, latent, latescent, perdu, unadmitted, unnamed.

7. **1. arcane** cabalistic, cabbalistic, cryptic, esoteric, hermetic, mysterious, mystic, mystical, occult, orphic, qabalistic, recondite, secret.

8. **1. secretive** clandestine, clever, cloak-and-dagger, collusive, deep-laid, feline, furtive, hole-and-corner, hugger-mugger, insidious, Jesuitical, sly, sneaking, stealthy, surreptitious, tiptoe, underhand, underhanded. *Informal:* cagey, carney, shifty, snaky, sneaky. **2. clandestine** backdoor, backstairs, bootleg *(Chiefly US)*, concealed, esoteric, furtive, hole-and-corner, hugger-mugger, private, secret, sly, sneaking, subterranean, under-the-counter, undercover, underground, underhand, underhanded, unlawful.

v. **9.** **1. keep secret** black out, bosom, classify, hide, hush up, secrete, sit on, smother, suppress, withhold. **2. keep a secret** detain, keep one's own counsel, let it go no further, not breathe a word. *Informal:* clam up, keep mum, keep one's mouth shut. **3. be secretive** cabal, collaborate, collude, compass, complot, concoct, connive, connive at, conspire, contrive, counterplot, hugger-mugger, intrigue, machinate, manoeuvre, plan, plot, pussyfoot, scheme, tick-tack with. *Informal:* work one's nut.

adv. **10.** **1. in secret** backstage, behind someone's back, behind the scenes, by (or through) the back door, cagily, clandestinely, close, closely, furtively, in the background, invisibly, on the quiet, on the side, on the sly, secretly, slyly, sneakily, sneakingly, stealthily, surreptitiously, through the back door, under one's hat, under the table, underhand, up one's sleeve. *Informal:* on the q.t. **2. covertly** clandestinely, collusively, under cover, underground. **3. confidentially** between ourselves, between you and me, entre nous, just quietly. **4. privately** behind closed doors, behind the scenes, confidentially, in confidence, intimately, sub rosa, under the rose.

RELATED KEYWORDS: HIDING, SILENCE, RETICENCE

SELFISHNESS

n. **1.** **1. selfishness** egocentricity, egoism, egomania, egotism, individualism, materialism, narcissism, self-absorption, self-awareness, self-interest, self-love, self-regard, self-seeking. **2. self-indulgence** hoggishness, inconsiderateness, inconsideration, possessiveness, self-pity. **3. mercenariness** baseness, careerism, cupboard love, opportunism, sordidness, venality. *Informal:* sleaze.

2. **1. self-seeker** egocentric, egoist, egomaniac, egotist, road-hog. *Informal:* brute, hog. **2. self-important person** spoilt brat. **3. mercenary** careerist, hireling, opportunist, soldier of fortune. **4. sponge** fortune-hunter, leech, parasite, sponger, trencherman. *Informal:* beat, bloodsucker, bludger, gimme girl, gold-digger, ten-per-center.

adj. **3.** **1. selfish** asocial, egocentric, egoistic, egoistical, egotistic, egotistical, hoggish, narcissistic, self-absorbed, self-aware, self-centred, self-loving, self-regarding, small-minded, spoilt. **2. self-indulgent** hoggish, incogitant, inconsiderate, possessive, self-pitying, selfish, spoilt, thoughtless, uncharitable, unchristian, ungenerous, unsympathetic. *Informal:* rude. **3. self-interested** base, calculating, greedy, hoggish, hoglike, mean-spirited, mercenary, open-mouthed, rapacious, ravenous, self-seeking, selfish, small, sordid, venal. *Informal:* gutsy.

v. **4.** **1. be selfish** care about number one, feather one's nest, have an axe to grind, keep an eye to the main chance, not care about anyone else, push one's barrow.

adv. **5.** **1. selfishly** egoistically, egotistically, in one's own interest, self-indulgently. **2. mercenarily** opportunistic, sordidly, venally.

RELATED KEYWORDS: MEANNESS, BADNESS, UNKINDNESS

SELLING

n. **1.** **1. selling** e-tailing, inertia selling, marketing, merchandising, pyramid selling, vendition. **2. auction** Bruce auction, crown auction, Dutch auction, public auction, vendue. **3. sale** bazaar, boot sale, car boot sale, clearance sale, clearing sale, closing-down sale, disposal, fete, fire sale, forward sale, garage sale, jumble sale, lawn sale, reduction sale, resale, rummage sale, runout campaign, sales promotion, sell-off, tie-in sale *(US)*, walk-in walk-out sale, wholesale, yard sale. **4. sales talk** colportage, hard sell, patter, pitch, sales pitch, salesmanship, sell, soft sell, spiel. *Informal:* plug. **5. vendorship** dealership, distributorship, retailership, wholesalership.

2. **1. seller** bourgeois, broker, cash and carry, chandler, commission agent, dealer, discounter, distributor, e-tailer, hawker *(SE Asian English)*, kerb broker, kulak, merchant, merchant prince, middleman, monger, pedlar, purveyor, regrater, reseller, retailer, shopkeeper, stockist, supplier, tallyman, trader, trafficker, vendor, warehouseman, wholesaler.

Informal: flogger. **2. travelling salesman** agent, cheapjack, colporteur, commercial traveller, hawker, higgler, huckster, packman, peddler, pedlar, pitchman, representative, sutler, traveller. *Informal:* faker *(US)*, Ghan, rep. **3. salesperson** bourgeois, cashier, checkout operator, clerk *(Chiefly US)*, keeper, merchant, sales assistant, salesclerk *(US)*, salesgirl, saleslady, salesman, saleswoman, shop assistant, shopgirl, shopkeeper, shopman, storekeeper. *Informal:* checkout chick, counterjumper. **4. spieler** *Informal:* barker, tout, touter. **5. auctioneer. 6. dishonest trader** black marketeer, blackbirder, bootlegger, peddler, pedlar, short, slaver. *Informal:* dud-dropper, fence.

adj. **3.** **1. saleable** alienable, for (or on) sale, marketable, resaleable, vendible. **2. commercial** retail, wholesale. **3. remaindered** marked down.

v. **4.** **1. sell** auction, dispose of, forward sell, hire, market, merchandise, offer, outsell, oversell, realise, regrate, resell, retail, sell off, sell out, sell short, sell up, traffic, turn over, wholesale. *Informal:* flog, hock, short. **2. peddle** hawk, push, put on the market, send to market, tout, traffic, vend. **3. hustle** hard-sell, push, soft-sell. **4. sell off** discount, dump, go, knock down, move, rediscount, remainder, sell like hotcakes, undersell, unload. **5. be sold** come (or go) under the hammer.

adv. **5.** **1. commercially** by auction, by mail order, by wholesale, door-to-door, on the market, over the counter, retail.

RELATED KEYWORDS: COST, EXPENSIVENESS, CHEAPNESS, FINANCE, MONEY, SHOP, COMMERCE

SEPARATION

n. **1.** **1. separation** diastasis, disarticulation, disassociation, disconnectedness, disconnection, discontinuity, discreteness, disjointedness, disjunction, disjuncture, dissociation, disunion, disunity, fragmentariness, non-union, separateness, unconnectedness.

2. **1. severance** cleavage, detachment, dilaceration, disengagement, dismemberment, disruption, disseveration, divulsion, fission, rupture, schism, scission, section, sunderance. *Informal:* bust-up. **2. brokenness** dissiliency. **3. disintegration** crumbling, nivation. **4. breakage** crash.

3. **1. division** bifurcation, bipartition, dichotomy, dualism, metamerism, partition, trifurcation. *Informal:* divide. **2. partitionment** compartmentalisation, demarcation, departmentalism, furcation, partition, repartition, segmentation, subdivision. **3. disassembly** decartelisation, disbandment, dismantlement, dispersion, dissolution, unravelment. **4. demodulation** detection. **5. political division** apartheid, class barriers, class distinction, colour-bar, demarcation, schism, segregation, zoning. **6. secession** partition, seceding, split. **7. sectionalisation** Balkanisation.

4. **1. crack** breach, break, burst, chap, chink, cleft, craze, crevasse, crevice, cut, diastema, fault plane, fissure, flaw, fracture, gash, laceration, parting, rent, rift, rip, rupture, sand-crack, slash, slit, split, spring, tear. **2. fault** cleat, fault line, fault plane, grain, joint, transcrystalline fracture. **3. separate group** cave *(English History)*, detachment, faction, fringe group, splinter group.

5. **1. filtration** biofiltration, centrifugation, cupellation, elutriation, floatation, flotation, fragmentation, screening, segregation, vacuum filtration. **2. chemical separation** atmolysis, chromatography, cracking, debourbage, dehydrogenation, desorption, dialysis, diffraction, dissection, distillation, distilment, electrolysation, electrolysis, electrowinning, fractional distillation, fractionation, haemodialysis, hydrolysis, ion exchange chromotography, precipitation, scorification, synersis, thin layer chromatography. **3. chemical disintegration** atomisation, breakdown, decomposition, deionisation, disassociation, dissociation, fission, nuclear fission, photodisintegration, photofission, photolysis.

6. **1. separator** breaker-down, detacher, disarticulator, dismemberer, disperser, divider, harrower, ripper, subdivider, sunderer, zootomist. **2. screener** cutter-out, dryblower, rippler, scutcher, thresher, winnower. **3. dag picker** dag, dagger. **4. splitter** mauler, river. **5. separatist** schismatic, seceder, secessionist, splittist.

7. **1. filter** colander, cullender, cupel, dryblower, riddle, riffle, ripple, ripper, screen, sieve, sifter, sluice, strainer, strake, tamis, tammy, ultrafilter, wirecloth. **2. chemical separator** catalytic cracker, cracker unit, deioniser, dialyser, dialysis machine, electrolyser, electrolytic cell, fractionator, insulator, macerator, precipitant, quicksilver cradle, scorifier, separator. **3. cradle** buddle, jig, puddler, puddling machine, puddling tub. **4. creamer** cream separator, elutriator, milk separator, separator. **5. centrifuge** microcentrifuge. **6. husker** brake, cotton gin, gin, scutch, winnow, winnowing machine.

adj. **8.** **1. separate** apart, detached, disconnected, discrete, disjoined, disjointed, disjunct, distinct, divided, loose, segregate, segregated, separable, separated, spaced, spiccato, staccato, unattached, unbundled. **2. loose** apart, distinct, free, separate, unattached, unconnected, yokeless. **3. adrift** castaway, cut loose, secluded. **4. alienated** disembodied, remote, removed, segregated. **5. freestanding** outstanding, singular. **6. unmixable** immiscible, incoherent, unmiscible. **7. separatist** schismatic, splittist.

9. **1. divided** cleft, cloven, compartmental, creviced, cut, diffractive, dipartite, disjointed, disjunct, disrupt, dissected, disunited, episodic, exploded, malapportioned, multifid, parted, partite, polytomous, ripped, riven, ruptured, separative, septempartite, split. **2. cleft in two** bifid, bifurcate, bilateral, bilobed, bilocular, bipartite, cloven, dichotomous, dimerous, dimidiate, fissile, forficate, forked, furcate, partitive, septate, swallowtailed. **3. trifurcate** trifid, triform, trifurcated, trimerous, triparted, tripartite.

10. **1. cracked** avulsed, broken, crazed, fractural, fractured, splintery. **2. fragmentary** clastic, fragmental, fragmented, green. **3. crumbly** exfoliative, flaky, splitting. **4. separating** dividing, parting.

v. **11.** **1. separate** delaminate, detach, disaggregate, disassociate, disconnect, disengage, disjoin, disrupt, dissever, dissociate, disunite, part, precipitate, rift, splay, split, unfasten. **2. divide** bifurcate, bisect, branch, canton, carve up, chap, chapter, compartment, cut up, departmentalise, dichotomise, dismember, dissect, dissever, factionalise, fissure, fork, fraction, furcate, halve, joint, paragraph, part, partition, quarter, ramify, rend, segment, separate, slice, slice up, slit, split, subdivide, sunder, trifurcate. **3. partition** Balkanise, compartmentalise, demarcate, divide and rule, fence off, hedge, isolate, lot, mark off, regionalise, sector, segregate, sequester, shut off, wall off.

12. **1. dissever** cleave, crack, cut, dismember, divide, maul *(US)*, open, part, rend, rip, rive, sever, shiver, slice, slit, split, sunder, unseam, wedge. **2. cut off** abscind, break off, chip, cut, dissever, hew off, rip off, sever, shear, slice, slice off, snip, splinter, split, tear off. **3. pull apart** cleave, dilacerate, disjoint, lancinate, rend, rip up, rive, scrap, shred, split, stave, tatter, tear, tear to pieces, tear up. **4. break** breach, crack, crash, dash, fracture, rupture, shatter, smash, snap, tear.

13. **1. disassemble** break up, decartelise, disaffiliate, disaggregate, disarticulate, disband, dismantle, dismember, dismount, disunite, knock down, separate, unglue, unravel, unsolder, unyoke. **2. unfasten** cast loose, cast off, detach, disconnect, loose, loosen, slip, unbend, unbind, unbuckle, unbutton, unclasp, uncouple, undo, unfix, unglue, unharness, unhasp, unhinge, unhitch, unhook, unknit, unlash, unlay, unlimber, unlink, unloose, unloosen, unmoor, unpeg, unpick, unpin, unplug, unreel, unscrew, unsolder, unstick, untie, untuck, unwind, unyoke.

14. **1. crumble** air-slake, break up, calve, chip, decompose, disintegrate, disperse, dissolve, explode, fall to pieces, moulder, separate, slake, spall, splinter, tetter. **2. flake** cast, exfoliate, foliate, husk, laminate, peel, shed, slough.

15. **1. part company** break up, cut loose, dissociate, divorce, grow apart, part. *Informal:* bust up, split up.

16. **1. separate mechanically** atomise, blanch, centrifugalise, centrifuge, cream, decompound, demulsify, desorb, dialyse, disassociate, dissociate, distil, electrolyse, fractionate, knap, liberate, liquate out, precipitate, screen, sift, sleave, tease, ultracentrifuge.

adv. **17.** **1. separately** apart, asunder, distantly, dividually, individually, loose, loosely, singly, singularly, unconnectedly. **2. disjunctively** divisively, partitively. **3. disconnectedly** bifidly, bipartitely, discretely, dispersedly, episodically, incoherently. **4. asunder** in pieces, in shreds, in two, to bits, to pieces, to shreds.

RELATED KEYWORDS: DIVERGENCE, DESTRUCTION, CUT, DAMAGE, GAP, DISPERSION

SERVANT

n. **1.** **1. servant** acolyte, altar boy, attendant, boy *(Asian English)*, dependant, follower, menial, muchacho, peon, punkah wallah *(Indian English)*, server, servitor, sommelier, underservant, waitperson, walla, wallah *(Indian English)*. *Informal:* pube, skivvy. **2. domestic** au pair, ayah *(Originally Indian English)*, bedmaker, boy, chambermaid, charlady, charwoman *(British)*, cleaning lady, daily, domestic help, handmaid, help, helper, home aid, home help, houseboy, housekeeper, housemaid, lady's maid, maid, maidservant, nursemaid, parlourmaid, soubrette, yardman. *Informal:* char *(British)*, cleaner upper, girl, greasy, old Dutch, sadie, slavey. **3. nursemaid** amah, ayah *(Originally Indian English)*, babysitter, caregiver, carer, careworker, childcare worker, childminder, dry nurse, duenna, housefather, housemother, houseparent, maid, mammy, minder, mother's help, nanny, nurse, OOSH worker, yaya *(Philippine English)*. **4. washerwoman** dhobi *(South Asian English)*, laundress, laundryman, laundrywoman, spotter, washerman, washwoman. **5. lady-in-waiting** gentlewoman, señora. **6. bondservant** assignee, blackbird, bondmaid, bondman, bondsman, bondwoman, cessionary, dependant, follower, galley slave, helot, hierodule, liegeman, man, nubian, peon, prisoner servant, serf, servant, slave, thrall, vassal, villain, villein. **7. concubine** comfort woman, hetaera, hetaira, odalisque. **8. attendant** acolyte, camp follower, follower, hatchet man, hireling, lackey, mercenary, page, servant, squire. *Informal:* roadie, traveller. **9. aide-de-camp** adc, aid *(US)*, aide, batman, medical orderly, orderly, squire. **10. armour-bearer** armiger, armourbearer, linkboy, squire, squireling. **11. beadle** verger. **12. retainer** body-servant, dependant, liege, liegeman, man, samurai, subject, vassal. **13. entourage** attendance, bodyguard, cortege, retinue, suite, tail, villeinage.

2. **1. butler** bailiff, chamberlain, factor, maître d', maître d'hôtel, major-domo, manciple, reeve, seneschal, sewer, steward. **2. valet** attendant, bearer *(Indian English)*, bellboy, bellhop *(US)*, body-servant, boots *(British)*, boy, buttons, cabin boy, callboy, devil, garcon, gentleman, gillie *(Scottish)*, jaga kereta boy *(Malaysian English)*, lackey, man, manservant, page, pageboy *(British)*, valet de chambre, watch-your-car boy *(Philippine English)*. *Informal:* fag *(British)*, leg man. **3. hotel attendant** bath butler, car valet, concierge, IT butler, page. **4. porter** bellboy, bellhop *(US)*, buttons, callboy, night porter, pageboy *(British)*. **5. flunkey** flunky, footboy, footman, lackey, page. **6. stableboy** equerry, groom, horsetailer, mafoo, ostler, strapper.

3. **1. waiter** attendant, bearer *(Indian English)*, busboy *(Originally US)*, ganymede, garcon, maître d'hôtel, server, waitress. **2. bartender** bar hostess *(SE Asian English)*, bar useful, barkeep *(US)*, barmaid, barman, cellarmaster, drink waiter, useful, wine waiter. *Informal:* bar girl *(SE Asian English)*, skimpy. **3. kitchen hand** bus boy, cupbearer, kitchener, kitchenman, tea lady. **4. flight attendant** cabin crew, hostess, steward, stewardess. *Informal:* hostie.

RELATED KEYWORDS: AGENT, EMPLOYMENT, REPRESSION, OBEDIENCE, WORKER

SEX

n. **1.** **1. sex** intersex. **2. gender** female, male, opposite sex. **3. bisexualism** androgyny, hermaphroditism, virilism. **4. sexlessness** asexuality. **5. lust** ardency, ardour, arousal, concupiscence, desire, erotism, excitement, fire, flame, heat, lechery, libido, passion, zeal. **6. sex drive** libido, oestrus.

2. **1. sexual intercourse** access, carnal knowledge, coition, coitus, commerce, congress, connection, consummation, copulation, favours, fulfilment, intercourse, intimacy, love-making, safe sex, sex, Tantric sex. **2. sexual behaviour** facts of life, love-life. **3. adultery** forbidden fruit, fornication, illicit sex, infidelity. **4. love-play** after-play, foreplay, lovemaking. *Informal:* fumble, hanky-panky, how's your father *(Chiefly British)*, slap-and-tickle. **5. orgy** group sex, ménage à trois. **6. virtual sex** cybersex. **7. masturbation** autoerotism, onanism. **8. orgasm** climax, ejaculation, nocturnal emission, wet dream.

3. **1. sexual relationship** affair, affaire de coeur, amour, eternal triangle, involvement, liaison, love affair, ménage à trois. **2. romance** flirtation, intrigue.

4. **1. rape** date rape, defilement, gang rape, marital rape, pack-rape, ravishment, sexual assault, statutory rape *(US)*, violation. **2. indecent assault** assault, interference, sexual assault. **3. incest 4. seduction** ruin.

5. **1. sexuality** alloerotism, carnality, earthiness, eroticisation, eroticism, erotics, lewdness, lubricity, sensuality. **2. sex appeal** allure, alluringness, animal magnetism, bed-worthiness, bedroom eyes, charm, erogeneity, seductiveness, sexinessit, oomph. **3. promiscuity** amorism, bawdry, bawdy, eroticism, lewdness, licence, sensuality, whorishness. **4. frigidity** coldness, frigidness. **5. heterosexuality** unisexuality. **6. homosexuality** gayness, homoeroticism, homosexualism, pederasty. **7. bisexuality** ambisexuality. **8. lesbianism** sapphism, tribadism. **9. transvestism** cross-dressing, eonism. **10. indecent exposure** exhibitionism. **11. paraphilia** algolagnia, fetishism, masochism, paedophilia, perversion, sadism, sadomasochism, voyeurism.

6. **1. sexual partner** amorist, beau, bedfellow, boyfriend, cohabitant, cohabiter, concubine, darling, dulcinea, girlfriend, hetaira, inamorata, inamorato, ladylove, lass, lover, nuba *(Aboriginal English)*, paramour, partner, sleeping partner, spark, sultana, swain *(Chiefly Poetic)*, sweetheart, tom. *Informal:* babe, babester, bash, bird, boy, fellow, floozy, girl, guy, man, missus, pick-up, potato peeler, sheila, squeeze, woman. **2. adulterer** adulteress, adultress, cicisbeo, co-respondent, fornicator, lover, swain *(Chiefly Poetic)*. **3. erotomaniac** eroticist, nymphomaniac, satyr. **4. lover** admirer, amorist, Romeo, suitor, swain *(Chiefly Poetic, British)*. *Informal:* daddy, fancy man, sugar daddy. **5. womaniser** Bluebeard, Casanova, debauchee, Don Juan, flirt, gay deceiver, ladies' man, lecher, libertine, Lothario, philanderer, profligate, rake, roué, ruiner, satyr, seducer, wencherlad, lady-killer, lech. **6. seductress** Circe, Delilah, enchantress, femme fatale, houri, kitten, kitty, man-eater, Mata Hari, minx, nymphette, siren, vampire, witchfoxy lady, mantrap, popsy, vamp. **8. teaser** charmer, coquette, tease. **9. cradle-snatcher** baby snatcher. **10. mistress** chatelaine, concubine, courtesan, de facto, demimondaine, hetaera, kept woman, number two *(Philippine English)*, paramour. *Informal:* kulasisi *(Philippine English)*, moll. **11. hussy** jezebel, nymphomaniac, scarlet woman, slut, wanton. *Informal:* floozy, goodtime girl, gunnie, slack. **12. groupie** band moll. **13. frigid person** *Informal:* fridge.

7.   **1. sexual identity. 2. heterosexual** straight. *Informal:* breeder, het, hetero, square. **3. bisexual** androgyne, epicene, hermaphrodite. *Informal:* bi. **4. homosexual** camp, catamite, cissy, effeminate, fascine, ganymede, gay, sis. *Informal:* fairy, homo, pansy, poof, poofter, poonce, queen, queer. **5. lesbian** femme, homosexual, tribade. *Informal:* butch, dyke, he-girl, lezzo. **6. transsexual** *Informal:* trannie. **7. transvestite** cross-dresser, drag queen. *Informal:* trannie. **8. exhibitionist** *Informal:* flasher. **9. masturbator** onanist. **10. paraphiliac** algolagnist, fetishist, kink, masochist, peeping tom, pervert, sadist, sadomasochist, voyeur.

8.   **1. sex symbol** a bit of all right, adonis, angel, Apollo, bathing beauty, beau ideal, beauty, belle, bombshell, cover girl, desirable, dream, drop-dead honey, enchanter, English rose, fascinator, goddess, head-turner, magnet, megababe, megahunk, nubile, nymph, peri, phoenix, picture, sex god, sex goddess, swan, tempter, Venus *(Poetic)*. *Informal:* a good sort, babe, chick magnet, chicky babe, cutie, cutie-pie *(Chiefly US)*, dish, doll, dolly, dreamboat, eyeful, good-looker, honey, knockout, looker, lovely, number, perv, pin-up, sex kitten, sexpot, smasher, sort, stunner.

9.   **1. sex shop** *Informal:* porn shop. **2. pornography** centrefold, filth, full-frontal, hard-core, hard-core pornography, obscenity, smut, soft-core pornography, yellow culture *(Singaporean and Malaysian English)*, yellowback. *Informal:* blue movie, cyberporn, pin-up, porn, porno, skin flick, soft porn, video nasty.

10.   **1. brothel** bagnio, bawdy house, bordello, disorderly house, escort agency, house of ill fame, house of ill repute, massage parlour, timothy, whorehouse. **2. red-light district**.

11.   **1. prostitute** callboy, callgirl, camp follower, cocotte, courtesan, drab, fallen woman, harlot, hussy, hustler, light-o'-love *(British, US)*, nightwalker, painted lady, painted woman, rake, scarlet woman, sex worker, streetwalker, taxi girl, trollop, white slave, whore, worker. **2. gigolo** walker. **3. procuress** madam. **4. pimp** go-between, pander, procurer, white-slaver. *Informal:* bludger, fancy man, hoon, ponce.

12.   **1. prostitution** harlotry, solicitation, streetwalking, the game, whoredom. *Informal:* business. **2. procuration** procurement. **3. sex industry**.

13.   **1. rapist** defiler, deflowerer, ravisher, violator.

adj. **14.**   **1. sexual** gamic, gendered, sexed. **2. genital** procreative, reproductive. **3. female** feminine. **4. male** masculine. **5. unisexual. 6. hermaphroditic** androgynous, epicene, hermaphrodite, hermaphroditical. **7. sexless** agamic, asexual. **8. heterosexual** straight. *Informal:* hetero, square. **9. bisexual** ambisexual. *Informal:* ac-dc, bi. **10. homosexual** camp, effeminate, emasculate, gay, high-camp, lesbian, Sapphic, unmanly, womanish, homo, lezzo, queer. **11. transsexual. 12. paraphiliac** algolagnic, masochistic, pederastic, perverted, swinish, voyeuristic. *Informal:* kinky. **13. incestuous**.

15.   **1. sexy** alluring, amorous, appetising, attractive, bosomy, busty, buxom, callipygian, captivating, catching, comely, cuddlesome, cuddly, curvaceous, curvy, cute, delectable, desirable, enchanting, enticing, erogenous, fascinating, fetching, flirtatious, full-bodied, glamorous, inviting, kittenish, nubile, oomphy, piquant, provocative, racy, ravishing, seductive, shapely, siren, sonsy *(Scottish, Irish)*, taking, tempting, thrilling, voluptuous, well-proportioned, well-rounded, winsomebuilt, hot, pin-up, spunky. **2. erotic** alloerotic, amatory, aphrodisiac, autoerotic, carnal, concupiscent, copulative, earthy, epicurean, erotogenic, fleshly, orgasmic, orgastic, sensual, sexual, supersensual, voluptuary, voluptuous. *Informal:* anatomical. **3. aroused** ablaze, aflame, agitated, concupiscent, excited. **4. lecherous** broad, cacky, concupiscent, Corinthian, Cyprian, dirty, dissipated, dissolute, earthy, evil-minded, fast, free, goatish, grimy, hircine, immoral, intemperate, lascivious, lewd, libertine, libidinous, licentious, lubricious, luxurious, mucky, oversexed, profane, profligate, raffish, rakish, ribald, riotous, salacious, salty, smutty, suggestive, vicious. **5. permissive** base, indecent, light, loose, nympho-maniac, promiscuous, sensual, swinging, trashy, unbecoming, unchaste, unseemly, wanton, whorish. *Informal:* easy, slack. **6. pornographic** adult, bawdy, bedroom, erotic, hardcore, ithyphallic, lewd, obscene, salacious, scabrous, X-rated. *Informal:* anatomical, blue, hot, perv, porno. **7. copulative** intimate, orgastic, venereal. **8. obscene** Fescennine, indecorous, lewd, nasty, naughty, salacious, vulgar. *Informal:* blue, green *(Philippine English)*, ripe. **9. suggestive** borderline, curious, spicy, steamy. **10. extra-marital. 11. psychosexual**.

  v. **16.**   **1. have sex** consummate a marriage, copulate, couple, fornicate, have intercourse, have relations, make love, mate. **2. have sex with** bed, get with, have, lie with, make love to (or with), make out with, sleep with, do. **3. commit adultery** cuckold. **4. cohabit** live together, live with. *Informal:* shack up (with). **5. proposition** come on to, make a pass at. *Informal:* chat up, crack onto, do a line for, put the hard word on. **6. come out**.

        17.   **1. rape** assault, defile, outrage, ravish, violate. **2. assault** interfere with, molest. **3. pack-rape** gang-rape. **4. seduce** ruin, wrong. **5. deflower**.

        18.   **1. sexually excite** arouse, eroticise, excite, titillate. *Informal:* fumble, turn on. **2. orgasm** ejaculate. **3. masturbate**.

        19.   **1. prostitute oneself** sell oneself, walk the streets, whore. **2. solicit** accost, ask, board, hustle. **3. procure** live on immoral earnings, pander, pimp. **4. whore** wench.

  adv. **20.**   **1. sexually** carnally, intimately, sensually. **2. sexily** alluringly, permissively. **3. sexlessly** asexually. **4. lasciviously** lecherously, lewdly, libidinously, lustfully, permissively, wantonly. **5. bisexually** ambisexually. **6. heterosexually**. **7. homosexually**. **8. voyeuristically**.

      RELATED KEYWORDS: BODY, DESIRE, ROMANCE, LOVE, PLEASURE, PROMISCUITY, REPRODUCTION, VOLUPTUOUSNESS, WOMAN, MAN

SHALLOWNESS

  n. **1.**   **1. shallowness** superficiality, superficialness. **2. shallows** bank, bar, barrier reef, bombora, coral reef, flat, ford, low-water mark, reef, sandbank, sandbar, shelf, shoal, spit, vlei *(South African)*. **3. scratch** pinprick. **4. thin coat** gloss, skin, veneer.

  adj. **2.**   **1. shallow** ankle-deep, flat, knee-deep, low, shoal, shoaly. **2. superficial** skin-deep, slight.

  v. **3.**   **1. shallow** flatten, shoal, silt up.

  adv. **4.**   **1. shallowly** on the surface, skin-deep, spread thin, superficially.

      RELATED KEYWORDS: SHORTNESS, THINNESS

SHAPE

  n. **1.**   **1. shape** fashion, figuration, figure, form, lines, mould, turn. **2. design** cogitation, conception, layout, pattern, plan, project, schematism, scheme. *Informal:* dart. **3. geometry** spherics, topology. **4. multiformity** dimorphism, diversity, heteromorphism, heteromorphy, metamorphism, metamorphosis, polymorphism, pseudomorphism, stereoisomerism, trimorphism. **5. polymorph** dimorph, habit, trimorph. **6. cast** casting, die, formwork, matrix, plaster cast, swage, swage block.

        2.   **1. structure** arrangement, array, build, cast, composition, constitution, contexture, form, make, make-up, microstructure, morphology, mould, ordonnance, workings. **2. build** body, frame, physique. *Informal:* anatomy, bod. **3. architecture** design, genre, mode, style, tone. **4. crystal lattice** lattice, macrostructure, space lattice. **5. formation** crystallisation, figuration.

        3.   **1. plane figure** decagon, dodecagon, enneagon, heptagon, hexagon, isogon, isogonic, nonagon, octagon, pentagon, polygon, quindecagon, re-entrant polygon, undecagon. **2. triangle** equilateral triangle, isosceles triangle, right triangle, right-angled triangle, scalene triangle, spherical triangle. **3. quadrilateral** diamond, lozenge, oblong, parallelogram, parallelogram of forces, quad, quadrangle, quadrum, rectangle, rhomb, rhombohedron, rhomboid, rhombus, square, tetragon, trapeze, trapezium, trapezoid. **4. curve** arc, bow, cardioid, circle, crook, ellipse, parabola, quadrant, sinus, sphere. **5. star** asterisk, hexagram, pentacle, pentagram, pentalpha, pentangle.

        4.   **1. solid** decahedron, dodecahedron, heptahedron, icosahedron, octahedron, pentahedron, polyhedron, prism, pyramid, trisoctahedron. **2. hexahedron** cube, cuboid, dice, parallelpiped, rhomb, rhombohedron, rhombus. **3. tesseract** hypercube. **4. sphere** ball, circle, cone, conoid, cylinder, globe, globoid, oblate spheroid, orb, orbit, prolate spheroid, solid of revolution, toroid, torus, tube, ungula. **5. helix** spiral, spire, thread, volute. **6. crystal** baguette, brilliant, rose.

        5.   **1. building** architecture, construction, edifice, erection, fabric, facility, place, structure, superstructure, work. **2. edifice** complex, dome, fabric, megastructure, pile. **3. outbuilding** additions, annexe, dependency, extension, finger, outhouse, shed, wing. **4. substructure** chassis, foundation, infrastructure, shell, substruction. **5. framework** cage, casing, cradling, fabric, frame, gantry, gauntry, matrix, roll cage, scaffold, scaffolding, skeleton, truss, trussing, undercarriage. **6. trellis** espalier, lattice, latticework, pergola, treillage.

6. 1. construction building, civil engineering, prefabrication, public works, reconstruction, restoration, structure. **2. architecture** architectonics, draughtsmanship, landscape architecture, structure, tectonics. **3. bricklaying** indenting, infilling, masonry, rubblework, stonemasonry, stonework, toothing. **4. carpentry** post-and-beam construction, timber-framing.

7. 1. builder architect, builder's labourer, checker *(US)*, civil engineer, draftsman, draughtsman, engineer, erecter, heritage architect, landscape architect, master builder, nipper, roofer. **2. mason** bricklayer, cowan, hodman, lather, master mason, muckshifter, stonecutter, stonemason. *Informal:* brickie. **3. rigger** dogman, scaffolder. **4. carpenter** *Informal:* chippie. **5. glazier** glass-cutter, glassman.

8. 1. shaper chiseller, fashioner, former, founder, sculptor.

adj. **9. 1. shaped** figurate, figured, formal, formed, set, wrought. **2. multiform** biform, dimorphous, diverse, heteromorphic, idiomorphic, morphologic, peloric, polymorphous, pseudomorphic, pseudomorphous, triform, trimorphic, trimorphous. **3. wrought** blown, cast, chiselled, molten, moulded, plastic, repoussé.

10. 1. shaped acicular, aciculate, aciform, actiniform, actinoid, alary, ampullaceal, anchor-like, arborescent, asteriated, asteroid, auriculate, bacciform, baculiform, bell-bottomed, bell-mouthed, bell-shaped, botryoidal, botryose, bottle-shaped, broom-shaped, brush-like, campanulate, castellated, columnar, coralloid, cordate, cordiform, coronoid, cuneal, deltaic, dendriform, dendritic, dendroid, denticulate, digitiform, fan-shaped, figured, flabellate, funnel-shaped, fusiform, galeiform, gull-wing, heart-shaped, helmet-shaped, horny, infundibular, infundibulate, infundibuliform, inswept, keratoid, kidney-shaped, knobbed, lambdoid, leg-of-mutton, mitred, mitriform, napiform, needle-shaped, obcordate, pear-shaped, petaline, petaloid, phylloid, pinnate, pyriform, radiate, ray-like, raylike, reniform, rhombic, rod-shaped, s-shaped, saddle-backed, scalariform, scaphoid, scopulate, scutiform, sphenic, sphenoid, spindle-shaped, star-shaped, starlike, stelliform, stellular, stilliform, t-shaped, torose, treelike, ungual, unguiculate, ungular, urceolate, v-shaped, wedgelike, wedgy.

11. 1. structural architectonic, architectural, constructional, constructive, tectonic. **2. skeletal** anatomical, bony, osteological, physiological. **3. prefabricated** demountable, modular.

12. 1. architectural styles Baroque, Bauhaus, Brutalist, Byzantine, Classical, Colonial, Corinthian, Cyclopean, Doric, Federation, Gothic, Ionic, Khmer, Norman, Palladian, Perpendicular, Plateresque, Renaissance, Rococo, Roman, Romanesque, Tuscan. **2. columned** amphiprostyle, dipteral, octastyle, peristylar, prostyle, pycnostyle.

v. **13. 1. structure** construct, define, develop, do, erect, fabricate, fashion, figure, forge, form, formalise, formulate, frame, incubate, make, model, pattern, sculpture, shape. **2. design** geometrise, round, square, style, tailor. **3. mould** block, cast, fashion, found, ingot, plaster cast, tree. **4. sculpt** carve, chisel, cut, engrave, etch, gouge, incise, rough-hew, sculp, trim, whittle. **5. forge** beat out, dolly, hammer out, smith. **6. turn** blow, cast, spin, throw, wrest. **7. stamp** die, swage, tool.

14. 1. build construct, devise, engineer, erect, form, frame, knock together, knock up, make, make up, manufacture, mock up, put up, raise, throw together, turn out, whip up. **2. mason** carpenter, riprap. **3. prefabricate** precast, preform.

15. 1. take shape crystallise, jell, shape up, take form.

RELATED KEYWORDS: BEND, BULGE, HOLLOW, CURVE, DWELLING, ROUNDNESS, STRAIGHTNESS, TWIST

SHAPELESSNESS

n. **1. 1. shapelessness** aggregation, amorphia, amorphism, amorphousness, formlessness. **2. lump** agglomeration, agglutination, aggregate, aggregation, bezoar, blur, bunch, chunk, clod, clot, cloud, clump, cumulation, divot *(Scottish)*, gob, grume, knot, mass, nub, nubbin *(US)*, nugget, smudge, smutch, tuft, wad. *Informal:* divvy, dollop, goolie, goozy *(WA, SA)*.

adj. **2. 1. shapeless** amorphous, aoristic, baggy, blobby, featureless, formless, inchoate, indefinable, indefinite, indescribable, indeterminate, indigested, indistinct, nondescript, obscure, unformed, uninteresting, unorganised, unshapen. **2. unshaped** elementary, embryo, embryonic, formless, germinal, nascent, rudimentary, seminal, shapeless, uncut, undeveloped, unformed, unhewn.

RELATED KEYWORDS: DISTORTION, DISORDER, IMPRECISION

SHARING

n. **1.**   **1. sharing** communalism, communism, Dutch shout, Dutch treat, profit sharing, socialism. **2. distribution** admeasurement, administration, allocation, allotment, apportionment, appropriation, assignation, assignment, assortment, canton, carve-up, cavel, cavil, dispensation, division, issue, malapportionment, participation, partition, partitionment, rationing, redistribution, repartition, share-out, sharing out. *Informal:* chop-up, divide. **3. job sharing** skillshare.

     2.   **1. share** a slice of the action, allotment, allowance, ante, apportionment, average, bit, bonus, chip, commission, contingent, darg, deal, distribution, dividend, dole, fraction, fragment, helping, interest, lay, lot, moiety, parcel, part, percentage, piece, portion, preallotment, proportion, quantum, quota, ration, round, scrap, section, slice, split, stint, time share. *Informal:* a slice of the cake, bunce *(British)*, chop, cut, divvy, rake-off, whack. **2. common fund** kitty, pool, tontine. **3. job share**.

     3.   **1. sharer** associate, bedfellow, bedmate, partner. **2. dispenser** administrator, allotter, almoner, dispensator, distributor, partitioner. **3. sharefarmer** cropper, sharecocky, sharecropper *(Chiefly US)*, sharemilker *(NZ)*, tenant farmer. **4. allottee** partaker, participant, participator.

adj. **4.**   **1. shared** bipartite, common, dipartite, disjunct, distributed, disunited, divided, joint, multifid, participable, partite, polytomous, quinquepartite, segmental, separate, separated, split. **2. distributable** apportionable, commonable, dividable, divisible. **3. distributive** distributional, respective.

v. **5.**   **1. share out** admeasure, administer, administrate, allocate, allot, apportion, assign, assort, average out, canton, circularise, circulate, deal, deal out, demark, detail, dish out, dismember, dispense, distribute, divide, divvy, divvy up, dole out, fractionise, give, give way to, halve, hand out, hypothecate, issue, joint, lot, mete out, mince, morsel, parcel out, partition, pass, portion, ration, redistribute, repartition, serve out, share, split, subdivide, unlock the land. *Informal:* carve up. **2. share** apportion, go Dutch, go halves, split. *Informal:* whack up. **3. participate** get one's share, partake, share. *Informal:* get in for one's chop, get one's corner, muscle in. **4. pool. 5. jobshare** skillshare.

adv. **6.**   **1. in common** jointly, severally, together. **2. one another** each to the other, respectively.

RELATED KEYWORDS: GENEROSITY, ACQUIREMENT, GIVING, UNSELFISHNESS

SHARPNESS

n. **1.**   **1. sharpness** acumination, acuteness, keenness. **2. pointedness** prickliness, spininess, spinosity, thorniness. **3. acuity** acuteness, bite.

     2.   **1. sharp point** cusp, mucro, neb, nib, pike, pinpoint, point, prickle, thorn, tip. **2. spire** flèche, minaret, steeple. **3. stylus** needle, scribe, scriber, style, stylo pen.

     3.   **1. piercer** aiguille, anlace, awl, barong, bowie knife, brochette, caltrop, crowfoot, dagger, dirk, eyeleteer, flick-knife, fork, glover's needle, hayfork, keris, knife, knitting needle, kris, kukri, machete, marlinespike, misericord, nail, panga, parang, pigsticker, point, poniard, prog, rapier, sheath-knife, skean, skewer, stiletto, stylet, tooth, toothpeg, ulu. *Informal:* shiv *(British)*. **2. needle** acicula, aciculate, aciculum, cock, pin, point, ram, rostellum, rostrum, spicula, spicule, spiculum, spine, spinule. **3. hypodermic needle** hypodermic, hypodermic syringe, injector, needle, point, spike, vaccine gun, vaccine point. *Informal:* hype, hypo. **4. spike** crampon, creeper, peg, pike, piton, pricket, prog, prong, punji stake, spit, sticker, tine. **5. spear** assegai, eelspear, gaff, gidgee, gig, grains, harpoon, iron, javelin, lance, leister, lily iron, shaft, spearhead, striker, woomera. **6. arrow** arrowhead, bolt, dart, flight arrow, pile, shaft. **7. horn** antler, claw, fang, nail, pin tooth, spike. **8. sting** aculeate, aculeus, emergence, stinger. **9. spur** ankus, goad, prod, prog, rowel, sting. **10. pick** ice-axe, icepick, pickaxe, spud stick. *Informal:* mad mick. **11. bit** borer, brace and bit, bradawl, broach, burin, cangkul, centre-bit, diamond point, drill, gimlet, grubber, jackhammer, mattock, miser, pneumatic drill, post-hole digger, power drill, sticker, stopper, twist drill, wimble. **12. punch** centre-punch, pirri pirri, puncheon. **13. barb** beard, fluke. **14. quill** barb, barbicel, barbule, barrel, calamus, flue, herl, pinnula, pinnule. **15. thorn** aculeus, prickle, snag, spica, spine. **16. hook** clamper *(Chiefly US)*, crampon, grapnel, grapple, grappling, grappling iron, tenaculum, tenterhook.

     4.   **1. sharpener** grinder, grinding wheel, grindstone, hone, oilstone, pencil-sharpener, slip, strap, strickle, strop, whetstone.

adj. **5.**   **1. sharp** acuate, acute, cultrate, edgy, fine, keen, keen-edged, knife-edged, sharp-edged, sharpened. **2. biting** mordacious, nipping. **3. acid** acidulous, acrid. **4. cutting** incisive, keen, trenchant *(Chiefly Poetic)*. **5. penetrating** bitter, piercing, pointed, pungent. **6. double-edged** two-edged. **7. self-sharpening**.

6. 1. pointed acuate, aculeate, acuminate, acute, bicorn, bicuspid, calcariferous, corniculate, cornuted, cultrate, cusp-like, cusped, cuspidal, cuspidate, ericoid, fastigiate, obeliscal, oxy, sharpened, subacute, superacute, tricorn, tricuspid. **2. barbed** pinnular, pinnulate, pinnulated. **3. beaked** beaky, lipped. **4. spearlike** harpoonlike, lanceolate, oblanceolate. **5. arrowy** pointed, sagittal, sagittate. **6. cone-shaped** coniform.

7. 1. spiny acanthoid, acanthous, bristly, echinate, echinated, echinoid, hispid, horrent, prickly, spiculate, spined, spinelike, spinescent, spiniferous, spinose, spinous, stubby. **2. prickly** acanthaceous, acanthoid, brambly, burr-like, burry, calcarate, echinate, horny, muricate, snaggy, spiniferous, spiny, spurred, thistlelike, thistly, thorny. **3. spiky** apiculate, mucronate, spicate, spikelike, spinal, spinelike, spinulose, spurlike, thornlike. **4. needle-shaped** acerose, acicular, aciculate, aciform, fanglike, needle-like, spiculate.

v. **8. 1. sharpen** acuminate, edge, grind, point, set, spike, whet. *Informal:* put kinchella on. **2. point** barb, hone, shag, sharpen, vandyke.

adv. **9. 1. sharply** acutely, finely, keenly, prickingly, sharp. **2. piercingly** cuttingly, penetratingly. **3. bitingly** acridly, bitterly.

RELATED KEYWORDS: LEVEL, ROUGHNESS

SHELTER

n. **1. 1. shelter** air-raid shelter, Anderson shelter, bunker, fallout shelter, hardened site, storm cellar *(US)*, watch-box, wiltja. **2. hut** apple hut, badger box *(Tasmania)*, beach hut, bothy *(Scottish)*, cabana *(US)*, cabane, cot, field hut, gundy, gunyah, humpy, hutch, lodge, melon hut, mia-mia, Nissen hut, portaloo, rancho *(Spanish America, south-western US)*, whare, wurley. **3. shed** bathing box *(Victoria)*, booth, box, bus-shelter, picnic shelter, press-box, sentry box, sentry-box, shelter shed, shelter-shed, telephone box, tollbooth, weathershed, woodshed. **4. tent** awning, bell tent, canvas, fly, gazebo, hoochie, hutchie, marquee, marquise, pavilion, pup tent, shelter, stock camp, stock-camp, tarpaulin, tilt. *Informal:* bivvy, tarp. **5. arbour** bower, mai mai *(NZ)*, pergola, summerhouse. **6. garage** boathouse, boatshed, bus station, car shed, carport, coach-house, depository, depot *(US)*, hangar, hoverport, lawn locker, lockup, magazine, pataka, repertory, running shed, shed, shelter, store, storehouse, toolshed, treasure-house, whata. **7. den** burrow, cote, doghouse, earth, lair, lodge, set, sett, tunnel. **8. ant hill** magnetic ant hill. **9. nest** eyrie. **10. kennel** birdcage, hive, hutch, stable.

2. 1. refuge asylum, bolthole, concealment, cot, cover, covert, coverture, disguise, hideout, hideaway, hidey-hole, hiding, home, mew, place of safety, protection, retreat, sacrarium, safety house, sanctuary, sanctum, shelter. *Informal:* funk-hole, lurk. **2. hospice** hideaway, home, hospitium, imaret, retreat. **3. traffic island**.

3. 1. harbour anchorage, assembly anchorage, harbour of refuge, harbourage, haven, mole, moorage, moorings, port, roads, roadstead, safe haven. **2. port** free port, haven, outport, seaport. **3. basin** marina, tidal basin, wet dock. **4. quay** breakwater, dock, jetty, pier, slip *(US)*, staithe, wharf. **5. quayage** wharfage.

v. **4. 1. shelter** ensconce, harbour, haven, house, hut, lodge, quarter. **2. garage** embower, shed. **3. kennel** hive, stable.

5. 1. take refuge go to ground, lay to, put in, take cover, take shelter.

RELATED KEYWORDS: DWELLING, PROTECTION, SAFETY

SHOP

n. **1. 1. shop** co-op, outlet, point of sale, store, tallyshop. **2. market** bazaar, exchange, fair, flea market, fort *(North American History)*, futures exchange, marketplace, mart, meat market, souk. **3. shopping centre** arcade, mall, pedestrian plaza, shopping complex, shopping mall, shopping precinct *(British)*, shoppingtown. **4. stall** applecart, bar, barrow, booth, counter, pie-cart, stand. **5. vending machine** automat, slot machine. **6. general store** chaff-and-grain store, convenience store, corner shop, corner store, duty-free shop, milk bar *(Chiefly Victoria)*, post, produce store, trading post. *Informal:* deli *(Chiefly WA and SA)*, prodgie. **7. supermarket** barn, cash and carry, hypermarket *(Chiefly US, British)*, market, mini-mart, rialto, superette *(NZ)*. **8. food shop** bakehouse, bakery, bevery, butcher's shop, charcuterie, continental delicatessen, dairy *(British, US)*, delicatessen, gelataria, grocery, macellaria, milk bar, pasticceria, patisserie, snack bar, soda fountain *(US)*, sweetshop. *Informal:* deli. **9. restaurant** brasserie, buffet, buffet car, cafeteria, canteen, chophouse *(British, US)*, diner, dining car, grill, grillroom, kiosk, luncheonette, pizzeria, pull-in *(British)*, restaurant car, roadhouse, saloon car, soup kitchen, steakhouse, take-out, takeaway, tavern, tuckshop. *Informal:* eatery, el cheapo, greasy spoon, hash house, noshery, ref, refec. **10. cafe** bistro, coffee bar, coffee house, coffee shop, eating house, espresso bar, estaminet, kiosk, tea-garden, tea-house, tearoom, teashop *(British)*. *Informal:* caff. **11. bar** beer garden, bistro, bodega, cocktail bar, cocktail lounge, hotel, ladies' lounge, ladies' parlour, liquor store, lounge, nightclub, nightspot, private bar, public bar, saloon, saloon bar, speak-easy *(US)*, taproom *(British)*, wine bar, wineshop. *Informal:* clipjoint, grog shop, groggery, joint, nineteenth hole. **12. nightclub** bunny club, hot spot, nightspot. **13. liquor store** bottle department, bottle shop, bottle store *(NZ)*, cellar door, cellars. *Informal:* bottlo, grog shop. **14. department store** chain store, emporium, megastore, retail store. **15. clothes shop** boutique, furriery, hosiery, jeanery, millinery, slopshop. **16. haberdashery** mercery. **17. bookshop** bibliopole, bookstall, bookstand. **18. newsagency** kiosk, newsstand, paper shop. **19. service station** gas station, self-service. *Informal:* servo. **20. tobacconist**. **21. pharmacy** all-night chemist, chemist, chemist's shop, dispensary, drugstore *(US)*, night chemist, pharmaceutics. **22. hardware store** ironmongery. **23. toyshop**. **24. florist**. **25. video library** toy library. **26. second-hand shop** family shop *(NZ)*, junk shop, op shop, opportunity shop. *Informal:* Vinnies. **27. pawnshop** mont-de-piété. *Informal:* hockshop *(US)*, Moscow, pop-shop. **28. army surplus store** army disposals store, disposals store. **29. salesroom** floor space, saleroom, shopwindow. **30. saleyard** caryard, timber yard. *Informal:* birdcage *(NZ)*. **31. booking office** box office, office. **32. betting shop** Footy Punt *(Tasmania)*, TAB. *Informal:* lucky shop *(Victoria)*.

RELATED KEYWORDS: ALCOHOL, BUYING, SELLING, FOOD, COMMERCE

SHORTNESS

n. **1. 1. shortness** littleness, stockiness. **2. podginess** stubbiness, tubbiness.

2. 1. short person diminutive, dwarf, elf, half-pint, homunculus, hop-o'-my-thumb, Lilliputian, little person, manikin, midget, mite, pigmy, PORG, runt, squab, stodge, Tom Thumb, wisp. *Informal:* midge, nugget, peanut, pipsqueak, pudding, pygmy, shortie, shrimp, snippet, tiddler.

adj. **3. 1. short** brief, cut-off, short and sweet, short-winded, truncate, truncated. **2. little** baby, diminutive, dwarf, dwarfed, dwarfish, knee-high to a grasshopper, Lilliputian, low, mini, minuscule, minute, petite, pint-size, pygmaean, pygmy, runty, short, snub, snubby, stunted, tiny, underdeveloped, undersized. *Informal:* dinky, ickle, itsy-bitsy, pint-sized, teeny, teeny-weeny, wee, weeny. **3. stocky** chunky, dumpy, squat, stodgy. **4. tubby** chubby, chunky, plump, podgy, pudgy, pyknic, rotund, stocky, stodgy, stumpy, thickset. *Informal:* fubsy, roly-poly. **5. low-rise** lowblocked.

v. **4. 1. shorten** abbreviate, abridge, condense, curtail, cut, diminish, reduce, telescope. *Informal:* axe. **2. cut down** crop, cut, detruncate, truncate. **3. cut across** cut corners, cut off a corner.

RELATED KEYWORDS: SHALLOWNESS, SMALLNESS

SHOUTING

n. **1. 1. shouting** call, calling, clamour, clangour, hue and cry, noise, vociferance, vociferation. *Informal:* row. **2. exclamation** ejaculation, interjection.

2. 1. shout bawl, bellow, call, cry, holler, scream, whoop, yell. *Informal:* kick. **2. howl** cry, squall, squawk, wail, whimper, whine, yelp, yowl. *Informal:* yawp. **3. shriek** scream, screech, squeal. **4. cheer** encore. *Informal:* huzza. **5. call** azan, bidding, calling, clarion *(Poetic)*, hoot, muster, mustering, note, page, rollcall, summons. **6. hail** oyez. *Informal:* cooee, cooey. **7. distress call** alarm. **8. war cry** battle cry, catchcry, catchphrase, cry, slogan, watchword. **9. outcry** ballyhoo, pillaloo *(British)*.

3. 1. shouter bawler, bellower, brayer, clamourer, hooter, howler, noisemaker, vociferant, vociferator, yeller. **2. screamer** screecher, shrieker, squaller, squealer, wailer, yawper, yelper. **3. exclaimer** caller, caller-out, cheerer, ejaculator, interjector. **4. crier** hailer, muezzin, musterer, summoner.

adj. **4. 1. shouting** boisterous, clamant, clamorous, clangorous, loud, noisy, obstreperous, open-mouthed, rackety, riotous, roaring, rorty, rowdy, rumbustious, stormy, tumultuary, tumultuous, turbulent, unquiet, uproarious, vociferant, vociferous. *Informal:* obstropolous, rambunctious *(US)*, rip-roaring. **2. exclamatory** interjectional, interjectory.

v. **5. 1. shout** bawl, bellow, blow, bluster, call, clamour, clangour, give tongue, hawk, holler, hoot, loudmouth, outcry, pipe, rave, roar, shout down, speak up, thunder, vociferate, yell.

Informal: pipe up, scream blue murder, sing out, sound off *(US)*. **2. whoop** crow, hoot, tally-ho, whistle, wolf whistle. **3. scream** caterwaul, outsing, pipe, screech, shriek, shrill, skirl *(Chiefly Scottish)*, squall, squawk, squeal. **4. howl** bark, bawl, bellow, bray, heehaw, keen, wail, yelp, yowl. *Informal:* yawp. **5. call out** cry out, ejaculate, exclaim, heckle, inject, interject, needle. **6. hail** call, cite, shout, summon. *Informal:* cooee, give a hoy, halloo, hallow, hollo, yo-ho, yoo-hoo. **7. cheer** encore. *Informal:* huzza.

adv. **6. 1. in a loud voice** at the top of one's lungs, at the top of one's voice, screamingly, vociferously. **2. clamorously** clangorously, noisily.

interj. **7. 1. alleluia** banzai, bravo, eureka, hallelujah, hip hip hooray (or hurrah), hooray, hosanna, hurray, rah, tiger *(US)*, viva. *Informal:* cowabunga, huzza, whoopee, woo hoo, yahoo, yeah, yippee. **2. hello** ahoy, hi, hoy, hulloo. *Informal:* cooee, halloo, hallow, hey, ho, hoicks, hollo, oi, yo-ho, yoo-hoo. **3. oyez** hear ye. **4. come on** *Informal:* carn, have a go. **5. tally-ho** tantivy, view halloo, yoicks.

RELATED KEYWORDS: ANIMAL NOISE, LOUDNESS, SHRILLNESS, SPEECH

SHOWINESS

n. **1. 1. showiness** beadledom, fineness, flashiness, gaiety, obtrusiveness, ostentation, ostentatiousness, pomposity, pompousness, pretension, pretentiousness, sharpness. **2. garishness** floridity, floridness, gaudiness, loudness, overelaborateness, sportiness, vulgarism, vulgarity, vulgarness.

2. 1. show demonstration, display, fanfare, fanfaron, gala performance, gold show, hikoi *(NZ)*, manifestation, ostentation, pageant, parade, peace march, showing, sight, spectacle, tattoo. *Informal:* demo, hoopla, razzamatazz, razzle-dazzle, spread. **2. pomp** display, eclat, gimmickry, glitter, pageant, pageantry, pomp and circumstance, pomposity, wallow. *Informal:* razzamatazz. **3. flourish** bravura, flash, flaunt. **4. style** chic, panache, pizazz *(Chiefly US)*. **5. flamboyance** flamboyancy, machismo. **6. finery** best, dress, fallal, fallalery, frippery, full dress, gaiety, gaudery, Sunday best. *Informal:* glad rags, one's best bib and tucker, war paint.

3. 1. show-off *(Informal)* actor, artiste, drama queen, exhibitionist, flaunter, gobbler, macho, peacock, pooh-bah, poser, poseur, turkey cock, wallower, Woolloomooloo Yank. *Informal:* boiled shirt, duchess, ham. **2. silvertail** *(Informal)* glitterati, social climber.

adj. **4. 1. showy** champagne, chocolate-box, clinquant, dashy, done for effect, dramatic, exhibitionistic, flashy, flaunty, florid, frilly, garish, gaudy, gay, gimcrack, gimmicky, gingerbread, glittering, loud, meretricious, obtrusive, ornate, raffish, rich, roxy, specious, tarted up, tawdry, tinsel, tinselly, trumpery, unsubtle, vulgar. *Informal:* arty-farty, flash, hifalutin, highfalutin, lairy, sporty, tizzy. **2. dressed to the nines** *Informal:* dressed fit to kill, dressed up like a sore toe, in one's glad rags. **3. ostentatious** arty-crafty, bombastic, chichi, consequential, extravagant, flamboyant, flatulent, high-camp, highflown, overelaborate, pompous, pretentious, puffy, swollen, up-market. *Informal:* jammy, swank, toplofty.

v. **5. 1. show off** bear, call attention to oneself, cut a dash, flounce, glitter, grandstand, hog the limelight, keep a high profile, maintain a high profile, make a figure, make a spectacle of oneself, showboat, strut. *Informal:* camp it up, lair it up, strut one's stuff. **2. flaunt** air, display, exhibit, flourish, parade, play to the gallery, show off to the best advantage, show one's wares, showcase. *Informal:* flash, sport. **3. dress up** array, bedeck, deck out, doll up in, dress, overdress, overelaborate, preen, primp, prink, titivate. *Informal:* lair up, poon up, tart up, tizzy up, trick out in, trick up in. **4. sensationalise** *Informal:* lairise.

adv. **6. 1. showily** flamboyantly, flash, flashily, flauntingly, floridly, gaily, garishly, gaudily, loud, loudly, obtrusively, vulgarly. **2. ostentatiously** overelaborately, pompously, pretentiously.

RELATED KEYWORDS: AFFECTEDNESS, ARROGANCE, BRAGGING, DECORATION, DISPLAY

SHRILLNESS

n. **1. 1. shrillness** creakiness, flutiness, high frequency, reediness, sharpness, squeakiness, stridor, stridulation, stridulousness, thinness, tinniness, wheeziness.

2. 1. scream caterwaul, screech, shriek, squawk. **2. whine** grizzle, pule, wail, waul. **3. toot** tootle. **4. whistle** bleep, chirp, chirrup, croak, peep, pip, squark, trill, tweet, twitter, wolf-whistle.

adj. **3. 1. shrill** acute, clarion, cutting, ear-piercing, ear-splitting, high, piercing, pipy, sharp, strident, stridulatory, stridulous. **2. screeching** screaming, screechy, wailsome. **3. piping** ear-piercing, ear-splitting, pipy, shrill. **4. squeaky** creaking, creaky, squeaking, unmelodious. **5. thin** reedy, tinny. **6. whining** puling. **7. high-pitched** altissimo, alto, falsetto, high, high-frequency, high-toned, pipy, soprano, treble.

v. **4.** **1. screech** caterwaul, scream, shriek, shrill, squall, squeal. **2. pipe** skirl *(Chiefly Scottish)*. **3. whistle** blow, wheeze, wolf-whistle. **4. toot** flute, tootle. **5. whine** grizzle, howl, mewl, pule, wail, waul, whimper. **6. squeak** beep, bleep, cheep, chirk, chirm, chirp, chirrup, chitter, creak, peep, pip, squawk, trill, tweet, twitter.

adv. **5.** **1. shrilly** sharply, shrill, stridently, stridulously. **2. creakily** squeakily, wheezily. **3. thinly** thin, tinnily.

RELATED KEYWORDS: ANIMAL NOISE, HISSING, MUSIC, DISSONANCE, SHOUTING, SOUND

SIDE

n. **1.** **1. side** border, cheek, corner, edge, flank, hand, hem, jowl, margin, rim, temple, van *(Poetic)*, wing. **2. jamb** hance, haunch. **3. profile** half-face, silhouette. **4. side-piece** edge. **5. winger** flanker, outrider, postilion. **6. weatherside** lee, leeside, leeward, sunny side. **7. starboard** beam, bowside, bulwarks, gunnel, gunwale, port, quarter, saxboard, wale, weatherboard. **8. closed side** inside, open side.

adj. **2.** **1. side** by, collateral, flanking, lateral, port, sidelong, sidling, skirting, starboard. **2. sideways** half-face, in silhouette, side-on, sideway *(US)*. **3. costal** parietal.

v. **3.** **1. flank** come alongside, go alongside, juxtapose, outflank, outskirt, skirt. **2. edge** crab, sidle.

adv. **4.** **1. sideways** askance, askew, broadside on, collaterally, edgeways, half-face, laterally, side-on, sideway *(US)*, to leeward, to windward. *Informal:* skew-whiff. **2. alongside** abeam, aboard, abreast, apart, aside, beside, by, ex parte, on all sides, on beam-ends, on the left, on the right, side by side. **3. side by side** cheek by jowl.

RELATED KEYWORDS: EDGE, FRONT, REAR, OUTSIDE, LEFT, RIGHT, TOP, BOTTOM

SIGHT

n. **1.** **1. sight** eye, eyesight, view, vision. **2. binocularity** stereopsis, stereoscopy, stereovision. **3. sharp-sightedness** far-sightedness, perspicuity. **4. normal vision** 20/20 vision, trichromatopsia. **5. day vision** photopia. **6. night vision** scotopia. **7. optics** ophthalmology, orthoptics. **8. observation** contemplation, espial, invigilation, lookout, notice, observance, scrutiny, surveillance, watch. **9. visualisation** envisagement, vision. **10. voyeurism** scopophilia.

2. **1. look** double take. *Informal:* bo-peep, butchers, Captain, Captain Cook, dek, dekko, eyeful, geek, gig, gink, look-see, optic, shoofty, squiz, sticky. **2. peek** peep, pry, squint. **3. glance** blink, eyebeam, eyewink, glimpse. **4. stare** gape, glare, goggle. **5. leer** ogle. **6. gaze** regard, view. **7. look of disdain** *Informal:* hairy eyeball, the glassy eye, the greasy eyeball. **8. inspection** look, look-over, reconnaissance, reconnoitre, review, scan, survey, trip-check, view. *Informal:* going-over, once-over, recce. **9. sheep's eyes**.

3. **1. looker** argus, beholder, bystander, contemplator, eyewitness, gazer, look on, looker-on, observer, onlooker, sightseer, spectator, watcher, witness, witnesser. *Informal:* gig. **2. starer** gaper. *Informal:* rubberneck, stickybeak. **3. descrier** espier, observer. **4. peeping Tom** gubba, leerer, ogler, peeper, spy, voyeur. **5. spotter** birdwatcher, racegoer, supertwitcher. *Informal:* twitcher. **6. lookout** watch. **7. inspector** invigilator, sentinel, spier, spyer. **8. audience** televiewer, theatregoer, viewer.

4. **1. lookout** captive balloon, conning tower, crow's nest, lookdown, observation post, observatory, outlook, viewpoint.

5. **1. telescope** binoculars, field glasses, panoramic sight, telescopic sight.

6. **1. view** landscape, lookout, outlook, panorama, prospect, scene, vista. **2. range of vision** command, eyeshot, ken, purview, sight, view. **3. sightline**.

adj. **7.** **1. sharp-eyed** clear-eyed, clear-sighted, eagle-eyed, far-seeing, far-sighted, hawk-eyed, long-sighted, lyncean, lynx-eyed, perspicuous, sharp-sighted, telescopic. **2. watchful** alert, argus-eyed, awake, observant, open-eyed, sharp, surveillant, unwinking, vigilant, wakeful. **3. voyeuristic**.

8. **1. optical** ocular, ophthalmic, optic, photopic, visual. **2. binocular** emmetropic, orthoptic, orthoscopic, stereoscopic, stereoscopical. **3. audiovisual**.

v. **9.** **1. see** behold, observe, view, witness. **2. catch sight of** clap eyes on, glance, glimpse, lay eyes on, look to, set eyes on, sight, view. *Informal:* twig. **3. discern** descry, distinguish, espy, notice, perceive, recognise, resolve, spot, spy. **4. visualise** envisage, vision. **5. vide** vide ante, vide infra, vide post, vide supra.

10. **1. look** eye, look after, look out, observe, preview, regard, spot, spy on, squint, stargaze, surveil, tout, view, watch. *Informal:* get a load of, gig, have a screw at, have an optic at, lamp, rubberneck, take (or have) a gander at, twig. **2. ogle** leer at, make (sheep's) eyes at. *Informal:* perv on. **3. inspect** eyeball, look over, rake, reconnoitre, review, scan, scout, scrutinise, see over, study, survey, sweep. *Informal:* case, squiz. **4. keep watch** invigilate, keep a weather eye open, keep one's eyes open, overlook, oversee, overwatch, sentinel, tout, watch, watch over. *Informal:* keep one's eyes peeled, keep one's eyes skinned. **5. glance at** glimpse at, look, run one's eye over, scan, skew, skim, squint. **6. peek** look in, peep, peer, pry. *Informal:* have a sticky, have a sticky beak. **7. stare** gape, gawp, gaze, glare, goggle. *Informal:* gawk, gig. **8. have a view of** command, overlook. **9. contemplate** have eyes only for, pore on (or over). **10. see through** pierce, see into. **11. look for** keep an eye out for, look out for, watch out for.

adv. **11.** **1. voyeuristically**.

interj. **12.** **1. lo** behold. **2. look** see here, watch this.

RELATED KEYWORDS: APPEARANCE, LIGHT, OPTICS, VISIBILITY

SIGN

n. **1.** **1. sign** colours, emblem, ensign, figure, image, indication, manifestation, mark, sacrament, segno, signage, signal, symbol, taw, tessera, token, totem. **2. character** colophon, hieroglyphic, hieroglyphics, hierogram, ideogram, ideograph, logogram, logograph, monogram, note. **3. mark** black mark, block, chalk, check *(US)*, cross, diacritic, dot, engram, erasure, fingermark, line, lineation, markings, note, points, print, score, seal, stamp, tick, tittle, trace, underline, underscore. **4. signature** autograph, countersignature, e-signature, sign. *Informal:* dhobi mark *(South Asian English)*, henry. **5. spoor** condensation trail, contrail, drag, fingerprint, footfall, footmark, footprint, footstep, ichnite, pug, scent, toeprint, track, tracks, trail, vapour trail. *Informal:* mundowie. **6. trace** cast, dab, dash, dreg, hint, mark, remnant, shadow, sign, smell, soupçon, suggestion, suspicion, thought, vestige, vestigium. **7. evidence** appearances, face, indication, show, sign, signal. **8. symptom** attribute, characteristic, denotation, determinative, diagnostic, indication, prodrome, show, sign, signal, signifier, trace. **9. sign of the times** straw in the wind. **10. stigma** arrow, broad arrow, mark of Cain.

2. **1. gesture** action, beau geste, business, gesticulation, motion, shrug, wave. **2. nod** beck, beckon, eyewink, nictation, nictitation, twinkle, wink. **3. mime** charades, dumb show, pantomime. **4. thumbs up** thumbs down, V-sign. **5. grimace** mouth, smack, snarl. *Informal:* mug *(British)*.

3. **1. signal** catchword, clue, cue, hint, lead, leading question, message, selah, sennet, tip-off, wind, word. *Informal:* heads-up, the office. **2. password** countersign, parole, secret sign, watchword, word. **3. warning signal** cone, double black diamond, red flag. **4. alarm** air alert, all clear, burglar alarm, car alarm, fire alarm, fog signal, foghorn, gong, horn, klaxon, shark bell, shark siren, siren, tocsin. **5. distress signal** distress call, distress rocket, Mayday, pan, SOS. **6. railway signal** distant signal, home signal. **7. light signal** Aldis lamp, amber, anchor light, beacon, Belisha beacon *(British)*, bonfire, flare, flash, heliograph, light, lighthouse, localiser beacon, magnesium light, maroon, pharos, pilot lamp, pilot light, red fire, riding light, rocket, storm signals, storm warning, tracer, Very light, watch-fire. **8. radio beam** beam, blip, localiser. **9. telephone ring** dial tone, engaged signal. **10. beep** bleep, gating signal, pinger, pip, time signal. **11. military signal** assembly, boots and saddles *(US)*, call, charge, clarion call, last post, last trump, lights out, reveille, rollcall, rouse *(US)*, standard, taps *(US Military)*, tattoo. **12. death knell** muffled drum, passing bell. **13. semaphore** waft, waif.

4. **1. indicator** barometer, guide, guidepost, index, indicant. **2. marker** benchmark, cairn, checkpoint, cue dot, guide-mark, landmark, matchmark, mile post, milestone, post, surface indication, target, term, terminus, tidemark, vigia, witness mark. **3. pointer** arrow, cock, fingerpost, guide, guidepost, hand, lodestar, signpost. **4. buoy** anchor buoy, bell buoy, cork. **5. buoyage** balisage. **6. weathercock** vane, weathervane, windsock, windvane. **7. traffic sign** give-way sign, stop sign, traffic dome, witch's hat. *Informal:* cop, fried egg, silent cop. **8. traffic lights** amber light, green light, red light. **9. indicator light** brakelight, hand signal, hazard lights, light, stoplight, trafficator, turning-indicator. *Informal:* blinker, clicker, flasher, flickers, winker.

5. **1. label** car sticker, sticker, tab, tag. **2. hallmark** audio watermark, countermark, digital watermark, frank, impress, imprint, plate-mark, postmark, remarque, seal, stamp, surcharge, touch, touchmark, watermark. **3. brand** blaze, chop, crop, earmark, fryingpan brand, graffiti tag, logo, logotype, mark, moko, raddle, reddle, rubber stamp, ruddle, tattoo, trademark, woolmark. **4. inscription** legend, rubric, writing.

425

5. identification badge, calling card, credentials, dog tag, ID card, identity disc, marking tape, name tag, ok card, papers, passport, place-card, ration-card, register, union card, visiting card. *Informal:* dead meat ticket, ID, meat (ticket), meat tag, OK card. **6. nameplate** bookmark, bookplate, doorplate, escutcheon, firemark, flag, marque, numberplate, registration plate, scutcheon, shingle. **7. serial number** box number, call number, dewey number, flight number, IBN, postcode, pressmark, shelf mark, telephone number, VIN number, zipcode *(US)*. **8. station identification** call sign, signature tune. **9. ticket** check *(US)*, docket, excursion ticket, gift token, jetton, meal ticket, platform ticket, price-tag, return ticket, round-trip ticket *(US)*, season, season ticket, security tag, shopper docket, transfer, transfer-ticket, voucher. **10. stamp** health stamp *(NZ)*, postage stamp, precancel, provisional. **11. noticeboard** bulletin board *(US)*, clapperboard, clappers, facia, fascia *(British)*, notice, notification, signboard. **12. tombstone** gravestone, headstone, ledger, stela, stele, stone.

   6. 1. signer marksman, signatory, the undersigned. **2. graphologist** hieroglyphist, hierogrammat, punctuator, rubricator, symbolist.

   7. 1. labeller brander, dotter, franker, impresser, marker, smoothing-iron, stamper, stigmatiser, tagger, tattooer. **2. brand** branding iron, die, stamp.

   8. 1. signaller flagman, gesticulator, gesturer, heliographer, indicator, marker, pointer, signalman, switchman *(US)*, waver, wigwagger. *Informal:* flaggie.

   9. 1. punctuation mark angle bracket, apostrophe, braces, brackets, check *(US)*, colon, comma, curly bracket, curly brackets, dash, exclamation mark, full point (stop), interrogation mark, inverted comma, mark, parenthesis, period, point, quark, question mark, quotation mark, quote, round bracket, semicolon, speech mark, square bracket, stop, turned comma. **2. diacritical mark** accent, acute, breve, cedilla, circumflex, diaeresis, dieresis, grave, macron, mutation, rough breathing, smooth breathing, soft breathing, spiritus asper, spiritus lenis, tilde, umlaut. **3. writing and printing sign** asterisk, at sign, caret, dagger, dash, diesis, ditto marks, double dagger, ellipsis, em rule, en rule, fist, hyphen, index sign, obelisk, obelus, paragraph, parallel, pilcrow, reference mark, section, slash, star, subindex, subscript, subscription, superior, superscription, suspension point *(Chiefly US)*, virgule. *Informal:* par, para. **4. mathematical sign** diagonal, division sign, equals sign, forward slash, minus, minus sign, multiplication sign, negative, plus sign, positive, sigma, solidus, stroke, virgule. **5. music sign** abbreviation, accidental, alto clef, bass clef, clef, direction, expression mark, F clef, fermata, flat, key signature, ligature, natural, pause, presa, rest, segno, sharp, sign, signature, slur, soprano clef, tenor clef, tenuto, time signature, treble clef.

adj. **10. 1. indicative** connotative, denotative, evincive, gesticulatory, indexical, indicant, indicatory, meaning, significant, significative, suggestive. **2. symbolic** emblematic, figurative, pantomimic, prime, representative, symbolical, symbolist, typical. **3. symptomatic** prodromal, semeiotic, semiotic, stigmatic.

  v. **11. 1. signify** bespeak, betoken, connote, denote, forebode, imply, import, index, indicate, involve, mean, point to, proclaim, purport, signalise, stand for. **2. symbolise** allegorise, betoken, emblematise, emblemise, figure, image, incarnate, indicate, prefigure, represent, sign, symbol, type, typify.

   12. 1. gesture beckon, gesticulate, motion, point, recognise, shrug, wave. **2. mime** pantomime, talk with one's hands. **3. cue** peter, telegraph one's punches, tick-tack. **4. nod** bob, give the nod, nictitate, shake one's head, wink. **5. grimace** mouth, raise one's eyebrows. *Informal:* mug *(British)*.

   13. 1. signal beacon, beam, flag, flag down, flare, semaphore, sign, wigwag. **2. sound the alarm** beat the drum, beat the gong, ring, whistle. **3. lower the flag** dip the flag, hail, half-mast, salute, strike. **4. show the way** blaze a trail, buoy, buoy off, demarcate, mark the way, point the way.

   14. 1. label identify, mark, personalise, tab, tag, ticket. **2. brand** badge, barcode, blaze, designate, earmark, fingerprint, notch, raddle, reddle, sear, stigmatise, tattoo. **3. stamp** enface, frank, hallmark, impress, imprint, incuse, postmark, print, roulette, rubricate, seal, surcharge, touch, trace, watermark. *Informal:* stomp. **4. sign** autograph, initial, put one's mark on, re-sign, signature. **5. countersign** countermark, ratify, undersign, underwrite.

   15. 1. mark chalk, chalk up, direct, dot, hatch, inscribe, mark up, overscore, pencil, redpencil, rule, score, touch, underline, underscore, write. **2. tick** check *(US)*, check off, cross, cross off, record, register, tally, tick off. **3. punctuate** accent, accentuate, acute, dagger, emphasise, hyphen, hyphenate, hyphenise, lemmatise, obelise, parenthesise, point, star, subscribe, superscribe.

RELATED KEYWORDS: SUGGESTION, ALPHABET, EMBLEM, MEANING, NAME, REPRESENTATION, WORD

SILENCE

n. **1.** **1. silence** acostic privacy, hush, lull, peace, quiescence, quiet, quietness, repose, reserve, still *(Poetic)*, stillness. **2. period of silence** cessation, interval, let-up, pause, rest, stop, tacet. **3. dead space** anechoic chamber, cone of silence, soundproof box. **4. soundlessness** inaudibility, noiselessness. **5. muteness** dumbness, voicelessness. **6. speechlessness** reticence, sullenness, tacitness, taciturnity.

2. **1. silencer** deadener, muffle, muffler, quieter, squasher.

adj. **3.** **1. silent** dark, hushed, mum, mute, quiescent, quiet, quiet as the grave, reticent, speechless, still, stilly *(Poetic)*. *Informal:* q.t. **2. unsounded** noteless, silent, tacit, unsaid, unspoken, unuttered, unvoiced, voiceless. **3. inaudible** infrasonic, mum, mute, noiseless, quiet, silent, soundless, subsonic, supersonic, ultrasonic, wordless. **4. silenced** muffled, muted, subdued. **5. soundproof** anechoic, echoless. **6. inarticulate** mousy, quiet as a mouse, tongue-tied. **7. speechless** dumb, mum, mute, noteless, silent, songless, surd, tacit, tuneless, unvoiced, voiceless, wordless. **8. tight-lipped** close-lipped, dark, farouche, mum, mute, pokerfaced, reserved, reticent, self-contained, silent, sullen, taciturn. *Informal:* po-faced.

v. **4.** **1. silence** hush, lull, mum, quiet, quieten, shush, still. **2. suppress** burke, choke back, crush, jugulate, play down, quell, quench, quiet, silence, smother, soft-pedal, stifle, subdue. *Informal:* squash, squelch. **3. mute** drown, drown the noise, gag, muffle, muzzle, tongue-tie. **4. soundproof** deaden.

5. **1. be silent** hold one's peace, hold one's tongue, keep one's mouth shut, rest, shush. *Informal:* ace it (up), belt up, can it, cut the cackle, pipe down, put a cork in it, put a sock in it, shut one's mouth, shut up, stow it. **2. refuse comment** keep mum, keep one's counsel, stand mute. *Informal:* button the lip. **3. lose one's tongue** save one's breath, waste no words on.

adv. **6.** **1. silently** inaudibly, noiselessly, quiescently, quietly, soundlessly, still, stilly, subduedly. **2. speechlessly** dumbly, mutely. **3. reticently** sullenly, tacitly, taciturnly, voicelessly.

interj. **7.** **1. silence** hist, hush, hushaby, mum, sh, shush, whist. *Informal:* mum's the word, shut up, shut your face, shut your mouth, shut your mouth there's a bus coming.

RELATED KEYWORDS: DEAFNESS, QUIETNESS, FAULTY SPEECH, RETICENCE

SIMILARITY

n. **1.** **1. similarity** analogousness, analogy, closeness, comparableness, conformableness, conformance, correspondence, isomorphism, likeness, parity, resemblance, resonance, semblance, similitude. **2. affinity** imitation, mimesis, nearness, parallelism, propinquity. **3. rhyme** alliteration, assonance, double entendre, equivoque, metaphor, onomatopoeia, paronomasia, play on words, pun, simile. **4. conformity** compatibility, equality, equivalence, equivalence relation, identity, parity.

2. **1. similar thing** approximation, close match, counterpart, like, look-alike, match, parallel. **2. perfect match** alter ego, carbon copy, clone, copy, counterpart, doppelganger, double, duplicate, duplication, ectype, image, match, mate, mirror image, repeat, replica, replicar, replication, reproduction, second self, twin, xerox. *Informal:* chip off the old block, dead spit, ditto, knock-off, spitting image. **3. analogue** counterpart, isomorph, obverse, opposite number, parallel. **4. class** category, community, family, subset. **5. set** birds of a feather, matching pair, matching set, pair, peas in a pod, pigeon pair, Siamese twins, twins, two of a kind. **6. peer** coequal, compeer, equal, fellow, peer group.

adj. **3.** **1. similar** akin, alike, all of a piece, analogical, cut from the same cloth, equal, look-alike, not unlike, reminiscent of, suggestive of, tarred with the same brush, twinned. **2. comparable** analogous, conformable, correspondent, homothetic, parallel. **3. assimilable** compatible, conformable. **4. approximate** approaching, bastard, close, counterfeit, much the same, near, pseudo, quasi, spurious. **5. congeneric** akin, cognate, congenerous, connatural, consanguineous. **6. isomorphic** isologous.

v. **4.** **1. be similar** agree, answer, be all one, be birds of a feather, be in the same boat, be much of a muchness, be nothing in it, be of the same kidney, be twins, conform, correspond, match, parallel. **2. approximate** approach, border on, come close to, counterfeit, remind of, resemble, savour of, smack of, take after.

adv. **5.** **1. similarly** analogically, analogously, comparably, connaturally, correspondently, correspondingly, nearly, semblably. **2. conformably** compatibly. **3. likewise** by the same token, in kind. **4. approximately** in the neighbourhood of, nearly.

RELATED KEYWORDS: ACCORD, EQUALITY, HOMOGENEITY, IMITATION

SIMPLICITY

n. **1.** **1. simplicity** elementariness, modesty, ordinariness, plainness, resolvability, resolvableness, rudimentariness, simpleness. **2. purity** homogeneity, homogeneousness, pureness, unsophisticatedness, unsophistication. **3. straightforwardness** directness, plainness, straightness.

2. **1. simplification** degradation, denouement, disembarrassment, disentanglement, resolution, solution, streamlining, unravelment. **2. simplism** oversimplification, reductionism.

adj. **3.** **1. simple** attic, bare, dry, ho-hum, homespun, mere, naked, obvious, plain, sheer, simplex, single, unostentatious, unpolished, very. **2. ordinary** common-or-garden, commonplace, day-to-day, everyday, household, humdrum, normal, philistine, plebeian, slow, stock, tasteless, trivial, unexceptional, uninteresting, unremarkable, workaday. *Informal:* random *(Chiefly US)*. **3. no-frills** bald, bare, bread-and-butter, cold-turkey, drab, dry, dull, literal, matter-of-fact, mousy, pedestrian, practical, primitive, prosaic, unadorned, undecorated, unfancy, unimaginative. *Informal:* vanilla. **4. elementary** abecedarian, back-to-basics, basal, baseline, basic *(Chiefly US)*, basilar, elemental, essential, fundamental, key, low, primary, rudimentary, ultimate, uncompounded, underlying. **5. pure** absolute, au naturel, clean, fresh, full, homogeneous, homogenous, native, natural, neat, perfect, pristine, sheer, stark, straight, unadulterated, unalloyed, uniform, unmingled, unmixed, unsophisticated, unvarying, utter. **6. straightforward** blunt, direct, downright, flat, forthright, perspicuous, plain, plain-speaking, point-blank, pure, resolvable, round, square, straight, unambiguous, uncomplicated, unequivocal. **7. simplistic** oversimplified.

v. **4.** **1. simplify** clarify, clear, make plain, streamline. **2. disentangle** disembarrass, disembroil, disentwine, extricate, sort out, uncoil, uncross, undo, unknit, unlay, unloose, unloosen, unmix, unplait, unravel, unscramble, unsnarl, untangle, unthread, untie, untwine, untwist, unwind. **3. resolve** break down, degrade, disassociate, disintegrate, dissociate. **4. oversimplify** popularise.

adv. **5.** **1. simply** alone, barely, downright, just, merely, only, ordinarily, plain, plainly, purely, semplice. **2. straightforwardly** commonly, elementarily, naturally, ordinarily, rudimentarily, unmixedly, unsophisticatedly. **3. simplistically**.

RELATED KEYWORDS: ARTLESSNESS, EASINESS, ORDER

SIMULTANEITY

n. **1.** **1. simultaneity** coeternity, coexistence, coextension, coincidence, concomitance, concurrence, concurrency, contemporaneousness, intercurrence, isochronism, simultaneousness, synchronisation, synchronism, synchronousness, synchrony, unison. *Informal:* sync.

adj. **2.** **1. simultaneous** accompanying, coetanious, coeternal, coeval, coexisting, coextensive, coincident, coincidental, coinciding, coinstantaneous, concomitant, concurrent, contemporaneous, contemporary, conterminous, coseismal, cotemporaneous, cotemporary, inseparable, intercurrent, isochronal, isochronous, synchronic, synchronistic, synchronous. **2. twin** didymous, geminate, hemitrope, twinborn, twinned.

adv. **3.** **1. simultaneously** at once, at the same moment, at the same time, coevally, coincidentally, coincidently, concurrently, contemporaneously, hand in hand, in concert, in step, in sync, in unison, isochronally, isochronously, jointly, neck and neck, synchronistically, synchronously, together.

RELATED KEYWORDS: ACCORD, TIMELINESS

SINGLE STATE

n. **1.** **1. single state** bachelorhood, bachelorship, celibacy, maidenhead, maidenhood, misogamy, single blessedness, singleness, spinsterhood, viduity, virginity, widowhood.

2. **1. divorce** annulment, divorcement, family break-up, legal separation, separation, sequestration, sunderance, voidance. **2. maintenance** aid, alimentation, alimony *(US)*, keep, keeping, subsistence, support, visiting rights. *Informal:* palimony *(US)*. **3. nullity of marriage** discretion statement.

3. **1. single person** bachelor, bachelor girl, bachelor-at-arms, feme sole, Fräulein, lonely heart, maid, maiden, misogamist, old maid, spinster, vestal virgin, virgin. *Informal:* bach, tabby. **2. divorcee** divorcer. **3. single parent**. **4. widow** dowager, grass widow, grass widower, queen dowager, widower.

4. **1. singles bar** dating service, lonely hearts' club, marriage bureau, parents without partners club. **2. internet dating service** online dating service.

adj. **5.** **1. single** celibate, lone, maiden, partnerless, unattached, unmarried, unwedded, virgin. **2. spinsterish** old-maidish. *Informal:* on the shelf. **3. widowed** vidual.

v. **6.** **1. be single** live alone. **2. divorce** divide, live separately, separate, split up, sunder.
RELATED KEYWORDS: SOLITUDE

SIZE

n. **1.** **1. size** capacity, dimensions, extent, magnitude, measure, proportions, scale, scope, volume. **2. hugeness** enormity, enormousness, giantism, giganticness, immenseness, immensity, mightiness, monstrousness, oversize, prodigiousness, sizeableness, vastitude, vastness, voluminosity. **3. amplitude** ampleness, breadth, extensiveness, spaciousness, spread, sweepingness. **4. bulk** bulkiness, buxomness, dumpiness, heftiness, massiness, massiveness, rotundness, steatopygia. **5. corpulence** beefiness, burliness, corpulency, embonpoint, fatness, flesh, fleshiness, grossness, obesity, plumpness, portliness, stoutness. *Informal:* chubbiness, tubbiness. **6. squatness** chunkiness, podginess, pudginess, stockiness, stodginess.

2. **1. giant** behemoth, bouncer, bumper, colossus, giantess, hulk, jumbo, leviathan, megalith, monster, monstrosity. *Informal:* biggie, boomer, husky *(US)*, snorter, the daddy of them all, the father and mother of a, whopper. **2. legendary giants** Ajax, Cyclops, Gargantua, Gog, Goliath, Hagrid, Jumbo, Magog, the BFG, Titan, Titaness, Ymir.

adj. **3.** **1. big** biggish, bull, decuman, double, family-size, full-scale, great, large, majuscule, massive, queen-size, sizeable, tall. **2. bulky** cyclopean, elephantine, gigantic, great, gross, heavy, imposing, large, massive, massy, megalithic, monumental, vast. **3. ample** capacious, expansive, voluminous. **4. huge** broad, colossal, enormous, herculean, jumbo, king, large, mammoth, mighty, titanic. *Informal:* king-size, old-man. **5. gigantic** Brobdingnagian, colossal, cyclopean, enormous, gargantuan, giant, gigantean, gigantesque, immense, mammoth, massive, monster, monstrous, prodigious, tremendous. *Informal:* strapping, whopping. **6. extensive** broad, large-scale, palatial, spacious, sweeping, wide. **7. vast** cosmic, immense, oceanic, vasty *(Poetic)*. **8. outsize** overgrown, oversize, oversized. **9. walloping** *Informal:* slashing, smacking, spanking, swingeing, thumping, thundering, whacking, whopping.

4. **1. fat** adipose, ample, beefy, big, big boned, bloated, burly, corpulent, fattish, fleshy, full-toned, gross, hulking, hulky, meaty, obese, overweight, plump, portly, pursy, rotund, steatopygous, stout, well-fed. *Informal:* chubby, husky, poddy *(British)*, porky, roly-poly, tubby, well-padded. **2. potbellied** abdominous, paunchy. **3. buxom** bosomy, busty, deep-bosomed, full-bodied, junoesque, sonsy *(Scottish, Irish)*, voluptuous, Wagnerian, well-stacked, well-upholstered. *Informal:* pneumatic, stacked. **4. squat** bullocky, chunky, dumpy, endomorphic, podgy, pudgy, pyknic, squab, squabby, squatty, stocky, stodgy, stubbed, stubby, stumpy, thickset, well built, well-built. *Informal:* fubsy, hefty, hippy.

adv. **5.** **1. sizeably** enormously, extensively, gigantically, hugely, immensely, massively, monstrously, prodigiously, sizably, sweepingly, vastly. **2. amply** capaciously, spaciously, voluminously. **3. exceedingly** *Informal:* ever so. **4. corpulently** bulkily, grossly, obesely, rotundly, squabbily, squatly. **5. monumentally** palatially. **6. wholesale** by wholesale, in bulk.

RELATED KEYWORDS: GREATNESS, HEIGHT, LENGTH, QUANTITY, THICKNESS

SKIN

n. **1.** **1. skin** bark, capsule, epicarp, exocarp, fur, genet, hide, hull, integument, rind, scalp, sheath, shell, tunic, utricle. **2. membrane** caul, cortex, film, fraenulum, fraenum, frenulum, furfur, indusium, lamella, pellicle, scale, scum, squama, tela, tunic, web, webbing. **3. corium** cuticle, cuticula, cutis, derma, dermatome, dermis, epidermis, hypoderm, Malpighian layer, matrix, scarfskin. **4. hangnail** agnail. **5. marsupium** epicanthus. **6. peel** husk, jacket, peeling, zest.

2. **1. hide** crop, fell, fur, greenhide, kid, kip, pelt, peltry, rawhide, seal. **2. animal skin** antelope, bearskin, broadtail, buckskin, busby, calf, calfskin, chinchilla, cowhide, cowskin, crimmer, deerskin, doeskin, fox, goatskin, hamster, horsehide, kidskin, krimmer, lambskin, nutria, pigskin, seal, sealskin, sheepskin, snakeskin, swanskin. **3. leather** buckskin, buff, cordovan, grain, levant, mocha, morocco leather, ooze leather, shagreen, suede, whitleather. **4. bootlaces** moult, pie piece, scarf, slough.

3. **1. currier** fellmonger, flesher, skinner.

4. **1. curriery** skinnery, tannery.

adj. **5.** **1. skin** cutaneous, cuticular, dermal, dermatomic, dermic, epicanthic, epidermal, epidermic, membranaceous, membranous, subcutaneous. **2. dermatoid** dermoid, skinlike. **3. fair-skinned**. **4. hypodermic** endermic, percutaneous. **5. cortical** corticate, lamellar, lamellate, lamellose, pellicular, scutellate. **6. crustaceous** crusty, furfuraceous, scurfy. **7. leather** buff, cordovan, coriaceous, shagreen, shagreened.

v. **6.** **1. skin** flay, peel.

RELATED KEYWORDS: BODY, COVERING, LAYER

SKY

n. **1.** **1. sky** aether, azure, canopy, celestial sphere, cope, empyrean, ether, firmament, heaven, skies, sphere, the blue. **2. atmosphere** aeropause, air, Appleton layers, chemosphere, E layer, exosphere, Heaviside layer, inversion layer, ionosphere, Kennelly-Heaviside layer, lower atmosphere, magnetosphere, mesosphere, stratosphere, troposphere, upper atmosphere, Van Allen belt. **3. space** aerospace, deep space, infinite, inner space, outer space, plenum. **4. cosmos** creation, macrocosm, nature, universe, world.

2. **1. heavenly body** Arian, ball, celestial body, dwarf planet, exoplanet, gas giant, globe, lord, luminary, moon, orb *(Chiefly Poetic)*, satellite, sphere, star, terrestrial planet, world. **2. solar system** asteroid, planet, satellite, sun. **3. the planets** Earth, Jupiter, Mars, Mercury, Neptune, Saturn, Uranus, Venus. **4. Earth** earth, lower world, marl, Mother Earth, planet Earth, Terra, terrene, the globe, world. **5. dwarf planets** Ceres, Eris, Pluto, Xena. **6. asteroid** asteroidean, minor planet, planetoid, small solar-system body, SSSB. **7. asteroids** Adonis, Apollo, Eros, Hermes, Icarus.

3. **1. star** cannibal star, collapsar, dark star, fixed star, magnetar, main-sequence star, protostar, sun, W star, Wolf-Rayet star, X-ray star. **2. giant star** red giant, supergiant. **3. dwarf star** brown dwarf, dwarf, red dwarf, starlet, white dwarf. **4. nova** supernova. **5. variable** Cepheid variable, eclipsing variable. **6. morning star** daystar, Lucifer, Venus. **7. evening star** Hesperus, Venus, Vesper. **8. lodestar** North Star, Polaris, Pole Star. **9. constellation** asterism, binary star, cluster, double star, globular cluster, multiple star, open cluster. **10. constellations** Aquarius, Archer, Aries, Big Dipper, Bull, Cancer, Capricorn, Capricornus, Carina, Crab, Fish, Gemini, Goat, Leo, Libra, Lion, Pisces, Plough, Pyxis, Ram, Sagittarius, Scales, Scorpio, Scorpion, Scorpius, Southern Cross, Taurus, the Dipper, Twins, Virgin, Virgo, Water bearer. **11. Southern Cross** Crater, Cross. **12. galaxy** Galaxy, island universe, metagalaxy, Milky Way, radio galaxy, spiral galaxy, spiral nebula. **13. nebula** irregular nebula, Magellanic cloud, planetary nebula, spiral nebula, starburst, stardust, stellar evolution. **14. aurora** aurora australis, aurora borealis, Haidinger's brush, northern lights, polar lights, southern lights, zodiacal light. **15. star motion** star drift, star stream. **16. black hole** pulsar, quasar.

4. **1. sun** annual, daystar *(Poetic)*, eye of the day *(Poetic)*, mean sun, midnight sun, Phoebus, sun disc. **2. corona** anthelion, aureole, chromosphere, halo, photosphere, rainband, sunglow. **3. parhelion** mock sun, sundog. **4. sunspot** facula, flocculus, penumbra, solar flare, solar wind, umbra.

5. **1. moon** blue moon, earth satellite, lamp *(Poetic)*, new moon, Phoebe. *Informal:* Paddy's lantern *(NZ)*. **2. moons** Amalthea, Callisto, Charon, Deimos, Europa, Galilean satellite, Ganymede, Io, Nereid, Phobos, Titan, Triton. **3. phase** crescent, first quarter, full moon, gibbous moon, half-moon, harvest moon, interlunation, mansion, moonrise, new moon, old moon, quadrature, waning moon, waxing moon. **4. paraselene** mock moon. **5. crater** mare, mascon, ray, rill, sea, walled plain.

6. **1. meteor** ball lightning, bolide, eta Aquarid meteor, eta Orionid meteor, falling star, fireball, shooting star. **2. meteorite** aerolite, meteor, meteoroid, siderite, siderolite. **3. comet** Halley's comet. **4. nucleus** coma, tail, trail, train.

7. **1. astronomic point** aberration, annual parallax, diurnal parallax, evection, geocentric parallax, heliocentric parallax, inequality. **2. magnitude**. **3. arc** amplitude, azimuth, ecliptic, epicycle, southing. **4. declination** celestial latitude, celestial longitude, degree, elongation, galactic coordinate, galactic latitude, galactic longitude, latitude, longitude, magnetic declination, magnetic variation, trigon, variation. **5. node** syzygy. **6. octant** opposition, quadrature, quartile, quintile, sextile, trine. **7. perigee** pericynthion, perihelion, perilune. **8. apogee** aphelion, apocynthion, apolune. **9. precession** precession of the equinoxes. **10. solstice** solstitial point, summer solstice, vertical circle, winter solstice. **11. equinox** autumnal equinox, equinoctial point, March equinox, September equinox, vernal equinox. **12. eclipse** annual eclipse, annular eclipse, dichotomy, emersion, occultation, partial eclipse, total eclipse. **13. rise** right ascension. **14. orbit** geostationary orbit, line of apsides, revolution, rotation, synchronous equatorial, true anomaly, variation. **15. equinoctial** celestial equator, equinoctial circle, equinoctial line, meridian. **16. galactic circle** colure, galactic equator, galactic plane. **17. tropic** Cancer, Capricorn. **18. pole** celestial pole, galactic pole, magnetic dipole, magnetic pole, North Pole, South Pole. **19. zenith** nadir, radiant, solar apex, vertex. **20. aclinic line** magnetic equator.

8. **1. astronomy** Almagest, almagest, areodesy, astrometry, astrophysics, radioastronomy, selenodesy, selenography, selenology, stargazing, uranography. **2. astrobiology** astrobotany, astrogeology. **3. big bang theory** expanding universe, nebular hypothesis, steady state theory, superdense theory. **4. Copernican system** Ptolemaic system.

9. **1. astronomer** astrologist, astrophysicist, lunarian, selenographer, selenologist, stargazer, uranographist, uranologer.

10. **1. observatory** tracking station. **2. planetarium** celestial globe, orrery, planisphere, tellurian, tellurion, zodiac.

adj. **11.** **1. cosmic** cosmical, galactic, macrocosmic, universal. **2. heavenly** celestial, empyreal, ethereal, firmamental, skyey *(Chiefly Poetic)*, sphery, superlunar, superlunary, supernal, superterrestrial, uranian, uranic. **3. extragalactic** intergalactic, interplanetary, intersidereal, interstellar.

12. **1. planetary** global, planetesimal, planetoidal, sublunar, sublunary, tellurian, telluric, terrene, terrestrial, translunary. **2. meteoric** cometic, meteoritic.

13. **1. astronomical** areodetic, astrophysical, radioastronomical, selenodetic, selenographic, uranographical, uranological, zodiacal. **2. areocentric** geocentric, geocentrical, heliocentric. **3. epicyclic** epicyclical, equinoctial, evectional, nodical, perigean, periodic, solstitial, syzygetic. **4. Copernican** Ptolemaic.

14. **1. solar** circumsolar, combust, heliac, heliacal, parheliacal, parhelic, solarian, subsolar. **2. lunisolar**

15. **1. stellar** asteriated, astral, sidereal, star-studded, starred, starry, stelliferous. **2. Sothic**.

16. **1. lunar** circumlunar, interlunar, lunarian, moony, sublunary, superlunary, translunary.

adv. **17.** **1. cosmically** ethereally, supernally. **2. geocentrically** heliacally, heliocentrically, stellately.

RELATED KEYWORDS: AIR, LIGHT, WEATHER

SLANDER

n. **1.** **1. slander** assassination, calumniation, calumny, character assassination, defamation, dirt, innuendo, insinuation, libel, malediction, scandal. *Informal:* defo. **2. denigration** aspersion, backbiting, decrial, disparagement, objurgation, revilement, sledging, smear, vilification. **3. disparagement** abuse, assailment, criticism, derogation, derogatoriness, detraction, excoriation, pejoration, personality, vituperation. *Informal:* bashing, flak. **4. muckraking** dirty tricks, mud-slinging, smear campaign. **5. invective** attack. **6. insult** backhander, barb, fling, jeer, nip, put-down, rub. **7. disparaging remark** aspersion, byword, epithet, pejorative, slur, smear, smear word.

2. **1. slanderer** backbiter, backstabber, belier, calumniator, defamer, libeller, maligner, traducer. **2. scandalmonger** blackener, muck-raker, mud-slinger. *Informal:* tabby. **3. disparager** decrier, denigrator, depreciator, detractor, dispraiser, vilipender. *Informal:* basher, knocker. **4. vilifier** abuser, asperser, assailant, assailer, assassinator, attacker, character assassin, railer, reviler, vituperator.

adj. **3.** **1. slanderous** calumnious, defamatory, libellous, scandalous. **2. abusive** denunciatory, insulting, invective, maledictory, objurgatory, opprobrious, vituperative. **3. disparaging** belittling, contemptuous, derogative, derogatory, detractive, pejorative, personal, slighting, snide.

v. **4.** **1. slander** asperse, backbite, badmouth, belie, bespatter, calumniate, defame, denigrate, discredit, libel, malign, put the knife into, squib, sully, traduce, vilify, vilipend. *Informal:* slag. **2. blacken** besmirch, bespatter, defame, denigrate, smear. *Informal:* empty the bucket on, muckrake, sling mud at, throw mud at, tip the bucket on. **3. revile** abuse, assail, attack, be personal, belabour, bullyrag, excoriate, fling out, fulminate against, insult, lash, objurgate, scarify, slam, slate, slur, snipe at, vituperate. *Informal:* bash, dump on, get stuck into, knock, slag, slag off at, sling off at, throw off at. **4. disparage** belittle, cheapen, cry down, damn, decry, degrade, demean, depreciate, diminish, dispraise, downgrade, lessen, make light of, make little of, pooh-pooh, riddle, slight, sneer at.

RELATED KEYWORDS: DISAPPROVAL, LOW REGARD, DISHONESTY

SLEEP

n. **1.** **1. sleep** slumber. *Informal:* beauty sleep, bye-byes, doss, shut-eye. **2. rest** reposal, repose. **3. dormancy** aestivation, coma, hibernation, inactivity, lethargy, sopor, suspended animation, torpor. **4. oblivion** dream, hypnosis, trance. **5. sandman** dreamland, land of Nod.

2. 1. nap bange, catnap, doze, lie-down, nod, rest, siesta. *Informal:* blow, camp, forty winks, kip, nanna nap, snooze, zizz. **2. sleep-in** lie-in.

3. 1. sleepiness doziness, drowse, drowsiness, oscitance, somnolence, yawn, yawning. **2. lethargy** inertia, sluggishness, torpor. **3. snoring** tossing and turning, zzz. **4. sleepwalking** noctambulism, somnambulation, somnambulism, somniloquy. **5. sleeping sickness** encephalitis lethargica, narcolepsy, narcosis, narcotism.

4. 1. sleeping-pill depressant, hypnotic, laudanum, mickey, narcotic, opiate, sedative, sleeping-draught, soporific, stupefacient. *Informal:* bromide, downer, knockout drop, mickey finn, sleeper, stopper. **2. lullaby** berceuse, cradlesong.

5. 1. sleeper dosser, dreamer, slumberer, snorer. **2. sleepyhead** dozer, napper. **3. sleepwalker** somnambulant, somnambulator, somnambulist.

6. 1. sleeping quarters barracks, bedroom, crash pad, crew's quarters, dorm, dormer, dormitory, dosshouse, flophouse, focsle, forecastle, glory hole. **2. sleeping car** couchette, sleeper. **3. bed** bassinette, berth, bosun's chair, box bed, bunk, camp stretcher, carry basket, carrycot, charpoy, cot, couch, cradle, cradle scythe, creeper, crib, day bed, divan, double bed, double-bunk, featherbed, folding bed, four-poster, humidicrib, lounge, night-and-day, pallet, rocker, shakedown, sofa bed, stretcher, studio couch, waterbed. *Informal:* doss, pad. **4. sleeping-bag. 5. mattress** air bed, air mattress, futon, paillasse, pallet, palliasse.

adj. **7. 1. asleep** dormant, fast asleep, in the arms of Morpheus, in the land of Nod, not awake, sleeping, sound asleep. *Informal:* dead, dead to the world, out to it. **2. dormant** dormient, latent, torpid. **3. sleepy** dozy, drowsy, exhausted, fatigued, heavy with sleep, heavy-laden, lethargic, oscitant, overweary, slumberous, somnolent, tired, weary, worn. *Informal:* clapped-out, jiggered, knocked-up, stuffed, wrecked, zonked. **4. drowsy** dozy, dreamy, inattentive, oscitant, somnolent, switched-off. *Informal:* out of it. **5. torpid** comatose, dead, dead-and-alive, dull, effortless, flat, idle, inactive, inanimate, indolent, inert, languid, languishing, languorous, lazy, lethargic, lifeless, listless, narcoleptic, numb, otiose, paralytic, phlegmatic, poppied, quiet, remiss, slack, slothful, slow, sluggard, sluggardly, sluggish, slumberous, somnolent, stagnant, supine, thick. *Informal:* stonkered. **6. somnambulant** somnambulate, somnambulistic.

8. 1. soporific dozy, drowsy, hypnotic, narcotic, opiate, oscitant, somniferous, somnific, somnolent, soporiferous, torporific.

v. **9. 1. sleep** be dead to the world, doze, dream, drowse, repose, rest, sleep like a log, sleep like a top, slumber, slumber away. *Informal:* push up (or stack) zeds. **2. nap** catnap, doze, drowse, rest, sit, slumber, take a nap. *Informal:* snooze, take forty winks. **3. hibernate** aestivate, estivate, lie dormant. **4. go to sleep** doss down, drop off, fall asleep, fall off, go to the land of Nod, nod off. *Informal:* crash, die on someone, flake, flake out. **5. go to bed** bed down, double-bunk, jump into bed, retire, roll in, roost, settle down for the night. *Informal:* bunk, camp, doss, get between the sheets, go to beddy-byes, hit the hay, hit the sack, kip down, turn in. **6. sleep in** lie in, oversleep.

10. 1. become sleepy begin to nod, feel one's eyelids become heavy, rub one's eyes, yawn.

11. 1. put to sleep bed down, hushaby, lull, lullaby, sedate, sing to sleep.

adv. **12. 1. asleep** to the land of Nod. **2. in bed** abed, bedward. *Informal:* in the sack. **3. sleepily** dozily, drowsily, somnolently. **4. soporifically** hypnotically, lethargically, somnolently, soporiferously.

RELATED KEYWORDS: REST, UNCONSCIOUSNESS

SLOPE

n. **1. 1. slope** bank, banking, brae *(Scottish)*, cant, escarp, glacis, grade, gradient, oblique, obliquity, pitch, ramp, side, slant, steep, superelevation, talus, tilt. **2. pitch** acclivity, anhedral, attitude, bank, batter, bearing, camber, cant, chandelle, dihedral, dip, inclination, knockdown, lean, leaning, list, rake, skew, slope, talus, tilt, wane. **3. incline** acclivity, ascent, bank, brae *(Scottish)*, dip, inclination, jump-up, pitch, rise, slopes, talus, upgrade *(US)*, uphill, upsweep. **4. declivity** anticline, anticlinorium, brae *(Scottish)*, declension, declination, decline, descent, dip, downgrade, downswing, drop, drop-off, fall, geanticline, icefall, isocline, magnetic declination, magnetic variation, monoclinal, monocline, nappe, preponderation, syncline, variation. **5. mountainside** crag-and-tail, hillside, versant. **6. ramp** camber, cattle ramp, caunter, chamfer, chute, counter, counterscarp, escarp, gangway, glacis, logway, nursery slope, raked floor, shaft, skate bowl, ski run, ski-jump, skidboard, skids *(NZ)*, skidway, skimboard, slide, slip, slipway, stepped floor, talus, tambour, trunk. **7. slippery-dip** slide *(Chiefly WA, Victoria,*

Tasmania and ACT, Chiefly NSW, SA, Qld and ACT, Chiefly Qld and Tasmania), slippery slide *(Chiefly Qld and Tasmania)*.

2. **1. slopingness** abruptness, dip, inclination, obliqueness, pitch, precipitousness, proneness, sharpness, sheerness, steepness.

adj. **3.** **1. sloping** acute, askew, aslant, bevel, cant, declivous, inclinatory, inclining, leaning, lopsided, oblique, on her beam ends, on its beam-ends, out of square, preponderating, sideling, skew, slanting, slantwise, tilted, weathered. **2. banking** anhedral, dihedral. **3. anticlinal** centroclinal, clinometric, dihedral, isoclinal, monoclinal, synclinal, unilateral. **4. aslant** aslope, atilt, backhanded, bevel, declivitous, gradient, inclined, oblique, prone, slanting, slantwise, sloping. **5. steep** abrupt, arduous, bold, critical, gorgy, hilly, precipitous, sharp, sheer, uphill.

v. **4.** **1. slope** bank, be at an angle, bevel, cant, careen, converge, decline, heel, incline, lean, list, lurch, oblique, shelve, slant, splay, steeve, sway, tend, tilt, tip, trip, verge, verge to (or towards). **2. grade** bank, batter, chamfer, decline, descend, escarp, hade, heel, pitch, rake, tilt, weather. **3. climb** incline, slant, steepen, uptilt. **4. fall** delve, descend, dip, droop *(Poetic)*, lower, plunge, preponderate, sink.

adv. **5.** **1. slopingly** aslant, bias, obliquely, preponderatingly, slantingly, slantwise. **2. aslope** aslant, atilt, obliquely, slantingly, slantwise, tilted. **3. steeply** abruptly, obliquely, precipitously, pronely, sharply, sheer, sheerly.

RELATED KEYWORDS: BEND, HEIGHT, OVERTURN

SLOWNESS

n. **1.** **1. slowness** deliberateness, deliberation, flat-footedness, lack of speed, laggardness, leadenness, listlessness, sluggishness. **2. delay** cunctation, deceleration, delaying action, dilatoriness, hold-up, lag, latency, latent period, loitering, pause, procrastination, retardation, tardiness, tarrying, waiting. **3. hesitation** breather, hesitancy, pause. **4. slackness** languidness, languor, leisureliness. **5. work-to-rule** *Informal:* go-slow. **6. deceleration** brakeage, calando, moderation, retardation, slowdown, slowup.

2. **1. slow person** ambler, crawler, dallier, dawdler, delayer, laggard, lagger, lingerer, plodder, potterer, slug, snail, straggler, tarrier, tortoise. *Informal:* shellback *(Chiefly Tasmania)*, slowcoach, slowpoke, Sunday driver. **2. slow animal** drongo *(Horseracing)*, non-chaser *(Greyhounds)*.

adj. **3.** **1. slow** at a snail's pace, deliberate, dull, languid, languorous, leisured, leisurely, low-geared, slack, sleepy, slow-moving, torpid, unhurried. **2. adagio** largo, lentamente, lentissimo, lento. **3. sluggish** coasty, drowsy, inactive, inert, lazy, leaden, phlegmatic, slack, sleepy, slow, sullen, torpid. **4. snail-like** bumper-to-bumper, lumbering, slow-motion, snail-paced, tardigrade. **5. dilatory** backward, laggard, lagging, slack, slow, tardy, unready. **6. retardative** retardatory.

v. **4.** **1. go slowly** amble, coast, crawl, drag, drift, inch, plod, stalk, trail, trudge. *Informal:* run like a hairy goat, schlep around *(Chiefly US)*, trundle. **2. lag** be slow off the mark, brake, compound, fall behind, lose time, run dead, slow, straggle, trail. **3. tarry** coquet, dally, dawdle, delay, dillydally, hang fire, hesitate, linger, loaf, loiter, lounge, lounge about, pause, perambulate, potter, putter *(US)*, ramble, retard, saunter, stall for time, stay, stop, stroll, take one's time, trifle. *Informal:* fiddle, mosey *(US)*. **4. work to rule** *Informal:* drag the chain.

adv. **5.** **1. slowly** at one's leisure, bumper-to-bumper, deliberately, languidly, languorously, lazily. **2. gradually** bit by bit, by degrees, by easy stages, by inches, inch by inch, inchmeal, leisurely, little by little, piecemeal, poco a poco, step by step. **3. dilatorily** dallyingly, laggardly, loiteringly, potteringly, tardily. **4. sluggishly** leadenly, lumberingly, ploddingly, slackly, sullenly. **5. adagio** lentardo, ritardando.

RELATED KEYWORDS: MOVEMENT, TRAVEL

SLUDGE

n. **1.** **1. sludge** grease, heavy mud, mire, muck, mud, ooze, scum, slime, slob *(Irish)*, slop, slosh, slush, spume, sullage. *Informal:* cack, glop, grunge, guck, guk, gunk, scunge. **2. bog** boghole, fen *(British)*, gluepot, marsh, mire, morass, ooze, quagmire, quicksand, slough, swamp, wash, wet ground. **3. magma** eruption. **4. viscosity** creaminess, gelatinousness, glairiness, glutinosity, glutinousness, gooiness, mucosity, ropiness, sloppiness, stringiness, thickness, threadiness, toughness, treacliness, viscidity, viscidness, viscousness. **5. gelatinisation** gelation, impastation, thickening.

2. **1. paste** clag, clobber, dope, mess. *Informal:* goo. **2. syrup** blackstrap, corn syrup *(US)*, flax honey *(NZ)*, golden syrup, honey, honey bee *(Aboriginal English)*, honeybag, honeybee sugar *(Aboriginal English)*, mel, molasses *(US)*, sirup *(US)*, sugarbag *(Aboriginal*

English), treacle. *Informal:* bullocky's joy, Bundaberg honey, cocky's joy, honey pot. **3. semifluid** colloid, semisolid. **4. gel** gelatinoid, glair, jelly.

adj. **3.**   **1. sludgy** muddy, oozy, plashy, roily, slimey, slimy, sloppy, slushy, splashy. *Informal:* goozy. **2. boggy** boggish, fenny *(British),* marshy, miry, quaggy, swampy. **3. viscous** adhesive, claggy, clotted, colloidal, curdled, gelatinoid, gelatinous, glairy, gluey, glutenous, glutinous, gummous, gummy, jelly-like, lyophilic, magmatic, melting, mucilaginous, mucous, oozy, semifluid, semisolid, soupy, sticky, syruplike, tacky, tenacious, thick, treacly, unset, viscid, viscoid. *Informal:* gluggy, gooey, goopy, icky. **4. stringy** ropy, thready, tough.

RELATED KEYWORDS: FLOW, LIQUID, PULP, SOLIDITY, SWAMP

SMALLNESS

n. **1.**   **1. smallness** diminutiveness, littleness, minuteness. **2. neatness** dapperness. **3. shortness** dwarfishness, squatness, stumpiness. **4. runtiness** puniness, scrubbiness. **5. exiguousness** scantiness, skimpiness, slightness, spareness, sparsity. **6. insubstantiality** inconsiderableness, negligibleness, triflingness. **7. pettiness** meanness, niggardliness, sparingness, stinginess.

2.   **1. small amount** ambs-ace, jot, least, little, low, minimum, minimus. *Informal:* pennorth. **2. next to nothing** *Informal:* a fat lot, cat's whisker, damn-all. **3. tinge** lick, relish, smack, strain, taste, tincture, touch. **4. trace** cast, cue, dab, dash, dreg, hint, pointer, remnant, shadow, show, sign, soupçon, suspicion, thought, vestige. **5. skerrick** bit, fragment, grain, inch, iota, jot, particle, patch, pea, peppercorn, rag, rap, scrap, straw, tap, tittle. **6. spark** blink, gleam, scintilla. **7. hair's-breadth** a struck match, hair, hairbreadth. *Informal:* whisker. **8. sprinkling** fistful, handful, sprinkle. **9. pittance** mess of pottage, starvation wages. *Informal:* peanuts. **10. modicum** bit, pennyworth, pinch, scantling, smidgin, snip, snippet, soupçon, stiver, tot, trifle. **11. drop** dribble, driblet, nip. **12. point** dot, pinhead. **13. crumb** chip, morceau, morsel, nibble. *Informal:* droob. **14. sliver** paring, shavings, snippet. **15. grain** granule, nubbin *(US),* nubble, pellet. **16. atom** molecule, mote, nanoparticle, particle, whit. **17. speck** fleck, spot. **18. mouthful** spoonful, thimbleful.

3.   **1. small thing** diminutive, feather, featherweight, fingerling, midget, miniature, mite, pygmy. *Informal:* pipsqueak. **2. minutiae** detail. **3. splinter** flinders, matchwood, shiver, splinters. **4. microcosm** Lilliput.

4.   **1. small person** diminutive, dwarf, elf, gamine, half-pint, homunculus, hop-o'-my-thumb, Lilliputian, little person, manikin, midget, mite, pigmy, PORG, pygmy, squab, Tom Thumb, tot, wisp. *Informal:* midge, nugget, peanut, pipsqueak, shortie, shrimp, snippet, tiddler. **2. elf** brownie, devilkin, dwarf, elfin, fairy, fay, gnome, goblin, gremlin, hob, hobgoblin, imp, kobold, leprechaun, little people, pixie, puck, sprite, water sprite. **3. lightweight** bantam, featherweight. *Informal:* skeeter, titch. **4. runt** stunt. *Informal:* squirt.

adj. **5.**   **1. small** baby, diminutive, insignificant, little, microscopic, microscopical, mini, miniature, minuscule, minute, peerie *(Scottish),* petit, petite, pygmaean, pygmy, tiny, wee. *Informal:* dinky, ickle, itsy-bitsy, itty-bitty, pint-sized, small-time, teensy-weensy, teeny, teeny-weeny, titchy, two-by-four *(US),* weeny. **2. petite** dainty, dapper, delicate, elfin, fine, gamin, light, little, mignon, slender, slight, slim, small, tenuous, tiny. **3. undersized** dwarfish, puny, runty, short, stunted, underdeveloped, undersize. **4. scant** abbreviated, abstemious, brief, exiguous, limited, meagre, narrow, scanty, scrimpy, skimpy, small, spare, sparing, sparse, stingy, threadbare, wispish, wisplike, wispy. **5. compact** close, desktop, microcosmical, pocket size, small-scale. **6. Lilliputian** diminutive, dwarf, dwarfish, gnomish, pygmaean, pygmy, runty, tiny. **7. squat** dumpy, squab, squabby, squatty, stumpy. **8. incommodious** poky. **9. beady** beadlike, grain-like, grainy, granular, granulose.

6.   **1. smallest** least, low, minim, minimal, minimum, slightest. **2. inconsiderable** fractional, inappreciable, inessential, infinitesimal, insignificant, insubstantial, lightweight, marginal, minimal, minor, negligible, partial, slight, teensy, vestigial. **3. measly** *(Informal)* halfpenny, lousy, mere, paltry, petit, pettifogging, petty, sixpenny, slight, trifling. *Informal:* piddling, piffling, potty *(British).* **4. mean** cheeseparing, close, close-fisted, near, niggardly, penurious, stingy, tight-fisted. *Informal:* mingy, tight. **5. slight** certain. **6. cursory** superficial, tenuous. **7. bare** mere, no more than, only, very.

adv. **7.**   **1. negligibly** inconsiderably, infinitesimally, microscopically, vestigially. **2. scantily** exiguously, skimpily, slightly, sparingly, sparsely. **3. merely** alone, just, only, simply. **4. at least** in the least. **5. just** by degrees, by inches, hardly, merely. *Informal:* by the skin of one's teeth. **6. in a nutshell** in miniature.

RELATED KEYWORDS: DECREASE, SHORTNESS, THINNESS

SMELL

n. **1.** **1. smell** aroma, bouquet, fragrance, fumes, nose, odour, scent, snuff. **2. waft** odour, vapour, whiff. **3. scent** contrail, drag, flair, remnant, show, sign, smell, sniff, snuff, trace, trail, vestige. **4. sense of smell** flair *(Hunting)*, hyperosmia, nose, olfaction, scent.

2. **1. fragrance** aromaticity, balminess, deliciousness, essence, odoriferousness, odorousness, perfume, perfumery, redolence, savor, savour, savouriness, scent, spice *(Poetic)*, spicery, spiciness, sweet, sweetness, tang. **2. perfume** anisole, aromatic, balm, bath cube, bath salts, essence, essential oil, incense, joss stick, perfumery, scent. **3. cologne** angel water, bay rum, eau de Cologne, eau de toilette, lavender water, pomade, rosewater, toilet water. **4. pomander** lavender bag, potpourri, sachet. **5. buttonhole** bouquet, boutonniere, corsage, garland, nosegay, posy, spray. **6. censer** thurible. **7. breath-sweetener** breath-freshener, pastille.

3. **1. stench** fetor, foetor, funk *(US)*, malodour, odour, reek, smell, snuff, stink. *Informal:* niff, pong. **2. body odour** *Informal:* BO. **3. bad breath** halitosis. **4. malodorousness** cheesiness, fetidity, fetidness, nastiness, noisomeness, offensiveness, rancidity, rankness, ripeness. **5. mustiness** frowziness, fustiness, stuffiness. **6. miasma** effluvium, emanon, exhalation, gas, maremma, mephitis, mofette, reek, vapour. **7. stink bomb** adamsite, arsine, cacodyl, diphosgene, mustard gas, poison gas, yperite. **8. stinker** reeker, smeller. *Informal:* stinkpot.

4. **1. type of perfume** aloes, ambergris, attar, balsam, bergamot, calamus, camphorwood, cassie-flower, castor, cineol, civet, essence, eucalyptol, eucalyptus oil, eugenol, frangipanni, frankincense, ilang-ilang, iris, lavender, lilac, magnolia, menthol, mignonette, musk, myrrh, neroli oil, olibanum, orrisroot, patchouli, peppermint, rose, sassafras oil, scent, spikenard, violet, wintergreen, ylang-ylang.

adj. **5.** **1. fragrant** aromatic, balmy, odoriferous, odorous, perfumed, redolent, spicy, sweet, sweet-scented, sweet-smelling. **2. spicy** aloetic, aromatic, balsamaceous, balsamic, fragrant, gingery, moschate, musky. **3. strong** avid, fruity, heady, intense, nappy *(British)*, rich, warm. **4. garlicky** alliaceous.

6. **1. smelly** acrid, bilgy, cacodylic, fetid, filthy, foetid, funky, high, malodorous, mephitic, nasty, offensive, poohey, putrid, rammish, rancid, rank, reeky, ripe, rotten, stinking. *Informal:* a bit on the nose, cheesy, festy, on the bugle, on the nose, perishing, pongo, pongy, stinko, stinky, whiffy, whoofy. **2. stuffy** airless, anoxia, close-smelling, frowsty, frowzy, fusty, ill-smelling, moldy *(US)*, mouldy, mucid, musty. **3. effluvial** miasmal, miasmatic, miasmatical, miasmic.

7. **1. olfactory**.

v. **8.** **1. smell** breathe, get wind of, inbreathe, inhale, inspire, savour, scent, smell out, sniff, snuff, whiff.

9. **1. be smelly** nose, reek, reek of, smell, stink, stink out. *Informal:* honk like a gaggle of geese, hum, pong, smell like dead horse gully.

SMOOTHNESS

n. **1.** **1. smoothness** evenness. **2. sleekness** glassiness, lubricity, shininess, silkiness, slickness, slipperiness, velvetiness. **3. creaminess** fluency, greasiness. **4. glissade** glide, glissando, portamento, slide. **5. polish** glare, glaze, lustre, shine.

2. **1. smooth object** alabaster, byssus, eyeglasses, glass, gossamer, ice, marble, plate, satin, silk, slickensides, smooth, velure, velvet.

3. **1. smoother** comber, filer, glazer, grinder, planer, planisher, surfacer, trimmer, troweller. **2. polisher** furbisher, lapper, waxer. **3. putty powder** rottenstone. **4. file** bastard file, bath brick, block plane, compass plane, cropper, crosscut file, drove, emery board, emery cloth, emery paper, emery wheel, facer, facing tool, floatstone, glasspaper, grinder, grinding wheel, grindstone, hone, jack plane, land plane, nailfile, oilstone, plane, rasp, riffler, rubber, sandblast, sander, sanding machine, sandpaper, smoothing plane, steel wool, stone, strop, trimmer, wet and dry, whetstone, wire wool. **5. abrasive** abradant, carborundum. **6. smoothing device** battledore, box iron, bulldozer, calender, calfdozer, clothes press, comb, dozer, float, glazing, grader, hot-press, iron, jointer, lap, mouldboard, overglaze, rake, rolling pin, slicker, smoothing-iron, supercalender. **7. varnish** glaze, glazing, glost, lacquer, overglaze, tiger's eye. **8. shoe polish** shoeshine.

adj. **4.** **1. smooth** alabaster, satiny, silken, silky, sleek, sleeky, smug, soft, velutinous, velvet, velvet-like, velvety. **2. sleek** ganoid, glacé, glossy, lustrous, polished, satin, satin-like, satiny, sericeous, sheeny, shiny, silken, silky, sleeky, slick, smooth, smug, soft.

3. **glassy** glare, glazy, icy. 4. **slippery** greasy, icy, slithery. 5. **streamlined** fastback, flowing, fluent, profluent. 6. **glissando** gliding, legato. 7. **creamy** lubricious, lubricous, slick. *Informal:* slippy. 8. **even** fair, flat, flush, lamellar, lamellate, level, plain, plane, platelike, smooth, straight, tabular, tabulate, undisturbed. 9. **bald** baldish, bare, glabrate, glabrous, smooth, waterworn. 10. **ratite**. 11. **cold-rolled** coated. 12. **crease-resistant** siroset.

v. 5. 1. **smooth** compress, even, face, fettle, flush, laser, level, lubricate, manicure, pat, plane, planish, pumice, re-press, rub down, sleek, slick, smoothen, square, strike. 2. **sandpaper** arris, crop, drove, file, glasspaper, grate, gride, grind, mill, plane, rasp, sand, scrape, shave, trim. 3. **comb** rake. 4. **coat** lay, plate, surface. 5. **glaze** lacquer. 6. **pave** concrete, macadamise, seal. 7. **flatten** bulldoze, float, grade, trowel. 8. **press** calender, iron, iron out, roll. 9. **unwrinkle** sironise. 10. **polish** beeswax, buff, burnish, dub, French-polish, furbish, lustre, planish, rub up, shine, wax.

6. 1. **glide** coast, free-fall, freewheel, glissade, plane, run, skate, skim, slide, slip, slur.

adv. 7. 1. **smoothly** smooth. 2. **silkily** glassily, sleekly, slickly. 3. **flowingly** fluently, glidingly, legato. 4. **evenly** even.

RELATED KEYWORDS: OIL, PRESSURE, REGULARITY, RUBBING, BLUNTNESS

SOCIABILITY

n. 1. 1. **sociability** companionableness, conviviality, good fellowship, gregariousness, hospitableness, hospitality, party spirit, sociableness, sociality. 2. **cordiality** advances, approachability, approachableness, backslapping, bonhomie, cordialness, expansiveness, gladhanding, good humour, jollity, joviality, mellowness, merriment. 3. **association** company, society. 4. **social relations** camaraderie, commerce, communion, companionship, comradeship, consociation, fellowship, social intercourse, socialness, sodality, solidarity. 5. **open house** welcome.

2. 1. **revelry** celebration, festivity, jollification, revelling, revels, routs and revels, shindy, social occasion. *Informal:* chevoo, shivoo. 2. **party** après-ski, at-home, bienvenida *(Philippine English)*, birthday party, bottle party, conversazione, cracker night, gala, house-warming, junket, masque, meet and greet, potlatch, preparty, reunion, singsong, social, soiree, spree, tea-party, the turn, turnout, wayzgoose. *Informal:* barney, beanfeast, do, drunk, get-together, send-off, show, third half. 3. **dance** ball, barn-dance, dinner-dance, fancy-dress ball, fandango *(US)*, hoedown, mask, masked ball, masque, masquerade, ridotto. *Informal:* hop. 4. **house party** blanket party, pyjama party, slumber party. 5. **rort** bust-up. *Informal:* destroy party, destructo, ding, hooley, hui *(NZ)*. 6. **picnic** outdoor meal. 7. **barbecue** barby, chop picnic, clambake *(US)*, cookout *(US)*, fry *(US)*, luau, picnic races. *Informal:* barbie, sausage sizzle. 8. **drinks party** bowl, carousal, carouse, cocktail party, conviviality, drinks, jamboree, wassail. *Informal:* beer-up, booze-up, boozeroo *(NZ)*, grog-on, grog-up. 9. **wedding breakfast** reception. 10. **bucks' party** bucks' night, stag party. 11. **hens' party** bridal shower, hens' night, kitchen tea, shower tea. *Informal:* girls' night out. 12. **baby shower**. 13. **launch** opening night, premiere.

3. 1. **greeting** beck *(Scottish)*, bonjour, bow, cheerio, cheerio call, congé, hail, hongi, mihi, salaam, salutation, the glad hand. 2. **regards** compliment, remembrances. 3. **introduction** debut, presentation *(British)*, presentment. *Informal:* intro, knockdown.

4. 1. **sociable person** backslapper, convivialist, good mixer, hail-fellow-well-met, man about town, partygoer, social butterfly, socialite. *Informal:* gadabout.

adj. 5. 1. **sociable** amiable, approachable, cheerful, chummy, clubbable, companionable, convivial, cordial, friendly, good-humoured, gregarious, hearty, hospitable, livable, neighbourly, outgoing, social, societal, warm. *Informal:* folksy *(US)*. 2. **convivial** Anacreontic, bacchic, backslapping, blithesome, boon, expansive, festive, hail-fellow-well-met, high, jocund *(Poetic)*, jolly, jovial, merry, sociable, unrestrained. *Informal:* slaphappy. 3. **welcoming** greeting, salutatory.

v. 6. 1. **be sociable** accost, bow, gladhand, greet, hail, have the flags out, hello, mingle, recognise, rub noses *(NZ)*, salaam, shake hands with, tin kettle, welcome, wring someone's hand. 2. **meet** bump into, find, run across, run into, run up against. 3. **introduce** acquaint *(US)*, bring out, debut, offer, present. 4. **associate** consociate, consort, forgather, go out, keep company, mate, neighbour with, rub elbows with, rub shoulders with. 5. **ask out** date, woo. 6. **entertain** do the honours, give a party, host a party, keep open house, lunch, receive, regale, throw a party, treat. 7. **invite** ask, bid, cultivate, have in, have over. 8. **regale** delight, dine, do someone proud, serve, sup, treat. 9. **party on** racket. *Informal:* make whoopee, rage. 10. **socialise** circulate, come out of one's shell, commix, get about, get around, go around, mingle, mix, step out *(US)*, table-hop.

436

adv. **7.** **1. sociably** chummily, companionably, convivially, cordially, expansively, gregariously, heartily, hospitably, kindly, sincerely, socially, with open arms.

interj. **8.** **1. hello** aloha, ave, bonjour, good afternoon, good day, good evening, good morning, greetings, haere mai *(NZ)*, haeremai, hallo, heil, how-do-you-do, hullo, kia-ora *(NZ)*, tenakoe *(NZ)*, welcome. *Informal:* g'day, gidday, gooday, hi, how, how ya goin' (mate), how're the bots biting, how're you going, how's things, how's tricks, how-de-do, howdy *(Chiefly US)*, whassup, yello, yickadee *(NT)*. **2. bon appétit** all the best, cheers, chin-chin, good health, l'haim, skol, to your health. **3. goodbye** adieu, adios, bon voyage, bye, farewell, haere ra *(NZ)*, vale. *Informal:* Abyssinia, cheerio, ciao, hooroo, pip-pip *(British)*, see you later, so long, ta, toodle-loo, toodle-oo *(Chiefly British)*, tooroo.

RELATED KEYWORDS: ALCOHOL, COMPANIONSHIP, FRIENDLINESS, JOY

SOCIETY

n. **1.** **1. society** civilisation, culture, humanity, humankind, the general public, the people, the population, the public. **2. community** hamlet *(British)*, kraal, street, town. *Informal:* burg *(US)*. **3. clan** colony, demographic, general muster, house, kindred, nationality, people, plantation, primary group, race, rod, tribe. **4. commune** ashram, collective, cooperative, kibbutz, kolkhoz, village settlement. **5. class** caste, genus, league, order, stratum. **6. social system** matriarchate, matriarchy, patriarchate, patriarchy. **7. social subset** underclass.

2. **1. association** auxiliary, club, foundation, group, movement, sewing circle, society, sodality, tong. **2. alliance** affiliation, affinity group, alignment, axis, bloc, camp, clachan, coalition, combination, confederation, consortium, front, party, solidarity, union, united front. **3. interest group** lobby. **4. federation** commonwealth, confederacy, confederation, consociation, federacy, league, umbrella organisation. **5. branch** chapter, local *(US)*.

3. **1. crowd** confluence, gathering, multitude, press, ruck, throng. **2. band** association, caravan, choir, chorus, companionship, company, consociation, crew, crowd, fellowship, flock, gang, squad, tribe, troupe. **3. corps** army, body, brigade, cohort, legion, phalange, phalanx, regiment. **4. meeting** assembly, ceilidh, corroboree, gathering, jamboree, mass meeting, muster, online meet, parade, rally, unlawful assembly. *Informal:* flesh meet, get-together. **5. congregation** association, church, communion, ecclesia, fellowship, flock, fold, parish council, vestry. **6. reception** audience, durbar, levee.

4. **1. institute** academy, college, faculty *(US)*, juniorate, university college *(British)*. **2. guild** chapel, confraternity, court, craft, craft guild, livery company, lodge, trade, trade union. **3. fellowship** brotherhood, college, company, consociation, corporation, fraternity, guild, sisterhood, sodality, sorority *(US)*. **4. friendly society** benevolent association, benevolent society, cooperative society, housing association, provident society, service club.

5. **1. committee** board, caucus *(British)*, comitia, commission, panel, qango, quango, shop committee, standing committee, subcommittee, vigilance committee *(Chiefly US)*, works council. **2. conference** colloquium, colloquy, convention, forum, parley, pourparler, round table, seminar, summit, symposiac, symposium, talk, think tank, workshop. **3. quorum** plenum. **4. faction** arm, caucus, left wing, right wing, wing. **5. conclave** conventicle. **6. gang** camorra, mafia, shift, squad, tong. **7. picket line** line-up.

6. **1. clique** bunch, circle, cluster, clutch, coterie, crew, crowd, in-crowd, knot, outfit, smart set. *Informal:* rat pack. **2. cult** cultus, persuasion, push, sect. **3. cell** cabal, cadre, inner circle, inside. **4. connections** old boy network, old school tie. **5. salon** conversazione, reunion.

7. **1. corporation** body corporate, business house, conglomerate, enterprise, no-liability company, owners' corporation, public corporation, unincorporated association, unlimited company. **2. establishment** organisation, set-up. **3. cartel** combine, conference, consortium, monopoly, pool, ring, syndicate. **4. trading bloc** co-op, common market, EEC, farmers' cooperative, OPEC. **5. company** cast, crew, firm, line-up, outfit. **6. partnership** duumvirate, group practice, joint venture, triumvirate. **7. team** line-up, side, squad, troupe.

8. **1. amalgamation** consolidation, embodiment, federalisation, fusion, integration, merger, transgenesis, unification. **2. affiliation** filiation, membership. **3. institutionalism** officialism, regimentation.

adj. **9.** **1. societal** collective, combined, common, communal, cooperative, joint, mutual, social. **2. associational** associative, comitial, congregational, curial, institutional, institutionary, organisational. **3. allied** agnate, associated, coalition, common, federate, joint. **4. federal** combined, confederative, federalist, fusionist, league, unitarian, unitary, united. **5. corporate** corporative, incorporate, incorporated. **6. fraternal** comradely. *Informal:* matey. **7. intercommunity** interclub, interdepartmental. **8. tribal** tribalist, tribalistic. **9. cliquey** clannish, cliquish, incestuous.

v. 10.   **1. associate** bear company, combine, consociate, consort, forgather with, hobnob, keep company, keep in touch, mate, mingle, partner, rub shoulders with, socialise, stay in touch, take up with, troop with. **2. rally** associate, forgather, meet, rendezvous. **3. club** band, band together, cartelise, clique, hang together, hold together, league, merge, organise, squadron, syndicate, troop, unite. *Informal:* gang, gang up. **4. affiliate** align, aline, ally, associate, enlist, filiate, fraternise, identify with, join, link, nail one's colours to the mast, take sides, unite. **5. federate** confederate, federalise, pull together. **6. unite** associate, coalesce, combine, consolidate, enter into, federate, merge, pool, syncretise. **7. organise** embody, incorporate, institutionalise, unionise. **8. join up** enlist, enrol, join the colours, sign on, take out membership. **9. jump on the band wagon** climb on the band wagon, get with the strength.

adv. 11.   **1. communally** associatively, collectively, jointly, mutually, reciprocally, shoulder to shoulder, together, unitedly. **2. federally** corporately. **3. clannishly** brotherly, cliquishly, fraternally, tribally.

RELATED KEYWORDS: COUNCIL, COOPERATION, PARTNER, COMMERCE, TRADE UNION

SOFTNESS

n. 1.   **1. softness** downiness, flocculence, silkiness, velvetiness. **2. suppleness** ductility, flexibleness, floppiness, malleableness, plasticity, pliableness, pliantness, tractableness, tractility. **3. delicateness** tenderness. **4. laxness** laxation, laxity, mellowness, mildness. **5. tenderness** soft-heartedness. **6. friableness** mealiness. **7. smooth texture** butteriness, creaminess. **8. mushiness** doziness, fleshiness, pulpiness, rottenness, sectility, sponginess. **9. stodginess** doughiness. **10. softening** emollition, laxation, maceration, mollescence.

    2.   **1. softener** macerator, plasticiser, tenderiser.

adj. 3.   **1. soft** cottony, downy, floccose, flocculent, flocky, flossy, pillow-like, pillowy, silken, silky, sleek, smooth, spongy, tender, velutinous, velvet, velvet-like, velvety. **2. delicate** lacerable, soft, tender. **3. crumbly** crumby, floury, friable, loose, mealy, mellow, powdery. **4. plastic** bendy, ductile, elastic, flexible, flexile, floppy, lax, limber, lissom, lithe, malleable, pliable, pliant, pulvinar, semiplastic, supple, thermoplastic, tractable, tractile, waxen, whippy, willowish, willowy. **5. smooth** buttery, creamy. **6. mushy** dozy, fenny *(British)*, fleshy, fluctuant, lush, marshy, mush-like, pithy, plashy, pulpy, sloppy, splashy, spongy, springy, unset. *Informal:* squidgy. **7. doughy** sodden, stodgy. **8. emollient** mollescent, softening. **9. mellowed** mild.

v. 4.   **1. soften** defreeze, defrost, emolliate, macerate, melt, pulp, repulp, tenderise, thaw, unfreeze. **2. cushion** ease, pad, pillow, upholster. **3. mellow** milden.

adv. 5.   **1. delicately** silkily, tenderly. **2. flexibly** floppily, laxly. **3. pliably** plastically, pliantly, supply, tractably. **4. mildly** mellowly. **5. mushily** lushly.

RELATED KEYWORDS: PLIABILITY, PULP, SLUDGE

SOLIDITY

n. 1.   **1. solidity** closeness, coagulation, cohesion, compaction, concretion, condensation, congealment, congelation, constringency, denseness, density, grossness, intensity, ply, relative density, solidness, specific gravity, thickness. **2. solidification** eburnation, freezing, gelation, inspissation, thickening. **3. impenetrability** impenetrableness, impermeability, impermeableness, imperviousness.

    2.   **1. solid body** adamant, amorphous, bezoar, body, bunch, cake, chunk, clod, clot, clump, cluster, concrete, concretion, condensate, conglomerate, conglomeration, gastrolith, gob, grume, hard core, hunk, lump, mass, nubbin *(US)*, phytobezoar, resinoid, sphacelus, substance, wad. *Informal:* dollop, gollion. **2. clot** blood clot, DVT, grume, lump, thrombosis. **3. curds** coagulation, coagulum, concretion, congelation.

    3.   **1. solidifier** alginic acid, coagulant, coagulator, condenser, congealer, thickener, thickening. **2. densimeter** Baumé scale, hydrometer, pycnometer, pyknometer, saccharometer, salinometer, spindle, vinometer.

adj. 4.   **1. solid** caked, close, close-grained, compact, condensed, dense, gross, heavy, thick, thickish. *Informal:* so thick you can cut it with a knife. **2. concretionary** constringent. **3. impenetrable** athermanous, concrete, impermeable, impervious, proof. **4. clotted** clotty, coagulated, curdy, grumous. **5. condensable** congealable.

v. **5.** **1. solidify** bind, cluster, cohere, conglomerate, full. **2. clot** coagulate, congeal, curd, curdle. **3. curdle** clabber, coagulate, congeal, curd. **4. thicken** cake, coagulate, concrete, condense, congeal, curd, curdle, inspissate, set, silt, silt up.

adv. **6.** **1. solidly** hard, impenetrably, impermeably, imperviously. **2. densely** grossly, heavily, stodgily, thick, thickly.

RELATED KEYWORDS: HARDNESS, MATTER, THICKNESS

SOLITUDE

n. **1.** **1. solitude** desolateness, desolation, disconsolateness, distance, friendlessness, isolation, loneliness, lonesomeness, obscureness, obscurity, reclusion, remoteness, secludedness, solitariness. **2. aloofness** distance, insularity, introversion, ivory tower, privacy, reserve, reticence, retirement, seclusion, secrecy, sequestration. **3. withdrawal** hibernation, relegation, retirement, rustication, seclusion, segregation, sequestration.

2. **1. seclusion** isolation, privacy, purdah, quarantine, retirement, secrecy, solitude. **2. private place** a world of one's own, cloister, closet, holy of holies, inner sanctum, ivory tower, nook, recesses, sanctum, sanctum sanctorum. **3. place of refuge** asylum, bolthole, harbour, hideaway, hidey-hole, refuge, retreat, sanctuary. *Informal:* funk-hole. **4. cloister** convent, hermitage, monastery, monkery, nunnery. **5. remote place** backwater, desert island, far(flung) corner of the earth, jumping-off place *(US)*, the end of the earth, ultima Thule. *Informal:* the back of beyond, the back of Bourke.

3. **1. solitary person** hatter, introvert, isolate, lone, lone wolf, loner, maverick, skulker. *Informal:* trog, troglodyte. **2. hermit** anchoress, anchoret, anchorite, ascetic, eremite, incluse, monk, recluse, seclusionist, solitary. **3. castaway** maroon. **4. lonely heart** wallflower. *Informal:* a lily on the dustbin, a rose on the rubbish tip. **5. isolationist** little Englander.

adj. **4.** **1. solitary** anchoritic, ascetic, ascetical, cloistered, eremitic, eremitical, eremitish, hermitic, hermitical, incommunicado, lonely, monkish, out of circulation, private, recluse, reclusive, remote, retired, secluded, separate, single, solo. **2. antisocial** asocial, coy, farouche, inimical, reclusive, reserved, retiring, shy, strange, troglodytic, unfriendly, unsociable, withdrawn. **3. aloof** abstracted, apart, disinterested, distant, ill-disposed, reclusive, remote, removed, stand-off, stand-offish, unapproachable, unfriendly, unsympathetic. *Informal:* offish. **4. lonely** friendless, insular, introversive, introvert, isolative, lone *(Poetic)*, lonesome *(Chiefly US)*, misanthropic, shy, single, solitary, unfriended. *Informal:* like a bandicoot on a burnt ridge, like a shag on a rock.

5. **1. secluded** claustral, cloister-like, cloistered, cloistral, in private, lonely, monachal, monasterial, monastic, monkish, on one's lonesome, out-of-the-way, outlying, remote, retired, seclusive, sequestered, single, solitary, withdrawn. **2. secret** closet, interior, private, privy. **3. remote** deserted, desolate, distant, far from the madding crowd, far-off, godforsaken, isolated, lonely, obscure, out-of-the-way, outlandish, removed, secluded, unmanned. **4. unfrequented** buried, concealed, hidden, latent, obscure, off the beaten track, off the map, sequestered, solitary, tucked-away.

v. **6.** **1. seclude** cloister, closet, cut adrift, dissever, insulate from, isolate, quarantine, relegate, rusticate, separate, sequester, shut away, sunder, warehouse. **2. retreat** beat a retreat, go to ground, hibernate, lie low, retire, shut out the world, skulk, withdraw. *Informal:* bunker, bunker down, hole up, pull one's head in, take to the hills. **3. repel** forbid, hold off, insulate oneself from, keep a low profile, keep at arm's length, keep away, withdraw from. **4. be isolated** be in a world of one's own, be off the beaten track. **5. be antisocial** go it alone, keep one's distance, keep one's own counsel, keep oneself to oneself.

adv. **7.** **1. solitarily** alone, lonelily, lonesomely, out on a limb, single-handed, solo. *Informal:* like a lily on a dustbin, on one's ace, on one's pat, on one's Pat Malone. **2. antisocially** aloof, aloofly, distantly, insularly, remotely.

8. **1. secludedly** ascetically, hermitically, monastically, monkishly, reclusively, seclusively. **2. privately** backstage, behind the scenes, in secret, on the side, on the sly, out of court, secretly. *Informal:* on the q.t.

RELATED KEYWORDS: ABSTINENCE, UNFRIENDLINESS, HIDING, ONE, SECRECY

SOMBRENESS

n. **1.** **1. sombreness** bleakness, dismalness, dullness, greyness, grimness, melancholy, pensiveness, sourness, wintriness. *Informal:* dismals. **2. austereness** austerity, harshness, rigorousness, rigour, severeness, severity. **3. sternness** dourness, mirthlessness. **4. soberness** demureness, sedateness, seriousness, sobermindedness, sobriety.

5. solemnity deepness, depth, earnestness, graveness, gravity, impressiveness, seriousness, severity, sobriety, solemness. **6. solemnification** solemnify, solemnisation.

2. 1. sobersides *(Informal)* Job's comforter, owl, straight man. *Informal:* boy scout. **2. wowser** damper, depressor, killjoy, spoilsport, wet blanket. *Informal:* party pooper, snufflebuster, sod, sourpuss, streak of misery.

adj. **3. 1. sombre** black, bleak, cheerless, crestfallen, dark, depressing, desolate, dismal, dispiriting, dour, drab, embittered, funereal, gaunt, gloomy, grey, grizzled, heavy, joyless, melancholic, melancholy, morose, mournful, murky, sad, serious, solemn, sour, stark, sulky, sunless, wintry, wistful. **2. solemn** awful, deep, grave, grim, heavy, severe. **3. sedate** austere, calm, composed, decorous, demure, disimpassioned, down-to-earth, impassive, low-key, museful, owl-like, owlish, possessed, quiet, regardful, self-composed, self-contained, self-controlled, sensible, serene, serious, sober, soberminded, staid, steady, subdued, thoughtful, tranquillo, unfussed, unmoved, unruffled. **4. stern** austere, dour, frowning, gloomy, hard, humourless, iron, joyless, lowering, mirthless, plutonian, severe.

adv. **4. 1. sombrely** gravely, gravemente, heavily, heavy, seriously, solemnly.

RELATED KEYWORDS: ABSTINENCE, UNHAPPINESS, GRIEF, HARSHNESS

SOUND

n. **1. 1. sound** beat, lull, noise, sonance, sonant, tone, voice, vox. **2. complex sound** chord, combination tone, harmonics. **3. sonority** concord, consonance, euphonicalness, euphoniousness, euphony, harmonisation, harmony, homophony, sonorousness, syntony. **4. assonance** alliteration, echoism, eye rhyme, onomatopoeia, rhyme. **5. melody** air, tune.

2. 1. acoustics acoustic, acoustic impedance, audio, phonics, subsonics, supersonics, tonometry, ultrasonics. **2. monophonic sound** mono, quadraphonics, quadrophony, stereo, stereophony. **3. soundwave** envelope, wave train. **4. audio frequency** amplitude, high frequency, wave number, wavelength. **5. diffraction** dispersal, dispersion, equalisation. **6. sonagraph** photospectroscope, Rayleigh disc, sound spectrograph, spectrograph, spectrogram, speech spectrogram, speech spectrograph, tonometer. **7. bel** decibel, phon. **8. magnetic sound** optical sound. **9. synthesiser** ondes Martenot, oscillator, tuning fork.

3. 1. sound system audio system, boom box, Dolby system, ghetto-blaster, hi-fi system, music system, playback, stereo. *Informal:* stack. **2. gramophone** changer, jukebox, nickelodeon, phonautograph, record-changer, record-player, stereogram, turntable. **3. stylus** cartridge, crystal, crystal pick-up, magnetic pick-up, pick-up, pick-up arm, soundbox. **4. radio** radio-cassette, radiogram, radiotelegraphy, radiotelephony, tuner, two-way, wireless, wireless set. *Informal:* rock box. **5. amplifier** lock-in amplifier, preamp, preamplifier, preselector. *Informal:* amp, box, brick. **6. speaker** exponential horn, horn, loudspeaker, tweeter, tweeter-woofer, woofer. **7. tone control** dolby system, fuzz box, graphic equaliser, mixer, VU meter. **8. tape-recorder** cassette deck, cassette recorder, dictaphone, magnetic recorder, recorder, recording head, reel-to-reel, tape deck, walkman, wire recorder. **9. reel** audiocassette, cartridge, cassette, pick-up, spool, take-up spool, video cassette. **10. electromagnetic tape** magnetic tape, tape, tape loop, tape recording.

4. 1. recording album, audio book, audiotape, cover version, digital recording, disc, gramophone record, LP, MIDI, MP3, pressing, record, soundtrack, take, telerecording, WAV, wild track. *Informal:* vinyl. **2. LP** 12-inch, 45, 7-inch, 78, A side, album, B side, black disc, cassingle, cd, compact disc, digital disc, DVD, EP, extended play, flip side, forty-five, laser disc, long-playing, mono, one-track, optical disc, quadradisc, seventy-eight, single, thirty-three. **3. track** cut, groove, microgroove, run-in groove. **4. smash-hit** bullet, chart-buster, gold, gold record, gorilla *(Chiefly US)*, platinum record, smash, top forty, top ten. **5. sound library** discography.

5. 1. microphone bug, contact microphone, hydrophone, pick-up, radiophone, thermophone, throat microphone. *Informal:* mic, mike. **2. resonator** cavity resonator, resonant cavity, reverb, reverberation unit, reverberator, rhumbatron, sound post, soundboard, sounding-board. **3. public-address system** bullhorn, loudhailer, loudspeaker, megaphone, PA, speaker, speaking trumpet, tannoy *(British)*.

adj. **6. 1. acoustic** bass, euphonic, phonic, sonant, sonantal, soniferous, syllabic, unplugged, vocal, voiced. **2. audible** articulate, candid, clear, distinct, heard, loud, plain, unmistakable. **3. sonic** infrasonic, subsonic, supersonic, ultrasonic. **4. homophonic** polyphonic, symphonic.

7. **1. audio** heterodyne, hi-fi, high-fidelity, laser, lo-fi, mono, monophonic, quadraphonic, quadrasonic, stereo, stereophonic. **2. gramophonic** phonautographic, phonographic. **3. megaphonic** microphonic.

v. 8. **1. sound** articulate, assonate, cipher, phonate, strike, strike up, vocalise. **2. attune** euphonise, pitch, syntonise, tone. **3. lower the pitch** depress, flatten, sink. **4. raise the pitch** sharpen. **5. record** lay down a track, mix.
RELATED KEYWORDS: EXPLOSION, HEARING, HISSING, LOUDNESS, QUIETNESS, MUSIC, DISSONANCE, RESONANCE, SHOUTING, SHRILLNESS

SOURNESS

n. 1. **1. sourness** acidity, astringency, austereness, sharpness, subacidity, subacidness, tartness. **2. bitterness** acerbity. **3. saltiness** brackishness, brininess, salinity. **4. acidulation** acidification. **5. acid** bitters, brine, gall, lemon, vinegar.

adj. 2. **1. sour** acerbic, acetous, acid, acidic, acidulous, acidy, astringent, bitter, lemon, sharp, sourish, subacid, tart, tartish, vinegar-like, vinegarish, vinegary. **2. bitter** acerbic, bitterish, bittersweet, sour. **3. salty** brackish, brinish, briny, saliferous, saline, salt, saltish, saltlike. **4. dry** brut, demi-sec, flinty, sec, unsweetened. **5. rough** austere, harsh. **6. unripe** green, immature.

v. 3. **1. sour** acerbate, acetify, acidify, acidulate, bitter, brine, embitter, envenom, pickle, salt, vinegar.
RELATED KEYWORDS: PLEASANT FLAVOUR, UNPLEASANT FLAVOUR, FOOD, TASTE

SPACE

n. 1. **1. space** air space, elbow-room, floor space, head room, heliosphere, houseroom, lebensraum, leg room, play, room, room to breathe, room to move, sea room, serene, standing room. **2. scope** ambit, area, compass, extent, free (or full) rein, range, room, verge. **3. expanse** acreage, area, continuum, field, open, vastitude. **4. storage** boxroom, lumber-room, magazine, roomage, stowage. **5. roominess** commodiousness, spaciousness, wideness, width. **6. spatiality** 3-d, three-dimensionality. **7. vacuum** blank, free space, vacuity, void. **8. space-time** continuum, four-dimensional continuum, hyperspace, Minkowski universe, Minkowski world, parallel universe, subspace.

2. **1. area** ambit, circumference, circumscription, compass, cubic measure, dimensions, extent, girth, length, magnitude, quantity, range, scope, solid geometry, specific volume, spread, third dimension, volume. **2. hectare** acre, are, hektare, hide, pole, square. **3. square measure** acreage, floor space, floorage.

adj. 3. **1. spacious** commodious, expansive, extended, extensive, immense, large, oceanic, open, roomy, unrestrained, vast, vasty *(Poetic)*, wide. *Informal:* ginormous, humungous. **2. spatial** 3-D, four-dimensional, space, three-dimensional, tridimensional, two-dimensional.

adv. 4. **1. spaciously** abroad, commodiously, expansively, roomily, spatially, three-dimensionally, widely.
RELATED KEYWORDS: THE BUSH, SKY, LENGTH, REGION

SPEECH

n. 1. **1. speech** breath, breathing, dialect, expression, language, locution, mouth, oration, speaking, talk, tongue, utterance, vocalisation, voice, word. **2. expression** accent, cadence, close, delivery, diction, imperfect cadence, intonation, note, phraseology, phrasing, reading, recital, tone, upspeak, wording. **3. talk** causerie, communion, conversation, language, small talk, words. *Informal:* lingo, pyalla, say, yabber. **4. comment** ejaculation, exclamation, interjection, observation, phrase, quip, remark. **5. whisper** aside, breath, stage whisper, susurration. **6. emphasis** accent, primary accent, primary stress, secondary accent, secondary stress, stress. **7. somniloquy** sleep talking. **8. pronunciation** accent, articulation, diction, distinctness, enouncement, enunciation, phonation, utterance. **9. fluency** articulateness, competence, competency, vocalism, vocality, vocalness. **10. loquacity** blab, cackle, chat, chatter, clack, claver *(Scottish)*, gibberish, humdrum, logorrhoea, palaver, patter, prattle, spiel, talkativeness. *Informal:* gab, gas, jabber, jaw, natter, yap. **11. gibberish** abracadabra, babble, blather, blither, burble, drivel, gabble, twaddle. *Informal:* double-dutch, doubletalk, gobbledegook, guff, slipslop, waffle. **12. phonetics** acoustic phonetics, articulatory phonetics, orthoepy, perceptual phonetics, phonemics, phonology, syllabism.

2. **1. accent** brogue, burr, drawl, flection, inflection, inflexion, talk, tongue. **2. dialect** dialecticism, foreignism *(US)*, localism, patois, talk, tongue. *Informal:* slanguage. **3. lect** acrolect,

basilect, mesolect. **4. Standard English**. **5. International English** Basic English. **6. British English** BBC English, Estuary English, Oxford English, Received Pronunciation, Received Standard English, RP, the King's English, the Queen's English. **7. Australian English** broad Australian, cultivated Australian, general Australian, modified Australian. *Informal:* Strine. **8. Aboriginal English**. **9. American English** African American English, Afro-American English, American Black English, Black English, Black English Vernacular, Valley speak *(Chiefly US)*, Valspeak. **10. Englishes** Chinglish, Denglish, Franglais, Japlish, Manglish, Singlish, Taglish.

3. **1. speaker** native speaker, sayer, talker, vocaliser, voicer. **2. exclaimer** ejaculator, quipster. **3. reciter** articulator, deliverer, elocutionist, enunciator. **4. drawler** snuffler. **5. babbler** blabber, gossip, patterer, tittle-tattle, twaddler, whisperer. *Informal:* blabbermouth, earbasher, motormouth. **6. ranter** blusterer, haranguer.

4. **1. speech sound** affricate, affricative, allomorph, allophone, alveolar, approximant, aspirate, atonic, bilabial, cacuminal, cerebral, click, consonant, dental, dentilingual, diaphone, diphthong, ejective, enclitic, fortis, fricative, gingival, glide, glottic, guttural, homophone, indeterminate vowel, ingressive, labial, labiodental, labionasal, labiovelar, laminal, lenis, liquid, monophthong, mouillé, mute, nasal, obstruent, occlusive, orinasal, palatal, phone, plosive, postvocalic, r-colour, retroflex, schwa, semivowel, sibilant, sonant, sonorant, stop, suction stop, supraglottal, surd, syllabic, syllable, systole, triphthong, ultima, uvular, velar, vocal, vowel, yogh.

5. **1. diacritic** acute, breve, cedilla, circumflex, diaeresis, dieresis, grave, háček, macron, mutation, primary stress, rough breathing, secondary stress, smooth breathing, soft breathing, spiritus asper, spiritus lenis, tilde, tonic accent, umlaut.

6. **1. pronunciation** affrication, aspiration, breath, breathing, closure, connected speech, devocalisation, diphthongisation, dissimilation, elision, enunciation, epenthesis, fainting, frication, glide, haplology, inversion, labialisation, lenition, nasalisation, occlusion, palatalisation, plosion, r-colour, retroflexion, rough breathing, semivowel, smooth breathing, syllabification, synaeresis, synaloepha, syncope, syneresis, synizesis, velarisation, velation. **2. voice quality** buzzing, drone, gruffness, gutturalness, hoarseness, humming, monotone, nasality, roup, shake, snuffle, trachyphonia, trill, twang.

adj. 7. **1. spoken** articulate, nuncupative, oral, parol, phonatory, pronounced, speaking, verbal, viva-voce, vocal, voiced. **2. speakable** effable, enunciable, pronounceable, utterable, vocable. **3. pronunciational** orthoepic. **4. interjectory** ejaculative, ejaculatory, exclamatory, interjectional. **5. phonal** phonemic, phonetic, phonic, phonogrammatic, phonologic, vocal, vocalic, vowel-like. **6. homophonous** dissimilative.

8. **1. articulated** back, broad, close, closed, dark, free, front, hard, high, labialised, low, narrow, neutral, rough, rounded, stopped, unilateral, unrounded, weak. **2. voiced** lenis, soft, vibrant, vocal. **3. unvoiced** breathed, fortis, surd, voiceless. **4. accented** sonant, sonantal, syllabic, tonic. **5. hoarse** gruff, guttural, ragged.

v. 9. **1. speak** articulate, babble, burr, cantillate, chant, confide, deadpan, dictate, drivel, drone, emit, enounce, enunciate, execrate, express, give tongue to, give voice to, groan, iterate, lilt, murmur, mutter, narrate, outspeak, phonate, platitudinise, pronounce, rave, relate, report, revile, rhapsodise, say, simper, sing, smirk, snigger, snivel, snort, snuffle, sob, soliloquise, sound, state, syllable, talk, tell, tongue, utter, vent, ventriloquise, vocalise, vociferate, voice, whimper, whisper, yaffle, yawn. *Informal:* give, go, pyalla, wisecrack, yabber. **2. think aloud** soliloquise. **3. recite** chant, cite, intonate, intone, rhapsodise, say, sing. **4. dictate** deliver, elocute, give out, intonate, pass, pronounce, proverb, read, say, speak, utter. *Informal:* trot out. **5. speak of** mention, name, relate, report, tell, tell of. **6. comment** advert, allow *(US)*, express, observe, outspeak, pass comment, pass comment on, pass comment upon, quote, rejoin, remark, say, state, talk off the top of one's head, vent, ventilate, weigh one's words. **7. said**. **8. talk** chatter, clatter, get on one's soapbox, get up on the stump, go on, gossip, harangue, mag, natter, prate, preach at, rattle, talk nineteen to the dozen, tongue, twaddle. *Informal:* bend someone's ear, blow down someone's lug, chew someone's ear, chinwag, crap, crap on, earbash, jaw, jawbone, yabber. **9. exclaim** ejaculate, gasp. **10. chatter** babble, blab, blabber, blather, blether *(British)*, burble, clack, dribble, drivel, footle, gabble, gossip, jabber, mag, natter, patter, prattle, talk, tattle, twaddle, yap, yip *(Chiefly US)*. *Informal:* gab, jaw. **11. blurt** blunder, bolt, come out with, drop, jerk out. **12. snap** hurl, rasp, snarl, spit, throw out. *Informal:* spit it out. **13. whine** bleat, blubber, cant, grizzle, grumble, mutter, snivel, snuffle, whinge. *Informal:* beef *(Chiefly US)*, bellyache, bitch, gripe, grouse, moan, yammer. **14. whisper** breathe, lip, mumble, murmur, peek, peep, sigh. **15. shout** raise one's voice, yell. **16. slur** burr, drawl, twang. **17. buzz** croak, drone, hum, purr, squark, thrum.

10. **1. pronounce** accidence, affricate, articulate, aspirate, assonate, conjugate, denasalise, devocalise, devoice, diphthongise, dissimilate, elide, enunciate, implode, inflect, labialise, monophthongise, nasalise, palatalise, pass, roll, round, sibilate, syllabicate, syllabify, syllabise, tongue, trill, unround, unvoice, velarise, velate.

RELATED KEYWORDS: ELOQUENCE, BOMBAST, LANGUAGE, NONSENSE, TALKATIVENESS, WORD

SPEED

n. **1.** **1. speed** celerity, fastness, fleetness, quickness, rapidity, speediness, swiftness. *Informal:* lick, toe. **2. promptness** dispatch, expedition, expeditiousness, immediateness, promptitude, smartness, summariness. **3. haste** cursoriness, hastiness, helter-skelter, hurriedness, hurry, hurry-scurry, precipitancies, precipitancy, precipitateness, precipitation, rush, stampede. **4. briskness** activeness, agility, alacrity, lightness, mercurialness, nimbleness, sharpness, slippiness, snappiness.

2. **1. rate** cadence, pace, rhythm, tempo, time. *Informal:* clip. **2. quick time** double time *(US Army)*, quick march. **3. rush** whirl. **4. scamper** bolt, dart, scud, scurry, whisk. *Informal:* scoot. **5. gallop** canter, lope, romp, sprint, stride, tantivy. **6. run** hit-out, schuss. *Informal:* burn, fang, spin. **7. walking pace** amble, footpace.

3. **1. velocity** airspeed, airspeed indicator, angular acceleration, angular momentum, angular velocity, burnout velocity, characteristic velocity, critical velocity, escape velocity, flap speed, geostrophic wind speed, gradient wind speed, ground speed, group velocity, line-of-sight velocity, motion, muzzle velocity, orbital velocity, phase velocity, radial velocity, stall speed, terminal velocity, velocity of light. **2. mach** mach number, sonic barrier, sound barrier, speed of sound. **3. knot** k.p.h.

4. **1. speedster** *(Informal)* darter, dasher, fleer, flier, flitter, galloper, Jehu, racer, rusher, speeder, speeler, sprinter. *Informal:* goer, speed-merchant. **2. pacesetter** pacemaker, pacer. **3. express** clipper, flier. *Informal:* blue streak, hot rod. **4. expediter** hastener, rusher.

5. **1. accelerator** pedal, quickener, tandem generator, throttle.

6. **1. speedometer** amphometer, dumaresq, log, log chip, log line, machmeter, Pitot tube, radar trap, tacheometer, tachograph, tachometer, tachymeter. *Informal:* speedo, tacho.

adj. **7.** **1. speedy** allegro, arrowy, blistering, cracking, express, fast, fast-forward, fast-track, fleet, high-speed, jet-propelled, meteoric, nimble, pacy, presto, quick, rapid, rapid-fire, swift, tantivy, ton-up, wingy. *Informal:* nippy, toey. **2. spanking** double-quick, furious, raking, tripping. *Informal:* clipping. **3. brisk** alacritous, briskish, expeditious, prompt, quick, sharp, smacking, smart, snappy. **4. hurried** hasty, headlong, helter-skelter, hurry-scurry, precipitant, precipitate, rush. *Informal:* go-go-go. **5. nimble** active, agile, alert, feathered, fleet, fleet-footed, flitting, flying, light on one's feet, meteoric, quick, rapid, swift, swift-footed, wingy. *Informal:* slippy, whippy, zippy. **6. clipper-built** racing, rakish, streamlined. **7. transonic** hypersonic, relativistic, subsonic, supersonic.

v. **8.** **1. speed** clip, dart, fast-track, flash, fleet, fly, hasten, hotfoot, hurry, hurtle, lope, pelt, post, romp, scud, scurry, skirr, skitter, slip, spank, spin, whip, whirl. *Informal:* bat, bat along, bowl along, go like the clappers, hightail it *(Chiefly US)*, hike along, pike, scoot, shift, spear, spear on, tear, travel, zap, zip. **2. drive fast** fang along, pelt, rocket, streak. *Informal:* barrel along, beetle along, belt along, break the sound barrier, burl, crack on sail, do a ton, fang, flat-chat, give it a rap, go like a bomb, go like a rocket, go through on the padre's bike, herb *(US)*, hunt along, rip, scorch. **3. dart** dive, flit, glint, leap, play, pounce. *Informal:* pop up, scoot. **4. scamper** chivvy, clatter, rattle, scramble, scurry, scutter, scuttle. **5. run** chivvy, course, double, double-time, hare, hotfoot it, make the running, pace, race, scamper, schuss, scour, sprint, step out. *Informal:* lam *(US)*, run like a hairy goat. **6. stampede** bolt, career, rampage.

9. **1. hurry** be quick off the mark, bicker, come along, come on, dash, drive, fast-track, flash, fling, hasten, hie, hurry-scurry, lash, look lively (or sharp), make haste, rack, run, rush, sally forth, shoot, swash. *Informal:* bust a gut, chase, get a move on, get a wriggle on, get one's skates on, get the hell out of, hop to it, jump to it, make it snappy, p.o.q., put one's best foot forward, shake a leg, thrash along. **2. expedite** express *(Chiefly US)*, hasten, hurry, speed. **3. spur** accelerate, brisk up, gee up, hurry, hustle, press, quicken. *Informal:* boot home, buck up.

10. **1. accelerate** gun, race. *Informal:* give it herbs *(US)*, put the pedal to the metal, rap, step on it, step on the gas. **2. quicken** pick up, rally.

adv. **11.** **1. speedily** apace, by leaps and bounds, fast, fleetly, hotfoot, meteorically, pell-mell, quickly, rapidly, swiftly. *Informal:* at a fair bat, at a rate of knots, at warp speed, lickety-split *(Chiefly US)*, like a bat out of hell, like a bird, like a house on fire, like a shot, like billyo, like greased lightning, like mad, like one thing, move like a scalded cat.

2. briskly actively, agilely, nimbly, quickly, sharp, snap, snappily. **3. flittingly** dartingly, trippingly. **4. flat out** *(Informal)* at full speed, full sail, headlong, tantivy. *Informal:* flat chat, flat out like a lizard drinking, flat strap, for the lick of one's life, full bore, full chat, full fling, full pelt, hell for leather, in nothing flat. **5. in double time** at the double, doppio movimento, double-quick. **6. accelerando** agitato, allegretto, allegro, mosso, prestissimo, presto, veloce.

12. 1. hurriedly cursorily, hastily, hectically, helter-skelter, hurryingly, in haste, on the fly *(US)*, precipitantly, precipitously, summarily. **2. all at once** pop, sharp, slam-bang, slap, subito, suddenly. *Informal:* slap-bang, smack. **3. promptly** activity, asap, at once, be quick off the mark, directly, forthwith, immediately, in short order, instantly, presto, pronto, quick smart, quickly, readily, right away, smartly, soon, straightaway, yarely. **4. express** expeditiously, posthaste.

interj. **13. 1. hurry up** look lively, look sharp. *Informal:* chop chop *(Chiefly British)*, get a move on, get a wriggle on, giddy-up, jump to it, look alive, make it snappy, mush, pull your finger out, rattle your dags, tantivy *(Chiefly British)*.

RELATED KEYWORDS: FLYING, MOVEMENT, TRAVEL

SPIN

n. **1. 1. spin** backspin, overspin, side, tail spin, top, top spin, turning, underspin. **2. twist** spin, turn, twiddle, twirl, whirl, whirlabout. **3. spinning** burling, centrifugation, gyration, revolution, rotation, twisting, whirling, winding. **4. swirl** eddy, puddle, purl, ripple, whirl. **5. eddy** maelstrom, vortex, whirlpool. **6. catherine-wheel** girandole, millwheel, pinwheel. **7. propeller** impeller, screw, screw-propeller. *Informal:* prop. **8. waterwheel** fly, flywheel, windmill. **9. spinner** gyro, gyroscope, gyrostat, peg top, reel, teetotum, top, twirler. **10. cyclone** cockeye bob, dust devil, tornado, tourbillion, twister *(US)*, typhoon, whirlwind, whirly wind, whirly-whirly, willy-willy.

2. 1. rotation autorotation, circulation, circumrotation, circumvolution, free rotation, precession, retortion, revolution, rolling, turning. **2. pronation** supination. **3. turning power** torc. **4. circuit** circle, cycle, equatorial, gyre, orbit, ring.

3. 1. spiral helix, screw, screw thread, spire, thread, turbinate, twist, volute. **2. curl** scroll, verticil, whorl. **3. convolution** circination, circumvolution, involution, obvolution, sinuation, whorl, winding.

4. 1. roll backflip, cartwheel, eskimo roll, esquimautage, flick-roll, flip, forward roll, handspring, neck roll, snap-roll, somersault, summersault, tumble.

5. 1. turn about, about-face, about-turn, caracole, christiania, facing *(Chiefly US Military)*, kick turn, left turn, pirouette, right about turn, right turn, tack, three-point turn, three-pointer, turnabout, volt, volte, volte-face, yaw, zigzag. *Informal:* 180 degrees, christie.

adj. **6. 1. spinning** circulative, circulatory, gyroscopic, gyrostatic, orbital, precessional, rotational, rotatory, trochal. **2. revolving** gyratory, planetary, rolling, rotary, rotating, rotative, swirling, swirly, swivel-like, trochoid, twisted, vertiginous, vortical, vorticose, vortiginous, whirlabout, whirling, whirly. **3. clockwise** anticlockwise, contraclockwise *(US)*, counterclockwise *(US)*, dextrogyrate, dextrorotatory, laevogyrate, laevorotatory, levogyrate *(US Optics)*, levorotatory *(US)*.

7. 1. spiral circinate, corkscrew, curled, involute, involutional, obvolute, obvolutive, rolled, scroll-like, spiry, turbinate, whorled.

v. **8. 1. spin** circle, gyrate, revolve, twiddle, twirl, whirl, whirr. **2. eddy** centrifugalise, centrifuge, swirl, whirl. **3. whip** stir. **4. dizzy** giddy.

9. 1. rotate brace, circumrotate, circumvolve, pivot, revolve, screw, turn, twist, wheel. *Informal:* windmill. **2. circle** circuit, circulate, circumnavigate, encircle, orb, orbit, round, turn. **3. spiral** corkscrew. **4. turn** about-face, about-turn, caracole, pirouette, rotate, turn around, twirl, wheel, whirl. **5. jibe** slew around, swing, yaw. **6. turn over** flip, pronate, supinate.

10. 1. roll cartwheel, somersault, troll, trundle, tumble. **2. wallow** labour. **3. bowl** rim, roll, roll down. *Informal:* burl *(US Timber Industry)*, roll along. **4. wheel** trundle.

RELATED KEYWORDS: BEND, CURVE, DEVIATION, OVERTURN, ROUNDNESS

SPORT

n. **1. 1. sport** spectator sport. **2. sporting match** cup final, cup tie, event, fixture, friendly, game, grand final, grudge match, international, match, match-of-the-day, play-off, preliminary final, replay, run-off, test, test match. **3. sports day** carnival, field day, games, meeting, rodeo, track meet. *Informal:* bangtail muster. **4. tournament** championship, competition, gymkhana, head of the river, jousts, knockout, local derby, meet, motorkhana, round robin, rubber, tilt, trial. *Informal:* comp. **5. doubles** four, four-some, singles, threesome, twosome.

2. 1. ball sports badminton, ball game *(Chiefly US)*, baseball, basketball, battledore and shuttlecock, beach, beach volleyball, bocce, boule, bowling, bowls, bumble puppy, captain ball, carpet bowls, clock-golf, court tennis *(US)*, croquet, curling, field hockey, fives, golf, hand tennis, handball, hockey, hurling, lawn bowls, lawn tennis, mall, miniature golf, minigolf, netball, netta, overhead ball, pall-mall, pelota, ping-pong, real tennis, rounders, royal tennis, shinty, shuttlecock, softball, sphairee, squash, squash racquets, squash tennis, table tennis, tennis, tether tennis, vigoro, volleyball. **2. football** American football, Association Football, Australian Football, Australian National Football, Australian Rules, gridiron, League, national code, Rugby football, Rugby League, Rugby Union, rugger, soccer, touch football. *Informal:* aerial ping-pong, Aussie Rules, footer, footie, footy, Rules, touch, wogball. **3. cricket** cricko, French cricket, hit-and-run, nick-and-run, tip-and-go, tip-and-run *(Especially Qld, NSW, Tasmania and WA)*, tippety cricket, tippety-run, tippy cricket, tippy-go-run, tippy-runs, tipsy.

3. 1. athletics broad jump, decathlon, discus, field event, hammer, heat, heptathlon, high jump, hop, step, and jump, hurdles, javelin, jump, long jump, marathon, medley relay, middle distance, pentathlon, pole vault, relay, running, shot-put, sprint, track, track event, triple jump.

4. 1. boxing noble art, prize-fighting, pugilism, savate, shadow-boxing. **2. wrestling** aikido, catch-as-catch-can, freestyle, sumo, tag-wrestling. **3. fighting** bullfighting, cockfighting, fence, fencing, foils, kendo, singlestick, swordplay, tauromachy. **4. martial arts** jiujitsu, judo, jujitsu, karate, kung-fu, tae kwon do, taekwondo, tai chi.

5. 1. water sports blue water sailing, boating, body-surfing, canoe polo, loxodromics, musical flags, polo, sailboarding, sailing, skindiving, surf-riding, surfboard riding, surfing, synchronised swimming, tow surfing, water-polo, wind-surfing, yachting.

6. 1. sports – miscellaneous – parachuting paraflying, parasailing, skydiving. **2. extreme sports** basejumping, buildering, urban climbing. **3. winter sports** alpine, ice hockey, ice-sailing, skating, skiing, skijoring. **4. marksmanship** archery, cockshy *(Chiefly British)*, darts, down-the-line shooting, postal shooting, roving, shooting, shy, skeet, toxophily. **5. horse-riding** dressage, equestrianism, haute école, hazard, manège, polo, polocrosse, showjumping, tent-pegging. **6. bushwalking** alpinism, mountaineering, orienteering, rogaining. **7. weight-lifting** .

7. 1. sports player amateur, athlete, biathlete, corinthian, decathlete, first string, gamesman, junior, Mack truck, man of the match, matchwinner, player, pothunter, reserve grade, senior, sporter, sportsman, sportswoman, tourneyer. *Informal:* jock *(Chiefly US)*. **2. international player** cap, international, tourist. **3. team** eighteen, eleven, fifteen, nine, side, squad.

8. 1. surfer aquanaut, natural foot, skindiver. *Informal:* boardie, clubbie, goofy-foot, hot-dogger, lemonhead, seaweed, surfie, water-baby, water-rat, waxhead, waxie.

9. 1. football and hockey positions back, back line *(Rugby)*, back man *(Australian Rules)*, back pocket *(Australian Rules)*, breakaway, centre, centre half-back, centre half-forward, centre three-quarter, centre-forward, centre-half, centre-line, centre-man, centreman, defence, emergency *(Australian Rules)*, first five-eighth *(NZ, Rugby)*, five-eighth *(Rugby)*, flank *(Australian Rules)*, flank forward *(NZ, Rugby Union)*, flanker *(Rugby, NZ, Rugby Union)*, fly half *(NZ, British)*, fly-half, follower *(Australian Rules)*, forward, forward line, forward pocket *(Australian Rules)*, front-row forward *(Rugby)*, full-back, full-forward *(Australian Rules, Soccer, Hockey)*, goalkeep, goalkeeper, guard *(American Football)*, half, half-back, half-back flanker *(Australian Rules)*, half-forward, half-forward flanker *(Australian Rules)*, head *(Rugby)*, hooker *(Rugby)*, inside *(Rugby, Soccer)*, inside centre *(Rugby)*, inside left, inside right *(Rugby)*, interchange *(Australian Rules)*, keeper, key position *(Australian Rules)*, kicker, left back, left half, left inner *(Hockey)*, left wing, lock *(Rugby Rugby, Rugby)*, lock forward *(Rugby)*, loose forward *(Rugby Union)*, loose man *(Australian Rules)*, loosehead, loosehead (prop) *(Rugby Union)*, nineteenth man *(Australian Rules)*, number eight forward *(NZ, Rugby)*, on-baller, outside *(Rugby)*, outside half *(Rugby)*, outside left *(Hockey)*, outside right *(Hockey)*, pack *(Rugby)*, pig *(Rugby Union)*, pivot, placed man *(Australian Rules)*, prop *(Rugby)*, prop-forward *(Rugby)*, rake, right inner *(Hockey)*, rover *(Australian Rules)*, ruck *(Australian Rules)*, ruck-rover *(Australian Rules)*, ruckman *(Australian Rules)*, scrum-half *(British, Rugby)*, second five-eighth *(NZ, Rugby)*, second rower *(Rugby)*, spearhead *(Australian Rules)*, stand-off *(British, Rugby)*, stand-off half *(British, Rugby)*, sweeper *(Soccer)*, three-quarter *(Rugby)*, tighthead (prop) *(Rugby)*, twentieth man *(Australian Rules)*, utility, utility player, wing, wing forward *(British Rugby Union)*, wing-forward, wing-half *(Rugby)*, wing-three-quarter *(Rugby)*, winger, wingman *(Australian Rules)*. *Informal:* goalie. **2. cricket positions**

all-rounder, attack, backstop, backward square leg, bat, batsman, bowler, change bowler, cover, cover point, cover-point, deep cover, deep extra cover, deep fine leg, deep mid wicket, deep mid-off, deep mid-on, deep square leg, deep third man, extra cover, fast bowler, fielder, fieldsman, fine leg, fly slip, forward short leg, grave-digger, gully, infielder, keeper, leg slip, leg spinner, long leg, long-off, long-on, long-stop, medium pacer, mid wicket, mid-off, mid-on, middle-order batsman, non-striker, off spinner, opener, opening batsman, outfielder, pace bowler, paceman, point, rabbit, seam bowler, short fine leg, short leg, short point, short third man, silly mid-off, silly mid-on, silly point, slip, spin bowler, spinner, square leg, stonewaller, straight hit, striker, swing bowler, switch *(Chiefly US)*, tail-ender, third man, topspinner, twelfth man, wicket-keeper, wicketkeeper. *Informal:* gloveman, leggie, nightwatchman, quickie, stumper. **3. baseball positions** catcher, first (second) (third) (fourth) base, outfield, pitcher, shortstop. **4. athlete** discobolus, gymnast, putter, runner, shot-putter, sprinter. **5. boxer** bruiser, infighter, junior middleweight, light flyweight, light heavyweight, light middleweight, light welterweight, prize-fighter, pugilist. *Informal:* dreadnought, ex-pug, pug, slugger. **6. wrestler** black belt, judoka. *Informal:* grappler. **7. archer** bowman, marksman, markswoman, toxophilite. *Informal:* deadeye. **8. skater** ice-skater, langlaufer, sleigher, snowshoer, tobogganer, tobogganist. **9. skateboarder** roller-skater, skater. *Informal:* woodpusher. **10. rower** sculler. **11. other sports** alpinist, bullfighter, bushwalker, cocker, curler, fencer, foilsman, free diver, golfer, hand-in, iceberg, matador, minute man, mountaineer, parachutist, picador, poloist, receiver, reinsman, reinswoman, reserve, showjumper, skydiver, skysurfer, striker, swordsman, tent-pegger, toreador, torero, weight-lifter.

10. 1. sportsground arena, cockpit, colosseum, field, pitch, playing field, sports complex, stadium. **2. playing area** ballpark *(US)*, bowling green, clay court *(Tennis)*, court, covered court, grass court, green, hard court, icerink, links *(Golf)*, net *(Cricket)*, paddock, piste *(Fencing)*, practice range *(Golf)*, prize ring, ring, rink, saddling paddock, shooting gallery, skate bowl, squared ring (circle), tennis court, velodrome *(Cycling)*. **3. gymnasium** gym. **4. pool** above-ground pool, lido *(British)*, natatorium *(US)*, spa, spa pool, swimming pool.

11. 1. playing areas – football behind line, by-line, centre, centre circle, centre diamond, corner area, dead-ball line, end, goal line, mark, penalty area, penalty spot, pocket, sideline, spot, three-quarter line, wing. *Informal:* touch. **2. cricket** boundary, bowler's end, end, infield, leg side, matting wicket, off side, on side, outfield, popping crease, striker's end, wicket. **3. golf** Ambrose event, bunker, fairway, green, hazard, hole, putting green, rough, sand trap, sand-trap, tee. **4. tennis** base, baseline, centre-line, dedans, grille, hazard, net, tramlines, winning gallery, winning opening. **5. boxing or wrestling** apron, blue corner, canvas, corner, mat, neutral corner, red corner, ringside, ropes, scratch.

12. 1. sports moves and strokes – football attack, balloon, banana kick, bicycle kick, bomb, breakaway, checkside kick *(Chiefly SA Australian Rules)*, coathanger, corner, cover defence, crosskick, disposal, dribble, drop goal, drop kick, drop-out, drop-punt, fair catch, field goal, flying tackle, forward pass, free kick, garryowen, grubber kick, hack, hand-off, handball, handpass, head-hunting, header, headhigh, hit-out, inswinger, kick, knockout, line-kick, mark, maul, penalty, penalty kick, placekick, punch, punt, ruckwork, rush, save, scissors kick, sliding tackle, smother tackle, snap, spear tackle, spiral punt, stab, stab kick, stab pass, stiff-arm, stiff-arm tackle, tackle, tap-kick, torpedo, torpedo punt, up-and-under. *Informal:* bonecrusher, boot, droppie, free, pass, rainmaker, screamer, spot kick, torp. **2. cricket** a dead bat, air shot, back cut, back play, back swing, boundary, cover drive, hook, leg glance, lolly, nick, pull, snick, square-cut, square-drive, straight bat, stroke. *Informal:* agricultural, cow shot, windy woof. **3. tennis** ace, air shot, backhand, bricole, chip, chip shot, chop, chop stroke, drop shot, forehand, ground stroke, half-volley, kill, lob, passing shot, power serve, scissors, serve, smash, smasher, stop volley, volley. **4. golf** address, air swing, approach, blind stroke, chip, chip shot, downswing, drive, hole-in-one, hook, iron shot, loft, putt, slice, wood shot, wrist shot. **5. other shots and strokes** air dribble, back swing, backspin, bouncer, bumper, bunt, cradling, draw, finesse, forehand, free hit, free throw, incurve, jump shot, matchwinner, rush, save, tag, underspin, walk, wide. **6. canoeing** draw, pushover, recovery, telemark. **7. skiing** assist, axel, bodycheck, christiania, jump turn, kick turn, main-range, telemark, vorlage. *Informal:* christie. **8. delivery** beamer, bean-ball, bodyline bowling, bouncer, break, bump ball, bumper, chinaman, creeper, dolly catch, flipper, floater, flyer, full pitch, full toss, googly, grounder, half-volley, inswinger, leg break, leg spinner, legcutter, lifter, lob, long hop, mollygrubber, mullygrubber, off break, off spinner, outswinger, overthrow, seam bowling, shooter, volley, yorker. *Informal:* bosie, donkey drop, gozunder, grubber, leggie, offie, wrong 'un. **9. gymnastics** acrobatics, forward roll, fosbury flop, gym, headstand, neck roll, piked hang, roll, scissors, scissors jump. **10. surfing** angle, angling, beach break, bottom turn, nose riding, pearling, surfboard riding. *Informal:* tiger. **11. swimming** aquaplane, Australian crawl, backstroke, beacher, breast stroke, butterfly, butterfly stroke, crawl, dog paddle, dolphin kick, fly, freestyle, frog kick, inside, jackknife, jackknife dive, pike, pike dive, scissors kick, sidestroke, trail foot. *Informal:* flutter-by, hodad. **12. fencing** appel, carte, engagement, hit, pass, prime, quart, quarte, quinte, recovery, redoublement, seconde, sixte, stop, terce, tierce, touch. **13. weight-lifting** bench press, dead lift, deep knees bend, jerk, press, snatch. **14. punch** body blow, bolo punch, buffet, clip, clock, clonk, cross, cuff, flick, hook, infighting, jab, left, one-two, pivot punch, right, round-arm, roundhouse, short-arm jab, sideswipe, uppercut. *Informal:* biff, haymaker, knuckle sandwich, plug, sidewinder *(US)*, sucker punch. **15. wrestling** aeroplane spin, body scissors, bodycheck, buttock, chip, full nelson, grapevine, grapple, half-nelson, hammer lock, headlock, knee drop, lock, maginnis, nelson, octopus clamp, scissors, stranglehold, throw, toehold, toss, wristlock.

13. **1. sports scoring – football** behind, conversion, drop goal, field goal, full points, goal, golden goal, minor, penalty goal, penalty try, point, single, touchdown, try. *Informal:* major, poster. **2. cricket** aggregate, boundary, bye, century, double, duck, extras, four, golden duck, hat-trick, king pair, knock, leg bye, maiden, maiden (over), maiden over, no-ball, overthrow, pairs, partnership, run, single, six, stand, sundries, wicket, wicket maiden, wide. *Informal:* blob, sixer. **3. golf** albatross, birdie, eagle, half, hole, hole in one, match play, medal play, Stableford, stroke play. **4. tennis** advantage, deuce, double-fault, doubles, game point, love game, love set, match point, service break, set point, van, vantage. *Informal:* ad. **5. other sports** basket, bisque, equalisation, home run, kill, matchwinner, rounder, strike. *Informal:* homer.

14. **1. sporting equipment – bats** bandy, cricket bat, hockey stick, mall, mallet, racket, racquet, shinty, stick, tennis racquet. *Informal:* willow. **2. balls** baseball, basketball, bowl, cricket ball, football, golf ball, handball, jack, kitty, mark, pilot ball, pioneer ball, softball, squash, tennis ball, volleyball, wood. *Informal:* cherry, pill, six-stitcher. **3. missiles** caber, discus, hammer, javelin, lead, shot, stone. **4. puck** shuttlecock. **5. surfboards** barge, boogie board, down-railer, kneeboard, malibu, malibu board, rail, stubby, surfboard. *Informal:* elephant gun, hot dog, pintail, pop-out, shooter, spear, stick. **6. golf clubs** blaster, brassy, broomstick putter, bulger, cleek, driver, iron, jigger, lofting iron, mashie, mid-iron, niblick, pitcher, putter, sand wedge, spoon, wedge, wood.

15. **1. sporting terms – football** advantage rule *(Soccer)*, all clear *(Australian Rules)*, behind post *(Australian Rules)*, best and fairest, big sticks *(Australian Rules)*, blind side *(Rugby)*, fairest and best *(Especially WA)*, helicopter punt, knock-on *(Rugby)*, league table, line-out *(Rugby Union)*, loosehead, man up, mark, net *(Soccer, Hockey)*, penalty, penalty kick *(Rugby, Soccer)*, point post *(Australian Rules)*, scrimmage, scrum *(Rugby)*, scrummage *(Rugby)*, sticks, throw-in *(Australian Rules)*, touch-in-goal *(Rugby)*, tunnel *(Rugby)*. *Informal:* spot kick. **2. cricket** bail, batting average, bowling crease, declaration, leg before wicket, leg stump, overspin, powerplay, screen, sightscreen, spin, sticky wicket, strike, supersub, the ashes, the covers, top spin, topspinner, twist, twister. **3. baseball** bag, ball game *(Chiefly US)*, base, batter, catcher, home, home base, home plate, lineball, plate. **4. golfing** blind hole, borrow, carry, hazard, hole, honour, leaderboard, lie, long game, nap, rub of the green, scare, short game, socket, tee, top. **5. tennis** chopper, eastern grip, en-tout-cas, handshake grip, lineball, rough, tie breaker. **6. boxing** belt, cestus *(Roman Antiquity)*, eight-second rule, point, punchball, punching bag, Queensberry rules, technical knockout. *Informal:* mittens. **7. bowling** alley, bowling alley, dead draw, dead length, grassing, head, headpin *(Tenpin Bowling)*, jack, kingpin, kitty, spare *(Tenpin Bowling)*, split *(Tenpin Bowling)*, the kill, toucher. **8. archery and shooting** bird, bull, bullseye, carton, clay pigeon, inner, magpie, nock, outer, red, rover *(Archery)*, target, yew. **9. miscellaneous sporting terms** bag, base *(Baseball)*, basket *(Basketball, Netball)*, baulk *(Croquet)*, blood bin, box *(Baseball, Squash)*, cage *(Hockey)*, cover-point *(Lacrosse)*, defence, draw, guard *(Basketball)*, hand-in *(Squash)*, hand-out *(Squash)*, held ball *(Basketball)*, match-up, moment of truth *(Bullfighting)*, penalty box, penalty seconds *(Showjumping)*, quintain *(Medieval History)*, roll in, roll-in *(Hockey)*, rover *(Australian Rules, Croquet)*, throw, undercut, veronica *(Bullfighting)*. *Informal:* sin-bin.

adj. **16.** **1. sports** athletic, fit, sportful, sporting. *Informal:* sporty. **2. sports grade** amateur, big league *(US Sport)*, expert, friendly, international, league, national, Olympic, pro-am, professional, representative, State.

17. **1. sportsmanlike** sporting. *Informal:* sporty.

v. **18.** **1. play sport** aquaplane, body-shoot, body-surf, bowl, bushwalk, cricket, croquet, curl *(Scottish)*, fence, golf, hang-glide, hike, ice-skate, lacrosse, mountaineer, roller-skate, row, run, sail, shinty, skydive, surf, surf-ride, tramp *(NZ)*, trampoline, water-ski, windsurf, wrestle.

19. **1. make a stroke – cricket** bat, block, cut, drive, edge, hook, nick, pull, snick, square-cut, square-drive, stonewall, sweep, tip. **2. tennis** ace, chop, half-volley, kill the ball, lob, serve, smash, spin, volley. **3. golf** borrow, drive, heel, hook, lip, loft, putt, slice, socket, toe, top. **4. other sports** boast, bunt, roquet, rush, scoop, undercut, wire.

20. **1. kick** convert, dribble, drop-kick, drop-punt, foot, handball, handpass, head, heel, kick a goal, knock on, left foot, net, palm, punch, punt, rush, snap. *Informal:* boot. **2. bowl** break the wicket, bump, lob, no-ball, overpitch, spin.

21. **1. football terms** break, break away, carry, chest-mark, goalscore, hand off, have the loosehead, hold the ball, mankad, mark, nod, pack, pack down, play on, ruck, run, screw, scrimmage, scrum, scrummage, spoil, stand off, the loose head, win against the head. *Informal:* hang on. **2. cricket terms** appeal, back up, break one's duck, carry one's bat, declare, draw stumps, farm the strike, field, hit for six, hold a catch, keep wicket, send back. **3. boxing terms** beat the count, beat the punch, carry the fight, draw the lead, hook, uppercut. *Informal:* hang on. **4. surfing moves** fade, kick off, make a wave, trim, walk the board. *Informal:* hang five, hang in, hang ten, hit the lip, hot dog, max out. **5. miscellaneous sporting terms** aim, airball, attack, birdie, bodycheck, bogey *(Golf)*, break service *(Tennis)*, break the wrists *(Golf)*, breast-stroke, bump *(British, Rowing)*, buttock *(Wrestling)*, catch a crab *(Rowing)*, cox, draw *(Archery)*, launch, net *(Tennis)*, pass, play through *(Golf)*, poach *(Tennis)*, recover, remise *(Fencing)*, roll in *(Hockey)*, save, shark, shoot, sink the ball *(Golf)*, snatch *(Rowing)*, square the blade *(Rowing)*, steal, throw, traverse *(Fencing)*, walk *(Baseball, Softball)*, wrong-foot. *Informal:* chuck, peg.

adv. **22.** **1. sportingly** athletically, sportfully.

RELATED KEYWORDS: AMUSEMENT, HITTING, THROW, TRAVEL

START

n. **1.** **1. start** alpha, beginning, commencement, conception, early days, epoch, exordium, inception, inchoation, incipiency, lead-off, morning, offset, onset, opening, origin, origination, outset. *Informal:* kick-off, square one. **2. initiative** first blow, first move, first step, opening gambit, opening move, undertaking. **3. dawn** advent, dawning, daybreak, morning, prime, spring, springtime, youth. *Informal:* zero hour. **4. dreamtime** alcheringa. **5. genesis** birth, birthplace, derivation, nascency, nativity, origin, origination, provenance, provenience, womb. **6. source** beginning, fount, fountain, fountainhead, head, headspring, headstream, origin, rise, riverhead, seminary, spring, springhead, wellhead, wellspring, womb. **7. germ** anlage, bud, conception, embryo, pippin, primordium, principle, protoplast, rudiment, seeder, seeds. **8. root** grassroots, radical, radix. **9. primitiveness** fundamentality. **10. first cause** big bang theory, causa sui, prime mover, primum movens. **11. cosmology** cosmogony.

2. **1. foundation** base, basic *(Chiefly US)*, basis, grounding, groundwork, substruction. **2. spadework** preparation. **3. baseline** base, datum level, datum plane, datum point.

3. **1. inauguration** establishment, induction, initiation, instigation, institution, introduction. **2. debut** coming out, first speech, inaugural, maiden speech, premiere.

4. **1. starting line** gate, grid, mark, mobile barrier, scratch, starting block, starting box, starting gate, starting grid, tape. **2. flying start** getaway, Le Mans start, standing start. *Informal:* kick-off, send-off. **3. jumping-off place** springboard, threshold.

5. **1. starter** commencer, instigator, launcher, opener, promoter. **2. beginner** abecedarian, abecedary, apprentice, cub, fresher, infant, initiate, Jacky Raw, Johnny Raw, neophyte, new chum, novice, novitiate, recruit, tenderfoot, tyro, youngling. *Informal:* kook, parcel-post man, rookie. **3. debutante** *Informal:* deb. **4. spearhead** apostle, pioneer, trendsetter, van, vanguard. **5. founder** antediluvian, father, founding father, inaugurator, initiator, institutor, introducer, originator, patriarch, progenitor. **6. firstling** aborigine, primogenitor.

adj. **6.** **1. original** conceptive, exordial, first, fontal, front-end, inaugural, inceptive, inchoative, incipient, initial, initiative, initiatory, instigative, institutive, primal, primary, primordial, proactive, radical, unprecedented. **2. germinal** elementary, embryo, embryonic, nascent, rudimentary, seminal, undeveloped, unformed. **3. rudimentary** abecedarian, basic *(Chiefly US)*, elementary, foundation, fundamental, introductory, primary. **4. primeval** early, early-stage, inchoate, primal, primigenial, primitive, primordial, pristine, protomorphic, protopathic. **5. cosmogonical** cosmologic.

v.   **7.**   **1. start** fall to, get away, get going, get off on the right foot, get off on the wrong foot, head start, hit off, kick off, lead off, ring up the curtain, set to, set to work, set up shop. *Informal:* bundy on, fire away, get cracking, get weaving, get-go, hoe in, kickstart, pitch in, strike a blow, wade in (or into). **2. begin** belt into, commence, ease into, embark on, enter into, germinate, get underway, go, launch, open, set about, set afloat, set on foot, start. *Informal:* get stuck into, rip into. **3. arise** burst forth, come, come into the world, crop up, dawn, originate, proceed, rise, set in, spring up, well up. **4. come out** debut, make one's debut. **5. start again** make a fresh start, resume, take up. **6. go back to the beginning** begin again. *Informal:* go back to square one, go back to taws.

  8.   **1. initiate** accede, birth, bring in, bring into use, create, father, float, give birth to, give rise to, handsel, hatch, inaugurate, initialise, innovate, instigate, institute, introduce, launch, phase in, pioneer, premiere, set on foot, spawn, start, trigger. **2. establish** erect, found, ground, institute, plant, set up. **3. baptise** anabaptise, blood, christen. **4. prime** clutch-start, crank, fetch, jump-start, kick-start, push-start, set going, turn over.

  9.   **1. derive from** come from, grow out of, hail from, originate in, stem from.

adv. **10.**   **1. firstly** basically, first, for starters, fundamentally, imprimis, initially, to begin with. **2. originally** anew, at first, at the first, da capo, de novo, from scratch, from the first, from the top, in limine, in the bud. *Informal:* from the word go, in the egg. **3. primevally** primitively, primordially.

phr. **11.**   **1. back to basics** *Informal:* back to the drawing board, here we go again.

     RELATED KEYWORDS: COMING BEFORE, CREATION, EARLINESS, NEWNESS

STATE

n.   **1.**   **1. state** condition, fettle, shape, state of repair, temper, trim. **2. appearance** appearances, aspect, complexion, dimension, facies, guise, shape, visage. **3. dimension** plane. **4. mode** feel, modality, phase, phasis, state, tone, turn, way.

  2.   **1. situation** case, circumstances, condition, conjuncture, lot, pass, place, plight, position, posture, predicament. *Informal:* spot. **2. circumstances** how it is, how things stand, terms, the state of affairs, the state of play, the state of the nation, the way of it. *Informal:* circs. **3. status** footing, place, position, quality, rank, sort, standing, station, status quo.

     RELATED KEYWORDS: CHARACTER, ESSENCE

STEADINESS

n.   **1.**   **1. steadiness** determinateness, entrenchment, firmness, foursquareness, secureness, sureness, tightness. **2. stability** anchor, anchorage, fastness, fixedness, fixity, indissolubleness, inexorableness, inextensibility, irreducibleness, poise, rootage, stableness, steadfastness, thermostability, unalterableness, viscosity. **3. fixture** attachment, installation. **4. climax** *(Ecology)* ground state *(Physics)*, node *(Physics)*. **5. statics** aerostatics, thermostatics.

  2.   **1. steadier** balancer, bracer, entrencher, mordant, securer, stabiliser, tightener. **2. stabilising device** aerofoil, aileron, air foil, anti-roll bar, anti-sway bar, automatic gain control, brace, cowcatcher, drag-anchor, drag-sheet, dragsail, drift anchor, drift sail, drogue, fiddle, guestrope, guy, gyroscope, gyrostabiliser, gyrostat, humidistat, hygrostat, pyrostat, sea-anchor, sponson, stabiliser, tailplane, thermostat, trim tab. **3. ballast** kentledge.

  3.   **1. steadying** fixation, impaction, stabilisation. **2. equilibrium** balance, conservation of physical quantity, homeostasis, homoeostasis, inertia, isostasy, poise, stable equilibrium.

adj. **4.**   **1. steady** earthbound, firm, foursquare, roadholding, secure, stabile, stable, sure, surefooted. **2. stable** critical, indissoluble, inextensible, irreducible, monostable, noble, sure, thermostable. **3. even** homeostatic, isostatic, magnetostatic. **4. fixed** fast, firm, hardset, impacted, rigid, set, static, steadfast, stiff, tight.

v.   **5.**   **1. steady** balance, ballast, compact, equilibrate, firm, fix, guy, level, poise, settle, stabilise. **2. firm** harden, set. **3. be steady** have one's sea legs, hold the road, retain one's equilibrium. **4. secure** brace, build on a rock, root.

adv. **6.**   **1. steadily** fixedly, indissolubly, irreducibly, steadfastly, surely, unblinkingly, unerringly. **2. stably** foursquarely, gyrostatically, securely, steady. **3. fast** firm, firmly, hard and fast, tight, tightly. **4. even** evenly, isostatically, on an even keel.

     RELATED KEYWORDS: CHANGELESSNESS, FASTENING, REGULARITY

STICKINESS

n. **1.** **1. stickiness** adhesiveness, glutinosity, glutinousness, tackiness, viscidity, viscidness, viscosity, viscousness. **2. cohesiveness** glueyness, stickiness, tack, tenaciousness, tenacity. **3. cohesion** adherence, adhesion, agglutination, binding, cementation, coherence, colligation, concretion, conglutination, fixation, fusion, fusion reaction, sizing, solidification, sorption.

2. **1. adhesive** adherer, agglutinant, binding, cohesive, fixative, stick. *Informal:* goo, goop. **2. binder** bind, bond, bonder. **3. uniter** binder, bonder, gluer. **4. burr** clinger. **5. adhesive tape** durex, gaffer tape, masking tape, Scotch tape, sellotape, sticky tape, wafer. **6. glue** acacia, alkyd resin, araldite, arming, birdlime, clag, clearcole, contact cement, contact glue, dextrin, fish glue, gluten, glyptal resin, glyptol, gum, lime, mucilage, original gum, paste, propolis, size, solder, spirit gum, starch gum, starch-gum, strass. **7. grout** luting, putty, sealant, sealing wax, wax, white lead. **8. cement** concrete, maltha, MDF, mortar, plaster, ready-mix. *Informal:* compo, mud.

adj. **3.** **1. sticky** adhesive, claggy, cloggy, gluey, glutenous, glutinous, gummy, mucilaginous, tacky, tenacious, viscid, viscoid, viscous. *Informal:* gluggy, gooey, goopy, icky. **2. cohesive** adherent, adhering, adhesive, agglutinant, agglutinate, agglutinative, clinging, clingy, coherent, cohering, conglutinate, conglutinative, stickfast, sticking, tenacious, viscid, viscous. **3. fast** bonded, fixed, secure, solid, tight. **4. cement-like** cementitious.

v. **4.** **1. stick together** agglutinate, agglutination, cement, cohere, conglutinate, fasten, glue, lute, paste, size. **2. solder** bind, bond, calcine, fix, flux, frit, fuse, sweat, unite, wattle. **3. cohere** adhere, cling, clog, gum, gum up, stick, stick together, take. **4. cling** adhere, cleave to, hold, hold on, stick.

adv. **5.** **1. stickily** clingingly, glutinously, tenaciously, viscidly, viscously. **2. cohesively** adherently, adhesively, coherently, en bloc, indivisibly. **3. tightly** fast, intently, solidly.

RELATED KEYWORDS: FASTENING, JOINING, SLUDGE

STOPPAGE

n. **1.** **1. stoppage** abatement, abruption, arrest, break-up, breakdown, check, close, closure, desistance, freeze, hold-up, shutdown, snarl-up, suppression, suspension, tie-up. **2. halt** abscission, break, catch, cessation, dead stop, deadlock, discontinuance, discontinuation, disuse, end, epistasis, full point, full stop, period, prop, stalemate, standstill, stay, stop, stopping, stunt, suppression. **3. respite** armistice, ceasefire, forbearance, intercept, interception, moratorium, pause, pretermission, prorogation, truce. **4. interruption** abeyance, break, intermission, interregnum, interval, lapse, let-up, lull, pause, remission, rest, spell, stay, suspension, truce. **5. stall** whipstall. **6. stagnation** stagnancy. **7. prevention** check, estoppage, inactivation, suppression, suspension. **8. preventive** gag, kangaroo closure, snub, walkout. **9. notice to quit** caveat, declaration, notice.

2. **1. stopper** agraffe, bathplug, bung, catch, cork, estoppel, impediment, inhibitor, lock, plug, shive, spigot, spile, spill, sticking point, stop. **2. tap** cock, cut-off, faucet *(Chiefly US)*, pillar cock, spigot. **3. brake** air brake, bandbrake, brake block, brake drum, brake parachute, brakes, communication cord, disc brake, drum brake, footbrake, handbrake, hydraulic brake, pneumatic brake, retro-rocket, retrograde rocket, speed brake, vacuum brake. **4. anchor** arrest, bower, chock, dogstick, drag-anchor, grapnel, kedge, kellick, killick, sheet anchor, sprag. *Informal:* mudhook, pick.

v. **3.** **1. stop** arrest, bail up, baulk, becalm, belay, blow up, bring up with a jolt, buttonhole, check, debar, enjoin, foil, gag, halt, hold up, inhibit, intercept, interrupt, lower the boom on, prop, pull the plug on, pull up, pull up short, rise, save, snub, staunch, suppress. **2. discontinue** abandon, abate, abort, break, break off, break up, choke, close, closure, cut, cut someone short, do away with, end, give pause, interrupt, knock on the head, pinch, prorogue, scotch, sideline, silence, sit on (or upon), snub *(US)*, suppress, suspend, wind up. *Informal:* kibosh, put the kibosh on. **3. desist** abort, break up, cease, cut it out, discontinue, draw up, drop, leave it at that, leave off, quit, sign off, stop, stop in one's tracks. *Informal:* fetch up, lay off, snatch one's time, stow. **4. cease** call it off, come to a halt, come to a standstill, conclude, declare, give up, give way to, quit, ring down the curtain on, stop, terminate. *Informal:* bundy off, call it a day, call it quits, chuck it (in), chuck one's hand in, come to a full stop, draw stumps, give it away, give up as a bad job, pack it in, pack the (whole) game in, shut down on (or upon), shut up shop. **5. staunch** stanch, stay, stem, stop. **6. interrupt** hesitate, intermit, pause, recess, respite, rest, stay, stop, stop off at (or in), wind down. *Informal:* hit the pause button, rest on one's oars. **7. hinder** cramp someone's style, estop, forbid, foreclose, forestall, hold up, impede, inhibit, prevent, respite, stonewall, stop, stunt. **8. prevent** avert, intercept, nip in the bud, outlaw, prohibit. **9. knock off** break off, down tools. *Informal:* knock it off. **10. deadlock** be at a standstill, stalemate.

4. 1. brake back and fill, kellick. *Informal:* anchor, hit the anchors. **2. switch off** shut off, turn off. **3. cast anchor** bring to, heave to, lay to, snub. **4. stall** whipstall.

interj. **5. 1. stop** avast, belay, halt, whoa, wo. **2. enough** come off it, cut it out, enough's enough, hold it, knock it off, lay off, steady on, stop it, stow it, turn it up. *Informal:* break it down.

RELATED KEYWORDS: INTERRUPTION, IRREGULARITY, FINISH

STRAIGHTNESS

n. **1. 1. straightness** alignment, directness, linage, rightness. **2. straightening** bracing, extension. **3. line** rank, row. **4. beeline** direttissimo, short cut. **5. straight** back straight, home straight.

2. 1. straight edge braces, plane, rod, rule, ruler, T-square, truing plane, trying plane.

adj. **3. 1. straight** agonic, direct, even, level, planar, rectilinear, right, true, virgate, waveless. **2. rigid** erect, inflexible, stiff, unbending, unbent, unbowed.

v. **4. 1. straighten** disentwine, extend, lock, set straight, unbend, uncoil, uncross, uncurl, unlay, unreel, untwine, untwist, unwind. **2. align** enqueue, line up.

adv. **5. 1. straight** directly, due, right. *Informal:* slap, smack. **2. in line** in a column, in a file, in a queue, in a row.

RELATED KEYWORDS: ERECTNESS, LEVEL, SMOOTHNESS

STRANGENESS

n. **1. 1. strangeness** abnormality, anomalousness, curiousness, eccentricity, exceptionalness, extraordinariness, irregularity, novelty, oddity, oddness, peculiarity, queerness, rareness, rarity, singularity, singularness, supernormality, uncommonness, unusualness, unwontedness. **2. foreignness** exoticism, unfamiliarity. **3. eccentricity** funniness, kinkiness, quaintness. *Informal:* ratbaggery. **4. bizarreness** fancifulness, freakiness, freakishness, grotesqueness, incongruity, incongruousness, outlandishness, uncouthness. **5. monstrousness** abnormity, enormity, enormousness, grotesqueness, grotesquerie, malformation, monstrosity, prodigiousness. **6. eeriness** feyness, preternaturalism, uncanniness, unearthliness, unnaturalness, weirdness. **7. teratology** teratologist.

2. 1. abnormality aberrancy, aberration, abnormity, anomaly, exception, incongruity, irregularity, isolated instance, oddity, peculiarity, singularity, special case, vagary. **2. perversion** deviation, kink, pica, twist.

3. 1. freak bastard, chimaera, chimera, freak of nature, grotesque, grotesquerie, lusus naturae, monster, monstrosity, mutant, mutation, neither fish nor fowl, odd, odd one out, oddity, perversion, prodigy, quip, rogue, sport. **2. rarity** exotica, novelty, oncer, one of a kind, wonder.

4. 1. strange person caution, character, eccentric, erratic, madman, madwoman, oddity, phrenetic, prodigy. *Informal:* a queer fish, basket case, bat, bird, card, case, crackbrain, crackpot, crank, crazy, dag, ding-a-ling, dingbat, freak, fruitcake, geek, geezer, hangman *(NZ)*, kook, loco *(US)*, nut, nut case, nutter, odd bod, oddball, old bat, poon, ratbag, schizo, screwball, trick, wacko, weirdo, whacker, whacko. **2. nonconformist** maverick, misfit, odd man out, odd one out, original, outside. **3. pervert** deviant, kink, monster.

adj. **5. 1. strange** abnormal, anomalous, different, eerie, exotic, heteroclite, heterodox, nonstandard, nonconformist, out of character, out-of-the-way, peculiar, queer, recherché, select, unaccustomed, unclassifiable, uncommon, unconformable, unorthodox, unusual. *Informal:* iffy, offbeat. **2. foreign** alien, exotic, unaccustomed, unfamiliar. **3. exceptional** amazing, extraordinary, freak, one-off, prodigious, rare, remarkable, singular, sui generis, unco *(Scottish)*, unexampled, unheard-of, unimaginable, unique, unparalleled, unprecedented, without parallel. *Informal:* raving, tremendous. **4. odd** curious, dilly, eccentric, fey, funny, maggoty, peculiar, Pickwickian, pixilated, quaint. *Informal:* barmy, barmy as a bandicoot, dingbats, dotty, far-out, gonzo, kinky, kooky, loony, magnoon, oddball, oddish, out to lunch, ratty, rum, rummy, screwball, wacko, wacky *(Chiefly US)*, way-out, weird, whacky. **5. bizarre** crazy, fanciful, fantastic, freakish, freaky, grotesque, incongruous, outlandish, outré, uncouth. *Informal:* screwy. **6. uncanny** eerie, eldritch *(Scottish)*, ghostly, metaphysical, phantasmal, phantom, supernatural, supernormal, surreal, transcendental, transnormal, unearthly, unworldly. *Informal:* spooky. **7. monstrous** absonant, bastard, crooked, deformed, grotesque, malformed, miscreated, misshapen, preterhuman, prodigious, teratoid. **8. abnormal** aberrant, atypical, deviate

(Chiefly US), perverted, preternatural, unnatural. *Informal:* bent. **9. erratic** improper, irregular, variable. **10. perverted** deviant, psychopathic, wayward. *Informal:* kinky. **11. teratological** teratogenic.

adv. **6.** **1. strangely** amazingly, exceptionally, extraordinarily, peculiarly, uncommonly, unusually, unwontedly. **2. bizarrely** crazily, funnily, oddly, quaintly, queerly, wildly. *Informal:* kookily. **3. fantastically** exotically, fancifully. **4. freakishly** grotesquely, monstrously, outlandishly. **5. abnormally** atypically, pathologically, pervertedly, unnaturally. **6. irregularly** anomalously, erratically. **7. supernaturally** eerily, preternaturally, supernormally, uncannily, weirdly.

RELATED KEYWORDS: NONCONFORMITY, FOREIGNNESS

STRENGTH

n. **1.** **1. strength** arm, brawn, force, manpower, might, mightiness, muscle, potence, potency, potentness, power, powerfulness, sinew. *Informal:* beef. **2. muscularity** brawn, brawniness, heftiness, huskiness, robustness, stalwartness, steeliness, sthenia *(Pathology)*. *Informal:* beef. **3. wiriness** athleticism, stringiness. **4. vigour** energy, fire, force, juice, jus, nerve, pith, sinew, spirit, strength. *Informal:* kick, oomph, pep, zip. **5. machismo** hardiness, lustiness, manliness, robustness, rudeness, ruggedness, vigorousness. **6. sturdiness** stockiness, stoutness.

2. **1. durability** durableness, serviceability, serviceableness. **2. fortitude** backbone, doughtiness, force, hardiness, manliness, marrow, nerve, resolution, resolve, robustness, sinew, stalwartness, staunchness, strength. **3. stamina** inexhaustibility, intestinal fortitude, relentlessness, staying power, tenacity, tirelessness. *Informal:* stay *(US)*. **4. indestructibility** imperishability, impregnability, inexpugnability, inexpugnableness, invincibility, inviolability.

3. **1. strong person** athlete, Atlas, ball of muscle, ball of strength, behemoth, bull, giant, goliath, hercules, iron man, juggernaut, lion, macho, Patagon, Rambo, Samson, stalwart, strongman, superman, Tarzan, telamon, titan. *Informal:* bruiser, butch, gangster *(NZ)*, heman, husky *(US)*, jock *(Chiefly US)*, muscle man, strapper. **2. muscular person** mesomorph. *Informal:* nugget. **3. giantess** amazon, Boadicea.

4. **1. strengthener** bands, brace, bracer, fortifier, reinforcement, stiffener, suspenders *(US)*. *Informal:* reo.

adj. **5.** **1. strong** barrel-chested, bearish, brawny, bull, bull-like, bullish, bullocky, burly, cast-iron, firm, indomitable, large, mesomorphic, muscly, muscular, nuggetty, powerful, sinewy, stanch, staunch, sthenic, stocky, stout, strong as an ox, sturdy, substantial, well-built. *Informal:* built like a brick, hefty, husky, strong as a mallee bull. **2. mighty** armipotent, potent. **3. herculean** Atlantean, titanic. **4. athletic** able-bodied, amazonian, hard-fisted, masculine, sinewy, strapping, stringy, thewy, tough, wiry. **5. robust** bouncing, cracking, doughty, full-blooded, hardy, hearty, robustious, rude, rugged *(US)*, sound, stalwart, stout, sturdy, valiant, vigorous, well-built. *Informal:* two-fisted *(US)*. **6. virile** full-blooded, hot-blooded, lusty, macho, manly, masculine, red-blooded. **7. inexhaustible** exhaustless, fatigueless, indefatigable, inexorable, infinite, relentless, staminal, tireless, unfailing, unrelenting, unstoppable, untiring, unwearied, weariless.

6. **1. durable** cast-iron, doughty, fortified, hard-wearing, hardy, heavy-duty, industrial-strength, knockabout, serviceable, stout, tough. **2. sturdy** cast-iron, firm, hardy, heavy-duty, indissoluble, indomitable, iron, irony, steel, steely, stout. **3. indestructible** enduring, imperishable, impregnable, indomitable, inexpugnable, inextinguishable, insuppressible, invincible, inviolable, irrefrangible, perdurable, persistent, sturdy, unconquerable. **4. tempered** case-hardened, post-tensioned, pre-tensioned, thermo-tensile.

v. **7.** **1. strengthen** fortify, harden, reinforce, season, sinew, steel, stiffen, tone up, toughen. **2. consolidate** build up, confirm, fortify, reinforce, solidify, strengthen. **3. brace up** brace, fortify, man, nerve, rally, rouse, steady. **4. reinforce** brace, buttress, pile, prop, rib, riprap, slab, stake, stay, strengthen, support, sustain, undergo, underpin. **5. fortify** arm, reinforce, stockade. **6. harden** anneal, season, steel, temper, toughen. **7. proof** prove, weatherproof.

adv. **8.** **1. strongly** athletically, doughtily, forcibly, heftily, lustily, mightily, muscularly, potently, powerfully, robustiously, robustly, rudely, ruggedly, stalwartly, stockily, stoutly, strong, sturdily, vigorously, with might and main. *Informal:* scone-hot. **2. tirelessly** inexhaustibly, relentlessly, unstoppably, unweariedly.

RELATED KEYWORDS: HARDNESS, POWER, SOLIDITY

STUBBORNNESS

n. **1.** **1. stubbornness** contumacy, difficultness, doggedness, impracticability, inconvincibility, inexorability, inexorableness, inflexibility, inflexibleness, intractability, intractableness, intransigence, intransigency, obduracy, obdurateness, obstinacy, obstinateness, recusancy, refractoriness, tenaciousness, tenacity. **2. self-will** pigheadedness, wilfulness. *Informal:* piggery, piggishness. **3. perverseness** incompliancy, perversity, restiveness, wrong-headedness. *Informal:* bloody-mindedness, cussedness. **4. asininity** mulishness.

2. **1. stubborn person** hardliner, incorrigible, intransigent, irreconcilable. *Informal:* bolshie, bonehead, bullet-head, bullhead, chump, crank, donk, donkey, hard case, hard nut to crack, hardnose, mule, pig, trac.

adj. **3.** **1. stubborn** adamant, adamantine, anal retentive, diehard, dogged, firm, hardline, immovable, impossible, incorrigible, inexorable, inflexible, intractable, ironbound, obdurate, obstinate, opinionated, opinionative, pertinacious, refractory, rigid, self-opinionated, self-willed, set, stalwart, steady, stern, stiff, stiff-necked, stout, strong-willed, tenacious, unalterable, unbending, uncompromising, unfeeling, unflinching, unshakeable, unswayed, unwavering, unyielding. *Informal:* bull-headed, bullish. **2. determined** determinate, fixed, hard-bitten, hard-set, hardened, hell-bent, persevering, persistent, recusant, resolute, resolved, risoluto, single-minded, steadfast, strong-willed, unrelenting. **3. perverse** awkward, cantankerous, contrary, contumacious, cross-grained, difficult, froward, gnarled, gnarly, headstrong, incontrollable, incorrigible, intractable, intransigent, irreconcilable, obstinate, obstructive, oppugnant, purposeful, refractory, restive, self-willed, stubborn, troublesome, uncontrollable, unhelpful, unmanageable, unreasonable, unruly, wilful, wrong-headed. *Informal:* bloody, bloody-minded, bolshie, cussed, piggish. **4. mulish** asinine, hard-set, intractable, obstinate, refractory, stiff-necked, stout, stubborn. *Informal:* bolshie, boneheaded, bull-headed, bullet-headed, bullish, ornery *(US)*, pig-headed, piggish.

adv. **4.** **1. stubbornly** contrariwise, determinedly, doggedly, inexorably, inflexibly, intractably, obdurately, obstinately, pertinaciously, stiffly, tenaciously. *Informal:* bull-headed. **2. perversely** incorrigibly, refractorily, restively, unmanageably, unreasonably, untowardly, wilfully, wrong-headedly. *Informal:* cussedly. **3. mulishly** asininely. *Informal:* bull-headedly, piggishly.

RELATED KEYWORDS: PERSISTENCE, INTENTION, WILLINGNESS

STUDENT

n. **1.** **1. student** bursar, collegian, day student, evening student, exchange student, exhibitioner, external student, mature age student, part-time student, postgraduate student, pupil, scholar, scholarship holder, underclassman *(US)*. **2. pupil** boarder, colegiala *(Philippine English)*, day pupil, dayboy, daygirl, high-schooler, scholar, schoolboy, schoolchild, schoolgirl, student. *Informal:* day bug, schoolkid. **3. prefect** head boy, head girl, praefect, school captain. **4. undergraduate** fresher, freshette, freshman, sophomore *(Chiefly US)*, underclassman *(US)*. *Informal:* undergrad. **5. graduate** diplomate, doctor, fellow, graduand, licentiate, matriculant, matriculate, postgraduate. **6. classmate** alumna *(Chiefly US)*, alumnus *(Chiefly US)*, fellow student, former student, old boy, old girl.

2. **1. learner** autodidact, bookworm, fast learner, good learner, imbiber, practiser, student. *Informal:* grind. **2. slow learner.**

3. **1. beginner** apprentice, cub, fresher, Johnny Raw, learner, new chum, novice, novitiate, raw recruit, tenderfoot, tiro, tyro, youngling. *Informal:* parcel-post man, rookie. **2. novice** abecedarian, abecedary, beginner, catechumen, neophyte. **3. trainee** apprentice, articled clerk, cadet, improver, learner, pupil-teacher.

4. **1. catechist** catechumen, chela, disciple, follower, neophyte, novice, proselyte, ritualist, scholastic, seminarian, seminarist. *Informal:* theolog.

5. **1. studentship** discipleship, fellowship, undergraduateship. **2. traineeship** apprenticeship, cadetship, licentiateship.

RELATED KEYWORDS: IGNORANCE, LEARNING, SCHOOL

STUPIDITY

n. **1.** **1. stupidity** asininity, barrenness, bluntness, boneheadedness, brainlessness, denseness, density, dullness, dumbness, half-wittedness, hebetude, mindlessness, oafishness, opacity, purblindness, silliness, simplicity, slowness, stupidness, thickheadedness, thickness, unaptness, unintelligence, unthinkingness, vacancy, vacuity, vacuousness, witlessness, woodenness. *Informal:* blockishness, cloddishness, crassitude, crassness, doltishness, gormlessness, loutishness, lubberliness, nuttiness, soddenness, soft-headedness, sogginess, wooden-headedness. **2. low intelligence** anility, defectiveness, dotage, feeblemindedness, idiotism, imbecility, insanity, insensateness, madness, mental deficiency, moronity, retardation, senility, simple-mindedness, simpleness, subnormality, unreason, weak-mindedness. **3. foolishness** dizziness, dogberryism, emptiness, folly, goofiness, idiocy, ignorance, impoliticness, imprudence, injudiciousness, insipience, lunacy, madness, unreason, unwisdom, unwiseness. **4. shallowness** fatuity, short-sightedness, superficialness. **5. act of stupidity** bêtise, brainless act, moronic thing to do, stupidity. **6. blonde moment**.

2. **1. stupid person** automaton, doter, dullard, dunce, featherbrain, featherhead, fool, gawk, ignoramus, innocent, lostie, lowbrow, muddle-head, simple, spaghetti-for-brains. *Informal:* airhead, ass, berk, bevan *(Especially Qld)*, bimbette, bimbo, bit of fluff, blockhead, blunderbuss, bonehead, boob, booby, boofhead, bozo *(Chiefly US)*, bullet-head, bullhead, butthead, cement head, charlie, chucklehead, chump, clod, clodpate, clodpoll *(British)*, clot, coot, cough drop *(British)*, cretin, deadhead, der, dill, dillpot, dimwit, ding-a-ling, dipstick, ditz, dodo, dogberry, dolt, donkey, doob, doofus, dope, doughhead *(Chiefly US)*, doughie, drip, drongo, droob, duffer, dumb Dora, dumbbell, dumbcluck, dumbo, dumdum, dummy, dunderhead, dunderpate, egg roll, fathead, flathead, Fred Nerk, gazob, gimp, git *(Chiefly British)*, goat, goober, goof, goon, great ape, gup, himbo *(US)*, hoon, idjut, imbecile, imbo, jackass, jay, jerk, joe, juggins, knucklehead, lamebrain *(US)*, lightweight, loggerhead, loghead, loon, lout, lubber, lummox, lump, lunk, lunkhead *(US)*, meat-head *(Chiefly US)*, meatball, melon, melonhead, mong, moo, mooncalf, mopoke, moron, mug, mug alec, mule, mutt, mutton-head, nig-nog, nincompoop, ning-nong, ninny, nit, nitwit, noddy, nong, noodle, numbskull, numskull, nut, nutter, oaf, one-ten, palooka, parrot, pea eater, peabrain, pinhead, poon, pudding, pudding head, pup, puppy, rabbit, random *(Chiefly US)*, rattlebrain, retard, Richard Cranium, rock ape, rock-ape, sap, saphead, sawney, scatterbrain, schlub *(US)*, schmo, schmuck, sheep, shmo, silly, sillybilly, simpleton, slob, slowcoach, slowpoke, spac, spastic, spaz, spinner, spoony, stem, stock, stumblebum, stupid, subman, subnormal, thickhead, trog, troglodyte, turkey, twerp, twirp, village idiot, weed, woodenhead, wooz. **2. person of low intelligence** amentum, cretin, defective, halfwit, idiot, imbecile, mental defective, oaf, subnormal. *Informal:* dubbo *(Chiefly NSW)*, eejit *(Chiefly Irish and Scottish)*, fruitloop, grommet, spacbrain.

adj. **3.** **1. stupid** addle, addlebrained, addlepated, anserine, asinine, blind, dense, dumb, empty, empty-headed, fatuitous, fatuous, foolish, inane, insensate, irrational, mad, mad as a two-bob watch, mindless, muddle-headed, obtuse, opaque, pig-headed, puerile, senseless, silly, soft-headed, thick, thick-skulled, thick-witted, thickheaded, thickish, tomfool, twitty, unthinking, vacuous. *Informal:* barmy, boneheaded, boobyish, boofheaded, brain dead, bull-headed, bullet-headed, bullish, cloddy, clottish, clueless, crass, cretinous, daggy, dead from the neck up, der, dippy, dizzy, doltish, drippy, drooby, dubbo *(Chiefly NSW)*, dunderheaded, fat, fat-witted, fatheaded, goofy, gormless, headless, idiotic, imbecile, loutish, lubberly, meatball, mug, nutty, oafish, off one's nut, pudding-headed, punch-drunk, punchy, scatterbrained, scatty, silly as a hatful of worms, silly as a snake, silly as a square wheel, silly as a two-bob watch, silly as a wet hen, silly as a wheel, soft in the head, soggy, spac, spastic, spaz, spoony, troglodytical, Uncle Willy, wooden-headed. **2. slow-witted** backward, barren, blunt, dimwitted, doting, dull, dullish, half-witted, inapt, lowbrow, purblind, slow, slow on the uptake, thick-witted, unapt, weak-minded, witless, wooden. *Informal:* a brick (or a few bricks) short (of a load), a brick short, blockish, boofy, brainless, dead-and-alive, dim, doltish, dopey, drooby, not the full quid, short a sheet of bark, thick as two short planks, three bangers short of a barbie, without enough brains to give oneself a headache. **3. unintelligent** anile, cretinous, defective, doddering, doting, feeble-minded, imbecilic, impolitic, in one's second childhood, ineducable, insensate, insipient, mentally deficient, mentally handicapped, mindless, moronic, retarded, senile, simple, simple-minded, subnormal, unteachable. *Informal:* a shingle short, gaga, weak in the upper storey. **4. ignorant** benighted, dark, illiterate, imprudent, incognisant, injudicious, uneducated, unenlightened, unformed, uninformed, unknowing, unlearned, unlettered, unread, unscholarly, unschooled, untaught, untutored, unwise. **5. unwise** impolitic, injudicious, short-sighted. **6. shallow-minded** facile, fatuitous, fluffy, frivolous, shallow, superficial.

v. **4.** **1. be stupid** dote, have no brains, take leave of one's senses. *Informal:* be a shingle short, have come down in the last shower, have kangaroos (loose) in the top paddock, have rocks in one's head, have slipped one's trolley, have whiteants, not know if it's Bourke Street or Tuesday, not know if it's Pitt Street or Christmas, not know the time of day, not know what day it is, not to know B from a bull's foot.

adv. **5. 1. stupidly** asininely, barrenly, blankly, blockishly, bluntly, crassly, defectively, densely, dizzily, doltishly, dully, dumbly, emptily, foolishly, glassily, goofily, half-wittedly, ignorantly, imbecilely, inaptly, insensately, insipiently, loutishly, lubberly, mindlessly, oafishly, purblindly, sillily, simple-mindedly, simply, slowly, soddenly, thickly, unaptly, unintelligently, unlearnedly, unthinkingly, unwisely, vacantly, vacuously, witlessly, woodenly. **2. unwisely** impoliticly, injudiciously, short-sightedly.

RELATED KEYWORDS: FOOLISHNESS, IGNORANCE, ILLOGICALITY, INSANITY, FOOL

SUBJECT MATTER

n. **1. 1. subject matter** angle, argument, article, barbecue stopper, cause célèbre, contention, controversy, dispute, issue, matter, question, subject, substance, talk of the town, talking point, thesis, topic, topic of the day. **2. theme** burden, leitmotiv, motif, topic. **3. text** article. **4. field** area, bailiwick, domain, field of interest, ground, major, orbit, realm, speciality, specialty, sphere, territory. *Informal:* scene. **5. quadrivium** trivium. **6. person referred to** party, subject. **7. thing referred to** object, referent.

adj. **2. 1. topical** apposite, bearing on the matter, germane, grist to the mill, in point, pertinent, relative, relevant, to the point.

3. 1. propositional arguable, debatable, doubtful, moot, problematic, questionable, quodlibetical, thematic, theorematic, uncertain.

adv. **4. 1. at issue** before the house, in mind, in question, on the table, under discussion.

RELATED KEYWORDS: NAME, QUESTION

SUBTRACTION

n. **1. 1. subtraction** abatement, attrition, curtailment, decrement, deduction, dockage, enucleation, evisceration, excision, expurgation, exsection, extirpation, removal, subduction, truncation. **2. amputation** mutilation. **3. castration** elastration, emasculation, the unkindest cut of all. **4. circumcision** clitoridectomy. **5. epilation** depilation.

adj. **2. 1. truncated** abrupt, castrated, couped, crop-eared, curt, cut, cut short, docked, lopped, poley, premorse, truncate.

v. **3. 1. subtract** abate, abridge, bate, deduct, diminish, lessen, minify, reduce, take, take away. **2. decrease** abridge, abscind, amputate, apocopate, bang, bobtail, clip, crop, curtail, cut, cut back, de-escalate, decimate, deplete, diminish, disbranch, dock, head, lessen, lop, pare down, pare off (or away), poll, prune, reduce, retrench, scant, snuff, trash, trim, trim off, truncate, whittle. **3. excise** core, cut out, enucleate, excide, exscind, exsect, extirpate, pit, remove. **4. discount** abate, allow, deduct, rebate, slash. *Informal:* knock off. **5. detract**.

4. 1. cut off amputate, clip, crop, decapitate, dehorn, head, mutilate, pinion, poll, shear, tail. **2. disembowel** eviscerate, exenterate, gut. **3. desex** castrate, cut, do, emasculate, fix, geld, mark, mutilate, neuter, spay, sterilise, unsex. *Informal:* alter, deknacker, doctor. **4. epilate** depilate, shave, shingle.

prep. **5. 1. less** 'cept, apart from, bar, except, excepting, excluding, failing, minus, omitting, save, wanting, without.

RELATED KEYWORDS: DECREASE, CALCULATION, CUT, DEFICIENCY, REMNANT

SUGGESTION

n. **1. 1. suggestion** allusion, hint, implication, innuendo, insinuation, intimation, rumour, undercurrent, word. **2. connotation** overtones, predication, subaudition, subtext. **3. indication** adumbration, prefigurement.

2. 1. suggestiveness allusiveness, implicitness, obliqueness, obliquity, tacitness. **2. latency** more than meets the eye, potentiality.

adj. **3. 1. suggestive** allusive, allusory, insinuative, oblique. **2. implicative** connotative, implicational, indicative, indicatory, predicative, suggestive. **3. implicit** half-spoken, implied, tacit, undeclared, understood, unexpressed, unspoken, unvoiced, unwritten. **4. latent** below the surface, hidden, potential, sleeping, underlying, undeveloped, unsuspected. **5. obscure** abstract, abstruse, ambiguous, arcane, cloudy, esoteric, mysterious, nubilous, opaque, rarefied, recondite, unexplored.

v. **4. 1. suggest** allude to, get at, hint at, imply, infer, insinuate, look, refer. **2. imply** connote, implicate, incriminate, involve, predicate.

adv. **5. 1. suggestively** allusively, insinuatingly, obliquely. **2. impliedly** connotatively, implicationally, implicatively, predicatively. **3. implicitly** tacitly.

RELATED KEYWORDS: OBSCURITY, FIGURE OF SPEECH, MEANING, SIGN

SUPERIORITY

n. **1.** **1. superiority** conspicuousness, distinction, eminence, excellence, excellency, meliority, note, pre-eminence, prominence, superlativeness. **2. matchlessness** divineness, divinity, inapproachability, incomparability, incomparableness, loftiness, sublimeness, sublimity, supremeness, surpassingness, transcendence, transcendentness, ultimateness, unapproachableness. **3. quality** goodness, merit, value, virtue, worth. **4. one-upmanship.**

     2. **1. precedence** advantage, ascendancy, ascendant, dominance, hegemony, pas, pre-eminence, predominance, predomination, pride of place, priority, privilege, seniority. **2. primacy** headship, hegemony, leadership, lordship, mastery, overlordship, paramountcy, predominance, regality, sovereignty, supereminence, supremacy. **3. preponderance** preponderation, prevailingness, prevalence.

     3. **1. advantage** account, benefit, gain, grist to the mill, profit, van, vantage. **2. upper hand** command, high ground, trump card, vantage ground, vantage point. **3. flying start** edge, jumps, lead, odds, start. *Informal:* pull. **4. privilege** favour, prerogative. **5. advantageousness** desirability, preferability, preferableness.

     4. **1. the best** the acme, the cap, the crème de la crème, the cream, the fat, the first, the pick, the pink, the pride, uppermost. **2. the ultimate** the crest, the height, the maximum, the noon, the noontide, the sublime of, the summit, the top, the tops. *Informal:* the glassy. **3. first choice** preference, primary. **4. nonpareil** beauty, classic, collector's item, nonesuch, nonsuch, paragon, plum, speciality, specialty, top-liner, topnotcher. *Informal:* bobby-dazzler, clinker, clipper, corker, crackajack, cracker, crackerjack, dilly, dinkum, dinnyhayser, doozey, dynamite, humdinger, one out of the box, purler, ringer, ripper, ripsnorter, ruby-dazzler, something else, something else again. **5. masterpiece** chef-d'oeuvre, magnum opus, masterwork.

adj. **5.** **1. superior** above, best, best in show, champion, excellent, extraordinaire, extraordinary, extreme, fine, first, first-class, first-rate, five-star, front rank, GAQ, giant, good, grand, greatest, high-class, high-grade, highest, in the first flight, magnificent, maximal, monumental, of the first water, optimal, optimum, overtopping, splendid, super, superfine, superlative, superordinate, supreme, top, top-flight, top-of-the-line, topmost, uttermost, well-made, world-class. *Informal:* A-1, ace, bitchin', crack, crackerjack, cracking, crash-hot, dope, elegant, exo, famous, great, killer, mickey mouse, phat, plum, purler, ripper, ripping, spiffing *(British)*, super-duper, swell *(Chiefly US)*, terrif, the cat's whiskers, tiptop, top-hole *(Chiefly British)*, topnotch, upscale, whizzbang. **2. above average** a cut above, head and shoulders above, in a different class, in a different league, more than a match for, streets ahead. **3. incomparable** beyond compare, inaccessible, inapproachable, inimitable, matchless, nonpareil, Olympian, out of this world, peerless, supereminent, superordinate, unapproachable, unbeatable, unequalled, unmatched, unparalleled, unrivalled, unsurpassed, untouchable, world-beating. **4. supreme** basilic, celestial, deiform, divine, extraordinary, extreme, magnificent, noble, perfect, sublime, superior, supernal, surpassing, transcendent, transcendental, transcending, utmost. **5. deluxe** aristocratic, blue-chip, blue-ribbon, champagne, choice, classic, elegant, export, fine, glamour, gourmet, highbrow, luxurious, polished, premium, prime, quality, rich, select, stylish, up-market. *Informal:* classy, high-toned *(US)*, posh, posh up, schmick, silk department, swanky, swell *(Chiefly US)*, swish. **6. elect** chosen. **7. prize** award-winning, premier, prize-winning, record, record-breaking, winning.

     6. **1. advantageous** beneficial, desirable, preferable, profitable, useful, valuable.

v. **7.** **1. surpass** cast (or put) in the shade, exceed, excel, get ahead, head, outbox, outdo, outfoot, outgo, outman, outmatch, outperform, outrun, outsail, outstrip, outweigh, overmatch, overpass, overstride, overtop, pass, rise to the occasion, top, tower over, trump. *Informal:* lick. **2. eclipse** blind, dominate, exceed, excel, extinguish, outmatch, outperform, outshine, outstrip, overmatch, overshadow, overshine, overtop, steal the show, surpass, transcend. **3. lead the way** break the record, exceed, gain ground, go ahead, not miss a trick, outpace, outrange, outrun, overrun, pull ahead, run. **4. show up** cast in the shade, put in the shade, take the shine out of. **5. outclass** knock spots off, outdo, outmatch, outperform, outrank, rank *(US)*, ring the board, ring the shed, run rings round, surpass. *Informal:* wipe the floor with. **6. outact** outbrave, outsing. **7. best** beat, circumvent, defeat, get the better of, have someone on the hip, have the laugh on, jump the gun, outfox, outjockey, outmanoeuvre, outplay, outsmart, outwit, overcome, overreach, overwhelm, quell, score off, steal a march on, trump, undercut, vanquish. *Informal:* euchre, floor, lick, roll, stonker. **8. better** cap, excel, outperform, outstrip, outwit, overtop, surpass, trump. **9. augment** exceed, improve on (or upon), increase, potentiate, up.

8. 1. take advantage benefit, profit. *Informal:* work a point. **2. get someone's measure** gain ascendancy over, get to the windward of, pull rank, pull the braid. *Informal:* be laughing, get the jump on.

adv. **9. 1. superiorly** best, excellently, sublimely, supereminently, superlatively, supernally, supremely, surpassingly, transcendentally, transcendently. **2. incomparably** inapproachably, matchlessly, unapproachably. *Informal:* champion *(British)*, first-rate. **3. above** beyond, far and away, head and shoulders above, out and away, over. **4. par excellence** beyond compare, pre-eminently. **5. in the ascendant** one jump ahead.

RELATED KEYWORDS: ARISTOCRACY, GOODNESS, IMPORTANCE, IMPROVEMENT, MANAGER, RULER, WINNING

THE SUPERNATURAL

n. **1. 1. the supernatural** alchemy, gnosis, magic, qabala, spiritism, the occult, the paranormal. **2. occultism** animalism, animatism, animism, Averroism, cabbalism, esotericism, esotery, kabbalism, magick, neo-paganism, spiritualism, supernaturalism, table-lifting, table-turning, theurgy, transcendentalism, white magic. **3. witchcraft** black magic, black mass, conjuration, demonism, demonology, devilry, deviltry, diablerie, diabolism, fetishism, glamourie *(Poetic)*, goditcha magic, hoodoo, incantation, kadaitja magic, kurdaitcha magic, magic, necromancy, obi, santeria, sciomancy, sorcery, sortilege, the black art, voodoo, voodooism, wish on (or upon), witchery, witching, wizardry. *Informal:* mozz, mumbo jumbo. **4. psychomancy** crystal-gazing, demonomancy, divination, mythology, necromancy, spirit-rapping. **5. ESP** channelling, clairaudience, clairsentience, clairvoyance, crystal-gazing, divination, extrasensory perception, foreknowledge, foresight, precognition, prediction, prescience, prevision, psychometry, second sight, sixth sense, spirit photography, vaticination. **6. telepathy** mind-reading, mind-readng, psi, psionics, thought transference, thought-reading. **7. psychic research** parapsychology, psychosophy. **8. unearthliness** ghostliness, spookiness, weirdness.

2. 1. supernatural event apparition, appearance, Fortean phenomena, invocation, manifestation, materialisation, precipitation, psychography, spirit writing, xenoglossia. **2. astral trip** astral travel, exteriorisation, imaginal realm, levitation. **3. bedevilment** bewitching, entrancement, incantation, invocation, possession, trance. **4. telekinesis** teleportation. **5. psychokinesis** psychokinetics, spirit-rapping, spiritualism, table-lifting, table-turning. **6. ouija** crystal ball, divining rod, dowsing rod, effigy, ouija board, ouija-board, psychograph, tarot cards, voodoo doll, wand. *Informal:* doodlebug. **7. miracle** mirabilia, thaumatology, wonder. **8. augury** aeromancy, alectryomancy, aleuromancy, alphitomancy, anthropomancy, apantomancy, arithmomancy, astromancy, belomancy, bibliomancy, botanomancy, capnomancy, cartomancy, catoptromancy, cephaleonomancy, ceromancy, chiromancy, cleromancy, clidomancy, coscinomancy, crithomancy, crystallomancy, dactyliomancy, divination, geomancy, hand-reading, hydromancy, metagnomy, numerology, oenomancy, oneiromancy, onomancy, ornithomancy, palmistry, pessomancy, prophecy, pyromancy, rhabdomancy, sciomancy, soothsaying, sortilege, sycomancy, tephramancy, vaticination, xylomancy. **9. spell** charm, conjuration, enchantment, hex, incantation. *Informal:* mojo *(Chiefly US)*, whammy. **10. amulet** charm, fetish, frontlet, grigri, juju, obeah, obi, palladium, periapt, talisman, voodoo. *Informal:* mojo *(Chiefly US)*.

3. 1. occultist alchemist, animalist, black witch, cabbalist, carline *(Chiefly Scottish)*, charmer, conjurer, demonologist, diviner, enchanter, enchantress, fetishist, fortune teller, hag, hellcat, illusionist, magician, magus, occulter, prophetess, Pythagorean, pythoness, rainmaker, Rosicrucian, shaman, sibyl, sorcerer, sorceress, spiritist, spiritualist, supernaturalist, transcendentalist, warlock, water diviner, water witch *(US)*, waterfinder, white witch, witch, wizard. **2. mind-reader** telepath, telepathist, thought-reader. **3. medium** augur, channel, channeller, clairaudient, clairsentient, clairvoyant, crystal-gazer, evocator, geomancer, necromancer, oracle, predictor, prophet, prophetess, psychic, seer, soothsayer, spirit-rapper, spiritist. **4. demoniac** energumen, zombie.

adj. **4. 1. supernatural** bedevilled, bewitched, enchanted, extramundane, extraordinary, hyperphysical, immaterial, magic, magical, miraculous, mythical, paranormal, possessed, preternatural, psychic, runic, superhuman, supernaturalist, supernaturalistic, superphysical, supersensual, transcendental, transmundane, unlaid. **2. occult** arcane, cabbalistic, Chaldaic, cryptic, esoteric, hermetic, Masonic, mystic, mystical, occultist, Orphic, orphic, Pythagorean, qabalistic, secret, transcendentalist. **3. spiritual** psychogenic, spiritistic, spiritualist, spiritualistic, unfleshly. **4. parapsychological. 5. unearthly** eerie, eldritch *(Scottish)*, ghostly, phantasmal, phantom, preternatural, spectral, supernatural, uncanny, unco *(Scottish)*, unnerving, unworldly, weird. *Informal:* spooky.

6. clairvoyant clairaudient, clairsentient, mediumistic, psionic, second-sighted, telepathic. **7. telekinetic** psychokinetic. **8. shamanic** sibylic, sibylline. **9. witching** sorcerous, thaumaturgic, wizard, wizardly. **10. haunted** ghost-ridden, hag-ridden. **11. charming** entrancing. **12. bedevilled** bewitched, enchanted, entranced, fey, possessed, spellbound, unlaid.

v. **5. 1. haunt** bedevil, bewitch, fright *(Poetic)*, frighten, ghost, possess, spook. **2. communicate from the dead** channel, divine, prophesy, rap out. **3. bewitch** charm, conjure, curse, enchant, ensorcell *(Poetic)*, hex, overlook, philtre, point the bone at, transmogrify, voodoo, witch. *Informal:* jinx, put the mozz on someone. **4. supernaturalise** mysticise. **5. lay a ghost. 6. levitate.**

adv. **6. 1. supernaturally** mystically, preternaturally, superhumanly, transcendentally, transcendently.

interj. **7. 1. abracadabra** hey-presto, hocus-pocus.

RELATED KEYWORDS: MAGIC, PREDICTION, SUPERNATURAL BEING

SUPERNATURAL BEING

n. **1. 1. supernatural being** apparition, appearance, astral, astral body, astral spirit, bogle, eidolon, embodiment, fantasm, ghost, invisible, kehua *(NZ)*, manifestation, materialisation, phantasm, phantasma, phantom, presence, shade, shadow, shape, spectre, spirit, supernatural, taipo *(NZ)*, wraith. *Informal:* spook. **2. ghost** doppleganger, kehua *(NZ)*, phantasm, phantom, poltergeist, revenant, shadow, spectre, spirit, taipo *(NZ)*, umbra, visitant, zombie. *Informal:* spook. **3. soul** anima, animus, dybbuk, inner nature, manes, psyche, shade, shades, spirit, wairua. **4. attendant spirit** familiar, familiar spirit, genius. **5. zombie** golem, undead.

2. 1. angel angelolatry, archangel, cherub, cherubim, guardian angel, houri, ministering spirit, morning star, pure spirit, seraph, spirit. **2. celestial hierarchy** Angels, Archangels, Cherubim, Dominations, Dominions, Powers, Principalities, Seraphim, seraphim, Thrones, Virtues. **3. angelhood** divinity.

3. 1. devil Adversary, Antichrist, archenemy, Beast, Beelzebub, cloven hoof, demon, deuce, dragon, evil, fiend, Lucifer, Old Nick, Prince of Darkness, Satan, serpent, the adversary, the devil, the evil one, the tempter. *Informal:* divil. **2. demon** archenemy, atua *(NZ)*, Azazel, Baphomet, belial, bugeen, cacodaemon, daemon, Davy Jones, debil-debil *(Aboriginal English)*, deil *(Scottish)*, demiurge, Demogorgon, devil, devil-devil, fiend, ghoul, hellhound, mammon, Mephistopheles, Satan, spirit, succubus. **3. vampire** Dracula, ghoul, incubus, lamia, mare, nightmare, Nosferatu, succuba, therianthrope, vampiress. **4. werewolf** loup-garou, lycanthrope. **5. devilishness** death, diabolicalness, diabolism, fiendishness, ghoulishness, lycanthropy, vampirism. **6. Death** the grim reaper.

4. 1. mythical being antihero, baresark, berserk, berserker, hero, psychopomp, superman, warlock, witch, wizard. **2. merpeople** blue men, Lorelei, merfolk, mermaid, merman, naiad, nereid, nix, nixie, ondine, seamaid *(Poetic)*, selkie, silkie, siren, undine, water nymph, water sprite. **3. Grace** Aglaia, Euphrosyne, Thalia. **4. nymph** dryad, hamadryad, numen, nymphette, oceanid, oread, satyr, silvan, sylvan, wood nymph, wood spirit. **5. genie** djinn, genius, jinn, jinnee. **6. giant** Aegir, Argus, Atlas, Brobdingnagian, Cyclops, Fafnir, Fasolt, Gog, Goliath, Heracles, Hercules, Juno, Magog, Orion, Pantagruel, Polyphemus, Titan, Ymir. **7. Furies** Alecto, Erinys, Eumenides, Magaera, Tisiphone. **8. alien being** alien, Alpha Centaurian, EBO, ET, extraterrestrial, grey, humanoid, Jovian, Jupiterian, Lunarian, man in the moon, Martian, Mercurian, Neptunian, Plutonian, Saturnian, saucerian, saucerman, Selenite, Solarian, spaceman, starseed, Uranian, Venusian.

5. 1. fairy banshee, brownie, elf, elfin, elle-folk, fairy godmother, fay, gnome, hob, huldre, leprechaun, little people, peri, pixie, pixy, sandman, sprite, sylph, tooth fairy, water sprite, white witch, will-o'-the-wisp. **2. specific fairies** Ariel, Jack Frost, Mab, Mimi, Morgan le Fay, Oberon, Puck, Robin Goodfellow, Sidhe, Tom Thumb, Wandjina. **3. imp** banshee, bogie, bogy, changeling, devilkin, elfchild, eudemon, goblin, gremlin, hob, hobgoblin, homunculus, kelpie, kobold, oaf, pixie, puck, Rumpelstiltskin, siren, sprite, sylph, sylphid. **4. ogre** carline *(Chiefly Scottish)*, dwarf, hag, hellcat, huldra, monopode, pigmy, PORG, pygmy, sibyl, troll. **5. bogyman** barguest, bogey, bogeyman, boggle, bogle, bogy, boogieman, bugaboo, headless horseman, hobgoblin, Jack Frost, scarecrow, spectre. **6. Santa Claus** Father Christmas, Kris Kringle, Saint Nicholas, Saint Nick, Santa, Santy.

6. 1. mythical beast aepyornis, androsphinx, barometz, basilisk, behemoth, bunyip, centaur, charybdis, chimaera, cockatrice, criosphinx, dragon, dragoness, drake, faun, firedrake, griffin, hippocampus, hippogriff, hoop snake, hydra, jubjub, kraken, manticore, mindi, mokele mbembe, monster, monstrosity, mummy, phoenix, roc, salamander, scylla, simurgh, snark, sphinx, taniwha, thunderbird, unicorn, vegetable lamb, wampus, wampus cat, wivern, wyvern, yowie. *Informal:* drop bear. **2. specific mythical beasts** Bandersnatch, Cerberus, Chiron, Easter bilby, Easter bunny, Echidna, Fenrir, Geryon, Gorgon, Grendel, Harpy, Jabberwocky, King Kong, Lambton worm, Medusa, Minotaur, Nemean lion, Pegasus, Pilliga yowie, Python. **3. abominable snowman** alma, Big Foot, sasquatch, yeti. **4. sea monster** cetus, Charybdis, Dagon, hippocampus, Hydra, kraken, leviathan, Loch Ness monster, Nessie, Ogopogo, orc, salamander, Scylla, sea serpent, seahorse. **5. movie monsters** Frankenstein, Frankenstein monster, Gamera, Ghidrah, Gigan, Godzilla, Golem, Megalon, Mothra, Rodan, Smog Monster.

adj. **7.** **1. supernatural** ghostly, ghoulish, illusive, phantasmal, phantom, shadowy, shady, spectral, spiritual, supersensual, superterrestrial, unearthly, unreal. *Informal:* spooky. **2. nymphal** chthonian, nymphean, satyric, sylphic. **3. impish** elfin, elfish, elvish, faery, fairy, gamin, puckish. **4. angelic** archangelic, celestial, cherubic, divine, ethereal, godly, heavenly, saintly, seraphic, spirit, spiritual, sublime, supernal.

8. **1. devilish** cloven-footed, cloven-hoofed, daemonic, demiurgeous, demiurgic, demoniac, demonian, demonic, diabolic, diabolical, evil-eyed, fiendish, infernal, satanic.

RELATED KEYWORDS: GOD, MAGIC, THE SUPERNATURAL

SUPPLY

n. **1.** **1. supply** aid, air support, assistance, endowment, fitment, furnishings, helping hand, maintenance, provision, purveyance, service, subvention, succour, suppliance, support, sustentation. **2. supply bill** advance, civil list *(British)*. **3. airdrop** airlift, space shuttle, tanker service.

2. **1. equipment** accessories, accoutrements, apparatus, appointments, appurtenances, baggage, caparison, equipage, gear, kit, manavelins, munitions, necessaries, outfit, paraphernalia, rig-out, tackle, tackling, turnout. *Informal:* the necessary. **2. personal effects** baggage, dunnage, luggage, paraphernalia, swag. *Informal:* stuff, things. **3. fittings** adornment, caparison, harness, ornament, rig, rigging, trappings, trim. **4. replacement** emergency, reinforcement, replacement part, spare, substitute.

3. **1. supply vehicle** articulated truck, baggage train, cargo ship, container ship, container terminal, freight ship, freighter, lorry *(Chiefly British)*, low-loader, rig, road train, semitrailer, supply train, transport *(British)*, truck. *Informal:* artic, biscuit bomber, semi.

4. **1. supplier** accommodator, caterer, endower, equipper, fitter, furnisher, maintainer, outfitter, provider, provisioner, purveyor. **2. quartermaster** camp follower, commissariat, commissary, feeder, licensed victualler, quartermaster sergeant, sutler, victualler, vivandière. **3. housekeeper** butler, cellarman, chamberlain, factor, maître d'hôtel, major-domo, manciple, manservant, reeve, seneschal, steward.

adj. **5.** **1. equipped** fitted, fitted out, full-rigged, ready, rigged out, supplied, well appointed, well-found. *Informal:* right.

v. **6.** **1. supply** fill, furnish, munition, plenish *(Chiefly Scottish)*, prime, produce, provide, provision, ration, reinforce, replenish, restock, stock, store, victual. **2. provide** afford, come to light with, come up with, enrich, feed, find, furnish, lay on, line up, minister to, ply, present, purvey, supply. *Informal:* bring home the bacon, rustle up. **3. provide for** allow for, cater for, do for, fend for, make provision for.

7. **1. equip** accommodate, accoutre, appoint, arm, fit, fit up, fix up, furnish, gear, grubstake, kit, mechanise, outfit, overpower, prime, refit, resource, set someone up. *Informal:* turn out. **2. endow** keep in, maintain, support, sustain.

RELATED KEYWORDS: SHOP, FOOD, COMMERCE, TRANSPORT, VEHICLE

SUPPORT

n. **1.** **1. support** Acrowprop, brace, bracing, crutch, fulcrum, prop, rest, stay, stull. **2. base** baseboard, basement, basis, bed, bedding, bedrock, drum, fantail, floor, footing, foundation, groundwork, hack, hardcore, hardpan, pedestal, pigsty, podium, predella, putlog, seat, socle, step, stereobate, stock, stylobate, sub-base, substrate, substratum, substruction, substructure, tholobate, understratum. **3. keystone** cornerstone, foundation stone. **4. wall** embankment, retaining wall. **5. float** hydrofoil, pontoon, raft. **6. fulcrum** arbor, axis, axle, hinge, monkey-block, oarlock, pivot, racer, rowlock, spindle, swivel, thole, tholepin, tholus, toggle joint, trunnion. **7. runner** cradle, rocker, trundle, undercarriage. **8. rest** arm, armrest, back rest, chinrest, headrest, ladder back, pillow. **9. bridge** jigger. **10. footrest** footboard, footing, footstool, hassock, horseblock, ottoman, plank, pouf, running board, scarcement, skid, step, stool, stretcher, tread, tuffet.

2. 1. beam arch bar, bar, baulk, bellcast batten, binder, bolster, box girder, cleat, crossbar, crossbeam, crosstree, dead shore, doorframe, fascine, fish, flying shore, gallows top, girder, hammerbeam, I-beam, jack, joist, lintel, manteltree, needle beam, noggin, nogging, open web joist, outrigger, pendant post, principal, purlin, rafter, rolled steel joist, rood beam, RSJ, shore, shoring, sill, sleeper, splat, stanchion, straining beam, stretcher, stringer, strut, subprincipal, summer, supporter, threshold, tie beam, timber, transom, traverse, tree, trestletree, trimmer, trussed beam, trussing, upholder, wall plate.

3. 1. stand bipod, coaster, crutch, easel, hallstand, hatstand, high hat, music stand, plane table, spider, stretcher, tank-stand, teapoy, triangle, tripod, trivet, valet. **2. holder** candelabra, candelabrum, candlestick, chandelier, flambeau, frog, gasolier, girandole, hold, menorah, pricket. **3. andiron** barbecue, dog, firedog, pothook, toast-rack, trammel. **4. shipway** chock, dogshore, saddle. **5. frame** armature, chassis, clothes drier, clothes hanger, clothes horse, clothes prop, coathanger, fadge frame, hanger, headframe, horse, lath, lathing, poppet head, sawhorse, skids, staddle, stocks, thorough brace *(US)*, tool-post, trestle, trestlework. **6. anvil** stithy.

4. 1. shelf étagère, bookrack, bookshelf, bookstand, chimneypiece, compactus, gradin, hob, luggage rack, mantel, mantelpiece, mantelshelf, mantle, mantlepiece, shelving, whatnot. **2. rack** hack, hayfeeder.

5. 1. platform apron, bandstand, barbette, bema, bridge, pageant, rotunda, stage, wavecut platform, wing. **2. podium** dais, footpace, hustings, pace, pulpit, rostrum, soapbox, tribune. **3. docking** boatswain's chair, bosun's chair, cradle, jiggerboard, springboard. **4. pallet** hack, skids *(NZ)*, skidway.

6. 1. floor ceiling, deck, flooring, promenade deck. **2. landing** fly gallery, fly-floor.

adj. **7. 1. supporting** sustentacular. **2. structural** skeletal. **3. base** foundation.

8. 1. supported backed, bolstered, mounted, ribbed, secured, transomed, trussed, walled. **2. highset** highblocked. **3. suspended** overhung, underhung, undershot.

v. **9. 1. support** bear, buoy, prop, shoulder, stay, sustain, take the strain, underpin, uphold. **2. bolster** buttress, chock, corbel, dowel, pile, pillar, rail, recruit, reinforce, rib, riprap, shore up, slab, spile, stake, stanchion, stick, strengthen, strut, timber, trig, truss, undergird, underlay, underpin, underprop, underset, uphold. **3. hold** pin. **4. brace** angle bracket, bracket, clamp, cleat, gusset, traverse. **5. mount** frame, set, step. **6. scaffold** espalier, trellis. **7. crutch** splint. **8. cushion** pillow, seat. **9. pivot** poise, stabilise.

RELATED KEYWORDS: FURNITURE, POLE, STEADINESS, BOTTOM

SURETY

n. **1. 1. surety** assurance, cover, coverage, indemnity, insurance, protection. **2. guarantee** avouchment, guaranty, warrant, warranty. **3. pledge** bail, bond, collateral, deposit, earnest, engagement, gage, hostage, parole, pawn, promise, security, word. **4. trust** discretionary trust, fixed trust, flexible trust, property trust, trust corporation, trust fund. **5. mortgage** equitable mortgage, hypothec *(Roman and Scottish Law)*, hypothecation, legal mortgage, stock mortgage. *Informal:* poultice. **6. suretyship** bailment, sponsion, sponsorship. **7. offsetting** covering, crossholding, safeguarding. **8. insurer** bailsman, bondsman, pledgee.

2. 1. type of insurance burial society, coinsurance, comprehensive insurance, consequential loss insurance, credit insurance, credit life insurance, disability insurance, endowment insurance, fire insurance, fire policy, life assurance, life insurance, marine insurance, mutual insurance, protective trust, provident fund, public liability insurance, reinsurance, self insurance, SMSF, super fund, superannuation, superannuation fund, term insurance, third-party insurance, tontine, valued policy, whole-life insurance.

RELATED KEYWORDS: CONTRACT, FINANCE

SURPRISE

n. **1. 1. surprise** admiration, amazement, astonishment, awe, stupefaction, surprisal, wonder, wonderment. **2. alarm** fright, shock, startle.

2. 1. wondrousness awesomeness, inexpressibleness, insaneness, marvellousness, miraculousness, prodigiousness, stupendousness, wonderfulness. **2. superbness** extraordinariness, remarkableness, sublimeness, sublimity.

3. 1. surpriser dumbfounder, eye-opener, shocker, startler. **2. bombshell** bolt out of or from the blue, thunderbolt. *Informal:* sucker punch. **3. bonus** dark horse, godsend, manna from heaven. **4. unexpected effect** bricole, irony, note, surprise ending, turn-up. *Informal:* turn-up for the books.

adj. **4.** **1. surprised** alarmed, amazed, startled, taken aback. *Informal:* like a stunned mullet. **2. astonished** agog, marvelling, open-eyed, open-mouthed, wondering. *Informal:* bug-eyed, bushwhacked, gobsmacked. **3. astounded** aghast, amazed, confounded, discomfited, dumbfounded, flabbergasted, staggered, stupefied, thunderstruck, unable to believe one's eyes. **4. awe-struck** blown away, overwhelmed, struck dumb, wonderstruck.

5. **1. surprising** abrupt, precipitant, precipitative, precipitous, sudden, unpremeditated. **2. astonishing** amazing, astounding, remarkable, shock, shocking, staggering, startling, stupendous. **3. overwhelming** awe-inspiring, awesome, awful, inexpressible, mind-boggling. **4. wonderful** extraordinaire, extraordinary, fantastic, fearful, incredible, marvellous, miraculous, phenomenal, prodigious, wondrous. *Informal:* fab, fabuloso, fabulous, fantabulous, fazzo, insane, tops. **5. superb** massive, singular, splendid, sublime, tremendous.

6. **1. surprise** accident, uncalculated, unexpected, unforeseen, unguessed, unheralded, unplanned. **2. bonus** too good to be true, unhoped-for, unlooked-for.

v. **7.** **1. surprise** amaze, astonish, bowl over, flabbergast, make someone open their eyes, overwhelm. *Informal:* throw. **2. shock** alarm, appal, stagger, startle, take aback. **3. take by surprise** ambush, blindside, catch, catch off-guard, catch out, catch unawares, overtake, take. *Informal:* bushwhack, get the jump on, king, king-hit. **4. dumbfound** astound, benumb, petrify, stun, stupefy. **5. awe** dazzle, take one's breath away. *Informal:* blow someone away, blow someone out. **6. stagger** shock. *Informal:* knock someone bandy, make someone's hair curl, strike all of a heap.

8. **1. be surprised** hit the ceiling, sit up, start. *Informal:* hit the roof, jump out of one's skin, not know what hit one. **2. wonder** gape, gawp, gaze, marvel.

adv. **9.** **1. surprisingly** amazingly, astonishingly, astoundingly, remarkably, startlingly, to one's astonishment, wondrous, wondrously. **2. unexpectedly** against all expectations, by surprise, contrary to all expectations, in an unguarded moment, like a thief in the night, out of the blue, unawares, without warning. **3. wonderfully** awesomely, extraordinarily, fabulously, fantastically, incredibly, inexpressibly, marvellously, miraculously, phenomenally. **4. sublimely** dazzlingly, singularly, superbly. **5. suddenly** all at once, all of a sudden, precipitantly, precipitately, precipitously, sudden *(Poetic)*. **6. strange to say** marvellous to relate.

10. **1. in astonishment** agape, amazedly, with open mouth, wonderingly.

interj. **11.** **1. oh** ah, dear me, fancy, ha-ha, hallo, heavens, heavens above, hello, indeed, oh my, well. *Informal:* (goodness) gracious (me), bejesus, bless me, bless my soul, blimey, blow me down, boy, by George, by gum, by hokey *(NZ)*, by Jove, can you beat that, Christ, coo *(British)*, cor, crikey, cripes, crumbs, egad, far out, for crying out loud, for the love of Mike, garn, gee, gee whiz, geez, Glory be, God almighty, golly, good grief, good heavens, good Lord, goodness, goodness gracious, gorblimey, gosh, great blistering blood oranges, great Caesar's ghost, Great Scott, heavens to Betsy, heavens to Murgatroyd, hell's bells, hell's teeth, holy cow, holy guacamole, holy mackerel, holy Moses, hoots, hot dog *(US)*, how about that, hullo, hush my mouth, I ask you, I declare, I say, I'll be a son of a gun *(Chiefly US)*, jeepers creepers *(Chiefly US)*, jeez, Jesus, Jesus Christ, jiminy, jingaloes, jumping Jehoshaphat, lawks amercy, lawks-a-mussy, lo and behold, lor, Lord, Losh, lumme, mamma mia, man alive!, mercy me, my hat, my sainted aunt, my word, oh boy, oops, phew, sheesh, shiver me timbers, starve the bardies, starve the crows, stiffen the crows, stone the crows, strewth, strike me dead, strike me lucky, strike me pink, strike-a-light, struth, the dickens, well I never, well, I'll be hornswoggled, what on earth, whew, whoops, will wonders never cease, woops, wow, wowzers, yikes, you wouldn't read about it, yow.

RELATED KEYWORDS: ANXIETY, ATTACK, SPEED

SURROUNDINGS

n. **1.** **1. surroundings** entourage, environment, environs, geographic environment, milieu, precincts, purlieu, surrounds. **2. environment** ambience, entourage, habitat, medium, milieu, niche. **3. element** sphere, world. **4. real world** lifeworld. *Informal:* meatspace. **5. ecosphere** bioregion, ecosystem, macrocosm. **6. setting** background, decor, location, lot, mise en scène, scene, scenery, set, stage, staging post. **7. context** frame of reference, reference. **8. atmosphere** aura, climate, vibrations. *Informal:* vibes. **9. ambience** circumambience, circumfluence, circumfusion.

    2. **1. encirclement** encincture, encompassment, enlacement. **2. aureole** border, contact aureole, contact zone, halo.

adj. **3.** **1. surrounding** all-round *(US)*, ambient, background, boundary, circumambient, circumfluent, circumfluous, circumjacent, circumvallate, encompassing, outward.

v. **4.** **1. surround** beset, box, box in, circumvallate, circumvent, close, close in, compass, embay, embrace, envelop, hem in, incarcerate, round, shut, shut in, stake out. **2. circle** embrace, encircle, enclose, encompass, halo, moat, round, surround, wreathe, zone. **3. engird** begird, cincture, clip, encincture, engirdle, enlace, gird, girdle, girth, hoop, loop, orb *(Poetic)*, picket, round, span. **4. enfold** bind, embosom, embrace, enrol, enwall, enwomb, fold, infold *(Chiefly US)*, swathe, twine, wrap.

    RELATED KEYWORDS: EDGE, ENCLOSURE, NATURE, ROUNDNESS

SWAMP

n. **1.** **1. swamp** alluvion, bog, flats, flow *(Scottish)*, gluepot, hanging swamp, innings, marsh, mire, morass, mudflat, ooze, quagmire, quicksand, salt marsh, slob *(Irish)*, slough, wallow, wash. **2. fen** bayou, everglade *(US)*, marsh, salina, salt, salt marsh, shott, wet ground. **3. swampland** maremma, marshland, wetland. **4. paddy field** paddy, paddy land. **5. mud** mire, morass, ooze, slime, sludge, slush.

    2. **1. swampiness** marshiness, squashiness.

adj. **3.** **1. swampy** boggy, fenny *(British)*, marshy, miry, paludal, plashy, quaggy, sloughy, wet. **2. oozy** slushy, splashy, squashy, squelchy. **3. muddy** miry.

    RELATED KEYWORDS: FLOOD, LAKE, SLUDGE, WETNESS

SWEARING

n. **1.** **1. swearing** abuse, abusiveness, bawdry, billingsgate *(Chiefly British)*, bullocky, cursing, damnation, dirt, filth, foul language, invective, language, obloquy, unparliamentary language, vilification, vituperation. **2. blasphemy** blasphemousness, profanity. **3. execration** anathema, anathematisation, ban, curse, excommunication, imprecation, malediction, proscription. **4. curse** commination, epithet, oath, profanity, scurrility, smear word. *Informal:* cuss *(Chiefly US)*. **5. swearword** byword, dirty word, four-letter word. *Informal:* blankety blank, the great Australian adjective.

    2. **1. swearer** abuser, blasphemer, curser, execrator, imprecator.

adj. **3.** **1. execratory** abusive, anathematic, blasphemous, damnatory, damning, execrative, foul, foul-mouthed, hard-mouthed, imprecatory, maledictory, thersitical. **2. coarse** abusive, bad, crass, crude, foul, indecent, offensive, rough, rude, strong, uncivil, uncivilised, unparliamentary, vulgar. *Informal:* rorty, snake-headed.

    4. **1. cursed** accursed, blasted, blighted, curst, damn, damnable, damned, detestable, goddamn *(US)*. *Informal:* b., bally, blamed *(US)*, blank, blankety, bleeding *(Chiefly British)*, blithering, bloody, blooming, confounded, cussed, darn, darned, doggone *(US)*, dratted, flaming, flogging, nbg, plurry, tarnation.

v. **5.** **1. swear** abuse, anathematise, bitch and bind, blacken, blackguard, blaspheme, confound, curse, damn, darken, darn, defame, denigrate, execrate, fling, imprecate, pelt, slander, swear at, thunder against, traduce, use bad language, use foul language, vilify, vilipend. *Informal:* blow, cuss *(Chiefly US)*, dis, drat, give curry, let rip, swear like a trooper. **2. put a curse on someone** blaspheme, curse, execrate, hex, imprecate. *Informal:* cuss *(Chiefly US)*, jinx, mozz, put the mozz on. **3. call down curses on** curse up hill and down dale.

interj. **6.** **1. my God** (for) Christ's sake, begob, begorrah *(Irish)*, by Jove, Christ almighty, egad, god, God almighty, goddamn *(US)*, Godsakes, gosh, Great Scott, gum *(British)*, Jesus Christ, perdie, strewth. *Informal:* blimey, by jingo, geez, gorblimey, jeez, Jesus. **2. curses** bah, blast, by George, Christ, confound it, damn, damnation, darn, dash, drat, faugh, fie, good heavens, rot. *Informal:* bejesus, bloody hell, blow, crikey, dammit, garn, golly, hell, hell's bells, hell's teeth, I'll be a son of a gun *(Chiefly US)*, phut, pigs, rats, sheesh, spew, spewing, spit, the blazes, the dickens, the hell with it. **3. I'll be damned** *Informal:* I'll be hanged, I'll be jiggered, man. **4. bloody oath** my oath. **5. nonsense**. **6. curse you** à bas, plague upon you. *Informal:* bash it, bore it up you, get knotted, go jump in the lake, go to blazes, go to hell, go to the devil, rack off, shove it, sod it, stick it, stick that for a lark, take a running jump, you can stick that for a joke. **7. may your chooks turn to emus** (and kick your dunny down).

    RELATED KEYWORDS: DISAPPROVAL, SLANDER, OBSCENITY

SWEETNESS

n. **1.** **1. sweetness** lusciousness, saccharinity, sickliness, sugariness, sweetishness. **2. sweetener** aspartame, honey, honeybee sugar *(Aboriginal English)*, sirup *(US)*, sorghum, stevioside, sweetening, syrup, topping. **3. sugar** aldose, coffee sugar, cyclamate, d-glucose, demerara sugar, dextroglucose, dextrose, fructose, fruit sugar, glucose, invert sugar, ketose, laevoglucose, laevulose, molasses, saccharide, saccharin, saccharine, saccharose, sucrose. **4. sweets** candy, chew *(NZ)*, chonk *(Gippsland)*, confection, confectionary, confectionery, junk food, lollipop, lolly, sugar candy, sweet, sweetmeats, taffy *(US)*, toffee. *Informal:* goodies, guk, gunk, sweetie. **5. types of lollies** acid drop, all-day sucker, barley sugar, blackball, bonbon, brandyball, brittle, bubblegum, bullseye, butterball, butterscotch, caramel, chewing gum, dolly mixture, fairy floss, fudge, gobstopper, gumdrop, hokey-pokey *(Chiefly NZ)*, humbug, jaw-breaker, jelly baby, jelly bean, jube, licorice, liquorice allsorts, marshmallow, nougat, panocha *(US)*, pear drop, rainbow ball, rock, rumball, snowball, Turkish delight. **6. sweet tooth. 7. sugar concentration** brix.

adj. **2.** **1. sweet** ambrosial, candied, delicious, honeyed, honeysweet, lipsmacking, luscious, nectareous, sugared, sugary. **2. syrupy** candied, cloying, rich, saccharine, sickly, sugary, sweet, sweetish, syruplike. **3. sweetened** candied, cream, glacé, honeyed.

v. **3.** **1. sweeten** candy *(US)*, crystallise, dulcify, ice, mull, sugar, syrup.

adv. **4.** **1. sweetly** lusciously, sweet.

RELATED KEYWORDS: PLEASANT FLAVOUR, UNPLEASANT FLAVOUR, FOOD, TASTE

TAKING

n. **1.** **1. taking** annexation, appropriation, arrogation, confiscation, conversion, dispossession, distraint, distress, escheatment, expropriation, impoundage, misappropriation, removal, reprises, resumption, sequestration, usurpation. **2. tax** contribution, custom, deduction, duty, excise, imposition, impost, levy, toll, tribute. **3. extortion** blackmail, exaction, grab, Rachmanism, rapacity, usury, vampirism. *Informal:* shakedown. **4. deprivation** bereavement, destitution, dispossession, divestiture, divesture, loss, privation.

2. **1. capture** apprehension, arrest, conquest, occupancy, occupation, seizing, seizure. **2. pillage** looting, ravishment, theft. **3. abduction** kidnappings.

3. **1. takings** booty, catch, grab, haul, loot, pillage, plunder, prize, proceeds, take. *Informal:* boodle *(Chiefly US)*, earn, snatch.

4. **1. taker** appropriator, enterer, grabber, harpy, Indian giver, snatcher, wrester. **2. depriver** confiscator, dispossessor, disseisor, distrainer, expropriator, impounder, sequestrator, usurper. **3. capturer** abductor, captor, catcher, conqueror, kidnapper, seizor. **4. pillager** ransacker. **5. rapist** ravisher.

5. **1. extortionist** blackmailer, extorter, extortioner, grafter *(Chiefly US)*, rack-renter, Shylock, usurer, vampire. *Informal:* bloodsucker. **2. swindler** carpetbagger, hawk, picklock, profiteer, sharper, thief. *Informal:* forty, Ned Kelly, peter thief, tea-leaf. **3. vulture** vampire, wolf. **4. parasite** cadger, leech, sponge, sponger, trencherman. *Informal:* beat, bloodsucker, bludger, droog, ten-per-center.

adj. **6.** **1. predatory** bloodsucking, confiscatory, dispossessory, predacious, prehensile, privative, raptorial, ravening. **2. extortionary** avaricious, covetous, extortionate, extortive, grasping, greedy, leechlike, parasitic, rapacious, vampirish, vulture-like. *Informal:* on the make, on the take.

7. **1. takable** adoptable, appropriable, assumable, attachable, confiscable, detachable, distrainable, escheatable, impoundable, pregnable, resumable, takeable. **2. deprivable** divestible, fleeceable.

8. **1. bereft** beggared, deprived, dispossessed, impoverished, pillaged, ransacked, ravished, stripped.

v. **9.** **1. possess** adopt, arrogate, enter, grab, jump, misappropriate, possess oneself of, run away with, seize, steal, take. *Informal:* snaffle. **2. retake** recapture, repossess, resume. **3. appropriate** annex, commandeer, confiscate, convert, escheat, expropriate, impound, impress, impropriate, possess oneself of, sequester, sequestrate, usurp. **4. adopt** assume, borrow. **5. tax** attach, distrain, garnishee, levy. **6. dispossess** disseise, divest, expropriate, forejudge, forjudge, oust. **7. disinherit** cut off, cut off without a cent. **8. deprive** alienate, bankrupt, beggar, beguile someone of something, bleed white, divest, fleece, impoverish, pauperise, pillage, rob, ruin, strip, take from. *Informal:* bust, clean out, do out of, shake, skin. **9. crop** cull, gather, reap, subtract.

10. **1. extort** blackmail, exact, extract, force, rack-rent, sweat. *Informal:* garnish *(British)*, put the nips in, put the screws on, screw, shake down. **2. cadge** beg, bleed dry. *Informal:* bite someone for, bludge, bludge off, bludge on, bot, bum, eat out of house and home, fang, hum, put the acid on, put the bite on, put the hooks into, scab, scunge.

11. **1. capture** apprehend, arrest, carry, catch, conquer, jump, plunder, seize, surprise, swoop down on, take, take by storm, take by surprise, take possession of, take prisoner, trap. *Informal:* bag, bounce, collar, knock off, lumber, nab, nick, pick up, pinch, pull in. **2. conquer** carry off, extend. **3. seize** help oneself to, plunder, take by storm, take possession of. *Informal:* jump at. **4. abduct** abduce, abstract, bear off, carry off, kidnap, make away with, remove, spirit away (or off), tear off with. **5. grab** bag, catch, catch at, catch up, clasp, clutch, clutch at, fist, foot, gobble, grasp, grip, gripe, help oneself, hook, lay by the heels, lay hold of (or on), make a grab for, pocket, pounce, reach, seize, snap, snatch, snavel, steal, swoop up, tail, take, take hold of, whisk, wrench, wrest. *Informal:* collar, jump at, nab, nail, scrag, snaffle.

RELATED KEYWORDS: ACQUIREMENT, IMPOSITION, ROBBERY

TALKATIVENESS

n. **1.** **1. talkativeness** chattiness, communicativeness, garrulity, garrulousness, gassiness, longwindedness, loquacity, verbosity, volubility, volubleness. *Informal:* jaw, verbal diarrhoea.

2. **1. talk** blat, causerie, chitchat, civilities, colloquy, commune, communication, communion, confabulation, conference, conversation, conversazione, converse, dialogue, discourse, give-and-take, intercourse, interlocution, parley, repartee, shoptalk, small talk, speech, table talk, whispering. *Informal:* chinwag, confab, yabber. **2. chat** causerie, conversation, natter, talk, yarn. *Informal:* chinwag, convo, rap, wongi, yabber. **3. interview** press conference. **4. heart-to-heart** dialogue, duologue, tete-a-tete, vis-a-vis. *Informal:* D & M. **5. telephone call** advocacy call, call, person-to-person. *Informal:* galah session. **6. chatter** babble, blab, blather, cackle, causerie, chat, chitchat, claver *(Scottish)*, drivel, malarky, moonshine, natter, palaver, pap, patter, persiflage, prate, prattle, twaddle. *Informal:* baloney, chinwag, gab, gas, guff, guyver, rave, slipslop, waffle, yak, yap. **7. gossip** ana, dirt, furphy, gossiping, hearsay, scandal, tattle, tittle-tattle. *Informal:* goss, scuttlebutt.

3. **1. discussion** academic, adjournment debate, argument, argumentation, colloquy, conference, consultation, controversy, cross-fire, cross-talk, debate, dialogism, disputation, dispute, korero *(NZ)*, parley, talk. **2. argument** altercation, bicker, catfight, contretemps, disputation, polemic, row, slanging match, squabble, tiff, words, wrangling. *Informal:* argy-bargy, barney, ding, hassle, high words, ruction, run-in. **3. conference** colloquium, colloquy, congress, convention, discussion, korero *(NZ)*, negotiation, palaver, parley, plea bargaining, pourparler, powwow, roundtable discussion, seminar, summit, symposiac, symposium, talk, teach-in, workshop. *Informal:* gabfest, talkfest.

4. **1. talker** collocutor, colloquist, conversationalist, converser, debater, dialogist, dialoguer, discourser, interlocutor, interlocutrice, interlocutrix. **2. big-mouth** waffler, yaffler. *Informal:* all guff 'n' guyver, bag of wind, fluter, gasbag, gusher, rattletrap, windbag, yabberer. **3. chatterbox** cackler, chatterer, flibbertigibbet, gabber, magger, magpie, prater, prattler. **4. gossip** gossiper, gossipmonger, newsmonger, scandalmonger, sneak, tale-bearer, tattler, telltale, tittle-tattle. *Informal:* scuttlebutt, tabby. **5. interviewer** interviewee. **6. negotiator** honest broker, negotiant.

adj. **5.** **1. talkative** chatty, communicable, communicative, conversational, diffuse, garrulous, gossipy, longwinded, loquacious, of many words, prolix, rambling, verbose, voluble, wordy. *Informal:* gabby, gassy, motormouth. **2. conversational** conferential, north-south interlocutory. **3. talkback** open-line.

v. **6.** **1. talk** burr, commune, confabulate, confer, consult, converse, dialogue, discourse, elocute, get together, have a word with, palaver, parley, rhapsodise, soliloquise, speak, talk shop, tongue, yaffle. *Informal:* confab, go into a huddle, pass the flute, pass the kip, pialla, powwow, pyalla, waffle, wongi, yabber. **2. negotiate** broker, talk over. *Informal:* talk turkey. **3. chat** blab, blabber, blather, blether *(British)*, chatter, claver *(Scottish)*, gossip, mag, palaver, pass the time of day, patter, powwow, talk, tattle, visit *(US)*, yarn. *Informal:* bat the breeze, earbash, natter, rap, schmooze, yak. **4. gossip** natter, rumour, tattle. *Informal:* chew the fat, chew the rag. **5. chinwag** chatter, go on, mag, prattle. *Informal:* bend someone's ear, chew someone's ear, gab, gasbag, jaw, jawbone. **6. chatter** babble, cackle, clatter, drivel, footle, gloze, gossip, jabber, mag, natter, prate, prattle, rattle, splutter, talk, twaddle. **7. discuss** address, advise with, argue, canvass, caucus, consult, controvert, debate, deliberate, have it out, kick about, kick around, korero *(NZ)*, review, talk, thrash out. *Informal:* barney, tangle with. **8. argue** bicker, chaffer, contend, debate, dispute, quarrel, wrangle. *Informal:* argle-bargle, argufy, argy-bargy, have words with, row.

RELATED KEYWORDS: DISAGREEMENT, VERBOSITY, CONTEST, ELOQUENCE, BOMBAST, NONSENSE, MEDIATION, QUESTION, SPEECH

TASTE

n. **1.**   **1. taste** aftertaste, degustation. **2. flavour** body, flavouring, race, relish, sapor, savour, substance. **3. tang** nip, smack, soupçon, suspicion, tinge. **4. tastiness** delicateness, flavoursomeness, freshness, mellowness, palatability, richness, sapidity, savouriness. **5. palate** relish, taste, tooth. **6. acquired taste** foretaste, prelibation. **7. gustation** tea-tasting, wine-tasting.

2.   **1. taster** savourer, tea-taster, wine-taster.

adj. **3.**   **1. tasty** ambrosial, appetising, delicate, delicious, flavorous, flavourful, flavoursome, fresh, lipsmacking, luscious, more-ish, mouth-watering, nectareous, palatable, pleasing, savorous *(Chiefly US)*, savory, savoury, sweet, tangy, toothsome, zestful. *Informal:* delish, easy-to-take, goluptious, nummy, scrummy, scrumptious, yummy. **2. full-bodied** aggressive, big, foxy, fruity, generous, intense, rancio, rich, strong, vintage, vivid. *Informal:* gutsy. **3. mellow** creamy, smooth. **4. plain** gentle, mild.

v. **4.**   **1. taste** eat, lick, relish, sample, savour, smack one's lips, test, try. **2. taste of** smack of. **3. mellow** age, maturate, mature, ripen, season. **4. flavour** tinge.

RELATED KEYWORDS: PUNGENCY, PLEASANT FLAVOUR, UNPLEASANT FLAVOUR, FOOD, SWEETNESS, SOURNESS

TEACHER

n. **1.**   **1. teacher** demonstrator, educationalist, educationist, educator, heurist, instructor, knowledge worker, preceptor, professor, schoolman, sensei, side, sir, Sophist, tutor. **2. schoolteacher** adviser, assistant teacher, careers adviser, counsellor, CRT *(Victoria)*, dominie *(Chiefly Scottish)*, form master, form mistress, governess, headmaster, headmistress, housemaster, housemistress, master, mistress, pedagogue, principal, PT instructor, remedial teacher, school-teacher, schoolmaster, schoolmistress, sportsmaster, sportsmistress, subprincipal, usher *(British History)*. *Informal:* beak, chalkie, guzinter, schoolie, schoolmarm. **3. relief teacher** casual teacher *(Especially NSW)*, emergency teacher *(Victoria)*, supply teacher *(Qld)*. **4. teacher aide. 5. professor** academic, associate professor, chancellor, dean, doctor, don, emeritus, pro-vice-chancellor, provost, reader, rector, senior lecturer, subdean, vice-chancellor, visiting professor. *Informal:* aspro, prof. **6. lecturer** docent *(US)*, senior tutor, supervisor, teaching fellow, tutor. **7. rhetor** rhetorician. **8. teaching staff** cadre, department, faculty, professoriate, school. **9. coach** coacher, drillmaster, gym instructor, mentor, personal trainer, riding master, trainer. **10. animal trainer** breaker, horse whisperer, horsebreaker, lion tamer. **11. disciplinarian** discipliner.

2.   **1. enlightener** apostle, Bodhisattva, civiliser, initiator, prophet, refiner, torchbearer. **2. mentor** adviser, counsellor, guru, mufti, sage. **3. apostle** evangelist, gospeller, missionary, preacher, prophet. *Informal:* hot-gospeller. **4. guru** maharishi, swami. **5. indoctrinator** agitprop, implanter, inculcator, promulgator, propagandist.

3.   **1. educational office** chair, deanship, headmastership, lectureship, proctorship, professoriate, professorship. **2. tutorship** instructorship, supervisorship.

RELATED KEYWORDS: GUIDANCE, MISGUIDANCE, LEARNING, SCHOOL, WISE PERSON

TEACHING

n. **1.**   **1. teaching** direction, drilling, education, exegesis, exercitation, explanation, guidance, implantation, inculcation, indoctrination, initiation, instruction, pedagogy, promulgation, reskilling, schooling, skilling, spoon-feeding, training, tuition, tutelage, tutorage. **2. catechesis** kerugma, preaching, preachment. **3. guidance** advice, consciousness raising, counsel, direction, edification, enlightenment, instruction. **4. rearing** breeding, bringing-up, civilisation, cultivation, education, nurture, parenting, up-bringing. **5. didacticism** didactics, doctrinism, educology, heurism, pedagogics, pedagogy, scholasticism, teaching. **6. toilet-training** *Informal:* house-training, potty-training.

2.   **1. type of education** adult education, coeducation, continuing education, day classes, distance learning, evening classes, further education, higher education, manual training, PE, physical education, physical training, primary education, re-education, remediation, schooling, secondary education, self-education, sex education, special education, technical education, tertiary education, three r's, vocational training.

3. **1. teaching method** chalk and talk, direct method, discovery method, heuristic method, hypnopaedia, Montessori method, Socratic method, team teaching. **2. teaching aid** Cuisenaire rods, epidiascope, language laboratory, overhead projector, teaching machine, visual aid.

4. **1. teachings** doctrine, doxy, koan, prescribed text, set book, text, textbook, workbook.

adj. 5. **1. teaching** catechetical, catechistic, consciousness-raising, didactic, edificatory, educational, exegetical, indoctrinatory, instructional, instructive, introductory, pedagogic, pedagogical, preceptive, tuitionary. **2. introductory** preliminary, preparatory, propaedeutic. *Informal:* prep, the bubs *(Chiefly Victoria)*. **3. advanced** difficult.

6. **1. teachable** docile, educable. **2. toilet-trained** *Informal:* potty-trained. **3. house-trained** housebroken.

v. 7. **1. induct** indoctrinate, indoctrinate in, induct to. **2. teach** apprentice, coach, cultivate, develop, disciple, drill, edify, educate, enlighten, familiarise, ground, illuminate, illumine, implant, inculcate, induct to, initiate, instil, instruct, introduce, learn *(Aboriginal English)*, manage, prepare, qualify, school, shape, sophisticate, spoon-feed, team-teach, train, tutor, upskill. *Informal:* cram. **3. lecture** evangelise, harangue, preach, preachify *(Chiefly US)*, promulgate, proselyte, proselytise, sermonise. *Informal:* earbash. **4. demonstrate** enlighten, prove, show. *Informal:* work at the chalkface. **5. examine** assess, catechise, evaluate, introspect, measure. **6. re-educate** rehabilitate, resocialise.

8. **1. rear** breed, bring up, discipline, drill, nurture, raise, teach manners to. **2. house-train** toilet-train. *Informal:* potty-train.

adv. 9. **1. didactically** exponentially, pedagogically, preachingly, preceptively.

RELATED KEYWORDS: GUIDANCE, MISGUIDANCE, LEARNING, SCHOOL, TEACHER, STUDENT

TELECOMMUNICATIONS

n. 1. **1. telecommunications** communications, electronic media, electronic publishing, mass media, media, telecine. **2. public broadcasting** community radio. **3. broadcast** colourcast, feature, newscast, newsradio, outside broadcast, phone-in, satellite broadcast, simulcast, talk radio, talkback, telecast, telethon, transcription, transmission. **4. telephone** answering machine, answerphone, car phone, cell phone, cellular car phone, cellular mobile phone, cellular telephone, extension, handpiece, handset, hot line, intercommunication system, interphone, mobile phone, party line, pay phone, pay telephone, payphone, processor, public telephone, radiotelephone, receiver, red phone, telefacsimile, tie line, videophone, vocoder. *Informal:* blower, dog and bone, eau de Cologne, intercom, mobie, phone, telling bone. **5. telephone call** international call, ISD call, person-to-person call, reverse-charge call, ring, SMS, STD call, text message, tinkle, trunk call. *Informal:* bell, buzz, tingle. **6. international subscriber dialling** ISD code, STD code, subscriber trunk dialling. **7. exchange** central *(US)*, PABX, PBX, private automatic branch exchange, private branch exchange, step-by-step, telephone exchange, trunks. **8. switchboard** crossbar switch. *Informal:* switch. **9. telephone box** callbox *(British)*, kiosk *(British)*, pay station *(US)*. **10. telegraphy** radiotelegraphy, telegraphics. **11. teleprinter** teletype, teletypewriter, telex.

2. **1. radio** crystal set, jigger, pedal wireless, radio receiver, radio set, radio-cassette, radiogram, radiotelephony, receiver, receiving set, sports ears, steam radio, transceiver, transistor, two-way, walkie-talkie, wireless, wireless set. *Informal:* gibson girl, trannie. **2. transmitter** matter transmitter, racon, radio beacon, radio transmitter, transmitting set, transponder. **3. modulator** tuner. **4. microphone** bug, cans, carbon microphone, cartridge, contact microphone, throat microphone. *Informal:* mic, mike. **5. valve** beam tube, cistern valve, diode, dynatron, electron tube *(US Electronics)*, pentagrid, pentode, radio valve, thermionic valve, tickler coil, triode, tube. **6. airplay** air, airshift, publicity. **7. interference** hash, noise, snow, whistler. *Informal:* jitter. **8. modulation** demodulation, diplexer, duplexer, heterodyne method, phase modulation, pulse-time modulation, superheterodyne method, synchrodyne method. **9. amplitude modulation** AM, FM, frequency modulation. **10. wireless technology** 3G, bluetooth wireless technology, wi-fi.

3. **1. television** black-and-white, cable television, cable TV, closed-circuit television, colour television, monitor, satellite television, set, tube, TV, valve. *Informal:* boob tube, cable, idiot box, small screen, telly, the box, vid, video *(US)*. **2. video cassette recorder** camcorder, PVR, recorder, teleplayer, VCP, VCR, video recorder, video tape recorder. **3. phototelegraphy** telephotography, teletext. **4. teleprompter** autocue.

4. **1. the internet** cyberspace, the Net, the Web, World Wide Web. **2. internet access** ADSL, bluetooth wireless technology, broadband, cable, cable modem, dialup. **3. website** commons, home page, internet portal, node, portal, web page, web portal. **4. blog** vlog, web log. **5. URL** bookmark, domain name. **6. cookie. 7. search engine** spambot, web browser, web crawler. **8. chat room** chat, internet relay chat, newsgroup. **9. email** flame mail, flame war. **10. posting** flame bait. **11. internet café** cyber café, games café. **12. internet user** hacker. *Informal:* cyberbabe, geekgirl, mouse potato, net chick, nethead, netizen, webhead. **13. netpreneur** technopreneur. **14. e-business** cybermall, cyberstore, dotcom, e-commerce, e-tailer, home shopping, internet banking, storefront. **15. netsurfing** ego-surfing, googling, surfing. **16. cybersex** cyberporn, netsex, teledildonics.

5. **1. telecommunications station** channel, citizen band radio, earth station, pirate radio, radio station, recording studio, relay station, sound studio, station, studio, television station. **2. network** circuit, hook-up, link-up, radio link, radio relay, video link. **3. landline** fixed line, transmission line. **4. communication satellite** comsat. **5. signal** air, airwaves, carrier, carrier wave, continuous waves, direct ray, direct wave, ground wave, long wave, medium wave, radio signal, radio wave, radiofrequency, sky wave, wavelength. **6. crystal** cat whisker, cat's whisker, crystal detector, crystal rectifier. **7. control room** studio.

6. **1. aerial** antenna, dipole, direction-finder, dish antenna, ferrite-rod aerial, monopole, radiator, radio direction-finder, Yagi aerial. *Informal:* rabbit ears.

7. **1. television equipment** camera, cartridge, cathode-ray tube, channel, cinecamera, cue card, floater, flying spot scanner, iconoscope, idiot board, image orthicon, microphone, orthicon, overlay, pick-up, picture tube, plumbicon, scanner, shadow-mask, video camera, videodisc, videotape, videotext, vidicon, vision mixer. *Informal:* mic, mike.

adj. **8.** **1. broadcast** airtime, beamed, live, live-action, on (the) air, prerecorded, recorded, transmitted.

v. **9.** **1. telecast** beam, broadcast, colourcast, datacast, multichannel, newscast, podcast, radio, satellite, televise, transmit, webcast.

10. **1. telephone** buzz, call, get through to, message, ring, ring up, signal, SMS, text, wireless. *Informal:* bell.

RELATED KEYWORDS: COMMUNICATION, ELECTRICITY, ENTERTAINMENT, MESSAGE, NEWS

TEMPORARINESS

n. **1.** **1. temporariness** changeableness, currency, impermanence, impermanency, temporality. **2. transitoriness** caducity, evanescence, fleetingness, fugacity, fugitiveness, transience, transientness, volatileness, volatility.

2. **1. temporary appointment** commendam, interim council, interregnum, regency, temporals. **2. casual** ad hoc committee, temporary, transient. *Informal:* floater, temp.

3. **1. temporary thing** breath, flash, instant, moment, second, split second, spurt, trice, twinkle, twinkling. *Informal:* a brace of shakes, crack, jiffy, shake, tick, whipstitch *(US)*. **2. ephemeron** ephemera, flash in the pan, nine day wonder. *Informal:* one-hit wonder.

adj. **4.** **1. temporary** acting, commendatory, de bene esse, fill-in, interim, jury, make-do, makeshift, mutable, on (or to) account, pro tem, pro tempore, provisional, provisory, stopgap, substitute, temporal, temporarily, tentative, transitory, working. **2. transitory** brief, cursory, disposable, ephemeral, evanescent, fleeting, fugacious, fugitive, hasty, in transit, like a dream, passing, shifting, summary, transient, volatile. **3. instant** ad hoc, extemporaneous, extempore, immediate, impromptu, instantaneous, momentary, split-second. **4. short-lived** earthborn, here today and gone tomorrow, mortal, perishable, primitive, short-life, spasmodic. **5. brief** acute, brisk, meteoric, quick, short. **6. impermanent** casual, catchy, deciduous, inordinate, irregular, labile, lapsable, movable, occasional, odd, ragged, semipermanent, spotty, transitory, uneven.

adv. **5.** **1. temporarily** ad hoc, for the moment, for the nonce, for the time being, in the interim, in the meantime, present, pro tem, pro tempore, provisionally. **2. transitorily** ephemerally, fleetingly, flickeringly, fugaciously, fugitively, transiently. **3. in passing** by the bye, by the way, casually, en passant, incidentally. **4. briefly** acutely, in the twinkling of an eye, meteorically.

RELATED KEYWORDS: CHANGE, CHANGEABLENESS, MOMENT, SPEED

TEST

n. **1.** **1. test** ascertainment, assay, bio-assay, check, crucible, essay, examination, experiment, herd testing, titration, touch, trial. **2. experiment** assay, control experiment, gedanken experiment, inquiry, leap in the dark, probe, test, thought experiment, trial, trial run. **3. trial** dress rehearsal, dry run, dummy run, field trial, pilot, pilot film, pilot study, rehearsal, road test, run-through, trial run, tryout, walk-through, war game, work-out. **4. trial by ordeal** acid test, baptism of fire, ordeal.

2. 1. tests – miscellaneous acid test, affluence test, aptitude test, Benedict's test, beta test, Binet test, blood alcohol test, blood cholesterol test, blood test, breath test, cholesterol test, crash test, drill stem test, driving test, fatigue test, flame test, Guthrie test, impact test, intelligence test, literacy test, litmus test, Mantoux test, nuchal translucency test, nuclear test, paternity test, performance test, pinch test, PKU test, PSA test, road test, screen test, stress test.

3. 1. empiricism empirical formula, experimentalism, experimentation, tentation, trial and error, verification.

4. 1. tester academic, analyst, assayer, empiricist, experimentalist, experimenter, gauger, herd tester, researcher, sampler, scientist. **2. testing agent** criteria, criterion, determinative, gage, gauge, key performance indicator, litmus paper, monitor, reagent, test, test paper, tide gauge, touchstone. **3. test group** guineapig, pilot plant, subject. **4. control group** canon, criterion, gauge, standard, touchstone, yardstick. **5. laboratory** insectary, phytotron, proving ground, test tube, wind-tunnel.

adj. **5. 1. test** dummy run, pilot, probative, trial. **2. experimental** a posteriori, conditional, empiric, empirical, hypothetical, provisional, tentative. **3. probational** on approval, on probation, on trial, verificatory. *Informal:* on appro. **4. tentative** experimental, speculative.

v. **6. 1. test** assay, endeavour, essay, put to the test, seek, trial, try out. **2. try** sample, test. **3. hypothesise** explore every avenue, try out an idea. *Informal:* fly a kite. **4. experiment** ascertain, assay, condition, determine, evaluate, prove, take, test, titrate, try. **5. monitor** assess, calibrate, cess, control, evaluate, measure.

RELATED KEYWORDS: ANALYSIS, ATTEMPT, MATTER, MEASUREMENT

TEXTILES

n. **1. 1. textiles** cloth, contexture, fabric, homespun, material, stuff, texture, tissue. **2. knit** knitting, stockinet. **3. cotton print** batik, battik, challis, chiné, futah, India print, persienne, sarong. **4. rag** bribe, fag end, flock, lock, necks, tag, tatter, tatters, thrum, waste. **5. lining** buckram, fleece, interfacing, interlining, venetian. **6. padding**. **7. suiting** blanketing, coating, sacking, shirting, skirting, skirting board, skirtings, towelling, vesting *(Chiefly US)*. **8. waterproof** camlet, japara, mackintosh, nettlecloth, oilcloth, oiled silk, oilskin, tammy. *Informal:* mac. **9. lint** gauze, jaconet. **10. crush fabric**. **11. swatch** bolt, length, piece, roll, web, weft.

2. 1. manchester dry goods, lingerie, mercery, napery, piece goods, soft goods. **2. drapes** arras, curtain, drapery, hangings, runner, swag, valance, wall-hanging. **3. soft furnishings** curtains, drapes, hangings, upholstery. **4. upholstery fabric** chintz, frisé, moquette, madras muslin, tabaret. **5. carpet** Aubusson carpet, Axminster carpet, body carpet, broadloom carpet, brussels carpet, carpet tile, carpeting, felting, hooked rug, Persian carpet, red carpet, shag pile, stair-carpet, velvet carpet, Wilton carpet.

3. 1. weave feel, pattern, stitch, wale, watering. **2. weft** pick, shoot, warp, woof. **3. nap** float, pile. **4. different weaves** basket weave, double cloth, double tabby, interlock, Jacquard weave, khaddar, locknit, plain weave, satin, tabby, twill, two-way stretch, union, waffle-weave, warp-face weave, whipping. **5. yarn** cabling, fibre, fibril, filament, fluff, noil, oakum, pack-thread, rope yarn, rove, roving, thread, tops, tram, twist.

4. 1. lace Alençon lace, all-over, Battenberg lace, binche lace, bobbin lace, bobbinet, brussels lace, cascade, chantilly, cluny lace, drawn-thread work, duchesse lace, filet lace, gauze, guipure, lacework, macramé, Mechlin lace, mesh, needle-point lace, net, orris, pillow lace, point, reseau, tatting, tiffany, torchon lace, valenciennes. **2. embossment** enlacement, moiré, morrie, pattern, print, watering. **3. trimmings** bias binding, elastic, flouncing, gauffer, goffer, insertion, lastings, material, piping, rickrack, ricrac, ruche, ruching, ruffle, soutache, stripe, tape, tinsel. *Informal:* fixings.

5. 1. sewing cutwork, darning, dressmaking, fancywork, overcasting, petit point, sampler, smocking, whipping. **2. spinning** beating-up, carding, combing, contexture, crabbing, filature, shedding. **3. lacing** tatting. **4. weaving** intertwining, interweaving, tapestry. **5. embroidery** appliqué, broderie anglaise, broidery, cornelli, couching, crewelwork, cutwork, needle point, needlepoint. **6. quilting** Florentine trapunto, patchwork, trapunto. **7. crochet. 8. knitting.**

6. 1. sewing machine charka, knitting machine, napper, overlocker, scutch. **2. sewing aid** bobbin, bodkin, buttonholer, card, clew, clue, comb, crochet hook, darner, darning needle, distaff, dobbie, dobby, godet, hemming foot, knitting needle, knitting wire, monkey, needle, pick, quill, reed, ripple, rippler, sacking needle, spindle, tacking needle, temple, thimble, three-cornered needle, upholsterer's needle. **3. spinning wheel** jenny, spinning jenny, throstle. **4. loom** Jacquard loom, power loom, scribbler. **5. flax mill** willower.

7. 1. sewer darner, dressmaker, hemmer, looper, machinist, needlewoman, seamstress, sempstress, tailer, tailor, taylor. **2. weaver** knitter, tatter. **3. textile worker** comber, napper, rippler, teaseller. *Informal:* flaxie *(NZ)*.

8. 1. yarn abb, acetate fibre, acrilan, alaska, berlin, berlin wool, bouclé, byssus, carpet wool, clothing wool, combed yarn, combing wool, cotton, crewel, filasse, fingering, flax, floss, floss silk, French combing (wool), gossamer, grease wool, hemp *(NZ)*, henequen, homespun, istle, ixtle, jute, Kevlar, linen, lint cotton, linters, lisle thread, lurex, lycra, maguey, manila hemp, manila rope, merino, mungo, organzine, plucked wool, poly-cotton, PVC, ramie, raw silk, rayon, rope yarn, schappe silk, scoured wool, shetland wool, shoddy, silk, skin wool, sleave, slipe, slub, spinner's type, staple, thrown silk, thrums, top maker's type, triacetate fibre, tussah, tusser, tussore, vegetable silk, wool, worsted, zephyr yarn.

9. 1. cotton aertex, alaska, balbriggan, batiste, bird's-eye, buckram, bunting, byssus, calico *(US)*, chambray, cheesecloth, cotton broadcloth, cotton flannel, cottonade, covert cloth, cretonne, crinoline, delaine, denim, dimity, dowlas, drabbet, drill, drilling, dun-garee, eiderdown, fustian, huckaback, jean, lawn, longcloth, monk's cloth, mousseline, mousseline de laine, mousseline de soie, mull, muslin, nainsook, nankeen, nankin, ninon, organdie, osnaburg, Oxford, percale, percaline, poplin, regatta, sateen, scrim, tarlatan, terry towelling, turkey red, winceyette. **2. linen** bird's-eye, cambric, damask, holland, scrim, toile. **3. silk** bombasine, byssus, gum silk, messaline, paduasoy, peau de soie, pongee, raw silk, samite, sarcenet, sarsenet, sendal, shantung, sleave, tabby, tussah, tusser, tussore, wild silk. **4. wool** alpaca, Angora, bearskin, beaver, calamanco, camelhair, camlet, cashmere, chinchilla, cilice, delaine, doeskin, duffel, duffle, flannel, flannelette, grogram, kashmir, kersey, kerseymere, Linsey-Woolsey, lisle, melton, merino, mocha, mohair, moreen, mousseline de laine, petersham, pilot-cloth, rateen, ratine, shalloon, stamin, swan's-down, tabbinet, Tasmanian bluey, toilinet, tweed, vicuña, whipcord, wincey, winsey, wonga bluey, woollen broadcloth, worsted, zibeline. **5. synthetics** acetate rayon, acrylic, art silk, artificial silk, banlon, bri-nylon, celanese, cellulose acetate, crimplene, dacron, grenadine, lurex, nylon, orlon, polyester, rayon, rayon broadcloth, sharkskin, taffeta, terylene.

10. 1. soft fabric astrakhan, chenille, duvetyn, foulard, kid, kidskin, lambskin, moquette, panne, plush, suede, velour, velure, velvet, velveteen. **2. sheer fabric** Canton crepe, chiffon, circassian, crepe, crepe de Chine, gauze, georgette, gossamer, madras, marocain, marquisette, milanese, nun's veiling, organza, piña cloth, pongee, romaine, Swiss muslin, tulle, viyella, voile, zephyr cloth. **3. heavy fabric** bagging, baize, bocking, boxcloth, burlap, canvas, duck, felt, fustian, gunny, harden, hessian, hopsack, jute, matting, sack-cloth, sailcloth, webbing, wigan. **4. haircloth** horsehair. **5. patterned fabric** argyle, brocade, brocatelle, calamanco, candy stripe, check, checker, diaper, gingham, grey goods, hairline, Harris tweed, hound's-tooth check, Jacquard weave, lampas, matelassé, mixture, overcheck, paisley, patchwork, pinstripe, piqué, plaid, plissé, polka dot, pom-padour, print, regatta, russet, seersucker, sett, shepherd's check, shepherd's plaid, stripe, tartan, tattersall, tweed. **6. shiny fabric** angelskin, brilliantine *(US)*, ciré, cloth of gold, diamanté, glaze, lamé, lurex, lustre, satin, satinet, slipper satin, taffeta.

11. 1. knitted fabric casinett, cassimere, jersey, jersey cloth, tricot. **2. cord** barathea, bedford cord, bengaline, chenille, cheviot, chino, corduroy, diagonal cloth, faille, gros-grain, ottoman, pinwale corduroy, serge. **3. twill** diagonal cloth, foulard, fustian, gabardine, gaberdine, jean, kerseymere, khaki, parramatta, regatta, shalloon, surah. **4. matted fabric** felt, tapa.

12. 1. stitches blanket stitch, Bokhara couching, buttonhole stitch, chain-stitch, couching stitch, coutil, cross-stitch, filling stitch, four-sided stitch, garter stitch, hemstitching, her-ringbone, lazy daisy stitch, needle stitch, outline stitch, overcasting, overhand stitch, Palestrina stitch, Parma stitch, petit point, Princess stitch, Richelieu stitch, Rodi stitch, running stitch, saddle stitch, satin stitch, shadow stitch, slip-stitch, smocking, Star stitch, stay stitching, stem stitch, tent stitch, Turkish stitch, whipping, whipstitch. **2. knitting stitches** cable stitch, garter stitch, moss stitch, plain, purl, rib stitch, ripple, stocking stitch.

v. **13. 1. sew** darn, fine-draw, hem. **2. stitch** buttonhole, run, saddle-stitch, sew. **3. embroider** appliqué, enlace, hook, tat, work. **4. interface** buckram, interline. **5. brocade** boss, damask, emboss, quilt. **6. pipe** goffer. **7. weave** beetle, bolt, card, comb, garnet, pick, ripple, scribble, scutch, spin, spindle, tease, teasel, throw, twill, willow. **8. felt** baste, nap, tack. **9. knit** purl, rib.

RELATED KEYWORDS: CLOTHES, HAIR

THICKNESS

n. **1.**   **1. thickness** amplitude, beam, breadth, crassitude, depth, largeness, latitude, ply, third dimension, tread, wideness, width. **2. diameter** bore, calibre, gauge, module, radius. **3. extent** amount, area, cubic measure, dimensions, expanse, extensiveness, gauge, immensity, magnitude, measure, measurement, quantity, scope, spread, vastitude, volume. **4. bulk** body, bulkiness, corpulence. **5. fullness** bagginess.

     2.   **1. thickening** callosity, callus, coagulation, dilatation, dilation, varicosis, varicosity. **2. chunk** cake, clod, clog, clot, clump, floc, gobbet, hunk, knot, lump, mass, nub, nubbin *(US)*, nugget, wad. *Informal:* chump, dollop, glob, gob.

adj. **3.**   **1. thick** blocky, bold, bold-face, deep, fat, full-faced, heavy, massive, thickish. **2. wide** broad, deep, expansive, extended, extensive, great, immense, large, large-scale, main, outspread, sizable, sizeable, spacious, spread, tabular, vast, vasty *(Poetic)*, widish. **3. spatular** spathulate, spatulate. **4. bloated** blown, blubber, blubbery, incrassate, puffy, sodden, swollen, tumid, turgid, varicose. **5. full** ample, baggy, generous, good, substantial, voluminous. **6. broad** beamy, broad-shouldered, broadish, wide-hipped. *Informal:* broad across the beam. **7. fat** adipose, ample, big, blubbery, bulky, chubby, corpulent, crass, dumpy, elephantine, fatly, fatted, fattish, fatty, fleshy, full-faced, gross, heavy, hefty, large, meaty, obese, overweight, paunchy, plump, podgy, porky, portly, pudgy, pursy, roly-poly, rotund, Rubenesque, steatopygic, well-fed, well-rounded. *Informal:* ginormous, poddy *(British)*, tubby, well-padded. **8. thickset** beefy, bulky, bull-necked, burly, chunky, endomorphic, gross, heavy-set, hulking, pyknic, robust, squab, squabby, squat, squatty, stocky, stodgy, stout, stubbed, stubby, stumpy, well-built. *Informal:* fubsy, husky. **9. solid** adamant, compact, dense, gross, heavy, intense, lump, massive, sodden, thick, thickset.

v. **4.**   **1. thicken** bloat, fatten *(Chiefly US)*, swell, widen.

adv. **5.**   **1. thickly** bulkily, crassly, podgily, solidly, stockily, stodgily, stoutly, stumpily, thick. **2. widely** abroad, broadly, extensively, spaciously, wide.

     6.   **1. widthwise** breadthways, broadside, broadways, laterally.

RELATED KEYWORDS: SIZE, LENGTH, SOLIDITY

THIEF

n. **1.**   **1. thief** abstracter, acquirer, appropriator, Autolycus *(Greek Legend)*, boodler, cribber, cutpurse, filcher, fingerer, flogger, frisker, hoister, jumper, kleptomaniac, lurcher, picaro, picaroon, picklock, pickpocket, pilferer, purloiner, robber, shoplifter, snowdropper, stealer, water-rat. *Informal:* dip, forty, head-puller, kway, light fingers, ratter, tea-and-sugar bushranger, tea-leaf. **2. burglar** cat-burglar, housebreaker, picklock, sneakthief. *Informal:* cracksman, pussy-footer, yegg *(US)*. **3. safebreaker** safeblower *(US)*, tank-man. **4. fence** receiver of stolen goods. **5. cattleduffer** duffer, horse-duffer, poacher, rustler. *Informal:* gully-raker, poddy-dodger.

     2.   **1. bandit** bravo, brigand, bushranger, dacoit *(Indian English)*, Dick Turpin, highwayman, mosstrooper, pad, ranger, Robin Hood, thug, waylayer. *Informal:* chokeman, goon, knight of the road, Ned Kelly, poofter-rorter. **2. pirate** buccaneer, corsair, filibuster, forayer, freebooter, hijacker, marauder, picaroon, sea robber, sea rover, sea-robber, sea-rover, skyjacker, viking, wrecker. **3. looter** depredator, despoiler, forayer, harpy, marauder, pillager, plunderer, predator, ransacker, rifler, robber baron, sacker, spoiler, spoliator. **4. kidnapper** baby snatcher. **5. body-snatcher** ghoul, resurrectionist.

RELATED KEYWORDS: DECEPTION, TAKING, UNLAWFULNESS, IMMORALITY, ROBBERY

THINKING

n. **1.**   **1. thinking** cerebration, cogitation, concentration, consideration, contemplation, deliberation, headwork, ideation, intellectualisation, introspection, lateral thinking, meditation, musing, philosophism, preoccupation, reconsideration, reflection, rumination, thought, thought experiment, wool-gathering. *Informal:* think. **2. thoughtfulness** contemplativeness, deliberativeness, introspectiveness, meditativeness, pensiveness, profoundness, reflectiveness, transcendentalism.

     2.   **1. thought** cerebration, cogitation, consideration, percept, reflection, thinking. **2. meditation** brown study, reflection, samadhi, thought. **3. free association** stream of consciousness.

3. **1. thinker** brooder, cogitator, concentrator, contemplator, deliberator, headworker, intellectual, meditator, muser, philosophiser, puzzler, ruminator. **2. think tank** brains trust.

adj. 4. **1. thinking** cogitative, considerate, contemplative, meditative, museful, musing, pensive, preoccupied, reflective, ruminant, ruminative, speculative, thoughtful.

v. 5. **1. think** be in a brown study, bethink oneself of, calculate, cast about, cerebrate, cogitate, compute, conceive of, conceptualise, figure, ideate, imagine, reckon, revolve in one's mind, suppose, view. *Informal:* bash one's brains out, use one's loaf, use one's noodle. **2. ponder** concentrate, consider, contemplate, cudgel one's brains, mull over, muse, reflect, speculate, take to heart, think, turn over in one's mind. *Informal:* put on one's thinking cap. **3. meditate** brood, chew over, introspect, muse, ponder, pore over (or on) (or upon), reflect, reflect on, reflect upon, ruminate, run upon. *Informal:* chew the cud, contemplate one's navel. **4. deliberate** agitate, consider, consult, ponder, premeditate, take into consideration, think out, think over, think through, weigh, weigh up. **5. envisage** augur, cogitate, dream of, forecast, speculate, take it into one's head, theorise, think, wonder. **6. opine** account, consider, express, reckon, suppose, take, think. **7. philosophise** intellectualise, theologise. **8. rethink** do a rethink, have second thoughts, reconsider, review. **9. brainstorm** free-associate.

adv. 6. **1. thoughtfully** cogitatively, contemplatively, in a brown study, meditatively, musingly, pensively, reflectively, ruminatingly, speculatively.

RELATED KEYWORDS: CONJECTURE, IDEA, JUDGEMENT, LOGICALITY, MIND

THINNESS

n. 1. **1. thinness** angularness, cadaverousness, emaciation, gauntness, gracility, lankness, lean and hungry look, marasmus, meagreness, peakiness, poorness, scragginess, scrawniness, skinniness, tabescence. **2. leanness** lankiness, slenderness, slightness, slimness, spareness, stalkiness, wiriness. **3. fineness** attenuation, foliation, maceration. **4. tenuousness** subtleness, subtlety, tenuity. **5. narrowing** contraction, intake. **6. narrowness** bottleneck, choke, flume *(US)*, narrows, neck, strait. **7. hairbreadth** hair's-breadth, hairline, hairstroke. **8. blade** lath, shim, slat, spline, taper, thong. **9. strip** band, belt, belting, facia, fascia, fillet, ray, slip, stripe, swathe. **10. tendril** ray, shaft, stem, thread.

2. **1. thin person** a mere shadow of one's former self, beanstalk, ectomorph, hatchet face, scarecrow, scrag, skin and bones, spindlelegs, spindleshanks, sylph, wasp, weed, wisp, wraith. *Informal:* bag of bones, beanpole, Belsen horror, lolly legs, ninety pound weakling, skeleton, snapper, streak. **2. slimmer** calorie counter, reducer, weight watcher.

3. **1. slimming** calorie-counting, dieting, reducing, slenderising, weight-watching. **2. diet** Atkins diet, biblical diet, CSIRO diet, yoyo diet. **3. starvation diet** subsistence diet.

adj. 4. **1. thin** angular, bony, cadaverous, gaunt, haggard, hatchet-faced, lank, lean, meagre, paper, peaked, peaky, poor, raw-boned, scraggy, scrawny, skinny, slight, spare, sparse, thin as a lath, thin as a rail, thin as a rake, virgate, weak. **2. slender** attenuate, attenuated, ectomorphic, gracile, lean, light, slight, slim, slimline, small, tenuous, wiry, wisplike, wispy, wraithlike. **3. svelte** hourglass, limber, lissom, lithe, sinuous, slinky, supple, waisted, wasp-waisted, waspish, willowish, willowy. **4. stalky** asthenic, gangling, gangly, lanky, rangy, spindle-legged, spindle-shanked, spindling, spindly, stalk-like. **5. skeletal** anorectic, atrophied, bony, emaciated, marasmic, peaked, tabescent, tabetic, wasted, weedy, wizened. **6. narrow** close, confined, contracted, cramped, near, pokey, poky, small. *Informal:* no room to swing a cat. **7. wafer-thin** eggshell, fine-drawn, paper, paper-like, papery, papyraceous, wafery. **8. threadlike** capreolate, filiform, spidery, tendrilous. **9. bladelike** lathlike, lathy. **10. fine** fine-spun, gossamer, hair's-breadth, hairbreadth, hairline, spiry, subtle, tenuous, terete, unsubstantial.

v. 5. **1. thin** attenuate, fall away, fine, fine-draw, rarefy, taper. **2. slim** bant, count calories, cut, diet, fine down, lose weight, reduce, slenderise, take off weight. **3. emaciate** macerate, peak, skeletonise. **4. narrow** confine, constrict, cramp, limit, restrict, squeeze.

adv. 6. **1. thinly** lankily, leanly, slenderly, slimly, stalkily, taperingly, thin. **2. gauntly** angularly, cadaverously, lankly, meagrely, peakily, scraggily. **3. narrowly** close, closely, straitly.

RELATED KEYWORDS: HINDRANCE, INTANGIBILITY, POLE

THREE

n. 1. **1. three** ternary, ternion, triad, trilogy, trine, trinity, trio, triunity. **2. triarchy** trimester, triumvirate, troika. **3. triplets** tercet, triplicate. **4. triennium. 5. threepiece** triplex. **6. threesome** hat-trick, leash.

    2.   **1. triplication** triad, triplicity. **2. triangularity**. **3. trisection** trichotomy, tripartism, tripartition. **4. trisector**.

adj.   3.   **1. third** ternary, tertiary, threefold, treble, triennial, trinal, trine, triple, triplex, triplicate. **2. antepenultimate** third last. **3. three** treble, trinal, trine, triplex, triplicate.

    4.   **1. tripartite** ternary, ternate, three-piece, three-ply, threesome, treble, triadic, trichotomic, trichotomous, trifid, triform, trifurcate, trilinear, trimerous, trinal, trinary, trine, trinomial, triparted, triplex, triplicate. **2. triangular** deltoid, three-cornered, three-square, triangulate, trifacial, trigonal, trigonous, trihedral, trilateral, triquetral, triquetrous. **3. tripedal** tripodal, tripodic.

v.   5.   **1. triple** cube, treble, triplicate. **2. trisect**.

    6.   **1. be third** come third, get a bronze, show.

adv.   7.   **1. triply** threefold, thrice, trebly. **2. tripartitely** ternately. **3. triangularly** trilaterally.

      RELATED KEYWORDS: SHAPE, PART

THRIFT

n.   1.   **1. thrift** abstemiousness, chariness, forehandedness, frugality, frugalness, saving, spareness, sparingness, thriftiness. **2. economy** carefulness, husbandry, providence, prudence. **3. economisation** costcutting, economies of scale, good housekeeping.

    2.   **1. saver** economiser, hoarder. *Informal:* squirrel. **2. stinter** sparer.

adj.   3.   **1. thrifty** economic, economical, frugal, money-conscious, no-frills, penny-wise, provident, saving, skimpy. **2. abstemious** careful, chary, forehanded (*US*), spare, sparing.

v.   4.   **1. save** make every penny work, scrape by on. *Informal:* put it all down south, squirrel. **2. skimp on** stint on. **3. economise** be sparing, cut one's coat according to one's cloth, husband, keep costs down, keep within one's budget, make both ends meet.

adv.   5.   **1. thriftily** economically, frugally, providently, savingly. **2. abstemiously** charily, sparingly, stintingly.

      RELATED KEYWORDS: ABSTINENCE, BUYING, CHEAPNESS, MEANNESS

THROW

n.   1.   **1. throw** cast, chuck, fling, heave, hurl, put, shy, toss, upcast. **2. bowl** delivery, incurve, pitch. **3. types of bowl** beamer, bean-ball, bouncer, bumper, chinaman, doosra, fin, flier, flipper, floater, flyer, full pitch, full toss, googly, half-volley, inswing, inswinger, leg break, leg spinner, lob, off break, off spinner, outswing, outswinger, top spin, topspinner, volley, yorker. *Informal:* bosie, gazunder, leggie, offie, wrong 'un. **4. pass** flick pass, flickback, flip pass. *Informal:* hospital pass.

    2.   **1. thrust** boost, detrusion, dig, dub, jab, jerk, jostle, poke, push, shove, stab, stick, upthrust. **2. impetus** drive, impulse, impulsion, jet propulsion, pressure, propulsion, reaction propulsion, rocket propulsion, sweep. **3. trundle** roll.

    3.   **1. shot** cannon shot, discharge, gunshot, long shot, pot, pot shot, round, shoot, shooting, snipe. **2. volley** bombardment, cannonade, cannonry, crossfire, fire, firing, friendly fire, fusillade, quick fire, rapid fire, salvo, shellfire.

    4.   **1. propellant** booster, impellent, propellent, solid propellant. **2. catapult** mangonel, onager, shanghai, sling, slingshot, trap, trebuchet. *Informal:* dinger, gat, ging, gonk. **3. launching pad** cosmodrome, pad, silo, slipway, ways. **4. paddle** float, oar, scull, sweep. **5. spur** ankus, crop, gad, goad, prod, riding crop, stockwhip, whip. *Informal:* gully-raker. **6. propeller** bow thruster, paddlewheel, pusher, rotor, screw, screw-propeller, tail rotor, tractor. *Informal:* prop.

    5.   **1. thrower** caster, flinger, heaver, hurler, impeller, pitcher, precipitator. **2. bowler** deliverer, fast bowler, leg spinner, off spinner, pace bowler, paceman, quick, spin bowler, spinner, topspinner. *Informal:* leggie.

adj.   6.   **1. propellent** impellent, impulsive, propelling, propulsive. **2. self-propelled** automobile, automotive, horseless, self-propelling.

v.   7.   **1. throw** battledore, bomb, cant, cast, chuck, dart, dash, fire, fling, flip, flirt, heave, hurl, hurtle, jerk, launch, let fly, lob, pass, pitch, pitchfork, quoit, send, shoot, shy, skim, sling, toss, tumble. *Informal:* bung, hoick, hoist, peg, piff *(Chiefly Victoria)*. **2. bowl** deliver, flight, lob, pitch, throw. **3. flop** dump, plunk, precipitate. *Informal:* flump, whop.

    8.   **1. thrust** crowd, detrude, dub, hustle, jab, jog, jolt, jostle, lunge, obtrude, poke, prod, push, ram, shoulder, shove, skewer. *Informal:* boot home. **2. propel** bullet, drive, force, impel, launch, precipitate, project, send, spurt. *Informal:* scoot. **3. roll** bowl, trundle, wheel. **4. edge** elbow, nudge, poke. **5. flick** fillip.

9. **1. shoot** blaze, bolt, discharge, empty, fire, let fly, loose, pepper, shanghai, twang, volley. *Informal:* ping, plug, pot. **2. gun** bombard, cannon, cannonade, carom, catapult, machine-gun, pot, snipe. *Informal:* fill someone full of lead. **3. catapult** bungee, bungy.

RELATED KEYWORDS: FLYING, HITTING, MOVEMENT, WEAPON

TIME

n. **1.** **1. time** Father Time, fourth dimension, geological time, kronos, sands of time, space-time, years. **2. fixed time** chronogram, date, hour, obit, operative date, pull date, zero hour. **3. office hours** after-hours, business hours, flex, flexi hours, flexiday, flexitime, gliding time, overtime, span of hours. *Informal:* fat.

adj. **2.** **1. temporal** chronological, datal, fourth-dimensional, space-time, time.

adv. **3.** **1. then** at that time. **2. during that time** the while. **3. sometime** anytime, around.

conj. **4.** **1. while** as, when, whilst. **2. when** once, whene'er, whenever, whensoever. **3. until** till. **4. whereupon** against.

RELATED KEYWORDS: INTERVAL, MOMENT, THE PAST, THE PRESENT, THE FUTURE, PERIOD, TIME MEASUREMENT

TIMELINESS

n. **1.** **1. timeliness** good timing, opportuneness, propitiousness, seasonableness. **2. punctuality** expedition, promptitude, promptness, punctualness.

2. **1. crucial moment** appropriate moment, climacteric, conjuncture, crisis, crux, great divide, juncture, moment of truth, one's hour, psychological moment, the crunch, the fullness of time, turning point, watershed. **2. deadline** eleventh hour, high time, last minute, term day. **3. time** day, hour, instant, minute, moment, opportunity, second, trice, turn. *Informal:* crack, mo, tick.

adj. **3.** **1. timely** apt, opportune, ready, ripe, seasonable, synchronised, well-timed. *Informal:* pat. **2. punctual** prompt, quick. **3. crucial** critical, decisive, make-or-break, vital. **4. last-minute** eleventh-hour.

v. **4.** **1. be timely** strike while the iron is hot, take time by the forelock. **2. live for the day** carpe diem, make hay while the sun shines.

adv. **5.** **1. timely** critically, in due course, in good time, in season, opportunely, seasonably. **2. punctually** on cue, on time, promptly, sharp. *Informal:* on the beat, on the dot, on the knocker, on the nail, on the tick. **3. in the nick of time** betimes, in the nick (of time), in time.

RELATED KEYWORDS: SIMULTANEITY, TIME, TIME MEASUREMENT

TIME MEASUREMENT

n. **1.** **1. time measurement** anachronism, chronology, chronometry, horology, measurement, timing. **2. dating** carbon dating, dendrochronology, fluorine dating, geochronology, potassium-argon dating, radiocarbon dating. **3. calendar** almanac, ephemeris, Gregorian calendar, Jewish calendar, Julian calendar, menology, Roman calendar. **4. date** date line, day, day of the month, year. **5. mean time** date line, daylight-saving, ephemeris time, local time, mean solar time, standard time, summertime, true time, universal time. *Informal:* zulu time. **6. Greenwich Mean Time** Central Standard Time, Eastern Standard Time, International Atomic Time, Western Standard Time. **7. intercalation** embolism.

2. **1. timepiece** chronometer, clepsydra, sundial, timekeeper, water clock. **2. clock** alarm clock, astronomical clock, atomic clock, caesium clock, carriage clock, chronograph, chronometer, cuckoo clock, digital clock, grandfather clock, grandmother clock, photochronograph. **3. watch** digital watch, hunter, hunting watch, pocket watch, repeater, stem-winder, wristwatch. *Informal:* ticker. **4. biological clock** biological timeclock. **5. timer** autotimer, bundy, chronopher, chronoscope, chronotron, eggtimer, hourglass, parking meter, sand-glass, stopwatch, time clock. **6. time signal** curfew, last post, lights out, pips, retreat, reveille, rouse *(US)*, taps *(US Military)*.

3. **1. time sheet** plod *(WA, Tasmania Mining)*, schedule, timebook, timecard, timetable. *Informal:* cheat sheet, sked.

4. **1. timekeeper** chronologist, clocker, timer. **2. clockmaker** horologist, watchmaker.

5. **1. parts of timepieces** albert, balance (wheel), balance spring, bezel, bob, calibre, centrewheel, chapter, clock, clockwork, crown wheel, dial, escapement, face, gnomon, hairspring, hour hand, mainspring, minute hand, pallet, pendulum, pinwheel, style, watch-chain, watch-glass, watch-guard, watchband, watchcase, watchstrap.

6. **1. hour** attosecond, bell, half-hour, man-hour, millisecond, nanosecond, second, sidereal hour. **2. day** astronomical day, civil day, mean solar day, sidereal day, solar day. **3. week** decan, fortnight, hebdomad, working week. **4. month** anomalistic month, calendar month, lunar month, lunation, moon, solar month, synodic month. **5. year** anomalistic year, astronomical year, bissextile, calendar year, epact, financial year, fiscal year, leap year, lunar year, sidereal year, solar year, tropical year, twelvemonth. **6. decade** centenary, centennial *(US, NZ)*, century, chiliad, decennary, decennium, generation, lustrum, olympiad, pentad, quadrennium, quadricentennial *(US)*, quatercentenary, quincentenary, quinquennial, quinquennium, septenary, sesquicentenary, sesquicentennial, sexcentenary, sexcentennial, sexennial *(US)*, siècle, tercentenary, tercentennial *(US)*, tricentennial, triennial, triennium, vicennium. **7. age** epoch, era, galactic year, millenary, millennium, siècle, sidereal period, solar period.

adj. 7. **1. chronometric** chronogrammatic, chronographic, chronological, datal, horary, horologic.

v. 8. **1. time** clock, keep time, minute. **2. bundy on** clock in, clock on. *Informal:* punch the bundy. **3. periodise** date.

RELATED KEYWORDS: INTERVAL, MOMENT, PERIOD, TIME

TIREDNESS

n. 1. **1. tiredness** fatigue, languor, lassitude, wearifulness, weariness. **2. jadedness** jadishness, staleness. **3. over-tiredness** frazzle, psychasthenia, strain. **4. exhaustion** breakdown, collapse, inanition, limit of endurance, prostration, wornness. *Informal:* crack-up. **5. battle fatigue** combat fatigue.

adj. 2. **1. tired** dozy, drowsy, dull, fatigued, footsore, heavy-eyed, heavy-laden, jaded, jadish, listless, oscitant, overweary, sleepy, somnolent, spiritless, toilworn, warweary, wayworn, wearied, weariful, wearisome, weary, worn. *Informal:* bug-eyed. **2. exhausted** bone-tired, fagged, knocked-up, overworked, overwrought, prostrate, psychasthenic, run-down, strained, stretched, strung-out, worn-out, wrung-out. *Informal:* dog-tired, knackered, pooped, punctured, whacked, zonked. **3. all in** *(Informal)* beaten, blown, broken, defeated, on one's last legs, ruined, spent, wasted, wrecked. *Informal:* beat, buggered, bushed, bushwhacked, cactus, clapped-out, dead, done for, done in, euchred, far gone, flat as a tack, flat out, jack, jiggered, jiggered up, kaput, munted, out for the count, rissoled, stonkered, stuffed, washed-out, washed-up, zapped. **4. like death** green at the gills, half-dead, like death warmed up, white at the gills.

3. **1. tiring** exhausting, exhaustive, gruelling, irksome, killing, tedious, tiresome, weariful, wearing, wearisome, weary, wearying.

v. 4. **1. be tired** die, droop, fade, faint, languish, pass out, reel, sink, stagger, swoon, vacillate. *Informal:* feel like a greasespot. **2. collapse** be fagged out, cark, crack up, crumple, drop, pack up. **3. do one's dash** have shot one's bolt, knock oneself out.

5. **1. tire** do in, exhaust, fatigue, prostrate, ruin, take it out of, use up, weary. *Informal:* fag, fag out, knock up, poop, puncture, tucker out. **2. jade** frazzle, irk. **3. overwork** drive, gruel, outwear, overdrive, overstrain, overtask, overwear, overweary, strain, task, tax, wear. *Informal:* put through the mangle.

adv. 6. **1. tiredly** jadedly, jadishly, wearifully, wearily.

RELATED KEYWORDS: BUSYNESS, EFFORT, WEAKNESS

TOBACCO

n. 1. **1. tobacco** nicotine. *Informal:* baccy, flat, weed. **2. stick of tobacco** plug, quid, twist. *Informal:* nailrod, nicki-nicki, niggerhead, pigtail. **3. type of tobacco** broadleaf, bush tobacco, caporal, cavendish, kapuka, native tobacco, perique, shag. **4. snuff** maccaboy, rappee. **5. cigarette** bidi *(Indian English)*, blue seal *(Philippine English)*, keretek, skag, smoke. *Informal:* african, cancer stick, ciggie, coffin nail, dart, durry, fag, gasper *(Chiefly British)*, OP, reefer, weed. **6. tailor-made** filter, filter tip, ready-made. **7. roll-your-own** *Informal:* greyhound, racehorse, rollie, roly. **8. the makings** cigarette paper, filler, wrapper. *Informal:* tissue. **9. fag-end** bumper, butt, dottle. **10. cigar** cheroot, cigarillo, claro, Havana, panatella, perfecto, Piramido. *Informal:* toby jug *(US)*, weed. **11. pipe** briar, briar-root, briarwood, chibouk, churchwarden, clay pipe, cob, corncob, cutty-pipe, dudeen, meerschaum. *Informal:* doodie, matchbox. **12. water pipe** bong, chillum, hookah, hubble-bubble, kalian, narghile. **13. peacepipe** calumet, pipe of peace. **14. pipestem** bowl. **15. drag** drawback, puff, pull, whiff. *Informal:* toke. **16. passive smoke.**

2. **1. smoker** chain smoker, inhaler. **2. passive smoker.**

   3. **1. smoking room** divan, smokeroom, smoking car, smoking carriage.

   4. **1. smoking accessories** ashtray, cigar box, cigar-cutter, cigarette case, cigarette-holder, humidor, pipe-cleaner, reamer, snuffbox, tar guard.

v. **5.** **1. smoke** aspirate, chain-smoke, do the drawback, draw, huff, inbreathe, inhale, inspire, puff, pull, suck, whiff.

   RELATED KEYWORDS: DRUG

TOLERANCE

n. **1.** **1. tolerance** anti-discrimination, broad-mindedness, cosmopolitanism, cosmopolitism, open-mindedness, receptiveness, receptivity, unbiasedness. **2. latitude** allowance, forbearance, forbearing, sufferance, toleration. **3. liberality** breadth, catholicity, generosity, generousness, large-mindedness, liberalness, universality. **4. liberalism** latitudinarianism, liberality, tolerationism.

adj. **2.** **1. tolerant** equal-opportunity, forbearing, generous, impartial, liberal, liberal-minded, open, open-minded, receptive, unbiased, unprejudiced. **2. broad-minded** catholic, cosmopolitan, large-minded, latitudinous, permissive. **3. liberal** freethinking, latitudinarian, liberalist, liberalistic.

adv. **3.** **1. tolerantly** broad-mindedly, generously, liberally, open-mindedly, receptively, unbiasedly.

   RELATED KEYWORDS: KINDNESS, LENIENCE, PITY

TOP

n. **1.** **1. top** acme, apex, apogee, apolune, cap, crest, crown, foreside, head, height, ne plus ultra, peak, pinnacle, roof, soprano, summit, tip, tiptop, upper limit, vertex, zenith. **2. climax** crescendo, crest of the wave, culmination, high point, high spot, meridian.

   2. **1. top piece** crown, crowner, crownpiece, headpiece. **2. top layer** ceiling, housetop, mountaintop, roof, rooftop, treetop. **3. topsides** bridge, topside, upperdeck. **4. topping** coating, surfacing. **5. capital** abacus, capstone, chapiter, cope, copestone, coping, crest, pediment, summer. **6. crest** arête, cap, cope, divide, lip, ridge, water parting, water-parting, watershed.

adj. **3.** **1. top** apical, apogean, ceiling, climactic, culminant, head, highest, meridian, supermedial, tiptop, topmost, upper, uppermost, zenithal. **2. overtopping** overlooking, superincumbent, transcendent, transcending.

v. **4.** **1. top** cap, crest, crown, head, overlook, overshadow, overtop. **2. surmount** bestraddle, bestride, exceed, mount, pinnacle, ride, transcend. **3. climax** culminate, peak.

adv. **5.** **1. above** aloft, atop, over, overhead.

   RELATED KEYWORDS: COVERING, HEIGHT, LAYER

TOUCH

n. **1.** **1. touch** contact, feel, handle, kiss, tact. **2. stroke** bob, brush, chuck, dab, flick, graze, pat, peck, tap, touch. **3. feeling** fingering, handling, manipulation, palpation. **4. massage** effleurage, embrocation, rub, rub-down, squeezing. **5. sense of touch** palpability, tact, tactility, touch. **6. touch sensation** itchiness, pins-and-needles, ticklishness. **7. tickle** itch, tingle.

   2. **1. texture** fabric, finish, wale. **2. viscosity** body, consistency. **3. unit of viscosity** centipoise, centistokes, stoke, stokes.

   3. **1. toucher** fingerer, fumbler, groper, handler, tickler, twiddler.

   4. **1. feeler** antenna, antennule, barbel, dactyl, digit, finger, hand, ommatophore, palp, palpus, pedipalp, tentacle. *Informal:* mitt, onkaparinga, paw.

adj. **5.** **1. tactile** haptic, tactual, tangible, textural. **2. palpable** corporeal, substantial, tangible, touchable. **3. touching** adjoining, conterminous, contiguous, tangent, tangential. **4. handled** affected, felt, moved, stirred, touched.

v. **6.** **1. touch** feel, finger, fumble, grope, palpate, pat. **2. handle** fiddle with, finger, manipulate, thumb, twiddle. **3. tickle** kittle *(Scottish)*, prickle, scratch, titillate. **4. pat** bob, chuck, dab, tap. **5. stroke** brush, caress, chafe, embrocate, graze, knead, massage, paddle, pat, pet, rake, rub, rub down, scrape. **6. grope** grabble, palm, paw.

   RELATED KEYWORDS: PAIN, PERCEPTION

TRADE UNION

n. **1.** **1. trade union** artel, brotherhood, gild, guild, guildhall *(British)*, Hanse, industrial union, labour union, mystery, union. *Informal:* stump office. **2. chapel** local *(US)*. **3. shop committee** works committee.

   2. **1. unionism** compulsory unionism, restrictive practice, syndicalism, trade unionism, unionisation. *Informal:* British disease. **2. union movement** organised labour.

   3. **1. industrial action** ban, bans and limitations, black ban, boycott, demarcation dispute, direct action, flying picket, general strike, green ban, lockout, picket, picket line, ring-the-tin boycott, rolling ban, rolling strike, secondary boycott, shutout, sit-down, sit-down strike, stop-work meeting, strike, sympathy strike, walk-off, walkout, wildcat strike, work-to-rule. *Informal:* go-slow. **2. collective bargaining** collective agreement.

   4. **1. trade unionist** agent, deputy, guildsman, labour, representative, secondary, syndicalist, unionist. *Informal:* redfed. **2. union delegate** delegate, organiser, shop steward. *Informal:* delo, rep. **3. striker** picketer.

   RELATED KEYWORDS: COOPERATION, SOCIETY

TRANSPARENCY

n. **1.** **1. transparency** diaphaneity, diaphanousness, pellucidity, pellucidness, penetrability, sheerness, transparence. **2. clearness** clarity, distinctness, limpidity, limpidness, liquidness, lucence, lucency, lucidity, lucidness. **3. glassiness** vitreosity, vitreousness. **4. semitransparency** translucence, translucency, translucidity.

   2. **1. transparent substance** china, crystal, eggshell china, glass, hyaline, porcelain, silica glass. **2. gossamer** gauze, sheer silk.

adj. **3.** **1. transparent** lucid, pellucid, see-through, sheer. **2. semitransparent** diaphanous, semitranslucent, translucent, translucid. **3. clear** bright, limpid, liquid, lucid, pellucid. **4. glasslike** cryptocrystalline, crystal, crystalline, glassy, hyaline, hyaloid, microcrystalline, vitreous, vitriform.

v. **4.** **1. be transparent** allow light, show through. **2. make transparent** clarify, clear.

adv. **5.** **1. transparently** diaphanously, pellucidly, translucently. **2. clearly** bright, brightly, limpidly, liquidly, lucidly. **3. glassily** vitreously.

   RELATED KEYWORDS: LIGHT, INTANGIBILITY, SIGHT, VISIBILITY

TRANSPORT

n. **1.** **1. transport** airlift, cabotage, carriage, cartage, commissariat, conveyance, drayage, entrainment, express, expressage, ferriage, forwarding, handling, haulage, passage, piggyback, pipage, portage, traffic, transit, transportation, truckage, trucking, waterage. **2. transfer** move, movement, passage, removal, remove, shift, shunt, transference, transferral, translation, translocation, transmittal, transmittance. *Informal:* shanghai. **3. logistics. 4. delivery** airdrop, collection, courier service, deliverance, dispatch, express delivery, forward delivery, paradrop, RD, special delivery. **5. lift** ride. **6. double** dink, donkey, double-bank, double-dink.

   2. **1. transportability** movability, movableness, portability, transferability, transmissibility. **2. clearance capacity** conductivity.

   3. **1. carrier** carter, common carrier, consignor, conveyor, courier, deliverer, dispatcher, fetcher, forwarder, freighter, haulier, milk carter, mover, packman *(NZ History)*, postman, remitter, removalist, remover, sender, shipper, transferrer, transmitter, trucker. *Informal:* postie, track. **2. porter** bearer, bheesti, grip, janitor, pallbearer, stretcher-bearer, watercarrier. **3. driver** Afghan, bull-puncher, bullock driver, bullock-puncher, bullocker, bullocky, cameleer, Ghan, mule-skinner, muleteer, offsider, swamper *(US)*. **4. stevedore** dock labourer, docker, loader, longshoreman *(US)*, waterside worker, wharf labourer, wharf lumper. *Informal:* disso, lumper, seagull *(NZ)*, wharfie. **5. coalman** coal-heaver. **6. beast of burden** ass, burro, camel, donkey, dromedary, jackass, mule, oont *(Indian English)*, packhorse, packtrain. *Informal:* dicky, donk, moke *(British)*.

   4. **1. conveyor** apron, auger, beef chain, belt, chain pump, conveyor belt, ship-loader, sushi train, the chain. *Informal:* racetrack. **2. escalator** moving pathway, moving staircase, travelator. **3. lift** dumb waiter, elevator, fork hoist *(NZ)*, forklift, goods lift, grain elevator, hoist, ladder lift, service lift.

adj. **5.** **1. transport** airborne, intermodal, lift-on, lift-off, logistic, overland, pack, portative, roll-on roll-off, windborne.

   6. **1. transportable** consignable, conveyable, deliverable, dischargeable, mobile, movable, moveable, portable, portative, remissible, remittable, transferable, translatable, transmissible, transmittable.

v. **7.** **1. transport** backload, carry, convey, dispatch, forward, frank, freight, lift, move, relocate, remove, run, shift, take, teleport, traffic, transfer, translate, translocate, transmit, uplift. *Informal:* shanghai. **2. send** check *(US)*, consign, containerise, despatch, dispatch, drop, forward, pass on, reconsign, relay, remit, resend, send ahead, transmit.

3. express rush. *Informal:* herb *(US)*. **4. deliver** bail, discharge, drop off, dump, hand-deliver, home-deliver, off-load, unlade, unload. **5. collect** bring, fetch, get, look something out, retrieve. *Informal:* fox. **6. manhandle** bear, carry, frogmarch, pack, pikau, port, shlep, stretcher. *Informal:* hump, lump, schlep *(Chiefly US)*, tote. **7. cart** barrow, chariot, dray, jitney *(US)*, motor, railroad *(US)*, sled, sledge, team *(US)*, telpher, tram, trolley, truck, wagon, wheelbarrow. **8. airfreight** airdrop, airlift, chopper, fly, parachute. **9. ship** barge, boat, canoe, ferry, flume *(US)*, lighter, lock, punt, raft, reship, row, wherry. **10. shunt** reship, switch *(Chiefly US)*, tranship, transship. **11. stevedore** lade, land, load, off-load, reload, unlade, unload. **12. convey** carry, ferry, give someone a lift, take, taxi. **13. double** dink, donkey, double-bank, double-dink.

RELATED KEYWORDS: FLYING, MOVEMENT, TRAVEL, VEHICLE, WATERCRAFT

TRAVEL

n. **1. 1. travel** itinerancy, itineration, journey, passage, peregrination, staging, travelling, trip, wayfaring. **2. commuting** commutation *(US)*, straphanging. **3. migration** immigration, nomadism, repatriation, transhumance. **4. vagabondism** excursiveness, fugitiveness, vagabondage, vagrancy, vagrantness. *Informal:* pink-eye, vag, walkabout. **5. wanderlust.**

2. 1. tourism globetrotting, sightseeing. **2. type of tourism** cultural tourism, dark tourism, destination tourism, ecotourism, envirotourism, event tourism.

3. 1. journey expedition, odyssey, safari, tramp *(British)*, travels, trip. **2. trip** daytrip, drive, excursion, expedition, jaunt, joy-ride, junket, outing, picnic, round trip. *Informal:* fang, sally, spin. **3. tour** grand tour, lecture tour, mystery tour, package tour. **4. pilgrimage** haj. **5. lift** *Informal:* hitch, pick-up. **6. patrol** round.

4. 1. walking ambulation, circumambulation, legwork, Nordic walking, pedestrianism, perambulation. **2. gait** amble, dogtrot, double time *(US Army)*, goosestep, hobble, jog, limp, lope, muddling pace, pace, plod, roll, romp, saunter, shamble, shuffle, skip, stalk, step, stride, stroll, strut, stump, swagger, toddle, totter, tread, waddle, walk.

5. 1. walk airing, constitutional, parade, promenade, ramble, roam, saunter, stroll, turn, wander. *Informal:* blow. **2. march** anabasis, cakewalk, forced march, route-march.

6. 1. traveller adventurer, backpacker, journeyer, passenger, peregrinator, pilgrim *(Poetic)*, voyager, wayfarer. **2. tourist** excursionist, jetsetter, joy-rider, junketer, tourer, touring car. *Informal:* globetrotter, rubberneck, tripper. **3. migrant** émigré, black hat, boat people, emigré, emigrant, immigrant, incomer, migrator, nominated migrant, refugee, repatriate. *Informal:* ethno, reffo, refo. **4. wanderer** Bedouin, Egyptian, gipsy, gypsy, Ishmaelite, nomad, peripatetic, pilgrim *(Poetic)*, rambler, ranger, roamer, rolling stone, Romani, rover, travelling labour, Wandering Jew. *Informal:* gippo, gyppo. **5. hiker** bushwalker. **6. itinerant** bird of passage, rogue, rolling stone, track man, vagrant, wanderer. *Informal:* bogtrotter, hobo, toe-ragger. **7. pilgrim** haji, palmer, visitant. **8. tramp** battler, beachcomber, coaster, drummer, itinerant *(British)*, outcast, overlander, rogue, sundowner, swagger, swagman, swamper *(US)*, track mate, tramper, vagabond, vagrant. *Informal:* bagman, beat, bum, Darling whaler, deadbeat, dero, hobo, knight of the road, Murray whaler, Murrumbidgee whaler, swaggie, tea-and-sugar bushranger, toe-ragger, vag, whaler. **9. explorer** trekker. **10. travelling salesman** agent, colporteur, commercial traveller, hawker, higgler, packman, peddler, pedlar, pitchman *(US)*, representative, roundsman, sutler. *Informal:* cheapjack, faker *(US)*, rep, shoddy dropper. **11. commuter** season ticket holder. *Informal:* kiss-and-ride commuter, straphanger. **12. drover** bull-puncher, bullock driver, bullock-puncher, bullocker, bullocky, cameleer, Ghan, mule-skinner, muleteer, offsider, overlander, swamper *(US)*. *Informal:* Afghan, mahout.

7. 1. driver bus driver, cabman *(Chiefly British)*, chauffeur, chauffeuse, defensive driver, motorist, road rider, road-hog, roadhog, syce, taxidriver. *Informal:* cabbie, hackie, Sunday driver, wheelman. **2. motorcyclist** biker, Hell's Angel. *Informal:* bikie, milk bar cowboy *(NZ)*. **3. cyclist** bicyclist, wheelman. **4. engine-driver** engineer *(US)*, engineman, gripman, shunter, train driver, tram driver. **5. charioteer** carter, coachman, wagoner, whip. **6. conductor** busman, motorman *(British)*, ticket inspector. *Informal:* connie *(Chiefly Victoria)*, trammie.

8. 1. walker ambler, cakewalker, foot-passenger, footer, marcher, passer-by, pedestrian, saunterer, stepper, strider, stroller, strutter, toddler, treader, trudger, waddler. *Informal:* footslogger. **2. jaywalker. 3. jogger** galloper, loper, pacer, runner. **4. limper** hobbler, shuffler, the walking wounded, totterer.

9. 1. passenger back-seat driver, cabbie's jockey, fare, hitcher, pillion. *Informal:* swinger. **2. hitchhiker** stowaway.

adj. **10.** **1. travelling** globetrotting, seafaring, touring. **2. migratory** anadromous, immigrant, migrant, migrational, nomad, nomadic, roving, transhumant, vagarious, vagrant. **3. expeditionary** odyssean. **4. peripatetic** ambulant, ambulatory, desultory, Egyptian, errant, excursive, gipsy, gipsy-like, itinerant, itinerating, journeying, nomadic, of no fixed address, planetary, rambling, roaming, Romany, vagabond, vagarious, vagrant, wandering. *Informal:* deadbeat, gippo.

11. **1. walking** ambulant, ambulatory, heel-and-toe, high-stepping, pedestrian, perambulatory, strutting, unmounted.

v. **12.** **1. travel** do, ford, gang *(Scottish)*, get about, get around, go, go around, journey, make one's way, pace, peregrinate, repair, run, run round, run up, see the world, step, take oneself, tour, wade, walk. *Informal:* bat along, buzz about, rock, slope. **2. migrate** come out, emigrate, immigrate. **3. gallivant** digress, excurse, gad about, jaunt, joy-ride, junket, wander. **4. roam** circumambulate, divagate, excurse, maunder, meander, ramble, range, rove, straggle, stray, stroll, swag, wander. *Informal:* go walkabout, have itchy feet, hump the bluey, knock about, knock around, waltz matilda. **5. ply** commute, itinerate, patrol, round, whistlestop. **6. hike** bushwalk, ramble, tramp, trek. *Informal:* footslog.

13. **1. walk** amble, ambulate, defile, foot, foot it, gang *(Scottish)*, goosestep, linger, march, mark time, mush, overstride, pace, pad, parade, ramble, saunter, shamble, shank *(Chiefly Scottish)*, shuffle, slouch, snowshoe, somnambulate, step, stride, stroll, strut, swagger, swamp, sweep, toddle, tramp, tread, troop, trudge, waddle, whisk. *Informal:* footslog, hoof it, leg it, mosey *(US)*, tootle, truck, trundle. **2. promenade** perambulate, stretch one's legs, stroll, take the air. *Informal:* do the block, mosey *(US)*. **3. jaywalk**. **4. mince** cakewalk, waltz. *Informal:* pansy, sashay. **5. limp** dot, hobble, hop, hopple, kangaroo-hop, lurch, scuff, shake, shuffle, stagger, stumble along, totter, wag, waver. *Informal:* dot and carry one. **6. plod** clamp, clump, lumber, march, pound, thump, toil, tramp, trample, trudge, walk. *Informal:* schlep around *(Chiefly US)*, slog, traipse. **7. run** bicker, breeze along, double, double-time, hasten, hurry, jog, lope, pat, put one's best foot forward, scour. *Informal:* chase. **8. scramble** grabble, slither, wriggle. **9. brachiate**.

adv. **14.** **1. wanderingly** errantly, excursively, from pillar to post, itinerantly, meanderingly, vagrantly. **2. on the road** off, on the track, on the wing. *Informal:* on the wallaby, on the wallaby track. **3. aboard**.

15. **1. on foot** afoot, on footback, on shanks's pony, walking.

RELATED KEYWORDS: FLYING, TRANSPORT, VEHICLE, WATERCRAFT

TRAVERSING

n. **1.** **1. traversing** crossing, crossover, perambulation, transit, traverse. **2. passage** flowthrough, passing.

2. **1. bridge** aerobridge, airbridge, Bailey bridge, box-girder bridge, chain-bridge, clapper bridge, crossover, drawbridge, floating bridge, flyover, gangway, humpback bridge, overbridge, overfly, overpass, pivot bridge, pontlevis, pontoon bridge, span, suspension bridge, swing bridge, toll bridge, transporter bridge, traversing bridge, trestle bridge, truss bridge. **2. gangplank**. **3. crossover** covered way, covert way, crosswalk *(Especially WA)*, flyover, footbridge, overpass, pedestrian crossing, scramble crossing, zebra crossing. **4. conduit** aqueduct, course, lockage, viaduct. **5. pass** access, defile. **6. tunnel** breezeway, corridor, crosscut, gallery, gangway, hall, hallway, passage, passageway, shaft. **7. pontoon** float. **8. ford** stepping stone.

v. **3.** **1. traverse** cross, crosscut, cut, cut across, cut through, do, ford, measure, navigate, overpass, pass, pass over, passage, peregrinate, run, voyage. **2. bridge** span.

4. **1. pass through** ferry, negotiate, pass, pick one's way, plough through, ply, thread one's way, transit. **2. percolate** infiltrate, perfuse, permeate.

adv. **5.** **1. across** angle, athwart, cross-country, crosswise, o'er, over, through, thwart, transversely.

prep. **6.** **1. across** along, athwart, o'er *(Poetic)*, over, per, round, through, thru, thwart, via. *Informal:* thro.

RELATED KEYWORDS: CROSSING, OVERTAKING, TRAVEL

TRUTH

n. **1.** **1. truth** actualities, fact, facts, reality, the Absolute, verity. *Informal:* what's what. **2. self-evident truth** axiom, first principle, truism. **3. the truth** the true, the whole truth and nothing but the truth. *Informal:* gospel, griff *(Chiefly NZ, British)*, the drum, the full two bob, the genuine article, the lowdown, the real McCoy, the real thing, the strong of it. **4. factuality** actualness, historicity, realness, trueness, verity. **5. correctness** accuracy, accurateness, exactness, fidelity, infallibleness, precision, rightness, rigorousness, soundness, tenableness, validity. **6. genuineness** authenticity, legitimacy, legitimateness.

2. **1. truthfulness** honesty, straightness, veracity. **2. sincerity** genuineness, unfeignedness. **3. candour** downrightness, frankness, plain-speaking.

adj. 3. **1. true** accurate, certain, correct, dead set, definite, faithful, inerrant, infallible, right, truthful, veracious. *Informal:* dinkum, dinky, dinky-di, fair dinkum, for real, ridge, ridgydidge, true dinks *(Especially Victoria)*. **2. genuine** actual, authentic, bona fide, factual, historical, legitimate, literal, real, true, veritable, very. *Informal:* dinkum, fair dinkum, legit. **3. verifiable** affirmable, authenticable, certifiable, checkable. **4. realistic** recognisable, three-dimensional, true to nature, true-to-life. **5. valid** just, logically true, rigorous, sound, straight, tenable, true, well-founded. **6. verified** authenticated, proved. **7. self-evident** axiomatic, tautological, truistical, undeniable.

4. **1. truthful** honest, veracious, veridical. **2. sincere** candid, downright, frank, genuine, guileless, plain-spoken, simple-hearted, true-hearted, unfeigned. *Informal:* on the up and up, open as the day (is long).

v. 5. **1. be true** be a fact, be the case, conform to fact, has the ring of truth, hold good, hold true, hold water, ring true, stand the test. **2. prove to be fact** authenticate, notarise, verify, vouch.

6. **1. be truthful** be in earnest, mean what one says, stick to the facts, tell the truth.

adv. 7. **1. truly** actually, certainly, definitely, for a fact, genuinely, in fact, in reality, in truth, indeed, just, quite, really, soothly, true, truthfully. *Informal:* dinkum. **2. factually** accurately, aright, correctly, justly, literally, properly. **3. genuinely** authentically, legitimately, veritably. **4. in effect** effectively, essentially, in substance, realistically. **5. validly** logically, rigorously, soundly, tenably. **6. self-evidently** axiomatically, undeniably.

8. **1. truthfully** dead set, honestly, veraciously, veridically. **2. sincerely** candidly, frankly, genuinely, unfeignedly.

interj. 9. **1. it's true** Amen, so help me. *Informal:* by jingo, dinkum, fair dinkum, honest Injun, my oath, straight up, struth, too right, too right!.

RELATED KEYWORDS: ACTUALITY, REALISM, HONESTY, LOGICALITY, PROPRIETY

TURBULENCE

n. 1. **1. turbulence** agitation, coil, convulsion, disquiet, disturbance, ferment, inquietude, moil, perturbation, restlessness, tempest, torment, trouble, turmoil, uneasiness, unquietness, unrest, vexedness. **2. commotion** ado, bobberie, brouhaha, bustle, carry-on, cataclysm, flurry, furore, fuss, hubbub, hullabaloo, hurly, hurly-burly, melee, much ado about nothing, pother, racket, tumult, uproar, welter. *Informal:* ballyhooly, botheration, hoo-ha, kafuffle, kerfuffle, row, ruckus, song and dance, stink. **3. convulsion** fit, palpitation, paroxysm, seizure, spasm, throe, welter. **4. flurry** fluster, jactation, jiggle, joggle, jounce, popple, shake, shaking, startle, succussion, tingle, toss. **5. excitement** ebullience, ebulliency, enthusiasm, fermentation, fire, get-up-and-go, tempestuousness. *Informal:* hoopla, razzle-dazzle, zing, zip. **6. boil** churning, ebullition, outburst, seethe, vortex. **7. quake** shudder. **8. the shakes** blue devils, delirium tremens. *Informal:* d.t.'s, heebie-jeebies, horrors, Joe Blakes, pink elephants, shakes, the dingbats.

adj. 2. **1. turbulent** agitated, churned up, disturbed, hurly-burly, restless, stormy, tempestuous, tumultuary, tumultuous, unquiet, uproarious, wild. **2. excited** ebullient, feverish, feverous, hectic, palpitant, spewing, wrought-up. *Informal:* hyped, steamed-up. **3. vexed** annoyed, disturbed, restless, troubled, turbid, unquiet. **4. fluttery** aflutter, fluttering, quaky, rocky, saltatory, shaky, shivery, trembling, trembly, tremulant, tremulous, twittery, wobbly. **5. jittery** fidgety, jumpy, like a cat on a hot tin roof, like a cat on hot bricks. **6. convulsant** convulsionary, convulsive, paroxysmal.

v. 3. **1. agitate** disjoint, disturb, perturb, pouter, roil, shock, startle, tousle, traumatise, trouble, unfix, unsettle, wimple. *Informal:* faze, muss *(Chiefly US)*. **2. shake** bucket about, fret, jiggle, joggle, jolt, quake, shog, stoke, succuss, toss about. **3. ferment** excite, hot up, inflame, innervate, rev. **4. beat** cheddar, churn, commingle, commix, cream, mill, mingle, mix, move, muddle *(US)*, paddle, popple, sjambok *(South African)*, slosh, stir, stoke, whip, whisk. **5. torment** bullyrag, fluster, fret, harass, harry, heckle, irritate, martyrise, pester, plague, put out, shake up, stir, unsettle, upset, vex, worry. *Informal:* discombobulate, rattle, rile *(US)*.

4. 1. toss roll about, toss and turn, twist, writhe. **2. seethe** boil, churn, fret, heave, torment. **3. flutter** flitter, quake, ripple, ruffle, wimple. **4. convulse** agitate, palpitate, throb.

adv. **5. 1. turbulently** disturbingly, ebulliently, excitedly, vexedly. **2. flutteringly** convulsively, shakily. **3. tempestuously** unquietly.

RELATED KEYWORDS: EXCITEMENT, VIBRATION, VIOLENCE

TWIST

n. **1. 1. twist** convolution, crinkle, curl, curlicue, gyrus, kink, marl, ring, slub, squiggle, torsade, tortuosity, turn, twine, twirl, verticil, volute, warp, whorl, wind, winding. **2. convolution** roll, sinuosities, whorl, winding. **3. coil** clew, curl, flake, hank, skein. **4. helix** double helix, helices, right-handed helix, right-handed spiral, screw, screw thread, scroll, spiral, spire, square thread, thread, twist, twisted pair, volute, worm. **5. coil spring** balance spring, hairspring.

2. 1. curl braid, crimp, crimps, frizz, frizzle, plat, ringlet. **2. permanent wave** body wave, cold wave, marcel, marcelling, perm, wave. **3. curler** braider, crimper, crisper, frizzler.

3. 1. circuitousness anfractuosity, circuity, circularity, circumvolution, convolution, crookedness, flexuosity, involution, meanders, sinuation, sinuosity, sinuousness, tortuosity, tortuousness, winding, wriggle. **2. intorsion** circumnutation, koru. **3. curliness** crispation, crispness, frizz. **4. torsion** wring, wringing, writhe. **5. entwinement** twine, wind, winding. **6. volution** dextrality, verticillation.

adj. **4. 1. twisting** anfractuous, bending, circuitous, circular, circumflex, crooked, flexuose, flexuous, labyrinthine, mazy, periphrastic, peristaltic, roundabout, serpentine, sinuate, sinuous, snakelike, snaky, tortuous, turning, winding, wry. **2. tendril-like** capreolate, tendrillar, vinelike. **3. curly** crimpy, crinkly, crisp, crispate, crispy, frizzy, undulant, undulate, wavy, wiggly. **4. wriggly** rolling, sigmate, squiggly, vermicular, vermiculate, volute, wiggly.

5. 1. twisted cochleate, coiled, convolute, convoluted, obvolute, spiral, spiry, tortile, turbinate, turreted, verticillate, whorled. *Informal:* snaily-horn. **2. spiral** coiled, corkscrew, dextral, dextrorse, helical, helicoid, helicoidal, screwed, scroll-like, sinistrorse, spiroid, tortile, turbinate, twisted, whorled.

v. **6. 1. twist** bend, circumflex, circumnutate, coil, contort, convolute, convolve, corkscrew, crimple, crinkle, curve, distort, inflect, intort, loop, ripple, screw, serve, slew, spiral, squirm, trundle, turn, twiddle, twine, warp, whip, wind, wrap, wrench, wrest, wring, wrinkle. **2. snake** squiggle, vermiculate, weave, wriggle, writhe. **3. curl** braid, crimp, crimple, crisp, frizz, frizzle, roll, wave.

7. 1. roll up belay, clew, marl, reel, rewind, scroll, spool. **2. entwine** entwist, enwind, intwine, intwist, inwind, pleach, twine, twirl. **3. convolve** circumflex, coil, enclose, fold, gnarl, spiral, twist.

adv. **8. 1. twistingly** circuitously, circularly, flexuously, round, sinuously, tortuously, vermicularly, windingly. **2. convolutely** dextrally, helically, helicoidally, verticillately.

RELATED KEYWORDS: BEND, CURVE, ROUNDNESS

TWO

n. **1. 1. two** binary, brace, couple, couplet, deuce, diad, doublet, duad, duumvirate, dyad, pair, twa *(Scottish)*, twain, twosome, yoke. *Informal:* pigeon pair. **2. twins** fellow, match, mate, pair. **3. twins** Castor and Pollux, fraternal twins, gemini, identical twins, Siamese twins, the Bobbsey twins, Tweedledum and Tweedledee.

2. 1. doubleness biformity, dimerism, dimorphism, dualism, duality, duplicity. **2. doublesidedness** bilateralism, bilateralness. **3. duplication** clone, counterpart, double, doubling, duplicate, gemination, repetition.

3. 1. second b, beta, number two, secondary, trail.

4. 1. half equal part, fifty per cent, moiety. **2. halving** bipartition, bisection, dichotomisation, dimidiation, division.

5. 1. bisector diagonal, diameter, dividers, dividing line, equator.

adj. **6. 1. two** binary, binate, both, conjugate, coupled, didymous, dizygotic, double, dual, duple, duplex, duplicate, dyad, dyadic, geminate, paired, twin, twinned, twofold, twosome. **2. double** binate, biparous, diploid, duple, duplex, duplicate, duplicative, twofold. **3. two-sided** amphibious, bicameral, biform, bilateral, bimanous, binucleate, dimorphous, double-sided, two-handed, two-piece. **4. second** alternate, alternative, every other, latter, secondary, subsidiary.

7. **1. halved** bisected, cleft, cloven, divided, half, riven, separate. **2. in two parts** bifid, bifurcate, bilateral, bilocular, bipartite, bisectional, dichotomous, dimerous, dimidiate.

v. **8.** **1. double** bracket, couple, duplicate, geminate, match, pair, redouble, twin.

9. **1. halve** divide by two. **2. bisect** cut in two, dichotomise, dimidiate, divide into halves, split in two. **3. go halves** share equally. *Informal:* go fifty-fifty.

adv. **10.** **1. in twos** à deux, bilaterally, binately, bipartitely, double, doubly, dually, geminately, in pairs, tete-a-tete. **2. double** as much again, bis, doubly, in duplicate, twice, twofold.

11. **1. in two. 2. half** halfway, midway.

RELATED KEYWORDS: EQUALITY, SEPARATION, COPY, PART

UGLINESS

n. **1.** **1. ugliness** dreadfulness, haggishness, hideousness, ill-favouredness, unsightliness. **2. unattractiveness** plainness, unhandsomeness, unloveliness. **3. grotesqueness** deformity, distortion, grotesquerie. **4. dowdiness** frumpiness, frumpishness, homeliness, manginess. **5. inelegance** gracelessness, horsiness, inelegancy, stiffness. **6. uglification** disfigurement.

2. **1. ugly person** eyesore, fright, gorgon, gorilla, hag, harpy, harridan, hellcat, scarecrow, toad, ugly duckling, witch. *Informal:* cow, face-ache, horror, lemon, old bag, old cow, sight, slapper *(Chiefly British)*, trout *(Chiefly British)*. **2. grotesque** guy, monster, monstrosity, Punchinello. **3. frump** dowdy, drab, hausfrau. *Informal:* fleabag, plain Jane.

adj. **3.** **1. ugly** abominable, awful, disagreeable, disgusting, dreadful, foul, frightful, grotesque, hideous, horrible, horrid, monstrous, not fit to be seen, odious, revolting, toadlike, ugly as sin, unpleasant. *Informal:* feral, festy, gross, ugly as a hatful of monkeys, with a face like the back of a bus, with a face that would stop a clock. **2. unprepossessing** blemished, coarse, coarse-grained, common, crooked, disfigured, distorted, favourless, gaunt, graceless, gross, haggard, hard-favoured, hard-featured, ill-favoured, ill-looking, ill-proportioned, ill-shaped, inelegant, lumbering, misshapen, repellent, repulsive, shapeless, stiff, unbeauteous, unbeautiful, unbecoming, uncomely, uncouth, ungainly, ungraceful, unhandsome, unlovely, unshapely, unsightly, vulgar. *Informal:* skanky. **3. squalid** clumsy, dingy, foul, mangy, mean, rickety, rough, rude, scrubby, shaggy. *Informal:* tacky. **4. ghastly** cadaverous, Gothic, grim, grisly, gruesome, macabre, shocking. *Informal:* erky. **5. plain** homely, ordinary, unattractive. **6. horsy** *(Informal)* horse-faced. **7. haggish** haggy. **8. dowdy** dowdyish, drack, dumpy, frumpish, frumpy, gawky, ill-dressed, shabby, shapeless, ungainly. **9. showy** crude, flashy, garish, gaudy, gross, overdecorated, overdone, roxy, sporty, tarty, tinsel, tinselly, tizzy. **10. unattractive** unaesthetic, unesthetic *(US)*, unpleasant.

v. **4.** **1. uglify** besmear, besmirch, blemish, contort, deface, deform, disfigure, distort, mangle, mar, smut, soil, spoil, vandalise.

adv. **5.** **1. uglily** dreadfully, grotesquely, hideously, ill-favouredly. **2. unattractively** plainly, unhandsomely. **3. inelegantly** gracelessly, stiffly. **4. dowdily** frumpily, frumpishly.

RELATED KEYWORDS: REPULSION, BLEMISH, IMPERFECTION, UNPLEASANTNESS

UNCERTAINTY

n. **1.** **1. uncertainty** ambivalence, bewilderment, confusion, doubtfulness, haltingness, hesitance, hesitancy, hesitation, incertitude, indecision, indecisiveness, indefiniteness, insecurity, misgiving, pendency, perplexity, puzzlement, query, self-distrust, undecidedness, unresolvedness, unsureness, vacillation, vagary. **2. doubt** agnosticism, doubtfulness, dubiety, dubiosity, dubitation, incertitude, uncertainty. **3. indeterminateness** incalculableness, indemonstrability, indiscernibleness, unknowableness, unpredictability, unpredictableness, untrustworthiness. **4. unreliableness** dubiousness. **5. chanciness** fortuitousness, fortuity, precariousness, suspense, uncertainness. **6. ambiguity** ambiguousness, amphibology, amphiboly, cloudiness, double meaning, equivocalness, obscureness, obscurity, vagueness.

2. **1. uncertain thing** a question of ..., borderland, borderline, cliffhanger, conjecture, contingency, contingent, hazard, jeopardy, loose cannon, possibility, rumour, uncertainty, unknowable, unknown, unknown factor, variable, x. *Informal:* lineball, neither fish nor fowl, the joker in the pack, what-if. **2. risk** chance, hazard, leap in the dark. *Informal:* a pig in a poke. **3. open question** enigma, koan, matter of opinion, moot point, mystery, puzzle, query, question, riddle, uncertainty. **4. quandary** dilemma, problem.

adj. **3.** **1. uncertain** amphibolic, arguable, at stake, changeable, debatable, doubtable, doubtful, dubious, dubitable, dubitative, exponible, facultative, fallible, in doubt, in the air,

481

insecure, obscure, open, precarious, problematic, questionable, random, rocky, rogue, slippery, suspenseful, ticklish, touch-and-go, unconfirmed, unpredictable, unreliable, unsourced, unstable, untrustworthy. **2. doubtful** agnostic, dubitative, moot, sceptical, uncertain. **3. unsure** aimless, ambivalent, at a loose end, at one's wits' (or wit's) end, dithery, double-minded, halting, hesitant, hesitative, indecisive, irresolute, nonplussed, on the horns of a dilemma, pendulous, perplexed, puzzled, shillyshally, stop-start, suspensive, tentative, unassured, undecided, undetermined, unresolved, unsettled, vacillating. **4. indeterminable** amphibolic, borderline, immeasurable, immensurable, incalculable, incomputable, indefinite, indemonstrable, indeterminate, indiscernible, indistinguishable, inestimable, innumerable, uncertain, unknowable, unmeasurable, vague. **5. unknown** hypothetical, incalculable, uncertain, uncounted, undetermined, unmeasured, unnumbered, unresolved, unsettled, unsure, untold, without number. **6. marginal** amphibolic, borderline, cliffhanging, indeterminate, uncertain. **7. conditional** aoristic, chancey, chancy, contingent, dependent on circumstances, eventual, hypothetical, possible, provisional, provisory, subject to, uncertain. **8. ambiguous** amphibological, amphibolous, apocryphal, borderline, cloudy, cryptic, Delphic, enigmatic, equivocal, indefinite, indeterminate, indistinct, inexplicable, inscrutable, left-handed, misty, mysterious, obscure, oracular, paradoxical, puzzling, uncertain, undefined, vague, veiled.

v. **4.**　**1. be uncertain** be in a quandary, boggle, change one's tune, dicker *(Chiefly US)*, dither, doubt, flounder, halt, hesitate, hover, lose the scent, lose the trail, misgive, not know which way to turn, sway, vacillate, waver, wobble, wonder. *Informal:* um and ah. **2. take a chance** bet, buy a pig in a poke, have a bet both ways, hazard, wager. **3. hang in the balance** be open to question, be touch and go, depend, hinge, suspend. *Informal:* be lineball.

adv. **5.**　**1. uncertainly** ambiguously, arguably, cloudily, contingently, dubitably, equivocally, haltingly, incalculably, indiscernibly, obscurely, precariously, problematically, unpredictably. **2. indeterminably** indemonstrably, inestimably, unknowably, unmeasurably. **3. indecisively** agnostically, doubtfully, dubiously, hesitantly, hesitatingly, hesitatively, in a state of uncertainty, indeterminately, perplexedly, suspensefully, undecidedly, unresolvedly.

RELATED KEYWORDS: DISBELIEF, CONJECTURE, INDECISION, UNLIKELIHOOD

UNCONDITIONALITY

n. **1.**　**1. unconditionality** absoluteness, categoricalness, definitiveness, implicitness, the Absolute, unconditionalness, unqualifiedness.

adj. **2.**　**1. unconditional** absolute, clear, round, straight, termless, unequivocal, unqualified, utter. *Informal:* straight-out. **2. categorical** conclusive, definitive, determining, unexceptional. **3. regardless** at all costs, independent, irrespective of. **4. utter** absolute, blank, downright, flat, implicit, out-and-out, outright, perfect, unconditional, unmitigated, unqualified. *Informal:* plumb. **5. total** arrant, complete, downright, perfect, positive, pure, sheer, stark, thorough, utter. *Informal:* crashing, full-on.

adv. **3.**　**1. unconditionally** categorically, clear, clearly, implicitly, unexceptionally, unmitigatedly, unqualifiedly, with no strings attached. *Informal:* come hell or high water. **2. utterly** absolutely, arrantly, beyond question, completely, definitively, easily, entirely, flat, flatly, full, fully, hundred-per-cent, positively, purely, stark, totally. *Informal:* plumb, properly. **3. independently** irrespectively. **4. unequivocally** explicitly, in so many words, unquestionably.

4.　**1. nevertheless** all the same, any way, anyhow, anyway, howbeit, however, irregardless, just the same, non obstante, nonetheless, notwithstanding, regardless, still, though, yet. **2. at all events** in (or under) the circumstances, in any case, in spite of everything, on all counts.

prep. **5.**　**1. notwithstanding** after, after all, despite, for all that, in (the) face of, in despite of, in spite of, non obstante.

conj. **6.**　**1. notwithstanding** by any means, e'en, even, for aught, no matter what, somehow or other, still, though, yet. **2. although** albeit, however. **3. though**.

UNCONSCIOUSNESS

n. **1.**　**1. unconsciousness** land of Nod, Lethe, oblivion, sleep, the arms of Morpheus. **2. grogginess** bleariness, concussion, daze, narcosis, stupefaction, stupidness, stupor, subconsciousness. **3. faint** attack, blackout, catalepsy, coma, convulsion, epilepsy, fit, grand mal, petit mal, seizure, swoon, syncopation, syncope, trance. **4. hypnosis** autohypnosis, hypnogenesis.

2.   **1. senselessness** blockishness, dullness, hypesthesia *(Chiefly US)*, impassiveness, impassivity, imperception, imperceptiveness, imperceptivity, impercipience, insensateness, insensitiveness, insensitivity, insentience, insusceptibility, obtuseness, unawareness. **2. insensibility** anosmia, hypaesthesia, numbness, paralysis, sensory deprivation.

3.   **1. anaesthesia** anaesthetisation, etherisation, thermanaesthesia. **2. analgesia** abirritation, deadening, desensitisation. **3. sedation** narcotisation, narcotism, twilight sleep. **4. anaesthesiology.**

4.   **1. anaesthetic** abirritant, anaesthesin, epidural, etheriser, fluothane, general, general anaesthetic, local, local anaesthetic, painkiller. *Informal:* knockout drop. **2. anaesthetic substances** alpha-eucaine, angel dust, benzamine, benzocaine, beta-eucaine, cyclopropane, diethyl ether, ether, ethyl ether, eucaine, halothane, morphine, novocaine, opioid, palfium, pethidine, phenacaine, phencyclidine, sulfuric ether, tribromoethanol, trichlorethylene, trilene. *Informal:* palf, peth. **3. analgesic** anodyne, deadener, painkiller, painkiller. **4. laughing gas** exhilarant, gas, nitrous oxide. **5. sedative** depressant, hypnotic, mickey, narcotic, sleeping-draught, sleeping-drug, sleeping-pill, soporific, stupefacient, stupefier, truth drug. *Informal:* bromide, mickey finn, sleeper, stopper. **6. sedative substances** acetal, chloral, laudanum, opiate.

adj.   **5.**   **1. unconscious** asleep, comatose, in the land of Nod, oblivious, out, out cold, senseless, syncopic, unaware. *Informal:* flakers, out like a light. **2. dazed** bleary, bleary-eyed, blurry, groggy, indistinct, silly, sottish, stunned, stupefied, stupid, stuporous. *Informal:* non compos. **3. concussed** punch-drunk. *Informal:* like a stunned mullet, punchy. **4. drugged** baited, blind. *Informal:* dopey. **5. hypnotic** autohypnotic, hypnagogic, hypnoid, hypnologic, hypnopompic, trancelike.

6.   **1. insensible** imperceptive, imperceptient, incognisant, insensate, insensitive, insentient, insusceptible, lost to, unaware. **2. numb** dead, inert, insensible, lifeless, paralysed, stonecold. **3. dull** dead-and-alive, dense, dullish, obtuse, thick-skinned, thick-skulled, thickwitted, thickheaded, unalive, witless, wooden. *Informal:* brain dead, dead from the neck up, wooden-headed. **4. senseless** anosmatic, tasteless.

7.   **1. anaesthetic** abirritant, analgesic, anodyne, calmative, deadening, depressant, knockout, sedative.

v.   **8.**   **1. become unconscious** black out, die, faint, pass out, swoon, swound. *Informal:* chuck a seven, throw a seven. **2. faint** go out like a light. *Informal:* conk out.

9.   **1. anaesthetise** chloroform, etherise, freeze, keep under. **2. narcotise** befuddle, besot, drug, opiate, stupefy. *Informal:* dope. **3. knock out** concuss, daze, knock endways, knock endwise, stun. *Informal:* flatten, k.o., kayo, king, king-hit, knock rotten, knock someone silly. **4. desensitise** abirritate, benumb, blur, cork, dampen, deaden, dull, numb, obtund. **5. hypnotise.**

adv.   **10.**   **1. unconsciously** blindly, comatosely, insensately, lifelessly, numbly, senselessly. **2. dazedly** blearily, dully, groggily, stupidly. **3. blockishly** impassively, obtusely.

RELATED KEYWORDS: ALCOHOL, INATTENTION, CALLOUSNESS, DRUG, ILL HEALTH, MEDICATION, PSYCHE, SLEEP

UNDERTAKING

n.   **1.**   **1. undertaking** affair, business, campaign, enterprise, matter, operation, program, show, venture. *Informal:* thing. **2. assignment** charge, commission, duty, engagement, errand, job, mission, project, task, work. **3. campaign** adventure, crusade, expedition, exploration, hunt, mission, operation, pursuit, quest, search. **4. forlorn hope** leap in the dark, tall order. **5. embarkation** assumption, candidature, commitment, embarcation, espousal.

adj.   **2.**   **1. enterprising** adventurous, daring, foolhardy, go-ahead, venturesome, venturous.

v.   **3.**   **1. undertake** assay, assume, attempt, come to holts with, do, endeavour, engage in, essay, execute, fix, go ahead with, perform, purpose, tackle, take on, take upon oneself. *Informal:* have a lash at. **2. break new ground** cross the Rubicon, embark, enter on, launch forth, venture upon. **3. have irons in the fire** have a lot on one's plate. **4. get on with the job** buckle (down) to, get a grip on, get one's teeth into, go at, go to it, make bold to, put one's hand to the plough, put one's shoulder to the wheel, square up to, take in hand, take the bit between one's teeth, take upon one's shoulders, throw oneself into, turn one's hand to. *Informal:* do someone's dirty work, get cracking, get stuck into, have a go, hoe into, hop into. **5. attempt the impossible** bite off more than one can chew, square the circle.

RELATED KEYWORDS: ATTEMPT, COURAGE, EFFORT, PLAN

UNFAIRNESS

n. **1.** **1. unfairness** inequality, inequity, iniquitousness, iniquity, injury, invidiousness. **2. discrimination** bias, cronyism, favouritism, leaning, nepotism, onesidedness, partiality, preferential treatment. **3. injustice** dirtiness, injury, inofficiousness, miscarriage of justice, unjustness, wrong. *Informal:* rum go. **4. oppression** abuse, bloodiness, injuriousness, oppressiveness, unrighteousness, wantonness. **5. head-hunting** kangaroo court, McCarthyism, Star Chamber, witch-hunting.

2. **1. undeservedness** gratuitousness, unfitness.

adj. **3.** **1. unfair** biased, hard, inofficious, invidious, loaded, undue, unjust, unjustified, unrighteous, wanton. *Informal:* a bit rough, bloody, raw. **2. discriminatory** biased, coloured, ex parte, hometown, nepotic, one-eyed, one-sided, partial, partisan, selective, unfair, unilateral. **3. unauthorised** unconstitutional, unsanctioned, unwarrantable, unwarranted. **4. foul** dirty, unsportsmanlike. **5. unpardonable** inexcusable, objectionable. **6. oppressive** extortionate, inequitable, iniquitous, injurious.

4. **1. undeserved** gratuitous, improper, uncalled-for, unearned, unexpected, unfitting, unmerited, unwarranted.

v. **5.** **1. act unfairly** take advantage, take unfair advantage. *Informal:* be on the grouter, come in on the grouter, pull (or put over) a fastie. **2. discriminate** discriminate against, favour, gerrymander, load the scales, rig, rob Peter to pay Paul, stack. **3. not play the game** break the rules, commit a foul, hit below the belt, overstep the mark.

adv. **6.** **1. unfairly** below the belt, dirtily, foul. **2. unjustly** extortionately, gratuitously, iniquitously, injuriously, inofficiously, invidiously, oppressively, unrighteously, wantonly. **3. undeservedly** unfitly.

RELATED KEYWORDS: BADNESS, UNKINDNESS, UNLAWFULNESS, IMMORALITY, INTOLERANCE

UNFAITHFULNESS

n. **1.** **1. unfaithfulness** disloyalty, faithlessness, falseness, falsity, infidelity, untrueness. **2. treacherousness** apostasy, doubleness, felinity, insidiousness, perfidiousness, recreancy, scabbery, tergiversation, traitorousness, treasonableness.

2. **1. betrayal** a knife in the back, breach of promise, breach of trust, give-away. *Informal:* sell-out. **2. defection** collaboration, double-dealing, doublecross, foul play, high treason, perfidy, treachery, treason. **3. adultery** extramarital sex, zinah. *Informal:* a bit on the side.

3. **1. betrayer** apostate, backstabber, belier, blackleg, Delilah, double-crosser, double-dealer, fair-weather friend, Iscariot, judas, Mata Hari, recreant, renegade, tergiversator, traditor, traitor, traitress. *Informal:* fink, ratter, scab, snake, snake in the grass, snitcher, viper, weasel, welsher. **2. informer** fizgig, intelligencer, pimp, stool pigeon *(Chiefly US)*. *Informal:* chocolate frog, copper's nark, dog, fizzer, golliwog, grass, grasser, nark, shelf, snitch, supergrass. **3. collaborator** collaborationist, fifth column, fifth columnist, quisling, security risk, Trojan Horse, turncoat. *Informal:* silvertail. **4. adulterer** adulteress, two-timer.

adj. **4.** **1. unfaithful** disloyal, faithless, false, forsworn, recreant, slippery, unreliable, untrue. **2. treacherous** apostate, double-dealing, false-hearted, feline, insidious, perfidious, renegade, snaky, traitorous, treasonable, treasonous. **3. adulterous** adulterant, adulterate, adulterine, two-timing.

v. **5.** **1. betray** doublecross, give away, knife in the back. *Informal:* sell down the river, sell out. **2. tell on** delate, give up, turn king's evidence on. *Informal:* blow the whistle on, dingo on, dob, dob in, dob on, drop someone in, finger, grass on, nark, put in, put someone's weights up, put the finger on, rat on, scab on, shelf, shelve, shop *(Chiefly British)*, snitch on, welsh on. **3. turn informer** inform. *Informal:* sing, squeak, squeal. **4. collaborate** collude, fraternise. **5. deceive** cheat on, play fast and loose, play someone false, two-time.

adv. **6.** **1. faithlessly** falsely, recreantly, untruly. **2. treacherously** felinely, perfidiously, traitorously, treasonably, treasonously.

RELATED KEYWORDS: CHANGE OF ALLEGIANCE, DISHONESTY, IMMORALITY

UNFRIENDLINESS

n. **1.** **1. unfriendliness** animosity, animus, bad blood, bad feeling, enmity, hostility, ill feeling, ill will, inimicality, malevolence, rivalry, virulence. **2. antipathy** adverseness, antagonism, defiantness, opposition, quarrelsomeness. *Informal:* allergy. **3. alienation** disaffection, estrangement, incompatibility. **4. bitterness** jealousy, rancorousness, rancour, resentment, spite, spitefulness. *Informal:* the sulks.

2. **1. unsociableness** exclusiveness, inhospitality. **2. surliness** bearishness, moroseness, spleen, sulkiness, sullenness. **3. coldness** chill, chillness, coolness, frostiness. **4. uncommunicativeness** offishness, silence, stand-offishness, unapproachableness, undemonstrativeness. **5. reserve** aloofness, distance, remoteness, reservedness, reticence.

3. **1. enemy** adversary, archenemy, ill-wisher, nemesis, opponent. **2. antagonist** adversary, combatant, foe, opponent, opposite side, the other side. **3. firebrand** incendiary, troublemaker. *Informal:* fighting cock. **4. traitor** judas. *Informal:* snake, snake in the grass. **5. snubber** iceberg, ostraciser. **6. persona non grata** castaway, exile, leper, outcast, pariah.

adj. **4.** **1. unfriendly** antagonistic, hostile, ill-disposed, ill-willed, inimical, malevolent, oppositional, unkindly, unsympathetic. **2. quarrelsome** aggressive, argumentative, bantam, belligerent, cantankerous, combative, currish, defiant, dissentious, feisty, pugnacious, truculent. **3. traitorous** disloyal, double-dealing, insidious, treacherous. *Informal:* snaky. **4. bitter** malevolent, malicious, rancorous, resentful, spiteful, spleenful, splenetic, venomous.

5. **1. unsociable** antisocial, dissociable, dissocial, inhospitable, insociable, unsocial, unwelcoming. **2. sullen** bearish, broody, moody, morose, sulky, surly. **3. reserved** farouche, in one's shell, indrawn, introspective, reticent, retiring, unforthcoming, withdrawn. **4. aloof** distant, exclusive, forbidding, inapproachable, remote, reserved, self-contained, stand-offish, unapproachable, uncommunicative, undemonstrative. *Informal:* offish. **5. cold** chill, cool, frigid, frosty, frozen, icy. **6. antipathetic** bigoted, disaffected, incompatible, intolerant, unsympathetic. **7. alienated** estranged, irreconcilable, isolated, outcast. *Informal:* on the coat.

v. **6.** **1. be unfriendly** be at daggers drawn, bear ill will, bear malice. *Informal:* be bad friends with, gun for, have a hate on (or against), have it in for. **2. quarrel** come to blows. **3. hound** crush, harass, oppress, persecute, spite. **4. snub** give someone the cold shoulder, ignore, keep at arm's length, turn one's back on. *Informal:* cut someone dead, give someone the deep freeze. **5. ostracise** boycott, exclude, excommunicate, have nothing to do with, send to Coventry, treat as a leper. **6. alienate** antagonise, cause bad blood, dissocialise, estrange, set at odds. **7. sulk** grudge. *Informal:* have a hate on, have a snout on, have the sulks.

adv. **7.** **1. hostilely** adversely, defiantly, quarrelsomely, rancorously. **2. sullenly** bearishly, spitefully, splenetically, sulkily, surlily. **3. reservedly** remotely, reticently, standoffishly, uncommunicatively, undemonstratively. **4. unsociably** antisocially, inhospitably, insociably, unapproachably. **5. coldly** coolly, frostily.

RELATED KEYWORDS: DISAGREEMENT, CALLOUSNESS, BADNESS, UNKINDNESS, HARSHNESS, HATE, SOLITUDE

UNGRATEFULNESS

n. **1.** **1. ungratefulness** inappreciativeness, indifference, ingratitude, thanklessness, unappreciativeness, unthankfulness. **2. grudging thanks** a show of gratitude. **3. ingrate** ungrateful wretch.

adj. **2.** **1. ungrateful** inappreciative, ingrate, insensible, insensible of benefits, unappreciative, unthankful, whingeing. **2. forgetful** oblivious, unmindful. **3. thankless** unappreciated.

v. **3.** **1. be ungrateful** look a gift-horse in the mouth, take as one's due, take for granted, turn one's nose up. **2. grumble** complain. *Informal:* moan, whinge. **3. omit to thank** forget to thank. **4. begrudge a thankyou** not be beholden to, see no reason to thank. **5. forget a kindness** return evil for good.

adv. **4.** **1. ungratefully** inappreciatively, unappreciatively, unthankfully. **2. thanklessly**.

interj. **5.** **1. thanks for nothing** *Informal:* big deal, no thanks to you.

RELATED KEYWORDS: UNKINDNESS

UNHAPPINESS

n. **1.** **1. unhappiness** cheerlessness, disconsolateness, downheartedness, dreariness, dumpishness, sadness, wistfulness. **2. misery** agony, comfortlessness, crestfallenness, distress, dolefulness, dolorousness, dolour, grief, lamentation, mournfulness, plaintiveness, ruefulness, ruthfulness, sorrow, sorrowfulness, tearfulness, woe, woefulness, wretchedness. **3. depression** blue devils, damp, dejectedness, dejection, despondence, despondency, gloom, gloominess, glumness, leadenness, low-spiritedness, maudlinness, melancholy, mopishness, pensiveness, pessimism, prostration, vallecula, vapourishness, Weltschmerz. *Informal:* blues, dumps. **4. midlife crisis** male menopause, MLC. **5. melancholy** atrabiliousness, byronism, melancholia, moodiness, pensiveness, tragic. *Informal:* dismals. **6. loneliness** forlornness, homesickness, lonesomeness, lovelornness. **7. dismalness** depressiveness, dreariness, gloominess, infelicity, joylessness, mirthlessness, miserableness, oppressiveness, sullenness, sunlessness, unblessedness. **8. distressfulness** pathos, poignancy. **9. heartache** anguish, heartbreak, heartbrokenness, heartsickness.

  2. **1. bad mood** fit of depression, fit of the blues, gloom, low spirits, megrims, moods, mopes, the miseries, the shits. *Informal:* blues, dismals, dumps, joes, lousy. **2. tears** *Informal:* waterworks. **3. long face** mournful mien, sad face.

  3. **1. wet blanket** damper, depressor, killjoy, languisher, lonely heart, martyr, Mater Dolorosa, misery, mope, moper. *Informal:* lemon, miseryguts, party pooper, sad sack, snufflebuster, sod, sourpuss, streak of misery. **2. melancholiac** brooder, depressive. **3. wretch** object of compassion, poor unfortunate.

 adj. **4.** **1. sad** cheerless, comfortless, disconsolate, distressful, doleful, dolorous, dour, drab, drear, droopy, dumpish, forlorn, gloomy, glum, grieved, grievous, heavy, heavy-hearted, heavy-laden, joyless, leaden, maudlin, miserable, mournful, sorrowful, sorry, unhappy, upset. *Informal:* blue, happy as a bastard on Father's Day, in the miseries, lonely as a bastard on Father's Day, miserable as a bandicoot. **2. dejected** chapfallen, chopfallen, crestfallen, depressed, despondent, disheartened, dispirited, down in the dumps, down in the mouth, downcast, downhearted, exanimate, hipped, hippish, leaden, low, low-spirited, melancholiac, melancholic, melancholy, mopey, mopish, prostrate, run-down, spiritless, wistful, world-weary. *Informal:* down, in the miseries. **3. lonely** homesick, lonesome *(Chiefly US)*, unfriended. *Informal:* like a bandicoot on a burnt ridge, like a shag on a rock. **4. broken-hearted** broken up, grief-stricken, heart-stricken, heart-struck, heartbroken, heartsick, heartsore, inconsolable, lovelorn, mourning. **5. weepy** in tears, lachrymal, lachrymose, lacrimal, misty-eyed, mournful, tearful, teary. **6. moody** atrabiliar, atrabilious, bilious, broody, byronic, morose, peevish, saturnine, splenetic, sulky, sullen, temperamental. **7. humourless** gloomy, joyless, mirthless. **8. unfortunate** abject, miserable, rueful, unblessed, woebegone, woeful, wretched. *Informal:* pathetic.

  5. **1. distressing** bitter, grievous, harrowing, heartbreaking, hurtful, lamentable, pathetic, pathetical, poignant, pungent, sorrowful, upsetting. **2. dismal** cheerless, chill, cloudy, dark, depressive, discouraging, drear, dreary, gloomy, joyless, murky, oppressive, sulky, sullen, sunless. **3. mournful** dismal, doleful, elegiac, epicedian, funereal, gloomy, lugubrious, plaintive, sepulchral, sorrowful, tragic, tragical.

  v. **6.** **1. be unhappy** be sad, have a lump in the throat, have one's heart in one's boots, hurt, sorrow. *Informal:* have a face as long as a fiddle, have a face as long as a wet week. **2. droop** languish, slump. **3. brood** moan, mope, ponder. *Informal:* chew the rag. **4. cry** bawl, blubber, boohoo, cry one's eyes out, cry one's heart out, have a good cry, have a good moan, snivel, snuffle, sob, weep, weep one's eyes out. *Informal:* blub. **5. pine** eat one's heart out, fret, grieve, pine away, pine for, repine.

  7. **1. make unhappy** break the heart of, darken, distress, fret, gloom, grieve, harrow, hurt, mope, rend, sadden, upset. **2. depress** dash, deject, discourage, dishearten, dismay, dispirit, get someone down, gloom, oppress, sadden. **3. darken** cloud, dampen, gloom, oppress.

 interj. **8.** **1. alas** alackaday, dear, deary me, heigh-ho, misery me, oh, oh dear, oh no, welladay, woe, woe is me.

      RELATED KEYWORDS: DISCONTENTEDNESS, EMOTION, DESPAIR, GRIEF, SOMBRENESS

UNIMPORTANCE

  n. **1.** **1. unimportance** immateriality, immaterialness, inessentiality, insignificance, irrelevance, worthlessness. **2. triviality** bathos, impertinence, inconsequentiality, irrelevance, puerility, triflingness, trivialness. **3. frivolity** frivolousness, frothiness, lightsomeness, Vanity Fair. *Informal:* fribble. **4. pettiness** futility, impertinence, insignificancy, littleness, nihility, nothingness, obscureness, obscurity, paltriness, puniness, tenuousness, triviality, veniality, venialness. **5. minimisation** trivialisation.

  2. **1. unimportant thing** adjunct, anybody, cipher, inessential, minim, non-essential, non-event, nothing, trivialism, unessential. **2. side issue** accident, accidental, afterthought, bye, circumstance, immateriality, indifference, insignificant, irrelevance, red herring, sideshow, subsidiary. **3. trifle** absurdity, bêtise, breath, falderal, folderol, frivolity, impertinence, joke, nonsense, petty detail, pinpoint, triviality. *Informal:* fiddle-faddle. **4. bagatelle** bauble, bit of tinsel, chip *(US)*, falderal, fiddlestick, flummery, frippery, frivolity, gee-gaw, gewgaw, gingerbread, knick-knack, nick-nack, pedlary, peppercorn, picayune, straw, toy, trinket, trumpery. *Informal:* doodads, gimcrack, whatnot. **5. cavil** fleabite, pinprick. **6. trivia** minutiae. **7. chickenfeed** *(Informal)* small change. *Informal:* kid-stakes, small beer, small potatoes. **8. peccadillo** venial sin. **9. insignificant place** backstreet, Bullamakanka, byway, sideway, whistlestop *(US)*. *Informal:* one-horse town, one-pub town.

3. **1. unimportant person** also-ran, cipher, figurehead, insignificancy, insignificant, jackstraw, man of straw, nobody, non-person, nonentity, nothing, obscurity. *Informal:* squit *(British)*. **2. trifler** amateur, dabbler, dallier, dilettante. *Informal:* piddler. **3. lightweight** minnow, nonentity, picayune, pygmy, small fry, twirp. *Informal:* peanut, pipsqueak, snippet, twerp, twit, zed.

adj. **4.** **1. unimportant** childish, forgettable, frivolous, frothy, good-for-nothing, impertinent, inappreciable, insignificant, light, ne'er-do-well, obscure, paltry, pint-size, silly, simple, small, soft-headed, tenuous, tuppeny, twopenny, unconsidered, uneventful, vagabond. *Informal:* flim-flam, no-good, not worth a whoop *(British)*, piffling, potty *(British)*, small-time, two-by-four *(US)*. **2. unessential** acritical, dispensable, expendable, extrinsic, inessential, non-essential, peripheral, unimportant. **3. inconsequential** immaterial, impertinent, inconsequent, irrelevant, mean, unimportant. **4. accidental** circumstantial, incidental. **5. superficial** shallow, skin-deep. **6. subordinate** halfpenny, less, minor, petit, sixpenny, small, trifling, venial. *Informal:* measly. **7. secondary** puisne, subordinate, subsidiary, under. **8. fiddling** insignificant, nonsensical, paltry, pettifogging, petty, picayune, pimping, small, trifling, trivial. *Informal:* crappy, mickey mouse, piddling, piffling, potty *(British)*, tinhorn *(US)*. **9. frivolous** frothy, idle, jesting, light, lightsome, lightweight, slight, trifling. **10. trivial** gewgaw, gingerbread, inconsiderable, nugatory, petty, puerile, puny, trifling, twopenny-halfpenny, worthless. *Informal:* footling, for the birds, frying pan, gimcrack, not worth a tinker's cuss (or damn).

v. **5.** **1. downplay** hose down, make light of, trivialise. **2. belittle** cry down, debunk, decry, demean, depreciate, detract from, devalue, disparage, dispraise, downgrade, lessen, make little of, minify, minimise, misprise, pooh-pooh, run down, set at naught, slight, vilipend. *Informal:* slag off at. **3. subordinate** overshadow.

6. **1. be unimportant** be nothing to boast about, make no odds. *Informal:* be no big deal, be no biggie, be no great shakes, be not worth a cracker, be not worth two bob, not be a row of beans, not matter a twopenny damn, not matter a twopenny dump. **2. be all the same** be neither here nor there. **3. play second fiddle** take a back seat.

adv. **7.** **1. unimportantly** circumstantially, immaterially, insignificantly, irrelevantly, peripherally, tenuously, unessentially, uneventfully, venially, worthlessly. **2. frivolously** dallyingly, frothily, jestingly, jokingly, lightsomely. **3. inconsequentially** inconsiderably, pettily, puerilely, punily, triflingly, trivially.

RELATED KEYWORDS: LOW REGARD, INFERIORITY

UNKINDNESS

n. **1.** **1. unkindness** disobligingness, harshness, meanness, nastiness, soullessness, uncharitableness, ungentleness, unkindliness. **2. inconsideration** insensitivity, thoughtlessness, unfeelingness. **3. cruelty** barbarity, bestiality, bloody-mindedness, brutality, brutishness, cold-bloodedness, cruelness, flintiness, heartlessness, inhumanity, mental cruelty, mercilessness, pitilessness, remorselessness, ruthlessness, sadism, savageness, savagery, tigerishness, unmercifulness, unrelentingness, viciousness. **4. fiendishness** atrociousness, fellness. **5. brutalisation** dehumanisation.

2. **1. ill will** animosity, enmity, hostility, malevolence, misanthropy. **2. malice** acrimony, cattiness, cattishness, despite, ill-naturedness, malevolence, maliciousness, malignity, poisonousness, rancour, schadenfreude, spite, venom, venomousness, virulence. **3. abuse** ill-treatment, maltreatment.

3. **1. unkind person** abuser, animal, beast, brute, demon, devil, fiend, gorilla, harmer, hellhound, monster, sadist, savage, Turk, victimiser, vulture. *Informal:* so-and-so. **2. job's comforter**. **3. cat** *(Informal)* adder, snake, tigress, viper.

adj. **4.** **1. unkind** cruel, disobliging, harsh, ill, ill nature, ill-natured, incogitant, inconsiderate, rude, thoughtless, uncharitable, unchristian, ungenerous, ungentle, unkindly, unpitying, unsympathetic, wry. **2. ill-willed** beastly, bitchy, bitter, cantankerous, cattish, catty, hostile, ill-natured, malevolent, malicious, malignant, mean, misanthropic, nasty, poisonous, rancorous, sharp-tongued, snaky, spiteful, spleenful, ugly, venomous, vicious, viper-like, viperish, viperous, virulent, wicked. **3. cruel** brutal, brutish, cold-blooded, cutthroat, flinty, grim, hard-hearted, harsh, heartless, implacable, inexorable, inhuman, inhumane, merciless, obdurate, pitiless, relentless, remorseless, ruthless, sadistic, steely, stony, stony-hearted, unfeeling, unmerciful, unrelenting, unsparing. *Informal:* bloody-minded. **4. brutal** atrocious, beastly, bestial, bloodthirsty, boarish, brute, brutish, butcherly, cruel, farouche, ferocious, fiendish, fierce, inhuman, lupine, sanguinary, savage, tigerish, tigrish, truculent, vicious, vulture-like.

v. **5.** **1. act unkindly** bear malice towards, cut, cut to the quick, do someone a bad turn, do someone an ill turn, offend. *Informal:* come the acid over *(NZ)*, go for the jugular. **2. bully** abuse, bludgeon, browbeat, brutalise, bullyrag, give curry, hector, martyrise, torment, tyrannise, victimise. *Informal:* heavy. **3. torment** badger, bait, bedevil, harass, harry, hound, keep at, persecute, plague, play cat and mouse with. *Informal:* devil, hassle. **4. maltreat** give no quarter, harm, hurt, ill-treat, ill-use, maul, mishandle, mistreat, misuse, ride roughshod over. *Informal:* give someone hell. **5. brutalise** brutify, dehumanise.

adv. **6.** **1. unkindly** soullessly, thoughtlessly, uncharitably, unfeelingly, ungently, unsympathetically. **2. maliciously** cattily, despitefully, ill-naturedly, malignantly, misanthropically, nastily, poisonously, venomously. **3. cruelly** cold-bloodedly, cuttingly, heartlessly, inhumanely, inhumanly, mercilessly, remorselessly, ruthlessly, sadistically, unmercifully. **4. brutally** brutishly, fiendishly, fiercely, savagely, tigerishly, viciously.

RELATED KEYWORDS: CALLOUSNESS, UNFRIENDLINESS, BADNESS

UNLAWFULNESS

n. **1.** **1. unlawfulness** illegality, illegalness, illegitimacy, illicitness, law-breaking, malfeasance, unconstitutionality, wrong side of the law, wrongfulness. **2. criminality** banditry, corruption, crookedness, delinquency, feloniousness, felony, gangsterism, lawlessness, mafia, outlawry, racketeering, recidivism, standover tactics. **3. lynch law** gang rule, kangaroo court, mob law, mob rule.

2. **1. unlawful act** crime, felony, illegal act, misprision. **2. infringement** breach, conspiracy, contempt, contravention, crime, delinquency, dereliction, encroachment, fault, infraction, misconduct, misdeed, misdemeanour, offence, transgression, trespass, violation, wrong. **3. wrong** injury, injustice, offence, tort, wrongdoing. **4. atrocity** malpractice, outrage, war crime. **5. capital crime** *Informal:* a hanging offence. **6. treason** lese-majesty. **7. corruption** malversation. **8. extortion** blacksmithing, cheat, collusion, collusiveness, fraud, protection racket, solicitation. *Informal:* inside job, racket, set-up, swiz. **9. blue-collar crime** white-collar crime. **10. e-crime** computer crime, cybercrime. **11. crime of passion. 12. crime wave. 13. crime scene** murder scene, scene of the crime.

3. **1. criminal** accessory, bandit, bravo, brigand, bushranger, confidence man, dacoit *(Indian English)*, desperado, felon, gangster, highwayman, hoodlum, hooligan, Mafioso, offender, outlaw, pad, principal, ranger, ruffian, standover man, thug. *Informal:* bruiser, con man, crim, crook, goon, gunnie, hood, knight of the road, perp *(US)*, pie-eater, punk, torch, villain, yegg *(US)*. **2. law-breaker** contravener, criminal, encroacher, infractor, malefactor, malfeasant, offender, trespasser, villain. *Informal:* crim. **3. recidivist** hardnose, lag. *Informal:* trac. **4. convict** canary, felon, gaolbird, inmate, jailbird, old chum, old hand, prisoner, prisoner of the crown, yellow jacket. *Informal:* con, jailie, lifer. **5. racketeer** black marketeer, colluder, mobster *(US)*, sokaiya. **6. Mafia** Cosa Nostra, Honourable Society. **7. underworld** gangland. **8. crime ring** razor gang.

adj. **4.** **1. unlawful** backstreet, backyard, bootleg *(Chiefly US)*, colorum *(Philippine English)*, illegal, illegitimate, illicit, improper, non-legal, racketeering, sly, unauthorised, unlicensed, wrongful. **2. contraband** black, black-market, bootleg *(Chiefly US)*. **3. law-breaking** corrupt, criminal, criminological, crooked, cross, dishonest, felonious, malfeasant, recidivistic, recidivous, rotten, Tammany-Hall, venal. *Informal:* bent, crim, crook, dodgy, shoofty. **4. indictable** actionable, culpable, punishable, tortious. **5. lawless** amoral, anarchic, chaotic. **6. above the law** absolute, arbitrary, autocratic, despotic, dictatorial, tyrannical, tyrannous. **7. outlawed** off limits, out of bounds, outside the law. **8. fraudulent** collusive, conspiratorial. **9. unconstitutional** extrajudicial, irregular, unstatutory.

v. **5.** **1. contravene** break, infract, infringe, transgress against, trespass, violate. **2. offend** break the law, err, transgress against. **3. racketeer** traffic, truck. **4. trespass** encroach. **5. sin** do wrong, transgress.

6. **1. outlaw** illegalise, illegitimise, put outside the law.

adv. **7.** **1. unlawfully** illegally, illegitimately, illicitly, lawlessly, unconstitutionally, wrongfully. **2. criminally** crookedly, feloniously. **3. red-handed** in flagrante delicto. *Informal:* dead to rights.

RELATED KEYWORDS: BADNESS, GUILT, IMMORALITY, WRONGDOING

UNLIKELIHOOD

n. **1.** **1. unlikelihood** improbability, unlikeliness. **2. an outside chance** bare possibility, half a chance, hundred to one, long chance, long shot, poor chance, remote possibility, small chance. *Informal:* a fat chance, Buckley's chance. **3. implausibility** improbability, inconceivability, inconceivableness, incredibility, incredibleness. **4. tall story** exaggeration. *Informal:* shaggy dog story, snake yarn, the story about the one that got away.

adj. **2.** **1. unlikely** at long odds, contrary to expectation. **2. implausible** far-fetched, improbable, inconceivable, incredible, unimaginable, unthinkable.

v. **3.** **1. be unlikely** be improbable, stand only a poor (or small) chance. **2. think unlikely** doubt, lack confidence about, take with a grain of salt, take with a pinch of salt.

adv. **4.** **1. unlikely** hardly, improbably, scarcely.

RELATED KEYWORDS: UNCERTAINTY, GAMBLING, LUCK, IMPOSSIBILITY

UNPLEASANT FLAVOUR

n. **1.** **1. unpleasant flavour** unpalatability, unpalatableness, unsavouriness. **2. nastiness** noisomeness, offensiveness, rankness, unwholesomeness. **3. rancidity** brackishness, gaminess, tinniness. **4. pig swill** *(Informal)* pigwash, slops, swill. *Informal:* guck, guk, gunk, pig-tucker *(NZ)*. **5. bread and water** prison fare. *Informal:* stodge.

adj. **2.** **1. unpalatable** beastly, disagreeable, distasteful, ill-flavoured, indigestible, inedible, repugnant, sour, unappetising, uneatable, unsavoury. *Informal:* poohey. **2. rough** astringent, austere, coarse, strong. **3. off** corked, corky, nauseous, noisome, on the turn, tinny. *Informal:* festy, nasty. **4. rank** acrid, brackish, earthy, foetid, gamey, gamy, high, mephitic, putrid, rammish, rancid, stinking.

v. **3.** **1. be unpalatable** nauseate, sicken, turn one's stomach. **2. pall** cloy, lose its appeal, lose its savour.

interj. **4.** **1. yuk** *Informal:* bleah, ergh, faugh, fie, gross, phew, poo, pooh, spew, ugh, yecch, yuck.

RELATED KEYWORDS: PUNGENCY, FOOD, SWEETNESS, SOURNESS, TASTE

UNPLEASANTNESS

n. **1.** **1. unpleasantness** awfulness, badness, disagreeableness, distastefulness, dreadfulness, frightfulness, harshness, insufferableness, intolerableness, irksomeness, lousiness, meanness, nastiness, poisonousness, unbearableness, uncomfortableness. **2. obnoxiousness** fulsomeness, repellency, repulsiveness. **3. gruesomeness** creepiness, ghastliness, ghoulishness, grimness, grisliness, horribleness, monstrousness. **4. bloody-mindedness** bitchery, cantankerousness, doggishness. **5. loathsomeness** abominableness, beastliness, filthiness, foulness, insalubrity, rottenness, vileness. **6. discomfort** irritation, pain.

2. **1. unpleasant person** bête noire, cad, coyote *(US)*, cur, dingo, ghoul, pimp, repeller, reptile, squib, swine, the (living) end, varmint, vermin, viper, wretch. *Informal:* bastard, bat, bathplug, blighter, blister *(British)*, bounder *(British)*, bugger, dog, drop kick, heavy, heel, hound, insect, louse, low-life, mongrel, old bag, old bat, pain, pill, ratfink, rotter *(Chiefly British)*, scumbag, shocker, skunk, so-and-so, sod, stinker, swab.

3. **1. unpleasant thing** a taste of one's own medicine, abomination, anathema, bitter cup, bitter pill, blow, dose, hell, horror, incubus, nightmare, sorry sight, thorn in one's flesh. *Informal:* a bad scene, a cow of a …, a fair cow, four-letter word, lemon, pain, pain in the behind, pain in the bum, pain in the neck. **2. chore** bonus work, dirty work, hackwork, nuisance, taskwork. **3. abomination** detestable action, shameful vice, wickedness. **4. unpleasant substance** foulness, grunge, muck, mud, ooze, slime, slob *(Irish)*, slop, slosh, sludge, slush, swill. *Informal:* glop, goo, guck, guk, gunk, scunge.

4. **1. unpleasant place** hell, purgatory. *Informal:* hellhole, the dead end, the end, the living end, the pits.

adj. **5.** **1. unpleasant** abominable, awful, bad, beastly, disagreeable, disgraceful, dislikeable, displeasing, distasteful, dreadful, enormous, forbidding, frightful, ghastly, hard, ill-favoured, nasty, objectionable, offensive, outrageous, painful, rotten, shocking, terrible, tough, ugly, unacceptable, uncomfortable, undesirable, unenviable, ungrateful, uninviting, unpalatable, unpleasing, unspeakable, vile. *Informal:* appalling, festy, filthy, God-awful, gory, hell of a, helluva, icky, low-life, perishing, poohey, poxy, rough, sticky, unreal, wicked, yucky. **2. offensive** abhorrent, abominable, damnable, detestable, distasteful, execrable, fearsome, filthy, foul, hateful, heinous, insulting, loathsome, nauseous, objectionable, obnoxious, odious, outrageous, poisonous, putrid, rank, rebarbative, repellent, repugnant, repulsive, unsavoury, vile. *Informal:* creepy, damned. **3. tasteless** in bad taste. *Informal:* on the nose.

6. 1. sickening dirty, disgusting, foul, frightful, messy, nauseating, odious, offensive, revolting, sickish, slimy, untouchable. *Informal:* chunderous, daggy, feral, gooey, gross, icky, scungy, scuzzy, yuck, yucky. **2. rank** bilgy, evil smelling, fetid, foetid, frowsty, funky, high, malodorous, mephitic, nasty, noisome, poohey, putrid, rancid, reeky, ripe, rotten, smelly, stinking. *Informal:* on the nose, stinko, stinky.

7. 1. unbearable enough to drive one mad, enough to try the patience of Job, insufferable, intolerable, more than flesh and blood can bear, not to be borne, not to be put up with, past bearing, unendurable, unsupportable. **2. distressing** afflicting, bitter, comfortless, depressing, disheartening, grievous, harrowing, heart-rending, heartbreaking, hurtful, poignant, pungent, sharp, sorrowful, upsetting.

8. 1. dreadful awful, bloodcurdling, chilling, crushing, demoralising, dire, direful, fearful, formidable, frightening, grim, hair-raising, horrible, horrid, spinechilling, terrific, terrifying, traumatic. *Informal:* creepy-crawly, hairy, scary. **2. gruesome** appalling, cadaverous, creepy, frightful, ghoulish, Gothic, grim, grisly, horrendous, horrific, macabre, monstrous, nightmarish, shocking. *Informal:* erky.

9. 1. troublesome annoying, bothersome, cumbersome, cumbrous, importunate, importune, irksome, mischievous, onerous, oppressive, pestering, pestilent, teasing, thorny, tormenting, vexatious, worrisome. *Informal:* pesky *(Chiefly US)*, pestiferous. **2. bloody-minded** *(Informal)* bad-tempered, bitchy, cantankerous, cattish, catty, doggish, ill-natured, liverish, livery, malevolent, malicious, malignant, mean, nasty, poisonous, spiteful, venomous, vicious, virulent. *Informal:* ornery *(US)*.

v. **10. 1. displease** appal, cause trouble, chagrin, discomfort, discontent, disgruntle, dissatisfy, make life unpleasant, offend, open Pandora's box, rankle, rub up the wrong way, sadden, stir up a hornet's nest, trouble, vex. *Informal:* bug. **2. sicken** be wormwood and gall, disgust, nauseate, offend, repel, revolt, turn off, turn one's stomach. **3. horrify** appal, chill the spine, consternate, curdle the blood, freeze the blood, fright *(Poetic)*, frighten, make one's hair stand on end, make someone's hair stand on end, make the flesh creep, scare, spook, terrify, terrorise. *Informal:* funk, give the heebie-jeebies, put the breeze up, put the wind up, scare (or frighten) the (living) daylights out of someone. **4. grate** jar, jar on, set the teeth on edge.

adv. **11. 1. unpleasantly** abhorrently, appallingly, awfully, disagreeably, distastefully, dreadfully, forbiddingly, hatefully, insufferably, intolerably, lousily, objectionably, rottenly, uncomfortably. **2. gruesomely** ghoulishly, horrendously, horribly, horridly, monstrously, obnoxiously, poisonously, vilely. **3. revoltingly** abominably, filthily, foully, loathsomely, repellently, repugnantly, repulsively, sickeningly. **4. noisomely** frowzily, mephitically, rankly, stinkingly. **5. bitchily** cantankerously, doggishly, ill-naturedly.

RELATED KEYWORDS: UGLINESS, DISCONTENTEDNESS, BADNESS, DISPLEASURE

UNPREPAREDNESS

n. **1. 1. unpreparedness** improvidence, lack of preparation, neglect, unreadiness. **2. rawness** crudeness, crudity, rudeness.

adj. **2. 1. unprepared** cold, ill-equipped, ill-prepared, out of order, unarmed, unarranged, unorganised, unready. *Informal:* flat-footed. **2. half-baked** *(Informal)* incomplete, sketchy. **3. on the anvil** on the drawing board, under discussion. **4. improvident** devil-may-care, happy-go-lucky, shiftless, unthrifty.

3. 1. raw crude, green, in the rough, incomplete, premature, rough, unrefined. **2. untreated** en déshabille, in a state of nature, natural, unconditioned, undressed, unlaid, untilled.

v. **4. 1. be unready** be caught napping. *Informal:* be caught short, be caught with one's pants down. **2. go off half-cocked**.

adv. **5. 1. off one's guard** unaware, unawares, unknowingly. *Informal:* on the hop, with one's pants down.

RELATED KEYWORDS: YOUTH, NATURE, NEWNESS, RAW MATERIALS, UNTIMELINESS

UNRELATEDNESS

n. **1. 1. unrelatedness** autonomy, distance, foreignism *(US)*, foreignness, immateriality, impertinence, impertinency, inconsequence, independence, irrelativeness, irrelevance, irrelevancy. **2. absoluteness** kinlessness, uniqueness.

adj. **2. 1. unrelated** disjointed, disjunct, dissociable, dissociated, distinct, far-off, far-out, foreign, immaterial, impertinent, inconsequent, inconsequential, independent, irrelevant, remote, separate, substantive, unconnected, unconstrained, unimportant, unsubstantial, wide. **2. beside the point** not to the purpose. **3. absolute** alone, apart, distinct, irrelative, positive, sole, unique.

RELATED KEYWORDS: DISCORD, SEPARATION, STRANGENESS, DIFFERENCE

UNSELFISHNESS

n. **1.** **1. unselfishness** altruism, disinterest, disinterestedness, self-devotion, self-renunciation, self-sacrifice. **2. generosity** bounty, charity, goodness, humanitarianism, largesse, liberality, magnanimity, philanthropy.

2. **1. unselfish person** almoner, altruist, humanitarian, lady bountiful, martyr, noble soul, philanthropist. *Informal:* saint.

adj. **3.** **1. unselfish** altruistic, beneficent, benevolent, bounteous, charitable, civic-minded, disinterested, eleemosynary, generous, great-hearted, high-minded, humanitarian, kind-hearted, kindly, large-hearted, magnanimous, non-profitmaking, open-hearted, public-spirited, self-devotional, self-effacing, self-forgetful, self-renunciatory, self-sacrificing, selfless, white. **2. generous** benevolent, big, big-hearted, bountiful, chivalric, chivalrous, free-handed, gallant, good-hearted, handsome, kind, liberal, magnanimous, munificent, noble, open, open-handed, philanthropic, profuse in, unselfish, white.

v. **4.** **1. be unselfish** be altruistic, be disinterested, bend over backwards, do as you would be done by, go out of one's way, live for others, make a sacrifice, observe the golden rule, put oneself out, sacrifice oneself.

adv. **5.** **1. unselfishly** altruistically, benevolently, chivalrously, disinterestedly, nobly.

RELATED KEYWORDS: FAIRNESS, GENEROSITY, GOODNESS, KINDNESS, MORALITY

UNTIMELINESS

n. **1.** **1. untimeliness** bad timing, inopportuneness, inopportunity, interruption, unseasonableness. **2. mistiming** asynchronism. **3. false start** miscue, wrong entry. **4. anachronism** archaism, prolepsis. **5. obsolescence** fustiness, obsoleteness.

adj. **2.** **1. untimely** abortive, behindhand, early, ill-timed, inopportune, interruptive, late, out of season, overhasty, premature, tardy, unseasonable. *Informal:* previous. **2. mistimed** asynchronous, fast, slow. **3. anachronous** anachronistic, antediluvian, antique, archaic, behind the times, dated, demoded, dinosaur, fusty, obsolescent, obsolete, old hat, old-fashioned, old-time, old-world, olde-worlde, out of fashion, out-of-date, outdated, outmoded, outworn, passé, primitive, superannuated, vintage. *Informal:* Dad's Army, trad.

v. **3.** **1. mistime** backfire, go off at half-cock, go off half-cocked, miscue, miss, overtime. *Informal:* shoot one's bolt. **2. lose an opportunity** let a chance slip through one's fingers, miss the boat, miss the bus. *Informal:* blow it. **3. misdate** antedate, foredate, postdate, predate.

adv. **4.** **1. untimely** inopportunely, out of turn. **2. out** behind, out of season, out of time, slow, unseasonably.

RELATED KEYWORDS: EARLINESS, LATENESS, IRREGULARITY

UNTRUTHFULNESS

n. **1.** **1. untruthfulness** double-dealing, duplicity, equivocation, evasion, insincerity, inveracity, lying, mendaciousness, mendacity, mountebankery, mythomania, prevarication, quackery, two-facedness. **2. falseness** artificiality, artificialness, delusiveness, fakery, falsity, spuriousness, supposititiousness, untrueness. **3. fraudulency** charlatanism, cheating, deceitfulness, disingenuousness, humbug, humbuggery, make-believe, pretence. *Informal:* barney, flim-flam. **4. deviousness** craftiness, cunningness, guile, insidiousness, tortuousness.

2. **1. fake** act, artifice, bluff, cheat, con, cozenage, deceit, deception, dissimulation, doubleness, feigning, fraud, hoax, hocus-pocus, hypocrisy, impersonation, imposture, pretence, ruse, scheme, sham, simulation, swindle. *Informal:* con trick, fastie, flim-flam, put-on, racket, scam, sell, swiz, swizzle, wangle. **2. frame-up** put-up job. *Informal:* verbal. **3. hypocrisy** cant, humbug, tokenism. **4. cupboard love** crocodile tears, Judas kiss.

3. **1. lie** alias, canard, cover-up, disinformation, distortion, equivocation, evasion, fable, fabrication, factoid, fairytale, falsehood, falsity, fiction, half-truth, invention, inveracity, legal fiction, mendacity, misinformation, misreport, misrepresentation, misstatement, perjury, pretext, prevarication, tale, tarradiddle, untruth, white lie. *Informal:* bodgie, bricking, cock-and-bull story, crammer, fib, porky, story *(Chiefly US)*, whopper.

4. **1. faker** cheat, confidence man, counterfeit, dissembler, dissimulator, fake, false-pretencer, four-flusher, fraud, front man, grifter *(US)*, imitation, impersonator, impostor, make-believe, malingerer, pretender, pseudo, shammer, whited sepulchre, wolf in sheep's clothing. *Informal:* bodgie, phoney, pseud *(Chiefly British)*. **2. charlatan** mountebank, quack, quacksalver. **3. hypocrite** boggler, equivocator, humbug, prevaricator.

5. **1. liar** belier, fabricator, fabulist, falsifier, fibber, fibster, forswearer, misinformer, mis-reporter, mythomaniac, pathological liar, perjurer. *Informal:* storyteller.

adj. **6.** **1. untruthful** bastard, crafty, deceitful, deceptive, delusive, devious, dishonest, dissim-ulative, double, double-faced, double-tongued, false, fast, fictitious, fraudulent, hollow, hypocritical, insidious, insincere, Janus-faced, knavish, lying, mendacious, misleading, pseudo, tortuous, two-timing, untrue. *Informal:* dodgy, shoofty. **2. hypocritical** phar-asaical. **3. insincere** deceptive, disingenuous, evasive, hollow, tricksy. **4. unfaithful** corrupt, dishonest, double-dealing, perfidious, recreant, two-timing, untrue. *Informal:* bent. **5. perjured** forsworn.

7. **1. fake** bastard, bogus, counterfeit, done with mirrors, dummy, faux, phony, pinchbeck, pseudo, sham, shoddy, suppositious, supposititious, suppositive, unauthentic. *Informal:* bodgie, persuado, phoney. **2. artificial** celluloid, ersatz, imitation, plastic. **3. pre-tended** alleged, assumed, counterfeit, feigned, imposturous, make-believe, ostensible, ostensive, professed, so-called, soi-disant, would-be. **4. meretricious** flash, painted. **5. false** adulterate, adulterine, apocryphal, fictitious, made out of whole cloth *(US)*, mendacious, spurious, untrue. **6. apocryphal** chimerical, fabled, fabulous, fairytale, fantastic, feigned, fictional, fictitious, imaginary, made-up, mythical, mythological, pre-tend, romantic, storybook. *Informal:* never-never.

v. **8.** **1. fake** fabricate, falsify, juggle, manipulate, rig, simulate, trump up. *Informal:* brick, cook, doctor, dud up, fiddle, wangle. **2. frame** *(Informal)* bear false witness against, libel. *Informal:* dolly, verbal.

9. **1. lie** cant, dissemble, fable, fabricate, fib, fluff, forswear oneself, lying, perjure oneself, twist. *Informal:* lie like a trooper. **2. equivocate** boggle, not give a straight answer, palter, prevaricate, quibble, stall. **3. exaggerate** embroider, overstate, strain the truth, understate. *Informal:* amplify *(US)*, big-mouth, bull, bulldust, skite. **4. distort** belie, bend the truth, contort, garble, misreport, misrepresent, oversimplify, pervert, skew, tell a white lie.

10. **1. pretend** act, assume, boggle, cry wolf, dissimulate, equivocate, fake, feign, fudge, keep up appearances, lead a double life, make as if (or as though), masquerade, pay lip-service to, play a part, play-act, posture, profess, put on an act, sham. *Informal:* bung (or stack) on an act. **2. impersonate** pass oneself off as. **3. malinger** *Informal:* swing the lead.

RELATED KEYWORDS: FANTASY, DISHONESTY, WRONGDOING

UNWILLINGNESS

n. **1.** **1. unwillingness** averseness, disinclination, indisposition, unenthusiasm. **2. reluc-tance** difficulty, hesitancy, hesitation, reservation, scruple, scrupulosity. **3. idleness** laziness, perfunctoriness, tardiness. **4. aimlessness** purposelessness. **5. backward-ness** bashfulness, shyness, timidity. **6. unintentionality** unconsciousness, unwitting-ness. **7. involuntariness** automatism, mechanicalness. **8. automatic response** compulsion, knee-jerk reaction.

adj. **2.** **1. unwilling** aloof, averse, difficult, disinclined, hesitant, hesitating, indisposed, loath, loth, negative, passive aggressive, reluctant, reserved, scrupulous, uncooperative, unde-monstrative, unenthusiastic, unforthcoming, uninclined. *Informal:* offside. **2. involun-tary** autokinetic, automatic, autonomic, compulsive, compulsory, matter-of-course, mechanical, mesmeric, reflex, self-acting, self-moving, semiautomatic. **3. back-ward** bashful, coy, diffident, hesitating, reluctant, retiring, shamefaced, sheepish, shy, timid, timorous, withdrawn.

3. **1. purposeless** aimless, careless, collar-proud, devil-may-care, idle, indifferent, lazy, objectless, perfunctory, shiftless, tardy, unambitious, unenterprising, work-shy.

4. **1. unintentional** inadvertent, involuntary, unconscious, unpremeditated, unwilled, unwitting.

v. **5.** **1. be unwilling** back off, baulk, baulk at, be disinclined, be reluctant, boggle, boggle at, disincline, fight shy of, have no stomach for, hesitate, jib, jib at, not be in the mood for, shake one's head, shy away from. **2. hang back** not cooperate, not pull one's weight, pussyfoot, shirk, slack, slack off. *Informal:* drag the chain. **3. grudge** begrudge.

adv. **6.** **1. unwillingly** aversely, grudgingly, hesitatingly, loathly, reluctantly, with a bad grace. **2. backwardly** bashfully, shyly, timidly. **3. purposelessly** idly, tardily.

492

7. **1. unintentionally** accidentally, in spite of oneself, unconsciously, unexpectedly, unwittingly. **2. involuntarily** automatically, autonomically, by rote, compulsively, mechanically, willy-nilly.

RELATED KEYWORDS: IDLENESS, APATHY, UNCONSCIOUSNESS

USE

n. **1.** **1. use** application, employment, exercise, usage. **2. deployment** optimisation, telesis, utilisation. **3. consumption** disbursement, enjoyment, exhaustion, expenditure, usufruct. **4. accession** access. **5. recovery** reclamation, resurrection, revival. **6. wear** wear and tear. **7. abuse** exploitation.

2. **1. usefulness** advantageousness, profitableness, valuableness, value, worth. **2. function** purpose, use. **3. advantage** avail, good, service. **4. practicableness** instrumentality, practicalness, viability. **5. usableness** serviceableness, utility. **6. availability** readiness.

3. **1. user** applier, exerciser, utiliser. **2. consumer** enjoyer, exhauster, expender, spender. **3. exploiter** *Informal:* urger.

adj. **4.** **1. useful** assistant, conducive, constructive, handy, helpful, of use, serviceable. **2. all-purpose** adaptable, convertible, flexible, general-purpose, multipurpose, purposive. **3. beneficial** advantageous, available, forthcoming, free, open, profitable, valuable.

5. **1. usable** applicative, applicatory, constructive, effective, exercisable, functional, practicable, practical, serviceable, subservient, utilisable, viable, workable. **2. exploitable** deployable, employable, tappable. **3. consumable** enjoyable, expendable. **4. available** disposable, ready, ready-made. **5. recoverable** reclaimable, recyclable. **6. valid** good, good for.

6. **1. in use** live, living. **2. occupied** busy, engaged.

7. **1. used up** exhausted, spent. **2. worn** second-hand.

v. **8.** **1. use** apply, employ, handle, make use of, manage, minister, ply, wield. **2. put to use** exploit, optimise, parlay *(Chiefly US)*, ply, utilise. **3. bring into use** deploy, find, mobilise, press into service. **4. apply** bring to bear, exercise, exert. **5. capitalise on** get the best out of, improve, make the most of, turn to account, use to the full. **6. avail oneself of** adopt, draw on, enjoy, seize. **7. resort to** fall back on, have recourse to, make do with, run to. **8. exploit** milk, take advantage of, tap, trade on. **9. recycle** recall *(Poetic)*, recover, renovate, resurrect, revive.

9. **1. use up** consume, expend, go through, run through, spend. *Informal:* do. **2. exhaust** beggar, clean out, finish up, work out.

10. **1. be of service** avail, come in handy, come into use, serve, stand in good stead, subserve.

adv. **11.** **1. usefully** constructively, serviceably. **2. advantageously** beneficially, profitably, valuably.

RELATED KEYWORDS: DAMAGE, EXPEDIENCE, MISUSE, PREPAREDNESS

USELESSNESS

n. **1.** **1. uselessness** bootlessness, inutility, unemployability, unserviceability. *Informal:* a fat lot of use. **2. unsuitableness** disservice, inconvenience, inoperativeness, unfitness. **3. worthlessness** drossiness, effeteness, inadequateness, inefficiency, trashiness, valuelessness. **4. futility** futileness, hollowness, idleness, otiosity, purposelessness, superfluousness, unnecessariness, vainness, vanity. **5. stultification** crippling, thwarting. **6. impracticableness** unpracticalness, unworkability. **7. disadvantage** drawback, loss. *Informal:* slug.

2. **1. waste** biosolid, chaff, debris, dregs, dross, effluent, fragments, husks, junk, leavings, lumber, mullock, offscourings, ruins, scrap, slag, slash *(NZ)*, tailings, wash, waste matter, waste product, wastewater. **2. garbage** culch, litter, muck, refuse, rubbish, trash, truck. *Informal:* dreck *(Chiefly US)*, gunk. **3. encumbrance** cumbrance, dead weight, deadwood, elephant, hamper, snuff, white elephant. **4. dead stock** cast-offs, delenda, rags, rejectamenta, rejects, remainders, stock.

3. **1. waste of time** waste of breath. *Informal:* fun and games. **2. fool's errand** lost cause, wild-goose chase. **3. a dead loss** *Informal:* a waste of space, dead duck.

4. **1. garbage dump** dump, junk-heap, junkyard, landfill, midden, mirrnyong, rubbish tip, slagheap, tip. **2. rubbish bin** ash can *(US)*, car tidy, dirt box, dustbin *(Chiefly British)*, garbage bin, garbage tin, hell, kitchen tidy, litter bin, litter-bin, pedal bin, rubbish tin, trash can *(US)*, wastebasket, wastepaper basket. *Informal:* w.p.b., w.p.b. file. **3. cesspit** cess, cesspool, grease trap.

5. **1. waster** futilitarian, wastrel.

adj. *6.* **1. useless** barren, functionless, ineffective, ineffectual, inept, infertile, inutile, non-effective, otiose, unemployable, unpractical, unusable, weak. **2. worthless** nugatory, trashy, valueless. *Informal:* two-bob. **3. good-for-nothing** fit for nothing, no-good. *Informal:* not worth a tinker's cuss (or damn), not worth a whoop *(British)*, not worth shucks, not worth the candle. **4. rubbishy** (of) no use, brashy, defective, draffy, dreggy, drossy, jerry-built, trumpery, unreliable, unsatisfactory. *Informal:* bodgie, bum, dud, grotty, pathetic, poxy, up to mud, up to putty, upter, warby. **5. worn-out** broken-down, condemnable, done, dysfunctional, effete, exhausted, inoperable, on the scrap heap, on the way out, out of joint, out of order, out of plumb, u/s, unfit, unserviceable. *Informal:* buggered, cactus, clapped-out, gone to Gundy, kaput, munted, on the blink, on the fritz, played-out. **6. obsolete** antediluvian, antiquated, obsolescent, out-of-date, outworn, superannuated. **7. ne'er-do-well** vagabond. *Informal:* fly-by-night, scummy. **8. waste** refuse, scrap. **9. futile** abortive, bootless, empty, fruitless, futilitarian, idle, impracticable, ineffective, ineffectual, no use, nugatory, of no use, purposeless, Sisyphean, unavailing, unprofitable, useless, vain. **10. invalid** informal, inoperative. **11. redundant** superfluous, unnecessary.

v. *7.* **1. waste one's time** cry for the moon, flog a dead horse, labour in vain, labour the obvious, whistle against the wind, whistle in the wind.

8. **1. throw out** put on the scrap-heap, remainder, scrap, toss on(to) the rubbish heap. *Informal:* file in the w.p.b.

adv. *9.* **1. uselessly** effetely, otiosely, potteringly. **2. futilely** bootlessly, emptily, idly, in vain, unavailingly, vainly.

RELATED KEYWORDS: BODILY DISCHARGE, DAMAGE, BADNESS, MISUSE, DISUSE

VANITY

n. *1.* **1. vanity** conceit, conceitedness, ego, egoism, egomania, egotism, immodesty, impudicity, narcissism, self-absorption, self-conceit, self-congratulation, self-esteem, self-importance, self-love, self-opinion, self-regard, self-satisfaction, smugness. *Informal:* swelled head. **2. pride** amour-propre, crest, heart, high spirit, mettle, self-esteem, self-respect, spirit. *Informal:* spunk. **3. conceitedness** boastfulness, vainness. **4. condescension** elevation, inflatedness, loftiness, lordliness, malapertness, overconfidence. **5. vainglory** boasting, bombast. *Informal:* skiting, wind.

adj. *2.* **1. vain** big-headed, bloated, complacent, conceited, condescending, consequential, dogmatic, full of oneself, grandiose, haughty, holier-than-thou, inflated, jumped-up, lofty, lordly, narcissistic, opinionated, overblown, overproud, overweening, parvenu, patronising, pharisaic, pompous, pragmatic, proud, puffed-up, puffy, sanctimonious, self-conceited, self-important, self-loving, self-opinionated, self-righteous, self-satisfied, smug, snubby, stuffy, swollen-headed, upperty, uppish, uppity, upstart, vainglorious. *Informal:* pi *(British)*, stuck-up. **2. vainglorious** boastful, bombastic, immodest, prideful, self-congratulatory, shameless, thrasonical. *Informal:* not backward in coming forward, swanky. **3. purse-proud** house-proud. **4. ostentatious** arty, arty-crafty, dramatic, flash, flatulent, gimcrack, high-flown, pompous, pretentious, showy, tinsel, tinselly, vulgar. *Informal:* arty-farty, hifalutin, highfalutin, jammy, tizzy, toffee-nosed, toplofty.

v. *3.* **1. be vain** be above oneself, be too big for one's boots, boast, fancy oneself, fish for compliments, get (a bit) above oneself, get a big (or swelled) head, have a good opinion of oneself, have a swelled head, overween. *Informal:* be up oneself, have tickets on oneself, skite, think oneself Christmas. **2. pride oneself** claim, credit to oneself. **3. talk down to** condescend, deign, lord it over, patronise. **4. lord it** pontificate, put on dog, put on side, stand on one's dignity. **5. preen** bloat, bluster, cock, cut a dash, flaunt, inflate, plume oneself, primp, prink, puff, put on airs, put on airs and graces, roister, strut, strut one's stuff, swagger, swank, swell with pride. *Informal:* grin (or smile) like a Cheshire cat.

adv. *4.* **1. vainly** conceitedly, immodestly, inflatedly, loftily, malapertly, proudly, smugly. **2. boastfully** pridefully.

RELATED KEYWORDS: AFFECTEDNESS, ARROGANCE, BEAUTY, BRAGGING, SHOWINESS

VEHICLE

n. *1.* **1. vehicle** commercial vehicle, conveyance, motor vehicle, wheel-horse, wheeler. **2. tracklaying vehicle** bulldozer, calfdozer, caterpillar, caterpillar tractor, crawler, dozer, front-end loader, halftrack, loader, tractor, tractor shovel, weasel. **3. amphibian** air cushion, duck, hovercraft, hovertrain.

2. **1. car** all-terrain vehicle, all-wheel drive, auto *(Chiefly US)*, automatic, automobile *(Chiefly US)*, brougham, buggy, courtesy car, demonstrator, electric car, four-door, hatchback, horseless carriage, manual, modaga *(Aboriginal English)*, motor car, motorbus, prime mover, rod, two-door, wheels, z-car. *Informal:* bus, flagon wagon, plagon wagon. **2. runabout** beetle, bubble car, three-wheeler. **3. sports car** coupé, fastback, g.t., gran turismo, hardtop, roadster, tourer, turbo, two-seater. **4. convertible** coupé, fastback. **5. jalopy** *(Informal)* flivver. *Informal:* bomb, chaffcutter, crate, crock, Lizzie, rattletrap, rust bucket, shandrydan, tin lizzie. **6. limousine** berlin, berline, limmo, phaeton, saloon, saloon car, sedan, touring car, v8. *Informal:* limo, yank tank. **7. station wagon** brake, break, estate car *(British)*. **8. utility** buckboard *(Chiefly SA)*, pick-up, utility truck. *Informal:* tilly *(Especially Qld and Rural Northern NSW)*, ute. **9. four-wheel drive** bobcat, buggy, four-wheeler, landrover, off-road vehicle, oversnow vehicle, snowcat, snowmobile, SUV *(Chiefly US)*, urban assault vehicle. *Informal:* beach buggy, dune buggy. **10. panel van. 11. campervan** camper, combi, kombi, RV. **12. police car** paddy wagon, paddy-wagon, patrol car, patrol wagon, prowl car *(US)*, squad car, wagon. *Informal:* black maria, bull car, bull wagon, bun wagon, divvy van *(Chiefly Victoria)*. **13. racing car** altered, dragster, go-cart, go-kart, high-riser, hot rod, kart, stock car. **14. taxicab** cab, taxi. *Informal:* hack *(US)*, jitney *(US)*.

3. **1. carriage** American buggy, barouche, berlin, britska, britzka, brougham, buckboard *(US)*, buggy, calash, car *(Poetic)*, cariole, caroche, carriole, carromata, chaise, chariot, coach, coach-and-four, cobb, coupé, curricle, diligence, dogcart, drag, droshky, equipage, fastback, fiacre, fly, four-in-hand, gharry, gig, hackney, hackney-carriage, hackney-coach, hansom, jaunting car, jingle, landau, phaeton, post-chaise, rig, shay, spider, stage, stagecoach, stanhope, sulky, surrey *(US)*, tally-ho, tandem, tilbury, trap, unicorn, vardo *(Romani English)*, victoria, vis-a-vis, wagonette. **2. caravan** covered wagon *(Chiefly US)*, prairie schooner *(US)*, trailer *(US)*.

4. **1. wagon** bullock dray, bullock wagon, camion, cart, dray, jinker, junker, lorry, oxcart, telega, timber jinker, truck, tumbrel, wain *(Chiefly Poetic)*. **2. sanitary cart** sullage tanker. *Informal:* dunny cart, honey cart, night cart, sanny cart, seventeen-door sedan. **3. trailer** band wagon, box-trailer, dog trailer, flat-top, float, horse float, horsebox, milk float, tandem trailer. **4. barrow** applecart, barouche *(SA)*, billycart, bogie, buggy, dolly, go-cart, golf buggy, golf trundle *(NZ)*, gurney, handbarrow, handcart, hill trolley *(Especially WA)*, hospital trolley, noddie *(NZ Railways)*, pushcart, shopping buggy, shopping jeep *(NZ)*, shopping stroller, shopping trolley, soapbox *(Especially WA and SA)*, stroller, tea-trolley, tea-wagon, teacart *(US)*, trolley, trundler *(NZ)*, washing dolly, wheelbarrow. *Informal:* wagon.

5. **1. truck** lorry *(Chiefly British)*, mini-van, pantechnicon, table-top, taxi truck, transit van, utility, utility van, van *(Poetic)*, wing. **2. semitrailer** articulated lorry, articulated truck, low-loader, prime mover, rig, road train, transport *(British)*. *Informal:* artic, semi. **3. tiptruck** dump truck, tip-cart. *Informal:* dumper. **4. convoy** autocade *(US)*, beef train, caravan, motorcade, safeguard, wagon train *(US History)*. **5. armoured car** blitz buggy, jeep, panzer, tank, troop-carrier, urban assault vehicle. **6. bus** charabanc *(British)*, coach, double-decker, minibus, motor coach, motorbus, omnibus, service car *(NZ)*, single-decker. *Informal:* green cart.

6. **1. tram** cable car, cable tram, dummy, inclinator, streetcar *(US)*, trailing tram, tramcar, trolley, trolley car *(US)*, trolleybus. *Informal:* dreadnought, toast-rack. **2. cable car** telfer, telpher.

7. **1. train** boat-train, cane train, container train, division, freight train, goods train, maglev, magnetic levitation train, mail, metro, mixed train, special, tube train *(British)*, unit *(NZ)*. *Informal:* choo choo, choofer, picker-up, rattler, sweeper, tin hare. **2. steam train** *Informal:* puffing billy. **3. express train** very fast train, VFT, XPT. **4. locomotive** bank engine, diesel, engine, loci *(NZ)*, loco. *Informal:* chuff-chuff, chuffer, puffer. **5. rolling stock** b.c.w., b.s.v., bogie cattle wagon, bogie sheep van, boxcar *(US Railways)*, brake, brake van, buffet car, caboose *(US)*, car, carriage, coach, couchette, day coach *(US)*, dining car, display van, dogbox carriage, flat-top, freight car *(US)*, goods wagon, guard's van, hopper car, louvre van, luggage van, observation car, railcar, rail-carriage, railcoach, railmotor, restaurant car, roomette *(US)*, saloon car, sleeper, sleeping car, smoker, tank wagon, tender, truck, van, wagon, wagon-lit, water-carrier. **6. section car** flivver, kalamazoo, quad, quadracycle, velocipede *(NZ)*. **7. specific trains** Chips, Fish, Ghan, Indian Pacific, Newcastle Flier, Overlander, Prospector, Rocket, Silver Fern, Southern Aurora, Spirit of Progress, Sunlander, the Alice.

8. **1. bicycle** bike, BMX, boneshaker, coaster, cycle, dragster, high-riser, pedal cycle, penny-farthing, pushbike, safety bicycle, tandem, velocipede. *Informal:* chopper, grid, pushie. **2. tricycle** pedicab, quadricycle, sidecar, three-wheeler, trishaw, unicycle. *Informal:* dinky, trike. **3. skateboard** mountainboard, roller-skate, scooter. *Informal:* skatie. **4. motorcycle** ag-bike, agricultural bike, moped, moto, motor scooter, motorbike, quad bike, scooter, solo, three-wheeler, trail bike, tricycle. *Informal:* easy rider, hog. **5. sidecar** chair, combination.

9. **1. pram** bathchair, crash trolley, jinrikisha, perambulator, pushchair, pusher *(Chiefly Victoria, Tasmania, SA and WA)*, rickshaw, stroller, wheelchair. *Informal:* crash cart.

10. **1. sledge** bob, bobsled, bobsleigh, cat, catamaran *(NZ)*, coaster *(US)*, hurdle, ice-yacht, iceboat, jumper, koneke *(NZ)*, luge, skibob, skidboard, skidoo, skids, skimboard, sled, sleigh, toboggan, troika. *Informal:* fart machine. **2. ski** ice skate, skate. **3. land yacht** land sailer, sandyacht.

11. **1. vehicles – miscellaneous** bloodmobile, bookmobile, bowser, cattle truck, concrete-mixer, dodgem, dustcart *(British)*, field ambulance, fire truck, fire-engine, float, garbage truck, grader, hearse, mail car, manriding transport, milk float, minitanker, oil tanker, petrol bowser, pie-cart, road-roller, sag wagon, snowplough, steamroller, stock car *(US)*, tanker, tow truck, traction engine, transporter, water cart, water wagon, water-cart. *Informal:* bonk wagon, chuck wagon, reefer.

12. **1. vehicle parts** ABS, active suspension, air dam, air suspension, align, anti-roll bar, anti-sway bar, atlantic, axle, axletree, bodywork, bonnet, boot, bumper, bumper bar, camping body, chassis, child restraint, coachbox, coachwork, cowcatcher, cowl, dash, dashboard, demister, fairing, fascia *(British)*, fender *(US)*, glove box, glove compartment, grill, grille, hood, IFS1, imperial, independent front suspension, inner tube, instrument panel, instrumentation, IRS, kangaroo bar, kingpin, knobbly, luggage rack, MacPherson strut suspension, mouldboard, mudflap, mudguard, multiple unit, odograph, odometer, overrider, pacific, panel, perch, pin, pneumatic tyre, recap, restraint, revolution counter, rim, roll bar, roll cage, roof-rack, rumble, shoe, strut suspension, stub axle, sun shield, sun visor, sunroof, sunshine roof, suspension, swingletree, swivel pin, tailboard, tailgate, tonneau, top, torsion bar, tow bar, track, track rod, tray, tread, tripmeter, tubeless tyre, tyre, weather shield, wheel, whippletree, windscreen, windshield *(Chiefly US)*, wing. *Informal:* mag wheel, roo bar, slick. **2. motor** accelerator, air-intake, big end, carburettor, connecting rod, crankcase, crankpin, crankshaft, cylinder, cylinder block, cylinder head, dip stick, distributor, driving wheel, dynamo, generator, head, ignition (coil), kickstart, kick-starter, muffler, pushrod, rotary engine, rotor, short engine, short motor, silencer, steering wheel, sump, suppressor, tailpipe, traction motor, valve gear. *Informal:* carbie, carby. **3. gears** automatic transmission, clutch, column shift, differential, differential gear, drive shaft, fluid drive, gate, gear-ratio, gearbox, gearstick, high, hydraulic torque converter, limited-slip differential, low, overdrive, preselector, propeller shaft, reverse, selective transmission, shift, shifter *(Chiefly Eastern States)*, synchro, synchromesh, tail shaft, torque converter, universal. *Informal:* diff, diffy *(NZ)*, four-on-the-floor, slush box, three-on-the-tree.

adj. **13.** **1. vehicular. 2. automotive** automobile, convertible, four-wheel drive, four-wheeler, gran turismo, hardtop, motor, multicylinder, multimotored, pre-crumple, souped-up, tracked, trackless, veteran, vintage. **3. table-top** flat-bed.

v. **14.** **1. drive** corner, guttercrawl, motor, ride, scramble. *Informal:* fang, tool, tootle. **2. wade** ford, slop. **3. taxi** bus, jitney *(US)*, post, stage, train, tram. **4. cycle** bicycle, scooter. **5. sledge** bobsled, bobsleigh, luge, skibob, sled, sleigh. **6. chariot** gig. **7. hitchhike** stowaway. *Informal:* bum a ride, hitch, jump the rattler, ringbolt *(NZ)*, scale.

RELATED KEYWORDS: FLYING, MACHINE, TRANSPORT, TRAVEL, WATERCRAFT

VERBOSITY

n. **1.** **1. verbosity** gabbiness, garrulity, garrulousness, longwindedness, loquaciousness, loquacity, overelaboration, prolixness, superfluity, surplusage, talkativeness, verboseness, volubleness, wordiness. *Informal:* gift of the gab, jaw, verbal diarrhoea. **2. diffuseness** diffusion, diffusiveness. **3. digressiveness** discursiveness, vagrancy.

2. **1. waffle** babble, blab, blather, burble, chatter, clack, drivel, empty words, gabble, gibberish, gush, jabber, load of old rubbish, mere words, mumbo jumbo, nonsense, padding, patter, prattle, rigmarole, rubbish, sermonising, sound and fury signifying nothing, trumpery, verbiage. *Informal:* doubletalk, gab, gabber, garbage, gas, slipslop, twaddle, yap. **2. amplification** expansion, expatiation. **3. digression** apostrophe, discursion, divagation, divergence, episode, excursion, excursus. **4. tautology** pleonasm, redundance, redundancy. **5. circumlocution** periphrase, periphrasis. **6. doublespeak**

3. **1. verbose person** expatiator, maunderer, tautologist. *Informal:* bag of wind, big mouth, bush lawyer, fluter, gasbag, gusher, motormouth, rattletrap, windbag.

adj. **4. 1. verbose** diffuse, diffusive, expansive, garrulous, gushing, lengthy, long-drawn, longwinded, loquacious, of many words, profusive, prolix, rambling, talkative, tedious, voluble, waffly, wordy. *Informal:* gabby, motormouth. **2. amplificatory** circumlocutory, overelaborated, periphrastic. **3. digressive** apostrophic, discursive, divergent, episodic, excursive, prolegomenous, roundabout. **4. redundant** empty, pleonastic, tautological.

v. **5. 1. waffle** chatter, gush, mag, maunder, rant, rant and rave, talk nonsense, talk off the top of one's head, verbalise. *Informal:* chinwag, gasbag, motormouth, piffle, rabbit on, rap on, run on, run on and on, talk someone blind, talk the leg off an iron pot, talk through one's hat, yack on, yaffle, yak. **2. expatiate** amplify, descant, dilate on (or upon), enlarge on, expand, harp on (or upon), overextend, sermonise. **3. overelaborate** draw out, pad, protract. *Informal:* beat about the bush. **4. digress** deviate, divagate, diverge, ramble, sidetrack, wander.

adv. **6. 1. verbosely** diffusely, diffusively, digressively, discursively, divergently, overelaborately, periphrastically. **2. garrulously** at great length, in extenso, longwindedly, loquaciously, prolixly, wordily. **3. redundantly** pleonastically, tautologically.

RELATED KEYWORDS: BOMBAST, SPEECH, TALKATIVENESS

VIBRATION

n. **1. 1. vibration** beat, beating, drumming, judder, pulsation, pulse, shaking, throb, throbbing, trepidation. **2. earthquake** aftershock, earth tremor, foreshock, microseism, moonquake, quake, seaquake, seiche, seism, sunquake, temblor *(Chiefly US)*, tremor. *Informal:* shake. **3. shiver** fremitus, frisson, shimmy, tremble, tremor, wobble. **4. quiver** buzz, dither, palpitation, quaver, roll, shake, thrill, tremolo, tremor, twang, twitter, vibrato, whirr. **5. vibrancy** shakiness, the shivers, tremulousness, vibratility, waviness. **6. buffeting** concussion, jar, joggle, jounce, shake-up.

2. 1. flutter flickers, fluctuation, nutation, seesaw, shake, sway, swing, teeter, totter, undulation, waddle, wag, waggle, wave, wiggle.

3. 1. vibrator buzzer, diaphragm, pulsator, rattle, reciprocator. **2. shaker** dodderer, flutterer, swayer, swinger, throbber, trembler, twitterer, waddler, waverer, wiggler, wobbler.

adj. **4. 1. vibrating** libratory, nutant, nutational, oscillating, oscillatory, pendulous, pulsatile, pulsating, pulsative, pulsatory, swinging, throbbing, undulatory, up-and-down, vacillating, vacillatory, wavering, wavy. **2. shaky** doddering, doddery, juddering, quaky, reeling, rocky, rolling, tottering, tottery, trembling, trembly, tremulous, unsteady, waggly, wobbling. **3. dithery** agitated, twittery. *Informal:* all a-twitter, antsy. **4. earthshaking** seismic.

5. 1. fluttery aflutter, asp, aspen, fly-away, palpitant, quavery, quivering, quivery, shivering, shivery, tremulant, tremulous, vibrant, vibratile, vibrating, vibrative, vibratory, vibronic, wavering, wavy. **2. resonant** thrilling.

v. **6. 1. vibrate** beat, dandle, jog, joggle, judder, oscillate, pulsate, pulse, pump, shog, shudder, thrill, throb, wobble. **2. shake** dither, dodder, flutter, palpitate, pant, quake, quaver, quiver, shimmy, shiver, totter, tremble, twitter. **3. go back and forth** come and go, fishtail, go backwards and forwards, go to and fro, go up and down, rock, seesaw, teeter. **4. shake up** bucket about, concuss, jar, jig, jolt, jounce, rattle. **5. buzz** chatter, pound, quaver, rattle, resonate, twang, whirr.

7. 1. flutter bat, beat, flap, flick, flicker, flitter. **2. oscillate** dicker *(Chiefly US)*, fluctuate, hunt, librate, reciprocate, shuttle, shuttlecock, sway, vacillate, vibrate, waver, wobble. **3. roll** seesaw, shake, sway, swing, teeter, toss, totter, waddle, wag, waggle, weave, wiggle, wriggle. **4. wave** brandish, flap, flourish, wag, wigwag.

adv. **8. 1. flutteringly** atremble, pantingly, tremulously, waveringly. **2. resonantly** thrillingly, throbbingly. **3. shakily** totteringly, waddlingly, wobblingly. **4. swayingly** back and forth, backwards and forwards, flip-flop, pendulously, to-and-fro.

RELATED KEYWORDS: SPIN, TURBULENCE

VICTIM

n. **1. 1. victim** injured party, kill, prey, sufferer, underdog. **2. the oppressed** the downtrodden. **3. martyr** protomartyr, sacrifice, sin offering, victim, willing sacrifice. **4. scapegoat** cat's paw, dupe, greenhorn, gudgeon, gull, lamb, new chum, pawn, puppet, tool, whipping boy. *Informal:* mug, patsy, pigeon, sucker.

2. 1. butt April fool, Aunt Sally, buffoon, byword, easy prey, fair game, figure of fun, guy, laughing-stock, object of ridicule, zany. *Informal:* clown, fall guy, patsy, stooge.

2. gullible person bumpkin, country bumpkin, innocent, innocent abroad, rustic, yokel. *Informal:* hayseed, hick, rube *(US)*, Simple Simon.

3. 1. victimisation discrimination, harassment, oppression, unfair treatment. *Informal:* frame-up. **2. discrimination** ableism, ageism, Jim Crowism, positive discrimination, racial discrimination, sexual discrimination. **3. persecution** oppression, torment. **4. genocide** crime against humanity, holocaust, massacre.

adj. **4. 1. victimised** discriminated against, hard done by, ill-treated, ill-used, persecuted, singled-out, stigmatised. **2. downtrodden** crushed, heavy-laden, oppressed, stricken, under the whip, under the yoke.

v. **5. 1. victimise** be a scourge, come down (heavily) on, crack down on, deal hardly by someone, discriminate, discriminate against, get tough, punish selectively, single out. **2. persecute** afflict, burden, burke, crush, decimate, domineer, give no quarter, grind, grind down, grind down the faces of the poor, gripe, harass, hound, impose hardship on (or upon), massacre, molest, oppress, scourge, spite, subdue, suppress, torment, tyrannise. *Informal:* flatten, kneel on.

RELATED KEYWORDS: DECEPTION, REPRESSION, PAIN

VIOLENCE

n. **1. 1. violence** bloodthirstiness, furiousness, fury, impetuosity, outrage, rabidity, rabidness, rampancy, sanguinariness, sanguineness, vehemence. *Informal:* blood and thunder, rough stuff. **2. boisterousness** rampageousness, severeness, severity, storminess, turbulence, volcanicity. **3. aggression** aggressiveness, hubris, hybris, rage, rowdiness. *Informal:* aggro, bovver *(British)*. **4. fierceness** barbarity, ferity, ferociousness, ferocity, forcibility, forcibleness, fury, grimness, savageness, savagery, shrewishness, truculence. **5. barbarianism** barbarism, barbarity, Gothicism, heathenism, heathenry, loutishness, rudeness, wildness. **6. brutality** beastliness, bestiality, ruffianism, toughness.

2. 1. violent person aggressor, assailant, assaulter, attacker, invader, pirate, terrorist, trespasser, violator. **2. bully** blusterer, bullyboy, dragon, swashbuckler. *Informal:* bruiser. **3. lout** *(Informal)* barbarian, boor, boyo, hoodlum, hooligan, hoon, juvenile delinquent. *Informal:* bovver boy *(British)*, yobbo. **4. turk** tartar. **5. ruffian** apache, brute, bull, goon, gorilla, muscle man, nightrider *(US)*, rowdy, street fighter, thug, tough, yahoo. *Informal:* chokeman, he-man, plug-ugly *(US)*, poofter-basher, poofter-rorter, rough, yegg *(US)*. **6. shrew** fury, harridan, hellcat, maenad, scold, spitfire, termagant, tigress, virago, vixen, xanthippe. *Informal:* cow.

3. 1. violent outburst bluster, fury, heat, rage, rampage. **2. force** brunt, shock, violence. **3. cataclysm** catastrophe. **4. storm** gale, hurricane, maelstrom, squall, tempest, whirlwind. **5. paroxysm** throes.

adj. **4. 1. violent** driving, forceful, forcible, sharp, strongarm, terrorist. **2. boisterous** blustery, disorderly, rampageous, riotous, robust, robustious, rorty, rough, rough-and-tumble, rowdy, tumultuous, turbulent, unruly, uproarious, wild. *Informal:* rip-roaring. **3. foul** dirty, furious, hard, rough, severe. **4. drastic** extreme, severe, slashing, sledgehammer, undue, violent. *Informal:* all-fired *(Chiefly US)*, OTT, over-the-top. **5. sensational** violent. *Informal:* blood-and-thunder. **6. cataclysmic** catastrophic, earth-shaking, earth-shattering. **7. stormy** tempestuous, torrential, turbulent.

5. 1. ferocious aggressive, bellicose, belligerent, cruel, cutthroat, dominating, militant, nasty, pugnacious, ruthless, savage, tigerish, truculent, vicious, wicked. *Informal:* aggro. **2. maenadic** shrewish, termagant. **3. fierce** acrid, farouche, fiendish, furious, grim, hot, mad, rabid, raging, rampant, red-hot, vehement. **4. bloodthirsty** murderous, sanguinary, sanguine, slaughterous, warlike. **5. berserk** paroxysmal. *Informal:* berko.

6. 1. brutal beastly, bestial, boarish, brute, bull, bull-like, bullish, ferocious, hubristic, inhuman, lupine, savage. **2. barbaric** barbarian, barbarous, brutish, loutish, rough, rude, uncivil, uncivilised, vandal, vandalic. **3. ruffianly** piratical, thuggish, tough. *Informal:* hard-boiled, plug-ugly *(US)*.

v. **7. 1. be violent** be on the rampage, dash, go on the rampage, lash out, let fly, let rip, rage, ramp, rampage, rant, storm, swash, unleash. **2. bluster** bellow, din, roar, storm, thunder. **3. run wild** break away, break bounds, run amuck, stampede. **4. riot** run riot. **5. see red** *(Informal)* get up, go beserk. *Informal:* go bananas, go off pop, go off the deep end, go postal *(Chiefly US)*. **6. brutalise** barbarise, bestialise, brutify. **7. assault** assail, attack, attempt, bash, beat up, bombard, go bull-headed at, maul, pelt, sool, storm. *Informal:* lace into, tear into. **8. manhandle** bemaul, do violence to, knock about, knock around, rumple, tousle. **9. bully** abuse, badger, browbeat, bullyrag, give someone the shock treatment, strongarm. *Informal:* chuck one's weight about. **10. violate** outrage, shock, sin against.

adv. **8.** **1. violently** ferociously, savagely, truculently. **2. fiercely** furiously, grimly, rabidly, rampantly, vehemently. *Informal:* like fury. **3. bloodthirstily** sanguinarily, sanguinely. **4. brutally** barbarically, bestially, ferociously, loutishly, rudely. **5. forcibly** heavily, vigorously, violently, with a vengeance. *Informal:* hammer and tongs, slam-bang, slap-bang. **6. stormily** turbulently. **7. wildly** harum-scarum, madly, roughly, wild. *Informal:* tooth and nail. **8. blusteringly** aggressively, boisterously, swashingly, uproariously.

RELATED KEYWORDS: ANGER, ATTACK, ENERGY, FIGHTER, HITTING, RETALIATION, TURBULENCE, WEAPON

VISIBILITY

n. **1.** **1. visibility** apparentness, perceptibleness, visibleness, visual range. *Informal:* vis. **2. focus** eyeshot, range, resolution, view. **3. conspicuousness** boldness, clearness, obviousness, plainness, prominence. **4. spotlight** centrepiece, feature, hallmark, highlight, limelight, pride of place, showcase.

   2. **1. visualisation** appearance, manifestation, materialisation, pentimento, reappearance.

adj. **3.** **1. visible** macroscopic, noticeable, objective, observable, overt, viewable. **2. perceivable** apparent, discernible, distinguishable, evident, identifiable, manifest, obvious, patent, perceptible, plain, transparent, visible. **3. in focus** as plain as a pikestaff, black-and-white, clear, clear-cut, definite, distinct, palpable, plain, unambiguous, unblurred, unclouded, undisguised, unmistakable. *Informal:* as plain as the nose on your face. **4. conspicuous** blatant, bold, distinguished, exposed, eye-catching, for all to see, in full view, in view, marked, on view, open, open to view, outstanding, plain as day, pointed, salient, uncovered, under one's nose, within range.

adv. **4.** **1. visibly** apparently, evidently, observably, obviously. **2. conspicuously** boldly, clear, clearly, obviously, plainly. **3. at sight** on sight.

RELATED KEYWORDS: APPEARANCE, DISPLAY, REVELATION, OBVIOUSNESS, OPTICS, SIGHT

VISIT

n. **1.** **1. visit** call, country visit *(Aboriginal English)*, gam *(Nautical and US)*, social call, visitation. **2. stopover** abode, sojourn, stay, stop, stop-off. **3. tour** eco-tour, package tour, round trip. **4. the rounds** *Informal:* the traps. **5. visitors day** open day. **6. tourism** cultural tourism, dark tourism, destination tourism, ecotourism, event tourism.

   2. **1. visitor** caller, company, first foot *(Scottish)*, guest, house guest, inquiline, manuhiri, stranger, tramontane, visitant. *Informal:* do-drop-in. **2. frequenter** habitué, haunter, roundsman. **3. tourer** globetrotter, tourist. *Informal:* rubberneck.

v. **3.** **1. visit** call, call on, drop across, drop by, drop in, drop over, first-foot *(Scottish)*, go and see, go over to, look in, look in on, look up, make a call, pay a call, pay a visit, pop in, pop over, run across to, run over to, run round to, see, stop by, wait on, wait upon. *Informal:* blow in. **2. return a visit** pay back the visit. **3. do the rounds** do the calls, keep in touch, tour. *Informal:* visit the traps. **4. stay** sojourn, stay with, stop off at, stop over, tarry. **5. frequent** ghost, habituate, haunt. **6. tour** globetrot, jetset.

RELATED KEYWORDS: ARRANGEMENT, SOCIABILITY, TRAVEL

VOLUPTUOUSNESS

n. **1.** **1. voluptuousness** bacchanalianism, carnality, earthiness, erotism, erotology, fleshliness, hedonism, luxuriousness, luxury, narcissism, pleasure, sensualism, sensuality, volupté, voluptuosity. **2. concupiscence** debauchery, dissipation, dissoluteness, goatishness, lecherousness, lechery, lewdness, libidinousness, licentiousness, lubricity, lustfulness, sensuality. **3. lust** eros, libido, sexual desire. **4. bestiality** animalism, animality, beastliness, debauchment, sensuality, swinishness. **5. orgy** bacchanal, bacchanalia. **6. fleshpots. 7. pleasure principle**.

   2. **1. voluptuary** bacchant, bacchante, boulevardier, epicure, epicurean, eroticist, hedonist, sensualist, sybarite. **2. lecher** beast, Casanova, Don Juan, ladies' man, satyr, swine. *Informal:* boudoir bandicoot, d.o.m., dirty old man, goat, pants man, slut, wolf. **3. earthmother** *(Informal)*.

adj. **3.** **1. voluptuous** carnal, earthy, epicurean, erotic, erotogenic, fleshly, hedonic, hedonistic, sensual, sensualistic, sensuous, supersensual, sybaritic, voluptuary. **2. concupiscent** fruity, hircine, hot, lascivious, lecherous, lewd, libidinous, lubricious, lustful, racy, rampant, raunchy, salacious. *Informal:* buaya *(Singaporean and Malaysian English),* randy. **3. bacchanalian** bacchanal, bacchic, dionysian. **4. bestial** beastly, boarish, brute, brutish, carnal, debauched, fleshly, porcine, swinish.

v. **4. 1. sensualise** eroticise, erotise. **2. animalise** bestialise, debauch.

RELATED KEYWORDS: OVERINDULGENCE, DESIRE, PLEASURE, PROMISCUITY, SEX

VULGARITY

n. **1. 1. vulgarity** cannibalism, commonness, grossness, heathendom, low-mindedness, lowness, rudeness, rusticity, uncivilness, uncouthness, vulgarism, vulgarness. **2. coarseness** crudity, earthiness, ribaldry, sensationalism, sensualness. **3. Philistinism** ill-breeding, illiberalness, plebeianism. **4. bad taste** tastelessness. **5. unmentionableness** unparliamentariness, unrepeatability. **6. garishness** blatancy, flashiness, fulsomeness, gaudiness, Gothicism, loudness, outlandishness, sensationalism. **7. tawdriness** dowdiness, frumpishness, unfashionableness, unkemptness. **8. indecorousness** gaucherie, impropriety, indecency, indecorum, indelicacy, obscenity, unbecomingness, unseemliness. **9. rowdiness** bawdiness, boorishness, buffoonery, loutishness, oafishness, rowdyism, swinishness. **10. barbarism** atrociousness, atrocity, barbarianism, barbarity, baseness, brutishness, harshness, heathenishness, heathenism, heathenness, heathenry, life in the raw.

2. 1. vulgarism burlesque, choice language, dirty word, profanity, ribaldry, slang. **2. kitsch** gingerbread, tinsel. **3. vulgarisation** barbarisation, brutalisation, rustication.

3. 1. vulgarian cad. *Informal:* bounder *(British),* low-life. **2. philistine** groundling, plebeian, rough diamond. *Informal:* mucker *(British),* pleb. **3. nouveau riche** arriviste, new-rich, parvenu, social climber, upstart. **4. peasant** *(Informal)* back-countryman, backwoodsman *(Chiefly US),* bumpkin, clodhopper, clown, cottager *(British),* cottier, country bumpkin, countryman, hatter, hillbilly *(Chiefly US),* muzhik, ploughboy, ploughman, plowman *(US),* rustic, ryot, villager, wench, yeoman *(British),* yokel. *Informal:* bushwhacker *(US),* hayseed, local yokel, redneck *(US),* rube *(US).* **5. boor** buffoon, churl, clown, harlequin, lout. *Informal:* alf, hick, ocker, ockerina, oik, rugger-bugger. **6. swine** oaf, yob. *Informal:* goon, slob, yobbo. **7. city slicker** *Informal:* hoon, lair, mug lair, show-off, teddy bear, two-bob lair. **8. lout** hoodlum, hooligan, oaf, rowdy, ruffian, thug. *Informal:* bodgie, bovver boy *(British),* gorilla, hoon, low-life, punk, rough, roughie, roughneck, widgie, yahoo, yegg *(US),* yeggman, yob, yobbo. **9. gang** the push. *Informal:* low-life. **10. barbarian** beast, brute, cave-dweller, savage, tramontane. *Informal:* apeman, caveman, trog, troglodyte. **11. vulgariser** ribald, sensationalist.

adj. **4. 1. vulgar** agrestic, banausic, broad, coarse, coarse-grained, common, crass, crude, earthy, foul-mouthed, gross, heavy, indelicate, inelegant, low, rorty, unpolished, unrefined. **2. indecent** bawdy, burlesque, earthy, Fescennine, filthy, lecherous, lewd, lubricious, obscene, profane, Rabelaisian, raunchy, ribald, scurrilous, strong. *Informal:* French. **3. unmentionable** unparliamentary, unprintable, unrepeatable, unspeakable. **4. tasteless** atrocious, outlandish, unaesthetic. **5. unfashionable** dowdy, shabby, tatty. *Informal:* budget, gay, nunty, tacky. **6. garish** cheap, clinquant, commercial, common, flashy, fulsome, gaudy, gingerbread, meretricious, raffish, roxy, showy, tarty, tawdry, tinsel, tinsel-like, tinselly. *Informal:* lairy, tizzy. **7. loud** blatant, obtrusive, showy. *Informal:* sporty. **8. kitschy** chocolate-box. **9. overdone** Gothic, rococo.

5. 1. ill-bred base, baseborn, ill-conditioned, illiberal, low, low-minded, lowbred, philistine, plebeian, underbred. *Informal:* pleb. **2. indecorous** improper, unbecoming, uncivil, uncivilised, unseemly, untoward. **3. parvenu** nouveau riche. *Informal:* non-U. **4. uncouth** improper, raw, rough, rough-and-ready, rough-spoken, rude, troglodytical, unkempt. **5. loutish** leery, oafish, rowdy, rowdyish. *Informal:* lairy, leary. **6. rustic** awkward, backwoods, barnyard, buffoonish, bush, clodhopping, country, gauche. *Informal:* gorblimey. **7. brutish** barbarian, barbaric, barbarous, beastlike, beastly, bestial, boarish, brutal, brute, harsh, heathenish, swinish.

v. **6. 1. vulgarise** cheapen, debase, lower. **2. coarsen** rusticate. **3. brutalise** barbarise, brutify. **4. tart up** *(Informal)* commercialise, tinsel. *Informal:* tizzy up. **5. be vulgar** have no taste whatsoever, show bad taste. *Informal:* lair it up.

adv. **7. 1. vulgarly** basely, bawdily, coarsely, commonly, grossly. **2. tastelessly** atrociously, indelicately, inelegantly, unaesthetically, unbecomingly. **3. unmentionably** unparliamentarily, unrepeatably, unspeakably. **4. blatantly** fulsomely, obtrusively, outlandishly. **5. garishly** flashily, gaudily, loud, loudly, tawdrily.

8. **1. uncouthly** loutishly, oafishly, rowdily. **2. awkwardly** broadly, rustically. **3. uncivilly** illiberally, indecorously, low-mindedly. **4. brutishly** barbarically, brutally, harshly, heathenishly, roughly, rudely, swinishly.

RELATED KEYWORDS: UGLINESS, DISCOURTESY, OBSCENITY

WAKING

n. **1.** **1. waking** arousal, awakening, rouse. **2. wakefulness** inquietude, insomnia, restlessness, sleeplessness, unrest, wake. *Informal:* the big eye. **3. reveille** early-morning call, rouse, wake-up call.

adj. **2.** **1. awake** wide-awake. **2. aware** analeptic, aroused, conscious. **3. wakeful** insomniac, insomnious, restless, sleepless. **4. alert** attentive, awake, on the alert, on the lookout, vigilant. **5. astir** about, abroad, afoot, up and about.

v. **3.** **1. wake up** awake, awaken, rouse, rub the sleep from one's eyes, wake, waken. **2. rise** arise, awake, get out of bed, get up, rouse, stir. *Informal:* hit the deck, surface, turn out. **3. arouse** call, knock up, rouse.

interj. **4.** **1. wake up** rise and shine, up you get, wakey-wakey.

WALL

n. **1.** **1. wall** ashlaring, brattice, bulkhead, cavity wall, curtain wall, dissepiment, enceinte, firewall, partition, party wall, walls, withe. **2. screen** iconostasis, jube, reredos, transenna, veil, veiling, velum. **3. curtain** air curtain, drop, drop curtain, drop scene, fire-curtain, safety curtain, tormentor. **4. diaphragm** dissepiment, interface, mediastinum, partition, septum, velum. **5. buffer** cushion, fender, pudding fender, shock absorber, stopping. **6. deflector** baffle plate, baffle plates, starling. **7. air-curtain** airlock. **8. shield** biological shield, butt, stone shield, washboard. **9. buffer zone** bamboo curtain, border, boundary, bounds, confines, fringe, frontier, iron curtain, limbo, no-man's-land, Rubicon.

2. **1. fence** barbwire fence, boundary, chock-and-log fence, cyclone fence, deadwood fence, dingo fence, dog fence, dog net, dogleg fence, dry-stone wall, electric fence, electrified fence, ha-ha, hedge, hedgerow, kangaroo fence, marsupial fence, pale, paling, paling fence, palisade, pest fence, picket fence, post-and-rail fence, rabbit fence, rabbit-proof fence, shark fence, shark net, snake fence *(Chiefly US)*, sunk fence, tick fence, wire, wire entanglement, worm fence *(Chiefly US)*. **2. netting** bird netting, cowl, flyscreen, flywire, fowling net. **3. gate** grate, grating, grille, starting gate. **4. bar** bail, balustrade, barriers, fiddle, ledge, rail, railings, tollbar, traverse. **5. fencing materials** barbed wire, barbwire, chain mesh, chain wire, chicken wire, cyclone wire, fencing panel, fencing wire, mesh, netting wire, palings, weldmesh, wire gauze, wire netting.

3. **1. embankment** baulk, bund, dam, dyke, flood bank, floodbank, floodgate, gate, levee, mound, retaining wall, revetment, sea bank, seawall, stopbank, tuffet, wall, water gate. **2. rampart** barricade, battery, bench, berm, bulwark, entrenchments, parapet, retrenchment, stockade, vallation.

adj. **4.** **1. intervenient** intercalary, intercurrent, interjacent, intermediate, intermissive, interposed, intervening, interventional, irruptive, mesne, middle, sandwiched.

v. **5.** **1. wall** bar, blockade, cordon off, curtain off, obstruct, partition, rope off. **2. come between** barricade, block, intercept, interlope, interpose, intervene, punctuate. *Informal:* sprag. **3. intercept** cut off, occult.

prep. **6.** **1. between** 'twixt and 'tween, amid, amidst, among, mid, midst *(Poetic)*. **2. 'tween**.

RELATED KEYWORDS: COVERING, ENCLOSURE

WAR

n. **1.** **1. war** civil war, discord, hostilities, shooting war, sword, total war, trench warfare, turf war, war of attrition, war of nerves, war to the knife, warfare, world war. **2. siege** war of attrition. **3. biological warfare** biowarfare, BW, chemical warfare, germ warfare. **4. atomic warfare** nuclear warfare. **5. unconventional warfare** evasion, guerilla warfare, subversion. **6. terrorism** bioterror, bioterrorism, cyberterrorism, ecoterrorism, homegrown terrorism. **7. psychological warfare** propaganda. **8. economic warfare** attrition, blockade, sanctions, scorched earth policy. **9. gigantomachia** theomachy. **10. holy war** crusade, jihad.

2. **1. warmongering** aggression, bellicosity, belligerence, combativeness, fight, hostilities, hostility, militancy, pugnaciousness, pugnacity, warfare, warlikeness. **2. militarism**. **3. jingoism** chauvinism, national prejudice.

3. **1. act of war** aggression, armed intervention, casus belli, declaration of war, invasion. **2. battle** action, armed conflict, attack, brush, charge, clash, combat, contest, dogfight, engagement, fight, fray, gunbattle, incident, pitched battle, raid, rencounter, sally, scrape, skirmish, sortie, storm, strife, struggle. **3. war manoeuvre** campaign, combined operations, framework operations, leaguer, operation, siege, tactic, wet work. *Informal:* op. **4. campaign** anabasis, crusade, expedition, mission, operation, sally. **5. call to arms** appeal to arms, battle cry, calling, cry, marching orders, summons, war cry. **6. strategy** battle-orders, commander's concept, concept of operations, deployment, generalship, manoeuvres, orders of the day, plan, power play, tactics. **7. war game** field day, naumachia, naumachy. **8. fortune of war** outcome of battle. **9. massacre** battue, blood, blood-letting, bloodbath, bloodshed, butchery, carnage, genocide, hecatomb, holocaust, maihem, mayhem, pillage, pogrom, slaughter. **10. barrage** bombardment, shelling. *Informal:* stonk. **11. militarisation** armament, mobilisation, rearmament, war footing, war measures.

4. **1. military service** active service, soldiering. *Informal:* hitch *(US)*. **2. recruitment** call-up, conscription, draft, national service, selective service. *Informal:* nasho.

5. **1. battleground** action stations, Armageddon, cockpit, field, field of battle, fire-zone, firing line, front, killing field, trenches. **2. enfilade** action stations, battlefront, battle-line, echelon, firing line, front, front line, line, line of battle. **3. minefield. 4. beach-head** bridgehead. **5. headquarters** base, camp, command post, G.H.Q., general headquarters, H.Q., operations room. *Informal:* oicery.

6. **1. warmonger** aggressor, assailant, campaigner, champion, chauvinist, combater, crusader, fighter, hawk, invader, militant, militarist.

7. **1. battle** Actium, Agincourt, Anzac Beach, Anzio, Ardennes, Austerlitz, Balaclava, Battle of Britain, Battle of the Bulge, Beersheba, Bismark Sea, Blenheim, Borodino, Boyne, Bunker Hill, Castle Hill rebellion, Coral Sea, Crécy, Dardanelles, Dienbienphu, Dunkirk, El Alamein, Eureka Stockade, Gallipoli, Gaza, Gettysburg, Guadalcanal, Iwo Jima, Java Sea, Jena-Auerstedt, Jutland, Khartoum, Kokada Trail, Leningrad, Lepanto, Lexington and Concord, Mafeking, Marathon, Marengo, Marne, Midway, Naseby, Okinawa, Omdurman, Passchendale, Pearl Harbour, Philippi, Plassey, Poitiers, Quebec, Rorke's Drift, Salerno, Saratoga, Sari Bair, Sevastopol, Singapore, Somme, Spanish Armada, Stalingrad, Tannenberg, Tet offensive, Teutoburger Wald, Thermopylae, Tobruk, Trafalgar, Verdun, Villers Bretonneux, Waterloo, Wounded Knee, Yalu River, Ypres, Zama.

adj. **8.** **1. warlike** aggressive, armipotent, bellicose, belligerent, bloodthirsty, bloody, combatant, combating, currish, cutthroat, hawkish, martial, militant, murderous, pugnacious, quarrelsome, sanguinary, sanguine, slaughterous, warring. **2. militaristic** chauvinist, chauvinistic, jingoistic.

v. **9.** **1. wage war** attack, commit hostilities, declare war, dig up the hatchet, engage in hostilities, give battle, go to war, invade, join battle, make war, raise one's banner, resort to arms, resort to war, take the offensive, take up arms, take up the cudgels. **2. pillage** burn, butcher, foray, lay waste, maraud, massacre, mow down, pirate, plunder, put to the sword, ravage, scorch, shed blood, slaughter, spoliate. **3. be at war** attack, battle, be at daggers drawn, be on the warpath, be rowing *(Aboriginal English)*, combat, commit hostilities, contest, declare war, dig up the hatchet, engage in hostilities, fight, give battle, go to war, invade, join battle, lay waste, make a stand, make war, put to the sword, raise one's banner, ravage, resort to war, shed blood, slaughter, stand by, strive, struggle, take the offensive, take up arms, take up the cudgels, wage war, war. **4. besiege** beleaguer, blockade, dig in, lay siege to, leaguer, move in on, siege. **5. barrage** blitz, bomb, bombard, bunker buster, creeping barrage, strafe, torpedo. *Informal:* stonk. **6. manoeuvre** brush, countermarch, flank, march, operate, outflank, overrun, rout, skirmish, sortie. *Informal:* footslog. **7. deploy** change front, darraign, deraign, enfilade, marshal.

10. **1. militarise** activate *(US Military)*, arm, crusade, embattle, mobilise, put on a war footing. **2. recruit** call up, conscript, draft. **3. enlist** enrol, join, join the colours, join up. **4. soldier** bear arms, campaign, go on active service. **5. prepare for action** clear the decks.

RELATED KEYWORDS: ATTACK, DEFENCE, CONTEST, FIGHTER, WEAPON

WARNING

n. **1.** **1. warning** alarm, alert, appel, caution, mayday, monitum, red alert, red flag, signal. **2. warning signal** beacon, blue light, danger signal, distant signal, exclamation mark

(British), fog signal, hazard flasher, hazard lights, klaxon, red light, seamark, skull and crossbones, storm signals, storm warning. **3. alarm bell** alarm clock, burglar alarm, curfew, fire alarm, foghorn, gong, horn, klaxon, shark bell, shark siren, siren, tocsin. **4. forewarning** boding, foreboding, forerunner, harbinger, hunch, omen, premonition, presage, presentiment, prognostic, sign, symptom, the writing on the wall. **5. admonition** caution, caveat, counsel, denunciation, exhortation, garnishment, heads-up, hint, intimation, lecture, memento mori, monition, notice, notification, object lesson, sabre-rattling, threat, tip, tip-off, warning, word. **6. example** deterrent, lesson, object lesson, warning.

2. 1. warner exhorter, lookout, monitor, night patrol, patrol, sentinel, sentry, shark patrol, vedette, vidette, watch, watchdog, watchman. *Informal:* cockatoo, nit-keeper. **2. picket** air picket, outrider. **3. monitor** airborne early warning system, distant early warning system *(Chiefly US)*, early warning system, indicator, radar, radiolocation, sonar, sonobuoy. **4. alarmist** Cassandra.

adj. **3. 1. warning** exemplary, instructive, monitory, premonitory, sematic, telltale. **2. threatening** boding, fateful, fatidic, ominous, oracular, portentous, prophetic. **3. admonitory** cautionary, exhortative.

v. **4. 1. warn** admonish, advise, caution, exhort, forewarn, garnish, give someone a tip, premonish, previse, recommend, tip off, tutor. *Informal:* put wise. **2. alarm** alert, gong. **3. keep watch** monitor, patrol. *Informal:* keep nit.

interj. **5. 1. beware** caveat emptor, look out, watch it, watch out. *Informal:* action stations, cave *(British)*.

RELATED KEYWORDS: MENACE, DANGER

WATERCRAFT

n. **1. 1. watercraft** boat, bottom, class boat, cockle, cockleshell, consort, craft, flatboat, flatiron, hog, launch, monohull, multihull, pink, prow *(Poetic)*, shallop, ship, shipboard, skiff, vessel, whaleboat, wherry *(US)*. *Informal:* greyhound. **2. log** *Informal:* tub. **3. jolly-boat** cockboat, cockleboat, hoy, tender. **4. barge** gondola, lighter, scow. **5. merchant vessel** argosy, bilander, bulk carrier, cargo boat, coaster, collier, container ship, factory ship, freighter, fruiter, indiaman, liner, merchantman, oil tanker, packet (boat), pearler, sealer, sixty-miler, slaver, supertanker, tanker, trader, tramp, tramp steamer, whaler. **6. shipping** flotage, marine, merchant navy, watercraft. **7. fleet** argosy, armada, column, convoy, fleet in being, flotilla, navy, screen, squadron, wing. **8. flagship** admiral. **9. warship** aircraft-carrier, assault craft, battle cruiser, battleship, capital ship, caravel, carrier, corsair, cruiser, cutter, destroyer, destroyer escort, dreadnought, e-boat, fire ship, flag, flagship, flat-top, frigate, gunboat, HMAS, HMS, ironclad, ironsides, landing craft, man-o'-war, man-of-war, mine-layer, minesweeper, minisub, monitor, pocket battleship, privateer, PT boat, q-ship, RAN, ship of the line, submarine, superdreadnought, three-decker, torpedo-boat, torpedo-boat destroyer, troop-carrier, trooper, troopship, U-boat, vedette. **10. pirate ship** corsair, sea-rover. **11. fishing vessel** crabber, drifter, fisherman, fishing smack, hooker, smack, trawler. **12. training ship** mother ship, school ship. **13. water taxi** aquacab. **14. ark. 15. miscellaneous** bumboat, cutter, dredger, fireboat, hospital ship, hulk, iceboat, icebreaker, lifeboat, lightship, revenue cutter *(British)*, showboat *(US)*, surf rescue boat, towboat, transport, tug, tugboat, victualler, weathership. *Informal:* snagger. **16. shipwreck** wreck.

2. 1. motor vessel flyboat, longtail boat, motor boat, oil-burner, powerboat, runabout, ski-boat, speedboat. *Informal:* hot-water boat, rubber duckie. **2. steamship** paddle-steamer, paddleboat, side-wheeler, steamboat, steamer, stern-wheeler. **3. cabin cruiser** cruiser, houseboat. **4. hydrofoil** float plane, hydro-aeroplane, seaplane *(US)*. **5. ferry** car ferry, ferryboat, punt, wherry *(US)*. **6. jet ski. 7. wetbike. 8. submarine** bathyscaphe, bathysphere, minisub, U-boat. *Informal:* sub. **9. hovercraft** airboat.

3. 1. sailing ship bark, barkentine, barque, barquentine, brig, brigantine, caravel, carvel, catboat, clipper, cutter, dandy, dogger, fore-and-after, galleon, hoy, jolly-boat, ketch, lugger, polacca, schooner, sloop, smack, tartan, three-decker, three-master, topsail schooner, two-master, xebec. **2. sailing boat** auxiliary, dhow, dory, drogher, dromond, felucca, galleon, junk, keel, keelboat, knockabout, maxi, maxi-yacht, pinnace, prau, proa, sabot, sail, sailboard, sailboat, sailer, sharpie, windjammer, windsurfer, yacht. **3. catamaran** cat, Hobie cat, trimaran.

4. 1. rowing boat bateau, caique, coble, dinghy, dingy, double scull, eight, felucca, gig, longboat, outrigger, pair, rowboat, scull, shell, skiff, surfboat, wherry *(US)*, whiff.

Informal: dinky, flattie, gun, toothpick. **2. canoe** dugout, faltboat, foldboat, kayak, piragua, pirogue, surf ski. **3. coracle** bidarka, oomiak, umiak. **4. punt** gondola, sampan. **5. galley** bireme, galleass, galliot, longship, quinquereme, trireme.

5. **1. raft** balsa, catboat, float, kon-tiki *(NZ)*, life raft, scow. **2. floating bridge** bateau, pontoon, stakeboat. **3. buoy** lifebuoy.

6. **1. surfboard** barge, body board, boogie board, down-railer, downrailer, hot dog, kickboard, kneeboard, longboard, mal, malibu, pin, rail, stubby, surf mat, surfoplane. *Informal:* elephant gun, pintail, pop-out, shooter, spear, stick.

7. **1. boat or ship parts – hull and superstructure** apron, back, beak, bilge, bilge keel, billboard, binnacle, body, bow, bowsprit, bulkhead, bulwarks, canoe stern, centreboard, centreplate, cheese-cutter, conning tower, counter stern, cutwater, dagger plate, dagger-board, daggerplate, deadwood, deckhouse, displacement hull, figurehead, fin, fin keel, forefoot, futtock plank, futtock plate, gunnel, gunwale, hance, harpings, hawse, hawse pipe, head, inwale, island, keel, lapstreak, leeboard, monkey island, nose, outrigger, pilot house, plank-sheer, prow, ram, rib, ribband, ribbon, rostrum, samson post, sheer, skeg, skids, stem, stemson, stern door, sternpost, strake, stretcher, stringer, superstructure, taffrail, thwart, timber, timberhead, topsides, transom stern, trunk, tuck, upper works, wale, washboard, water-level, waterline, wheelhouse. **2. deck** admiral's walk, after peak, afterdeck, bay, boat-deck, bottom, cabin, canvas, channel, charthouse, chartroom, coach-house, coal-bunker, cockpit, counter, cuddy, engine-room, eye, fighting top, flight deck, flotage, fly-bridge, flying bridge, focsle, forecastle, forecastle head, foredeck, forepeak, foresheets, foretop, freeboard deck, gallery, galley, head, hold, hurricane deck, lower deck, lubber's hole, main deck, mess deck, orlop, poop, poop deck, promenade deck, prow, quarterdeck, roundhouse, spar deck, stateroom, steerage, stern, stern sheets, stokehold, stokehole, sun-deck, tonnage deck, upper deck, vehicle deck, waist, wale, weather deck, welldeck, wing. **3. spars** boom, bumpkin, channel, dolphin striker, fore, fore-topgallant mast, fore-topmast, foremast, foreyard, futtock band, gaff, jack, jackyard, jib boom, jigger, jiggermast, jockey pole, jury mast, main, main-topgallant mast, main-topmast, mainbrace, mainmast, maintop, mainyard, martingale, mast, masthead, mizzen, mizzenmast, monkey-gaff, out-rigger, royal mast, sailyard, spar, sprit, steeve, stick, tack, top, topgallant, tophamper, topmast, trestletree, truck, whisker, whisker boom, whisker pole, yard, yardarm. **4. sails** balloon jib, bonnet, bunt, canvas, course, crossjack, flying jib, flying kite, fore-and-aft sail, fore-topsail, forecourse, foresail, forestay sail, gaff-topsail, genoa, headsail, jib, jigger, lateen sail, lug, lugsail, main, main-topgallant, main-topsail, mainsail, mizzen, miz-zenmast, moonraker, moonsail, press of sail, ringtail, royal, sail, skysail, spanker, spencer, spinnaker, spritsail, square sail, staysail, storm jib, storm sail, studdingsail, stunsail, topsail, trysail. *Informal:* ballooner, kite. **5. sail part** clew, foot, head, leech, luff, nock, peak, reef, tack, throat. **6. rigging** boltrope, boom vang, brail, breeching, buntline, cable, cat, chainplate, clew line, footrope, foresheet, forestay, futtock shrouds, gantline, grabrope, guestrope, halyard, inhaul, jackstay, mainsheet, mainstay, outhaul, pendant, preventer, roband, robbin, robin, running rigging, seizing, sheet, shrouds, slings, snotter, spring, standing rigging, stay, stirrup, stop, stopper, swifter, tack, tackle, tripping line, vang, warp. **7. steering gear** rudder, rudderhead, rudderpost, tiller, wheel, yoke.

8. **1. sailing dinghies: Australian design** 12-(16)-(18)-foot skiff, 29er, 49er, Australian Sharpie, Contender, Flying Eleven, Laser II, Manly Junior, Minnow, Moth, NS 14, Pelican, Tasar, VJ, VS. **2. dinghies: non-Australian design** 14 foot, 420, 470, 505, Cadet, Cherub, Enterprise, Europe, Finn, Fireball, Flying Ant, Flying Dutchman, Flying Junior, GP 14, Heron, Laser, Lazy E, Lightning, Mirror, OK, Optimist, P-class, Pacer, RS, Sabot, Snipe, Splash, Sunfish, Topper, Vaurien, Zoom 8.

adj. **9.** **1. nautical** marine, maritime, naval, sailing, shipboard, waterborne. **2. floating** afloat, waterborne. **3. seaworthy** A1 at Lloyd's, fit for sea, shipshape and Bristol fashion, watertight. **4. ocean-going.**

v. **10.** **1. set sail** cast off, get under way, put off, put out, put to sea, sail, weigh anchor. **2. go to sea** cruise, follow the sea, ship, voyage. **3. picaroon** buccaneer. **4. make way** beat, luff, make heavy weather, pinch, point, sail close to the wind, scud, thrash. **5. tack** bear away, broach, ease off, go about, harden sheets, overstand. *Informal:* haul up. **6. shorten sail** back and fill, blanket, fill away, jibe, reef. **7. make sail** overhaul, sheet home. **8. dismast** unrig.

RELATED KEYWORDS: MARINER, TRANSPORT, TRAVEL, VEHICLE

WEAKNESS

n. **1.** **1. weakness** adynamia, anaemia, anergy, asthenia, atony, consumption, debility, decrepitude, delicateness, dotage, effeteness, failing, faintness, fecklessness, feebleness, frailness, helplessness, impotence, inanition, infirmity, infirmness, littleness, lowness, malaise, mushiness, nervelessness, paleness, powerlessness, puniness, senility, sickliness, tremulousness. **2. enfeeblement** anility, atrophy, break-up, brokenness, debilitation, devitalisation, disablement, disintegration, enervation, intolerance. **3. frailty** caducity, destructibility, destructibleness, infirmity, pregnability, shakiness, transitoriness, unsubstantiality, vincibility, vincibleness, violability. **4. paleness** colourlessness, peakiness. **5. looseness** flabbiness, flaccidity, flaccidness, flimsiness, languidness, languishing, limpness, slackness, tenuousness. **6. droop** languish, tremor, wilt. **7. fatigue** exhaustion, languor, lassitude, prostration.

2. **1. weakling** asthenic, broken reed, dotard, milquetoast *(US)*, subman, wreck. *Informal:* cry-baby, doormat, gutless wonder, jelly blubber, jellyfish, paper tiger, softie, sook, sop, weakie, wimp, wuss. **2. effeminate male** milksop. *Informal:* cream puff, gussie, pansy, poof, poofter, sis, sissy.

3. **1. weak spot** Achilles heel, breaking point, disability, failing, foible, shortcoming, spot, vice, weak link, weakness. **2. blemish** defect, failure, fault. *Informal:* bugs.

4. **1. weakener** deadener, enervator, enfeebler, softener, underminer.

adj. **5.** **1. weak** adynamic, asthenic, atonic, atrophic, atrophied, dependent, doddered, effeminate, effete, enervate, enervated, expugnable, fatigable, feeble, flimsy, helpless, impotent, impuissant, incapable, infirm, invalid, lily-livered, nerveless, on one's last legs, pimping, powerless, rickety, sickish, sickly, sinewless, subduable, unable, unmanly, wan, weak as water, weak-minded, weakling. *Informal:* limp-wristed, pooncey, sawney, sicko, wimpy. **2. frail** delicate, diminutive, faint, feckless, feeble, flimsy, gentle, helpless, languishing, languorous, limp, little, low, malnourished, pimping, puny, rickety, sickly, slight, small, spiritless, tender, tenuous, thewless, thready, valetudinarian, weak, weakling, weakly, weedy, wishy-washy. *Informal:* dicky, hothouse, mushy, soft, wet. **3. pale** ailing, anaemic, anemic, ashy, colourless, faint, feeble, green, impuissant, mealy, pallid, pasty, pasty-faced, peaky, pimping, sallow, sick, sickly, thin, wan, wannish, weak-looking, white, white-faced, white-livered, wisplike, wispy. *Informal:* washed-out. **4. effeminate** anile, camp, doting, emasculate, feminine, namby-pamby, petticoat, sawney, sorney, unmanly, womanish. *Informal:* dotty, poofy, trissy. **5. rickety** doddered, doddering, doddery, groggy, infirm, rocky, senile, shaking, shaky, shickery, shivery, tottering, tottery, trembling, trembly, tremulant, tremulous, twittery, unsound, wobbling, wobbly. *Informal:* dodgy, wonky. **6. broken** beaten, broken-down, collapsed, decrepit, droopy, exhausted, fatigued, feeble, gone, knocked-up, prostrate, run-down, shattered, spent, tired, wasted, weary, worn, worn-out, wrung-out. *Informal:* beat, buggered, bushed, bushwhacked, cactus, clapped-out, dead, dog-tired, done for, done in, euchred, far gone, fizzer, flat as a tack, flat out, jiggered, kaput, knackered, munted, out for the count, perished, pooped, punctured, rissoled, stonkered, stretched, washed-out, washed-up, whacked, wrecked, zapped, zonked. **7. loose** drooping, failing, feeble, flabby, flaccid, flagging, flaggy, flimsy, languid, limp, loose-jointed, slack, slight, tenuous, vague, weakening. *Informal:* sloppy. **8. debilitative** enervative, exhaustive.

v. **6.** **1. weaken** attenuate, blunt, break, cripple, deaden, debilitate, demoralise, devitalise, disable, dull, enervate, enfeeble, hamstring, hock, incapacitate, prostrate, sap, shake, shatter, swamp, unbrace, undermine, wilt, wither. **2. collapse** break down, crack, crash, crumple, fail, fall down, fold up, give way. **3. waste** atrophy, decay, decline, die, die away, dilapidate, disintegrate, droop, dwindle, ebb, emaciate, enfeeble, fade, fail, fall away, falter, flag, go soft, go to seed, invalid, languish, lose, miff, pass out, peak, pine, rot away, sink, subside, tetter, turn to jelly, wither on the vine, wizen. *Informal:* lose the plot. **4. soften** emolliate, shrivel, tame, wilt, wither. **5. loosen** check, loose, open, slack, slacken, unclasp, unlace, unlash, unloose, unstrap, unstring. *Informal:* mellow. **6. shake** dodder, palpitate, quake, quiver, shiver, shudder, sway, totter, tremble, wobble.

adv. **7.** **1. weakly** airily, delicately, frailly, helplessly, impotently, infirmly. **2. faintly** dotingly, effetely, fecklessly, feebly, languidly, languishingly, mushily, nervelessly. **3. palely** bloodlessly, colourlessly, peakily, punily. **4. femininely** languorously, tenderly, womanishly.

8. **1. limply** droopingly, flabbily, flaccidly, flaggingly, flimsily, loosely, slack, slackly, tenuously. **2. shakily** groggily, totteringly, tremulously.

RELATED KEYWORDS: COWARDICE, SOFTNESS, PLIABILITY, POWERLESSNESS

WEALTH

n. **1.** **1. wealth** cash in hand, dollars, filthy lucre, gold, gumtree money, lucre, mammon, means, money, opulence, pelf, petrodollars, riches, silver, the readies, the ready, worth. *Informal:* spondulicks. **2. fortune** a pretty penny, blood money, king's ransom, mega-dollars, tidy sum, wad. *Informal:* big bickies, big bucks, big dollars, megabucks, mint, motser, motza, pile. **3. resources** land, means, natural resources. **4. boom** minerals boom, resources boom. **5. treasure** blue chip, bonanza, bullion, capital, goldmine, independent means, nest egg, private means, treasure-trove, trove. **6. affluence** prosperousness, solidness, soundness, substantialness. **7. richness** abundance, affluence, opulence, riches, sumptuousness, wealth. **8. enrichment** aggrandisement, self-aggrandisement. **9. el dorado** Babylon, Golconda, land of milk and honey.

2. 1. wealthy person billionaire, Croesus, dollar millionaire, hustler, man of means, man of substance, megamillionaire, Midas, millionaire, millionairess, moneyed man, multi-millionaire, pound millionaire. *Informal:* a whale in the bay, fat cat, moneybags, sugar daddy. **2. nouveau riche** arriviste, new-rich, parvenu, upstart. **3. tycoon** aggrandiser, baron, capitalist, king, magnate, merchant prince, mogul, money-maker, nabob, plutocrat. *Informal:* plute. **4. mammonite** mammonist. **5. playboy** gilded youth, jetsetter, sybarite. *Informal:* silvertail, toff. **6. the rich** plutocracy, the haves, the idle rich, the other half, the ruling classes. **7. high society** beautiful people, fashionable, jet set, society.

adj. **3. 1. wealthy** affluent, afloat, brownstone *(US)*, copper-bottomed, flush, forehanded *(US)*, in funds, in pocket, made of money, moneyed, monied, opulent, prosperous, rich, rolling, solid, substantial, well-endowed, well-lined, well-to-do. *Informal:* filthy rich, in the money, loaded, on easy street, pluty *(NZ)*, stinking, well-fixed, well-heeled. **2. nouveau riche** new-rich. *Informal:* cashed-up. **3. opulent** Edwardian, palatial, palatine, ritzy, sumptuous, sybaritic. **4. capitalist** capitalistic, chrematistic, mammonistic, nabobish, plutocratic. **5. wealth producing** get-rich-quick.

v. **4. 1. be wealthy** be born with a silver spoon in one's mouth. *Informal:* be rolling in it, have a quid, have money to burn. **2. make money** coin money, make a mint. *Informal:* clean up. **3. prosper** mint it, strike it rich, thrive. *Informal:* coin it. **4. enrich oneself** accumulate wealth, aggrandise, batten on, enrich, feather one's nest, line one's pocket, stash it away.

adv. **5. 1. wealthily** affluently, fatly, plentifully, profitably, richly, substantially. **2. opulently** in the lap of luxury, luxuriously, palatially, sumptuously, sybaritically. **3. prosperously** successfully, thrivingly.

RELATED KEYWORDS: ARISTOCRACY, MIDDLE CLASS, EXTRAVAGANCE, GOOD FORTUNE, MONEY, OWNERSHIP, PROFIT, PROPERTY

WEAPON

n. **1. 1. weapon** atomic weapon, biological weapon, blast weapon, BW, clean weapon, deadly weapon, death ray, deterrent, fragmentation weapon, kiloton weapon, megaton weapon, nominal weapon, nuclear weapon, offensive weapon, salted weapon, secret weapon, thermonuclear weapon. *Informal:* nuke. **2. weaponry** artillery, cannonry, enginery, field artillery, field gun, gunnery, ordnance, rocketry. *Informal:* ack-ack. **3. arms** ammunition, armament, armoury, artillery, battery, cannonry, hardware, heavy metal, matériel, militaria, munitions, ordnance.

2. 1. gun automatic, field piece, firearm, firelock, firer, flintlock, ironmongery, magnum, matchlock, muzzle-loader, over-under, piece, pump action, rapid-firer, repeater, scattergun, semiautomatic, side-arm, small arms, smoothbore. *Informal:* equaliser, gat, joint, roscoe, shooter, shooting iron. **2. pistol** automatic, automatic pistol, bulldog, Colt, derringer, handgun, horse pistol, Luger, magnum, Mauser, revolver, smart gun, Smith and Wesson. *Informal:* cannon, heater *(US)*, iron *(British)*, rod, six-shooter, squirt. **3. rifle** 22 rifle, AK-47, armalite, assault rifle, automatic, automatic rifle, breech-loader, carabin, carbine, chassepot, elephant gun, Enfield rifle, Kalashnikov, machine gun, Mauser, submachine gun, Winchester rifle. **4. shotgun** chokebore, fowling-piece, Manton, petronel, pump gun, sawn-off shotgun. *Informal:* double, shotty, side-by-side. **5. machine gun** anti-aircraft gun, Bofors gun, Bren gun, Gatling gun, Lewis gun, Owen gun, pom-pom, pounder, sten gun, Thompson machine gun, Uzi. *Informal:* Tommy gun. **6. cannon** basilisk, Big Bertha, bombard, canon bit, chase-gun, chaser, culverin, falconet, field-gun, field-piece, howitzer, mortar, stern-chaser, trench mortar. **7. musket** arquebus, blunderbuss, culverin, fusil, hackbut, harquebus. **8. blowgun** blowpipe, pipe gun. **9. airgun** air rifle, BB gun, daisy gun, pea-shooter. **10. ray gun. 11. spear gun. 12. swivel gun. 13. toy gun** cap gun, popgun, supersoaker, water pistol.

3. 1. gun part air cylinder, barrel, breech, breechblock, butt, chamber, chase, chassis, chokebore, cock, cylinder, ejector, flask, foresight, guncarriage, gunflint, gunstock, hairtrigger, half-cock, hammer, muzzle, muzzle brake, pull-through, ramrod, rear sight, rib, safety catch, sear, sight, stock, touch-hole, trail, trigger, tumbler. **2. gunlock** firelock, flintlock, matchlock, percussion lock, wheel-lock. **3. fuse** boresafe fuse, proximity fuse.

4. **1. gunfire** firepower, flak. **2. gunshot** snapshot. **3. penetration** gunshot, shot. *Informal:* pop. **4. bombardment** barrage, blitz, broadside, burst, dispersal, dispersion, fusillade, round, salvo.

5. **1. ammunition** magazine, powder magazine. *Informal:* ammo, mag. **2. bullet** blank cartridge, cartridge, dumdum, pellet, rubber bullet, slow bullet, slug, tracer, tracer bullet. *Informal:* pick-up. **3. projectile** cannonball, round-shot, shell, torpedo. *Informal:* fish. **4. gunpowder** guncotton, potassium nitrate, saltpetre, smokeless powder. **5. shot** ball, BB shot, buckshot, bullets, canister, cannon shot, case shot, chain shot, chain-shot, drop shot, dust-shot, langrage, lead, load, round-shot, shrapnel. **6. shell** firebomb, gas shell, gezumpher, grenade, hand grenade, hang-fire, incendiary, rifle grenade, sabot, starshell, stun grenade, whiz-bang. *Informal:* firebug. **7. detonator** booster, cap, percussion cap, primer. **8. cannelure** twist. **9. nuclear warhead** nose-cone, payload, war nose, warhead. **10. chemical weapon** adamsite, air burst, arsine, blister gas, diphosgene, gas, lewisite, mustard gas, nerve gas, phosgene, poison gas, stinkpot, vesicant, yellow rain, yperite. **11. fireball** flamethrower, gas, Greek fire, liquid fire, napalm.

6. **1. bomb** A-bomb, air-fuel bomb, atomic bomb, blockbuster, bombshell, booby trap, bunker buster, buzzbomb, car bomb, clean bomb, cluster bomb, depth charge, fire bomb, fission bomb, flying bomb, fragmentation bomb, fusion bomb, H-bomb, hydrogen bomb, incendiary, landmine, laser-guided bomb, letter bomb, LGB, Mills bomb, mine, Molotov cocktail, neutron bomb, nuclear bomb, petard, pipe bomb, plastic bomb, rocket bomb, smokebomb, stick, stink bomb, time bomb. *Informal:* doodlebug, pineapple. **2. missile** aerodynamic missile, air-to-air missile, air-to-surface missile, antiballistic missile, Atlas, ballistic missile, barrage rocket, cruise missile, guided missile, intercontinental ballistic missile, intermediate range ballistic missile, mangonel, MX missile, Pershing II missile, Polaris, rocket, surface-to-air missile, surface-to-surface missile, theatre missile, torpedo, V-1, V-2. **3. mine** acoustic mine, antenna mine, contact mine, girandole, influence mine, landmine, magnetic mine. **4. launcher** anti-tank gun, bazooka, rocket gun, rocket-launcher, silo.

7. **1. knife** anlace, barong, bolo knife, bowie knife, crease, creese, dagger, dirk, flick-knife, kris, kukri, machete, misericord, panga, parang, poniard, sheath-knife, skean, stiletto, stiletto heel, stylet, ulu. *Informal:* shiv *(British)*. **2. sword** épée, ataghan, backsword, bayonet, blade, broadsword, claymore, cold steel, cutlass, estoc, falchion, foil, hanger, pigsticker, prog, rapier, sabre, scimitar, simitar, smallsword, snickersnee, steel, sticker, sword bayonet, Toledo, yataghan. **3. sword part** chape, cross-guard, faible, foible, forte, quillon, roundel. **4. axe** battleaxe, broadaxe, celt, chopper, cleaver, Douglas, fasces, hack, hatchet, ice-axe, kelly, meataxe, mogo, palstave, poleaxe, sax, scutch, tomahawk, tommyaxe, twibill. *Informal:* tommyhawk.

8. **1. spear** assegai, atlatl, dart, eelspear, gaff, gidgee, gig, harpoon, iron, javelin, leister, lily iron, spear-thrower, striker, woomera. **2. lance** bill, gisarme, halberd, partisan, pike, prog, shaft, spike, spontoon, trident, vouge. **3. boomerang** kylie, throwing stick. **4. flail** thunderbolt.

9. **1. arsenal** armoury, arms chest, caisson, dump, gun rack, magazine, pile, stack. **2. guncarriage** caisson, limber. **3. magazine** powder keg. *Informal:* mag. **4. holster** pistol-case. **5. bandolier** cartridge belt, clip. **6. scabbard** baldric, sheath. **7. arrow-case** quiver. **8. rifle range** practice range, rocket range. **9. bomb bay** bomb rack, gun emplacement.

10. **1. armourer** ballistics expert, bowyer, fletcher. **2. bombmaker**.

adj. **11.** **1. armed** under arms, weapon-carrying. **2. heavily-armed** capital, heavy-armed. **3. armoured** armour-plated, bombproof, bulletproof, helmeted, mailed, panzer.

RELATED KEYWORDS: ATTACK, DEFENCE, FIGHTER, THROW, VIOLENCE, WAR

WEATHER

n. **1.** **1. weather** the elements. **2. climate** clime *(Poetic)*, regime, seasonal pattern. **3. regional climate** continental climate, equatorial climate, insular climate, maritime climate, Mediterranean climate, microclimate, polar climate, temperate climate, tropical climate. **4. fair weather** balminess, calm weather, clemency, fairness, fineness, halcyon days, shine, sunniness, sunshine. **5. rough weather** inclemency, intemperateness, raininess, storminess, sultriness, unsettledness, windiness, wintriness. **6. storm** blow, cyclone, hailstorm, hurricane, rainstorm, snowstorm, squall, tempest, thunder, tornado, twister *(US)*, typhoon. **7. dust storm** dust squall, sandstorm. *Informal:* Bedourie shower, Bogan shower, Cobar shower, cockeye bob, Darling shower, Wilcannia shower, Wimmera shower.

2. **1. atmospheric pressure** air pressure, air-pressure, free air overpressure. **2. high** anticyclone. **3. low** cyclone. **4. cold front** depression, low area, trough. **5. warm front** heatwave, warm sector. **6. occluded front** occlusion. **7. eye** front, ridge, storm centre, wedge. **8. convergence** divergence, frontogenesis, frontolysis.

3. **1. climatology** bioclimatology, hygrometry, microclimatology. **2. meteorology** anemology, met report, meteorological report, micro-meteorology, synoptic meteorology, weather forecasting. **3. weather map** aerograph, synoptic chart, weather chart. **4. isobar** isallobar, isochor, isopiestic. **5. isotherm** isallotherm, isocheim, isothere, isothermal. **6. isoneph**.

4. **1. weather bureau** pilot balloon, sounding balloon, sounding rocket, weather station, weathership.

5. **1. weather device** aerometer, barograph, barometer, baroscope, Fortin's barometer, glass, hygrogram, hygrograph, hygrometer, hygroscope, maximum and minimum thermometer, mercury thermometer, meteorograph, microbarograph, psychrometer, radio-meteorograph, radiosonde, thermobarometer, thermoelectric thermometer, thermometer, weatherglass, wet-and-dry bulb hygrometer. **2. weathervane** cyclonoscope, vane, weather eye, weathercock.

6. **1. meteorologist** climatologist, weather forecaster, weatherman. *Informal:* skywonkie.

adj. **7.** **1. climatic** climatological, meteorological. **2. fair** balmy, bright, calm, fair-weather, fine, mild, sunny, temperate. **3. intemperate** boisterous, dirty, drastic, inclement, rainy, rough, severe, soppy, squally, stormy, tempestuous, tornadic, unsettled, windy. **4. weathered** weather-beaten. **5. weatherwise**.

RELATED KEYWORDS: CLOUD, SKY, HEAT, COLDNESS, RAINFALL, WIND

WETNESS

n. **1.** **1. wetness** clamminess, dewiness, moistness, ooziness, sloppiness, soddenness, sogginess, soppiness, stickiness, wet. **2. dampness** dankness, humidness, sweatiness. **3. lushness** succulence, succulency. **4. humidity** absolute humidity, dampness, regain, relative humidity, vapour concentration. **5. moisture** damp, rising damp. **6. bog** everglade *(US)*, fen *(British)*, marsh, mire, morass, ooze, quagmire, salt marsh, slob *(Irish)*, slough, swamp, wash, wet ground. **7. seepage** leakage, seep *(US)*.

2. **1. wetting** drench, marinade, soak, soakage, souse, steep. **2. saturation** calcification, inundation, rinsing. **3. irrigation** aspersion, drip irrigation, flood irrigation, subirrigation, watering, wild flooding. **4. immersion** affusion, baptism, bath, bogey, duck, immergence, plunge, rinse, submergence, submersion. **5. fomentation** embrocation, humidification, imbuement. **6. maceration** marination. **7. splash** dash, plash, splosh.

3. **1. wetter** baptiser, bather, douser, drencher, ducker, inundator, splasher, steeper, waterer. **2. dampener** damper, humidifier, macerater, moistener, moisturiser, rinser. **3. irrigator** soaker.

adj. **4.** **1. wet** damp, dripping wet, humid, hydric, moist, pluvial, pluvious, rainy, soaked, sodden, soggy, sopping, sticky, sweaty. **2. damp** clammy, dampish, dank, humid, hygric, mesic, moist, oozy. *Informal:* squidgy. **3. dewy** lachrymose, rainy, slobbery, wet. **4. lush** juicy, sappy, succulent. **5. boggy** fenny *(British)*, marshy, muddy, oozy, plashy, sloppy, sloshy, slushy, splashy. **6. irrigational** irrigative. **7. hygrophilous** deliquescent. **8. sodden** dozy, drenched, impregnate, soaked, soggy, sopping, sopping wet, soppy, waterlogged, wringing wet. **9. awash** swimming, water-sick, watery. **10. immersed** submerged, submersed.

v. **5.** **1. wet** baptise, dip, water. **2. bedew** dew. **3. moisten** baste, damp, dampen, dip, embrocate, foment, humidify, irrigate, moisturise, water down. **4. impregnate** imbue, saturate, soak. **5. sweat** cry, drip, reek, slobber, weep. **6. sprinkle** asperse, hose, shower. **7. splash** dabble, dash, plash, slop, spat, spatter, splatter, squirt. **8. drench** ret, rot, soak, sop, steep, swamp, waterlog. **9. soak** macerate, marinade, marinate, sodden, sop, souse, steep, water-soak. **10. deliquesce** **11. irrigate** deluge, drown, float, flood, inundate, overflow, subirrigate, water. **12. immerse** bathe, dip, douse, dowse, duck, dunk, engulf, ingulf, sink, souse, submerge, submerse. **13. dip** dap, puddle, sop. **14. go for a swim** bathe *(Chiefly British)*, have a dip, swim.

adv. **6.** **1. wetly** damply, dankly, humidly, moistly. **2. soggily** sloppily. **3. soddenly** soppily. **4. succulently** lushly. **5. dewily** sweatily.

RELATED KEYWORDS: BODILY DISCHARGE, FLOOD, FLOW, SEA, LAKE, LIQUID, RAINFALL, SLUDGE, SWAMP

WHITE

n. **1.** **1. white** alabaster, chalk, cream, ivory, milk, off-white, pearl, snow. **2. silver** Luna. **3. blond** albino, blonde, platinum blonde.

2. **1. whiteness** blondeness, blondness, creaminess, frostiness, hoariness, lactescence, milkiness, opalescence, pearliness, silveriness, snowiness, whitishness. **2. lightness** brightness. **3. blondness** albinism, fairness.

3. **1. whitening** albescence, blanching, etiolation.

4. **1. whitener** blancher, bleach, bleacher, blue, blue-bag, blueing, bluing, calcimine, kalsomine, washing blue, whitening, whitewash, whiting. **2. white pigment** Chinese white, flake white, lithopone, pipeclay, Venetian white, white lead, whiting, zinc white.

adj. **5.** **1. white** blank, floury, lilied, lily, lilywhite, pale, white as a ghost, white as a sheet. **2. snowy** frosty, snow-white, snowlike. **3. creamy** cream, cream-coloured, eggshell. **4. ivory** alabaster, chalky, eburnean. **5. milky** lacteous, milk-white, opalescent, opaline. **6. off-white** albescent, broken white, fair, light, oyster, oyster white, whitish, whity. **7. foaming** sudsy. **8. silver** argent, silvery, silvery-white. **9. blond** albino, ash-blond, bald, blonde, blonded, canescent, hoary, platinum blonde, towheaded, white-haired, white-headed. **10. pearly** nacreous.

v. **6.** **1. whiten** blanch, bleach, blench, etiolate, peroxide. **2. chalk** calcimine, kalsomine, pipeclay, powder one's face, powder one's nose, whitewash.

RELATED KEYWORDS: CLEANLINESS, COLOURLESSNESS, HAIR, INNOCENCE, LIGHT

WHOLE

n. **1.** **1. whole** aggregate, all, alpha and omega, altogether, entire, entirety, synthesis, synthesisation, total, totality. *Informal:* tot. **2. the lot** the whole lot. *Informal:* the full monty, the whole (kit and) caboodle, the whole box and dice, the whole enchilada, the whole schmear, the whole shebang, the whole shooting match, the works, whole hog. **3. whole amount** aggregation, continuity, ensemble, full amount, sum, summation, whole. **4. full set** complement, corpus, full board, full house, series, system. **5. gamut** circle, continuum, cycle, range.

2. **1. wholeness** absoluteness, completeness, entireness, entirety. **2. intactness** integrality, integrity, perfection, soundness, unbrokenness, undividedness, uninterruptedness, unity. **3. completion** finish, finishing touches, follow-through, follow-up, last touch, totalisation. **4. consummation** fruition, fulfilment, matureness, maturity, ne plus ultra. **5. supplementation** complement, filling. **6. thoroughness** clean sweep, exhaustiveness, extensiveness, sweepingness. **7. comprehensiveness** circumstantiality, circumstantiation, inclusiveness.

3. **1. completer** clincher, closer, finisher, fulfiller, supplementer. **2. integrator** synthesist, synthetiser.

adj. **4.** **1. whole** clean, complete, entire, full, plenary, total. **2. intact** acatalectic, entire, full-length, inedited, inviolate, unabbreviated, unabridged, unbroken, uncensored, uncut, undivided, unexpurgated, uninterrupted, unmoderated, whole, whole-length. **3. absolute** complete, consummate, dead, diametric, living, perfect, plenipotentiary, strict, unconditional, unconditioned, unqualified, utter. **4. finished** all over, complete, made-up, mature, over, well-rounded. **5. hundred-per-cent** complete, full, full on, full out, perfect, undamped. **6. inclusive** full, harmonious, integrated, integrative, plenary, round, sum, tutti, tutto, whole. **7. self-contained** autonomous, independent, self-sufficient, self-sufficing.

5. **1. thorough** all-out, all-up, deep-dyed, dyed-in-the-wool, in-depth, out-and-out, outright, overall, resounding, thorough-going, thoroughgoing, thoroughpaced, total, wholehearted, wholesale. *Informal:* boots-and-all, regular. **2. utter** arrant, complete, downright, extreme, grand, gross, stark, thorough, unmitigated. *Informal:* crashing, proper. **3. extensive** across-the-board, all-embracing, broad, clear, comprehensive, detailed, far-reaching, full-scale, fulsome, global, house-to-house, macroscopic, panoptic, sweeping, thorough, umbrella, universal, wall-to-wall. **4. comprehensive** detailed, encyclopedic, exhaustive, expansive, extensive, intensive, thorough. **5. completive** complemental, complementary, consummative, suppletory.

v. **6.** **1. make whole** complement, fill a gap, fill in, fill out, make good, round off, supplement. **2. integrate** piece together, synthesise, synthetise, totalise. **3. complete** accomplish, conclude, consummate, do, finish, perfect, perform, polish off, put the finishing touches, stop, wrap up. **4. follow through** carry through, explore every avenue, follow up, go through with, tie up the loose ends. *Informal:* go the whole hog, go the whole nine yards. **5. finalise** clench, clinch, close, come full circle, settle. **6. mature** flower, fulfil.

adv. **7. 1. wholly** absolutely, altogether, completely, consummately, entirely, every inch, first and last, full, fully, grossly, heartily, hundred-per-cent, on the whole, out, perfectly, quite, thoroughly, totally, unconditionally, unreservedly, utterly. *Informal:* every bit, good and proper, properly. **2. unbrokenly** continuously, undividedly, uninterruptedly. **3. altogether** all, all in all, all told, as a whole, bodily, in all, in full, in sum, in the aggregate, in toto, inclusively, integrally, overall, tout ensemble, wholly. **4. to the full** bag and baggage, body and soul, boots and all, down to the ground, from head to foot, holus-bolus, lock stock and barrel, neck and crop, root and branch, to the backbone, to the bitter end, to the hilt, to the letter, to the teeth. **5. head over heels** heart and soul, hook, line, and sinker. **6. downright** absolutely, deathly, fairly, hard, outright, quite, simply, stark, starkly, straight, utterly. *Informal:* dead, fair. **7. with a vengeance** and then some, in full force. **8. radically** diametrically.

8. 1. thoroughly broadly, comprehensively, exhaustively, extensively, in depth, intensively, sweepingly. **2. throughout** across-the-board, all along, from A to Z, from beginning to end, from end to end, from head to foot, from top to bottom, from top to toe, over, through, through and through. **3. clear** clean, hands down, well.

RELATED KEYWORDS: ADEQUACY, UNCONDITIONALITY, FULLNESS, GENERALITY, ONE, PERFECTION, FINISH

WILLINGNESS

n. **1. 1. willingness** alacrity, desire, eagerness, ebullience, enthusiasm, fire, get-up-and-go, inclination, promptness, readiness, wholeheartedness, zeal. **2. agreeability** a willing heart, complaisance. **3. free will** ultroneousness, voluntariness.

adj. **2. 1. willing** acquiescent, agreeable, agreeably disposed, amenable, bent upon, complacent, complaisant, compliable, compliant, complying, conformable, consenting, desirous, disposed, easy, easygoing, favourably disposed, inclined to, minded, obliging, of a mind to, pliant, predisposed. **2. happy to** assenting, content, glad, nothing loath, prepared, ready, sporting. **3. wholehearted** ungrudging, unmurmuring. **4. prompt** alacritous, forward, spontaneous. **5. voluntary** free, gratuitous, unasked for, unforced, volunteer.

v. **3. 1. be willing** be disposed, be inclined, be of a mind to, enthuse, have a mind to, have no scruples, lean towards, see fit, think fit. **2. agree** accede, accept, acquiesce, agree to, assent, concur, consent, fall in with, give one's consent, go along with, lend a willing ear, meet, say yes to, turn a willing ear. *Informal:* be a sport. **3. volunteer** offer, offer oneself.

adv. **4. 1. willingly** as lief, as soon, gladly, lief, lieve, readily, soon, with a will, with open arms. **2. voluntarily** of one's own accord, of one's own free will, ultroneously. **3. wholeheartedly** con amore, heart and soul, ungrudgingly, unmurmuringly, with all one's heart, with good grace.

RELATED KEYWORDS: AGREEMENT, CHOICE, ENTHUSIASM, INTENTION

WIND

n. **1. 1. wind** advection, air current, airflow, airstream, convection, cross-wind, crosswind, current, current of air, down draught, draught, gale, headwind, hurricane, overdraught, standing wave, storm, tail wind, up draught, windage. **2. breeze** air, breath, cat's paw, doctor, fresh breeze, gale *(Poetic)*, gentle breeze, land breeze, moderate breeze, sea breeze, slight breeze, strong breeze, trade wind, variable wind, zephyr. **3. strong wind** blow, gale, high wind, near gale, stiff wind, strong gale, whole gale, wind, windstorm. *Informal:* buster. **4. gust** blast, flaw, flurry, puff, waft. **5. whirlwind** dust devil, tornado, tourbillion, twister *(US)*, waterspout, whirly wind, whirly-whirly, williwaw *(NZ, Antarctica)*, willy-willy. **6. storm** blizzard, blow, buran, cyclone, dust squall, dust storm, hurricane, magnetic storm, monsoon, rainstorm, squall, tempest, typhoon, white squall. *Informal:* Bedourie shower, Bogan shower, cockeye bob, Darling shower, Wilcannia shower, Wimmera shower. **7. seasonal winds** equinoctial, etesian winds, nor'-easter, nor'-wester, north-easter, north-wester, northerly, sou', sou'-wester, sou'wester, south *(Chiefly Poetic)*, south-easter, south-wester, south-westerly, southerly, westerly. **8. directional wind** easterly, nor'-wester, north-easter, north-wester, northerly, sou'-wester, southerly, westerly. **9. Australian winds** Albany doctor, bora, brickfielder, Esperance doctor, Fremantle doctor, southerly buster. **10. regional winds** barber *(NZ)*, chili, föhn, foehn, gregale, levanter, mistral, nor', north *(Chiefly Poetic)*, samiel, simoom, sirocco. **11. trade wind** antitrade, antitrades, roaring forties, trades. **12. easterly** zephyrus.

2. 1. windiness breeziness, draughtiness, gustiness.

3.   **1. wind gauge** airsock, anemometer, anemoscope, wind cone, wind sleeve, windsock.
2. anemogram anemograph, wind rose. **3. wind speed** geostrophic wind speed, gradient wind speed. **4. Beaufort scale** wind scale.

adj.   4.   **1. windy** airy, blowy, breezy, draughty, puffy. **2. blustery** Aeolian, boreal, favonian, flawy, gusty, monsoonal, squally. **3. fair** free. **4. stiff** cyclonal, cyclonic, cyclonical, strong, tempestuous, tornadic, tornado-like, typhonic. **5. windswept** windblown.

v.   5.   **1. blow** blast, bluster, gust, howl, overblow, rage, squall, storm.

adv.   6.   **1. windward** alee, aweather, downwind, upwind. **2. before the wind** close to the wind, downwind, in the teeth of the wind, large, near, upwind, windrode. **3. onshore** alongshore, katabatic, offshore, quartering. **4. windily** breezily.

RELATED KEYWORDS: AIR, WEATHER

WINNING

n.   1.   **1. winning** successfulness, victoriousness. **2. first place** first, honours, line honours. **3. favourable issue**.

2.   **1. winner** ace, champion, conqueror, giant-killer, knockout, master, scorer, vanquisher, victor, victress. *Informal:* champ, champeen, gun, sleeper. **2. placegetter** minor premier. **3. whiz-kid** enfant terrible, marvel, portent, prodigy, talent, wunderkind. *Informal:* natural. **4. bolter** goer, mudlark, mudrunner. *Informal:* boom galloper, knocktaker, skinner. **5. winning hit** score, trump card. *Informal:* boomer, bottler.

3.   **1. championship** ascendancy, mastery.

4.   **1. win** conquest, defeat, game set and match, mastery, success, triumph, vanquishment, victory. **2. walkover** pushover, snip, walkaway. *Informal:* armchair ride, breeze, cinch, gift, picnic, sitter, snack, soda, walk-up start. **3. success** do *(NZ)*, hit, winner. **4.** Pyrrhic victory. **5. landslide** *Informal:* whitewash.

adj.   5.   **1. winning** conquering, first-past-the-post, fruitful, home and hosed, made, on top, premier, successful, triumphal, triumphant, unbeaten, up, victorious. *Informal:* home on the pig's back, in like Flynn. **2. winnable** gettable.

v.   6.   **1. win** carry off, carve out, conquer, gain, medal, score, sew up, take. *Informal:* crack. **2. succeed** arrive, bring home the bacon, carry all before one, carry the day, come through, make every post a winner, make good, make the grade, pass, pull oneself up by the bootstraps, put it across, ride it out, set the world on fire, shine, steal the show, triumph, win one's spurs. *Informal:* be in the box seat, crack it, curl the mo, do the trick, get a guernsey, get it together, have it made, take the cake. **3. clean up** get it in one, guess it in one, have it in one, romp home, romp home (or in), romp in, scoop the pool, sweep the board, walk away with, walk off with, win at a canter. *Informal:* go great guns, go like a bomb. **4. land on one's feet** *(Informal)* be on to a good thing, hit the jackpot, strike pay-dirt. **5. have it both ways** *Informal:* kill two birds with one stone. **6. outmatch** beat, best, come off best, defeat, dominate, get the better of, have the better of, have the last laugh on, one-up, outbox, outclass, outdo, outflank, outgo, outperform, outrank, outrun, outsail, outstrip, outweigh, outwit, overcome, overmaster, overmatch, overpower, overreach, overtop, trump. *Informal:* lick, run rings round, wipe the floor with. **7. get ahead** be ahead, be going places, distance, draw first blood, gain ground, go far, go places, go to town, head, lead, overtake, pass, rise, soar, surpass, take off, top. *Informal:* leave someone for dead.

adv.   7.   **1. successfully** conqueringly, effectually, like a charm, swimmingly, with a bang, with flying colours. *Informal:* great. **2. triumphantly** victoriously.

RELATED KEYWORDS: ACCOMPLISHMENT, CONTEST, SPORT, SUPERIORITY, WAR

WISE PERSON

n.   1.   **1. wise person** doctor, elder, greybeard, hakim, level-head, light, luminary, owl, philosopher, sage, savant, seer, Solon, tohunga, wise virgin, wise woman. **2. genius** mastermind, prodigy, wunderkind. *Informal:* brain, whiz. **3. oracle** brains trust, elder statesman, expert, guru, master. **4. intelligentsia** illuminati.

2.   **1. know-all** know-it-all, wiseacre. *Informal:* alec, clever dick, smart alec, smartie, smartypants, wise guy *(Chiefly US)*.

RELATED KEYWORDS: COMPETENCE, INTELLECTUAL, INTELLIGENCE, KNOWLEDGE

WOMAN

n.   1.   **1. woman** earthmother, female, feme, femme, Fräulein, Frau, gentlewoman, grisette, lady, señora, she. *Informal:* girl. **2. womankind** distaff side, fair sex, gentle sex, womenfolk. *Informal:* weaker sex. **3. girl** colleen, debutante, demoiselle, hussy, lass, lassie, mademoiselle, maid, maiden, mesdemoiselles, miss, missy, moppet, nymph *(Chiefly Poetic)*, virgin, young woman. *Informal:* chicken, chook, deb, filly, gal, girlie, puss. **4. old woman** carline *(Chiefly Scottish)*, crone, dowager, grandam, grandmother, hag, harpy, harridan, hellcat, kuia *(NZ)*, matron, mother of vinegar, nanny, nonna, old chook, old maid, queen mother, sibyl, witch. *Informal:* biddy, boiler, cow, granny, l.o.l., nanna, old bag, old cow, old duck, old girl *(Chiefly British)*, tabby. **5. black woman** Mary *(Aboriginal English)*, wahine *(NZ)*. **6. white woman** *Informal:* albino *(Northern Australian)*. **7. virgin** bachelor girl, spinster, vestal virgin. **8. ladylove** dulcinea, girlfriend, inamorata, lass, sweetheart. *Informal:* squeeze. **9. sheila** *(Informal)* donna, nuba *(Aboriginal English)*, quean *(Scottish)*, wench. *Informal:* babe, baby, bint, bird, charlie, charlie wheeler, chick, dame *(Chiefly US)*, flapper, floozy, heifer, hen, jane, judy *(British)*, mole, moll, nubile, ockerina, petticoat, potato, potato peeler, puss, tabo, totty *(Originally British)*, trout *(Chiefly British)*, widgie. **10. wife** feme covert, feme sole, lady, Madam Kerfoops, mate, nuba, sultana. *Informal:* little woman, missis, missus, old lady, rib, the old ball and chain, trouble and strife, woman. **11. concubine** harem, minor wife. **12. beauty** angel, bathing beauty, bathing belle, beauty queen, belle, bombshell, charmer, dream, English rose, goddess, juno, nymph, picture, swan, sylph, Venus *(Poetic)*, witch. *Informal:* a good sort, dish, doll, dolly, dreamboat, eyeful, glamour girl, good-looker, headturner, knockout, looker, lush, smasher, sort, stunner. **13. trollop** jade, lost woman. *Informal:* slapper *(Chiefly British)*. **14. seductress** Circe, coquette, Delilah, enchantress, femme fatale, flirt, houri, kitten, Lolita, man-eater, Mata Hari, minx, nymphette, sexpot, siren, sorceress, tease, temptress, vamper. *Informal:* foxy lady, mantrap, popsy, sex kitten, teaser, vamp. **15. grrl** *(Informal)* riot grrl. *Informal:* dragon lady, net chick. **16. tomboy** hoyden, romp. **17. amazon** lesbian, tribade. *Informal:* butch, dyke, he-girl. **18. two-ton Tessie** *(Informal)*. **19. feminist** femocrat, suffragette, suffragist, women's libber. *Informal:* feminazi, femmo.

2. **1. womanliness** anima, femaleness, femineity, feminineness, femininity, gentlewomanliness, ladylikeness, matronliness, muliebrity, womanhood, womanishness. **2. feminisation. 3. feminism** women's liberation.

adj. **3.** **1. female** gynaecomorphous, yin. **2. feminine** distaff, female, gentlewomanly, lady, ladylike, muliebral, petticoat, spindle *(US)*, womanish, womanlike, womanly. **3. matronly** housewifely, matronal. **4. old-womanish** anile, old-maidish, spinsterish. **5. girlish** girly-girly, maiden, maidenly. **6. amazonian** butch, mannish, masculine, unfeminine, unwomanly, viraginous. **7. tomboyish** hoydenish.

v. **4.** **1. feminise** effeminise, womanise.

RELATED KEYWORDS: OFFSPRING, RELATIVE, REPRODUCTION, SEX, MARRIAGE

WORD

n. **1.** **1. word** adjunct, content word, element, expression, function word, heteronym, lexeme, particle, substitute, term, vocable. **2. part of speech** adjective, adverb, article, conjunction, copula, determiner, intensifier, interjection, modifier, noun, preposition, pronoun, substantive, verb. **3. monosyllable** tetragram, triliteral. **4. polysyllable** oxytone, paroxytone, proparoxytone, sesquipedalian, tonguetwister. *Informal:* jaw-breaker. **5. coinage** back formation, ghost word, neologism, neology, non-word, nonce word. **6. inkhorn term** Latinism. **7. euphemism** genteelism, hypocorism, weasel word. **8. blend** contraction, haplography, portmanteau word. **9. malapropism** catachresis, corruption, parapraxis. **10. archaism** counterword, literalism. **11. colloquialism** dialecticism, vernacularism, vulgarism. **12. Australianism** Americanism, Britishism. **13. expletive** exclamation, interjection, swearword. **14. catchcry** battle cry, buzz word, buzzword, call, catchphrase, catchword, cry, epithet, keyword, slogan, war cry, watchword. **15. byword** household word. **16. qualifier** adherent, attributive, complement, definitive, distributive, prepositive.

2. **1. vocabulary** accents, dictionary, gloss, glossary, language, lexicogrammar, lexicon, lexis, syllabary, synonymy, text, thesaurus, wordage. *Informal:* vocab.

3. **1. word part** affix, agglutination, antepenult, bound form, combining form, formative, formative element, infix, morpheme, syllable, word element. **2. prefix** proclitic. **3. suffix**.

4. **1. noun** abstract noun, adverbial noun, appellative, collective noun, common name, common noun, diminutive, gerund, gerundive, mass noun, neuter, nominative, nominative of address, non-count noun, personal pronoun, predicate noun, preposition, pronoun, proper name, proper noun, relative, relative pronoun, substantive, uncount noun, verbal, verbal noun. **2. gender** feminine, masculine, neuter. **3. adjective** participial, participle, perfect participle, predicative adjective. **4. verb** auxiliary, auxiliary verb, copula, copular verb, denominative, deponent verb, desiderative, finite verb, frequentative, impersonal, impersonal verb, infinitive, intransitive, intransitive verb, linking verb, reflexive, transitive, transitive verb, verbid. **5. adverb** conjunct. **6. conjunction** conjunctive, connective, coordinating conjunction, subordinating conjunction, suppositive. **7. determiner** article, definite article, demonstrative, indefinite article.

RELATED KEYWORDS: ALPHABET, LANGUAGE, NAME, WRITING, SIGN, SPEECH

WORK

n. **1.** **1. work** avocation, business, calling, employment, life's work, metier, occupation, practice, profession, pursuit, trade, vocation, walk of life, wet work. *Informal:* game. **2. labour** toil. *Informal:* yakka. **3. workload** darg. **4. piecework** bonus work, day labour, dirty work, hackwork, jobbing, journeywork, legwork, mixed functions, overwork, session work, taskwork. **5. job** assignment, care, career, charge, chore, commission, detail, duty, errand, fool's errand, job of work, mission, office, piece of work, project, role, task, undertaking. *Informal:* bludge, gig, lurk, racket, ready. **6. government work**. **7. craft** handiwork. **8. working bee** corvée, fatigue, fatigue duty, fatigue party, working party. **9. working holiday** busman's holiday. **10. industry** guild, trade union, union.

adj. **2.** **1. working** at work, busy, employed, engaged, in a job, in harness, labouring, occupied, on duty, on fatigue. *Informal:* on the job. **2. blue-collar** factory-floor, manual, mechanical, sweated. **3. white-collar** clerical, managerial, professional. *Informal:* pro.

v. **3.** **1. work** devil, do hackwork, drudge, labour, moil, outwork, overwork, toil. *Informal:* fag, sweat. **2. be employed** carry on a business, drive a trade, have a steady job, have an honest job, ply one's trade, turn an honest penny. *Informal:* carry a cut-lunch, turn an honest quid. **3. serve** lackey, lacquey. **4. freelance** job, job-share, moonlight.

RELATED KEYWORDS: BUSYNESS, ACTION, EFFORT, EMPLOYMENT

WORKER

n. **1.** **1. worker** guest worker, industrial, OCW, operative, spalpeen, tradesman, tradesperson, tradeswoman, workingman, workman. **2. employee** breadwinner, jobholder, wage-earner. *Informal:* wage slave. **3. casual** day labourer, extra *(US)*, journeyman, supernumerary, temporary. *Informal:* floater, hobo, temp. **4. freelance** freelancer, independent contractor. *Informal:* backyarder, moonlighter. **5. pieceworker** jobber, outworker. **6. toiler** battler, drudge, drudger, moiler, slave. *Informal:* dogsbody, old soldier, slogger. **7. hard worker** compulsive worker, grafter, wheel-horse, willing horse, workaholic, workhorse. *Informal:* a beggar for punishment, a glutton for punishment, a tiger for punishment. **8. bad worker** clock-watcher, cobbler, slopworker. *Informal:* dilutee.

2. **1. workers** labour, labour force, labour market, shop floor, workfolk, workpeople. **2. staff** cadre, general staff, office, personnel. **3. shift** afternoon shift, coor, day shift, night shift, quick shift. **4. gang** aircrew, assembly line, chain gang, chain-gang, crew, learners' chain, shift, squad, the chain, working party. **5. coworker** accomplice, assistant, associate, colleague, compeer, comrade, confrère, copartner, fellow servant, fellow worker, offsider, partner, peer. *Informal:* pardner *(US)*.

3. **1. blue-collar worker** assistant, coolie, day labourer, hand, labourer, manual labourer, offsider, operative, partner, unskilled worker, worker. *Informal:* bohunk *(US)*, fellah, hunky *(US)*. **2. handyman** factotum, farmhand, fix-it man, help, jack-of-all-trades, knockabout, odd-job man, rouseabout, roustabout, station hand. *Informal:* blue-tongue, bogtrotter, leatherneck, loppy, rouser, rousie, wood-and-water joey. **3. fettler** jobber, permanent-way man, platelayer, sleeper cutter, trackman, trackwalker *(US)*. *Informal:* hairy-legs, snake-charmer, woollynose. **4. wharf lumper** dock labourer, docker, loader, longshoreman *(US)*, lumper, make-up, stevedore, waterside worker, wharf labourer. *Informal:* disso, seagull *(NZ)*, wharfie. **5. housekeeper** hausfrau, home-maker, home-maker, housemaid, housewife. **6. plumber** drainer. *Informal:* blackjack merchant, turd strangler. **7. servant** cleaner, man Friday, messenger, room boy *(Philippine English)*, runner, yardman. **8. unskilled labourer** assembler, cottager *(British)*, detailer, ditcher, dustman *(Chiefly British)*, flagman, garbageman, gripman, labourer, lamplighter, limeburner, maltster, moulder, navigator *(British)*, navvy, oiler, packer, paver, paviour, peon, platemaker, process worker, pumpman, removalist, roadman, rubbish collector, sanitary man, signalman, sprag, stoker, stonehand, switchman *(US)*, wrecker. *Informal:* Dan, dunny man, flaggie, flaxie *(NZ)*, garbo, garbologist, roughneck *(Chiefly US)*, sanny man, sano man, spudder, trashy.

4. **1. farm worker** boundary rider, culler, farmer, farmhand, grazier, station hand, stockman. *Informal:* dag picker, snagger. **2. hunter** fisherman, gatherer, gleaner, trapper.

5. **1. meatworker** boner, butcher, chainman, flesher, freezing-worker, slaughterman, tripeman.

6. **1. timberman** axeman, bush-faller *(NZ)*, busher, bushman, cedar-getter, crosscutter *(NZ)*, cutter, emu-bobber, faller, gooseman, jacker, logger, lumberjack *(Chiefly US, Canadian)*, lumberman, sandalwooder, sawyer, scrub-cutter, skiddy, splitter, swamper *(US)*, timber-getter, top dog, topnotch, topnotcher, tree-surgeon, underdog, woodcutter, woodman, woodsman. *Informal:* bushwhacker *(NZ)*, jarrah jerker *(WA)*, slabby *(NZ)*, stick-picker.

7. **1. miner** alluvial miner, balmaiden, black-sander *(NZ)*, coalminer, collier, digger, dryblower, dryblower, gold-digger, goldfielder, goldminer, gouger, gum-digger *(NZ)*, mineworker, picker, pitman, pitworker, reefer, tributer. *Informal:* Cousin Jack, Geordie, grass captain.

8. **1. wright** cartwright, chandler, coachbuilder, cooper, cutler, fencer, glassmaker, millwright, shipbuilder, shipwright, shoemaker, spurrier, wainwright, wheelwright.

9. **1. metalworker** arc welder, armourer, bell-founder, blacksmith, boilermaker, coppersmith, electrometallurgist, electroplater, farrier, founder, foundryworker, galvaniser, goldsmith, gunman, gunsmith, ironmaster, ironsmith, ironworker, locksmith, metal fabricator, pewterer, plater, plumber, shipwright, shoer, silversmith, smelter, smith, solderer, steelworker, tinker, tinman, tinner, tinsmith, turner, welder, whitesmith.

10. **1. furniture-maker** cabinet-maker, French-polisher, inlayer, joiner, upholsterer, veneerer.

11. **1. engineer** aeronautical engineer, chemical engineer, electrical engineer, flight engineer, industrial designer, mechanical engineer, systems engineer.

12. **1. builder** bricklayer, builder's labourer, bush carpenter, carpenter, cementer, civil engineer, cowan, dogman, floorer, Freemason, glass-cutter, glassman, glassworker, glazer, glazier, hodman, housepainter, lather, mason, master builder, master mason, nipper, paperer, paperhanger, plasterer, rigger, roofer, shopfitter, spiderman *(British)*, steeplejack, stonecutter, stonemason, stoneworker, thatcher, tiler. *Informal:* brickie, brickie's labourer, chaser, chippie, hoddie, muckshifter, seagull *(NZ)*, tradie. **2. architect** draftsman, draughtsman, heritage architect, interior designer, landscape architect, planner.

13. **1. mariner** cockswain, cox, harbourmaster, helmsman, sailor, steersman.

14. **1. guard** air-raid warden, archivist, beach inspector, caretaker, catchpole, chief superintendent, coastguard, collector, concierge, conductor *(US)*, conservator, custodian, doorkeeper, fighter, firefighter, game warden, gamekeeper, gatekeeper, gateman, guard commander, guardian, gunjabal *(Aboriginal English)*, health inspector, hutkeeper, inspector, janitor, jerquer, keeper, lifeguard, night watch, nightwatchman, ostiary, patrolman, porter, portress, ranger, security guard, security officer, security police, sentinel, sentry, sky marshal, station agent *(US)*, stationmaster, superintendent, ticket-inspector, tipstaff, tollkeeper, usherette, warden, warrener, watchman, woodman, yard-master. *Informal:* clippie, connie, firey, grey meanie, meter maid *(British)*, minder, sticker licker, ticket snapper.

15. **1. technician** aeromechanic, auto-electrician, electrician, engine-room artificer, engineman, fireman, fitter, gasfitter, gasman, jerker, laboratory technician, lineman, linesman, master mechanic, mechanic, mechanician, miller, panelbeater, rigger, spray painter, turner, wireworker. *Informal:* grease monkey. **2. driver** motorman, pilot, railman, railwayman, wheelman *(US)*. *Informal:* fly-boy *(US)*, truckie.

16. **1. craftsperson** artisan, artist, basketweaver, candlestick-maker, craftsman, die-sinker, jeweller, matchmaker, violin-maker, watchmaker. **2. artist** artificer, designer, fabricant, fashion designer, fashion-designer, graphic designer, photographer, printer. *Informal:* camera-pointer. **3. cook** baker, caterer, chef, pastrycook, sous-chef. **4. beautician** hairdresser, handicraftsman, mannequin, master-craftsman, model, tattooer.

17. **1. entertainer** actor, announcer, contortionist, dancer, director, dramatist, filmmaker, musician, playwright, presenter, producer. **2. backstage hand** dresser, projectionist, prompt, scene-shifter, stage manager, stagehand.

18. **1. white-collar worker** accountant, adjuster, agent, alienor, amanuensis, banker, book editor, careworker, chemist, clergyman, company secretary, editor, editor-in-chief, finance editor, instructor, interpreter, judge, lawyer, librarian, manager, managing

director, officer, operator, pay officer, paymaster, penman, politician, social worker, teacher, writer. **2. professional** paraprofessional. **3. career woman** career girl.

19. 1. office worker bank clerk, bookkeeper, clerical assistant, clerk, copy typist, filing clerk, girl friday, girl Friday, keyboard operator, office boy, private secretary, salaryman *(Japan)*, secretary, shorthand typist, sorter, stamper, stenographer, switchboard operator, teller, typist, undersecretary. *Informal:* bagboy, desk jockey, pen-pusher.

20. 1. health worker ambulanceman, chemist, dentist, doctor, general practitioner, nurse, optometrist, paramedic, pharmacist, pharmacologist, physician, physiotherapist, specialist, surgeon, therapist. *Informal:* medic, the men in white coats.

21. 1. salesperson bailor, bar attendant, barrowman, bourgeois, cashier, chandler, cheapjack, clerk, clothier, coalman, colporteur, commercial traveller, coster, costermonger *(British)*, cutler, fellmonger, fishmonger, fishwife, fletcher, floorwalker, flower girl, haberdasher, hawker, higgler, huckster, ironmonger, keeper, merchant, milkman, oilman, oysterman, packman, paperboy, pedlar, pitchman, representative, saddler, salesclerk *(US)*, salesgirl, saleslady, salesman, saleswoman, scrap merchant, seller, shop assistant, shopgirl, shopkeeper, shopman, shopwalker, skinner, storekeeper, storeman, sutler, traveller, travelling salesman, vendor, water-carrier. *Informal:* checkout chick, counter-jumper, faker *(US)*, Ghan, milkie *(NZ)*, milko, rep.

22. 1. sex worker camp follower, nightwalker, prostitute, streetwalker. *Informal:* battler, pro, worker. **2. hooker** *(Informal)* callgirl, courtesan, drab, harlot, hospitality girl *(Philippine English)*, light-o'-love *(British, US)*, painted woman, quean, scarlet woman, taxi girl, trollop, whore. *Informal:* moll, tart. **3. gigolo** callboy.

RELATED KEYWORDS: WORKING CLASS, EFFORT, EMPLOYMENT, COMMERCE, WORK

WORKING CLASS

n. **1. 1. working class** lower class, lumpenproletariat, poor white trash, proletariat, rank and file, the lower orders, the masses, third estate. **2. commonfolk** all the world and his wife, commonage, commonalty, commons, crowd, demos, every man and his dog, folk, mobile vulgus, plebs, populace, small fry, the have-nots, the many, the multitude, Tom, Dick, and Harry. **3. the rabble** canaille, cattle, doggery, gutter, herd, mob, ragtag and bobtail, riffraff, rout, ruck, scum, the dregs (of society), the herd, vermin. *Informal:* the great unwashed. **4. commoner** coppertail, plebeian, proletarian. *Informal:* pleb, prole.

2. 1. public body politic, commonalty, commonwealth, community at large, democracy, people, people in general, the community. *Informal:* peepz. **2. society** age, everyone, real world, world.

3. 1. democratisation communisation, socialisation. **2. populism** communism.

4. 1. plebeianism humbleness, ignobleness, low birth. **2. popularisation** vulgarisation.

adj. **5. 1. working-class** lower-class, lumpenproletarian, plebeian, underprivileged. **2. low-born** baseborn, ceorlish, churlish, dunghill, from the wrong side of the tracks, humble, ignoble, low, lowbred, of low birth, of low parentage, of mean birth, of mean parentage, peasant, simple.

6. 1. public common, communal, demotic, mob, popular, vernacular, vulgar. **2. folk** grassroots, local, parish-pump, parochial.

v. **7. 1. democratise** communise, give to the people, socialise. **2. popularise** debase, lower, vernacularise, vulgarise.

RELATED KEYWORDS: POVERTY, WORKER

WRITING

n. **1. 1. writing** calligraphy, chirography, manuscript, script, stylography. **2. hand-writing** hand, lettering. *Informal:* fist. **3. longhand** copperplate, court hand, cursive, prescription, roundhand, running writing, script. **4. shorthand** dictation, logography, phonography, stenography, stenotypy, tachygraphy. **5. word processing** typewriting, typing. **6. writing style** character, expression, fluency, language, literariness, stylisation, stylistics. **7. palaeography**.

2. 1. writing form boustrophedon, cuneiform, graffiti, notation, ogham, script, syllabism. **2. picture writing** demotic, hieratic, hieroglyphic, idiography, monogram, pictography. **3. cipher** mirror writing. **4. braille** point system. **5. alphabet** ABC, Cyrillic alphabet, futhorc, International Phonetic Alphabet, IPA, Kufic, morse code, phonetic alphabet, Pinyin. **6. Greek alphabet** alpha, beta, chi, delta, digamma, epsilon, eta, gamma, iota, kappa, lambda, mu, nu, omega, omicron, phi, pi, psi, rho, sigma, tau, theta, upsilon, xi, zeta. **7. old English character** ash, eth, thorn.

3. **1. writing materials**   cabinet, continuous stationery, daybook, fanfold, foolscap, jotter, letter paper, manifold, notebook, notepad, notepaper, onion skin, pad, papyrus, parchment, pocketbook, quad, quarto, scratchpad *(US)*, scribble block, scribble pad, scroll, stationery, table-book, vellum, writing pad, writing paper. **2. tablet** diptych, slate, triptych. **3. board** blackboard, chalkboard, slate, whiteboard. **4. pencil** lead pencil, propelling pencil, red pencil. **5. typewriter** stenograph, stenotype.

4. **1. manuscript** autograph, codex, document, draft, inedita, MS., prescription, schedule, script, treatise, typescript. **2. scroll** palimpsest, parchment. **3. jottings** adversaria, notes. **4. extract** analects, chapter, citation, epigraph, excerpt, gobbet, paragraph, passage, pericope, quotation, quote, selection, tag, tirade. *Informal:* par. **5. annotation** apostil, appendix, casenotes, comment, commentary, crib, critical apparatus, cross-index, cross-reference, end note, epexegesis, excursus, footnote, gloss, glossary, interlineation, interlining, marginalia, note, preface, protocol, rubric, scholium, scholiums, sidenote, subtitle, superscription, vermiform appendix. **6. rewrite** adaptation, redaction, revision, rifacimento. **7. caption** balloon, banderol, chronogram, circumscription, epigraph, inscription.

5. **1. writer** amorist, annotator, architect, author, authoress, co-author, columnist, composer, contributor, copywriter, futurist, gnomist, inditer, littérateur, parent, pen, penman, scribe, stylist, typist, wordsmith. **2. portrayer** depicter, describer. **3. dialogist** colloquist, librettist. **4. scriptwriter** screenwriter. **5. penman** calligrapher, calligraphist, hieroglyphist. **6. scribe** amanuensis, clerk *(Chiefly US)*, copier, copy typist, copyist, court reporter, Hansard reporter, inscriber, penciller, stenographer, stenographist, tachygrapher, tachygraphist, transcriber. *Informal:* pen-pusher, steno. **7. scrawler** cacographer, scratcher, scribbler. **8. secretary** private secretary, secretariat. **9. typist** keyboard operator.

adj. **6.** **1. written** chirographic, handwritten, longhand, stylographic. **2. calligraphic** copperplate, round, roundhand. **3. scrawly** cacographic, scratchy, scrawled, scribbly. **4. italic** engrossed, italicised. **5. inscriptional** epigraphic, inscriptive, lapidary.

7. **1. authorial** auctorial, editorial, subeditorial. **2. under one's hand** holographic, manuscript.

v. **8.** **1. write** doodle, inscribe, lower-case, narrate, print, scratch, scrawl, scribble, scribe, scrive, scroll, trace, write out. **2. pencil** chalk, charcoal, pen. **3. type** compose, touch-type, typewrite. **4. write down** dash down, dash off, draft, jot down, minute, set down, take down, write up. *Informal:* knock off. **5. portray** depict, express.

adv. **9.** **1. in writing** in black and white, on paper.

RELATED KEYWORDS: ENTERTAINMENT, ESSAY, NARRATIVE, POETRY, BOOK

WRONGDOING

n. **1.** **1. wrongdoing** aberration, error, fault, misdeed, misdemeanour, misprision, misstep, offence, wrong. **2. crime** breach, conspiracy, contravention, delict, delinquency, felony, infringement, malefaction, misdemeanour, offence, outrage, tort, wrong. **3. kind of crime** appropriation, assault, assault and battery, bag snatching, computer crime, crime of passion, cybercrime, date rape, encroachment, extortion, heist, housebreaking, identity theft, incest, indecent assault, libel, maid abuse, multicide, murder, murder-suicide, organised crime, piracy, rape, robbery, sacrilege, solicitation, subreption, tax evasion, theft, thievery, treason, trespass, victimless crime, violation, white-collar crime. *Informal:* five-finger discount, hoist. **4. transgression** abuse, malpractice. **5. minor transgression** indiscretion, peccadillo, slip, stumble, trip, venial sin. **6. misbehaviour** misconduct. **7. sin** actual sin, cardinal sin, deadly sin, debt, mortal sin, original sin, seven deadly sins, trespass, venial sin. **8. vice** bad habit, besetting sin, weakness.

2. **1. impropriety** bad form, improperness, incorrectness, inexcusableness, irregularity, offensiveness, shabbiness, unacceptableness, unbecomingness. **2. wrongfulness** badness, blameworthiness, censurability, peccancy. **3. wickedness** depravity, sinfulness, sordidness, uncleanliness, unregeneracy. **4. evil** evilness, flagitiousness, foulness, heinousness, outrageousness, viciousness. **5. immorality** aberrancy, delinquency, disgracefulness, obliquity, perverseness, perversity, unconscionableness, unprincipledness, unscrupulousness. **6. baseness** blackguardism, contemptibleness, currishness, damnableness, despicableness, turpitude, villainousness, villainy. **7. criminality** illegality, reprehensibleness, suability. **8. evil intent** cold-blooded murder, malice, malice aforethought, mens rea, premeditated murder. **9. frailty** caducity.

3. **1. wrongdoer** blackguard, evildoer, malpractitioner, miscreant, scoundrel, the bad guys, villain, villein. **2. transgressor** sinner, trespasser. **3. criminal** accessory, bushranger, culprit, desperado, felon, first offender, gangster, hoodlum, malfeasor, misfeasor, outlaw, recidivist, tortfeasor. *Informal:* crim, crook, gunnie, hood, lag, perp *(US)*, punk, torch, yoggy. **4. murderer** killer, multiple killer, serial killer, thrill killer. **5. assassin** bravo, hatchet man, hired gun *(US)*, hit squad, poisoner. *Informal:* hit man. **6. sex offender** child molester, paedophile, pedophile, rapist. **7. thief** bandit, buccaneer, corsair, forayer, freebooter, picaroon, pilferer, pirate, privateer, purloiner, robber, sea robber, sea rover, wrecker. **8. swindler** embezzler, impersonator, money launderer. *Informal:* con man. **9. dealer** drug dealer. *Informal:* mule. **10. accomplice** accessory. *Informal:* bagman, cockatoo.

adj. **4.** **1. improper** unacceptable, uncalled-for. **2. incorrect** abroad, amiss. **3. questionable** censurable, reproachable. **4. immoral** aberrational, conscienceless, inofficious, unethical, unprincipled, unscrupulous, villainous, wrong. **5. unworthy**. **6. criminal** illegal. *Informal:* crim. **7. unjustified**. **8. outrageous** heinous, reprehensible. **9. villainous** black-hearted, blackguardly, conscienceless. **10. vicious** debauched, depraved, uncleanly. **11. unrepentant**. **12. evil** corrupt, evildoing, harmful, maleficent. **13. bad** sinful. **14. base** abject, abominable, contemptible, currish, deplorable, despicable, detestable, discreditable, disgraceful, dishonourable, disreputable, execrable, ignoble, ignominious, inexpiable, inglorious, lumpen, mean, opprobrious, shameful, slavish, sordid, vile, wretched. *Informal:* bastard, bastardly, low-down, rotten, scumbag, scummy, scurvy.

v. **5.** **1. wrong** aggrieve, backstab, harm, offend against. *Informal:* do the dirty on. **2. offend** sail close to the wind, scandalise. **3. debauch** corrupt. **4. err** go to the bad. **5. compound one's error** add insult to injury.

adv. **6.** **1. improperly** badly, inadequately, incorrectly, unacceptably, unseemly, wrongly.

RELATED KEYWORDS: MISBEHAVIOUR, ERROR, BADNESS, GUILT, UNLAWFULNESS, IMMORALITY, DISOBEDIENCE, OBSCENITY

YOUTH

n. **1.** **1. youth** freshness, immaturity, juvenescence, tenderness, youngness. **2. early years** salad days, tender age, youth, youthhood. **3. infancy** babyhood, infanthood, swaddling clothes, the cradle. **4. childhood** boyhood, girlhood, preadolescence. **5. adolescence** awkward age, nonage, puberty, pubescence, sweet sixteen, teens, the awkward age, youth. **6. minority** nonage.

2. **1. youthfulness** adolescence, boyishness, coltishness, girlishness, juvenility, rejuvenescence. **2. callowness** greenness, immatureness, inexperience. **3. agelessness** rejuvenescence.

3. **1. childishness** babyishness, cubbishness, juvenileness, puerilism, puerility.

4. **1. young person** juvenile, minor, slip of a thing, whelp, youngling, youth. *Informal:* spring chicken. **2. infant** a babe in arms, babe, baby, bottle baby, child, neonate, papoose, test-tube baby. *Informal:* bub, little stranger. **3. premature baby** *Informal:* prem, premmie. **4. child** bairn *(Chiefly Scottish)*, bambino, brat, chiel *(Scottish)*, little ones, moppet, piccaninny, toddler, tot, tweeny, youngster. *Informal:* anklebiter, billy, joey, kid, kiddie, littlie, nipper, sprog, tiddler, tin lid, young'un, youngie. **5. adolescent** teen, teenager. *Informal:* teeny-bopper.

adj. **5.** **1. young** juvenescent, of tender age (or years), prentice, small, vernal, youngish, youngling, youthful. **2. youthful** boyish, coltish, cubbish, girlish. **3. ageless** evergreen, fresh, rejuvenescent, young-eyed. **4. callow** beardless, green, immature, tender, undeveloped, unfledged, wet behind the ears. **5. infant** in arms, neonatal, preschool, yeanling. **6. school-age** preadolescent, prepubescent. **7. adolescent** hebetic, juvenile, minor, preadult, pubescent, teen, teenage, under-age. **8. younger** cadet, junior, puisne. *Informal:* kid. **9. youngest** minimus *(British)*. **10. kidult**.

6. **1. childish** baby, babyish, infantile, infantine, juvenile, puerile, younger.

adv. **7.** **1. youthfully** boyishly, coltishly, girlishly. **2. childishly** babyishly, immaturely, juvenilely, puerilely.

RELATED KEYWORDS: EARLINESS, INNOCENCE, IGNORANCE, OFFSPRING

aubergine *adj.*
  purple 3.1
aubergine *n.*
  food 9.1
auburn *adj.*
  brown 3.4
  orange 5.1
  red 6.11
auburn *n.*
  brown 1.4
auction *n.*
  selling 1.2
auction *v.*
  selling 4.1
auctioneer *n.*
  selling 2.5
audacious *adj.*
  arrogance 4.1, 5.1
  courage 4.4
  discourtesy 3.3
  low regard 6.3
  obscenity 3.8
  rashness 3.5
audacity *n.*
  arrogance 1.3, 2.1
  courage 1.4
  low regard 1.4
  rashness 1.3
audible *adj.*
  hearing 4.3
  loudness 5.2
  obviousness 2.3
  precision 3.2
  sound 6.2
audience *n.*
  entertainment 11.1
  hearing 1.1, 2.1
  music 11.2
  presence 1.2
  sight 3.8
  society 3.6
audio *adj.*
  hearing 4.5
  sound 7.1
audio *n.*
  sound 2.1
audiovisual *adj.*
  hearing 4.2
  sight 8.3
audit *n.*
  accounting 1.3
  question 5.6
audit *v.*
  accounting 4.1
  question 12.3
audition *n.*
  hearing 1.1
  question 5.1
audition *v.*
  entertainment 17.2
  question 11.2
auditor *n.*
  accounting 3.3
  hearing 2.1
  question 7.4
auditorium *n.*
  entertainment 8.1
  rooms 5.2
augment *v.*
  increase 7.1
  superiority 7.9

augur *n.*
  prediction 4.1
  the supernatural
    3.3
augur *v.*
  anticipation 3.5
  conjecture 6.1
  prediction 8.1
  thinking 5.5
august *adj.*
  importance 4.10
  maturity 4.10
  repute 5.4
aunt *n.*
  relative 1.6
aura *n.*
  character 1.7
  perception 1.3
  surroundings 1.8
aural *adj.*
  hearing 4.2
aurora *n.*
  light 1.10
  sky 3.14
auspices *n.*
  help 1.3
  influence 1.4
  protection 1.3
auspicious *adj.*
  good fortune 3.1,
    3.3
  hope 5.1
  prediction 7.3
Aussie *n.*
  nation 6.1
austere *adj.*
  abstinence 4.2
  harshness 3.8
  intolerance 3.3
  sombreness 3.3,
    3.4
  sourness 2.5
  unpleasant flavour
    2.2
austerity *n.*
  abstinence 1.2
  harshness 1.6
  sombreness 1.2
Australian Rules *n.*
  sport 2.2
Australian values *n.*
  nation 3.4
authentic *adj.*
  belief 6.1
  faithfulness 3.6
  honesty 3.3
  propriety 4.4
  truth 3.2
authenticate *v.*
  evidence 9.1
  propriety 7.3
  truth 5.2
authenticity *n.*
  faithfulness 1.5
  truth 1.6
author *n.*
  creation 5.1, 5.2
  writing 5.1
author *v.*
  creation 8.1
authorisation *n.*
  agreement 3.2

authority 1.1
  permission 1.1, 1.2
authorise *v.*
  agent 8.1
  agreement 10.2
  authority 8.1
  evidence 9.1
  justification 6.2
  lawfulness 6.1
  permission 5.1
  rights 5.3
authoritarian *adj.*
  authority 7.1
  command 4.3
  force 6.4
  power 5.4
  repression 5.3
authoritarian *n.*
  repression 3.1
authoritative *adj.*
  authority 6.1
  command 4.1
  power 5.3, 6.1
  propriety 4.3
authority *n.*
  authority 1.1
  competence 3.2
  evidence 1.3, 2.5
  government 1.1
  guidance 2.3
  influence 1.2, 5.1
  information 4.3
  knowledge 4.1
  lawfulness 2.6
  nation 1.7
  power 1.1
  rights 1.2
autistic *adj.*
  psyche 11.12
autobiography *n.*
  narrative 2.7
  record 1.1
  remembering 2.3
autocracy *n.*
  government 2.1
  nation 1.5
  power 2.3
autocrat *n.*
  power 4.2
  ruler 1.10
autocratic *adj.*
  arrogance 4.1
  authority 7.1
  power 5.4
  unlawfulness 4.6
autograph *n.*
  book 1.2
  name 2.2
  sign 1.4
  writing 4.1
autograph *v.*
  name 8.3
  sign 14.4
automate *v.*
  machine 24.1
automated *adj.*
  controlling device
    7.1
automatic *adj.*
  machine 23.3
  unwillingness 2.2
automatic *n.*
  machine 1.9

  vehicle 2.1
  weapon 2.1, 2.2,
    2.3
automatically *adv.*
  unwillingness 7.2
automation *n.*
  controlling device
    1.2
  machine 22.1
automobile *adj.*
  movement 3.1
  throw 6.2
  vehicle 13.2
automobile *n.*
  vehicle 2.1
autonomous *adj.*
  exclusion 5.1
  independence 3.1,
    3.2, 4.1
  whole 4.7
autonomy *n.*
  independence 1.1,
    1.5
  liberation 2.1
  unrelatedness 1.1
autopsy *n.*
  analysis 1.5
  question 6.2
autumn *adj.*
  season 2.5
autumn *n.*
  maturity 2.2
  season 1.5
auxiliary *adj.*
  addition 5.3
  help 5.6
  inferiority 3.1, 3.2
auxiliary *n.*
  help 2.1, 4.3
  partner 2.2
  society 2.1
  watercraft 3.2
  word 4.4
auxiliary verb *n.*
  word 4.4
avail *n.*
  use 2.3
avail *v.*
  profit 3.1
  use 10.1
availability *n.*
  use 2.6
available *adj.*
  use 4.3, 5.4
avail oneself of *v.*
  use 8.6
avalanche *n.*
  coldness 3.3
  descent 4.1
  destruction 2.7
avalanche *v.*
  descent 9.3
avaricious *adj.*
  desire 7.1
  meanness 3.2
  overindulgence 7.1
  taking 6.2
avenge *v.*
  retaliation 4.1,
    4.3
avenue *n.*
  entrance 1.1

  method 1.3
  route 2.3, 2.6, 4.6
average *adj.*
  mediocrity 2.7
  ordinariness 5.1,
    5.3, 5.4
average *n.*
  cost 3.3
  ordinariness 2.1
  sharing 2.1
average *v.*
  ordinariness 6.1
averse *adj.*
  divergence 3.2
  unwillingness 2.1
aversion *n.*
  displeasure 2.1
  hate 1.1, 4.1
  repulsion 1.1
avert *v.*
  avoidance 5.1
  divergence 4.2
  exclusion 8.4
  repulsion 3.1
  stoppage 3.8
aviary *n.*
  dwelling 10.8
aviation *n.*
  flying 1.1
aviator *n.*
  flying 3.1
avid *adj.*
  desire 4.3
  enthusiasm 3.1
  smell 5.3
avocado *n.*
  food 9.1
avoid *v.*
  abstinence 5.2
  avoidance 5.1
  cancellation 3.2
  counteraction 6.1
  denial 5.3
  retreat 5.5
avoidance *n.*
  avoidance 1.1
  cancellation 1.3
  counteraction 1.2
  denial 1.3
  non-payment 1.1
avowed *adj.*
  assertion 5.1
await *v.*
  expectation 5.2
awake *adj.*
  attention 5.1
  sight 7.2
  waking 2.1, 2.4
awake *v.*
  action 6.2
  emotion 7.2
  encouragement 6.3
  waking 3.1, 3.2
awaken *v.*
  action 6.2
  life 3.2
  waking 3.1
awakening *n.*
  encouragement 1.3
  waking 1.1
award *n.*
  award 1.1

brittle *adj.*
brittleness 2.1, 2.2
irritableness 5.1
brittle *n.*
food 20.1
sweetness 1.5
broach *n.*
decoration 6.3
opening 5.1
pole 5.4
rubbing 3.2
sharpness 3.11
broach *v.*
deviation 8.2
increase 7.1
opening 7.2
watercraft 10.5
broad *adj.*
generality 6.1
importance 4.9
informality 2.3
liberation 7.5
obscenity 3.2
obviousness 2.2
sex 15.4
size 3.4, 3.6
speech 8.1
thickness 3.2, 3.6
vulgarity 4.1
whole 5.3
broad *n.*
lake 1.1
broadcast *adj.*
dispersion 5.1
generality 6.4
telecommunica-
tions 8.1
broadcast *adv.*
dispersion 7.1
broadcast *n.*
publicity 1.3
telecommunica-
tions 1.3
broadcast *v.*
communication
2.1
dispersion 6.8,
6.17
farming 16.13
generality 8.2
news 6.3
publicity 4.4
telecommunica-
tions 9.1
broad-minded *adj.*
tolerance 2.2
broadside *adv.*
thickness 6.1
broadside *n.*
attack 1.4
disapproval 2.4
publicity 2.6
weapon 4.4
brocade *n.*
textiles 10.5
brocade *v.*
textiles 13.5
broccoli *n.*
food 9.1
brochure *n.*
book 1.9
essay 1.8
publicity 2.6

brogue *n.*
clothes 29.2
speech 2.1
broke *adj.*
absence 3.2
non-payment 4.1
poverty 4.3
broken *adj.*
absence 3.2
cooperation 7.3
damage 7.1
deficiency 2.2
destruction 5.1
disorder 6.3
faulty speech 3.1
gap 2.1
illogicality 2.8
indebtedness 5.3
interruption 3.1
irregularity 2.1
non-payment 4.1
part 2.2
poverty 4.4
roughness 3.1, 3.2,
3.4, 4.2
separation 10.1
tiredness 2.3
weakness 5.6
broker *n.*
commerce 5.2, 5.4
finance 5.3
selling 2.1
broker *v.*
commerce 9.2
talkativeness 6.2
brokerage *n.*
commerce 1.1
finance 1.5
payment 3.2
bronchitis *n.*
ill health 6.1
bronze *adj.*
brown 3.4
orange 5.1
red 6.11
bronze *n.*
brown 1.4
fine arts 5.3
metal 3.2
representation 2.3
bronze *v.*
brown 4.1
brooch *n.*
decoration 6.3
brood *adj.*
reproduction 11.2
brood *n.*
classification 2.3
habitation 3.3
offspring 4.15
parentage 2.6, 2.11
relative 1.2
brood *v.*
reproduction 14.8
thinking 5.3
unhappiness 6.3
brook *n.*
flow 3.2
brook *v.*
pain 7.1
patience 7.3
possibility 4.1

broom *n.*
cleanliness 6.3
machine 11.1
broom *v.*
cleanliness 11.4
broth *n.*
food 11.1
brothel *n.*
disorder 2.2
sex 10.1
brother *n.*
companionship 2.1
friendliness 4.2
name 6.4
partner 1.5
relative 1.10, 4.1,
4.3
religion 3.6
religious leader 4.2
brother *v.*
friendliness 6.2
brother-in-law *n.*
relative 4.3
brow *n.*
body 2.4, 4.6
edge 1.1
height 3.2
browbeat *v.*
arrogance 6.6
force 7.3
menace 4.2
repression 7.7
unkindness 5.2
violence 7.9
brown *adj.*
brown 3.1
brown *n.*
brown 1.1
brown *v.*
brown 4.1
cookery 6.5
browse *n.*
food 31.1
browse *v.*
farming 16.4
food 40.2, 44.2
reading 4.2
bruise *n.*
blemish 1.5
damage 3.2
ill health 16.3
bruise *v.*
damage 12.4
powder 7.1
brumby *adj.*
animals 78.5
brumby *n.*
animals 69.1
brunch *n.*
day 2.4
food 3.3
brunette *adj.*
brown 3.1, 3.7
hair 10.4
brunette *n.*
brown 1.7
hair 6.4
brunt *n.*
violence 3.2
brush *n.*
animals 53.10
cleanliness 2.3, 6.1

contact 1.1
contest 3.1
disorder 3.1
electricity 1.11, 2.3
hitting 4.1
machine 16.1
plants 3.4, 8.2
the bush 1.2
touch 1.2
war 3.2
brush *v.*
cleanliness 11.4
contact 3.6
hair 12.1
touch 6.5
war 9.6
brusque *adj.*
discourtesy 3.2
brussels sprout *n.*
food 9.1
brutal *adj.*
animals 78.1
callousness 2.3
pain 5.3
unkindness 4.3, 4.4
violence 6.1
vulgarity 5.7
brutality *n.*
callousness 1.2
misbehaviour 1.8
unkindness 1.3
violence 1.6
brute *adj.*
animals 78.1
unkindness 4.4
violence 6.1
voluptuousness 3.4
vulgarity 5.7
brute *n.*
animals 1.2
badness 3.7
disorder 5.2
selfishness 2.1
unkindness 3.1
violence 2.5
vulgarity 3.10
bubble *n.*
bubbliness 2.1
deception 2.1
delusion 1.2
finance 1.6
gas 1.5
hissing 2.5
intangibility 2.3
robbery 2.2
roundness 4.1, 4.6
bubble *v.*
bubbliness 6.1
bubblegum *n.*
bubbliness 3.4
food 20.1
sweetness 1.5
bubbler *n.*
flow 4.7
buccaneer *n.*
fighter 1.11
mariner 3.1
thief 2.2
wrongdoing 3.7
buccaneer *v.*
robbery 5.5
watercraft 10.3

buck *adj.*
man 3.1, 3.3
buck *n.*
jump 1.4
man 1.3, 1.9
money 1.4
buck *v.*
jump 5.4
misplacement 4.2
bucket *n.*
container 11.6
buckle *n.*
distortion 1.2
fastening 6.2
fold 1.1
buckle *v.*
contest 11.2
distortion 6.1
fold 6.4
buckle down *v.*
preparedness 4.7
buck up *v.*
happiness 4.2, 5.1
pleasure 8.3
speed 9.3
bucolic *adj.*
farming 14.1
poetry 7.4
the bush 4.4, 5.4
bucolic *n.*
farming 8.15
poetry 1.9
the bush 3.4
bud *n.*
bulge 3.4
friendliness 3.1
growth 2.1
name 6.4
offspring 3.5
plants 6.2, 8.1
relative 4.3
start 1.7
bud *v.*
growth 6.1, 7.1
buddy *n.*
friendliness 3.1
name 6.4
partner 1.5
budge *v.*
movement 4.11
budget *adj.*
vulgarity 4.5
budget *n.*
accounting 2.7
gathering 2.2
plan 1.3
budget *v.*
accounting 4.1
plan 7.2
buff *adj.*
brown 3.2
orange 6.4
skin 5.7
buff *n.*
brown 1.2
clothes 19.1
desire 3.2
enthusiasm 2.1
hitting 2.2
knowledge 4.2
orange 2.2
punishment 2.4
skin 2.3

cunning 1.1
dishonesty 1.4
illogicality 1.6, 1.8
indecision 1.6
chick *n.*
food 8.1
relative 3.1
woman 1.9
chicken *adj.*
cowardice 3.1
chicken *n.*
cowardice 2.1
food 8.1
man 1.7
offspring 2.10, 4.8
woman 1.3
chicken out *v.*
cowardice 4.2
refusal 5.2
chickenpox *n.*
ill health 4.1, 17.1
chide *v.*
disapproval 7.1,
7.3
irritableness 7.2
punishment 10.2
chief *adj.*
importance 4.9,
4.11
influence 6.2
power 6.1
repute 5.2
chief *n.*
emblem 8.1
importance 3.1
manager 1.1, 1.2,
1.3, 2.1
repute 4.1
ruler 1.1, 1.4, 2.1
chieftain *n.*
ruler 1.1
chiffon *n.*
textiles 10.2
child *n.*
obedience 2.1
offspring 1.2, 1.6,
2.2
relative 3.1
youth 4.2, 4.4
childbirth *n.*
reproduction 4.1
childhood *n.*
youth 1.4
childish *adj.*
foolishness 3.1
unimportance 4.1
youth 6.1
chill *adj.*
coldness 5.6
unfriendliness 5.5
unhappiness 5.2
chill *n.*
coldness 1.2, 2.1
fastening 10.2
ill health 5.1, 7.2
unfriendliness 2.3
chill *v.*
coldness 6.2
cooling 4.2
despair 8.1
discouragement 4.2
fright 7.2
hardness 4.1, 4.3

chilli *n.*
food 5.1
chilly *adj.*
coldness 5.6
chime *n.*
edge 1.6
music 1.2
musical instrument
7.14, 10.3
peace 1.1
resonance 5.3
chime *v.*
accord 7.1
music 23.15
resonance 10.1
chimney *n.*
channel 2.3
exit 1.4
fire 6.1
gap 1.4
heating 3.2
chimpanzee *n.*
animals 56.1
china *adj.*
brittleness 2.1
china *n.*
container 14.1
fine arts 6.1
friendliness 3.1
name 6.4
transparency 2.1
chin *n.*
body 3.3
chink *n.*
gap 1.4
hollow 3.3
opening 1.3
resonance 3.1
separation 4.1
chink *v.*
fullness 5.5
resonance 10.2
chintz *n.*
textiles 2.4
chip *n.*
computing 3.1
cut 1.2
disapproval 2.2
food 9.3
gambling 5.5
hitting 3.1
hold 1.2
part 1.9, 1.10
punishment 1.3
quantity 2.1
rock 3.2
sharing 2.1
smallness 2.13
sport 12.3, 12.4,
12.15
unimportance 2.4
chip *v.*
cookery 6.11
cut 14.11
farming 16.10
fine arts 13.7
separation 12.2,
14.1
chip in *v.*
giving 4.2
help 6.14
interruption 5.4

chip on the shoulder
n.
discontentedness
2.1
chiropodist *n.*
healing 6.13
chiropractor *n.*
healing 6.14
chirp *n.*
animal noise 2.1,
3.1
shrillness 2.4
chirp *v.*
animal noise 6.1,
7.1
shrillness 4.6
chirpy *adj.*
happiness 3.3
life 2.5
chirrup *n.*
animal noise 2.1
shrillness 2.4
chirrup *v.*
animal noise 6.1
shrillness 4.6
chisel *n.*
cut 8.1
furrow 2.2
chisel *v.*
cut 14.5
deception 5.1
dishonesty 4.1
misbehaviour 5.2
non-payment 6.2
shape 13.4
chivalrous *adj.*
courage 4.3
courtesy 4.1
man 3.4
unselfishness 3.2
chivalry *n.*
courage 1.3
courtesy 1.2
chive *n.*
food 23.2
chlorine *n.*
cleanliness 7.6
colourlessness 2.2
chloroform *n.*
matter 9.1
chloroform *v.*
unconsciousness
9.1
chlorophyll *n.*
colour 1.9
green 2.4
matter 10.1
chock *adv.*
closeness 5.2
chock *n.*
hindrance 3.7
restraints 1.5
stoppage 2.4
support 3.4
chock *v.*
hindrance 8.4
support 9.2
chock-a-block *adj.*
fullness 4.1
chocolate *adj.*
brown 3.3

chocolate *n.*
brown 1.3
food 2.8, 20.1
choice *adj.*
choice 6.1
goodness 5.6
superiority 5.5
choice *n.*
choice 1.1, 1.3
difference 2.5
intention 1.2
choir *n.*
musician 3.9
place of worship
2.5
rooms 1.18
society 3.2
choir *v.*
music 24.2
choke *n.*
controlling device
4.1
electricity 7.2
thinness 1.6
choke *v.*
air 15.1
death 7.3
fullness 5.7
hindrance 8.3
killing 9.4
punishment 11.4
restraints 8.2
reticence 3.4
stoppage 3.2
choko *n.*
food 9.1
cholesterol *n.*
matter 10.1
chook *n.*
food 8.1
offspring 2.10
woman 1.3
choose *v.*
choice 7.1
desire 10.3
intention 6.1, 6.4
chop *n.*
emblem 1.3
food 4.1
hitting 2.5, 3.1, 3.2
part 1.5
quantity 2.1
roughness 2.2
sharing 2.1
sign 5.3
sport 12.3
chop *v.*
cookery 6.11
cut 14.11
dismissal 5.1
disuse 6.5
hitting 10.1
sport 19.2
chopper *n.*
cut 5.1, 10.1
flying 5.2
sport 15.5
vehicle 8.1
weapon 7.4
chopper *v.*
transport 7.8
chopsticks *n.*
machine 20.1

choral *adj.*
music 22.6
choral *n.*
music 12.8
musician 3.9
religious ceremony
2.7
chord *n.*
cord 5.5
length 2.3
music 18.1
musical instrument
10.2
sound 1.2
chore *n.*
difficulty 1.5
effort 2.3
job 1.8
obligation 1.4
unpleasantness 3.2
work 1.5
choreograph *v.*
dancing 8.6
choreographer *n.*
dancing 3.4
entertainment 10.2
choreography *n.*
dancing 1.3
chortle *n.*
humour 4.5
chortle *v.*
humour 9.1
chorus *n.*
dancing 4.1
entertainer 6.3
music 2.8
musical instrument
9.3
musician 3.9
repetition 1.4
society 3.2
chorus *v.*
music 24.2
chose *n.*
property 2.2
chowder *n.*
food 11.1
christen *v.*
name 8.1
reverence 8.1
start 8.3
chrome *v.*
colour 9.1
chromosome *n.*
organism 2.2
reproduction 6.6
chronic *adj.*
badness 4.3
changelessness 2.3,
2.5
eternity 3.2
frequency 2.1
ill health 39.9
repetition 3.2
chronicle *n.*
narrative 1.1
record 1.1
remembering 2.3
chronicle *v.*
narrative 7.1
record 7.1
remembering 9.3

damask *v.*
  textiles 13.5
dame *n.*
  aristocracy 2.2
  entertainer 2.7
  woman 1.9
damn *adj.*
  swearing 4.1
damn *interj.*
  swearing 6.2
damn *v.*
  disapproval 6.2
  irreverence 4.2
  punishment 10.7
  slander 4.4
  swearing 5.1
damnable *adj.*
  badness 4.8
  disrepute 5.1, 5.2
  guilt 2.3
  hate 7.1
  swearing 4.1
  unpleasantness 5.2
damnation *interj.*
  swearing 6.2
damnation *n.*
  afterworld 3.3
  disapproval 1.5
  immorality 1.5
  swearing 1.1
damned *adj.*
  badness 4.8
  disrepute 5.2
  guilt 2.2
  hate 7.1
  punishment 8.2
  swearing 4.1
  unpleasantness 5.2
damned *adv.*
  greatness 9.1
damning *adj.*
  disapproval 5.7
  punishment 7.5
  swearing 3.1
damp *adj.*
  wetness 4.1, 4.2
damp *n.*
  despair 1.3
  discouragement 2.1
  hindrance 1.9
  unhappiness 1.3
  wetness 1.5
damp *v.*
  controlling device 8.1
  decrease 4.4
  discouragement 4.2
  hindrance 7.7
  quietness 6.2
  restraints 8.1
  reticence 3.4
  wetness 5.3
damper *n.*
  controlling device 1.1
  food 18.2
  hindrance 4.5
  moderation 3.2
  quietness 3.1
  sombreness 2.2
  unhappiness 3.1
  wetness 3.2

dance *adj.*
  dancing 7.1
dance *n.*
  dancing 2.1
  sociability 2.3
dance *v.*
  dancing 8.1
  jump 5.2
dance music *n.*
  music 12.6
dancer *n.*
  dancing 3.1
  worker 17.1
dandruff *n.*
  dirtiness 2.7
dandy *adj.*
  affectedness 4.7
  fashion 3.2
  goodness 5.1
dandy *n.*
  affectedness 3.2
  fashion 2.5
  goodness 3.1
  man 1.10
  watercraft 3.1
danger *n.*
  danger 1.1
dangerous *adj.*
  danger 5.1, 5.4
dangle *n.*
  hanging 1.3, 2.5
dangle *v.*
  companionship 4.3
  hanging 5.1
  killing 12.1
dank *adj.*
  wetness 4.2
dapper *adj.*
  busyness 4.2
  fashion 3.2
  good taste 3.2
  happiness 3.3
  order 6.1
  smallness 5.2
dappled *adj.*
  multicolour 2.4
dare *v.*
  courage 5.2
  danger 7.2
daredevil *adj.*
  rashness 3.5
daredevil *n.*
  courage 3.1
  rashness 2.2
dare say *v.*
  certainty 1.2
  likelihood 3.2
dark *adj.*
  anger 5.1, 5.3, 6.2
  badness 4.5
  dark 6.1
  displeasure 3.1
  hiding 5.1
  ignorance 4.1
  immorality 5.6
  irreverence 3.2
  obscurity 5.1
  reticence 2.1, 2.3
  secrecy 6.1
  silence 3.1, 3.8
  sombreness 3.1
  speech 8.1

  stupidity 3.4
  unhappiness 5.2
dark *n.*
  dark 1.1
  night 2.2
  secrecy 1.1
darling *adj.*
  approval 6.4
  love 7.1, 7.2
darling *n.*
  friendliness 3.6, 3.9
  love 4.1, 4.3, 5.1
  sex 6.1
darn *adj.*
  swearing 4.1
darn *interj.*
  swearing 6.2
darn *n.*
  repair 1.1
darn *v.*
  irreverence 4.2
  repair 6.4
  swearing 5.1
  textiles 13.1
dart *n.*
  clothes 1.2
  plan 1.5
  shape 1.2
  sharpness 3.6
  speed 2.4
  tobacco 1.5
  weapon 8.1
dart *v.*
  speed 8.1, 8.3
  throw 7.1
dash *interj.*
  swearing 6.2
dash *n.*
  busyness 2.1, 2.2
  competence 2.5
  contest 4.2
  discouragement 2.1
  disenchantment 1.2
  energy 2.3
  explosion 3.1
  hindrance 1.9
  impulsiveness 2.2
  length 2.1
  sign 1.6, 9.1, 9.3
  smallness 2.4
  vehicle 12.1
  wetness 2.7
dash *v.*
  discouragement 4.1
  disenchantment 3.1
  fright 7.2
  hindrance 7.4
  hitting 10.6
  meekness 5.1
  mixture 7.1
  separation 12.4
  speed 9.1
  throw 7.1
  unhappiness 7.2
  violence 7.1
  wetness 5.7
dashboard *n.*
  vehicle 12.1
dashing *adj.*
  beauty 3.8
  busyness 4.4
  display 6.2
  fashion 3.3

  impulsiveness 4.1
  rashness 3.2
  repute 5.4
data *n.*
  evidence 2.4
  information 1.2, 2.1, 2.5
database *n.*
  book 10.4
  computing 5.1
  information 1.9, 2.1
  record 4.2
date *n.*
  arrangement 1.2
  food 10.1
  love 2.2
  romance 3.1, 4.4
  time 1.2
  time measurement 1.4
date *v.*
  arrangement 4.3
  romance 6.4
  sociability 6.5
  time measurement 8.3
daub *n.*
  covering 8.1
  raw materials 11.2
daub *v.*
  covering 13.3, 13.7
  dirtiness 7.2
  fine arts 13.3
daughter *n.*
  offspring 1.2
  relative 3.1
daughter-in-law *n.*
  relative 3.3
daughterly *adj.*
  relative 7.5
dawdle *v.*
  idleness 7.2
  incompetence 7.4
  slowness 4.3
dawn *n.*
  day 2.2
  light 1.9
  start 1.3
dawn *v.*
  start 7.3
day *n.*
  day 1.1
  light 1.8
  period 1.6
  time measurement 1.4, 6.2
  timeliness 2.3
daydream *n.*
  delusion 1.3
  fantasy 3.2
daydream *v.*
  delusion 4.3
  fantasy 7.1
  idleness 7.3
  inattention 4.1
daze *n.*
  confusion 1.1
  unconsciousness 1.2
daze *v.*
  complexity 5.2
  confusion 6.1

  unconsciousness 9.3
dazzle *n.*
  faulty sight 2.2
  light 2.1
  repute 2.4
dazzle *v.*
  complexity 5.2
  confusion 6.1
  faulty sight 6.3
  high regard 10.1
  surprise 7.5
deaconess *n.*
  religious leader 2.2
dead *adj.*
  closeness 2.1
  death 4.1
  disuse 4.2
  dullness 2.5
  emptiness 3.1
  extinguishing 6.1
  hiding 5.1
  idleness 6.5
  infertility 5.1, 5.2, 5.4, 6.1
  insipidity 2.2
  invisibility 2.3
  oldness 2.3
  quietness 5.9
  sleep 7.1, 7.5
  the past 7.1
  tiredness 2.3
  unconsciousness 6.2
  weakness 5.6
  whole 4.3
dead *adv.*
  greatness 7.7
  precision 5.2
  whole 7.6
deaden *v.*
  bluntness 3.1
  callousness 3.4
  moderation 5.5
  quietness 6.2
  silence 4.4
  unconsciousness 9.4
  weakness 6.1
dead end *n.*
  hindrance 1.13
  route 4.10
deadline *n.*
  edge 2.4
  timeliness 2.2
deadlock *n.*
  fastening 9.3
  hindrance 1.11
  impossibility 1.4
  stoppage 1.2
deadlock *v.*
  fastening 15.12
  stoppage 3.10
deadly *adj.*
  death 6.1
  excess 4.2
  goodness 5.1
  killing 7.1
  poison 6.1
deadly *adv.*
  excess 9.1
deadpan *adj.*
  composure 2.4

deadpan v.
speech 9.1
dead set adj.
truth 3.1
dead set adv.
truth 8.1
dead spit n.
similarity 2.2
deaf adj.
deafness 3.1
deafen v.
deafness 4.4
loudness 7.1
deafness n.
deafness 1.1
deal n.
arrangement 1.1
buying 1.5
contract 1.1
drug 1.3
obligation 1.2
pole 3.3
raw materials 11.1
sharing 2.1
deal v.
behaviour 3.1
commerce 9.1
dispersion 6.8
sharing 5.1
dealer n.
amusement 2.4
commerce 5.2
drug 12.1
selling 2.1
wrongdoing 3.9
deal with v.
action 5.4
dean n.
manager 2.5
religious leader 1.4
teacher 1.5
dear adj.
excess 4.1
expensiveness 3.1
high regard 6.1
love 7.1
dear adv.
love 9.1
dear interj.
unhappiness 8.1
dear n.
love 5.1
dearth n.
inadequacy 1.2
death n.
death 1.1
destruction 1.1
ill health 2.5
killing 1.2
non-existence 1.4
supernatural being 3.5
debacle n.
destruction 2.7
failure 2.2
flow 1.3
misfortune 1.4
debase v.
damage 14.2
dismissal 8.1
irreverence 4.1
low regard 7.2

misuse 3.3
mixture 7.8
vulgarity 6.1
working class 7.2
debasing adj.
disrepute 5.4
inferiority 3.3
debatable adj.
indecision 4.2
subject matter 3.1
uncertainty 3.1
debate n.
contest 3.2
logicality 2.1
talkativeness 3.1
debate v.
influence 7.4
logicality 6.1
talkativeness 6.7, 6.8
debater n.
logicality 4.1
talkativeness 4.1
debauched adj.
immorality 5.1
overindulgence 6.2
voluptuousness 3.4
wrongdoing 4.10
debauchery n.
immorality 1.1
overindulgence 1.1
voluptuousness 1.2
debilitate v.
weakness 6.1
debility n.
ill health 1.2
powerlessness 1.1
weakness 1.1
debit n.
accounting 2.4
indebtedness 2.1
non-payment 2.1
debit v.
accounting 4.2
debonair adj.
courtesy 4.1
happiness 3.3
hope 4.2
pleasure 4.3
debriefing n.
information 3.3
question 2.1
debris n.
remnant 1.8
rock 1.7, 1.8
uselessness 2.1
debt n.
immorality 2.2
indebtedness 2.1
non-payment 2.1
wrongdoing 1.7
debunk v.
disrepute 7.5
mockery 4.1
unimportance 5.2
debut n.
entertainment 6.2
sociability 3.3
start 3.2
debut v.
sociability 6.3
start 7.4

decade n.
five 6.1
period 3.1
time measurement 6.6
decadent adj.
deterioration 2.1, 2.2
immorality 5.1
decadent n.
immorality 3.1
decanter n.
container 12.4
decapitate v.
cut 14.17
killing 9.4
punishment 11.6
subtraction 4.1
decathlete n.
sport 7.1
decathlon n.
sport 3.1
decay n.
deterioration 1.4
ill health 18.1
powerlessness 1.2
decay v.
decrease 5.3
deterioration 5.3, 5.4
ill health 40.5
weakness 6.3
decease n.
death 1.1
decease v.
death 7.1
finish 9.5
deceased adj.
death 4.1, 4.2
deceit n.
cunning 2.1
deception 1.1, 2.1
error 2.2, 2.4
untruthfulness 2.1
deceitful adj.
dishonesty 3.1
untruthfulness 6.1
deceive v.
cunning 5.1
deception 4.1
dishonesty 4.3
misguidance 4.4
unfaithfulness 5.5
decency n.
courtesy 1.1
modesty 1.3
propriety 1.1
decent adj.
accord 6.3
adequacy 3.2
courtesy 4.1
high regard 6.2
honesty 3.1
kindness 3.1
mediocrity 2.2
modesty 3.1, 3.3
morality 5.3
pleasantness 2.2
propriety 4.1
relation 3.5
repute 5.1
satisfaction 3.1

decentralisation n.
dispersion 1.4
deception n.
cunning 2.1
deception 1.1
hiding 2.5
untruthfulness 2.1
deceptive adj.
delusion 3.1
error 3.3
illogicality 3.1
untruthfulness 6.1, 6.3
decibel n.
sound 2.7
decide v.
choice 7.4
influence 8.1
judgement 8.1
mediation 4.1
decided adj.
certainty 4.1
intention 5.3
persistence 3.1
deciduous adj.
descent 6.2
irregularity 2.1
temporariness 4.6
decimal adj.
five 18.1
number 7.9
decimal n.
five 6.1
decimal fraction n.
number 1.5
decimal point n.
number 1.19
decimate v.
destruction 6.1
killing 9.1, 11.2
subtraction 3.2
victim 5.2
decipher v.
clarity 6.3
interpretation 8.3, 9.2
decision n.
intention 2.1
judgement 1.1, 1.2
decisive adj.
answer 4.2
certainty 4.2
command 4.1
influence 6.1
intention 5.2
persistence 3.3
timeliness 3.3
deck n.
amusement 4.2
drug 1.3
support 6.1
watercraft 7.2
deck v.
descent 10.3
hitting 15.1
declaim v.
eloquence 6.2
declamatory adj.
eloquence 5.2
declaration n.
assertion 1.1
gambling 2.5

judgement 1.3
publicity 2.1, 2.9
sport 15.2
stoppage 1.9
declaratory adj.
assertion 4.1
clarity 5.1
interpretation 6.1
declare v.
assertion 6.1
payment 6.6
publicity 4.2
revelation 7.2
sport 21.2
stoppage 3.4
declension n.
descent 1.1
deterioration 1.1
deviation 1.1
refusal 1.1
slope 1.4
decline n.
decrease 1.4
descent 1.1
deterioration 1.1
night 2.2
slope 1.4
decline v.
decrease 5.3
deterioration 5.1, 5.3
finish 9.5
maturity 5.2
refusal 5.4
slope 4.1, 4.2
weakness 6.3
decode v.
clarity 6.3
interpretation 8.3, 9.2
decompose v.
deterioration 5.4
dirtiness 8.3
separation 14.1
decomposition n.
destruction 1.1, 1.7
deterioration 1.4
separation 5.3
decongestant n.
medication 7.1
decor n.
decoration 1.1
entertainment 9.3
surroundings 1.6
decorate v.
award 3.2
beauty 4.1
decoration 12.1
fine arts 13.5
decoration n.
award 1.14
decoration 1.1
emblem 1.2
high regard 3.6, 4.3
decorative adj.
beauty 3.2
decoration 11.1
decorator n.
decoration 10.1
decorous adj.
conformity 5.1
courtesy 4.1
high regard 6.2

degraded adj.
deterioration 2.1
immorality 5.1
degree n.
bend 3.5
classification 2.4
gradation 1.2, 1.5
length 1.9
measurement 4.13
sky 7.4
dehydrate v.
dryness 6.4
preservation 6.1
dehydration n.
dryness 2.1
preservation 1.1
deign v.
disrepute 6.3
meekness 4.3
vanity 3.3
deity n.
god 1.2, 2.1
dejected adj.
unhappiness 4.2
delay n.
idleness 2.2, 2.5
lateness 1.3, 1.4
slowness 1.2
delay v.
idleness 7.2
indecision 5.4
lateness 7.3, 8.1, 8.2
slowness 4.3
delectable adj.
allure 4.1
pleasant flavour 2.1
pleasantness 2.5
pleasure 4.1
sex 15.1
delegate n.
agent 2.1
inferiority 2.1
trade union 4.2
delegate v.
agent 8.1
giving 4.4
delete v.
cancellation 3.1
exclusion 6.2
deletion n.
cancellation 1.1
exclusion 1.7
deliberate adj.
cautiousness 2.1
composure 2.1
intention 4.1
slowness 3.1
deliberate v.
guidance 5.1
intention 6.3
judgement 7.3
talkativeness 6.7
thinking 5.4
deliberation n.
slowness 1.1
thinking 1.1
deliberative adj.
guidance 3.1
delicacy n.
beauty 1.8
competence 2.1

emotion 2.2
food 1.4
good taste 1.7
ill health 1.1
perception 2.1
pleasure 1.4
delicate adj.
beauty 3.11
brittleness 2.2
colourlessness 3.2
discernment 4.3
emotion 5.6
good taste 4.4
intangibility 7.5
lightness 4.1
perception 4.3
pleasant flavour 2.2
smallness 5.2
softness 3.2
taste 3.1
weakness 5.2
delicatessen n.
shop 1.8
delicious adj.
pleasant flavour 2.1
pleasantness 2.5
sweetness 2.1
taste 3.1
delight n.
happiness 1.1
joy 1.1
pleasure 1.1, 1.2
delight v.
happiness 4.5, 5.1
joy 8.1
pleasantness 4.1
pleasure 8.3
sociability 6.8
delightful adj.
pleasantness 2.5
delineate v.
fine arts 13.2
narrative 5.2
representation 7.1
delinquency n.
disobedience 1.2
guilt 1.2
misbehaviour 1.1
neglect 1.1
unlawfulness 1.2, 2.2
wrongdoing 1.2, 2.5
delinquent adj.
disobedience 3.5
guilt 2.3
neglect 3.2
delinquent n.
disobedience 2.3
misbehaviour 3.6
delirious adj.
excitement 4.3
ill health 35.2
insanity 3.1
pleasure 5.4
psyche 11.2
deliver v.
alleviation 5.3
giving 4.4
liberation 8.1
reproduction 14.1
speech 9.4

throw 7.2
transport 7.4
deliverance n.
alleviation 1.2
help 1.6
liberation 1.1, 1.2
publicity 2.9
transport 1.4
delivery n.
liberation 1.1
message 4.4
reproduction 4.1
speech 1.2
sport 12.8
throw 1.2
transport 1.4
delta n.
land 1.6
writing 2.6
delude v.
cunning 5.1
deception 4.1
misrepresentation 4.3
deluge n.
excess 1.1
flood 1.1
flow 2.3
rainfall 1.5
deluge v.
excess 7.2
flood 4.1
flow 10.6
growth 6.5
many 4.1, 4.2
rainfall 4.4
wetness 5.11
delusion n.
deception 1.1
delusion 1.1, 1.2
psyche 2.3
deluxe adj.
good taste 3.4
goodness 5.6
superiority 5.5
delve v.
slope 4.4
demand n.
command 1.1
desire 1.1
entreaty 2.1
imposition 2.1
indebtedness 3.1
insistence 1.2
obligation 1.1
question 1.1
demand v.
command 5.1
force 7.7
imposition 4.4
insistence 4.1
necessity 4.1
question 11.1
demanding adj.
difficulty 3.7
harshness 3.3
insistence 3.1
demarcation n.
edge 2.2
separation 3.2, 3.5
demean v.
irreverence 4.1
low regard 7.2

slander 4.4
unimportance 5.2
demeanour n.
behaviour 1.1, 1.4
pose 1.2
demented adj.
insanity 3.1
psyche 11.2
demise n.
death 1.1
demise v.
loan 5.2
demister n.
air 3.2
heating 3.8
vehicle 12.1
democracy n.
equality 1.4
government 2.1
nation 1.2
politics 6.1
working class 2.1
democrat n.
politician 3.1
democratic adj.
equality 3.12
fairness 4.2
demolish v.
destruction 6.1
food 40.1
intake 4.3
overindulgence 9.2
demolition n.
defeat 1.2
destruction 1.1
demon n.
authority 4.1
badness 3.7
god 1.1
immorality 3.4
supernatural being 3.1, 3.2
unkindness 3.1
demoniac adj.
immorality 5.8
supernatural being 8.1
demoniac n.
insanity 2.1
psyche 5.1
the supernatural 3.4
demonic adj.
immorality 5.8
supernatural being 8.1
demonstrate v.
attack 6.6
display 8.1
evidence 9.2
teaching 7.4
demonstration n.
display 1.1
evidence 1.5
showiness 3.1
demonstrative adj.
display 5.3
emotion 5.4
demonstrative n.
word 4.7
demoralise v.
despair 8.1

discouragement 4.1
fright 7.2
weakness 6.1
demote v.
dismissal 8.1
demotion n.
dismissal 3.1
demur n.
disagreement 1.3
demur v.
disagreement 6.2, 6.3
demure adj.
abstinence 4.6
modesty 3.1
sombreness 3.3
demurral n.
disagreement 1.3
den n.
dwelling 5.8, 10.10
hiding 3.1
hollow 4.3
rooms 1.9, 4.1
shelter 1.7
denial n.
abstinence 1.1
denial 1.1, 1.2
disagreement 1.3, 1.4
disbelief 1.1
refusal 1.1
denigrate v.
black 4.1
disrepute 7.3, 7.4
slander 4.1, 4.2
swearing 5.1
denim n.
textiles 9.1
denomination n.
classification 2.1
gradation 1.5
name 1.3
religion 1.1
denominator n.
name 4.1
number 1.21
denotation n.
meaning 1.3
sign 1.8
denote v.
meaning 1.3
name 8.2
sign 11.1
denounce v.
accusation 5.2, 5.3
disapproval 7.3
punishment 10.2
dense adj.
greatness 6.1
hardness 3.6
opacity 3.1
pressure 7.1
solidity 4.1
stupidity 3.1
thickness 3.9
unconsciousness 6.3
density n.
opacity 1.1
photography 5.9
solidity 1.1
stupidity 1.1

joy 2.2
robbery 2.2
sociability 2.2
winning 4.3
do v.
accomplishment
5.1
action 5.1
adequacy 5.2
behaviour 3.1
cause 5.1
creation 9.1, 9.2
deception 5.1
direction 9.3
dishonesty 4.1
expedience 7.2
finish 9.1
imprisonment 8.1
infertility 8.2
job 2.3
learning 7.1
non-payment 6.2
satisfaction 6.1
sex 16.2
shape 13.1
subtraction 4.3
travel 12.1
traversing 3.1
undertaking 3.1
use 9.1
whole 6.3
dob v.
hitting 10.1
information 10.1
revelation 6.7
unfaithfulness 5.2
dob in v.
giving 4.2
information 10.1
unfaithfulness 5.2
docile adj.
composure 2.7
obedience 3.5
teaching 6.1
dock n.
court of law 1.7
imprisonment 2.4
shelter 3.4
dock v.
arrival 4.4
cut 14.13, 15.1
removal 3.10
subtraction 3.2
docket n.
accounting 2.6
list 1.6, 2.1
sign 5.9
docket v.
list 5.2
doctor n.
cookery 2.1
healing 6.3
intellectual 1.1
student 1.5
teacher 1.5
wind 1.2
wise person 1.1
worker 20.1
doctor v.
damage 14.1
healing 12.1
infertility 8.2
medication 16.2

misrepresentation
4.1
mixture 7.9
repair 6.1
subtraction 4.3
untruthfulness 8.1
doctoral adj.
healing 11.1
doctrine n.
belief 3.1
rule 1.3
teaching 4.1
document n.
book 1.2
information 1.5
record 1.1
writing 4.1
document v.
evidence 9.2
documentary adj.
evidence 6.1
information 7.1
documentary n.
entertainment 4.8
dodge n.
avoidance 1.3
cunning 2.1
deception 2.1
dishonesty 1.5
expedience 3.3
resonance 2.4
dodge v.
avoidance 5.3
dodgy adj.
cunning 4.2
danger 5.2
difficulty 3.1, 3.6
dishonesty 3.1
unlawfulness 4.3
untruthfulness 6.1
weakness 5.5
doff v.
disuse 6.6
repulsion 3.4
dog n.
animals 73.1
badness 3.2
book 1.8
evidence 4.3
information 4.7
machine 13.1
man 1.3
news 5.3
support 3.3
unfaithfulness 3.2
unpleasantness 2.1
dog v.
pursuit 9.1, 9.2,
10.1
doggerel n.
nonsense 1.3
poetry 1.6
dogma n.
belief 3.1
rule 1.3
dogmatic adj.
arrogance 5.2
assertion 4.2, 4.3
certainty 4.4
command 4.3
intolerance 3.2
power 5.4
vanity 2.1

dole n.
help 2.5
payment 2.1, 2.14
sharing 2.1
doleful adj.
grief 4.2
unhappiness 4.1,
5.3
doll n.
amusement 14.1
beauty 2.1
representation 2.4
sex 8.1
woman 1.12
dollar n.
money 1.4, 8.1, 9.1
doll up v.
clothes 38.2
dolphin n.
fastening 12.1
domain n.
dwelling 11.1
job 1.5
nation 2.2
number 1.18
ownership 1.1
power 1.2
property 3.1
region 1.1, 2.1
subject matter 1.4
dome n.
body 2.1
covering 3.1
curve 3.2
fastening 6.1
height 6.1
shape 5.2
dome v.
bulge 7.3
domestic adj.
dwelling 13.1, 13.3
habitation 8.4
inside 2.2, 2.4
nation 8.3
domestic n.
cleanliness 8.1
contest 3.1
disorder 3.1
help 4.5
servant 1.2
domesticate v.
repression 7.5
domesticity n.
dwelling 12.1
dominant adj.
authority 6.1
greatness 5.2
importance 4.9,
4.11
influence 6.2
power 6.1
dominant n.
music 17.2
dominate v.
height 12.1
management 3.2
power 8.1
superiority 7.2
winning 6.6
domination n.
authority 1.3
height 1.2
influence 1.3

obedience 1.3
power 1.2
domineering adj.
arrogance 5.2
authority 7.1
command 4.3
imposition 3.1
power 5.4
repression 5.1
dominion n.
authority 1.4
government 1.1
influence 1.2, 1.3,
1.4
nation 2.3
power 1.2, 2.2
domino n.
amusement 12.1
clothes 7.1
hiding 2.7
don n.
aristocracy 2.3
intellectual 1.1, 1.2
ruler 2.2
teacher 1.5
don v.
clothes 38.2
donate v.
giving 4.1
donation n.
generosity 1.3
giving 2.4
done adj.
accomplishment
3.1
cookery 5.3
finish 6.1
uselessness 6.5
doner kebab n.
food 5.1
donkey n.
animals 69.4
fool 1.1
stubbornness 2.1
stupidity 2.1
transport 1.6, 3.6
donkey v.
transport 7.13
donor n.
giving 3.1
help 4.8
doodle v.
writing 8.1
doom n.
death 1.10
destruction 2.1
inevitability 1.4,
2.1
judgement 1.3
luck 1.7
prediction 2.3
punishment 1.6
doom v.
inevitability 5.2
judgement 8.2
doomed adj.
death 4.4
inevitability 3.2
doona n.
covering 6.3
do one's dash v.
tiredness 4.3

do one's homework
v.
preparedness 4.6
door n.
closure 3.1
entrance 1.1, 2.3
opening 3.1
route 2.3
doover n.
defence 2.9
generality 5.5
matter 1.3
dope adj.
goodness 5.1
superiority 5.1
dope n.
covering 8.1
drug 1.1, 2.1
fool 1.1
ignorance 3.1
information 1.1
intake 2.2
news 1.1
raw materials 11.2
sludge 2.1
stupidity 2.1
dope v.
unconsciousness
9.2
dork n.
fool 1.1
incompetence 3.2
dormant adj.
idleness 6.4
sleep 7.1, 7.2
dormitory n.
city 1.3
dwelling 9.3
region 2.4
rooms 4.1
sleep 6.1
dose n.
ill health 2.3
medication 1.2
quantity 1.6
unpleasantness 3.1
dose v.
medication 16.1
dossier n.
book 10.1
information 1.9
dot n.
blemish 1.3
giving 2.9
marriage 2.14
multicolour 1.11
music 7.4
property 1.2
sign 1.3
smallness 2.12
dot v.
dispersion 6.10
hitting 10.1, 10.7
sign 15.1
travel 13.5
dotage n.
foolishness 1.3
love 1.2
maturity 2.5
powerlessness 1.1
psyche 3.10
stupidity 1.2
weakness 1.1

dote v.
  stupidity 4.1
dotty adj.
  insanity 3.1
  nonconformity 3.5
  psyche 11.2
  strangeness 5.4
  weakness 5.4
double adj.
  fold 4.1
  size 3.1
  two 6.1, 6.2
  untruthfulness 6.1
double adv.
  two 10.1, 10.2
double n.
  amusement 4.3
  copy 1.1
  cunning 2.1
  entertainer 2.1, 2.5
  gambling 2.3
  imitation 1.4
  repetition 1.5
  rock 3.1
  similarity 2.2
  sport 13.2
  transport 1.6
  two 2.3
  weapon 2.4
double v.
  increase 7.1, 8.5
  music 23.19
  relation 4.1
  repetition 4.1
  speed 8.5
  transport 7.13
  travel 13.7
  two 8.1
double bass n.
  musical instrument 4.5
doublecross n.
  unfaithfulness 2.2
doublecross v.
  cunning 5.9
  unfaithfulness 5.1
doubt n.
  disbelief 1.1
  irreverence 1.4
  uncertainty 1.2
doubt v.
  disbelief 4.1
  uncertainty 4.1
  unlikelihood 3.2
doubtful adj.
  disbelief 3.1
  disrepute 5.1, 5.9
  imprecision 2.2
  indecision 3.1, 3.4, 4.2
  irreverence 3.4
  subject matter 3.1
  uncertainty 3.1, 3.2
douche n.
  cleanliness 2.1, 4.1
douche v.
  cleanliness 12.2
dough n.
  food 18.1
  money 1.1
  pulp 1.2

doughnut n.
  atom 4.4
  food 17.4
dour adj.
  abstinence 4.2
  anger 6.2
  harshness 3.2, 3.8
  sombreness 3.1, 3.4
  unhappiness 4.1
douse v.
  descent 10.1
  dive 4.2
  extinguishing 7.2
  wetness 5.12
dove n.
  emblem 3.1
  goodness 4.1
  innocence 2.1
  peace 2.2, 4.1
dowdy adj.
  clothes 36.4
  ugliness 3.8
  vulgarity 4.5
dowdy n.
  disorder 5.1
  ugliness 2.3
down adj.
  cooperation 7.3
  defeat 4.1
  descent 6.1
  despair 4.3
  disrepute 5.10
  idleness 6.7
  ill health 34.1
  unhappiness 4.2
down adv.
  bottom 4.2
  decrease 2.1
  descent 12.1
  idleness 11.1
down n.
  descent 1.1
  feather 1.6
  hair 1.1, 1.3, 4.1
down v.
  alcohol 26.1
  defeat 4.2
  descent 10.3
  food 40.1, 43.1
  hitting 15.2
  intake 4.3
  repression 7.5
downfall n.
  defeat 1.1
  destruction 2.1
  dismissal 1.3
down in the dumps adj.
  unhappiness 4.2
downpour n.
  rainfall 1.4
downstairs adj.
  bottom 2.1
downstairs adv.
  descent 12.1
downstairs n.
  bottom 1.6
downward adj.
  descent 6.1
downward adv.
  descent 12.2
downwards adv.
  descent 12.2

dowry n.
  giving 2.9
  marriage 2.14
  property 1.2
doyen n.
  maturity 3.6
doze n.
  machine 7.1
  sleep 2.1
doze v.
  sleep 9.1, 9.2
dozen n.
  five 8.1
drab adj.
  boredom 4.7
  brown 3.2
  colourlessness 3.7
  dullness 2.1
  grey 2.7
  simplicity 3.3
  sombreness 3.1
  unhappiness 4.1
drab n.
  brown 1.2
  dirtiness 4.1
  disorder 5.1
  grey 1.4
  promiscuity 2.1
  sex 11.1
  ugliness 2.3
  worker 22.2
draft n.
  book 1.2
  diagram 1.2
  fine arts 4.3
  force 2.3
  war 4.2
  writing 4.1
draft v.
  diagram 6.1
  fine arts 13.2
  force 7.4
  war 10.2
  writing 8.4
draftsman n.
  artist 1.4
  diagram 2.1
  shape 7.1
  worker 12.2
drag n.
  boredom 3.1, 3.6
  clothes 7.1
  contest 4.6
  digging 2.6
  farming 12.1
  hindrance 1.3
  imprisonment 1.7
  intake 1.1
  machine 10.1
  period 1.9
  pulling 2.1
  remnant 1.4
  route 4.1
  rubbing 2.2
  sign 1.5
  smell 1.3
  tobacco 1.15
  vehicle 3.1
drag v.
  hanging 5.5
  pulling 5.1
  slowness 4.1

dragon n.
  supernatural being 3.1, 6.1
  violence 2.2
drain n.
  channel 3.1, 5.2
  exit 1.4
  healing 9.3
  losing 1.6
drain v.
  dryness 6.3
  emptiness 4.4
  exit 4.1
  extraction 4.5
  flow 10.1, 10.11
  food 43.1
  intake 4.3
drainage n.
  dirtiness 2.5
  dryness 2.2
  exit 1.3
  extraction 1.3
  healing 3.3
  removal 1.6
drake n.
  supernatural being 6.1
drama n.
  entertainment 3.1
dramatic adj.
  affectedness 4.1, 4.2
  display 6.2
  entertainment 13.1
  showiness 4.1
  vanity 2.4
drape n.
  hanging 1.3
drape v.
  covering 12.2
  fold 6.7
drapery n.
  covering 1.9
  hanging 2.6
  textiles 2.2
drastic adj.
  violence 4.4
  weather 7.3
draught adj.
  pulling 4.1
draught n.
  air 2.1
  alcohol 2.1, 3.1
  amusement 5.1, 5.2
  diagram 1.2
  extraction 1.3
  food 2.1
  medication 1.2
  pulling 1.1
  quantity 1.3, 2.2
  wind 1.1
draughtsman n.
  amusement 5.2
  artist 1.4
  diagram 2.1
  shape 7.1
  worker 12.2
draw v.
  air 5.5
  allure 1.2
  attraction 1.1, 2.1
  equality 2.3
  intake 1.1

  length 1.8
  pulling 2.1
  sport 12.5, 12.6, 15.9
draw v.
  advance 3.3
  answer 6.1
  attraction 6.1
  contest 10.2
  contraction 3.2
  cookery 6.9
  creation 8.4
  equality 4.2
  exit 4.1
  extraction 4.1, 4.6
  fine arts 13.2
  liquid 8.4
  money 11.1
  narrative 5.2
  placement 3.1
  position 4.1
  pulling 5.1
  representation 7.1
  sport 21.5
  tobacco 5.1
drawback n.
  hindrance 1.1
  inexpedience 1.3
  intake 1.1
  payment 1.1, 1.8
  tobacco 1.15
  uselessness 1.7
drawbridge n.
  route 3.10
  traversing 2.1
drawer n.
  artist 1.5
  extraction 2.1
  furniture 8.4
drawing-pin n.
  fastening 7.1
drawl n.
  speech 2.1
drawl v.
  speech 9.16
drawn adj.
  anxiety 3.1
  closure 4.1
  equality 3.11
dray n.
  vehicle 4.1
dray v.
  transport 7.7
dread adj.
  fright 6.1
  high regard 6.4
dread n.
  fright 1.2
  high regard 1.4
dread v.
  fright 8.2
dreadful adj.
  badness 4.3
  disrepute 5.2
  fright 6.1
  greatness 4.3
  high regard 6.4
  misfortune 5.1
  ugliness 3.1
  unpleasantness 5.1, 8.1
dreadful n.
  book 3.2, 7.2

sky 11.2
supernatural being 7.4
ethical *adj.*
  medication 15.8
  morality 5.1
ethics *n.*
  conjecture 4.2
  morality 1.2
  rule 1.2
ethnic *adj.*
  foreignness 3.2
  habitation 8.5
  humanity 8.4
ethnic *n.*
  foreignness 2.3
  habitation 4.7
ethos *n.*
  character 1.1, 1.2
etiquette *n.*
  custom 1.3
  formality 1.2
etymology *n.*
  language 2.1
eulogise *v.*
  approval 7.2
  religious ceremony 8.1
  repute 7.1
eulogistic *adj.*
  approval 5.2
eulogy *n.*
  approval 2.2
  eloquence 2.5
  high regard 3.5
euphemism *n.*
  bodily discharge 6.1
  eloquence 3.1
  word 1.7
euphemistic *adj.*
  figure of speech 3.7
euphoria *n.*
  pleasure 1.13
euphoric *adj.*
  pleasure 5.4
euthanasia *n.*
  death 1.7
  killing 1.7
evacuate *v.*
  abandonment 5.2
  bodily discharge 12.1
  departure 5.1, 5.8
  emission 5.3
  emptiness 4.1
  retreat 5.1
evade *v.*
  avoidance 5.1, 5.3, 5.4, 6.1
  escape 5.4
  indecision 5.3
  neglect 5.1
evaluate *v.*
  analysis 3.1
  cost 9.1
  judgement 7.2
  measurement 8.2
  question 12.4
  teaching 7.5
  test 6.4, 6.5

evangelical *adj.*
  religion 7.3
  religious leader 7.2
  scripture 4.1, 5.1
evangelical *n.*
  religion 3.3
  religious leader 2.1
evangelism *n.*
  belief 3.2
evangelist *n.*
  eloquence 4.4
  religion 3.3
  religious leader 1.2, 2.1
  teacher 2.3
evaporate *v.*
  disappearance 5.1
  dryness 6.4
  gas 5.3
evaporation *n.*
  disappearance 1.1
  dryness 2.1
  gas 2.2
evasion *n.*
  avoidance 1.1, 2.3
  cunning 2.2
  escape 1.2
  indecision 1.6
  non-payment 1.1
  untruthfulness 1.1, 3.1
  war 1.5
evasive *adj.*
  avoidance 4.1, 4.4
  disappearance 3.1
  indecision 3.5
  untruthfulness 6.3
even *adj.*
  accord 5.3
  composure 2.2
  equality 3.2
  fairness 4.3
  homogeneity 2.1
  level 4.1
  moderation 4.3
  neutrality 2.1
  number 7.5
  precision 3.6
  regularity 3.1
  smoothness 4.8
  steadiness 4.3
  straightness 3.1
even *adv.*
  addition 8.3
  fairness 7.2
  level 7.1
  smoothness 7.4
  steadiness 6.4
  the present 3.5
even *conj.*
  unconditionality 6.1
even *v.*
  level 5.2
  smoothness 5.1
evening *adj.*
  night 4.3
evening *n.*
  dark 1.3
  day 4.1
  finish 1.13
  night 2.1

event *n.*
  occurrence 1.1
  result 1.3
  sport 1.2
eventful *adj.*
  importance 4.3
eventual *adj.*
  conditionality 2.1
  finish 7.1
  the future 2.1
  uncertainty 3.7
eventuality *n.*
  possibility 1.1
ever *adv.*
  continuation 9.3
  eternity 5.3
evergreen *adj.*
  eternity 3.4
  youth 5.3
evergreen *n.*
  offspring 3.9
  plants 2.1
everybody *n.*
  generality 5.2
everyday *adj.*
  conformity 5.2
  homogeneity 2.3
  ordinariness 5.2
  repetition 3.3
  simplicity 3.2
everyone *n.*
  generality 5.2
  working class 2.2
every other *adj.*
  regularity 3.2
  two 6.4
everything *n.*
  generality 5.4
  importance 2.4
everywhere *adv.*
  generality 9.1
evict *v.*
  exclusion 7.3
eviction *n.*
  exclusion 1.6
evidence *n.*
  evidence 1.1
  sign 1.7
evidence *v.*
  display 8.2
  evidence 10.1
evident *adj.*
  clarity 4.1
  display 7.1
  loudness 5.1
  obviousness 2.1
  precision 3.2
  visibility 3.2
evil *adj.*
  anger 5.3
  badness 4.5
  damage 10.1
  immorality 5.1, 5.6
  irreverence 3.2
  misfortune 1.1
  wrongdoing 4.12
evil *n.*
  damage 2.2
  ill health 2.1
  immorality 1.4, 2.1
  misfortune 1.1

supernatural being 3.1
  wrongdoing 2.4
evince *v.*
  display 8.2
  evidence 10.1
evocation *n.*
  cause 1.1
evocative *adj.*
  cause 4.4
  meaning 2.2
  remembering 6.3
  the past 6.2
evoke *v.*
  cause 5.2
  encouragement 7.1
  remembering 10.4
evolution *n.*
  calculation 3.1
  evolution 1.1
  gas 2.2
  growth 1.1
  movement 1.2
  result 1.5
evolve *v.*
  creation 8.4
  evolution 5.1
  improvement 7.2
ewe *n.*
  animals 71.1
exacerbate *v.*
  annoyance 5.2
  increase 7.2
  irritableness 7.1
exact *adj.*
  particularity 4.1
  precision 3.1, 3.4, 3.10
  propriety 4.2
exact *v.*
  force 7.5
  imposition 4.1
  insistence 4.3
  taking 10.1
exacting *adj.*
  harshness 3.3
  imposition 3.1
  insistence 3.1
  power 5.4
exactitude *n.*
  precision 1.2
exactness *n.*
  precision 1.1, 1.2
  truth 1.5
exaggerate *v.*
  exaggeration 4.1, 4.3, 4.4
  increase 7.2
  untruthfulness 9.3
exaggerated *adj.*
  exaggeration 3.1
  misjudgement 4.2
exaggeration *n.*
  exaggeration 1.1, 1.3
  increase 1.2
  misrepresentation 1.1
  nonsense 1.2
  unlikelihood 1.4
exalt *v.*
  approval 7.2, 7.3
  ascent 11.2

employment 9.2
  importance 5.3
  photography 8.3
  religious ceremony 8.1, 8.2, 8.5
  repute 7.1
  reverence 7.1
exaltation *n.*
  approval 1.3
  ascent 4.1
  joy 1.1
  pleasure 1.10
  repute 1.7, 3.2
exam *n.*
  question 5.1
examination *n.*
  analysis 1.2
  question 2.1, 3.2, 3.4, 5.1
  test 1.1
examine *v.*
  analysis 3.3
  judgement 7.2
  question 11.2, 12.1, 13.1
  teaching 7.5
example *n.*
  model 2.1
  part 1.4
  warning 1.6
exasperate *v.*
  annoyance 5.1, 5.2
  irritableness 7.1
exasperated *adj.*
  annoyance 4.2
exasperating *adj.*
  annoyance 3.3
  irritableness 6.1
exasperation *n.*
  annoyance 1.1
  displeasure 1.1
  irritableness 1.1
  pain 1.2
excavate *v.*
  digging 6.2
  hollow 10.2
excavation *n.*
  digging 1.3, 4.2
  hollow 5.1
exceed *v.*
  superiority 7.1, 7.2, 7.3, 7.9
  top 4.2
excel *v.*
  competence 6.1
  superiority 7.1, 7.2, 7.8
excellent *adj.*
  approval 6.2
  goodness 5.1
  repute 5.1
  satisfaction 3.2
  superiority 5.1
excellent *interj.*
  goodness 5.1
excellently *adv.*
  goodness 6.1
  superiority 9.1
except *prep.*
  exclusion 9.1
  subtraction 5.1
except *v.*
  exclusion 6.1

golf v.
  sport 18.1, 19.3
golfer n.
  sport 9.11
gonad n.
  body 15.3, 15.5,
    24.1
  reproduction 5.4
gone adj.
  death 4.1
  departure 4.4
  excitement 4.1
  ill health 35.3
  love 6.3
  reproduction 11.1
  romance 5.2
  weakness 5.6
gong n.
  award 1.14
  emblem 1.2
  musical instrument
    7.12
  sign 3.4
  warning 1.3
gong v.
  warning 4.2
gonorrhoea n.
  ill health 13.1
good adj.
  adequacy 4.2
  allure 4.1
  beauty 3.3, 3.5
  behaviour 2.1
  competence 4.1
  courtesy 4.2
  faithfulness 3.2
  goodness 5.1
  greatness 3.1
  happiness 3.1
  health 5.1
  high regard 6.1
  honesty 3.3
  operation 3.3
  order 6.3
  perfection 4.4
  pleasantness 2.1
  pleasure 4.2
  satisfaction 3.2
  superiority 5.1
  thickness 3.5
  use 5.6
good interj.
  approval 10.2
good n.
  goodness 2.1
  importance 1.7
  reverence 1.2
  use 2.3
goodbye interj.
  departure 7.1
  sociability 8.3
goodbye n.
  departure 2.1, 2.2
good deed n.
  generosity 1.3
good for adj.
  use 5.6
good for you interj.
  approval 10.1
good-looking adj.
  beauty 3.2, 3.3
good luck n.
  luck 1.4

good-natured adj.
  happiness 3.2
  kindness 3.5
  pleasantness 2.2
good on you interj.
  approval 10.1
  high regard 13.1
goods n.
  commerce 2.2
  property 2.1
  result 3.2
goodwill n.
  finance 3.3
  friendliness 2.3
  happiness 1.4
  kindness 1.2
go off v.
  departure 5.1
  deterioration 5.4
  emission 6.3
  excitement 7.3
  explosion 9.1
  marriage 8.2
  occurrence 5.2
goose n.
  dissonance 1.9
  food 8.1
  fool 1.1
  hitting 4.3
go over v.
  change of alle-
    giance 4.2
  question 13.2
  reading 4.1
  repetition 4.7
gore n.
  bodily discharge
    1.5
  clothes 1.2
gore v.
  insertion 7.1
gorge n.
  body 8.2
  entrance 2.2
  food 3.1
  gap 1.5
  overindulgence 2.1
  rear 1.1
gorge v.
  food 40.1
  hindrance 8.3
  intake 4.3
  overindulgence 9.1,
    9.2
gorgeous adj.
  beauty 3.1, 3.8
  goodness 5.1
  pleasantness 2.5
  repute 5.4
gorilla n.
  animals 56.1
  disorder 5.2
  hair 5.5
  sound 4.4
  ugliness 2.1
  unkindness 3.1
  violence 2.5
  vulgarity 3.8
gory adj.
  blemish 2.6
  red 6.4
  unpleasantness 5.1

gosling n.
  offspring 4.8
gospel adj.
  religion 7.3
  scripture 4.1
gospel n.
  belief 3.1
  certainty 2.3
  truth 1.3
gossamer adj.
  intangibility 7.5
  lightness 4.1
  thinness 4.10
gossamer n.
  cord 5.5
  raw materials 5.1
  smoothness 2.1
  textiles 8.1, 10.2
  transparency 2.2
gossip n.
  news 1.2, 5.1, 5.2
  speech 3.5
  talkativeness 2.7,
    4.4
gossip v.
  news 7.2
  speech 9.8, 9.10
  talkativeness 6.3,
    6.4, 6.6
gouge n.
  channel 1.8
  cut 8.1
  furrow 1.1, 2.2
  hollow 2.2
gouge v.
  cut 14.5
  digging 6.1
  hollow 10.1
  shape 13.4
go under v.
  cooperation 9.1
  defeat 5.1, 5.3
  destruction 8.1
  failure 4.1, 4.2
  misfortune 6.2
gourd n.
  container 13.4
gourmet adj.
  superiority 5.5
gourmet n.
  food 32.2
  good taste 2.1
  overindulgence 5.2
gout n.
  ill health 24.3
govern v.
  controlling device
    8.1
  government 8.1
  management 3.2
  restraints 8.1
governess n.
  teacher 1.2
government adj.
  government 7.1
government n.
  authority 1.5, 1.6
  government 1.1
  management 1.1
  operation 1.4
  power 1.2
governor n.
  agent 1.4

controlling device
  1.1
  manager 1.1, 1.2
  relative 2.5
  ruler 1.4, 2.1
governor-general n.
  agent 1.4
  manager 1.1
  ruler 1.4
gown n.
  clothes 3.1, 22.1
gown v.
  clothes 37.1
GP n.
  healing 6.3
grab n.
  amusement 4.1
  hold 1.1
  robbery 3.1
  taking 1.3, 3.1
grab v.
  approval 8.3
  emotion 7.2
  hold 7.3
  influence 8.1, 8.4
  robbery 5.3
  taking 9.1, 11.5
grace n.
  beauty 1.7
  competence 2.2
  forgiveness 1.1
  god 1.7
  gratefulness 1.6
  kindness 1.2, 1.6
  lenience 1.2
  music 15.1
  pity 1.2
  pleasantness 1.3
grace v.
  congratulation 4.5
graceful adj.
  allure 4.1
  beauty 3.9
  competence 5.1
  pleasantness 2.3
gracious adj.
  affectedness 4.3
  arrogance 4.1
  courtesy 4.1
  generosity 3.1
  kindness 3.2, 3.4,
    3.7
  lenience 3.1
  pity 4.2
gradation n.
  colour 1.12
  continuation 4.1
  gradation 1.1
grade n.
  animals 1.5
  classification 2.4
  gradation 2.1
  measurement 4.13
  parentage 4.5
  repute 1.2
  slope 1.1
grade v.
  classification 5.1
  gradation 4.2
  judgement 7.2
  level 5.2
  measurement 8.2
  order 7.4

plan 7.5
  reproduction 12.5
  slope 4.2
  smoothness 5.7
gradient adj.
  slope 3.4
gradient n.
  ascent 1.4
  curve 1.2
  slope 1.1
gradual adj.
  gradation 3.2
gradual n.
  answer 1.4
  music 7.1, 12.8
  religious ceremony
    2.7
graduate n.
  imprisonment 5.1
  intellectual 1.4
  student 1.5
graduate v.
  gradation 4.1
graduation n.
  gradation 1.3
graffiti n.
  fine arts 3.6
  writing 2.1
graft n.
  bribery 1.1
  dishonesty 1.3, 1.5
  effort 2.1
  healing 3.4
  insertion 1.2
  joining 3.8
  profit 1.2
graft v.
  effort 7.4
  exchange 7.3
  insertion 4.3
  joining 8.9
  reproduction 12.6
grain n.
  character 1.2, 1.4
  food 25.1
  fuel 1.13
  heaviness 3.1
  length 2.5
  matter 1.2
  powder 1.9
  quantity 2.1
  reproduction 6.2
  roughness 1.5
  roundness 4.1
  separation 4.2
  skin 2.3
  smallness 2.5, 2.15
grain v.
  bareness 10.6
  powder 7.4
  roughness 5.1
gram n.
  food 9.1, 31.1
  heaviness 3.1
  measurement 4.4
grammar n.
  book 5.1
  essence 1.3
  language 2.1
grammarian n.
  language 3.1
grammatical adj.
  language 4.1

hapless adj.
luck 6.1
misfortune 4.1, 4.2
pity 5.1
happen adv.
indecision 6.5
luck 9.1
possibility 6.1
happen v.
actuality 5.3
luck 8.2
occurrence 5.1, 5.2
happiness n.
accord 2.1
contentedness 1.3
good fortune 1.1
happiness 1.1
joy 1.1
pleasure 1.1
happy adj.
accord 5.1
contentedness 2.4
good fortune 3.1, 3.3
happiness 3.1
joy 5.1
luck 5.1
pleasure 5.1
harangue n.
bombast 2.1
eloquence 2.1
harangue v.
eloquence 6.4
speech 9.8
teaching 7.3
harass v.
annoyance 5.4
attack 5.4
menace 4.1
turbulence 3.5
unfriendliness 6.3
unkindness 5.3
victim 5.2
harbinger n.
anticipation 1.5
coming before 2.1
prediction 2.1
warning 1.4
harbinger v.
prediction 8.1
harbour n.
arrival 3.2
dwelling 1.1
hiding 3.1
sea 2.1
secrecy 5.1
shelter 3.1
solitude 2.3
harbour v.
hiding 6.3, 6.4
shelter 4.1
hard adj.
alcohol 22.1
badness 4.4
callousness 2.1, 2.5
difficulty 3.1
effort 5.1
hardness 3.1
harshness 3.1
impenitence 3.2
misfortune 1.2
sombreness 3.4
speech 8.1
unfairness 3.1

unpleasantness 5.1
violence 4.3
hard adv.
effort 8.2
enthusiasm 5.1
hardness 5.1
harshness 5.1
solidity 6.1
whole 7.6
hard disk n.
computing 4.3
harden n.
textiles 10.3
harden v.
callousness 3.4
custom 6.1
hardness 4.1, 4.3
harshness 4.3
increase 8.2
steadiness 5.2
strength 7.1, 7.6
hardened adj.
callousness 2.1
hardness 3.7
harshness 3.5
impenitence 3.2
stubbornness 3.2
hardline adj.
changelessness 2.3
harshness 3.4
stubbornness 3.1
hardly adv.
smallness 7.5
unlikelihood 4.1
hardship n.
difficulty 1.6, 1.8
misfortune 1.2
hardware n.
computing 4.3
result 3.2
weapon 1.3
hardworking adj.
busyness 4.6
patience 4.2
persistence 3.2
hard-working adj.
effort 5.3
hardy adj.
courage 4.8
health 5.3
persistence 3.4
rashness 3.1
strength 5.5, 6.1, 6.2
hardy n.
cut 8.1
furrow 2.2
hare v.
speed 8.5
harem n.
dwelling 9.6
woman 1.11
hark v.
hearing 5.2
hark back v.
pursuit 10.2
retreat 5.2
harm n.
damage 2.1
pain 1.1
harm v.
damage 12.1

unkindness 5.4
wrongdoing 5.1
harmonic adj.
accord 5.2
music 22.1
order 5.3
harmonica n.
musical instrument 2.6, 7.14
harmonic n.
music 17.6
harmonious adj.
accord 5.2
agreement 5.1
music 22.2
order 5.3
peace 5.1
whole 4.6
harmonise v.
accord 7.1
agreement 8.1
music 23.19, 24.2
harmony n.
accord 1.2
agreement 1.3
music 1.1, 13.1
order 2.1
peace 1.1
scripture 1.5
sound 1.3
harness n.
cord 4.1
restraints 2.1
supply 2.3
harp n.
musical instrument 2.6, 5.4, 7.14
harpoon n.
sharpness 3.5
weapon 8.1
harpoon v.
killing 10.2
harpsichord n.
musical instrument 6.2
harrowing adj.
pain 5.1
pity 5.1
unhappiness 5.1
unpleasantness 7.2
harsh adj.
callousness 2.2, 2.3, 2.5
difficulty 3.5
dissonance 2.3, 2.5
harshness 3.1
repression 5.2
sourness 2.5
unkindness 4.1, 4.3
vulgarity 5.7
harvest n.
farming 1.13
result 2.4
season 1.5
harvest v.
farming 17.1
gathering 5.1
hash n.
complexity 2.1
disorder 4.1
drug 2.1
failure 1.6
food 5.1

telecommunica-
tions 2.7
hash v.
cookery 6.1
cut 14.9
hashish n.
drug 2.1
hassle n.
contest 3.2
disagreement 1.2
talkativeness 3.2
hassle v.
annoyance 5.4, 5.5
menace 4.1
unkindness 5.3
haste n.
rashness 1.2
speed 1.3
hasten v.
speed 8.1, 9.1, 9.2
travel 13.7
hasty adj.
anger 5.3
impulsiveness 4.1
irritableness 5.2
neglect 3.1
rashness 3.1, 3.4
speed 7.4
temporariness 4.2
hat n.
clothes 13.1
employment 2.2
hatch n.
covering 1.12
entrance 2.2, 2.3
length 2.1
offspring 4.15
opening 1.5
hatch v.
creation 8.2
dark 8.5
fine arts 13.4
length 7.1
plan 7.4
preparedness 4.4
reproduction 14.8
sign 15.1
start 8.1
hatchback n.
vehicle 2.1
hatchet n.
cut 5.1
weapon 7.4
hate n.
displeasure 2.1
hate 1.1, 4.1
hate v.
displeasure 4.1
hate 8.1
hateful adj.
hate 7.1
unpleasantness 5.2
hatred n.
anger 2.1
displeasure 2.1
hate 1.1, 1.2
haughty adj.
arrogance 4.1, 4.2
discourtesy 3.5
vanity 2.1
haul n.
profit 1.3
pulling 1.1, 2.1

quantity 1.3
robbery 3.1
taking 3.1
haul v.
ascent 11.8
deviation 8.2
pulling 5.1
haunch n.
body 14.2
curve 3.1
food 4.1
side 1.2
haunt v.
partner 4.3
presence 3.2
remembering 8.5
the supernatural 5.1
visit 3.5
haunted adj.
fright 5.2
the supernatural 4.10
have n.
cunning 2.1
deception 2.1
delusion 2.2
dishonesty 1.5
have v.
acquirement 4.1
buying 4.1
cause 5.3
deception 4.1
hold 7.8
inclusion 3.2
ownership 5.1
permission 5.1
profit 4.1
reproduction 14.1
sex 16.2
have a go interj.
shouting 7.4
have a go v.
attempt 4.6
busyness 7.1
luck 7.1
undertaking 3.4
haven n.
arrival 3.1
shelter 3.1, 3.2
haven v.
shelter 4.1
havoc n.
damage 2.3
destruction 1.2
havoc v.
destruction 7.1
hawk n.
attack 3.1
fighter 1.9
politician 3.9
taking 5.2
war 6.1
hawk v.
bodily discharge 11.3
loudness 7.4
pursuit 10.2
selling 4.2
shouting 5.1
hay n.
dancing 4.1
money 1.1

imbue v.
blemish 3.1
colour 9.2
insertion 6.6
wetness 5.4

imitate v.
copy 5.1
imitation 4.1
pose 4.1
repetition 4.8
representation 6.2

imitation adj.
imitation 3.2
untruthfulness 7.2

imitation n.
copy 1.1, 1.2
imitation 1.1
repetition 1.4, 1.5
similarity 1.2
untruthfulness 4.1

immaculate adj.
abstinence 4.3
cleanliness 10.1
colour 8.2
homogeneity 2.4
innocence 3.2
perfection 4.4

immaterial adj.
intangibility 6.1
the supernatural 4.1
unimportance 4.3
unrelatedness 2.1

immediacy n.
actuality 1.1
closeness 1.1
moment 2.2
perception 2.1
the present 1.2

immediate adj.
closeness 2.2
coming after 4.2
moment 3.2
newness 5.3
region 8.5
temporariness 4.3
the present 2.1, 2.2

immemorial adj.
oldness 2.2
the past 6.7

immense adj.
goodness 5.1
greatness 4.1, 4.3
height 11.2
infinity 2.1
many 3.1
size 3.5, 3.7
space 3.1
thickness 3.2

immerse v.
dive 4.2
insertion 6.4, 6.6
inside 3.1
wetness 5.12

immersion n.
dive 1.2
invisibility 1.3
religious ceremony 1.3
wetness 2.4

immigrant adj.
entrance 4.1
travel 10.2

immigrant n.
arrival 2.2
entrance 3.1
habitation 4.7
nation 6.2
travel 6.3

immigrate v.
entrance 5.1
travel 12.2

immigration n.
foreignness 1.3
travel 1.3

imminent adj.
bulge 4.2
danger 5.3
expectation 4.1
hanging 4.2
the future 2.4

immoral adj.
immorality 5.1
obscenity 3.1
promiscuity 3.1
sex 15.4
wrongdoing 4.4

immorality n.
immorality 1.1, 2.1
wrongdoing 2.5

immortal adj.
changelessness 2.6
continuation 5.2
eternity 3.2, 3.4
repute 6.3

immortal n.
eternity 2.1

immortalise v.
eternity 4.2
remembering 11.1
repute 7.2

immortality n.
changelessness 1.4
eternity 1.2

immune adj.
protection 4.1

immunisation n.
healing 2.13

immunise v.
protection 6.3

immunity n.
acquittal 1.4
liberation 1.5
protection 1.1
safety 1.5

immutable adj.
changelessness 2.2

imp n.
humour 5.3
misbehaviour 3.1
smallness 4.2
supernatural being 5.3

impact n.
hitting 6.1

impact v.
hitting 14.1
pressure 8.3

impair v.
damage 11.1

impale v.
damage 12.5
insertion 7.1
punishment 11.5

impart v.
communication 2.1
information 8.4
publicity 4.2
revelation 6.1

impartial adj.
fairness 4.1
honesty 3.5
neutrality 2.1
tolerance 2.1

impasse n.
danger 1.4
difficulty 2.1
hindrance 1.11
impossibility 1.4

impassive adj.
apathy 3.3
callousness 2.7
composure 2.4
moderation 4.3
sombreness 3.3

impatience n.
irritableness 1.1

impatient adj.
desire 4.2
irritableness 5.1
rashness 3.2

impeach v.
accusation 6.1
imputation 4.2
litigation 5.2

impeccable adj.
perfection 4.4, 4.5

impeccable n.
goodness 4.1

impede v.
difficulty 7.1
hindrance 7.1, 7.2
stoppage 3.7

impediment n.
closure 1.1
damage 3.4
hindrance 1.1, 3.1
prohibition 1.6
stoppage 2.1

impel v.
encouragement 6.1
importance 6.1
influence 9.2
throw 8.2

impending adj.
danger 5.3
expectation 4.1
hanging 4.2
the future 2.4

imperative adj.
authority 6.1
command 4.1, 4.2
importance 4.1
insistence 3.1
necessity 3.2
obligation 3.1

imperative n.
command 1.1
insistence 1.3
necessity 2.3

imperfect adj.
deficiency 2.2
imperfection 2.1
part 2.1, 2.2
powerlessness 5.1

imperial adj.
aristocracy 3.3

authority 6.1, 7.1
beauty 3.8
imposition 3.1
nation 8.2
power 5.4, 6.1
repute 5.4

imperial n.
container 2.2
fighter 4.1
hair 4.1
measurement 4.17
ruler 1.9
vehicle 12.1

imperial system n.
gradation 1.4
measurement 3.1

imperious adj.
arrogance 5.2
authority 7.1
command 4.3
importance 4.1
imposition 3.1
power 5.4

impersonal adj.
generality 7.1

impersonal n.
word 4.4

impersonate adj.
humanity 8.2

impersonate v.
entertainment 16.2
imitation 4.3
representation 6.2
untruthfulness 10.2

impertinent adj.
arrogance 4.1
discord 3.5
discourtesy 3.3
foolishness 3.3
inexpedience 4.1, 4.4
low regard 6.3
unimportance 4.1, 4.3
unrelatedness 2.1

impervious adj.
callousness 2.7
closure 4.3
hardness 3.6
solidity 4.3

impetuous adj.
anarchy 4.4
energy 4.4
impulsiveness 4.1
rashness 3.1, 3.2, 3.4

impetus n.
encouragement 1.2, 2.3, 4.1
energy 1.1
throw 2.2

impinge v.
hitting 14.1

implacable adj.
callousness 2.4
unkindness 4.3

implant v.
insertion 1.2

implant n.
farming 16.12
insertion 6.1, 6.6, 6.7
preparedness 4.5

reproduction 12.7
teaching 7.2

implement n.
machine 2.1
method 1.4

implicate v.
accusation 5.5, 6.1
imputation 4.2
participation 5.1
suggestion 4.2

implication n.
accusation 1.5
logicality 3.1
meaning 1.2
participation 1.1
suggestion 1.1

implicit adj.
suggestion 3.3
unconditionality 2.4

implore v.
entreaty 6.1

imply v.
accusation 5.4
likelihood 3.3
meaning 3.1
prediction 8.3
sign 11.1
suggestion 4.1, 4.2

impolite adj.
discourtesy 3.1
low regard 6.2

import n.
entrance 3.1
importance 1.1, 1.6
meaning 1.1
repute 1.5

import v.
commerce 9.1
importance 6.3
meaning 3.1
obligation 6.2
sign 11.1

importance n.
importance 1.1, 1.7
repute 1.1, 1.5

important adj.
importance 4.1, 4.4, 4.8
repute 5.1, 5.2

importunate adj.
annoyance 3.2
entreaty 5.1
unpleasantness 9.1

importunate n.
insistence 1.1

importune v.
annoyance 3.2
unpleasantness 9.1

importune v.
entreaty 6.1
influence 9.2

impose v.
imposition 4.1

imposing adj.
imposition 3.1
influence 6.1
power 5.4
repute 6.1
size 3.2

imposition n.
cost 2.9
imposition 1.1

jury *adj.*
expedience 5.6
impulsiveness 4.3
temporariness 4.1

jury *n.*
judge 3.1
judgement 3.1

just *adj.*
fairness 4.5
honesty 3.1
lawfulness 5.1
modesty 3.3
neutrality 2.1
permission 4.2
propriety 4.1, 4.2
rights 4.1
truth 3.5

just *adv.*
precision 5.1, 5.2
simplicity 5.1
smallness 7.3, 7.5
truth 7.1

justice *n.*
fairness 1.2
judge 1.1
judgement 1.4

justification *n.*
conformity 2.1
forgiveness 1.4
justification 1.1

justify *v.*
acquittal 3.2
forgiveness 6.3
justification 6.1,
6.2, 6.3
liberation 8.2
order 8.3
printing 9.5

jut *n.*
bulge 1.6

jut *v.*
bulge 8.1

jute *n.*
raw materials 5.1
textiles 8.1, 10.3

juvenile *adj.*
youth 5.7, 6.1

juvenile *n.*
contest 6.2
entertainer 2.7
offspring 3.1, 4.1,
4.8
youth 4.1

juxtapose *v.*
closeness 4.1
contact 3.3
side 3.1

juxtaposition *n.*
closeness 1.5

kaleidoscope *n.*
multicolour 1.3
optics 4.1

kaleidoscopic *adj.*
changeableness 3.7
complexity 4.1
mixture 1.5

kangaroo *n.*
emblem 3.7
food 4.5
imprisonment 4.1

kangaroo *v.*
bodily discharge
12.2
jump 5.4
pose 5.5

karate *n.*
sport 4.4

kayak *n.*
watercraft 4.2

kebab *n.*
food 5.1

keel *n.*
ill health 32.1
quantity 1.4
red 2.1
watercraft 3.2, 7.1

keel *v.*
overturn 5.1

keel over *v.*
descent 9.1
overturn 5.3

keen *adj.*
cut 13.3
desire 4.2, 4.3
emotion 5.2
enthusiasm 3.1
greatness 6.1
intelligence 3.3
pain 5.3
perception 5.2
sharpness 5.1, 5.4

keen *n.*
grief 2.2

keen *v.*
grief 5.4
shouting 5.4

keep *n.*
defence 3.1
help 2.9
single state 2.2

keep *v.*
carefulness 6.3
continuation 7.3,
8.2
defence 6.2
hold 7.8
imprisonment 7.2
obedience 4.2
preservation 6.1,
6.2
protection 6.1
restraints 8.1
reticence 3.4
safety 12.1

keep an eye on *v.*
attention 7.1
carefulness 6.2

keeping *n.*
carefulness 1.3
conformity 1.1
help 2.9
imprisonment 1.5
protection 1.3
restraints 1.4
single state 2.2

keepsake *n.*
giving 2.1
remembering 4.1

keg *n.*
alcohol 10.1
container 10.1

kelpie *n.*
supernatural being
5.3

kennel *n.*
dwelling 10.1
imprisonment 3.4
shelter 1.10

kennel *v.*
habitation 9.10
shelter 4.3

kerb *n.*
edge 3.1
finance 2.2
region 6.1
restraints 2.2
route 3.2
safety 5.4

kerb *v.*
edge 11.3

kernel *n.*
centre 1.1
inside 1.3
plants 9.2, 10.1

kernel *v.*
enclosure 4.1

kerosene *n.*
fuel 1.12

ketchup *n.*
food 22.2

kettle *n.*
cookery 4.8
hollow 1.2
musical instrument
7.3

key *adj.*
essence 5.1
importance 4.5, 4.9
simplicity 3.4

key *n.*
answer 2.1
book 4.1
clarity 2.7
classification 1.4
computing 5.1
fastening 7.3
interpretation 1.4
joining 3.13
land 2.3, 4.1
music 5.2, 5.5
musical instrument
10.4
opening 5.1
pole 5.4
restraints 1.4
roughness 1.2

key *v.*
computing 9.1
roughness 5.2

keyboard *n.*
computing 4.3
controlling device
5.1
musical instrument
10.4

keyboarder *n.*
musician 2.7

keynote *n.*
importance 2.7
music 17.2

keynote *v.*
information 8.4
publicity 4.2

keystone *n.*
joining 3.13
support 1.3

khaki *adj.*
brown 3.2

khaki *n.*
brown 1.2
green 1.5
textiles 11.3

kibbutz *n.*
farming 4.3
society 1.4

kick *n.*
alcohol 5.1
busyness 2.2
competence 2.5
discontentedness
2.1
energy 2.3
excitement 1.4
hitting 5.1
money 8.1
pleasure 1.14
reaction 1.3
shouting 2.1
sport 12.1
strength 1.4

kick *v.*
hitting 13.1
reaction 3.4
refusal 5.2
sport 20.1

kick out *v.*
exclusion 6.4

kick the bucket *v.*
death 7.1
finish 9.5

kid *adj.*
youth 5.8

kid *n.*
animals 71.3
offspring 1.2, 2.2,
4.5
relative 3.1
skin 2.1
textiles 10.1
youth 4.4

kid *v.*
deception 4.2
humour 8.4
mockery 4.4
reproduction
14.6

kidnap *v.*
robbery 5.6
taking 11.4

kidnapper *n.*
taking 4.3
thief 2.4

kidney *n.*
body 24.1
character 1.2, 1.3
classification 2.1
food 4.6

kill *n.*
hitting 3.1
killing 1.1
sport 12.3, 13.5
victim 1.1

kill *v.*
death 7.11
destruction 6.1
killing 9.1, 9.2

prohibition 5.3
removal 3.4

kiln *n.*
heating 3.11

kiln *v.*
heating 8.7

kilo *n.*
heaviness 3.1

kilogram *n.*
heaviness 3.1
measurement 4.4

kilojoule *n.*
energy 1.6

kilometre *n.*
length 1.9
measurement 4.2

kilt *n.*
clothes 22.3

kilt *v.*
ascent 11.7
fold 6.5

kimono *n.*
clothes 6.2, 22.1

kin *adj.*
relative 6.1

kin *n.*
parentage 2.11
relative 1.1, 1.2,
1.10

kind *adj.*
courtesy 4.1
generosity 3.1
kindness 3.1
pleasantness 2.2
unselfishness 3.2

kind *n.*
classification 2.1,
2.2, 2.3

kindergarten *n.*
carefulness 3.1
school 1.12

kindle *v.*
fire 8.1
light 11.2

kindliness *n.*
kindness 1.2

kindly *adj.*
generosity 3.1
happiness 3.2
kindness 3.1, 3.2,
3.4
lenience 3.1
moderation 4.2
pleasantness 2.2
unselfishness
3.1

kindly *adv.*
kindness 4.1
sociability 7.1

kindness *n.*
generosity 1.1
kindness 1.1

kindred *adj.*
relative 6.1

kindred *n.*
classification
2.3
parentage 2.11
relative 1.2
society 1.3

kinetic *adj.*
movement 3.6

reproduction 6.2,
6.3
roundness 5.2
owe *v.*
indebtedness 7.1
owing *adj.*
indebtedness 6.1
non-payment 5.1
owing to *adv.*
imputation 5.3
owing to *conj.*
cause 7.2
owl *n.*
night 3.1
sombreness 2.1
wise person 1.1
own *adj.*
ownership 3.1
own *v.*
guilt 4.3
honesty 4.3
ownership 5.1
ownership *n.*
ownership 1.1
own up *v.*
guilt 4.3
honesty 4.3
revelation 7.1
ox *n.*
animals 70.1
oxygen *n.*
air 1.5
gas 1.2
oyster *adj.*
white 5.6
oyster *n.*
food 6.2
grey 1.6
quietness 4.1
ozone *n.*
air 1.2
gas 1.2
poison 4.1

pace *n.*
length 1.5
measurement 4.12
movement 2.3
speed 2.1
support 5.2
travel 4.2
pace *v.*
measurement 8.4
speed 8.5
travel 12.1, 13.1
pacemaker *n.*
body 20.2
healing 10.1
model 2.3
speed 4.2
pacific *adj.*
mediation 3.1
peace 5.1
quietness 5.5
pacific *n.*
vehicle 12.1
pacifist *adj.*
peace 5.2
pacifist *n.*
peace 4.1
pacify *v.*
idleness 9.1

mediation 4.3
moderation 5.2, 5.3
peace 7.2, 7.3
satisfaction 6.2
pack *adj.*
transport 5.1
pack *n.*
amusement 4.2
container 17.1
gathering 1.4, 1.11,
2.7
heaviness 2.6
placement 1.5
quantity 1.4
sport 9.1
pack *v.*
computing 9.1
covering 12.6
fullness 5.3, 5.7
gathering 5.4
heaviness 7.1
many 4.1
pressure 8.3
sport 21.1
transport 7.6
package *n.*
container 4.5
gathering 2.7
package *v.*
covering 12.6
management 3.5
packet *n.*
container 4.5
gathering 2.7
hitting 2.3
misfortune 1.5
packet *v.*
covering 12.6
pact *n.*
agreement 1.2
arrangement 1.1
contract 1.3
obligation 1.2
pad *n.*
animals 53.7, 69.1
dwelling 1.1
furniture 4.1
habitation 1.1
record 1.5
region 7.4
resonance 3.6
rooms 1.1, 4.1
route 3.15
safety 2.11
sleep 6.3
thief 1.7
throw 4.3
unlawfulness 3.1
writing 3.1
pad *v.*
closure 5.6
fullness 5.5
increase 7.1
protection 6.1
safety 12.1
softness 4.2
travel 13.1
verbosity 5.3
paddle *n.*
animals 28.3
closure 3.1
computing 4.3
mixture 4.2
punishment 2.5

roundness 8.2
throw 4.4
paddle *v.*
disorder 8.1
hitting 10.5
mixture 7.1
touch 6.5
turbulence 3.4
paddock *n.*
enclosure 2.1
farming 6.1
region 3.1, 3.2
sport 10.2
paddock *v.*
enclosure 4.7
imprisonment 7.7
padlock *n.*
fastening 9.3
padlock *v.*
fastening 15.12
paediatrician *n.*
healing 6.5
paediatrics *n.*
healing 7.1
paedophile *n.*
wrongdoing 3.6
paedophilia *n.*
psyche 4.5
sex 5.11
pagan *adj.*
foreignness 3.3
immorality 5.7
irreverence 3.5
religious ceremony
6.4
pagan *n.*
irreverence 2.3
religious ceremony
5.7
page *n.*
book 2.3
period 1.7
printing 2.4
servant 1.8, 2.2,
2.3, 2.5
shouting 2.5
page *v.*
number 9.2
pageant *n.*
entertainment 1.2,
9.1
joy 3.1
religious ceremony
2.8
representation 3.1
showiness 2.1, 2.2
support 5.1
pageantry *n.*
display 1.3
showiness 2.2
pagoda *n.*
height 6.1
place of worship
2.2
pail *n.*
container 11.6
pain *n.*
annoyance 1.5
boredom 3.1
pain 1.1, 2.1
unpleasantness 1.6,
2.1, 3.1

pain *v.*
pain 6.1, 6.5
punishment 10.8
painkiller *n.*
alleviation 2.3
medication 6.1
unconsciousness
4.1, 4.3
painstaking *adj.*
attention 5.4
busyness 4.6
carefulness 5.1
effort 5.1
painstaking *n.*
effort 1.1
paint *n.*
colour 5.3, 5.4
covering 8.1
decoration 9.1
raw materials 11.2
paint *v.*
colour 9.1
covering 13.3
fine arts 13.3
narrative 5.2
placement 3.4
representation 7.1
painter *n.*
artist 1.2
colour 4.1
cord 1.6
painting *n.*
colour 3.1
fine arts 1.4, 3.1
pair *n.*
amusement 4.3
animals 69.5
combination 2.4
love 4.2
marriage 4.7
similarity 2.5
two 1.1, 1.2
watercraft 4.1
pair *v.*
gap 3.2
two 8.1
pal *n.*
cooperation 5.3
friendliness 3.1
help 4.11
name 6.4
partner 1.5, 2.1
pal *v.*
friendliness 6.1
palace *n.*
dwelling 1.1,
2.13
entertainment
8.2
palatable *adj.*
pleasant flavour
2.3
pleasantness 2.1
taste 3.1
palatal *adj.*
body 27.2
palatal *n.*
speech 4.1
palate *n.*
body 7.7
good taste 1.2
pleasure 1.7
taste 1.5

palatial *adj.*
size 3.6
wealth 3.3
pale *adj.*
colourlessness 3.4,
3.5, 3.6
dullness 2.2
ill health 34.3
weakness 5.3
white 5.1
pale *n.*
edge 2.1
pole 3.1
region 1.1
wall 2.1
pale *v.*
colourlessness 4.2
enclosure 4.6
palette *n.*
colour 1.3
fine arts 1.5, 3.10
safety 2.10
palindrome *n.*
figure of speech
1.9
overturn 2.1
paling *n.*
pole 3.1
wall 2.1
pall *n.*
clothes 3.4
dark 2.3
emblem 7.1
funeral rites 2.2
pall *v.*
covering 12.1
excess 7.1
satisfaction 6.4, 6.5
unpleasant flavour
3.2
pallbearer *n.*
funeral rites 6.2
transport 3.2
pallet *n.*
bulge 1.6
fine arts 3.1
furniture 4.1, 4.4
machine 9.1, 16.1
sleep 6.3, 6.5
support 5.4
time measurement
5.1
palliative *adj.*
alleviation 3.1
moderation 4.4
palliative *n.*
alleviation 2.2
moderation 3.2
pallid *adj.*
colourlessness 3.1,
3.4, 3.5
ill health 34.3
weakness 5.3
pallor *n.*
colourlessness 1.5
palm *n.*
award 1.4
body 10.3
clothes 26.2
emblem 3.1
high regard 3.6
length 1.5
measurement 4.12

position 4.2
travel 12.4
ranger *n.*
authority 4.1
badness 3.5
classification 3.1
length 3.1
manager 1.8
pursuit 4.1
thief 2.1
travel 6.4
unlawfulness 3.1
worker 14.1
rank *adj.*
badness 4.10
growth 4.6
hate 7.1
immorality 5.9
obscenity 3.5
pungency 2.4
smell 6.1
unpleasant flavour
2.4
unpleasantness 5.2,
6.2
rank *n.*
classification 2.4
continuation 4.2
gradation 2.1
job 1.2
length 2.2
musical instrument
10.3
repute 1.2
state 2.3
straightness 1.3
rank *v.*
analysis 3.1
classification 5.1
gradation 4.2
judgement 7.2
length 7.2
order 7.4
plan 7.5
question 13.1
superiority 7.5
rankle *v.*
annoyance 5.1
irritableness 7.1
pain 6.4
unpleasantness
10.1
ransack *v.*
attack 5.6
question 14.1
robbery 5.4
ransom *n.*
liberation 1.1, 2.9
repair 1.6
ransom *v.*
buying 4.3
compensation 6.3
liberation 8.2
repair 6.7
rant *n.*
anger 3.3
bombast 1.1
nonsense 1.1
rant *v.*
anger 8.1
entertainment 16.6
nonsense 5.1
verbosity 5.1
violence 7.1

rap *n.*
accusation 1.2
hitting 4.1
imputation 1.2
money 2.3
resonance 4.3
smallness 2.5
talkativeness 2.2
rap *v.*
hitting 10.2, 10.4
resonance 11.1
speed 10.1
talkativeness 6.3
rapacious *adj.*
desire 7.1
meanness 3.2
overindulgence 7.1,
7.2
robbery 4.3
selfishness 3.3
taking 6.2
rape *n.*
attack 1.8
force 2.2
remnant 1.14
sex 4.1
wrongdoing 1.3
rape *v.*
destruction 6.2
promiscuity 4.4
sex 17.1
rapid *adj.*
speed 7.1, 7.5
rapidity *n.*
speed 1.1
rapier *n.*
cut 4.1
sharpness 3.1
weapon 7.2
rapport *n.*
accord 1.2
agreement 1.3
relation 1.1
rapt *adj.*
approval 5.3
attention 5.3
emotion 5.5
joy 5.1
pleasure 5.1, 5.3
rapture *n.*
happiness 1.2
joy 1.1, 1.4
pleasure 1.1, 1.10,
1.12
rare *adj.*
a few 2.1
cookery 5.2
goodness 5.3
lightness 4.2
nonconformity
3.3
rareness 2.1
strangeness 5.3
rarefied *adj.*
lightness 4.2
obscurity 5.1
rareness 2.1
suggestion 3.5
rarity *n.*
air 1.4
goodness 1.6
lightness 1.2
nonconformity 2.6

rareness 1.1, 1.4
strangeness 1.1, 3.2
rascal *n.*
dishonesty 2.1
rash *adj.*
foolishness 3.4
impulsiveness 4.1
rashness 3.1, 3.2,
3.4, 3.5
rash *n.*
ill health 16.4
increase 1.3
rasher *n.*
food 7.2
rasp *n.*
dissonance 1.11
powder 4.1
rubbing 3.2
smoothness 3.4
rasp *v.*
annoyance 5.1
dissonance 3.5
irritableness 7.1
powder 7.1, 7.3
roughness 5.1
rubbing 5.2, 5.4
smoothness 5.2
speech 9.12
raspberry *n.*
disapproval 3.1
food 10.1
low regard 2.3
purple 1.1
rat *n.*
abandonment 2.1
badness 3.3
fighter 4.1
rat *v.*
pursuit 10.5
robbery 5.3
rate *n.*
cost 1.1
gradation 2.3
payment 1.2
repute 1.2
speed 2.1
rate *v.*
classification 5.1
cost 9.1, 10.1
disapproval 7.3
fairness 6.1
gradation 4.2
judgement 7.2
measurement 8.2
order 7.4
plan 7.5
punishment 10.2
rather *adv.*
choice 9.3
comparison 8.1
oppositeness 5.2
rather *interj.*
agreement 12.1
ratify *v.*
agreement 10.2
approval 7.9
permission 5.1
sign 14.5
rating *n.*
classification 1.1
disapproval 2.2
gradation 2.3
mariner 2.1

measurement 1.3
punishment 1.3
repute 1.2
ratio *n.*
cost 5.5
interaction 1.4
number 1.20
relation 2.4
ration *n.*
food 1.3
part 1.5
sharing 2.1
ration *v.*
restraints 9.2
sharing 5.1
supply 6.1
rational *adj.*
logicality 5.1
mind 2.3
number 7.4
sanity 2.1
rationale *n.*
cause 1.2
logicality 2.1
rationalise *v.*
calculation 7.3
clarity 6.1
justification 6.4
order 7.3
psyche 12.2
rationality *n.*
logicality 1.1
mind 1.2
sanity 1.1
rattle *n.*
air 5.7
amusement 14.1
explosion 2.1
loudness 2.5
musical instrument
7.11
resonance 3.2
vibration 3.1
rattle *v.*
anxiety 5.1
complexity 5.2
confusion 6.1
loudness 7.6
resonance 12.2
speech 9.8
speed 8.4
talkativeness 6.6
turbulence 3.5
vibration 6.4, 6.5
raucous *adj.*
dissonance 2.6, 2.8
ravage *n.*
damage 2.3
destruction 1.2
ravage *v.*
damage 11.2
destruction 6.2
robbery 5.4
war 9.2, 9.3
rave *adj.*
approval 5.2
rave *n.*
approval 1.2
dancing 2.1
joy 2.2
nonsense 1.1
overindulgence 2.1
talkativeness 2.6

rave *v.*
enthusiasm 4.3
excitement 7.1
loudness 7.4
nonsense 5.1
pleasure 7.3
shouting 5.1
speech 9.1
raven *adj.*
black 3.1
dark 6.2
raven *n.*
robbery 1.6, 1.8
raven *v.*
food 40.1
overindulgence 9.2
ravenous *adj.*
desire 7.1
overindulgence 7.1,
7.2
selfishness 3.3
rave party *n.*
dancing 2.1
ravine *n.*
channel 1.7
depth 1.2
gap 1.5
hollow 1.6
ravioli *n.*
food 13.5
ravishing *adj.*
allure 4.1
beauty 3.10
sex 15.1
raw *adj.*
coldness 5.6
cookery 5.2
essence 5.3
ignorance 4.5
incompetence 5.5
pain 5.5
unfairness 3.1
unpreparedness 3.1
vulgarity 5.4
ray *n.*
atom 5.1, 5.2
length 2.1
light 1.4
sky 5.5
thinness 1.9, 1.10
ray *v.*
dispersion 6.5
length 7.1
light 10.5
rayon *n.*
cord 5.3
raw materials 5.1,
7.1
textiles 8.1, 9.5
raze *v.*
destruction 6.8
level 5.1
razoo *n.*
gambling 5.5
razor *n.*
cut 3.6
razor *v.*
cut 15.2, 15.3
powder 7.3
rubbing 5.2
reach *n.*
channel 1.1
length 1.1

sago n.
food 25.1

said adj.
coming before 5.2
repetition 3.6

said v.
speech 9.7

sail n.
watercraft 3.2, 7.4

sail v.
departure 5.2
movement 4.7
sport 18.1
watercraft 10.1

sailboard n.
watercraft 3.2

sailboarder n.
mariner 1.4

sailboarding n.
sport 5.1

sailor n.
mariner 1.1, 1.4
worker 13.1

saint n.
goodness 4.1
reverence 3.1
unselfishness 2.1

saint v.
religious ceremony
8.5
repute 7.1
reverence 7.1, 8.2

sake n.
alcohol 17.1
plan 3.4

salad n.
food 9.3

salamander n.
cookery 3.4, 3.5
remnant 1.16
supernatural being
6.1, 6.4

salami n.
food 7.3

salary n.
payment 2.1, 2.4

sale n.
cheapness 2.3
selling 1.3

salesperson n.
encouragement 3.6
selling 2.3
worker 21.1

salient adj.
bulge 4.2
jump 4.1
obviousness 2.4
visibility 3.4

salient n.
defence 2.3

saline adj.
sourness 2.3

saliva n.
bodily discharge
2.7

sallow adj.
colourlessness 3.4
orange 6.7
weakness 5.3

sallow v.
colourlessness 4.1
orange 7.2

salmon adj.
red 6.8

salmon n.
food 6.1

salon n.
rooms 2.1
society 6.5

salt adj.
cookery 5.6
preservation 5.1
sourness 2.3

salt n.
food 23.1
humour 1.4
mariner 1.1
matter 3.3
pungency 1.2
rock 9.1
swamp 1.2

salt v.
cookery 6.15, 6.18
preservation 6.1
sourness 3.1

salutary adj.
goodness 5.8, 5.9
health 6.1

salute n.
congratulation 1.3
emblem 3.3
high regard 3.4

salute v.
congratulation 4.4
courtesy 5.1
funeral rites 8.1
high regard 9.1, 9.2
pose 5.4
sign 13.3

salvage n.
compensation 1.3
property 1.5
repair 1.4

salvage v.
safety 13.1

same adj.
accord 5.3

same adv.
accord 9.3

sample adj.
model 3.2

sample n.
model 1.1, 2.2

sample v.
question 13.2
taste 4.1
test 6.2

sanatorium n.
healing 4.5, 4.6
health 4.1

sanctimonious adj.
vanity 2.1

sanction n.
agreement 3.1, 3.2
approval 1.5
command 1.1, 2.1
force 1.4
permission 1.1,
1.2

sanction v.
agreement 10.2
approval 7.9
authority 8.1
lawfulness 6.1

permission 5.1
rights 5.4

sanctity n.
god 1.7
reverence 1.2, 2.1,
2.3

sanctuary n.
liberation 2.7
place of worship
1.1, 4.1
preservation 3.1
shelter 2.1
solitude 2.3

sand n.
land 5.6
matter 1.2
orange 2.2
powder 1.3
rock 9.1

sand v.
dispersion 6.12
powder 7.3
rubbing 5.2
smoothness 5.2

sandal n.
clothes 32.1
cord 3.2

sandalwood n.
raw materials 2.4

sandpaper n.
rubbing 3.1
smoothness 3.4

sandpaper v.
rubbing 5.2
smoothness 5.2

sandshoe n.
clothes 29.6

sandstone n.
raw materials
11.1
rock 7.1

sandwich n.
food 19.1

sandwich v.
addition 7.4
insertion 6.2

sane adj.
mind 2.3
sanity 2.1

sanger n.
food 19.1

sanguine adj.
blemish 2.6
expectation 3.1
happiness 3.5
hope 4.2, 5.1
killing 8.1
red 6.1, 6.4, 7.1
violence 5.4
war 8.1

sanitary adj.
cleanliness 10.4
health 6.1

sanitary pad n.
intake 2.2

sanity n.
mind 1.2
sanity 1.1

satire n.
figure of speech 1.3
humour 2.5
misrepresentation
1.2

liquid 1.1
stupidity 2.1

sap v.
advance 3.3
closeness 3.1
defence 6.3
digging 6.3
furrow 6.3
weakness 6.1

sapling n.
offspring 3.2
plants 2.1

sapphire adj.
blue 4.1

sapphire n.
blue 1.1
rock 8.1

sarcasm n.
humour 2.5
mockery 1.2
oppositeness 2.4

sarcastic adj.
disapproval 5.4,
5.8
humour 7.8
mockery 3.1

sardonic adj.
figure of speech 3.4
mockery 3.1

sari n.
clothes 22.2

sarong n.
clothes 22.2
textiles 1.3

satanic adj.
badness 4.7
immorality 5.8
supernatural being
8.1

sate v.
excess 7.1
food 40.1
overindulgence 9.2
satisfaction 6.2, 6.4

satellite n.
companionship 2.3
dependence 2.1, 2.2
flattery 2.1
flying 8.1
inferiority 2.1
meekness 2.1
partner 1.3, 2.5
repression 4.5
sky 2.1, 2.2

satellite v.
dispersion 6.17
news 6.3
telecommunica-
tions 9.1

satiate v.
excess 7.1
satisfaction 6.4, 6.5

satin adj.
light 8.7
smoothness 4.2

satin n.
smoothness 2.1
textiles 3.4, 10.6

mockery 1.6
poetry 1.2

satiric adj.
mockery 3.3
poetry 7.5

satirical adj.
mockery 3.3

satisfaction n.
adequacy 1.1
compensation 1.1
contentedness 1.1,
1.4
payment 1.1
pleasure 1.3
punishment 1.5
retaliation 1.1
satisfaction 1.1, 1.3

satisfactory adj.
adequacy 3.2
expedience 5.5
goodness 5.10
satisfaction 3.1

satisfied adj.
contentedness 2.1
satisfaction 4.1

satisfy v.
accomplishment
5.1
accord 7.2
action 5.2
answer 6.3
compensation 6.1
expedience 7.2
obligation 7.1
payment 6.3
pleasure 8.1
satisfaction 6.1,
6.2, 6.4

saturate adj.
fullness 4.7

saturate v.
attack 6.2
fullness 5.6
wetness 5.4

satyr n.
overindulgence 3.2
promiscuity 2.2
psyche 5.5
sex 6.3, 6.5
supernatural being
4.4
voluptuousness 2.2

sauce n.
arrogance 1.3
discourtesy 1.3
food 2.2
low regard 1.4

sauce v.
cookery 6.19
energy 5.1
excitement 6.1
low regard 8.6
pleasantness 3.1

saucepan n.
cookery 4.8

saucer n.
container 14.3

saucy adj.
arrogance 4.1
discourtesy 3.3
fashion 3.3
low regard 6.3

senate *n.*
government 3.1,
3.3

senator *n.*
alcohol 3.1
politician 2.1

send *v.*
excitement 6.3
throw 7.1, 8.2
transport 7.2

send up *v.*
enclosure 4.6
imprisonment 7.1
mockery 4.6
punishment 10.3

senile *adj.*
ill health 34.2
maturity 4.8
powerlessness 4.4
psyche 11.12
stupidity 3.3
weakness 5.5

senior *adj.*
importance 4.10
maturity 4.4, 4.14
repute 5.4

senior *n.*
lawyer 1.3
maturity 3.2, 3.6
ruler 2.1
sport 7.1

senior citizen *n.*
maturity 3.2

seniority *n.*
maturity 2.2
superiority 2.1

sensation *n.*
emotion 1.1
excitement 1.5
goodness 3.1
news 2.1
perception 1.1

sensationalise *v.*
excitement 6.4
showiness 5.4

sense *n.*
competence 1.6
direction 1.2
intelligence 2.3
interpretation 2.4
knowledge 3.2
logicality 1.2
meaning 1.1
perception 1.1
realism 1.1

sense *v.*
knowledge 9.2
perception 7.1

sensibility *n.*
emotion 2.2
good taste 1.8
influence 3.1
knowledge 3.3
perception 2.1

sensible *adj.*
intelligence 4.3
knowledge 7.3
logicality 5.1
mind 2.2
perception 4.1, 6.2
sanity 2.1
sombreness 3.3

sensitive *adj.*
emotion 5.6
good taste 4.3
influence 7.2
perception 4.2, 4.3
reaction 2.1

sensory *adj.*
perception 6.3

sensual *adj.*
allure 4.1
obscenity 3.1
perception 6.3
promiscuity 3.1
sex 15.2, 15.5
voluptuousness 3.1

sensuous *adj.*
perception 6.3
voluptuousness 3.1

sentence *n.*
judgement 1.3

sentence *v.*
court of law 5.4
judgement 8.2
punishment 10.3

sentiment *n.*
belief 2.1
emotion 1.1

sentimental *adj.*
affectedness 4.9
desire 4.6
emotion 5.8

sentinel *n.*
defence 4.2
fighter 4.11
protection 3.2
sight 3.7
warning 2.1
worker 14.1

sentinel *v.*
sight 10.4

sentry *n.*
defence 4.2
fighter 4.11
protection 3.2
warning 2.1
worker 14.1

separate *adj.*
difference 3.3
exclusion 5.1
independence 3.3,
3.6
one 3.2
part 2.3
particularity 4.2
separation 8.1, 8.2
sharing 4.1
solitude 4.1
two 7.1
unrelatedness 2.1

separate *v.*
gap 3.2
separation 11.1,
11.2, 13.1, 14.1
single state 6.2
solitude 6.1

separated *adj.*
exclusion 5.2
part 2.3
separation 8.1
sharing 4.1

sepia *adj.*
brown 3.3
colourlessness 3.3

sepia *n.*
brown 1.3
photography 2.4

septic *adj.*
badness 4.10
dirtiness 5.7
ill health 39.3

septic *n.*
bodily discharge
6.7

septicaemia *n.*
ill health 27.1

septic tank *n.*
bodily discharge
6.7

sepulchre *n.*
death 2.1
funeral rites 3.2
place of worship
2.9
rooms 1.17

sepulchre *v.*
funeral rites 8.2

sequel *n.*
coming after 1.4,
2.1, 2.4
entertainment 4.9
result 1.2, 1.4

sequence *n.*
amusement 4.3
classification 1.4
coming after 2.1
continuation 4.1
entertainment 7.1
music 12.8
number 5.3
repetition 1.8
result 1.4
scripture 1.6

sequin *n.*
decoration 5.6

serenade *n.*
music 8.4, 12.3

serenade *v.*
music 24.4

serene *adj.*
composure 2.2
moderation 4.3
peace 5.1
quietness 5.1
sombreness 3.3

serene *n.*
space 1.1

serenity *n.*
peace 1.2

serf *n.*
repression 4.2
servant 1.6

sergeant *n.*
authority 4.1
fighter 9.1

serial *adj.*
continuation 6.1
regularity 3.1
repetition 3.2

serial *n.*
book 1.16
entertainment 5.1

serial killer *n.*
wrongdoing 3.4

series *n.*
book 1.4

coming after 2.1
continuation 4.1
entertainment 5.1
layer 1.4
music 6.4
repetition 1.8
rock 2.9
whole 1.4

serious *adj.*
importance 4.8
intention 5.1
sombreness 3.1,
3.3

seriously *adv.*
importance 7.3
intention 8.3
sombreness 4.1

sermon *n.*
bombast 2.1
boredom 3.4
eloquence 2.1
essay 1.12
figure of speech 1.3
learning 2.1

serpent *n.*
badness 3.3
cunning 3.4
explosion 5.2
musical instrument
3.6
supernatural being
3.1

serpentine *adj.*
animals 82.2
complexity 3.2
cunning 4.2
deviation 5.3
twist 4.1

serpentine *n.*
rock 8.3

serrated *adj.*
bend 5.5
bulge 5.5
cut 13.1
roughness 4.1

serum *n.*
bodily discharge
2.1
body 22.1
medication 1.12

servant *n.*
help 4.5
repression 4.4
servant 1.1, 1.6, 1.8
worker 3.7

serve *n.*
disapproval 2.2
hitting 3.1
punishment 1.3
sport 12.3

serve *v.*
adequacy 5.2
covering 12.7
expedience 7.2
food 41.3
help 6.1, 6.9
obedience 4.1
obligation 7.1
operation 4.1
religious leader 9.1
satisfaction 6.1
sociability 6.8
sport 19.2
twist 6.1

use 10.1
work 3.3

service *n.*
employment 1.2
help 1.7, 1.9
job 1.1
kindness 2.1
machine 20.1
music 12.8
religious ceremony
2.7
repair 1.2
supply 1.1
use 2.3

service *v.*
repair 6.1
reproduction 13.4

serviceable *adj.*
persistence 3.4
strength 6.1
use 4.1, 5.1

service station *n.*
repair 4.2
shop 1.19

serviette *n.*
cleanliness 5.4

servile *adj.*
cooperation 7.1
flattery 3.2
meekness 3.3
obedience 3.2
repression 6.2, 6.3

sesame *n.*
food 23.1

session *n.*
busyness 3.3
court of law 3.1
drug 10.1
learning 2.1
period 1.3, 1.4

set *adj.*
changelessness 2.5
conformity 5.1
faithfulness 3.5
hardness 3.7
harshness 3.4
intention 5.2, 5.3
persistence 3.1
preparedness 2.1
shape 9.1
steadiness 4.4
stubbornness 3.1

set *n.*
book 1.4
character 3.2
classification 2.1
dancing 5.2
desire 1.6
difference 1.4
direction 1.1
distortion 1.2
entertainment 9.3
gathering 2.6
hanging 1.3
intolerance 1.7
plants 6.4
pose 1.2
position 1.1
sea 3.4
shelter 1.7
similarity 2.5
surroundings 1.6
telecommunica-
tions 3.1

set *v.*
  command 5.4
  conformity 8.3
  cost 8.4
  creation 9.1
  dancing 8.4
  decoration 12.3
  descent 7.1
  direction 9.2, 9.3
  flow 10.1
  hardness 4.1, 4.3
  music 23.19
  order 7.1, 8.2
  placement 3.1
  position 4.1
  printing 9.4
  reproduction 14.5
  sharpness 8.1
  solidity 5.4
  steadiness 5.2
  support 9.5
set about *v.*
  attack 5.1
  start 7.2
setback *n.*
  discouragement 2.1
  disenchantment 1.2
  hindrance 1.9
  hollow 2.1
  length 1.8
  misfortune 1.1
set off *v.*
  accounting 4.3
  beauty 4.1
  departure 5.2
  explosion 9.2
set out *v.*
  clarity 6.2
  departure 5.2
  order 8.2
  plan 7.3
set square *n.*
  bend 4.1
settee *n.*
  furniture 3.1
setting *n.*
  entertainment 9.3
  hair 7.1
  hardness 2.1
  music 2.3
  placement 1.1
  position 1.3
  surroundings 1.6
settle *n.*
  furniture 2.5
settle *v.*
  accomplishment 5.3
  accounting 4.3
  agreement 8.1
  arrangement 4.1
  contract 5.4
  descent 8.2, 9.5
  finish 9.1
  giving 4.6
  habitation 10.3
  mediation 4.3
  order 7.1
  payment 6.3
  rest 5.1
  steadiness 5.1
  whole 6.5
settlement *n.*
  accord 4.1

  arrangement 1.1
  changelessness 1.7
  city 2.2
  contract 1.1
  descent 4.2
  dwelling 1.4
  finish 1.14
  help 3.1
  payment 1.6
  placement 1.1
  property 1.1
settler *n.*
  habitation 4.6
set to *v.*
  contest 11.3
  effort 7.7
  start 7.1
seven *adj.*
  five 15.1
seven *n.*
  five 3.1
sever *v.*
  cut 15.1
  separation 12.1, 12.2
several *adj.*
  a few 2.1
  many 3.1
  particularity 4.2
severance *n.*
  cut 2.2
  ownership 1.2
  separation 2.1
severe *adj.*
  abstinence 4.2
  callousness 2.2, 2.5
  difficulty 3.5
  greatness 6.1
  harshness 3.3, 3.8
  precision 3.8
  repression 5.2
  sombreness 3.2, 3.4
  violence 4.3, 4.4
  weather 7.3
severity *n.*
  callousness 1.1
  greatness 1.2
  harshness 1.1, 1.3
  importance 1.2
  pain 3.1
  precision 1.8
  sombreness 1.2, 1.5
  violence 1.2
sew *v.*
  joining 8.8
  repair 6.4
  textiles 13.1, 13.2
sewage *n.*
  bodily discharge 1.7
  dirtiness 2.4
  remnant 1.20
sewer *n.*
  bodily discharge 6.7
  channel 3.1
  clothes 10.1
  dirtiness 3.4
  manager 1.6
  servant 2.1
  textiles 7.1

sewerage *n.*
  bodily discharge 6.7
  remnant 1.20
sewing machine *n.*
  machine 18.1
  textiles 6.1
sex *n.*
  sex 1.1, 2.1
sexist *adj.*
  intolerance 3.6
sexist *n.*
  intolerance 2.2
sexual *adj.*
  reproduction 10.2
  sex 14.1, 15.2
sexual intercourse *n.*
  sex 2.1
sexy *adj.*
  allure 4.1
  beauty 3.6
  desire 5.2
  obscenity 3.4
  romance 5.1
  sex 15.1
shabby *adj.*
  damage 9.1
  dirtiness 6.3
  disorder 7.1
  meanness 3.3
  ugliness 3.8
  vulgarity 4.5
shack *n.*
  dwelling 5.1, 5.7
shade *n.*
  afterworld 1.2
  colour 1.2
  dark 2.1, 5.2
  fright 2.1
  intangibility 3.3
  safety 5.2
  secrecy 1.1
  supernatural being 1.1, 1.3
shade *v.*
  covering 12.11
  dark 8.3, 8.5
  fine arts 13.4
  hiding 6.3
  protection 6.1
  safety 12.1
shadow *n.*
  black 1.2, 1.4
  companionship 2.3
  danger 1.3
  dark 2.1
  fine arts 4.6
  friendliness 3.5
  fright 2.1
  imprecision 1.4
  intangibility 3.3
  partner 2.5
  sign 1.6
  smallness 2.4
  supernatural being 1.1, 1.2
shadow *v.*
  cloud 5.1
  dark 8.5
  partner 4.3
  protection 6.1

  pursuit 9.1
  safety 12.1
shadowy *adj.*
  dark 7.1
  delusion 3.3
  imprecision 2.3
  intangibility 7.1
  invisibility 2.4
  supernatural being 7.1
shady *adj.*
  dark 7.1
  delusion 3.3
  dishonesty 3.1
  disrepute 5.1, 5.9
  imprecision 2.2
  intangibility 7.1
  invisibility 2.4
  supernatural being 7.1
shaft *n.*
  channel 2.1
  digging 4.7
  feather 1.2
  hollow 5.2
  light 1.4
  pole 2.5, 3.1, 6.10
  sharpness 3.5, 3.6
  slope 1.6
  thinness 1.10
  traversing 2.6
  weapon 8.2
shag *n.*
  hair 1.1
  tobacco 1.3
shag *v.*
  roughness 5.1
  sharpness 8.2
shaggy *adj.*
  dirtiness 6.1
  disorder 7.1
  hair 9.1
  roughness 3.1
  ugliness 3.3
shake *n.*
  dancing 4.1
  food 2.5
  moment 1.1
  music 15.1
  raw materials 2.2
  speech 6.2
  temporariness 3.1
  turbulence 1.4
  vibration 1.2, 1.4, 2.1
shake *v.*
  agreement 8.1
  display 8.7
  escape 5.4
  fright 8.4
  mixture 7.1
  movement 4.5
  music 23.4
  pose 5.1
  robbery 5.3
  taking 9.8
  travel 13.5
  turbulence 3.2
  vibration 6.2, 7.3
  weakness 6.1, 6.6
shale *n.*
  layer 2.7
  rock 7.1

shallot *n.*
  food 9.1
shallow *adj.*
  foolishness 3.1
  shallowness 2.1
  stupidity 3.6
  unimportance 4.5
shallow *v.*
  shallowness 3.1
sham *adj.*
  untruthfulness 7.1
sham *n.*
  imitation 1.5
  untruthfulness 2.1
sham *v.*
  affectedness 6.1
  imitation 4.1
  untruthfulness 10.1
shamble *n.*
  travel 4.2
shamble *v.*
  travel 13.1
shambles *n.*
  confusion 2.1
  disorder 2.1
  failure 1.6
  killing 5.1
shame *n.*
  disapproval 1.7
  disrepute 1.4
  guilt 1.3
  low regard 3.1
  penitence 1.2
shame *v.*
  disrepute 7.2
shampoo *n.*
  cleanliness 2.1, 7.1
shampoo *v.*
  cleanliness 11.2
shamrock *n.*
  emblem 3.7
shandy *n.*
  alcohol 3.1, 19.1
shank *n.*
  body 16.1
  food 4.1
  incompetence 2.4
  musical instrument 10.1
  printing 7.4
shank *v.*
  deterioration 5.3
  incompetence 7.8
  travel 13.1
shape *n.*
  fantasy 2.2
  model 1.2
  order 1.1
  shape 1.1
  state 1.1, 1.2
  supernatural being 1.1
shape *v.*
  accord 8.1
  change 5.2
  creation 9.1
  shape 13.1
  teaching 7.2
shapeless *adj.*
  imprecision 2.5

shudder *n.*
coldness 2.2
fright 1.4
turbulence 1.7

shudder *v.*
coldness 6.4
fright 8.4
vibration 6.1
weakness 6.6

shuffle *n.*
avoidance 1.3
dancing 4.1, 5.1
travel 4.2

shuffle *v.*
complexity 6.1
dancing 8.1
disorder 9.1
mixture 7.6
travel 13.1, 13.5

shun *v.*
avoidance 5.1, 5.2

shunt *n.*
deviation 2.2
electricity 7.2
healing 3.1
route 5.1
transport 1.2

shunt *v.*
deviation 7.4
divergence 4.2
removal 3.8
transport 7.10

shut *adj.*
closure 4.1

shut *n.*
joining 3.10

shut *v.*
closure 5.1
enclosure 4.1
exclusion 6.1, 8.1
hindrance 8.3
prohibition 5.2
surroundings 4.1

shut in *v.*
closure 5.3
enclosure 4.1
imprisonment 7.1, 7.3
punishment 10.3
surroundings 4.1

shut out *v.*
exclusion 7.1
prohibition 5.2

shutter *n.*
closure 3.1
covering 1.12
crossing 1.10
photography 5.5

shutter *v.*
closure 5.2

shuttle *v.*
vibration 7.2

shuttlecock *n.*
sport 2.1, 14.4

shuttlecock *v.*
vibration 7.2

shut up *interj.*
silence 7.1

shut up *v.*
closure 5.3
enclosure 4.6
imprisonment 7.1, 7.3

punishment 10.3
silence 5.1

shy *adj.*
cowardice 3.1
deficiency 2.1
fright 5.2
inadequacy 2.1
infertility 5.4
modesty 3.1
reticence 2.2
solitude 4.2, 4.4
unwillingness 2.3

shy *n.*
reaction 1.2
sport 6.4
throw 1.1

shy *v.*
anxiety 5.2
cowardice 4.3
deviation 8.2
fright 8.4
reaction 3.2
throw 7.1

sibling *n.*
relative 4.1, 4.2, 4.3

sick *adj.*
anger 5.2
approval 6.2
boredom 5.3
colourlessness 3.4
damage 7.2
ill health 34.1, 38.1
infertility 5.2
weakness 5.3

sick *n.*
emission 2.2

sickie *n.*
absence 1.2
rest 2.4

sickle *n.*
curve 1.9
cut 3.4
machine 11.1

sickly *adj.*
affectedness 4.9
colourlessness 3.4
cookery 5.4
emotion 5.8
ill health 34.3
sweetness 2.2
weakness 5.1, 5.2, 5.3

side *adj.*
inferiority 3.1
side 2.1

side *n.*
affectedness 2.2
amusement 6.2
arrogance 1.4
ascent 1.4
parentage 2.8
part 1.3
side 1.1
slope 1.1
society 7.7
spin 1.1
sport 7.3
teacher 1.1

sideboard *n.*
furniture 8.2

side effect *n.*
result 1.6

sidelong *adj.*
side 2.1

sidelong *adv.*
deviation 10.1

sideways *adj.*
deviation 5.1
side 2.2

sideways *adv.*
deviation 10.1
side 4.1

sidle *v.*
ascent 10.7
deception 4.4
deviation 7.5
side 3.2

siege *n.*
war 1.2, 3.3

siege *v.*
attack 5.3
war 9.4

siesta *n.*
sleep 2.1

sieve *n.*
machine 19.1
news 5.2
revelation 3.3
separation 7.1

sift *v.*
analysis 3.1
dispersion 6.7
question 13.1
separation 16.1

sigh *n.*
air 5.6
grief 2.3
hissing 2.1
quietness 2.3

sigh *v.*
desire 10.4
grief 5.4
hissing 5.2
speech 9.14

sight *n.*
showiness 2.1
sight 1.1, 6.2
ugliness 2.1
weapon 3.1

sight *v.*
direction 9.3
sight 9.2

sightseeing *n.*
travel 2.1

sign *n.*
alphabet 2.1
anticipation 1.5
emblem 1.1
evidence 1.2
prediction 2.1, 3.3
remnant 1.4
sign 1.1, 1.4, 1.6, 1.7, 1.8, 9.5
smallness 2.4
smell 1.3
warning 1.4

sign *v.*
agreement 10.2
deafness 5.1
name 8.3
permission 5.1
sign 11.2, 13.1, 14.4

signal *adj.*
importance 4.2, 4.4

remembering 5.1
repute 5.1

signal *n.*
command 1.1
evidence 1.2
remembering 3.3
sign 1.1, 1.7, 1.8, 3.1
telecommunications 5.5
warning 1.1

signal *v.*
communication 2.4
direction 9.2
sign 13.1
telecommunications 10.1

signature *n.*
book 2.4
music 4.10, 7.5
name 2.2
printing 2.5
sign 1.4, 9.5

signature *v.*
sign 14.4

significance *n.*
importance 1.1, 1.6, 2.4
meaning 1.1, 1.3
repute 1.5

significant *adj.*
importance 4.1, 4.4
meaning 2.1, 2.3
repute 5.1
sign 10.1

signify *v.*
importance 6.1
meaning 3.1
prediction 8.3
sign 11.1

silence *interj.*
silence 7.1

silence *n.*
forgetting 2.1
reticence 1.2
secrecy 1.1
silence 1.1
unfriendliness 2.4

silence *v.*
answer 5.3
restraints 8.3
silence 4.1, 4.2
stoppage 3.2

silent *adj.*
faulty speech 3.2
idleness 6.1
reticence 2.1, 2.3, 2.4, 2.5
silence 3.1, 3.2, 3.3, 3.7, 3.8

silhouette *n.*
fine arts 3.3
outside 1.4
representation 2.1
side 1.3

silhouette *v.*
dark 8.5

silk *adj.*
cord 7.5

silk *n.*
lawyer 1.3
raw materials 5.1

smoothness 2.1
textiles 8.1, 9.3

silken *adj.*
beauty 3.5
good taste 3.4
smoothness 4.1, 4.2
softness 3.1

silk-screen *v.*
fine arts 14.2

sill *n.*
layer 1.3
pole 3.4
rock 2.7
support 2.1

silly *adj.*
closeness 2.1
foolishness 3.1, 3.3
humour 7.1
illogicality 2.6
nonsense 4.1
stupidity 3.1
unconsciousness 5.2
unimportance 4.1

silly *n.*
fool 1.1
stupidity 2.1

silo *n.*
farming 5.3
height 6.1
throw 4.3
weapon 6.4

silo *v.*
preservation 6.1

silt *v.*
fullness 5.5
solidity 5.4

silver *adj.*
eloquence 5.1
grey 2.10
influence 6.4
metal 7.8
white 5.8

silver *n.*
grey 1.12
machine 20.1
money 2.1
wealth 1.1
white 1.2

silver *v.*
grey 4.1

silverfish *n.*
food 6.1

similar *adj.*
similarity 3.1

simile *n.*
comparison 1.1
figure of speech 1.2
similarity 1.3

simmer *v.*
cookery 6.6
heating 8.10

simmer down *phr.*
patience 8.1

simmer down *v.*
composure 3.1

simper *n.*
affectedness 2.6

simper *v.*
affectedness 6.2
speech 9.1

Acanthocephala → animals 7.3
acids → matter 8.1
aerobatical manoeuvres → flying 2.4
aeroplanes → flying 6.1
Agnatha → animals 31.1
agricultural implements → machine 10.1
ailments, cardiovascular ailments → 12.1
ailments, animal → ill health 31.1
ailments, blood → ill health 27.1
ailments, bone → ill health 26.1
ailments, congenital → ill health 29.2
ailments, eye → ill health 19.1
ailments, gastrointestinal → ill health 10.1
ailments, infectious → ill health 4.1
ailments, liver → ill health 28.1
ailments, muscular → ill health 25.1
ailments, neurological → ill health 23.1
ailments, plants → ill health 32.1
ailments, respiratory → ill health 6.1
ailments, secretion → ill health 29.1
ailments, skin → ill heath 17.1
air force ranks → fighter 11.1
aircraft body, parts of → flying 7.1
aircraft instrumentation → flying 7.4
algae → plants 44.1
alloys → metal 3.2
amoebae → animals 4.2
amphibians → animals 33.1
anaesthetics → medication 5.1
analgesics → medication 6.1
anemones → animals 6.2
animal ailments → ill health 31.1
antibiotics → medication 8.1
anti-inflammatory steroids → medication 9.1
antiseptics → medication 8.2
aphrodisiacs → medication 16.1
aquatic plants, Australian → plants 39.1
aquatic plants, non-Australian → plants 40.1
Arachnida → animals 10.1
army ranks → fighter 9.1
art movements → fine arts 10.1
Artiodactyla → animals 55.1
aschelminthes → animals 8.8
asteroids → sky 2.7
athletics events → sport 3.1
Australasian birds, indigenous → animals 44.1
Australasian carnivorous marsupials → animals 54.2
Australasian insects → animals 17.1
Australasian lizards → animals 35.1
Australasian mammals (monotremes) → animals 54.1

Australasian ocean birds → animals 47.1
Australasian parrots → animals 45.1
Australasian shore birds → animals 48.1
Australasian snakes → animals 37.1
Australasian tortoises → animals 39.1
Australasian water birds → animals 49.1
Australian aquatic plants → plants 39.1
Australian birds, introduced → animals 50.1
Australian bulbs → plants 26.1
Australian climbing plants → plants 41.1
Australian conifers → plants 15.1
Australian corms → plants 26.1
Australian grasses → plants 28.1
Australian herbaceous legumes → plants 24.1
Australian herbaceous plants → plants 36.1
Australian legumes (shrubs) → plants 22.1
Australian legumes (trees) → plants 14.1
Australian orchids → plants 31.1
Australian palms → plants 16.1
Australian prehistoric animals → animals 75.5
Australian Rules terms → sport 15.1
Australian rushes → plants 30.1
Australian sedges → plants 30.1
Australian shrubs → plants 20.1
Australian succulents → plants 33.1
Australian tubers → plants 26.1

bacteria → plants 43.1
ball games → amusement 11.1
ball sports → sport 2.1
balms → medication 2.1
bandicoots → animals 54.3
base course materials → raw materials 4.1
baseball positions → sport 9.3
battles → war 7.1
bearings → machine 12.1
beetles → animals 19.1
beverage plants → plants 52.1
bilbies → animals 54.3
billiard terms → amusement 6.2
biochemicals → matter 10.1
biological cycles → matter 14.1
birds, Australasian indigenous → animals 44.1
birds, Australian introduced → animals 50.1
birds, non-Australian → animals 51.1
birds, ocean, Australasian → animals 47.1
birds, shore, Australasian → animals 48.1
biscuits → food 17.2
bivalves → animals 24.3
blood ailments → ill health 27.1

blood vessels → body 21.2
blue bottles (hydrozoans) → animals 6.7
board games → amusement 5.1
bone ailments → ill health 26.1
bones, arm → 17.11
bones, leg → 17.12
bones, pectoral girdle → 17.7
bones, pelvic girdle → 17. 8
bones, skull → 17.4
bones, vertebral column → 17.10
booms → pole 1.5
botany disciplines → plants 64.1
bowling deliveries, cricket → sport 12.8
box jellyfish → animals 6.6
Brachiopoda → animals 23.1
breads → food 18.1
brittle stars → animals 26.2
building materials → raw materials 10.1
building tools → machine 13.1
bulbs, Australian → plants 26.1
bulbs, non-Australian → plants 27.1
butterflies → animals 18.1

cakes → food 17.1
canoeing moves → sport 12.6
card games → amusement 4.1
card hands → amusement 4.3
cardiovascular ailments → ill health 12.1
Carnivora → animals 58.1
carnivorous marsupials, Australasian → animals
   54.2
cattle breeds → animals 70.2
cells → organism 3.1
centipedes → animals 13.1
cephalopods → animals 24.4
cereals → plants 47.1
cetaceans → animals 61.1
chamber music, type of → music 12.3
cheeses → food 12.1
Chelicerata (Arachnida) → animals 10.1
chemical measurement methods → measurement
   2.3
chemical processes → matter 13.1
chess terms → amusement 5.3
chicken dishes → food 8.3
children's games → amusement 10.1
Chiroptera → animals 62.1
chitons → animals 24.1
Chordata (Protochordata) → animals 32.1
chords → music 18.1
ciliates → animals 4.3
circular measures → measurement 4.13

clays → raw materials 12.1
clefs → music 20.1
climbing plants, Australian → plants 41.1
climbing plants, non-Australian → plants 42.1
cocktails → alcohol 19.1
coins → money 8.1
common compounds → matter 9.1
complexes → psyche 9.2
computer applications → computing 6.1
computer elements → computing 3.1
computer terms → computing 5.1, 9.1
confectionery → food 20.1
congenital ailments → ill health 29.2
conifers, Australian → plants 15.1
conifers, non-Australasian → plants 12.3
conifers, NZ → plants 15.2
constellations → sky 3.10
contemporary music genres → music 12.4
contraceptive devices → infertility 3.4
contracts → contract 2.1
corals, hard → animals 6.4
corals, soft → animals 6.3
corms, Australian → plants 26.1
corms, non-Australian → plants 27.1
cotton materials → textiles 9.1
courts → court of law 1.3
crabs → animals 11.1
cricket field positions → sport 9.2
cricket scores → sport 13.2
cricket strokes → sport 12.2
crocodiles → animals 41.1
Crustacea → animals 12.1
Ctenophores → animals 7.1
cultural periods → period 3.8
cutlery → machine 20.1
cycads → plants 46.1

dance movements → dancing 5.1
dance music, types of → music 12.6
dance, types of → dancing 4.1
decks → watercraft 6.2
decongestants → medication 7.1
depression, types of → psyche 4.2
depth measurement instruments → measurement
   5.2
desserts → food 15.1
diagnostic procedures → healing 8.1
diagrams, types of → diagram 4.1
digestive tract medications → medication 11.1
dilators → medication 7.2
dinosaurs → animals 75.1
diseases See ailments

disorders See ailments
distance measuring instruments → measurement 5.1
divination methods → prediction 6.1
dog breeds → animals 73.3
drum parts → musical instrument 10.5
dugongs → animals 61.2
dye plants → plants 55.1

earth-moving machinery → machine 7.1
earthworms → animals 25.2
Echinodermata (sea-lilies) → animals 26.1
Ectoprocta → animals 22.1
Edentata → animals 57.1
egg dishes → food 13.3
electrical measuring devices → electricity 8.1
electric motors → electricity 7.1
electric units → electricity 9.1
electronic devices → electricity 7.2
elementary particles → atom 2.1
elements → matter 7.1
elements of computation → calculation 5.1
emblems → emblem 3.1
engines → machine 3.1
engines, reaction → machine 3.2
eucalyptus, types of → plants 11.1
eye diseases → ill health 19.1

fabrics, heavy → textiles 10.3
fabrics, knitted → textiles 11.1
fabrics, patterned → textiles 10.5
fabrics, sheer → textiles 10.2
fabrics, shiny → textiles10.6
fabrics, soft → textiles 10.1
fencing moves → sport 12.12
fermented drinks → alcohol 17.1
ferns → plants 45.1
ferns, NZ → plants 45.2
fertilisers → fertility 4.1
fevers→ ill health 8.1
fibre plants → plants 56.1
fish → animals 29.1
fish dishes → food 6.3
flagellates → animals 4.5
flags → emblem 5.1
flatworms → animals 21.1
flies → animals 20.1
flukes → animals 21.2
fodder → food 31.1
fodder plants → plants 59.1
football field positions → sport 9.1
football moves → sport 12.1

football scores → sport 13.1
football terms → sport 15.1
football, types of → sport 2.2
fossil birds → animals 75.3
Freudian terminology → psyche 9.1
fruits → plants 49.1
fungi → plants 43.1

garden tools → machine 11.1
gastrointestinal ailments → ill health 10.1
gears → vehicle 12.3
gears → vehicle 12.3
gemstones → rock 8.1
genital diseases → ill health 14.1
glass, types of → raw materials 14.1
gliders → animals 54.5
golf scores → sport 13.3
golf strokes → sport 12.4
grains → plants 47.1
grape varieties → alcohol 15.1
grasses, Australian → plants 28.1
grasses, non-Australian → plants 29.1
gymnastic moves → sport 12.9

hard corals → animals 6.4
hardware → computing 4.3
heavy fabrics → textiles 10.3
height measurement instruments → measurement 5.2
heraldic devices → emblem 7.1
heraldic points → emblem 8.1
herbaceous legumes, Australian → plants 24.1
herbaceous legumes, non-Australian → plants 25.1
herbaceous plants, Australian → plants 36.1
herbaceous plants, non-Australasian → plants 38.1
herbaceous plants, NZ → plants 37.1
herbal medicine → medication 15.1
herbs → plants 51.1
hockey positions → sport 9.1
hormones → reproduction 5.5
horse-riding events→ sport 6.5
horseshoe crabs → animals 11.1
household appliances → machine 18.1
hull and superstructure, parts of → 6.1
hyracoideans → animals 65.2

ice-creams → food 15.2
igneous rocks → rock 7.1
illnesses See ailments
illumination measures → measurement 4.14
imaginary substances → matter 12.1

sponges → animals 5.1
Sporifera (sponges) → animals 5.1
Sporozoa → animals 4.1
stanza, types of → poetry 2.1
starfish → animals 26.2
steroids, anti-inflammatory → medication 9.1
stimulants → medication 3.2
stitches → textiles 12.1
stone age tools → machine 21.1
string instrument parts → musical instrument 10.2
succulents, Australian → plants 33.1
succulents, non-Australian → plants 34.1
sugars → food 24.1
surfers → sport 8.1
surfing moves → sport 12.10
surgery, types of → healing 3.1
surgical tools → healing 9.5
swimming strokes → sport 12.11
symphonic music, types of → music 12.2
synthetics → textiles 9.5

tapeworms → animals 21.3
temperature measuring instruments → measurement 5.8
tennis scores → sport 13.4
tennis strokes → sport 12.3
theorists → conjecture 3.1
timber plants → plants 57.1
timepieces, parts of → time measurement 5.1
tonics → medication 3.1
tortoises, Australasian → animals 39.1
tortoises, non-Australasian → animals 40.1
toys → amusement 14.1
traders → commerce 5.2
trains → vehicle 7.1
transmission, types of → machine 5.1
trees, NZ → plants 18.1
tubers, Australian → plants 26.1

tubers, non-Australian → plants 71.1
tunicates → animals 32.1

upper houses (chambers) → government 4.3
urchins → animals 26.3
urinary ailments → ill health 15.1

vegetable crops → plants 48.1
vegetable dishes → food 9.3
vehicle parts → vehicle 12.1
vitamins → medication 13.1
volume measuring instrument → measurement 5.4

wallabies → animals 54.7
water birds, Australasian → animals 49.1
water sports → sport 5.1
wattles (acacia) → plants 12.1
waxes → raw material 8.1
weeds → plants 61.1
weight measuring instruments → measurement 5.3
weight, units of → heaviness3.1
weightlifting moves → sport 12.13
welders → joining 5.2
welding, types of → joining 5.1
wind instrument parts → musical instrument 10.1
wind speed measuring instruments → measurement 5.9
wine, types of → alcohol 14.1
winter sports → sport 6.3
wombats → animals 54.4
wood, types of → raw material 2.4
wool, types of → textiles 9.4
wrestling moves → sport 12.15
wrestling, types of → sport 4.2
writing signs → sign 9.3

yarn, types of → textiles 8.1